# Wood
# Design
# Manual

## 2005

# Wood
# Design
# Manual

# 2005

The complete
reference
for wood design
in Canada

Canadian
Wood
Council

Conseil
canadien
du bois

© 2005 Copyright
Canadian Wood Council
Conseil canadien du bois
Ottawa, Ontario, Canada
www.cwc.ca

ISBN 0-921628-75-7
(ISBN 0-921628-62-5. 4th revised edition, 2001
ISBN 0-921628-50-1. 3rd revised edition, 1997
ISBN 0-921628-33-1. 2nd revised edition, 1995
ISBN 0-921628-04-8. 1st edition, 1990)


2.0M05-12



Illustrations:
RJS ID Inc., Ottawa, ON


Book design and production:
Eton Systems, Nepean, ON


Printing:
Friesens, Altona, MB

 Printed in Canada on recycled paper.

# Preface

The Canadian Wood Council (CWC) is the association responsible for the development and dissemination of technical information on the use of wood products in construction. Ensuring that this information is in tune with technical change and users' needs requires constant vigilance.

The purpose of this fifth edition of the *Wood Design Manual* is to help the Canadian design community – architects, engineers, specification writers, teachers and students of these disciplines – to design wood structures with efficiency, economy and safety. It brings together, in a comprehensive but concise format, the essential information a designer needs for a wide range of wood structural elements and systems.

The information in the *Wood Design Manual* is based on the latest information available from the *National Building Code of Canada (2005)* and from *CSA Standard O86-01 (2005) Engineering Design in Wood*. Every effort has been made to ensure that the data and information in the *Manual* are accurate and complete. The CWC does not, however, assume any responsibility for errors or omissions in the *Manual* nor for engineering designs or plans prepared from it.

The CWC would like to thank the individuals who were instrumental in the development of this manual: Stephen J. Boyd, Quaile Engineering Ltd., and Gary C. Williams, President, Timber Systems Limited.

Pauline Rochefort
President

November 2005

*For information on CWC's other design tools, call this toll-free number: 1-800-463-5091 or visit the CWC web site at www.cwc.ca

# Sustainable Building Materials – Wood is the Natural Choice

Sustainable Buildings and Green Buildings are gaining interest of designers looking to conserve energy and minimize the environmental impact of buildings using four generally accepted objectives to reduce the global impact of a particular product or system:
- Reduced energy and resource use in extraction and processing
- Reduced energy consumption in processing and end use
- Minimized external pollution and environmental damage throughout the life cycle
- Minimized internal pollution in the built environment.

Wood is the best environmental choice to meet these four principles based on the following:
- Wood is the only renewable major construction material
- Wood is energy efficient in manufacture and use
- Wood is easily recycled or re-used
- Wood minimizes environmental impact
- Canadian wood products are produced from well managed forests that are regulated by sustainable forestry policy.

## Life-Cycle Assessment

Life Cycle Assessment is a performance-based approach to assessing the impacts that building products or systems have on the environment over their lifetime. This includes all activities from material extraction or harvesting through manufacturing, transportation, installation, use, maintenance, and final disposal or re-use. LCA is the best available tool to compare sustainability of building materials.

When considering environmental impact using Life Cycle Assessment, wood outperforms other major building materials in the following ways:
- Requires less embodied energy in production
- Reduces greenhouse gas emissions
- Releases fewer pollutants into the air
- Discharges less water pollutants
- Generates fewer solid wastes.

## Sustainable Forest Management

Canada is a world leader in forest conservation, protection and sustainable use. 94% of Canada's forests are on crown land and provincial governments enforce strict guidelines on harvesting, regenerating and sustaining these publicly owned forests.

For example:
• Canada has the largest area of legally protected forests in the world
• Canada has the largest area of original forest cover in the world (over 90%)
• Only one-quarter of Canada's forests are managed for commercial use
• Annually, Canada harvests less than one-half of 1% of its forest
• Canada has the largest area of independently certified forests in the world
    Canada's history of caring for our resource base and our desire to continually improve has made these facts a reality. Canadian law, as it now stands, has some of the most progressive legislation for forest management in the world.
    Public concerns focus on the highly visible effects of wood resource extraction. To address these concerns, Canadian wood product manufacturers are using certification by qualified, 3rd party, independent bodies to attest that they meet the requirements of a rigorous and independent forest management standard. Canadian companies have achieved third-party certification on over 100 million hectares (250 million acres) of forests, the largest area of certified forests in the world.

# Table of Contents

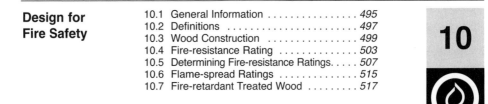

# Introduction

**1.**

**i**

# 1.1 General Information

The design information provided in this manual is based on the Canadian Standards Association (CSA) Standard CSA O86 *Engineering Design in Wood (Limit States Design)*.

## Member Design

The chapters that deal with the design of members provide selection tables listing factored resistances and stiffnesses for common sizes. The tabulated values have been calculated from CSA O86 using modification factors for conditions most often encountered in the design of wood structures. The designer must verify that the tabulated values are appropriate for a particular structure being designed by reviewing the checklist provided before each set of tables. In most chapters, modification factors are provided so that the tabulated values may be adjusted for different conditions. Where a direct modification of the tabulated value is not possible, a simplified design equation is provided to calculate the resistance; however, the tables may be used to select a trial section.

Chapters are arranged so that the lightest load-carrying element is presented first and the heaviest last. For example, Chapter 2 *Bending Members* begins with sheathing and decking followed by joists and beams. This arrangement should assist the designer in making economical choices for an efficient design.

## Fastenings Design

The design approach for fastenings is somewhat different since the resistance of a particular fastener often depends on a larger number of variables. For each fastener, a simplified formula for factored resistance is provided. The formula generally includes a number of modification factors which may be determined using a checklist. The checklist indicates the conditions where each factor is equal to unity, and where it is not. This enables the designer to quickly adjust the nominal resistance for the actual conditions and also ensures that all of the factors have been considered. Where applicable, diagrams are provided showing edge distance, end distance and spacings for different sizes of fasteners in order to assist the designer in detailing the connections.

## Reference Material

Chapter 11 *Reference Information* provides background material on a variety of topics. Of particular importance to the design of members and fasteners is the description of duration of load and service conditions. In addition, information on species combinations, grades and sizes of lumber is included. Chapter 11 also contains beam diagrams and formulae, deflection factors and standard dimensions of fastening hardware.

# 1.2    Limit States Design

### General

The limit states design approach is to provide adequate resistance to certain limit states, namely strength and serviceability. Strength limit states refer to the maximum load-carrying capacity of the structure. Serviceability limit states are those that restrict the normal use and occupancy of the structure such as excessive deflection or vibration.

The *National Building Code of Canada (NBCC)* applies factors of safety to both the resistance side and the load side of the design equation. The design criterion to be satisfied then becomes the following:

Factored resistance ≥ factored load effect

The factored resistance is the product of a resistance factor $\phi$ and the nominal resistance, both of which are given in CSA O86 for wood materials and fasteners. The resistance factor takes into account the variability of dimensions and material properties, workmanship, type of failure, and uncertainty in the prediction of resistance.

The factored load effect is calculated in accordance with the *NBCC* by multiplying the actual loads on the structure (specified loads) by load factors that account for the variability of the load. A summary of the *NBCC* loading is given below.

### Specified Loads and Combinations

Revisions have been made to the limit states requirements in the 2005 edition of the *NBCC*: These include:

- Adoption of the companion action format for load combinations.
- Separation of load due to snow and rain from live load due to use and occupancy.
- Use of importance factors to determine the specified snow and rain, wind and earthquake loads. The importance factors are dependant on the type of load and the building use and occupancy. Separate importance factors are used to determine serviceability loads.
- Modification of the return period for snow, rain and wind loads from 1/30 to 1/50 probability of exceedence per year.

## Specified Loads
Loads to be considered are:

D – dead load due to the weight of building components

E – load due to earthquake, including the effect of the importance factors

L – live load due to use and occupancy

S – load due to snow and rain, including the effect of the importance factors

W – load due to wind, including the effect of the importance factors

H – load due to lateral earth pressure

P – permanent effects caused by prestress

T – load due to temperature, shrinkage and settlement effects

Specified earthquake load, E; snow load, S; and wind load, W incorporate the importance factors shown in Table 1.1.

| Table 1.1 **Importance factors for determining S, W, and E loads** | | Importance factors for snow loads, $I_S$ | | Importance factors for wind loads, $I_W$ | | Importance factors for earthquake loads, $I_E$ | |
|---|---|---|---|---|---|---|---|
| Importance category | | Ultimate limit state | Serviceability limit state | Ultimate limit state | Serviceability limit state | Ultimate limit state | Serviceability limit state |
| Low | | 0.8 | 0.9 | 0.8 | 0.75 | 0.8 | N/A |
| Normal | | 1.0 | 0.9 | 1.0 | 0.75 | 1.0 | N/A |
| High | | 1.15 | 0.9 | 1.15 | 0.75 | 1.3 | N/A |
| Post-disaster | | 1.25 | 0.9 | 1.25 | 0.75 | 1.5 | N/A |

Importance categories for buildings are based on intended use and occupancy as follows:

Low – Buildings that represent a hazard to human life in the event of failure

Normal – All buildings except those listed as low, high or post-disaster

High – Buildings that are likely to be used as post-disaster shelters, including schools and community centres

Post-disaster – Buildings that are essential to provide services in the event of a disaster

## Load Combinations for Ultimate Limit States
The effect of principal plus companion loads is determined using the load combinations in the building code as shown in Table 1.2. The load effect should be in the same units as the resistance (i.e., kN, kN•m) and should be the most unfavourable effect considering all possible load combinations.

| Table 1.2 | Case | Principal loads | Companion loads |
|---|---|---|---|
| **Load combinations for ultimate limit states** | 1 | 1.4D | |
| | 2 | (1.25D or 0.9D) + 1.5L[2] | 0.5S or 0.4W |
| | 3 | (1.25D or 0.9D) + 1.5S | 0.5L[3] or 0.4W |
| | 4 | (1.25D or 0.9D) + 1.4W | 0.5L[3] or 0.5S |
| | 5 | 1.0D + 1.0E | 0.5L[3] + 0.25S |

Notes:
1. Refer to the *NBCC* for;
   • dead load, D, for soil,
   • guidance on combining snow load, S, and live load, L, on exterior areas,
   • loads due to lateral earth pressure, H, prestress, P, and imposed deformation, T.
2. The principal load factor of 1.5 for a live load, L, may be reduced to 1.25 for liquids in tanks.
3. The companion load factor of 0.5 for a live load, L, shall be increased to 1.0 for storage occupancies, equipment areas and service rooms.

## Load Combinations for Serviceability Limit States

The effect of principal plus companion loads is determined using the load combinations specified in CSA O86 as shown in Table 1.3.

| Table 1.3 | Case | Principal loads | Companion loads |
|---|---|---|---|
| **Load combinations for serviceability limit states** | 1 | 1.0D | |
| | 2 | 1.0D + 1.0L | 0.5S or 0.4W |
| | 3 | 1.0D + 1.0S | 0.5L or 0.4W |
| | 4 | 1.0D + 1.0W | 0.5L or 0.5S |

Notes:
1. Dead loads include permanent loads due to lateral earth pressure, H, and prestress, P.
2. Refer to the *NBCC* for guidance on combining snow load, S, and live load, L, on exterior areas.

## Example: Lintel Loads

Determine the design loads for the following conditions

- lintel supporting roof and one floor of a school
- lintel span = 3 m
- tributary width of roof = 3 m
- tributary width of floor = 3 m
- specified roof dead load = 1 kPa
- specified floor dead load = 1.5 kPa
- 1 in 50 year ground snow load, $S_s$ = 1.8 kPa
- 1 in 50 year associated rain load, $S_r$ = 0.2 kPa
- basic snow load factor, $C_b$ = 0.8; snow load wind exposure factor, $C_w$ = 1.0; snow load slope factor, $C_s$ = 1.0; snow load shape factor, $C_a$ = 1.0
- specified floor live load = 2.4 kPa

**1**

**Introduction**

## Calculation

Ultimate limit states:

Uniform specified dead load
$$w_D = (1 \times 3) + (1.5 \times 3) = 7.5 \text{ kN/m}$$

Uniform specified live load
$$w_L = (3 \times 2.4) = 7.2 \text{ kN/m}$$

Specified snow load
$$S = I_S[S_s(C_bC_wC_sC_a) + S_r]$$
$$= 1.15[1.8(0.8 \times 1.0 \times 1.0 \times 1.0) + 0.2] = 1.89 \text{ kPa}$$

Uniform specified snow load
$$w_S = 3 \times 1.89 = 5.67 \text{ kN/m}$$

D:
$$w_f = 1.4 \times 7.5 = 10.5 \text{ kN/m}$$

D+S+L:
$$w_f = (1.25 \times 7.5) + (1.5 \times 7.2) + (0.5 \times 5.67) = 23.01 \text{ kN/m} \quad \textit{Governs D+S+L}$$
$$w_f = (1.25 \times 7.5) + (1.5 \times 5.67) + (0.5 \times 7.2) = 21.48 \text{ kN/m}$$

Serviceability limit state:

Specified snow load
$$S = I_S[S_s(C_bC_wC_sC_a) + S_r]$$
$$= 0.9[1.8(0.8 \times 1.0 \times 1.0 \times 1.0) + 0.2] = 1.48 \text{ kPa}$$

Uniform specified snow load
$$w_S = 3 \times 1.48 = 4.43 \text{ kN/m}$$

D:
$$w = 7.5 \text{ kN/m}$$

D+S+L:
$$w = 7.5 + 7.2 + (0.5 \times 4.43) = 16.92 \text{ kN/m} \quad \textit{Governs D+S+L}$$
$$w = 7.5 + 4.43 + (0.5 \times 7.2) = 15.53 \text{ kN/m}$$

S+L:
$$w = 7.2 + (0.5 \times 4.43) = 9.41 \text{ kN/m} \quad \textit{Governs S+L}$$
$$w = 4.43 + (0.5 \times 7.2) = 8.03 \text{ kN/m}$$

**Use the following loads for design:**
**Ultimate limit states – 10.5 kN/m, D; and 23.0 kN/m, D+S+L**
**Serviceability limit states – 7.5 kN/m, D; 16.9 kN/m, D+S+L; and 9.4 kN/m, S+L**

# Bending
# Members

2

The sweeping form of these 50 m span arches provides a dramatic structure for this skating arena. The frame, purlins and decking satisfy the *NBCC* "Heavy Timber Construction" requirements for fire safety.

*Top left:* Tongue and groove decking is manufactured from several species, and usually has a vee joint on the exposed face.

*Top right:* Double tongue and groove 64 mm and 89 mm thick decking is pre-drilled at 760 mm on centre for side nailing with 200 mm spikes.

*Middle left:* Structural Composite Lumber (SCL) and glulam beams provide significantly higher design values than sawn lumber.

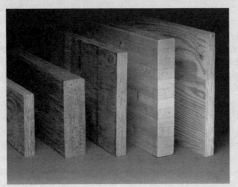

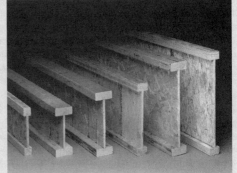

*Middle right:* Wood I-joists are stocked in long lengths and a range of depths for use as secondary framing members.

*Bottom:* Non-residential applications may be framed very competitively with glulam beams and a number of sheathing materials, including steel decking.

Glulam beams and wood I-joists are readily integrated with steel columns in this structure.

Joists in the typical floor layout shown here are usually provided in No.1 or No.2 grade, both of which have the same specified strengths.

Glulam beams are commonly used as primary framing members and can be left exposed to form an architectural feature.

## 2.1     General Information

The following sections contain design information for members that are used in bending or flexure. These members include sheathing and decking, joists, beams and purlins. Additional design information is included for built-up beams, oblique purlins and cantilevered beams. While the tables in this chapter deal only with bending moment, shear resistance and stiffness, the designer must also be concerned with bearing of the bending members on their supports. Chapter 6 provides design information for bearing and compression loads perpendicular to the grain.

The Sheathing Selection Tables provide the recommended thicknesses of waferboard, oriented strandboard and plywood for use on floors and roofs for various joist spacings. These thicknesses are recommended by Part 9 of the *National Building Code of Canada (NBCC)*, the Canadian Plywood Association (CanPly) and the Structural Board Association (SBA).

Selection tables for joists, beams and purlins are arranged to provide moment and shear resistances, and bending stiffnesses ($E_S I$) for given species, grades and size combinations. The design tables presented in this chapter are based upon conditions that are typical for most building structures. Checklists are also given before each set of tables. The designer should review these checklists to be sure that the tabulated resistance is appropriate for the actual conditions of use.

### Serviceability

Adequate bending stiffness should be provided so that the maximum deflection ($\Delta_{max}$) of the member does not exceed the values given in Table 2.1. A serviceability table is provided in Section 2.3 to assist in determining the required bending stiffness for a deflection criterion of L/360. For conditions outside the scope of the serviceability table, the designer should calculate a required $E_S I$ and compare it with the tabulated $E_S I$ values. The tabulated $E_S I$ values are based on bending about the strong axis (depth) except as noted.

**Table 2.1**
**Deflection**
**Criteria**

|  |  | Loading | $\Delta_{max}$ | Limitation |
|---|---|---|---|---|
| Roofs and floors |  | Total load | L/180 | CSA O86 |
| Plastered or gypsum ceilings: | Glulam | Live load | L/360 | Suggested |
|  | Lumber | Total load | L/360[1] | Suggested |
| Roofs |  | Live load | L/240[2] | Suggested |
| Floors |  | Live load[3] | L/360 | Suggested |
| Wind columns |  | Wind load | L/180 | Suggested |

Notes:
1. Part 9 of the *NBCC* permits L/360 deflection limitation based on live load for all roofs and floors with plaster or gypsum board.
2. In Part 9, this is required for roofs with ceilings other than plaster or gypsum. Where no ceilings exist, L/180 based on live load is permitted.
3. For floor beams supporting floors with concrete topping, L/360 based on total specified load is recommended.
4. For curved glulam members, refer to Section 8.2 and clause 4.5.2 of CSA O86.

2

Bending Members

The serviceability of structures subject to ponding should be investigated, and guidance is given in CSA O86 Section 4.5.4.

Consideration should also be given to structures subject to vibration. Although CSA O86 provides no specific guidelines, the designer may refer to Appendix A-9.23.4.2 of the *NBCC*. This article of the *NBCC* contains span tables for joists in Part 9 buildings which incorporate vibration criteria (see Chapter 11). Additional guidance on floor vibration can be found in the Commentaries to Part 4 of the NBCC and the CSA 086 Commentary.

# 2.2 Sheathing & Decking

Structural sheathing is manufactured from a wide variety of wood-based materials. Plywood, oriented strandboard (OSB) and waferboard are the most commonly used panel products for structural roof, wall and floor sheathing. They are generally used on joists or light frame trusses spaced no more than 610 mm apart.

Plank decking may be used to span farther and carry greater loads than panel products. Decking is generally used in combination with heavy timber or glulam structures and often where fire performance must meet the heavy timber construction requirements of Part 3 of the *National Building Code of Canada.*

## Plywood Sheathing

Plywood panels are built-up from sheets of softwood veneer glued together with a waterproof resin adhesive. Typically the grain direction and thickness about the panel centreline is balanced. Douglas Fir Plywood (DFP) and Canadian Softwood Plywood (CSP) are the two most common softwood plywoods produced conforming respectively to CSA Standard O121, *Douglas Fir Plywood*, and O151, *Canadian Softwood Plywood.* Typical sizes of plywood are shown in Table 2.2.

Tongue and groove (T&G) plywood is a standard panel with a factory-machined tongue along one of the long edges and a groove along the other. During installation, T&G plywood provides effective load transfer between adjacent panels.

These metric panel thicknesses are similar to the imperial sizes, which have been established through experience and traditional usage. The length and width of panels are typically used with supporting members spaced at 305 mm (12"), 406 mm (16"), 488 mm (19.2") or 610 mm (24").

Table 2.2
**Typical plywood sizes[1], nominal thicknesses[2]**

| Sheathing and selected grades mm | Sanded grades mm |
|---|---|
| 7.5 | 6.0 |
| 9.5 | 8.0 |
| 11.0[3] | - |
| 12.5[3] | 11.0 |
| 15.5[4] | 14.0 |
| 18.5[4] | 17.0[4] |
| 20.5[4] | 19.0[4] |
| 22.5[4] | 21.0[4] |
| 25.5[4] | 24.0[4] |
| 28.5[4] | 27.0[4] |
| 31.5[4] | 30.0[4] |

Notes:
1. Nominal panel sizes of 1220 × 2440 mm (4' × 8') or cut to size.
   Larger panel sizes may be available on a limited special order basis.
2. All thicknesses are metric. Some, but not all, thicknesses approximate imperial dimensions, namely: 6 mm (1/4"), 9.5 mm (3/8"), 12.5 mm (1/2"), 15.5 mm (5/8"), 19 mm (3/4"), 22.5 mm (7/8"), 25.5 mm (1"), 28.5 mm (1-1/8"), and 31.5 mm (1-1/4").
3. Available as square edge (except 11.0 mm) or with EASY T&G Roof edge profile.
4. Available as square edge or with EASY T&G Floor edge profile.

**2**

**Bending Members**

## Oriented Strandboard (OSB) and Waferboard

Oriented strandboard (OSB) and waferboard are structural mat-formed panel products made of thin strands or wafers, sliced from small-diameter round wood logs or blocks, and bonded with exterior-type binder under heat and pressure.

OSB is manufactured with the surface layer strands aligned in the long panel direction, while the inner layers have random or cross alignment. Waferboard on the other hand has all the wafers randomly aligned throughout the panel.

OSB and waferboard panels are manufactured in both imperial and metric sizes, and are either square-edged or tongue-and-grooved on the long edges for panels 15 mm (19/32") or thicker. The sizes shown in Table 2.3 are most common.

The general product standard is CSA O437, *OSB and Waferboard.* The product standard contains three designations: O-1 and O-2 indicate alignment of the strands as in OSB; while R-1 indicates random alignment, and is less common.

Another standard that applies to OSB and waferboard, as well as to plywood, is a performance standard: CSA O325, *Construction Sheathing.* This standard sets performance ratings (Table 2.4) for specific end uses such as floor, roof and wall sheathing in light-frame construction. It is referenced in Part 9 of the *NBCC,* and provides an alternative way of specifying products for these applications without referencing product standards. In addition to the Part 9 reference, design values for construction sheathing OSB conforming to CSA O325 are listed in CSA O86 allowing engineering design of roof sheathing, wall sheathing and floor sheathing using CSA O325 rated OSB.

OSB can be certified specifically for engineered design applications, in accordance with CSA Standard O452, *Design Rated OSB* (Table 2.5). This standard contains certification and grade-marking requirements for three types of design-rated OSB panels:

- Type 1 (STANDARD):
  products consisting of three different rating grades (A, B or C), with design values listed in CSA O86.

- Type 2 (PLUS):
  products exceeding Type 1 rating grade levels by 10% or more (noted on grade mark).

- Type 3 (PROPRIETARY):
  products for which a certification organization certifies specified design capacities, different from STANDARD or PLUS capacities.

Designers should ensure the availability of design-rated OSB before specifying.

| Table 2.3 CSA O437 sizes for OSB and waferboard | Imperial thickness (in.) | Metric thicknesses for the following grades (mm) | | |
|---|---|---|---|---|
| | | O-2 | O-1 | R-1 |
| | 1/4 | 6.00 | 6.35 | 6.35 |
| | 5/16 | 7.50 | 7.90 | 7.90 |
| | 3/8 | 9.50 | 9.50 | 9.50 |
| | 7/16 | 11.0 | 11.1 | 11.1 |
| | 15/32 | 12.0 | | |
| | 1/2 | 12.5 | 12.7 | 12.7 |
| | 19/32 | 15.0 | | |
| | 5/8 | 15.5 | 15.9 | 15.9 |
| | 23/32 | 18.0 | | |
| | 3/4 | 18.5 | 19.0 | 19.0 |
| | 7/8 | 22.5 | | |
| | 1-1/8 | 28.5 | | |

Note:
Panel sizes are 4' × 8' (1220 × 2440 mm) or cut to size.
Larger sizes up to 8' × 24' (2440 × 7320 mm) are available on special order.

| Table 2.4 CSA O325 performance marks | | | Spacing in inches (mm) | | | | | |
|---|---|---|---|---|---|---|---|---|
| | Assumed end use | | 16 (400) | 20 (500) | 24 (600) | 32 (800) | 40 (1000) | 48 (1200) |
| | Subflooring | (1F) | 1F16 | 1F20 | 1F24 | 1F32 | – [3] | 1F48 |
| | Subflooring used with a panel-type underlay | (2F) | 2F16 | 2F20 | 2F24 | – [3] | – [3] | – [3] |
| | Roof sheathing used without edge support | (1R) | 1R16 | 1R20 | 1R24 | 1R32 | 1R40 | 1R48 |
| | Roof sheathing used with edge support | (2R) | 2R16 | 2R20 | 2R24 | 2R32 | 2R40 | 2R48 |
| | Wall sheathing | (W) | W16 | W20 | W24 | – [3] | – [3] | – [3] |

Notes:
1. Panel marks consist of an end use mark followed by the appropriate span mark.
2. Multiple panel marks may be used on panels qualified for more than one end use, e.g., 1R24/2F16 or 2R48/2F24/1F24.
3. Not covered by this Standard.

| Table 2.5 CSA O452 design-rated OSB | Product type | Design rating grade | Nominal thickness (mm) |
|---|---|---|---|
| | 1 (STANDARD) | A | 9.5 |
| | 2 (PLUS) | B | to |
| | | C | 28.5 |
| | 3 (PROPRIETARY) | – | unspecified |

Note:
Structural properties (strength and stiffness) are given for bending, axial (tension and compression) and shear (in-plane and through-the-thickness). Values are listed for forces applied parallel and perpendicular to major axis (or length) of the panel.

## Sheathing Selection Tables

The roof and floor Sheathing Selection Tables provide the recommended panel thickness for the most common support spacings. These thicknesses conform to NBCC requirements for Part 9 buildings when applicable, reflecting past experience. The tables have been extended to meet the same criteria. The plywood, OSB and waferboard thickness for floors with live loads of up to 4.8 kPa are recommended by the Canadian Plywood Association and the Structural Board Association, respectively.

# Sheathing Selection Tables

## Floors

F

2

▼

Bending Members

Minimum nominal required panel thickness or panel mark for specified live floor loads 2.4 kPa or less

| Support spacing mm | Plywood[4,5] CSA O121 DFP,or CSA O151 CSP,or CSA O153 Poplar[6] mm | OSB and waferboard[4,5] CSA O437 O-2 grade[6] mm | O-1,R-1 grades[6] mm | Construction sheathing CSA O325 panel mark |
|---|---|---|---|---|
| 400 | 15.5 | 15.5 | 15.9 | 1F16 |
| 500 | 15.5 | 15.5 | 15.9 | 1F20 |
| 600 | 18.5 | 18.5 | 19.0 | 1F24 |

Minimum nominal required panel thickness or panel mark

| Support spacing mm | Floor live load up to 4.8 kPa | | | Floor live load up to 4.8 kPa Specified Concentrated Live load 9 kN | | | |
|---|---|---|---|---|---|---|---|
| | Plywood CSA O121 DFP,or CSA O151 CSP mm | OSB CSA O452 Type 1 Rated grade C mm | CSA O325 panel mark | Plywood CSA O121 DFP mm | CSA O151 CSP mm | OSB CSA O452 Type 1 Rated grade C mm | CSA O325 panel mark |
| 400 | 15.5 | 15.5 | 1F16 | 15.5 | 15.5 | 18.5 | 1F24 |
| 500 | 15.5 | 18.5 | 1F20 | 18.5 | 20.5 | 22 | 1F32 |
| 600 | 20.5 | 22 | 1F32 | 22.5 | 25.5 | 28.5 | 1F48 |

Notes:
1. Edge support is required except where a separate panel-type underlay is applied to a subfloor. Edge support must consist of not less than 38 × 38 mm blocking securely nailed between framing members, or tongue and groove edge joint.
2. Install plywood or OSB (O grades) with strong axis at right angles to joists. End joints parallel to joists must be staggered.
3. Where panel-type underlay is installed over the sheathing, offset the underlay end joints at least 200 mm from the sheathing end joints.
4. Where the finished flooring consists of at least 19 mm matched wood strip flooring laid at right angles to the joists, sheathing thickness for joists spaced up to 600 mm may be:
   12.5 mm for plywood and O-2 grade OSB, and
   12.7 mm for O-1 grade OSB and R-1 grade waferboard.
5. Where a separate panel-type underlay or concrete topping is applied over the subfloor, sheathing thickness for joists spaced up to 400 mm may be:
   12.5 mm for plywood and O-2 grade OSB, and
   12.7 mm for O-1 grade OSB and R-1 grade waferboard.
   (except where ceramic tiles applied with adhesive are used for flooring).
6. Published design values do not exist for these products. Tabulated thicknesses are accepted under Part 9 of the NBCC. Check availability of CSA O437 Grades before specifying.

# Sheathing Selection Tables

## R  Roofs

Minimum nominal required panel thickness or panel mark for specified roof loads ≤ 2.0 kPa.

| | Edges unsupported | | | | Edges supported | | | |
|---|---|---|---|---|---|---|---|---|
| | Plywood | OSB and waferboard | | Construction sheathing | Plywood | OSB and waferboard | | Construction sheathing |
| Support spacing mm | CSA O121 DFP, or CSA O151 CSP, or CSA O153 Poplar[6] mm | CSA O437 O-2 grade[6] mm | O-1, R-1 grades[6] mm | CSA O325 panel mark | CSA O121 DFP, or CSA O151 CSP, or CSA O153 Poplar[6] mm | CSA O437 O-2 grade[6] mm | O-1, R-1 grades[6] mm | CSA O325 panel mark |
| 300 | 7.5 | 7.5 | 9.5 | 1R16 | 7.5 | 7.5 | 9.5 | 2R16 |
| 400 | 9.5 | 9.5 | 11.1 | 1R16 | 7.5 | 9.5[7] | 9.5 | 2R16 |
| 500 | 12.5 | 12.5 | 12.7 | 1R20 | 9.5 | 9.5 | 11.1 | 2R20 |
| 600 | 12.5 | 12.5 | 12.7 | 1R24 | 9.5 | 11[7] | 11.1 | 2R24 |

Minimum nominal required panel thickness or panel mark for specified roof loads ≤ 4.0 kPa.

| | Edges unsupported | | | Edges supported | | |
|---|---|---|---|---|---|---|
| | Plywood | OSB | | Plywood | OSB | |
| Support spacing mm | CSA O121 DFP, or CSA O151 CSP mm | CSA O452 Type 1 Rated grade C mm | CSA O325 panel mark | CSA O121 DFP, or CSA O151 CSP mm | CSA O452 Type 1 Rated grade C mm | CSA O325 panel mark |
| 300 | 7.5 | 9.5 | 1R20 | 7.5 | 9.5 | 1R20 |
| 400 | 9.5 | 9.5 | 2R24 | 9.5 | 9.5 | 2R24 |
| 500 | 12.5 | 12.5 | 1R24 | 12.5 | 11 | 1R24 |
| 600 | 12.5 | 15.5 | 2R40 | 12.5 | 15.5 | 2R40 |

Notes:
1. These recommendations include consideration of the 1.3 kN point load specified in Part 4 of the NBCC.
2. Install plywood or OSB (O grades) with strong axis at right angles to roof framing.
3. Install sheathing with at least a 2 mm gap between panel edges.
4. Where sheathing requires edge support, the support may consist of metal H-clips, a tongue and groove joint, or not less than 38 x 38 mm blocking securely nailed between framing members.
5. For a flat roof used as a walking deck, use the recommended thicknesses for floor sheathing.
6. Published design values do not exist for these products. Tabulated thicknesses are accepted under Part 9 of the NBCC. Check availability of CSA O437 Grades before specifying.
7. The NBCC allows use of 7.5 mm thickness for 9.5 mm, and 9.5 mm for 11 mm thickness in these cases. The tabular values are recommended for enhanced performance.

## Plank Decking

### General

Plank decking consists of lumber members kiln dried to an average moisture content of 15% (maximum 19%). The correct specification for lumber dried to a maximum of 19% is S-Dry (surfaced dry). Decking is normally produced in three thicknesses: 38, 64 and 89 mm. 38 mm (nominal) decking may be manufactured using 38 mm lumber resulting in slightly thinner decking. The 38 mm decking has a single tongue and groove while the thicker sizes have a double tongue and groove. The 64 and 89 mm decking also have 6 mm diameter holes at 760 mm spacing so that each piece may be nailed to the adjacent one with 8" No.3 gauge decking spikes. The standard sizes and profiles are shown below.

Figure 2.1
**Plank decking**

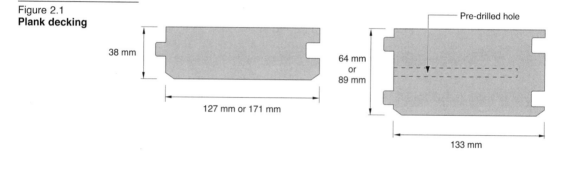

Decking is generally manufactured from the following species:

- Douglas fir (Douglas Fir-Larch combination)
- Pacific coast hemlock (Hem-Fir combination)
- Various species from the Spruce-Pine-Fir combination
- Western red cedar (Northern combination)

### Availability

Plank decking is available in two grades:

- Select grade (Sel)
- Commercial grade (Com)

Select grade has a higher quality appearance than Commercial grade and is also stronger and stiffer. A complete description of the characteristics of each grade is provided in Chapter 11.

Plank decking is most readily available in random lengths of 1.8 m to 6.1 m and longer. Decking may be ordered in specific lengths but designers should expect limited availability and extra costs. It is usual to specify that at least 90% of decking be 3.0 m and longer, and between 40 and 50% be 4.9 m and longer.

## Installation

Decking may be laid in any one of the following patterns:

### 1. Controlled random

This is the most convenient and economical pattern since random length material may be used. Controlled random decking must be laid in the following manner:

- The entire deck must extend over at least three spans.
- End joints are not permitted in the outer half of end spans.
- Where end joints occur in adjacent courses they must be staggered by 610 mm or more.
- Where end joints occur in the same general line they must be separated by at least two intervening courses.
- In floors and roofs, planks that do not span over one support must be flanked by courses resting on both supports of that span and must, in addition, be separated from the next unsupported plank by at least six courses, each of which extends over at least one support. This is only permitted for double tongue and groove planks more than 36 mm thick.
- In bridges, each plank or lamination must extend over at least one support.

This pattern is illustrated in the following figure:

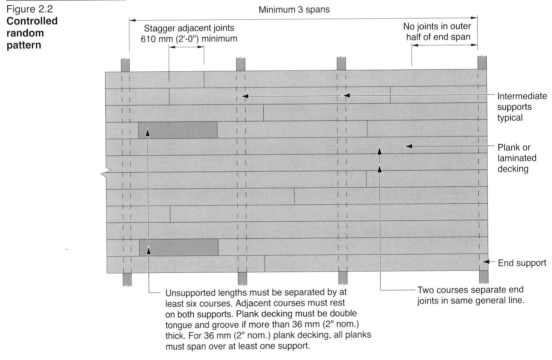

Figure 2.2
**Controlled random pattern**

Minimum 3 spans

Stagger adjacent joints 610 mm (2'-0") minimum

No joints in outer half of end span

Intermediate supports typical

Plank or laminated decking

End support

Unsupported lengths must be separated by at least six courses. Adjacent courses must rest on both supports. Plank decking must be double tongue and groove if more than 36 mm (2" nom.) thick. For 36 mm (2" nom.) plank decking, all planks must span over at least one support.

Two courses separate end joints in same general line.

Notes:
1. Random pattern is not permitted for bridges.
2. The other methods, Simple Span and Two Span Continous installation patterns, require that all butt joints occur over a support.

Alternative patterns require decking of specified lengths, which is more costly.

2. Simple span – all pieces rest on two supports

3. Two-span continuous – all pieces rest on three supports

Nails are used to fasten the deck to its supports. The following nailing schedule is recommended:

Figure 2.3
**Nailing
arrangement
for decking**

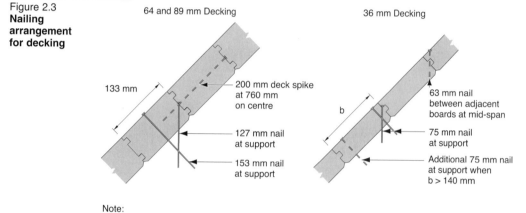

64 and 89 mm Decking

36 mm Decking

133 mm

200 mm deck spike
at 760 mm
on centre

127 mm nail
at support

153 mm nail
at support

b

63 mm nail
between adjacent
boards at mid-span

75 mm nail
at support

Additional 75 mm nail
at support when
b > 140 mm

Note:
1. Planks 140 mm or less in width shall be nailed with 2 nails to each support.
   Planks more than 140 mm in width shall be nailed with 3 nails to each support.

## Design

Decking must be designed so that the following criteria are satisfied:

1. Factored moment resistance $M_r$ ≥ maximum factored moment $M_f$

2. Maximum deflection under specified loads ≤ deflection criteria

Deflection usually governs the design unless the decking is heavily loaded and on a short span.
    For each grade and size of decking, the selection tables provide the maximum uniform factored load $w_{FR}$ and maximum uniform specified load $w_{\Delta R}$ that may be applied to a controlled random deck to ensure that the design criteria are met.
    Occasionally decking may have to be designed for concentrated loads or other non-uniform loading. In these cases refer to CSA O86 Clause 5.5.11.

**2**

Bending Members

## Modification Factors

The tabulated maximum uniform loads for plank decking are based upon the following formulae and modification factors. When using the tables, be certain the member conforms exactly to the modification factors used in the tables; if not, use the factors below and make the necessary adjustments to the tabulated values.

$$w_{FR} = \frac{8 \times 10^{-3} \; \phi \, F_b \, K_{Zb} \, d^2}{6 \, L^2} \quad (kPa)$$

$$w_{\Delta R} = \frac{34.6 \times 10^{-9} \; E_s \, d^3 \, K_\Delta \, K_{span}}{L^3} \quad (kPa)$$

where:

$w_{FR}$ = maximum factored load capacity (kPa)

$w_{\Delta R}$ = maximum specified load capacity based on deflection limitations (kPa)

$F_b$ = $f_b \, (K_D \, K_H \, K_{Sb} \, K_T)$ (MPa)

$f_b$ = specified strength in bending (MPa)

$\phi$ = 0.9

$d$ = thickness (mm)

$L$ = span (m)

$E_s$ = $E \, (K_{SE} \, K_T)$ (MPa)

$E$ = specified modulus of elasticity (MPa)

$K_D$ is a load duration factor. The tables are based on a standard term load ($K_D$ = 1.0), which includes the effects of dead loads plus live loads due to use and occupancy, and snow loads. For decking used in roof or floor structures intended to support permanent loads the tabulated $w_{FR}$ values must be multiplied by 0.65. For decking intended to support short term loads such as wind, the tabulated $w_{FR}$ values may be multiplied by 1.15.

$K_H$ is a system factor. Systems are defined in Section 2.3. The tabulated $w_{FR}$ values are based on a Case 1 system ($K_H$ = 1.1).

$K_S$ is a service condition factor. The tables are based on dry service conditions ($K_{Sb} = K_{SE}$ = 1.0). For wet service conditions, multiply the values by the following factors:

$K_{Sb}$ = 0.84 for $w_{FR}$

$K_{SE}$ = 0.94 for $w_{\Delta R}$

$K_T$ is a treatment factor. The tables are based on untreated decking ($K_T$ = 1.0). If the decking is impregnated with a fire retardant chemical, see the Commentary for further guidance.

# Checklist: **Plank Decking** ✔

To verify that the Decking Selection Tables are appropriate for the structure being designed, the following questions should be asked (the appropriate modification factor is given in brackets):

1. Is load duration "standard" ($K_D$)?

2. Is the service condition "dry" ($K_S$)?

3. Is the material free of incising and/or strength-reducing chemicals ($K_T$)?

4. Is the width of the decking 127 or 133 mm ($K_{Zb}$)?

5. Is L/240, based on live load, the applicable deflection limitation ($K_\Delta$)?

6. Is the decking laid in a controlled random pattern ($K_{span}$)?

7. Is the loading of a uniform nature?

If the answer to any of these questions is no, refer to the description of modification factors below and make the necessary adjustments to the tabulated values. Otherwise, the Decking Selection Tables may be used directly.

**2**

**Bending Members**

$K_{Zb}$ is a size factor in bending that is incorporated in the tables for a maximum plank width of 140 mm. If 178 × 38 mm deck is used multiply the $w_{FR}$ values by 0.86.

$K_\Delta$ is a deflection factor. The tables are based on a deflection limit of span/240 ($K_\Delta$ = 1.0) under specified live load. Decking may also be checked for a deflection limit for specified total load. For other deflection limits multiply the $w_{\Delta R}$ values by the following:

$$K_\Delta = 1.33 \text{ for span/180}$$
$$= 0.80 \text{ for span/300}$$
$$= 0.67 \text{ for span/360}$$

$K_{span}$ is a factor for deflection depending on the pattern in which the decking is laid. The tables are based on a controlled random pattern ($K_{span}$ = 1.0). For other patterns multiply the $w_{\Delta R}$ values by the following factors:

$$K_{span} = 0.77 \text{ for single span}$$
$$= 1.83 \text{ for two-span continuous}$$

## Example: Decking

Determine the plank decking thickness required for the following conditions:

- roof deck
- specified dead load = 1.5 kPa
- specified snow load for strength calculations = 2.2 kPa
- specified snow load for serviceability calculations = 2.0 kPa
- purlin spacing (deck span) = 1.6 m

- dry service condition
- untreated
- deflection limitations: L/240 based on live load
                          L/180 based on total load
- use controlled random pattern western red cedar (Northern species group)
- Select grade

**Calculation**

Factored loading $w_f = (1.25 \times 1.5) + (1.5 \times 2.2) = 5.18$ kPa

Specified live load $w_L = 2.0$ kPa

Total specified loading $w = 1.5 + 2.0 = 3.5$ kPa

From Decking Selection Tables select 38 mm thickness:

$w_{FR} = 9.92$ kPa $> 5.18$ kPa                                              *Acceptable*

$w_{\Delta R} = 2.96$ kPa $> 2.0$ kPa for L/240 deflection                    *Acceptable*

$w_{\Delta R} = 2.96 \times 1.33 = 3.94$ kPa $> 3.50$ kPa for L/180 deflection   *Acceptable*

**Use 38 mm thick western red cedar Select grade decking.**

# Decking Selection Tables

## Select Grade                                              Sel

**W_FR** Maximum factored uniform load $W_{FR}$ (kPa)

| Span m | D.Fir-L Thickness, mm 38* | 64 | 89 | Hem-Fir Thickness, mm 38* | 64 | 89 | S-P-F Thickness, mm 38* | 64 | 89 | Northern Thickness, mm 38* | 64 | 89 |
|---|---|---|---|---|---|---|---|---|---|---|---|---|
| 1.0 | 39.5 | | | 38.3 | | | 39.5 | | | 25.4 | | |
| 1.2 | 27.4 | | | 26.6 | | | 27.4 | | | 17.6 | | |
| 1.4 | 20.2 | | | 19.6 | | | 20.2 | | | 13.0 | | |
| 1.6 | 15.4 | | | 15.0 | | | 15.4 | | | 9.92 | 31.3 | |
| 1.8 | 12.2 | | | 11.8 | | | 12.2 | 38.5 | | 7.84 | 24.8 | |
| 2.0 | 9.88 | 31.2 | | 9.58 | 30.3 | | 9.88 | 31.2 | | 6.35 | 20.1 | |
| 2.2 | 8.16 | 25.8 | | 7.92 | 25.0 | | 8.16 | 25.8 | | 5.25 | 16.6 | |
| 2.4 | 6.86 | 21.7 | | 6.65 | 21.0 | | 6.86 | 21.7 | | 4.41 | 13.9 | 28.9 |
| 2.6 | 5.85 | 18.5 | | 5.67 | 17.9 | | 5.85 | 18.5 | 38.3 | | 11.9 | 24.6 |
| 2.8 | 5.04 | 15.9 | 33.0 | 4.89 | 15.4 | 32.0 | 5.04 | 15.9 | 33.0 | | 10.2 | 21.2 |
| 3.0 | 4.39 | 13.9 | 28.8 | | 13.5 | 27.9 | | 13.9 | 28.8 | | 8.92 | 18.5 |
| 3.2 | | 12.2 | 25.3 | | 11.8 | 24.5 | | 12.2 | 25.3 | | 7.84 | 16.2 |
| 3.4 | | 10.8 | 22.4 | | 10.5 | 21.7 | | 10.8 | 22.4 | | 6.94 | 14.4 |
| 3.6 | | 9.64 | 20.0 | | 9.34 | 19.4 | | 9.64 | 20.0 | | 6.19 | 12.8 |
| 3.8 | | 8.65 | 17.9 | | 8.39 | 17.4 | | 8.65 | 17.9 | | 5.56 | 11.5 |
| 4.0 | | 7.81 | 16.2 | | 7.57 | 15.7 | | | 16.2 | | | 10.4 |
| 4.2 | | | 14.7 | | | 14.2 | | | 14.7 | | | 9.42 |
| 4.4 | | | 13.4 | | | 13.0 | | | 13.4 | | | 8.59 |
| 4.6 | | | 12.2 | | | 11.9 | | | 12.2 | | | 7.86 |
| 4.8 | | | 11.2 | | | 10.9 | | | 11.2 | | | 7.22 |
| 5.0 | | | 10.4 | | | 10.0 | | | 10.4 | | | 6.65 |
| 5.2 | | | 9.57 | | | 9.28 | | | 9.57 | | | 6.15 |
| 5.4 | | | 8.87 | | | 8.61 | | | 8.87 | | | 5.70 |
| 5.6 | | | 8.25 | | | 8.00 | | | 8.25 | | | 5.30 |
| 5.8 | | | 7.69 | | | 7.46 | | | 7.69 | | | 4.94 |

**W_ΔR** Maximum specified uniform load for L/240 deflection $W_{\Delta R}$ (kPa)

| Span m | D.Fir-L Thickness, mm 38* | 64 | 89 | Hem-Fir Thickness, mm 38* | 64 | 89 | S-P-F Thickness, mm 38* | 64 | 89 | Northern Thickness, mm 38* | 64 | 89 |
|---|---|---|---|---|---|---|---|---|---|---|---|---|
| 1.0 | 20.2 | | | 19.4 | | | 17.0 | | | 12.1 | | |
| 1.2 | 11.7 | | | 11.2 | | | 9.81 | | | 7.01 | | |
| 1.4 | 7.35 | | | 7.06 | | | 6.18 | | | 4.41 | | |
| 1.6 | 4.93 | | | 4.73 | | | 4.14 | | | 2.96 | 16.6 | |
| 1.8 | 3.46 | | | 3.32 | | | 2.91 | 16.3 | | 2.08 | 11.7 | |
| 2.0 | 2.52 | 14.2 | | 2.42 | 13.6 | | 2.12 | 11.9 | | 1.51 | 8.50 | |
| 2.2 | 1.90 | 10.6 | | 1.82 | 10.2 | | 1.59 | 8.94 | | 1.14 | 6.39 | |
| 2.4 | 1.46 | 8.20 | | 1.40 | 7.87 | | 1.23 | 6.89 | | 0.88 | 4.92 | 13.2 |
| 2.6 | 1.15 | 6.45 | | 1.10 | 6.19 | | 0.96 | 5.42 | 14.6 | | 3.87 | 10.4 |
| 2.8 | 0.92 | 5.16 | 13.9 | 0.88 | 4.96 | 13.3 | 0.77 | 4.34 | 11.7 | | 3.10 | 8.33 |
| 3.0 | 0.75 | 4.20 | 11.3 | | 4.03 | 10.8 | | 3.53 | 9.49 | | 2.52 | 6.78 |
| 3.2 | | 3.46 | 9.30 | | 3.32 | 8.93 | | 2.91 | 7.82 | | 2.08 | 5.58 |
| 3.4 | | 2.88 | 7.76 | | 2.77 | 7.45 | | 2.42 | 6.52 | | 1.73 | 4.65 |
| 3.6 | | 2.43 | 6.54 | | 2.33 | 6.27 | | 2.04 | 5.49 | | 1.46 | 3.92 |
| 3.8 | | 2.07 | 5.56 | | 1.98 | 5.33 | | 1.74 | 4.67 | | 1.24 | 3.33 |
| 4.0 | | 1.77 | 4.76 | | 1.70 | 4.57 | | | 4.00 | | | 2.86 |
| 4.2 | | | 4.12 | | | 3.95 | | | 3.46 | | | 2.47 |
| 4.4 | | | 3.58 | | | 3.44 | | | 3.01 | | | 2.15 |
| 4.6 | | | 3.13 | | | 3.01 | | | 2.63 | | | 1.88 |
| 4.8 | | | 2.76 | | | 2.65 | | | 2.32 | | | 1.65 |
| 5.0 | | | 2.44 | | | 2.34 | | | 2.05 | | | 1.46 |
| 5.2 | | | 2.17 | | | 2.08 | | | 1.82 | | | 1.30 |
| 5.4 | | | 1.94 | | | 1.86 | | | 1.63 | | | 1.16 |
| 5.6 | | | 1.74 | | | 1.67 | | | 1.46 | | | 1.04 |
| 5.8 | | | 1.56 | | | 1.50 | | | 1.31 | | | 0.94 |

\* Thinner decking may result from remanufacturing. Loads are based on 36 mm thick decking and may be increased when the actual decking thickness is 38 mm.

2

Bending Members

# Decking Selection Tables

## Com Commercial Grade

### $W_{FR}$ Maximum factored uniform load $W_{FR}$ (kPa)

| Span m | D.Fir-L 38* | 64 | 89 | Hem-Fir 38* | 64 | 89 | S-P-F 38* | 64 | 89 | Northern 38* | 64 | 89 |
|---|---|---|---|---|---|---|---|---|---|---|---|---|
| 1.0 | 24.0 | | | 26.3 | | | 28.3 | | | 18.2 | | |
| 1.2 | 16.6 | | | 18.3 | | | 19.6 | | | 12.6 | | |
| 1.4 | 12.2 | | | 13.4 | | | 14.4 | | | 9.29 | | |
| 1.6 | 9.36 | | | 10.3 | | | 11.0 | | | 7.11 | 22.5 | |
| 1.8 | 7.39 | | | 8.13 | | | 8.72 | 27.6 | | 5.62 | 17.8 | |
| 2.0 | 5.99 | 18.9 | | 6.59 | 20.8 | | 7.07 | 22.3 | | 4.55 | 14.4 | |
| 2.2 | 4.95 | 15.6 | | 5.44 | 17.2 | | 5.84 | 18.5 | | 3.76 | 11.9 | |
| 2.4 | 4.16 | 13.1 | | 4.57 | 14.5 | | 4.91 | 15.5 | | 3.16 | 9.99 | 20.7 |
| 2.6 | 3.54 | 11.2 | | 3.90 | 12.3 | | 4.18 | 13.2 | 27.4 | | 8.51 | 17.6 |
| 2.8 | 3.05 | 9.65 | 20.0 | 3.36 | 10.6 | 22.0 | | 11.4 | 23.6 | | 7.34 | 15.2 |
| 3.0 | | 8.41 | 17.4 | | 9.25 | 19.2 | | 9.92 | 20.6 | | 6.39 | 13.2 |
| 3.2 | | 7.39 | 15.3 | | 8.13 | 16.8 | | 8.72 | 18.1 | | 5.62 | 11.6 |
| 3.4 | | 6.55 | 13.6 | | 7.20 | 14.9 | | 7.73 | 16.0 | | 4.98 | 10.3 |
| 3.6 | | 5.84 | 12.1 | | 6.42 | 13.3 | | 6.89 | 14.3 | | 4.44 | 9.20 |
| 3.8 | | 5.24 | 10.9 | | 5.77 | 11.9 | | 6.19 | 12.8 | | 3.98 | 8.25 |
| 4.0 | | 4.73 | 9.80 | | 5.20 | 10.8 | | 5.58 | 11.6 | | 3.60 | 7.45 |
| 4.2 | | | 8.89 | | | 9.78 | | | 10.5 | | | 6.76 |
| 4.4 | | | 8.10 | | | 8.91 | | | 9.56 | | | 6.16 |
| 4.6 | | | 7.41 | | | 8.15 | | | 8.75 | | | 5.63 |
| 4.8 | | | 6.81 | | | 7.49 | | | 8.03 | | | 5.17 |
| 5.0 | | | 6.27 | | | 6.90 | | | 7.40 | | | 4.77 |
| 5.2 | | | 5.80 | | | 6.38 | | | 6.84 | | | 4.41 |
| 5.4 | | | 5.38 | | | 5.92 | | | 6.35 | | | 4.09 |
| 5.6 | | | 5.00 | | | 5.50 | | | 5.90 | | | 3.80 |
| 5.8 | | | 4.66 | | | 5.13 | | | 5.50 | | | 3.54 |

### $W_{\Delta R}$ Maximum specified uniform load for L/240 deflection $W_{\Delta R}$ (kPa)

| Span m | D.Fir-L 38* | 64 | 89 | Hem-Fir 38* | 64 | 89 | S-P-F 38* | 64 | 89 | Northern 38* | 64 | 89 |
|---|---|---|---|---|---|---|---|---|---|---|---|---|
| 1.0 | 17.8 | | | 17.8 | | | 15.3 | | | 11.3 | | |
| 1.2 | 10.3 | | | 10.3 | | | 8.87 | | | 6.54 | | |
| 1.4 | 6.47 | | | 6.47 | | | 5.59 | | | 4.12 | | |
| 1.6 | 4.34 | | | 4.34 | | | 3.74 | | | 2.76 | 15.5 | |
| 1.8 | 3.04 | | | 3.04 | | | 2.63 | 14.8 | | 1.94 | 10.9 | |
| 2.0 | 2.22 | 12.5 | | 2.22 | 12.5 | | 1.92 | 10.8 | | 1.41 | 7.94 | |
| 2.2 | 1.67 | 9.37 | | 1.67 | 9.37 | | 1.44 | 8.09 | | 1.06 | 5.96 | |
| 2.4 | 1.28 | 7.22 | | 1.28 | 7.22 | | 1.11 | 6.23 | | 0.82 | 4.59 | 12.4 |
| 2.6 | 1.01 | 5.68 | | 1.01 | 5.68 | | 0.87 | 4.90 | 13.2 | | 3.61 | 9.71 |
| 2.8 | 0.81 | 4.55 | 12.2 | 0.81 | 4.55 | 12.2 | | 3.93 | 10.6 | | 2.89 | 7.78 |
| 3.0 | | 3.70 | 9.94 | | 3.70 | 9.94 | | 3.19 | 8.58 | | 2.35 | 6.32 |
| 3.2 | | 3.04 | 8.19 | | 3.04 | 8.19 | | 2.63 | 7.07 | | 1.94 | 5.21 |
| 3.4 | | 2.54 | 6.83 | | 2.54 | 6.83 | | 2.19 | 5.90 | | 1.62 | 4.34 |
| 3.6 | | 2.14 | 5.75 | | 2.14 | 5.75 | | 1.85 | 4.97 | | 1.36 | 3.66 |
| 3.8 | | 1.82 | 4.89 | | 1.82 | 4.89 | | 1.57 | 4.22 | | 1.16 | 3.11 |
| 4.0 | | 1.56 | 4.19 | | 1.56 | 4.19 | | 1.35 | 3.62 | | 0.99 | 2.67 |
| 4.2 | | | 3.62 | | | 3.62 | | | 3.13 | | | 2.30 |
| 4.4 | | | 3.15 | | | 3.15 | | | 2.72 | | | 2.00 |
| 4.6 | | | 2.76 | | | 2.76 | | | 2.38 | | | 1.75 |
| 4.8 | | | 2.43 | | | 2.43 | | | 2.10 | | | 1.54 |
| 5.0 | | | 2.15 | | | 2.15 | | | 1.85 | | | 1.37 |
| 5.2 | | | 1.91 | | | 1.91 | | | 1.65 | | | 1.21 |
| 5.4 | | | 1.70 | | | 1.70 | | | 1.47 | | | 1.08 |
| 5.6 | | | 1.53 | | | 1.53 | | | 1.32 | | | 0.97 |
| 5.8 | | | 1.38 | | | 1.38 | | | 1.19 | | | 0.88 |

* Thinner decking may result from remanufacturing. Loads are based on 36 mm thick decking and may be increased when the actual decking thickness is 38 mm.

# 2.3　　Lumber Joists

### General

Lumber products are manufactured in accordance with CSA Standard O141, *Softwood Lumber.* The permitted characteristics of structural dimension lumber grades contained in the National Lumber Grades Authority *Standard Grading Rules for Canadian Lumber* are uniform throughout Canada and the United States.

Sawn lumber used as joists ranges in common thicknesses from 38 to 89 mm and in depths from 89 to 286 mm. They are commonly used for spans up to approximately 7 m. The selection tables in this section provide bending moment and shear resistances along with stiffnesses for a range of joist sizes and grades. Although 38 × 89 mm members are not classified as joists, they are frequently used in bending applications and are included with these tables.

### Availability

The selection tables for joists include three thicknesses (38, 64 and 89 mm), three visual grade categories (Select Structural, No.1 and No.2 grade) and several Machine Stress-Rated (MSR) grades.

In the 38 mm thickness, the most readily obtainable material is No.1 or No.2 grade. S-P-F, Hem-Fir and D.Fir-L are most likely to be stocked by lumber yards, but other species in the Northern species combination may also be on hand. Some MSR grades are also readily available in widths up to 184 mm; wider material may not be available and suppliers tend to carry a limited range of grades. Joists in 38 mm thickness can usually be obtained kiln-dried (specify S-Dry) to a moisture content of 19% or less.

In the 64 and 89 mm thicknesses, choice of species and grade is more limited. These thicknesses are generally surfaced in the green condition (S-Grn) and are not obtainable as MSR lumber.

### Systems

In the Joist Selection Tables, resistances are given for single members, Case 2 systems and (in the footnote) Case 1 systems.

#### Case 1 System
Case 1 systems are composed of three or more essentially parallel members spaced no more than 610 mm apart and arranged so that they mutually support the load. However, Case 1 systems lack the sheathing and fastening requirements to qualify as Case 2 systems; or they may include a more complex structural component such as a wood truss.

#### Case 2 System
Case 2 systems are intended to represent most floors, roofs and walls where three or more essentially parallel lumber joists, rafters or studs are spaced at not more than 610 mm and are arranged to mutually support the applied load. In addition, the lumber members must be covered with minimum 9.5 mm

panel sheathing, or 17 mm lumber sheathing that is overlaid with panel sheathing or wood finish flooring. In all cases the sheathing must be fastened to the joists to provide a minimum stiffness equivalent to that provided by 2" common nails at 150 mm centres at the edges of sheathing panels and 300 mm centres elsewhere.

## Design

Sawn lumber joists must be designed so that the following criteria are satisfied:

1. Factored moment resistance $M_r \geq$ maximum factored moment $M_f$.

2. Factored shear resistance $V_r \geq$ maximum factored shear force $V_f$
   In the calculation of maximum shear force, the loads within a distance from the support equal to the depth of the member may be neglected.

3. Factored notch shear resistance for members with end notches on the tension side at supports $F_r \geq$ maximum factored reaction force $Q_f$.

4. Factored bearing resistance $Q_r \geq$ maximum factored reaction $Q_f$
   (refer to Chapter 6).

5. Maximum deflection under specified loads $\leq$ deflection criteria
   (actual $E_s I \geq$ required $E_s I$).

The Joist Selection Tables provide $M_r$, $V_r$ and $E_s I$ values. In addition, the Serviceability Table provides the required $E_s I$ value for uniform loading and a maximum deflection of L/360.
   Floor joists in Part 9 buildings should be designed using the tables in Appendix A-9.23.4.1 of the *NBCC* since many spans are limited by vibration. Further information on the *NBCC* vibration criterion is given in Chapter 11 and the Commentary.

# Checklist: **Joists** ✔

To verify that the tabulated resistances and $E_s I$ values are appropriate for the structure being designed, the following questions should be asked (the appropriate modification factor is given in brackets):

1. Is load duration "standard" $(K_D)$?

2. Is the service condition "dry" $(K_S)$?

3. Is the material free of incising and/or strength reducing chemicals $(K_T)$?

4. Are the joists free of notches $(K_N)$?

5. Does the construction provide lateral stability to the joists $(K_L)$?

If the answer to any of these questions is no, refer to the description of modification factors below and make the necessary adjustments to tabulated resistances and $E_s I$ values. Otherwise, the Joist Selection Tables may be used directly.

## Modification Factors

The tabulated resistances for joists are based upon the following formulae and modification factors. When using the tables, be certain that the member conforms exactly to the modification factors used in the tables; if not, use the factors below and make the necessary adjustments to the tabulated values.

$$M_r = \phi \, F_b \, S \, K_{Zb} \, K_L \quad (\text{N} \cdot \text{mm})$$

$$V_r = \phi \, F_v \, \frac{2 \, A}{3} \, K_{Zv} \quad (\text{N})$$

$$E_s I = E \, (K_{SE} \, K_T) \, I \quad (\text{N} \cdot \text{mm}^2)$$

$$F_r = \phi \, F_f \, A \, K_N \quad (\text{N}) \quad (\text{for joists with notches on the tension side at supports})$$

where:

$$\phi = 0.9$$
$$F_b = f_b \, (K_D \, K_H \, K_{Sb} \, K_T) \quad (\text{MPa})$$
$$f_b = \text{specified bending strength (MPa)}$$
$$S = \text{section modulus (mm}^3)$$
$$F_v = f_v \, (K_D \, K_H \, K_{Sv} \, K_T) \quad (\text{MPa})$$
$$f_v = \text{specified shear strength (MPa)}$$
$$A = \text{gross cross-section area (mm}^2)$$
$$E = \text{specified modulus of elasticity (MPa)}$$
$$I = \text{moment of inertia (mm}^4)$$

and for joists with notches on the tension side at supports:

$$F_f = f_f (K_D K_H K_{Sf} K_T) \text{ (MPa)}$$

$f_f$ = specified notch shear force resistance, 0.5 MPa for all sawn members

$K_D$ is a load duration factor. The tabulated resistances are based on a "standard" term load, which includes the effects of dead loads plus live loads due to use and occupancy, and snow loads. ($K_D$ = 1.0). For structures intended to support permanent loads the $M_r$ and $V_r$ values must be multiplied by 0.65. For joists intended to support short term loads such as wind and earthquakes, $M_r$ and $V_r$ may be multiplied by 1.15.

$K_H$ is a system factor. The factor is incorporated in the tables as noted.

$K_S$ is a service condition factor. The tabulated values (and $E_S I$ values) are based on dry service ($K_S$ = 1.0). For wet service conditions, multiply the tabulated values by the following factors:

$K_{Sb}$ = 0.84 for $M_r$

$K_{Sv}$ = 0.96 for $V_r$

$K_{Sf}$ = 0.70 for $F_r$

$K_{SE}$ = 0.94 for $E_S I$

$K_T$ is a treatment factor. The tabulated resistances are based on joists that are either untreated or treated with a non-strength-reducing chemical ($K_T$ = 1.0). Most wood preservatives do not reduce strength unless the lumber has been incised. However, most fire retardants will reduce strength. If the material is treated with a fire retardant or if it is incised prior to preservative treatment, multiply the tabulated values by the following factors:

Table 2.6
**Treatment factor $K_T$**

| Treatment type | $K_T$ for $M_r$ and $V_r$ | | $K_T$ for $E_S I$ | |
| --- | --- | --- | --- | --- |
| | Dry service | Wet service | Dry service | Wet service |
| Preservative treated, incised lumber | 0.75 | 0.85 | 0.90 | 0.95 |
| Fire-retardant treated lumber | refer to Commentary | | | |

$K_Z$ is a size factor incorporated in the tables for given material dimensions.

$K_N$ is a notch factor for notches located on the tension side of the member at a support:

$$K_N = \left[ 0.006\, d \left[ 1.6 \left[ \frac{1}{\alpha} - 1 \right] + \eta^2 \left[ \frac{1}{\alpha^3} - 1 \right] \right] \right]^{-0.5}$$

where:

d   = depth of joist (mm)

$d_n$  = depth of notch (mm), must not exceed 0.25d

$\alpha$  = 1 - $(d_n/d)$

$\eta$  = e/d

e   = length of notch (mm), from centre of nearest support to reentrant corner of notch. Length of support may be taken as the minimum required bearing length.

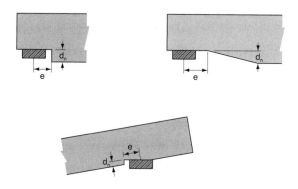

Note: Where a member is notched, the tabulated shear resistance values, $V_r$, must be adjusted by $A_n/A$ where $A_n$ is the net cross-sectional area at the notch and A is the gross cross-sectional area.

$K_L$ is a lateral stability factor. The tables are based on joists that are restrained against lateral displacement and rotation at their ends, the compressive edges are held in line by the sheathing, and bridging is provided at intervals not exceeding 8 times the member depth ($K_L$ = 1.0). For depth to width ratios of 6.5:1 or less, the bridging may be omitted. If the joists lack this restraint, refer to CSA O86 (Clauses 5.5.4.2 and 6.5.6.4) for the appropriate adjustment factor.

## Example 1: Joists

Design single span floor joists for the following conditions:

- joist spacing = 400 mm
- joist span = 3.0 m
- specified dead load = 1.5 kPa (includes partitions)
- specified live load = 2.4 kPa (commercial use and occupancy)
- standard load duration
- dry service condition
- untreated
- fully laterally supported by subfloor
- Case 2 system

Use S-P-F No.1/No.2 sawn lumber.

## Calculation

Total factored load = (1.25 × 1.5) + (1.5 × 2.4) = 5.48 kPa
Total specified load = 1.5 + 2.4 = 3.90 kPa

$$w_f = 5.48 \times 0.40 = 2.19 \text{ kN/m}$$

$$w = 3.90 \times 0.40 = 1.56 \text{ kN/m}$$

$$w_L = 2.40 \times 0.40 = 0.96 \text{ kN/m}$$

$$M_f = \frac{w_f L^2}{8} = \frac{2.19 \times 3.0^2}{8} = 2.46 \text{ kN} \Sigma \text{m}$$

$$V_f = \frac{w_f L}{2} = \frac{2.19 \times 3.0}{2} = 3.29 \text{ kN}$$

Calculate a required $E_s I$ for the specified live load or select the required $E_s I$ from the Serviceability Table.

$$E_s I_{REQ'D} = 122 \times 10^9 \text{ N} \cdot \text{mm}^2 \text{ for L/360 deflection based on live load } (w_L)$$

From Joist Selection Tables select 38 × 184 mm:

| | | |
|---|---|---|
| $M_r$ = 3.83 > 2.46 kN·m | | *Acceptable* |
| $V_r$ = 10.6 > 3.29 kN | | *Acceptable* |
| $E_s I$ = 187 × 10⁹ > 122 × 10⁹ N·mm² | | *Acceptable* |

Note: Verify acceptable bearing capacity as per Chapter 6

**Use 38 × 184 mm No.1/No.2 S-P-F sawn lumber.**

### Example 2: Joists notched on tension side at supports

Verify that the Hem-Fir No.1/No.2 38 × 286 mm floor joists (see drawing) notched at the supports are adequate for the following conditions :

- joist spacing = 600 mm
- joist span = 4.0 m
- specified dead load = 1.2 kPa
- specified live load = 2.4 kPa
- standard load duration
- dry service conditions
- untreated
- fully laterally supported by subfloor
- Case 2 system

### Calculation

Total factored load = (1.25 × 1.20) + (1.5 × 2.40) = 5.10 kPa
Total specified load = 1.20 + 2.40 = 3.60 kPa

$$w_f = 5.10 \times 0.6 = 3.06 \text{ kN/m}$$

$$w = 3.60 \times 0.6 = 2.16 \text{ kN/m}$$

$$w_L = 2.40 \times 0.6 = 1.44 \text{ kN/m}$$

$$M_f = \frac{w_f L^2}{8} = \frac{3.06 \times 4.0^2}{8} = 6.12 \text{ kN} \cdot \text{m}$$

$$V_f = \frac{w_f L}{2} = \frac{3.06 \times 4.0}{2} = 6.12 \text{ kN}$$

$$A_n = 9424 \text{ mm}^2$$

$$A = 10870 \text{ mm}^2$$

$$A_n/A = 0.87$$

Note: In this example, the maximum factored reaction force $Q_f$ is equal to $V_f$.

From the Serviceability Table:

$$E_S I_{REQ'D} = 432 \times 10^9 \text{ N} \cdot \text{mm}^2 \text{ for } L/360 \text{ deflection based on live load } (w_L)$$

From Joist Selection Tables:

$M_r = 7.18 > 6.12$ kN•m                              *Acceptable*
$V_r = 14.6 \times 0.87 = 12.70 > 6.12$ kN            *Acceptable*
$E_S I = 815 \times 10^9 > 432 \times 10^9$ N•mm²      *Acceptable*

The factored notch shear force resistance at the support:

$$F_r = \phi\, F_f\, A\, K_N$$

$$\phi = 0.9$$

$$F_f = 0.5 \times 1.4 = 0.7 \text{ MPa}$$

$$A = 38 \times 286 = 10868 \text{ mm}^2$$

$$K_N = \left[0.006\, d\left[1.6\left[\frac{1}{\alpha}-1\right]+\eta^2\left[\frac{1}{\alpha^3}-1\right]\right]\right]^{-0.5}$$

$$\alpha = 1-\frac{d_n}{d} = 1-\frac{38}{286} = 0.87$$

$$\eta = \frac{e}{d} = \frac{70}{286} = 0.24$$

$$K_N = \left[0.006 \times 286\left[1.6\left[\frac{1}{0.87}-1\right]+0.24^2\left[\frac{1}{0.87^3}-1\right]\right]\right]^{-0.5} = 1.45$$

Note: As an alternative, $K_N$ may also be calculated using Table 5.5.5.4 of CSA O86.

Therefore:

$$F_r = 0.9 \times 0.7 \times 10868 \times 1.45$$
$$= 9.93 \text{ kN} > Q_f = 6.12 \text{ kN} \qquad \textit{Acceptable}$$

Note : Also verify acceptable bearing capacity as per Chapter 6.

# Joist Selection Tables

## Sawn Lumber

**38** mm

| | | | Single member | | System Case 2 | | $E_sI$ |
|---|---|---|---|---|---|---|---|
| | Species | Size (b × d) mm | $M_r$ kN·m | $V_r$ kN | $M_r$ kN·m | $V_r$ kN | ×10⁹ N·mm² |
| Select Structural | D.Fir-L | 38 × 89 | 1.27 | 6.55 | 1.77 | 9.18 | 27.9 |
| | | 38 × 114 | 1.83 | 7.41 | 2.57 | 10.4 | 58.6 |
| | | 38 × 140 | 2.58 | 8.49 | 3.61 | 11.9 | 109 |
| | | 38 × 184 | 3.82 | 9.57 | 5.35 | 13.4 | 247 |
| | | 38 × 235 | 5.71 | 11.2 | 8.00 | 15.7 | 514 |
| | | 38 × 286 | 7.69 | 12.4 | 10.8 | 17.3 | 926 |
| | Hem-Fir | 38 × 89 | 1.23 | 5.52 | 1.72 | 7.73 | 26.8 |
| | | 38 × 114 | 1.78 | 6.24 | 2.49 | 8.73 | 56.3 |
| | | 38 × 140 | 2.50 | 7.15 | 3.50 | 10.0 | 104 |
| | | 38 × 184 | 3.71 | 8.05 | 5.19 | 11.3 | 237 |
| | | 38 × 235 | 5.54 | 9.43 | 7.76 | 13.2 | 493 |
| | | 38 × 286 | 7.46 | 10.4 | 10.4 | 14.6 | 889 |
| | S-P-F | 38 × 89 | 1.27 | 5.17 | 1.77 | 7.24 | 23.4 |
| | | 38 × 114 | 1.83 | 5.85 | 2.57 | 8.19 | 49.3 |
| | | 38 × 140 | 2.58 | 6.70 | 3.61 | 9.38 | 91.2 |
| | | 38 × 184 | 3.82 | 7.55 | 5.35 | 10.6 | 207 |
| | | 38 × 235 | 5.71 | 8.84 | 8.00 | 12.4 | 432 |
| | | 38 × 286 | 7.69 | 9.78 | 10.8 | 13.7 | 778 |
| | Northern | 38 × 89 | 0.814 | 4.48 | 1.14 | 6.28 | 16.7 |
| | | 38 × 114 | 1.18 | 5.07 | 1.65 | 7.10 | 35.2 |
| | | 38 × 140 | 1.66 | 5.81 | 2.32 | 8.13 | 65.2 |
| | | 38 × 184 | 2.45 | 6.54 | 3.44 | 9.16 | 148 |
| | | 38 × 235 | 3.67 | 7.66 | 5.14 | 10.7 | 308 |
| | | 38 × 286 | 4.94 | 8.48 | 6.92 | 11.9 | 556 |
| No.1/No.2 | D.Fir-L | 38 × 89 | 0.768 | 6.55 | 1.07 | 9.18 | 24.6 |
| | | 38 × 114 | 1.11 | 7.41 | 1.56 | 10.4 | 51.6 |
| | | 38 × 140 | 1.56 | 8.49 | 2.19 | 11.9 | 95.6 |
| | | 38 × 184 | 2.32 | 9.57 | 3.24 | 13.4 | 217 |
| | | 38 × 235 | 3.46 | 11.2 | 4.85 | 15.7 | 452 |
| | | 38 × 286 | 4.66 | 12.4 | 6.53 | 17.3 | 815 |
| | Hem-Fir | 38 × 89 | 0.844 | 5.52 | 1.18 | 7.73 | 24.6 |
| | | 38 × 114 | 1.22 | 6.24 | 1.71 | 8.73 | 51.6 |
| | | 38 × 140 | 1.72 | 7.15 | 2.41 | 10.0 | 95.6 |
| | | 38 × 184 | 2.55 | 8.05 | 3.57 | 11.3 | 217 |
| | | 38 × 235 | 3.81 | 9.43 | 5.33 | 13.2 | 452 |
| | | 38 × 286 | 5.13 | 10.4 | 7.18 | 14.6 | 815 |
| | S-P-F | 38 × 89 | 0.906 | 5.17 | 1.27 | 7.24 | 21.2 |
| | | 38 × 114 | 1.31 | 5.85 | 1.84 | 8.19 | 44.6 |
| | | 38 × 140 | 1.85 | 6.70 | 2.58 | 9.38 | 82.5 |
| | | 38 × 184 | 2.73 | 7.55 | 3.83 | 10.6 | 187 |
| | | 38 × 235 | 4.09 | 8.84 | 5.72 | 12.4 | 390 |
| | | 38 × 286 | 5.50 | 9.78 | 7.70 | 13.7 | 704 |
| | Northern | 38 × 89 | 0.583 | 4.48 | 0.817 | 6.28 | 15.6 |
| | | 38 × 114 | 0.844 | 5.07 | 1.18 | 7.10 | 32.8 |
| | | 38 × 140 | 1.19 | 5.81 | 1.66 | 8.13 | 60.8 |
| | | 38 × 184 | 1.76 | 6.54 | 2.46 | 9.16 | 138 |
| | | 38 × 235 | 2.63 | 7.66 | 3.68 | 10.7 | 288 |
| | | 38 × 286 | 3.54 | 8.48 | 4.96 | 11.9 | 519 |

Note:
For Case 1 System multiply single member $M_r$ and $V_r$ values by 1.10.

# Joist Selection Tables

**64 mm**

## Sawn Lumber

| | Species | Size (b × d) mm | Single member $M_r$ kN•m | Single member $V_r$ kN | System Case 2 $M_r$ kN•m | System Case 2 $V_r$ kN | $E_S I$ ×10⁹ N•mm² |
|---|---|---|---|---|---|---|---|
| Select Structural | D.Fir-L | 64 × 89 | 2.13 | 11.0 | 2.99 | 15.5 | 47.0 |
| | | 64 × 114 | 3.09 | 12.5 | 4.32 | 17.5 | 98.8 |
| | | 64 × 140 | 4.35 | 14.3 | 6.09 | 20.0 | 183 |
| | | 64 × 184 | 6.44 | 16.1 | 9.01 | 22.6 | 415 |
| | | 64 × 235 | 9.62 | 18.9 | 13.5 | 26.4 | 865 |
| | | 64 × 286 | 13.0 | 20.9 | 18.1 | 29.2 | 1560 |
| | Hem-Fir | 64 × 89 | 2.07 | 9.30 | 2.90 | 13.0 | 45.1 |
| | | 64 × 114 | 2.99 | 10.5 | 4.19 | 14.7 | 94.8 |
| | | 64 × 140 | 4.21 | 12.0 | 5.90 | 16.9 | 176 |
| | | 64 × 184 | 6.24 | 13.6 | 8.74 | 19.0 | 399 |
| | | 64 × 235 | 9.33 | 15.9 | 13.1 | 22.2 | 831 |
| | | 64 × 286 | 12.6 | 17.6 | 17.6 | 24.6 | 1500 |
| | S-P-F | 64 × 89 | 2.13 | 8.71 | 2.99 | 12.2 | 39.5 |
| | | 64 × 114 | 3.09 | 9.85 | 4.32 | 13.8 | 83.0 |
| | | 64 × 140 | 4.35 | 11.3 | 6.09 | 15.8 | 154 |
| | | 64 × 184 | 6.44 | 12.7 | 9.01 | 17.8 | 349 |
| | | 64 × 235 | 9.62 | 14.9 | 13.5 | 20.8 | 727 |
| | | 64 × 286 | 13.0 | 16.5 | 18.1 | 23.1 | 1310 |
| | Northern | 64 × 89 | 1.37 | 7.55 | 1.92 | 10.6 | 28.2 |
| | | 64 × 114 | 1.98 | 8.54 | 2.78 | 12.0 | 59.3 |
| | | 64 × 140 | 2.79 | 9.78 | 3.91 | 13.7 | 110 |
| | | 64 × 184 | 4.13 | 11.0 | 5.79 | 15.4 | 249 |
| | | 64 × 235 | 6.18 | 12.9 | 8.65 | 18.1 | 519 |
| | | 64 × 286 | 8.32 | 14.3 | 11.7 | 20.0 | 936 |
| No.1/No.2 | D.Fir-L | 64 × 89 | 1.29 | 11.0 | 1.81 | 15.5 | 41.4 |
| | | 64 × 114 | 1.87 | 12.5 | 2.62 | 17.5 | 86.9 |
| | | 64 × 140 | 2.63 | 14.3 | 3.69 | 20.0 | 161 |
| | | 64 × 184 | 3.90 | 16.1 | 5.46 | 22.6 | 365 |
| | | 64 × 235 | 5.83 | 18.9 | 8.16 | 26.4 | 761 |
| | | 64 × 286 | 7.85 | 20.9 | 11.0 | 29.2 | 1370 |
| | Hem-Fir | 64 × 89 | 1.42 | 9.30 | 1.99 | 13.0 | 41.4 |
| | | 64 × 114 | 2.06 | 10.5 | 2.88 | 14.7 | 86.9 |
| | | 64 × 140 | 2.90 | 12.0 | 4.06 | 16.9 | 161 |
| | | 64 × 184 | 4.29 | 13.6 | 6.01 | 19.0 | 365 |
| | | 64 × 235 | 6.41 | 15.9 | 8.98 | 22.2 | 761 |
| | | 64 × 286 | 8.64 | 17.6 | 12.1 | 24.6 | 1370 |
| | S-P-F | 64 × 89 | 1.53 | 8.71 | 2.14 | 12.2 | 35.7 |
| | | 64 × 114 | 2.21 | 9.85 | 3.09 | 13.8 | 75.1 |
| | | 64 × 140 | 3.11 | 11.3 | 4.35 | 15.8 | 139 |
| | | 64 × 184 | 4.60 | 12.7 | 6.44 | 17.8 | 316 |
| | | 64 × 235 | 6.88 | 14.9 | 9.63 | 20.8 | 658 |
| | | 64 × 286 | 9.27 | 16.5 | 13.0 | 23.1 | 1190 |
| | Northern | 64 × 89 | 0.980 | 7.55 | 1.30 | 10.6 | 26.3 |
| | | 64 × 114 | 1.42 | 8.54 | 1.99 | 12.0 | 55.3 |
| | | 64 × 140 | 2.00 | 9.78 | 2.80 | 13.7 | 102 |
| | | 64 × 184 | 2.96 | 11.0 | 4.15 | 15.4 | 233 |
| | | 64 × 235 | 4.43 | 12.9 | 6.20 | 18.1 | 485 |
| | | 64 × 286 | 5.97 | 14.3 | 8.35 | 20.0 | 873 |

Note:
For Case 1 System multiply single member $M_r$ and $V_r$ values by 1.10.

# Joist Selection Tables

## Sawn Lumber

**89** mm

| Species | Size (b × d) mm | Single member $M_r$ kN·m | $V_r$ kN | System Case 2 $M_r$ kN·m | $V_r$ kN | $E_S I$ ×10⁹ N·mm² |
|---|---|---|---|---|---|---|
| **Select Structural** | | | | | | |
| D.Fir-L | 89 × 89 | 2.97 | 15.4 | 4.15 | 21.5 | 65.4 |
| | 89 × 114 | 4.58 | 18.5 | 6.41 | 25.9 | 137 |
| | 89 × 140 | 6.48 | 21.3 | 9.07 | 29.8 | 254 |
| | 89 × 184 | 9.69 | 24.3 | 13.6 | 34.0 | 578 |
| | 89 × 235 | 14.6 | 28.6 | 20.4 | 40.1 | 1200 |
| | 89 × 286 | 19.8 | 31.9 | 27.7 | 44.7 | 2170 |
| Hem-Fir | 89 × 89 | 2.88 | 12.9 | 4.03 | 18.1 | 62.7 |
| | 89 × 114 | 4.44 | 15.6 | 6.22 | 21.8 | 132 |
| | 89 × 140 | 6.28 | 17.9 | 8.79 | 25.1 | 244 |
| | 89 × 184 | 9.40 | 20.4 | 13.2 | 28.6 | 554 |
| | 89 × 235 | 14.2 | 24.1 | 19.8 | 33.7 | 1160 |
| | 89 × 286 | 19.2 | 26.9 | 26.9 | 37.6 | 2080 |
| S-P-F | 89 × 89 | 2.97 | 12.1 | 4.15 | 17.0 | 54.9 |
| | 89 × 114 | 4.58 | 14.6 | 6.41 | 20.5 | 115 |
| | 89 × 140 | 6.48 | 16.8 | 9.07 | 23.5 | 214 |
| | 89 × 184 | 9.69 | 19.2 | 13.6 | 26.8 | 485 |
| | 89 × 235 | 14.6 | 22.6 | 20.4 | 31.6 | 1010 |
| | 89 × 286 | 19.8 | 25.2 | 27.7 | 35.3 | 1820 |
| Northern | 89 × 89 | 1.91 | 10.5 | 2.67 | 14.7 | 39.2 |
| | 89 × 114 | 2.94 | 12.7 | 4.12 | 17.7 | 82.4 |
| | 89 × 140 | 4.16 | 14.6 | 5.82 | 20.4 | 153 |
| | 89 × 184 | 6.23 | 16.6 | 8.72 | 23.2 | 347 |
| | 89 × 235 | 9.38 | 19.6 | 13.1 | 27.4 | 722 |
| | 89 × 286 | 12.7 | 21.8 | 17.8 | 30.6 | 1300 |
| **No.1/No.2** | | | | | | |
| D.Fir-L | 89 × 89 | 1.80 | 15.4 | 2.52 | 21.5 | 57.5 |
| | 89 × 114 | 2.78 | 18.5 | 3.89 | 25.9 | 121 |
| | 89 × 140 | 3.92 | 21.3 | 5.49 | 29.8 | 224 |
| | 89 × 184 | 5.88 | 24.3 | 8.23 | 34.0 | 508 |
| | 89 × 235 | 8.85 | 28.6 | 12.4 | 40.1 | 1060 |
| | 89 × 286 | 12.0 | 31.9 | 16.8 | 44.7 | 1910 |
| Hem-Fir | 89 × 89 | 1.98 | 12.9 | 2.77 | 18.1 | 57.5 |
| | 89 × 114 | 3.05 | 15.6 | 4.27 | 21.8 | 121 |
| | 89 × 140 | 4.32 | 17.9 | 6.04 | 25.1 | 224 |
| | 89 × 184 | 6.46 | 20.4 | 9.05 | 28.6 | 508 |
| | 89 × 235 | 9.73 | 24.1 | 13.6 | 33.7 | 1060 |
| | 89 × 286 | 13.2 | 26.9 | 18.5 | 37.6 | 1910 |
| S-P-F | 89 × 89 | 2.12 | 12.1 | 2.97 | 17.0 | 49.7 |
| | 89 × 114 | 3.28 | 14.6 | 4.59 | 20.5 | 104 |
| | 89 × 140 | 4.63 | 16.8 | 6.48 | 23.5 | 193 |
| | 89 × 184 | 6.93 | 19.2 | 9.71 | 26.8 | 439 |
| | 89 × 235 | 10.4 | 22.6 | 14.6 | 31.6 | 914 |
| | 89 × 286 | 14.2 | 25.2 | 19.8 | 35.3 | 1650 |
| Northern | 89 × 89 | 1.37 | 10.5 | 1.91 | 14.7 | 36.6 |
| | 89 × 114 | 2.11 | 12.7 | 2.95 | 17.7 | 76.9 |
| | 89 × 140 | 2.98 | 14.6 | 4.18 | 20.4 | 142 |
| | 89 × 184 | 4.47 | 16.6 | 6.25 | 23.2 | 323 |
| | 89 × 235 | 6.72 | 19.6 | 9.41 | 27.4 | 674 |
| | 89 × 286 | 9.13 | 21.8 | 12.8 | 30.6 | 1210 |

Note:
For Case 1 System multiply single member $M_r$ and $V_r$ values by 1.10.

# Joist Selection Tables

**38** mm

## Machine Stress-Rated Lumber (MSR)

| Species | Grade | Size (b × d) mm | Single member M_r kN·m | V_r* kN | System Case 2 M_r kN·m | V_r* kN | $E_s I$ ×10⁹ N·mm² |
|---------|-------|-----------------|------------------------|---------|------------------------|---------|--------------------|
| MSR | 1450F_b-1.3E | 38 × 89 | 0.948 | 5.17 | 1.14 | 6.21 | 20.1 |
| | | 38 × 114 | 1.56 | 5.85 | 1.87 | 7.02 | 42.2 |
| | | 38 × 140 | 2.35 | 6.70 | 2.82 | 8.04 | 78.2 |
| | | 38 × 184 | 4.05 | 7.55 | 4.86 | 9.06 | 178 |
| | | 38 × 235 | 6.61 | 8.84 | 7.93 | 10.6 | 370 |
| | | 38 × 286 | 9.80 | 9.78 | 11.7 | 11.7 | 667 |
| | 1650F_b-1.5E | 38 × 89 | 1.08 | 5.17 | 1.30 | 6.21 | 23.0 |
| | | 38 × 114 | 1.78 | 5.85 | 2.13 | 7.02 | 48.3 |
| | | 38 × 140 | 2.68 | 6.70 | 3.22 | 8.04 | 89.5 |
| | | 38 × 184 | 4.63 | 7.55 | 5.56 | 9.06 | 203 |
| | | 38 × 235 | 7.52 | 8.84 | 9.03 | 10.6 | 423 |
| | | 38 × 286 | 11.1 | 9.78 | 13.4 | 11.7 | 763 |
| | 1800F_b-1.6E | 38 × 89 | 1.17 | 5.17 | 1.41 | 6.21 | 24.6 |
| | | 38 × 114 | 1.93 | 5.85 | 2.31 | 7.02 | 51.6 |
| | | 38 × 140 | 2.90 | 6.70 | 3.49 | 8.04 | 95.6 |
| | | 38 × 184 | 5.02 | 7.55 | 6.02 | 9.06 | 217 |
| | | 38 × 235 | 8.22 | 8.84 | 9.86 | 10.6 | 452 |
| | | 38 × 286 | 12.2 | 9.78 | 14.6 | 11.7 | 815 |
| | 2100F_b-1.8E | 38 × 89 | 1.38 | 5.17 | 1.65 | 6.21 | 27.7 |
| | | 38 × 114 | 2.26 | 5.85 | 2.71 | 7.02 | 58.2 |
| | | 38 × 140 | 3.41 | 6.70 | 4.09 | 8.04 | 108 |
| | | 38 × 184 | 5.89 | 7.55 | 7.06 | 9.06 | 245 |
| | | 38 × 235 | 9.57 | 8.84 | 11.5 | 10.6 | 510 |
| | | 38 × 286 | 14.2 | 9.78 | 17.0 | 11.7 | 919 |
| | 2400F_b-2.0E | 38 × 89 | 1.57 | 5.17 | 1.88 | 6.21 | 30.8 |
| | | 38 × 114 | 2.57 | 5.85 | 3.08 | 7.02 | 64.7 |
| | | 38 × 140 | 3.88 | 6.70 | 4.65 | 8.04 | 120 |
| | | 38 × 184 | 6.70 | 7.55 | 8.04 | 9.06 | 272 |
| | | 38 × 235 | 10.9 | 8.84 | 13.1 | 10.6 | 567 |
| | | 38 × 286 | 16.2 | 9.78 | 19.4 | 11.7 | 1020 |

Note:
For Case 1 System multiply single member $M_r$ and $V_r$ values by 1.10.
* Species factors to be applied to $V_r$ :   1.0 for S-P-F
                                 1.1 for D.Fir-L
                                 0.9 for all other species

# Serviceability Table

Required $E_S I$ (N•mm$^2$ × 10$^9$) for L/360 deflection

| Span m | Uniform specified load kN/m | | | | | | | | |
|---|---|---|---|---|---|---|---|---|---|
| | 0.4 | 0.6 | 0.8 | 1.0 | 1.2 | 1.4 | 1.6 | 1.8 | 2.0 |
| 1.0 | 1.88 | 2.81 | 3.75 | 4.69 | 5.63 | 6.56 | 7.50 | 8.44 | 9.38 |
| 1.2 | 3.24 | 4.86 | 6.48 | 8.10 | 9.72 | 11.3 | 13.0 | 14.6 | 16.2 |
| 1.4 | 5.15 | 7.72 | 10.3 | 12.9 | 15.4 | 18.0 | 20.6 | 23.2 | 25.7 |
| 1.6 | 7.68 | 11.5 | 15.4 | 19.2 | 23.0 | 26.9 | 30.7 | 34.6 | 38.4 |
| 1.8 | 10.9 | 16.4 | 21.9 | 27.3 | 32.8 | 38.3 | 43.7 | 49.2 | 54.7 |
| 2.0 | 15.0 | 22.5 | 30.0 | 37.5 | 45.0 | 52.5 | 60.0 | 67.5 | 75.0 |
| 2.2 | 20.0 | 29.9 | 39.9 | 49.9 | 59.9 | 69.9 | 79.9 | 89.8 | 99.8 |
| 2.4 | 25.9 | 38.9 | 51.8 | 64.8 | 77.8 | 90.7 | 104 | 117 | 130 |
| 2.6 | 33.0 | 49.4 | 65.9 | 82.4 | 98.9 | 115 | 132 | 148 | 165 |
| 2.8 | 41.2 | 61.7 | 82.3 | 103 | 123 | 144 | 165 | 185 | 206 |
| 3.0 | 50.6 | 75.9 | 101 | 127 | 152 | 177 | 203 | 228 | 253 |
| 3.2 | 61.4 | 92.2 | 123 | 154 | 184 | 215 | 246 | 276 | 307 |
| 3.4 | 73.7 | 111 | 147 | 184 | 221 | 258 | 295 | 332 | 368 |
| 3.6 | 87.5 | 131 | 175 | 219 | 262 | 306 | 350 | 394 | 437 |
| 3.8 | 103 | 154 | 206 | 257 | 309 | 360 | 412 | 463 | 514 |
| 4.0 | 120 | 180 | 240 | 300 | 360 | 420 | 480 | 540 | 600 |
| 4.2 | 139 | 208 | 278 | 347 | 417 | 486 | 556 | 625 | 695 |
| 4.4 | 160 | 240 | 319 | 399 | 479 | 559 | 639 | 719 | 799 |
| 4.6 | 183 | 274 | 365 | 456 | 548 | 639 | 730 | 821 | 913 |
| 4.8 | 207 | 311 | 415 | 518 | 622 | 726 | 829 | 933 | 1040 |
| 5.0 | 234 | 352 | 469 | 586 | 703 | 820 | 938 | 1050 | 1170 |
| 5.2 | 264 | 395 | 527 | 659 | 791 | 923 | 1050 | 1190 | 1320 |
| 5.4 | 295 | 443 | 590 | 738 | 886 | 1030 | 1180 | 1330 | 1480 |
| 5.6 | 329 | 494 | 659 | 823 | 988 | 1150 | 1320 | 1480 | 1650 |
| 5.8 | 366 | 549 | 732 | 915 | 1100 | 1280 | 1460 | 1650 | 1830 |
| 6.0 | 405 | 608 | 810 | 1010 | 1220 | 1420 | 1620 | 1820 | 2030 |

Note:
Chapter 11 provides a procedure for calculating the vibration controlled spans of lumber floor joists.

2

Bending Members

# 2.4 Engineered Joists

### General

This section describes prefabricated wood I-joists and parallel chord light frame trusses. The reader is referred to the product manufacturers' literature for design equations and for additional framing details.

Prefabricated wood I-joists are proprietary engineered wood products manufactured by gluing lumber or engineered wood flanges to structural panel webs. CSA O86 provides for the use of wood I-joists that have been certified to meet the strength and stiffness requirements of ASTM Standard D 5055. Flanges are commonly made of laminated veneer lumber, MSR or visually graded lumber, although glulam or parallel strand lumber may also be used. Webs are normally 9.5 mm (3/8") or 11 mm (7/16") OSB, although plywood may also be used.

Parallel chord light frame trusses, for use as joists, are prefabricated shallow flat trusses. They are designed according to CSA O86 and to the Truss Plate Institute of Canada's *Truss Design Procedures and Specifications for Light Metal Plate Connected Wood Trusses – Limit States Design*. Top and bottom chords are either MSR or visually graded lumber. The web material may be MSR lumber, visually graded lumber or steel. Light frame trusses are described in more detail in Section 8.7.

Engineered joists are available in longer lengths than traditional lumber joists and can achieve greater spans. They are light–weight, easily installed and can readily accommodate plumbing, electrical wiring and HVAC ducts.

### Availability

Prefabricated wood I-joists were introduced to the marketplace over thirty years ago and are readily available and commonly used throughout North America. Depths of I-joists range from 241 mm (9.5") to 610 mm (24"). They are supplied to retailers in lengths up to 18 m but the length available at the job site may be limited by transportation requirements. Joists are normally cut to approximate length at the yard and trimmed to fit on site.

Parallel chord light frame trusses are built to specification for a particular job. They can be ordered directly from truss manufacturers or through lumber retailers. Depths of trusses used as floor joists typically range from 254 mm (10") to 610 mm (24"). Parallel chord trusses can have either flat or upright chords. Flat chord trusses are primarily used in floors where depth is a consideration.

### I-Joist Detailing

### Definitions

1. *Rim boards* are structural composite lumber, plywood or OSB panels used to transfer loads vertically from upper to lower bearing walls and to provide lateral restraint to the ends of joists.

2. *Rim joists* are joists that transfer loads vertically from upper to lower bearing walls. They may run either parallel or perpendicular to other joists.

3.  A *web stiffener*, also known as a *strong back, backer block* or *bearing block* is wood or panel blocking nailed to the web of an I-joist to increase the allowed reaction or to fill in the space between a hanger and the I- joist web. Web stiffeners should be 3 mm shorter than the web height to prevent damaging the joist during installation.

4.  A *squash block*, or *cripple block*, is wood blocking installed alongside an I–joist to transfer loads from an upper to a lower bearing wall. Squash blocks should be 2 mm deeper than the I-joist and are nailed to the outside of the flanges.

5.  *Filler blocking* is wood blocking installed between adjacent I-joists in a multiple ply I-joist application. Filler blocking is normally required for headers made up of multiple ply I-joists.

**Installation Details**

The following details should be considered for all I-joist installations. Note that in addition to these general recommendations, each manufacturer provides framing details and installation procedures. The designer should review the manufacturer's literature when specifying a particular product.

1.  Top and bottom flanges must be laterally restrained against rotation at the ends of the joists. This can be accomplished with specially design joist hangers as shown in Figure 2.4.

2.  Adequate I-joist bearing length is required as per the manufacturer's literature. Web stiffeners, as shown in Figure 2.5 may be required to increase allowable bearing reaction.

3.  Special details are required where I-joists support concentrated loads:
    • For I-joists installed beneath bearing walls perpendicular to the joists, rim joists (or rim boards), I-joist blocking panels, or squash blocks are required to transfer loads from upper to lower bearing walls. Refer to Figure 2.6
    • Squash blocks are required where I-joists support columns.

4.  Continuous lateral support of the I-joist's compression flange is required to prevent rotation and buckling. For simple spans, the floor sheathing normally supports the top flange. The bottom flange should be braced in accordance with the manufacturer's literature when it is in compression. For example:
    • Bracing of the I-joist bottom flange is required at interior supports of multiple span joists.
    • I-joist bottom flange bracing is required where the joist is cantilevered.

5.  Each I-joist manufacturer publishes unique hole charts specifying allowable sizes and location of web holes. Follow the manufacturer's specifications for web holes for the specific I-joist being used.

Figure 2.4
**I-joist hangers
to restrain
against
rotation**

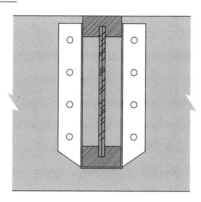

Figure 2.5
**I-joist bearing**

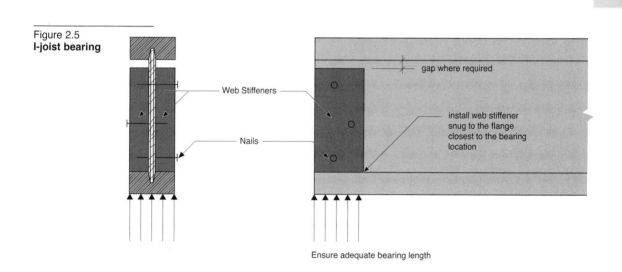

Web Stiffeners

Nails

gap where required

install web stiffener
snug to the flange
closest to the bearing
location

Ensure adequate bearing length

Figure 2.6
**Vertical load
transfer details
for I-joists**

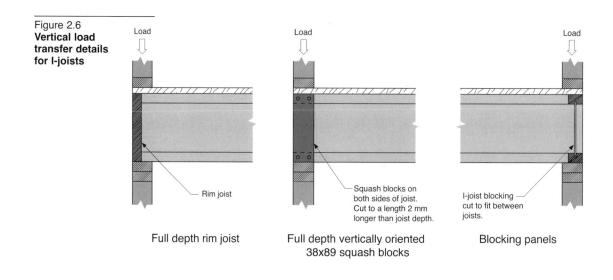

Full depth rim joist          Full depth vertically oriented          Blocking panels
                                    38x89 squash blocks

## Parallel Chord Truss Detailing

### Definitions

1. *Strongbacks* (or load sharing bridging) are sawn lumber or structural composite lumber members installed perpendicular to the joist direction so that concentrated loads are shared among several joists. In floor applications strongbacks may be specified to reduce vibration. Strongback detailing (spacing, location etc.) is specified by the truss manufacturer.

2. *Bracing* consists of sawn lumber or SCL members fastened to truss webs or chords to prevent local buckling of truss members.

### Installation Details

The truss drawings for the parallel chord trusses will contain installation details that need to be followed. Further information about truss installation can be found in Chapter 8.

# 2.5    Beams and Purlins

### General

This section covers three types of wood beams:

- Sawn Timbers
- Glued Laminated Timber (Glulam)
- Structural Composite Lumber (SCL)

Built-up beams, composed of two or more lumber members, are covered in Section 2.6.

Sawn timbers are produced in accordance with CSA Standard O141, *Softwood Lumber.* The rules for the grading of timbers are outlined in the National Lumber Grades Authority, *Standard Grading Rules for Canadian Lumber.* Sawn timbers range in size from 140 to 394 mm.

Glued-laminated timber is an engineered wood product manufactured by gluing together lumber laminations with a waterproof adhesive. Glulam is manufactured to meet CSA Standard O122, *Structural Glued Laminated Timber,* and the manufacturers of glulam must be certified in accordance with CSA Standard O177, *Qualification Code for Manufacturers of Structural Glued Laminated Timber.* Glulam beams range in thickness from 80 to 365 mm and in depth from 114 mm to approximately 2128 mm.

Structural composite lumber (SCL) may be either laminated veneer lumber (LVL) or parallel strand lumber (PSL). Laminated veneer lumber is a structural composite manufactured by gluing veneers together to produce a lumber product. In LVL the grain direction of each veneer layer is parallel to the length of the piece. Parallel strand lumber is similar to laminated veneer lumber except that strips of veneer rather than sheets of veneer are glued together. Both types of products are proprietary and currently no manufacturing standard exists, but the processes are under the supervision of a quality control agency. SCL products are usually 45 mm (1-3/4" actual) thick and 241 to 606 mm deep. PSL and some LVL products are also available in widths up to 178 mm as shown in the Beam Selection Tables for structural composite lumber.

### Availability

**Sawn Timber**

The Beam Selection Tables for sawn timber include design information for the following grades and beam thicknesses:

**Table 2.7**
**Grades and thicknesses of sawn timbers**

| Grades | Beam thickness for all grades mm |
|---|---|
| Select Structural, No.1, No.2 | 140 |
| | 190 |
| | 242 |
| | 292 |
| | 343 |
| | 394 |

**2**

**Bending Members**

D.Fir-L and Hem-Fir are the species groups most readily available in timber sizes, but S-P-F and Northern species may also be obtained. The selection tables provide design values for timbers up to 394 × 394 mm in size; however, availability of large sizes should be checked before specifying. Timbers may be obtained in lengths up to 9.1 m, but this should also be confirmed with local suppliers.

The most readily available grades are No.1 and No.2; however, Select Structural may be ordered. Materials available from lumber yard stock are usually resawn to order from large timbers and should be re-graded after cutting. Verification of the grade may be obtained in writing from the supplier, or a qualified grading agency may be retained to check the supplied material. Specific sizes graded at the mill are usually available by special order, but delivery time will be longer.

Timbers are always dressed green since their large size makes kiln-drying impractical. As a result, some amount of shrinkage and checking can be expected after dressing. These effects are already taken into account in the specified strengths. Shrinkage should also be considered when designing connections.

**Glulam**

The Beam Selection Tables for glulam include design information for straight beams (refer to Chapter 8 for design information on curved glulam beams and arches) of the following species, grades and beam thicknesses:

| Table 2.8 **Species, grades and thicknesses of glulam beams** | Species and stress grades | Beam thickness for all species and stress grades mm |
|---|---|---|
| | **D.Fir-L:** 20f-E, 20f-EX, 24f-E, 24f-EX | 80 |
| | | 130 |
| | **Spruce-Pine:** 20f-E, 20f-EX | 175 |
| | **Hem-Fir:** 24f-E, 24f-EX | 215 |
| | | 265 |
| | | 315 |
| | | 365 |

Most fabricators produce either D.Fir-L or Spruce-Pine glulam. Hem-Fir glulam may be available in certain areas. The beam thicknesses shown above are industry standards, but some fabricators can produce slightly different sizes. Most fabricators use 38 mm thick laminations for straight beams, and 19 mm and 38 mm thick laminations for curved beams.

The 20f-E grade should be specified for most applications other than long span or heavily loaded beams since fabricators do not produce large amounts of the 24f-E grade glulam. This is due to the limited availability of the high quality laminating stock used in the 24f-E lay-up.

Glulam beams are also available in the 20f-EX and 24f-EX grades. These grades have higher quality laminations on the top and bottom face so that the bending resistance is the same for negative or positive moment. The EX grade should only be used whenever the negative moments exceed the capacity of the E grade, such as may occur in a cantilevered system.

In addition to different stress grades, glulam is available in three appearance grades. Information on appearance grades as well as other finishing and sealing data is provided in Chapter 11.

### Structural Composite Lumber (SCL)

Structural composite lumber (SCL) refers to proprietary engineered wood products which are composites of wood veneer sheets or wood strand elements joined with adhesives. This term encompasses laminated veneer lumber (LVL) and parallel strand lumber (PSL).

Laminated veneer lumber (LVL) is a layered composite of wood veneers and adhesive. The grain of each layer of veneer runs in the same (long) direction with the result that it is strong when edge loaded as a beam or face loaded as a plank. This kind of lamination is called parallel-lamination, and it produces a material with greater uniformity and predictability than the same dimension material made by cross-lamination. LVL is fabricated into large billets and then cut at the factory into stock for headers and beams, flanges for prefabricated wood I-joists, or for other specific uses. LVL is used primarily as structural framing for residential and commercial construction and is well suited to applications where open web steel joists and light steel beams might be considered.

Parallel strand lumber (PSL) is a high strength structural composite lumber product manufactured by gluing strands of wood together under pressure. This results in a product having consistent properties and high load carrying ability. It is available in lengths up to (66 ft.) and longer if transportation permits. PSL is manufactured to a moisture content of 11 percent, making it less prone to shrinking, warping, cupping, bowing or splitting. PSL is well suited for use as beams and columns for post and beam construction, and for beams, headers, and lintels for light framing construction. It is used for large members in residential construction and as intermediate and large members in commercial building construction.

The Beam Selection Tables for structural composite lumber provide design information for typical sizes and strength values in limit states design format. These tables are provided for illustration purposes only. Although the design values are in the range of manufacturers' published values, proprietary differences can result in discrepancies. The SCL manufacturer should be contacted for actual sizes and design values, due to the proprietary nature of these products. A list of manufacturers is available from the Canadian Wood Council.

### Design

Sawn timber, glulam and SCL beams must be designed so that the following criteria are satisfied:

1. Factored moment resistance $M_r \geq$ maximum factored moment $M_f$

2. Adequate shear resistance must be provided

   a) For sawn timber and SCL:

   Factored shear resistance $V_r \geq$ maximum factored shear force $V_f$

   In the calculation of $V_f$, loads within a distance from the support equal to the depth of the member may be neglected.

   For sawn timber only, factored notch shear force resistance $F_r \geq$ maximum reaction force $Q_f$ when a member has a notch on the tension side at a support.

   b) For glulam only:

   i) Beams with a volume less than 2.0 m$^3$
   If the beam volume is less than 2.0 m$^3$, shear resistance may be checked by the procedure described in ii) or the tabulated shear resistance $V_r$ may simply be compared to the maximum factored shear force $V_f$. In the calculation of $V_f$, loads within a distance from the support equal to the depth of the member may be neglected.

   ii) Beams of any volume
   Shear resistance $W_r \geq$ total of all factored loads acting on beam $W_f$
   where:
   $$W_r = (W_r L^{0.18}) L_o^{-0.18}$$
   $(W_r L^{0.18})$ = unit factored shear resistance from Beam Selection Tables
   $L_o$ = beam length in m

3. Factored bearing resistance $Q_r \geq$ maximum factored reaction $Q_f$ (refer to Chapter 6)

4. Maximum deflection under specified loads < deflection criteria
   (actual $E_s I >$ required $E_s I$)

   Examples:

   For L/180 deflection limit based on total load:

   $$E_s I_{REQ'D} = 180 \left[ \frac{5\, w\, L^3}{384} \right]$$

   For L/360 deflection limit based on live load:

   $$E_s I_{REQ'D} = 360 \left[ \frac{5\, w_L\, L^3}{384} \right]$$

   where:
   $w$ = total specified load
   $w_L$ = specified live load

# Checklist: **Beams** ✔

To verify that the tabulated resistances and $E_S I$ values are appropriate for the structure being designed, the following questions should be asked (the appropriate modification factor is given in brackets):

**For sawn timbers:**

1. Is load duration "standard" ($K_D$)?

2. Is the material free of strength reducing chemicals ($K_T$)?

3. Is the beam free of notches?

**For straight glulam beams:**

1. Is the beam subject to positive bending moments only ($f_b$)?

2. Is load duration "standard" ($K_D$)?

3. Is the service condition "dry" ($K_S$)?

4. Is the material free of strength-reducing chemicals ($K_T$)?

5. Does the construction provide lateral stability for the beam ($K_L$)?

6. Is a size factor applicable ($K_{Zbg}$)?

7. Is the beam free of notches ($K_N$)?

8. For $W_r L^{0.18}$ only, is the beam simply supported and the loading uniformly distributed ($C_V$)?

If the answer to any of these questions is no, refer to the description of modification factors below and make the necessary adjustments to tabulated resistances and $E_S I$ values. Note that the $M'_r$ values for glulam must be adjusted by the lesser of $K_L$ or $K_{Zbg}$. Otherwise, the Beam Selection Tables may be used directly.

**2**

**Bending Members**

The Beam Selection Tables for sawn timbers and SCL provide $M_r$, $V_r$ and $E_s I$ values.

The Beam Selection Tables for glulam provide $M'_r$, $V_r$ and $E_s I$ values. To obtain $M_r$, for glulam, multiply $M'_r$ (from the Glulam Beam Selection Tables) by the lesser of $K_L$ (from Table 2.10) or $K_{Zbg}$ (from Table 2.11).

Note that in certain cases the *National Building Code of Canada* permits a reduction in the loads due to use and occupancy depending upon the size of the tributary area (refer to Article 4.1.6.9 of the *NBCC*).

## Modification Factors

The tabulated resistances for sawn timber and glulam are based upon the following formulae and modification factors. When using the tables, be certain that the member conforms exactly to the modification factors used in the tables; if not, use the factors below and make the necessary adjustments to the tabulated values.
For sawn timbers:

$$M_r = \phi F_b S K_{zb} K_L \text{ (N·mm)}$$

$$V_r = \phi F_v \frac{2 A_n}{3} K_{Zv} \text{ (N)}$$

$$F_r = \phi F_f A K_N \text{ (N)} \quad \text{for beams with notches on the tension side at supports}$$

For glulam:

$$M_r = \text{lesser of } M'_r K_L \text{ or } M'_r K_{Zbg} \text{ (N·mm)}$$

$$M'_r = \phi F_b S \text{ (N·mm)}$$

$$V_r = \phi F_v \frac{2 A}{3} K_N \text{ (N)}$$

$$W_r = \phi F_v 0.48 A K_N C_v Z^{-0.18} \text{ (N)}$$

which may be expressed as:

$$W_r L^{0.18} = \phi F_v 0.48 A K_N C_v (b\,d)^{-0.18} \text{ (N·m}^{0.18})$$

(as shown in the Beam Selection Tables)

For sawn timber and glulam:

$$E_s I = E (K_{SE} K_T) I \text{ (N·mm}^2)$$

where:

$\phi = 0.9$

$F_b = f_b\ (K_D\ K_H\ K_{Sb}\ K_T)$ (MPa)

$f_b$ = specified bending strength (MPa)

$F_v = f_v\ (K_D\ K_H\ K_{Sv}\ K_T)$ (MPa)

$f_v$ = specified shear strength (MPa)

$A_n$ = net cross-section area (mm²)

$F_f = f_f\ (K_D\ K_H\ K_{Sf}\ K_T)$ (MPa)

$f_f$ = specified notch shear force strength, 0.5 MPa for all sawn members

$A$ = gross cross-section area (mm²)

For 20f-E and 24f-E glulam the tabulated $M'_r$ values are calculated using the specified strength for positive bending moment. To determine the negative bending moment strength, multiply the tabulated values by the ratio of bending strengths that are listed in Table 6.3 of CSA O86.

For 20f-EX and 24f-EX grade, the tabulated $M'_r$ values apply to both positive and negative bending.

* b and d are expressed in metres for this calculation only

$S$ = section modulus (mm³)

$E$ = specified modulus of elasticity (MPa)

$I$ = moment of inertia (mm⁴)

$Z$ = beam volume (m³)

$L$ = length of beam (m)

$b$ = width of beam (m) *

$d$ = depth of beam (m) *

$K_D$ is a load duration factor. The tabulated resistances are based on a standard term load ($K_D = 1.0$), which includes the effects of dead loads plus loads due to use and occupancy and snow loads. For members intended to support permanent loads, the $M_r$, $M'_r$ and $V_r$ values must be multiplied by 0.65. For beams or purlins intended to support short term loads such as wind and earthquakes, $M_r$, $M'_r$ and $V_r$ may be multiplied by 1.15.

$K_H$ is a system factor. The tabulated resistances are based on a single member configuration ($K_H = 1.0$). For a configuration consisting of 3 or more parallel beams or purlins spaced not more than 610 mm apart, $M_r$, $M'_r$ and $V_r$ may be multiplied by 1.10.

$K_S$ is a service condition factor. The tabulated values are based on dry service conditions ($K_S = 1.0$). For wet conditions, only one change is required for sawn timbers, where $K_{Sf} = 0.7$ for $F_r$. However, for glulam multiply the tabulated values by the following factors:

$K_{Sb} = 0.80$ for $M'_r$

$K_{Sv} = 0.87$ for $V_r$ and $W_r$ $L^{0.18}$

$K_{SE} = 0.90$ for $E_S I$

$K_T$ is a treatment factor. The tabulated resistances are based on beams and purlins that are untreated ($K_T = 1.0$). If either sawn timbers or glulam is treated with a fire retardant, multiply $M_r$ and $V_r$ and $E_S I$ values by $K_T$ as described in the Commentary. No modification is required for preservative treatment.

$K_Z$ is a size factor applicable only to sawn timbers. It is incorporated into the tables for given material dimensions. No further adjustments are required.

$K_{Zbg}$ is a size factor for bending applied to gluam beams and is only applicable if it is less than the value of $K_L$. The values of $M'_r$ in the Beam Selection Tables for glulam do not include $K_{Zbg}$. Values of $K_{Zbg}$ are given in Table 2.11.

$K_L$ is a lateral stability factor. The tables are based on beams that are restrained against lateral displacement and rotation at their ends ($K_L = 1.0$). Since all sawn timbers in the selection tables have a d/b ratio less than 4, no intermediate support is required.

For glulam, it is assumed that the compressive edge of the bending member is supported throughout its length by decking so as to provide a rigid diaphragm. If glulam lacks this restraint, then use the following procedure to modify the tabulated $M'_r$ value:

1. Determine the effective length $L_e$ from Table 2.9

2. Calculate $C_b = \sqrt{\dfrac{L_e d}{b^2}}$

3. Determine $K_L$ from Table 2.10

4. If $K_L$ is less than $K_{Zbg}$, multiply the tabulated value of $M'_r$ by $K_L$

$K_N$ is a notch factor. The tables are based on beams that are not notched ($K_N = 1.0$). If the members are notched, refer to page 34 for sawn timbers. For glulam, if members are notched on the tension side at supports, multiply the tabulated $V_r$ values by:

$$K_N = \left[1 - \frac{d_n}{d}\right]^2$$

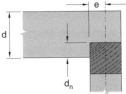

If members are notched on the compression side, multiply the tabulated $V_r$ values by:

$$\text{(if } e > d) \quad K_N = 1 - \frac{d_n}{d}$$

$$\text{(if } e < d) \quad K_N = 1 - \frac{d_n\, e}{d\left(d - d_n\right)}$$

where:

$d$ = depth of beam (mm)

$d_n$ = depth of notch (mm), which must not exceed 0.25d

$e$ = length of notch (mm), from inner edge of closest support to farthest edge of notch

$C_v$ is a shear load coefficient. The tables are based on a simply supported beam with a uniformly distributed load, therefore $C_v = 3.69$. If the beam is not simply supported or the loading is not uniformly distributed, select the appropriate $C_v$ value from Clause 6.5.7.4 of CSA O86 and multiply the tabulated $W_r L^{0.18}$ value by $C_v / 3.69$.

Table 2.9
**Effective length $L_e$ for bending members**

| Beams | Intermediate support Yes | No |
|---|---|---|
| Any loading | 1.92 a | $1.92\, l_u$ |
| Uniformly distributed load | 1.92 a | $1.92\, l_u$ |
| Concentrated load at centre | 1.11 a | $1.61\, l_u$ |
| Concentrated loads at 1/3 points | 1.68 a | |
| Concentrated loads at 1/4 points | 1.54 a | |
| Concentrated loads at 1/5 points | 1.68 a | |
| Concentrated loads at 1/6 points | 1.73 a | |
| Concentrated loads at 1/7 points | 1.78 a | |
| Concentrated loads at 1/8 points | 1.84 a | |

| Cantilevers | |
|---|---|
| Any loading | $1.92\, l_u$ |
| Uniformly distributed load | $1.23\, l_u$ |
| Concentrated load at free end | $1.69\, l_u$ |

where:
$l_u$ = unsupported length = distance between points of bearing or the length of the cantilever, mm.
a = maximum purlin spacing when purlins provide lateral support for the compressive edge of the beam, mm.

| Table 2.10 Values of $K_L$ for glulam beams | | 20f-E stress grade | | 24f-E stress grade |
|---|---|---|---|---|
| | $C_b$ | D.Fir-L | Spruce-Pine | D.Fir-L, Hem-Fir |
| | 10 | 1.00 | 1.00 | 1.00 |
| | 12 | 0.969 | 0.955 | 0.960 |
| | 14 | 0.942 | 0.916 | 0.926 |
| | 16 | 0.901 | 0.857 | 0.873 |
| | 18 | 0.841 | 0.770 | 0.797 |
| | 20 | 0.758 | 0.654 | 0.691 |
| | 22 | 0.651 | 0.540 | 0.575 |
| | 24 | 0.547 | 0.454 | 0.483 |
| | 26 | 0.466 | 0.387 | 0.412 |
| | 28 | 0.402 | 0.334 | 0.355 |
| | 30 | 0.350 | 0.291 | 0.309 |
| | 32 | 0.307 | 0.255 | 0.272 |
| | 34 | 0.272 | 0.226 | 0.241 |
| | 36 | 0.243 | 0.202 | 0.215 |
| | 38 | 0.218 | 0.181 | 0.193 |
| | 40 | 0.197 | 0.163 | 0.174 |
| | 42 | 0.178 | 0.148 | 0.158 |
| | 44 | 0.163 | 0.135 | 0.144 |
| | 46 | 0.149 | 0.124 | 0.132 |
| | 48 | 0.137 | 0.114 | 0.121 |
| | 50 | 0.126 | 0.105 | 0.111 |

Notes:

1. $C_b = \sqrt{L_e d / b^2}$ where $L_e$ = effective length, mm (Table 2.9); d = depth, mm; b = width, mm.

2. $K_L$ values are valid when $K_D = K_H = K_S = 1.0$. For other conditions, use Clause 6.5.6.4.4 of CSA O86.

3. Use the lesser of $K_L$ and $K_{Zbg}$ to determine $M_r$.

Table 2.11
**Values of $K_{Zbg}$ for glulam beams**

| L m | B (mm) | | | | | | |
|-----|--------|-----|-----|-----|-----|-----|-----|
|      | 80    | 130 | 175 | 215 | 265 | 315 | 365 |
| 3    | 1     | 1   | 1   | 1   | 1   | 1   | 1     |
| 3.5  | 1     | 1   | 1   | 1   | 1   | 1   | 0.986 |
| 4    | 1     | 1   | 1   | 1   | 1   | 0.988 | 0.962 |
| 4.5  | 1     | 1   | 1   | 1   | 0.998 | 0.967 | 0.942 |
| 5    | 1     | 1   | 1   | 1   | 0.979 | 0.949 | 0.924 |
| 5.5  | 1     | 1   | 1   | 1   | 0.962 | 0.933 | 0.909 |
| 6    | 1     | 1   | 1   | 0.984 | 0.948 | 0.918 | 0.894 |
| 6.5  | 1     | 1   | 1   | 0.970 | 0.934 | 0.905 | 0.882 |
| 7    | 1     | 1   | 0.993 | 0.957 | 0.922 | 0.893 | 0.870 |
| 7.5  | 1     | 1   | 0.981 | 0.945 | 0.910 | 0.882 | 0.859 |
| 8    | 1     | 1   | 0.969 | 0.934 | 0.900 | 0.872 | 0.849 |
| 8.5  | 1     | 1   | 0.959 | 0.924 | 0.890 | 0.863 | 0.840 |
| 9    | 1     | 1   | 0.949 | 0.915 | 0.881 | 0.854 | 0.831 |
| 9.5  | 1     | 0.992 | 0.940 | 0.906 | 0.872 | 0.846 | 0.823 |
| 10   | 1     | 0.982 | 0.931 | 0.897 | 0.864 | 0.838 | 0.816 |
| 10.5 | 1     | 0.974 | 0.923 | 0.890 | 0.857 | 0.830 | 0.809 |
| 11   | 1     | 0.966 | 0.915 | 0.882 | 0.850 | 0.824 | 0.802 |
| 11.5 | 1     | 0.958 | 0.908 | 0.875 | 0.843 | 0.817 | 0.796 |
| 12   | 1     | 0.951 | 0.901 | 0.868 | 0.836 | 0.811 | 0.790 |
| 12.5 | 1     | 0.944 | 0.895 | 0.862 | 0.830 | 0.805 | 0.784 |
| 13   | 1     | 0.937 | 0.888 | 0.856 | 0.824 | 0.799 | 0.778 |
| 13.5 | 1     | 0.931 | 0.882 | 0.850 | 0.819 | 0.794 | 0.773 |
| 14   | 1     | 0.925 | 0.877 | 0.845 | 0.813 | 0.789 | 0.768 |
| 14.5 | 1     | 0.919 | 0.871 | 0.839 | 0.808 | 0.784 | 0.763 |
| 15   | 0.997 | 0.913 | 0.866 | 0.834 | 0.803 | 0.779 | 0.758 |

**2**

Bending Members

Notes:
1. B is the member width for single piece laminations, mm. For laminations consisting of multiple pieces, B is the width of the widest piece. Glulam laminations wider than 175 mm are typically constructed with multiple pieces. Check with glulam supplier.
2. L is the length of the glulam from point of zero moment to zero moment, m. For simple span beams, L is the span of the beam.
3. $K_{Zgb} = 1.03(B/1000 \times L)^{-0.18}$ but not greater than 1.0.
4. Use the lesser of $K_{Zbg}$ and $K_L$ to determine $M_r$.

## Example 1: Beams

Design single span floor beams for the following conditions:

- beam spacing = 3.0 m
- beam span = 6.0 m
- specified dead load = 1.5 kPa (includes partitions and self weight)
- specified live load = 2.4 kPa (commercial use and occupancy)
- gypsum ceiling
- standard load duration
- dry service condition
- untreated

Use D.Fir-L No.1 sawn timber.

## Calculation

Tributary area = $3.0 \times 6.0 = 18.0 \text{ m}^2 < 20.0 \text{ m}^2$
Therefore, no live load reduction is permitted by the *NBCC*.

Total Factored Load = $(1.25 \times 1.5) + (1.5 \times 2.4) = 5.48$ kPa
Total Specified Load = $1.5 + 2.4 = 3.90$ kPa

$$w_f = 5.48 \times 3.0 = 16.4 \text{ kN/m}$$

$$w = 3.90 \times 3.0 = 11.7 \text{ kN/m}$$

$$w_L = 2.40 \times 3.0 = 7.20 \text{ kN/m}$$

$$M_f = \frac{w_f L^2}{8} = \frac{16.4 \times 6.0^2}{8} = 73.8 \text{ kN} \Sigma\text{m}$$

$$V_f = \frac{w_f L}{2} = \frac{16.4 \times 6.0}{2} = 49.2 \text{ kN}$$

For L/180 deflection limit based on total load:

$$E_S I_{REQ'D} = 180 \left[ \frac{5 \, w \, L^3}{384} \right] = 180 \left[ \frac{5 \times 11.7 \times 6000^3}{384} \right]$$

$$= 5920 \times 10^9 \text{ N} \cdot \text{mm}^2$$

For L/360 deflection limit based on live load:

$$E_S I_{REQ'D} = 360 \left[ \frac{5 \, w_L \, L^3}{384} \right] = 360 \left[ \frac{5 \times 7.20 \times 6000^3}{384} \right]$$

$$= 7290 \times 10^9 \text{ N} \cdot \text{mm}^2 \quad \text{(governs stiffness calculation)}$$

From Beam Selection Tables for sawn timber try 241 × 394 mm:

$M_r$ = 79.8 kN·m > 73.8 kN·m $\quad\quad\quad$ *Acceptable*
$V_r$ = 76.9 kN > 49.2 kN $\quad\quad\quad\quad$ *Acceptable*

**Use 241 × 394 mm No.1 D.Fir-L.**

**Example 2: Beams**

Design single span floor beams for the following conditions:

- beam spacing = 5.0 m
- beam span = 7.5 m
- specified dead load = 2.0 kPa (includes partitions and self-weight)
- specified live load = 2.4 kPa (office area above first floor)
- gypsum ceiling

- standard load duration
- dry service condition
- untreated
- compression edge assumed fully laterally supported by joists framed in by joist hangers and spaced at 400 mm on centre.

Use D.Fir-L 20f-E glulam.

**Calculation**

Tributary area = 5.0 × 7.5 = 37.5 m$^2$ > 20 m$^2$
Live load reduction factor (LLRF) = 0.3 + $\sqrt{(9.8/37.5)}$ = 0.81
(from Article 4.1.6.9, *NBCC*)

Live Load = 2.4 × 0.81 = 1.94 kPa
Total Factored Load = (1.25 × 2.0) + (1.5 × 0.81 × 2.4) = 5.42 kPa
Total Specified Load = 2.0 + (2.4 × 0.81) = 3.94 kPa

$w_f$ = 5.42 × 5.0 = 27.1 kN/m
$w$ = 3.94 × 5.0 = 19.7 kN/m
$w_L$ = 1.94 × 5.0 = 9.7 kN/m

2

Bending Members

$$M_f = \frac{w_f L^2}{8} = \frac{27.1 \times 7.5^2}{8} = 191 \text{kN} \cdot \text{m}$$

$$V_f = \frac{w_f L}{2} = \frac{27.1 \times 7.5}{2} = 102 \text{ kN}$$

For L/180 deflection limit based on total load:

$$E_S I_{REQ'D} = 180 \left[ \frac{5 \, w \, L^3}{384} \right] = 180 \left[ \frac{5 \times 19.7 \times 7500^3}{384} \right]$$

$$= 19500 \times 10^9 \text{ N} \cdot \text{mm}^2 \text{ (governs stiffness calculation)}$$

For L/360 deflection limit based on live load:

$$E_S I_{REQ'D} = 360 \left[ \frac{5 \, w_L \, L^3}{384} \right] = 360 \left[ \frac{5 \times 9.7 \times 7500^3}{384} \right]$$

$$= 19200 \times 10^9 \text{ N} \cdot \text{mm}^2$$

From Beam Selection Tables for glulam try 130 × 646 mm:

$M'_r$ = 208 KN·m
$M_r$ = lesser of $M'_r$ $K_L$ or $M'_r$ $K_{Zbg}$
$K_L$ = 1 (compression edge laterally supported)
$K_{Zbg}$ = 1 (Table 2.11)
$M_r$ = 208 kN·m > 191 kN·m          *Acceptable*

For beam volumes < 2 m³, $V_r$ may be used as a simplified method of checking shear resistance.

beam volume = 0.630 m³
$V_r$ = 101 kN < 102 kN          *Not Acceptable*

For beams < 2 m³, $W_r$ may be used to check beam shear capacity.
For beam volumes ≥ 2 m³, $W_r$ must be used to check beam shear capacity.
Calculate $W_r$ and compare to $W_f$ to check shear resistance:

$W_r$ = 418 × (7.5)$^{-0.18}$ = 291 kN
$W_f$ = 27.1 × 7.5 = 203 kN          *Acceptable*
$E_S I$ = 36200 × 10⁹ N·mm² > 19500 × 10⁹ N·mm²     *Acceptable*

Note: Verify acceptable bearing capacity as per Chapter 6

**Use 130 × 646 mm 20f-E D.Fir-L glulam.**

# Beam Selection Tables

## Sawn Timbers

**140** mm

| Species | Size (b × d) mm | Select Structural $M_r$ kN·m | $V_r$ kN | $E_sI$ ×10⁹ N·mm² | No.1 Grade $M_r$ kN·m | $V_r$ kN | $E_sI$ ×10⁹ N·mm² | No.2 Grade $M_r$ kN·m | $V_r$ kN | $E_sI$ ×10⁹ N·mm² |
|---|---|---|---|---|---|---|---|---|---|---|
| D.Fir-L | 140 × 140 | 9.79 | 22.9 | 384 | 7.38 | 22.9 | 336 | 3.21 | 22.9 | 304 |
| | 140 × 191 | 18.2 | 31.3 | 976 | 13.7 | 31.3 | 854 | 5.98 | 31.3 | 772 |
| | 140 × 241 | 28.5 | 36.4 | 1960 | 23.1 | 36.4 | 1960 | 13.2 | 36.4 | 1550 |
| | 140 × 292 | 38.4 | 40.5 | 3490 | 31.1 | 40.5 | 3490 | 17.7 | 40.5 | 2760 |
| | 140 × 343 | 48.2 | 43.2 | 5650 | 39.0 | 43.2 | 5650 | 22.2 | 43.2 | 4470 |
| | 140 × 394 | 57.2 | 44.7 | 8560 | 46.4 | 44.7 | 8560 | 26.4 | 44.7 | 6780 |
| Hem-Fir | 140 × 140 | 7.28 | 18.3 | 320 | 5.46 | 18.3 | 288 | 2.41 | 18.3 | 256 |
| | 140 × 191 | 13.5 | 25.0 | 813 | 10.2 | 25.0 | 732 | 4.48 | 25.0 | 650 |
| | 140 × 241 | 21.2 | 29.2 | 1630 | 17.1 | 29.2 | 1630 | 9.81 | 29.2 | 1310 |
| | 140 × 292 | 28.6 | 32.4 | 2900 | 23.0 | 32.4 | 2900 | 13.2 | 32.4 | 2320 |
| | 140 × 343 | 35.8 | 34.6 | 4710 | 28.9 | 34.6 | 4710 | 16.6 | 34.6 | 3770 |
| | 140 × 394 | 42.5 | 35.7 | 7140 | 34.3 | 35.7 | 7140 | 19.7 | 35.7 | 5710 |
| S-P-F | 140 × 140 | 6.80 | 18.3 | 272 | 5.14 | 18.3 | 240 | 2.25 | 18.3 | 208 |
| | 140 × 191 | 12.6 | 25.0 | 691 | 9.56 | 25.0 | 610 | 4.18 | 25.0 | 528 |
| | 140 × 241 | 19.9 | 29.2 | 1390 | 16.1 | 29.2 | 1390 | 9.22 | 29.2 | 1060 |
| Northern | 140 × 140 | 6.42 | 15.3 | 256 | 4.82 | 15.3 | 224 | 2.09 | 15.3 | 192 |
| | 140 × 191 | 12.0 | 20.9 | 650 | 8.96 | 20.9 | 569 | 3.88 | 20.9 | 488 |
| | 140 × 241 | 18.7 | 24.3 | 1310 | 15.1 | 24.3 | 1310 | 8.64 | 24.3 | 980 |

**191** mm

| Species | Size (b × d) mm | Select Structural $M_r$ kN·m | $V_r$ kN | $E_sI$ ×10⁹ N·mm² | No.1 Grade $M_r$ kN·m | $V_r$ kN | $E_sI$ ×10⁹ N·mm² | No.2 Grade $M_r$ kN·m | $V_r$ kN | $E_sI$ ×10⁹ N·mm² |
|---|---|---|---|---|---|---|---|---|---|---|
| D.Fir-L | 191 × 191 | 24.9 | 42.7 | 1330 | 18.8 | 42.7 | 1160 | 8.15 | 42.7 | 1050 |
| | 191 × 241 | 36.5 | 49.7 | 2670 | 27.6 | 49.7 | 2340 | 12.0 | 49.7 | 2120 |
| | 191 × 292 | 52.4 | 55.2 | 4760 | 42.5 | 55.2 | 4760 | 24.2 | 55.2 | 3760 |
| | 191 × 343 | 65.7 | 59.0 | 7710 | 53.3 | 59.0 | 7710 | 30.3 | 59.0 | 6100 |
| | 191 × 394 | 78.1 | 61.0 | 11700 | 63.2 | 61.0 | 11700 | 36.0 | 61.0 | 9250 |
| Hem-Fir | 191 × 191 | 18.5 | 34.1 | 1110 | 13.9 | 34.1 | 998 | 6.11 | 34.1 | 887 |
| | 191 × 241 | 27.2 | 39.8 | 2230 | 20.4 | 39.8 | 2010 | 8.99 | 39.8 | 1780 |
| | 191 × 292 | 39.0 | 44.2 | 3960 | 31.4 | 44.2 | 3960 | 18.0 | 44.2 | 3170 |
| | 191 × 343 | 48.9 | 47.2 | 6420 | 39.4 | 47.2 | 6420 | 22.6 | 47.2 | 5140 |
| | 191 × 394 | 58.0 | 48.8 | 9740 | 46.8 | 48.8 | 9740 | 26.8 | 48.8 | 7790 |
| S-P-F | 191 × 191 | 17.3 | 34.1 | 943 | 13.0 | 34.1 | 832 | 5.71 | 34.1 | 721 |
| | 191 × 241 | 25.3 | 39.8 | 1890 | 19.1 | 39.8 | 1670 | 8.38 | 39.8 | 1450 |
| Northern | 191 × 191 | 16.3 | 28.5 | 887 | 12.2 | 28.5 | 776 | 5.30 | 28.5 | 665 |
| | 191 × 241 | 24.0 | 33.1 | 1780 | 18.0 | 33.1 | 1560 | 7.79 | 33.1 | 1340 |

**2** Bending Members

# Beam Selection Tables

## 241 mm    Sawn Timbers

| Species | Size (b × d) mm | Select Structural | | | No.1 Grade | | | No.2 Grade | | |
|---|---|---|---|---|---|---|---|---|---|---|
| | | $M_r$ kN·m | $V_r$ kN | $E_S I$ ×10⁹ N·mm² | $M_r$ kN·m | $V_r$ kN | $E_S I$ ×10⁹ N·mm² | $M_r$ kN·m | $V_r$ kN | $E_S I$ ×10⁹ N·mm² |
| D.Fir-L | 241 × 241 | 46.1 | 62.7 | 3370 | 34.8 | 62.7 | 2950 | 15.1 | 62.7 | 2670 |
| | 241 × 292 | 62.0 | 69.7 | 6000 | 46.8 | 69.7 | 5250 | 20.3 | 69.7 | 4750 |
| | 241 × 343 | 82.9 | 74.4 | 9730 | 67.2 | 74.4 | 9730 | 38.3 | 74.4 | 7700 |
| | 241 × 394 | 98.5 | 76.9 | 14700 | 79.8 | 76.9 | 14700 | 45.5 | 76.9 | 11700 |
| Hem-Fir | 241 × 241 | 34.3 | 50.2 | 2810 | 25.7 | 50.2 | 2530 | 11.3 | 50.2 | 2250 |
| | 241 × 292 | 46.1 | 55.7 | 5000 | 34.6 | 55.7 | 4500 | 15.3 | 55.7 | 4000 |
| | 241 × 343 | 61.7 | 59.5 | 8100 | 49.8 | 59.5 | 8100 | 28.5 | 59.5 | 6480 |
| | 241 × 394 | 73.2 | 61.5 | 12300 | 59.1 | 61.5 | 12300 | 33.8 | 61.5 | 9830 |
| S-P-F | 241 × 241 | 32.0 | 50.2 | 2390 | 24.2 | 50.2 | 2110 | 10.6 | 50.2 | 1830 |
| Northern | 241 × 241 | 30.2 | 41.8 | 2250 | 22.7 | 41.8 | 1970 | 9.83 | 41.8 | 1690 |

## 292-394 mm

| Species | Size (b × d) mm | Select Structural | | | No.1 Grade | | | No.2 Grade | | |
|---|---|---|---|---|---|---|---|---|---|---|
| D.Fir-L | 292 × 292 | 75.2 | 84.4 | 7270 | 56.7 | 84.4 | 6360 | 24.6 | 84.4 | 5760 |
| | 292 × 343 | 94.3 | 90.1 | 11800 | 71.1 | 90.1 | 10300 | 30.9 | 90.1 | 9330 |
| | 292 × 394 | 119 | 93.2 | 17900 | 96.7 | 93.2 | 17900 | 55.1 | 93.2 | 14100 |
| | 343 × 343 | 111 | 106 | 13800 | 83.5 | 106 | 12100 | 36.3 | 106 | 11000 |
| | 343 × 394 | 132 | 110 | 21000 | 99.2 | 110 | 18400 | 43.1 | 110 | 16600 |
| | 394 × 394 | 151 | 126 | 24100 | 114 | 126 | 21100 | 49.5 | 126 | 19100 |
| Hem-Fir | 292 × 292 | 55.9 | 67.5 | 6060 | 41.9 | 67.5 | 5450 | 18.5 | 67.5 | 4850 |
| | 292 × 343 | 70.1 | 72.1 | 9820 | 52.6 | 72.1 | 8840 | 23.2 | 72.1 | 7860 |
| | 292 × 394 | 88.7 | 74.6 | 14900 | 71.6 | 74.6 | 14900 | 41.0 | 74.6 | 11900 |
| | 343 × 343 | 82.3 | 84.7 | 11500 | 61.7 | 84.7 | 10400 | 27.2 | 84.7 | 9230 |

# Beam Selection Tables

## Glulam

**80** mm

| Size (b × d) mm | Spruce-Pine 20f-E Stress Grade | | | | D.Fir-L 20f-E Stress Grade | | | | D.Fir-L 24f-E Stress Grade | | | |
|---|---|---|---|---|---|---|---|---|---|---|---|---|
| | $M'_r$ | $V_r$ | $W_rL^{0.18}$ | $E_sI$ | $M'_r$ | $V_r$ | $W_rL^{0.18}$ | $E_sI$ | $M'_r$ | $V_r$ | $W_rL^{0.18}$ | $E_sI$ |
| | | | | $\times 10^9$ | | | | $\times 10^9$ | | | | $\times 10^9$ |
| | kN·m | kN | kN·m$^{0.18}$ | N·mm$^2$ | kN·m | kN | kN·m$^{0.18}$ | N·mm$^2$ | kN·m | kN | kN·m$^{0.18}$ | N·mm$^2$ |
| 80 × 114 | 3.99 | 9.58 | 59.3 | 102 | 3.99 | 10.9 | 67.7 | 122 | 4.77 | 10.9 | 67.7 | 129 |
| 80 × 152 | 7.10 | 12.8 | 75.0 | 241 | 7.10 | 14.6 | 85.7 | 290 | 8.48 | 14.6 | 85.7 | 307 |
| 80 × 190 | 11.1 | 16.0 | 90.1 | 471 | 11.1 | 18.2 | 103 | 567 | 13.3 | 18.2 | 103 | 599 |
| 80 × 228 | 16.0 | 19.2 | 105 | 814 | 16.0 | 21.9 | 120 | 980 | 19.1 | 21.9 | 120 | 1040 |
| 80 × 266 | 21.7 | 22.3 | 119 | 1290 | 21.7 | 25.5 | 136 | 1560 | 26.0 | 25.5 | 136 | 1640 |
| 80 × 304 | 28.4 | 25.5 | 132 | 1930 | 28.4 | 29.2 | 151 | 2320 | 33.9 | 29.2 | 151 | 2450 |
| 80 × 342 | 35.9 | 28.7 | 146 | 2750 | 35.9 | 32.8 | 167 | 3310 | 42.9 | 32.8 | 167 | 3490 |
| 80 × 380 | 44.4 | 31.9 | 159 | 3770 | 44.4 | 36.5 | 182 | 4540 | 53.0 | 36.5 | 182 | 4790 |
| 80 × 418 | 53.7 | 35.1 | 172 | 5020 | 53.7 | 40.1 | 197 | 6040 | 64.2 | 40.1 | 197 | 6380 |
| 80 × 456 | 63.9 | 38.3 | 185 | 6510 | 63.9 | 43.8 | 211 | 7840 | 76.4 | 43.8 | 211 | 8280 |
| 80 × 494 | 75.0 | 41.5 | 197 | 8280 | 75.0 | 47.4 | 225 | 9970 | 89.6 | 47.4 | 225 | 10500 |
| 80 × 532 | 86.9 | 44.7 | 210 | 10300 | 86.9 | 51.1 | 240 | 12400 | 104 | 51.1 | 240 | 13100 |
| 80 × 570 | 99.8 | 47.9 | 222 | 12700 | 99.8 | 54.7 | 253 | 15300 | 119 | 54.7 | 253 | 16200 |

**130** mm

| Size (b × d) mm | $M'_r$ | $V_r$ | $W_rL^{0.18}$ | $E_sI \times 10^9$ | $M'_r$ | $V_r$ | $W_rL^{0.18}$ | $E_sI \times 10^9$ | $M'_r$ | $V_r$ | $W_rL^{0.18}$ | $E_sI \times 10^9$ |
|---|---|---|---|---|---|---|---|---|---|---|---|---|
| 130 × 152 | 11.5 | 20.7 | 112 | 392 | 11.5 | 23.7 | 128 | 472 | 13.8 | 23.7 | 128 | 498 |
| 130 × 190 | 18.0 | 25.9 | 134 | 765 | 18.0 | 29.6 | 153 | 921 | 21.5 | 29.6 | 153 | 973 |
| 130 × 228 | 26.0 | 31.1 | 156 | 1320 | 26.0 | 35.6 | 178 | 1590 | 31.0 | 35.6 | 178 | 1680 |
| 130 × 266 | 35.3 | 36.3 | 177 | 2100 | 35.3 | 41.5 | 202 | 2530 | 42.2 | 41.5 | 202 | 2670 |
| 130 × 304 | 46.1 | 41.5 | 197 | 3130 | 46.1 | 47.4 | 225 | 3770 | 55.1 | 47.4 | 225 | 3990 |
| 130 × 342 | 58.4 | 46.7 | 217 | 4460 | 58.4 | 53.4 | 248 | 5370 | 69.8 | 53.4 | 248 | 5680 |
| 130 × 380 | 72.1 | 51.9 | 237 | 6120 | 72.1 | 59.3 | 271 | 7370 | 86.2 | 59.3 | 271 | 7790 |
| 130 × 418 | 87.2 | 57.1 | 256 | 8150 | 87.2 | 65.2 | 293 | 9810 | 104 | 65.2 | 293 | 10400 |
| 130 × 456 | 104 | 62.2 | 275 | 10600 | 104 | 71.1 | 314 | 12700 | 124 | 71.1 | 314 | 13500 |
| 130 × 494 | 122 | 67.4 | 294 | 13500 | 122 | 77.1 | 336 | 16200 | 146 | 77.1 | 336 | 17100 |
| 130 × 532 | 141 | 72.6 | 312 | 16800 | 141 | 83.0 | 357 | 20200 | 169 | 83.0 | 357 | 21400 |
| 130 × 570 | 162 | 77.8 | 330 | 20700 | 162 | 88.9 | 377 | 24900 | 194 | 88.9 | 377 | 26300 |
| 130 × 608 | 185 | 83.0 | 348 | 25100 | 185 | 94.8 | 398 | 30200 | 221 | 94.8 | 398 | 31900 |
| 130 × 646 | 208 | 88.2 | 366 | 30100 | 208 | 101 | 418 | 36200 | 249 | 101 | 418 | 38300 |
| 130 × 684 | 234 | 93.4 | 383 | 35700 | 234 | 107 | 438 | 43000 | 279 | 107 | 438 | 45400 |
| 130 × 722 | 260 | 98.6 | 401 | 42000 | 260 | 113 | 458 | 50600 | 311 | 113 | 458 | 53400 |
| 130 × 760 | 288 | 104 | 418 | 49000 | 288 | 119 | 478 | 59000 | 345 | 119 | 478 | 62300 |
| 130 × 798 | 318 | 109 | 435 | 56700 | 318 | 124 | 497 | 68300 | 380 | 124 | 497 | 72100 |
| 130 × 836 | 349 | 114 | 452 | 65200 | 349 | 130 | 517 | 78500 | 417 | 130 | 517 | 82900 |
| 130 × 874 | 381 | 119 | 469 | 74500 | 381 | 136 | 536 | 89700 | 456 | 136 | 536 | 94700 |
| 130 × 912 | 415 | 124 | 485 | 84600 | 415 | 142 | 555 | 102000 | 496 | 142 | 555 | 108000 |
| 130 × 950 | 451 | 130 | 502 | 95700 | 451 | 148 | 574 | 115000 | 539 | 148 | 574 | 122000 |

Notes:
1. 24f-E Hem-Fir values are identical to 24f-E D.Fir-L for $M_r$ and $E_sI$, and are identical to 20f-E Spruce-Pine for $V_r$ and $W_rL^{0.18}$.
2. All values apply to EX grades also.
3. $V_r$ may only be used as a simplified check of shear capacity if the beam volume is < 2 m$^3$.
4. $W_rL^{0.18}$ may be used for all beam volumes to check shear capacity. See Example 2: Beams.
5. Some plant manufacturing processes may result in small variations from the standard member widths shown.

2

Bending Members

# Beam Selection Tables

## Glulam

| Size (b × d) mm | Spruce-Pine 20f-E Stress Grade | | | | D.Fir-L 20f-E Stress Grade | | | | D.Fir-L 24f-E Stress Grade | | | |
|---|---|---|---|---|---|---|---|---|---|---|---|---|
| | $M'_r$ | $V_r$ | $W_r L^{0.18}$ | $E_s I$ | $M'_r$ | $V_r$ | $W_r L^{0.18}$ | $E_s I$ | $M'_r$ | $V_r$ | $W_r L^{0.18}$ | $E_s I$ |
| | kN·m | kN | kN·m$^{0.18}$ | ×10⁹ N·mm² | kN·m | kN | kN·m$^{0.18}$ | ×10⁹ N·mm² | kN·m | kN | kN·m$^{0.18}$ | ×10⁹ N·mm² |
| 175 × 190 | 24.3 | 34.9 | 171 | 1030 | 24.3 | 39.9 | 196 | 1240 | 29.0 | 39.9 | 196 | 1310 |
| 175 × 228 | 34.9 | 41.9 | 199 | 1780 | 34.9 | 47.9 | 227 | 2140 | 41.8 | 47.9 | 227 | 2260 |
| 175 × 266 | 47.5 | 48.9 | 226 | 2830 | 47.5 | 55.9 | 258 | 3400 | 56.8 | 55.9 | 258 | 3600 |
| 175 × 304 | 62.1 | 55.9 | 252 | 4220 | 62.1 | 63.8 | 288 | 5080 | 74.2 | 63.8 | 288 | 5370 |
| 175 × 342 | 78.6 | 62.8 | 277 | 6010 | 78.6 | 71.8 | 317 | 7230 | 94 | 71.8 | 317 | 7640 |
| 175 × 380 | 97.0 | 69.8 | 302 | 8240 | 97.0 | 79.8 | 345 | 9920 | 116 | 79.8 | 345 | 10500 |
| 175 × 418 | 117 | 76.8 | 327 | 11000 | 117 | 87.8 | 373 | 13200 | 140 | 87.8 | 373 | 14000 |
| 175 × 456 | 140 | 83.8 | 351 | 14200 | 140 | 95.8 | 401 | 17100 | 167 | 95.8 | 401 | 18100 |
| 175 × 494 | 164 | 90.8 | 375 | 18100 | 164 | 104 | 428 | 21800 | 196 | 104 | 428 | 23000 |
| 175 × 532 | 190 | 97.8 | 398 | 22600 | 190 | 112 | 455 | 27200 | 227 | 112 | 455 | 28800 |
| 175 × 570 | 218 | 105 | 421 | 27800 | 218 | 120 | 482 | 33500 | 261 | 120 | 482 | 35400 |
| 175 × 608 | 248 | 112 | 444 | 33800 | 248 | 128 | 508 | 40600 | 297 | 128 | 508 | 42900 |
| 175 × 646 | 280 | 119 | 467 | 40500 | 280 | 136 | 534 | 48800 | 335 | 136 | 534 | 51500 |
| 175 × 684 | 314 | 126 | 489 | 48100 | 314 | 144 | 559 | 57900 | 376 | 144 | 559 | 61100 |
| 175 × 722 | 350 | 133 | 511 | 56500 | 350 | 152 | 585 | 68100 | 419 | 152 | 585 | 71900 |
| 175 × 760 | 388 | 140 | 533 | 65900 | 388 | 160 | 610 | 79400 | 464 | 160 | 610 | 83900 |
| 175 × 798 | 428 | 147 | 555 | 76300 | 428 | 168 | 635 | 91900 | 512 | 168 | 635 | 97100 |
| 175 × 836 | 470 | 154 | 577 | 87800 | 470 | 176 | 659 | 106000 | 561 | 176 | 659 | 112000 |
| 175 × 874 | 513 | 161 | 598 | 100000 | 513 | 184 | 684 | 121000 | 614 | 184 | 684 | 128000 |
| 175 × 912 | 559 | 168 | 619 | 114000 | 559 | 192 | 708 | 137000 | 668 | 192 | 708 | 145000 |
| 175 × 950 | 606 | 175 | 641 | 129000 | 606 | 200 | 732 | 155000 | 725 | 200 | 732 | 164000 |
| 175 × 988 | 656 | 182 | 662 | 145000 | 656 | 207 | 756 | 174000 | 784 | 207 | 756 | 184000 |
| 175 × 1026 | 707 | 189 | 682 | 162000 | 707 | 215 | 780 | 195000 | 846 | 215 | 780 | 206000 |
| 175 × 1064 | 761 | 196 | 703 | 181000 | 761 | 223 | 803 | 218000 | 909 | 223 | 803 | 230000 |
| 175 × 1102 | 816 | 202 | 723 | 201000 | 816 | 231 | 827 | 242000 | 975 | 231 | 827 | 256000 |
| 175 × 1140 | 873 | 209 | 744 | 223000 | 873 | 239 | 850 | 268000 | 1040 | 239 | 850 | 283000 |
| 175 × 1178 | 933 | 216 | 764 | 246000 | 933 | 247 | 873 | 296000 | 1110 | 247 | 873 | 312000 |
| 175 × 1216 | 994 | 223 | 784 | 270000 | 994 | 255 | 896 | 325000 | 1190 | 255 | 896 | 344000 |
| 175 × 1254 | 1060 | 230 | 804 | 296000 | 1060 | 263 | 919 | 357000 | 1260 | 263 | 919 | 377000 |

Notes:
1. 24f-E Hem-Fir values are identical to 24f-E D.Fir-L for $M_r$ and $E_s I$, and are identical to 20f-E Spruce-Pine for $V_r$ and $W_r L^{0.18}$.
2. All values apply to EX grades also.
3. $V_r$ may only be used as a simplified check of shear capacity if the beam volume is < 2 m³.
4. $W_r L^{0.18}$ may be used for all beam volumes to check shear capacity. See Example 2: Beams.
5. Some plant manufacturing processes may result in small variations from the standard member widths shown.

# Beam Selection Tables

## Glulam

**215** mm

| Size (b × d) mm | Spruce-Pine 20f-E Stress Grade | | | | D.Fir-L 20f-E Stress Grade | | | | D.Fir-L 24f-E Stress Grade | | | |
|---|---|---|---|---|---|---|---|---|---|---|---|---|
| | $M'_r$ kN·m | $V_r$ kN | $W_r L^{0.18}$ kN·m$^{0.18}$ | $E_S I$ ×10$^9$ N·mm$^2$ | $M'_r$ kN·m | $V_r$ kN | $W_r L^{0.18}$ kN·m$^{0.18}$ | $E_S I$ ×10$^9$ N·mm$^2$ | $M'_r$ kN·m | $V_r$ kN | $W_r L^{0.18}$ kN·m$^{0.18}$ | $E_S I$ ×10$^9$ N·mm$^2$ |
| 215 × 266 | 58.4 | 60.0 | 267 | 3470 | 58.4 | 68.6 | 305 | 4180 | 69.8 | 68.6 | 305 | 4420 |
| 215 × 304 | 76.3 | 68.6 | 298 | 5180 | 76.3 | 78.4 | 340 | 6240 | 91.2 | 78.4 | 340 | 6590 |
| 215 × 342 | 96.6 | 77.2 | 328 | 7380 | 96.6 | 88.2 | 375 | 8890 | 115 | 88.2 | 375 | 9390 |
| 215 × 380 | 119 | 85.8 | 358 | 10100 | 119 | 98.0 | 409 | 12200 | 143 | 98.0 | 409 | 12900 |
| 215 × 418 | 144 | 94.4 | 387 | 13500 | 144 | 108 | 442 | 16200 | 172 | 108 | 442 | 17100 |
| 215 × 456 | 172 | 103 | 415 | 17500 | 172 | 118 | 475 | 21100 | 205 | 118 | 475 | 22300 |
| 215 × 494 | 201 | 112 | 444 | 22200 | 201 | 127 | 507 | 26800 | 241 | 127 | 507 | 28300 |
| 215 × 532 | 234 | 120 | 471 | 27800 | 234 | 137 | 539 | 33500 | 279 | 137 | 539 | 35300 |
| 215 × 570 | 268 | 129 | 499 | 34200 | 268 | 147 | 570 | 41100 | 321 | 147 | 570 | 43500 |
| 215 × 608 | 305 | 137 | 526 | 41500 | 305 | 157 | 601 | 49900 | 365 | 157 | 601 | 52800 |
| 215 × 646 | 345 | 146 | 553 | 49700 | 345 | 167 | 632 | 59900 | 412 | 167 | 632 | 63300 |
| 215 × 684 | 386 | 154 | 579 | 59100 | 386 | 176 | 662 | 71100 | 462 | 176 | 662 | 75100 |
| 215 × 722 | 430 | 163 | 606 | 69500 | 430 | 186 | 692 | 83600 | 514 | 186 | 692 | 88300 |
| 215 × 760 | 477 | 172 | 632 | 81000 | 477 | 196 | 722 | 97500 | 570 | 196 | 722 | 103000 |
| 215 × 798 | 526 | 180 | 657 | 93800 | 526 | 206 | 751 | 113000 | 628 | 206 | 751 | 119000 |
| 215 × 836 | 577 | 189 | 683 | 108000 | 577 | 216 | 780 | 130000 | 690 | 216 | 780 | 137000 |
| 215 × 874 | 631 | 197 | 708 | 123000 | 631 | 225 | 809 | 148000 | 754 | 225 | 809 | 157000 |
| 215 × 912 | 687 | 206 | 733 | 140000 | 687 | 235 | 838 | 169000 | 821 | 235 | 838 | 178000 |
| 215 × 950 | 745 | 214 | 758 | 158000 | 745 | 245 | 867 | 190000 | 891 | 245 | 867 | 201000 |
| 215 × 988 | 806 | 223 | 783 | 178000 | 806 | 255 | 895 | 214000 | 963 | 255 | 895 | 226000 |
| 215 × 1026 | 869 | 232 | 808 | 199000 | 869 | 265 | 923 | 240000 | 1040 | 265 | 923 | 253000 |
| 215 × 1064 | 935 | 240 | 832 | 222000 | 935 | 275 | 951 | 268000 | 1120 | 275 | 951 | 283000 |
| 215 × 1102 | 1000 | 249 | 857 | 247000 | 1000 | 284 | 979 | 297000 | 1200 | 284 | 979 | 314000 |
| 215 × 1140 | 1070 | 257 | 881 | 273000 | 1070 | 294 | 1010 | 329000 | 1280 | 294 | 1010 | 348000 |
| 215 × 1178 | 1150 | 266 | 905 | 302000 | 1150 | 304 | 1030 | 363000 | 1370 | 304 | 1030 | 384000 |
| 215 × 1216 | 1220 | 275 | 929 | 332000 | 1220 | 314 | 1060 | 399000 | 1460 | 314 | 1060 | 422000 |
| 215 × 1254 | 1300 | 283 | 952 | 364000 | 1300 | 324 | 1090 | 438000 | 1550 | 324 | 1090 | 463000 |
| 215 × 1292 | 1380 | 292 | 976 | 398000 | 1380 | 333 | 1120 | 479000 | 1650 | 333 | 1120 | 506000 |
| 215 × 1330 | 1460 | 300 | 999 | 434000 | 1460 | 343 | 1140 | 523000 | 1750 | 343 | 1140 | 552000 |
| 215 × 1368 | 1550 | 309 | 1020 | 472000 | 1550 | 353 | 1170 | 569000 | 1850 | 353 | 1170 | 601000 |
| 215 × 1406 | 1630 | 317 | 1050 | 513000 | 1630 | 363 | 1200 | 617000 | 1950 | 363 | 1200 | 652000 |
| 215 × 1444 | 1720 | 326 | 1070 | 556000 | 1720 | 373 | 1220 | 669000 | 2060 | 373 | 1220 | 707000 |
| 215 × 1482 | 1810 | 335 | 1090 | 601000 | 1810 | 382 | 1250 | 723000 | 2170 | 382 | 1250 | 764000 |
| 215 × 1520 | 1910 | 343 | 1110 | 648000 | 1910 | 392 | 1270 | 780000 | 2280 | 392 | 1270 | 824000 |
| 215 × 1558 | 2000 | 352 | 1140 | 698000 | 2000 | 402 | 1300 | 840000 | 2400 | 402 | 1300 | 888000 |
| 215 × 1596 | 2100 | 360 | 1160 | 750000 | 2100 | 412 | 1330 | 903000 | 2510 | 412 | 1330 | 954000 |

Notes:
1. 24f-E Hem-Fir values are identical to 24f-E D.Fir-L for $M_r$ and $E_S I$, and are identical to 20f-E Spruce-Pine for $V_r$ and $W_r L^{0.18}$.
2. All values apply to EX grades also.
3. $V_r$ may only be used as a simplified check of shear capacity if the beam volume is < 2 m$^3$.
4. $W_r L^{0.18}$ may be used for all beam volumes to check shear capacity. See Example 2: Beams.
5. Some plant manufacturing processes may result in small variations from the standard member widths shown.

2

Bending Members

# Beam Selection Tables

 **Glulam**

| Size (b × d) mm | Spruce-Pine 20f-E Stress Grade | | | | D.Fir-L 20f-E Stress Grade | | | | D.Fir-L 24f-E Stress Grade | | | |
|---|---|---|---|---|---|---|---|---|---|---|---|---|
| | $M'_r$ | $V_r$ | $W_r L^{0.18}$ | $E_S I$ ×10⁹ | $M'_r$ | $V_r$ | $W_r L^{0.18}$ | $E_S I$ ×10⁹ | $M'_r$ | $V_r$ | $W_r L^{0.18}$ | $E_S I$ ×10⁹ |
| | kN·m | kN | kN·m$^{0.18}$ | N·mm² | kN·m | kN | kN·m$^{0.18}$ | N·mm² | kN·m | kN | kN·m$^{0.18}$ | N·mm² |
| 265 × 342 | 119 | 95.2 | 390 | 9100 | 119 | 109 | 445 | 11000 | 142 | 109 | 445 | 11600 |
| 265 × 380 | 147 | 106 | 425 | 12500 | 147 | 121 | 485 | 15000 | 176 | 121 | 485 | 15900 |
| 265 × 418 | 178 | 116 | 459 | 16600 | 178 | 133 | 525 | 20000 | 213 | 133 | 525 | 21100 |
| 265 × 456 | 212 | 127 | 493 | 21600 | 212 | 145 | 564 | 26000 | 253 | 145 | 564 | 27400 |
| 265 × 494 | 248 | 137 | 527 | 27400 | 248 | 157 | 602 | 33000 | 297 | 157 | 602 | 34900 |
| 265 × 532 | 288 | 148 | 560 | 34200 | 288 | 169 | 640 | 41200 | 344 | 169 | 640 | 43600 |
| 265 × 570 | 331 | 159 | 592 | 42100 | 331 | 181 | 677 | 50700 | 395 | 181 | 677 | 53600 |
| 265 × 608 | 376 | 169 | 624 | 51100 | 376 | 193 | 714 | 61500 | 450 | 193 | 714 | 65000 |
| 265 × 646 | 425 | 180 | 656 | 61300 | 425 | 205 | 750 | 73800 | 508 | 205 | 750 | 78000 |
| 265 × 684 | 476 | 190 | 688 | 72800 | 476 | 218 | 786 | 87600 | 569 | 218 | 786 | 92600 |
| 265 × 722 | 530 | 201 | 719 | 85600 | 530 | 230 | 821 | 103000 | 634 | 230 | 821 | 109000 |
| 265 × 760 | 588 | 211 | 750 | 99800 | 588 | 242 | 857 | 120000 | 703 | 242 | 857 | 127000 |
| 265 × 798 | 648 | 222 | 780 | 116000 | 648 | 254 | 892 | 139000 | 775 | 254 | 892 | 147000 |
| 265 × 836 | 711 | 233 | 811 | 133000 | 711 | 266 | 926 | 160000 | 850 | 266 | 926 | 169000 |
| 265 × 874 | 777 | 243 | 841 | 152000 | 777 | 278 | 961 | 183000 | 929 | 278 | 961 | 193000 |
| 265 × 912 | 846 | 254 | 871 | 173000 | 846 | 290 | 995 | 208000 | 1010 | 290 | 995 | 219000 |
| 265 × 950 | 918 | 264 | 900 | 195000 | 918 | 302 | 1030 | 235000 | 1100 | 302 | 1030 | 248000 |
| 265 × 988 | 993 | 275 | 930 | 219000 | 993 | 314 | 1060 | 264000 | 1190 | 314 | 1060 | 279000 |
| 265 × 1026 | 1070 | 285 | 959 | 246000 | 1070 | 326 | 1100 | 296000 | 1280 | 326 | 1100 | 312000 |
| 265 × 1064 | 1150 | 296 | 988 | 274000 | 1150 | 338 | 1130 | 330000 | 1380 | 338 | 1130 | 348000 |
| 265 × 1102 | 1240 | 307 | 1020 | 304000 | 1240 | 350 | 1160 | 366000 | 1480 | 350 | 1160 | 387000 |
| 265 × 1140 | 1320 | 317 | 1050 | 337000 | 1320 | 363 | 1190 | 406000 | 1580 | 363 | 1190 | 429000 |
| 265 × 1178 | 1410 | 328 | 1070 | 372000 | 1410 | 375 | 1230 | 448000 | 1690 | 375 | 1230 | 473000 |
| 265 × 1216 | 1500 | 338 | 1100 | 409000 | 1500 | 387 | 1260 | 492000 | 1800 | 387 | 1260 | 520000 |
| 265 × 1254 | 1600 | 349 | 1130 | 449000 | 1600 | 399 | 1290 | 540000 | 1910 | 399 | 1290 | 570000 |
| 265 × 1292 | 1700 | 359 | 1160 | 491000 | 1700 | 411 | 1320 | 591000 | 2030 | 411 | 1320 | 624000 |
| 265 × 1330 | 1800 | 370 | 1190 | 535000 | 1800 | 423 | 1360 | 644000 | 2150 | 423 | 1360 | 681000 |
| 265 × 1368 | 1900 | 381 | 1210 | 582000 | 1900 | 435 | 1390 | 701000 | 2280 | 435 | 1390 | 741000 |
| 265 × 1406 | 2010 | 391 | 1240 | 632000 | 2010 | 447 | 1420 | 761000 | 2400 | 447 | 1420 | 804000 |
| 265 × 1444 | 2120 | 402 | 1270 | 685000 | 2120 | 459 | 1450 | 824000 | 2540 | 459 | 1450 | 871000 |
| 265 × 1482 | 2230 | 412 | 1300 | 740000 | 2230 | 471 | 1480 | 891000 | 2670 | 471 | 1480 | 942000 |
| 265 × 1520 | 2350 | 423 | 1320 | 799000 | 2350 | 483 | 1510 | 962000 | 2810 | 483 | 1510 | 1020000 |
| 265 × 1558 | 2470 | 434 | 1350 | 860000 | 2470 | 495 | 1540 | 1040000 | 2950 | 495 | 1540 | 1090000 |
| 265 × 1596 | 2590 | 444 | 1380 | 925000 | 2590 | 508 | 1570 | 1110000 | 3100 | 508 | 1570 | 1180000 |
| 265 × 1634 | 2720 | 455 | 1400 | 992000 | 2720 | 520 | 1600 | 1190000 | 3250 | 520 | 1600 | 1260000 |
| 265 × 1672 | 2840 | 465 | 1430 | 1060000 | 2840 | 532 | 1640 | 1280000 | 3400 | 532 | 1640 | 1350000 |
| 265 × 1710 | 2980 | 476 | 1460 | 1140000 | 2980 | 544 | 1670 | 1370000 | 3560 | 544 | 1670 | 1450000 |
| 265 × 1748 | 3110 | 486 | 1480 | 1210000 | 3110 | 556 | 1700 | 1460000 | 3720 | 556 | 1700 | 1550000 |
| 265 × 1786 | 3250 | 497 | 1510 | 1300000 | 3250 | 568 | 1730 | 1560000 | 3880 | 568 | 1730 | 1650000 |
| 265 × 1824 | 3390 | 508 | 1540 | 1380000 | 3390 | 580 | 1760 | 1660000 | 4050 | 580 | 1760 | 1760000 |
| 265 × 1862 | 3530 | 518 | 1560 | 1470000 | 3530 | 592 | 1790 | 1770000 | 4220 | 592 | 1790 | 1870000 |
| 265 × 1900 | 3670 | 529 | 1590 | 1560000 | 3670 | 604 | 1820 | 1880000 | 4390 | 604 | 1820 | 1980000 |
| 265 × 1938 | 3820 | 539 | 1620 | 1660000 | 3820 | 616 | 1850 | 1990000 | 4570 | 616 | 1850 | 2110000 |
| 265 × 1976 | 3970 | 550 | 1640 | 1750000 | 3970 | 628 | 1880 | 2110000 | 4750 | 628 | 1880 | 2230000 |

Notes: See page 67.

# Beam Selection Tables

## Glulam

**315** mm

| Size (b × d) mm | Spruce-Pine 20f-E Stress Grade | | | | D.Fir-L 20f-E Stress Grade | | | | D.Fir-L 24f-E Stress Grade | | | |
|---|---|---|---|---|---|---|---|---|---|---|---|---|
| | $M'_r$ | $V_r$ | $W_r L^{0.18}$ | $E_s I$ | $M'_r$ | $V_r$ | $W_r L^{0.18}$ | $E_s I$ | $M'_r$ | $V_r$ | $W_r L^{0.18}$ | $E_s I$ |
| | | | | $\times 10^9$ | | | | $\times 10^9$ | | | | $\times 10^9$ |
| | kN·m | kN | kN·m$^{0.18}$ | N·mm² | kN·m | kN | kN·m$^{0.18}$ | N·mm² | kN·m | kN | kN·m$^{0.18}$ | N·mm² |
| 315 × 380 | 175 | 126 | 489 | 14800 | 175 | 144 | 559 | 17900 | 209 | 144 | 559 | 18900 |
| 315 × 418 | 211 | 138 | 529 | 19700 | 211 | 158 | 605 | 23800 | 253 | 158 | 605 | 25100 |
| 315 × 456 | 252 | 151 | 568 | 25600 | 252 | 172 | 649 | 30900 | 301 | 172 | 649 | 32600 |
| 315 × 494 | 295 | 163 | 607 | 32600 | 295 | 187 | 693 | 39200 | 353 | 187 | 693 | 41500 |
| 315 × 532 | 342 | 176 | 645 | 40700 | 342 | 201 | 737 | 49000 | 409 | 201 | 737 | 51800 |
| 315 × 570 | 393 | 189 | 682 | 50100 | 393 | 215 | 780 | 60300 | 470 | 215 | 780 | 63700 |
| 315 × 608 | 447 | 201 | 719 | 60800 | 447 | 230 | 822 | 73200 | 534 | 230 | 822 | 77300 |
| 315 × 646 | 505 | 214 | 756 | 72900 | 505 | 244 | 864 | 87800 | 603 | 244 | 864 | 92700 |
| 315 × 684 | 566 | 226 | 792 | 86500 | 566 | 259 | 906 | 104000 | 676 | 259 | 906 | 110000 |
| 315 × 722 | 631 | 239 | 828 | 102000 | 631 | 273 | 947 | 123000 | 754 | 273 | 947 | 129000 |
| 315 × 760 | 699 | 251 | 864 | 119000 | 699 | 287 | 987 | 143000 | 835 | 287 | 987 | 151000 |
| 315 × 798 | 770 | 264 | 899 | 137000 | 770 | 302 | 1030 | 165000 | 921 | 302 | 1030 | 175000 |
| 315 × 836 | 845 | 277 | 934 | 158000 | 845 | 316 | 1070 | 190000 | 1010 | 316 | 1070 | 201000 |
| 315 × 874 | 924 | 289 | 969 | 181000 | 924 | 330 | 1110 | 217000 | 1100 | 330 | 1110 | 230000 |
| 315 × 912 | 1010 | 302 | 1000 | 205000 | 1010 | 345 | 1150 | 247000 | 1200 | 345 | 1150 | 261000 |
| 315 × 950 | 1090 | 314 | 1040 | 232000 | 1090 | 359 | 1190 | 279000 | 1300 | 359 | 1190 | 295000 |
| 315 × 988 | 1180 | 327 | 1070 | 261000 | 1180 | 373 | 1220 | 314000 | 1410 | 373 | 1220 | 332000 |
| 315 × 1026 | 1270 | 339 | 1100 | 292000 | 1270 | 388 | 1260 | 352000 | 1520 | 388 | 1260 | 371000 |
| 315 × 1064 | 1370 | 352 | 1140 | 326000 | 1370 | 402 | 1300 | 392000 | 1640 | 402 | 1300 | 414000 |
| 315 × 1102 | 1470 | 364 | 1170 | 362000 | 1470 | 417 | 1340 | 436000 | 1760 | 417 | 1340 | 460000 |
| 315 × 1140 | 1570 | 377 | 1200 | 401000 | 1570 | 431 | 1380 | 482000 | 1880 | 431 | 1380 | 509000 |
| 315 × 1178 | 1680 | 390 | 1240 | 442000 | 1680 | 445 | 1410 | 532000 | 2010 | 445 | 1410 | 562000 |
| 315 × 1216 | 1790 | 402 | 1270 | 486000 | 1790 | 460 | 1450 | 585000 | 2140 | 460 | 1450 | 618000 |
| 315 × 1254 | 1900 | 415 | 1300 | 533000 | 1900 | 474 | 1490 | 642000 | 2270 | 474 | 1490 | 678000 |
| 315 × 1292 | 2020 | 427 | 1330 | 583000 | 2020 | 488 | 1530 | 702000 | 2410 | 488 | 1530 | 742000 |
| 315 × 1330 | 2140 | 440 | 1370 | 636000 | 2140 | 503 | 1560 | 766000 | 2560 | 503 | 1560 | 809000 |
| 315 × 1368 | 2260 | 452 | 1400 | 692000 | 2260 | 517 | 1600 | 833000 | 2710 | 517 | 1600 | 880000 |
| 315 × 1406 | 2390 | 465 | 1430 | 751000 | 2390 | 531 | 1630 | 905000 | 2860 | 531 | 1630 | 956000 |
| 315 × 1444 | 2520 | 478 | 1460 | 814000 | 2520 | 546 | 1670 | 980000 | 3010 | 546 | 1670 | 1040000 |
| 315 × 1482 | 2660 | 490 | 1490 | 880000 | 2660 | 560 | 1710 | 1060000 | 3180 | 560 | 1710 | 1120000 |
| 315 × 1520 | 2790 | 503 | 1530 | 950000 | 2790 | 575 | 1740 | 1140000 | 3340 | 575 | 1740 | 1210000 |
| 315 × 1558 | 2940 | 515 | 1560 | 1020000 | 2940 | 589 | 1780 | 1230000 | 3510 | 589 | 1780 | 1300000 |
| 315 × 1596 | 3080 | 528 | 1590 | 1100000 | 3080 | 603 | 1810 | 1320000 | 3680 | 603 | 1810 | 1400000 |
| 315 × 1634 | 3230 | 540 | 1620 | 1180000 | 3230 | 618 | 1850 | 1420000 | 3860 | 618 | 1850 | 1500000 |
| 315 × 1672 | 3380 | 553 | 1650 | 1260000 | 3380 | 632 | 1880 | 1520000 | 4040 | 632 | 1880 | 1610000 |
| 315 × 1710 | 3540 | 566 | 1680 | 1350000 | 3540 | 646 | 1920 | 1630000 | 4230 | 646 | 1920 | 1720000 |
| 315 × 1748 | 3700 | 578 | 1710 | 1440000 | 3700 | 661 | 1950 | 1740000 | 4420 | 661 | 1950 | 1840000 |
| 315 × 1786 | 3860 | 591 | 1740 | 1540000 | 3860 | 675 | 1990 | 1850000 | 4610 | 675 | 1990 | 1960000 |
| 315 × 1824 | 4020 | 603 | 1770 | 1640000 | 4020 | 689 | 2020 | 1980000 | 4810 | 689 | 2020 | 2090000 |
| 315 × 1862 | 4190 | 616 | 1800 | 1750000 | 4190 | 704 | 2060 | 2100000 | 5010 | 704 | 2060 | 2220000 |
| 315 × 1900 | 4370 | 628 | 1830 | 1850000 | 4370 | 718 | 2090 | 2230000 | 5220 | 718 | 2090 | 2360000 |
| 315 × 1938 | 4540 | 641 | 1860 | 1970000 | 4540 | 733 | 2130 | 2370000 | 5430 | 733 | 2130 | 2500000 |
| 315 × 1976 | 4720 | 654 | 1890 | 2090000 | 4720 | 747 | 2160 | 2510000 | 5650 | 747 | 2160 | 2650000 |
| 315 × 2014 | 4910 | 666 | 1920 | 2210000 | 4910 | 761 | 2200 | 2660000 | 5860 | 761 | 2200 | 2810000 |
| 315 × 2052 | 5090 | 679 | 1950 | 2340000 | 5090 | 776 | 2230 | 2810000 | 6090 | 776 | 2230 | 2970000 |
| 315 × 2090 | 5280 | 691 | 1980 | 2470000 | 5280 | 790 | 2260 | 2970000 | 6320 | 790 | 2260 | 3140000 |
| 315 × 2128 | 5480 | 704 | 2010 | 2610000 | 5480 | 804 | 2300 | 3140000 | 6550 | 804 | 2300 | 3310000 |

Notes: See page 67.

# Beam Selection Tables

## 365 mm    Glulam

| Size (b × d) mm | Spruce-Pine 20f-E Stress Grade | | | | D.Fir-L 20f-E Stress Grade | | | | D.Fir-L 24f-E Stress Grade | | | |
|---|---|---|---|---|---|---|---|---|---|---|---|---|
| | $M'_r$ | $V_r$ | $W_r L^{0.18}$ | $E_s I$ | $M'_r$ | $V_r$ | $W_r L^{0.18}$ | $E_s I$ | $M'_r$ | $V_r$ | $W_r L^{0.18}$ | $E_s I$ |
| | | | | $\times 10^9$ | | | | $\times 10^9$ | | | | $\times 10^9$ |
| | kN·m | kN | kN·m$^{0.18}$ | N·mm$^2$ | kN·m | kN | kN·m$^{0.18}$ | N·mm$^2$ | kN·m | kN | kN·m$^{0.18}$ | N·mm$^2$ |
| 365 × 380 | 202 | 146 | 552 | 17200 | 202 | 166 | 631 | 20700 | 242 | 166 | 631 | 21900 |
| 365 × 418 | 245 | 160 | 597 | 22900 | 245 | 183 | 682 | 27500 | 293 | 183 | 682 | 29100 |
| 365 × 456 | 291 | 175 | 641 | 29700 | 291 | 200 | 733 | 35800 | 348 | 200 | 733 | 37800 |
| 365 × 494 | 342 | 189 | 685 | 37800 | 342 | 216 | 782 | 45500 | 409 | 216 | 782 | 48000 |
| 365 × 532 | 397 | 204 | 728 | 47200 | 397 | 233 | 832 | 56800 | 474 | 233 | 832 | 60000 |
| 365 × 570 | 455 | 218 | 770 | 58000 | 455 | 250 | 880 | 69800 | 544 | 250 | 880 | 73800 |
| 365 × 608 | 518 | 233 | 812 | 70400 | 518 | 266 | 928 | 84800 | 619 | 266 | 928 | 89600 |
| 365 × 646 | 585 | 248 | 853 | 84500 | 585 | 283 | 975 | 102000 | 699 | 283 | 975 | 107000 |
| 365 × 684 | 656 | 262 | 894 | 100000 | 656 | 300 | 1020 | 121000 | 784 | 300 | 1020 | 128000 |
| 365 × 722 | 731 | 277 | 935 | 118000 | 731 | 316 | 1070 | 142000 | 873 | 316 | 1070 | 150000 |
| 365 × 760 | 810 | 291 | 975 | 138000 | 810 | 333 | 1110 | 166000 | 968 | 333 | 1110 | 175000 |
| 365 × 798 | 893 | 306 | 1010 | 159000 | 893 | 350 | 1160 | 192000 | 1070 | 350 | 1160 | 202000 |
| 365 × 836 | 980 | 320 | 1050 | 183000 | 980 | 366 | 1200 | 220000 | 1170 | 366 | 1200 | 233000 |
| 365 × 874 | 1070 | 335 | 1090 | 209000 | 1070 | 383 | 1250 | 252000 | 1280 | 383 | 1250 | 266000 |
| 365 × 912 | 1170 | 350 | 1130 | 238000 | 1170 | 399 | 1290 | 286000 | 1390 | 399 | 1290 | 302000 |
| 365 × 950 | 1260 | 364 | 1170 | 269000 | 1260 | 416 | 1340 | 323000 | 1510 | 416 | 1340 | 342000 |
| 365 × 988 | 1370 | 379 | 1210 | 302000 | 1370 | 433 | 1380 | 364000 | 1640 | 433 | 1380 | 384000 |
| 365 × 1026 | 1480 | 393 | 1250 | 338000 | 1480 | 449 | 1420 | 407000 | 1760 | 449 | 1420 | 430000 |
| 365 × 1064 | 1590 | 408 | 1280 | 377000 | 1590 | 466 | 1470 | 454000 | 1900 | 466 | 1470 | 480000 |
| 365 × 1102 | 1700 | 422 | 1320 | 419000 | 1700 | 483 | 1510 | 505000 | 2030 | 483 | 1510 | 533000 |
| 365 × 1140 | 1820 | 437 | 1360 | 464000 | 1820 | 499 | 1550 | 559000 | 2180 | 499 | 1550 | 590000 |
| 365 × 1178 | 1940 | 451 | 1400 | 512000 | 1940 | 516 | 1600 | 617000 | 2320 | 516 | 1600 | 651000 |
| 365 × 1216 | 2070 | 466 | 1430 | 563000 | 2070 | 533 | 1640 | 678000 | 2480 | 533 | 1640 | 716000 |
| 365 × 1254 | 2200 | 481 | 1470 | 618000 | 2200 | 549 | 1680 | 744000 | 2630 | 549 | 1680 | 786000 |
| 365 × 1292 | 2340 | 495 | 1510 | 676000 | 2340 | 566 | 1720 | 813000 | 2800 | 566 | 1720 | 859000 |
| 365 × 1330 | 2480 | 510 | 1540 | 737000 | 2480 | 583 | 1760 | 887000 | 2960 | 583 | 1760 | 937000 |
| 365 × 1368 | 2620 | 524 | 1580 | 802000 | 2620 | 599 | 1800 | 966000 | 3140 | 599 | 1800 | 1020000 |
| 365 × 1406 | 2770 | 539 | 1610 | 871000 | 2770 | 616 | 1840 | 1050000 | 3310 | 616 | 1840 | 1110000 |
| 365 × 1444 | 2920 | 553 | 1650 | 943000 | 2920 | 632 | 1890 | 1140000 | 3490 | 632 | 1890 | 1200000 |
| 365 × 1482 | 3080 | 568 | 1690 | 1020000 | 3080 | 649 | 1930 | 1230000 | 3680 | 649 | 1930 | 1300000 |
| 365 × 1520 | 3240 | 583 | 1720 | 1100000 | 3240 | 666 | 1970 | 1320000 | 3870 | 666 | 1970 | 1400000 |
| 365 × 1558 | 3400 | 597 | 1760 | 1180000 | 3400 | 682 | 2010 | 1430000 | 4070 | 682 | 2010 | 1510000 |
| 365 × 1596 | 3570 | 612 | 1790 | 1270000 | 3570 | 699 | 2050 | 1530000 | 4270 | 699 | 2050 | 1620000 |
| 365 × 1634 | 3740 | 626 | 1830 | 1370000 | 3740 | 716 | 2090 | 1650000 | 4470 | 716 | 2090 | 1740000 |
| 365 × 1672 | 3920 | 641 | 1860 | 1460000 | 3920 | 732 | 2130 | 1760000 | 4680 | 732 | 2130 | 1860000 |
| 365 × 1710 | 4100 | 655 | 1900 | 1570000 | 4100 | 749 | 2170 | 1890000 | 4900 | 749 | 2170 | 1990000 |
| 365 × 1748 | 4280 | 670 | 1930 | 1670000 | 4280 | 766 | 2210 | 2010000 | 5120 | 766 | 2210 | 2130000 |
| 365 × 1786 | 4470 | 684 | 1960 | 1780000 | 4470 | 782 | 2240 | 2150000 | 5340 | 782 | 2240 | 2270000 |
| 365 × 1824 | 4660 | 699 | 2000 | 1900000 | 4660 | 799 | 2280 | 2290000 | 5570 | 799 | 2280 | 2420000 |
| 365 × 1862 | 4860 | 714 | 2030 | 2020000 | 4860 | 816 | 2320 | 2430000 | 5810 | 816 | 2320 | 2570000 |
| 365 × 1900 | 5060 | 728 | 2070 | 2150000 | 5060 | 832 | 2360 | 2590000 | 6050 | 832 | 2360 | 2730000 |
| 365 × 1938 | 5260 | 743 | 2100 | 2280000 | 5260 | 849 | 2400 | 2750000 | 6290 | 849 | 2400 | 2900000 |
| 365 × 1976 | 5470 | 757 | 2130 | 2420000 | 5470 | 865 | 2440 | 2910000 | 6540 | 865 | 2440 | 3070000 |
| 365 × 2014 | 5690 | 772 | 2170 | 2560000 | 5690 | 882 | 2480 | 3080000 | 6800 | 882 | 2480 | 3260000 |
| 365 × 2052 | 5900 | 786 | 2200 | 2710000 | 5900 | 899 | 2520 | 3260000 | 7050 | 899 | 2520 | 3440000 |
| 365 × 2090 | 6120 | 801 | 2230 | 2860000 | 6120 | 915 | 2550 | 3440000 | 7320 | 915 | 2550 | 3640000 |
| 365 × 2128 | 6350 | 816 | 2270 | 3020000 | 6350 | 932 | 2590 | 3630000 | 7590 | 932 | 2590 | 3840000 |

Notes: See page 67.

# Beam Selection Tables

## Structural Composite Lumber

**2.0E SCL**

(For preliminary sizing only – Consult with manufacturer for actual capacities)

| Size (b x d) mm | $M_r$ kN·m | $V_r$ kN | $E_s I$ x $10^9$ N·mm² | $Q_r$ kN/mm of bearing length |
|---|---|---|---|---|
| 44 x 140 | 5.2 | 14 | 140 | 0.33 |
| 44 x 184 | 8.7 | 18 | 310 | 0.33 |
| 44 x 241 | 15 | 24 | 710 | 0.33 |
| 44 x 302 | 22 | 29 | 1400 | 0.33 |
| 44 x 356 | 30 | 35 | 2300 | 0.33 |
| 44 x 406 | 39 | 40 | 3400 | 0.33 |
| 68 x 140 | 8.1 | 21 | 220 | 0.51 |
| 68 x 184 | 14 | 28 | 490 | 0.51 |
| 68 x 241 | 23 | 36 | 1100 | 0.51 |
| 68 x 302 | 34 | 46 | 2200 | 0.51 |
| 68 x 356 | 47 | 54 | 3500 | 0.51 |
| 68 x 406 | 60 | 61 | 5200 | 0.51 |
| 68 x 476 | 81 | 72 | 8400 | 0.51 |
| 68 x 606 | 130 | 91 | 17000 | 0.51 |
| 89 x 140 | 11 | 28 | 280 | 0.67 |
| 89 x 184 | 18 | 36 | 640 | 0.67 |
| 89 x 241 | 29 | 48 | 1400 | 0.67 |
| 89 x 302 | 45 | 60 | 2800 | 0.67 |
| 89 x 356 | 62 | 70 | 4600 | 0.67 |
| 89 x 406 | 79 | 80 | 6900 | 0.67 |
| 89 x 476 | 110 | 94 | 11000 | 0.67 |
| 89 x 606 | 170 | 120 | 23000 | 0.67 |

**2**

Bending Members

Notes:
1. Tabulated values were calculated based on the following typical values of specified strength:
   $f_b$ = 37 MPa
   $f_v$ = 3.7 MPa
   $E$ = 13 800 MPa
   $f_{cp}$ = 9.4 MPa
2. Values of $M_r$ include a typical size factor in bending, $K_{zb}$ = $(305/d)^{1/9}$. Consult manufacturer for actual $K_{zb}$.
3. These values are suggested for the following conditions:
   • dry service conditions
   • full lateral support
   • no preservative or fire-retardant treatment
   • no notches
   • standard duration of load
   • single member use
4. Not all sizes are available in all products or locations. Up to four plies of 45 mm (1-3/4") SCL may be fastened together to support loads in beam applications. Depths of 400 mm (16") or greater are not recommended for single ply applications. When each ply is equally top loaded, minimal fastening of plies is required, as per the manufacturer's recommendations. Multiple-ply SCL beams may be used in applications where the loads are introduced at the faces of the beam, however, more stringent fastening is required and the manufacturer's recommendations should be followed.
5. Values are listed in two significant digits and are to be used as preliminary estimates only. Consult manufacturer for actual design values.

# Beam Selection Tables

## Structural Composite Lumber

(For preliminary sizing only – Consult with manufacturer for actual capacities)

| Size (b × d) mm | $M_r$ kN·m | $V_r$ kN | $E_s I$ ×10⁹ N·mm² | $Q_r$ kN/mm of bearing length |
|---|---|---|---|---|
| 133 x 140 | 16 | 41 | 420 | 1.0 |
| 133 x 184 | 26 | 54 | 950 | 1.0 |
| 133 x 241 | 44 | 71 | 2100 | 1.0 |
| 133 x 302 | 67 | 89 | 4200 | 1.0 |
| 133 x 356 | 92 | 100 | 6900 | 1.0 |
| 133 x 406 | 120 | 120 | 10000 | 1.0 |
| 133 x 476 | 160 | 140 | 16000 | 1.0 |
| 133 x 606 | 250 | 180 | 34000 | 1.0 |
| 178 x 140 | 21 | 55 | 560 | 1.3 |
| 178 x 184 | 35 | 73 | 1300 | 1.3 |
| 178 x 241 | 59 | 95 | 2900 | 1.3 |
| 178 x 302 | 90 | 120 | 5600 | 1.3 |
| 178 x 356 | 120 | 140 | 9200 | 1.3 |
| 178 x 406 | 160 | 160 | 14000 | 1.3 |
| 178 x 476 | 210 | 190 | 22000 | 1.3 |
| 178 x 606 | 340 | 240 | 46000 | 1.3 |

Notes:
1. Tabulated values were calculated based on the following typical values of specified strength:
   $f_b$ = 37 MPa
   $f_v$ = 3.7 MPa
   E = 13 800 MPa
   $f_{cp}$ = 9.4 MPa
2. Values of $M_r$ include a typical size factor in bending, $K_{zb}$ = (305/d)$^{1/9}$. Consult manufacturer for actual $K_{zb}$.
3. These values are suggested for the following conditions:
   • dry service conditions
   • full lateral support
   • no preservative or fire-retardant treatment
   • no notches
   • standard duration of load
   • single member use
4. Not all sizes are available in all products or locations. Up to four plies of 45 mm (1-3/4") SCL may be fastened together to support loads in beam applications. Depths of 400 mm (16") or greater are not recommended for single ply applications. When each ply is equally top loaded, minimal fastening of plies is required, as per the manufacturer's recommendations. Multiple-ply SCL beams may be used in applications where the loads are introduced at the faces of the beam, however, more stringent fastening is required and the manufacturer's recommendations should be followed.
5. Values are listed in two significant digits and are to be used as preliminary estimates only. Consult manufacturer for actual design values.

# 2.6     Built-up Beams

### General

Built-up beams are composed of two or more lumber members fastened together side by side with bolts or nails. Built-up beams are often used in situations where the loading is light and dimension lumber is used for secondary framing, thus simplifying the type of materials required for the structure.

### Design

Selection tables are provided for built-up sawn lumber beams consisting of 2 to 5 plies. The tables assume that there are no butt joints in the beam, except at supports. The formulae used to develop these tables are identical to those in the joist section; therefore, the joist checklist and modification factors should be reviewed prior to using the tables.

In Part 9 of the *NBCC,* maximum spans for built-up beams are based on serviceability experience. Therefore, the spans in Part 9 may differ from those calculated using the design data provided in this section.

Where possible, built-up beams should be top loaded. When side loaded, fastening between plies is more critical. Bolts or nails may be used and the following design procedure is recommended:

1. Determine the loading that must be transfered from the outer ply to the inner plies. For instance, for a 3-ply beam loaded on one side, 2/3 of the load must be transfered from the outer ply to the two adjacent plies.

2. Calculate the lateral resistance of the nails or bolts to be used.

3. Determine the spacing of bolts or nails required by dividing the loading in Step 1 by the resistance in Step 2.

Nails are not recommended for side-loaded beams with more than 4 plies. Furthermore, 4- and 5-ply beams are recommended only when the loads are applied from both sides.

For top-loaded beams, the individual plies should also be nailed or bolted together. The fastener spacing should be no greater than four times the beam depth. This is to assure that the beam will act as a unit.

# Built-up Beam Selection Tables

**38** mm    ## Sawn Lumber

| Species | Size (b × d) mm | 2-Ply $M_r$ kN·m | $V_r$ kN | $E_sI$ ×10⁹ N·mm² | 3-Ply $M_r$ kN·m | $V_r$ kN | $E_sI$ ×10⁹ N·mm² | 4-Ply $M_r$ kN·m | $V_r$ kN | $E_sI$ ×10⁹ N·mm² | 5-Ply $M_r$ kN·m | $V_r$ kN | $E_sI$ ×10⁹ N·mm² |
|---|---|---|---|---|---|---|---|---|---|---|---|---|---|
| **Select Structural** | | | | | | | | | | | | | |
| D.Fir-L | 38 × 140 | 5.68 | 18.7 | 217 | 8.52 | 28.0 | 326 | 11.4 | 37.4 | 434 | 14.2 | 46.7 | 543 |
| | 38 × 184 | 8.41 | 21.0 | 493 | 12.6 | 31.6 | 740 | 16.8 | 42.1 | 986 | 21.0 | 52.6 | 1230 |
| | 38 × 235 | 12.6 | 24.6 | 1030 | 18.9 | 37.0 | 1550 | 25.1 | 49.3 | 2060 | 31.4 | 61.6 | 2580 |
| | 38 × 286 | 16.9 | 27.3 | 1850 | 25.4 | 40.9 | 2780 | 33.8 | 54.5 | 3700 | 42.3 | 68.1 | 4630 |
| Hem-Fir | 38 × 140 | 5.51 | 15.7 | 209 | 8.26 | 23.6 | 313 | 11.0 | 31.5 | 417 | 13.8 | 39.3 | 521 |
| | 38 × 184 | 8.15 | 17.7 | 473 | 12.2 | 26.6 | 710 | 16.3 | 35.4 | 947 | 20.4 | 44.3 | 1180 |
| | 38 × 235 | 12.2 | 20.7 | 986 | 18.3 | 31.1 | 1480 | 24.4 | 41.5 | 1970 | 30.5 | 51.9 | 2470 |
| | 38 × 286 | 16.4 | 23.0 | 1780 | 24.6 | 34.4 | 2670 | 32.8 | 45.9 | 3560 | 41.0 | 57.4 | 4450 |
| S-P-F | 38 × 140 | 5.68 | 14.7 | 182 | 8.52 | 22.1 | 274 | 11.4 | 29.5 | 365 | 14.2 | 36.9 | 456 |
| | 38 × 184 | 8.41 | 16.6 | 414 | 12.6 | 24.9 | 621 | 16.8 | 33.2 | 829 | 21.0 | 41.5 | 1040 |
| | 38 × 235 | 12.6 | 19.4 | 863 | 18.9 | 29.2 | 1290 | 25.1 | 38.9 | 1730 | 31.4 | 48.6 | 2160 |
| | 38 × 286 | 16.9 | 21.5 | 1560 | 25.4 | 32.3 | 2340 | 33.8 | 43.0 | 3120 | 42.3 | 53.8 | 3900 |
| Northern | 38 × 140 | 3.65 | 12.8 | 130 | 5.47 | 19.3 | 196 | 7.29 | 25.6 | 261 | 9.12 | 32.0 | 326 |
| | 38 × 184 | 5.40 | 14.4 | 296 | 8.10 | 21.6 | 444 | 10.8 | 28.8 | 592 | 13.5 | 36.0 | 740 |
| | 38 × 235 | 8.07 | 16.9 | 616 | 12.1 | 25.3 | 925 | 16.1 | 33.7 | 1230 | 20.2 | 42.1 | 1540 |
| | 38 × 286 | 10.9 | 18.6 | 1110 | 16.3 | 28.0 | 1670 | 21.7 | 37.3 | 2220 | 27.2 | 46.6 | 2780 |
| **No.1/No.2 Grades** | | | | | | | | | | | | | |
| D.Fir-L | 38 × 140 | 3.44 | 18.7 | 191 | 5.16 | 28.0 | 287 | 6.88 | 37.4 | 382 | 8.60 | 46.7 | 478 |
| | 38 × 184 | 5.09 | 21.0 | 434 | 7.64 | 31.6 | 651 | 10.2 | 42.1 | 868 | 12.7 | 52.6 | 1080 |
| | 38 × 235 | 7.62 | 24.6 | 904 | 11.4 | 37.0 | 1360 | 15.2 | 49.3 | 1810 | 19.0 | 61.6 | 2260 |
| | 38 × 286 | 10.3 | 27.3 | 1630 | 15.4 | 40.9 | 2450 | 20.5 | 54.5 | 3260 | 25.6 | 68.1 | 4080 |
| Hem-Fir | 38 × 140 | 3.79 | 15.7 | 191 | 5.68 | 23.6 | 287 | 7.57 | 31.5 | 382 | 9.46 | 39.3 | 478 |
| | 38 × 184 | 5.60 | 17.7 | 434 | 8.41 | 26.6 | 651 | 11.2 | 35.4 | 868 | 14.0 | 44.3 | 1080 |
| | 38 × 235 | 8.38 | 20.7 | 904 | 12.6 | 31.1 | 1360 | 16.8 | 41.5 | 1810 | 20.9 | 51.9 | 2260 |
| | 38 × 286 | 11.3 | 23.0 | 1630 | 16.9 | 34.4 | 2450 | 22.6 | 45.9 | 3260 | 28.2 | 57.4 | 4080 |
| S-P-F | 38 × 140 | 4.06 | 14.7 | 165 | 6.09 | 22.1 | 248 | 8.12 | 29.5 | 330 | 10.2 | 36.9 | 413 |
| | 38 × 184 | 6.01 | 16.6 | 375 | 9.02 | 24.9 | 562 | 12.0 | 33.2 | 750 | 15.0 | 41.5 | 937 |
| | 38 × 235 | 8.99 | 19.4 | 781 | 13.5 | 29.2 | 1170 | 18.0 | 38.9 | 1560 | 22.5 | 48.6 | 1950 |
| | 38 × 286 | 12.1 | 21.5 | 1410 | 18.2 | 32.3 | 2120 | 24.2 | 43.0 | 2820 | 30.3 | 53.8 | 3530 |
| Northern | 38 × 140 | 2.62 | 12.8 | 122 | 3.92 | 19.2 | 182 | 5.23 | 25.6 | 243 | 6.54 | 32.0 | 304 |
| | 38 × 184 | 3.87 | 14.4 | 276 | 5.81 | 21.6 | 414 | 7.74 | 28.8 | 552 | 9.68 | 36.0 | 690 |
| | 38 × 235 | 5.79 | 16.9 | 575 | 8.68 | 25.3 | 863 | 11.6 | 33.7 | 1150 | 14.5 | 42.1 | 1440 |
| | 38 × 286 | 7.80 | 18.6 | 1040 | 11.7 | 28.0 | 1560 | 15.6 | 37.3 | 2080 | 19.5 | 46.6 | 2600 |

# 2.7    Two-way Bending Members

## General

Two-way bending members (sometimes called oblique purlins) are secondary framing members used in curved or pitched roofs that are subjected to two-way bending moments. As shown in the figure below, two-way bending is created by the action of the tangential and normal components of the vertical load where purlins are installed perpendicular to the sloped roof.

Figure 2.7
**Two-way
bending
member**

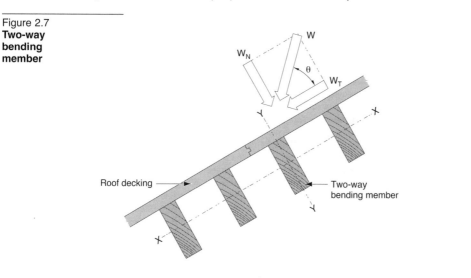

The purlins are designed for two-way bending when the roof sheathing cannot effectively transfer tangential loads to the member ends. When panel sheathing is installed over purlins, it is usually capable of resisting the tangential loads without depending upon the purlin stiffness. Similarly, plank decking installed in a diagonal pattern may adequately resist these loads. However, the scale of the structure and its members can affect this capability.

Purlins sized for two-way bending are larger than those sized for the normal component only. In order to avoid the need for tangential bending resistance, the following alternatives may be considered:

1. Use of panel sheathing over the decking.

2. Attachment of the decking to heavy ridge and eave purlins that are designed to resist the tangential loads.

3. The introduction of intermediate struts or trussing in the tangential plane to provide lateral restraint to the purlins.

For cost-effective structures, two-way bending members should be single-ply members. In the detailing of connections the two-way bending member ends must be fastened so that forces tangential and normal to the roof plane as well as overturning forces may be safely resisted.

## Design

Two-way bending members must be designed to satisfy the same criteria as regular purlins and joists, but with the following special provisions:

1. Member design must satisfy moment requirements

$$\frac{M_{fx}}{M_{rx}} + \frac{M_{fy}}{M_{ry}} \leq 1$$

where:

$M_{fx}$ = factored bending moment about X-X axis

$M_{fy}$ = factored bending moment about Y-Y axis

$M_{rx}$ = moment resistance about X-X axis

$M_{ry}$ = moment resistance about Y-Y axis

2. Total deflection is calculated as

$$\Delta = \sqrt{\Delta_x^2 + \Delta_y^2}$$

where:

$\Delta$   = total deflection

$\Delta_x$ = deflection normal to X-X axis

$\Delta_y$ = deflection normal to Y-Y axis

Two-way Bending Member Selection Tables provide $M_r$ and $E_s I$ values in the X-X and Y-Y plane for common sawn timber and $M'_{rx}$, $M_{ry}$, $E_s I_x$ and $E_s I_y$ for glulam purlin sizes. The tabulated values for sawn timber are based on the same formulae and modification factors as the Joist and Beam Selection Tables. Therefore, the checklists and modification factors in the joist and beam sections should be reviewed prior to using the tables.

For glulam, the specified bending strength and modulus of elasticity values provided in CSA O86 only apply for bending about the X-X axis (load perpendicular to the gluebond). When glulam is bent about the Y-Y axis, its bending resistance and stiffness is equivalent to a beam built up of No.2 grade laminations. Therefore, the $M_{ry}$ and $E_s I_y$ values for glulam are based on No.2 grade lumber properties, and the checklists and modification factors in the joist section should be reviewed prior to using these values. For $M'_{rx}$ and $E_s I_x$, review the checklist and modification factors for glulam. The two-way Bending Member Selection tables for glulam list values of $M'_{rx}$. To obtain $M_{rx}$, multiply $M'_{rx}$ by the lesser of $K_L$ (from Table 2.10) or $K_{Zbg}$ (from Table 2.11).

## Example: Two-way Bending Members

Design single span oblique roof purlins for the following conditions:

- purlin spacing = 2.0 m
- purlin span = 4.8 m
- roof pitch = 4/12 = 18.4°
- specified dead load = 0.60 kPa (includes purlin weight)
- specified snow load for strength calculations = 2.0 kPa
- specified snow load for serviceability calculations = 1.8 kPa

- standard load duration
- dry service condition
- untreated

Use 20f-E D.Fir-L glulam.

## Calculation

Total factored load = (1.25 × 0.60) + (1.5 × 2.0) = 3.75 kPa

$$w_f = 3.75 \times 2.0 = 7.5 \text{ kN/m}$$
$$w_S = 1.8 \times 2.0 = 3.6 \text{ kN/m}$$

Resolving the above loads into normal and tangential components:

$$w_{fN} = 7.5 \times \cos 18.4° = 7.12 \text{ kN/m}$$
$$w_{fT} = 7.5 \times \sin 18.4° = 2.37 \text{ kN/m}$$
$$w_{SN} = 3.6 \times \cos 18.4° = 3.42 \text{ kN/m}$$
$$w_{ST} = 3.6 \times \sin 18.4° = 1.14 \text{ kN/m}$$

$$M_{fx} = \frac{w_{fN} L^2}{8} = \frac{7.12 \times 4.8^2}{8} = 20.5 \text{ kN·m}$$

$$M_{fy} = \frac{w_{fT} L^2}{8} = \frac{2.37 \times 4.8^2}{8} = 6.83 \text{ kN·m}$$

For the first trial, select a section having an $M'_{rx}$ approximately 20% greater than the sum of $M_{fx}$ and $M_{fy}$ = 1.20 × (20.5 + 6.83) = 32.8 kN·m.

From Two-way Bending Member Selection Tables for glulam, try 175 × 228 mm:

$K_L$ = 1.0 (compression edge laterally restrained by decking)

$K_{Zbg}$ = 1.0 (Table 2.11)

$M'_{rx}$ = 34.9 kN·m

$M_{rx}$ = 34.9 kN·m

$M_{ry}$ = 14.3 kN·m

$$\frac{M_{fx}}{M_{rx}} + \frac{M_{fy}}{M_{ry}} = \frac{20.5}{34.9} + \frac{6.83}{14.3} = 1.07 \qquad \text{Not Acceptable}$$

Try the next larger section, 175 × 266 mm:

$M_{rx}$ = 47.5 kN·m

$M_{ry}$ = 16.7 kN·m

$$\frac{M_{fx}}{M_{rx}} + \frac{M_{fy}}{M_{ry}} = \frac{20.5}{47.5} + \frac{6.83}{16.7} = 0.84 \leq 1.00 \qquad \text{Acceptable}$$

Check purlin deflection for L/240 based on snow load:

$$\Delta_{max} = \frac{L}{240} = \frac{4800}{240} = 20 \text{ mm}$$

$$\Delta_x = \frac{5\,w_{SN}L^4}{384\,E_S I_x} = \frac{5 \times 3.42 \times 4800^4}{384 \times 3400 \times 10^9} = 6.93 \text{ mm}$$

$$\Delta_y = \frac{5\,w_{ST}L^4}{384\,E_S I_y} = \frac{5 \times 1.14 \times 4800^4}{384 \times 1310 \times 10^9} = 5.97 \text{ mm}$$

$$\Delta = \sqrt{\Delta_x^2 + \Delta_y^2} = \sqrt{6.93^2 + 5.97^2} = 10.1 \text{ mm} < 20 \text{ mm} \quad \text{Acceptable}$$

Note: Verify acceptable shear and bearing capacity as per Section 2.5 and Chapter 6.

**Use 175 × 266 mm 20f-E D.Fir-L glulam.**

# Two-way Bending Member Selection Tables

## Sawn Lumber

**38** mm

| Species | Size (b×d) mm | Select Structural | | | | No.1/No.2 | | | |
|---|---|---|---|---|---|---|---|---|---|
| | | $M_{rx}$ kN·m | $M_{ry}$ kN·m | $E_sI_x$ ×10⁹ N·mm² | $E_sI_y$ ×10⁹ N·mm² | $M_{rx}$ kN·m | $M_{ry}$ kN·m | $E_sI_x$ ×10⁹ N·mm² | $E_sI_y$ ×10⁹ N·mm² |
| D.Fir-L | 38 × 89 | 1.27 | 0.541 | 27.9 | 5.09 | 0.768 | 0.328 | 24.6 | 4.48 |
| | 38 × 114 | 1.83 | 0.611 | 58.6 | 6.52 | 1.11 | 0.370 | 51.6 | 5.73 |
| | 38 × 140 | 2.58 | 0.700 | 109 | 8.00 | 1.56 | 0.425 | 95.6 | 7.04 |
| | 38 × 184 | 3.82 | 0.789 | 247 | 10.5 | 2.32 | 0.478 | 217 | 9.26 |
| | 38 × 235 | 5.71 | 0.924 | 514 | 13.4 | 3.46 | 0.560 | 452 | 11.8 |
| | 38 × 286 | 7.69 | 1.02 | 926 | 16.4 | 4.66 | 0.619 | 815 | 14.4 |
| Hem-Fir | 38 × 89 | 1.23 | 0.524 | 26.8 | 4.88 | 0.844 | 0.360 | 24.6 | 4.48 |
| | 38 × 114 | 1.78 | 0.593 | 56.3 | 6.26 | 1.22 | 0.407 | 51.6 | 5.73 |
| | 38 × 140 | 2.50 | 0.679 | 104 | 7.68 | 1.72 | 0.467 | 95.6 | 7.04 |
| | 38 × 184 | 3.71 | 0.765 | 237 | 10.1 | 2.55 | 0.526 | 217 | 9.26 |
| | 38 × 235 | 5.54 | 0.896 | 493 | 12.9 | 3.81 | 0.616 | 452 | 11.8 |
| | 38 × 286 | 7.46 | 0.991 | 889 | 15.7 | 5.13 | 0.681 | 815 | 14.4 |
| S-P-F | 38 × 89 | 1.27 | 0.541 | 23.4 | 4.27 | 0.906 | 0.387 | 21.2 | 3.87 |
| | 38 × 114 | 1.83 | 0.611 | 49.3 | 5.47 | 1.31 | 0.437 | 44.6 | 4.95 |
| | 38 × 140 | 2.58 | 0.700 | 91.2 | 6.72 | 1.85 | 0.501 | 82.5 | 6.08 |
| | 38 × 184 | 3.82 | 0.789 | 207 | 8.83 | 2.73 | 0.564 | 187 | 7.99 |
| | 38 × 235 | 5.71 | 0.924 | 432 | 11.3 | 4.09 | 0.661 | 390 | 10.2 |
| | 38 × 286 | 7.69 | 1.02 | 778 | 13.7 | 5.50 | 0.731 | 704 | 12.4 |
| Northern | 38 × 89 | 0.814 | 0.347 | 16.7 | 3.05 | 0.583 | 0.249 | 15.6 | 2.85 |
| | 38 × 114 | 1.18 | 0.393 | 35.2 | 3.91 | 0.844 | 0.281 | 32.8 | 3.65 |
| | 38 × 140 | 1.66 | 0.450 | 65.2 | 4.80 | 1.19 | 0.323 | 60.8 | 4.48 |
| | 38 × 184 | 2.45 | 0.507 | 148 | 6.31 | 1.76 | 0.363 | 138 | 5.89 |
| | 38 × 235 | 3.67 | 0.594 | 308 | 8.06 | 2.63 | 0.426 | 288 | 7.52 |
| | 38 × 286 | 4.94 | 0.657 | 556 | 9.81 | 3.54 | 0.471 | 519 | 9.15 |

**64** mm

| Species | Size (b×d) mm | Select Structural | | | | No.1/No.2 | | | |
|---|---|---|---|---|---|---|---|---|---|
| | | $M_{rx}$ kN·m | $M_{ry}$ kN·m | $E_sI_x$ ×10⁹ N·mm² | $E_sI_y$ ×10⁹ N·mm² | $M_{rx}$ kN·m | $M_{ry}$ kN·m | $E_sI_x$ ×10⁹ N·mm² | $E_sI_y$ ×10⁹ N·mm² |
| D.Fir-L | 64 × 89 | 2.13 | 1.53 | 47.0 | 24.3 | 0.760 | 0.547 | 41.4 | 21.4 |
| | 64 × 114 | 3.09 | 1.73 | 98.8 | 31.1 | 1.87 | 1.05 | 86.9 | 27.4 |
| | 64 × 140 | 4.35 | 1.99 | 183 | 38.2 | 2.63 | 1.20 | 161 | 33.6 |
| | 64 × 184 | 6.44 | 2.24 | 415 | 50.2 | 3.90 | 1.36 | 365 | 44.2 |
| | 64 × 235 | 9.62 | 2.62 | 865 | 64.2 | 5.83 | 1.59 | 761 | 56.5 |
| | 64 × 286 | 13.0 | 2.90 | 1560 | 78.1 | 7.85 | 1.76 | 1370 | 68.7 |
| Hem-Fir | 64 × 89 | 2.07 | 1.49 | 45.1 | 23.3 | 0.836 | 0.601 | 41.4 | 21.4 |
| | 64 × 114 | 2.99 | 1.68 | 94.8 | 29.9 | 2.06 | 1.16 | 86.9 | 27.4 |
| | 64 × 140 | 4.21 | 1.93 | 176 | 36.7 | 2.90 | 1.32 | 161 | 33.6 |
| | 64 × 184 | 6.24 | 2.17 | 399 | 48.2 | 4.29 | 1.49 | 365 | 44.2 |
| | 64 × 235 | 9.33 | 2.54 | 831 | 61.6 | 6.41 | 1.75 | 761 | 56.5 |
| | 64 × 286 | 12.6 | 2.81 | 1500 | 75.0 | 8.64 | 1.93 | 1370 | 68.7 |
| S-P-F | 64 × 89 | 2.13 | 1.53 | 39.5 | 20.4 | 0.897 | 0.645 | 35.7 | 18.5 |
| | 64 × 114 | 3.09 | 1.73 | 83.0 | 26.2 | 2.21 | 1.24 | 75.1 | 23.7 |
| | 64 × 140 | 4.35 | 1.99 | 154 | 32.1 | 3.11 | 1.42 | 139 | 29.1 |
| | 64 × 184 | 6.44 | 2.24 | 349 | 42.2 | 4.60 | 1.60 | 316 | 38.2 |
| | 64 × 235 | 9.62 | 2.62 | 727 | 53.9 | 6.88 | 1.87 | 658 | 48.8 |
| | 64 × 286 | 13.0 | 2.90 | 1310 | 65.6 | 9.27 | 2.07 | 1190 | 59.4 |
| Northern | 64 × 89 | 1.37 | 0.985 | 28.2 | 14.6 | 0.578 | 0.416 | 26.3 | 13.6 |
| | 64 × 114 | 1.98 | 1.11 | 59.3 | 18.7 | 1.42 | 0.798 | 55.3 | 17.4 |
| | 64 × 140 | 2.79 | 1.28 | 110 | 22.9 | 2.00 | 0.915 | 102 | 21.4 |
| | 64 × 184 | 4.13 | 1.44 | 249 | 30.2 | 2.96 | 1.03 | 233 | 28.1 |
| | 64 × 235 | 6.18 | 1.68 | 519 | 38.5 | 4.43 | 1.21 | 485 | 35.9 |
| | 64 × 286 | 8.32 | 1.86 | 936 | 46.9 | 5.97 | 1.34 | 873 | 43.7 |

**2**

Bending Members

# Two-way Bending Member Selection Tables

## 89 mm    Sawn Lumber

| Species | Size (b×d) mm | Select Structural | | | | No.1/No.2 | | | |
|---|---|---|---|---|---|---|---|---|---|
| | | $M_{rx}$ kN·m | $M_{ry}$ kN·m | $E_S I_x$ ×10⁹ N·mm² | $E_S I_y$ ×10⁹ N·mm² | $M_{rx}$ kN·m | $M_{ry}$ kN·m | $E_S I_x$ ×10⁹ N·mm² | $E_S I_y$ ×10⁹ N·mm² |
| D.Fir-L | 89 × 140 | 6.48 | 4.12 | 254 | 103 | 3.92 | 2.50 | 224 | 90.5 |
| | 89 × 184 | 9.69 | 4.69 | 578 | 135 | 5.88 | 2.84 | 508 | 119 |
| | 89 × 235 | 14.6 | 5.53 | 1200 | 173 | 8.85 | 3.35 | 1060 | 152 |
| | 89 × 286 | 19.8 | 6.17 | 2170 | 210 | 12.0 | 3.74 | 1910 | 185 |
| Hem-Fir | 89 × 140 | 6.28 | 3.99 | 244 | 98.7 | 4.32 | 2.74 | 224 | 90.5 |
| | 89 × 184 | 9.40 | 4.55 | 554 | 130 | 6.46 | 3.13 | 508 | 119 |
| | 89 × 235 | 14.2 | 5.36 | 1160 | 166 | 9.73 | 3.69 | 1060 | 152 |
| | 89 × 286 | 19.2 | 5.98 | 2080 | 202 | 13.2 | 4.11 | 1910 | 185 |
| S-P-F | 89 × 140 | 6.48 | 4.12 | 214 | 86.4 | 4.63 | 2.94 | 193 | 78.1 |
| | 89 × 184 | 9.69 | 4.69 | 485 | 114 | 6.93 | 3.35 | 439 | 103 |
| | 89 × 235 | 14.6 | 5.53 | 1010 | 145 | 10.4 | 3.95 | 914 | 131 |
| | 89 × 286 | 19.8 | 6.17 | 1820 | 176 | 14.2 | 4.41 | 1650 | 160 |
| Northern | 89 × 140 | 4.16 | 2.64 | 153 | 61.7 | 2.98 | 1.90 | 142 | 57.6 |
| | 89 × 184 | 6.23 | 3.01 | 347 | 81.1 | 4.47 | 2.16 | 323 | 75.7 |
| | 89 × 235 | 9.38 | 3.55 | 722 | 104 | 6.72 | 2.55 | 674 | 96.6 |
| | 89 × 286 | 12.7 | 3.96 | 1300 | 126 | 9.13 | 2.84 | 1210 | 118 |

Note:
All values are for single member application ($K_H$ = 1.0).

# Two-way Bending Member Selection Tables

## Sawn Timbers

**140** mm
**191** mm

| Species | Size (b×d) mm | Select Structural | | | | No.1 | | | | No.2 | | | |
|---|---|---|---|---|---|---|---|---|---|---|---|---|---|
| | | $M_{rx}$ kN·m | $M_{ry}$ kN·m | $E_SI_x$ ×10⁹ N·mm² | $E_SI_y$ ×10⁹ N·mm² | $M_{rx}$ kN·m | $M_{ry}$ kN·m | $E_SI_x$ ×10⁹ N·mm² | $E_SI_y$ ×10⁹ N·mm² | $M_{rx}$ kN·m | $M_{ry}$ kN·m | $E_SI_x$ ×10⁹ N·mm² | $E_SI_y$ ×10⁹ N·mm² |
| D.Fir-L | 140 × 140 | 9.79 | 9.79 | 384 | 384 | 7.38 | 7.38 | 336 | 336 | 3.21 | 3.21 | 304 | 304 |
| | 140 × 191 | 18.2 | 13.4 | 976 | 524 | 13.7 | 10.1 | 854 | 459 | 5.98 | 4.38 | 772 | 415 |
| | 140 × 241 | 28.5 | 14.6 | 1960 | 661 | 23.1 | 10.3 | 1960 | 595 | 13.2 | 5.89 | 1550 | 471 |
| | 140 × 292 | 38.4 | 16.2 | 3490 | 801 | 31.1 | 11.5 | 3490 | 721 | 17.7 | 6.54 | 2760 | 571 |
| | 140 × 343 | 48.2 | 17.3 | 5650 | 941 | 39.0 | 12.3 | 5650 | 847 | 22.2 | 6.99 | 4470 | 671 |
| | 140 × 394 | 57.2 | 17.9 | 8560 | 1080 | 46.4 | 12.7 | 8560 | 973 | 26.4 | 7.22 | 6780 | 770 |
| | 191 × 191 | 24.9 | 24.9 | 1330 | 1330 | 18.8 | 18.8 | 1160 | 1160 | 8.15 | 8.15 | 1050 | 1050 |
| | 191 × 241 | 36.5 | 29.0 | 2670 | 1680 | 27.6 | 21.8 | 2340 | 1470 | 12.0 | 9.50 | 2120 | 1330 |
| | 191 × 292 | 52.4 | 30.2 | 4760 | 2030 | 42.5 | 21.4 | 4760 | 1830 | 24.2 | 12.2 | 3760 | 1450 |
| | 191 × 343 | 65.7 | 32.2 | 7710 | 2390 | 53.3 | 22.8 | 7710 | 2150 | 30.3 | 13.0 | 6100 | 1700 |
| | 191 × 394 | 78.1 | 33.3 | 11700 | 2750 | 63.2 | 23.6 | 11700 | 2470 | 36.0 | 13.4 | 9250 | 1960 |
| Hem-Fir | 140 × 140 | 7.28 | 7.28 | 320 | 320 | 5.46 | 5.46 | 288 | 288 | 2.41 | 2.41 | 256 | 256 |
| | 140 × 191 | 13.5 | 9.93 | 813 | 437 | 10.2 | 7.45 | 732 | 393 | 4.48 | 3.29 | 650 | 349 |
| | 140 × 241 | 21.2 | 10.8 | 1630 | 551 | 17.1 | 7.66 | 1630 | 496 | 9.81 | 4.39 | 1310 | 397 |
| | 140 × 292 | 28.6 | 12.0 | 2900 | 668 | 23.0 | 8.51 | 2900 | 601 | 13.2 | 4.87 | 2320 | 481 |
| | 140 × 343 | 35.8 | 12.9 | 4710 | 784 | 28.9 | 9.08 | 4710 | 706 | 16.6 | 5.20 | 3770 | 565 |
| | 140 × 394 | 42.5 | 13.3 | 7140 | 901 | 34.3 | 9.39 | 7140 | 811 | 19.7 | 5.38 | 5710 | 649 |
| | 191 × 191 | 18.5 | 18.5 | 1110 | 1110 | 13.9 | 13.9 | 998 | 998 | 6.11 | 6.11 | 887 | 887 |
| | 191 × 241 | 27.2 | 21.5 | 2230 | 1400 | 20.4 | 16.1 | 2010 | 1260 | 8.99 | 7.12 | 1780 | 1120 |
| | 191 × 292 | 39.0 | 22.4 | 3960 | 1700 | 31.4 | 15.8 | 3960 | 1530 | 18.0 | 9.07 | 3170 | 1220 |
| | 191 × 343 | 48.9 | 23.9 | 6420 | 1990 | 39.4 | 16.9 | 6420 | 1790 | 22.6 | 9.68 | 5140 | 1430 |
| | 191 × 394 | 58.0 | 24.8 | 9740 | 2290 | 46.8 | 17.5 | 9740 | 2060 | 26.8 | 10.0 | 7790 | 1650 |
| S-P-F | 140 × 140 | 6.80 | 6.80 | 272 | 272 | 5.14 | 5.14 | 240 | 240 | 2.25 | 2.25 | 208 | 208 |
| | 140 × 191 | 12.6 | 9.27 | 691 | 371 | 9.56 | 7.01 | 610 | 328 | 4.18 | 3.07 | 528 | 284 |
| | 140 × 241 | 19.9 | 10.2 | 1390 | 468 | 16.1 | 7.20 | 1390 | 422 | 9.22 | 4.12 | 1060 | 322 |
| | 191 × 191 | 17.3 | 17.3 | 943 | 943 | 13.0 | 13.0 | 832 | 832 | 5.71 | 5.71 | 721 | 721 |
| | 191 × 241 | 25.4 | 20.1 | 1890 | 1190 | 19.2 | 15.2 | 1670 | 1050 | 8.39 | 6.65 | 1450 | 910 |
| Northern | 140 × 140 | 6.42 | 6.42 | 256 | 256 | 4.82 | 4.82 | 224 | 224 | 2.09 | 2.09 | 192 | 192 |
| | 140 × 191 | 12.0 | 8.76 | 650 | 349 | 8.96 | 6.57 | 569 | 306 | 3.88 | 2.85 | 488 | 262 |
| | 140 × 241 | 18.7 | 9.58 | 1310 | 441 | 15.1 | 6.74 | 1310 | 397 | 8.64 | 3.86 | 980 | 331 |
| | 191 × 191 | 16.3 | 16.3 | 887 | 887 | 12.2 | 12.2 | 776 | 776 | 5.30 | 5.30 | 665 | 665 |
| | 191 × 241 | 24.0 | 19.0 | 1780 | 1120 | 18.0 | 14.2 | 1560 | 980 | 7.79 | 6.17 | 1340 | 840 |

Note:
All values are for single member application ($K_H$ = 1.0).

# Two-way Bending Member Selection Tables

## Glulam

| Size (b×d) mm | D.Fir-L 20f-E Stress Grade | | | | Spruce-Pine 20f-E Stress Grade | | | | D.Fir-L 24f-E Stress Grade | | | |
|---|---|---|---|---|---|---|---|---|---|---|---|---|
| | $M'_{rx}$ kN·m | $M_{ry}$ kN·m | $E_S I_x$ ×10⁹ N·mm² | $E_S I_y$ ×10⁹ N·mm² | $M'_{rx}$ kN·m | $M_{ry}$ kN·m | $E_S I_x$ ×10⁹ N·mm² | $E_S I_y$ ×10⁹ N·mm² | $M'_{rx}$ kN·m | $M_{ry}$ kN·m | $E_S I_x$ ×10⁹ N·mm² | $E_S I_y$ ×10⁹ N·mm² |
| 80 × 152 | 7.10 | 2.73 | 290 | 71.3 | 7.10 | 3.22 | 241 | 61.6 | 8.48 | 2.73 | 307 | 71.3 |
| 80 × 190 | 11.1 | 3.41 | 567 | 89.2 | 11.1 | 4.02 | 471 | 77.0 | 13.3 | 3.41 | 599 | 89.2 |
| 80 × 228 | 16.0 | 4.09 | 980 | 107 | 16.0 | 4.83 | 814 | 92.4 | 19.1 | 4.09 | 1040 | 107 |
| 130 × 152 | 11.5 | 6.10 | 472 | 306 | 11.5 | 7.20 | 392 | 264 | 13.8 | 6.10 | 498 | 306 |
| 130 × 190 | 18.0 | 7.63 | 921 | 383 | 18.0 | 9.00 | 765 | 330 | 21.5 | 7.63 | 973 | 383 |
| 175 × 190 | 24.3 | 11.9 | 1240 | 933 | 24.3 | 14.0 | 1030 | 806 | 29.0 | 11.9 | 1310 | 933 |
| 175 × 228 | 34.9 | 14.3 | 2140 | 1120 | 34.9 | 16.9 | 1780 | 967 | 41.8 | 14.3 | 2260 | 1120 |
| 175 × 266 | 47.5 | 16.7 | 3400 | 1310 | 47.5 | 19.7 | 2830 | 1130 | 56.8 | 16.7 | 3600 | 1310 |
| 175 × 304 | 62.1 | 19.0 | 5080 | 1490 | 62.1 | 22.5 | 4220 | 1290 | 74.2 | 19.0 | 5370 | 1490 |
| 175 × 342 | 78.6 | 21.4 | 7230 | 1680 | 78.6 | 25.3 | 6010 | 1450 | 94.0 | 21.4 | 7640 | 1680 |
| 175 × 380 | 97.0 | 23.8 | 9920 | 1870 | 97.0 | 28.1 | 8240 | 1610 | 116 | 23.8 | 10500 | 1870 |
| 175 × 418 | 117 | 26.2 | 13200 | 2050 | 117 | 30.9 | 11000 | 1770 | 140 | 26.2 | 14000 | 2050 |
| 175 × 456 | 140 | 28.6 | 17100 | 2240 | 140 | 33.7 | 14200 | 1930 | 167 | 28.6 | 18100 | 2240 |

Note:
All values are for single member application.

# 2.8    Cantilevered Beams

## General

Cantilevered beam systems can provide an economical structure in multi-span buildings. A typical cantilevered system consists of a series of beams extending over one or two supports, with suspended beams supported by the cantilevered ends.

A number of common cantilevered systems are shown in Figure 2.8. The hinge points are located so that the maximum negative moment at the support is equal to the maximum positive moment at mid-span, which will be approximately 67% of a simple-span bending moment. This usually permits the use of smaller beams in a cantilevered system than in a simple-span system.

The cantilevered system also has advantages over a continuous beam system. These include easier handling and erection due to shorter components, and less adverse effects due to support settlement.

## Materials and Applications

Glued-laminated timber is commonly used in cantilevered systems due to the variety of sizes available. Generally the 20f-EX or 24f-EX grade is used since the resistance to negative and positive moments is equal.

Sawn beams may also be used in cantilevered systems, but they must be graded for continuity. This means that the grading restrictions that normally apply to the middle third of the length for beams and stringers must be applied to the full length.

## Design

### Hinge Locations

For a uniform load case, the optimum hinge location is approximately 17% of the span from the support for equal span layouts. However, the *National Building Code of Canada* specifies that both roof and floor structures be designed for the following unbalanced load cases in addition to the balanced case:

1. Floors

    Full live load plus dead load on any portion of the area, with dead load on the remainder of the area.

2. Roofs

    Full dead load plus snow load on any portion of the area, with dead plus one half of full snow load on the remainder.

Optimum hinge locations are then governed by the unbalanced load cases. Figure 2.8 provides the optimum hinge locations for a number of typical cantilevered systems.

Figure 2.8
**Typical
cantilevered
beam systems**

| Factored load ratio n | Optimum hinge locations (× length of span) | | | | | |
|---|---|---|---|---|---|---|
| | a | b | c | d | e | f |
| 0.10 | 0.238 | 0.227 | 0.392 | 0.374 | 0.363 | 0.349 |
| 0.20 | 0.228 | 0.208 | 0.351 | 0.331 | 0.311 | 0.296 |
| 0.30 | 0.218 | 0.192 | 0.322 | 0.301 | 0.275 | 0.260 |
| 0.40 | 0.210 | 0.179 | 0.300 | 0.279 | 0.248 | 0.233 |
| 0.50 | 0.202 | 0.167 | 0.281 | 0.261 | 0.225 | 0.211 |
| 0.60 | 0.195 | 0.156 | 0.265 | 0.246 | 0.207 | 0.194 |
| 0.70 | 0.188 | 0.147 | 0.252 | 0.233 | 0.192 | 0.179 |
| 0.80 | 0.182 | 0.139 | 0.240 | 0.222 | 0.179 | 0.167 |
| 0.90 | 0.177 | 0.132 | 0.229 | 0.212 | 0.167 | 0.156 |

Note:
For floors $n = \dfrac{D}{D+L}$ ; For roofs $n = \dfrac{D+0.5S}{D+S}$   where  D = factored dead load
L = factored live load
S = factored snow load

● = Hinge location (see below)
▭ = Suspended beam
▨ = Cantilevered beam
All spans are equal

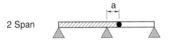
2 Span

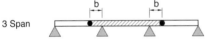
3 Span

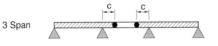
3 Span

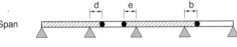
4 Span

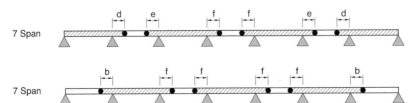
5 Span

5 Span

6 Span

7 Span

7 Span

## Design Procedure

1. Sketch the building bay arrangement as shown in Figure 2.8 using as many double cantilevered beams as possible.

2. Determine the factored load ratio n.

For floors: $n = \dfrac{D}{D+L}$

For roofs: $n = \dfrac{D+0.5S}{D+S}$

where:

$\quad$ D $\;=\;$ factored dead load

$\quad$ L $\;=\;$ factored live load

$\quad$ S $\;=\;$ factored snow load

3. Dimension the hinge points from Figure 2.8.

4. Determine the maximum factored moments and reactions on the suspended beams using D + L or D + S.

5. Determine the maximum factored moments and shears on the cantilevered beams for both balanced and unbalanced loading.

6. Use the Beam Selection Tables to select a trial beam size with a moment resistance $M_r$ or $M'_r$ greater than the maximum factored moment $M_f$. Calculate the lateral stability factor $K_L$ if continuous lateral support is not provided for the compression edge (particularly where the beam is subjected to negative moment) and adjust the tabulated $M_r$ value. For glulam, adjust $M'_r$ by the lesser of $K_L$ or $K_{Zbg}$. If $M_r$ is less than $M_f$, select a larger section. Alternatively, increase the amount of lateral support so that $M_r$ will exceed $M_f$.

7. Compare the shear resistance $V_r$ to the maximum factored shear force $V_f$. If $V_f$ exceeds $V_r$ (or, for glulam, if beam size is greater than 2.0 m³) then:

a) For glulam, calculate the total shear resistance $W_r$ by multiplying the tabulated $W_r L^{0.18}$ value by $\left[\dfrac{L^{-0.18}\, C_v}{3.69}\right]$

If $W_r$ is greater than $W_f$, the sum of all factored loads acting on the beam, then the section is adequate for shear. Otherwise select a larger section with adequate shear resistance.

b) For sawn timber, select a larger size with adequate shear resistance.

2

Bending Members

8. Compare the deflection at the centre of the cantilevered beams to the maximum allowable deflection.

9. Compare the maximum deflection of the suspended beams to the maximum allowable deflection. Deflections in cantilevered systems are always less than in simply supported beams and greater than in continuous beams. Maximum deflection may be calculated as follows:

    a) For a suspended beam supported by a cantilever and an exterior support, the maximum deflection is approximately equal to the deflection of the suspended beam plus half of the deflection of the cantilever.

    b) For a suspended beam supported by a cantilever at each end, the maximum deflection is approximately equal to the deflection of the suspended beam plus the deflection of the cantilever.

Formulae for calculating deflections are provided in Chapter 11.

### Other Design Considerations

Adequate lateral stability for the cantilevered beams must be provided at each column. This may be done by providing a purlin (with a purlin-to-beam connection) at each column. Knee bracing at the column purlin may be added if necessary.

At the hinge points the suspended member must be attached to the supporting member so that the full depth of the beam is available for shear resistance. Connection details are described in Chapter 7.

The roof should be sloped to minimize the possibility of ponding.

### Example: Cantilevered Beams

Design a cantilevered roof beam system for the following conditions:

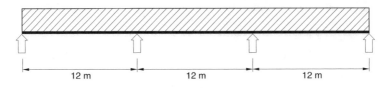

* beam spacing = 6.0 m
* three equal spans of 12.0 m (each)
* specified dead load = 1.0 kPa (includes self weight)
* specified snow load for strength calculations = 1.30 kPa
* specified snow load for serviceability calculations = 1.17 kPa

- standard load duration
- dry service condition
- untreated
- flat roof with no ceiling

Use 20f-EX D.Fir-L glulam.

**Calculation**

Total factored load = $(1.25 \times 1.0) + (1.5 \times 1.30) = 3.20$ kPa
Total specified load = $1.0 + 1.17 = 2.17$ kPa

$w_f = 3.20 \times 6.0 = 19.2$ kN/m

$w = 2.17 \times 6.0 = 13.02$ kN/m

Following the design procedure outlined above:

1. Sketch building bay elevations.

Select configuration with hinges in outside bays as shown in Figure 2.8.

2. Determine factored load ratio, n.
   For roofs:

$$n = \frac{D+0.5S}{D+S} = \frac{1.25+0.5 \times 1.95}{1.25+1.95} = 0.7$$

3. Dimension hinge points, from Figure 2.5. Use:

$b = 0.147 \times \text{span} = 0.147 \times 12.0 = 1.76$ m

4. Determine the maximum factored moments and shears on the suspended beams (governed by uniformly distributed load).

$$M_f = \frac{w_f L^2}{8} = \frac{19.2 \times (12.0-1.76)^2}{8} = 252 \text{ kN} \cdot \text{m}$$

$$V_f = \frac{w_f L}{2} = \frac{19.2 \times (12.0-1.76)}{2} = 98.3 \text{ kN}$$

5. Determine the maximum factored moments and shears on the cantilevered beam. By examining all possible loading patterns, it is found that the maximum factored moment and shear occur at the support when the cantilevered end is fully loaded (the concentrated loads are the end shears from the suspended beams). The most critical load occurs in the centre span.

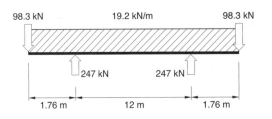

98.3 kN          19.2 kN/m          98.3 kN

247 kN          247 kN

1.76 m          12 m          1.76 m

$$M_f = 98.3 \times 1.76 + \frac{19.2 \times 1.76^2}{2} = 203 \text{ kN} \cdot \text{m}$$

$$V_f = 98.3 + (19.2 \times 1.76) = 132 \text{ kN}$$

6. Use the Beam Selection Tables to select trial sections.

   a) For the suspended beams select 130 × 722 mm:

   | | | |
   |---|---|---|
   | $M'_r$ | = | 260 kN·m |
   | $K_L$ | = | 1.0 |
   | $K_{Zbg}$ | = | 0.978 (Table 2.11) |
   | $M_r$ | = | 254 kN·m > 252 kN·m |
   | $V_r$ | = | 113 kN > 98.3 kN |

   $M_r$ = 254 kN·m > 252 kN·m          *Acceptable*
   $V_r$ = 113 kN > 98.3 kN          *Acceptable*

   b) For the cantilevered beams select 130 × 722 mm:

   $M'_r$ = 260 kN·m

In this case, $K_L$ is not equal to 1 since the lower edge of the cantilevered beam is in compression along part of its length and will not be fully supported. The maximum unsupported length is found to be 2.14 m at the ends of the interior span. Using Tables 2.9 and 2.10, $K_L$ is calculated to be 0.95. From a bending moment diagram L, the length from zero moment to zero moment, was found to be 7.71 m. Using Table 2.11, $K_{Zbg}$ = 1.

Therefore:

   $M_r$ = 260 × 0.95 = 248 kN·m > 203 kN·m          *Acceptable*

7. Check shear on the cantilevered beam.

$$V_r = 113 \text{ kN} < 132 \text{ kN} \qquad \textit{Not Acceptable}$$

Therefore, check $W_r$:

$$W_f = 2 \times 98.3 + (19.2 \times 15.5) = 494 \text{ kN}$$

$$C_V = 6.61 \text{ (From Table 6.5.7.4C of CSA O86)}$$

$$W_r = 458 (15.5)^{-0.18} \left[ \frac{6.61}{3.69} \right] = 501 \text{ kN} > 494 \text{ kN} \qquad \textit{Acceptable}$$

8. Check deflection at the centre of the cantilevered beam. This occurs when full snow load extends over the centre span and half of full snow load on the outside spans. Maximum allowable deflection is governed by L/180 based on total load. Using the deflection formulae in Chapter 11:

$$\Delta = 33 \text{ mm}$$

$$\Delta_{max} = \frac{L}{180} = \frac{12000}{180} = 66.7 \text{ mm} > 33 \text{ mm} \qquad \textit{Acceptable}$$

9. Check deflection of the suspended beam. This occurs when full snow load is on the suspended beam and supporting cantilever, and half of full snow load on the other spans. Using the deflection formulae in Chapter 11:

$$\Delta = \text{deflection of suspended beam} + 1/2 \text{ deflection of cantilever} = 42 \text{ mm}$$

$$\Delta_{max} = \frac{L}{180} = 67 \text{ mm} > 42 \text{ mm} \qquad \textit{Acceptable}$$

**Use 130 × 722 mm glulam for the cantilevered beam and the suspended beams.**

2

Bending Members

# Compression
# Members

Wood columns are elegantly integrated into this version of a post and beam frame for a clubhouse structure.

Stud grade lumber is used together with plywood sheathing in bearing wall applications such as this gable wall.

Continuous columns form an integral part of this attractive glulam frame.

Heavy loads are supported by this spaced glulam column. A unique architectural detail is used for the base shoe shown to transfer the loads to the foundation.

# 3.1     General Information

The following sections contain design information for members that are used in compression parallel to grain. These members include sawn lumber studs, posts, truss chords, single member glulam and sawn timber columns, and nailed built-up sawn lumber columns.

The design information is for concentrically loaded members; however, the designer must consider eccentricity where it occurs. Chapter 5 provides design information for members subjected to bending due to eccentricity or lateral loading combined with compression. In addition, Chapter 6 provides design information for compression perpendicular to grain.

Selection tables are arranged to provide compressive resistances, $P_r$, for given species, grades and sizes. Checklists are given in each section. The designer should review these checklists to be sure that the tabulated resistance is appropriate for the actual conditions of use.

**3**

**⌀**

Compression Members

# 3.2 Stud Walls and Posts

## General

Lumber products are produced in accordance with CSA Standard O141 *Softwood Lumber.* The characteristics of structural grades are outlined in the National Lumber Grades Authority *Standard Grading Rules for Canadian Lumber.* "Stud" grade lumber, which is manufactured specifically for use in stud wall systems, is assigned the same strength values as No.3 grade lumber, but other grades may also be used.

Sawn lumber used in stud wall systems has a common thickness of 38 mm and ranges in depth from 89 to 184 mm. Stud grade lumber, however, ranges in depth from 38 to 140 mm; the smaller sizes are used mainly in partitions. For depths greater than 140 mm, another grade must be specified.

In stud walls, the members are spaced no farther apart than 610 mm to take advantage of load-sharing. Usually the spacing is 406 mm or less. Stud wall systems are usually sheathed by plywood, waferboard, oriented strandboard or drywall. The sheathing is nailed to the narrow faces of the studs (on at least one side) along the entire length of the stud, thereby preventing buckling about the weak axis. Studs are susceptible to buckling if heavy loads are applied prior to installation of the sheathing.

Members supporting stud walls or posts must provide adequate bearing resistance to prevent crushing. Bearing considerations are covered in Chapter 6. For walls with combined vertical and lateral loading, refer to Chapter 5. Shearwall design considerations are covered in Chapter 9 and fire resistance ratings for stud wall assemblies are discussed in Chapter 10.

Sawn lumber posts are generally 89 × 89 mm or larger No.1 grade members. Posts may also be built up from 38 mm lumber (refer to Section 3.4).

## Availability

The Stud Wall Selection Tables provide design information for the sizes and grades shown in Table 3.1.

Table 3.1
**Grades, available sizes and common stud and post sizes for sawn lumber**

| Grade | Available sizes | Common stud and post sizes (mm) |
|---|---|---|
| Select Structural, No.1, No.2, No.3 | 38 to 89 mm in thickness and 38 to 286 mm in depth | 38 × 89 |
| | | 38 × 140 |
| | | 38 × 184 |
| | | 89 × 89 |
| Stud | 38 to 89 mm in thickness and 38 to 140 mm in depth | 38 × 89 |
| | | 38 × 140 |

S-P-F, Hem-Fir and D.Fir-L are most likely to be stocked by lumber yards, but species in the Northern species combination may also be on hand.

Lumber can usually be obtained kiln- or air-dried to a moisture content of 19% or less (specify S-Dry) in 38 mm thickness. The 64 and 89 mm thicknesses are generally surfaced in the green condition (S-Grn).

**3**

▼
Ô

Compression Members

## Design

Sawn lumber members subjected to axial loading must be designed so that the following criterion is satisfied:

Factored compressive resistance parallel to grain $P_r \geq$ factored compressive load $P_f$

The factored compressive resistance, $P_r$, may be determined as follows:

1. When the conditions of use meet the requirements given in the following checklist, $P_r$ may be taken directly from the Stud Wall Selection Tables.

2. When the conditions of use do not meet the requirements of the checklist, the value of $P_r$ given in the selection tables is not valid. Furthermore, the tabulated values cannot be adjusted by a factor that will apply throughout the entire unsupported length range. Therefore, $P_r$ should be calculated from the following formula. This formula may also be used for lumber sizes not given in the selection tables.

$$P_r = \phi F_c A K_{Zc} K_C \text{ (N)}$$

where:

$\phi F_c$ = factored compressive strength, given in Table 3.2 (MPa)

$A$ = cross-sectional area (mm²)

$K_{Zc}$ = size factor

= $6.3 (d L_d)^{-0.13} \leq 1.3$ for buckling in direction of d

or

= $6.3 (b L_b)^{-0.13} \leq 1.3$ for buckling in direction of b

$K_C$ = slenderness factor

$$= \left[1.0 + \frac{F_c}{E'} K_{Zc} C_c^3\right]^{-1}$$

$F_c / E'$ = strength to stiffness ratio, given in Table 3.3

$C_c$ = the greater of $\dfrac{K_e L_d}{d}$ or $\dfrac{K_e L_b}{b}$ ($C_c > 50$ is not permitted)

$K_e$ = effective length factor, given in Figure 3.1

$L_d, L_b$ = unsupported length associated with d or b (mm)

$d$ = depth of member (mm)

$b$ = thickness of member (mm)

In addition to axial loading, bearing considerations must also be taken into account. The stud selection tables provide bearing resistance values for a sill plate of the same grade, species and cross-sectional dimensions as the studs. Bearing is described in more detail in Chapter 6.

# Checklist: **Stud Walls** ✅

To verify that the tabulated resistances given in the Stud Wall Selection Tables are appropriate for the structure being designed, the following questions should be asked:

1. Is load duration "standard" term (dead load plus loads due to snow or occupancy)?

2. Is the service condition "dry"?

3. Is the material free of incising and/or strength reducing chemicals?

4. Are the studs effectively pinned and laterally restrained at both ends, and prevented from buckling about the weak axis by wall sheathing?

5. Does the stud wall system consist of at least 3 studs spaced no farther apart than 610 mm?

6. Is the stud concentrically loaded?

If the answer to any of these questions is no, the Stud Wall Selection Tables should not be used. If conditions 1 to 5 are not met, calculate $P_r$ from the formula given on page 98. Adjust $Q_r$ using the $K_D$, $K_{Zcp}$ and $K_T$ modification factors described in Chapter 6. See Chapter 5 for design information on eccentrically loaded compression members.

To prevent crushing, sill plates should be designed so that the following criterion is satisfied:

Factored compressive resistance perpendicular to grain, $Q_r \geq$ Factored compressive force, $Q_f$.

The factored compressive force bearing on the sill plate, $Q_f$, is equivalent to the factored axial load on the stud.

Factored compressive resistance perpendicular to grain, $Q_r$, of the sill plates may be determined as follows:

1. When the conditions of use meet the requirements of the checklist, $Q_r$ may be taken directly from the Stud Wall Selection Tables.

2. When the conditions of use do not meet the requirements of the checklist, the value of $Q_r$ given in the tables should be multiplied by the $K_D$, $K_{Scp}$, or $K_T$ modification factors described in Chapter 6.

$Q_r$ includes a length of bearing factor, $K_B = 1.25$ and a size factor for bearing, $K_{Zcp} = 1.15$.

## Example 1: Stud Wall Systems

Design bearing wall studs for the following conditions:

- stud spacing = 600 mm
- stud length = limited to 3 m for Stud grade
- specified dead load = 6.0 kN/m
- specified snow load for strength calculations = 13.2 kN/m
- dry service condition
- untreated
- studs effectively held in position by roof joists at top, and foundation at bottom
- wall sheathing prevents buckling about weak axis

Use Stud grade S-P-F sawn lumber.

## Calculation
Total factored load per stud:

$$P_f = (1.25 \times 6.0 + 1.5 \times 13.2) \times 0.60$$
$$= 16.4 \text{ kN}$$

From Stud Wall Selection Tables select 38 × 140 mm:

$$P_r = 26.3 \text{ kN} > 16.4 \text{ kN} \qquad\qquad Acceptable$$
$$Q_r = 32.4 \text{ kN} > 16.4 \text{ kN} \qquad\qquad Acceptable$$

**Use 38 × 140 mm Stud grade S-P-F sawn lumber at 600 mm spacing.**

## Example 2: Stud Wall Systems

Check the bearing wall in Example 1 for wet service conditions.

## Calculation

$$P_r = \phi F_c A K_{Zc} K_C$$

$\phi F_c$ = 4.25 MPa from Table 3.2

$A$ = $38 \times 140 = 5320 \text{ mm}^2$

$K_{Zc}$ = $6.3 (140 \times 3000)^{-0.13} = 1.17$

$C_c$ = $3000 / 140 = 21.4$

$F_c / E'$ = $29.4 \times 10^{-6}$ from Table 3.3

$K_C$ = $[1.0 + 29.4 \times 10^{-6} \times 1.17 \times (21.4)^3]^{-1}$

= 0.748

$P_r$ = $4.25 \times 5320 \times 1.17 \times 0.748$

= 19.8 kN > 16.4 kN                     *Acceptable*

$Q_{r(wet)}$ = $Q_{r\ (dry)}\ K_{Scp}$

= 32.4 kN x 0.67                     (refer to Chapter 6)

= 21.7 kN > 16.4 kN                     *Acceptable*

**38 × 140 mm Stud grade S-P-F studs can be used under wet service conditions provided sheathing is adequate for wet service.**

**3**

Compression Members

| Figure 3.1 **Effective length factor for compression members** | Degree of end restraint of compression member | Effective length factor $K_e$ | Symbol |
|---|---|---|---|
| | Effectively held in position and restrained against rotation at both ends | 0.65 |  |
| | Effectively held in position at both ends, restrained against rotation at one end | 0.80 |  |
| | Effectively held in position at both ends, but not restrained against rotation | 1.00 |  |
| | Effectively held in position and restrained against rotation at one end, and at the other restrained against rotation but not held in position | 1.20 | 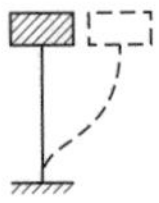 |
| | Effectively held in position and restrained against rotation at one end, and at the other partially restrained against rotation but not held in position | 1.50 | 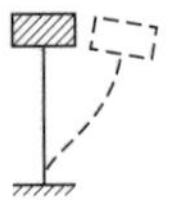 |
| | Effectively held in position at one end but not restrained against rotation, and at the other end restrained against rotation but not held in position | 2.00 | 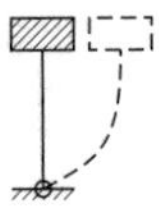 |
| | Effectively held in position and restrained against rotation at one end but not held in position nor restrained against rotation at the other end | 2.00 | 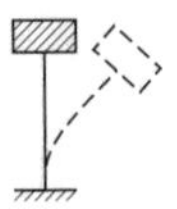 |

Note:
Effective length $L_e = K_e L$ where L is the distance between centres of lateral supports of the compression member in the place in which buckling is being considered. At a base or cap detail, the distance should be measured from the outer surface of the base or cap plate. The effective length factor $K_e$ should be not less than what would be indicated by rational analysis. Where conditions of end restraint cannot be evaluated closely, a conservative value for $K_e$ should be used.

Table 3.2
**Factored compressive strength for dimension lumber in wall systems[1] $\phi F_c$ (MPa)**

| Service conditions | | Dry service | | | Wet service | | | Wet service | | |
|---|---|---|---|---|---|---|---|---|---|---|
| Preservative treatment[2] | | Untreated | | | Untreated or treated with preservative without incising | | | Treated with preservative and incised | | |
| Load Duration[3] | | Std. | Perm. | Short term | Std. | Perm. | Short term | Std. | Perm. | Short term |
| Species | Grade | | | | | | | | | |
| D.Fir-L | Sel Str | 16.7 | 10.9 | 19.2 | 11.5 | 7.50 | 13.3 | 9.81 | 6.37 | 11.3 |
| | No.1/No.2 | 12.3 | 8.01 | 14.2 | 8.50 | 5.53 | 9.78 | 7.23 | 4.70 | 8.31 |
| | No.3/Stud | 4.05 | 2.63 | 4.66 | 2.79 | 1.82 | 3.21 | 2.37 | 1.54 | 2.73 |
| Hem-Fir | Sel Str | 15.5 | 10.1 | 17.8 | 10.7 | 6.95 | 12.3 | 9.08 | 5.90 | 10.4 |
| | No.1/No.2 | 13.0 | 8.47 | 15.0 | 8.99 | 5.84 | 10.3 | 7.64 | 4.97 | 8.78 |
| | No.3/Stud | 6.16 | 4.00 | 7.08 | 4.25 | 2.76 | 4.89 | 3.61 | 2.35 | 4.15 |
| S-P-F | Sel Str | 12.8 | 8.29 | 14.7 | 8.80 | 5.72 | 10.1 | 7.48 | 4.86 | 8.61 |
| | No.1/No.2 | 10.1 | 6.58 | 11.6 | 6.98 | 4.54 | 8.03 | 5.94 | 3.86 | 6.83 |
| | No.3/Stud | 6.16 | 4.00 | 7.08 | 4.25 | 2.76 | 4.89 | 3.61 | 2.35 | 4.15 |
| Northern | Sel Str | 11.4 | 7.44 | 13.2 | 7.89 | 5.13 | 9.08 | 6.71 | 4.36 | 7.72 |
| | No.1/No.2 | 9.15 | 5.95 | 10.5 | 6.31 | 4.10 | 7.26 | 5.37 | 3.49 | 6.17 |
| | No.3/Stud | 3.96 | 2.57 | 4.55 | 2.73 | 1.78 | 3.14 | 2.32 | 1.51 | 2.67 |

**3**

**⊙**

Compression Members

Notes:
1. For a system consisting of at least 3 studs spaced no further than 610 mm apart to develop load-sharing. For single members divide tabulated values by 1.1.
2. For fire-retardant treated material, multiply by a treatment factor $K_T$. See the Commentary for further guidance.
3. Standard term loading = dead loads plus snow or occupancy loads
   Permanent loading = dead loads alone
   Short term loading = dead plus wind loads
4. $\phi F_c = \phi f_c K_D K_H K_{Sc} K_T$ (refer to Clause 5.5.6 of CSA O86)
5. Dimension lumber has a thickness of less than 102 mm.

Table 3.3
**Strength to stiffness ratio for dimension lumber in wall systems[1] $F_c / E'$ ($\times 10^{-6}$)**

| Service conditions | | Dry service | | | Wet service | | | Wet service | | |
|---|---|---|---|---|---|---|---|---|---|---|
| Preservative treatment | | Untreated | | | Untreated or treated with preservative without incising | | | Treated with preservative and incised | | |
| Load Duration[2] | | Std. | Perm. | Short term | Std. | Perm. | Short term | Std. | Perm. | Short term |
| Species | Grade | | | | | | | | | |
| D.Fir-L | Sel Str | 70.3 | 45.7 | 80.8 | 51.6 | 33.5 | 59.3 | 46.1 | 30.0 | 53.1 |
| | No.1/No.2 | 62.9 | 40.9 | 72.3 | 46.1 | 30.0 | 53.1 | 41.3 | 26.8 | 47.5 |
| | No.3/Stud | 26.3 | 17.1 | 30.2 | 19.3 | 12.5 | 22.2 | 17.3 | 11.2 | 19.9 |
| Hem-Fir | Sel Str | 65.1 | 42.3 | 74.8 | 47.8 | 31.0 | 54.9 | 42.7 | 27.8 | 49.2 |
| | No.1/No.2 | 62.0 | 40.3 | 71.3 | 45.5 | 29.6 | 52.4 | 40.7 | 26.5 | 46.8 |
| | No.3/Stud | 36.7 | 23.8 | 42.2 | 26.9 | 17.5 | 31.0 | 24.1 | 15.7 | 27.7 |
| S-P-F | Sel Str | 60.8 | 39.5 | 69.9 | 44.6 | 29.0 | 51.3 | 39.9 | 25.9 | 45.9 |
| | No.1/No.2 | 55.6 | 36.1 | 63.9 | 40.8 | 26.5 | 46.9 | 36.5 | 23.7 | 42.0 |
| | No.3/Stud | 40.0 | 26.0 | 46.0 | 29.4 | 19.1 | 33.8 | 26.3 | 17.1 | 30.2 |
| Northern | Sel Str | 74.3 | 48.3 | 85.4 | 54.5 | 35.4 | 62.7 | 48.8 | 31.7 | 56.1 |
| | No.1/No.2 | 65.4 | 42.5 | 75.2 | 48.0 | 31.2 | 55.2 | 42.9 | 27.9 | 49.4 |
| | No.3/Stud | 35.4 | 23.0 | 40.7 | 26.0 | 16.9 | 29.8 | 23.2 | 15.1 | 26.7 |

Notes:
1. For a system consisting of at least 3 studs spaced no further than 610 mm apart to develop load-sharing. For single members divide tabulated values by 1.1.
2. Standard term loading = dead loads plus snow or occupancy loads
   Permanent loading = dead loads alone
   Short term loading = dead plus wind loads
3. $F_c / E' = (f_c K_D K_H K_{Sc} K_T) / (35 E_{05} K_{SE} K_T)$ (refer to Clause 5.5.6 of CSA O86)
4. Dimension lumber has a thickness of less than 102 mm.

# Stud Wall Selection Tables

## DF-L
### b = 38 mm

## Sawn Lumber

Factored compressive resistance per stud $P_r$ (kN)

| D.Fir-L | Select Structural | | | No.1/No.2 | | | No.3/Stud | | |
|---|---|---|---|---|---|---|---|---|---|
| L m | d mm 89 | 140 | 184 | 89 | 140 | 184 | 89 | 140 | 184* |
| 2.0 | 36.1 | 87.6 | 126 | 28.1 | 65.9 | 93.6 | 12.8 | 24.3 | 32.4 |
| 2.2 | 30.8 | 81.4 | 120 | 24.2 | 61.6 | 89.9 | 11.7 | 23.3 | 31.6 |
| 2.4 | 26.2 | 75.1 | 115 | 20.7 | 57.2 | 86.2 | 10.5 | 22.4 | 30.8 |
| 2.6 | 22.2 | 69.0 | 110 | 17.7 | 52.8 | 82.3 | 9.47 | 21.4 | 30.0 |
| 2.8 | 18.9 | 63.1 | 104 | 15.1 | 48.6 | 78.4 | 8.47 | 20.4 | 29.2 |
| 3.0 | 16.2 | 57.5 | 98.3 | 13.0 | 44.5 | 74.4 | 7.55 | 19.3 | 28.3 |
| 3.2 | 13.9 | 52.3 | 92.6 | 11.2 | 40.7 | 70.4 | 6.73 | 18.3 | 27.5 |
| 3.4 | 11.9 | 47.4 | 87.0 | 9.64 | 37.1 | 66.4 | 5.99 | 17.3 | 26.6 |
| 3.6 | 10.3 | 43.0 | 81.6 | 8.36 | 33.7 | 62.5 | 5.34 | 16.3 | 25.7 |
| 3.8 | 8.98 | 38.9 | 76.3 | 7.28 | 30.7 | 58.7 | 4.76 | 15.3 | 24.7 |
| 4.0 | 7.84 | 35.2 | 71.2 | 6.37 | 27.9 | 55.0 | 4.25 | 14.4 | 23.8 |
| 4.2 | 6.88 | 31.9 | 66.4 | 5.59 | 25.3 | 51.5 | 3.80 | 13.4 | 22.9 |
| 4.4 | 6.06 | 28.9 | 61.8 | 4.94 | 23.0 | 48.1 | 3.40 | 12.6 | 21.9 |
| 4.6 | | 26.2 | 57.5 | | 20.9 | 44.9 | | 11.7 | 21.0 |
| 4.8 | | 23.8 | 53.4 | | 19.0 | 41.9 | | 10.9 | 20.1 |
| 5.0 | | 21.6 | 49.6 | | 17.4 | 39.0 | | 10.2 | 19.2 |
| 5.2 | | 19.7 | 46.1 | | 15.8 | 36.4 | | 9.51 | 18.3 |
| 5.4 | | 18.0 | 42.8 | | 14.5 | 33.9 | | 8.86 | 17.5 |
| 5.6 | | 16.4 | 39.8 | | 13.2 | 31.5 | | 8.25 | 16.6 |
| 5.8 | | 15.0 | 36.9 | | 12.1 | 29.4 | | 7.69 | 15.8 |
| 6.0 | | 13.8 | 34.3 | | 11.1 | 27.4 | | 7.17 | 15.1 |
| 6.2 | | 12.6 | 31.9 | | 10.2 | 25.5 | | 6.68 | 14.3 |
| 6.4 | | 11.6 | 29.7 | | 9.43 | 23.8 | | 6.23 | 13.6 |
| 6.6 | | 10.7 | 27.7 | | 8.70 | 22.2 | | 5.82 | 12.9 |
| 6.8 | | 9.88 | 25.8 | | 8.04 | 20.7 | | 5.43 | 12.2 |
| 7.0 | | 9.14 | 24.1 | | 7.44 | 19.4 | | 5.08 | 11.6 |
| $Q_r$(kN) | 27.2 | 42.8 | 56.3 | 27.2 | 42.8 | 56.3 | 27.2 | 42.8 | 56.3 |

Note:
Tabulated values are valid for the following conditions:
• standard term loading (dead plus snow or occupancy)
• dry service conditions
• untreated lumber, or preservative treated but not incised
• studs effectively pinned and laterally restrained at both ends and prevented from buckling about weak axis by wall sheathing
• wall system consisting of at least 3 studs spaced no farther apart than 610 mm apart
• studs concentrically loaded

* 38 × 184 mm lumber is available as No.3, but not as Stud grade.

# Stud Wall Selection Tables

## Sawn Lumber

**H-F**
b = 38 mm

Factored compressive resistance per stud $P_r$ (kN)

| Hem-Fir | Select Structural | | | No.1/No.2 | | | No.3/Stud | | |
|---|---|---|---|---|---|---|---|---|---|
| L<br>m | d<br>mm<br>89 | 140 | 184 | 89 | 140 | 184 | 89 | 140 | 184* |
| 2.0 | 34.7 | 82.4 | 117 | 29.9 | 69.9 | 99.0 | 17.6 | 35.7 | 48.6 |
| 2.2 | 29.8 | 76.8 | 113 | 25.8 | 65.3 | 95.2 | 15.7 | 34.0 | 47.2 |
| 2.4 | 25.4 | 71.2 | 108 | 22.0 | 60.6 | 91.3 | 13.9 | 32.3 | 45.8 |
| 2.6 | 21.7 | 65.6 | 103 | 18.8 | 56.1 | 87.2 | 12.2 | 30.5 | 44.3 |
| 2.8 | 18.5 | 60.3 | 97.8 | 16.1 | 51.6 | 83.1 | 10.7 | 28.7 | 42.8 |
| 3.0 | 15.9 | 55.1 | 92.8 | 13.8 | 47.3 | 78.9 | 9.43 | 27.0 | 41.2 |
| 3.2 | 13.7 | 50.3 | 87.7 | 11.9 | 43.2 | 74.7 | 8.28 | 25.2 | 39.7 |
| 3.4 | 11.8 | 45.8 | 82.6 | 10.3 | 39.4 | 70.5 | 7.28 | 23.5 | 38.1 |
| 3.6 | 10.2 | 41.6 | 77.7 | 8.94 | 35.9 | 66.4 | 6.41 | 21.9 | 36.5 |
| 3.8 | 8.88 | 37.8 | 72.9 | 7.78 | 32.7 | 62.4 | 5.65 | 20.3 | 34.8 |
| 4.0 | 7.77 | 34.3 | 68.2 | 6.81 | 29.7 | 58.5 | 5.00 | 18.8 | 33.2 |
| 4.2 | 6.82 | 31.1 | 63.7 | 5.99 | 27.0 | 54.8 | 4.44 | 17.4 | 31.6 |
| 4.4 | 6.01 | 28.2 | 59.5 | 5.28 | 24.5 | 51.2 | 3.95 | 16.1 | 30.1 |
| 4.6 | | 25.7 | 55.5 | | 22.3 | 47.8 | | 14.9 | 28.5 |
| 4.8 | | 23.3 | 51.7 | | 20.3 | 44.6 | | 13.7 | 27.1 |
| 5.0 | | 21.2 | 48.1 | | 18.5 | 41.6 | | 12.7 | 25.6 |
| 5.2 | | 19.4 | 44.8 | | 16.9 | 38.7 | | 11.7 | 24.2 |
| 5.4 | | 17.7 | 41.6 | | 15.5 | 36.1 | | 10.8 | 22.9 |
| 5.6 | | 16.2 | 38.7 | | 14.2 | 33.6 | | 10.0 | 21.6 |
| 5.8 | | 14.8 | 36.1 | | 13.0 | 31.3 | | 9.26 | 20.4 |
| 6.0 | | 13.6 | 33.6 | | 11.9 | 29.2 | | 8.58 | 19.2 |
| 6.2 | | 12.5 | 31.3 | | 11.0 | 27.2 | | 7.95 | 18.1 |
| 6.4 | | 11.5 | 29.1 | | 10.1 | 25.4 | | 7.37 | 17.1 |
| 6.6 | | 10.6 | 27.2 | | 9.31 | 23.7 | | 6.84 | 16.1 |
| 6.8 | | 9.80 | 25.4 | | 8.60 | 22.1 | | 6.36 | 15.2 |
| 7.0 | | 9.07 | 23.7 | | 7.96 | 20.7 | | 5.92 | 14.3 |
| $Q_r$(kN) | 17.9 | 28.1 | 37.0 | 17.9 | 28.1 | 37.0 | 17.9 | 28.1 | 37.0 |

**3**

Compression Members

Note:
Tabulated values are valid for the following conditions:
• standard term loading (dead plus snow or occupancy)
• dry service conditions
• untreated lumber, or preservative treated but not incised
• studs effectively pinned and laterally restrained at both ends and prevented from buckling about weak axis by wall sheathing
• wall system consisting of at least 3 studs spaced no farther apart than 610 mm apart
• studs concentrically loaded

* 38 × 184 mm lumber is available as No.3, but not as Stud grade,

# Stud Wall Selection Tables

**S-P-F**
b = 38 mm

# Sawn Lumber

Factored compressive resistance per stud $P_r$ (kN)

| S-P-F | Select Structural | | | No.1/No.2 | | | No.3/Stud | | |
|---|---|---|---|---|---|---|---|---|---|
| | d | | | | | | | | |
| L | mm | | | | | | | | |
| m | 89 | 140 | 184 | 89 | 140 | 184 | 89 | 140 | 184* |
| 2.0 | 29.6 | 68.7 | 97.2 | 24.4 | 55.4 | 77.6 | 17.0 | 35.3 | 48.3 |
| 2.2 | 25.5 | 64.3 | 93.5 | 21.2 | 51.9 | 74.8 | 15.1 | 33.6 | 46.9 |
| 2.4 | 21.9 | 59.7 | 89.7 | 18.3 | 48.5 | 72.0 | 13.3 | 31.8 | 45.4 |
| 2.6 | 18.7 | 55.3 | 85.7 | 15.7 | 45.1 | 69.0 | 11.7 | 29.9 | 43.9 |
| 2.8 | 16.0 | 50.9 | 81.7 | 13.5 | 41.7 | 65.9 | 10.2 | 28.1 | 42.3 |
| 3.0 | 13.8 | 46.7 | 77.7 | 11.7 | 38.4 | 62.8 | 8.91 | 26.3 | 40.7 |
| 3.2 | 11.9 | 42.8 | 73.6 | 10.1 | 35.3 | 59.7 | 7.80 | 24.5 | 39.0 |
| 3.4 | 10.3 | 39.0 | 69.5 | 8.73 | 32.3 | 56.6 | 6.83 | 22.7 | 37.4 |
| 3.6 | 8.90 | 35.6 | 65.5 | 7.60 | 29.6 | 53.5 | 6.00 | 21.1 | 35.7 |
| 3.8 | 7.76 | 32.4 | 61.6 | 6.63 | 27.0 | 50.4 | 5.28 | 19.5 | 34.0 |
| 4.0 | 6.79 | 29.5 | 57.8 | 5.82 | 24.7 | 47.5 | 4.66 | 18.0 | 32.4 |
| 4.2 | 5.97 | 26.8 | 54.2 | 5.12 | 22.5 | 44.6 | 4.13 | 16.6 | 30.8 |
| 4.4 | 5.27 | 24.4 | 50.7 | 4.52 | 20.5 | 41.8 | 3.67 | 15.3 | 29.2 |
| 4.6 | | 22.2 | 47.3 | | 18.7 | 39.2 | | 14.1 | 27.6 |
| 4.8 | | 20.2 | 44.2 | | 17.1 | 36.7 | | 13.0 | 26.1 |
| 5.0 | | 18.4 | 41.2 | | 15.6 | 34.3 | | 12.0 | 24.6 |
| 5.2 | | 16.8 | 38.4 | | 14.3 | 32.1 | | 11.0 | 23.2 |
| 5.4 | | 15.4 | 35.8 | | 13.1 | 30.0 | | 10.2 | 21.9 |
| 5.6 | | 14.1 | 33.4 | | 12.0 | 28.0 | | 9.40 | 20.6 |
| 5.8 | | 12.9 | 31.1 | | 11.0 | 26.1 | | 8.68 | 19.4 |
| 6.0 | | 11.9 | 29.0 | | 10.1 | 24.4 | | 8.02 | 18.3 |
| 6.2 | | 10.9 | 27.1 | | 9.33 | 22.8 | | 7.43 | 17.2 |
| 6.4 | | 10.1 | 25.2 | | 8.61 | 21.3 | | 6.88 | 16.2 |
| 6.6 | | 9.28 | 23.6 | | 7.95 | 19.9 | | 6.38 | 15.2 |
| 6.8 | | 8.58 | 22.0 | | 7.35 | 18.7 | | 5.92 | 14.3 |
| 7.0 | | 7.94 | 20.6 | | 6.81 | 17.5 | | 5.50 | 13.5 |
| $Q_r$(kN) | 20.6 | 32.4 | 42.6 | 20.6 | 32.4 | 42.6 | 20.6 | 32.4 | 42.6 |

Note:
Tabulated values are valid for the following conditions:
• standard term loading (dead plus snow or occupancy)
• dry service conditions
• untreated lumber, or preservative treated but not incised
• studs effectively pinned and laterally restrained at both ends and prevented from buckling about weak axis by wall sheathing
• wall system consisting of at least 3 studs spaced no farther apart than 610 mm apart
• studs concentrically loaded

\* 38 × 184 mm lumber is available as No.3, but not as Stud grade,

# Stud Wall Selection Tables

## Sawn Lumber

**Nor**

b = 38 mm

**3**

▼O

Compression Members

Factored compressive resistance per stud $P_r$ (kN)

| Northern | Select Structural | | | No.1/No.2 | | | No.3/Stud | | |
|---|---|---|---|---|---|---|---|---|---|
| L m | d mm 89 | 140 | 184 | 89 | 140 | 184 | 89 | 140 | 184* |
| 2.0 | 24.0 | 59.3 | 85.5 | 20.5 | 48.6 | 69.3 | 11.4 | 23.1 | 31.3 |
| 2.2 | 20.4 | 54.9 | 81.8 | 17.6 | 45.3 | 66.5 | 10.2 | 22.0 | 30.4 |
| 2.4 | 17.3 | 50.5 | 78.0 | 15.0 | 42.0 | 63.7 | 9.07 | 20.9 | 29.5 |
| 2.6 | 14.6 | 46.3 | 74.2 | 12.8 | 38.7 | 60.7 | 8.01 | 19.8 | 28.6 |
| 2.8 | 12.4 | 42.2 | 70.2 | 10.9 | 35.5 | 57.8 | 7.05 | 18.6 | 27.6 |
| 3.0 | 10.6 | 38.4 | 66.3 | 9.35 | 32.5 | 54.8 | 6.20 | 17.5 | 26.7 |
| 3.2 | 9.07 | 34.8 | 62.3 | 8.04 | 29.6 | 51.7 | 5.45 | 16.4 | 25.7 |
| 3.4 | 7.80 | 31.5 | 58.4 | 6.93 | 27.0 | 48.8 | 4.80 | 15.3 | 24.7 |
| 3.6 | 6.74 | 28.5 | 54.7 | 6.01 | 24.5 | 45.8 | 4.23 | 14.3 | 23.6 |
| 3.8 | 5.85 | 25.7 | 51.0 | 5.23 | 22.2 | 43.0 | 3.74 | 13.3 | 22.6 |
| 4.0 | 5.10 | 23.2 | 47.5 | 4.57 | 20.2 | 40.2 | 3.31 | 12.3 | 21.6 |
| 4.2 | 4.47 | 21.0 | 44.2 | 4.01 | 18.3 | 37.6 | 2.94 | 11.4 | 20.6 |
| 4.4 | 3.94 | 19.0 | 41.1 | 3.54 | 16.6 | 35.1 | 2.62 | 10.6 | 19.6 |
| 4.6 | | 17.2 | 38.2 | | 15.1 | 32.7 | | 9.76 | 18.6 |
| 4.8 | | 15.6 | 35.4 | | 13.7 | 30.4 | | 9.03 | 17.6 |
| 5.0 | | 14.2 | 32.8 | | 12.5 | 28.3 | | 8.35 | 16.7 |
| 5.2 | | 12.9 | 30.4 | | 11.4 | 26.4 | | 7.72 | 15.8 |
| 5.4 | | 11.7 | 28.2 | | 10.4 | 24.5 | | 7.14 | 15.0 |
| 5.6 | | 10.7 | 26.2 | | 9.53 | 22.8 | | 6.61 | 14.1 |
| 5.8 | | 9.80 | 24.3 | | 8.73 | 21.2 | | 6.12 | 13.4 |
| 6.0 | | 8.97 | 22.6 | | 8.01 | 19.8 | | 5.67 | 12.6 |
| 6.2 | | 8.23 | 21.0 | | 7.36 | 18.4 | | 5.25 | 11.9 |
| 6.4 | | 7.57 | 19.5 | | 6.77 | 17.2 | | 4.88 | 11.2 |
| 6.6 | | 6.97 | 18.1 | | 6.25 | 16.0 | | 4.53 | 10.6 |
| 6.8 | | 6.43 | 16.9 | | 5.77 | 14.9 | | 4.21 | 10.0 |
| 7.0 | | 5.94 | 15.7 | | 5.34 | 13.9 | | 3.92 | 9.43 |
| $Q_r$(kN) | 13.6 | 21.4 | 28.1 | 13.6 | 21.4 | 28.1 | 13.6 | 21.4 | 28.1 |

Note:
Tabulated values are valid for the following conditions:
• standard term loading (dead plus snow or occupancy)
• dry service conditions
• untreated lumber, or preservative treated but not incised
• studs effectively pinned and laterally restrained at both ends and prevented from buckling about weak axis by wall sheathing
• wall system consisting of at least 3 studs spaced no farther apart than 610 mm apart
• studs concentrically loaded

* 38 × 184 mm lumber is available as No.3, but not as Stud grade,

# Checklist: **Posts**    ✅

To verify that the tabulated resistances given in the Post Selection Table are adequate for the structure being designed, the following questions should be asked:

1. Is the load duration "standard" term (dead load plus snow load or occupancy loads)?

2. Is the service condition "dry"?

3. Is the material free of strength reducing chemicals such as fire retardants?

4. Is the effective length factor $K_e$ equal to 1.0 or 2.0 as shown in the Post Selection Table?

If the answer to any of these questions is no, the Post Selection Table may not be used. Instead, calculate $P_r$ from the formulae given on page 98.

### Example 3: Post

Check the resistance of a single 89 × 89 mm No.1/No.2 grade S-P-F post for the following conditions:

- specified dead load = 1.5 kPa
- specified live load = 2.4 kPa
- tributary area = 4.5 m$^2$
- unbraced length = 3.0 m

- dry service conditions
- untreated
- post effectively pinned at both ends

### Calculation
Total factored load:

$$P_f = (1.25 \times 1.5 + 1.5 \times 2.4) \times 4.5$$
$$= 24.6 \text{ kN}$$

From the Post Selection Table:

$$P_r = 26.6 > 24.6 \text{ kN} \qquad \qquad \textit{Acceptable}$$

**The 89 × 89 mm No.1/No.2 grade S-P-F Post is adequate.**

# Post Selection Table

## Sawn Lumber

**Post**
89 × 89 mm

Factored compressive resistance per post $P_r$ (kN)

| L m | D.Fir-L | | Hem-Fir | | S-P-F | | Northern | |
|---|---|---|---|---|---|---|---|---|
| | Sel Str | No.1/No.2 | Sel Str | No.1/No.2 | Sel Str | No.1/No.2 | Sel Str | No.1/No.2 |
| where $K_e$ = 1.0 | | | | | | | | |
| 1.0 | 140 | 104 | 131 | 110 | 108 | 86.7 | 95.2 | 77.2 |
| 1.5 | 112 | 85.1 | 106 | 90.3 | 88.9 | 72.1 | 75.4 | 62.5 |
| 2.0 | 80.6 | 62.6 | 77.4 | 66.6 | 65.8 | 54.3 | 53.7 | 45.7 |
| 2.5 | 54.7 | 43.2 | 53.2 | 46.1 | 45.7 | 38.2 | 36.1 | 31.3 |
| 3.0 | 37.0 | 29.6 | 36.3 | 31.6 | 31.5 | 26.6 | 24.3 | 21.4 |
| 3.5 | 25.6 | 20.7 | 25.2 | 22.1 | 22.0 | 18.7 | 16.7 | 14.9 |
| 4.0 | 18.2 | 14.7 | 18.0 | 15.8 | 15.7 | 13.4 | 11.8 | 10.6 |
| where $K_e$ = 2.0 | | | | | | | | |
| 1.0 | 80.6 | 62.6 | 77.4 | 66.6 | 65.8 | 54.3 | 53.7 | 45.7 |
| 1.5 | 37.5 | 30.0 | 36.8 | 32.0 | 31.9 | 26.9 | 24.6 | 21.6 |
| 2.0 | 18.3 | 14.9 | 18.2 | 15.9 | 15.9 | 13.6 | 11.9 | 10.7 |

Note:
Tabulated values are valid for the following conditions:
• standard term loading (dead plus snow or occupancy)
• dry service conditions
• untreated lumber
• $K_e$ = 1.0 or $K_e$ = 2.0
• L = unsupported length
• concentrically loaded

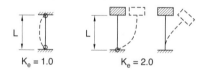

$K_e$ = 1.0          $K_e$ = 2.0

3

Compression Members

# 3.3    Columns

### General

This section provides design procedures and selection tables for two types of wood columns:

- Sawn timbers
- Glued-laminated timber (glulam)

Sawn timbers are produced in accordance with CSA Standard O141 *Softwood Lumber*. The rules for the grading of timbers are outlined in the National Lumber Grades Authority *Standard Grading Rules for Canadian Lumber*. Generally, timber columns fall into the Post and Timber size and end use category.

Glued-laminated timber is an engineered wood product manufactured by gluing together 38 or 19 mm thick lumber laminations with a waterproof adhesive. Glulam is manufactured to meet CSA Standard O122 *Structural Glued-Laminated Timber* and the manufacturers of glulam must be certified in accordance with CSA Standard O177 *Qualification Code for Manufacturers of Structural Glued-Laminated Timber*. Generally, the 16c-E or 12c-E stress grade is used for compression members. The 24f-EX and 20f-EX grades are used for members subjected to combined axial and bending loads and design information is provided in Chapter 5.

### Availability

**Sawn Timber**
The Column Selection Tables for sawn timber provide resistance values for the following grades and sizes:

| Table 3.4 **Grades and sizes of sawn timber columns** | Grades | Column sizes for all grades (mm) |
|---|---|---|
| | Select Structural, No.1, No.2 | 140 × 140 |
| | | 191 × 191 |
| | | 241 × 241 |
| | | 292 × 292 |
| | | 140 × 191 |
| | | 191 × 241 |
| | | 241 × 292 |

D.Fir-L and Hem-Fir are the species groups most readily available in lumber yards, but S-P-F and Northern species may also be obtained.

All the sizes listed above should be available; however, the availability of large sizes should be checked before specifying. Timbers may be obtained in lengths up to 9.1 m, but this should also be confirmed with local suppliers.

The most readily available grades are No.1 and No.2 but Select Structural may be ordered.

Timbers are always dressed green as their large size makes kiln-drying impractical. As a result, some amount of shrinkage and checking can be expected after
dressing. These effects should be considered when detailing members and
connections.

### Glulam

The Column Selection Tables for glulam provide resistance values for the following species, grades and thicknesses:

Table 3.5
**Species,
grades and
thicknesses of
glulam
columns**

| Species and stress grades | Column thickness for all species and grades mm |
|---|---|
| **D.Fir-L:** 16c-E<br>**Spruce-Pine:** 12c-E | 80 |
| | 130 |
| | 175 |
| | 215 |
| | 265 |
| | 315 |
| | 365 |

Most fabricators produce either D.Fir-L or Spruce-Pine glulam. The thicknesses
shown in Table 3.5 are industry standards, but some fabricators can produce
slightly different sizes. Most fabricators use 38 mm thick laminations for straight
columns.

### Design

Sawn timber and glulam columns subjected to axial loading must be designed
so that the following criterion is satisfied:

Factored compressive resistance parallel to grain $P_r \geq$ factored
compressive load $P_f$

The factored compressive resistance, $P_r$, may be determined as follows:

1. When the conditions of use meet the restrictions listed in the following checklist, $P_r$ may be taken directly from the Column Selection Tables for sawn
   timber or glulam.

2. When the conditions of use do not meet the requirements of the checklist, the
   value of $P_r$ given in the selection tables is not valid. Furthermore, the tabulated
   values cannot be adjusted by a factor that will apply throughout the entire
   unsupported length range. Therefore, $P_r$ should be calculated from the
   following formula:

$$P_r = \phi\, F_c\, A\, K_{Zc}\, K_C \ (N)$$

where:

$\phi\, F_c$ = factored compressive strength (MPa), given in
Table 3.6 for sawn timber and
Table 3.8 for glulam

$A$ = cross-sectional area (mm²)

$K_{Zc}$ = size factor

for sawn timber
$K_{Zc} = 6.3\,(d\, L_d)^{-0.13} < 1.3$ for buckling in direction of d
$\phantom{K_{Zc}} = 6.3\,(b\, L_b)^{-0.13} < 1.3$ for buckling in direction of b

for glulam
$K_{Zc} = 0.68\,(Z)^{-0.13} < 1.0$, where Z = member volume in m³

$K_C$ = slenderness factor

$$= \left[1.0 + \frac{F_c}{E'}\, K_{Zc}\, C_c^3\right]^{-1}$$

$F_c / E'$ = strength to stiffness ratio, given in
Table 3.7 for sawn timber and
Table 3.9 for glulam

$C_c$ = the greater of $\dfrac{K_e\, L_d}{d}$ or $\dfrac{K_e\, L_b}{b}$ ($C_c > 50$ is not permitted)

$K_e$ = effective length factor, given in Figure 3.1

$L_d, L_b$ = unsupported length associated with d or b (mm)

$d$ = depth of member (mm)

$b$ = thickness of member (mm)

Since column design is an iterative process, the Column Selection Tables may be used to select a trial section. When designing a sawn timber column with an effective length factor $K_e$ other than 1.0 or 2.0, a preliminary section may be selected by using the table for $K_e = 1.0$ with the length L equal to the actual effective length $K_e L$. The preliminary section can then be checked using the formula above (note the difference between the estimated resistance and the actual resistance will not usually exceed 5%).

## Additional Design Considerations

Where a column must be drilled or notched, the cross-sectional area removed must not exceed 25% of the gross area of the member (refer to Section 7.1 for information on net area). As long as the drilling or notching does not occur near the point of maximum buckling stress, the tabulated resistances given in the following sections may not need to be adjusted. However, the designer should check the resistance at net section assuming an unsupported length of zero.

In certain cases the *National Building Code of Canada (NBCC)* permits the loads due to use and occupancy to be reduced depending upon the size of the tributary area the member supports. Refer to Article 4.1.6.9 of the *NBCC* for the appropriate reduction factor.

## Example 1: Sawn Timber Columns

Design columns for the following conditions:

- specified dead load = 2.0 kPa
- specified live load = 2.4 kPa
- tributary area = 25 m²
- unbraced length = 5 m

- dry service conditions
- untreated
- column effectively pinned at both ends ($K_e$ = 1.0)

Use No.1 D.Fir-L.

### Calculation
Tributary area > 20 m²
Therefore, live load reduction factor from Part 4 of the *NBCC* is:

$$= \ 0.3 + \sqrt{\frac{9.8}{25}} = 0.926$$

Total factored load:
$$P_f \ = \ (1.25 \times 2.0 + 1.5 \times 0.926 \times 2.4) \times 25$$
$$= \ 146 \ kN$$

From Column Selection Tables select 191 × 191 mm:
$$P_r \ = \ 186 \ kN > 146 \ kN \qquad\qquad \textit{Acceptable}$$

**Use 191 × 191 mm No.1 D.Fir-L column.**

# Checklist: **Columns**

To verify that the tabulated resistances given in the Column Selection Tables are appropriate for the structure being designed, the following questions should be asked:

1. Is load duration "standard" term (dead load plus snow or occupancy loads)?

2. Is the service condition "dry"?

3. Is the material free of strength reducing chemicals such as fire retardants?

4. For sawn timber columns only:
   Is the effective length factor $K_e$ equal to 1.0 or 2.0 as shown in the Column Selection Tables?
   For glulam columns only:
   Is the effective length factor $K_e$ equal to 1.0 and the effective column length in the direction of buckling equal to the total column length?

5. Are the columns concentrically loaded?

If the answer to any of these questions is no, the Column Selection Tables may not be used. Instead, calculate $P_r$ from the formula given on page 113. Information on eccentrically loaded columns is provided in Chapter 5.

### Example 2: Sawn Timber Columns

Design a column for the following conditions:

- specified dead load = 1.0 kPa
- specified live load = 1.9 kPa
- specified snow load = 2.0 kPa
- tributary area = 25 m² (for both snow and live load)
- unbraced length = 5 m

- wet service conditions
- treated with a preservative
- column effectively pinned at both ends ($K_e$ = 1.0)

Use No.2 D.Fir-L.

### Calculation
Live load reduction factor = 0.926

Total factored load:

$$P_f = (1.25 \times 1.0 + 1.5 \times 0.926 \times 1.9 + 0.5 \times 2.0) \times 25 = 122 \text{ kN or}$$
$$P_f = (1.25 \times 1.0 + 0.5 \times 0.926 \times 1.9 + 1.5 \times 2.0) \times 25 = 128 \text{ kN } \textit{Governs}$$

Since service conditions are wet, the Column Selection Tables cannot be used to select final size. However, the selection tables may be used to obtain a trial section.

Select 191 × 191 mm as a trial section since it is the smallest section with $P_r > 128$ kN.

Calculate $P_r$ for wet service conditions:

$$P_r = \phi F_c A K_{Zc} K_C$$
$$\phi F_c = 5.46 \text{ MPa from Table 3.6}$$
$$A = 191 \times 191 = 36.5 \times 10^3 \text{ mm}^2$$
$$K_{Zc} = 6.3 (191 \times 5000)^{-0.13} = 1.05$$
$$F_c / E' = 32.5 \times 10^{-6} \text{ from Table 3.7}$$
$$C_c = 5000 / 191 = 26.2$$
$$K_C = [1.0 + 32.5 \times 10^{-6} \times 1.05 \times (26.2)^3]^{-1}$$
$$= 0.62$$
$$P_r = 5.46 \times 36.5 \times 10^3 \times 1.05 \times 0.62$$
$$= 130 \text{ kN} > 128 \text{ kN} \qquad\qquad \textit{Acceptable}$$

**Use a 191 × 191 mm No.2 D. Fir-L column.**

### Example 3: Glulam Columns

Is a 175 × 228 mm 12c-E Spruce-Pine glulam column adequate for the following conditions?

- specified dead load = 1.5 kPa
- specified snow load = 3.5 kPa
- tributary area = 30 m²
- total length = 7 m

- dry service condition
- untreated

The column is effectively pinned at both ends and braced at mid-height in the narrow dimension as shown below.

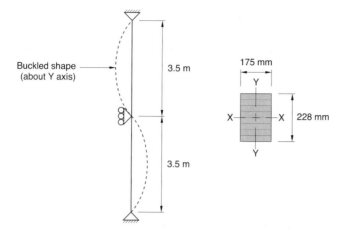

Buckled shape (about Y axis)

3.5 m

3.5 m

175 mm

228 mm

**Calculation**

Since the column supports dead plus snow loads only, the *NBCC* live load reduction factor does not apply.

Total factored load:

$$P_f = (1.25 \times 1.5 + 1.5 \times 3.5) \times 30$$
$$= 214 \text{ kN}$$

Slenderness ratio, $C_c$

$$C_{cx} = K_e \times L_d / d$$
$$= 1.0 \times 7000 / 228 = 30.7 \qquad \textit{Governs}$$
$$C_{cy} = K_e \times L_b / b$$
$$= 1.0 \times 3500 / 175 = 20.0$$

Since buckling about X axis governs, Column Selection Tables may be used because $K_e L_d = L$.

From Column Selection Tables:

$$P_{rx} = 217 \text{ kN} > 214 \text{ kN} \qquad \textit{Acceptable}$$

**The 175 × 228 mm 12c-E Spruce-Pine glulam section is adequate.**

3

Compression Members

## Example 4 : Glulam Columns

Is a 175 × 228 mm Spruce-Pine glulam column adequate for the following conditions?

- specified dead load = 1.5 kPa
- specified snow load = 3.5 kPa
- tributary area = 30 m$^2$
- total length = 9 m

- dry service conditions
- untreated

The column is effectively pinned at both ends and braced at mid-height in all directions.

### Calculation

Although the effective length factor $K_e$ is equal to 1.0 in both X and Y directions, the Column Selection Tables cannot be used because the effective column length about X and Y axis ($K_e \times L_{d,b} = 1.0 \times 4.5 = 4.5$ m) is not equal to the total column length (L = 9.0 m).

Total factored load:

$$P_f = (1.25 \times 1.5 + 1.5 \times 3.5) \times 30$$
$$= 214 \text{ kN}$$

Calculate $P_r$ :

$$P_r = \phi F_c A K_{Zc} K_C$$
$$\phi F_c = 20.16 \text{ MPa from Table 3.8}$$
$$A = 175 \times 228 = 39.9 \times 10^3 \text{ mm}^2$$
$$K_{Zc} = 0.68 \times (0.175 \times 0.228 \times 9.0)^{-0.13} = 0.78$$
$$F_c / E' = 85.32 \times 10^{-6} \text{ from Table 3.9}$$
$$C_{cx} = 1.0 \times 4500 / 228 = 19.7$$
$$C_{cy} = 1.0 \times 4500 / 175 = 25.7 \text{ (governs)}$$
$$K_C = [1.0 + 85.32 \times 10^{-6} \times 0.78 \times (25.7)^3]^{-1} = 0.47$$
$$P_r = 20.2 \times 39.9 \times 10^3 \times 0.78 \times 0.47$$
$$= 295 \text{ kN} > 214 \text{ kN} \qquad\qquad \textit{Acceptable}$$

**The 175 × 228 mm 12c-E Spruce-Pine glulam section is adequate.**

Table 3.6
**Factored compressive strength for sawn timbers**
$\phi\ F_c$ **(MPa)**[1]

| Service conditions | | Dry service | | | Wet service | | |
|---|---|---|---|---|---|---|---|
| Load duration[2] | | Std. | Perm. | Short term | Std. | Perm. | Short term |
| Species | Grade | | | | | | |
| D.Fir-L | Sel Str | 11.0 | 7.18 | 12.7 | 10.0 | 6.53 | 11.6 |
| | No.1 | 9.76 | 6.34 | 11.2 | 8.88 | 5.77 | 10.2 |
| | No.2 | 6.00 | 3.90 | 6.90 | 5.46 | 3.55 | 6.28 |
| Hem-Fir | Sel Str | 9.04 | 5.88 | 10.4 | 8.23 | 5.35 | 9.46 |
| | No.1 | 8.00 | 5.20 | 9.20 | 7.28 | 4.73 | 8.37 |
| | No.2 | 4.88 | 3.17 | 5.61 | 4.44 | 2.89 | 5.11 |
| S-P-F | Sel Str | 7.92 | 5.15 | 9.11 | 7.21 | 4.68 | 8.29 |
| | No.1 | 6.96 | 4.52 | 8.00 | 6.33 | 4.12 | 7.28 |
| | No.2 | 4.32 | 2.81 | 4.97 | 3.93 | 2.56 | 4.52 |
| Northern | Sel Str | 6.00 | 3.90 | 6.90 | 5.46 | 3.55 | 6.28 |
| | No.1 | 5.36 | 3.48 | 6.16 | 4.88 | 3.17 | 5.61 |
| | No.2 | 3.28 | 2.13 | 3.77 | 2.98 | 1.94 | 3.43 |

Notes:
1. For fire-retardant treated material, multiply by a treatment factor $K_T$. See the Commentary for further guidance.
2. Standard term loading = dead loads plus snow or occupancy loads
   Permanent loading = dead loads alone
   Short term loading = dead plus wind loads
3. $\phi\ F_c = \phi\ f_c\ K_D\ K_H\ K_{Sc}\ K_T$ (refer to Clause 5.5.6 of CSA O86).
4. Sawn timbers have a smaller dimension of at least 114 mm and a larger dimension not more than 51 mm greater than the smaller dimension.

Table 3.7
**Strength to stiffness ratio for sawn timbers**
$F_c\ /\ E'$ ($\times 10^{-6}$)

| Service conditions | | Dry service | | | Wet service | | |
|---|---|---|---|---|---|---|---|
| Load duration[1] | | Std. | Perm. | Short term | Std. | Perm. | Short term |
| Species | Grade | | | | | | |
| D.Fir-L | Sel Str | 49.3 | 32.0 | 56.7 | 44.9 | 29.2 | 51.6 |
| | No.1 | 53.6 | 34.9 | 61.7 | 48.8 | 31.7 | 56.1 |
| | No.2 | 35.7 | 23.2 | 41.1 | 32.5 | 21.1 | 37.4 |
| Hem-Fir | Sel Str | 46.1 | 30.0 | 53.0 | 42.0 | 27.3 | 48.3 |
| | No.1 | 47.6 | 31.0 | 54.8 | 43.3 | 28.2 | 49.8 |
| | No.2 | 31.7 | 20.6 | 36.4 | 28.8 | 18.7 | 33.2 |
| S-P-F | Sel Str | 47.1 | 30.6 | 54.2 | 42.9 | 27.9 | 49.3 |
| | No.1 | 49.7 | 32.3 | 57.2 | 45.2 | 29.4 | 52.0 |
| | No.2 | 34.3 | 22.3 | 39.4 | 31.2 | 20.3 | 35.9 |
| Northern | Sel Str | 39.0 | 25.3 | 44.8 | 35.5 | 23.0 | 40.8 |
| | No.1 | 38.3 | 24.9 | 44.0 | 34.8 | 22.6 | 40.1 |
| | No.2 | 29.3 | 19.0 | 33.7 | 26.7 | 17.3 | 30.6 |

Notes:
1. Standard term loading = dead loads plus snow or occupancy loads
   Permanent loading = dead loads alone
   Short term loading = dead plus wind loads
2. $F_c\ /\ E' = (f_c\ K_D\ K_H\ K_{Sc}\ K_T)\ /\ (35\ E_{05}\ K_{SE}\ K_T)$ (refer to Clause 5.5.6 of CSA O86).

| Table 3.8 | Service conditions | Dry service | | | Wet service | | |
|---|---|---|---|---|---|---|---|
| **Factored compressive strength for glulam** $\phi\ F_c$ **(MPa)** | Load duration[2] | Std. | Perm. | Short term | Std. | Perm. | Short term |
| | Compression grades | | | | | | |
| | D.Fir-L 16c-E | 24.2 | 15.7 | 27.8 | 18.1 | 11.8 | 20.8 |
| | Spruce-Pine 12c-E | 20.2 | 13.1 | 23.2 | 15.1 | 9.83 | 17.4 |

Notes:
1. For fire-retardant treated material, multiply by a treatment factor $K_T$. See the Commentary for further guidance.
2. Standard term loading = dead loads plus snow or occupancy loads
   Permanent loading = dead loads alone
   Short term loading = dead plus wind loads
3. $\phi\ F_c = \phi\ f_c\ K_D\ K_H\ K_{Sc}\ K_T$ (refer to Clause 6.5.8 of CSA O86).

| Table 3.9 | Service conditions | Dry service | | | Wet service | | |
|---|---|---|---|---|---|---|---|
| **Modified strength to stiffness ratio for glulam** $F_c / E'$ **(×10⁻⁶)** | Load duration[1] | Std. | Perm. | Short term | Std. | Perm. | Short term |
| | Compression grades | | | | | | |
| | D.Fir-L 16c-E | 80.0 | 52.0 | 92.0 | 66.7 | 43.3 | 76.7 |
| | Spruce-Pine 12c-E | 85.3 | 55.5 | 98.1 | 71.1 | 46.2 | 81.8 |

Notes:
1. Standard term loading = dead loads plus snow or occupancy loads
   Permanent loading = dead loads alone
   Short term loading = dead plus wind loads
2. $F_c / E' = (f_c\ K_D\ K_H\ K_{Sc}\ K_T) / (35\ E_{05}\ K_{SE}\ K_T)$ (refer to Clause 6.5.8 of CSA O86).

# Column Selection Tables

## Sawn Timbers

**DF-L Sel**

| | Square timbers | | | | Rectangular timbers | | | | | |
|---|---|---|---|---|---|---|---|---|---|---|
| b (mm) | 140 | 191 | 241 | 292 | 140 | | 191 | | 241 | |
| d (mm) | 140 | 191 | 241 | 292 | 191 | | 241 | | 292 | |
| L | $P_r$ | $P_r$ | $P_r$ | $P_r$ | $P_{rx}$ | $P_{ry}$ | $P_{rx}$ | $P_{ry}$ | $P_{rx}$ | $P_{ry}$ |
| m | kN | kN | kN | kN | kN | kN | kN | kN | kN | kN |
| 2.0 | 227 | 447 | 714 | 1040 | 328 | 309 | 566 | 564 | 856 | 865 |
| 2.5 | 194 | 411 | 675 | 992 | 301 | 265 | 535 | 519 | 819 | 817 |
| 3.0 | 162 | 373 | 634 | 947 | 273 | 220 | 502 | 470 | 782 | 768 |
| 3.5 | 132 | 333 | 590 | 902 | 244 | 180 | 468 | 420 | 744 | 715 |
| 4.0 | 106 | 293 | 545 | 854 | 215 | 145 | 432 | 369 | 705 | 660 |
| 4.5 | 85.3 | 255 | 498 | 804 | 187 | 116 | 395 | 321 | 663 | 603 |
| 5.0 | 68.5 | 219 | 452 | 752 | 161 | 93.5 | 358 | 277 | 620 | 547 |
| 5.5 | 55.3 | 188 | 406 | 699 | 138 | 75.4 | 322 | 238 | 577 | 492 |
| 6.0 | 44.9 | 161 | 364 | 646 | 118 | 61.3 | 288 | 203 | 533 | 440 |
| 6.5 | 36.8 | 138 | 324 | 595 | 101 | 50.2 | 257 | 174 | 491 | 392 |
| 7.0 | 30.4 | 118 | 287 | 545 | 86.3 | 41.5 | 228 | 149 | 449 | 348 |
| 7.5 | | 101 | 255 | 497 | 74.1 | | 202 | 127 | 410 | 308 |
| 8.0 | | 86.9 | 225 | 452 | 63.7 | | 179 | 110 | 373 | 273 |
| 8.5 | | 75.1 | 200 | 411 | 55.1 | | 158 | 94.8 | 339 | 242 |
| 9.0 | | 65.1 | 177 | 372 | 47.7 | | 140 | 82.2 | 307 | 214 |
| 2.0 | 110 | 311 | 585 | 920 | 228 | 151 | 464 | 392 | 763 | 709 |
| 2.5 | 70.3 | 230 | 480 | 810 | 168 | 95.9 | 380 | 290 | 667 | 582 |
| 3.0 | 45.7 | 167 | 382 | 688 | 122 | 62.4 | 303 | 210 | 568 | 463 |
| 3.5 | 30.8 | 121 | 299 | 575 | 88.6 | 42.0 | 237 | 152 | 474 | 362 |
| 4.0 | | 88.6 | 233 | 473 | 65.0 | | 184 | 112 | 391 | 282 |
| 4.5 | | 66.1 | 181 | 387 | 48.4 | | 144 | 83.4 | 319 | 220 |
| 5.0 | | | 142 | 315 | | | 113 | | 260 | 173 |
| 5.5 | | | 113 | 258 | | | 89.5 | | 213 | 137 |
| 6.0 | | | 90.5 | 212 | | | 71.7 | | 175 | 110 |
| 6.5 | | | | 175 | | | | | 144 | |
| 7.0 | | | | 145 | | | | | 120 | |

**D.Fir-L Select Structural**

$K_e = 1.0$

$K_e = 2.0$

**3**

**Compression Members**

Notes:

1. $P_{rx}$ is the factored resistance to buckling about the x-x (strong) axis.
   $P_{ry}$ is the factored resistance to buckling about the y-y (weak) axis.
2. For $L \leq 2.0$ m, use $P_r$ for $L = 2.0$ m.
   Where $P_r$ values are not given, the slenderness ratio exceeds 50 (maximum permitted).
3. Tabulated values are valid for the following conditions:
   - standard term load (dead plus snow or occupancy loads)
   - dry service conditions
   - no fire-retardant treatment
   - $K_e = 1.0$ or $K_e = 2.0$
   - concentrically loaded.

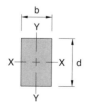

# Column Selection Tables

## DF-L No.1

## Sawn Timbers

| D.Fir-L No.1 | L | Square timbers | | | | Rectangular timbers | | | | | |
|---|---|---|---|---|---|---|---|---|---|---|---|
| b (mm) | | 140 | 191 | 241 | 292 | 140 | | 191 | | 241 | |
| d (mm) | | 140 | 191 | 241 | 292 | 191 | | 241 | | 292 | |
| | | $P_r$ | $P_r$ | $P_r$ | $P_r$ | $P_{rx}$ | $P_{ry}$ | $P_{rx}$ | $P_{ry}$ | $P_{rx}$ | $P_{ry}$ |
| | m | kN | kN | kN | kN | kN | kN | kN | kN | kN | kN |
| $K_e = 1.0$ | 2.0 | 198 | 393 | 629 | 915 | 288 | 270 | 499 | 496 | 756 | 763 |
| | 2.5 | 168 | 360 | 593 | 874 | 264 | 229 | 470 | 454 | 722 | 719 |
| | 3.0 | 138 | 324 | 556 | 834 | 238 | 189 | 440 | 409 | 688 | 673 |
| | 3.5 | 112 | 288 | 515 | 791 | 211 | 153 | 409 | 363 | 653 | 625 |
| | 4.0 | 89.5 | 251 | 474 | 747 | 184 | 122 | 375 | 317 | 617 | 574 |
| | 4.5 | 71.3 | 217 | 431 | 701 | 159 | 97.3 | 341 | 274 | 578 | 522 |
| | 5.0 | 57.0 | 186 | 389 | 653 | 136 | 77.8 | 308 | 235 | 539 | 471 |
| | 5.5 | 45.8 | 159 | 348 | 605 | 116 | 62.5 | 276 | 200 | 499 | 421 |
| | 6.0 | 37.1 | 135 | 310 | 557 | 99.0 | 50.6 | 245 | 170 | 460 | 375 |
| | 6.5 | 30.3 | 115 | 274 | 510 | 84.3 | 41.3 | 217 | 145 | 421 | 332 |
| | 7.0 | 25.0 | 98.0 | 242 | 465 | 71.8 | 34.1 | 192 | 124 | 384 | 294 |
| | 7.5 | | 83.8 | 214 | 423 | 61.4 | | 170 | 106 | 349 | 259 |
| | 8.0 | | 71.9 | 189 | 383 | 52.7 | | 150 | 90.7 | 316 | 229 |
| | 8.5 | | 62.0 | 167 | 347 | 45.4 | | 132 | 78.2 | 286 | 202 |
| | 9.0 | | 53.6 | 147 | 313 | 39.3 | | 117 | 67.7 | 259 | 178 |
| $K_e = 2.0$ | 2.0 | 92.8 | 266 | 508 | 808 | 195 | 127 | 403 | 336 | 667 | 616 |
| | 2.5 | 58.4 | 194 | 412 | 701 | 143 | 79.6 | 327 | 245 | 578 | 500 |
| | 3.0 | 37.7 | 140 | 325 | 592 | 102 | 51.4 | 258 | 176 | 489 | 394 |
| | 3.5 | 25.3 | 100 | 252 | 490 | 73.6 | 34.5 | 200 | 127 | 405 | 305 |
| | 4.0 | | 73.2 | 195 | 400 | 53.7 | | 154 | 92.4 | 330 | 236 |
| | 4.5 | | 54.4 | 151 | 325 | 39.9 | | 120 | 68.6 | 268 | 183 |
| | 5.0 | | | 118 | 263 | | | 93.4 | | 217 | 143 |
| | 5.5 | | | 93.1 | 214 | | | 73.8 | | 177 | 113 |
| | 6.0 | | | 74.4 | 175 | | | 58.9 | | 145 | 90.1 |
| | 6.5 | | | | 144 | | | | | 119 | |
| | 7.0 | | | | 120 | | | | | 98.7 | |

Notes:
1. $P_{rx}$ is the factored resistance to buckling about the x-x (strong) axis.
   $P_{ry}$ is the factored resistance to buckling about the y-y (weak) axis.
2. For L ≤ 2.0 m, use $P_r$ for L = 2.0 m.
   Where $P_r$ values are not given, the slenderness ratio exceeds 50 (maximum permitted).
3. Tabulated values are valid for the following conditions:
   • standard term load (dead plus snow or occupancy loads)
   • dry service conditions
   • no fire-retardant treatment
   • $K_e = 1.0$ or $K_e = 2.0$
   • concentrically loaded.

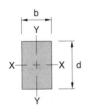

# Column Selection Tables

## Sawn Timbers

**DF-L No.2**

| | | Square timbers | | | | Rectangular timbers | | | | | |
|---|---|---|---|---|---|---|---|---|---|---|---|
| | b (mm) | 140 | 191 | 241 | 292 | 140 | | 191 | | 241 | |
| | d (mm) | 140 | 191 | 241 | 292 | 191 | | 241 | | 292 | |
| **D.Fir-L No.2** | L m | $P_r$ kN | $P_r$ kN | $P_r$ kN | $P_r$ kN | $P_{rx}$ kN | $P_{ry}$ kN | $P_{rx}$ kN | $P_{ry}$ kN | $P_{rx}$ kN | $P_{ry}$ kN |
| $K_e = 1.0$ | 2.0 | 129 | 247 | 391 | 566 | 181 | 175 | 310 | 312 | 467 | 474 |
| | 2.5 | 113 | 231 | 373 | 544 | 169 | 155 | 295 | 291 | 449 | 451 |
| | 3.0 | 97.5 | 213 | 353 | 523 | 156 | 133 | 280 | 269 | 431 | 428 |
| | 3.5 | 82.3 | 194 | 334 | 501 | 142 | 112 | 264 | 245 | 414 | 404 |
| | 4.0 | 68.4 | 175 | 312 | 479 | 128 | 93.3 | 248 | 221 | 395 | 379 |
| | 4.5 | 56.4 | 156 | 291 | 456 | 114 | 76.9 | 230 | 197 | 376 | 352 |
| | 5.0 | 46.3 | 138 | 268 | 432 | 101 | 63.2 | 213 | 174 | 357 | 325 |
| | 5.5 | 38.1 | 121 | 246 | 407 | 88.4 | 51.9 | 195 | 152 | 336 | 298 |
| | 6.0 | 31.4 | 105 | 224 | 382 | 77.1 | 42.8 | 178 | 133 | 315 | 272 |
| | 6.5 | 26.0 | 91.5 | 203 | 357 | 67.1 | 35.5 | 161 | 115 | 295 | 246 |
| | 7.0 | 21.7 | 79.6 | 184 | 332 | 58.3 | 29.6 | 145 | 100 | 274 | 222 |
| | 7.5 | | 69.2 | 165 | 307 | 50.7 | | 131 | 87.3 | 254 | 200 |
| | 8.0 | | 60.2 | 148 | 284 | 44.1 | | 118 | 76.0 | 234 | 180 |
| | 8.5 | | 52.5 | 133 | 261 | 38.5 | | 106 | 66.3 | 216 | 161 |
| | 9.0 | | 46.0 | 119 | 240 | 33.7 | | 94.7 | 58.0 | 198 | 145 |
| $K_e = 2.0$ | 2.0 | 71.6 | 187 | 337 | 520 | 137 | 97.6 | 267 | 236 | 429 | 409 |
| | 2.5 | 47.8 | 145 | 287 | 466 | 106 | 65.2 | 227 | 183 | 385 | 348 |
| | 3.0 | 32.1 | 110 | 237 | 409 | 80.3 | 43.8 | 188 | 138 | 338 | 288 |
| | 3.5 | 22.0 | 82.1 | 192 | 353 | 60.2 | 30.1 | 153 | 104 | 291 | 233 |
| | 4.0 | | 61.7 | 154 | 299 | 45.2 | | 122 | 77.8 | 247 | 187 |
| | 4.5 | | 46.8 | 123 | 251 | 34.3 | | 97.7 | 59.1 | 207 | 149 |
| | 5.0 | | | 98.7 | 210 | | | 78.2 | | 173 | 120 |
| | 5.5 | | | 79.4 | 175 | | | 62.9 | | 144 | 96.2 |
| | 6.0 | | | 64.4 | 146 | | | 51.0 | | 120 | 78.0 |
| | 6.5 | | | | 122 | | | | | 101 | |
| | 7.0 | | | | 103 | | | | | 84.7 | |

Notes:
1. $P_{rx}$ is the factored resistance to buckling about the x-x (strong) axis.
   $P_{ry}$ is the factored resistance to buckling about the y-y (weak) axis.
2. For L ≤ 2.0 m, use $P_r$ for L = 2.0 m.
   Where $P_r$ values are not given, the slenderness ratio exceeds 50 (maximum permitted).
3. Tabulated values are valid for the following conditions:
   • standard term load (dead plus snow or occupancy loads)
   • dry service conditions
   • no fire-retardant treatment
   • $K_e = 1.0$ or $K_e = 2.0$
   • concentrically loaded.

**3**

**Compression Members**

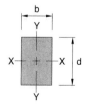

# Column Selection Tables

**H-F Sel**

## Sawn Timbers

| | | Square timbers | | | | Rectangular timbers | | | | | |
|---|---|---|---|---|---|---|---|---|---|---|---|
| b (mm) | | 140 | 191 | 241 | 292 | 140 | | 191 | | 241 | |
| d (mm) | | 140 | 191 | 241 | 292 | 191 | | 241 | | 292 | |
| **Hem-Fir Select Structural** | L m | $P_r$ kN | $P_r$ kN | $P_r$ kN | $P_r$ kN | $P_{rx}$ kN | $P_{ry}$ kN | $P_{rx}$ kN | $P_{ry}$ kN | $P_{rx}$ kN | $P_{ry}$ kN |
| $K_e = 1.0$ | 2.0 | 187 | 368 | 586 | 850 | 270 | 256 | 464 | 464 | 702 | 710 |
| | 2.5 | 162 | 339 | 554 | 814 | 249 | 220 | 439 | 428 | 672 | 672 |
| | 3.0 | 135 | 309 | 522 | 778 | 226 | 185 | 414 | 389 | 642 | 632 |
| | 3.5 | 111 | 277 | 488 | 742 | 203 | 152 | 386 | 349 | 613 | 591 |
| | 4.0 | 90.3 | 245 | 452 | 704 | 179 | 123 | 358 | 309 | 581 | 547 |
| | 4.5 | 72.8 | 214 | 414 | 665 | 157 | 99.4 | 328 | 270 | 549 | 502 |
| | 5.0 | 58.8 | 185 | 377 | 623 | 136 | 80.2 | 299 | 234 | 515 | 457 |
| | 5.5 | 47.6 | 160 | 341 | 582 | 117 | 65.0 | 270 | 202 | 480 | 413 |
| | 6.0 | 38.8 | 137 | 306 | 539 | 101 | 52.9 | 243 | 173 | 445 | 371 |
| | 6.5 | 31.9 | 118 | 274 | 498 | 86.3 | 43.5 | 217 | 149 | 411 | 332 |
| | 7.0 | 26.4 | 101 | 244 | 457 | 74.1 | 36.0 | 193 | 128 | 378 | 295 |
| | 7.5 | | 86.9 | 217 | 419 | 63.7 | | 172 | 110 | 346 | 263 |
| | 8.0 | | 75.0 | 192 | 382 | 54.9 | | 152 | 94.6 | 315 | 233 |
| | 8.5 | | 64.9 | 171 | 348 | 47.5 | | 135 | 81.9 | 287 | 207 |
| | 9.0 | | 56.4 | 152 | 317 | 41.3 | | 120 | 71.1 | 261 | 184 |
| $K_e = 2.0$ | 2.0 | 93.9 | 260 | 486 | 763 | 191 | 128 | 385 | 328 | 630 | 589 |
| | 2.5 | 60.4 | 194 | 402 | 670 | 143 | 82.3 | 318 | 245 | 553 | 487 |
| | 3.0 | 39.5 | 142 | 322 | 575 | 104 | 53.9 | 255 | 179 | 475 | 391 |
| | 3.5 | 26.7 | 104 | 254 | 483 | 76.1 | 36.4 | 201 | 131 | 399 | 308 |
| | 4.0 | | 76.5 | 199 | 401 | 56.1 | | 158 | 96.5 | 331 | 241 |
| | 4.5 | | 57.2 | 156 | 329 | 41.9 | | 124 | 72.2 | 272 | 189 |
| | 5.0 | | | 123 | 270 | | | 97.3 | | 223 | 149 |
| | 5.5 | | | 97.6 | 221 | | | 77.4 | | 183 | 118 |
| | 6.0 | | | 78.4 | 182 | | | 62.1 | | 150 | 95.0 |
| | 6.5 | | | | 151 | | | | | 125 | |
| | 7.0 | | | | 126 | | | | | 104 | |

Notes:
1. $P_{rx}$ is the factored resistance to buckling about the x-x (strong) axis.
   $P_{ry}$ is the factored resistance to buckling about the y-y (weak) axis.
2. For $L \le 2.0$ m, use $P_r$ for $L = 2.0$ m.
   Where $P_r$ values are not given, the slenderness ratio exceeds 50 (maximum permitted).
3. Tabulated values are valid for the following conditions:
   • standard term load (dead plus snow or occupancy loads)
   • dry service conditions
   • no fire-retardant treatment
   • $K_e = 1.0$ or $K_e = 2.0$
   • concentrically loaded.

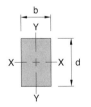

# Column Selection Tables

## Sawn Timbers

**H-F No.1**

**3**

**Ⓞ Compression Members**

| | | Square timbers | | | | Rectangular timbers | | | | | |
|---|---|---|---|---|---|---|---|---|---|---|---|
| | b (mm) | 140 | 191 | 241 | 292 | 140 | | 191 | | 241 | |
| | d (mm) | 140 | 191 | 241 | 292 | 191 | | 241 | | 292 | |
| **Hem-Fir No.1** | L m | $P_r$ kN | $P_r$ kN | $P_r$ kN | $P_r$ kN | $P_{rx}$ kN | $P_{ry}$ kN | $P_{rx}$ kN | $P_{ry}$ kN | $P_{rx}$ kN | $P_{ry}$ kN |
| $K_e = 1.0$ | 2.0 | 165 | 325 | 518 | 752 | 238 | 225 | 410 | 410 | 621 | 628 |
| | 2.5 | 142 | 299 | 490 | 720 | 219 | 193 | 388 | 377 | 594 | 593 |
| | 3.0 | 119 | 272 | 461 | 688 | 199 | 162 | 365 | 343 | 568 | 558 |
| | 3.5 | 97.0 | 243 | 430 | 655 | 178 | 132 | 341 | 307 | 541 | 521 |
| | 4.0 | 78.5 | 214 | 397 | 621 | 157 | 107 | 315 | 271 | 513 | 481 |
| | 4.5 | 63.2 | 187 | 364 | 585 | 137 | 86.2 | 288 | 236 | 483 | 441 |
| | 5.0 | 50.9 | 162 | 331 | 548 | 119 | 69.4 | 262 | 204 | 453 | 401 |
| | 5.5 | 41.1 | 139 | 298 | 511 | 102 | 56.1 | 236 | 175 | 422 | 361 |
| | 6.0 | 33.5 | 119 | 267 | 473 | 87.3 | 45.7 | 212 | 150 | 390 | 324 |
| | 6.5 | 27.5 | 102 | 239 | 436 | 74.8 | 37.5 | 189 | 129 | 360 | 289 |
| | 7.0 | 22.7 | 87.4 | 212 | 400 | 64.1 | 31.0 | 168 | 110 | 330 | 257 |
| | 7.5 | | 75.1 | 188 | 366 | 55.1 | | 149 | 94.8 | 302 | 228 |
| | 8.0 | | 64.7 | 167 | 333 | 47.4 | | 132 | 81.7 | 275 | 202 |
| | 8.5 | | 56.0 | 148 | 303 | 41.0 | | 117 | 70.6 | 250 | 179 |
| | 9.0 | | 48.6 | 131 | 275 | 35.6 | | 104 | 61.3 | 227 | 159 |
| $K_e = 2.0$ | 2.0 | 81.6 | 228 | 427 | 673 | 167 | 111 | 339 | 287 | 555 | 518 |
| | 2.5 | 52.2 | 169 | 352 | 589 | 124 | 71.2 | 279 | 214 | 487 | 426 |
| | 3.0 | 34.1 | 123 | 281 | 504 | 90.4 | 46.5 | 223 | 156 | 416 | 341 |
| | 3.5 | 23.0 | 89.8 | 221 | 422 | 65.8 | 31.3 | 175 | 113 | 349 | 268 |
| | 4.0 | | 66.0 | 172 | 349 | 48.4 | | 137 | 83.3 | 288 | 209 |
| | 4.5 | | 49.3 | 135 | 286 | 36.1 | | 107 | 62.2 | 236 | 163 |
| | 5.0 | | | 106 | 234 | | | 84.0 | | 193 | 128 |
| | 5.5 | | | 84.2 | 191 | | | 66.7 | | 158 | 102 |
| | 6.0 | | | 67.5 | 157 | | | 53.5 | | 130 | 81.8 |
| | 6.5 | | | | 130 | | | | | 107 | |
| | 7.0 | | | | 108 | | | | | 89.4 | |

Notes:
1. $P_{rx}$ is the factored resistance to buckling about the x-x (strong) axis.
   $P_{ry}$ is the factored resistance to buckling about the y-y (weak) axis.
2. For L ≤ 2.0 m, use $P_r$ for L = 2.0 m.
   Where $P_r$ values are not given, the slenderness ratio exceeds 50 (maximum permitted).
3. Tabulated values are valid for the following conditions:
   • standard term load (dead plus snow or occupancy loads)
   • dry service conditions
   • no fire-retardant treatment
   • $K_e = 1.0$ or $K_e = 2.0$
   • concentrically loaded.

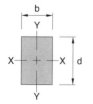

# Column Selection Tables

## Sawn Timbers

**H-F No.2**

| Hem-Fir No.2 | | Square timbers | | | | Rectangular timbers | | | | | |
|---|---|---|---|---|---|---|---|---|---|---|---|
| b (mm) | | 140 | 191 | 241 | 292 | 140 | | 191 | | 241 | |
| d (mm) | | 140 | 191 | 241 | 292 | 191 | | 241 | | 292 | |
| L m | | $P_r$ kN | $P_r$ kN | $P_r$ kN | $P_r$ kN | $P_{rx}$ kN | $P_{ry}$ kN | $P_{rx}$ kN | $P_{ry}$ kN | $P_{rx}$ kN | $P_{ry}$ kN |
| **$K_e = 1.0$** | 2.0 | 106 | 202 | 319 | 461 | 148 | 145 | 253 | 255 | 381 | 387 |
| | 2.5 | 94.2 | 189 | 304 | 444 | 139 | 129 | 241 | 239 | 366 | 369 |
| | 3.0 | 82.0 | 176 | 290 | 427 | 129 | 112 | 230 | 222 | 352 | 351 |
| | 3.5 | 70.0 | 161 | 274 | 410 | 118 | 95.5 | 218 | 204 | 339 | 333 |
| | 4.0 | 58.8 | 147 | 258 | 393 | 107 | 80.2 | 205 | 185 | 325 | 313 |
| | 4.5 | 49.0 | 132 | 242 | 376 | 96.5 | 66.8 | 192 | 166 | 310 | 293 |
| | 5.0 | 40.6 | 117 | 224 | 358 | 85.9 | 55.4 | 178 | 148 | 295 | 272 |
| | 5.5 | 33.6 | 104 | 207 | 339 | 75.9 | 45.9 | 164 | 131 | 279 | 251 |
| | 6.0 | 27.9 | 91.0 | 190 | 319 | 66.7 | 38.1 | 151 | 115 | 263 | 230 |
| | 6.5 | 23.2 | 79.7 | 173 | 300 | 58.4 | 31.7 | 137 | 101 | 247 | 210 |
| | 7.0 | 19.5 | 69.7 | 157 | 280 | 51.1 | 26.5 | 125 | 88.0 | 231 | 191 |
| | 7.5 | | 61.0 | 143 | 261 | 44.7 | | 113 | 76.9 | 215 | 173 |
| | 8.0 | | 53.3 | 129 | 242 | 39.1 | | 102 | 67.3 | 200 | 156 |
| | 8.5 | | 46.7 | 116 | 224 | 34.2 | | 92.1 | 58.9 | 185 | 141 |
| | 9.0 | | 41.0 | 105 | 207 | 30.1 | | 82.9 | 51.7 | 171 | 127 |
| **$K_e = 2.0$** | 2.0 | 61.7 | 157 | 279 | 427 | 115 | 84.2 | 221 | 198 | 353 | 338 |
| | 2.5 | 42.0 | 124 | 241 | 386 | 90.8 | 57.3 | 191 | 156 | 319 | 291 |
| | 3.0 | 28.6 | 95.1 | 202 | 342 | 69.7 | 39.0 | 160 | 120 | 283 | 244 |
| | 3.5 | 19.8 | 72.1 | 166 | 298 | 52.9 | 27.0 | 131 | 91.0 | 246 | 201 |
| | 4.0 | | 54.7 | 134 | 256 | 40.1 | | 106 | 69.1 | 211 | 163 |
| | 4.5 | | 41.9 | 108 | 217 | 30.7 | | 85.8 | 52.8 | 179 | 131 |
| | 5.0 | | | 87.4 | 183 | | | 69.3 | | 151 | 106 |
| | 5.5 | | | 70.8 | 153 | | | 56.1 | | 127 | 85.7 |
| | 6.0 | | | 57.7 | 129 | | | 45.7 | | 106 | 69.9 |
| | 6.5 | | | | 108 | | | | | 89.5 | |
| | 7.0 | | | | 91.6 | | | | | 75.6 | |

Notes:
1. $P_{rx}$ is the factored resistance to buckling about the x-x (strong) axis.
   $P_{ry}$ is the factored resistance to buckling about the y-y (weak) axis.
2. For $L \leq 2.0$ m, use $P_r$ for $L = 2.0$ m.
   Where $P_r$ values are not given, the slenderness ratio exceeds 50 (maximum permitted).
3. Tabulated values are valid for the following conditions:
   • standard term load (dead plus snow or occupancy loads)
   • dry service conditions
   • no fire-retardant treatment
   • $K_e = 1.0$ or $K_e = 2.0$
   • concentrically loaded.

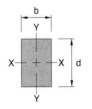

# Column Selection Tables

## Sawn Timbers

| S-P-F Select Structural | | Square timbers | | | Rectangular timbers | | | |
|---|---|---|---|---|---|---|---|---|
| b (mm) | | 140 | 191 | 241 | 140 | | 191 | |
| d (mm) | | 140 | 191 | 241 | 191 | | 241 | |
| | L | $P_r$ | $P_r$ | $P_r$ | $P_{rx}$ | $P_{ry}$ | $P_{rx}$ | $P_{ry}$ |
| | m | kN | kN | kN | kN | kN | kN | kN |
| $K_e = 1.0$ | 2.0 | 164 | 322 | 513 | 236 | 223 | 407 | 406 |
| | 2.5 | 141 | 296 | 485 | 217 | 192 | 385 | 374 |
| | 3.0 | 118 | 269 | 456 | 197 | 161 | 362 | 340 |
| | 3.5 | 96.5 | 241 | 426 | 177 | 132 | 338 | 304 |
| | 4.0 | 78.1 | 213 | 394 | 156 | 107 | 312 | 269 |
| | 4.5 | 62.9 | 186 | 361 | 136 | 85.9 | 286 | 235 |
| | 5.0 | 50.7 | 161 | 328 | 118 | 69.2 | 260 | 203 |
| | 5.5 | 41.0 | 138 | 296 | 101 | 56.0 | 235 | 175 |
| | 6.0 | 33.4 | 119 | 266 | 87.0 | 45.6 | 211 | 150 |
| | 6.5 | 27.4 | 102 | 237 | 74.5 | 37.4 | 188 | 128 |
| | 7.0 | 22.7 | 87.2 | 211 | 63.9 | 30.9 | 167 | 110 |
| | 7.5 | | 74.9 | 187 | 54.9 | | 149 | 94.5 |
| | 8.0 | | 64.6 | 166 | 47.3 | | 132 | 81.5 |
| | 8.5 | | 55.8 | 148 | 40.9 | | 117 | 70.5 |
| | 9.0 | | 48.5 | 131 | 35.5 | | 104 | 61.2 |
| | 2.0 | 81.3 | 226 | 424 | 166 | 111 | 336 | 285 |
| | 2.5 | 52.1 | 169 | 349 | 124 | 71.0 | 277 | 213 |
| | 3.0 | 34.0 | 123 | 280 | 90.1 | 46.4 | 222 | 155 |
| | 3.5 | 22.9 | 89.5 | 220 | 65.6 | 31.3 | 174 | 113 |
| | 4.0 | | 65.9 | 172 | 48.3 | | 136 | 83.1 |
| | 4.5 | | 49.2 | 134 | 36.1 | | 107 | 62.1 |
| | 5.0 | | | 106 | | | 83.8 | |
| | 5.5 | | | 84.0 | | | 66.6 | |
| | 6.0 | | | 67.4 | | | 53.4 | |

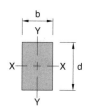

$K_e = 2.0$

Notes:
1. $P_{rx}$ is the factored resistance to buckling about the x-x (strong) axis.
   $P_{ry}$ is the factored resistance to buckling about the y-y (weak) axis.
2. For L ≤ 2.0 m, use $P_r$ for L = 2.0 m.
   Where $P_r$ values are not given, the slenderness ratio exceeds 50 (maximum permitted).
3. Tabulated values are valid for the following conditions:
   • standard term load (dead plus snow or occupancy loads)
   • dry service conditions
   • no fire-retardant treatment
   • $K_e = 1.0$ or $K_e = 2.0$
   • concentrically loaded.

**3**

**Compression Members**

# Column Selection Tables

## Sawn Timbers

**S-P-F No.1**

| | | Square timbers | | | Rectangular timbers | | | |
|---|---|---|---|---|---|---|---|---|
| b (mm) | | 140 | 191 | 241 | 140 | | 191 | |
| d (mm) | | 140 | 191 | 241 | 191 | | 241 | |
| S-P-F No.1 | L m | $P_r$ kN | $P_r$ kN | $P_r$ kN | $P_{rx}$ kN | $P_{ry}$ kN | $P_{rx}$ kN | $P_{ry}$ kN |
| | 2.0 | 143 | 282 | 450 | 207 | 195 | 357 | 356 |
| | 2.5 | 122 | 259 | 425 | 190 | 167 | 337 | 327 |
| | 3.0 | 102 | 235 | 399 | 172 | 139 | 316 | 296 |
| | 3.5 | 82.8 | 209 | 372 | 153 | 113 | 295 | 264 |
| | 4.0 | 66.7 | 184 | 343 | 135 | 90.9 | 272 | 232 |
| | 4.5 | 53.5 | 160 | 313 | 117 | 72.9 | 248 | 202 |
| | 5.0 | 42.9 | 138 | 284 | 101 | 58.6 | 225 | 174 |
| | 5.5 | 34.6 | 118 | 255 | 86.6 | 47.3 | 202 | 149 |
| | 6.0 | 28.1 | 101 | 228 | 74.0 | 38.4 | 181 | 127 |
| | 6.5 | 23.0 | 86.3 | 203 | 63.2 | 31.4 | 161 | 109 |
| | 7.0 | 19.0 | 73.8 | 180 | 54.1 | 26.0 | 143 | 93.1 |
| | 7.5 | | 63.3 | 160 | 46.4 | | 127 | 79.9 |
| | 8.0 | | 54.4 | 141 | 39.9 | | 112 | 68.7 |
| | 8.5 | | 47.0 | 125 | 34.5 | | 99.2 | 59.3 |
| | 9.0 | | 40.8 | 111 | 29.9 | | 87.8 | 51.4 |
| | 2.0 | 69.2 | 195 | 368 | 143 | 94.5 | 292 | 246 |
| | 2.5 | 44.0 | 144 | 302 | 106 | 60.1 | 239 | 182 |
| | 3.0 | 28.6 | 104 | 240 | 76.6 | 39.0 | 190 | 132 |
| | 3.5 | 19.3 | 75.7 | 188 | 55.5 | 26.3 | 149 | 95.5 |
| | 4.0 | | 55.5 | 146 | 40.7 | | 116 | 70.0 |
| | 4.5 | | 41.4 | 114 | 30.3 | | 90.1 | 52.2 |
| | 5.0 | | | 89.2 | | | 70.7 | |
| | 5.5 | | | 70.7 | | | 56.0 | |
| | 6.0 | | | 56.6 | | | 44.9 | |

$K_e = 1.0$

$K_e = 2.0$

Notes:
1. $P_{rx}$ is the factored resistance to buckling about the x-x (strong) axis.
   $P_{ry}$ is the factored resistance to buckling about the y-y (weak) axis.
2. For L ≤ 2.0 m, use $P_r$ for L = 2.0 m.
   Where $P_r$ values are not given, the slenderness ratio exceeds 50 (maximum permitted).
3. Tabulated values are valid for the following conditions:
   • standard term load (dead plus snow or occupancy loads)
   • dry service conditions
   • no fire-retardant treatment
   • $K_e$ = 1.0 or $K_e$ = 2.0
   • concentrically loaded.

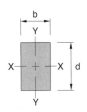

# Column Selection Tables

## Sawn Timbers

**S-P-F No.2**

|  |  | Square timbers | | | Rectangular timbers | | | |
|---|---|---|---|---|---|---|---|---|
| | b (mm) | 140 | 191 | 241 | 140 | | 191 | |
| | d (mm) | 140 | 191 | 241 | 191 | | 241 | |
| S-P-F No.2 | L m | $P_r$ kN | $P_r$ kN | $P_r$ kN | $P_{rx}$ kN | $P_{ry}$ kN | $P_{rx}$ kN | $P_{ry}$ kN |
| | 2.0 | 93.0 | 178 | 282 | 131 | 127 | 224 | 225 |
| | 2.5 | 82.2 | 167 | 269 | 122 | 112 | 213 | 210 |
| $K_e = 1.0$ | 3.0 | 71.0 | 154 | 255 | 113 | 96.9 | 202 | 194 |
| | 3.5 | 60.2 | 141 | 241 | 103 | 82.1 | 191 | 178 |
| | 4.0 | 50.2 | 127 | 226 | 93.3 | 68.5 | 179 | 161 |
| | 4.5 | 41.5 | 114 | 211 | 83.3 | 56.6 | 167 | 143 |
| | 5.0 | 34.2 | 101 | 195 | 73.8 | 46.7 | 155 | 127 |
| | 5.5 | 28.2 | 88.5 | 179 | 64.9 | 38.5 | 142 | 112 |
| | 6.0 | 23.3 | 77.4 | 164 | 56.7 | 31.8 | 130 | 97.7 |
| | 6.5 | 19.3 | 67.5 | 149 | 49.5 | 26.4 | 118 | 85.2 |
| | 7.0 | 16.2 | 58.8 | 135 | 43.1 | 22.0 | 107 | 74.2 |
| | 7.5 | | 51.2 | 121 | 37.5 | | 96.2 | 64.6 |
| | 8.0 | | 44.6 | 109 | 32.7 | | 86.6 | 56.3 |
| | 8.5 | | 39.0 | 98.2 | 28.6 | | 77.9 | 49.2 |
| | 9.0 | | 34.2 | 88.2 | 25.0 | | 69.9 | 43.1 |
| $K_e = 2.0$ | 2.0 | 52.6 | 136 | 244 | 100 | 71.7 | 194 | 172 |
| | 2.5 | 35.3 | 106 | 209 | 77.8 | 48.2 | 165 | 134 |
| | 3.0 | 23.8 | 80.7 | 174 | 59.2 | 32.5 | 138 | 102 |
| | 3.5 | 16.4 | 60.7 | 141 | 44.5 | 22.4 | 112 | 76.6 |
| | 4.0 | | 45.8 | 114 | 33.6 | | 90.1 | 57.8 |
| | 4.5 | | 34.8 | 91.2 | 25.5 | | 72.3 | 43.9 |
| | 5.0 | | | 73.2 | | | 58.0 | |
| | 5.5 | | | 59.0 | | | 46.8 | |
| | 6.0 | | | 47.9 | | | 38.0 | |

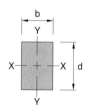

Notes:
1. $P_{rx}$ is the factored resistance to buckling about the x-x (strong) axis.
   $P_{ry}$ is the factored resistance to buckling about the y-y (weak) axis.
2. For L ≤ 2.0 m, use $P_r$ for L = 2.0 m.
   Where $P_r$ values are not given, the slenderness ratio exceeds 50 (maximum permitted).
3. Tabulated values are valid for the following conditions:
   • standard term load (dead plus snow or occupancy loads)
   • dry service conditions
   • no fire-retardant treatment
   • $K_e = 1.0$ or $K_e = 2.0$
   • concentrically loaded.

**3**

Compression Members

# Column Selection Tables

**Nor Sel**

## Sawn Timbers

**Northern Select Structural**

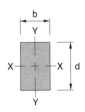

| | | Square timbers | | | Rectangular timbers | | | |
|---|---|---|---|---|---|---|---|---|
| b (mm) | | 140 | 191 | 241 | 140 | | 191 | |
| d (mm) | | 140 | 191 | 241 | 191 | | 241 | |
| | L m | $P_r$ kN | $P_r$ kN | $P_r$ kN | $P_{rx}$ kN | $P_{ry}$ kN | $P_{rx}$ kN | $P_{ry}$ kN |
| $K_e = 1.0$ | 2.0 | 127 | 246 | 391 | 181 | 174 | 310 | 311 |
| | 2.5 | 111 | 229 | 371 | 168 | 152 | 294 | 289 |
| | 3.0 | 95.0 | 210 | 351 | 154 | 130 | 278 | 265 |
| | 3.5 | 79.4 | 191 | 330 | 140 | 108 | 262 | 241 |
| | 4.0 | 65.5 | 171 | 308 | 125 | 89.3 | 244 | 216 |
| | 4.5 | 53.6 | 151 | 286 | 111 | 73.1 | 226 | 191 |
| | 5.0 | 43.8 | 133 | 262 | 97.3 | 59.7 | 208 | 167 |
| | 5.5 | 35.8 | 116 | 239 | 84.8 | 48.8 | 190 | 146 |
| | 6.0 | 29.4 | 100 | 217 | 73.6 | 40.1 | 172 | 127 |
| | 6.5 | 24.3 | 86.9 | 196 | 63.7 | 33.1 | 155 | 110 |
| | 7.0 | 20.2 | 75.2 | 176 | 55.1 | 27.5 | 140 | 94.9 |
| | 7.5 | | 65.1 | 158 | 47.7 | | 125 | 82.2 |
| | 8.0 | | 56.5 | 141 | 41.4 | | 112 | 71.3 |
| | 8.5 | | 49.2 | 126 | 36.0 | | 100 | 62.0 |
| | 9.0 | | 42.9 | 113 | 31.4 | | 89.5 | 54.1 |
| $K_e = 2.0$ | 2.0 | 68.4 | 182 | 333 | 133 | 93.3 | 264 | 230 |
| | 2.5 | 45.1 | 140 | 280 | 102 | 61.5 | 222 | 176 |
| | 3.0 | 30.0 | 104 | 230 | 76.5 | 40.9 | 182 | 132 |
| | 3.5 | 20.5 | 77.5 | 184 | 56.8 | 27.9 | 146 | 97.7 |
| | 4.0 | | 57.8 | 147 | 42.4 | | 116 | 72.9 |
| | 4.5 | | 43.7 | 116 | 32.0 | | 92.2 | 55.1 |
| | 5.0 | | | 92.6 | | | 73.4 | |
| | 5.5 | | | 74.2 | | | 58.8 | |
| | 6.0 | | | 59.9 | | | 47.5 | |

Notes:
1. $P_{rx}$ is the factored resistance to buckling about the x-x (strong) axis.
   $P_{ry}$ is the factored resistance to buckling about the y-y (weak) axis.
2. For L ≤ 2.0 m, use $P_r$ for L = 2.0 m.
   Where $P_r$ values are not given, the slenderness ratio exceeds 50 (maximum permitted).
3. Tabulated values are valid for the following conditions:
   • standard term load (dead plus snow or occupancy loads)
   • dry service conditions
   • no fire-retardant treatment
   • $K_e = 1.0$ or $K_e = 2.0$
   • concentrically loaded.

# Column Selection Tables

## Sawn Timbers

| | | Square timbers | | | Rectangular timbers | | | |
|---|---|---|---|---|---|---|---|---|
| b (mm) | | 140 | 191 | 241 | 140 | | 191 | |
| d (mm) | | 140 | 191 | 241 | 191 | | 241 | |
| **Northern No.1** | L m | $P_r$ kN | $P_r$ kN | $P_r$ kN | $P_{rx}$ kN | $P_{ry}$ kN | $P_{rx}$ kN | $P_{ry}$ kN |
| | 2.0 | 114 | 220 | 349 | 161 | 155 | 277 | 278 |
| | 2.5 | 100 | 205 | 332 | 150 | 136 | 263 | 258 |
| | 3.0 | 85.3 | 188 | 314 | 138 | 116 | 249 | 238 |
| | 3.5 | 71.5 | 171 | 296 | 125 | 97.5 | 234 | 216 |
| | 4.0 | 59.0 | 153 | 276 | 112 | 80.5 | 219 | 193 |
| | 4.5 | 48.4 | 136 | 256 | 100 | 66.0 | 203 | 172 |
| | 5.0 | 39.5 | 119 | 236 | 87.5 | 53.9 | 187 | 151 |
| | 5.5 | 32.4 | 104 | 215 | 76.4 | 44.2 | 170 | 131 |
| | 6.0 | 26.6 | 90.5 | 195 | 66.3 | 36.3 | 155 | 114 |
| | 6.5 | 22.0 | 78.4 | 176 | 57.5 | 30.0 | 140 | 99.0 |
| | 7.0 | 18.3 | 67.9 | 159 | 49.8 | 25.0 | 126 | 85.7 |
| | 7.5 | | 58.9 | 142 | 43.2 | | 113 | 74.3 |
| | 8.0 | | 51.1 | 127 | 37.5 | | 101 | 64.5 |
| | 8.5 | | 44.5 | 114 | 32.6 | | 90.4 | 56.2 |
| | 9.0 | | 38.9 | 102 | 28.5 | | 80.8 | 49.0 |
| | 2.0 | 61.7 | 164 | 298 | 120 | 84.1 | 236 | 206 |
| | 2.5 | 40.7 | 126 | 252 | 92.1 | 55.6 | 199 | 159 |
| | 3.0 | 27.2 | 94.2 | 206 | 69.0 | 37.1 | 164 | 119 |
| | 3.5 | 18.6 | 70.0 | 166 | 51.3 | 25.3 | 132 | 88.4 |
| | 4.0 | | 52.3 | 132 | 38.4 | | 105 | 66.0 |
| | 4.5 | | 39.6 | 105 | 29.0 | | 83.3 | 49.9 |
| | 5.0 | | | 83.8 | | | 66.4 | |
| | 5.5 | | | 67.2 | | | 53.3 | |
| | 6.0 | | | 54.3 | | | 43.1 | |

$K_e = 1.0$

$K_e = 2.0$

Notes:
1. $P_{rx}$ is the factored resistance to buckling about the x-x (strong) axis.
   $P_{ry}$ is the factored resistance to buckling about the y-y (weak) axis.
2. For L ≤ 2.0 m, use $P_r$ for L = 2.0 m.
   Where $P_r$ values are not given, the slenderness ratio exceeds 50 (maximum permitted).
3. Tabulated values are valid for the following conditions:
   • standard term load (dead plus snow or occupancy loads)
   • dry service conditions
   • no fire-retardant treatment
   • $K_e$ = 1.0 or $K_e$ = 2.0
   • concentrically loaded.

**3**

**Compression Members**

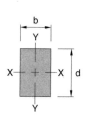

# Column Selection Tables

## Sawn Timbers

| | | Square timbers | | | Rectangular timbers | | | |
|---|---|---|---|---|---|---|---|---|
| b (mm) | | 140 | 191 | 241 | 140 | | 191 | |
| d (mm) | | 140 | 191 | 241 | 191 | | 241 | |
| **Northern**<br>**No.2** | L<br>m | $P_r$<br>kN | $P_r$<br>kN | $P_r$<br>kN | $P_{rx}$<br>kN | $P_{ry}$<br>kN | $P_{rx}$<br>kN | $P_{ry}$<br>kN |
| | 2.0 | 71.8 | 136 | 215 | 100 | 97.9 | 170 | 172 |
| | 2.5 | 64.2 | 128 | 205 | 93.9 | 87.6 | 163 | 162 |
| | 3.0 | 56.3 | 119 | 196 | 87.4 | 76.8 | 155 | 151 |
| | 3.5 | 48.4 | 110 | 186 | 80.6 | 66.0 | 147 | 139 |
| | 4.0 | 40.9 | 100 | 175 | 73.5 | 55.9 | 139 | 127 |
| | 4.5 | 34.3 | 90.6 | 165 | 66.4 | 46.8 | 130 | 114 |
| | 5.0 | 28.6 | 81.1 | 153 | 59.4 | 39.0 | 122 | 102 |
| | 5.5 | 23.8 | 72.0 | 142 | 52.8 | 32.5 | 113 | 90.9 |
| | 6.0 | 19.8 | 63.6 | 131 | 46.6 | 27.1 | 104 | 80.3 |
| | 6.5 | 16.6 | 56.0 | 120 | 41.0 | 22.6 | 95.0 | 70.6 |
| | 7.0 | 13.9 | 49.1 | 109 | 36.0 | 19.0 | 86.7 | 62.0 |
| | 7.5 | | 43.1 | 99.4 | 31.6 | | 78.8 | 54.4 |
| | 8.0 | | 37.8 | 90.2 | 27.7 | | 71.5 | 47.7 |
| | 8.5 | | 33.2 | 81.6 | 24.4 | | 64.7 | 41.9 |
| | 9.0 | | 29.3 | 73.8 | 21.4 | | 58.5 | 36.9 |
| | 2.0 | 43.0 | 108 | 190 | 78.8 | 58.7 | 150 | 136 |
| | 2.5 | 29.6 | 85.8 | 165 | 62.9 | 40.4 | 130 | 108 |
| | 3.0 | 20.3 | 66.6 | 139 | 48.8 | 27.8 | 110 | 84.0 |
| | 3.5 | 14.2 | 50.9 | 115 | 37.3 | 19.4 | 91.3 | 64.3 |
| | 4.0 | | 38.9 | 94.2 | 28.5 | | 74.6 | 49.1 |
| | 4.5 | | 29.9 | 76.5 | 21.9 | | 60.6 | 37.7 |
| | 5.0 | | | 62.0 | | | 49.1 | |
| | 5.5 | | | 50.4 | | | 40.0 | |
| | 6.0 | | | 41.2 | | | 32.7 | |

Notes:
1. $P_{rx}$ is the factored resistance to buckling about the x-x (strong) axis.
   $P_{ry}$ is the factored resistance to buckling about the y-y (weak) axis.
2. For L ≤ 2.0 m, use $P_r$ for L = 2.0 m.
   Where $P_r$ values are not given, the slenderness ratio exceeds 50 (maximum permitted).
3. Tabulated values are valid for the following conditions:
   • standard term load (dead plus snow or occupancy loads)
   • dry service conditions
   • no fire-retardant treatment
   • $K_e$ = 1.0 or $K_e$ = 2.0
   • concentrically loaded.

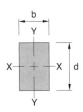

# Column Selection Tables

## Glulam
**80** mm

**3**

Ō

Compression Members

| | Spruce-Pine 12c-E | | | | | | | | D.Fir-L 16c-E | | | | | | | |
|---|---|---|---|---|---|---|---|---|---|---|---|---|---|---|---|---|
| d (mm) | 114 | | 152 | | 190 | | 228 | | 114 | | 152 | | 190 | | 228 | |
| L m | $P_{rx}$ kN | $P_{ry}$ kN | $P_{rx}$ kN | $P_{ry}$ kN | $P_{rx}$ kN | $P_{ry}$ kN | $P_{rx}$ kN | $P_{ry}$ kN | $P_{rx}$ kN | $P_{ry}$ kN | $P_{rx}$ kN | $P_{ry}$ kN | $P_{rx}$ kN | $P_{ry}$ kN | $P_{rx}$ kN | $P_{ry}$ kN |
| 2.0 | 126 | 78.8 | 205 | 105 | 279 | 131 | 348 | 158 | 154 | 97.9 | 249 | 131 | 336 | 163 | 418 | 196 |
| 2.5 | 96.8 | 51.0 | 178 | 68.0 | 257 | 85.0 | 331 | 102 | 120 | 64.0 | 217 | 85.4 | 311 | 107 | 399 | 128 |
| 3.0 | 72.0 | 33.4 | 148 | 44.6 | 229 | 55.7 | 306 | 66.8 | 89.7 | 42.2 | 182 | 56.3 | 279 | 70.4 | 370 | 84.3 |
| 3.5 | 53.0 | 22.6 | 120 | 30.1 | 199 | 37.6 | 275 | 45.0 | 66.5 | 28.6 | 149 | 38.2 | 244 | 47.7 | 334 | 57.0 |
| 4.0 | 39.2 | 15.8 | 96.0 | 21.0 | 169 | 26.2 | 244 | 31.4 | 49.5 | 20.0 | 120 | 26.7 | 208 | 33.3 | 298 | 39.9 |
| 4.5 | 29.4 | | 76.1 | | 141 | | 214 | | 37.2 | | 95.3 | | 175 | | 263 | |
| 5.0 | 22.4 | | 60.4 | | 118 | | 186 | | 28.4 | | 75.9 | | 146 | | 229 | |
| 5.5 | 17.4 | | 48.3 | | 97.8 | | 161 | | 22.1 | | 60.9 | | 122 | | 199 | |
| 6.0 | | | 38.9 | | 81.4 | | 138 | | | | 49.2 | | 102 | | 172 | |
| 6.5 | | | 31.7 | | 68.0 | | 119 | | | | 40.2 | | 85.6 | | 148 | |
| 7.0 | | | 26.1 | | 57.1 | | 102 | | | | 33.1 | | 72.0 | | 128 | |
| 7.5 | | | 21.6 | | 48.2 | | 88.1 | | | | 27.5 | | 60.9 | | 111 | |
| 8.0 | | | | | 40.9 | | 76.1 | | | | | | 51.8 | | 95.8 | |
| 8.5 | | | | | 35.0 | | 66.0 | | | | | | 44.3 | | 83.2 | |
| 9.0 | | | | | 30.0 | | 57.4 | | | | | | 38.1 | | 72.5 | |
| 9.5 | | | | | 26.0 | | 50.1 | | | | | | 33.0 | | 63.3 | |
| 10.0 | | | | | | | 43.9 | | | | | | | | 55.6 | |

Notes:
1. $P_{rx}$ is the factored resistance to buckling about the x-x (strong) axis.
   $P_{ry}$ is the factored resistance to buckling about the y-y (weak) axis.
2. For L ≤ 2.0 m, use $P_r$ for L = 2.0 m.
   Where $P_r$ values are not given, the slenderness ratio exceeds 50 (maximum permitted).
3. Tabulated values are valid for the following conditions:
   • standard term load (dead plus snow or occupancy loads)
   • dry service conditions
   • no fire-retardant treatment
   • $K_e$ = 1.0
   • concentrically loaded
4. L = unsupported length

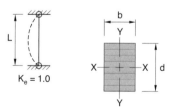

# Column Selection Tables

## 130 mm  Glulam

| | Spruce-Pine 12c-E | | | | | | | | D.Fir-L 16c-E | | | | | | | |
|---|---|---|---|---|---|---|---|---|---|---|---|---|---|---|---|---|
| d (mm) | 114 | | 152 | | 190 | | 228 | | 114 | | 152 | | 190 | | 228 | |
| L m | $P_{rx}$ kN | $P_{ry}$ kN | $P_{rx}$ kN | $P_{ry}$ kN | $P_{rx}$ kN | $P_{ry}$ kN | $P_{rx}$ kN | $P_{ry}$ kN | $P_{rx}$ kN | $P_{ry}$ kN | $P_{rx}$ kN | $P_{ry}$ kN | $P_{rx}$ kN | $P_{ry}$ kN | $P_{rx}$ kN | $P_{ry}$ kN |
| 2.0 | 205 | 228 | 334 | 304 | 453 | 380 | 555 | 450 | 250 | 277 | 404 | 370 | 546 | 462 | 668 | 547 |
| 2.5 | 157 | 186 | 289 | 248 | 409 | 305 | 515 | 361 | 194 | 228 | 352 | 304 | 495 | 375 | 621 | 443 |
| 3.0 | 117 | 146 | 238 | 193 | 360 | 237 | 471 | 282 | 146 | 181 | 292 | 239 | 438 | 294 | 570 | 348 |
| 3.5 | 86.1 | 112 | 191 | 147 | 311 | 182 | 426 | 216 | 108 | 140 | 237 | 184 | 380 | 227 | 517 | 270 |
| 4.0 | 63.5 | 85.3 | 153 | 112 | 264 | 139 | 379 | 166 | 80.0 | 107 | 190 | 141 | 325 | 175 | 463 | 208 |
| 4.5 | 47.6 | 65.3 | 121 | 86.4 | 222 | 107 | 334 | 128 | 60.1 | 82.3 | 152 | 109 | 275 | 135 | 410 | 161 |
| 5.0 | 36.2 | 50.6 | 96.6 | 67.0 | 186 | 83.3 | 292 | 99.6 | 45.9 | 63.9 | 121 | 84.7 | 231 | 105 | 360 | 126 |
| 5.5 | 28.1 | 39.7 | 77.4 | 52.7 | 155 | 65.6 | 253 | 78.4 | 35.6 | 50.3 | 97.6 | 66.7 | 194 | 83.0 | 313 | 99.2 |
| 6.0 | | 31.6 | 62.6 | 41.9 | 130 | 52.2 | 219 | 62.5 | | 40.1 | 79.1 | 53.2 | 163 | 66.2 | 272 | 79.2 |
| 6.5 | | 25.4 | 51.1 | 33.8 | 109 | 42.1 | 189 | 50.4 | | 32.3 | 64.7 | 42.9 | 137 | 53.5 | 236 | 64.0 |
| 7.0 | | | 42.1 | | 91.6 | | 163 | | | | 53.3 | | 115 | | 204 | |
| 7.5 | | | 35.0 | | 77.5 | | 141 | | | | 44.4 | | 97.8 | | 177 | |
| 8.0 | | | | | 65.9 | | 122 | | | | | | 83.3 | | 153 | |
| 8.5 | | | | | 56.3 | | 106 | | | | | | 71.4 | | 133 | |
| 9.0 | | | | | 48.5 | | 92.1 | | | | | | 61.5 | | 116 | |
| 9.5 | | | | | 41.9 | | 80.5 | | | | | | 53.2 | | 102 | |
| 10.0 | | | | | | | 70.7 | | | | | | | | 89.5 | |
| 10.5 | | | | | | | 62.3 | | | | | | | | 78.9 | |
| 11.0 | | | | | | | 55.1 | | | | | | | | 69.8 | |

Notes:
1. $P_{rx}$ is the factored resistance to buckling about the x-x (strong) axis.
   $P_{ry}$ is the factored resistance to buckling about the y-y (weak) axis.
2. For L ≤ 2.0 m, use $P_r$ for L = 2.0 m.
   Where $P_r$ values are not given, the slenderness ratio exceeds 50 (maximum permitted).
3. Tabulated values are valid for the following conditions:
   • standard term load (dead plus snow or occupancy loads)
   • dry service conditions
   • no fire-retardant treatment
   • $K_e$ = 1.0
   • concentrically loaded
4. L = unsupported length

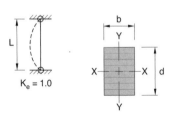

# Column Selection Tables

## Glulam

**175** mm

**3**

⊙

Compression Members

| L m | Spruce-Pine 12c-E | | | | | | | | D.Fir-L 16c-E | | | | | | | |
|---|---|---|---|---|---|---|---|---|---|---|---|---|---|---|---|---|
| d (mm) | 152 | | 190 | | 228 | | 266 | | 152 | | 190 | | 228 | | 266 | |
| | $P_{rx}$ kN | $P_{ry}$ kN | $P_{rx}$ kN | $P_{ry}$ kN | $P_{rx}$ kN | $P_{ry}$ kN | $P_{rx}$ kN | $P_{ry}$ kN | $P_{rx}$ kN | $P_{ry}$ kN | $P_{rx}$ kN | $P_{ry}$ kN | $P_{rx}$ kN | $P_{ry}$ kN | $P_{rx}$ kN | $P_{ry}$ kN |
| 2.0 | 447 | 474 | 591 | 577 | 721 | 678 | 841 | 777 | 542 | 572 | 713 | 697 | 866 | 818 | 1010 | 938 |
| 2.5 | 379 | 418 | 533 | 511 | 669 | 601 | 793 | 690 | 462 | 507 | 644 | 619 | 807 | 729 | 954 | 836 |
| 3.0 | 313 | 360 | 470 | 441 | 614 | 520 | 744 | 598 | 384 | 440 | 572 | 538 | 743 | 635 | 897 | 730 |
| 3.5 | 253 | 304 | 407 | 374 | 556 | 442 | 692 | 509 | 312 | 374 | 498 | 459 | 675 | 542 | 837 | 624 |
| 4.0 | 202 | 253 | 348 | 312 | 497 | 369 | 638 | 426 | 251 | 313 | 428 | 385 | 606 | 456 | 774 | 526 |
| 4.5 | 161 | 209 | 294 | 258 | 439 | 306 | 582 | 354 | 201 | 260 | 363 | 320 | 538 | 380 | 708 | 439 |
| 5.0 | 129 | 172 | 246 | 212 | 384 | 253 | 526 | 293 | 162 | 214 | 306 | 265 | 473 | 315 | 643 | 365 |
| 5.5 | 103 | 141 | 206 | 175 | 334 | 209 | 473 | 242 | 130 | 177 | 258 | 219 | 414 | 261 | 580 | 303 |
| 6.0 | 83.7 | 117 | 173 | 145 | 290 | 173 | 422 | 200 | 106 | 147 | 216 | 182 | 360 | 217 | 520 | 252 |
| 6.5 | 68.4 | 96.8 | 145 | 120 | 251 | 143 | 375 | 167 | 86.5 | 122 | 182 | 151 | 312 | 181 | 464 | 210 |
| 7.0 | 56.4 | 80.7 | 122 | 100 | 217 | 120 | 332 | 139 | 71.5 | 102 | 154 | 127 | 271 | 151 | 412 | 176 |
| 7.5 | 46.9 | 67.8 | 104 | 84.4 | 187 | 101 | 294 | 117 | 59.5 | 85.8 | 131 | 107 | 235 | 128 | 366 | 148 |
| 8.0 | | 57.3 | 88.1 | 71.4 | 162 | 85.4 | 260 | 99.4 | | 72.7 | 111 | 90.5 | 204 | 108 | 324 | 126 |
| 8.5 | | 48.8 | 75.4 | 60.8 | 141 | 72.8 | 230 | 84.7 | | 61.9 | 95.5 | 77.1 | 178 | 92.3 | 287 | 107 |
| 9.0 | | | 64.9 | | 123 | | 203 | | | | 82.3 | | 155 | | 255 | |
| 9.5 | | | 56.2 | | 108 | | 180 | | | | 71.3 | | 136 | | 226 | |
| 10.0 | | | | | 94.6 | | 160 | | | | | | 120 | | 202 | |
| 10.5 | | | | | 83.4 | | 142 | | | | | | 106 | | 180 | |
| 11.0 | | | | | 73.8 | | 127 | | | | | | 93.6 | | 161 | |
| 11.5 | | | | | | | 114 | | | | | | | | 144 | |
| 12.0 | | | | | | | 102 | | | | | | | | 129 | |
| 12.5 | | | | | | | 91.8 | | | | | | | | 116 | |
| 13.0 | | | | | | | 82.8 | | | | | | | | 105 | |

Notes:
1. $P_{rx}$ is the factored resistance to buckling about the x-x (strong) axis.
   $P_{ry}$ is the factored resistance to buckling about the y-y (weak) axis.
2. For $L \leq 2.0$ m, use $P_r$ for $L = 2.0$ m.
   Where $P_r$ values are not given, the slenderness ratio exceeds 50 (maximum permitted).
3. Tabulated values are valid for the following conditions:
   • standard term load (dead plus snow or occupancy loads)
   • dry service conditions
   • no fire-retardant treatment
   • $K_e = 1.0$
   • concentrically loaded
4. L = unsupported length

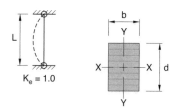

# Column Selection Tables

## 215 mm   Glulam

| L m | Spruce-Pine 12c-E 190 $P_{rx}$ kN | 190 $P_{ry}$ kN | 228 $P_{rx}$ kN | 228 $P_{ry}$ kN | 266 $P_{rx}$ kN | 266 $P_{ry}$ kN | 304 $P_{rx}$ kN | 304 $P_{ry}$ kN | D.Fir-L 16c-E 190 $P_{rx}$ kN | 190 $P_{ry}$ kN | 228 $P_{rx}$ kN | 228 $P_{ry}$ kN | 266 $P_{rx}$ kN | 266 $P_{ry}$ kN | 304 $P_{rx}$ kN | 304 $P_{ry}$ kN |
|---|---|---|---|---|---|---|---|---|---|---|---|---|---|---|---|---|
| 2.0 | 709 | 728 | 863 | 855 | 1010 | 979 | 1140 | 1100 | 854 | 876 | 1040 | 1030 | 1210 | 1180 | 1370 | 1320 |
| 2.5 | 640 | 671 | 802 | 788 | 951 | 903 | 1090 | 1020 | 774 | 810 | 967 | 951 | 1140 | 1090 | 1310 | 1230 |
| 3.0 | 566 | 610 | 737 | 717 | 893 | 823 | 1040 | 927 | 688 | 738 | 892 | 869 | 1080 | 996 | 1250 | 1120 |
| 3.5 | 492 | 545 | 669 | 643 | 831 | 739 | 980 | 833 | 601 | 664 | 812 | 782 | 1000 | 898 | 1180 | 1010 |
| 4.0 | 421 | 481 | 599 | 568 | 767 | 654 | 922 | 738 | 517 | 588 | 730 | 695 | 930 | 799 | 1110 | 902 |
| 4.5 | 356 | 420 | 530 | 496 | 701 | 572 | 861 | 647 | 440 | 516 | 650 | 610 | 853 | 703 | 1040 | 794 |
| 5.0 | 299 | 363 | 465 | 430 | 635 | 496 | 798 | 562 | 372 | 448 | 573 | 531 | 776 | 613 | 970 | 693 |
| 5.5 | 251 | 312 | 405 | 370 | 571 | 428 | 735 | 485 | 313 | 387 | 501 | 459 | 701 | 531 | 897 | 601 |
| 6.0 | 211 | 267 | 352 | 318 | 510 | 368 | 673 | 417 | 264 | 333 | 437 | 396 | 629 | 458 | 824 | 519 |
| 6.5 | 177 | 229 | 305 | 273 | 454 | 316 | 613 | 359 | 222 | 286 | 380 | 341 | 562 | 394 | 753 | 448 |
| 7.0 | 149 | 196 | 264 | 234 | 403 | 271 | 556 | 308 | 188 | 246 | 329 | 293 | 500 | 340 | 685 | 386 |
| 7.5 | 127 | 169 | 228 | 201 | 357 | 233 | 503 | 266 | 160 | 212 | 286 | 253 | 444 | 293 | 621 | 333 |
| 8.0 | 108 | 145 | 198 | 173 | 316 | 201 | 453 | 229 | 136 | 183 | 249 | 218 | 394 | 254 | 562 | 289 |
| 8.5 | 92.3 | 126 | 172 | 150 | 280 | 174 | 408 | 199 | 117 | 159 | 217 | 189 | 350 | 220 | 508 | 250 |
| 9.0 | 79.5 | 109 | 150 | 130 | 248 | 152 | 367 | 173 | 101 | 138 | 190 | 165 | 311 | 191 | 458 | 218 |
| 9.5 | 68.8 | 95.1 | 132 | 114 | 220 | 132 | 331 | 151 | 87.4 | 120 | 166 | 144 | 276 | 167 | 413 | 191 |
| 10.0 | | 83.2 | 116 | 99.6 | 195 | 116 | 298 | 132 | | 105 | 146 | 126 | 246 | 147 | 373 | 167 |
| 10.5 | | 73.2 | 102 | 87.6 | 174 | 102 | 268 | 116 | | 92.8 | 129 | 111 | 219 | 129 | 336 | 147 |
| 11.0 | | | 90.3 | | 155 | | 242 | | | | 115 | | 196 | | 304 | |
| 11.5 | | | | | 139 | | 218 | | | | | | 176 | | 275 | |
| 12.0 | | | | | 125 | | 197 | | | | | | 158 | | 249 | |
| 12.5 | | | | | 112 | | 179 | | | | | | 142 | | 226 | |
| 13.0 | | | | | 101 | | 162 | | | | | | 129 | | 205 | |
| 13.5 | | | | | | | 148 | | | | | | | | 187 | |
| 14.0 | | | | | | | 135 | | | | | | | | 170 | |
| 14.5 | | | | | | | 123 | | | | | | | | 156 | |
| 15.0 | | | | | | | 112 | | | | | | | | 143 | |

Notes:
1. $P_{rx}$ is the factored resistance to buckling about the x-x (strong) axis.
   $P_{ry}$ is the factored resistance to buckling about the y-y (weak) axis.
2. For L ≤ 2.0 m, use $P_r$ for L = 2.0 m.
   Where $P_r$ values are not given, the slenderness ratio exceeds 50 (maximum permitted).
3. Tabulated values are valid for the following conditions:
   • standard term load (dead plus snow or occupancy loads)
   • dry service conditions
   • no fire-retardant treatment
   • $K_e = 1.0$
   • concentrically loaded
4. L = unsupported length

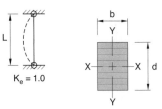

# Column Selection Tables

## Glulam

**265** mm

| | Spruce-Pine 12c-E | | | | | | | | D.Fir-L 16c-E | | | | | | | |
|---|---|---|---|---|---|---|---|---|---|---|---|---|---|---|---|---|
| d (mm) | 266 | | 304 | | 342 | | 380 | | 266 | | 304 | | 342 | | 380 | |
| L m | $P_{rx}$ kN | $P_{ry}$ kN | $P_{rx}$ kN | $P_{ry}$ kN | $P_{rx}$ kN | $P_{ry}$ kN | $P_{rx}$ kN | $P_{ry}$ kN | $P_{rx}$ kN | $P_{ry}$ kN | $P_{rx}$ kN | $P_{ry}$ kN | $P_{rx}$ kN | $P_{ry}$ kN | $P_{rx}$ kN | $P_{ry}$ kN |
| 2.0 | 1210 | 1210 | 1370 | 1360 | 1530 | 1500 | 1680 | 1650 | 1450 | 1450 | 1650 | 1630 | 1830 | 1810 | 2020 | 1980 |
| 2.5 | 1140 | 1140 | 1310 | 1280 | 1470 | 1420 | 1620 | 1560 | 1370 | 1370 | 1570 | 1540 | 1760 | 1710 | 1940 | 1880 |
| 3.0 | 1070 | 1070 | 1240 | 1210 | 1410 | 1340 | 1560 | 1470 | 1290 | 1290 | 1500 | 1450 | 1690 | 1610 | 1870 | 1770 |
| 3.5 | 1000 | 999 | 1180 | 1120 | 1350 | 1250 | 1500 | 1370 | 1210 | 1210 | 1420 | 1360 | 1620 | 1510 | 1810 | 1660 |
| 4.0 | 924 | 922 | 1110 | 1040 | 1280 | 1150 | 1440 | 1270 | 1120 | 1120 | 1340 | 1260 | 1550 | 1400 | 1740 | 1540 |
| 4.5 | 846 | 844 | 1040 | 952 | 1220 | 1060 | 1380 | 1160 | 1030 | 1030 | 1260 | 1160 | 1470 | 1290 | 1670 | 1420 |
| 5.0 | 768 | 765 | 963 | 864 | 1150 | 962 | 1320 | 1060 | 938 | 935 | 1170 | 1060 | 1390 | 1170 | 1590 | 1290 |
| 5.5 | 692 | 689 | 888 | 779 | 1080 | 868 | 1250 | 956 | 848 | 845 | 1080 | 955 | 1310 | 1060 | 1520 | 1170 |
| 6.0 | 619 | 616 | 815 | 698 | 1000 | 778 | 1180 | 857 | 763 | 759 | 997 | 859 | 1220 | 957 | 1440 | 1060 |
| 6.5 | 552 | 549 | 743 | 622 | 933 | 694 | 1120 | 766 | 682 | 679 | 912 | 769 | 1140 | 858 | 1360 | 946 |
| 7.0 | 491 | 488 | 675 | 553 | 863 | 618 | 1050 | 682 | 608 | 605 | 831 | 686 | 1060 | 766 | 1280 | 845 |
| 7.5 | 435 | 432 | 611 | 490 | 795 | 548 | 979 | 606 | 541 | 538 | 755 | 610 | 977 | 682 | 1200 | 753 |
| 8.0 | 386 | 383 | 552 | 435 | 730 | 486 | 912 | 537 | 481 | 478 | 684 | 542 | 900 | 606 | 1120 | 670 |
| 8.5 | 342 | 339 | 497 | 385 | 669 | 431 | 847 | 477 | 427 | 424 | 618 | 482 | 826 | 539 | 1040 | 596 |
| 9.0 | 303 | 301 | 448 | 342 | 612 | 383 | 785 | 423 | 380 | 377 | 558 | 428 | 758 | 480 | 968 | 531 |
| 9.5 | 269 | 267 | 404 | 304 | 559 | 340 | 726 | 376 | 338 | 335 | 504 | 381 | 694 | 427 | 897 | 473 |
| 10.0 | 239 | 237 | 364 | 270 | 510 | 303 | 671 | 335 | 301 | 299 | 455 | 340 | 634 | 381 | 830 | 422 |
| 10.5 | 213 | 211 | 328 | 241 | 465 | 270 | 619 | 299 | 269 | 267 | 411 | 303 | 580 | 340 | 768 | 377 |
| 11.0 | 191 | 189 | 296 | 215 | 424 | 241 | 570 | 267 | 241 | 238 | 372 | 272 | 530 | 305 | 709 | 337 |
| 11.5 | 171 | 169 | 267 | 193 | 387 | 216 | 525 | 240 | 216 | 214 | 336 | 244 | 484 | 273 | 655 | 303 |
| 12.0 | 153 | 152 | 242 | 173 | 353 | 194 | 484 | 215 | 194 | 192 | 305 | 219 | 443 | 246 | 604 | 272 |
| 12.5 | 138 | 137 | 219 | 156 | 323 | 175 | 446 | 194 | 175 | 173 | 277 | 197 | 405 | 221 | 558 | 246 |
| 13.0 | 125 | 123 | 199 | 141 | 295 | 158 | 411 | 175 | 158 | 156 | 252 | 178 | 371 | 200 | 515 | 222 |
| 13.5 | | | 181 | | 270 | | 379 | | | | 229 | | 341 | | 475 | |
| 14.0 | | | 165 | | 248 | | 350 | | | | 209 | | 313 | | 439 | |
| 14.5 | | | 151 | | 228 | | 323 | | | | 191 | | 287 | | 406 | |
| 15.0 | | | 138 | | 209 | | 299 | | | | 175 | | 264 | | 376 | |

Notes:
1. $P_{rx}$ is the factored resistance to buckling about the x-x (strong) axis.
   $P_{ry}$ is the factored resistance to buckling about the y-y (weak) axis.
2. For $L \le 2.0$ m, use $P_r$ for L = 2.0 m.
   Where $P_r$ values are not given, the slenderness ratio exceeds 50 (maximum permitted).
3. Tabulated values are valid for the following conditions:
   • standard term load (dead plus snow or occupancy loads)
   • dry service conditions
   • no fire-retardant treatment
   • $K_e = 1.0$
   • concentrically loaded
4. L = unsupported length

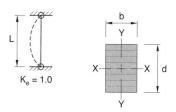

# Column Selection Tables

**315** mm    ## Glulam

| | Spruce-Pine 12c-E | | | | | | | | D.Fir-L 16c-E | | | | | | | |
|---|---|---|---|---|---|---|---|---|---|---|---|---|---|---|---|---|
| d (mm) | 304 | | 342 | | 380 | | 418 | | 304 | | 342 | | 380 | | 418 | |
| L m | $P_{rx}$ kN | $P_{ry}$ kN | $P_{rx}$ kN | $P_{ry}$ kN | $P_{rx}$ kN | $P_{ry}$ kN | $P_{rx}$ kN | $P_{ry}$ kN | $P_{rx}$ kN | $P_{ry}$ kN | $P_{rx}$ kN | $P_{ry}$ kN | $P_{rx}$ kN | $P_{ry}$ kN | $P_{rx}$ kN | $P_{ry}$ kN |
| 2.0 | 1590 | 1600 | 1780 | 1770 | 1960 | 1940 | 2130 | 2110 | 1910 | 1920 | 2130 | 2120 | 2350 | 2330 | 2550 | 2530 |
| 2.5 | 1520 | 1530 | 1710 | 1690 | 1880 | 1860 | 2060 | 2020 | 1830 | 1830 | 2050 | 2030 | 2260 | 2230 | 2470 | 2420 |
| 3.0 | 1450 | 1460 | 1640 | 1620 | 1820 | 1770 | 1990 | 1930 | 1740 | 1750 | 1970 | 1940 | 2180 | 2130 | 2390 | 2320 |
| 3.5 | 1370 | 1390 | 1570 | 1540 | 1750 | 1690 | 1920 | 1830 | 1660 | 1670 | 1880 | 1850 | 2100 | 2030 | 2310 | 2210 |
| 4.0 | 1290 | 1310 | 1490 | 1450 | 1680 | 1600 | 1860 | 1740 | 1560 | 1580 | 1800 | 1760 | 2020 | 1930 | 2240 | 2100 |
| 4.5 | 1210 | 1230 | 1420 | 1370 | 1610 | 1500 | 1790 | 1640 | 1470 | 1490 | 1710 | 1660 | 1940 | 1820 | 2160 | 1980 |
| 5.0 | 1130 | 1150 | 1340 | 1280 | 1540 | 1410 | 1720 | 1530 | 1370 | 1400 | 1620 | 1550 | 1860 | 1710 | 2080 | 1860 |
| 5.5 | 1040 | 1070 | 1260 | 1190 | 1460 | 1310 | 1650 | 1420 | 1270 | 1300 | 1530 | 1450 | 1770 | 1590 | 2000 | 1730 |
| 6.0 | 954 | 986 | 1170 | 1100 | 1380 | 1210 | 1580 | 1320 | 1170 | 1200 | 1430 | 1340 | 1680 | 1470 | 1910 | 1610 |
| 6.5 | 871 | 905 | 1090 | 1010 | 1300 | 1110 | 1510 | 1210 | 1070 | 1110 | 1330 | 1240 | 1590 | 1360 | 1830 | 1480 |
| 7.0 | 792 | 828 | 1010 | 923 | 1220 | 1020 | 1430 | 1110 | 975 | 1020 | 1240 | 1130 | 1490 | 1250 | 1740 | 1360 |
| 7.5 | 718 | 754 | 932 | 841 | 1150 | 928 | 1350 | 1010 | 887 | 930 | 1140 | 1040 | 1400 | 1140 | 1650 | 1250 |
| 8.0 | 649 | 685 | 857 | 765 | 1070 | 844 | 1280 | 922 | 804 | 847 | 1060 | 946 | 1310 | 1040 | 1560 | 1140 |
| 8.5 | 586 | 621 | 786 | 694 | 994 | 766 | 1200 | 838 | 728 | 770 | 971 | 860 | 1220 | 950 | 1470 | 1040 |
| 9.0 | 528 | 562 | 719 | 629 | 922 | 694 | 1130 | 760 | 658 | 699 | 891 | 782 | 1140 | 863 | 1380 | 944 |
| 9.5 | 476 | 509 | 657 | 569 | 853 | 629 | 1060 | 689 | 594 | 634 | 816 | 709 | 1050 | 784 | 1300 | 858 |
| 10.0 | 429 | 461 | 600 | 515 | 789 | 570 | 986 | 624 | 537 | 575 | 747 | 644 | 976 | 712 | 1210 | 779 |
| 10.5 | 387 | 417 | 548 | 467 | 728 | 516 | 920 | 566 | 485 | 522 | 683 | 584 | 903 | 646 | 1140 | 708 |
| 11.0 | 350 | 378 | 500 | 423 | 672 | 468 | 857 | 513 | 439 | 473 | 625 | 530 | 835 | 587 | 1060 | 643 |
| 11.5 | 316 | 342 | 457 | 383 | 619 | 425 | 797 | 465 | 398 | 430 | 572 | 482 | 771 | 533 | 989 | 584 |
| 12.0 | 286 | 311 | 417 | 348 | 571 | 386 | 742 | 423 | 361 | 391 | 523 | 438 | 712 | 485 | 921 | 532 |
| 12.5 | 260 | 282 | 381 | 317 | 526 | 351 | 689 | 385 | 327 | 356 | 479 | 399 | 658 | 442 | 858 | 484 |
| 13.0 | 236 | 257 | 349 | 288 | 485 | 319 | 641 | 350 | 298 | 324 | 439 | 364 | 608 | 403 | 799 | 442 |
| 13.5 | 215 | 234 | 320 | 263 | 448 | 291 | 595 | 320 | 271 | 296 | 403 | 332 | 561 | 368 | 743 | 404 |
| 14.0 | 196 | 214 | 293 | 240 | 413 | 266 | 553 | 292 | 248 | 271 | 370 | 304 | 519 | 336 | 692 | 369 |
| 14.5 | 179 | 196 | 269 | 220 | 382 | 244 | 514 | 268 | 227 | 248 | 340 | 278 | 480 | 308 | 644 | 338 |
| 15.0 | 164 | 180 | 248 | 202 | 353 | 223 | 478 | 245 | 207 | 227 | 313 | 255 | 444 | 283 | 600 | 311 |

Notes:
1. $P_{rx}$ is the factored resistance to buckling about the x-x (strong) axis.
   $P_{ry}$ is the factored resistance to buckling about the y-y (weak) axis.
2. For L ≤ 2.0 m, use $P_r$ for L = 2.0 m.
   Where $P_r$ values are not given, the slenderness ratio exceeds 50 (maximum permitted).
3. Tabulated values are valid for the following conditions:
   • standard term load (dead plus snow or occupancy loads)
   • dry service conditions
   • no fire-retardant treatment
   • $K_e = 1.0$
   • concentrically loaded
4. L = unsupported length

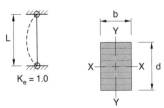

# Column Selection Tables

## Glulam

**365** mm

| L m | Spruce-Pine 12c-E | | | | | | | | D.Fir-L 16c-E | | | | | | | |
|---|---|---|---|---|---|---|---|---|---|---|---|---|---|---|---|---|
| d (mm) | 342 | | 380 | | 418 | | 456 | | 342 | | 380 | | 418 | | 456 | |
| | $P_{rx}$ kN | $P_{ry}$ kN | $P_{rx}$ kN | $P_{ry}$ kN | $P_{rx}$ kN | $P_{ry}$ kN | $P_{rx}$ kN | $P_{ry}$ kN | $P_{rx}$ kN | $P_{ry}$ kN | $P_{rx}$ kN | $P_{ry}$ kN | $P_{rx}$ kN | $P_{ry}$ kN | $P_{rx}$ kN | $P_{ry}$ kN |
| 2.0 | 2020 | 2030 | 2220 | 2220 | 2420 | 2410 | 2620 | 2600 | 2420 | 2430 | 2670 | 2660 | 2900 | 2890 | 3140 | 3120 |
| 2.5 | 1940 | 1950 | 2140 | 2140 | 2340 | 2320 | 2530 | 2500 | 2330 | 2340 | 2570 | 2560 | 2800 | 2790 | 3030 | 3010 |
| 3.0 | 1860 | 1880 | 2060 | 2060 | 2260 | 2240 | 2450 | 2410 | 2240 | 2250 | 2480 | 2470 | 2710 | 2680 | 2940 | 2900 |
| 3.5 | 1780 | 1800 | 1990 | 1980 | 2190 | 2150 | 2380 | 2320 | 2140 | 2170 | 2390 | 2380 | 2630 | 2590 | 2860 | 2790 |
| 4.0 | 1700 | 1730 | 1910 | 1900 | 2120 | 2060 | 2310 | 2230 | 2050 | 2080 | 2300 | 2280 | 2540 | 2480 | 2780 | 2680 |
| 4.5 | 1610 | 1650 | 1830 | 1810 | 2040 | 1970 | 2240 | 2130 | 1950 | 1990 | 2210 | 2190 | 2460 | 2380 | 2690 | 2570 |
| 5.0 | 1530 | 1570 | 1750 | 1720 | 1960 | 1880 | 2170 | 2030 | 1850 | 1900 | 2110 | 2080 | 2370 | 2270 | 2610 | 2450 |
| 5.5 | 1430 | 1490 | 1670 | 1630 | 1880 | 1780 | 2090 | 1920 | 1740 | 1800 | 2020 | 1980 | 2280 | 2150 | 2520 | 2330 |
| 6.0 | 1340 | 1400 | 1580 | 1540 | 1800 | 1680 | 2020 | 1810 | 1630 | 1700 | 1910 | 1870 | 2180 | 2040 | 2430 | 2200 |
| 6.5 | 1250 | 1320 | 1490 | 1450 | 1720 | 1580 | 1940 | 1710 | 1520 | 1600 | 1810 | 1760 | 2080 | 1920 | 2340 | 2080 |
| 7.0 | 1160 | 1230 | 1400 | 1350 | 1630 | 1480 | 1860 | 1600 | 1420 | 1500 | 1710 | 1650 | 1980 | 1800 | 2250 | 1950 |
| 7.5 | 1070 | 1140 | 1310 | 1260 | 1550 | 1380 | 1770 | 1490 | 1310 | 1400 | 1600 | 1540 | 1880 | 1680 | 2150 | 1820 |
| 8.0 | 982 | 1060 | 1220 | 1170 | 1460 | 1280 | 1690 | 1380 | 1210 | 1300 | 1500 | 1440 | 1780 | 1570 | 2050 | 1700 |
| 8.5 | 901 | 983 | 1140 | 1080 | 1370 | 1180 | 1600 | 1280 | 1110 | 1210 | 1400 | 1330 | 1680 | 1460 | 1960 | 1580 |
| 9.0 | 826 | 908 | 1060 | 1000 | 1290 | 1090 | 1520 | 1190 | 1020 | 1120 | 1300 | 1240 | 1580 | 1350 | 1860 | 1460 |
| 9.5 | 755 | 837 | 979 | 923 | 1210 | 1010 | 1440 | 1090 | 937 | 1040 | 1210 | 1140 | 1480 | 1250 | 1760 | 1350 |
| 10.0 | 690 | 770 | 905 | 850 | 1130 | 930 | 1360 | 1010 | 858 | 955 | 1120 | 1050 | 1390 | 1150 | 1670 | 1250 |
| 10.5 | 630 | 708 | 836 | 782 | 1050 | 856 | 1280 | 929 | 786 | 880 | 1040 | 972 | 1300 | 1060 | 1570 | 1150 |
| 11.0 | 576 | 651 | 772 | 719 | 983 | 787 | 1200 | 855 | 719 | 810 | 959 | 895 | 1220 | 980 | 1480 | 1060 |
| 11.5 | 526 | 598 | 712 | 661 | 916 | 724 | 1130 | 786 | 658 | 746 | 887 | 825 | 1130 | 903 | 1390 | 980 |
| 12.0 | 481 | 549 | 657 | 607 | 852 | 665 | 1060 | 723 | 603 | 687 | 819 | 759 | 1060 | 831 | 1310 | 903 |
| 12.5 | 440 | 505 | 606 | 559 | 793 | 612 | 994 | 665 | 552 | 632 | 757 | 699 | 986 | 766 | 1230 | 833 |
| 13.0 | 403 | 464 | 559 | 514 | 737 | 563 | 931 | 612 | 506 | 582 | 700 | 644 | 918 | 706 | 1160 | 767 |
| 13.5 | 369 | 427 | 516 | 473 | 685 | 518 | 872 | 564 | 464 | 537 | 647 | 594 | 855 | 651 | 1080 | 708 |
| 14.0 | 339 | 393 | 476 | 436 | 637 | 478 | 816 | 520 | 427 | 495 | 598 | 548 | 796 | 601 | 1020 | 653 |
| 14.5 | 311 | 363 | 440 | 402 | 592 | 441 | 764 | 479 | 392 | 457 | 554 | 506 | 742 | 555 | 953 | 603 |
| 15.0 | 286 | 335 | 407 | 371 | 551 | 407 | 715 | 443 | 361 | 422 | 513 | 467 | 691 | 513 | 893 | 558 |

**3**

**O**

Compression Members

Notes:
1. $P_{rx}$ is the factored resistance to buckling about the x-x (strong) axis.
   $P_{ry}$ is the factored resistance to buckling about the y-y (weak) axis.
2. For L ≤ 2.0 m, use $P_r$ for L = 2.0 m.
   Where $P_r$ values are not given, the slenderness ratio exceeds 50 (maximum permitted).
3. Tabulated values are valid for the following conditions:
   • standard term load (dead plus snow or occupancy loads)
   • dry service conditions
   • no fire-retardant treatment
   • $K_e$ = 1.0
   • concentrically loaded
4. L = unsupported length

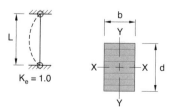

# 3.4 Built-up Columns

## General

Built-up columns are composed of two or more lumber members fastened together side by side with nails, bolts or split rings. Built-up columns are often constructed from the same grade and size of lumber used in roof, floor or wall framing. This simplifies the type of materials required for the structure.

This section provides design information for nailed built-up columns only. For the design of bolted or split ring connected columns, refer to Clause 5.5.6.4 of CSA O86. For spliced built-up columns, refer to Clause 5.5.6.6.

## Nailing Requirements

The individual laminations of a nailed built-up column must be fastened together as shown in Figure 3.2 in order for the tabulated resistances and design formulae to be valid.

Where large diameter nails are used, pre-drilling of the holes may be necessary to avoid splitting. Nailing may be omitted where the built-up column is incorporated into a stud wall and the sheathing is adequately nailed to the members.

## Design

Built-up columns must be designed so that the following criterion is satisfied:

Factored compressive resistance parallel to grain $P_r \geq$ factored compressive load $P_f$

The compressive resistance, $P_r$, for nailed built-up columns may be determined as follows:

1. When the conditions of use meet the requirements given in the following checklist, $P_r$ may be taken directly from the Built-up Column Selection Tables.

2. When the conditions of use do not meet the requirements of the checklist, the value of $P_r$ given in the selection tables is not valid. Furthermore, the tabulated values cannot be adjusted by a factor that will apply throughout the entire unsupported length range. Therefore, $P_r$ should be calculated as the lesser of:

$$P_{rd} = \phi F_c A K_{Zcd} K_{Cd} \text{ (N)}$$

or

$$P_{rb} = 0.6 \phi F_c A K_{Zcb} K_{Cb} \text{ (N)}$$

where:

$\phi F_c$ = factored specified compressive strength, given in Table 3.2 (divide by 1.1 since system action has already been considered in the above equation) (MPa)

$A$ = cross-sectional area (mm$^2$)

Figure 3.2
**Nailing for built-up columns (dimensions in mm)**

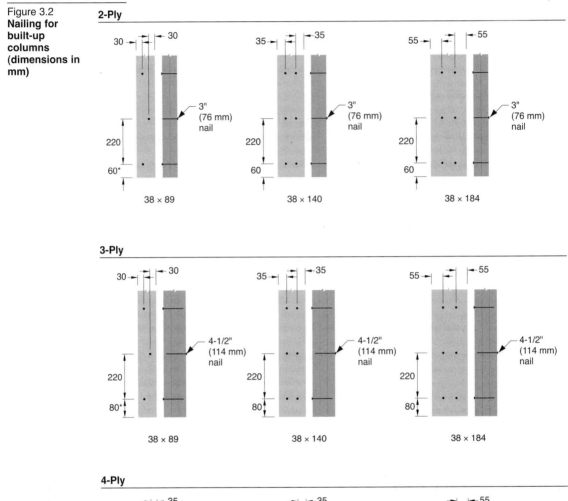

**2-Ply**

38 × 89     38 × 140     38 × 184

**3-Ply**

38 × 89     38 × 140     38 × 184

**4-Ply**

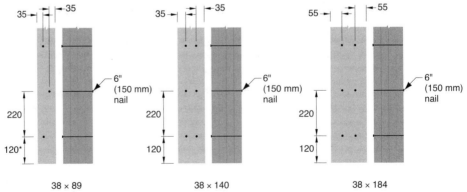

38 × 89     38 × 140     38 × 184

Note:
\* End distance values are shown for D.Fir-L, Hem-Fir, and Western cedar.
  For S-P-F and Northern, distances may be decreased to 80% of those shown.

## Checklist: **Built-up Columns** ✓

To verify that the tabulated resistances given in the Built-up Column Selection Tables are appropriate for the conditions of use, the following questions should be asked:

1. Is the load duration "standard" term (dead loads plus snow or occupancy loads)?

2. Is the service condition "dry"?

3. Is the material free of incisions and/or fire retardants?

4. Is the column effectively pinned at each end ($K_e$ =1.0)?

5. Is the column concentrically loaded?

If the answer to questions 1 to 4 is no, the selection tables should not be used. Instead, calculate $P_r$ from the formula given on page 141. Information on eccentrically loaded columns is provided in Chapter 5.

$K_{Zc}$ = size factor
= 6.3 $(d\ L_d)^{-0.13} \leq 1.3$ for buckling in direction of d
or
= 6.3 $(b\ L_b)^{-0.13} \leq 1.3$ for buckling in direction of b

$K_C$ = slenderness factor

$$= \left[1.0 + \frac{F_c}{E'} K_{Zc}\ C_c^3\right]^{-1}$$

$F_c$ / $E'$ = strength to stiffness ratio, given in Table 3.3
(divide by 1.1 for non-load-sharing)

$C_c$ = slenderness ratio ($C_c$ > 50 is not permitted)

$C_{cd} = \dfrac{K_e\ L_d}{d}$   $C_{cb} = \dfrac{K_e\ L_b}{b}$

$L_d$, $L_b$ = unsupported length associated with total member depth d or width b (mm)

b = total width of column, which is the thickness of an individual ply multiplied by the number of plies (mm)

d = depth of column, which is the depth of an individual ply (mm)

Where the column is short, or where sheathing prevents buckling about the weak axis of the plies, $P_r$ may calculated as the combined factored resistance of the individual pieces taken as independent members. This will provide a larger factored resistance than calculated from the formula given above for these cases. The resistance of an individual piece may be calculated from the design formula given in Section 3.1.

### Example 1: Built-up Columns

Design a built-up column for the following conditions:

- specified dead load = 1.0 kPa
- specified snow load = 2.4 kPa
- tributary area = 9 m$^2$
- unsupported length = 3 m

- dry service conditions
- untreated
- column effectively pinned at both ends

Use Stud grade S-P-F.

### Calculation
Total factored load:

$$P_f = (1.25 \times 1.0 + 1.5 \times 2.4) \times 9$$
$$= 43.6 \text{ kN}$$

From Built-up Column Selection Tables select 4-ply 38 × 140 mm:

$$P_r = 62.5 \text{ kN} > 43.6 \text{ kN} \qquad\qquad \textit{Acceptable}$$

**Use 4-ply 38 × 140 mm Stud grade S-P-F built-up columns nailed together as shown in Figure 3.2.**

# Built-up Column Selection Tables

## Nailed Built-up

**38** mm × **89** mm

Factored compressive resistance $P_r$ (kN)

| Grade | L m | D.Fir-L 2-Ply | 3-Ply | 4-Ply | Hem-Fir 2-Ply | 3-Ply | 4-Ply | S-P-F 2-Ply | 3-Ply | 4-Ply | Northern 2-Ply | 3-Ply | 4-Ply |
|---|---|---|---|---|---|---|---|---|---|---|---|---|---|
| **Select** | 2.0 | 31.9 | 81.6 | 128 | 30.9 | 77.3 | 120 | 26.5 | 64.9 | 99.6 | 21.1 | 54.9 | 86.7 |
| **Structural** | 2.2 | 26.6 | 73.6 | 118 | 25.9 | 70 | 113 | 22.3 | 59.0 | 94.4 | 17.5 | 49.3 | 78.4 |
| | 2.4 | 22.2 | 65.9 | 101 | 21.7 | 63 | 98 | 18.8 | 53.4 | 84.1 | 14.6 | 44.0 | 66.8 |
| | 2.6 | 18.5 | 58.8 | 86.3 | 18.2 | 56.4 | 84.1 | 15.8 | 48.0 | 72.4 | 12.1 | 39.1 | 56.9 |
| | 2.8 | 15.5 | 52.3 | 73.8 | 15.3 | 50.4 | 72.1 | 13.3 | 43.0 | 62.3 | 10.1 | 34.7 | 48.5 |
| | 3.0 | 13.1 | 46.4 | 63.2 | 12.9 | 44.9 | 62.0 | 11.2 | 38.4 | 53.7 | 8.54 | 30.7 | 41.5 |
| | 3.2 | 11.1 | 40.8 | 54.4 | 11.0 | 39.9 | 53.5 | 9.57 | 34.3 | 46.4 | 7.23 | 26.7 | 35.6 |
| | 3.4 | 9.46 | 35.2 | 47.0 | 9.37 | 34.7 | 46.3 | 8.19 | 30.2 | 40.3 | 6.16 | 23.0 | 30.7 |
| | 3.6 | 8.12 | 30.5 | 40.7 | 8.05 | 30.1 | 40.2 | 7.05 | 26.3 | 35.0 | 5.29 | 19.9 | 26.6 |
| | 3.8 | 7.01 | 26.6 | 35.4 | 6.96 | 26.3 | 35.0 | 6.10 | 22.9 | 30.6 | 4.56 | 17.3 | 23.1 |
| | 4.0 | | 23.2 | 31.0 | | 23.0 | 30.7 | | 20.1 | 26.8 | | 15.1 | 20.2 |
| **No.1/No.2** | 2.0 | 25.1 | 62.1 | 95.7 | 26.7 | 65.9 | 101 | 22.1 | 52.7 | 79.9 | 18.2 | 45.6 | 70.7 |
| | 2.2 | 21.1 | 56.4 | 90.7 | 22.5 | 59.9 | 96.1 | 18.7 | 48.2 | 76.0 | 15.3 | 41.3 | 66.9 |
| | 2.4 | 17.7 | 50.8 | 79.6 | 18.9 | 54.0 | 84.8 | 15.8 | 43.8 | 70.2 | 12.8 | 37.2 | 57.8 |
| | 2.6 | 14.8 | 45.6 | 68.4 | 15.8 | 48.5 | 72.9 | 13.3 | 39.5 | 60.7 | 10.7 | 33.3 | 49.5 |
| | 2.8 | 12.5 | 40.8 | 58.8 | 13.3 | 43.4 | 62.7 | 11.3 | 35.6 | 52.5 | 8.99 | 29.7 | 42.5 |
| | 3.0 | 10.6 | 36.4 | 50.6 | 11.3 | 38.8 | 54.0 | 9.58 | 31.9 | 45.4 | 7.60 | 26.4 | 36.5 |
| | 3.2 | 8.98 | 32.4 | 43.7 | 9.60 | 34.6 | 46.7 | 8.17 | 28.6 | 39.4 | 6.45 | 23.5 | 31.5 |
| | 3.4 | 7.68 | 28.4 | 37.8 | 8.21 | 30.3 | 40.4 | 7.01 | 25.6 | 34.2 | 5.51 | 20.4 | 27.2 |
| | 3.6 | 6.61 | 24.7 | 32.9 | 7.07 | 26.4 | 35.2 | 6.04 | 22.4 | 29.8 | 4.74 | 17.7 | 23.7 |
| | 3.8 | 5.71 | 21.5 | 28.7 | 6.11 | 23.0 | 30.7 | 5.23 | 19.6 | 26.1 | 4.10 | 15.5 | 20.6 |
| | 4.0 | | 18.9 | 25.2 | | 20.2 | 26.9 | | 17.2 | 22.9 | | 13.5 | 18.1 |
| **No.3/Stud** | 2.0 | 12.4 | 24.4 | 34.2 | 16.5 | 35.2 | 50.8 | 15.9 | 34.6 | 50.4 | 10.8 | 22.8 | 32.7 |
| | 2.2 | 11.1 | 23.1 | 33.1 | 14.4 | 32.8 | 48.8 | 13.8 | 32.1 | 48.4 | 9.43 | 21.3 | 31.5 |
| | 2.4 | 9.81 | 21.7 | 32.0 | 12.5 | 30.5 | 46.9 | 11.9 | 29.7 | 46.3 | 8.20 | 19.8 | 30.3 |
| | 2.6 | 8.63 | 20.4 | 30.9 | 10.8 | 28.1 | 44.8 | 10.2 | 27.3 | 44.1 | 7.09 | 18.3 | 29.0 |
| | 2.8 | 7.55 | 19.0 | 29.7 | 9.28 | 25.9 | 41.3 | 8.74 | 25.0 | 39.2 | 6.11 | 16.8 | 27.1 |
| | 3.0 | 6.61 | 17.7 | 28.5 | 8.00 | 23.7 | 36.4 | 7.51 | 22.8 | 34.5 | 5.28 | 15.5 | 23.9 |
| | 3.2 | 5.79 | 16.4 | 25.9 | 6.92 | 21.6 | 32.1 | 6.47 | 20.7 | 30.3 | 4.57 | 14.1 | 21.1 |
| | 3.4 | 5.08 | 15.1 | 23.1 | 6.00 | 19.7 | 28.3 | 5.60 | 18.8 | 26.6 | 3.97 | 12.9 | 18.7 |
| | 3.6 | 4.46 | 14.0 | 20.7 | 5.22 | 17.9 | 25.0 | 4.86 | 17.1 | 23.4 | 3.46 | 11.8 | 16.5 |
| | 3.8 | 3.93 | 12.9 | 18.5 | 4.56 | 16.3 | 22.1 | 4.24 | 15.5 | 20.7 | 3.02 | 10.7 | 14.6 |
| | 4.0 | | 11.8 | 16.6 | | 14.7 | 19.6 | | 13.7 | 18.3 | | 9.73 | 13.0 |

Notes:
1. Tabulated values are valid for the following conditions:
    • standard term load (dead load plus snow or occupancy)
    • dry service conditions
    • no fire-retardant treatment or preservative treated without incising
    • column effectively pinned at each end ($K_e$ = 1.0)
    • concentrically loaded
2. Where values are not given, $C_c$ > 50

**3**

**O**

Compression Members

# Built-up Column Selection Tables

## Nailed Built-up

Factored compressive resistance $P_r$ (kN)

| Grade | L m | D.Fir-L 2-Ply | 3-Ply | 4-Ply | Hem-Fir 2-Ply | 3-Ply | 4-Ply | S-P-F 2-Ply | 3-Ply | 4-Ply | Northern 2-Ply | 3-Ply | 4-Ply |
|---|---|---|---|---|---|---|---|---|---|---|---|---|---|
| **Select Structural** | 2.0 | 50.2 | 128 | 201 | 48.7 | 122 | 188 | 41.7 | 102 | 157 | 33.2 | 86.3 | 136 |
| | 2.2 | 41.9 | 116 | 190 | 40.8 | 110 | 178 | 35.1 | 92.9 | 149 | 27.6 | 77.5 | 128 |
| | 2.4 | 34.9 | 104 | 178 | 34.1 | 99.1 | 168 | 29.5 | 83.9 | 140 | 22.9 | 69.2 | 120 |
| | 2.6 | 29.1 | 92.5 | 166 | 28.6 | 88.8 | 157 | 24.8 | 75.5 | 132 | 19.1 | 61.6 | 112 |
| | 2.8 | 24.4 | 82.2 | 155 | 24.0 | 79.3 | 147 | 20.9 | 67.6 | 123 | 16.0 | 54.6 | 104 |
| | 3.0 | 20.6 | 72.9 | 143 | 20.3 | 70.6 | 136 | 17.7 | 60.4 | 115 | 13.4 | 48.3 | 96.0 |
| | 3.2 | 17.4 | 64.6 | 132 | 17.2 | 62.8 | 126 | 15.1 | 53.9 | 107 | 11.4 | 42.7 | 88.5 |
| | 3.4 | 14.9 | 57.3 | 122 | 14.7 | 55.8 | 117 | 12.9 | 48.1 | 99.0 | 9.69 | 37.8 | 81.3 |
| | 3.6 | 12.8 | 50.8 | 112 | 12.7 | 49.7 | 108 | 11.1 | 42.9 | 91.5 | 8.31 | 33.4 | 74.5 |
| | 3.8 | 11.0 | 45.2 | 103 | 11.0 | 44.2 | 99.1 | 9.59 | 38.3 | 84.5 | 7.17 | 29.6 | 68.2 |
| | 4.0 | | 40.2 | 94.2 | | 39.4 | 91.0 | | 34.2 | 77.8 | | 26.3 | 62.4 |
| **No.1/No.2** | 2.0 | 39.5 | 97.7 | 151 | 42.1 | 104 | 160 | 34.7 | 82.9 | 126 | 28.7 | 71.8 | 111 |
| | 2.2 | 33.2 | 88.7 | 143 | 35.4 | 94.1 | 151 | 29.4 | 75.8 | 120 | 24.0 | 65.0 | 105 |
| | 2.4 | 27.8 | 80.0 | 134 | 29.7 | 85.0 | 142 | 24.9 | 68.8 | 113 | 20.1 | 58.5 | 99.0 |
| | 2.6 | 23.3 | 71.8 | 126 | 24.9 | 76.3 | 134 | 21.0 | 62.2 | 107 | 16.8 | 52.4 | 92.8 |
| | 2.8 | 19.6 | 64.2 | 118 | 21.0 | 68.3 | 125 | 17.7 | 56.0 | 100 | 14.1 | 46.7 | 86.5 |
| | 3.0 | 16.6 | 57.3 | 110 | 17.8 | 61.0 | 117 | 15.1 | 50.3 | 93.8 | 12.0 | 41.6 | 80.4 |
| | 3.2 | 14.1 | 51.0 | 102 | 15.1 | 54.4 | 108 | 12.9 | 45.0 | 87.5 | 10.2 | 37.0 | 74.5 |
| | 3.4 | 12.1 | 45.4 | 94.2 | 12.9 | 48.4 | 100 | 11.0 | 40.3 | 81.4 | 8.67 | 32.9 | 68.9 |
| | 3.6 | 10.4 | 40.5 | 87.0 | 11.1 | 43.2 | 92.6 | 9.50 | 36.1 | 75.5 | 7.46 | 29.3 | 63.5 |
| | 3.8 | 8.99 | 36.1 | 80.2 | 9.61 | 38.5 | 85.3 | 8.23 | 32.3 | 69.9 | 6.44 | 26.0 | 58.4 |
| | 4.0 | | 32.2 | 73.8 | | 34.4 | 78.6 | | 28.9 | 64.6 | | 23.2 | 53.7 |
| **No.3/Stud** | 2.0 | 19.5 | 38.4 | 53.8 | 26.0 | 55.3 | 79.9 | 25.0 | 54.4 | 79.3 | 17.0 | 35.8 | 51.5 |
| | 2.2 | 17.4 | 36.3 | 52.1 | 22.7 | 51.6 | 76.8 | 21.7 | 50.6 | 76.1 | 14.8 | 33.5 | 49.6 |
| | 2.4 | 15.4 | 34.2 | 50.4 | 19.7 | 47.9 | 73.7 | 18.7 | 46.7 | 72.8 | 12.9 | 31.1 | 47.6 |
| | 2.6 | 13.6 | 32.0 | 48.6 | 16.9 | 44.2 | 70.5 | 16.0 | 43.0 | 69.4 | 11.1 | 28.8 | 45.6 |
| | 2.8 | 11.9 | 29.9 | 46.7 | 14.6 | 40.7 | 67.2 | 13.7 | 39.3 | 66.0 | 9.62 | 26.5 | 43.5 |
| | 3.0 | 10.4 | 27.8 | 44.9 | 12.6 | 37.3 | 63.8 | 11.8 | 35.9 | 62.5 | 8.31 | 24.3 | 41.4 |
| | 3.2 | 9.11 | 25.8 | 43.0 | 10.9 | 34.0 | 60.5 | 10.2 | 32.6 | 59.1 | 7.19 | 22.2 | 39.3 |
| | 3.4 | 7.99 | 23.8 | 41.0 | 9.44 | 31.0 | 57.2 | 8.81 | 29.6 | 55.7 | 6.25 | 20.3 | 37.1 |
| | 3.6 | 7.02 | 22.0 | 39.1 | 8.22 | 28.2 | 53.9 | 7.65 | 26.9 | 52.3 | 5.44 | 18.5 | 35.1 |
| | 3.8 | 6.18 | 20.2 | 37.2 | 7.18 | 25.6 | 50.7 | 6.67 | 24.3 | 49.0 | 4.76 | 16.8 | 33.0 |
| | 4.0 | | 18.6 | 35.3 | | 23.3 | 47.5 | | 22.0 | 45.9 | | 15.3 | 31.0 |

Notes:
1. Tabulated values are valid for the following conditions:
   • standard term load (dead load plus snow or occupancy)
   • dry service conditions
   • no fire-retardant treatment or preservative treated without incising
   • column effectively pinned at each end ($K_e = 1.0$)
   • concentrically loaded
2. Where values are not given, $C_c > 50$

# Built-up Column Selection Tables

## Nailed Built-up

Factored compressive resistance $P_r$ (kN)

| Grade | L m | D.Fir-L | | | Hem-Fir | | | S-P-F | | | Northern | | |
|---|---|---|---|---|---|---|---|---|---|---|---|---|---|
| | | 2-Ply | 3-Ply | 4-Ply | 2-Ply | 3-Ply | 4-Ply | 2-Ply | 3-Ply | 4-Ply | 2-Ply | 3-Ply | 4-Ply |
| **Select** | 2.0 | 66.0 | 169 | 264 | 63.9 | 160 | 248 | 54.8 | 134 | 206 | 43.6 | 113 | 179 |
| **Structural** | 2.2 | 55.0 | 152 | 249 | 53.6 | 145 | 234 | 46.1 | 122 | 195 | 36.2 | 102 | 169 |
| | 2.4 | 45.9 | 136 | 234 | 44.9 | 130 | 220 | 38.8 | 110 | 184 | 30.1 | 91.0 | 158 |
| | 2.6 | 38.3 | 122 | 219 | 37.6 | 117 | 207 | 32.6 | 99.2 | 173 | 25.1 | 80.9 | 147 |
| | 2.8 | 32.1 | 108 | 203 | 31.6 | 104 | 193 | 27.5 | 88.9 | 162 | 21.0 | 71.7 | 137 |
| | 3.0 | 27.0 | 95.9 | 188 | 26.7 | 92.8 | 179 | 23.2 | 79.4 | 151 | 17.7 | 63.5 | 126 |
| | 3.2 | 22.9 | 85.0 | 174 | 22.7 | 82.5 | 166 | 19.8 | 70.8 | 140 | 14.9 | 56.1 | 116 |
| | 3.4 | 19.6 | 75.3 | 160 | 19.4 | 73.4 | 153 | 16.9 | 63.2 | 130 | 12.7 | 49.6 | 107 |
| | 3.6 | 16.8 | 66.8 | 147 | 16.6 | 65.3 | 141 | 14.6 | 56.3 | 120 | 10.9 | 43.9 | 98.0 |
| | 3.8 | 14.5 | 59.3 | 135 | 14.4 | 58.1 | 130 | 12.6 | 50.3 | 111 | 9.43 | 39.0 | 89.7 |
| | 4.0 | | 52.8 | 124 | | 51.8 | 120 | | 44.9 | 102 | | 34.6 | 82.0 |
| **No.1/No.2** | 2.0 | 51.9 | 128 | 198 | 55.3 | 136 | 210 | 45.7 | 109 | 165 | 37.7 | 94.3 | 146 |
| | 2.2 | 43.6 | 117 | 187 | 46.5 | 124 | 199 | 38.7 | 99.6 | 157 | 31.6 | 85.4 | 138 |
| | 2.4 | 36.6 | 105 | 177 | 39.0 | 112 | 187 | 32.7 | 90.5 | 149 | 26.4 | 76.8 | 130 |
| | 2.6 | 30.7 | 94.3 | 166 | 32.8 | 100 | 176 | 27.6 | 81.8 | 140 | 22.1 | 68.8 | 122 |
| | 2.8 | 25.8 | 84.3 | 155 | 27.6 | 89.8 | 164 | 23.3 | 73.6 | 132 | 18.6 | 61.4 | 114 |
| | 3.0 | 21.8 | 75.2 | 144 | 23.3 | 80.1 | 153 | 19.8 | 66.0 | 123 | 15.7 | 54.7 | 106 |
| | 3.2 | 18.6 | 67.0 | 134 | 19.9 | 71.4 | 142 | 16.9 | 59.2 | 115 | 13.3 | 48.6 | 97.9 |
| | 3.4 | 15.9 | 59.7 | 124 | 17.0 | 63.6 | 132 | 14.5 | 53.0 | 107 | 11.4 | 43.2 | 90.5 |
| | 3.6 | 13.7 | 53.2 | 114 | 14.6 | 56.7 | 122 | 12.5 | 47.4 | 99.2 | 9.80 | 38.4 | 83.4 |
| | 3.8 | 11.8 | 47.4 | 105 | 12.6 | 50.6 | 112 | 10.8 | 42.4 | 91.9 | 8.47 | 34.2 | 76.7 |
| | 4.0 | | 42.3 | 97.0 | | 45.2 | 103 | | 38.0 | 84.9 | | 30.5 | 70.5 |
| **No.3/Stud** | 2.0 | 25.6 | 50.4 | 70.7 | 34.1 | 72.7 | 105 | 32.8 | 71.5 | 104 | 22.3 | 47.1 | 67.7 |
| | 2.2 | 22.9 | 47.7 | 68.5 | 29.8 | 67.9 | 101 | 28.5 | 66.5 | 100 | 19.5 | 44.0 | 65.2 |
| | 2.4 | 20.3 | 44.9 | 66.2 | 25.8 | 63.0 | 96.9 | 24.5 | 61.4 | 95.7 | 17.0 | 40.9 | 62.6 |
| | 2.6 | 17.8 | 42.1 | 63.8 | 22.3 | 58.1 | 92.6 | 21.1 · | 56.5 | 91.3 | 14.7 | 37.8 | 59.9 |
| | 2.8 | 15.6 | 39.3 | 61.4 | 19.2 | 53.5 | 88.3 | 18.1 | 51.7 | 86.8 | 12.6 | 34.8 | 57.2 |
| | 3.0 | 13.7 | 36.5 | 59.0 | 16.5 | 49.0 | 83.9 | 15.5 | 47.2 | 82.2 | 10.9 | 32.0 | 54.4 |
| | 3.2 | 12.0 | 33.9 | 56.5 | 14.3 | 44.7 | 79.5 | 13.4 | 42.9 | 77.7 | 9.45 | 29.2 | 51.6 |
| | 3.4 | 10.5 | 31.3 | 53.9 | 12.4 | 40.7 | 75.1 | 11.6 | 38.9 | 73.1 | 8.21 | 26.7 | 48.8 |
| | 3.6 | 9.22 | 28.9 | 51.4 | 10.8 | 37.1 | 70.8 | 10.1 | 35.3 | 68.7 | 7.15 | 24.3 | 46.1 |
| | 3.8 | 8.12 | 26.6 | 48.9 | 9.43 | 33.7 | 66.6 | 8.77 | 32.0 | 64.4 | 6.25 | 22.1 | 43.4 |
| | 4.0 | | 24.4 | 46.4 | | 30.6 | 62.5 | | 29.0 | 60.3 | | 20.1 | 40.8 |

**38** mm × **184** mm

**3**

**Compression Members**

Notes:
1. Tabulated values are valid for the following conditions:
   • standard term load (dead load plus snow or occupancy)
   • dry service conditions
   • no fire-retardant treatment or preservative treated without incising
   • column effectively pinned at each end ($K_e = 1.0$)
   • concentrically loaded
2. Where values are not given, $C_c > 50$

# Tension
# Members

**4**

The chords and
webs of light
frame trusses
are the most
common appli-
cations of wood
members in
tension.

A special stress grade of glulam may be used for tension members such as the bracing members in this roof system. Appearance grade specifications have no influence on material strengths.

Photo credit: Farrow Partner Architects Inc.

# 4.1 General Information

The following sections contain design information for members that are used in tension parallel to grain. This section provides design information and selection tables for sawn lumber, sawn timber and glulam tension members.

Lumber and timber products are produced in accordance with CSA Standard O141 *Softwood Lumber.* The characteristics of structural grades are outlined in the National Lumber Grades Authority *Standard Grading Rules for Canadian Lumber.* Common grades and thickness of sawn lumber and timber are shown in Tables 4.1 and 4.2 respectively.

Glulam is manufactured to meet CSA Standard O122 *Structural Glued-Laminated Timber* and the manufacturers of glulam must be certified in accordance with CSA Standard O177 *Qualification Code for Manufacturers of Structural Glued-Laminated Timber.* Generally, the 20f-EX or 24f-EX grades are suitable for use as tension members; however, the 18t-E or 14t-E grades may be ordered for high stress applications. The grade selected depends on the species combination as shown in Table 4.3.

Common tension members include webs and bottom chords of trusses, bottom flanges in wood I-joists, chord members in diaphragms and occasionally bracing members. The bottom chords of trusses are often loaded in tension combined with bending, which is covered in Chapter 5. This chapter deals only with axially loaded members.

Often the dimensions of tension members are governed by the connections rather than the tensile resistance of the section alone. The tension member must be large enough so that the spacing, and both end and edge distances for the fasteners are adequate. Also, the amount of material removed due to fastener holes and grooves must not exceed 25% of the gross area of the member. Section 7.1 contains information on net area.

**4**

Tension Members

# 4.2      Lumber and Glulam

## Availability

### Sawn Lumber

The selection tables for sawn lumber tension members provide resistance values for the following visual grades and lumber thicknesses:

Table 4.1
**Grades and thicknesses of sawn lumber**

| Visual grades | Thickness (all grades) mm |
|---|---|
| Select Structural, No.1, No.2 | 38 |
| | 64 |
| | 89 |

The most readily obtainable material is No.1 or No.2 grade. S-P-F, Hem-Fir and D.Fir-L are the species groups most likely to be stocked by lumber yards, but other species in the Northern species combination may also be on hand. In the 64 and 89 mm thicknesses, choice is more limited.

Some machine stress-rated (MSR) grades are also available in sizes ranging from 38 × 89 mm to 38 × 184 mm. The Tension Member Selection Tables provide resistance values for the following stress grades:

$1450F_b$-1.3E
$1650F_b$-1.5E
$1800F_b$-1.6E
$2100F_b$-1.8E
$2400F_b$-2.0E

All of the 38 mm visually graded and MSR material can be obtained dried to a moisture content of 19% (specify S-Dry).

### Sawn Timber

The Tension Member Selection Tables for sawn timber include resistance values for the following grades and thicknesses:

Table 4.2
**Grades and thicknesses of sawn timber**

| Grades | Thickness (all grades) mm |
|---|---|
| Select Structural, No.1 | 140 |
| | 191 |
| | 241 |

D.Fir-L and Hem-Fir are the species groups most readily available, but certain sizes of S-P-F and Northern species may also be obtained. The most readily available grade is No.1; however, Select Structural may be ordered.

Timbers are always dressed green since their large size makes kiln drying impractical. As a result, some shrinkage and checking can be expected after dressing. These effects should be considered when designing connections.

## Glulam

The Tension Member Selection Tables for glulam provide resistance values for the following species, grades and thicknesses:

Table 4.3
**Species, grades and thicknesses of glulam**

| Species and stress grades | Thickness (all species and grades) mm |
|---|---|
| **D.Fir-L:** 18t-E / 20f-EX / 24f-EX  **Spruce-Pine:** 14t-E / 20f-EX | 80 |
|  | 130 |
|  | 175 |
|  | 215 |

Most fabricators produce either D.Fir-L or Spruce-Pine glulam. The thicknesses shown above are industry standards, but some fabricators can produce slightly different sizes. Generally, 38 mm thick laminations are used for straight members.

## Design

### Sawn Lumber and Timber

Sawn lumber and sawn timber tension members must be designed so that the following criterion is met:

Factored tensile resistance at net section $T_{rN}$ ≥ factored tensile force $T_f$

The Tension Member Selection Tables provide tensile resistance values based on both gross area, $T_r$, and net area, $T_{rN}$. The $T_{rN}$ values are for members connected by shear plates or split rings where appropriate, so the designer need not calculate the area reduction in the member.

For members connected with other fasteners such as bolts, the resistance at net section may be obtained as follows:

$$T_{rN} = T_r \frac{A_N}{A_G}$$

where:

$T_{rN}$ = factored tensile resistance at net section

$T_r$ = factored tensile resistance based on gross section

$A_N$ = net area, which is the gross area less the area removed due to drilling or boring (refer to Section 7.1). Net area must be greater than 0.75 $A_G$.

$A_G$ = gross area

## Checklist: **Lumber and Glulam** ✔

To verify that the tabulated resistances are appropriate for the structure being designed, the following questions should be asked (the appropriate modification factor is given in brackets):

1. Is the load duration "standard" ($K_D$)?

2. Is the tension member acting as a single member ($K_H$)?

3. Is the service condition "dry" ($K_{St}$)?

4. Is the material free of incisions and/or strength reducing chemicals ($K_T$)?

If the answer to any of these questions is no, refer to the description of modification factors below and make the necessary adjustments to the tabulated resistances. Otherwise, the Tension Member Selection Tables may be used directly.

**4**

Tension Members

### Glulam
The design of glulam tension members differs from sawn timber since CSA O86 assigns different specified strengths for gross and net section. The specified strength at net section is slightly higher than the strength of the gross section. Therefore, glulam tension members must be designed so that the following criteria are met:

1. Factored tensile resistance of gross section $T_{rG} \geq$ factored tensile force $T_f$

2. Factored tensile resistance at net section $T_{rN} \geq$ maximum factored tensile force $T_f$

The resistance at gross section will always govern the design of a member as long as the net area is no less than 0.78 of the gross area for 18t-E glulam, and 0.75 of the gross area for 14t-E, 20f-EX and 24f-EX glulam. The minimum permitted net area is 0.75 of the gross area in either case.

The Tension Member Selection Tables provide $T_{rG}$ values for some common glulam sizes. The tables also provide the maximum number of shear plates that may be used so that the resistance at gross section governs the design.

## Modification Factors

The tabulated resistances for sawn lumber, sawn timber and glulam tension members are based upon the following formulae and modification factors. When using the tables be certain that the member conforms exactly with the modification factors used in the tables; if not, use the factors below and make the necessary adjustments to the tabulated values.

For sawn lumber or sawn timber:

$T_{rN} = \phi\, F_t\, A_N\, K_{zt}$ (N)

$F_t = f_t\, (K_D\, K_H\, K_{St}\, K_T)$ (MPa)

$f_t$ = specified tensile strength (MPa)

$A_N$ = net area of cross section (mm$^2$)

$\phi$ = 0.9

For glulam:

$T_{rN} = \phi\, F_{tn}\, A_N$ (N)

$T_{rG} = \phi\, F_{tg}\, A_G$ (N)

$F_{tN} = f_{tn}\, (K_D\, K_H\, K_{St}\, K_T)$ (MPa)

$F_{tG} = f_{tg}\, (K_D\, K_H\, K_{St}\, K_T)$ (MPa)

$f_{tN}$ = specified tensile strength at net section (MPa)

$f_{tG}$ = specified tensile strength at gross section (MPa)

$A_N$ = net area of cross section (mm$^2$)

$A_G$ = gross area of cross section (mm$^2$)

$\phi$ = 0.9

$K_D$ is a load duration factor. The tabulated resistances are based on a "standard" term load, which includes the effects of dead loads plus such live loads as snow and occupancy ($K_D = 1.0$). For structures intended to support permanent loads the tabulated resistances must be multiplied by 0.65. For tension members intended to support short term loads such as wind and earthquake, the tabulated resistances may be multiplied by 1.15.

$K_H$ is a system factor. The tabulated resistances are based on single member action ($K_H = 1.0$). For Case 1 Systems (refer to Section 2.3 for description) multiply the tabulated values by 1.10.

$K_{St}$ is a service condition factor. The tabulated resistances assume dry service ($K_{St} = 1.0$). For wet service conditions, tabulated values for sawn lumber of least dimension less than or equal to 89 mm only must be multiplied by 0.84. For glulam used in wet service conditions, multiply by 0.75.

$K_T$ is a treatment factor. The tabulated resistances are based on material that is either untreated or treated with a non-strength-reducing chemical ($K_T = 1.0$). Most wood preservatives do not reduce strength unless the lumber has been incised. However, most fire retardants will reduce strength. If the material is treated with a fire retardant or if it is incised prior to preservative treatment, multiply the tabulated values by the following factors:

Table 4.4
**Treatment factor $K_T$**

| Treatment type | Sawn lumber | | Glulam, sawn timber |
|---|---|---|---|
| | Dry service | Wet service | Wet or dry service |
| Preservative treated, incised lumber (89 mm thick or less) | 0.75 | 0.85 | 1.0 |
| Fire-retardant treated material | refer to the Commentary | | |

$K_{Zt}$ is a size factor (sawn lumber and sawn timber only), which is incorporated in the tabulated resistances for lumber and timber. No further adjustments are required.

**Example 1: Sawn Lumber**

Design the bottom chords of light-frame, metal plate connected trusses for the following conditions:

- factored tensile force = 30 kN (dead plus snow load)
- dry service condition
- untreated
- trusses spaced at 600 mm on centre

Use No.1 or No.2 grade S-P-F.

**Calculation**

$$T_f = 30 \text{ kN}$$

Since the chord is connected with truss plates, the tensile resistance may be based on gross area. From the Tension Member Selection Tables try 38 × 140 mm. A review of the checklist indicates that the tabulated resistance may be multiplied by $K_H = 1.1$ for a Case 1 system.

$$T_r = 34.2 \times 1.10 = 37.6 \text{ kN} > 30 \text{ kN} \qquad \textit{Acceptable}$$

**Use 38 × 140 mm No.1 or No.2 grade S-P-F.**

**4**

Tension Members

## Example 2: Sawn Timber

Check the adequacy of the bottom chord member shown in Example 1 of Section 7.7. The member is 140 × 191 mm No.1 grade D.Fir-L, connected with a single row of 4" diameter shear plates with 3/4" diameter bolts. The conditions are as follows:

- factored tensile force = 144 kN (dead plus snow load)
- dry service conditions
- untreated
- truss spacing exceeds 610 mm

### Calculation

$$T_f = 144 \text{ kN}$$

Since the chord is connected with shear plates, the tensile resistance at net section must be checked. From the Tension Member Selection Tables:

$$T_r = 185 \text{ kN} > 144 \text{ kN} \qquad \textit{Acceptable}$$

**Use 140 × 191 mm No.1 grade D.Fir-L.**

## Example 3: Glulam

Design the bottom chord of a bowstring roof truss for the following conditions:

- factored tensile force = 250 kN (dead plus snow load)
- dry service condition
- untreated
- truss spacing exceeds 610 mm

Use 80 mm 14t-E Spruce-Pine glulam connected with a single row of 4" diameter shear plates with 3/4" diameter bolts.

**Calculation**

$T_f$ = 250 kN

Since shear plates are used, the resistance at both the net and gross sections must be checked. From the Tension Member Selection Tables, try 80 × 266 mm:

$T_{rG}$ = 257 kN

$T_{rN}$ > $T_{rG}$ for a single row of 4" diameter shear plates

Therefore:

$T_r$ = 257 kN > 250 kN                                              *Acceptable*

**Use 80 × 266 mm 14t-E Spruce-Pine glulam.**

**4**

Tension Members

# Tension Member Selection Tables

## 38 mm    Sawn Lumber

Factored tensile resistance based on gross area, $T_r$ (kN)

| Species | Size (b × d) mm | Visually graded | | | Machine Stress-Rated (MSR) | | | | |
|---|---|---|---|---|---|---|---|---|---|
| | | Select Structural | No.1/ No.2 | No.3/ Stud | 1450$F_b$- 1.3E | 1650$F_b$- 1.5E | 1800$F_b$- 1.6E | 2100$F_b$- 1.8E | 2400$F_b$- 2.0E |
| D.Fir-L | 38 × 89 | 48.4 | 26.5 | 9.59 | 27.4 | 34.7 | 40.2 | 53.9 | 66.1 |
| | 38 × 140 | 66.0 | 36.1 | 13.1 | 43.1 | 54.6 | 63.2 | 84.7 | 104 |
| | 38 × 184 | 80.0 | 43.8 | 15.9 | 56.6 | 71.7 | 83.1 | 111 | 137 |
| | 38 × 235 | 93.7 | 51.3 | 18.6 | | | | | |
| | 38 × 286 | 104 | 56.7 | 20.5 | | | | | |
| Hem-Fir | 38 × 89 | 44.3 | 28.3 | 14.6 | 27.4 | 34.7 | 40.2 | 53.9 | 66.1 |
| | 38 × 140 | 60.4 | 38.6 | 19.9 | 43.1 | 54.6 | 63.2 | 84.7 | 104 |
| | 38 × 184 | 73.2 | 46.8 | 24.2 | 56.6 | 71.7 | 83.1 | 111 | 137 |
| | 38 × 235 | 85.8 | 54.8 | 28.3 | | | | | |
| | 38 × 286 | 94.9 | 60.6 | 31.3 | | | | | |
| S-P-F | 38 × 89 | 39.3 | 25.1 | 14.6 | 27.4 | 34.7 | 40.2 | 53.9 | 66.1 |
| | 38 × 140 | 53.5 | 34.2 | 19.9 | 43.1 | 54.6 | 63.2 | 84.7 | 104 |
| | 38 × 184 | 64.9 | 41.5 | 24.2 | 56.6 | 71.7 | 83.1 | 111 | 137 |
| | 38 × 235 | 76.0 | 48.6 | 28.3 | | | | | |
| | 38 × 286 | 84.1 | 53.8 | 31.3 | | | | | |
| Northern | 38 × 89 | 28.3 | 18.3 | 9.13 | 27.4 | 34.7 | 40.2 | 53.9 | 66.1 |
| | 38 × 140 | 38.6 | 24.9 | 12.4 | 43.1 | 54.6 | 63.2 | 84.7 | 104 |
| | 38 × 184 | 46.8 | 30.2 | 15.1 | 56.6 | 71.7 | 83.1 | 111 | 137 |
| | 38 × 235 | 54.8 | 35.4 | 17.7 | | | | | |
| | 38 × 286 | 60.6 | 39.1 | 19.6 | | | | | |

# Tension Member Selection Tables

## Sawn Lumber

**64** mm

| Species | Size (b × d) mm | Select Structural $T_r$ kN | $T_{rN}$ for use with shear plates or split rings (kN) 2-5/8" SH PL | 4" SH PL | 2-1/2" SR | No.1/No.2 $T_r$ kN | $T_{rN}$ for use with shear plates or split rings (kN) 2-5/8" SH PL | 4" SH PL | 2-1/2" SR |
|---|---|---|---|---|---|---|---|---|---|
| D.Fir-L | 64 × 89 | 81.5 | | | | 44.6 | | | |
| | 64 × 140 | 111 | | | 85.7 | 60.8 | | | 46.9 |
| | 64 × 184 | 135 | 108 | | 111 | 73.8 | 58.9 | | 60.9 |
| | 64 × 235 | 158 | 133 | | 136 | 86.4 | 72.7 | | 74.6 |
| | 64 × 286 | 175 | 152 | 137 | 155 | 95.5 | 83.2 | 74.7 | 84.8 |
| Hem-Fir | 64 × 89 | 74.6 | | | | 47.7 | | | |
| | 64 × 140 | 102 | | | 78.4 | 65.0 | | | 50.1 |
| | 64 × 184 | 123 | 98.5 | | 102 | 78.9 | 63.0 | | 65.1 |
| | 64 × 235 | 144 | 122 | | 125 | 92.3 | 77.8 | | 79.7 |
| | 64 × 286 | 160 | 139 | 125 | 142 | 102 | 88.9 | 79.9 | 90.7 |
| S-P-F | 64 × 89 | 66.1 | | | | 42.3 | | | |
| | 64 × 140 | 90.2 | | | 69.5 | 57.7 | | | 44.4 |
| | 64 × 184 | 109 | 87.3 | | 90.3 | 69.9 | 55.9 | | 57.8 |
| | 64 × 235 | 128 | 108 | | 111 | 81.9 | 69.0 | | 70.7 |
| | 64 × 286 | 142 | 123 | 111 | 126 | 90.6 | 78.9 | 70.9 | 80.4 |
| Northern | 64 × 89 | 47.7 | | | | 30.8 | | | |
| | 64 × 140 | 65.0 | | | 50.1 | 41.9 | | | 32.3 |
| | 64 × 184 | 78.9 | 63.0 | | 65.1 | 50.9 | 40.6 | | 42.0 |
| | 64 × 235 | 92.3 | 77.8 | | 79.7 | 59.6 | 50.2 | | 51.4 |
| | 64 × 286 | 102 | 88.9 | 79.9 | 90.7 | 65.9 | 57.4 | 51.5 | 58.5 |

Notes:
1. $T_r$ = Factored tensile resistance based on gross area
   $T_{rN}$ = Factored tensile resistance based on net area with a single shear plate or split ring on each side of member at a given cross section:

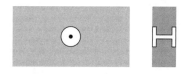

2. SH PL = Shear Plate, SR = Split Ring
3. Where $T_r$ values are not shown, area removed exceeds 25% of gross area.
4. For 4" diameter shear plates, values are based on the use of 3/4" diameter bolts.

**4**

Tension Members

# Tension Member Selection Tables

## 89 mm  Sawn Lumber

| Species | Size (b × d) mm | Select Structural $T_r$ kN | $T_{rN}$ for use with shear plates or split rings (kN) 2-5/8" SH PL | 4" SH PL | 2-1/2" SR | 4" SR | No.1/No.2 $T_r$ kN | $T_{rN}$ for use with shear plates or split rings (kN) 2-5/8" SH PL | 4" SH PL | 2-1/2" SR | 4" SR |
|---|---|---|---|---|---|---|---|---|---|---|---|
| D.Fir-L | 89 × 89 | 113 | | | | | 62.0 | | | | |
| | 89 × 140 | 155 | 119 | | 125 | | 84.6 | 65.0 | | 68.2 | |
| | 89 × 184 | 187 | 154 | | 160 | | 103 | 84 | | 87.5 | |
| | 89 × 235 | 219 | 189 | 172 | 194 | 175 | 120 | 104 | 94.3 | 106 | 95.9 |
| | 89 × 286 | 243 | 215 | 200 | 220 | 203 | 133 | 118 | 109 | 120 | 111 |
| Hem-Fir | 89 × 89 | 104 | | | | | 66.3 | | | | |
| | 89 × 140 | 141 | 109 | | 114 | | 90.4 | 69.4 | | 72.9 | |
| | 89 × 184 | 172 | 141 | | 146 | | 110 | 90.3 | | 93.5 | |
| | 89 × 235 | 201 | 173 | 158 | 178 | 160 | 128 | 111 | 101 | 114 | 103 |
| | 89 × 286 | 222 | 197 | 183 | 201 | 185 | 142 | 126 | 117 | 129 | 119 |
| S-P-F | 89 × 89 | 92.0 | | | | | 58.8 | | | | |
| | 89 × 140 | 125 | 96.3 | | 101 | | 80.2 | 61.6 | | 64.7 | |
| | 89 × 184 | 152 | 125 | | 130 | | 97.3 | 80.1 | | 83.0 | |
| | 89 × 235 | 178 | 153 | 140 | 158 | 142 | 114 | 98.2 | 89.4 | 101 | 91.0 |
| | 89 × 286 | 197 | 175 | 162 | 178 | 164 | 126 | 112 | 104 | 114 | 105 |
| Northern | 89 × 89 | 66.3 | | | | | 42.8 | | | | |
| | 89 × 140 | 90.4 | 69.4 | | 72.9 | | 58.3 | 44.8 | | 47.0 | |
| | 89 × 184 | 110 | 90.3 | | 93.5 | | 70.7 | 58.3 | | 60.3 | |
| | 89 × 235 | 128 | 111 | 101 | 114 | 103 | 82.8 | 71.4 | 65.0 | 73.3 | 66.1 |
| | 89 × 286 | 142 | 126 | 117 | 129 | 119 | 91.6 | 81.2 | 75.4 | 83.0 | 76.5 |

Notes:
1. $T_r$ = Factored tensile resistance based on gross area
   $T_{rN}$ = Factored tensile resistance based on net area with a single shear plate or split ring on each side of member at a given cross section:

2. SH PL = Shear Plate, SR = Split Ring
3. Where $T_r$ values are not shown, area removed exceeds 25% of gross area.
4 For 4" diameter shear plates, values are based on the use of 3/4" diameter bolts.

# Tension Member Selection Tables

## Sawn Timber                                              140 mm

| Species | Size (b × d) mm | Select Structural T_r kN | $T_{rN}$ for use with shear plates or split rings (kN) 2-5/8" SH PL 1 row | 2-5/8" SH PL 2 rows | 4" SH PL 1 row | 4" SH PL 2 rows | No.1 T_r kN | $T_{rN}$ for use with shear plates or split rings (kN) 2-5/8" SH PL 1 row | 2-5/8" SH PL 2 rows | 4" SH PL 1 row | 4" SH PL 2 rows |
|---|---|---|---|---|---|---|---|---|---|---|---|
| D.Fir-L | 140 × 140 | 245 | 196 | | | | 186 | 148 | | | |
| | 140 × 191 | 309 | 264 | | 245 | | 234 | 199 | | 185 | |
| | 140 × 241 | 334 | 295 | 256 | 279 | | 234 | 207 | 179 | 195 | |
| | 140 × 292 | 368 | 332 | 297 | 318 | | 258 | 233 | 208 | 223 | |
| | 140 × 343 | 389 | 357 | 325 | 344 | 299 | 272 | 250 | 228 | 241 | 209 |
| | 140 × 394 | 397 | 369 | 340 | 357 | 317 | 278 | 258 | 238 | 250 | 222 |
| Hem-Fir | 140 × 140 | 181 | 145 | | | | 138 | 110 | | | |
| | 140 × 191 | 228 | 195 | | 181 | | 173 | 148 | | 137 | |
| | 140 × 241 | 247 | 218 | 189 | 207 | | 174 | 153 | 133 | 145 | |
| | 140 × 292 | 272 | 246 | 220 | 235 | | 191 | 173 | 154 | 165 | |
| | 140 × 343 | 288 | 264 | 241 | 255 | 221 | 202 | 186 | 169 | 179 | 156 |
| | 140 × 394 | 294 | 273 | 252 | 264 | 235 | 207 | 192 | 177 | 186 | 165 |
| S-P-F | 140 × 140 | 170 | 136 | | | | 128 | 103 | | | |
| | 140 × 191 | 214 | 182 | | 169 | | 162 | 138 | | 128 | |
| | 140 × 241 | 234 | 207 | 179 | 195 | | 164 | 145 | 125 | 137 | |
| Northern | 140 × 140 | 161 | 128 | | | | 122 | 97.1 | | | |
| | 140 × 191 | 202 | 172 | | 160 | | 153 | 131 | | 121 | |
| | 140 × 241 | 217 | 192 | 166 | 181 | | 154 | 136 | 118 | 128 | |

4

Tension Members

Notes:
1. $T_r$ = Factored tensile resistance based on gross area
   $T_{rN}$ = Factored tensile resistance based on net area with one or two single shear plates or split rings on each side of member at a given cross section

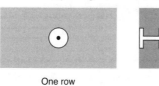

One row                                    Two rows

2. SH PL = Shear Plate, SR = Split Ring
3. Where $T_r$ values are not shown, area removed exceeds 25% of gross area.
4  For 4" diameter shear plates, values are based on the use of 3/4" diameter bolts.

# Tension Member Selection Tables

## 191 mm   Sawn Timber

| Species | Size (b × d) mm | Select Structural $T_r$ kN | $T_{rN}$ for use with shear plates or split rings (kN) 2-5/8" SH PL 1 row | 2 rows | 4" SH PL 1 row | 2 rows | No.1 $T_r$ kN | $T_{rN}$ for use with shear plates or split rings (kN) 2-5/8" SH PL 1 row | 2 rows | 4" SH PL 1 row | 2 rows |
|---|---|---|---|---|---|---|---|---|---|---|---|
| D.Fir-L | 191 × 191 | 422 | 364 | | 345 | | 319 | 276 | | 261 | |
| | 191 × 241 | 488 | 435 | 382 | 418 | | 369 | 329 | 289 | 316 | |
| | 191 × 292 | 502 | 457 | 412 | 443 | 383 | 351 | 320 | 289 | 310 | 268 |
| | 191 × 343 | 531 | 490 | 450 | 477 | 424 | 371 | 343 | 315 | 334 | 297 |
| | 191 × 394 | 542 | 506 | 470 | 494 | 447 | 379 | 354 | 329 | 346 | 313 |
| Hem-Fir | 191 × 191 | 311 | 269 | | 255 | | 236 | 204 | | 194 | |
| | 191 × 241 | 360 | 321 | 282 | 308 | | 273 | 244 | 214 | 234 | |
| | 191 × 292 | 371 | 338 | 305 | 327 | 284 | 261 | 238 | 214 | 230 | 199 |
| | 191 × 343 | 393 | 363 | 333 | 353 | 314 | 276 | 255 | 234 | 248 | 220 |
| | 191 × 394 | 401 | 374 | 348 | 366 | 331 | 282 | 263 | 244 | 257 | 232 |
| S-P-F | 191 × 191 | 292 | 252 | | 239 | | 221 | 190 | | 181 | |
| | 191 × 241 | 337 | 301 | 264 | 289 | | 255 | 227 | 200 | 219 | |
| Northern | 191 × 191 | 276 | 238 | | 226 | | 209 | 180 | | 171 | |
| | 191 × 241 | 319 | 284 | 250 | 273 | | 242 | 215 | 189 | 207 | |

Notes:
1. $T_r$ = Factored tensile resistance based on gross area
   $T_{rN}$ = Factored tensile resistance based on net area with one or two single shear plates or split rings on each side of member at a given cross section

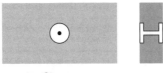

One row

Two rows

2. SH PL = Shear Plate, SR = Split Ring
3. Where $T_r$ values are not shown, area removed exceeds 25% of gross area.
4  For 4" diameter shear plates, values are based on the use of 3/4" diameter bolts.

# Tension Member Selection Tables

## Sawn Timber

**241** mm

| Species | Size (b × d) mm | $T_r$ kN | Select Structural | | | | No.1 | | | | |
|---|---|---|---|---|---|---|---|---|---|---|---|
| | | | $T_{rN}$ for use with shear plates or split rings (kN) | | | | $T_r$ kN | $T_{rN}$ for use with shear plates or split rings (kN) | | | |
| | | | 2-5/8" SH ₽ | | 4" SH ₽ | | | 2-5/8" SH ₽ | | 4" SH ₽ | |
| | | | 1 row | 2 rows | 1 row | 2 rows | | 1 row | 2 rows | 1 row | 2 rows |
| D.Fir-L | 241 × 241 | 615 | 552 | 488 | 534 | | 466 | 417 | 369 | 405 | |
| | 241 × 292 | 678 | 620 | 562 | 604 | 531 | 513 | 469 | 425 | 457 | 402 |
| | 241 × 343 | 670 | 621 | 572 | 608 | 546 | 469 | 435 | 400 | 425 | 382 |
| | 241 × 394 | 684 | 640 | 597 | 629 | 574 | 479 | 448 | 418 | 440 | 402 |
| Hem-Fir | 241 × 241 | 454 | 407 | 360 | 395 | | 345 | 309 | 274 | 300 | |
| | 241 × 292 | 500 | 458 | 415 | 446 | 392 | 380 | 348 | 315 | 339 | 298 |
| | 241 × 343 | 495 | 459 | 423 | 450 | 404 | 348 | 323 | 297 | 316 | 284 |
| | 241 × 394 | 506 | 474 | 442 | 465 | 425 | 356 | 333 | 310 | 327 | 298 |
| S-P-F | 241 × 241 | 426 | 382 | 337 | 370 | | 322 | 288 | 256 | 280 | |
| Northern | 241 × 241 | 403 | 361 | 319 | 350 | | 305 | 273 | 242 | 265 | |

Notes:
1. $T_r$ = Factored tensile resistance based on gross area
   $T_{rN}$ = Factored tensile resistance based on net area with one or two single shear plates or split rings on each side of member at a given cross section

 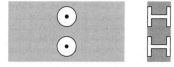

One row        Two rows

2. SH ₽ = Shear Plate, SR = Split Ring
3. Where $T_r$ values are not shown, area removed exceeds 25% of gross area.
4 For 4" diameter shear plates, values are based on the use of 3/4" diameter bolts.

**4**

Tension Members

# Tension Member Selection Tables

**18** t-E
**14** t-E

## Glulam

| Size (b × d) mm | 18t-E D.Fir-L | | | 14t-E Spruce-Pine | | |
|---|---|---|---|---|---|---|
| | Factored tensile resistance based on gross area | Maximum number of shear plates per side for $T_{rN} \geq T_{rG}$ | | Factored tensile resistance based on gross area | Maximum number of shear plates per side for $T_{rN} \geq T_{rG}$ | |
| | $T_{rG}$ kN | 2-5/8" | 4" | $T_{rG}$ kN | 2-5/8" | 4" |
| 80 × 152 | 196 | 1 | | 147 | 1 | |
| 80 × 190 | 245 | 1 | | 183 | 1 | |
| 80 × 228 | 294 | 1 | | 220 | 1 | 1 |
| 80 × 266 | 343 | 1 | 1 | 257 | 1 | 1 |
| 80 × 304 | 392 | 1 | 1 | 293 | 2 | 1 |
| 130 × 152 | 318 | 1 | | 238 | 1 | |
| 130 × 190 | 398 | 1 | 1 | 298 | 1 | 1 |
| 130 × 228 | 478 | 1 | 1 | 357 | 1 | 1 |
| 130 × 266 | 557 | 2 | 1 | 417 | 2 | 1 |
| 130 × 304 | 637 | 2 | 1 | 477 | 2 | 1 |
| 130 × 342 | 716 | 2 | 1 | 536 | 2 | 2 |
| 130 × 380 | 796 | 2 | 2 | 596 | 3 | 2 |
| 130 × 418 | 875 | 3 | 2 | 655 | 3 | 2 |
| 130 × 456 | 955 | 3 | 2 | 715 | 3 | 2 |
| 130 × 494 | 1030 | 3 | 2 | 774 | 4 | 3 |
| 175 × 190 | 536 | 1 | 1 | 401 | 1 | 1 |
| 175 × 228 | 643 | 1 | 1 | 481 | 2 | 1 |
| 175 × 266 | 750 | 2 | 1 | 561 | 2 | 1 |
| 175 × 304 | 857 | 2 | 1 | 642 | 2 | 2 |
| 175 × 342 | 964 | 2 | 2 | 722 | 3 | 2 |
| 175 × 380 | 1070 | 3 | 2 | 802 | 3 | 2 |
| 175 × 418 | 1180 | 3 | 2 | 882 | 3 | 2 |
| 175 × 456 | 1290 | 3 | 2 | 962 | 4 | 3 |
| 175 × 494 | 1390 | 4 | 3 | 1040 | 4 | 3 |
| 215 × 266 | 921 | 2 | 1 | 690 | 2 | 2 |
| 215 × 304 | 1050 | 2 | 2 | 788 | 2 | 2 |
| 215 × 342 | 1180 | 2 | 2 | 887 | 3 | 2 |
| 215 × 380 | 1320 | 3 | 2 | 985 | 3 | 2 |
| 215 × 418 | 1450 | 3 | 2 | 1080 | 4 | 3 |
| 215 × 456 | 1580 | 3 | 3 | 1180 | 4 | 3 |
| 215 × 494 | 1710 | 4 | 3 | 1280 | 4 | 3 |

Notes:

1. Number of shear plates per side at a given cross section:

One per side          Two per side

2. For 4" diameter shear plates, values are based on the use of 3/4" diameter bolts.

# Tension Member Selection Tables

## Glulam

**20** f-EX
**24** f-EX

| Size (b × d) mm | 20f-EX and 24f-EX D.Fir-L | | | 20f-EX Spruce-Pine | | |
|---|---|---|---|---|---|---|
| | Factored tensile resistance based on gross area $T_{rG}$ kN | Maximum number of shear plates per side for $T_{rN} \geq T_{rG}$ 2-5/8" | 4" | Factored tensile resistance based on gross area $T_{rG}$ kN | Maximum number of shear plates per side for $T_{rN} \geq T_{rG}$ 2-5/8" | 4" |
| 80 × 152 | 167 | 1 | | 139 | 1 | |
| 80 × 190 | 209 | 1 | | 174 | 1 | |
| 80 × 228 | 251 | 1 | | 208 | 1 | 1 |
| 80 × 266 | 293 | 1 | 1 | 243 | 1 | 1 |
| 80 × 304 | 335 | 2 | 1 | 278 | 2 | 1 |
| 130 × 152 | 272 | 1 | | 226 | 1 | |
| 130 × 190 | 340 | 1 | 1 | 282 | 1 | 1 |
| 130 × 228 | 408 | 1 | 1 | 339 | 2 | 1 |
| 130 × 266 | 476 | 2 | 1 | 395 | 2 | 1 |
| 130 × 304 | 544 | 2 | 1 | 452 | 2 | 1 |
| 130 × 342 | 612 | 2 | 2 | 508 | 3 | 2 |
| 130 × 380 | 680 | 3 | 2 | 565 | 3 | 2 |
| 130 × 418 | 748 | 3 | 2 | 621 | 3 | 2 |
| 130 × 456 | 816 | 3 | 2 | 678 | 4 | 2 |
| 130 × 494 | 880 | 4 | 3 | 734 | 4 | 3 |
| 175 × 190 | 458 | 1 | 1 | 380 | 1 | 1 |
| 175 × 228 | 549 | 2 | 1 | 456 | 2 | 1 |
| 175 × 266 | 641 | 2 | 1 | 532 | 2 | 1 |
| 175 × 304 | 733 | 2 | 2 | 608 | 2 | 2 |
| 175 × 342 | 824 | 3 | 2 | 684 | 3 | 2 |
| 175 × 380 | 920 | 3 | 2 | 760 | 3 | 2 |
| 175 × 418 | 1010 | 3 | 2 | 836 | 3 | 2 |
| 175 × 456 | 1100 | 4 | 3 | 912 | 4 | 3 |
| 175 × 494 | 1190 | 4 | 3 | 990 | 4 | 3 |
| 215 × 266 | 788 | 2 | 2 | 654 | 2 | 2 |
| 215 × 304 | 900 | 2 | 2 | 747 | 2 | 2 |
| 215 × 342 | 1010 | 3 | 2 | 840 | 3 | 2 |
| 215 × 380 | 1130 | 3 | 2 | 934 | 3 | 2 |
| 215 × 418 | 1240 | 4 | 3 | 1030 | 4 | 3 |
| 215 × 456 | 1350 | 4 | 3 | 1120 | 4 | 3 |
| 215 × 494 | 1460 | 4 | 3 | 1210 | 4 | 3 |

**4**

Tension Members

Notes:

1. Number of shear plates per side at a given cross section:

One per side

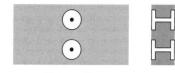

Two per side

2. For 4" diameter shear plates, values are based on the use of 3/4" diameter bolts.

# Combined
# Loads

The top chords and often the bottom chords of trusses are subjected to combined bending and axial stresses.

The high stud walls used in applications such as this church require that the designer consider deflection limitations as well as combined bending and axial stresses.

# 5.1  General Information

This chapter contains design information for members that are subjected to combined bending and axial load. Combined bending and axial compression often occurs in glulam arches and the top chords of trusses, as well as in laterally loaded studs and columns. Members loaded in bending combined with tension are less common, and include the bottom chords of trusses or top chords of trusses subject to uplift loading. Permanent wood foundations are also subjected to combined loading, and design information is provided in Section 8.8.

Generally, the 20f-EX or 24f-EX stress grades are used for glulam subjected to combined loads; however, 18t-E, 14t-E, 16c-E or 12c-E grades may be used. This section provides design information for the 20f-EX and 24f-EX grades only.

**5**

**Combined Loads**

### Design

Members subjected to combined bending and axial compressive or tensile loads must be designed to satisfy the appropriate strength interaction equation. With the exception of stud walls for permanent wood foundations and specific truss configurations, the following interaction equations are applicable:

$$\frac{P_f}{P_r} + \frac{M_f}{M_r} \leq 1.0$$

$$\frac{T_f}{T_r} + \frac{M_f}{M_r} \leq 1.0$$

where:

$P_f$ = factored axial compressive load

$T_f$ = factored axial tensile load

$M_f$ = factored bending moment, taking into account end moments and amplified moments due to axial loads in laterally loaded members (see below)

$P_r$ = factored compressive resistance parallel to grain

$T_r$ = factored tensile resistance parallel to grain

$M_r$ = factored bending moment resistance

The interaction equation applicable to the design of stud walls for permanent wood foundations is given in Section 8.8 of this manual. Refer to clause 5.5.13 of CSA O86 for the interaction equation applicable to specific truss applications.

When checking the interaction equation for bending and compression, the compressive resistance $P_r$ is calculated as if only compressive loads were present. Therefore, it is always based on buckling in the weakest direction.

The factored resistances $P_r$, $T_r$ and $M_r$ may be found in the appropriate sections of this manual as indicated in Table 5.1. In addition, selection tables for stud walls subjected to combined lateral wind loading and axial loading are provided in Section 5.2.

| Material | $P_r$ | $T_r$ | $M_r$ |
|---|---|---|---|
| Sawn Lumber | Section 3.2 | Tension Member Selection Tables, Section 4.2 | Joist Selection Tables, Section 2.3 |
| Sawn Timber | Section 3.3 | Tension Member Selection Tables, Section 4.2 | Beam Selection Tables, Section 2.4 |
| 20f-EX, 24f-EX Glulam | Section 5.1 | Tension Member Selection Tables, Section 4.2 | Beam Selection Tables, Section 2.4 |

**Table 5.1 Factored resistances for combined bending and axial load**

## Bending Moments in Laterally Loaded Compression Members

When a compression member is laterally loaded, a secondary bending moment is created by the product of the axial load and the total lateral deflection (P$\Delta$ effect). The total moment is then calculated as follows:

$$M_f = M'_f + P_f \Delta_T$$

where:

$M'_f$ = factored bending moment due to lateral loading only

$P_f$ = factored axial load

$\Delta_T$ = total lateral deflection

The total lateral deflection $\Delta_T$ consists of the deflection due to the lateral loading $\Delta_L$ plus additional deflections caused by the secondary moment. This may be calculated by multiplying $\Delta_L$ by an amplification factor as follows:

$$\Delta_T = \Delta_L \left[ \frac{1}{1 - \dfrac{P_f}{P_E}} \right]$$

where:

$P_f$ = factored axial compressive load

$P_E$ = Euler buckling load in direction of applied moment

$$= \frac{\pi^2 E_S I}{(K_e L)^2}$$

$E_S I$ = bending stiffness, given in Joist and Beam Selection Tables

$K_e$ = effective length factor, given in Figure 3.1

$L$ = unsupported length in the direction of the applied bending moment

As an alternative, the total bending moment for simply supported members may be estimated with reasonable accuracy by amplifying the bending moment due to lateral loading as follows:

$$M_f = M'_f \left[ \frac{1}{1 - \dfrac{P_f}{P_E}} \right]$$

For other support conditions, this expression may slightly underestimate the total moment.

**Bending Moments in Eccentrically Loaded Compression Members**

When a load is not applied in the center of the vertical axis of a compression member, the eccentricity will create a moment. At the location where the load is applied (typically the top of the column) there is no deflection and the moment is calculated as:

$$M_f = P_f e$$

where:

$M_f$ = factored bending moment due to eccentricity

$P_f$ = factored axial load

$e$ = load eccentricity

= distance between the center of the column and the centroid of the applied load

Midway between the location where the load is applied (typically mid-height of the column) and the column support the total moment is calculated as:

$$M_f = M'_f + P_f \Delta_E$$

where:

$M'_f$ = factored bending moment due to eccentricity at the mid point between the applied load and the column base

$$= \frac{1}{2} P_f e$$

$\Delta_E$ = total lateral deflection at mid height due to the eccentric load

The total bending moment at the mid point on the compression member may be estimated as:

$$M_f = \frac{1}{2} P_f e \left[ \frac{1}{1 - \dfrac{P_f}{P_E}} \right]$$

## Lateral Restraint

In the calculation of moment resistance for combined bending and compression, the lateral stability factor $K_L$ may be taken as unity where lateral support is provided at points of bearing and the depth to width ratio of the member does not exceed the following values:

4:1     if no additional intermediate support is provided

5:1     if the member is held in line by purlins or tie rods

6.5:1  if the compressive edge is held in line by direct connection of decking or joists spaced not more than 610 mm apart

7.5:1  if the compressive edge is held in line by direct connection of decking or joists spaced not more than 610 mm apart and adequate bridging or blocking is installed at intervals not exceeding 8 times the depth of the member

9:1     if both edges are held in line

These rules apply to glulam members as well as sawn lumber and timber. If the above limits are exceeded, $K_L$ may be calculated in accordance with CSA O86 Clause 6.5.6.4.

## Example 1: Glulam Column

Design the glulam column shown below. Use untreated 20f-EX Spruce-Pine glulam in dry service conditions. The axial load consists of 10 kN dead load and 40 kN snow load. The specified wind load is 10 kN for strength calculations and 7.5 for serviceability calculations. The specified wind loads are based on the $q_{1/50}$ hourly wind pressure, wind importance factors, internal and external pressure coefficients and the tributary wind load area.

**Calculation**

Load Case 1: (1.25D + 1.5S)

$$P_f = (1.25 \times 10) + (1.5 \times 40) = 72.5 \text{ kN}$$

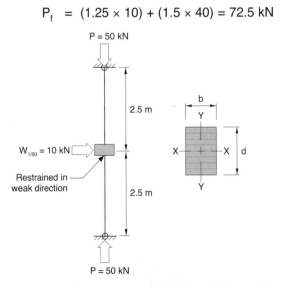

Load Case 2: (1.25D + 1.4W + 0.5S)

$$P_f = (1.25 \times 10) + (0.5 \times 40) = 32.5 \text{ kN}$$
$$W_f = 1.4 \times 10 = 14 \text{ kN}$$

Load Case 3: (1.25D + 1.5S + 0.4W)

$$P_f = (1.25 \times 10) + (1.5 \times 40) = 72.5 \text{ kN}$$
$$W_f = 0.4 \times 10 = 4 \text{ kN}$$

1. For Load Case 1 (standard term load)

Select initial trial section 130 × 152 mm:

$$C_{cx} = \frac{K_e L_d}{d} = \frac{1.0 \times 5000}{152} = 32.9 \qquad Governs$$

$$C_{cy} = \frac{K_e L_b}{b} = \frac{1.0 \times 2500}{130} = 19.2$$

Since buckling about X axis governs, Column Selection Tables may be used because $K_e L_d = L$.

Therefore, from Column Selection Tables:

$$P_r = P_{rx} = 101 \text{ kN} > 72.5 \text{ kN} \qquad Acceptable$$

The 130 × 152 mm section is adequate for Load Case 1.

2. Check 130 × 152 mm section for Load Case 2 (short term load)

a) Calculate $P_r$

For short term loads Column Selection Tables cannot be used.

$$P_r = \phi F_{cb} A K_{Zc} K_C$$
$$\phi F_{cb} = 23.2 \text{ MPa from Table 5.2}$$
$$A = 130 \times 152 = 19760 \text{ mm}^2$$
$$K_{Zc} = 0.68 (0.130 \times 0.152 \times 5.0)^{-0.13} = 0.92$$

$$K_C = \left[1.0 + \frac{F_{cb}}{E'} K_{Zc} C_c^3\right]^{-1}$$

$$C_{cx} = 32.9 \qquad Governs$$
$$F_{cb} / E' = 92.4 \times 10^{-6} \text{ from Table 5.3}$$
$$K_C = [1.0 + 92.4 \times 10^{-6} \times 0.92 \times (32.9)^3]^{-1} = 0.25$$
$$P_r = 23.2 \times 19760 \times 0.92 \times 0.25 = 105 \text{ kN}$$

**5**

Combined Loads

b) Determine $M_r$ using Beam Selection Tables:

A review of the checklist for beams indicates that the tabulated $M'_r$ values may be multiplied by 1.15 for short term loading. (note that $K_L = K_{Zbg} = 1$)

$M_r = 1.15 \times 11.5 = 13.2$ kN•m

$M_f = \dfrac{W_f L}{4} = \dfrac{14.0 \times 5.0}{4}$

     $= 17.5$ kN•m $> 13.2$ kN•m          *Not Acceptable*

c) Select a larger section:

Try 130 × 228 mm section

$C_{cx} = 1.0 \times 5000 / 228 = 21.9$          *Governs*

$A = 130 \times 228 = 29640$ mm$^2$

$K_{Zc} = 0.68 (0.13 \times 0.228 \times 5.0)^{-0.13} = 0.87$

$K_C = [1 + 92.4 \times 10^{-6} \times 0.87 \times (21.9)^3]^{-1} = 0.54$

$P_r = 23.2 \times 29640 \times 0.87 \times 0.54 = 323$ kN

$M_r = 1.15 \times 26.0 = 29.9$ kN•m

Note that since $d / b < 4$, the factor $K_L$ may be taken as unity. According to Table 2.11, $K_{Zbg} = 1.0$.

d) Calculate amplified bending moment and verify interaction equation:

$E_s I = 1320 \times 10^9$ N•mm$^2$

$P_E = \dfrac{\pi^2 E_s I}{(K_e L)^2} = \dfrac{\pi^2 \times 1320 \times 10^9}{(5000)^2} = 521$ kN

$M_f = \dfrac{W_f L}{4}\left[1 - \dfrac{P_f}{P_E}\right]^{-1}$    $\left\{ \text{where}: \left[1 - \dfrac{P_f}{P_E}\right]^{-1} = \left[1 - \dfrac{32.5}{521}\right]^{-1} = 1.07 \right\}$

$M_f = \dfrac{14.0 \times 5.0}{4} \times 1.07 = 18.7$ kN•m

$\dfrac{P_f}{P_r} + \dfrac{M_f}{M_r} = \dfrac{32.5}{323} + \dfrac{18.7}{29.9} = 0.73$          *Acceptable*

e) Check shear

$V_f = 14/2 = 7.0$ kN

beam volume = $0.130 \times 0.228 \times 5.00 = 0.148$ m$^3 < 2.0$ m$^3$

Check $V_r$ from the Beam Selection Tables. A review of the checklist indicates that $V_r$ values may be multiplied by 1.15 for short term loading.

$V_r = 1.15 \times 31.1 = 35.6$ kN $> 7.0$ kN          *Acceptable*

## Checklist: **Glulam Columns** (Combined Loading)

To verify that the tabulated resistances given in the Column Selection Tables are appropriate for the structure being designed, the following questions should be asked:

1. Is load duration "standard" term (dead load plus snow or occupancy loads)?

2. Is the service condition "dry"?

3. Is the material free of strength reducing chemicals such as fire retardants?

4. Is the effective length factor $K_e$ equal to 1.0 and the effective column length in the direction of buckling equal to the total column length?

If the answer to any of these questions is no, the Column Selection Tables may not be used. Instead, calculate $P_r$ as shown in Example 1: Glulam Column.

**5**

**Combined Loads**

f) Check L/180 deflection limit based on serviceability wind load

$$E_s I_{REQ'D} = 180 \left[ \frac{W_{1/50} L^2}{48} \right] = 180 \left[ \frac{7500 \times 5000^2}{48} \right]$$

$$= 703 \times 10^9 \text{ N} \cdot \text{mm}^2 < 1320 \times 10^9 \text{ N} \cdot \text{mm}^2 \text{ } Acceptable$$

3. Check 130 × 228 mm for Load Case 3 (short term load)

$$M_f = \frac{W_f L}{4} \left[ 1 - \frac{P_f}{P_E} \right]^{-1} \quad \left\{ where : \left[ 1 - \frac{P_f}{P_E} \right]^{-1} = \left[ 1 - \frac{72.5}{521} \right]^{-1} = 1.16 \right\}$$

$$M_f = \frac{4 \times 5.0}{4} \times 1.16 = 5.80 \text{ kN} \cdot \text{m}$$

$$\frac{P_f}{P_r} + \frac{M_f}{M_r} = \frac{72.5}{323} + \frac{5.80}{29.9} = 0.42 \qquad\qquad Acceptable$$

**Use 130 × 228 mm 20f-EX Spruce-Pine glulam.**

## Example 2:  Eccentrically Loaded Glulam Column

Design a glulam column supporting a glulam roof beam. The roof beam is supported on a bracket attached to the narrow face of the column. The width of both the beam and the column is 130 mm. The distance between the edge of the column and the center of the bracket is 60 mm and the distance between the underside of the bracket and the base of the column is 4 m. Use untreated 20f-EX D.Fir-L glulam in dry service conditions. The axial load consists of 10 kN dead load and 40 kN snow load.

### Calculation
Load Case: Dead plus snow:

$$P_f = (1.25 \times 10) + (1.5 \times 40) = 72.5 \text{ kN}$$

Select trial section 130 x 190 mm:

a) From Column Selection Tables (combined loading), check axial capacity in the Y axis:

$$P_{ry} = 175 \text{ kN} > 72.5 \text{ kN} \qquad \qquad \textit{Acceptable}$$

b) Check combined axial and moment resistance in the X axis at the top of the column. Since there is no deflection at the top of the column moment amplification is not considered:

Calculate eccentricity, e:

$$e = 228/2 + 60 = 174 \text{ mm}$$

$$M_f = 72.5 \times \frac{174}{1000} = 12.6 \text{ kN·m}$$

From Beam Selection Tables:

$$M_r = 18.0 \text{ kN·m}$$

From Column Selection Tables (combined loading):

$$P_{rx} = 325 \text{ kN}$$

$$\frac{P_f}{P_r} + \frac{M_f}{M_r} = \frac{72.5}{325} + \frac{12.6}{18.0} = 0.92 \qquad \qquad \textit{Acceptable}$$

c) Check combined axial and moment resistance in the X axis at the mid-height of the column:

Calculate the amplified bending moment and verify the interaction equation:

$$E_s I = 1320 \times 10^9 \text{ N·mm}^2$$

$$P_E = \frac{\pi^2 E_s I}{(K_e L)^2} = \frac{\pi^2 \times 921 \times 10^9}{(4000)^2} = 568 \text{ kN}$$

$$P_E = \frac{1}{2} P_f e \left[ \frac{1}{1 - \dfrac{P_f}{P_E}} \right] = \frac{1}{2} \times 72.5 \times \frac{174}{1000} \left[ \frac{1}{1 - \dfrac{72.5}{568}} \right] = 7.23 \text{ kN·m}$$

$$\frac{P_f}{P_r} + \frac{M_f}{M_r} = \frac{72.5}{325} + \frac{7.23}{18.0} = 0.62 \qquad \qquad \textit{Acceptable}$$

**Use 130 x 190 mm 20f-EX D.Fir-L glulam.**

**Table 5.2**
**Factored compressive strength for glulam subjected to combined bending and axial compression $\phi\, F_{cb}$ (MPa)**

|  | Dry service | | | Wet service | | |
|---|---|---|---|---|---|---|
|  | Load duration | | | Load duration | | |
| Grade | Std. | Perm. | Short term | Std. | Perm. | Short term |
| D.Fir-L 24f-EX and D.Fir-L 20f-EX | 24.2 | 15.7 | 27.8 | 18.1 | 11.8 | 20.8 |
| Spruce-Pine 20f-EX | 20.2 | 13.1 | 23.2 | 15.1 | 9.83 | 17.4 |

Notes:
1. $\phi\, F_{cb} = \phi\, f_{cb}\, K_D\, K_H\, K_{Sc}\, K_T$ (Refer to Clause 6.5.8.4 of CSA O86)
2. For fire-retardant treatment, multiply by a treatment factor $K_T$.
   See the Commentary for further guidance.
3. Standard term loading = dead loads plus snow or occupancy loads
   Permanent loading = dead loads alone
   Short term loading = dead plus wind loads

**Table 5.3**
**Modified strength to stiffness ratio for glulam $F_{cb}\,/\,E'\ (\times10^{-6})$**

|  | Dry service | | | Wet service | | |
|---|---|---|---|---|---|---|
|  | Load duration | | | Load duration | | |
| Grade | Std. | Perm. | Short term | Std. | Perm. | Short term |
| D.Fir-L 24f-EX | 75.7 | 49.2 | 87.1 | 63.1 | 41.0 | 72.5 |
| D.Fir-L 20f-EX | 80.0 | 52.0 | 92.0 | 66.7 | 43.3 | 76.7 |
| Spruce-Pine 20f-EX | 80.4 | 52.2 | 92.4 | 67.0 | 43.5 | 77.0 |

Notes:
1. $F_{cb}\,/\,E' = (f_{cb}\, K_D\, K_H\, K_{Sc}\, K_T)\,/\,(35\, E_{05}\, K_{SE}\, K_T)$ (Refer to Clause 6.5.8 of CSA O86).
2. Standard term loading = dead loads plus snow or occupancy loads.
   Permanent loading = dead loads alone.
   Short term loading = dead plus wind loads.

## Example 3: Sawn Timber Chord

Design the bottom chord of a heavy timber truss that has a maximum factored tensile force of 100 kN combined with a factored bending moment of 8 kN·m. The loading is due to a combination of dead plus snow loads. The service conditions are dry. Use No.1 grade Northern Species with area reduction due to one row of 4" diameter shear plates.

## Calculation

A review of the checklist for the Tension Member and Beam Selection Tables indicates that the tabulated values may be used without modification. Therefore select a series of sections and check the interaction equation as follows:

| Section (b × d) mm | $T_{rN}$ kN | $M_r$ kN·m | $\dfrac{T_f}{T_r} + \dfrac{M_f}{M_r}$ | Acceptable |
|---|---|---|---|---|
| 140 × 241 | 128 | 15.1 | 1.31 | No |
| 191 × 191 | 171 | 12.2 | 1.24 | No |
| 191 × 241 | 207 | 18.0 | 0.93 | Yes |

**Use 191 × 241 mm No.1 grade Northern Species.**

**5**

Combined Loads

# Column Selection Tables (Combined Loading)

## 80 mm    Glulam

### Spruce-Pine 20f-EX      D.Fir-L 20f-EX

| d (mm) | 114 | | 152 | | 190 | | 228 | | 114 | | 152 | | 190 | | 228 | |
|---|---|---|---|---|---|---|---|---|---|---|---|---|---|---|---|---|
| L m | $P_{rx}$ kN | $P_{ry}$ kN | $P_{rx}$ kN | $P_{ry}$ kN | $P_{rx}$ kN | $P_{ry}$ kN | $P_{rx}$ kN | $P_{ry}$ kN | $P_{rx}$ kN | $P_{ry}$ kN | $P_{rx}$ kN | $P_{ry}$ kN | $P_{rx}$ kN | $P_{ry}$ kN | $P_{rx}$ kN | $P_{ry}$ kN |
| 2.0 | 128 | 81.5 | 207 | 109 | 280 | 136 | 349 | 163 | 154 | 97.9 | 249 | 131 | 336 | 163 | 418 | 196 |
| 2.5 | 99.5 | 53.3 | 181 | 71.0 | 259 | 88.8 | 332 | 107 | 120 | 64.0 | 217 | 85.4 | 311 | 107 | 399 | 128 |
| 3.0 | 74.6 | 35.1 | 152 | 46.8 | 233 | 58.5 | 309 | 70.1 | 89.7 | 42.2 | 182 | 56.3 | 279 | 70.4 | 370 | 84.3 |
| 3.5 | 55.3 | 23.8 | 124 | 31.7 | 203 | 39.6 | 279 | 47.4 | 66.5 | 28.6 | 149 | 38.2 | 244 | 47.7 | 334 | 57.0 |
| 4.0 | 41.1 | 16.6 | 99.5 | 22.2 | 173 | 27.7 | 248 | 33.2 | 49.5 | 20.0 | 120 | 26.7 | 208 | 33.3 | 298 | 39.9 |
| 4.5 | 30.9 | | 79.3 | | 146 | | 219 | | 37.2 | | 95.3 | | 175 | | 263 | |
| 5.0 | 23.6 | | 63.2 | | 122 | | 191 | | 28.4 | | 75.9 | | 146 | | 229 | |
| 5.5 | 18.3 | | 50.6 | | 102 | | 166 | | 22.1 | | 60.9 | | 122 | | 199 | |
| 6.0 | | | 40.9 | | 84.9 | | 143 | | | | 49.2 | | 102 | | 172 | |
| 6.5 | | | 33.4 | | 71.2 | | 124 | | | | 40.2 | | 85.6 | | 148 | |
| 7.0 | | | 27.5 | | 59.9 | | 107 | | | | 33.1 | | 72.0 | | 128 | |
| 7.5 | | | 22.8 | | 50.6 | | 92.0 | | | | 27.5 | | 60.9 | | 111 | |
| 8.0 | | | | | 43.1 | | 79.7 | | | | | | 51.8 | | 95.8 | |
| 8.5 | | | | | 36.8 | | 69.2 | | | | | | 44.3 | | 83.2 | |
| 9.0 | | | | | 31.7 | | 60.2 | | | | | | 38.1 | | 72.5 | |
| 9.5 | | | | | 27.4 | | 52.7 | | | | | | 33.0 | | 63.3 | |
| 10.0 | | | | | | | 46.2 | | | | | | | | 55.6 | |

### D.Fir-L 24f-EX

| d (mm) | 114 | | 152 | | 190 | | 228 | |
|---|---|---|---|---|---|---|---|---|
| L m | $P_{rx}$ kN | $P_{ry}$ kN | $P_{rx}$ kN | $P_{ry}$ kN | $P_{rx}$ kN | $P_{ry}$ kN | $P_{rx}$ kN | $P_{ry}$ kN |
| 2.0 | 156 | 101 | 251 | 135 | 337 | 168 | 419 | 202 |
| 2.5 | 123 | 66.6 | 220 | 88.7 | 313 | 111 | 401 | 133 |
| 3.0 | 92.6 | 44.1 | 186 | 58.8 | 283 | 73.6 | 373 | 88.1 |
| 3.5 | 69.1 | 30.0 | 153 | 40.0 | 249 | 50.0 | 338 | 59.8 |
| 4.0 | 51.6 | 21.1 | 123 | 28.1 | 212 | 35.0 | 303 | 41.9 |
| 4.5 | 39.0 | | 98.8 | | 180 | | 268 | |
| 5.0 | 29.8 | | 79.0 | | 151 | | 235 | |
| 5.5 | 23.2 | | 63.6 | | 127 | | 205 | |
| 6.0 | | | 51.5 | | 106 | | 177 | |
| 6.5 | | | 42.1 | | 89.1 | | 154 | |
| 7.0 | | | 34.7 | | 75.2 | | 133 | |
| 7.5 | | | 28.9 | | 63.7 | | 115 | |
| 8.0 | | | | | 54.2 | | 99.8 | |
| 8.5 | | | | | 46.5 | | 86.8 | |
| 9.0 | | | | | 40.0 | | 75.7 | |
| 9.5 | | | | | 34.6 | | 66.3 | |
| 10.0 | | | | | | | 58.2 | |

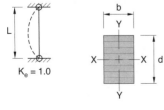

$K_e = 1.0$

Notes:
1. $P_r = \phi F_{cb} A K_{Zc} K_C$
2. $P_{rx}$ is the factored resistance to buckling about the x-x (strong) axis.
   $P_{ry}$ is the factored resistance to buckling about the y-y (weak) axis.
3. For L ≤ 2.0 m, use $P_r$ for L = 2.0 m. Where $P_r$ values are not given, the slenderness ratio exceeds 50 (maximum permitted).
4. Tabulated values are valid for the following conditions:
   - standard term load (dead plus snow or occupancy loads)
   - dry service conditions
   - no fire-retardant treatment
   - $K_e = 1.0$
5. L = unsupported length

# Column Selection Tables (Combined Loading)

## Glulam

**130** mm

### Spruce-Pine 20f-EX / D.Fir-L 20f-EX

| L m | SP 114 $P_{rx}$ kN | SP 114 $P_{ry}$ kN | SP 152 $P_{rx}$ kN | SP 152 $P_{ry}$ kN | SP 190 $P_{rx}$ kN | SP 190 $P_{ry}$ kN | SP 228 $P_{rx}$ kN | SP 228 $P_{ry}$ kN | DF 114 $P_{rx}$ kN | DF 114 $P_{ry}$ kN | DF 152 $P_{rx}$ kN | DF 152 $P_{ry}$ kN | DF 190 $P_{rx}$ kN | DF 190 $P_{ry}$ kN | DF 228 $P_{rx}$ kN | DF 228 $P_{ry}$ kN |
|---|---|---|---|---|---|---|---|---|---|---|---|---|---|---|---|---|
| 2.0 | 208 | 231 | 337 | 308 | 455 | 385 | 557 | 456 | 250 | 277 | 404 | 370 | 546 | 462 | 668 | 547 |
| 2.5 | 162 | 190 | 293 | 254 | 413 | 312 | 518 | 369 | 194 | 228 | 352 | 304 | 495 | 375 | 621 | 443 |
| 3.0 | 121 | 150 | 243 | 199 | 365 | 245 | 475 | 290 | 146 | 181 | 292 | 239 | 438 | 294 | 570 | 348 |
| 3.5 | 89.8 | 116 | 197 | 153 | 317 | 189 | 431 | 224 | 108 | 140 | 237 | 184 | 380 | 227 | 517 | 270 |
| 4.0 | 66.6 | 88.9 | 158 | 117 | 271 | 145 | 386 | 173 | 80.0 | 107 | 190 | 141 | 325 | 175 | 463 | 208 |
| 4.5 | 50.0 | 68.4 | 126 | 90.4 | 229 | 112 | 342 | 134 | 60.1 | 82.3 | 152 | 109 | 275 | 135 | 410 | 161 |
| 5.0 | 38.2 | 53.2 | 101 | 70.4 | 193 | 87.5 | 300 | 104 | 45.9 | 63.9 | 121 | 84.7 | 231 | 105 | 360 | 126 |
| 5.5 | 29.6 | 41.8 | 81.2 | 55.4 | 161 | 69.0 | 261 | 82.5 | 35.6 | 50.3 | 97.6 | 66.7 | 194 | 83.0 | 313 | 99.2 |
| 6.0 | | 33.3 | 65.8 | 44.2 | 135 | 55.0 | 226 | 65.8 | | 40.1 | 79.1 | 53.2 | 163 | 66.2 | 272 | 79.2 |
| 6.5 | | 26.8 | 53.8 | 35.7 | 114 | 44.4 | 196 | 53.2 | | 32.3 | 64.7 | 42.9 | 137 | 53.5 | 236 | 64.0 |
| 7.0 | | | 44.3 | | 96.0 | | 170 | | | | 53.3 | | 115 | | 204 | |
| 7.5 | | | 36.9 | | 81.3 | | 147 | | | | 44.4 | | 97.8 | | 177 | |
| 8.0 | | | | | 69.3 | | 127 | | | | | | 83.3 | | 153 | |
| 8.5 | | | | | 59.3 | | 111 | | | | | | 71.4 | | 133 | |
| 9.0 | | | | | 51.1 | | 96.7 | | | | | | 61.5 | | 116 | |
| 9.5 | | | | | 44.2 | | 84.6 | | | | | | 53.2 | | 102 | |
| 10.0 | | | | | | | 74.4 | | | | | | | | 89.5 | |
| 10.5 | | | | | | | 65.6 | | | | | | | | 78.9 | |
| 11.0 | | | | | | | 58.0 | | | | | | | | 69.8 | |

### D.Fir-L 24f-EX

| L m | 114 $P_{rx}$ kN | 114 $P_{ry}$ kN | 152 $P_{rx}$ kN | 152 $P_{ry}$ kN | 190 $P_{rx}$ kN | 190 $P_{ry}$ kN | 228 $P_{rx}$ kN | 228 $P_{ry}$ kN |
|---|---|---|---|---|---|---|---|---|
| 2.0 | 254 | 281 | 407 | 384 | 548 | 468 | 669 | 553 |
| 2.5 | 199 | 233 | 357 | 310 | 499 | 382 | 624 | 451 |
| 3.0 | 150 | 185 | 298 | 245 | 443 | 302 | 575 | 357 |
| 3.5 | 112 | 144 | 243 | 190 | 387 | 234 | 523 | 278 |
| 4.0 | 83.5 | 111 | 196 | 146 | 332 | 181 | 470 | 216 |
| 4.5 | 62.9 | 85.8 | 157 | 113 | 283 | 141 | 418 | 168 |
| 5.0 | 48.1 | 66.9 | 126 | 88.5 | 239 | 110 | 368 | 131 |
| 5.5 | 37.4 | 52.7 | 102 | 69.8 | 201 | 86.9 | 322 | 104 |
| 6.0 | | 42.0 | 82.7 | 55.8 | 169 | 69.5 | 280 | 83.1 |
| 6.5 | | 33.9 | 67.7 | 45.1 | 142 | 56.2 | 243 | 67.2 |
| 7.0 | | | 56.0 | | 120 | | 211 | |
| 7.5 | | | 46.6 | | 102 | | 183 | |
| 8.0 | | | | | 87.2 | | 159 | |
| 8.5 | | | | | 74.8 | | 139 | |
| 9.0 | | | | | 64.5 | | 121 | |
| 9.5 | | | | | 55.9 | | 107 | |
| 10.0 | | | | | | | 93.7 | |
| 10.5 | | | | | | | 82.7 | |
| 11.0 | | | | | | | 73.3 | |

**5**

**Combined Loads**

Notes: See page 184.

# Column Selection Tables (Combined Loading)

## 175 mm  Glulam

### Spruce-Pine 20f-EX  and  D.Fir-L 20f-EX

| L (m) | 152 Prx (kN) | 152 Pry (kN) | 190 Prx (kN) | 190 Pry (kN) | 228 Prx (kN) | 228 Pry (kN) | 266 Prx (kN) | 266 Pry (kN) | 152 Prx (kN) | 152 Pry (kN) | 190 Prx (kN) | 190 Pry (kN) | 228 Prx (kN) | 228 Pry (kN) | 266 Prx (kN) | 266 Pry (kN) |
|---|---|---|---|---|---|---|---|---|---|---|---|---|---|---|---|---|
| | Spruce-Pine 20f-EX | | | | | | | | D.Fir-L 20f-EX | | | | | | | |
| 2.0 | 452 | 477 | 594 | 581 | 723 | 683 | 842 | 782 | 542 | 572 | 713 | 697 | 866 | 818 | 1010 | 938 |
| 2.5 | 385 | 423 | 537 | 516 | 673 | 608 | 796 | 697 | 462 | 507 | 644 | 619 | 807 | 729 | 954 | 836 |
| 3.0 | 320 | 366 | 477 | 448 | 619 | 529 | 748 | 608 | 384 | 440 | 572 | 538 | 743 | 635 | 897 | 730 |
| 3.5 | 260 | 311 | 415 | 382 | 563 | 452 | 698 | 520 | 312 | 374 | 498 | 459 | 675 | 542 | 837 | 624 |
| 4.0 | 209 | 261 | 356 | 321 | 505 | 380 | 645 | 438 | 251 | 313 | 428 | 385 | 606 | 456 | 774 | 526 |
| 4.5 | 168 | 216 | 302 | 267 | 448 | 316 | 591 | 366 | 201 | 260 | 363 | 320 | 538 | 380 | 708 | 439 |
| 5.0 | 134 | 178 | 255 | 221 | 394 | 262 | 536 | 304 | 162 | 214 | 306 | 265 | 473 | 315 | 643 | 365 |
| 5.5 | 108 | 147 | 214 | 182 | 344 | 217 | 483 | 252 | 130 | 177 | 258 | 219 | 414 | 261 | 580 | 303 |
| 6.0 | 87.9 | 122 | 180 | 151 | 300 | 180 | 433 | 209 | 106 | 147 | 216 | 182 | 360 | 217 | 520 | 252 |
| 6.5 | 71.9 | 101 | 152 | 126 | 260 | 150 | 386 | 175 | 86.5 | 122 | 182 | 151 | 312 | 181 | 464 | 210 |
| 7.0 | 59.4 | 84.8 | 128 | 105 | 225 | 126 | 343 | 146 | 71.5 | 102 | 154 | 127 | 271 | 151 | 412 | 176 |
| 7.5 | 49.4 | 71.3 | 109 | 88.8 | 195 | 106 | 304 | 123 | 59.5 | 85.8 | 131 | 107 | 235 | 128 | 366 | 148 |
| 8.0 | | 60.4 | 92.6 | 75.2 | 170 | 89.9 | 270 | 105 | | 72.7 | 111 | 90.5 | 204 | 108 | 324 | 126 |
| 8.5 | | 51.5 | 79.4 | 64.1 | 148 | 76.7 | 239 | 89.3 | | 61.9 | 95.5 | 77.1 | 178 | 92.3 | 287 | 107 |
| 9.0 | | | 68.4 | | 129 | | 212 | | | | 82.3 | | 155 | | 255 | |
| 9.5 | | | 59.3 | | 113 | | 188 | | | | 71.3 | | 136 | | 226 | |
| 10.0 | | | | | 99.5 | | 168 | | | | | | 120 | | 202 | |
| 10.5 | | | | | 87.8 | | 149 | | | | | | 106 | | 180 | |
| 11.0 | | | | | 77.8 | | 133 | | | | | | 93.6 | | 161 | |
| 11.5 | | | | | | | 120 | | | | | | | | 144 | |
| 12.0 | | | | | | | 107 | | | | | | | | 129 | |
| 12.5 | | | | | | | 96.7 | | | | | | | | 116 | |
| 13.0 | | | | | | | 87.2 | | | | | | | | 105 | |

### D.Fir-L 24f-EX

| L (m) | 152 Prx (kN) | 152 Pry (kN) | 190 Prx (kN) | 190 Pry (kN) | 228 Prx (kN) | 228 Pry (kN) | 266 Prx (kN) | 266 Pry (kN) |
|---|---|---|---|---|---|---|---|---|
| 2.0 | 546 | 575 | 716 | 700 | 869 | 823 | 1010 | 943 |
| 2.5 | 469 | 512 | 650 | 625 | 810 | 736 | 957 | 844 |
| 3.0 | 392 | 446 | 579 | 546 | 748 | 644 | 902 | 740 |
| 3.5 | 321 | 381 | 507 | 468 | 683 | 553 | 843 | 636 |
| 4.0 | 259 | 321 | 437 | 395 | 615 | 467 | 781 | 539 |
| 4.5 | 209 | 267 | 373 | 330 | 548 | 391 | 718 | 452 |
| 5.0 | 168 | 222 | 316 | 274 | 484 | 326 | 654 | 377 |
| 5.5 | 136 | 184 | 266 | 228 | 425 | 271 | 592 | 314 |
| 6.0 | 111 | 153 | 225 | 189 | 371 | 226 | 532 | 262 |
| 6.5 | 90.6 | 127 | 190 | 158 | 323 | 189 | 476 | 219 |
| 7.0 | 74.9 | 107 | 161 | 133 | 280 | 158 | 424 | 184 |
| 7.5 | 62.5 | 89.9 | 137 | 112 | 244 | 134 | 377 | 155 |
| 8.0 | | 76.2 | 117 | 94.8 | 212 | 113 | 335 | 132 |
| 8.5 | | 65.0 | 100 | 81.0 | 185 | 96.9 | 298 | 113 |
| 9.0 | | | 86.3 | | 162 | | 265 | |
| 9.5 | | | 74.9 | | 142 | | 236 | |
| 10.0 | | | | | 125 | | 210 | |
| 10.5 | | | | | 111 | | 188 | |
| 11.0 | | | | | 98.1 | | 168 | |
| 11.5 | | | | | | | 150 | |
| 12.0 | | | | | | | 135 | |
| 12.5 | | | | | | | 122 | |
| 13.0 | | | | | | | 110 | |

Notes: See page 184.

# Column Selection Tables (Combined Loading)

## Glulam

**215 mm**

### Spruce-Pine 20f-EX / D.Fir-L 20f-EX

| L (m) | Spruce-Pine 20f-EX d=190 $P_{rx}$ kN | $P_{ry}$ kN | d=228 $P_{rx}$ kN | $P_{ry}$ kN | d=266 $P_{rx}$ kN | $P_{ry}$ kN | d=304 $P_{rx}$ kN | $P_{ry}$ kN | D.Fir-L 20f-EX d=190 $P_{rx}$ kN | $P_{ry}$ kN | d=228 $P_{rx}$ kN | $P_{ry}$ kN | d=266 $P_{rx}$ kN | $P_{ry}$ kN | d=304 $P_{rx}$ kN | $P_{ry}$ kN |
|---|---|---|---|---|---|---|---|---|---|---|---|---|---|---|---|---|
| 2.0 | 713 | 731 | 866 | 858 | 1010 | 982 | 1140 | 1100 | 854 | 876 | 1040 | 1030 | 1210 | 1180 | 1370 | 1320 |
| 2.5 | 645 | 675 | 807 | 793 | 954 | 909 | 1090 | 1020 | 774 | 810 | 967 | 951 | 1140 | 1090 | 1310 | 1230 |
| 3.0 | 574 | 616 | 743 | 724 | 897 | 831 | 1040 | 936 | 688 | 738 | 892 | 869 | 1080 | 996 | 1250 | 1120 |
| 3.5 | 501 | 553 | 677 | 652 | 838 | 749 | 986 | 844 | 601 | 664 | 812 | 782 | 1000 | 898 | 1180 | 1010 |
| 4.0 | 431 | 490 | 609 | 579 | 775 | 666 | 929 | 752 | 517 | 588 | 730 | 695 | 930 | 799 | 1110 | 902 |
| 4.5 | 366 | 430 | 541 | 508 | 711 | 585 | 870 | 662 | 440 | 516 | 650 | 610 | 853 | 703 | 1040 | 794 |
| 5.0 | 310 | 373 | 477 | 442 | 647 | 510 | 809 | 577 | 372 | 448 | 573 | 531 | 776 | 613 | 970 | 693 |
| 5.5 | 261 | 322 | 417 | 382 | 584 | 442 | 747 | 501 | 313 | 387 | 501 | 459 | 701 | 531 | 897 | 601 |
| 6.0 | 219 | 277 | 364 | 329 | 524 | 381 | 686 | 432 | 264 | 333 | 437 | 396 | 629 | 458 | 824 | 519 |
| 6.5 | 185 | 238 | 316 | 283 | 468 | 328 | 627 | 373 | 222 | 286 | 380 | 341 | 562 | 394 | 753 | 448 |
| 7.0 | 156 | 205 | 274 | 244 | 416 | 283 | 571 | 321 | 188 | 246 | 329 | 293 | 500 | 340 | 685 | 386 |
| 7.5 | 133 | 176 | 238 | 210 | 370 | 244 | 517 | 277 | 160 | 212 | 286 | 253 | 444 | 293 | 621 | 333 |
| 8.0 | 113 | 152 | 207 | 182 | 328 | 211 | 468 | 240 | 136 | 183 | 249 | 218 | 394 | 254 | 562 | 289 |
| 8.5 | 97.2 | 132 | 180 | 157 | 291 | 183 | 422 | 208 | 117 | 159 | 217 | 189 | 350 | 220 | 508 | 250 |
| 9.0 | 83.8 | 115 | 158 | 137 | 258 | 159 | 381 | 181 | 101 | 138 | 190 | 165 | 311 | 191 | 458 | 218 |
| 9.5 | 72.6 | 100 | 138 | 120 | 230 | 139 | 344 | 158 | 87.4 | 120 | 166 | 144 | 276 | 167 | 413 | 191 |
| 10.0 | | 87.7 | 122 | 105 | 205 | 122 | 310 | 139 | | 105 | 146 | 126 | 246 | 147 | 373 | 167 |
| 10.5 | | 77.1 | 107 | 92.3 | 182 | 107 | 280 | 122 | | 92.8 | 129 | 111 | 219 | 129 | 336 | 147 |
| 11.0 | | | 95.2 | | 163 | | 253 | | | | 115 | | 196 | | 304 | |
| 11.5 | | | | | 146 | | 228 | | | | | | 176 | | 275 | |
| 12.0 | | | | | 131 | | 207 | | | | | | 158 | | 249 | |
| 12.5 | | | | | 118 | | 188 | | | | | | 142 | | 226 | |
| 13.0 | | | | | 107 | | 171 | | | | | | 129 | | 205 | |
| 13.5 | | | | | | | 155 | | | | | | | | 187 | |
| 14.0 | | | | | | | 142 | | | | | | | | 170 | |
| 14.5 | | | | | | | 129 | | | | | | | | 156 | |
| 15.0 | | | | | | | 119 | | | | | | | | 143 | |

### D.Fir-L 24f-EX

| L (m) | d=190 $P_{rx}$ kN | $P_{ry}$ kN | d=228 $P_{rx}$ kN | $P_{ry}$ kN | d=266 $P_{rx}$ kN | $P_{ry}$ kN | d=304 $P_{rx}$ kN | $P_{ry}$ kN |
|---|---|---|---|---|---|---|---|---|
| 2.0 | 858 | 879 | 1040 | 1030 | 1210 | 1180 | 1370 | 1330 |
| 2.5 | 780 | 814 | 971 | 956 | 1150 | 1100 | 1310 | 1230 |
| 3.0 | 696 | 745 | 898 | 876 | 1080 | 1000 | 1250 | 1130 |
| 3.5 | 611 | 672 | 821 | 792 | 1010 | 909 | 1190 | 1020 |
| 4.0 | 528 | 598 | 741 | 706 | 939 | 812 | 1120 | 917 |
| 4.5 | 452 | 527 | 662 | 623 | 864 | 717 | 1050 | 810 |
| 5.0 | 383 | 459 | 585 | 544 | 788 | 627 | 982 | 710 |
| 5.5 | 324 | 398 | 514 | 472 | 714 | 546 | 910 | 618 |
| 6.0 | 273 | 344 | 450 | 408 | 643 | 472 | 838 | 536 |
| 6.5 | 231 | 296 | 392 | 353 | 576 | 408 | 768 | 463 |
| 7.0 | 196 | 256 | 341 | 304 | 515 | 353 | 701 | 401 |
| 7.5 | 167 | 221 | 297 | 263 | 458 | 305 | 637 | 347 |
| 8.0 | 143 | 191 | 259 | 228 | 408 | 264 | 578 | 301 |
| 8.5 | 122 | 166 | 226 | 198 | 363 | 230 | 523 | 261 |
| 9.0 | 106 | 144 | 198 | 172 | 323 | 200 | 473 | 228 |
| 9.5 | 91.7 | 126 | 174 | 151 | 287 | 175 | 428 | 200 |
| 10.0 | | 111 | 153 | 132 | 256 | 154 | 386 | 175 |
| 10.5 | | 97.4 | 135 | 116 | 229 | 136 | 349 | 155 |
| 11.0 | | | 120 | | 205 | | 316 | |
| 11.5 | | | | | 184 | | 286 | |
| 12.0 | | | | | 165 | | 260 | |
| 12.5 | | | | | 149 | | 236 | |
| 13.0 | | | | | 135 | | 215 | |
| 13.5 | | | | | | | 196 | |
| 14.0 | | | | | | | 178 | |
| 14.5 | | | | | | | 163 | |
| 15.0 | | | | | | | 150 | |

**5**

**Combined Loads**

Notes: See page 184.

# Column Selection Tables (Combined Loading)

## 265 mm    Glulam

| | Spruce-Pine 20f-EX | | | | | | | | D.Fir-L 20f-EX | | | | | | | |
|---|---|---|---|---|---|---|---|---|---|---|---|---|---|---|---|---|
| d (mm) | 266 | | 304 | | 342 | | 380 | | 266 | | 304 | | 342 | | 380 | |
| L m | $P_{rx}$ kN | $P_{ry}$ kN | $P_{rx}$ kN | $P_{ry}$ kN | $P_{rx}$ kN | $P_{ry}$ kN | $P_{rx}$ kN | $P_{ry}$ kN | $P_{rx}$ kN | $P_{ry}$ kN | $P_{rx}$ kN | $P_{ry}$ kN | $P_{rx}$ kN | $P_{ry}$ kN | $P_{rx}$ kN | $P_{ry}$ kN |
| 2.0 | 1210 | 1210 | 1370 | 1360 | 1530 | 1510 | 1680 | 1650 | 1450 | 1450 | 1650 | 1630 | 1830 | 1810 | 2020 | 1980 |
| 2.5 | 1150 | 1150 | 1310 | 1290 | 1470 | 1430 | 1620 | 1570 | 1370 | 1370 | 1570 | 1540 | 1760 | 1710 | 1940 | 1880 |
| 3.0 | 1080 | 1080 | 1250 | 1210 | 1410 | 1350 | 1560 | 1480 | 1290 | 1290 | 1500 | 1450 | 1690 | 1610 | 1870 | 1770 |
| 3.5 | 1010 | 1010 | 1190 | 1130 | 1350 | 1260 | 1510 | 1380 | 1210 | 1210 | 1420 | 1360 | 1620 | 1510 | 1810 | 1660 |
| 4.0 | 935 | 933 | 1120 | 1050 | 1290 | 1170 | 1450 | 1280 | 1120 | 1120 | 1340 | 1260 | 1550 | 1400 | 1740 | 1540 |
| 4.5 | 858 | 856 | 1050 | 965 | 1220 | 1070 | 1390 | 1180 | 1030 | 1030 | 1260 | 1160 | 1470 | 1290 | 1670 | 1420 |
| 5.0 | 782 | 779 | 976 | 880 | 1160 | 979 | 1330 | 1080 | 938 | 935 | 1170 | 1060 | 1390 | 1170 | 1590 | 1290 |
| 5.5 | 707 | 704 | 903 | 796 | 1090 | 886 | 1260 | 976 | 848 | 845 | 1080 | 955 | 1310 | 1060 | 1520 | 1170 |
| 6.0 | 635 | 632 | 830 | 715 | 1020 | 797 | 1200 | 879 | 763 | 759 | 997 | 859 | 1220 | 957 | 1440 | 1060 |
| 6.5 | 568 | 565 | 760 | 640 | 949 | 714 | 1130 | 788 | 682 | 679 | 912 | 769 | 1140 | 858 | 1360 | 946 |
| 7.0 | 506 | 503 | 692 | 571 | 881 | 637 | 1060 | 703 | 608 | 605 | 831 | 686 | 1060 | 766 | 1280 | 845 |
| 7.5 | 450 | 448 | 629 | 508 | 813 | 567 | 997 | 627 | 541 | 538 | 755 | 610 | 977 | 682 | 1200 | 753 |
| 8.0 | 400 | 397 | 569 | 451 | 749 | 505 | 931 | 558 | 481 | 478 | 684 | 542 | 900 | 606 | 1120 | 670 |
| 8.5 | 355 | 353 | 515 | 401 | 688 | 449 | 867 | 496 | 427 | 424 | 618 | 482 | 826 | 539 | 1040 | 596 |
| 9.0 | 316 | 313 | 465 | 356 | 631 | 399 | 806 | 441 | 380 | 377 | 558 | 428 | 758 | 480 | 968 | 531 |
| 9.5 | 281 | 279 | 419 | 317 | 577 | 355 | 747 | 393 | 338 | 335 | 504 | 381 | 694 | 427 | 897 | 473 |
| 10.0 | 250 | 248 | 379 | 283 | 528 | 317 | 691 | 351 | 301 | 299 | 455 | 340 | 634 | 381 | 830 | 422 |
| 10.5 | 224 | 222 | 342 | 252 | 483 | 283 | 639 | 313 | 269 | 267 | 411 | 303 | 580 | 340 | 768 | 377 |
| 11.0 | 200 | 198 | 309 | 226 | 441 | 253 | 590 | 281 | 241 | 238 | 372 | 272 | 530 | 305 | 709 | 337 |
| 11.5 | 179 | 178 | 280 | 202 | 403 | 227 | 545 | 252 | 216 | 214 | 336 | 244 | 484 | 273 | 655 | 303 |
| 12.0 | 161 | 160 | 254 | 182 | 369 | 204 | 503 | 226 | 194 | 192 | 305 | 219 | 443 | 246 | 604 | 272 |
| 12.5 | 145 | 144 | 230 | 164 | 337 | 184 | 464 | 204 | 175 | 173 | 277 | 197 | 405 | 221 | 558 | 246 |
| 13.0 | 131 | 130 | 209 | 148 | 309 | 166 | 428 | 184 | 158 | 156 | 252 | 178 | 371 | 200 | 515 | 222 |
| 13.5 | | | 191 | | 283 | | 395 | | | | 229 | | 341 | | 475 | |
| 14.0 | | | 174 | | 260 | | 365 | | | | 209 | | 313 | | 439 | |
| 14.5 | | | 159 | | 239 | | 338 | | | | 191 | | 287 | | 406 | |
| 15.0 | | | 146 | | 220 | | 313 | | | | 175 | | 264 | | 376 | |

| | | | | | | | | | D.Fir-L 24f-EX | | | | | | | |
|---|---|---|---|---|---|---|---|---|---|---|---|---|---|---|---|---|
| 2.0 | | | | | | | | | 1450 | 1450 | 1650 | 1630 | 1840 | 1810 | 2020 | 1980 |
| 2.5 | | | | | | | | | 1380 | 1380 | 1570 | 1550 | 1760 | 1720 | 1950 | 1880 |
| 3.0 | | | | | | | | | 1300 | 1300 | 1500 | 1460 | 1690 | 1620 | 1880 | 1780 |
| 3.5 | | | | | | | | | 1220 | 1220 | 1430 | 1370 | 1620 | 1520 | 1810 | 1670 |
| 4.0 | | | | | | | | | 1130 | 1130 | 1350 | 1270 | 1550 | 1410 | 1740 | 1550 |
| 4.5 | | | | | | | | | 1040 | 1040 | 1270 | 1170 | 1480 | 1300 | 1670 | 1430 |
| 5.0 | | | | | | | | | 953 | 950 | 1180 | 1070 | 1400 | 1190 | 1600 | 1310 |
| 5.5 | | | | | | | | | 865 | 861 | 1100 | 973 | 1320 | 1080 | 1530 | 1190 |
| 6.0 | | | | | | | | | 780 | 776 | 1010 | 878 | 1240 | 979 | 1450 | 1080 |
| 6.5 | | | | | | | | | 700 | 696 | 930 | 788 | 1160 | 879 | 1370 | 970 |
| 7.0 | | | | | | | | | 626 | 622 | 850 | 705 | 1080 | 787 | 1300 | 869 |
| 7.5 | | | | | | | | | 558 | 555 | 774 | 629 | 997 | 703 | 1220 | 776 |
| 8.0 | | | | | | | | | 497 | 494 | 703 | 561 | 920 | 627 | 1140 | 693 |
| 8.5 | | | | | | | | | 443 | 440 | 637 | 499 | 847 | 559 | 1060 | 618 |
| 9.0 | | | | | | | | | 394 | 391 | 577 | 445 | 779 | 498 | 990 | 551 |
| 9.5 | | | | | | | | | 352 | 349 | 522 | 397 | 714 | 444 | 920 | 491 |
| 10.0 | | | | | | | | | 314 | 311 | 472 | 354 | 655 | 397 | 853 | 439 |
| 10.5 | | | | | | | | | 281 | 278 | 427 | 317 | 600 | 355 | 790 | 393 |
| 11.0 | | | | | | | | | 251 | 249 | 387 | 284 | 549 | 318 | 731 | 352 |
| 11.5 | | | | | | | | | 226 | 224 | 350 | 255 | 503 | 286 | 676 | 317 |
| 12.0 | | | | | | | | | 203 | 201 | 318 | 229 | 460 | 257 | 625 | 285 |
| 12.5 | | | | | | | | | 183 | 181 | 289 | 207 | 422 | 232 | 578 | 257 |
| 13.0 | | | | | | | | | 165 | 164 | 263 | 187 | 387 | 210 | 534 | 233 |
| 13.5 | | | | | | | | | | | 240 | | 355 | | 494 | |
| 14.0 | | | | | | | | | | | 219 | | 326 | | 457 | |
| 14.5 | | | | | | | | | | | 200 | | 300 | | 423 | |
| 15.0 | | | | | | | | | | | 184 | | 277 | | 392 | |

Notes: See page 184.

# Column Selection Tables (Combined Loading)

## Glulam

**315** mm

### Spruce-Pine 20f-EX  /  D.Fir-L 20f-EX

| L (m) | 304 $P_{rx}$ kN | 304 $P_{ry}$ kN | 342 $P_{rx}$ kN | 342 $P_{ry}$ kN | 380 $P_{rx}$ kN | 380 $P_{ry}$ kN | 418 $P_{rx}$ kN | 418 $P_{ry}$ kN | 304 $P_{rx}$ kN | 304 $P_{ry}$ kN | 342 $P_{rx}$ kN | 342 $P_{ry}$ kN | 380 $P_{rx}$ kN | 380 $P_{ry}$ kN | 418 $P_{rx}$ kN | 418 $P_{ry}$ kN |
|---|---|---|---|---|---|---|---|---|---|---|---|---|---|---|---|---|
| 2.0 | 1600 | 1600 | 1780 | 1770 | 1960 | 1940 | 2130 | 2110 | 1910 | 1920 | 2130 | 2120 | 2350 | 2330 | 2550 | 2530 |
| 2.5 | 1530 | 1530 | 1710 | 1700 | 1890 | 1860 | 2060 | 2020 | 1830 | 1830 | 2050 | 2030 | 2260 | 2230 | 2470 | 2420 |
| 3.0 | 1450 | 1460 | 1640 | 1620 | 1820 | 1780 | 1990 | 1930 | 1740 | 1750 | 1970 | 1940 | 2180 | 2130 | 2390 | 2320 |
| 3.5 | 1380 | 1390 | 1570 | 1550 | 1750 | 1700 | 1930 | 1840 | 1660 | 1670 | 1880 | 1850 | 2100 | 2030 | 2310 | 2210 |
| 4.0 | 1300 | 1320 | 1500 | 1460 | 1690 | 1610 | 1860 | 1750 | 1560 | 1580 | 1800 | 1760 | 2020 | 1930 | 2240 | 2100 |
| 4.5 | 1220 | 1240 | 1430 | 1380 | 1620 | 1520 | 1800 | 1650 | 1470 | 1490 | 1710 | 1660 | 1940 | 1820 | 2160 | 1980 |
| 5.0 | 1140 | 1160 | 1350 | 1290 | 1550 | 1420 | 1730 | 1550 | 1370 | 1400 | 1620 | 1550 | 1860 | 1710 | 2080 | 1860 |
| 5.5 | 1060 | 1080 | 1270 | 1210 | 1470 | 1330 | 1670 | 1440 | 1270 | 1300 | 1530 | 1450 | 1770 | 1590 | 2000 | 1730 |
| 6.0 | 972 | 1000 | 1190 | 1120 | 1400 | 1230 | 1600 | 1340 | 1170 | 1200 | 1430 | 1340 | 1680 | 1470 | 1910 | 1610 |
| 6.5 | 890 | 924 | 1110 | 1030 | 1320 | 1130 | 1520 | 1240 | 1070 | 1110 | 1330 | 1240 | 1590 | 1360 | 1830 | 1480 |
| 7.0 | 812 | 848 | 1030 | 945 | 1240 | 1040 | 1450 | 1140 | 975 | 1020 | 1240 | 1130 | 1490 | 1250 | 1740 | 1360 |
| 7.5 | 738 | 774 | 953 | 864 | 1170 | 952 | 1370 | 1040 | 887 | 930 | 1140 | 1040 | 1400 | 1140 | 1650 | 1250 |
| 8.0 | 669 | 705 | 879 | 787 | 1090 | 869 | 1300 | 949 | 804 | 847 | 1060 | 946 | 1310 | 1040 | 1560 | 1140 |
| 8.5 | 606 | 641 | 808 | 716 | 1020 | 791 | 1220 | 864 | 728 | 770 | 971 | 860 | 1220 | 950 | 1470 | 1040 |
| 9.0 | 547 | 582 | 742 | 651 | 945 | 718 | 1150 | 786 | 658 | 699 | 891 | 782 | 1140 | 863 | 1380 | 944 |
| 9.5 | 494 | 528 | 679 | 590 | 877 | 652 | 1080 | 714 | 594 | 634 | 816 | 709 | 1050 | 784 | 1300 | 858 |
| 10.0 | 447 | 479 | 622 | 536 | 813 | 592 | 1010 | 648 | 537 | 575 | 747 | 644 | 976 | 712 | 1210 | 779 |
| 10.5 | 404 | 434 | 569 | 486 | 752 | 532 | 946 | 589 | 485 | 522 | 683 | 584 | 903 | 646 | 1140 | 708 |
| 11.0 | 365 | 394 | 520 | 441 | 695 | 488 | 883 | 535 | 439 | 473 | 625 | 530 | 835 | 587 | 1060 | 643 |
| 11.5 | 331 | 358 | 476 | 401 | 642 | 443 | 823 | 486 | 398 | 430 | 572 | 482 | 771 | 533 | 989 | 584 |
| 12.0 | 300 | 325 | 435 | 364 | 593 | 403 | 767 | 442 | 361 | 391 | 523 | 438 | 712 | 485 | 921 | 532 |
| 12.5 | 272 | 296 | 398 | 332 | 547 | 367 | 714 | 403 | 327 | 356 | 479 | 399 | 658 | 442 | 858 | 484 |
| 13.0 | 248 | 270 | 365 | 302 | 505 | 335 | 665 | 367 | 298 | 324 | 439 | 364 | 608 | 403 | 799 | 442 |
| 13.5 | 226 | 246 | 335 | 276 | 467 | 306 | 619 | 336 | 271 | 296 | 403 | 332 | 561 | 368 | 743 | 404 |
| 14.0 | 206 | 225 | 307 | 252 | 432 | 280 | 576 | 307 | 248 | 271 | 370 | 304 | 519 | 336 | 692 | 369 |
| 14.5 | 188 | 206 | 283 | 231 | 399 | 256 | 536 | 281 | 227 | 248 | 340 | 278 | 480 | 308 | 644 | 338 |
| 15.0 | 172 | 189 | 260 | 212 | 370 | 235 | 499 | 258 | 207 | 227 | 313 | 255 | 444 | 283 | 600 | 311 |

### D.Fir-L 24f-EX

| L (m) | 304 $P_{rx}$ kN | 304 $P_{ry}$ kN | 342 $P_{rx}$ kN | 342 $P_{ry}$ kN | 380 $P_{rx}$ kN | 380 $P_{ry}$ kN | 418 $P_{rx}$ kN | 418 $P_{ry}$ kN |
|---|---|---|---|---|---|---|---|---|
| 2.0 | 1920 | 1920 | 2130 | 2130 | 2350 | 2330 | 2560 | 2530 |
| 2.5 | 1830 | 1840 | 2050 | 2040 | 2260 | 2230 | 2470 | 2430 |
| 3.0 | 1750 | 1760 | 1970 | 1950 | 2180 | 2140 | 2390 | 2320 |
| 3.5 | 1660 | 1680 | 1890 | 1860 | 2110 | 2040 | 2320 | 2220 |
| 4.0 | 1570 | 1590 | 1810 | 1770 | 2030 | 1940 | 2240 | 2110 |
| 4.5 | 1480 | 1500 | 1720 | 1670 | 1950 | 1830 | 2170 | 1990 |
| 5.0 | 1380 | 1410 | 1630 | 1570 | 1870 | 1720 | 2090 | 1880 |
| 5.5 | 1280 | 1320 | 1540 | 1460 | 1780 | 1610 | 2010 | 1750 |
| 6.0 | 1190 | 1220 | 1450 | 1360 | 1690 | 1500 | 1930 | 1630 |
| 6.5 | 1090 | 1130 | 1350 | 1260 | 1600 | 1380 | 1840 | 1510 |
| 7.0 | 997 | 1040 | 1260 | 1160 | 1510 | 1280 | 1760 | 1390 |
| 7.5 | 909 | 952 | 1170 | 1060 | 1420 | 1170 | 1670 | 1280 |
| 8.0 | 826 | 870 | 1080 | 970 | 1330 | 1070 | 1580 | 1170 |
| 8.5 | 750 | 793 | 995 | 885 | 1250 | 977 | 1490 | 1070 |
| 9.0 | 679 | 721 | 915 | 806 | 1160 | 890 | 1410 | 973 |
| 9.5 | 615 | 656 | 840 | 733 | 1080 | 810 | 1320 | 886 |
| 10.0 | 557 | 596 | 771 | 666 | 1000 | 736 | 1240 | 806 |
| 10.5 | 504 | 541 | 706 | 606 | 929 | 670 | 1160 | 733 |
| 11.0 | 457 | 492 | 647 | 551 | 861 | 609 | 1090 | 667 |
| 11.5 | 414 | 447 | 593 | 501 | 796 | 554 | 1020 | 608 |
| 12.0 | 376 | 407 | 543 | 456 | 737 | 505 | 949 | 554 |
| 12.5 | 342 | 371 | 498 | 416 | 681 | 460 | 885 | 505 |
| 13.0 | 311 | 339 | 457 | 380 | 630 | 420 | 825 | 461 |
| 13.5 | 284 | 309 | 420 | 347 | 583 | 384 | 769 | 422 |
| 14.0 | 259 | 283 | 386 | 317 | 540 | 352 | 717 | 386 |
| 14.5 | 237 | 259 | 355 | 291 | 500 | 323 | 668 | 354 |
| 15.0 | 218 | 238 | 327 | 267 | 463 | 296 | 623 | 325 |

Notes: See page 184.

5

Combined Loads

# Column Selection Tables (Combined Loading)

## 365 mm   Glulam

### Spruce-Pine 20f-EX     D.Fir-L 20f-EX

| L m | 342 $P_{rx}$ kN | 342 $P_{ry}$ kN | 380 $P_{rx}$ kN | 380 $P_{ry}$ kN | 418 $P_{rx}$ kN | 418 $P_{ry}$ kN | 456 $P_{rx}$ kN | 456 $P_{ry}$ kN | 342 $P_{rx}$ kN | 342 $P_{ry}$ kN | 380 $P_{rx}$ kN | 380 $P_{ry}$ kN | 418 $P_{rx}$ kN | 418 $P_{ry}$ kN | 456 $P_{rx}$ kN | 456 $P_{ry}$ kN |
|---|---|---|---|---|---|---|---|---|---|---|---|---|---|---|---|---|
| 2.0 | 2020 | 2030 | 2230 | 2220 | 2420 | 2420 | 2620 | 2610 | 2420 | 2430 | 2670 | 2660 | 2900 | 2890 | 3140 | 3120 |
| 2.5 | 1940 | 1950 | 2140 | 2140 | 2340 | 2320 | 2530 | 2510 | 2330 | 2340 | 2570 | 2560 | 2800 | 2790 | 3030 | 3010 |
| 3.0 | 1870 | 1880 | 2070 | 2060 | 2260 | 2240 | 2460 | 2420 | 2240 | 2250 | 2480 | 2470 | 2710 | 2680 | 2940 | 2900 |
| 3.5 | 1790 | 1810 | 2000 | 1980 | 2190 | 2160 | 2380 | 2330 | 2140 | 2170 | 2390 | 2380 | 2630 | 2590 | 2860 | 2790 |
| 4.0 | 1710 | 1740 | 1920 | 1900 | 2120 | 2070 | 2320 | 2240 | 2050 | 2080 | 2300 | 2280 | 2540 | 2480 | 2780 | 2680 |
| 4.5 | 1630 | 1660 | 1840 | 1820 | 2050 | 1980 | 2250 | 2140 | 1950 | 1990 | 2210 | 2190 | 2460 | 2380 | 2690 | 2570 |
| 5.0 | 1540 | 1580 | 1760 | 1740 | 1980 | 1890 | 2180 | 2040 | 1850 | 1900 | 2110 | 2080 | 2370 | 2270 | 2610 | 2450 |
| 5.5 | 1450 | 1500 | 1680 | 1650 | 1900 | 1800 | 2100 | 1940 | 1740 | 1800 | 2020 | 1980 | 2280 | 2150 | 2520 | 2330 |
| 6.0 | 1360 | 1420 | 1600 | 1560 | 1820 | 1700 | 2030 | 1840 | 1630 | 1700 | 1910 | 1870 | 2180 | 2040 | 2430 | 2200 |
| 6.5 | 1270 | 1340 | 1510 | 1470 | 1740 | 1600 | 1950 | 1730 | 1520 | 1600 | 1810 | 1760 | 2080 | 1920 | 2340 | 2080 |
| 7.0 | 1180 | 1250 | 1420 | 1380 | 1650 | 1500 | 1870 | 1620 | 1420 | 1500 | 1710 | 1650 | 1980 | 1800 | 2250 | 1950 |
| 7.5 | 1090 | 1170 | 1330 | 1290 | 1570 | 1400 | 1790 | 1520 | 1310 | 1400 | 1600 | 1540 | 1880 | 1680 | 2150 | 1820 |
| 8.0 | 1010 | 1090 | 1250 | 1200 | 1480 | 1310 | 1710 | 1410 | 1210 | 1300 | 1500 | 1440 | 1780 | 1570 | 2050 | 1700 |
| 8.5 | 927 | 1010 | 1160 | 1110 | 1400 | 1210 | 1630 | 1310 | 1110 | 1210 | 1400 | 1330 | 1680 | 1460 | 1960 | 1580 |
| 9.0 | 851 | 933 | 1080 | 1030 | 1320 | 1120 | 1550 | 1220 | 1020 | 1120 | 1300 | 1240 | 1580 | 1350 | 1860 | 1460 |
| 9.5 | 780 | 862 | 1010 | 951 | 1240 | 1040 | 1470 | 1130 | 937 | 1040 | 1210 | 1140 | 1480 | 1250 | 1760 | 1350 |
| 10.0 | 714 | 795 | 932 | 877 | 1160 | 959 | 1390 | 1040 | 858 | 955 | 1120 | 1050 | 1390 | 1150 | 1670 | 1250 |
| 10.5 | 654 | 732 | 863 | 809 | 1080 | 885 | 1310 | 960 | 786 | 880 | 1040 | 972 | 1300 | 1060 | 1570 | 1150 |
| 11.0 | 598 | 674 | 798 | 745 | 1010 | 815 | 1230 | 885 | 719 | 810 | 959 | 895 | 1220 | 980 | 1480 | 1060 |
| 11.5 | 548 | 621 | 738 | 686 | 945 | 751 | 1160 | 816 | 658 | 746 | 887 | 825 | 1130 | 903 | 1390 | 980 |
| 12.0 | 501 | 571 | 682 | 632 | 881 | 692 | 1090 | 752 | 603 | 687 | 819 | 759 | 1060 | 831 | 1310 | 903 |
| 12.5 | 459 | 526 | 630 | 582 | 821 | 637 | 1030 | 693 | 552 | 632 | 757 | 699 | 986 | 766 | 1230 | 833 |
| 13.0 | 421 | 484 | 582 | 536 | 764 | 587 | 962 | 638 | 506 | 582 | 700 | 644 | 918 | 706 | 1160 | 767 |
| 13.5 | 386 | 446 | 538 | 494 | 712 | 541 | 902 | 589 | 464 | 537 | 647 | 594 | 855 | 651 | 1080 | 708 |
| 14.0 | 355 | 412 | 497 | 456 | 663 | 500 | 846 | 543 | 427 | 495 | 598 | 548 | 796 | 601 | 1020 | 653 |
| 14.5 | 326 | 380 | 460 | 421 | 617 | 461 | 793 | 502 | 392 | 457 | 554 | 506 | 742 | 555 | 953 | 603 |
| 15.0 | 300 | 351 | 426 | 389 | 575 | 426 | 743 | 464 | 361 | 422 | 513 | 467 | 691 | 513 | 893 | 558 |

### D.Fir-L 24f-EX

| L m | 342 $P_{rx}$ kN | 342 $P_{ry}$ kN | 380 $P_{rx}$ kN | 380 $P_{ry}$ kN | 418 $P_{rx}$ kN | 418 $P_{ry}$ kN | 456 $P_{rx}$ kN | 456 $P_{ry}$ kN |
|---|---|---|---|---|---|---|---|---|
| 2.0 | 2430 | 2430 | 2670 | 2670 | 2910 | 2900 | 3140 | 3120 |
| 2.5 | 2330 | 2340 | 2570 | 2570 | 2810 | 2790 | 3040 | 3010 |
| 3.0 | 2240 | 2260 | 2480 | 2470 | 2720 | 2690 | 2950 | 2900 |
| 3.5 | 1660 | 1680 | 1640 | 1630 | 1840 | 1820 | 2040 | 2010 |
| 4.0 | 1600 | 1620 | 1590 | 1580 | 1790 | 1760 | 1990 | 1940 |
| 4.5 | 1540 | 1560 | 1540 | 1520 | 1740 | 1700 | 1940 | 1870 |
| 5.0 | 1470 | 1500 | 1480 | 1470 | 1690 | 1640 | 1890 | 1810 |
| 5.5 | 1400 | 1440 | 1430 | 1410 | 1640 | 1570 | 1840 | 1740 |
| 6.0 | 1330 | 1380 | 1380 | 1360 | 1580 | 1510 | 1790 | 1660 |
| 6.5 | 1260 | 1310 | 1320 | 1300 | 1530 | 1440 | 1730 | 1590 |
| 7.0 | 1190 | 1240 | 1260 | 1240 | 1470 | 1370 | 1680 | 1510 |
| 7.5 | 1110 | 1170 | 1210 | 1170 | 1420 | 1310 | 1620 | 1440 |
| 8.0 | 1040 | 1110 | 1150 | 1110 | 1360 | 1240 | 1570 | 1360 |
| 8.5 | 971 | 1040 | 1090 | 1050 | 1300 | 1170 | 1510 | 1280 |
| 9.0 | 904 | 975 | 1030 | 990 | 1240 | 1100 | 1450 | 1210 |
| 9.5 | 839 | 912 | 972 | 931 | 1180 | 1030 | 1390 | 1140 |
| 10.0 | 778 | 852 | 915 | 873 | 1120 | 968 | 1330 | 1060 |
| 10.5 | 720 | 794 | 861 | 818 | 1060 | 906 | 1270 | 996 |
| 11.0 | 666 | 739 | 808 | 765 | 1010 | 847 | 1210 | 930 |
| 11.5 | 616 | 687 | 758 | 714 | 953 | 791 | 1160 | 868 |
| 12.0 | 569 | 639 | 710 | 667 | 900 | 738 | 1100 | 810 |
| 12.5 | 526 | 593 | 665 | 622 | 849 | 688 | 1050 | 755 |
| 13.0 | 486 | 551 | 622 | 580 | 800 | 641 | 992 | 703 |
| 13.5 | 449 | 512 | 581 | 540 | 754 | 597 | 941 | 655 |
| 14.0 | 415 | 475 | 543 | 504 | 710 | 557 | 891 | 610 |
| 14.5 | 384 | 442 | 508 | 469 | 668 | 519 | 844 | 568 |
| 15.0 | 356 | 411 | 475 | 438 | 628 | 483 | 798 | 529 |

Notes: See page 184.

# 5.2      Stud Walls

The Stud Wall Selection Tables (Combined Loading) provide combinations of the factored compressive load $P'_r$ and maximum factored lateral wind load $w'_r$ that satisfy the interaction equation. The tabulated values are valid only for the conditions outlined in the Stud Walls (Combined Loading) checklist.

The values of $P'_r$ are fixed percentages of the maximum compressive resistance $P_r$. These percentages represent the range in which the combined load case governs strength; therefore the compressive resistance for vertical loading alone need not be checked. However, the resistance to dead plus wind loads should be verified. Deflection under specified loads, shear capacity and the bearing capacity of the sill plate should also be checked. The Stud Wall Selection Tables (Combined Loads) include resistance values for $E_s I$, $V_r$ and $Q_r$.

**5**

**Combined Loads**

### Example 1: Stud Wall System

Design an exterior bearing wall stud system for the following conditions:

- stud spacing = 600 mm
- stud length = 3.0 m
- specified vertical dead load = 10 kN/m
- specified vertical snow load = 25 kN/m
- specified wind pressure for strength calculations based on $q_{1/50}$ hourly wind pressure = 0.833 kPa
- specified wind pressure for serviceability calculations based on $q_{1/50}$ hourly wind pressure = 0.625 kPa
  (Note: the specified wind pressures include adjustments for external and internal wind pressure coefficients.)

- dry service condition
- untreated
- studs effectively held in position by roof joists at top and by foundation at bottom
- buckling prevented about weak axis by wall sheathing and fastened to meet the requirements for a Case 2 system

Use S-P-F sawn lumber.

**Calculation**
Load Case 1: (1.25D + 1.5S + 0.4W)

$$
\begin{aligned}
P_f &= \text{total factored axial load per stud} \\
    &= \text{total factored axial load} \times \text{spacing} \\
    &= [(1.25 \times 10) + (1.5 \times 25)] \times 0.60 \\
    &= 30.0 \text{ kN}
\end{aligned}
$$

$$
\begin{aligned}
w_f &= \text{total factored horizontal wind load per stud} \\
    &= \text{total factored horizontal wind pressure} \times \text{spacing} \\
    &= 0.4 \times 0.833 \times 0.60 \\
    &= 0.200 \text{ kN/m}
\end{aligned}
$$

Load Case 2: (1.25D + 1.4W + 0.5S)

$P_f$ = total factored axial load × spacing

= [(1.25 x 10) + (0.5 x 25)] x 0.60

= 15 kN

For strength:

$w_f$ = 1.4 × 0.833 × 0.60

= 0.70 kN/m

For deflection:

= 0.625 × 0.60

= 0.375 kN/m

1. From the Stud Wall Selection Tables (Combined Loading) select a size that satisfies the strength interaction equation for Load Case 1.
   A review of the checklist indicates that the selection tables may be used. Therefore select 38 × 140 mm No.1/No.2 S-P-F.

   $P'_r$ = 33.4 > 30.0 kN                                          *Acceptable*

   $w'_r$ = 0.333 > 0.20 kN/m                                       *Acceptable*

2. Check interaction equation for Load Case 2.

   $P'_r$ = 16.7 > 15 kN                                            *Acceptable*

   $w'_r$ = 1.29 > 0.70 kN/m                                        *Acceptable*

3. Check shear

   $$V_f = \frac{0.75 \times 3}{2} = 1.13 \text{ kN}$$

   $V_r$ = 10.8 kN > 1.13 kN                                        *Acceptable*

4. Check L/180 deflection based on wind load

   $$E_s I_{REQ'D} = 180 \left[ \frac{5w_{1/50}\, L^3}{384} \right] = 180 \left[ \frac{5 \times 0.375 \times 3000^3}{384} \right]$$

   = 27.3 × 10⁹ N·mm² < 82.5 × 10⁹ N·mm²             *Acceptable*

**Use 38 × 140 mm No.1/No.2 S-P-F spaced at 600 mm.**

# Checklist: **Stud Walls** (Combined Loading)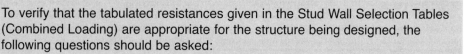

To verify that the tabulated resistances given in the Stud Wall Selection Tables (Combined Loading) are appropriate for the structure being designed, the following questions should be asked:

1. Is the load duration "short term" (for the combined load condition)?

2. Is the service condition "dry"?

3. Is the material free of incisions and/or fire retardants?

4. Are the studs effectively pinned and laterally restrained at both ends and prevented from buckling about the weak axis by wall sheathing?

5. Does the stud wall meet the requirements for a Case 2 system (refer to page 31)?

6. Is the stud concentrically loaded?

If the answer to any of these questions is no, the selection tables should not be used directly. Instead, the designer should pick a trial section, determine the resistances in accordance with Sections 2.3 and 3.2, and recheck the interaction equation.

**5**

Combined Loads

# Stud Wall Selection Tables (Combined Loading)

**DF-L Sel**

# Sawn Lumber

Maximum combined compressive load $P'_r$ (kN) and
lateral load $w'_r$ (kN/m) per stud

| Select Structural | $\dfrac{P'_r}{P_r}$ | 38 × 89 mm | | 38 × 140 mm | | 38 × 184 mm | |
|---|---|---|---|---|---|---|---|
| L<br>m | | $P'_r$<br>kN | $w'_r$<br>kN/m | $P'_r$<br>kN | $w'_r$<br>kN/m | $P'_r$<br>kN | $w'_r$<br>kN/m |
| 3.0 | 0.2 | 3.34 | 1.29 | 12.4 | 2.65 | 21.8 | 4.02 |
| | 0.3 | 5.00 | 1.06 | 18.6 | 2.18 | 32.6 | 3.37 |
| | 0.4 | 6.67 | 0.850 | 24.8 | 1.75 | 43.5 | 2.75 |
| | 0.5 | 8.34 | 0.659 | 31.0 | 1.37 | 54.4 | 2.18 |
| | 0.6 | 10.0 | 0.488 | 37.2 | 1.02 | 65.3 | 1.66 |
| | 0.7 | 11.7 | 0.336 | 43.4 | 0.704 | 76.2 | 1.18 |
| | 0.8 | 13.3 | 0.204 | 49.6 | 0.431 | 87.1 | 0.742 |
| 4.0 | 0.2 | 1.59 | 0.740 | 7.38 | 1.48 | 15.4 | 2.21 |
| | 0.3 | 2.39 | 0.615 | 11.1 | 1.21 | 23.1 | 1.83 |
| | 0.4 | 3.18 | 0.499 | 14.8 | 0.972 | 30.7 | 1.47 |
| | 0.5 | 3.98 | 0.392 | 18.5 | 0.753 | 38.4 | 1.15 |
| | 0.6 | 4.78 | 0.295 | 22.1 | 0.556 | 46.1 | 0.857 |
| | 0.7 | 5.57 | 0.207 | 25.8 | 0.383 | 53.8 | 0.596 |
| | 0.8 | 6.37 | 0.128 | 29.5 | 0.232 | 61.5 | 0.366 |
| 5.0 | 0.2 | | | 4.45 | 0.953 | 10.5 | 1.41 |
| | 0.3 | | | 6.68 | 0.786 | 15.7 | 1.16 |
| | 0.4 | | | 8.91 | 0.632 | 20.9 | 0.927 |
| | 0.5 | | | 11.1 | 0.492 | 26.2 | 0.720 |
| | 0.6 | | | 13.4 | 0.366 | 31.4 | 0.533 |
| | 0.7 | | | 15.6 | 0.254 | 36.7 | 0.368 |
| | 0.8 | | | 17.8 | 0.155 | 41.9 | 0.224 |
| 6.0 | 0.2 | | | 2.80 | 0.669 | 7.13 | 0.978 |
| | 0.3 | | | 4.21 | 0.555 | 10.7 | 0.806 |
| | 0.4 | | | 5.61 | 0.450 | 14.3 | 0.647 |
| | 0.5 | | | 7.01 | 0.353 | 17.8 | 0.503 |
| | 0.6 | | | 8.41 | 0.265 | 21.4 | 0.374 |
| | 0.7 | | | 9.82 | 0.186 | 25.0 | 0.259 |
| | 0.8 | | | 11.2 | 0.115 | 28.5 | 0.158 |
| 7.0 | 0.2 | | | 1.85 | 0.497 | 4.95 | 0.723 |
| | 0.3 | | | 2.78 | 0.415 | 7.42 | 0.598 |
| | 0.4 | | | 3.70 | 0.338 | 9.89 | 0.483 |
| | 0.5 | | | 4.63 | 0.267 | 12.4 | 0.377 |
| | 0.6 | | | 5.55 | 0.202 | 14.8 | 0.282 |
| | 0.7 | | | 6.48 | 0.143 | 17.3 | 0.196 |
| | 0.8 | | | 7.40 | 0.090 | 19.8 | 0.121 |
| $Q_r$ (kN) | | 27.2 | | 42.8 | | 56.3 | |
| $V_r$ (kN) | | | 10.6 | | 13.7 | | 15.4 |
| $E_s I \times 10^9$ N·mm² | | | 27.9 | | 109 | | 247 |

Notes:
1. Values of $P'_r$ are fixed percentages of the maximum compressive
   resistance, and are based on short term load duration ($K_D = 1.15$).
2. $w'_r$ is the maximum factored uniform wind load that satisfies the
   interaction equation for each $P'_r$ value.
3. Where values are not given, $C_c$ exceeds 50.

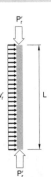

# Stud Wall Selection Tables (Combined Loading)

## Sawn Lumber

**DF-L
No.1
No.2**

Maximum combined compressive load P'$_r$ (kN) and
lateral load w'$_r$ (kN/m) per stud

| No.1/No.2 | $\frac{P'_r}{P_r}$ | 38 × 89 mm | | 38 × 140 mm | | 38 × 184 mm | |
|---|---|---|---|---|---|---|---|
| L m | | P'$_r$ kN | w'$_r$ kN/m | P'$_r$ kN | w'$_r$ kN/m | P'$_r$ kN | w'$_r$ kN/m |
| 3.0 | 0.2 | 2.68 | 0.791 | 9.63 | 1.63 | 16.5 | 2.47 |
| | 0.3 | 4.02 | 0.654 | 14.4 | 1.35 | 24.8 | 2.08 |
| | 0.4 | 5.36 | 0.528 | 19.3 | 1.10 | 33.1 | 1.71 |
| | 0.5 | 6.70 | 0.413 | 24.1 | 0.862 | 41.3 | 1.37 |
| | 0.6 | 8.04 | 0.308 | 28.9 | 0.649 | 49.6 | 1.05 |
| | 0.7 | 9.38 | 0.215 | 33.7 | 0.456 | 57.9 | 0.753 |
| | 0.8 | 10.7 | 0.132 | 38.5 | 0.283 | 66.1 | 0.479 |
| 4.0 | 0.2 | 1.30 | 0.452 | 5.86 | 0.907 | 11.9 | 1.36 |
| | 0.3 | 1.94 | 0.377 | 8.79 | 0.750 | 17.9 | 1.13 |
| | 0.4 | 2.59 | 0.307 | 11.7 | 0.605 | 23.8 | 0.919 |
| | 0.5 | 3.24 | 0.243 | 14.6 | 0.473 | 29.8 | 0.725 |
| | 0.6 | 3.89 | 0.184 | 17.6 | 0.353 | 35.8 | 0.546 |
| | 0.7 | 4.53 | 0.130 | 20.5 | 0.246 | 41.7 | 0.385 |
| | 0.8 | 5.18 | 0.081 | 23.4 | 0.152 | 47.7 | 0.240 |
| 5.0 | 0.2 | | | 3.58 | 0.583 | 8.27 | 0.862 |
| | 0.3 | | | 5.38 | 0.484 | 12.4 | 0.714 |
| | 0.4 | | | 7.17 | 0.392 | 16.5 | 0.578 |
| | 0.5 | | | 8.96 | 0.307 | 20.7 | 0.453 |
| | 0.6 | | | 10.8 | 0.230 | 24.8 | 0.339 |
| | 0.7 | | | 12.5 | 0.161 | 28.9 | 0.237 |
| | 0.8 | | | 14.3 | 0.100 | 33.1 | 0.147 |
| 6.0 | 0.2 | | | 2.28 | 0.409 | 5.70 | 0.599 |
| | 0.3 | | | 3.41 | 0.341 | 8.55 | 0.497 |
| | 0.4 | | | 4.55 | 0.277 | 11.4 | 0.402 |
| | 0.5 | | | 5.69 | 0.219 | 14.3 | 0.315 |
| | 0.6 | | | 6.83 | 0.166 | 17.1 | 0.236 |
| | 0.7 | | | 7.96 | 0.117 | 20.0 | 0.165 |
| | 0.8 | | | 9.10 | 0.073 | 22.8 | 0.102 |
| 7.0 | 0.2 | | | 1.51 | 0.303 | 3.99 | 0.443 |
| | 0.3 | | | 2.26 | 0.254 | 5.98 | 0.368 |
| | 0.4 | | | 3.02 | 0.208 | 7.98 | 0.299 |
| | 0.5 | | | 3.77 | 0.165 | 10.0 | 0.235 |
| | 0.6 | | | 4.53 | 0.126 | 12.0 | 0.177 |
| | 0.7 | | | 5.28 | 0.090 | 14.0 | 0.124 |
| | 0.8 | | | 6.04 | 0.056 | 16.0 | 0.077 |
| Q$_r$ (kN) | | 27.2 | | 42.8 | | 56.3 | |
| V$_r$ (kN) | | | 10.6 | | 13.7 | | 15.4 |
| E$_s$I x 10$^9$ N·mm$^2$ | | | 24.6 | | 95.6 | | 217 |

Notes:
1. Values of P'$_r$ are fixed percentages of the maximum compressive
   resistance, and are based on short term load duration (K$_D$ = 1.15).
2. w'$_r$ is the maximum factored uniform wind load that satisfies the
   interaction equation for each P'$_r$ value.
3. Where values are not given, C$_c$ exceeds 50.

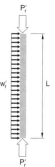

**5**

Combined Loads

# Stud Wall Selection Tables (Combined Loading)

## DF-L No.3 Stud

## Sawn Lumber

Maximum combined compressive load P′$_r$ (kN) and
lateral load w′$_r$ (kN/m) per stud

| No.3/Stud | | 38 × 89 mm | | 38 × 140 mm | | 38 × 184 mm | |
|---|---|---|---|---|---|---|---|
| L m | $\frac{P'_r}{P_r}$ | P′$_r$ kN | w′$_r$ kN/m | P′$_r$ kN | w′$_r$ kN/m | P′$_r$ kN | w′$_r$ kN/m |
| 3.0 | 0.2 | 1.60 | 0.378 | 4.30 | 0.787 | 6.41 | 1.18 |
|     | 0.3 | 2.41 | 0.319 | 6.45 | 0.672 | 9.61 | 1.02 |
|     | 0.4 | 3.21 | 0.263 | 8.60 | 0.562 | 12.8 | 0.861 |
|     | 0.5 | 4.01 | 0.211 | 10.8 | 0.457 | 16.0 | 0.706 |
|     | 0.6 | 4.81 | 0.162 | 12.9 | 0.356 | 19.2 | 0.556 |
|     | 0.7 | 5.61 | 0.117 | 15.1 | 0.260 | 22.4 | 0.410 |
|     | 0.8 | 6.42 | 0.075 | 17.2 | 0.169 | 25.6 | 0.269 |
| 4.0 | 0.2 | 0.879 | 0.213 | 3.11 | 0.436 | 5.29 | 0.656 |
|     | 0.3 | 1.32 | 0.180 | 4.67 | 0.370 | 7.94 | 0.561 |
|     | 0.4 | 1.76 | 0.149 | 6.22 | 0.307 | 10.6 | 0.470 |
|     | 0.5 | 2.20 | 0.119 | 7.78 | 0.248 | 13.2 | 0.382 |
|     | 0.6 | 2.64 | 0.092 | 9.33 | 0.191 | 15.9 | 0.298 |
|     | 0.7 | 3.08 | 0.066 | 10.9 | 0.138 | 18.5 | 0.218 |
|     | 0.8 | 3.52 | 0.042 | 12.4 | 0.089 | 21.2 | 0.142 |
| 5.0 | 0.2 | | | 2.16 | 0.278 | 4.19 | 0.415 |
|     | 0.3 | | | 3.24 | 0.235 | 6.29 | 0.353 |
|     | 0.4 | | | 4.33 | 0.194 | 8.39 | 0.294 |
|     | 0.5 | | | 5.41 | 0.156 | 10.5 | 0.237 |
|     | 0.6 | | | 6.49 | 0.120 | 12.6 | 0.184 |
|     | 0.7 | | | 7.57 | 0.087 | 14.7 | 0.134 |
|     | 0.8 | | | 8.65 | 0.055 | 16.8 | 0.086 |
| 6.0 | 0.2 | | | 1.49 | 0.193 | 3.23 | 0.287 |
|     | 0.3 | | | 2.24 | 0.163 | 4.84 | 0.243 |
|     | 0.4 | | | 2.99 | 0.135 | 6.46 | 0.201 |
|     | 0.5 | | | 3.74 | 0.109 | 8.07 | 0.162 |
|     | 0.6 | | | 4.48 | 0.084 | 9.68 | 0.125 |
|     | 0.7 | | | 5.23 | 0.060 | 11.3 | 0.090 |
|     | 0.8 | | | 5.98 | 0.039 | 12.9 | 0.058 |
| 7.0 | 0.2 | | | 1.05 | 0.142 | 2.45 | 0.210 |
|     | 0.3 | | | 1.57 | 0.121 | 3.68 | 0.178 |
|     | 0.4 | | | 2.09 | 0.100 | 4.91 | 0.147 |
|     | 0.5 | | | 2.62 | 0.080 | 6.13 | 0.118 |
|     | 0.6 | | | 3.14 | 0.062 | 7.36 | 0.091 |
|     | 0.7 | | | 3.66 | 0.045 | 8.59 | 0.066 |
|     | 0.8 | | | 4.19 | 0.029 | 9.82 | 0.042 |
| Q$_r$ (kN) | | 27.2 | | 42.8 | | 56.3 | |
| V$_r$ (kN) | | | 10.6 | | 13.7 | | 15.4 |
| E$_s$I x 10$^9$ N•mm$^2$ | | | 22.3 | | 86.9 | | 197 |

Notes:
1. Values of P′$_r$ are fixed percentages of the maximum compressive
   resistance, and are based on short term load duration (K$_D$ = 1.15).
2. w′$_r$ is the maximum factored uniform wind load that satisfies the
   interaction equation for each P′$_r$ value.
3. Where values are not given, C$_c$ exceeds 50.

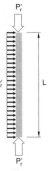

# Stud Wall Selection Tables (Combined Loading)

## Sawn Lumber

**H-F Sel**

Maximum combined compressive load P′$_r$ (kN) and
lateral load w′$_r$ (kN/m) per stud

**Select Structural**

| L m | $\dfrac{P'_r}{P_r}$ | 38 × 89 mm P′$_r$ kN | w′$_r$ kN/m | 38 × 140 mm P′$_r$ kN | w′$_r$ kN/m | 38 × 184 mm P′$_r$ kN | w′$_r$ kN/m |
|---|---|---|---|---|---|---|---|
| 3.0 | 0.2 | 3.28 | 1.25 | 11.9 | 2.57 | 20.6 | 3.91 |
|  | 0.3 | 4.92 | 1.02 | 17.9 | 2.12 | 30.9 | 3.27 |
|  | 0.4 | 6.56 | 0.819 | 23.8 | 1.70 | 41.2 | 2.68 |
|  | 0.5 | 8.20 | 0.633 | 29.8 | 1.32 | 51.5 | 2.13 |
|  | 0.6 | 9.84 | 0.467 | 35.7 | 0.985 | 61.8 | 1.62 |
|  | 0.7 | 11.5 | 0.321 | 41.7 | 0.683 | 72.1 | 1.15 |
|  | 0.8 | 13.1 | 0.194 | 47.7 | 0.418 | 82.4 | 0.724 |
| 4.0 | 0.2 | 1.58 | 0.715 | 7.20 | 1.43 | 14.8 | 2.15 |
|  | 0.3 | 2.37 | 0.593 | 10.8 | 1.17 | 22.1 | 1.77 |
|  | 0.4 | 3.16 | 0.480 | 14.4 | 0.938 | 29.5 | 1.43 |
|  | 0.5 | 3.95 | 0.376 | 18.0 | 0.725 | 36.9 | 1.11 |
|  | 0.6 | 4.74 | 0.282 | 21.6 | 0.535 | 44.3 | 0.831 |
|  | 0.7 | 5.53 | 0.197 | 25.2 | 0.368 | 51.6 | 0.578 |
|  | 0.8 | 6.32 | 0.122 | 28.8 | 0.223 | 59.0 | 0.355 |
| 5.0 | 0.2 |  |  | 4.38 | 0.922 | 10.2 | 1.36 |
|  | 0.3 |  |  | 6.58 | 0.758 | 15.3 | 1.12 |
|  | 0.4 |  |  | 8.77 | 0.609 | 20.4 | 0.896 |
|  | 0.5 |  |  | 11.0 | 0.473 | 25.4 | 0.695 |
|  | 0.6 |  |  | 13.2 | 0.351 | 30.5 | 0.514 |
|  | 0.7 |  |  | 15.3 | 0.243 | 35.6 | 0.354 |
|  | 0.8 |  |  | 17.5 | 0.148 | 40.7 | 0.216 |
| 6.0 | 0.2 |  |  | 2.78 | 0.647 | 6.99 | 0.946 |
|  | 0.3 |  |  | 4.16 | 0.535 | 10.5 | 0.778 |
|  | 0.4 |  |  | 5.55 | 0.433 | 14.0 | 0.624 |
|  | 0.5 |  |  | 6.94 | 0.339 | 17.5 | 0.484 |
|  | 0.6 |  |  | 8.33 | 0.254 | 21.0 | 0.359 |
|  | 0.7 |  |  | 9.72 | 0.177 | 24.5 | 0.248 |
|  | 0.8 |  |  | 11.1 | 0.110 | 28.0 | 0.151 |
| 7.0 | 0.2 |  |  | 1.84 | 0.480 | 4.88 | 0.699 |
|  | 0.3 |  |  | 2.76 | 0.400 | 7.31 | 0.577 |
|  | 0.4 |  |  | 3.68 | 0.326 | 9.75 | 0.465 |
|  | 0.5 |  |  | 4.60 | 0.257 | 12.2 | 0.362 |
|  | 0.6 |  |  | 5.52 | 0.194 | 14.6 | 0.270 |
|  | 0.7 |  |  | 6.43 | 0.137 | 17.1 | 0.188 |
|  | 0.8 |  |  | 7.35 | 0.085 | 19.5 | 0.115 |
| Q$_r$ (kN) |  | 17.9 |  | 28.1 |  | 37.0 |  |
| V$_r$ (kN) |  |  | 8.89 |  | 11.5 |  | 13.0 |
| E$_s$I x 10$^9$ N·mm$^2$ |  |  | 26.8 |  | 104 |  | 237 |

**5**

**Combined Loads**

Notes:
1. Values of P′$_r$ are fixed percentages of the maximum compressive resistance, and are based on short term load duration (K$_D$ = 1.15).
2. w′$_r$ is the maximum factored uniform wind load that satisfies the interaction equation for each P′$_r$ value.
3. Where values are not given, C$_c$ exceeds 50.

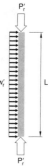

# Stud Wall Selection Tables (Combined Loading)

**H-F No.1 No.2**

## Sawn Lumber

Maximum combined compressive load P'$_r$ (kN) and
lateral load w'$_r$ (kN/m) per stud

| No.1/No.2 | | 38 × 89 mm | | 38 × 140 mm | | 38 × 184 mm | |
|---|---|---|---|---|---|---|---|
| L<br>m | $\dfrac{P'_r}{P_r}$ | P'$_r$<br>kN | w'$_r$<br>kN/m | P'$_r$<br>kN | w'$_r$<br>kN/m | P'$_r$<br>kN | w'$_r$<br>kN/m |
| 3.0 | 0.2 | 2.86 | 0.864 | 10.2 | 1.78 | 17.5 | 2.70 |
|  | 0.3 | 4.30 | 0.711 | 15.4 | 1.47 | 26.3 | 2.27 |
|  | 0.4 | 5.73 | 0.571 | 20.5 | 1.19 | 35.1 | 1.86 |
|  | 0.5 | 7.16 | 0.444 | 25.6 | 0.930 | 43.8 | 1.49 |
|  | 0.6 | 8.59 | 0.329 | 30.7 | 0.696 | 52.6 | 1.14 |
|  | 0.7 | 10.0 | 0.228 | 35.8 | 0.486 | 61.4 | 0.812 |
|  | 0.8 | 11.5 | 0.139 | 41.0 | 0.300 | 70.1 | 0.514 |
| 4.0 | 0.2 | 1.39 | 0.494 | 6.25 | 0.991 | 12.7 | 1.49 |
|  | 0.3 | 2.08 | 0.410 | 9.37 | 0.815 | 19.0 | 1.23 |
|  | 0.4 | 2.77 | 0.333 | 12.5 | 0.655 | 25.4 | 1.00 |
|  | 0.5 | 3.46 | 0.262 | 15.6 | 0.509 | 31.7 | 0.782 |
|  | 0.6 | 4.16 | 0.197 | 18.7 | 0.378 | 38.0 | 0.587 |
|  | 0.7 | 4.85 | 0.139 | 21.9 | 0.261 | 44.4 | 0.411 |
|  | 0.8 | 5.54 | 0.086 | 25.0 | 0.160 | 50.7 | 0.255 |
| 5.0 | 0.2 |  |  | 3.83 | 0.637 | 8.81 | 0.942 |
|  | 0.3 |  |  | 5.74 | 0.526 | 13.2 | 0.777 |
|  | 0.4 |  |  | 7.66 | 0.424 | 17.6 | 0.625 |
|  | 0.5 |  |  | 9.57 | 0.331 | 22.0 | 0.487 |
|  | 0.6 |  |  | 11.5 | 0.247 | 26.4 | 0.363 |
|  | 0.7 |  |  | 13.4 | 0.171 | 30.8 | 0.252 |
|  | 0.8 |  |  | 15.3 | 0.105 | 35.2 | 0.154 |
| 6.0 | 0.2 |  |  | 2.43 | 0.447 | 6.09 | 0.655 |
|  | 0.3 |  |  | 3.65 | 0.371 | 9.13 | 0.540 |
|  | 0.4 |  |  | 4.87 | 0.301 | 12.2 | 0.435 |
|  | 0.5 |  |  | 6.08 | 0.236 | 15.2 | 0.339 |
|  | 0.6 |  |  | 7.30 | 0.178 | 18.3 | 0.253 |
|  | 0.7 |  |  | 8.52 | 0.125 | 21.3 | 0.176 |
|  | 0.8 |  |  | 9.73 | 0.077 | 24.3 | 0.108 |
| 7.0 | 0.2 |  |  | 1.61 | 0.331 | 4.26 | 0.483 |
|  | 0.3 |  |  | 2.42 | 0.277 | 6.39 | 0.400 |
|  | 0.4 |  |  | 3.23 | 0.226 | 8.52 | 0.323 |
|  | 0.5 |  |  | 4.04 | 0.179 | 10.7 | 0.253 |
|  | 0.6 |  |  | 4.84 | 0.135 | 12.8 | 0.190 |
|  | 0.7 |  |  | 5.65 | 0.096 | 14.9 | 0.132 |
|  | 0.8 |  |  | 6.46 | 0.060 | 17.0 | 0.082 |
| Q$_r$ (kN) | | 17.9 | | 28.1 | | 37.0 | |
| V$_r$ (kN) | | | 8.89 | | 11.5 | | 13.0 |
| E$_s$I x 10$^9$ N•mm$^2$ | | | 24.6 | | 95.6 | | 217 |

Notes:
1. Values of P'$_r$ are fixed percentages of the maximum compressive
   resistance, and are based on short term load duration (K$_D$ = 1.15).
2. w'$_r$ is the maximum factored uniform wind load that satisfies the
   interaction equation for each P'$_r$ value.
3. Where values are not given, C$_c$ exceeds 50.

# Stud Wall Selection Tables (Combined Loading)

## Sawn Lumber

**H-F No.3 Stud**

Maximum combined compressive load P'$_r$ (kN) and
lateral load w'$_r$ (kN/m) per stud

| No.3/Stud L m | $\dfrac{P'_r}{P_r}$ | 38 × 89 mm P'$_r$ kN | 38 × 89 mm w'$_r$ kN/m | 38 × 140 mm P'$_r$ kN | 38 × 140 mm w'$_r$ kN/m | 38 × 184 mm P'$_r$ kN | 38 × 184 mm w'$_r$ kN/m |
|---|---|---|---|---|---|---|---|
| 3.0 | 0.2 | 1.98 | 0.565 | 5.94 | 1.18 | 9.27 | 1.78 |
|  | 0.3 | 2.97 | 0.473 | 8.91 | 0.994 | 13.9 | 1.52 |
|  | 0.4 | 3.96 | 0.387 | 11.9 | 0.823 | 18.5 | 1.27 |
|  | 0.5 | 4.95 | 0.307 | 14.8 | 0.661 | 23.2 | 1.04 |
|  | 0.6 | 5.94 | 0.233 | 17.8 | 0.510 | 27.8 | 0.809 |
|  | 0.7 | 6.93 | 0.165 | 20.8 | 0.368 | 32.5 | 0.592 |
|  | 0.8 | 7.92 | 0.104 | 23.8 | 0.235 | 37.1 | 0.384 |
| 4.0 | 0.2 | 1.03 | 0.320 | 4.03 | 0.652 | 7.33 | 0.981 |
|  | 0.3 | 1.54 | 0.269 | 6.04 | 0.547 | 11.0 | 0.831 |
|  | 0.4 | 2.05 | 0.221 | 8.06 | 0.449 | 14.7 | 0.689 |
|  | 0.5 | 2.57 | 0.176 | 10.1 | 0.358 | 18.3 | 0.554 |
|  | 0.6 | 3.08 | 0.134 | 12.1 | 0.273 | 22.0 | 0.428 |
|  | 0.7 | 3.60 | 0.096 | 14.1 | 0.195 | 25.6 | 0.309 |
|  | 0.8 | 4.11 | 0.061 | 16.1 | 0.123 | 29.3 | 0.198 |
| 5.0 | 0.2 |  |  | 2.66 | 0.416 | 5.53 | 0.621 |
|  | 0.3 |  |  | 3.99 | 0.349 | 8.29 | 0.522 |
|  | 0.4 |  |  | 5.32 | 0.286 | 11.1 | 0.430 |
|  | 0.5 |  |  | 6.65 | 0.227 | 13.8 | 0.343 |
|  | 0.6 |  |  | 7.98 | 0.173 | 16.6 | 0.263 |
|  | 0.7 |  |  | 9.31 | 0.123 | 19.3 | 0.188 |
|  | 0.8 |  |  | 10.6 | 0.078 | 22.1 | 0.120 |
| 6.0 | 0.2 |  |  | 1.77 | 0.290 | 4.08 | 0.429 |
|  | 0.3 |  |  | 2.66 | 0.244 | 6.11 | 0.360 |
|  | 0.4 |  |  | 3.54 | 0.200 | 8.15 | 0.296 |
|  | 0.5 |  |  | 4.43 | 0.159 | 10.2 | 0.235 |
|  | 0.6 |  |  | 5.32 | 0.122 | 12.2 | 0.180 |
|  | 0.7 |  |  | 6.20 | 0.087 | 14.3 | 0.128 |
|  | 0.8 |  |  | 7.09 | 0.055 | 16.3 | 0.081 |
| 7.0 | 0.2 |  |  | 1.21 | 0.214 | 2.99 | 0.315 |
|  | 0.3 |  |  | 1.82 | 0.181 | 4.49 | 0.265 |
|  | 0.4 |  |  | 2.42 | 0.149 | 5.99 | 0.217 |
|  | 0.5 |  |  | 3.03 | 0.119 | 7.48 | 0.173 |
|  | 0.6 |  |  | 3.63 | 0.091 | 8.98 | 0.132 |
|  | 0.7 |  |  | 4.24 | 0.065 | 10.5 | 0.094 |
|  | 0.8 |  |  | 4.84 | 0.042 | 12.0 | 0.060 |
| Q$_r$ (kN) |  | 17.9 |  | 28.1 |  | 37.0 |  |
| V$_r$ (kN) |  |  | 8.89 |  | 11.5 |  | 13.0 |
| E$_s$I x 10$^9$ N•mm$^2$ |  |  | 22.3 |  | 86.9 |  | 197 |

**5**

Combined Loads

Notes:
1. Values of P'$_r$ are fixed percentages of the maximum compressive resistance, and are based on short term load duration (K$_D$ = 1.15).
2. w'$_r$ is the maximum factored uniform wind load that satisfies the interaction equation for each P'$_r$ value.
3. Where values are not given, C$_c$ exceeds 50.

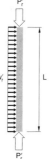

# Stud Wall Selection Tables (Combined Loading)

## S-P-F Sel

# Sawn Lumber

Maximum combined compressive load P'$_r$ (kN) and
lateral load w'$_r$ (kN/m) per stud

| Select Structural | $\frac{P'_r}{P_r}$ | 38 × 89 mm | | 38 × 140 mm | | 38 × 184 mm | |
|---|---|---|---|---|---|---|---|
| L m | | P'$_r$ kN | w'$_r$ kN/m | P'$_r$ kN | w'$_r$ kN/m | P'$_r$ kN | w'$_r$ kN/m |
| 3.0 | 0.2 | 2.85 | 1.29 | 10.1 | 2.66 | 17.3 | 4.04 |
| | 0.3 | 4.28 | 1.06 | 15.2 | 2.19 | 25.9 | 3.39 |
| | 0.4 | 5.70 | 0.846 | 20.3 | 1.77 | 34.5 | 2.78 |
| | 0.5 | 7.13 | 0.655 | 25.3 | 1.38 | 43.2 | 2.21 |
| | 0.6 | 8.55 | 0.484 | 30.4 | 1.03 | 51.8 | 1.69 |
| | 0.7 | 10.0 | 0.333 | 35.4 | 0.716 | 60.4 | 1.20 |
| | 0.8 | 11.4 | 0.202 | 40.5 | 0.440 | 69.1 | 0.761 |
| 4.0 | 0.2 | 1.38 | 0.738 | 6.20 | 1.48 | 12.5 | 2.22 |
| | 0.3 | 2.07 | 0.611 | 9.31 | 1.21 | 18.8 | 1.84 |
| | 0.4 | 2.76 | 0.495 | 12.4 | 0.972 | 25.1 | 1.48 |
| | 0.5 | 3.46 | 0.388 | 15.5 | 0.752 | 31.3 | 1.16 |
| | 0.6 | 4.15 | 0.291 | 18.6 | 0.556 | 37.6 | 0.868 |
| | 0.7 | 4.84 | 0.204 | 21.7 | 0.383 | 43.9 | 0.606 |
| | 0.8 | 5.53 | 0.126 | 24.8 | 0.232 | 50.1 | 0.374 |
| 5.0 | 0.2 | | | 3.81 | 0.951 | 8.74 | 1.41 |
| | 0.3 | | | 5.72 | 0.783 | 13.1 | 1.16 |
| | 0.4 | | | 7.62 | 0.629 | 17.5 | 0.929 |
| | 0.5 | | | 9.53 | 0.489 | 21.8 | 0.721 |
| | 0.6 | | | 11.4 | 0.363 | 26.2 | 0.535 |
| | 0.7 | | | 13.3 | 0.251 | 30.6 | 0.370 |
| | 0.8 | | | 15.2 | 0.153 | 35.0 | 0.225 |
| 6.0 | 0.2 | | | 2.43 | 0.667 | 6.05 | 0.977 |
| | 0.3 | | | 3.64 | 0.552 | 9.08 | 0.804 |
| | 0.4 | | | 4.85 | 0.447 | 12.1 | 0.645 |
| | 0.5 | | | 6.07 | 0.350 | 15.1 | 0.501 |
| | 0.6 | | | 7.28 | 0.262 | 18.2 | 0.372 |
| | 0.7 | | | 8.49 | 0.183 | 21.2 | 0.257 |
| | 0.8 | | | 9.70 | 0.113 | 24.2 | 0.157 |
| 7.0 | 0.2 | | | 1.61 | 0.495 | 4.24 | 0.722 |
| | 0.3 | | | 2.42 | 0.412 | 6.36 | 0.596 |
| | 0.4 | | | 3.22 | 0.336 | 8.49 | 0.480 |
| | 0.5 | | | 4.03 | 0.265 | 10.6 | 0.374 |
| | 0.6 | | | 4.83 | 0.200 | 12.7 | 0.279 |
| | 0.7 | | | 5.64 | 0.141 | 14.9 | 0.194 |
| | 0.8 | | | 6.45 | 0.088 | 17.0 | 0.119 |
| Q$_r$ (kN) | | 20.6 | | 32.4 | | 42.6 | |
| V$_r$ (kN) | | | 8.33 | | 10.8 | | 12.2 |
| E$_s$I x 10$^9$ N•mm$^2$ | | | 23.4 | | 91.2 | | 207 |

Notes:
1. Values of P'$_r$ are fixed percentages of the maximum compressive resistance, and are based on short term load duration (K$_D$ = 1.15).
2. w'$_r$ is the maximum factored uniform wind load that satisfies the interaction equation for each P'$_r$ value.
3. Where values are not given, C$_c$ exceeds 50.

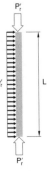

# Stud Wall Selection Tables (Combined Loading)

## Sawn Lumber

**S-P-F No.1 No.2**

Maximum combined compressive load P′$_r$ (kN) and
lateral load w′$_r$ (kN/m) per stud

| No.1/No.2 L m | $\dfrac{P'_r}{P_r}$ | 38 × 89 mm P′$_r$ kN | w′$_r$ kN/m | 38 × 140 mm P′$_r$ kN | w′$_r$ kN/m | 38 × 184 mm P′$_r$ kN | w′$_r$ kN/m |
|---|---|---|---|---|---|---|---|
| 3.0 | 0.2 | 2.42 | 0.929 | 8.35 | 1.92 | 14.0 | 2.92 |
|  | 0.3 | 3.63 | 0.766 | 12.5 | 1.59 | 21.0 | 2.46 |
|  | 0.4 | 4.84 | 0.616 | 16.7 | 1.29 | 28.0 | 2.03 |
|  | 0.5 | 6.05 | 0.480 | 20.9 | 1.02 | 35.0 | 1.62 |
|  | 0.6 | 7.26 | 0.357 | 25.0 | 0.764 | 42.0 | 1.24 |
|  | 0.7 | 8.47 | 0.247 | 29.2 | 0.537 | 49.0 | 0.893 |
|  | 0.8 | 9.67 | 0.151 | 33.4 | 0.333 | 56.0 | 0.569 |
| 4.0 | 0.2 | 1.19 | 0.530 | 5.21 | 1.07 | 10.3 | 1.60 |
|  | 0.3 | 1.78 | 0.441 | 7.81 | 0.881 | 15.5 | 1.33 |
|  | 0.4 | 2.37 | 0.358 | 10.4 | 0.709 | 20.7 | 1.08 |
|  | 0.5 | 2.96 | 0.282 | 13.0 | 0.553 | 25.8 | 0.854 |
|  | 0.6 | 3.56 | 0.212 | 15.6 | 0.412 | 31.0 | 0.644 |
|  | 0.7 | 4.15 | 0.149 | 18.2 | 0.286 | 36.1 | 0.454 |
|  | 0.8 | 4.74 | 0.093 | 20.8 | 0.176 | 41.3 | 0.283 |
| 5.0 | 0.2 |  |  | 3.24 | 0.685 | 7.30 | 1.02 |
|  | 0.3 |  |  | 4.85 | 0.566 | 11.0 | 0.840 |
|  | 0.4 |  |  | 6.47 | 0.457 | 14.6 | 0.678 |
|  | 0.5 |  |  | 8.09 | 0.357 | 18.3 | 0.530 |
|  | 0.6 |  |  | 9.71 | 0.267 | 21.9 | 0.396 |
|  | 0.7 |  |  | 11.3 | 0.186 | 25.6 | 0.276 |
|  | 0.8 |  |  | 12.9 | 0.115 | 29.2 | 0.170 |
| 6.0 | 0.2 |  |  | 2.07 | 0.480 | 5.11 | 0.704 |
|  | 0.3 |  |  | 3.11 | 0.399 | 7.66 | 0.582 |
|  | 0.4 |  |  | 4.15 | 0.324 | 10.2 | 0.470 |
|  | 0.5 |  |  | 5.19 | 0.254 | 12.8 | 0.367 |
|  | 0.6 |  |  | 6.22 | 0.191 | 15.3 | 0.274 |
|  | 0.7 |  |  | 7.26 | 0.135 | 17.9 | 0.191 |
|  | 0.8 |  |  | 8.30 | 0.084 | 20.4 | 0.118 |
| 7.0 | 0.2 |  |  | 1.38 | 0.356 | 3.61 | 0.520 |
|  | 0.3 |  |  | 2.08 | 0.297 | 5.41 | 0.431 |
|  | 0.4 |  |  | 2.77 | 0.243 | 7.22 | 0.349 |
|  | 0.5 |  |  | 3.46 | 0.192 | 9.02 | 0.273 |
|  | 0.6 |  |  | 4.15 | 0.146 | 10.8 | 0.205 |
|  | 0.7 |  |  | 4.84 | 0.103 | 12.6 | 0.143 |
|  | 0.8 |  |  | 5.54 | 0.065 | 14.4 | 0.089 |
| Q$_r$ (kN) |  | 20.6 |  | 32.4 |  | 42.6 |  |
| V$_r$ (kN) |  |  | 8.33 |  | 10.8 |  | 12.2 |
| E$_s$I x 10$^9$ N•mm$^2$ |  |  | 21.2 |  | 82.5 |  | 187 |

**5**

Combined Loads

Notes:
1. Values of P′$_r$ are fixed percentages of the maximum compressive resistance, and are based on short term load duration (K$_D$ = 1.15).
2. w′$_r$ is the maximum factored uniform wind load that satisfies the interaction equation for each P′$_r$ value.
3. Where values are not given, C$_c$ exceeds 50.

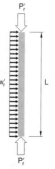

# Stud Wall Selection Tables (Combined Loading)

**S-P-F No.3 Stud**

## Sawn Lumber

Maximum combined compressive load $P'_r$ (kN) and
lateral load $w'_r$ (kN/m) per stud

| No.3/Stud | | 38 × 89 mm | | 38 × 140 mm | | 38 × 184 mm | |
|---|---|---|---|---|---|---|---|
| L m | $\dfrac{P'_r}{P_r}$ | $P'_r$ kN | $w'_r$ kN/m | $P'_r$ kN | $w'_r$ kN/m | $P'_r$ kN | $w'_r$ kN/m |
| 3.0 | 0.2 | 1.87 | 0.563 | 5.77 | 1.17 | 9.13 | 1.77 |
|  | 0.3 | 2.80 | 0.470 | 8.65 | 0.986 | 13.7 | 1.51 |
|  | 0.4 | 3.73 | 0.383 | 11.5 | 0.814 | 18.3 | 1.26 |
|  | 0.5 | 4.67 | 0.303 | 14.4 | 0.652 | 22.8 | 1.02 |
|  | 0.6 | 5.60 | 0.229 | 17.3 | 0.500 | 27.4 | 0.797 |
|  | 0.7 | 6.53 | 0.162 | 20.2 | 0.359 | 32.0 | 0.582 |
|  | 0.8 | 7.47 | 0.102 | 23.1 | 0.229 | 36.5 | 0.377 |
| 4.0 | 0.2 | 0.956 | 0.319 | 3.85 | 0.649 | 7.12 | 0.976 |
|  | 0.3 | 1.43 | 0.268 | 5.77 | 0.543 | 10.7 | 0.824 |
|  | 0.4 | 1.91 | 0.219 | 7.69 | 0.444 | 14.2 | 0.681 |
|  | 0.5 | 2.39 | 0.175 | 9.61 | 0.353 | 17.8 | 0.546 |
|  | 0.6 | 2.87 | 0.133 | 11.5 | 0.268 | 21.4 | 0.420 |
|  | 0.7 | 3.35 | 0.095 | 13.5 | 0.191 | 24.9 | 0.302 |
|  | 0.8 | 3.82 | 0.060 | 15.4 | 0.120 | 28.5 | 0.193 |
| 5.0 | 0.2 |  |  | 2.51 | 0.415 | 5.30 | 0.618 |
|  | 0.3 |  |  | 3.76 | 0.347 | 7.95 | 0.518 |
|  | 0.4 |  |  | 5.01 | 0.284 | 10.6 | 0.425 |
|  | 0.5 |  |  | 6.26 | 0.225 | 13.2 | 0.339 |
|  | 0.6 |  |  | 7.52 | 0.171 | 15.9 | 0.258 |
|  | 0.7 |  |  | 8.77 | 0.121 | 18.5 | 0.184 |
|  | 0.8 |  |  | 10.0 | 0.076 | 21.2 | 0.117 |
| 6.0 | 0.2 |  |  | 1.65 | 0.289 | 3.86 | 0.427 |
|  | 0.3 |  |  | 2.48 | 0.242 | 5.80 | 0.358 |
|  | 0.4 |  |  | 3.31 | 0.199 | 7.73 | 0.293 |
|  | 0.5 |  |  | 4.14 | 0.158 | 9.66 | 0.232 |
|  | 0.6 |  |  | 4.96 | 0.120 | 11.6 | 0.177 |
|  | 0.7 |  |  | 5.79 | 0.086 | 13.5 | 0.126 |
|  | 0.8 |  |  | 6.62 | 0.054 | 15.5 | 0.079 |
| 7.0 | 0.2 |  |  | 1.12 | 0.214 | 2.81 | 0.314 |
|  | 0.3 |  |  | 1.69 | 0.180 | 4.22 | 0.263 |
|  | 0.4 |  |  | 2.25 | 0.148 | 5.63 | 0.215 |
|  | 0.5 |  |  | 2.81 | 0.118 | 7.03 | 0.171 |
|  | 0.6 |  |  | 3.37 | 0.090 | 8.44 | 0.130 |
|  | 0.7 |  |  | 3.94 | 0.065 | 9.85 | 0.093 |
|  | 0.8 |  |  | 4.50 | 0.041 | 11.3 | 0.058 |
| $Q_r$ (kN) | | 20.6 | | 32.4 | | 42.6 | |
| $V_r$ (kN) | | | 8.33 | | 10.8 | | 12.2 |
| $E_s I \times 10^9$ N·mm² | | | 20.1 | | 78.2 | | 178 |

Notes:
1. Values of $P'_r$ are fixed percentages of the maximum compressive resistance, and are based on short term load duration ($K_D = 1.15$).
2. $w'_r$ is the maximum factored uniform wind load that satisfies the interaction equation for each $P'_r$ value.
3. Where values are not given, $C_c$ exceeds 50.

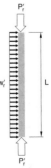

# Stud Wall Selection Tables (Combined Loading)

## Sawn Lumber

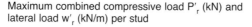

**Nor Sel**

Maximum combined compressive load P′$_r$ (kN) and
lateral load w′$_r$ (kN/m) per stud

**Select Structural**

| L m | $\frac{P'_r}{P_r}$ | 38 × 89 mm P′$_r$ kN | w′$_r$ kN/m | 38 × 140 mm P′$_r$ kN | w′$_r$ kN/m | 38 × 184 mm P′$_r$ kN | w′$_r$ kN/m |
|-----|------|------|------|------|------|------|------|
| 3.0 | 0.2 | 2.19 | 0.820 | 8.35 | 1.68 | 14.9 | 2.55 |
|     | 0.3 | 3.29 | 0.669 | 12.5 | 1.37 | 22.3 | 2.12 |
|     | 0.4 | 4.38 | 0.532 | 16.7 | 1.09 | 29.8 | 1.72 |
|     | 0.5 | 5.48 | 0.408 | 20.9 | 0.840 | 37.2 | 1.35 |
|     | 0.6 | 6.58 | 0.299 | 25.1 | 0.616 | 44.7 | 1.02 |
|     | 0.7 | 7.67 | 0.203 | 29.2 | 0.421 | 52.1 | 0.715 |
|     | 0.8 | 8.77 | 0.122 | 33.4 | 0.253 | 59.6 | 0.445 |
| 4.0 | 0.2 | 1.04 | 0.471 | 4.90 | 0.938 | 10.4 | 1.40 |
|     | 0.3 | 1.56 | 0.389 | 7.34 | 0.764 | 15.5 | 1.15 |
|     | 0.4 | 2.08 | 0.314 | 9.79 | 0.606 | 20.7 | 0.916 |
|     | 0.5 | 2.59 | 0.245 | 12.2 | 0.464 | 25.9 | 0.708 |
|     | 0.6 | 3.11 | 0.183 | 14.7 | 0.339 | 31.1 | 0.521 |
|     | 0.7 | 3.63 | 0.127 | 17.1 | 0.230 | 36.3 | 0.357 |
|     | 0.8 | 4.15 | 0.078 | 19.6 | 0.137 | 41.4 | 0.216 |
| 5.0 | 0.2 |      |       | 2.93 | 0.606 | 6.97 | 0.891 |
|     | 0.3 |      |       | 4.39 | 0.496 | 10.5 | 0.727 |
|     | 0.4 |      |       | 5.85 | 0.396 | 13.9 | 0.578 |
|     | 0.5 |      |       | 7.31 | 0.306 | 17.4 | 0.444 |
|     | 0.6 |      |       | 8.78 | 0.225 | 20.9 | 0.325 |
|     | 0.7 |      |       | 10.2 | 0.154 | 24.4 | 0.221 |
|     | 0.8 |      |       | 11.7 | 0.093 | 27.9 | 0.132 |
| 6.0 | 0.2 |      |       | 1.83 | 0.426 | 4.71 | 0.621 |
|     | 0.3 |      |       | 2.75 | 0.351 | 7.06 | 0.508 |
|     | 0.4 |      |       | 3.67 | 0.283 | 9.41 | 0.405 |
|     | 0.5 |      |       | 4.58 | 0.221 | 11.8 | 0.312 |
|     | 0.6 |      |       | 5.50 | 0.164 | 14.1 | 0.229 |
|     | 0.7 |      |       | 6.41 | 0.114 | 16.5 | 0.156 |
|     | 0.8 |      |       | 7.33 | 0.070 | 18.8 | 0.094 |
| 7.0 | 0.2 |      |       | 1.21 | 0.317 | 3.24 | 0.460 |
|     | 0.3 |      |       | 1.81 | 0.263 | 4.87 | 0.378 |
|     | 0.4 |      |       | 2.41 | 0.213 | 6.49 | 0.303 |
|     | 0.5 |      |       | 3.01 | 0.168 | 8.11 | 0.235 |
|     | 0.6 |      |       | 3.62 | 0.126 | 9.73 | 0.174 |
|     | 0.7 |      |       | 4.22 | 0.089 | 11.4 | 0.120 |
|     | 0.8 |      |       | 4.82 | 0.055 | 13.0 | 0.073 |
| Q$_r$ (kN) |  | 13.6 |      | 21.4 |      | 28.1 |      |
| V$_r$ (kN) |  |      | 7.22 |      | 9.35 |      | 10.5 |
| E$_s$I x 10$^9$ N·mm$^2$ |  |      | 16.7 |      | 65.2 |      | 148 |

**5**

**Combined Loads**

Notes:
1. Values of P′$_r$ are fixed percentages of the maximum compressive resistance, and are based on short term load duration (K$_D$ = 1.15).
2. w′$_r$ is the maximum factored uniform wind load that satisfies the interaction equation for each P′$_r$ value.
3. Where values are not given, C$_c$ exceeds 50.

# Stud Wall Selection Tables (Combined Loading)

**Nor No.1 No.2**

## Sawn Lumber

Maximum combined compressive load P′$_r$ (kN) and
lateral load w′$_r$ (kN/m) per stud

| No.1/No.2 L m | $\dfrac{P'_r}{P_r}$ | 38 × 89 mm P′$_r$ kN | w′$_r$ kN/m | 38 × 140 mm P′$_r$ kN | w′$_r$ kN/m | 38 × 184 mm P′$_r$ kN | w′$_r$ kN/m |
|---|---|---|---|---|---|---|---|
| 3.0 | 0.2 | 1.93 | 0.593 | 7.02 | 1.22 | 12.2 | 1.85 |
|     | 0.3 | 2.90 | 0.486 | 10.5 | 1.00 | 18.2 | 1.55 |
|     | 0.4 | 3.86 | 0.388 | 14.0 | 0.806 | 24.3 | 1.27 |
|     | 0.5 | 4.83 | 0.300 | 17.6 | 0.627 | 30.4 | 1.01 |
|     | 0.6 | 5.80 | 0.221 | 21.1 | 0.465 | 36.5 | 0.765 |
|     | 0.7 | 6.76 | 0.152 | 24.6 | 0.322 | 42.5 | 0.543 |
|     | 0.8 | 7.73 | 0.092 | 28.1 | 0.197 | 48.6 | 0.342 |
| 4.0 | 0.2 | 0.929 | 0.339 | 4.24 | 0.679 | 8.70 | 1.02 |
|     | 0.3 | 1.39 | 0.281 | 6.36 | 0.556 | 13.1 | 0.840 |
|     | 0.4 | 1.86 | 0.227 | 8.48 | 0.444 | 17.4 | 0.676 |
|     | 0.5 | 2.32 | 0.178 | 10.6 | 0.343 | 21.8 | 0.527 |
|     | 0.6 | 2.79 | 0.134 | 12.7 | 0.253 | 26.1 | 0.393 |
|     | 0.7 | 3.25 | 0.093 | 14.8 | 0.173 | 30.5 | 0.273 |
|     | 0.8 | 3.72 | 0.058 | 17.0 | 0.105 | 34.8 | 0.168 |
| 5.0 | 0.2 |  |  | 2.58 | 0.437 | 6.00 | 0.646 |
|     | 0.3 |  |  | 3.87 | 0.360 | 8.99 | 0.530 |
|     | 0.4 |  |  | 5.16 | 0.288 | 12.0 | 0.424 |
|     | 0.5 |  |  | 6.45 | 0.224 | 15.0 | 0.329 |
|     | 0.6 |  |  | 7.74 | 0.166 | 18.0 | 0.243 |
|     | 0.7 |  |  | 9.04 | 0.115 | 21.0 | 0.167 |
|     | 0.8 |  |  | 10.3 | 0.070 | 24.0 | 0.102 |
| 6.0 | 0.2 |  |  | 1.63 | 0.307 | 4.12 | 0.449 |
|     | 0.3 |  |  | 2.45 | 0.254 | 6.17 | 0.369 |
|     | 0.4 |  |  | 3.27 | 0.205 | 8.23 | 0.296 |
|     | 0.5 |  |  | 4.09 | 0.161 | 10.3 | 0.229 |
|     | 0.6 |  |  | 4.90 | 0.120 | 12.3 | 0.170 |
|     | 0.7 |  |  | 5.72 | 0.084 | 14.4 | 0.117 |
|     | 0.8 |  |  | 6.54 | 0.052 | 16.5 | 0.071 |
| 7.0 | 0.2 |  |  | 1.08 | 0.228 | 2.87 | 0.332 |
|     | 0.3 |  |  | 1.62 | 0.190 | 4.31 | 0.274 |
|     | 0.4 |  |  | 2.16 | 0.154 | 5.74 | 0.220 |
|     | 0.5 |  |  | 2.70 | 0.122 | 7.18 | 0.172 |
|     | 0.6 |  |  | 3.25 | 0.092 | 8.61 | 0.128 |
|     | 0.7 |  |  | 3.79 | 0.065 | 10.0 | 0.089 |
|     | 0.8 |  |  | 4.33 | 0.040 | 11.5 | 0.054 |
| Q$_r$ (kN) |  | 13.6 |  | 21.4 |  | 28.1 |  |
| V$_r$ (kN) |  |  | 7.22 |  | 9.35 |  | 10.5 |
| E$_s$I x 10$^9$ N•mm$^2$ |  |  | 15.6 |  | 60.8 |  | 138 |

Notes:
1. Values of P′$_r$ are fixed percentages of the maximum compressive
   resistance, and are based on short term load duration (K$_D$ = 1.15).
2. w′$_r$ is the maximum factored uniform wind load that satisfies the
   interaction equation for each P′$_r$ value.
3. Where values are not given, C$_c$ exceeds 50.

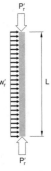

# Stud Wall Selection Tables (Combined Loading)

## Sawn Lumber

**Nor
No.3
Stud**

Maximum combined compressive load P'$_r$ (kN) and
lateral load w'$_r$ (kN/m) per stud

| No.3/Stud L m | $\dfrac{P'_r}{P_r}$ | 38 × 89 mm P'$_r$ kN | 38 × 89 mm w'$_r$ kN/m | 38 × 140 mm P'$_r$ kN | 38 × 140 mm w'$_r$ kN/m | 38 × 184 mm P'$_r$ kN | 38 × 184 mm w'$_r$ kN/m |
|---|---|---|---|---|---|---|---|
| 3.0 | 0.2 | 1.30 | 0.363 | 3.86 | 0.756 | 6.00 | 1.14 |
|  | 0.3 | 1.96 | 0.303 | 5.79 | 0.639 | 9.00 | 0.977 |
|  | 0.4 | 2.61 | 0.248 | 7.72 | 0.529 | 12.0 | 0.818 |
|  | 0.5 | 3.26 | 0.197 | 9.66 | 0.425 | 15.0 | 0.666 |
|  | 0.6 | 3.91 | 0.149 | 11.6 | 0.328 | 18.0 | 0.520 |
|  | 0.7 | 4.56 | 0.106 | 13.5 | 0.236 | 21.0 | 0.381 |
|  | 0.8 | 5.21 | 0.066 | 15.4 | 0.151 | 24.0 | 0.247 |
| 4.0 | 0.2 | 0.680 | 0.206 | 2.64 | 0.419 | 4.76 | 0.631 |
|  | 0.3 | 1.02 | 0.172 | 3.96 | 0.352 | 7.15 | 0.534 |
|  | 0.4 | 1.36 | 0.141 | 5.28 | 0.288 | 9.53 | 0.443 |
|  | 0.5 | 1.70 | 0.113 | 6.60 | 0.230 | 11.9 | 0.356 |
|  | 0.6 | 2.04 | 0.086 | 7.92 | 0.175 | 14.3 | 0.275 |
|  | 0.7 | 2.38 | 0.061 | 9.24 | 0.125 | 16.7 | 0.199 |
|  | 0.8 | 2.72 | 0.039 | 10.6 | 0.079 | 19.1 | 0.127 |
| 5.0 | 0.2 |  |  | 1.75 | 0.267 | 3.61 | 0.399 |
|  | 0.3 |  |  | 2.63 | 0.224 | 5.42 | 0.336 |
|  | 0.4 |  |  | 3.50 | 0.183 | 7.23 | 0.276 |
|  | 0.5 |  |  | 4.38 | 0.146 | 9.04 | 0.221 |
|  | 0.6 |  |  | 5.26 | 0.111 | 10.8 | 0.169 |
|  | 0.7 |  |  | 6.13 | 0.079 | 12.6 | 0.121 |
|  | 0.8 |  |  | 7.01 | 0.050 | 14.5 | 0.077 |
| 6.0 | 0.2 |  |  | 1.17 | 0.186 | 2.68 | 0.276 |
|  | 0.3 |  |  | 1.76 | 0.156 | 4.02 | 0.231 |
|  | 0.4 |  |  | 2.34 | 0.128 | 5.35 | 0.190 |
|  | 0.5 |  |  | 2.93 | 0.102 | 6.69 | 0.151 |
|  | 0.6 |  |  | 3.51 | 0.078 | 8.03 | 0.115 |
|  | 0.7 |  |  | 4.10 | 0.056 | 9.37 | 0.082 |
|  | 0.8 |  |  | 4.69 | 0.035 | 10.7 | 0.052 |
| 7.0 | 0.2 |  |  | 0.803 | 0.138 | 1.97 | 0.202 |
|  | 0.3 |  |  | 1.20 | 0.116 | 2.96 | 0.170 |
|  | 0.4 |  |  | 1.61 | 0.095 | 3.95 | 0.139 |
|  | 0.5 |  |  | 2.01 | 0.076 | 4.93 | 0.111 |
|  | 0.6 |  |  | 2.41 | 0.058 | 5.92 | 0.084 |
|  | 0.7 |  |  | 2.81 | 0.042 | 6.91 | 0.060 |
|  | 0.8 |  |  | 3.21 | 0.027 | 7.89 | 0.038 |
| Qr (kN) |  | 13.6 |  | 21.4 |  | 28.1 |  |
| Vr (kN) |  |  | 7.22 |  | 9.35 |  | 10.5 |
| Esl x 109 N mm2 |  |  | 14.5 |  | 56.5 |  | 128 |

**5**

**Combined Loads**

Notes:
1. Values of P'$_r$ are fixed percentages of the maximum compressive resistance, and are based on short term load duration ($K_D$ = 1.15).
2. w'$_r$ is the maximum factored uniform wind load that satisfies the interaction equation for each P'$_r$ value.
3. Where values are not given, $C_c$ exceeds 50.

# Bearing

Large reactions require significant bearing connections. The effects of any eccentricities at these connections must be reviewed.

The length of bearing required for both the supporting and supported member must be investigated in a connection such as this.

# 6.1     General Information

The following sections contain design information for wood members subjected to bearing stress. Bearing, or compression perpendicular to grain stress, occurs at the supported ends of bending members and under concentrated loads. Steel bearing plates are often used in many beam-to-column, beam-to-support, and beam-to-beam connections (refer to Section 7.11). This section provides design information for cantilevered bearing plates, plates supported on two sides and plates supported on three sides.

**6**

Bearing

# 6.2 Bearing Resistance of Wood

## Bearing Perpendicular to Grain

Wood members subjected to compression perpendicular to grain must be designed to satisfy the following criteria:

For bearing under the effect of all factored applied loads:

Factored compressive resistance perpendicular to grain under all factored applied loads $Q_r \geq$ factored compressive force $Q_f$

For bearing under the effect of loads applied only near a support:

Factored compressive resistance perpendicular to grain near a support $Q'_r \geq$ factored compressive force $Q_f$

$Q_r$ and $Q'_r$ may be determined as follows:

1. Effect of all applied loads:

$$Q_r = q_r L_b$$

where:

$q_r$ = factored compressive resistance perpendicular to grain per mm of bearing length given in the Bearing Selection Tables (kN/mm)

$L_b$ = bearing length (mm)

2. Effect of loads near a support only:

$$Q'_r = \frac{2\,q_r\,L'_b}{3}$$

where:

$q_r$ = factored compressive resistance perpendicular to grain per mm of bearing length given in the Bearing Selection Tables

$L'_b$ = average bearing length (see Figure 6.1)

Note: This case applies only to loads located within a distance from the centre of the support equal to the depth of the member (see Figure 6.1).

6

Bearing

Figure 6.1
**Loads applied
near support**

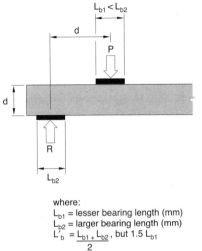

where:
$L_{b1}$ = lesser bearing length (mm)
$L_{b2}$ = larger bearing length (mm)
$L'_b = \dfrac{L_{b1} + L_{b2}}{2}$, but 1.5 $L_{b1}$

## Bearing at an Angle to Grain

Where wood members are subjected to compression at an angle to the grain, the compressive resistance $N_r$ may be determined as follows:

$$N_r = \frac{P_r Q_r}{P_r \sin^2 \theta + Q_r \cos^2 \theta}$$

where:

$Q_r$ = factored compressive resistance perpendicular to grain (kN)

$P_r$ = factored compressive resistance parallel to grain (kN)
(see Chapter 3)

$\theta$ = angle of load to grain (degrees)

## Modification Factors

The tabulated values are based upon the following formulae and modification factors. When using the tables, be certain that the member conforms exactly with the modification factors used in the tables; if not, use the factors below to make the necessary adjustments.

For all applied loads, including loads applied near a support (for sawn lumber and glulam):

$$q_r = \phi\, F_{cp}\, b \text{ (N/mm)}$$

$$\phi\, F_{cp} = \phi\, f_{cp}\, (K_D\, K_{Scp}\, K_T\, K_B\, K_{Zcp})$$

where:

$\phi$ = 0.8

$f_{cp}$ = specified strength in compression perpendicular to grain (MPa)

$b$ = width of beam (mm)

**$K_D$** is a load duration factor. The tabulated resistances are based on a "standard" term load, which includes the effects of dead loads plus live loads due to use and occupancy and snow loads ($K_D = 1.0$). For members intended to support permanent loads the tabulated resistances must be multiplied by 0.65. For members supporting short term loads such as wind and earthquake, the tabulated values may be multiplied by 1.15.

**$K_{Scp}$** is a service condition factor. The tabulated values are based on dry service ($K_{Scp} = 1.0$). For wet service conditions, multiply the tabulated values by 0.67 for both sawn lumber and glulam.

**$K_T$** is a treatment factor. The tabulated resistances are based on material that is either untreated or treated with a non-strength reducing chemical ($K_T = 1.0$). Most wood preservatives do not reduce strength unless the lumber has been incised. However, most fire retardants will reduce strength. If the material is treated with a fire retardant or if it is incised prior to treatment, multiply the tabulated values by the appropriate $K_T$ factor given in Table 6.1.

6

Bearing

Table 6.1
**Treatment factor $K_T$**

| Treatment type | Sawn lumber of thickness 89 mm or less | | Sawn lumber greater than 89 mm in thickness & glulam |
|---|---|---|---|
| | Dry service | Wet service | Dry or wet service |
| Preservative treated, incised | 0.75 | 0.85 | 1.0 |
| Fire retardant treatment | refer to Commentary | | |

$K_B$ is a length of bearing factor. The tabulated resistances have been developed for bearing at the end of a member (bearing area located within 75 mm from end of member) or in a area of relatively high bending stresses ($K_B = 1.0$). For other conditions, designers may multiply the tabulated resistances by the appropriate $K_B$ factor shown in Figure 6.2.

Figure 6.2
**Length of bearing factor $K_B$**

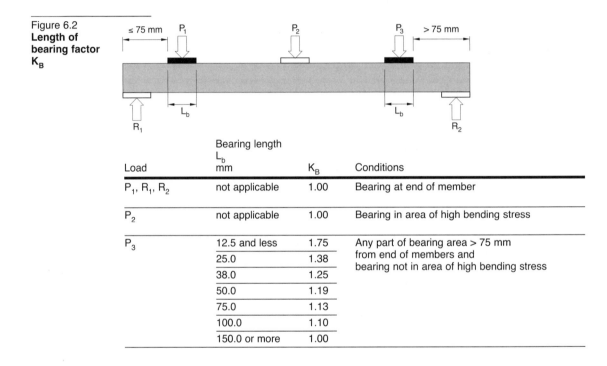

| Load | Bearing length $L_b$ mm | $K_B$ | Conditions |
|---|---|---|---|
| $P_1$, $R_1$, $R_2$ | not applicable | 1.00 | Bearing at end of member |
| $P_2$ | not applicable | 1.00 | Bearing in area of high bending stress |
| $P_3$ | 12.5 and less | 1.75 | Any part of bearing area > 75 mm from end of members and bearing not in area of high bending stress |
| | 25.0 | 1.38 | |
| | 38.0 | 1.25 | |
| | 50.0 | 1.19 | |
| | 75.0 | 1.13 | |
| | 100.0 | 1.10 | |
| | 150.0 or more | 1.00 | |

$K_{Zcp}$ is a size factor for bearing. It reflects the member width to member depth ratio. The tabulated resistances are based on ratios equal to 1.0 or less ($K_{Zcp} = 1.0$). For other conditions, the designers may multiply the tabulated values by the $K_{Zcp}$ factor given in Table 6.2. For Glulam, the depth is equal to the thickness of lamination.

Table 6.2
**Size factor for bearing $K_{Zcp}$**

| Member width / member depth [1] | $K_{Zcp}$ |
|---|---|
| 1.0 or less | 1.0 |
| 2.0 or greater | 1.15 |

Note:
1. For intermediate ratios, interpolation may be applied

# Checklist: **Bearing** ✔

To verify that the tabulated $q_r$ and $\phi\, F_{cp}$ values are appropriate for the structure being designed, the following questions should be asked (the appropriate modification factor is given in brackets):

1. Is the load duration "standard" ($K_D$)?

2. Is the service condition "dry" ($K_{Scp}$)?

3. Is the material free of incisions and/or strength reducing chemicals ($K_T$)?

4. Is the bearing area at the end of a member or in an area of high bending stress ($K_B$)?

5. Is the member width to member depth ratio less than or equal to 1.0 ($K_{Zcp}$)?

If the answer to any of these questions is no, refer to the description of modification factors and make the necessary adjustments to the tabulated values.Otherwise, the Bearing Selection Tables may be used directly.

6

Bearing

# Bearing Selection Tables

## Sawn Lumber

| Species | Factored compressive resistance perpendicular to grain per mm of bearing length $q_r$ (kN/mm) | | | | | | | | Factored compressive strength perpendicular to grain $\phi F_{cp}$ |
|---|---|---|---|---|---|---|---|---|---|
| | Width of beam mm | | | | | | | | |
| | 38 | 64 | 89 | 114 | 140 | 191 | 241 | 292 | MPa |
| D.Fir-L | 0.213 | 0.358 | 0.498 | 0.638 | 0.784 | 1.07 | 1.35 | 1.64 | 5.60 |
| Hem-Fir | 0.140 | 0.236 | 0.328 | 0.420 | 0.515 | 0.703 | 0.887 | 1.07 | 3.68 |
| S-P-F | 0.161 | 0.271 | 0.377 | 0.483 | 0.594 | 0.900 | 1.02 | 1.24 | 4.24 |
| Northern | 0.106 | 0.179 | 0.249 | 0.319 | 0.392 | 0.535 | 0.675 | 0.818 | 2.80 |

Note:
$q_r$ does not vary with grade.

## Glulam

| Species | Factored compressive resistance perpendicular to grain per mm of bearing length $q_r$ (kN/mm) | | | | | | | Factored compressive strength perpendicular to grain $\phi F_{cp}$ |
|---|---|---|---|---|---|---|---|---|
| | Width of beam mm | | | | | | | |
| | 80 | 130 | 175 | 215 | 265 | 315 | 365 | MPa |
| D.Fir-L | 0.448 | 0.728 | 0.980 | 1.20 | 1.48 | 1.76 | 2.04 | 5.60 |
| Spruce-Pine | 0.371 | 0.603 | 0.812 | 0.998 | 1.23 | 1.46 | 1.69 | 4.64 |

Note:
1.  For Hem-Fir 24f-E glulam bearing on tension face, use D.Fir-L values.
    For bearing on compression face, $\phi F_{cp}$ = 3.68 MPa.
2.  For Hem-Fir 24f-Ex glulam bearing on compression or tension face use D.Fir-L values.

# 6.3    Bearing Plates

The Bearing Plate Selection Tables provide the required steel plate thickness for cantilevered bearing plates, plates supported on two sides and plates supported on three sides. The tables are based on the use of CSA G40.21 Grade 300W steel ($F_y$ = 300 MPa).

The thicknesses are calculated so that the factored moment due to bearing pressure ($\phi\, F_{cp}$) does not exceed the moment resistance of the steel plate based on the plastic section modulus. In addition, the thickness of cantilevered plates was not permitted to be less than 1/5 of the length of the overhang for deflection. The length of the overhang should also be limited to that shown in the figure below each table so that the compressive resistance of the column is not exceeded.

The tabulated plate thicknesses were obtained by rounding up the calculated thicknesses to the nearest first or second preference size listed in CAN3-G312.1.

**6**

Bearing

### Example 1: Bearing Plates

Determine the required bearing length for a 130 × 304 mm 20f-E Spruce-Pine glulam beam on a beam hanger with a factored reaction of 30 kN. Also determine the bearing plate thickness required for the beam hanger. The plate is to be supported on two sides. The conditions are:

- standard load duration
- dry service
- untreated

### Calculation

$Q_f$ = 30 kN

$q_r$ = 0.603 kN/mm from Bearing Selection Tables

$$L_{b\ req'd} = \frac{Q_f}{q_r} = \frac{30}{0.603}$$

$$= 49.8 \text{ mm}$$

Therefore, use a bearing length of 50 mm.

From Bearing Plate Selection Tables, the required thickness of steel plate is 14 mm.

**Use 50 mm bearing length and 14 mm steel bearing plate.**

# Bearing Plate Selection Tables

| CP | **Cantilevered Plate** |
| --- | --- |

| | Minimum bearing plate thickness mm | |
| --- | --- | --- |
| Overhang (a) mm | D. Fir-L sawn lumber and glulam | All other species |
| 25 | 6 | 5 |
| 30 | 7 | 6 |
| 35 | 8 | 7 |
| 40 | 9 | 8 |
| 45 | 10 | 9 |
| 50 | 11 | 10 |
| 55 | 12 | 11 |
| 60 | 14 | 12 |
| 65 | 14 | 14 |
| 70 | 16 | 14 |
| 75 | 16 | 16 |
| 80 | 18 | 16 |
| 85 | 18 | 18 |
| 90 | 20 | 18 |
| 95 | 20 | 20 |
| 100 | 22 | 20 |
| 105 | 22 | 22 |
| 110 | 25 | 22 |
| 115 | 25 | 25 |
| 120 | 25 | 25 |
| 125 | 28 | 25 |
| 130 | 28 | 28 |
| 135 | 28 | 28 |
| 140 | 30 | 28 |
| 145 | 30 | 30 |
| 150 | 32 | 30 |

Notes:
1. Thickness limited to 0.2 × overhang
2. Maximum overhang "a" should be limited to the values shown below.
3. Values assume full bearing pressure.

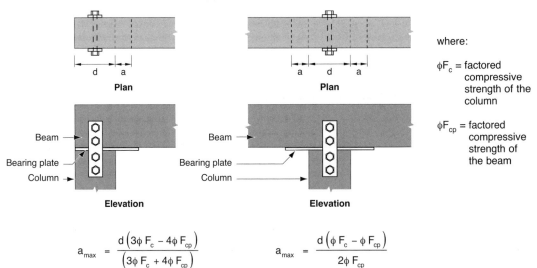

**Plan**      **Plan**

Beam
Bearing plate
Column

Beam
Bearing plate
Column

**Elevation**      **Elevation**

where:

$\phi F_c$ = factored compressive strength of the column

$\phi F_{cp}$ = factored compressive strength of the beam

$$a_{max} = \frac{d\left(3\phi F_c - 4\phi F_{cp}\right)}{\left(3\phi F_c + 4\phi F_{cp}\right)}$$

$$a_{max} = \frac{d\left(\phi F_c - \phi F_{cp}\right)}{2\phi F_{cp}}$$

# Bearing Plate Selection Tables

## Plate Supported Two Sides

**P-2S**

| Purlin width (b) mm | Minimum bearing plate thickness mm | | | |
|---|---|---|---|---|
| | D.Fir-L | Hem-Fir | S-P-F | Northern |
| **Sawn Lumber** | | | | |
| 64 | 7 | 6 | 6 | 5 |
| 89 | 10 | 8 | 9 | 7 |
| 140 | 16 | 12 | 14 | 11 |
| 191 | 20 | 18 | 18 | 14 |
| 241 | 25 | 22 | 22 | 18 |
| 292 | 32 | 25 | 28 | 22 |

| Purlin width (b) mm | | | | |
|---|---|---|---|---|
| | D.Fir-L | Spruce-Pine | | |
| **Glulam** | | | | |
| 80 | 9 | 8 | | |
| 130 | 14 | 14 | | |
| 175 | 20 | 18 | | |
| 215 | 25 | 22 | | |
| 265 | 28 | 25 | | |

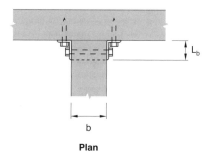

**Plan**

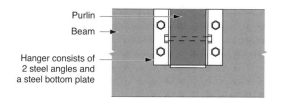

Purlin
Beam
Hanger consists of 2 steel angles and a steel bottom plate

**Elevation**

6

Bearing

# Bearing Plate Selection Tables

## P-3S  Plate Supported Three Sides

| Species / Sawn lumber | Purlin width (b) mm | Minimum plate thickness mm — Bearing length $L_b$ (mm) | | | | | | | | | | | |
|---|---|---|---|---|---|---|---|---|---|---|---|---|---|
| | | 40 | 50 | 60 | 70 | 80 | 90 | 100 | 110 | 120 | 130 | 140 | 150 |
| D.Fir-L | 64 | 6 | 6 | 7 | 7 | 7 | 7 | 7 | 7 | 7 | 7 | 7 | 7 |
| | 89 | 6 | 7 | 8 | 9 | 9 | 9 | 9 | 10 | 10 | 10 | 10 | 10 |
| | 140 | 8 | 9 | 10 | 10 | 11 | 12 | 14 | 14 | 14 | 14 | 14 | 14 |
| | 191 | 9 | 10 | 11 | 12 | 14 | 14 | 14 | 16 | 16 | 18 | 18 | 18 |
| | 241 | 10 | 11 | 12 | 14 | 14 | 16 | 16 | 18 | 18 | 18 | 20 | 20 |
| | 292 | 11 | 12 | 14 | 16 | 16 | 16 | 18 | 18 | 20 | 20 | 20 | 22 |
| Hem-Fir | 64 | 5 | 5 | 6 | 6 | 6 | 6 | 6 | 6 | 6 | 6 | 6 | 6 |
| | 89 | 5 | 6 | 7 | 7 | 7 | 8 | 8 | 8 | 8 | 8 | 8 | 8 |
| | 140 | 6 | 7 | 8 | 8 | 9 | 10 | 10 | 11 | 11 | 11 | 12 | 12 |
| | 191 | 7 | 8 | 9 | 10 | 10 | 11 | 12 | 12 | 14 | 14 | 14 | 14 |
| | 241 | 8 | 9 | 10 | 11 | 12 | 12 | 14 | 14 | 14 | 16 | 16 | 16 |
| | 292 | 9 | 10 | 11 | 12 | 14 | 14 | 14 | 16 | 16 | 16 | 18 | 18 |
| S-P-F | 64 | 5 | 6 | 6 | 6 | 6 | 6 | 6 | 6 | 7 | 7 | 7 | 7 |
| | 89 | 6 | 6 | 7 | 7 | 8 | 8 | 8 | 8 | 9 | 9 | 9 | 9 |
| | 140 | 7 | 8 | 8 | 9 | 10 | 10 | 11 | 11 | 12 | 12 | 12 | 14 |
| | 191 | 8 | 9 | 10 | 10 | 11 | 12 | 12 | 14 | 14 | 14 | 16 | 16 |
| | 241 | 9 | 10 | 11 | 12 | 12 | 14 | 14 | 14 | 16 | 16 | 18 | 18 |
| | 292 | 10 | 11 | 12 | 14 | 14 | 14 | 16 | 16 | 18 | 18 | 18 | 20 |
| Northern | 64 | 4 | 5 | 5 | 5 | 5 | 5 | 5 | 5 | 5 | 5 | 5 | 5 |
| | 89 | 5 | 5 | 6 | 6 | 6 | 7 | 7 | 7 | 7 | 7 | 7 | 7 |
| | 140 | 6 | 6 | 7 | 7 | 8 | 9 | 9 | 9 | 10 | 10 | 10 | 10 |
| | 191 | 7 | 7 | 8 | 9 | 9 | 10 | 10 | 11 | 11 | 12 | 12 | 14 |
| | 241 | 7 | 8 | 9 | 10 | 10 | 11 | 11 | 12 | 12 | 14 | 14 | 14 |
| | 292 | 8 | 9 | 10 | 10 | 11 | 12 | 12 | 14 | 14 | 14 | 16 | 16 |
| **Glulam** | | | | | | | | | | | | | |
| D.Fir-L | 80 | 6 | 7 | 8 | 8 | 8 | 9 | 9 | 9 | 9 | 9 | 9 | 9 |
| | 130 | 8 | 8 | 9 | 10 | 11 | 12 | 12 | 14 | 14 | 14 | 14 | 14 |
| | 175 | 9 | 10 | 11 | 11 | 12 | 14 | 14 | 16 | 16 | 16 | 16 | 18 |
| | 215 | 10 | 11 | 12 | 14 | 14 | 14 | 16 | 16 | 18 | 18 | 18 | 20 |
| | 265 | 11 | 12 | 14 | 14 | 16 | 16 | 18 | 18 | 18 | 20 | 20 | 20 |
| Spruce-Pine | 80 | 6 | 6 | 7 | 7 | 8 | 8 | 8 | 8 | 8 | 8 | 8 | 8 |
| | 130 | 7 | 8 | 8 | 9 | 10 | 11 | 11 | 11 | 11 | 12 | 12 | 12 |
| | 175 | 8 | 9 | 10 | 10 | 11 | 12 | 14 | 14 | 14 | 14 | 16 | 16 |
| | 215 | 9 | 10 | 11 | 11 | 12 | 14 | 14 | 16 | 16 | 16 | 18 | 18 |
| | 265 | 10 | 11 | 12 | 14 | 14 | 14 | 16 | 16 | 16 | 18 | 18 | 20 |

Note: The bearing plate is supported on three sides, on third side by weld to back plate.

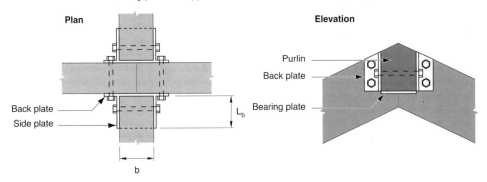

Plan — Back plate, Side plate, $L_b$, b

Elevation — Purlin, Back plate, Bearing plate

# Fastenings

**7**

The selection of fastener type for exposed applications will include architectural considerations as well as structural requirements. Here, connections are used to add interest and texture to the glulam purlins and trusses.

*Top left:*
Shear plates
are seated
in grooves
machined by a
special dapping
tool which may
be rented on
a job-by-job
basis.

*Top right:*
Loads are
transferred from
the steel side
plates to the
bolts, then by
bearing to the
flanges of the
shear plates
embedded
in the wood
member.

*Bottom left:*
Split rings are
set in grooves
machined in
opposing faces
of the wood
members,
similar to
shear plates.

*Bottom right:*
Attention must
be paid to end
and edge
distances as
well as connec-
tor spacing in
the design of
both shear
plates and split
rings. Large
washers must
be used with
the bolts to
clamp the
assembly.

The connection of members such as these ribs of a domed roof include a welded compression ring, which is detailed to facilitate the installation of fasteners.

The peak connection of these glulam trusses utilizes split rings in the wood members and a bearing weldment to be installed between abutting chords. The bearing weldment is used to prevent locking of end grain which may lead to splitting.

The timber rivet is a "flattened oval" nail driven through 7 mm diameter pre-drilled holes in steel side plates. This photograph is of a section cut through the rivet hole, and shows the rivet at various stages of penetration and final seating.

Timber rivets are used to provide efficient, compact connections such as this beam hanger.

A wide range of stock hangers is available, but custom hangers may be required for special loadings or member configurations. Hangers may be either top mounted *(above)* or face mounted *(below)*.

Modern timber
connectors can
be readily
concealed,
providing the
appearance
of traditional
timber framing.

Photo credit: Danny Signer

# 7.1 General Information

### Types of Fasteners

This section provides design information for the following fasteners:

- nails and spikes
- bolts
- drift pins
- lag screws
- timber rivets
- shear plates and split rings
- truss plates
- joist hangers
- framing anchors

Note that some of the symbols used in Chapter 7 differ from those used in CSA O86.

### Connection Geometry

#### Spacing, End and Edge Distance
The arrangement of fasteners in a connection is defined in terms of end distance, edge distance and spacing as shown in Figure 7.1. CSA O86 defines spacing differently depending on the particular fastener.

Figure 7.1
**Connection geometry**

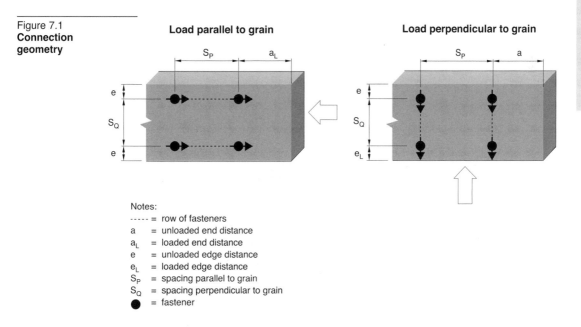

Notes:
- ----- = row of fasteners
- a    = unloaded end distance
- $a_L$   = loaded end distance
- e    = unloaded edge distance
- $e_L$   = loaded edge distance
- $S_P$   = spacing parallel to grain
- $S_Q$   = spacing perpendicular to grain
- ● = fastener

**7**

**Fastenings**

## Rows of Fasteners

A row is defined as one or more bolts, lag screws, shear plates or split rings aligned in the direction of the load (see Figure 7.1). When fasteners are used in staggered lines, the number of rows should be determined as shown in Figure 7.2.

Figure 7.2
**Staggered
lines of
fasteners**

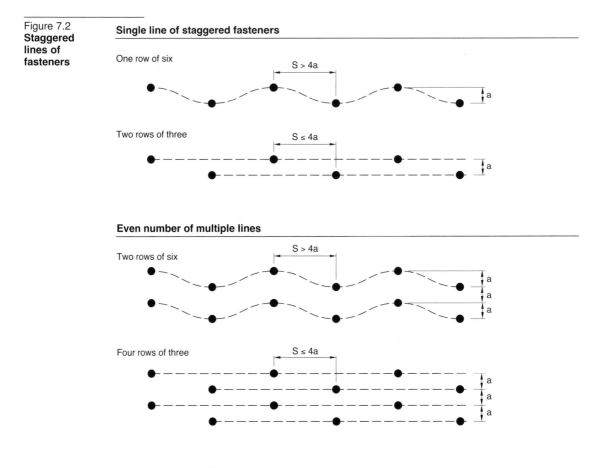

**Single line of staggered fasteners**

One row of six

$S > 4a$

$a$

Two rows of three

$S \leq 4a$

$a$

**Even number of multiple lines**

Two rows of six

$S > 4a$

$a$
$a$
$a$

Four rows of three

$S \leq 4a$

$a$
$a$
$a$

**Odd number of multiple lines**

One row of six and one row of three (where total capacity = lowest fastener capacity × number of
fasteners in joint) or three rows of three (whichever has the least factored resistance)

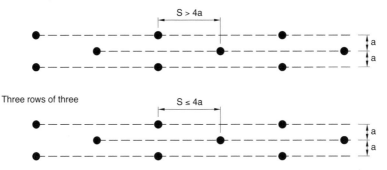

$S > 4a$

$a$
$a$

Three rows of three

$S \leq 4a$

$a$
$a$

## General Design Considerations

### Loading at an Angle to Grain

The lateral resistance of most fasteners depends upon the angle of load to grain. The angle is 0° when the load is parallel to grain, and 90° when the load is perpendicular to grain. Loading at an intermediate angle to grain may be calculated from the following empirical equation:

$$N_r = \frac{P_r Q_r}{P_r \sin^2 \theta + Q_r \cos^2 \theta}$$

where:

$N_r$ = factored resistance at an angle $\theta$ to grain

$P_r$ = factored resistance parallel to grain

$Q_r$ = factored resistance perpendicular to grain

$\theta$ = angle between grain direction and direction of load

$N_r$ may also be determined from Table 7.1.

### Service Condition Factors

The service condition factors for each of the connections reflect two aspects of connection resistance that may be affected by service conditions and the moisture content of the wood material. First, wood is generally weaker when wet so wood connections used in wet service conditions will have less resistance than those used in dry service conditions.

Second, when fasteners are installed in wood that will dry in service or where wood moisture contents fluctuate seasonally, shrinkage damage may occur. Wood has low resistance to tension forces perpendicular to the grain and splitting may occur when wood is restrained from moving across the grain. In fastenings, shrinkage damage may result in splits at the connections. Adopting good connection details, such as those illustrated in Section 7.11, will help to eliminate splitting at connections.

**7**

Fastenings

Table 7.1
**Coefficient of resistance X for loading at an angle to grain**

| Angle of load to grain $\theta°$ | $Q_r/P_r$ | | | | | | | | |
|---|---|---|---|---|---|---|---|---|---|
| | 0.2 | 0.3 | 0.4 | 0.5 | 0.6 | 0.7 | 0.8 | 0.9 | 1 |
| 0 | 1 | 1 | 1 | 1 | 1 | 1 | 1 | 1 | 1 |
| 5 | 0.97 | 0.98 | 0.99 | 0.99 | 0.99 | 1 | 1 | 1 | 1 |
| 10 | 0.89 | 0.93 | 0.96 | 0.97 | 0.98 | 0.99 | 0.99 | 1 | 1 |
| 15 | 0.79 | 0.86 | 0.91 | 0.94 | 0.96 | 0.97 | 0.98 | 0.99 | 1 |
| 20 | 0.68 | 0.79 | 0.85 | 0.90 | 0.93 | 0.95 | 0.97 | 0.99 | 1 |
| 25 | 0.58 | 0.71 | 0.79 | 0.85 | 0.89 | 0.93 | 0.96 | 0.98 | 1 |
| 30 | 0.50 | 0.63 | 0.73 | 0.80 | 0.86 | 0.90 | 0.94 | 0.97 | 1 |
| 35 | 0.43 | 0.57 | 0.67 | 0.75 | 0.82 | 0.88 | 0.92 | 0.96 | 1 |
| 40 | 0.38 | 0.51 | 0.62 | 0.71 | 0.78 | 0.85 | 0.91 | 0.96 | 1 |
| 45 | 0.33 | 0.46 | 0.57 | 0.67 | 0.75 | 0.82 | 0.89 | 0.95 | 1 |
| 50 | 0.30 | 0.42 | 0.53 | 0.63 | 0.72 | 0.80 | 0.87 | 0.94 | 1 |
| 55 | 0.27 | 0.39 | 0.50 | 0.60 | 0.69 | 0.78 | 0.86 | 0.93 | 1 |
| 60 | 0.25 | 0.36 | 0.47 | 0.57 | 0.67 | 0.76 | 0.84 | 0.92 | 1 |
| 65 | 0.23 | 0.34 | 0.45 | 0.55 | 0.65 | 0.74 | 0.83 | 0.92 | 1 |
| 70 | 0.22 | 0.33 | 0.43 | 0.53 | 0.63 | 0.73 | 0.82 | 0.91 | 1 |
| 75 | 0.21 | 0.31 | 0.42 | 0.52 | 0.62 | 0.71 | 0.81 | 0.91 | 1 |
| 80 | 0.20 | 0.31 | 0.41 | 0.51 | 0.61 | 0.71 | 0.80 | 0.90 | 1 |
| 85 | 0.20 | 0.30 | 0.40 | 0.50 | 0.60 | 0.70 | 0.80 | 0.90 | 1 |
| 90 | 0.20 | 0.30 | 0.40 | 0.50 | 0.60 | 0.70 | 0.80 | 0.90 | 1 |

Note:
Determine the resistance at an angle to grain $N_r$ as follows:
a) Calculate $Q_r/P_r$ = Perpendicular to grain resistance/Parallel to grain resistance.
b) Select coefficient X for given $Q_r/P_r$ ratio and angle $\theta$.
c) $N_r = X P_r$

## Shear Effects Due to Joint Configuration

Where a fastener or group of fasteners exerts a shear force on a member, such as an eccentric connection or where a connection supports a wood member, the factored shear resistance of the member must be checked using the dimension $d_e$ rather than the full depth as shown in Figure 7.3. The shear depth $d_e$ is the distance from the extremity of the fastener or group of fasteners to the loaded edge of the member.

To obtain the factored shear resistance of a member based on $d_e$, multiply the tabulated resistances given in Chapter 2 by the ratio $d_e/d$ where d is the actual depth of the member. Be sure to review the checklist for the particular table and make any other necessary modifications to the tabulated shear resistance.

The factored shear resistance at the connection must be greater than the factored shear stress in the member at the connection. For bending members, the shear force at the connection can be obtained from the shear force diagram.

Figure 7.3
**Shear depth $d_e$**

**7**

**Fastenings**

**Shear plates and split rings**

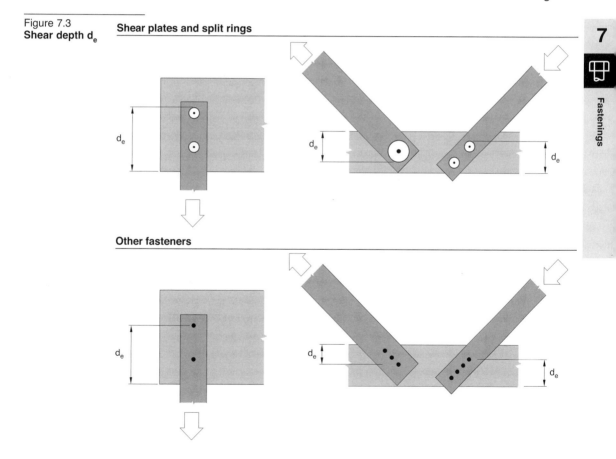

**Other fasteners**

Note: Suspending loads from the lower portion of a beam is not recommended, regardless of the shear depth provided. (See detail 7.51 for the preferred method.)

## Net Area

Members that have been drilled or bored must be designed using the net cross-sectional area. The net area $A_N$ is calculated as follows:

$$A_N = A_G - A_R$$

where:

$A_G$ = gross cross-sectional area

$A_R$ = area removed due to drilling, boring, grooving or other means
$A_R$ must not exceed $0.25\,A_G$

Only the following fasteners are considered to cause an area reduction:

- split rings
- shear plates
- bolts
- lag screws
- drift pins

The area reduction due to bolt, lag screw or drift pin holes is equal to the diameter of the hole multiplied by the thickness of the member. Table 7.2 contains area reduction information for shear plates and split rings.

Where staggered rows of fasteners are used, adjacent fasteners must be considered to occur at the same cross-sectional plane when the centre-to-centre spacing along the grain is less than the following values:

$\quad$ 2 × fastener diameter for split rings and shear plates

$\quad$ 8 × fastener diameter for bolts, lag screws or drift pins

Table 7.2
**Area removed for shear plate and split ring joints** $A_R$ (mm² × 10³)

| Diameter in. Connector | Bolt | Number of faces with connector | Member thickness mm 38 | 64 | 80 | 89 | 130 | 140 | 175 | 191 | 215 | 241 |
|---|---|---|---|---|---|---|---|---|---|---|---|---|
| **Split rings** | | | | | | | | | | | | |
| 2-1/2 | 1/2 | 1 | 1.11 | 1.48 | 1.71 | 1.84 | 2.43 | 2.57 | 3.07 | 3.30 | 3.65 | 4.02 |
| | | 2 | 1.68 | 2.05 | 2.28 | 2.41 | 3.00 | 3.14 | 3.64 | 3.87 | 4.22 | 4.58 |
| 4 | 3/4 | 1 | 1.97 | 2.51 | 2.84 | 3.02 | 3.87 | 4.07 | 4.79 | 5.12 | 5.61 | 6.15 |
| | | 2 | 3.16 | 3.70 | 4.02 | 4.21 | 5.06 | 5.26 | 5.98 | 6.31 | 6.80 | 7.34 |
| **Shear plates** | | | | | | | | | | | | |
| 2-5/8 | 3/4 | 1 | 1.31 | 1.85 | 2.18 | 2.36 | 3.20 | 3.41 | 4.13 | 4.46 | 4.95 | 5.49 |
| | | 2 | 1.84 | 2.37 | 2.70 | 2.89 | 3.73 | 3.94 | 4.66 | 4.99 | 5.48 | 6.02 |
| 4 | 3/4 | 1 | 2.12 | 2.65 | 2.98 | 3.17 | 4.01 | 4.22 | 4.94 | 5.27 | 5.76 | 6.30 |
| | | 2 | - | 3.99 | 4.32 | 4.50 | 5.34 | 5.55 | 6.27 | 6.60 | 7.09 | 7.63 |
| | 7/8 | 1 | 2.19 | 2.80 | 3.18 | 3.40 | 4.38 | 4.61 | 5.45 | 5.83 | 6.40 | 7.02 |
| | | 2 | - | 4.09 | 4.47 | 4.68 | 5.66 | 5.89 | 6.73 | 7.11 | 7.68 | 8.30 |

Note:
Net area for split rings and shear plates has been included in the Tension Member Selection Tables.

# 7.2   Nails and Spikes

## General

Nails and spikes are manufactured in many different sizes and styles. However, design information provided in CSA O86 is applicable only for common round steel wire nails and spikes and common spiral nails spiralled to head as defined in CSA Standard B111 *Wire Nails, Spikes and Staples.*

Common nails and spiral nails are used for general construction. However, spiral nails have greater withdrawal resistance than common nails and can also reduce splitting. Spikes are longer and thicker than nails and are generally used to fasten heavy pieces of timber.

## Availability

Nails are usually specified by the type and length in inches. Nails are available in lengths from 1/2 to 6 inches and spikes range in size from 4 to 14 inches.

## Design

Nails and spikes must be designed so that the factored lateral resistance is greater than or equal to the factored lateral load.

The factored lateral resistance for loading at any angle to grain is calculated from the following formula:

$$N_r = \phi\, n_u\, J_Y\, n_F\, n_{Se}\, K'\, J'$$

where:

$\phi\, n_u\, J_Y$ is the basic factored lateral resistance, given in Table 7.3

$J_Y$ = side plate factor (factor of 1.25 for metal side plates is included in Table 7.3)

$n_F$ = number of nails or spikes

$n_{Se}$ = the effective number of shear planes, given in Table 7.4

$K'$ and $J'$ are composite modification factors given below

In addition, Table 7.3 lists the minimum acceptable length of penetration into the main member and the minimum permissible thickness of wood side plates, which must be provided. Figure 7.4 gives the minimum required end distance, edge distance and nail spacing.

Nails and spikes may be designed for withdrawal under wind or earth-quake loading only. Design requirements for withdrawal are given in CSA O86 Clause 10.9.5. Withdrawal resistances for nails and spikes are also given in Table 7.5.

For nailed joints made up of two different species, the resistance of the joint must be based on the weaker species.

Pre-drilled holes are recommended when nails greater than 4.88 mm in diameter are used. This will reduce the occurrence of splitting. These pre-drilled holes should roughly be equal to 75% of the nail diameter.

7

Fastenings

## Modification Factors

The composite modification factors $K'$ and $J'$ adjust the basic factored lateral resistance for the actual conditions of use and are calculated as follows:

$$K' = K_D K_{SF} K_T$$
$$J' = J_E J_A J_B J_D$$

where:

$K_D$ = duration of load factor

$K_{SF}$ = service condition factor

$K_T$ = fire-retardant treatment factor

$J_E$ = factor for nailing into end grain

$J_A$ = factor for toe nailing

$J_B$ = factor for nail clinching

$J_D$ = factor for diaphragm construction

In many cases $K'$ and $J'$ will equal 1.0. Review the following checklist to determine if each factor is equal to 1.0. Where a factor does not equal 1.0 determine the appropriate value and calculate $K'$ and $J'$.

Note that the side plate factor, $J_y$, is incorporated into the values in Table 7.3

# Checklist: **Nails and Spikes** ✓

1. $K_D$ = 1.0 when the loading is "standard" term
   = 1.15 for short term loading (e.g., dead plus wind)
   = 0.65 for permanent loads (e.g., dead loads alone)

2. $K_{SF}$ = 1.0 when the service conditions are "dry" and the lumber is seasoned (moisture content ≤ 15%) prior to fabrication
   = 0.8 for unseasoned lumber in dry service conditions
   = 0.67 for wet service conditions, regardless of seasoning

3. $K_T$ = 1.0 when the wood is not treated with a fire retardant or other strength-reducing chemical.

   For wood treated with a fire retardant or other strength-reducing chemicals, see the Commentary for further guidance.

4. $J_E$ = 1.0 when the nails are used in side grain
   = 0.67 for end grain use

5. $J_A$ = 1.0 when the nails are not used as toe nails
   = 0.83 for toe nailing provided the nail is started at approximately 1/3 the nail length from the end of the piece and at an angle of 30° to the grain

6. $J_B$ = 1.0 for unclinched nails in single shear
   = 1.0 for clinched or unclinched nails in double shear
   = 1.6 when nails are in single shear and clinched on the far side

   (Note: The clinched portion of the nail should be at least three nail diameters long.)

7. $J_D$ = 1.0 when nails are not used as a fastener in shearwalls or diaphragms
   = 1.3 when nails are used to fasten sheathing in shearwall and diaphragm construction

**7**

Fastenings

## Example 1: Nails

Determine the size and number of nails required for the plywood tension splice shown below (dimensions in mm). The lumber members are kiln dried, untreated 38 × 140 mm S-P-F and the plywood is 12.5 mm sheathing grade Douglas Fir. The factored load is 14 kN due to dead plus snow loads. Service conditions are dry.

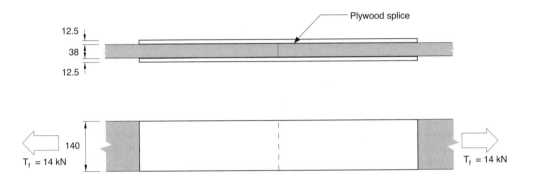

### Modification Factors

$K_D$ = 1.0 (standard term load)

$K_{SF}$ = 1.0 (dry service condition)

$K_T$ = 1.0 (untreated)

$J_E$ = 1.0 (nailed in side grain)

$J_A$ = 1.0 (not toe nailed)

$J_B$ = 1.0 (clinch factor does not apply)

$J_D$ = 1.0 (not a shearwall or diaphragm)

Therefore,

$K'$ = 1.0

$J'$ = 1.0

**Calculation**

Try 2-1/2" common nails since they will fully penetrate all members and develop double shear when driven from alternate sides of the splice or clinched:

Thickness of centre member/nail diameter $= \dfrac{38}{3.25} = 11.7$

Therefore, $n_{Se} = 2.0$ from Table 7.4

Plywood thickness = 12.5 mm > 10 mm from Table 7.3      *Acceptable*

$N_r = \phi\, n_u\, J_Y\, n_F\, n_{Se}\, K'\, J'$

$\phi\, n_u\, J_Y = 0.462$ kN for S-P-F from Table 7.3 (wood side plates)

$N_r = 0.462 \times n_F \times 2 \times 1.0 \times 1.0 = 0.924\, n_F$ kN

$n_F$ required $= \dfrac{14}{0.924} = 15.2$

Therefore, use sixteen 2-1/2" nails per side.

Determine minimum spacing, end distance and edge distance from Figure 7.4:

minimum spacing perpendicular to grain c = 26 mm

minimum edge distance d = 13 mm

Therefore, use two rows of nails spaced at 70 mm, with 35 mm edge distance:

minimum spacing parallel to grain a = 52 mm, use 60 mm

minimum end distance b = 39 mm, use 60 mm

The final connection geometry is shown below (dimensions in mm). Note that the tensile resistance of the plywood and lumber members should also be checked.

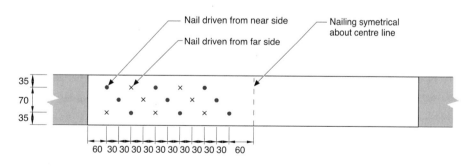

Use sixteen 2-1/2" common nails.

| Table 7.3 Basic factored lateral resistance for nails and spikes $\phi\, n_u\, J_Y$ | | | | Minimum penetration into main member[2] | Minimum thickness of side plates[3] | | Basic factored lateral resistance, $\phi\, n_u\, J_Y$ kN | | | | | |
|---|---|---|---|---|---|---|---|---|---|---|---|---|
| | | | | | | | Wood side plates | | | Steel side plates | | |
| Type | Length in. | Diameter mm | mm | | Wood mm | Plywood & OSB mm | D.Fir-L | Hem-Fir | S-P-F, North. | D.Fir-L | Hem-Fir | S-P-F, North. |
| Common wire nails | 2-1/2 | 3.25 | 26 | | 17 | 10 | 0.660 | 0.552 | 0.462 | 0.825 | 0.690 | 0.578 |
| | 3 | 3.66 | 29 | | 19 | 11 | 0.840 | 0.720 | 0.600 | 1.05 | 0.900 | 0.750 |
| | 3-1/2 | 4.06 | 33 | | 21 | 12.5 | 1.02 | 0.900 | 0.720 | 1.28 | 1.13 | 0.900 |
| | 4 | 4.88 | 39 | | 25 | 15 | 1.44 | 1.20 | 1.02 | 1.80 | 1.50 | 1.28 |
| | 5 | 5.89 | 47 | | 30 | 18 | 2.16 | 1.74 | 1.44 | 2.70 | 2.18 | 1.80 |
| | 6 | 7.01 | 56 | | 36 | 21.5 | 3.00 | 2.46 | 1.98 | 3.75 | 3.08 | 2.48 |
| Common spikes | 4 | 6.40 | 51 | | 32 | 19.5 | 2.52 | 2.10 | 1.68 | 3.15 | 2.63 | 2.10 |
| | 6 | 7.62 | 61 | | 39 | 23 | 3.30 | 2.70 | 2.22 | 4.13 | 3.37 | 2.78 |
| Common spiral nails | 2-1/2 | 2.77 | 22 | | 14 | 8.5 | 0.432 | 0.360 | 0.306 | 0.540 | 0.450 | 0.383 |
| | 3 | 3.10 | 25 | | 16 | 9.5 | 0.552 | 0.474 | 0.414 | 0.690 | 0.593 | 0.518 |
| | 3-1/2 | 3.86 | 31 | | 20 | 12 | 0.960 | 0.780 | 0.660 | 1.20 | 0.975 | 0.825 |
| | 4 | 4.33 | 35 | | 22 | 13 | 1.20 | 0.960 | 0.840 | 1.50 | 1.20 | 1.05 |
| | 5 | 4.88 | 39 | | 25 | 15 | 1.44 | 1.20 | 1.02 | 1.80 | 1.50 | 1.28 |

Notes:
1. $N_r = \phi\, n_u\, J_Y\, n_F\, n_{Se}\, K'\, J'$
2. The minimum penetration into main member that must be provided to attain full lateral resistance (where $n_{Se} = 1.0$)
3. The minimum required thickness of wood side plates to attain full lateral resistance
4. Minimum required spacing, end and edge distances are given in Figure 7.4.

| Table 7.4 Effective number of shear planes $n_{Se}$ | Thickness of centre member | Two member single shear connection | Three member double shear connection |
|---|---|---|---|
| | 11 × nail diameter | 1.0 | 2.0 |
| | 8 × nail diameter | 1.0 | 1.8 |

Notes:
1. Nails must fully penetrate each member and be either clinched on far side or driven alternately from both sides.
2. In CSA O86, the effective number of shear planes is referred to as $J_s$, rather than $n_{Se}$.
3. When thickness of centre member is between 8 and 11 nail diameters, interpolate linearly.

| Figure 7.4 **Minimum required spacing, end and edge distances for nails and spikes** | | D.Fir-L Hem-Fir | | | | S-P-F Northern | | | |
|---|---|---|---|---|---|---|---|---|---|
| | | Min. spacing parallel to grain | Min. end distance | Min. spacing perp. to grain | Min. edge distance | Min. spacing parallel to grain | Min. end distance | Min. spacing perp. to grain | Min. edge distance |
| Type | Length in. | a mm | b mm | c mm | d mm | a mm | b mm | c mm | d mm |
| Common wire nails | 2-1/2 | 65 | 49 | 33 | 17 | 52 | 39 | 26 | 13 |
| | 3 | 74 | 55 | 37 | 19 | 59 | 44 | 30 | 15 |
| | 3-1/2 | 82 | 61 | 41 | 21 | 65 | 49 | 33 | 17 |
| | 4 | 98 | 74 | 49 | 25 | 79 | 59 | 39 | 20 |
| | 5 | 118 | 89 | 59 | 30 | 95 | 71 | 48 | 24 |
| | 6 | 141 | 106 | 71 | 35 | 113 | 85 | 57 | 28 |
| Common spikes | 4 | 128 | 96 | 64 | 32 | 103 | 77 | 52 | 26 |
| | 6 | 153 | 115 | 77 | 39 | 122 | 92 | 61 | 31 |
| Common spiral nails | 2-1/2 | 56 | 42 | 28 | 14 | 45 | 34 | 23 | 12 |
| | 3 | 62 | 47 | 31 | 16 | 50 | 38 | 25 | 13 |
| | 3-1/2 | 78 | 58 | 39 | 20 | 62 | 47 | 31 | 16 |
| | 4 | 87 | 65 | 44 | 22 | 70 | 52 | 35 | 18 |
| | 5 | 98 | 74 | 49 | 25 | 79 | 59 | 39 | 20 |

**7**

Fastenings

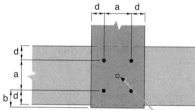
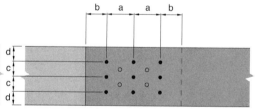

Additional nails staggered diagonally between rows are permitted

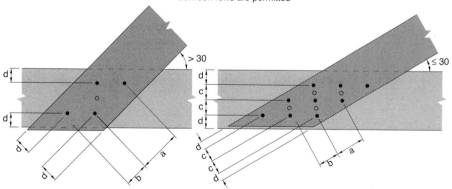

| Table 7.5 **Unit withdrawal resistance $\phi\,y_w$ (N/mm) for common wire nails, spikes and spiral nails** | Type | Length in. | Diameter mm | Douglas Fir-Larch | Hem-Fir | S-P-F | Northern |
|---|---|---|---|---|---|---|---|
| | Common wire nails | 2-1/2 | 3.25 | 5.4 | 4.7 | 3.8 | 2.6 |
| | | 3 | 3.66 | 5.9 | 5.2 | 4.2 | 2.8 |
| | | 3-1/2 | 4.06 | 6.5 | 5.6 | 4.6 | 3.1 |
| | | 4 | 4.88 | 7.5 | 6.5 | 5.4 | 3.6 |
| | | 5 | 5.89 | 8.8 | 7.6 | 6.2 | 4.2 |
| | | 6 | 7.01 | 10.1 | 8.8 | 7.2 | 4.8 |
| | Common spikes | 4 | 6.40 | 9.4 | 8.2 | 6.7 | 4.5 |
| | | 6 | 7.62 | 10.8 | 9.4 | 7.7 | 5.2 |
| | Common spiral nails | 2-1/2 | 2.77 | 4.7 | 4.1 | 3.4 | 2.3 |
| | | 3 | 3.10 | 5.2 | 4.5 | 3.7 | 2.5 |
| | | 3-1/2 | 3.86 | 6.2 | 5.4 | 4.4 | 3.0 |
| | | 4 | 4.33 | 6.8 | 5.9 | 4.9 | 3.2 |
| | | 5 | 4.88 | 7.5 | 6.5 | 5.4 | 3.6 |

Notes:
1. $P'_{rw} = \phi\,y_w\,L_p\,K_{sf}\,K_T\,n_F\,J_A\,J_B$
2. The use of nails and spikes loaded in withdrawal is permitted only for wind or earthquake loading (see Clause 10.9.5.1 of CSA O86).

# 7.3    Bolts

### General

Design information provided in CSA O86 is based on bolts conforming to the requirements of ASTM Standard A307. Threaded rods meeting the requirements of ASTM A307, except those made of mild steel, may be designed and used in lieu of bolts provided the rod is threaded at the ends only.

Cut washers are commonly used with bolted connections loaded laterally. When bolts are loaded in tension, round or square plate washers, designed to provide adequate resistance, are typically used.

### Availability

A307 bolts are commonly available as either square-headed machine bolts or more commonly as finished hexagon bolts. Information on standard sizes, weights and lengths of hexagon bolts is provided in Chapter 11. Bolts are generally available in imperial sizes.

A307 threaded rod is sometimes used in place of bolts because it is readily available in long lengths and can easily be cut to the required size.

### Design

Bolted connections must be designed so that the factored resistance of the connection is greater than or equal to the applied factored load.

**Lateral Resistance**

The factored lateral resistance depends upon the angle of load to grain and is calculated as follows:

$$P_r = P'_r\, n_s\, n_F\, K'\, J' \qquad \text{for parallel to grain loading}$$

$$Q_r = Q'_r\, n_s\, n_F\, K'\, J_R \qquad \text{for perpendicular to grain loading}$$

$$N_r = \frac{P_r\, Q_r}{P_r \sin^2 \theta + Q_r \cos^2 \theta} \qquad \begin{array}{l}\text{for loading at an angle } \theta \text{ to grain.}\\ N_r \text{ may also be determined from Table 7.1.}\end{array}$$

where:

$P'_r\, n_s$ and $Q'_r\, n_s$ are factored lateral resistances per bolt given in the Bolt Selection Tables

$n_s$ = number of shear planes and is included in the Bolt Selection Tables

$n_F$ = number of bolts

$K'$ and $J'$ are composite modification factors given below

$J_R$ = factor for number of rows

Edge distance, end distance and spacing for bolts are shown in Figure 7.5.

**7**

Fastenings

## Tensile Resistance

The factored tensile resistance for common bolt sizes is provided in Table 7.6. In addition, the washers or plates used with the bolts must be large enough to withstand the tensile loads as well as provide enough contact area so that the bearing resistance of the wood is not exceeded. Chapter 11 contains information on washers.

Table 7.6
**Factored tensile resistance of A307 bolts**

| Bolt diameter in. | Tensile resistance, $T_r$ kN |
| --- | --- |
| 1/2 | 26.4 |
| 5/8 | 41.2 |
| 3/4 | 59.3 |
| 7/8 | 80.7 |
| 1 | 105 |

Note:
$T_r = 0.75\ \phi_s\ A_b\ F_u$ where $\phi_s = 0.67$ (from CSA S16)
$A_b$ = area of bolt (mm$^2$)
$F_u$ = minimum specified tensile strength = 414 MPa

## Modification Factors

The composite modification factors K′ and J′ adjust the unit factored lateral resistances for the actual conditions of use and are calculated as follows:

$$K' = K_D\ K_{SF}\ K_T$$
$$J' = J_G\ J_L\ J_R$$

where:

$K_D$ = duration of load factor

$K_{SF}$ = service condition factor

$K_T$ = fire-retardant treatment factor

$J_G$ = factor for 2 to max. 12 bolts in a row

$J_L$ = factor for loaded end distance

$J_R$ = factor for number of rows

In some cases K′ and J′ will equal 1.0. Review the following checklist to determine if each modification factor is equal to 1.0 for the actual conditions of use. Where a factor does not equal 1.0 determine the value and calculate K′ and J′.

# Checklist: **Bolts**

1. $K_D$ = 1.0 when the loading is "standard" term
   = 1.15 for short term loading (e.g., dead plus wind)
   = 0.65 for permanent loads (e.g., dead loads alone)

2. $K_{SF}$ = 1.0 when the service conditions are "dry" and the lumber is seasoned
   (moisture content ≤ 15%) prior to fabrication

   For other conditions, determine $K_{SF}$ from Table 7.7

3. $K_T$ = 1.0 when the wood is not treated with a fire retardant or other strength
   reducing chemical. For wood treated with a fire retardant or other strength
   reducing chemical see the Commentary for further guidance.

4. $J_G$ = 1.0 for cases with one bolt per row, and all wood-to-concrete connections

   Otherwise,

   $$J_G = 0.33 \left[\frac{\ell}{d}\right]^{0.5} \left[\frac{s}{d}\right]^{0.2} N^{-0.3} < 1.0$$

   where:
   $\ell$ = thickness of the thinnest wood member in the connection, mm
   s = spacing of the bolts in a row, mm
   d = bolt diameter, mm
   N = number of bolts in a row

5. $J_L$ = 1.0 when the minimum loaded end distance (parallel to grain loading only)
   is at least 10 bolt diameters as shown in Figure 7.5
   = 0.75 for a minimum permitted end distance of 7 diameters

   Linear interpolation may be used for intermediate values

6. $J_R$ = 1.0 for 1 row or 1 bolt per row
   = 0.8 for 2 rows (2 or more bolts in a row)
   = 0.6 for 3 rows (2 or more bolts in a row)

**7**

Fastenings

## Steel Side Plates

Steel side plates must be designed to adequately resist the factored loading in accordance with CSA S16. However, the plate must be at least 6 mm thick in order for the tabulated bolt resistances to be valid. Thinner side plates may be used, but the lateral resistance of the bolts must be calculated in accordance with Clause 10.4.4 of CSA O86. The Clause may also be used to calculate resistances based on thicker side plates.

When the distance between rows of bolts in parallel to grain connections greater than 125 mm, single steel splice plates should not be used. Instead, provide a separate splice plate for each row.

Long rows of bolts loaded perpendicular to grain should be avoided where shrinkage of the wood is anticipated.

## Additional Design Considerations

The amount of material removed due to bolt holes must be considered in the design of wood members. Information on net area is given in Section 7.1.

Where bolts are used in eccentric connections or where the connection exerts a shear force on a wood member, the shear resistance of the member must be checked as outlined in Section 7.1.

| Table 7.7 **Service condition factor for bolts $K_{SF}$** | | | Condition of lumber | | |
|---|---|---|---|---|---|
| | | | Seasoned (moisture content ≤ 15%) | | Unseasoned (moisture content > 15%) |
| | Joint detail | Angle of load to grain | Wet service | Dry service | Wet service |
| | A | all | 0.67 | 1.00 | 0.67 |
| | B | 0° | 0.67 | 1.00 | 0.67 |
| | B | 90° | 0.67 | 0.40 | 0.27 |
| | C | all | 0.67 | 0.40 | 0.27 |

Note:
A = single fastening or a single row parallel to grain with steel side plates
B = single row parallel to grain with wood side plates or 2 rows parallel to grain not more than 125 mm apart with a common wood splice plate or multiple rows with separate wood or steel splice plates for each row
C = all other arrangements

## Example 1: Bolts

Determine if one row of two 1" bolts is adequate for the beam-to-column connection shown below (dimensions in mm). The column is 175 × 190 mm D.Fir-L glulam and the steel hanger is made from 6 mm steel plate. The factored reaction from each beam is 38.1 kN due to dead loads plus live loads for use and occupancy. The service conditions are dry.

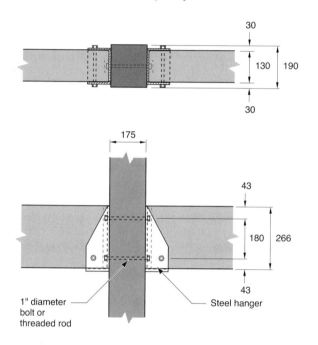

### Modification Factors

$K_D$ = 1.0 (loading is standard term)

$K_{SF}$ = 1.0 (service conditions are dry, material is seasoned)

$K_T$ = 1.0 (glulam is not treated)

$$J_G = 0.33 \left[\frac{175}{25.4}\right]^{0.5} \left[\frac{180}{25.4}\right]^{0.2} [2]^{-0.3} = 1.04 > 1.0$$

$$= 1.0$$

$J_L$ = 1.0 (end distance is very large)

$J_R$ = 1.0 (one row of bolts)

Therefore:

$K'$ = 1.0

$J'$ = 1.0

**Calculation**

$$P_f = 38.1 \times 2 = 76.2 \text{ kN}$$

Try one row of two 1" diameter bolts:

$$P_r = P'_r \, n_s \, n_F \, K' \, J'$$

$P'_r n_s = 49.5 \text{ kN from Bolt Selection Tables}$

$n_F = 2$

$P_r = 49.5 \times 2 \times 1.0 \times 1.0 = 99.0 \text{ kN}$          *Acceptable*

Check spacing and edge distances from Figure 7.5:

The use of a 180 mm spacing parallel to grain is greater than the 102 mm acceptable minimum. This leaves an end distance of 43 mm on the steel plate, which must be checked in accordance with CSA S16.

edge distance in the timber column = 190/2 = 95 mm
1.5 bolt diameter = 1.5 × 25.4 = 38 mm

95 mm > 38 mm          *Acceptable*

Note that since this loading is subject to both full and partial live loading, single shear checks are also required.
    The net area of the column satisfies the requirement of being greater than or equal to 75% of the gross area (see Clause 4.3.8.2 of CSA O86).

**Use two 1" diameter bolts.**

# Bolt Selection Tables

## Joint Configurations

### Single Shear, Wood Side Plates

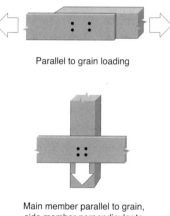

Parallel to grain loading

Main member parallel to grain,
side member perpendicular to
grain loading

Main member perpendicular
to grain, side member
parallel to grain loading

### Double Shear, Wood Side Plates

Parallel to grain loading

Main member parallel to grain,
side member perpendicular to
grain loading

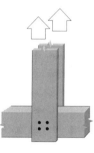

Main member perpendicular
to grain, side member
parallel to grain loading

7

Fastenings

# Bolt Selection Tables
## Joint Configurations

### Single Shear, Steel Side Plates

Parallel to grain loading                    Perpendicular to grain loading

### Double Shear, Steel Side Plates

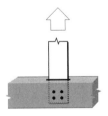

Parallel to grain loading                    Perpendicular to grain loading

### Double Shear, Steel Internal Plates

Parallel to grain loading                    Perpendicular to grain loading

### Single Shear, Wood to Concrete

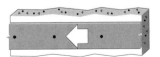

Parallel to grain loading                    Perpendicular to grain loading

# Bolt Selection Tables

## Single Shear, Wood Side Plate

**1S**

Factored lateral resistance

| Species **Sawn lumber** | Side plate thickness mm | Member thickness mm | 1/2" bolt | | | 5/8" bolt | | |
|---|---|---|---|---|---|---|---|---|
| | | | $P'_r\, n_s$ kN | $Q'^4_r\, n_s$ kN | $Q'^5_r\, n_s$ kN | $P'_r\, n_s$ kN | $Q'^4_r\, n_s$ kN | $Q'^5_r\, n_s$ kN |
| D.Fir-L | 38 | 38 | 2.91 | 2.09 | 2.09 | 3.51 | 2.52 | 2.52 |
| | 38 | 64 | 3.84 | 2.52 | 2.49 | 4.71 | 3.04 | 3.61 |
| | 38 | 89 | 3.84 | 2.94 | 2.49 | 5.41 | 3.54 | 3.61 |
| | 38 | 140 | 3.84 | 3.31 | 2.49 | 5.41 | 4.57 | 3.61 |
| | 38 | 191 | 3.84 | 3.31 | 2.49 | 5.41 | 4.60 | 3.61 |
| | 89 | 89 | 4.77 | 3.71 | 3.34 | 7.31 | 5.69 | 4.63 |
| | 89 | 140 | 4.77 | 3.71 | 3.34 | 7.31 | 5.69 | 4.63 |
| | 89 | 191 | 4.77 | 3.71 | 3.34 | 7.31 | 5.69 | 4.63 |
| Hem-Fir | 38 | 38 | 2.73 | 1.96 | 1.96 | 3.29 | 2.36 | 2.36 |
| | 38 | 64 | 3.67 | 2.37 | 2.39 | 4.42 | 2.85 | 3.47 |
| | 38 | 89 | 3.68 | 2.76 | 2.39 | 5.19 | 3.33 | 3.47 |
| | 38 | 140 | 3.68 | 3.17 | 2.39 | 5.19 | 4.29 | 3.47 |
| | 38 | 191 | 3.68 | 3.17 | 2.39 | 5.19 | 4.40 | 3.47 |
| | 89 | 89 | 4.62 | 3.60 | 3.19 | 7.08 | 5.52 | 4.44 |
| | 89 | 140 | 4.62 | 3.60 | 3.19 | 7.08 | 5.52 | 4.44 |
| | 89 | 191 | 4.62 | 3.60 | 3.19 | 7.08 | 5.52 | 4.44 |
| S-P-F | 38 | 38 | 2.50 | 1.79 | 1.79 | 3.01 | 2.16 | 2.16 |
| | 38 | 64 | 3.35 | 2.16 | 2.26 | 4.04 | 2.61 | 3.19 |
| | 38 | 89 | 3.45 | 2.52 | 2.26 | 4.89 | 3.04 | 3.27 |
| | 38 | 140 | 3.45 | 2.97 | 2.26 | 4.89 | 3.91 | 3.27 |
| | 38 | 191 | 3.45 | 2.97 | 2.26 | 4.89 | 4.14 | 3.27 |
| | 89 | 89 | 4.41 | 3.44 | 2.99 | 6.77 | 5.05 | 4.17 |
| | 89 | 140 | 4.41 | 3.44 | 2.99 | 6.77 | 5.27 | 4.17 |
| | 89 | 191 | 4.41 | 3.44 | 2.99 | 6.77 | 5.27 | 4.17 |
| Northern | 38 | 38 | 2.08 | 1.49 | 1.49 | 2.51 | 1.80 | 1.80 |
| | 38 | 64 | 2.79 | 1.80 | 2.02 | 3.36 | 2.17 | 2.66 |
| | 38 | 89 | 3.05 | 2.10 | 2.02 | 4.19 | 2.53 | 2.73 |
| | 38 | 140 | 3.05 | 2.61 | 2.02 | 4.34 | 3.26 | 2.73 |
| | 38 | 191 | 3.05 | 2.61 | 2.02 | 4.34 | 3.66 | 2.73 |
| | 89 | 89 | 4.03 | 3.14 | 2.63 | 5.87 | 4.21 | 3.68 |
| | 89 | 140 | 4.03 | 3.14 | 2.63 | 6.02 | 4.81 | 3.68 |
| | 89 | 191 | 4.03 | 3.14 | 2.63 | 6.02 | 4.81 | 3.68 |

Notes:
1. $P_r = P'_r\, n_s\, n_F\, K'\, J'$
   $Q_r = Q'_r\, n_s\, n_F\, K'\, J_R$
   $n_s = 1$ in the Table
2. Spacing, end and edge distances for bolted connections are shown in Figure 7.5.
3. Tabulated values are valid for cases where the wood side member is of same density as main member.
4. Main member perpendicular and side member parallel to grain loading.
5. Side member perpendicular and main member parallel to grain loading.
6. Tabulated values are based on A307 steel grade bolts.

7

Fastenings

# Bolt Selection Tables

## 1S    Single Shear, Wood Side Plate

Factored lateral resistance

| Species | Side plate thickness | Member thickness | 1/2" bolt | | | 5/8" bolt | | |
|---|---|---|---|---|---|---|---|---|
| **Glulam** | | | $P'_r\,n_s$ | $Q'^4_r\,n_s$ | $Q'^5_r\,n_s$ | $P'_r\,n_s$ | $Q'^4_r\,n_s$ | $Q'^5_r\,n_s$ |
| | mm | mm | kN | kN | kN | kN | kN | kN |
| D.Fir-L | 38 | 80 | 3.84 | 2.79 | 2.49 | 5.41 | 3.36 | 3.61 |
| | 38 | 130 | 3.84 | 3.31 | 2.49 | 5.41 | 4.37 | 3.61 |
| | 38 | 175 | 3.84 | 3.31 | 2.49 | 5.41 | 4.60 | 3.61 |
| | 38 | 215 | 3.84 | 3.31 | 2.49 | 5.41 | 4.60 | 3.61 |
| | 89 | 130 | 4.77 | 3.71 | 3.34 | 7.31 | 5.69 | 4.63 |
| | 89 | 175 | 4.77 | 3.71 | 3.34 | 7.31 | 5.69 | 4.63 |
| | 89 | 215 | 4.77 | 3.71 | 3.34 | 7.31 | 5.69 | 4.63 |
| Spruce-Pine | 38 | 80 | 3.48 | 2.45 | 2.27 | 4.82 | 2.95 | 3.27 |
| | 38 | 130 | 3.48 | 2.99 | 2.27 | 4.93 | 3.85 | 3.27 |
| | 38 | 175 | 3.48 | 2.99 | 2.27 | 4.93 | 4.18 | 3.27 |
| | 38 | 215 | 3.48 | 2.99 | 2.27 | 4.93 | 4.18 | 3.27 |
| | 89 | 130 | 4.46 | 3.49 | 3.00 | 6.85 | 5.36 | 4.19 |
| | 89 | 175 | 4.46 | 3.49 | 3.00 | 6.85 | 5.36 | 4.19 |
| | 89 | 215 | 4.46 | 3.49 | 3.00 | 6.85 | 5.36 | 4.19 |
| **MSR (MEL) lumber** | | | | | | | | |
| S-P-F | | | | | | | | |
| 2.0E to 2.1E | 38 | 38 | 2.97 | 2.13 | 2.13 | 3.58 | 2.57 | 2.57 |
| 1.8E to 1.9E | 38 | 38 | 2.79 | 2.00 | 2.00 | 3.37 | 2.41 | 2.41 |
| 1.2E to 1.7E | 38 | 38 | 2.50 | 1.79 | 1.79 | 3.01 | 2.16 | 2.16 |

Notes:
1. $P_r = P'_r\,n_s\,n_F\,K'\,J'$
   $Q_r = Q'_r\,n_s\,n_F\,K'\,J_R$
   $n_s = 1.0$ in the Table
2. Spacing, end and edge distances for bolted connections are shown in Figure 7.5.
3. Tabulated values are valid for cases where the wood side member is of same density as main member.
4. Main member perpendicular and side member parallel to grain loading.
5. Side member perpendicular and main member parallel to grain loading.
6. Tabulated values are based on A307 steel grade bolts.

# Bolt Selection Tables

## Single Shear, Wood Side Plate  `1S`

Factored lateral resistance

| Species Sawn lumber | Side plate thickness mm | Member thickness mm | 3/4" bolt $P'_r n_s$ kN | $Q'^4_r n_s$ kN | $Q'^5_r n_s$ kN | 7/8" bolt $P'_r n_s$ kN | $Q'^4_r n_s$ kN | $Q'^5_r n_s$ kN | 1" bolt $P'_r n_s$ kN | $Q'^4_r n_s$ kN | $Q'^5_r n_s$ kN |
|---|---|---|---|---|---|---|---|---|---|---|---|
| D.Fir-L | 38 | 38 | 4.05 | 2.91 | 2.91 | 4.54 | 3.26 | 3.26 | 4.98 | 3.57 | 3.57 |
|  | 38 | 64 | 5.44 | 3.51 | 4.29 | 6.10 | 3.93 | 4.81 | 6.68 | 4.31 | 5.28 |
|  | 38 | 89 | 6.77 | 4.09 | 4.41 | 7.59 | 4.58 | 4.94 | 8.32 | 5.03 | 5.41 |
|  | 38 | 140 | 7.19 | 5.27 | 4.41 | 9.16 | 5.91 | 4.94 | 11.3 | 6.48 | 5.41 |
|  | 38 | 191 | 7.19 | 6.05 | 4.41 | 9.16 | 7.24 | 4.94 | 11.3 | 7.93 | 5.41 |
|  | 38 | 241 | 7.19 | 6.05 | 4.41 | 9.16 | 7.63 | 4.94 | 11.3 | 9.35 | 5.41 |
|  | 38 | 292 |  |  |  | 9.16 | 7.63 | 4.94 | 11.3 | 9.35 | 5.41 |
|  | 89 | 89 | 9.49 | 6.81 | 6.08 | 10.6 | 7.63 | 7.63 | 11.7 | 8.37 | 8.37 |
|  | 89 | 140 | 9.91 | 7.99 | 6.08 | 12.2 | 8.96 | 7.68 | 14.6 | 9.82 | 9.40 |
|  | 89 | 191 | 9.91 | 8.04 | 6.08 | 12.2 | 10.3 | 7.68 | 14.6 | 11.3 | 9.40 |
|  | 89 | 241 | 9.91 | 8.04 | 6.08 | 12.2 | 10.7 | 7.68 | 14.6 | 12.7 | 9.40 |
|  | 89 | 292 |  |  |  | 12.2 | 10.7 | 7.68 | 14.6 | 12.7 | 9.40 |
| Hem-Fir | 38 | 38 | 3.80 | 2.73 | 2.73 | 4.26 | 3.06 | 3.06 | 4.67 | 3.35 | 3.35 |
|  | 38 | 64 | 5.11 | 3.30 | 4.03 | 5.72 | 3.69 | 4.52 | 6.27 | 4.05 | 4.95 |
|  | 38 | 89 | 6.36 | 3.84 | 4.14 | 7.13 | 4.30 | 4.64 | 7.81 | 4.72 | 5.08 |
|  | 38 | 140 | 6.90 | 4.95 | 4.14 | 8.81 | 5.55 | 4.64 | 10.9 | 6.08 | 5.08 |
|  | 38 | 191 | 6.90 | 5.80 | 4.14 | 8.81 | 6.79 | 4.64 | 10.9 | 7.45 | 5.08 |
|  | 38 | 241 | 6.90 | 5.80 | 4.14 | 8.81 | 7.33 | 4.64 | 10.9 | 8.78 | 5.08 |
|  | 38 | 292 |  |  |  | 8.81 | 7.33 | 4.64 | 10.9 | 8.98 | 5.08 |
|  | 89 | 89 | 8.91 | 6.39 | 5.83 | 9.99 | 7.16 | 7.16 | 10.9 | 7.85 | 7.85 |
|  | 89 | 140 | 9.46 | 7.50 | 5.83 | 11.7 | 8.41 | 7.37 | 14.0 | 9.22 | 9.03 |
|  | 89 | 191 | 9.46 | 7.79 | 5.83 | 11.7 | 9.65 | 7.37 | 14.0 | 10.6 | 9.03 |
|  | 89 | 241 | 9.46 | 7.79 | 5.83 | 11.7 | 10.2 | 7.37 | 14.0 | 11.9 | 9.03 |
|  | 89 | 292 |  |  |  | 11.7 | 10.2 | 7.37 | 14.0 | 12.1 | 9.03 |
| S-P-F | 38 | 38 | 3.47 | 2.49 | 2.49 | 3.89 | 2.79 | 2.79 | 4.27 | 3.06 | 3.06 |
|  | 38 | 64 | 4.66 | 3.01 | 3.68 | 5.23 | 3.37 | 4.13 | 5.73 | 3.70 | 4.52 |
|  | 38 | 89 | 5.80 | 3.51 | 3.78 | 6.51 | 3.93 | 4.23 | 7.13 | 4.31 | 4.64 |
|  | 38 | 140 | 6.52 | 4.52 | 3.78 | 8.32 | 5.07 | 4.23 | 10.0 | 5.55 | 4.64 |
|  | 38 | 191 | 6.52 | 5.46 | 3.78 | 8.32 | 6.20 | 4.23 | 10.3 | 6.80 | 4.64 |
|  | 38 | 241 | 6.52 | 5.46 | 3.78 | 8.32 | 6.91 | 4.23 | 10.3 | 8.02 | 4.64 |
|  | 38 | 292 |  |  |  | 8.32 | 6.91 | 4.23 | 10.3 | 8.49 | 4.64 |
|  | 89 | 89 | 8.13 | 5.84 | 5.49 | 9.12 | 6.54 | 6.54 | 10.0 | 7.17 | 7.17 |
|  | 89 | 140 | 8.85 | 6.85 | 5.49 | 10.9 | 7.68 | 6.95 | 12.9 | 8.42 | 8.53 |
|  | 89 | 191 | 8.85 | 7.44 | 5.49 | 10.9 | 8.81 | 6.95 | 13.2 | 9.66 | 8.53 |
|  | 89 | 241 | 8.85 | 7.44 | 5.49 | 10.9 | 9.52 | 6.95 | 13.2 | 10.9 | 8.53 |
|  | 89 | 292 |  |  |  | 10.9 | 9.52 | 6.95 | 13.2 | 11.3 | 8.53 |
| Northern | 38 | 38 | 2.89 | 2.08 | 2.08 | 3.24 | 2.33 | 2.33 | 3.56 | 2.55 | 2.55 |
|  | 38 | 64 | 3.88 | 2.51 | 3.07 | 4.35 | 2.81 | 3.44 | 4.77 | 3.08 | 3.77 |
|  | 38 | 89 | 4.84 | 2.92 | 3.15 | 5.42 | 3.27 | 3.53 | 5.94 | 3.59 | 3.87 |
|  | 38 | 140 | 5.81 | 3.77 | 3.15 | 7.44 | 4.22 | 3.53 | 8.33 | 4.63 | 3.87 |
|  | 38 | 191 | 5.81 | 4.61 | 3.15 | 7.44 | 5.17 | 3.53 | 8.89 | 5.67 | 3.87 |
|  | 38 | 241 | 5.81 | 4.84 | 3.15 | 7.44 | 6.10 | 3.53 | 8.89 | 6.68 | 3.87 |
|  | 38 | 292 |  |  |  | 7.44 | 6.16 | 3.53 | 8.89 | 7.58 | 3.87 |
|  | 89 | 89 | 6.78 | 4.86 | 4.86 | 7.60 | 5.45 | 5.45 | 8.33 | 5.98 | 5.98 |
|  | 89 | 140 | 7.75 | 5.71 | 4.87 | 9.62 | 6.40 | 6.19 | 10.7 | 7.01 | 7.61 |
|  | 89 | 191 | 7.75 | 6.55 | 4.87 | 9.62 | 7.35 | 6.19 | 11.6 | 8.05 | 7.61 |
|  | 89 | 241 | 7.75 | 6.79 | 4.87 | 9.62 | 8.27 | 6.19 | 11.6 | 9.07 | 7.61 |
|  | 89 | 292 |  |  |  | 9.62 | 8.33 | 6.19 | 11.6 | 9.96 | 7.61 |

7

Fastenings

Notes: see page 253

# Bolt Selection Tables

## 1S    Single Shear, Wood Side Plate

Factored lateral resistance

| Species | Side plate thickness | Member thickness | 3/4" bolt | | | 7/8" bolt | | | 1" bolt | | |
|---|---|---|---|---|---|---|---|---|---|---|---|
| | | | $P'_r n_s$ | $Q'^4_r n_s$ | $Q'^5_r n_s$ | $P'_r n_s$ | $Q'^4_r n_s$ | $Q'^5_r n_s$ | $P'_r n_s$ | $Q'^4_r n_s$ | $Q'^5_r n_s$ |
| **Glulam** | mm | mm | kN | kN | kN | kN | kN | kN | kN | kN | kN |
| D.Fir-L | 38 | 80 | 6.29 | 3.88 | 4.41 | 7.05 | 4.35 | 4.94 | 7.73 | 4.77 | 5.41 |
| | 38 | 130 | 7.19 | 5.04 | 4.41 | 9.16 | 5.65 | 4.94 | 11.0 | 6.19 | 5.41 |
| | 38 | 175 | 7.19 | 6.05 | 4.41 | 9.16 | 6.82 | 4.94 | 11.3 | 7.48 | 5.41 |
| | 38 | 215 | 7.19 | 6.05 | 4.41 | 9.16 | 7.63 | 4.94 | 11.3 | 8.62 | 5.41 |
| | 38 | 265 | 7.19 | 6.05 | 4.41 | 9.16 | 7.63 | 4.94 | 11.3 | 9.35 | 5.41 |
| | 38 | 315 | | | | | | | 11.3 | 9.35 | 5.41 |
| | 89 | 130 | 9.91 | 7.76 | 6.08 | 12.2 | 8.70 | 7.68 | 14.3 | 9.53 | 9.40 |
| | 89 | 175 | 9.91 | 8.04 | 6.08 | 12.2 | 9.87 | 7.68 | 14.6 | 10.8 | 9.40 |
| | 89 | 215 | 9.91 | 8.04 | 6.08 | 12.2 | 10.7 | 7.68 | 14.6 | 12.0 | 9.40 |
| | 89 | 265 | 9.91 | 8.04 | 6.08 | 12.2 | 10.7 | 7.68 | 14.6 | 12.7 | 9.40 |
| | 89 | 315 | | | | | | | 14.6 | 12.7 | 9.40 |
| Spruce-Pine | 38 | 80 | 5.57 | 3.40 | 3.78 | 6.24 | 3.81 | 4.23 | 6.84 | 4.18 | 4.64 |
| | 38 | 130 | 6.57 | 4.44 | 3.78 | 8.40 | 4.98 | 4.23 | 9.78 | 5.46 | 4.64 |
| | 38 | 175 | 6.57 | 5.38 | 3.78 | 8.40 | 6.03 | 4.23 | 10.4 | 6.61 | 4.64 |
| | 38 | 215 | 6.57 | 5.52 | 3.78 | 8.40 | 6.96 | 4.23 | 10.4 | 7.63 | 4.64 |
| | 38 | 265 | 6.57 | 5.52 | 3.78 | 8.40 | 6.99 | 4.23 | 10.4 | 8.59 | 4.64 |
| | 38 | 315 | | | | | | | 10.4 | 8.59 | 4.64 |
| | 89 | 130 | 8.90 | 6.77 | 5.52 | 11.0 | 7.59 | 6.98 | 12.6 | 8.32 | 8.57 |
| | 89 | 175 | 8.90 | 7.56 | 5.52 | 11.0 | 8.64 | 6.98 | 13.3 | 9.48 | 8.57 |
| | 89 | 215 | 8.90 | 7.56 | 5.52 | 11.0 | 9.58 | 6.98 | 13.3 | 10.5 | 8.57 |
| | 89 | 265 | 8.90 | 7.56 | 5.52 | 11.0 | 9.61 | 6.98 | 13.3 | 11.5 | 8.57 |
| | 89 | 315 | | | | | | | 13.3 | 11.5 | 8.57 |
| **MSR (MEL) lumber** | | | | | | | | | | | |
| **S-P-F** | | | | | | | | | | | |
| 2.0E to 2.1E | 38 | 38 | 4.13 | 2.97 | 2.97 | 4.63 | 3.33 | 3.33 | 5.08 | 3.65 | 3.65 |
| 1.8E to 1.9E | 38 | 38 | 3.89 | 2.79 | 2.79 | 4.36 | 3.13 | 3.13 | 4.78 | 3.43 | 3.43 |
| 1.2E to 1.7E | 38 | 38 | 3.47 | 2.49 | 2.49 | 3.89 | 2.79 | 2.79 | 4.27 | 3.06 | 3.06 |

Notes:
1. $P_r = P'_r n_s n_F K' J'$
   $Q_r = Q'_r n_s n_F K' J_R$
   $n_s = 1.0$ in the Table
2. Spacing, end and edge distances for bolted connections are shown in Figure 7.5.
3. Tabulated values are valid for cases where the wood side member is of same density as main member.
4. Main member perpendicular and side member parallel to grain loading.
5. Side member perpendicular and main member parallel to grain loading.
6. Tabulated values are based on A307 steel grade bolts.

# Bolt Selection Tables

## Double Shear, Wood Side Plates 2S

Factored lateral resistance

| Species | Side plate thickness | Member thickness | 1/2" bolt | | | 5/8" bolt | | |
|---|---|---|---|---|---|---|---|---|
| | | | $P'_r n_s$ | $Q'^4_r n_s$ | $Q'^5_r n_s$ | $P'_r n_s$ | $Q'^4_r n_s$ | $Q'^5_r n_s$ |
| **Sawn lumber** | mm | mm | kN | kN | kN | kN | kN | kN |
| D.Fir-L | 38 | 38 | 7.28 | 3.17 | 4.98 | 8.77 | 3.82 | 7.22 |
| | 38 | 64 | 7.68 | 5.33 | 4.98 | 10.8 | 6.43 | 7.22 |
| | 38 | 89 | 7.68 | 6.62 | 4.98 | 10.8 | 8.94 | 7.22 |
| | 38 | 140 | 7.68 | 6.62 | 4.98 | 10.8 | 9.20 | 7.22 |
| | 38 | 191 | 7.68 | 6.62 | 4.98 | 10.8 | 9.20 | 7.22 |
| | 89 | 89 | 9.53 | 7.42 | 6.68 | 14.6 | 8.94 | 9.27 |
| | 89 | 140 | 9.53 | 7.42 | 6.68 | 14.6 | 11.4 | 9.27 |
| | 89 | 191 | 9.53 | 7.42 | 6.68 | 14.6 | 11.4 | 9.27 |
| Hem-Fir | 38 | 38 | 6.84 | 2.97 | 4.79 | 8.24 | 3.58 | 6.95 |
| | 38 | 64 | 7.35 | 5.01 | 4.79 | 10.4 | 6.03 | 6.95 |
| | 38 | 89 | 7.35 | 6.33 | 4.79 | 10.4 | 8.39 | 6.95 |
| | 38 | 140 | 7.35 | 6.33 | 4.79 | 10.4 | 8.81 | 6.95 |
| | 38 | 191 | 7.35 | 6.33 | 4.79 | 10.4 | 8.81 | 6.95 |
| | 89 | 89 | 9.24 | 6.96 | 6.38 | 14.2 | 8.39 | 8.87 |
| | 89 | 140 | 9.24 | 7.19 | 6.38 | 14.2 | 11.0 | 8.87 |
| | 89 | 191 | 9.24 | 7.19 | 6.38 | 14.2 | 11.0 | 8.87 |
| S-P-F | 38 | 38 | 6.24 | 2.72 | 4.52 | 7.52 | 3.27 | 6.54 |
| | 38 | 64 | 6.91 | 4.57 | 4.52 | 9.78 | 5.51 | 6.54 |
| | 38 | 89 | 6.91 | 5.93 | 4.52 | 9.78 | 7.66 | 6.54 |
| | 38 | 140 | 6.91 | 5.93 | 4.52 | 9.78 | 8.28 | 6.54 |
| | 38 | 191 | 6.91 | 5.93 | 4.52 | 9.78 | 8.28 | 6.54 |
| | 89 | 89 | 8.83 | 6.36 | 5.98 | 13.5 | 7.66 | 8.33 |
| | 89 | 140 | 8.83 | 6.87 | 5.98 | 13.5 | 10.5 | 8.33 |
| | 89 | 191 | 8.83 | 6.87 | 5.98 | 13.5 | 10.5 | 8.33 |
| Northern | 38 | 38 | 5.20 | 2.26 | 4.04 | 6.27 | 2.73 | 5.45 |
| | 38 | 64 | 6.11 | 3.81 | 4.04 | 8.69 | 4.59 | 5.45 |
| | 38 | 89 | 6.11 | 5.22 | 4.04 | 8.69 | 6.38 | 5.45 |
| | 38 | 140 | 6.11 | 5.22 | 4.04 | 8.69 | 7.32 | 5.45 |
| | 38 | 191 | 6.11 | 5.22 | 4.04 | 8.69 | 7.32 | 5.45 |
| | 89 | 89 | 8.06 | 5.30 | 5.26 | 12.0 | 6.38 | 7.36 |
| | 89 | 140 | 8.06 | 6.27 | 5.26 | 12.0 | 9.62 | 7.36 |
| | 89 | 191 | 8.06 | 6.27 | 5.26 | 12.0 | 9.62 | 7.36 |

Notes:
1. $P_r = P'_r n_s n_F K' J'$
   $Q_r = Q'_r n_s n_F K' J_R$
   $n_s = 2$ in the Table
2. Spacing, end and edge distances for bolted connections are shown in Figure 7.5.
3. Tabulated values are valid for cases where the wood side member is of same density as main member.
4. Main member perpendicular and side member parallel to grain loading.
5. Side member perpendicular and main member parallel to grain loading.
6. Tabulated values are based on A307 steel grade bolts.

7

Fastenings

# Bolt Selection Tables

## Double Shear, Wood Side Plates

Factored lateral resistance

| Species Glulam | Side plate thickness mm | Member thickness mm | 1/2" bolt | | | 5/8" bolt | | |
|---|---|---|---|---|---|---|---|---|
| | | | $P'_r\, n_s$ kN | $Q'^4_r\, n_s$ kN | $Q'^5_r\, n_s$ kN | $P'_r\, n_s$ kN | $Q'^4_r\, n_s$ kN | $Q'^5_r\, n_s$ kN |
| D.Fir-L | 38 | 80 | 7.68 | 6.62 | 4.98 | 10.8 | 8.03 | 7.22 |
| | 38 | 130 | 7.68 | 6.62 | 4.98 | 10.8 | 9.20 | 7.22 |
| | 38 | 175 | 7.68 | 6.62 | 4.98 | 10.8 | 9.20 | 7.22 |
| | 38 | 215 | 7.68 | 6.62 | 4.98 | 10.8 | 9.20 | 7.22 |
| | 89 | 130 | 9.53 | 7.42 | 6.68 | 14.6 | 11.4 | 9.27 |
| | 89 | 175 | 9.53 | 7.42 | 6.68 | 14.6 | 11.4 | 9.27 |
| | 89 | 215 | 9.53 | 7.42 | 6.68 | 14.6 | 11.4 | 9.27 |
| Spruce-Pine | 38 | 80 | 7.13 | 5.99 | 4.65 | 10.1 | 7.21 | 6.76 |
| | 38 | 130 | 7.13 | 6.13 | 4.65 | 10.1 | 8.54 | 6.76 |
| | 38 | 175 | 7.13 | 6.13 | 4.65 | 10.1 | 8.54 | 6.76 |
| | 38 | 215 | 7.13 | 6.13 | 4.65 | 10.1 | 8.54 | 6.76 |
| | 89 | 130 | 9.03 | 7.03 | 6.18 | 13.9 | 10.8 | 8.60 |
| | 89 | 175 | 9.03 | 7.03 | 6.18 | 13.9 | 10.8 | 8.60 |
| | 89 | 215 | 9.03 | 7.03 | 6.18 | 13.9 | 10.8 | 8.60 |
| **MSR (MEL) lumber** | | | | | | | | |
| S-P-F | | | | | | | | |
| 2.0E to 2.1E | 38 | 38 | 7.43 | 3.23 | 5.04 | 8.95 | 3.89 | 7.31 |
| 1.8E to 1.9E | 38 | 38 | 6.99 | 3.04 | 4.85 | 8.41 | 3.66 | 7.04 |
| 1.2E to 1.7E | 38 | 38 | 6.24 | 2.72 | 4.52 | 7.52 | 3.27 | 6.54 |

Notes:
1. $P_r = P'_r\, n_s\, n_F\, K'\, J'$
   $Q_r = Q'_r\, n_s\, n_F\, K'\, J_R$
   $n_s = 2$ in the Table
2. Spacing, end and edge distances for bolted connections are shown in Figure 7.5.
3. Tabulated values are valid for cases where the wood side member is of same density as main member.
4. Main member perpendicular and side member parallel to grain loading.
5. Side member perpendicular and main member parallel to grain loading.
6. Tabulated values are based on A307 steel grade bolts.

# Bolt Selection Tables

## Double Shear, Wood Side Plates　2S

Factored lateral resistance

| Species Sawn lumber | Side plate thickness mm | Member thickness mm | 3/4" bolt $P'_r n_s$ kN | $Q'^4_r n_s$ kN | $Q'^5_r n_s$ kN | 7/8" bolt $P'_r n_s$ kN | $Q'^4_r n_s$ kN | $Q'^5_r n_s$ kN | 1" bolt $P'_r n_s$ kN | $Q'^4_r n_s$ kN | $Q'^5_r n_s$ kN |
|---|---|---|---|---|---|---|---|---|---|---|---|
| D.Fir-L | 38 | 38 | 10.1 | 4.41 | 8.81 | 11.4 | 4.94 | 9.88 | 12.4 | 5.41 | 10.8 |
|  | 38 | 64 | 14.4 | 7.42 | 8.81 | 18.3 | 8.32 | 9.88 | 21.0 | 9.12 | 10.8 |
|  | 38 | 89 | 14.4 | 10.3 | 8.81 | 18.3 | 11.6 | 9.88 | 22.6 | 12.7 | 10.8 |
|  | 38 | 140 | 14.4 | 12.1 | 8.81 | 18.3 | 15.3 | 9.88 | 22.6 | 18.7 | 10.8 |
|  | 38 | 191 | 14.4 | 12.1 | 8.81 | 18.3 | 15.3 | 9.88 | 22.6 | 18.7 | 10.8 |
|  | 38 | 241 | 14.4 | 12.1 | 8.81 | 18.3 | 15.3 | 9.88 | 22.6 | 18.7 | 10.8 |
|  | 38 | 292 |  |  |  | 18.3 | 15.3 | 9.88 | 22.6 | 18.7 | 10.8 |
|  | 89 | 89 | 19.8 | 10.3 | 12.2 | 24.4 | 11.6 | 15.4 | 29.2 | 12.7 | 18.8 |
|  | 89 | 140 | 19.8 | 16.1 | 12.2 | 24.4 | 18.2 | 15.4 | 29.3 | 19.9 | 18.8 |
|  | 89 | 191 | 19.8 | 16.1 | 12.2 | 24.4 | 21.4 | 15.4 | 29.3 | 25.4 | 18.8 |
|  | 89 | 241 | 19.8 | 16.1 | 12.2 | 24.4 | 21.4 | 15.4 | 29.3 | 25.4 | 18.8 |
|  | 89 | 292 |  |  |  | 24.4 | 21.4 | 15.4 | 29.3 | 25.4 | 18.8 |
| Hem-Fir | 38 | 38 | 9.51 | 4.14 | 8.27 | 10.7 | 4.64 | 9.27 | 11.7 | 5.08 | 10.2 |
|  | 38 | 64 | 13.8 | 6.97 | 8.27 | 17.6 | 7.81 | 9.27 | 19.7 | 8.56 | 10.2 |
|  | 38 | 89 | 13.8 | 9.69 | 8.27 | 17.6 | 10.9 | 9.27 | 21.8 | 11.9 | 10.2 |
|  | 38 | 140 | 13.8 | 11.6 | 8.27 | 17.6 | 14.7 | 9.27 | 21.8 | 18.0 | 10.2 |
|  | 38 | 191 | 13.8 | 11.6 | 8.27 | 17.6 | 14.7 | 9.27 | 21.8 | 18.0 | 10.2 |
|  | 38 | 241 | 13.8 | 11.6 | 8.27 | 17.6 | 14.7 | 9.27 | 21.8 | 18.0 | 10.2 |
|  | 38 | 292 |  |  |  | 17.6 | 14.7 | 9.27 | 21.8 | 18.0 | 10.2 |
|  | 89 | 89 | 18.9 | 9.69 | 11.7 | 23.3 | 10.9 | 14.7 | 27.4 | 11.9 | 18.1 |
|  | 89 | 140 | 18.9 | 15.2 | 11.7 | 23.3 | 17.1 | 14.7 | 28.0 | 18.7 | 18.1 |
|  | 89 | 191 | 18.9 | 15.6 | 11.7 | 23.3 | 20.4 | 14.7 | 28.0 | 24.2 | 18.1 |
|  | 89 | 241 | 18.9 | 15.6 | 11.7 | 23.3 | 20.4 | 14.7 | 28.0 | 24.2 | 18.1 |
|  | 89 | 292 |  |  |  | 23.3 | 20.4 | 14.7 | 28.0 | 24.2 | 18.1 |
| S-P-F | 38 | 38 | 8.68 | 3.78 | 7.55 | 9.73 | 4.23 | 8.47 | 10.7 | 4.64 | 9.28 |
|  | 38 | 64 | 13.0 | 6.36 | 7.55 | 16.4 | 7.13 | 8.47 | 18.0 | 7.82 | 9.28 |
|  | 38 | 89 | 13.0 | 8.84 | 7.55 | 16.6 | 9.91 | 8.47 | 20.6 | 10.9 | 9.28 |
|  | 38 | 140 | 13.0 | 10.9 | 7.55 | 16.6 | 13.8 | 8.47 | 20.6 | 17.0 | 9.28 |
|  | 38 | 191 | 13.0 | 10.9 | 7.55 | 16.6 | 13.8 | 8.47 | 20.6 | 17.0 | 9.28 |
|  | 38 | 241 | 13.0 | 10.9 | 7.55 | 16.6 | 13.8 | 8.47 | 20.6 | 17.0 | 9.28 |
|  | 38 | 292 |  |  |  | 16.6 | 13.8 | 8.47 | 20.6 | 17.0 | 9.28 |
|  | 89 | 89 | 17.7 | 8.84 | 11.0 | 21.9 | 9.91 | 13.9 | 25.0 | 10.9 | 17.1 |
|  | 89 | 140 | 17.7 | 13.9 | 11.0 | 21.9 | 15.6 | 13.9 | 26.3 | 17.1 | 17.1 |
|  | 89 | 191 | 17.7 | 14.9 | 11.0 | 21.9 | 19.0 | 13.9 | 26.3 | 22.7 | 17.1 |
|  | 89 | 241 | 17.7 | 14.9 | 11.0 | 21.9 | 19.0 | 13.9 | 26.3 | 22.7 | 17.1 |
|  | 89 | 292 |  |  |  | 21.9 | 19.0 | 13.9 | 26.3 | 22.7 | 17.1 |
| Northern | 38 | 38 | 7.24 | 3.15 | 6.29 | 8.11 | 3.53 | 7.06 | 8.89 | 3.87 | 7.73 |
|  | 38 | 64 | 11.6 | 5.30 | 6.29 | 13.7 | 5.94 | 7.06 | 15.0 | 6.51 | 7.73 |
|  | 38 | 89 | 11.6 | 7.37 | 6.29 | 14.9 | 8.26 | 7.06 | 17.8 | 9.06 | 7.73 |
|  | 38 | 140 | 11.6 | 9.69 | 6.29 | 14.9 | 12.3 | 7.06 | 17.8 | 14.2 | 7.73 |
|  | 38 | 191 | 11.6 | 9.69 | 6.29 | 14.9 | 12.3 | 7.06 | 17.8 | 15.2 | 7.73 |
|  | 38 | 241 | 11.6 | 9.69 | 6.29 | 14.9 | 12.3 | 7.06 | 17.8 | 15.2 | 7.73 |
|  | 38 | 292 |  |  |  | 14.9 | 12.3 | 7.06 | 17.8 | 15.2 | 7.73 |
|  | 89 | 89 | 15.5 | 7.37 | 9.74 | 19.0 | 8.26 | 12.4 | 20.8 | 9.06 | 15.2 |
|  | 89 | 140 | 15.5 | 11.6 | 9.74 | 19.2 | 13.0 | 12.4 | 23.2 | 14.2 | 15.2 |
|  | 89 | 191 | 15.5 | 13.6 | 9.74 | 19.2 | 16.7 | 12.4 | 23.2 | 19.4 | 15.2 |
|  | 89 | 241 | 15.5 | 13.6 | 9.74 | 19.2 | 16.7 | 12.4 | 23.2 | 19.9 | 15.2 |
|  | 89 | 292 |  |  |  | 19.2 | 16.7 | 12.4 | 23.2 | 19.9 | 15.2 |

Notes: see page 258

7

Fastenings

# Bolt Selection Tables

## Double Shear, Wood Side Plates

Factored lateral resistance

| Species | Side plate thickness | Member thickness | 3/4" bolt | | | 7/8" bolt | | | 1" bolt | | |
|---|---|---|---|---|---|---|---|---|---|---|---|
| | | | $P'_r\,n_s$ | $Q'^4_r\,n_s$ | $Q'^5_r\,n_s$ | $P'_r\,n_s$ | $Q'^4_r\,n_s$ | $Q'^5_r\,n_s$ | $P'_r\,n_s$ | $Q'^4_r\,n_s$ | $Q'^5_r\,n_s$ |
| **Glulam** | mm | mm | kN | kN | kN | kN | kN | kN | kN | kN | kN |
| D.Fir-L | 38 | 80 | 14.4 | 9.28 | 8.81 | 18.3 | 10.4 | 9.88 | 22.6 | 11.4 | 10.8 |
| | 38 | 130 | 14.4 | 12.1 | 8.81 | 18.3 | 15.3 | 9.88 | 22.6 | 18.5 | 10.8 |
| | 38 | 175 | 14.4 | 12.1 | 8.81 | 18.3 | 15.3 | 9.88 | 22.6 | 18.7 | 10.8 |
| | 38 | 215 | 14.4 | 12.1 | 8.81 | 18.3 | 15.3 | 9.88 | 22.6 | 18.7 | 10.8 |
| | 38 | 265 | 14.4 | 12.1 | 8.81 | 18.3 | 15.3 | 9.88 | 22.6 | 18.7 | 10.8 |
| | 38 | 315 | | | | | | | 22.6 | 18.7 | 10.8 |
| | 89 | 130 | 19.8 | 15.1 | 12.2 | 24.4 | 16.9 | 15.4 | 29.3 | 18.5 | 18.8 |
| | 89 | 175 | 19.8 | 16.1 | 12.2 | 24.4 | 21.4 | 15.4 | 29.3 | 24.9 | 18.8 |
| | 89 | 215 | 19.8 | 16.1 | 12.2 | 24.4 | 21.4 | 15.4 | 29.3 | 25.4 | 18.8 |
| | 89 | 265 | 19.8 | 16.1 | 12.2 | 24.4 | 21.4 | 15.4 | 29.3 | 25.4 | 18.8 |
| | 89 | 315 | | | | | | | 29.3 | 25.4 | 18.8 |
| Spruce-Pine | 38 | 80 | 13.4 | 8.33 | 7.91 | 17.1 | 9.34 | 8.87 | 21.2 | 10.2 | 9.72 |
| | 38 | 130 | 13.4 | 11.3 | 7.91 | 17.1 | 14.2 | 8.87 | 21.2 | 16.6 | 9.72 |
| | 38 | 175 | 13.4 | 11.3 | 7.91 | 17.1 | 14.2 | 8.87 | 21.2 | 17.5 | 9.72 |
| | 38 | 215 | 13.4 | 11.3 | 7.91 | 17.1 | 14.2 | 8.87 | 21.2 | 17.5 | 9.72 |
| | 38 | 265 | 13.4 | 11.3 | 7.91 | 17.1 | 14.2 | 8.87 | 21.2 | 17.5 | 9.72 |
| | 38 | 315 | | | | | | | 21.2 | 17.5 | 9.72 |
| | 89 | 130 | 18.3 | 13.5 | 11.3 | 22.6 | 15.2 | 14.3 | 27.2 | 16.6 | 17.6 |
| | 89 | 175 | 18.3 | 15.2 | 11.3 | 22.6 | 19.7 | 14.3 | 27.2 | 22.4 | 17.6 |
| | 89 | 215 | 18.3 | 15.2 | 11.3 | 22.6 | 19.7 | 14.3 | 27.2 | 23.5 | 17.6 |
| | 89 | 265 | 18.3 | 15.2 | 11.3 | 22.6 | 19.7 | 14.3 | 27.2 | 23.5 | 17.6 |
| | 89 | 315 | | | | | | | 27.2 | 23.5 | 17.6 |

**MSR (MEL) lumber**

| Species | Side plate thickness | Member thickness | 3/4" bolt | | | 7/8" bolt | | | 1" bolt | | |
|---|---|---|---|---|---|---|---|---|---|---|---|
| S-P-F | | | | | | | | | | | |
| 2.0E to 2.1E | 38 | 38 | 10.3 | 4.50 | 8.99 | 11.6 | 5.04 | 10.1 | 12.7 | 5.52 | 11.0 |
| 1.8E to 1.9E | 38 | 38 | 9.72 | 4.23 | 8.45 | 10.9 | 4.74 | 9.47 | 11.9 | 5.19 | 10.4 |
| 1.2E to 1.7E | 38 | 38 | 8.68 | 3.78 | 7.55 | 9.73 | 4.23 | 8.47 | 10.7 | 4.64 | 9.28 |

Notes:
1. $P_r = P'_r\,n_s\,n_F\,K'\,J'$
   $Q_r = Q'_r\,n_s\,n_F\,K'\,J_R$
   $n_s = 2$ in the Table
2. Minimum spacing, end and edge distances for bolted connections are shown in Figure 7.5.
3. Tabulated values are valid for cases where the wood side member is of same density as main member.
4. Main member perpendicular and side member parallel to grain loading.
5. Side member perpendicular and main member parallel to grain loading.
6. Tabulated values are based on A307 steel grade bolts.

# Bolt Selection Tables

## Single Shear, 6 mm Steel Side Plates 1S

Factored lateral resistance based on A36 steel grade plates

| Species Sawn lumber | Member thickness mm | 1/2" bolt $P'_r\,n_s$ kN | $Q'_r\,n_s$ kN | 5/8" bolt $P'_r\,n_s$ kN | $Q'_r\,n_s$ kN | 3/4" bolt $P'_r\,n_s$ kN | $Q'_r\,n_s$ kN | 7/8" bolt $P'_r\,n_s$ kN | $Q'_r\,n_s$ kN | 1" bolt $P'_r\,n_s$ kN | $Q'_r\,n_s$ kN |
|---|---|---|---|---|---|---|---|---|---|---|---|
| D.Fir-L | 38 | 6.68 | 3.17 | 8.77 | 3.82 | 10.1 | 4.41 | 11.4 | 4.94 | 12.4 | 5.41 |
|  | 64 | 6.68 | 4.43 | 10.2 | 6.43 | 14.5 | 7.42 | 19.1 | 8.32 | 21.0 | 9.12 |
|  | 89 | 6.68 | 4.43 | 10.2 | 6.79 | 14.5 | 9.60 | 19.3 | 11.6 | 24.7 | 12.7 |
|  | 140 | 6.68 | 4.43 | 10.2 | 6.79 | 14.5 | 9.60 | 19.3 | 12.8 | 24.7 | 16.4 |
|  | 191 | 6.68 | 4.43 | 10.2 | 6.79 | 14.5 | 9.60 | 19.3 | 12.8 | 24.7 | 16.4 |
|  | 241 |  |  |  |  | 14.5 | 9.60 | 19.3 | 12.8 | 24.7 | 16.4 |
|  | 292 |  |  |  |  |  |  | 19.3 | 12.8 | 24.7 | 16.4 |
| Hem-Fir | 38 | 6.47 | 2.97 | 8.24 | 3.58 | 9.51 | 4.14 | 10.7 | 4.64 | 11.7 | 5.08 |
|  | 64 | 6.47 | 4.29 | 9.93 | 6.03 | 14.0 | 6.97 | 18.0 | 7.81 | 19.7 | 8.56 |
|  | 89 | 6.47 | 4.29 | 9.93 | 6.58 | 14.0 | 9.30 | 18.7 | 10.9 | 24.0 | 11.9 |
|  | 140 | 6.47 | 4.29 | 9.93 | 6.58 | 14.0 | 9.30 | 18.7 | 12.4 | 24.0 | 15.9 |
|  | 191 | 6.47 | 4.29 | 9.93 | 6.58 | 14.0 | 9.30 | 18.7 | 12.4 | 24.0 | 15.9 |
|  | 241 |  |  |  |  | 14.0 | 9.30 | 18.7 | 12.4 | 24.0 | 15.9 |
|  | 292 |  |  |  |  |  |  | 18.7 | 12.4 | 24.0 | 15.9 |
| S-P-F | 38 | 6.19 | 2.72 | 7.52 | 3.27 | 8.68 | 3.78 | 9.73 | 4.23 | 10.7 | 4.64 |
|  | 64 | 6.19 | 4.10 | 9.50 | 5.51 | 13.4 | 6.36 | 16.4 | 7.13 | 18.0 | 7.82 |
|  | 89 | 6.19 | 4.10 | 9.50 | 6.29 | 13.4 | 8.84 | 17.9 | 9.91 | 22.9 | 10.9 |
|  | 140 | 6.19 | 4.10 | 9.50 | 6.29 | 13.4 | 8.89 | 17.9 | 11.9 | 22.9 | 15.2 |
|  | 191 | 6.19 | 4.10 | 9.50 | 6.29 | 13.4 | 8.89 | 17.9 | 11.9 | 22.9 | 15.2 |
|  | 241 |  |  |  |  | 13.4 | 8.89 | 17.9 | 11.9 | 22.9 | 15.2 |
|  | 292 |  |  |  |  |  |  | 17.9 | 11.9 | 22.9 | 15.2 |
| Northern | 38 | 5.20 | 2.26 | 6.27 | 2.73 | 7.24 | 3.15 | 8.11 | 3.53 | 8.89 | 3.87 |
|  | 64 | 5.66 | 3.75 | 8.68 | 4.59 | 12.2 | 5.30 | 13.7 | 5.94 | 15.0 | 6.51 |
|  | 89 | 5.66 | 3.75 | 8.68 | 5.75 | 12.3 | 7.37 | 16.4 | 8.26 | 20.8 | 9.06 |
|  | 140 | 5.66 | 3.75 | 8.68 | 5.75 | 12.3 | 8.12 | 16.4 | 10.8 | 20.9 | 13.9 |
|  | 191 | 5.66 | 3.75 | 8.68 | 5.75 | 12.3 | 8.12 | 16.4 | 10.8 | 20.9 | 13.9 |
|  | 241 |  |  |  |  | 12.3 | 8.12 | 16.4 | 10.8 | 20.9 | 13.9 |
|  | 292 |  |  |  |  |  |  | 16.4 | 10.8 | 20.9 | 13.9 |
| **Glulam** |  |  |  |  |  |  |  |  |  |  |  |
| D.Fir-L | 80 | 6.68 | 4.43 | 10.2 | 6.79 | 14.5 | 9.28 | 19.3 | 10.4 | 24.7 | 11.4 |
|  | 130 | 6.68 | 4.43 | 10.2 | 6.79 | 14.5 | 9.60 | 19.3 | 12.8 | 24.7 | 16.4 |
|  | 175 | 6.68 | 4.43 | 10.2 | 6.79 | 14.5 | 9.60 | 19.3 | 12.8 | 24.7 | 16.4 |
|  | 215 | 6.68 | 4.43 | 10.2 | 6.79 | 14.5 | 9.60 | 19.3 | 12.8 | 24.7 | 16.4 |
|  | 265 |  |  |  |  | 14.5 | 9.60 | 19.3 | 12.8 | 24.7 | 16.4 |
|  | 315 |  |  |  |  |  |  |  |  | 24.7 | 16.4 |
| Spruce-Pine | 80 | 6.33 | 4.20 | 9.72 | 6.44 | 13.7 | 8.33 | 18.3 | 9.34 | 23.5 | 10.2 |
|  | 130 | 6.33 | 4.20 | 9.72 | 6.44 | 13.7 | 9.10 | 18.3 | 12.1 | 23.5 | 15.5 |
|  | 175 | 6.33 | 4.20 | 9.72 | 6.44 | 13.7 | 9.10 | 18.3 | 12.1 | 23.5 | 15.5 |
|  | 215 | 6.33 | 4.20 | 9.72 | 6.44 | 13.7 | 9.10 | 18.3 | 12.1 | 23.5 | 15.5 |
|  | 265 |  |  |  |  | 13.7 | 9.10 | 18.3 | 12.1 | 23.5 | 15.5 |
|  | 315 |  |  |  |  |  |  |  |  | 23.5 | 15.5 |
| **MSR (MEL) lumber** |  |  |  |  |  |  |  |  |  |  |  |
| S-P-F | | | | | | | | | | | |
| 2.0E to 2.1E | 38 | 6.74 | 3.23 | 8.95 | 3.89 | 10.3 | 4.50 | 11.6 | 5.04 | 12.7 | 5.52 |
| 1.8E to 1.9E | 38 | 6.54 | 3.04 | 8.41 | 3.66 | 9.72 | 4.23 | 10.9 | 4.74 | 11.9 | 5.19 |
| 1.2E to 1.7E | 38 | 6.19 | 2.72 | 7.52 | 3.27 | 8.68 | 3.78 | 9.73 | 4.23 | 10.7 | 4.64 |

Notes: see page 260 (1, 2, 6 only).

7

Fastenings

# Bolt Selection Tables

## Double Shear, 6 mm Steel Side Plates

Factored lateral resistance based on A36 steel grade plates

| Species | Member thickness | 1/2" bolt | | 5/8" bolt | | 3/4" bolt | | 7/8" bolt | | 1" bolt | |
|---|---|---|---|---|---|---|---|---|---|---|---|
| **Sawn lumber** | mm | $P'_r\,n_s$ kN | $Q'_r\,n_s$ kN | $P'_r\,n_s$ kN | $Q'_r\,n_s$ kN | $P'_r\,n_s$ kN | $Q'_r\,n_s$ kN | $P'_r\,n_s$ kN | $Q'_r\,n_s$ kN | $P'_r\,n_s$ kN | $Q'_r\,n_s$ kN |
| D.Fir-L | 38 | 7.28 | 3.17 | 8.77 | 3.82 | 10.1 | 4.41 | 11.4 | 4.94 | 12.4 | 5.41 |
| | 64 | 12.3 | 5.33 | 14.8 | 6.43 | 17.1 | 7.42 | 19.1 | 8.32 | 21.0 | 9.12 |
| | 89 | 13.4 | 7.42 | 20.5 | 8.94 | 23.7 | 10.3 | 26.6 | 11.6 | 29.2 | 12.7 |
| | 140 | 13.4 | 8.85 | 20.5 | 13.6 | 29.0 | 16.2 | 38.6 | 18.2 | 45.9 | 19.9 |
| | 191 | 13.4 | 8.85 | 20.5 | 13.6 | 29.0 | 19.2 | 38.6 | 24.8 | 49.5 | 27.2 |
| | 241 | | | | | 29.0 | 19.2 | 38.6 | 25.6 | 49.5 | 32.8 |
| | 292 | | | | | | | 38.6 | 25.6 | 49.5 | 32.8 |
| Hem-Fir | 38 | 6.84 | 2.97 | 8.24 | 3.58 | 9.51 | 4.14 | 10.7 | 4.64 | 11.7 | 5.08 |
| | 64 | 11.5 | 5.01 | 13.9 | 6.03 | 16.0 | 6.97 | 18.0 | 7.81 | 19.7 | 8.56 |
| | 89 | 12.9 | 6.96 | 19.3 | 8.39 | 22.3 | 9.69 | 25.0 | 10.9 | 27.4 | 11.9 |
| | 140 | 12.9 | 8.58 | 19.9 | 13.2 | 28.1 | 15.2 | 37.5 | 17.1 | 43.1 | 18.7 |
| | 191 | 12.9 | 8.58 | 19.9 | 13.2 | 28.1 | 18.6 | 37.5 | 23.3 | 47.9 | 25.5 |
| | 241 | | | | | 28.1 | 18.6 | 37.5 | 24.8 | 47.9 | 31.7 |
| | 292 | | | | | | | 37.5 | 24.8 | 47.9 | 31.7 |
| S-P-F | 38 | 6.24 | 2.72 | 7.52 | 3.27 | 8.68 | 3.78 | 9.73 | 4.23 | 10.7 | 4.64 |
| | 64 | 10.5 | 4.57 | 12.7 | 5.51 | 14.6 | 6.36 | 16.4 | 7.13 | 18.0 | 7.82 |
| | 89 | 12.4 | 6.36 | 17.6 | 7.66 | 20.3 | 8.84 | 22.8 | 9.91 | 25.0 | 10.9 |
| | 140 | 12.4 | 8.20 | 19.0 | 12.0 | 26.8 | 13.9 | 35.8 | 15.6 | 39.3 | 17.1 |
| | 191 | 12.4 | 8.20 | 19.0 | 12.6 | 26.8 | 17.8 | 35.8 | 21.3 | 45.8 | 23.3 |
| | 241 | | | | | 26.8 | 17.8 | 35.8 | 23.7 | 45.8 | 29.4 |
| | 292 | | | | | | | 35.8 | 23.7 | 45.8 | 30.3 |
| Northern | 38 | 5.20 | 2.26 | 6.27 | 2.73 | 7.24 | 3.15 | 8.11 | 3.53 | 8.89 | 3.87 |
| | 64 | 8.76 | 3.81 | 10.6 | 4.59 | 12.2 | 5.30 | 13.7 | 5.94 | 15.0 | 6.51 |
| | 89 | 11.3 | 5.30 | 14.7 | 6.38 | 16.9 | 7.37 | 19.0 | 8.26 | 20.8 | 9.06 |
| | 140 | 11.3 | 7.49 | 17.4 | 10.0 | 24.5 | 11.6 | 29.9 | 13.0 | 32.8 | 14.2 |
| | 191 | 11.3 | 7.49 | 17.4 | 11.5 | 24.5 | 15.8 | 32.7 | 17.7 | 41.9 | 19.4 |
| | 241 | | | | | 24.5 | 16.2 | 32.7 | 21.7 | 41.9 | 24.5 |
| | 292 | | | | | | | 32.7 | 21.7 | 41.9 | 27.7 |
| **Glulam** | | | | | | | | | | | |
| D.Fir-L | 80 | 13.4 | 6.67 | 18.5 | 8.03 | 21.3 | 9.28 | 23.9 | 10.4 | 26.2 | 11.4 |
| | 130 | 13.4 | 8.85 | 20.5 | 13.1 | 29.0 | 15.1 | 38.6 | 16.9 | 42.6 | 18.5 |
| | 175 | 13.4 | 8.85 | 20.5 | 13.6 | 29.0 | 19.2 | 38.6 | 22.7 | 49.5 | 24.9 |
| | 215 | 13.4 | 8.85 | 20.5 | 13.6 | 29.0 | 19.2 | 38.6 | 25.6 | 49.5 | 30.6 |
| | 265 | | | | | 29.0 | 19.2 | 38.6 | 25.6 | 49.5 | 32.8 |
| | 315 | | | | | | | | | 49.5 | 32.8 |
| Spruce-Pine | 80 | 12.7 | 5.99 | 16.6 | 7.21 | 19.2 | 8.33 | 21.5 | 9.34 | 23.5 | 10.2 |
| | 130 | 12.7 | 8.39 | 19.4 | 11.7 | 27.5 | 13.5 | 34.9 | 15.2 | 38.2 | 16.6 |
| | 175 | 12.7 | 8.39 | 19.4 | 12.9 | 27.5 | 18.2 | 36.7 | 20.4 | 46.9 | 22.4 |
| | 215 | 12.7 | 8.39 | 19.4 | 12.9 | 27.5 | 18.2 | 36.7 | 24.3 | 46.9 | 27.5 |
| | 265 | | | | | 27.5 | 18.2 | 36.7 | 24.3 | 46.9 | 31.1 |
| | 315 | | | | | | | | | 46.9 | 31.1 |
| **MSR (MEL) lumber** | | | | | | | | | | | |
| S-P-F | | | | | | | | | | | |
| 2.0E to 2.1E | 38 | 7.43 | 3.23 | 8.95 | 3.89 | 10.3 | 4.50 | 11.6 | 5.04 | 12.7 | 5.52 |
| 1.8E to 1.9E | 38 | 6.99 | 3.04 | 8.41 | 3.66 | 9.72 | 4.23 | 10.9 | 4.74 | 11.9 | 5.19 |
| 1.2E to 1.7E | 38 | 6.24 | 2.72 | 7.52 | 3.27 | 8.68 | 3.78 | 9.73 | 4.23 | 10.7 | 4.64 |

Notes: see page 260 (1, 2, 6 only).

# Bolt Selection Tables

## Double Shear, 6 mm Steel Internal Plate 2S

Factored lateral resistance based on A36 steel grade plate

| Species | Thickness of thinnest wood member | 1/2" bolt | | 5/8" bolt | | 3/4" bolt | | 7/8" bolt | | 1" bolt | |
|---|---|---|---|---|---|---|---|---|---|---|---|
| **Sawn lumber** | mm | $P'_r n_s$ kN | $Q'_r n_s$ kN | $P'_r n_s$ kN | $Q'_r n_s$ kN | $P'_r n_s$ kN | $Q'_r n_s$ kN | $P'_r n_s$ kN | $Q'_r n_s$ kN | $P'_r n_s$ kN | $Q'_r n_s$ kN |
| D.Fir-L | 38 | 9.59 | 5.69 | 13.8 | 7.63 | 18.5 | 8.81 | 22.7 | 9.88 | 24.9 | 10.8 |
| | 64 | 11.6 | 6.56 | 16.2 | 9.36 | 21.3 | 12.6 | 27.0 | 16.1 | 33.1 | 18.2 |
| | 89 | 13.4 | 7.39 | 18.5 | 10.4 | 24.0 | 13.7 | 30.0 | 17.4 | 36.4 | 21.5 |
| | 140 | 13.4 | 8.85 | 20.5 | 12.4 | 29.0 | 16.1 | 36.1 | 20.1 | 43.1 | 24.4 |
| | 191 | 13.4 | 8.85 | 20.5 | 13.6 | 29.0 | 18.5 | 38.6 | 22.7 | 49.5 | 27.3 |
| | 241 | | | | | 29.0 | 19.2 | 38.6 | 25.3 | 49.5 | 30.1 |
| | 292 | | | | | | | 38.6 | 25.6 | 49.5 | 32.8 |
| Hem-Fir | 38 | 9.21 | 5.48 | 13.2 | 7.16 | 17.8 | 8.27 | 21.3 | 9.27 | 23.4 | 10.2 |
| | 64 | 11.1 | 6.29 | 15.5 | 9.00 | 20.4 | 12.1 | 25.9 | 15.5 | 31.8 | 17.1 |
| | 89 | 12.9 | 7.08 | 17.6 | 9.94 | 22.9 | 13.2 | 28.7 | 16.8 | 34.9 | 20.6 |
| | 140 | 12.9 | 8.58 | 19.9 | 11.9 | 28.1 | 15.4 | 34.4 | 19.2 | 41.2 | 23.4 |
| | 191 | 12.9 | 8.58 | 19.9 | 13.2 | 28.1 | 17.6 | 37.5 | 21.7 | 47.5 | 26.1 |
| | 241 | | | | | 28.1 | 18.6 | 37.5 | 24.2 | 47.9 | 28.8 |
| | 292 | | | | | | | 37.5 | 24.8 | 47.9 | 31.5 |
| S-P-F | 38 | 8.69 | 5.19 | 12.5 | 6.54 | 16.9 | 7.55 | 19.5 | 8.47 | 21.3 | 9.28 |
| | 64 | 10.4 | 5.93 | 14.6 | 8.49 | 19.3 | 11.4 | 24.5 | 14.3 | 30.1 | 15.6 |
| | 89 | 12.0 | 6.64 | 16.5 | 9.36 | 21.6 | 12.4 | 27.0 | 15.8 | 32.9 | 19.5 |
| | 140 | 12.4 | 8.10 | 19.0 | 11.1 | 26.2 | 14.5 | 32.3 | 18.1 | 38.6 | 22.0 |
| | 191 | 12.4 | 8.20 | 19.0 | 12.6 | 26.8 | 16.5 | 35.8 | 20.4 | 44.4 | 24.5 |
| | 241 | | | | | 26.8 | 17.8 | 35.8 | 22.6 | 45.8 | 26.9 |
| | 292 | | | | | | | 35.8 | 23.7 | 45.8 | 29.4 |
| Northern | 38 | 7.74 | 4.53 | 11.2 | 5.45 | 14.5 | 6.29 | 16.2 | 7.06 | 17.8 | 7.73 |
| | 64 | 9.16 | 5.27 | 12.9 | 7.58 | 17.1 | 10.2 | 21.8 | 11.9 | 26.9 | 13.0 |
| | 89 | 10.5 | 5.87 | 14.6 | 8.30 | 19.0 | 11.1 | 24.0 | 14.1 | 29.3 | 17.5 |
| | 140 | 11.3 | 7.08 | 17.4 | 9.76 | 22.9 | 12.8 | 28.3 | 16.0 | 34.0 | 19.6 |
| | 191 | 11.3 | 7.49 | 17.4 | 11.2 | 24.5 | 14.4 | 32.7 | 17.9 | 38.8 | 21.6 |
| | 241 | | | | | 24.5 | 16.1 | 32.7 | 19.8 | 41.9 | 23.7 |
| | 292 | | | | | | | 32.7 | 21.7 | 41.9 | 25.7 |
| **Glulam** | | | | | | | | | | | |
| D.Fir-L | 80 | 12.8 | 7.09 | 17.6 | 10.0 | 23.0 | 13.3 | 28.9 | 17.0 | 35.2 | 20.9 |
| | 130 | 13.4 | 8.76 | 20.5 | 12.0 | 28.3 | 15.6 | 34.9 | 19.6 | 41.8 | 23.8 |
| | 175 | 13.4 | 8.85 | 20.5 | 13.6 | 29.0 | 17.7 | 38.6 | 21.9 | 47.7 | 26.4 |
| | 215 | 13.4 | 8.85 | 20.5 | 13.6 | 29.0 | 19.2 | 38.6 | 24.0 | 49.5 | 28.6 |
| | 265 | | | | | 29.0 | 19.2 | 38.6 | 25.6 | 49.5 | 31.5 |
| | 315 | | | | | | | | | 49.5 | 32.8 |
| Spruce-Pine | 80 | 11.8 | 6.59 | 16.4 | 9.32 | 21.4 | 12.4 | 26.9 | 15.9 | 32.9 | 19.6 |
| | 130 | 12.7 | 8.09 | 19.4 | 11.1 | 26.2 | 14.5 | 32.3 | 18.2 | 38.7 | 22.2 |
| | 175 | 12.7 | 8.39 | 19.4 | 12.7 | 27.5 | 16.4 | 36.7 | 20.3 | 44.0 | 24.5 |
| | 215 | 12.7 | 8.39 | 19.4 | 12.9 | 27.5 | 18.0 | 36.7 | 22.2 | 46.9 | 26.5 |
| | 265 | | | | | 27.5 | 18.2 | 36.7 | 24.3 | 46.9 | 29.1 |
| | 315 | | | | | | | | | 46.9 | 31.1 |
| **MSR (MEL) lumber** | | | | | | | | | | | |
| S-P-F | | | | | | | | | | | |
| 2.0E to 2.1E | 38 | 9.72 | 5.76 | 13.9 | 7.79 | 18.8 | 8.99 | 23.2 | 10.1 | 25.4 | 11.0 |
| 1.8E to 1.9E | 38 | 9.34 | 5.55 | 13.4 | 7.32 | 18.1 | 8.45 | 21.8 | 9.47 | 23.9 | 10.4 |
| 1.2E to 1.7E | 38 | 8.69 | 5.19 | 12.5 | 6.54 | 16.9 | 7.55 | 19.5 | 8.47 | 21.3 | 9.28 |

Notes: see page 260 (1, 2, 6 only).

**7**

Fastenings

# Bolt Selection Tables

## 1S    Single Shear, Wood to Concrete

Factored lateral resistance based on 100 mm bolt penetration in concrete

| Species Sawn Lumber | Member thickness mm | 1/2" bolt | | 5/8" bolt | | 3/4" bolt | | 7/8" bolt | | 1" bolt | |
|---|---|---|---|---|---|---|---|---|---|---|---|
| | | $P'_r\, n_s$ kN | $Q'_r\, n_s$ kN | $P'_r\, n_s$ kN | $Q'_r\, n_s$ kN | $P'_r\, n_s$ kN | $Q'_r\, n_s$ kN | $P'_r\, n_s$ kN | $Q'_r\, n_s$ kN | $P'_r\, n_s$ kN | $Q'_r\, n_s$ kN |
| D.Fir-L | 38 | 4.51 | 2.76 | 6.46 | 3.82 | 8.69 | 4.41 | 11.2 | 4.94 | 12.4 | 5.41 |
| | 64 | 5.51 | 3.19 | 7.66 | 4.55 | 10.1 | 6.10 | 12.7 | 7.84 | 15.6 | 9.12 |
| | 89 | 6.11 | 3.61 | 8.81 | 5.05 | 11.4 | 6.68 | 14.2 | 8.49 | 17.3 | 10.4 |
| | 140 | 6.11 | 3.79 | 9.32 | 5.27 | 12.0 | 6.94 | 14.9 | 8.77 | 18.0 | 10.8 |
| Hem-Fir | 38 | 4.35 | 2.66 | 6.23 | 3.58 | 8.39 | 4.14 | 10.7 | 4.64 | 11.7 | 5.08 |
| | 64 | 5.28 | 3.07 | 7.36 | 4.38 | 9.70 | 5.88 | 12.3 | 7.56 | 15.1 | 8.56 |
| | 89 | 5.96 | 3.46 | 8.44 | 4.85 | 10.9 | 6.42 | 13.7 | 8.17 | 16.6 | 10.1 |
| | 140 | 5.96 | 3.63 | 8.92 | 5.06 | 11.5 | 6.66 | 14.3 | 8.43 | 17.3 | 10.4 |
| S-P-F | 38 | 4.12 | 2.52 | 5.91 | 3.27 | 7.98 | 3.78 | 9.73 | 4.23 | 10.7 | 4.64 |
| | 64 | 4.97 | 2.89 | 6.94 | 4.14 | 9.17 | 5.57 | 11.6 | 7.13 | 14.3 | 7.82 |
| | 89 | 5.73 | 3.25 | 7.93 | 4.57 | 10.3 | 6.07 | 12.9 | 7.73 | 15.7 | 9.53 |
| | 140 | 5.73 | 3.41 | 8.37 | 4.76 | 10.8 | 6.29 | 13.5 | 7.97 | 16.3 | 9.80 |
| Northern | 38 | 3.69 | 2.26 | 5.33 | 2.73 | 7.22 | 3.15 | 8.11 | 3.53 | 8.89 | 3.87 |
| | 64 | 4.40 | 2.58 | 6.19 | 3.71 | 8.21 | 5.01 | 10.5 | 5.94 | 12.9 | 6.51 |
| | 89 | 5.09 | 2.88 | 7.01 | 4.07 | 9.16 | 5.42 | 11.5 | 6.93 | 14.1 | 8.57 |
| | 140 | 5.30 | 3.01 | 7.38 | 4.23 | 9.58 | 5.61 | 12.0 | 7.13 | 14.6 | 8.79 |
| **MSR (MEL) lumber** | | | | | | | | | | | |
| S-P-F | | | | | | | | | | | |
| 2.0E to 2.1E | 38 | 4.57 | 2.79 | 6.53 | 3.89 | 8.79 | 4.50 | 11.3 | 5.04 | 12.7 | 5.52 |
| 1.8E to 1.9E | 38 | 4.40 | 2.69 | 6.31 | 3.66 | 8.49 | 4.23 | 10.9 | 4.74 | 11.9 | 5.19 |
| 1.2E to 1.7E | 38 | 4.12 | 2.52 | 5.91 | 3.27 | 7.98 | 3.78 | 9.73 | 4.23 | 10.7 | 4.64 |

Notes:
1. $P_r = P'_r\, n_s\, n_F\, K'\, J_L\, J_R$
   $Q_r = Q'_r\, n_s\, n_F\, K'\, J_R$
   $n_s = 1$ in the Table
2. Spacing, end and edge distances for bolted connections are shown in Figure 7.5.
3. Tabulated values are based on A307 steel grade bolts.

Figure 7.5
**Minimum spacing, end and edge distances for bolted connections (mm)**

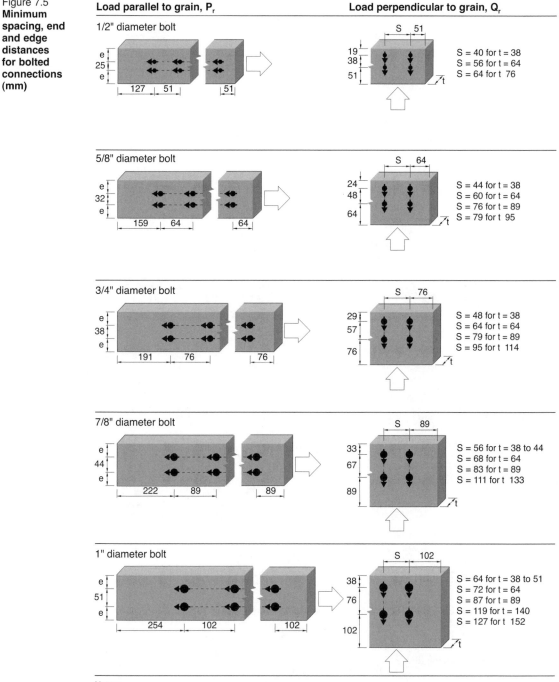

Load parallel to grain, $P_r$    Load perpendicular to grain, $Q_r$

1/2" diameter bolt

S = 40 for t = 38
S = 56 for t = 64
S = 64 for t  76

5/8" diameter bolt

S = 44 for t = 38
S = 60 for t = 64
S = 76 for t = 89
S = 79 for t  95

3/4" diameter bolt

S = 48 for t = 38
S = 64 for t = 64
S = 79 for t = 89
S = 95 for t  114

7/8" diameter bolt

S = 56 for t = 38 to 44
S = 68 for t = 64
S = 83 for t = 89
S = 111 for t  133

1" diameter bolt

S = 64 for t = 38 to 51
S = 72 for t = 64
S = 87 for t = 89
S = 119 for t = 140
S = 127 for t  152

**7**

Fastenings

Notes:
1. e = the greater of 1.5 times bolt diameter or half of actual spacing between rows
2. Loaded end distances are minimum permitted for $J_L$ = 1.0

# 7.4    Drift Pins

## General

Design information provided in CSA O86 is based on 16 mm (5/8") to 25 mm (1") diameter drift pins made from round mild steel conforming to ASTM Standard A307 or CSA Standard CAN3-G40.21.

As shown in Figure 7.6, drift pins are round steel dowels that do not have heads and are not threaded. The ends are tapered or shaped so that the pin may be easily driven into pre-bored holes with minimal damage to the wood.

Figure 7.6
**Typical drift pin**

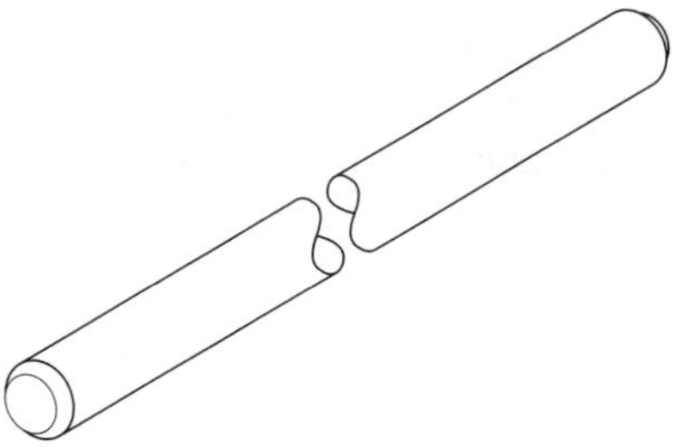

Drift pins are primarily used to fasten timbers in cribwork, and to anchor beams and columns to steel shoes (see Section 7.11).

## Installation

Drift pins are installed by driving them into pre-drilled holes. The holes must be between 0.8 mm and 1 mm smaller than the diameter of the drift pin. As shown in Figure 7.7, drift pins should be long enough to fully penetrate the top member and penetrate all but 15 mm of the lower member. Figure 7.7 also provides the minimum end distance, edge distance and spacing for drift pins.

## Design

Drift pins must be designed so that the factored lateral resistance is greater than or equal to the factored lateral applied load. Drift pins should only be used where mechanical restraint prevents axial tensile stress.

The factored lateral resistance of a drift pin is equivalent to 60% of the resistance of a bolt of the same diameter in single shear. Therefore the resistance may be calculated from the following formulae:

$$P_r = 0.6\ P'_r\ n_F\ K' \quad \text{for parallel to grain loading}$$
$$Q_r = 0.6\ Q'_r\ n_F\ K' \quad \text{for perpendicular to grain loading}$$

**7**

Fastenings

$$N_r = \frac{P_r Q_r}{P_r \sin^2 \theta + Q_r \cos^2 \theta}$$

for loading at an angle $\theta$ to grain. $N_r$ may also be determined from Table 7.1.

where:

$P'_r$ and $Q'_r$ are unit factored lateral resistances for a single bolt, loaded in single shear, given in the Bolt Selection Tables in Section 7.3

$n_F$ = the number of drift pins

$K'$ = composite modification factors for bolts given in Section 7.3

An additional design requirement is that the diameter of the drift pins must not exceed 1/10 the width of the timbers being connected. Also, in any shear plane between two overlapping timbers, only two pins shall be counted as resisting the shear force.

Figure 7.7
**Drift pin connection**

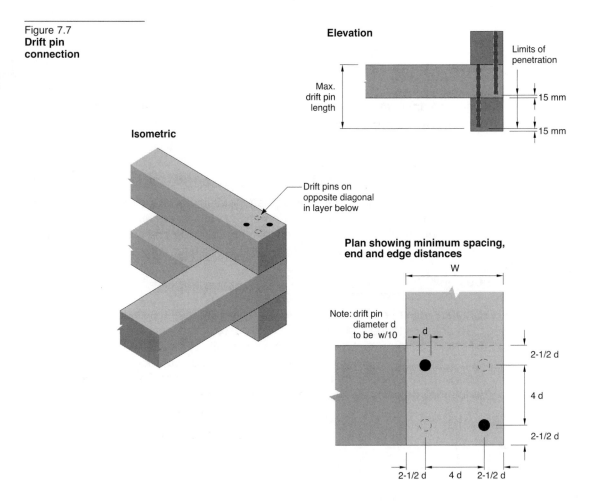

# 7.5 Lag Screws

### General

Lag screws may be used alone or with timber connectors in situations where through bolts are undesirable or impractical (Detail 7.24a). Lag screw materials and dimensions are specified in CSA Standard B34 *Miscellaneous Bolts and Screws.*

Usually lag screws are manufactured with regular square heads and cone points, but they can be obtained with hexagon heads and gimlet points. A typical lag screw joint is shown in Figure 7.8.

Figure 7.8
**Typical lag screw joint**

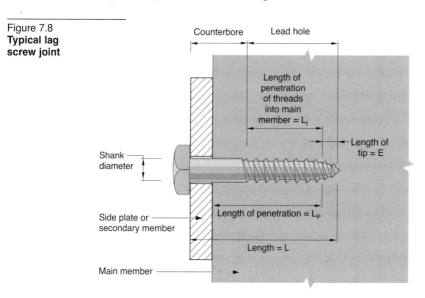

Lag screws may be used with wood or steel side plates. Since lag screws are threaded, they may be designed to resist withdrawal loads as well as lateral loads.

### Availability

Lag screws are generally available in imperial sizes. Typical sizes range from 3" to 12" in length and from 1/4" to 1" in diameter. However, the availability of long lengths should be confirmed before specifying. Chapter 11 contains information on standard lag screw dimensions.

### Installation

Lag screw holes consisting of a lead hole for the threaded portion and a counterbore for the unthreaded portion, must be drilled as shown in Table 7.8. The screw must be turned with a wrench, not driven with a hammer. Soap or any non-petroleum-based lubricant can be used to make turning easier.

These installation procedures must be strictly followed, or the load-carrying capacity of the joint will be seriously reduced.

7

Fastenings

| Drilling dimensions for lag screw holes | Counterbore | Lead hole | | |
|---|---|---|---|---|
| | | Dense hardwoods | D.Fir-L | Hem-Fir, S-P-F Northern |
| Diameter | same as shank | 65 to 85% of shank | 60 to 75% of shank | 40 to 70% of shank |
| Depth | same as shank | threaded length | threaded length | threaded length |

Note: For lead hole diameter, the larger percentage applies to larger lag screws.

## Design

Lag screw joints must be designed so that the following criteria are satisfied:

1. For lateral loading:
   Factored lateral strength resistance ≥ factored lateral load

2. For withdrawal loading:
   Factored withdrawal resistance ≥ factored withdrawal (tensile) load

In addition, adequate spacing between lag screws and adequate end distance and edge distance must be provided. Figure 7.9 provides minimum values for common lag screw sizes.

### Lateral Strength Resistance

The factored lateral strength resistance depends upon the angle of load to grain and is calculated from the following formulae:

$P_r = P'_r \, n_{Fe} \, n_R \, K'$    for parallel to grain loading

$Q_r = Q'_r \, n_{Fe} \, n_R \, K'$    for perpendicular to grain loading

$$N_r = \frac{P_r \, Q_r}{P_r \sin^2 \theta + Q_r \cos^2 \theta}$$    for loading at an angle $\theta$ to grain.
$N_r$ may also be determined from Table 7.1.

where:

$P'_r$ and $Q'_r$ are unit factored lateral resistances given in the Lag Screw Selection Tables.

$n_{Fe}$ = number of effective fasteners per row, given in Tables 7.17 and 7.18

$n_R$ = number of rows of fasteners

$K'$ is a modification factor given below

## Checklist: **Lag Screws** ✓

1. $K_D$ = 1.0 when the loading is "standard" term
   = 1.15 for short term loading (e.g., dead plus wind)
   = 0.65 for permanent loads (e.g., dead loads alone)

2. $K_{SF}$ = 1.0 when the service conditions are "dry" and the lumber is seasoned (moisture content ≤ 15%) prior to fabrication

   For other conditions, determine $K_{SF}$ from Table 7.9

3. $K_T$ = 1.0 when the wood is not treated with a fire retardant or other strength-reducing chemical.

   For wood treated with a fire retardant or other strength-reducing chemicals, see the Commentary for further guidance.

4. $J_E$ = 1.0 when lag screws are installed in side grain
   = 0.75 for end grain use (for withdrawal only)

   However, the use of lag screws in end grain should be avoided wherever possible.

**7**

Fastenings

### Withdrawal Resistance

The factored withdrawal resistance of lag screws is calculated as follows:

$$P_{rw} = P'_{rw} L_t n_F K' J_E$$

where:

$P'_{rw}$ = the factored withdrawal resistance per mm of penetration given in Table 7.11

$L_t$ = length of penetration of threaded portion into the main member, not including the point. In order to assure that the resistance of the steel is not exceeded, $L_t$ is limited to the standard length of penetration $L_P$ shown in Table 7.10. Threaded lengths for standard lag screw sizes are given in Table 7.12.

$n_F$ = number of fasteners

$K'$ and $J_E$ are modification factors given below

### Modification Factors

The following modification factors adjust the unit factored resistances of lag screw connections for the actual conditions of use:

$J_E$ = factor for lag screws installed in end grain

$K'$ = $K_D K_{SF} K_T$

where:

$K_D$ = duration of load factor

$K_{SF}$ = service condition factor

$K_T$ = fire-retardant treatment factor

In many cases the modification factors will equal 1.0. Review the checklist to determine if the factors equal 1.0 for the actual conditions of use. Where a factor does not equal 1.0, calculate the appropriate value as described.

### Example 1: Lag Screws

Determine the size of lag screws required in the purlin to beam connection shown below (dimensions in mm). The beam and purlins are D.Fir-L glulam. The service conditions are dry and the uplift force is due to the combination of dead plus wind loads.

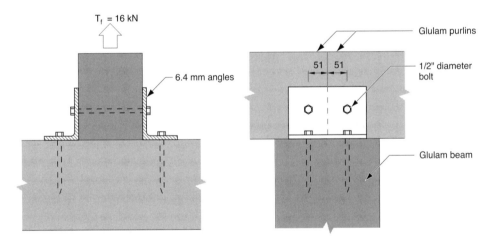

### Modification Factors

$K_D$ = 1.15 (short term duration of load)

$K_{SF}$ = 1.0 (service conditions are dry, material is seasoned)

$K_T$ = 1.0 (material is not treated with a fire retardant)

$J_E$ = 1.0 (installed in side grain)

Therefore, $K' = 1.15 \times 1.0 \times 1.0 = 1.15$

## Calculation

$$T_f = 16 \text{ kN}$$

Try four 3/8" diameter lag screws

$$P_{rw} = P'_{rw} L_t n_F K' J_E$$
$$P'_{rw} = 72.0 \text{ N/mm from Table 7.11}$$
$$n_F = 4$$
$$P_{rw} = 72.0 \times L_t \times 4 \times 1.15 \times 1.0$$
$$= 331 L_t \text{ (N)}$$

Required $L_t = \dfrac{16 \times 10^3}{331} = 48.3 \text{ mm} < 86 \text{ mm } (L_p)$      *Acceptable*

Determine required lag screw length from Table 7.12:

$$L_{REQ'D} = (48.3 + 6.4 - 12.7) \times 2$$
$$= 84 \text{ mm } (3.31")$$

Therefore, try four 3/8" × 3-1/2" lag screws

Check geometry of connection from Figure 7.9:

     unloaded edge distance > 38 mm      *Acceptable*

     spacing = 102 mm > 29 mm      *Acceptable*

     end distance > 50 mm      *Acceptable*

**Use four 3/8" × 3-1/2" lag screws.**

7

Fastenings

Table 7.9
**Service condition factor for lag screws $K_{SF}$**

| Joint detail | Angle of load to grain | Condition of lumber | | |
| | | Seasoned (moisture content ≤ 15%) | Unseasoned (moisture content >15%) | |
| | | Wet service | Dry service | Wet service |
|---|---|---|---|---|
| A | all | 0.67 | 1.0 | 0.67 |
| B | 0° | 0.67 | 1.0 | 0.67 |
| B | 90° | 0.67 | 0.40 | 0.27 |
| C | all | 0.67 | 0.40 | 0.27 |

Notes:
A = single fastening or a single row parallel to grain with steel side plates
B = single row parallel to grain with wood side plates or 2 rows parallel to grain not more than 125 mm apart with a common wood splice plate or multiple rows with separate wood or steel splice plates for each row
C = all other arrangements

**Table 7.10**
**Length of penetration $L_p$ (mm)**

|  |  | Lag screw diameter | | | | |
|---|---|---|---|---|---|---|
|  | Species | 1/4" | 3/8" | 1/2" | 5/8" | 3/4" |
| Minimum $L_p$ for lateral loading | All Species | 32 | 48 | 64 | 79 | 95 |
| Standard $L_p$ | D.Fir-L | 57 | 86 | 114 | 143 | 171 |
|  | Hem-Fir | 64 | 95 | 127 | 159 | 191 |
|  | S-P-F | 70 | 105 | 140 | 175 | 210 |
|  | Northern | 70 | 105 | 140 | 175 | 210 |

Notes:
1. Where the actual length of penetration into main member (excluding tip) is greater than the standard $L_p$, no increase in capacity is permitted.
2. Minimum required spacing, end and edge distances are shown in Figure 7.9.

**Table 7.11**
**Factored withdrawal resistance $P'_{rw}$ (N/mm)**

| Species | Lag screw diameter | | | | |
|---|---|---|---|---|---|
|  | 1/4" | 3/8" | 1/2" | 5/8" | 3/4" |
| D.Fir-L | 44.4 | 72.0 | 102 | 120 | 144 |
| Hem-Fir | 22.2 | 42.0 | 60.0 | 78.0 | 90.0 |
| S-P-F | 18.6 | 36.6 | 54.6 | 72.0 | 84.0 |
| Northern | 16.2 | 34.8 | 50.4 | 66.0 | 78.0 |

Notes:
1. $P_{rw} = P'_{rw} \, L_t \, n_F \, K' \, J_E$
2. When the length of penetration of thread (excluding tip) is greater than the standard $L_p$, the designer must ensure that the tensile capacity of the steel is not exceeded.

**Table 7.12**
**Threaded length of lag screws**

| Effective threaded length mm | Lag screw diameter in. | Length of tip, E mm |
|---|---|---|
| L/2 + 12.7 - E or 152 mm - E (whichever is less) | 1/4 | 4.8 |
|  | 3/8 | 6.4 |
|  | 1/2 | 7.9 |
|  | 5/8 | 9.5 |
|  | 3/4 | 11.1 |

Notes:
1. See Figure 7.8 for explanation of terms.
2. Effective threaded length = length of threads minus length of tip E.

# Lag Screw Selection Tables

## Single Shear, Wood Side Plate

**1S**

Factored lateral resistance

| Lag screw diameter in. | Side plate thickness mm | $L_p$ mm | Sawn lumber | | | | | |
|---|---|---|---|---|---|---|---|---|
| | | | D.Fir-L | | | Hem-Fir | | |
| | | | $P'_r$ kN | $Q'^3_r$ kN | $Q'^4_r$ kN | $P'_r$ kN | $Q'^3_r$ kN | $Q'^4_r$ kN |
| 1/4 | 38 | 32 | 0.761 | 0.571 | 0.472 | 0.721 | 0.536 | 0.453 |
| | 38 | 38 | 0.987 | 0.721 | 0.603 | 0.944 | 0.677 | 0.577 |
| | 38 | 44 | 1.15 | 0.884 | 0.703 | 1.11 | 0.830 | 0.674 |
| | 38 | 51 | 1.32 | 1.02 | 0.804 | 1.27 | 0.993 | 0.770 |
| | 89 | 32 | 0.761 | 0.641 | 0.472 | 0.727 | 0.621 | 0.453 |
| | 89 | 38 | 0.987 | 0.769 | 0.603 | 0.951 | 0.745 | 0.578 |
| | 89 | 44 | 1.15 | 0.897 | 0.747 | 1.12 | 0.869 | 0.714 |
| | 89 | 51 | 1.32 | 1.02 | 0.902 | 1.28 | 0.993 | 0.862 |
| 3/8 | 38 | 48 | 1.34 | 0.937 | 0.833 | 1.28 | 0.880 | 0.799 |
| | 38 | 57 | 1.61 | 1.20 | 1.00 | 1.53 | 1.13 | 0.959 |
| | 38 | 67 | 1.87 | 1.50 | 1.17 | 1.79 | 1.41 | 1.12 |
| | 38 | 76 | 2.14 | 1.82 | 1.33 | 2.04 | 1.71 | 1.28 |
| | 89 | 48 | 1.46 | 1.14 | 0.900 | 1.42 | 1.10 | 0.862 |
| | 89 | 57 | 1.75 | 1.37 | 1.16 | 1.70 | 1.32 | 1.11 |
| | 89 | 67 | 2.05 | 1.59 | 1.44 | 1.98 | 1.54 | 1.38 |
| | 89 | 76 | 2.34 | 1.82 | 1.76 | 2.27 | 1.76 | 1.68 |
| 1/2 | 38 | 64 | 2.06 | 1.35 | 1.33 | 1.96 | 1.26 | 1.28 |
| | 38 | 76 | 2.47 | 1.75 | 1.60 | 2.36 | 1.65 | 1.54 |
| | 38 | 89 | 2.88 | 2.20 | 1.87 | 2.76 | 2.07 | 1.79 |
| | 38 | 102 | 3.29 | 2.70 | 2.13 | 3.15 | 2.54 | 2.05 |
| | 89 | 64 | 2.55 | 1.99 | 1.56 | 2.46 | 1.93 | 1.50 |
| | 89 | 76 | 3.06 | 2.39 | 2.01 | 2.97 | 2.31 | 1.92 |
| | 89 | 89 | 3.57 | 2.78 | 2.50 | 3.46 | 2.70 | 2.39 |
| | 89 | 102 | 4.09 | 3.18 | 2.86 | 3.96 | 3.08 | 2.73 |
| 5/8 | 38 | 79 | 2.90 | 1.79 | 1.93 | 2.73 | 1.68 | 1.86 |
| | 38 | 95 | 3.48 | 2.36 | 2.32 | 3.34 | 2.21 | 2.23 |
| | 38 | 111 | 4.06 | 2.99 | 2.71 | 3.89 | 2.81 | 2.61 |
| | 38 | 127 | 4.64 | 3.69 | 3.09 | 4.45 | 3.46 | 2.98 |
| | 89 | 79 | 3.92 | 3.05 | 2.38 | 3.74 | 2.87 | 2.28 |
| | 89 | 95 | 4.70 | 3.66 | 2.98 | 4.55 | 3.55 | 2.85 |
| | 89 | 111 | 5.48 | 4.27 | 3.48 | 5.31 | 4.14 | 3.33 |
| | 89 | 127 | 6.27 | 4.88 | 3.97 | 6.07 | 4.73 | 3.80 |
| 3/4 | 38 | 95 | 3.81 | 2.27 | 2.36 | 3.57 | 2.13 | 2.22 |
| | 38 | 114 | 4.62 | 3.01 | 2.83 | 4.44 | 2.82 | 2.66 |
| | 38 | 133 | 5.39 | 3.84 | 3.30 | 5.18 | 3.60 | 3.10 |
| | 38 | 152 | 6.16 | 4.77 | 3.78 | 5.92 | 4.47 | 3.55 |
| | 89 | 95 | 5.26 | 3.73 | 3.26 | 4.94 | 3.50 | 3.12 |
| | 89 | 114 | 6.37 | 4.75 | 3.91 | 6.08 | 4.46 | 3.75 |
| | 89 | 133 | 7.43 | 5.88 | 4.56 | 7.09 | 5.52 | 4.37 |
| | 89 | 152 | 8.49 | 6.89 | 5.21 | 8.11 | 6.66 | 5.00 |

**7**

Fastenings

Notes:
1. $P_r = P'_r \, n_{Fe} \, n_R \, K'$
   $Q_r = Q'_r \, n_{Fe} \, n_R \, K'$
2. Tabulated values are valid for cases where the wood side member is of same density as main member.
3. Main member perpendicular and side member parallel to grain loading.
4. Side member perpendicular and main member parallel to grain loading.

# Lag Screw Selection Tables

## 1S    Single Shear, Wood Side Plate

Factored lateral resistance

| Lag screw diameter in. | Side plate thickness mm | $L_p$ mm | Sawn lumber | | | | | |
|---|---|---|---|---|---|---|---|---|
| | | | S-P-F | | | Northern | | |
| | | | $P'_r$ kN | $Q'^3_r$ kN | $Q'^4_r$ kN | $P'_r$ kN | $Q'^3_r$ kN | $Q'^4_r$ kN |
| 1/4 | 38 | 32 | 0.659 | 0.489 | 0.427 | 0.549 | 0.408 | 0.379 |
| | 38 | 38 | 0.862 | 0.618 | 0.543 | 0.718 | 0.515 | 0.481 |
| | 38 | 44 | 1.04 | 0.758 | 0.634 | 0.905 | 0.631 | 0.561 |
| | 38 | 51 | 1.18 | 0.908 | 0.724 | 1.03 | 0.756 | 0.641 |
| | 89 | 32 | 0.681 | 0.593 | 0.427 | 0.597 | 0.520 | 0.379 |
| | 89 | 38 | 0.889 | 0.712 | 0.544 | 0.777 | 0.650 | 0.481 |
| | 89 | 44 | 1.07 | 0.830 | 0.671 | 0.973 | 0.758 | 0.592 |
| | 89 | 51 | 1.22 | 0.949 | 0.808 | 1.11 | 0.866 | 0.711 |
| 3/8 | 38 | 48 | 1.17 | 0.803 | 0.753 | 0.976 | 0.669 | 0.670 |
| | 38 | 57 | 1.44 | 1.03 | 0.904 | 1.26 | 0.860 | 0.803 |
| | 38 | 67 | 1.68 | 1.28 | 1.05 | 1.47 | 1.07 | 0.937 |
| | 38 | 76 | 1.91 | 1.56 | 1.20 | 1.68 | 1.30 | 1.07 |
| | 89 | 48 | 1.33 | 1.05 | 0.810 | 1.16 | 0.962 | 0.717 |
| | 89 | 57 | 1.62 | 1.26 | 1.04 | 1.48 | 1.15 | 0.917 |
| | 89 | 67 | 1.90 | 1.48 | 1.29 | 1.73 | 1.35 | 1.14 |
| | 89 | 76 | 2.17 | 1.69 | 1.57 | 1.98 | 1.54 | 1.37 |
| 1/2 | 38 | 64 | 1.79 | 1.15 | 1.21 | 1.49 | 0.962 | 1.08 |
| | 38 | 76 | 2.22 | 1.50 | 1.45 | 1.96 | 1.25 | 1.30 |
| | 38 | 89 | 2.59 | 1.89 | 1.70 | 2.29 | 1.57 | 1.52 |
| | 38 | 102 | 2.96 | 2.31 | 1.94 | 2.62 | 1.93 | 1.73 |
| | 89 | 64 | 2.30 | 1.84 | 1.41 | 2.01 | 1.68 | 1.25 |
| | 89 | 76 | 2.84 | 2.21 | 1.80 | 2.59 | 2.02 | 1.59 |
| | 89 | 89 | 3.31 | 2.58 | 2.24 | 3.02 | 2.35 | 1.97 |
| | 89 | 102 | 3.78 | 2.94 | 2.56 | 3.45 | 2.69 | 2.25 |
| 5/8 | 38 | 79 | 2.49 | 1.54 | 1.75 | 2.07 | 1.28 | 1.46 |
| | 38 | 95 | 3.14 | 2.02 | 2.10 | 2.79 | 1.68 | 1.75 |
| | 38 | 111 | 3.67 | 2.56 | 2.45 | 3.26 | 2.14 | 2.04 |
| | 38 | 127 | 4.19 | 3.16 | 2.80 | 3.72 | 2.64 | 2.34 |
| | 89 | 79 | 3.50 | 2.62 | 2.14 | 2.97 | 2.18 | 1.90 |
| | 89 | 95 | 4.35 | 3.32 | 2.68 | 3.87 | 2.77 | 2.37 |
| | 89 | 111 | 5.08 | 3.95 | 3.13 | 4.52 | 3.40 | 2.76 |
| | 89 | 127 | 5.80 | 4.52 | 3.57 | 5.16 | 4.08 | 3.16 |
| 3/4 | 38 | 95 | 3.26 | 1.94 | 2.02 | 2.72 | 1.62 | 1.69 |
| | 38 | 114 | 4.19 | 2.58 | 2.43 | 3.73 | 2.15 | 2.02 |
| | 38 | 133 | 4.89 | 3.29 | 2.83 | 4.36 | 2.74 | 2.36 |
| | 38 | 152 | 5.59 | 4.08 | 3.24 | 4.98 | 3.40 | 2.70 |
| | 89 | 95 | 4.51 | 3.19 | 2.94 | 3.76 | 2.66 | 2.61 |
| | 89 | 114 | 5.69 | 4.08 | 3.53 | 4.98 | 3.40 | 3.13 |
| | 89 | 133 | 6.64 | 5.04 | 4.12 | 5.82 | 4.20 | 3.65 |
| | 89 | 152 | 7.58 | 6.08 | 4.71 | 6.65 | 5.07 | 4.18 |

Notes:
1. $P_r = P'_r \, n_{Fe} \, n_R \, K'$
   $Q_r = Q'_r \, n_{Fe} \, n_R \, K'$
2. Tabulated values are valid for cases where the wood side member is of same density as main member.
3. Main member perpendicular and side member parallel to grain loading.
4. Side member perpendicular and main member parallel to grain loading.

# Lag Screw Selection Tables

## Single Shear, Wood Side Plate

**1S**

Factored lateral resistance

| Lag screw diameter in. | Side plate thickness mm | $L_p$ mm | Glulam D.Fir-L $P'_r$ kN | $Q'^3_r$ kN | $Q'^4_r$ kN | Spruce-Pine $P'_r$ kN | $Q'^3_r$ kN | $Q'^4_r$ kN |
|---|---|---|---|---|---|---|---|---|
| 1/4 | 38 | 32 | 0.761 | 0.571 | 0.472 | 0.673 | 0.495 | 0.429 |
|  | 38 | 38 | 0.987 | 0.721 | 0.603 | 0.883 | 0.627 | 0.546 |
|  | 38 | 44 | 1.15 | 0.884 | 0.703 | 1.04 | 0.770 | 0.636 |
|  | 38 | 51 | 1.32 | 1.02 | 0.804 | 1.19 | 0.924 | 0.727 |
|  | 89 | 32 | 0.761 | 0.641 | 0.472 | 0.685 | 0.601 | 0.429 |
|  | 89 | 38 | 0.987 | 0.769 | 0.603 | 0.894 | 0.723 | 0.546 |
|  | 89 | 44 | 1.15 | 0.897 | 0.747 | 1.08 | 0.844 | 0.674 |
|  | 89 | 51 | 1.32 | 1.02 | 0.902 | 1.23 | 0.964 | 0.811 |
| 3/8 | 38 | 48 | 1.34 | 0.937 | 0.833 | 1.20 | 0.817 | 0.757 |
|  | 38 | 57 | 1.61 | 1.20 | 1.00 | 1.45 | 1.05 | 0.908 |
|  | 38 | 67 | 1.87 | 1.50 | 1.17 | 1.69 | 1.31 | 1.06 |
|  | 38 | 76 | 2.14 | 1.82 | 1.33 | 1.93 | 1.59 | 1.21 |
|  | 89 | 48 | 1.46 | 1.14 | 0.900 | 1.34 | 1.07 | 0.814 |
|  | 89 | 57 | 1.75 | 1.37 | 1.16 | 1.64 | 1.29 | 1.04 |
|  | 89 | 67 | 2.05 | 1.59 | 1.44 | 1.92 | 1.50 | 1.30 |
|  | 89 | 76 | 2.34 | 1.82 | 1.76 | 2.19 | 1.71 | 1.57 |
| 1/2 | 38 | 64 | 2.06 | 1.35 | 1.33 | 1.84 | 1.18 | 1.22 |
|  | 38 | 76 | 2.47 | 1.75 | 1.60 | 2.24 | 1.54 | 1.46 |
|  | 38 | 89 | 2.88 | 2.20 | 1.87 | 2.61 | 1.93 | 1.70 |
|  | 38 | 102 | 3.29 | 2.70 | 2.13 | 2.98 | 2.37 | 1.95 |
|  | 89 | 64 | 2.55 | 1.99 | 1.56 | 2.31 | 1.87 | 1.41 |
|  | 89 | 76 | 3.06 | 2.39 | 2.01 | 2.87 | 2.24 | 1.81 |
|  | 89 | 89 | 3.57 | 2.78 | 2.50 | 3.35 | 2.62 | 2.25 |
|  | 89 | 102 | 4.09 | 3.18 | 2.86 | 3.83 | 2.99 | 2.57 |
| 5/8 | 38 | 79 | 2.90 | 1.79 | 1.93 | 2.57 | 1.57 | 1.75 |
|  | 38 | 95 | 3.48 | 2.36 | 2.32 | 3.17 | 2.07 | 2.10 |
|  | 38 | 111 | 4.06 | 2.99 | 2.71 | 3.70 | 2.63 | 2.45 |
|  | 38 | 127 | 4.64 | 3.69 | 3.09 | 4.22 | 3.25 | 2.80 |
|  | 89 | 79 | 3.92 | 3.05 | 2.38 | 3.52 | 2.65 | 2.15 |
|  | 89 | 95 | 4.70 | 3.66 | 2.98 | 4.40 | 3.37 | 2.69 |
|  | 89 | 111 | 5.48 | 4.27 | 3.48 | 5.14 | 4.02 | 3.14 |
|  | 89 | 127 | 6.27 | 4.88 | 3.97 | 5.87 | 4.59 | 3.59 |
| 3/4 | 38 | 95 | 3.81 | 2.27 | 2.36 | 3.37 | 1.99 | 2.02 |
|  | 38 | 114 | 4.62 | 3.01 | 2.83 | 4.23 | 2.65 | 2.43 |
|  | 38 | 133 | 5.39 | 3.84 | 3.30 | 4.93 | 3.38 | 2.83 |
|  | 38 | 152 | 6.16 | 4.77 | 3.78 | 5.63 | 4.21 | 3.24 |
|  | 89 | 95 | 5.26 | 3.73 | 3.26 | 4.62 | 3.24 | 2.96 |
|  | 89 | 114 | 6.37 | 4.75 | 3.91 | 5.72 | 4.14 | 3.55 |
|  | 89 | 133 | 7.43 | 5.88 | 4.56 | 6.68 | 5.13 | 4.14 |
|  | 89 | 152 | 8.49 | 6.89 | 5.21 | 7.63 | 6.21 | 4.73 |

Notes:
1. $P_r = P'_r \, n_{Fe} \, n_R \, K'$
   $Q_r = Q'_r \, n_{Fe} \, n_R \, K'$
2. Tabulated values are valid for cases where the wood side member is of same density as main member.
3. Main member perpendicular and side member parallel to grain loading.
4. Side member perpendicular and main member parallel to grain loading.

7

Fastenings

# Lag Screw Selection Tables

## 1S    Single Shear, 4mm Steel Side Plate

Factored lateral resistance based on A36 steel grade plates

| Lag screw diameter in. | $L_p$ mm | Sawn lumber D.Fir-L $P'_r$ kN | $Q'_r$ kN | Hem-Fir $P'_r$ kN | $Q'_r$ kN | S-P-F $P'_r$ kN | $Q'_r$ kN | Northern $P'_r$ kN | $Q'_r$ kN |
|---|---|---|---|---|---|---|---|---|---|
| 1/4 | 32 | 1.15 | 0.760 | 1.12 | 0.714 | 1.07 | 0.652 | 0.977 | 0.543 |
|  | 38 | 1.38 | 0.917 | 1.34 | 0.889 | 1.28 | 0.850 | 1.17 | 0.776 |
|  | 44 | 1.62 | 1.07 | 1.57 | 1.04 | 1.50 | 0.991 | 1.37 | 0.905 |
|  | 51 | 1.85 | 1.22 | 1.79 | 1.19 | 1.71 | 1.13 | 1.56 | 1.03 |
| 3/8 | 48 | 2.05 | 1.36 | 1.99 | 1.32 | 1.90 | 1.26 | 1.74 | 1.15 |
|  | 57 | 2.46 | 1.63 | 2.39 | 1.58 | 2.28 | 1.51 | 2.08 | 1.38 |
|  | 67 | 2.87 | 1.90 | 2.78 | 1.84 | 2.66 | 1.76 | 2.43 | 1.61 |
|  | 76 | 3.28 | 2.17 | 3.18 | 2.11 | 3.04 | 2.01 | 2.78 | 1.84 |
| 1/2 | 64 | 3.58 | 2.37 | 3.47 | 2.30 | 3.32 | 2.20 | 3.03 | 2.01 |
|  | 76 | 4.30 | 2.85 | 4.17 | 2.76 | 3.98 | 2.64 | 3.64 | 2.41 |
|  | 89 | 5.02 | 3.32 | 4.86 | 3.22 | 4.65 | 3.08 | 4.25 | 2.81 |
|  | 102 | 5.73 | 3.80 | 5.56 | 3.68 | 5.31 | 3.52 | 4.86 | 3.21 |
| 5/8 | 79 | 5.50 | 3.64 | 5.33 | 3.53 | 5.09 | 3.37 | 4.66 | 3.05 |
|  | 95 | 6.60 | 4.37 | 6.39 | 4.23 | 6.11 | 4.05 | 5.59 | 3.70 |
|  | 111 | 7.69 | 5.10 | 7.46 | 4.94 | 7.13 | 4.72 | 6.52 | 4.31 |
|  | 127 | 8.79 | 5.82 | 8.52 | 5.64 | 8.15 | 5.40 | 7.45 | 4.93 |
| 3/4 | 95 | 7.77 | 5.14 | 7.53 | 4.98 | 7.20 | 4.76 | 6.58 | 4.23 |
|  | 114 | 9.32 | 6.17 | 9.03 | 5.98 | 8.64 | 5.72 | 7.89 | 5.22 |
|  | 133 | 10.9 | 7.20 | 10.5 | 6.98 | 10.1 | 6.67 | 9.21 | 6.09 |
|  | 152 | 12.4 | 8.23 | 12.0 | 7.97 | 11.5 | 7.62 | 10.5 | 6.96 |

Notes:
1. $P_r = P'_r \, n_{Fe} \, n_R \, K'$
   $Q_r = Q'_r \, n_{Fe} \, n_R \, K'$

# Lag Screw Selection Tables

## Single Shear, 4mm Steel Side Plate  `1S`

Factored lateral resistance based on A36 steel grade plates

| Lag screw diameter in. | $L_p$ mm | Glulam | | | |
|---|---|---|---|---|---|
| | | D.Fir-L | | Spruce-Pine | |
| | | $P'_r$ kN | $Q'_r$ kN | $P'_r$ kN | $Q'_r$ kN |
| 1/4 | 32 | 1.15 | 0.760 | 1.09 | 0.683 |
| | 38 | 1.38 | 0.917 | 1.31 | 0.870 |
| | 44 | 1.62 | 1.07 | 1.53 | 1.01 |
| | 51 | 1.85 | 1.22 | 1.75 | 1.16 |
| 3/8 | 48 | 2.05 | 1.36 | 1.95 | 1.29 |
| | 57 | 2.46 | 1.63 | 2.33 | 1.55 |
| | 67 | 2.87 | 1.90 | 2.72 | 1.80 |
| | 76 | 3.28 | 2.17 | 3.11 | 2.06 |
| 1/2 | 64 | 3.58 | 2.37 | 3.40 | 2.25 |
| | 76 | 4.30 | 2.85 | 4.08 | 2.70 |
| | 89 | 5.02 | 3.32 | 4.76 | 3.15 |
| | 102 | 5.73 | 3.80 | 5.44 | 3.60 |
| 5/8 | 79 | 5.50 | 3.64 | 5.21 | 3.45 |
| | 95 | 6.60 | 4.37 | 6.25 | 4.14 |
| | 111 | 7.69 | 5.10 | 7.30 | 4.83 |
| | 127 | 8.79 | 5.82 | 8.34 | 5.52 |
| 3/4 | 95 | 7.77 | 5.14 | 7.36 | 4.88 |
| | 114 | 9.32 | 6.17 | 8.84 | 5.85 |
| | 133 | 10.9 | 7.20 | 10.3 | 6.83 |
| | 152 | 12.4 | 8.23 | 11.8 | 7.80 |

Notes:
1. $P_r = P'_r \, n_{Fe} \, n_R \, K'$
   $Q_r = Q'_r \, n_{Fe} \, n_R \, K'$

7

Fastenings

Figure 7.9
**Minimum
spacing, end
and edge
distances
for lag screw
connections
(mm)**

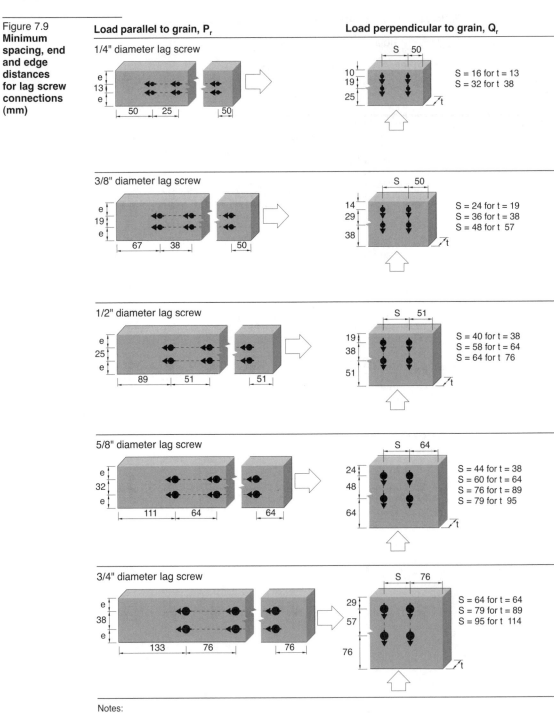

**Load parallel to grain, $P_r$**

1/4" diameter lag screw

3/8" diameter lag screw

1/2" diameter lag screw

5/8" diameter lag screw

3/4" diameter lag screw

**Load perpendicular to grain, $Q_r$**

S = 16 for t = 13
S = 32 for t  38

S = 24 for t = 19
S = 36 for t = 38
S = 48 for t  57

S = 40 for t = 38
S = 58 for t = 64
S = 64 for t  76

S = 44 for t = 38
S = 60 for t = 64
S = 76 for t = 89
S = 79 for t  95

S = 64 for t = 64
S = 79 for t = 89
S = 95 for t  114

Notes:
1. e = the greater of 1.5 times lag screw diameter or half of actual spacing between rows
2. Loaded end distance is the minimum permitted for tension members

# 7.6 Timber Rivets

## General

Timber rivets (formerly known as glulam rivets) are high strength fasteners originally developed for glued-laminated timber construction and now used for glulam and heavy timber construction. As shown in Figure 7.10, rivets have a flattened-oval shank with a wedge shaped head and are similar in appearance to nails.

Figure 7.10
Timber rivets

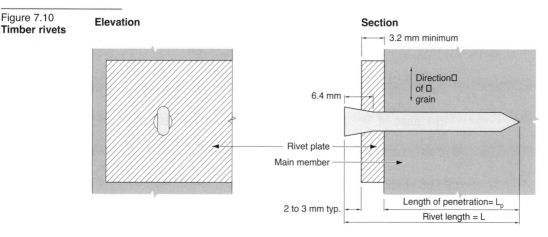

Timber rivets have adequate corrosion resistance for most service conditions but under extreme corrosion conditions where water combined with salts or acid can fall on the connection, or where steam is present, timber rivets should not be used.

Timber rivets are commonly available in lengths of 40, 65 and 90 mm. Rivets are used with steel side plates conforming to either CSA Standard CAN3-G40.21 or ASTM Standard A36. Side plates must be at least 3.2 mm thick and must be hot-dip galvanized for use in wet service conditions. Steel plates are pre-drilled (not punched) with 6.7 to 7 mm diameter holes to accommodate the rivets.

## Installation

Timber rivets are driven until the tapered head is firmly seated in the pre-drilled holes in the steel side plate while maintaining a minimum 2 mm head projection above the plate. Either a standard or pneumatic hammer may be used to drive the rivet.

Rivets must be installed so that the flat face is parallel to grain. If possible, each job should use only one length of timber rivet to avoid using the wrong length in a particular connection. Care should be taken to ensure that the connection is properly placed, as a completed connection is extremely difficult to remove.

When driving timber rivets, safety glasses should be worn to guard against particles of the galvanizing and because the hardened rivet can break if struck wrongly.

7

Fastenings

## Advantages

Timber rivets (commonly marketed as Griplam Nails) have many advantages over bolts and other connectors. These include:

- Timber rivet connections are much stiffer and transfer greater loads for a given connector area than any other timber fastener.
- The wood members need not be pre-drilled. This reduces shop fabrication time and costs. It also permits the integration of stock glulam beams into site-framed projects. Glulam fabricators are able to provide assistance in the design and sourcing of connection hardware.
- Ease of construction readily accommodates discrepancies on the site.
- The typically smaller connection size is considered a favourable feature by many architects.
- The ease of on-site installation of the rivet permits glulam and heavy timber trusses to be shipped knocked-down and assembled by the contractor.

Timber rivets have become the fastener of choice for the glulam industry and may be obtained from fabricators.

## Design

Timber rivet connections must be designed so that the factored resistance is greater than the factored lateral load.

This section provides design information and selection tables for the following two common timber rivet connections:

- double-sided splice plate loaded parallel to grain
- beam hanger loaded perpendicular to grain

For other configurations, refer to Clause 10.7.2 of CSA O86.

### Double-sided Splice Plate

The double-sided splice plate is shown in Figure 7.11 with design values tabulated on pages 290 to 296. It consists of a pair of steel splice plates fastened with timber rivets to both sides of the member. The rivets are loaded parallel to the grain and the total resistance of the connection (the sum of both sides) $P_r$ is the lesser of:

$$P_{ry} = P'_r K_{SF} K_T J_Y J_O H \quad \text{for rivet capacity}$$
$$P_{rw} = P'_r K_D K_{SF} K_T J_O H \quad \text{for wood capacity}$$

where:

$P'_r$, given in the Timber Rivet Selection Tables, is the capacity for two identical side plates and rivet groups

$K_D$, $K_{SF}$, $K_T$, $J_Y$, $J_O$ and $H$ are modification factors given below

The values of $P'_r$ given in bold type in the selection tables are governed by rivet yielding, otherwise wood capacity governs.

The rivet spacing, end distance and edge distance are shown in Figure 7.11.

**Figure 7.11**
**Double-sided splice plate (dimensions in mm)**

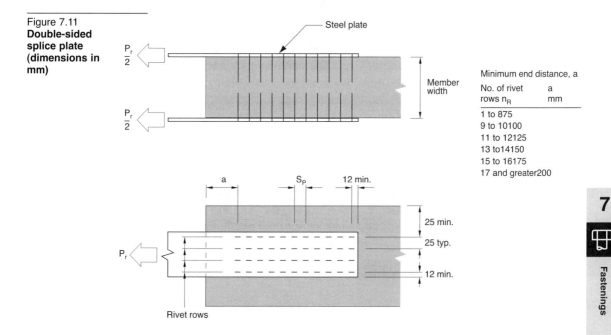

Minimum end distance, a

| No. of rivet rows $n_R$ | a mm |
|---|---|
| 1 to 8 | 75 |
| 9 to 10 | 100 |
| 11 to 12 | 125 |
| 13 to 14 | 150 |
| 15 to 16 | 175 |
| 17 and greater | 200 |

**Beam Hanger Connection**

This connection is shown in the figure below the Timber Rivet Selection Tables for beam hangers on pages 297 to 299. It consists of two back plates fastened to a beam with 2 rows of 4 to 16 rivets in each plate. The rivets are loaded perpendicular to the grain and the total resistance of the connection (the sum of both rivet groups) $Q_r$ is the lesser of:

$$Q_{ry} = Q'_y \, K_{SF} \, K_T \, J_Y \, J_O \, H \quad \text{for rivet capacity}$$
$$Q_{rw} = Q'_w \, K_D \, K_{SF} \, K_T \, J_O \, H \text{ for wood capacity}$$

where:

$Q'_y$ and $Q'_w$ are given in the Timber Rivet Selection Tables

$K_D$, $K_{SF}$, $K_T$, $J_Y$, $J_O$ and $H$ are modification factors given below

The required rivet spacings ($S_p$ and $S_q$), end distance (a) and edge distances ($e_p$ and $e_q$) are shown in or below the selection tables. The tabulated resistance values do not account for possible lateral or withdrawal forces arising from the eccentricity between the applied load and the centroid of each rivet group. The designer should give consideration to eccentricity and provide additional resistance when the effects are found to be significant. Examples providing such resistance include continuous back plates on hangers to counter the effects of in-plane eccentricity, and additional rivets in the supporting member to counter the effects of out-of-plane eccentricity.

**Steel Plates**

The steel plates must be designed to adequately resist the factored loading in accordance with CSA S16. However, if the required thickness of steel plate exceeds 6.3 mm, the factored lateral resistance $P_r$ or $Q_r$ must be calculated directly from Clause 10.7.2 of CSA O86 rather than using the selection tables. This is necessary since the tabulated basic resistances have been developed for a minimum length of penetration equal to the rivet length less 9.5 mm. A plate thickness greater than 6.3 mm will result in a lower length of penetration and, therefore, a lower lateral resistance.

**Modification Factors**

The modification factors adjust the basic factored lateral resistances for the actual conditions of use and are defined as follows:

$K_D$ = duration of load factor

$K_{SF}$ = service condition factor

$K_T$ = fire-retardant treatment factor

$J_Y$ = side plate factor

$J_O$ = factor for rivet orientation in grain

H = material factor

In many cases the modification factors will equal 1.0. Review the following checklist to determine if each modification factor is equal to 1.0 for the actual conditions of use. Where a factor does not equal 1.0, determine the appropriate value.

# Checklist: **Timber Rivets** ✓

1. $K_D$ = 1.0 when the loading is "standard" term
   = 1.15 for short term loading (dead plus wind)
   = 0.65 for permanent loads (dead loads alone)

2. $K_{SF}$ = 1.0 when the service conditions are "dry" and rivets are assembled in seasoned material
   = 0.80 for wet service conditions
   = 0.90 for connections assembled in unseasoned wood but used in dry conditions

3. $K_T$ = 1.0 when the wood is not treated with a fire retardant or other strength-reducing chemical.

   For wood treated with a fire retardant or other strength-reducing chemicals, see the Commentary for further guidance.

4. $J_Y$ = 1.0 when the steel side plates are 6.3 mm or thicker
   = 0.9 for side plates between 4.7 and 6.3 mm
   = 0.8 for side plates between 3.2 and 4.7 mm

5. $J_O$ = 1.0 when the rivets are installed into side grain
   = 0.5 when rivets are used in end grain with the slope of the cut 90° to the side grain, making the load perpendicular to grain

   For sloping end cuts the resistance of the connection may be increased linearly from 50% of $Q_r$ ($J_O$ = 0.5) to the full value of $P_r$ or $Q_r$ ($J_O$ = 1.0), whichever is applicable.

6. H = 1.0 for D.Fir-L glulam
   = 0.8 for Spruce-Pine glulam
   = 0.50 for D.Fir-L sawn lumber
   = 0.45 for Hem-Fir sawn lumber
   = 0.40 for S-P-F sawn lumber
   = 0.35 for Northern sawn lumber

**7**

**Fastenings**

## Example 1: Timber Rivets

Determine the number of rivets required for the tension splice shown below (dimensions in mm). The sawn lumber members are 89 × 235 mm D.Fir-L. The factored tensile force due to dead plus snow loads is 95 kN. The service conditions are wet. Use 40 mm rivets and 4.8 mm steel side plates.

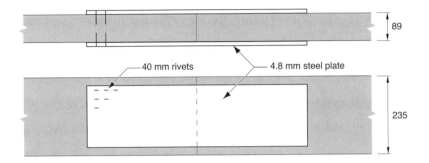

40 mm rivets                    4.8 mm steel plate

89

235

## Modification factors

$K_D$ = 1.0 (standard term load)

$K_{SF}$ = 0.80 (wet service conditions)

$K_T$ = 1.0 (untreated)

$J_Y$ = 0.9 (4.8 mm plates)

$J_O$ = 1.0 (side grain use)

H = 0.5 (D.Fir-L sawn lumber)

## Calculation

$T_f$ = 95 kN

Calculate the maximum number of rows $n_R$

$n_R$ = (235 / 25) - 1 = 8.40

Try 8 rows of 10 rivets each side, spaced at 25 mm parallel to grain

$P'_r$ = 279 kN from Timber Rivet Selection Tables (for sawn lumber)

$P_r$ is the lesser of:

$P_{ry}$ = $P'_r K_{SF} K_T J_Y J_O$ H
= 279 × 0.8 × 1.0 × 0.9 × 1.0 × 0.5 = 100 kN

$P_{rw}$ = $P'_r K_D K_{SF} K_T J_O$ H
= 279 × 1.0 × 0.8 × 1.0 × 1.0 × 0.5 = 112 kN

Therefore, $P_r$ = 100 kN > 95 kN                    *Acceptable*

Note that $P_{ry}$ is slightly conservative. A more accurate solution can be determined using Clause 10.7.2.3 of CSA O86

Check end and edge distances from Figure 7.11:

    edge distance for wood = 30 mm > 25 mm                 *Acceptable*

    minimum end distance for wood = 75 mm

    minimum end and edge distance for steel = 12 mm

**Using these values, the final connection geometry is shown below.**

Note that the resistance of the steel side plates must also be checked in accordance with CSA S16.

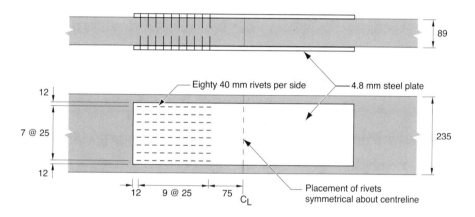

**7**

**Fastenings**

## Example 2: Timber Rivets

Design the beam hangers connection shown below (dimensions in mm). The glulam beam and girder are untreated Spruce-Pine glulam. The factored beam reaction is 30 kN due to dead plus snow loads. The service conditions are wet. Use 65 mm rivets.

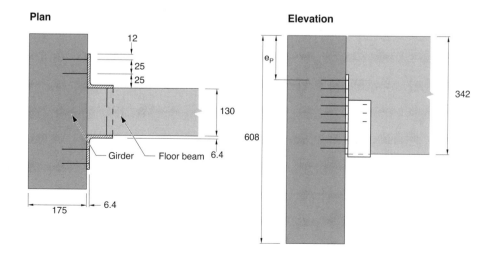

## Modification Factors

$K_D$ = 1.0 (standard term load)
$K_{SF}$ = 0.80 (wet service conditions)
$K_T$ = 1.0 (untreated)
$J_Y$ = 1.0 (6.4 mm plates)
$J_O$ = 1.0 (side grain use)
$H$ = 0.8 (Spruce-Pine glulam)

## Calculation

$Q_f$ = 30 kN

$Q_r$ is the lesser of:

$$Q_{ry} = Q'_y \, K_{SF} \, K_T \, J_Y \, J_O \, H$$
$$= Q'_y \times 0.8 \times 1.0 \times 1.0 \times 1.0 \times 0.8 = 0.64 \, Q'_y$$

$$Q_{rw} = Q'_w \, K_D \, K_{SF} \, K_T \, J_O \, H$$
$$= Q'_w \times 1.0 \times 0.8 \times 1.0 \times 1.0 \times 0.8 = 0.64 \, Q'_w$$

From Timber Rivet Selection Tables, estimate the required number of rivets per row using a 25 mm spacing perpendicular to grain ($S_Q$):

| Number of rivets per row $n_c$ | $e_p$ | $Q'_y$ | $Q'_w$ |
|---|---|---|---|
| | mm | kN | kN |
| 7 | 180 | 37.7 | 29.7 |
| 8 | 155 | 43.1 | 39.0 |
| 9 | 130 | 48.5 | 48.9 |
| 10 | 105 | 53.9 | 62.6 |

Note:
$e_p$ = 342 - 12 - 25($n_c$ - 1)

Try 10 rivets per row:

$$Q_{ry} = 0.64 \times 53.9 = 34.5 \text{ kN}$$
$$Q_{rw} = 0.64 \times 62.6 = 40.1 \text{ kN}$$

Therefore, $Q_r$ = 34.5 kN > 30 kN                    *Acceptable*

In this example the effects of eccentricity are assumed to be negligible, 10 rivets per row are sufficient.

Check end and edge distances from the selection tables:

    loaded edge distance for wood > 50 mm          *Acceptable*

    end distance for wood > 50 mm              *Acceptable*

    minimum end and edge distance for steel = 12 mm

**Using two rows of ten 65 mm rivets in each back plate, the final connection geometry is shown below (dimensions in mm).**

Note that the resistance of the plates should be checked in accordance with CSA S16.

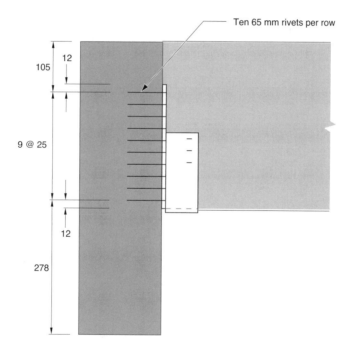

Ten 65 mm rivets per row

105

12

9 @ 25

12

278

7

Fastenings

# Timber Rivet Selection Tables

**L = 40mm**
**S$_p$ = 25mm**
**S$_q$ = 25mm**

## Double-sided Splice Plate

**P$'_r$ (kN) for Glulam**

| Member dimension mm | Rivets per row, n$_c$ | Number of rows | | | | | | | | | |
|---|---|---|---|---|---|---|---|---|---|---|---|
| | | 2 | 4 | 6 | 8 | 10 | 12 | 14 | 16 | 18 | 20 |
| 80 | 2 | **15.6** | **31.2** | **46.9** | **62.5** | **78.1** | **93.7** | **109** | **125** | **141** | **156** |
| | 4 | **31.2** | **62.5** | **93.7** | **125** | **156** | **187** | **219** | **250** | **281** | **312** |
| | 6 | **46.9** | **93.7** | **141** | **187** | **234** | **281** | **328** | **375** | **422** | **469** |
| | 8 | **62.5** | **125** | **187** | **250** | **312** | **375** | **437** | 492 | 552 | 624 |
| | 10 | **78.1** | 150 | 216 | 294 | 372 | 444 | 492 | 552 | 612 | 696 |
| | 12 | 91.2 | 168 | 246 | 324 | 408 | 480 | 540 | 612 | 684 | 768 |
| | 14 | 101 | 186 | 264 | 360 | 444 | 528 | 588 | 672 | 756 | 852 |
| | 16 | 106 | 204 | 294 | 384 | 492 | 576 | 636 | 720 | 816 | 924 |
| | 18 | 118 | 222 | 324 | 420 | 516 | 612 | 684 | 768 | 876 | 972 |
| | 20 | 125 | 246 | 336 | 444 | 552 | 648 | 720 | 816 | 924 | 1020 |
| 130 | 2 | **15.6** | **31.2** | **46.9** | **62.5** | **78.1** | **93.7** | **109** | **125** | **141** | **156** |
| | 4 | **31.2** | **62.5** | **93.7** | **125** | **156** | **187** | **216** | **250** | **281** | **312** |
| | 6 | **46.9** | **93.7** | 134 | 156 | 198 | 228 | 258 | 300 | 372 | 432 |
| | 8 | **62.5** | **125** | 156 | 180 | 228 | 258 | 294 | 336 | 408 | 468 |
| | 10 | **78.1** | **156** | 180 | 210 | 258 | 294 | 324 | 372 | 444 | 528 |
| | 12 | **93.7** | 180 | 204 | 234 | 288 | 324 | 360 | 420 | 492 | 576 |
| | 14 | **109** | 204 | 222 | 258 | 312 | 360 | 396 | 456 | 540 | 624 |
| | 16 | **125** | 222 | 246 | 282 | 348 | 396 | 432 | 492 | 600 | 696 |
| | 18 | **141** | 240 | 270 | 300 | 372 | 420 | 468 | 540 | 648 | 732 |
| | 20 | **156** | 264 | 288 | 324 | 396 | 456 | 504 | 588 | 708 | 792 |
| 175 | 2 | **15.6** | **31.2** | **46.9** | **62.5** | **78.1** | **93.7** | **109** | **125** | **141** | **156** |
| | 4 | **31.2** | **62.5** | **93.7** | 120 | 150 | 180 | 204 | 240 | **281** | **312** |
| | 6 | **46.9** | **93.7** | 122 | 144 | 180 | 210 | 240 | 282 | 336 | 396 |
| | 8 | **62.5** | **125** | 144 | 168 | 210 | 240 | 270 | 312 | 372 | 432 |
| | 10 | **78.1** | 150 | 168 | 192 | 240 | 270 | 300 | 348 | 420 | 492 |
| | 12 | **93.7** | 168 | 186 | 216 | 264 | 300 | 336 | 396 | 468 | 540 |
| | 14 | **109** | 186 | 210 | 240 | 294 | 336 | 372 | 432 | 504 | 588 |
| | 16 | **125** | 204 | 228 | 258 | 324 | 360 | 396 | 468 | 552 | 648 |
| | 18 | **141** | 222 | 246 | 282 | 348 | 396 | 432 | 504 | 612 | 684 |
| | 20 | **156** | 246 | 270 | 300 | 372 | 420 | 468 | 552 | 660 | 744 |
| 215 and greater | 2 | **15.6** | **31.2** | **46.9** | **62.5** | **78.1** | **93.7** | **109** | **125** | **141** | **156** |
| | 4 | **31.2** | **62.5** | **93.7** | 118 | 150 | 174 | 198 | 234 | **281** | **312** |
| | 6 | **46.9** | **93.7** | 120 | 142 | 180 | 204 | 234 | 276 | 336 | 384 |
| | 8 | **62.5** | **125** | 142 | 168 | 204 | 234 | 270 | 312 | 372 | 420 |
| | 10 | **78.1** | 144 | 162 | 186 | 234 | 270 | 300 | 348 | 408 | 480 |
| | 12 | **93.7** | 162 | 186 | 210 | 258 | 300 | 324 | 384 | 456 | 528 |
| | 14 | **109** | 186 | 204 | 234 | 288 | 324 | 360 | 420 | 492 | 576 |
| | 16 | **125** | 204 | 222 | 252 | 312 | 360 | 396 | 456 | 552 | 636 |
| | 18 | **141** | 222 | 240 | 276 | 336 | 384 | 432 | 492 | 600 | 672 |
| | 20 | **156** | 240 | 264 | 294 | 360 | 420 | 468 | 540 | 648 | 732 |

Notes:
1. Tabulated P$'_r$ values are for a connection consisting of a pair of riveted gusset plates on opposite sides of the member. Values in bold type indicate P$'_r$ is governed by rivet yielding. Values in regular type indicate P$'_r$ is governed by wood failure.
2. P$_r$ is the lesser of: $P_{ry} = P'_r K_{SF} K_T J_Y J_O H$ (rivet capacity)
   $P_{rw} = P'_r K_D K_{SF} K_T J_O H$ (wood capacity)
3. Rivet spacing, minimum end and edge distances are shown in Figure 7.11. For other connection configurations refer to Clause 10.7 of CSA O86.
4. L = rivet length, S$_p$ = spacing parallel to grain, S$_q$ = spacing perpendicular to grain

# Timber Rivet Selection Tables

## Double-sided Splice Plate

L = **40**mm
S$_p$ = **40**mm
S$_q$ = **25**mm

### P'$_r$ (kN) for Glulam

| Member dimension mm | Rivets per row, n$_c$ | Number of rows | | | | | | | | | |
|---|---|---|---|---|---|---|---|---|---|---|---|
| | | 2 | 4 | 6 | 8 | 10 | 12 | 14 | 16 | 18 | 20 |
| 80 | 2 | 15.6 | 31.2 | 46.9 | 62.5 | 78.1 | 93.7 | 109 | 125 | 141 | 156 |
| | 4 | 31.2 | 62.5 | 93.7 | 125 | 156 | 187 | 219 | 250 | 281 | 312 |
| | 6 | 46.9 | 93.7 | 141 | 187 | 234 | 281 | 328 | 375 | 422 | 469 |
| | 8 | 62.5 | 125 | 187 | 250 | 312 | 375 | 437 | 500 | 562 | 625 |
| | 10 | 78.1 | 156 | 234 | 312 | 390 | 469 | 547 | 625 | 703 | 781 |
| | 12 | 93.7 | 187 | 281 | 372 | 468 | 552 | 636 | 708 | 780 | 876 |
| | 14 | 109 | 216 | 300 | 408 | 504 | 612 | 696 | 768 | 864 | 972 |
| | 16 | 120 | 234 | 336 | 444 | 552 | 660 | 744 | 840 | 936 | 1060 |
| | 18 | 132 | 258 | 372 | 480 | 588 | 708 | 804 | 888 | 996 | 1120 |
| | 20 | 142 | 282 | 396 | 504 | 624 | 744 | 852 | 948 | 1040 | 1160 |
| 130 | 2 | 15.6 | 31.2 | 46.9 | 62.5 | 78.1 | 93.7 | 109 | 125 | 141 | 156 |
| | 4 | 31.2 | 62.5 | 93.7 | 125 | 156 | 187 | 219 | 250 | 281 | 312 |
| | 6 | 46.9 | 93.7 | 141 | 187 | 234 | 281 | 328 | 375 | 422 | 469 |
| | 8 | 62.5 | 125 | 187 | 250 | 312 | 375 | 437 | 500 | 562 | 625 |
| | 10 | 78.1 | 156 | 234 | 312 | 390 | 469 | 547 | 625 | 703 | 781 |
| | 12 | 93.7 | 187 | 281 | 348 | 468 | 562 | 656 | 750 | 843 | 937 |
| | 14 | 109 | 219 | 324 | 384 | 516 | 636 | 744 | 875 | 984 | 1090 |
| | 16 | 125 | 250 | 360 | 432 | 576 | 696 | 816 | 996 | 1120 | 1250 |
| | 18 | 141 | 281 | 384 | 468 | 624 | 756 | 900 | 1090 | 1270 | 1410 |
| | 20 | 156 | 312 | 420 | 504 | 672 | 816 | 972 | 1190 | 1370 | 1520 |
| 175 | 2 | 15.6 | 31.2 | 46.9 | 62.5 | 78.1 | 93.7 | 109 | 125 | 141 | 156 |
| | 4 | 31.2 | 62.5 | 93.7 | 125 | 156 | 187 | 219 | 250 | 281 | 312 |
| | 6 | 46.9 | 93.7 | 141 | 187 | 234 | 281 | 328 | 375 | 422 | 469 |
| | 8 | 62.5 | 125 | 187 | 246 | 312 | 375 | 437 | 500 | 562 | 625 |
| | 10 | 78.1 | 156 | 234 | 288 | 384 | 468 | 547 | 625 | 703 | 781 |
| | 12 | 93.7 | 187 | 270 | 324 | 432 | 528 | 624 | 750 | 843 | 937 |
| | 14 | 109 | 219 | 300 | 360 | 480 | 588 | 696 | 852 | 984 | 1090 |
| | 16 | 125 | 250 | 336 | 396 | 528 | 648 | 756 | 924 | 1120 | 1250 |
| | 18 | 141 | 281 | 360 | 432 | 576 | 696 | 840 | 1020 | 1270 | 1410 |
| | 20 | 156 | 312 | 396 | 468 | 624 | 756 | 912 | 1100 | 1410 | 1560 |
| 215 and greater | 2 | 15.6 | 31.2 | 46.9 | 62.5 | 78.1 | 93.7 | 109 | 125 | 141 | 156 |
| | 4 | 31.2 | 62.5 | 93.7 | 125 | 156 | 187 | 219 | 250 | 281 | 312 |
| | 6 | 46.9 | 93.7 | 141 | 187 | 234 | 281 | 328 | 375 | 422 | 469 |
| | 8 | 62.5 | 125 | 187 | 246 | 312 | 375 | 437 | 500 | 562 | 625 |
| | 10 | 78.1 | 156 | 228 | 282 | 384 | 456 | 547 | 625 | 703 | 781 |
| | 12 | 93.7 | 187 | 264 | 312 | 432 | 528 | 612 | 750 | 843 | 937 |
| | 14 | 109 | 219 | 294 | 360 | 480 | 576 | 684 | 840 | 984 | 1090 |
| | 16 | 125 | 250 | 324 | 384 | 516 | 636 | 744 | 912 | 1120 | 1250 |
| | 18 | 141 | 281 | 348 | 432 | 564 | 684 | 816 | 996 | 1270 | 1410 |
| | 20 | 156 | 312 | 384 | 456 | 612 | 744 | 888 | 1090 | 1400 | 1560 |

**7**

Fastenings

Notes:

1. Tabulated P'$_r$ values are for a connection consisting of a pair of riveted gusset plates on opposite sides of the member. Values in bold type indicate P'$_r$ is governed by rivet yielding. Values in regular type indicate P'$_r$ is governed by wood failure.

2. P$_r$ is the lesser of: P$_{ry}$ = P'$_r$ K$_{SF}$ K$_T$ J$_Y$ J$_O$ H (rivet capacity)
   P$_{rw}$ = P'$_r$ K$_D$ K$_{SF}$ K$_T$ J$_O$ H (wood capacity)

3. Rivet spacing, minimum end and edge distances are shown in Figure 7.11. For other connection configurations refer to Clause 10.7 of CSA O86.

4. L = rivet length, S$_p$ = spacing parallel to grain, S$_q$ = spacing perpendicular to grain

# Timber Rivet Selection Tables

## Double-sided Splice Plate (Sawn Timber)

**P'r (kN) for Sawn Timber**

| Member dimension mm | Rivets per row, $n_c$ | Number of rows | | | | |
|---|---|---|---|---|---|---|
| | | 2 | 4 | 6 | 8 | 10 |
| 89 | 2 | **15.6** | **31.2** | **46.9** | **62.5** | **78.1** |
| | 4 | **31.2** | **62.5** | **93.7** | **125** | **156** |
| | 6 | **46.9** | **93.7** | **141** | **187** | **234** |
| | 8 | **62.5** | **125** | 186 | 244 | 307 |
| | 10 | **78.1** | 152 | 210 | 279 | 351 |
| 89 | 12 | **93.7** | 170 | 238 | 308 | 386 |
| | 14 | 106 | 189 | 256 | 342 | 420 |
| | 16 | 111 | 207 | 285 | 366 | 466 |
| | 18 | 123 | 225 | 314 | 398 | 490 |
| | 20 | 131 | 249 | 327 | 422 | 524 |

**P'r (kN) for Sawn Timber**

| Member dimension mm | Rivets per row, $n_c$ | Number of rows | | | | |
|---|---|---|---|---|---|---|
| | | 2 | 4 | 6 | 8 | 10 |
| 89 | 2 | **15.6** | **31.2** | **46.9** | **62.5** | **78.1** |
| | 4 | **31.2** | **62.5** | **93.7** | **125** | **156** |
| | 6 | **46.9** | **93.7** | **141** | **187** | **234** |
| | 8 | **62.5** | **125** | **187** | **250** | **312** |
| | 10 | **78.1** | **156** | **234** | **312** | **390** |
| 89 | 12 | **93.7** | **187** | **281** | **368** | **468** |
| | 14 | **109** | **219** | 304 | **404** | 506 |
| | 16 | **125** | **246** | 340 | 442 | 556 |
| | 18 | **140** | 270 | 374 | 478 | 594 |
| | 20 | 149 | 294 | 400 | 504 | 633 |

Notes:
1. Tabulated $P'_r$ values are for a connection consisting of a pair of riveted gusset plates on opposite sides of the member. Values in bold type indicate $P'_r$ is governed by rivet yielding. Values in regular type indicate $P'_r$ is governed by wood failure.
2. $P_r$ is the lesser of: $P_{ry} = P'_r\, K_{SF}\, K_T\, J_Y\, J_O\, H$ (rivet capacity)
   $P_{rw} = P'_r\, K_D\, K_{SF}\, K_T\, J_O\, H$ (wood capacity)
   $H$   = 0.50 for D. Fir-L sawn timber
   = 0.45 for Hem-Fir sawn timber
   = 0.40 for S-P-F sawn timber
   = 0.35 for Northern sawn timber
3. Rivet spacing, minimum end and edge distances are shown in Figure 7.11. For other connection configurations refer to Clause 10.7 of CSA O86.
4. L = rivet length, $S_p$ = spacing parallel to grain, $S_q$ = spacing perpendicular to grain
5. For "wet" lumber at time of installation, the maximum overall dimension of a rivet group perpendicular to grain shall not exceed 200 mm (see Clause 10.7.1.10 of CSA O86).

# Timber Rivet Selection Tables

## Double-sided Splice Plate

$L = 65$mm
$S_p = 25$mm
$S_q = 25$mm

$P'_r$ (kN) for Glulam

| Member dimension mm | Rivets per row, $n_c$ | Number of rows 2 | 4 | 6 | 8 | 10 | 12 | 14 | 16 | 18 | 20 |
|---|---|---|---|---|---|---|---|---|---|---|---|
| 130 | 2 | 18.9 | 37.8 | 56.7 | 75.7 | 94.6 | 113 | 132 | 151 | 170 | 189 |
|  | 4 | 37.8 | 75.7 | 113 | 151 | 189 | 227 | 265 | 303 | 340 | 378 |
|  | 6 | 56.7 | 113 | 170 | 227 | 284 | 340 | 397 | 454 | 511 | 567 |
|  | 8 | 75.7 | 144 | 216 | 294 | 372 | 432 | 492 | 552 | 624 | 696 |
|  | 10 | 91.2 | 168 | 246 | 336 | 420 | 492 | 552 | 624 | 696 | 780 |
|  | 12 | 103 | 186 | 276 | 372 | 468 | 540 | 612 | 684 | 768 | 864 |
|  | 14 | 113 | 210 | 300 | 408 | 504 | 600 | 672 | 756 | 852 | 960 |
|  | 16 | 118 | 234 | 336 | 432 | 552 | 648 | 720 | 816 | 924 | 1030 |
|  | 18 | 132 | 252 | 360 | 468 | 588 | 684 | 780 | 864 | 984 | 1100 |
|  | 20 | 139 | 276 | 384 | 504 | 624 | 732 | 816 | 924 | 1030 | 1150 |
| 175 | 2 | 18.9 | 37.8 | 56.7 | 75.7 | 94.6 | 113 | 132 | 151 | 170 | 189 |
|  | 4 | 37.8 | 75.7 | 113 | 151 | 189 | 227 | 265 | 303 | 340 | 378 |
|  | 6 | 56.7 | 113 | 170 | 227 | 284 | 340 | 397 | 454 | 511 | 567 |
|  | 8 | 75.7 | 151 | 227 | 303 | 378 | 444 | 504 | 576 | 672 | 757 |
|  | 10 | 94.6 | 189 | 284 | 360 | 432 | 492 | 540 | 612 | 720 | 828 |
|  | 12 | 113 | 216 | 324 | 384 | 468 | 528 | 576 | 660 | 768 | 888 |
|  | 14 | 132 | 246 | 348 | 420 | 504 | 564 | 612 | 708 | 816 | 936 |
|  | 16 | 137 | 270 | 384 | 444 | 540 | 600 | 648 | 744 | 876 | 1010 |
|  | 18 | 150 | 294 | 420 | 480 | 564 | 636 | 696 | 792 | 948 | 1040 |
|  | 20 | 162 | 324 | 444 | 504 | 600 | 672 | 732 | 840 | 996 | 1120 |
| 215 | 2 | 18.9 | 37.8 | 56.7 | 75.7 | 94.6 | 113 | 132 | 151 | 170 | 189 |
|  | 4 | 37.8 | 75.7 | 113 | 151 | 189 | 227 | 265 | 303 | 340 | 378 |
|  | 6 | 56.7 | 113 | 170 | 227 | 284 | 336 | 384 | 444 | 511 | 567 |
|  | 8 | 75.7 | 151 | 227 | 270 | 336 | 372 | 420 | 468 | 564 | 636 |
|  | 10 | 94.6 | 189 | 258 | 294 | 360 | 408 | 444 | 504 | 600 | 696 |
|  | 12 | 113 | 227 | 288 | 324 | 384 | 444 | 480 | 552 | 648 | 744 |
|  | 14 | 132 | 265 | 312 | 348 | 420 | 468 | 516 | 588 | 684 | 780 |
|  | 16 | 151 | 294 | 336 | 372 | 444 | 504 | 540 | 624 | 732 | 852 |
|  | 18 | 170 | 324 | 348 | 396 | 468 | 528 | 576 | 660 | 792 | 876 |
|  | 20 | 180 | 336 | 372 | 420 | 504 | 564 | 612 | 708 | 840 | 936 |
| 265 | 2 | 18.9 | 37.8 | 56.7 | 75.7 | 94.6 | 113 | 132 | 151 | 170 | 189 |
|  | 4 | 37.8 | 75.7 | 113 | 151 | 189 | 227 | 265 | 303 | 340 | 378 |
|  | 6 | 56.7 | 113 | 170 | 222 | 270 | 312 | 348 | 408 | 480 | 564 |
|  | 8 | 75.7 | 151 | 216 | 246 | 300 | 336 | 372 | 432 | 516 | 576 |
|  | 10 | 94.6 | 189 | 240 | 270 | 324 | 372 | 408 | 468 | 552 | 636 |
|  | 12 | 113 | 227 | 258 | 294 | 360 | 396 | 432 | 504 | 588 | 684 |
|  | 14 | 132 | 258 | 282 | 312 | 384 | 432 | 468 | 540 | 624 | 720 |
|  | 16 | 151 | 276 | 300 | 336 | 408 | 456 | 492 | 564 | 672 | 780 |
|  | 18 | 170 | 300 | 324 | 360 | 432 | 480 | 528 | 612 | 720 | 804 |
|  | 20 | 189 | 312 | 348 | 384 | 456 | 516 | 564 | 648 | 768 | 864 |
| 315 and greater | 2 | 18.9 | 37.9 | 56.8 | 75.8 | 94.7 | 114 | 133 | 152 | 170 | 189 |
|  | 4 | 37.9 | 75.8 | 114 | 152 | 189 | 227 | 265 | 303 | 341 | 379 |
|  | 6 | 56.8 | 114 | 170 | 210 | 258 | 294 | 336 | 384 | 456 | 528 |
|  | 8 | 75.8 | 152 | 204 | 234 | 288 | 324 | 360 | 408 | 492 | 552 |
|  | 10 | 94.7 | 189 | 228 | 258 | 312 | 348 | 384 | 444 | 516 | 600 |
|  | 12 | 114 | 222 | 246 | 276 | 336 | 384 | 420 | 480 | 564 | 648 |
|  | 14 | 133 | 246 | 270 | 300 | 360 | 408 | 444 | 516 | 600 | 684 |
|  | 16 | 152 | 264 | 288 | 324 | 384 | 432 | 468 | 540 | 648 | 744 |
|  | 18 | 170 | 288 | 312 | 348 | 408 | 456 | 504 | 576 | 696 | 768 |
|  | 20 | 189 | 300 | 324 | 360 | 432 | 492 | 540 | 624 | 744 | 828 |

Notes: see page 290

7

Fastenings

# Timber Rivet Selection Tables

L = **65**mm
$S_p$ = **40**mm
$S_q$ = **25**mm

## Double-sided Splice Plate

$P'_r$ (kN) for Glulam

| Member dimension mm | Rivets per row, $n_c$ | Number of rows | | | | | | | | | |
|---|---|---|---|---|---|---|---|---|---|---|---|
| | | 2 | 4 | 6 | 8 | 10 | 12 | 14 | 16 | 18 | 20 |
| 130 | 2 | 18.9 | 37.8 | 56.7 | 75.7 | 94.6 | 113 | 132 | 151 | 170 | 189 |
| | 4 | 37.8 | 75.7 | 113 | 151 | 189 | 227 | 265 | 303 | 340 | 378 |
| | 6 | 56.7 | 113 | 170 | 227 | 284 | 340 | 397 | 454 | 511 | 567 |
| | 8 | 75.7 | 151 | 227 | 303 | 378 | 454 | 530 | 605 | 681 | 757 |
| | 10 | 94.6 | 189 | 282 | 372 | 468 | 567 | 648 | 720 | 792 | 900 |
| | 12 | 113 | 216 | 312 | 420 | 528 | 624 | 720 | 792 | 876 | 996 |
| | 14 | 130 | 240 | 348 | 468 | 576 | 696 | 780 | 864 | 972 | 1090 |
| | 16 | 134 | 264 | 384 | 504 | 624 | 744 | 840 | 948 | 1060 | 1190 |
| | 18 | 150 | 288 | 420 | 540 | 672 | 804 | 912 | 1010 | 1130 | 1260 |
| | 20 | 156 | 312 | 444 | 576 | 708 | 840 | 960 | 1070 | 1190 | 1320 |
| 175 | 2 | 18.9 | 37.8 | 56.7 | 75.7 | 94.6 | 113 | 132 | 151 | 170 | 189 |
| | 4 | 37.8 | 75.7 | 113 | 151 | 189 | 227 | 265 | 303 | 340 | 378 |
| | 6 | 56.7 | 113 | 170 | 227 | 284 | 340 | 397 | 454 | 511 | 567 |
| | 8 | 75.7 | 151 | 227 | 303 | 378 | 454 | 530 | 605 | 681 | 757 |
| | 10 | 94.6 | 189 | 284 | 378 | 473 | 567 | 662 | 757 | 851 | 946 |
| | 12 | 113 | 227 | 340 | 454 | 567 | 681 | 794 | 908 | 1020 | 1130 |
| | 14 | 132 | 265 | 396 | 530 | 662 | 794 | 912 | 1010 | 1130 | 1270 |
| | 16 | 151 | 303 | 444 | 576 | 720 | 876 | 972 | 1090 | 1220 | 1380 |
| | 18 | 170 | 336 | 480 | 624 | 780 | 924 | 1060 | 1160 | 1310 | 1460 |
| | 20 | 186 | 372 | 516 | 660 | 816 | 984 | 1120 | 1240 | 1380 | 1520 |
| 215 | 2 | 18.9 | 37.8 | 56.7 | 75.7 | 94.6 | 113 | 132 | 151 | 170 | 189 |
| | 4 | 37.8 | 75.7 | 113 | 151 | 189 | 227 | 265 | 303 | 340 | 378 |
| | 6 | 56.7 | 113 | 170 | 227 | 284 | 340 | 397 | 454 | 511 | 567 |
| | 8 | 75.7 | 151 | 227 | 303 | 378 | 454 | 530 | 605 | 681 | 757 |
| | 10 | 94.6 | 189 | 284 | 378 | 473 | 567 | 662 | 757 | 851 | 946 |
| | 12 | 113 | 227 | 340 | 454 | 567 | 681 | 794 | 908 | 1020 | 1130 |
| | 14 | 132 | 265 | 397 | 492 | 648 | 768 | 900 | 1060 | 1190 | 1320 |
| | 16 | 151 | 303 | 454 | 528 | 684 | 828 | 960 | 1150 | 1360 | 1510 |
| | 18 | 170 | 340 | 480 | 564 | 732 | 876 | 1030 | 1240 | 1480 | 1640 |
| | 20 | 189 | 378 | 516 | 600 | 780 | 936 | 1090 | 1320 | 1550 | 1720 |
| 265 | 2 | 18.9 | 37.8 | 56.7 | 75.7 | 94.6 | 113 | 132 | 151 | 170 | 189 |
| | 4 | 37.8 | 75.7 | 113 | 151 | 189 | 227 | 265 | 303 | 340 | 378 |
| | 6 | 56.7 | 113 | 170 | 227 | 284 | 340 | 397 | 454 | 511 | 567 |
| | 8 | 75.7 | 151 | 227 | 303 | 378 | 454 | 530 | 605 | 681 | 757 |
| | 10 | 94.6 | 189 | 284 | 372 | 473 | 567 | 662 | 757 | 851 | 946 |
| | 12 | 113 | 227 | 340 | 408 | 540 | 648 | 756 | 908 | 1020 | 1130 |
| | 14 | 132 | 265 | 384 | 444 | 588 | 708 | 828 | 996 | 1190 | 1320 |
| | 16 | 151 | 303 | 408 | 480 | 636 | 756 | 876 | 1060 | 1360 | 1510 |
| | 18 | 170 | 340 | 444 | 516 | 672 | 804 | 948 | 1140 | 1450 | 1700 |
| | 20 | 189 | 378 | 468 | 552 | 720 | 852 | 1010 | 1220 | 1560 | 1860 |
| 315 and greater | 2 | 18.9 | 37.9 | 56.8 | 75.8 | 94.7 | 114 | 133 | 152 | 170 | 189 |
| | 4 | 37.8 | 75.8 | 114 | 152 | 189 | 227 | 265 | 303 | 341 | 379 |
| | 6 | 56.7 | 114 | 170 | 227 | 284 | 341 | 398 | 455 | 511 | 568 |
| | 8 | 75.7 | 152 | 227 | 303 | 379 | 455 | 530 | 606 | 682 | 758 |
| | 10 | 94.6 | 189 | 284 | 360 | 473 | 568 | 663 | 758 | 852 | 947 |
| | 12 | 113 | 227 | 336 | 396 | 516 | 624 | 732 | 888 | 1020 | 1140 |
| | 14 | 132 | 265 | 360 | 432 | 564 | 672 | 780 | 948 | 1190 | 1330 |
| | 16 | 151 | 303 | 396 | 456 | 600 | 720 | 840 | 1010 | 1300 | 1520 |
| | 18 | 170 | 341 | 420 | 492 | 636 | 768 | 900 | 1090 | 1390 | 1670 |
| | 20 | 189 | 379 | 444 | 516 | 684 | 816 | 960 | 1160 | 1490 | 1790 |

Notes: see page 290

# Timber Rivet Selection Tables

## Double-sided Splice Plate

$$L = 90\,mm$$
$$S_p = 25\,mm$$
$$S_q = 25\,mm$$

$P'_r$ (kN) for Glulam

| Member dimension mm | Rivets per row, $n_c$ | Number of rows | | | | | | | | | |
|---|---|---|---|---|---|---|---|---|---|---|---|
| | | 2 | 4 | 6 | 8 | 10 | 12 | 14 | 16 | 18 | 20 |
| 175 | 2 | 21.3 | 42.6 | 63.9 | 85.2 | 107 | 128 | 149 | 170 | 192 | 213 |
| | 4 | 42.6 | 85.2 | 128 | 170 | 213 | 256 | 298 | 341 | 384 | 426 |
| | 6 | 63.9 | 128 | 192 | 256 | 320 | 384 | 447 | 504 | 575 | 639 |
| | 8 | 81.6 | 150 | 228 | 300 | 384 | 456 | 516 | 576 | 648 | 732 |
| | 10 | 96.0 | 174 | 258 | 348 | 432 | 516 | 576 | 648 | 720 | 816 |
| | 12 | 108 | 198 | 288 | 384 | 480 | 564 | 648 | 720 | 804 | 900 |
| | 14 | 118 | 216 | 312 | 420 | 528 | 624 | 696 | 780 | 888 | 996 |
| | 16 | 125 | 240 | 348 | 456 | 576 | 672 | 744 | 852 | 960 | 1080 |
| | 18 | 137 | 264 | 372 | 492 | 612 | 720 | 804 | 912 | 1030 | 1150 |
| | 20 | 144 | 288 | 408 | 516 | 648 | 756 | 852 | 972 | 1080 | 1200 |
| 215 | 2 | 21.3 | 42.6 | 63.9 | 85.2 | 107 | 128 | 149 | 170 | 192 | 213 |
| | 4 | 42.6 | 85.2 | 128 | 170 | 213 | 256 | 298 | 341 | 384 | 426 |
| | 6 | 63.9 | 128 | 192 | 256 | 320 | 384 | 447 | 511 | 575 | 639 |
| | 8 | 85.2 | 168 | 246 | 336 | 420 | 504 | 564 | 636 | 708 | 804 |
| | 10 | 106 | 192 | 282 | 384 | 480 | 564 | 636 | 708 | 792 | 900 |
| | 12 | 118 | 216 | 312 | 420 | 528 | 624 | 708 | 792 | 876 | 996 |
| | 14 | 130 | 240 | 348 | 468 | 576 | 684 | 768 | 864 | 972 | 1090 |
| | 16 | 137 | 264 | 384 | 504 | 624 | 744 | 828 | 936 | 1060 | 1190 |
| | 18 | 150 | 288 | 408 | 540 | 672 | 792 | 888 | 996 | 1140 | 1260 |
| | 20 | 162 | 312 | 444 | 576 | 708 | 828 | 936 | 1070 | 1190 | 1320 |
| 265 | 2 | 21.3 | 42.6 | 63.9 | 85.2 | 107 | 128 | 149 | 170 | 192 | 213 |
| | 4 | 42.6 | 85.2 | 128 | 170 | 213 | 256 | 298 | 341 | 384 | 426 |
| | 6 | 63.9 | 128 | 192 | 256 | 320 | 384 | 447 | 511 | 575 | 639 |
| | 8 | 85.2 | 170 | 256 | 341 | 426 | 511 | 597 | 682 | 767 | 852 |
| | 10 | 107 | 213 | 312 | 420 | 528 | 600 | 660 | 732 | 840 | 960 |
| | 12 | 128 | 240 | 348 | 468 | 564 | 624 | 660 | 756 | 864 | 984 |
| | 14 | 144 | 270 | 384 | 492 | 588 | 648 | 684 | 780 | 888 | 1010 |
| | 16 | 150 | 294 | 420 | 516 | 600 | 660 | 708 | 792 | 936 | 1060 |
| | 18 | 168 | 324 | 456 | 528 | 624 | 684 | 732 | 828 | 972 | 1070 |
| | 20 | 180 | 348 | 492 | 552 | 648 | 708 | 768 | 864 | 1020 | 1120 |
| 315 | 2 | 21.3 | 42.6 | 63.9 | 85.2 | 107 | 128 | 149 | 170 | 192 | 213 |
| | 4 | 42.6 | 85.2 | 128 | 170 | 213 | 256 | 298 | 341 | 384 | 426 |
| | 6 | 63.9 | 128 | 192 | 256 | 320 | 384 | 447 | 511 | 575 | 639 |
| | 8 | 85.2 | 170 | 256 | 341 | 426 | 511 | 564 | 624 | 732 | 816 |
| | 10 | 107 | 213 | 320 | 396 | 480 | 528 | 564 | 636 | 732 | 840 |
| | 12 | 128 | 256 | 372 | 408 | 492 | 540 | 576 | 648 | 756 | 864 |
| | 14 | 149 | 294 | 384 | 432 | 504 | 564 | 600 | 672 | 780 | 876 |
| | 16 | 168 | 324 | 408 | 444 | 528 | 576 | 612 | 696 | 816 | 924 |
| | 18 | 186 | 360 | 432 | 468 | 540 | 588 | 636 | 720 | 852 | 936 |
| | 20 | 198 | 384 | 444 | 480 | 564 | 612 | 672 | 756 | 888 | 984 |
| 365 and greater | 2 | 21.3 | 42.6 | 64.0 | 85.3 | 107 | 128 | 149 | 171 | 192 | 213 |
| | 4 | 42.6 | 85.3 | 128 | 171 | 213 | 256 | 299 | 341 | 384 | 426 |
| | 6 | 64.0 | 128 | 192 | 256 | 320 | 384 | 448 | 512 | 576 | 640 |
| | 8 | 85.3 | 171 | 256 | 341 | 426 | 480 | 516 | 588 | 684 | 768 |
| | 10 | 107 | 213 | 320 | 372 | 444 | 492 | 528 | 588 | 684 | 780 |
| | 12 | 128 | 256 | 348 | 384 | 456 | 504 | 540 | 612 | 708 | 804 |
| | 14 | 149 | 299 | 372 | 408 | 480 | 528 | 552 | 624 | 720 | 828 |
| | 16 | 171 | 336 | 384 | 420 | 492 | 540 | 576 | 648 | 756 | 864 |
| | 18 | 192 | 360 | 396 | 432 | 504 | 552 | 600 | 672 | 804 | 888 |
| | 20 | 210 | 372 | 420 | 444 | 528 | 576 | 624 | 708 | 840 | 924 |

Notes: see page 290

7

Fastenings

# Timber Rivet Selection Tables

## Double-sided Splice Plate

L = **90**mm
S$_p$ = **40**mm
S$_q$ = **25**mm

P$'_r$ (kN) for Glulam

| Member dimension mm | Rivets per row, n$_c$ | Number of rows | | | | | | | | | |
|---|---|---|---|---|---|---|---|---|---|---|---|
| | | 2 | 4 | 6 | 8 | 10 | 12 | 14 | 16 | 18 | 20 |
| 175 | 2 | 21.3 | 42.6 | 63.9 | 85.2 | 107 | 128 | 149 | 170 | 192 | 213 |
| | 4 | 42.6 | 85.2 | 128 | 170 | 213 | 256 | 298 | 341 | 384 | 426 |
| | 6 | 63.9 | 128 | 192 | 256 | 320 | 384 | 447 | 511 | 575 | 639 |
| | 8 | 85.2 | 170 | 256 | 341 | 426 | 511 | 597 | 660 | 744 | 840 |
| | 10 | 107 | 204 | 294 | 396 | 492 | 600 | 672 | 744 | 828 | 936 |
| | 12 | 122 | 228 | 324 | 444 | 552 | 660 | 756 | 828 | 912 | 1030 |
| | 14 | 134 | 252 | 360 | 480 | 600 | 720 | 816 | 900 | 1010 | 1140 |
| | 16 | 142 | 276 | 396 | 516 | 648 | 780 | 876 | 984 | 1090 | 1240 |
| | 18 | 156 | 300 | 432 | 564 | 696 | 840 | 948 | 1040 | 1180 | 1310 |
| | 20 | 168 | 336 | 468 | 600 | 732 | 876 | 996 | 1120 | 1240 | 1380 |
| 215 | 2 | 21.3 | 42.6 | 63.9 | 85.2 | 107 | 128 | 149 | 170 | 192 | 213 |
| | 4 | 42.6 | 85.2 | 128 | 170 | 213 | 256 | 298 | 341 | 384 | 426 |
| | 6 | 63.9 | 128 | 192 | 256 | 320 | 384 | 447 | 511 | 575 | 639 |
| | 8 | 85.2 | 170 | 256 | 341 | 426 | 511 | 597 | 682 | 767 | 852 |
| | 10 | 107 | 213 | 320 | 426 | 533 | 639 | 744 | 816 | 912 | 1030 |
| | 12 | 128 | 246 | 360 | 480 | 600 | 720 | 828 | 912 | 1010 | 1140 |
| | 14 | 144 | 276 | 396 | 528 | 660 | 792 | 900 | 996 | 1120 | 1260 |
| | 16 | 156 | 300 | 432 | 576 | 720 | 864 | 960 | 1080 | 1200 | 1360 |
| | 18 | 174 | 336 | 480 | 612 | 768 | 912 | 1040 | 1150 | 1300 | 1440 |
| | 20 | 180 | 360 | 504 | 648 | 804 | 972 | 1090 | 1220 | 1360 | 1510 |
| 265 | 2 | 21.3 | 42.6 | 63.9 | 85.2 | 107 | 128 | 149 | 170 | 192 | 213 |
| | 4 | 42.6 | 85.2 | 128 | 170 | 213 | 256 | 298 | 341 | 384 | 426 |
| | 6 | 63.9 | 128 | 192 | 256 | 320 | 384 | 447 | 511 | 575 | 639 |
| | 8 | 85.2 | 170 | 256 | 341 | 426 | 511 | 597 | 682 | 767 | 852 |
| | 10 | 107 | 213 | 320 | 426 | 533 | 639 | 746 | 852 | 959 | 1070 |
| | 12 | 128 | 256 | 384 | 511 | 639 | 767 | 895 | 1020 | 1130 | 1270 |
| | 14 | 149 | 298 | 444 | 597 | 732 | 888 | 1010 | 1120 | 1240 | 1400 |
| | 16 | 170 | 336 | 492 | 636 | 804 | 960 | 1080 | 1210 | 1340 | 1520 |
| | 18 | 192 | 372 | 528 | 684 | 852 | 1020 | 1160 | 1280 | 1450 | 1610 |
| | 20 | 204 | 408 | 564 | 720 | 900 | 1080 | 1220 | 1370 | 1510 | 1690 |
| 315 | 2 | 21.3 | 42.6 | 63.9 | 85.2 | 107 | 128 | 149 | 170 | 192 | 213 |
| | 4 | 42.6 | 85.2 | 128 | 170 | 213 | 256 | 298 | 341 | 384 | 426 |
| | 6 | 63.9 | 128 | 192 | 256 | 320 | 384 | 447 | 511 | 575 | 639 |
| | 8 | 85.2 | 170 | 256 | 341 | 426 | 511 | 597 | 682 | 767 | 852 |
| | 10 | 107 | 213 | 320 | 426 | 533 | 639 | 746 | 852 | 959 | 1070 |
| | 12 | 128 | 256 | 384 | 511 | 639 | 767 | 895 | 1020 | 1150 | 1280 |
| | 14 | 149 | 298 | 447 | 552 | 708 | 840 | 948 | 1140 | 1340 | 1490 |
| | 16 | 170 | 341 | 504 | 576 | 732 | 864 | 996 | 1190 | 1490 | 1680 |
| | 18 | 192 | 384 | 528 | 600 | 768 | 900 | 1040 | 1250 | 1580 | 1780 |
| | 20 | 213 | 426 | 552 | 624 | 804 | 948 | 1100 | 1320 | 1670 | 1860 |
| 365 and greater | 2 | 21.3 | 42.6 | 64.0 | 85.3 | 107 | 128 | 149 | 171 | 192 | 213 |
| | 4 | 42.6 | 85.3 | 128 | 171 | 213 | 256 | 299 | 341 | 384 | 426 |
| | 6 | 64.0 | 128 | 192 | 256 | 320 | 384 | 448 | 512 | 576 | 640 |
| | 8 | 85.3 | 171 | 256 | 341 | 426 | 512 | 597 | 682 | 768 | 853 |
| | 10 | 107 | 213 | 320 | 426 | 533 | 640 | 746 | 853 | 960 | 1070 |
| | 12 | 128 | 256 | 384 | 492 | 636 | 744 | 852 | 1020 | 1150 | 1280 |
| | 14 | 149 | 299 | 448 | 516 | 660 | 780 | 900 | 1070 | 1320 | 1490 |
| | 16 | 171 | 341 | 480 | 540 | 696 | 816 | 936 | 1120 | 1400 | 1710 |
| | 18 | 192 | 384 | 492 | 564 | 720 | 840 | 984 | 1180 | 1490 | 1760 |
| | 20 | 213 | 426 | 516 | 588 | 756 | 888 | 1030 | 1240 | 1570 | 1860 |

Notes: see page 290

# Timber Rivet Selection Tables

## Beam Hanger

L = **40**mm

$Q'_w{}^1$ (kN)

Rivets per row, $n_c$

| $S_q$ | $e_p$ | 4 | 5 | 6 | 7 | 8 | 9 | 10 | 11 | 12 | 13 | 14 | 15 | 16 |
|---|---|---|---|---|---|---|---|---|---|---|---|---|---|---|
| 15 | 50 | 12.8 | 15.6 | 20.0 | 24.0 | 29.1 | 33.2 | 38.0 | 43.7 | 49.7 | 59.5 | 71.8 | 80.1 | 89.9 |
| | 60 | 11.7 | 14.0 | 17.9 | 21.7 | 26.4 | 29.9 | 34.2 | 39.0 | 45.1 | 52.4 | 61.5 | 69.1 | 78.8 |
| | 70 | 10.8 | 13.1 | 16.5 | 19.8 | 24.2 | 27.7 | 31.4 | 36.0 | 41.2 | 47.7 | 56.6 | 62.4 | 69.4 |
| | 80 | 10.3 | 12.2 | 15.4 | 18.4 | 22.4 | 25.6 | 29.2 | 33.5 | 38.2 | 44.4 | 52.1 | 57.6 | 64.6 |
| | 90 | 9.92 | 11.6 | 14.5 | 17.2 | 21.0 | 23.9 | 27.3 | 31.4 | 35.9 | 41.4 | 49.0 | 53.9 | 59.8 |
| | 100 | 9.67 | 11.1 | 13.8 | 16.4 | 19.8 | 22.5 | 25.7 | 29.6 | 33.9 | 39.3 | 46.1 | 50.8 | 56.7 |
| | 125 | 9.05 | 10.3 | 12.5 | 14.7 | 17.6 | 19.9 | 22.7 | 26.0 | 29.8 | 34.6 | 40.9 | 45.1 | 50.3 |
| | 150 | 8.73 | 9.83 | 11.7 | 13.5 | 16.2 | 18.3 | 20.6 | 23.4 | 26.9 | 31.2 | 36.8 | 40.5 | 45.4 |
| | 175 | 8.50 | 9.41 | 11.3 | 12.8 | 15.1 | 16.9 | 19.1 | 21.8 | 24.8 | 28.6 | 33.8 | 37.1 | 41.4 |
| | 200 | 8.27 | 9.17 | 10.9 | 12.4 | 14.4 | 16.0 | 17.9 | 20.4 | 23.2 | 26.8 | 31.3 | 34.5 | 38.5 |
| 25 | 50 | 19.7 | 24.0 | 30.5 | 37.4 | 46.5 | 54.6 | 63.1 | 72.7 | 90.8 | 111 | 135 | 152 | 171 |
| | 60 | 17.7 | 21.8 | 27.7 | 33.4 | 41.4 | 46.5 | 55.3 | 64.8 | 75.1 | 87.6 | 110 | 128 | 147 |
| | 70 | 16.3 | 19.9 | 25.5 | 30.9 | 37.5 | 42.9 | 48.7 | 57.2 | 67.6 | 79.5 | 93.8 | 104 | 123 |
| | 80 | 15.2 | 18.4 | 23.7 | 28.7 | 35.1 | 39.4 | 45.3 | 51.8 | 60.2 | 72.0 | 86.0 | 96.0 | 107 |
| | 90 | 14.3 | 17.4 | 22.1 | 26.9 | 32.8 | 37.1 | 42.0 | 48.6 | 55.9 | 64.4 | 78.2 | 88.3 | 99.3 |
| | 100 | 13.6 | 16.3 | 20.7 | 25.4 | 31.1 | 34.8 | 39.8 | 45.3 | 52.6 | 61.2 | 71.5 | 80.6 | 91.6 |
| | 125 | 12.3 | 14.6 | 18.3 | 22.3 | 27.3 | 31.0 | 35.3 | 40.1 | 46.3 | 53.6 | 63.0 | 70.0 | 77.8 |
| | 150 | 11.6 | 13.4 | 16.8 | 20.1 | 24.7 | 27.9 | 31.8 | 36.5 | 41.9 | 48.3 | 57.0 | 62.9 | 69.5 |
| | 175 | 11.1 | 12.6 | 15.5 | 18.7 | 22.5 | 25.6 | 29.1 | 33.3 | 38.5 | 44.7 | 52.4 | 57.5 | 64.1 |
| | 200 | 10.7 | 12.1 | 14.6 | 17.5 | 21.2 | 23.6 | 27.1 | 30.8 | 35.6 | 41.4 | 48.7 | 53.8 | 59.6 |
| 40 | 50 | 37.2 | 45.6 | 61.3 | 75.4 | 101 | 123 | 145 | 168 | 194 | 223 | 262 | 290 | 323 |
| | 60 | 33.5 | 41.1 | 52.2 | 67.0 | 82.7 | 100 | 123 | 147 | 173 | 202 | 239 | 263 | 290 |
| | 70 | 31.0 | 37.7 | 48.2 | 58.7 | 74.7 | 86.2 | 102 | 126 | 152 | 181 | 217 | 241 | 268 |
| | 80 | 28.7 | 34.8 | 44.2 | 54.1 | 66.8 | 78.9 | 91.0 | 105 | 131 | 160 | 195 | 220 | 247 |
| | 90 | 26.8 | 32.9 | 41.7 | 50.5 | 61.5 | 71.5 | 84.0 | 97.5 | 112 | 139 | 173 | 198 | 225 |
| | 100 | 25.3 | 31.0 | 39.1 | 47.4 | 58.0 | 65.8 | 77.0 | 90.7 | 106 | 123 | 151 | 177 | 204 |
| | 125 | 22.3 | 27.2 | 34.8 | 41.9 | 51.0 | 57.8 | 66.3 | 75.7 | 88.9 | 106 | 127 | 141 | 157 |
| | 150 | 20.5 | 24.6 | 31.3 | 38.0 | 46.1 | 52.3 | 59.4 | 68.3 | 78.9 | 91.2 | 109 | 123 | 139 |
| | 175 | 19.0 | 22.7 | 28.7 | 34.7 | 42.4 | 48.2 | 54.6 | 62.6 | 71.6 | 83.8 | 98.9 | 109 | 122 |
| | 200 | 17.9 | 21.3 | 26.5 | 32.2 | 39.2 | 44.8 | 50.9 | 57.9 | 66.8 | 77.2 | 91.2 | 101 | 112 |
| $Q'_y{}^1$ (kN) | | 17.8 | 22.3 | 26.7 | 31.2 | 35.6 | 40.1 | 44.5 | 49.0 | 53.4 | 57.9 | 62.3 | 66.8 | 71.2 |

Notes:
1. $Q_r$ is the lesser of: $Q_{ry} = Q'_y\, K_{SF}\, K_T\, J_Y\, J_O\, H$ (rivet capacity)
   $\quad\quad\quad\quad\quad\quad\quad Q_{rw} = Q'_w\, K_D\, K_{SF}\, K_T\, J_O\, H$ (wood capacity)
2. $Q_r$ is the factored lateral resistance for 2 groups of 2 rows of rivets as shown below. Rivet spacing, minimum end and edge distances (mm) are also shown below. For other connection configurations refer to Clause 10.7 of CSA O86. Minimum unloaded end distance is 50 mm.
3. L = rivet length

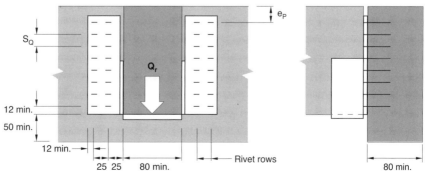

7

Fastenings

# Timber Rivet Selection Tables

## Beam Hanger

  L = **65**mm

**$Q'_w{}^1$ (kN)**

Rivets per row, $n_c$

| $S_q$ | $e_p$ | 4 | 5 | 6 | 7 | 8 | 9 | 10 | 11 | 12 | 13 | 14 | 15 | 16 |
|---|---|---|---|---|---|---|---|---|---|---|---|---|---|---|
| 15 | 50 | 20.5 | 25.1 | 32.2 | 38.7 | 46.9 | 53.4 | 61.1 | 70.4 | 80.1 | 95.9 | 116 | 129 | 145 |
| | 60 | 18.8 | 22.6 | 28.9 | 34.9 | 42.6 | 48.2 | 55.1 | 62.8 | 72.7 | 84.4 | 99.1 | 111 | 127 |
| | 70 | 17.5 | 21.0 | 26.6 | 31.9 | 39.0 | 44.6 | 50.5 | 58.0 | 66.3 | 76.9 | 91.2 | 101 | 112 |
| | 80 | 16.6 | 19.7 | 24.8 | 29.7 | 36.1 | 41.3 | 47.1 | 53.9 | 61.5 | 71.5 | 84.0 | 92.8 | 104 |
| | 90 | 16.0 | 18.7 | 23.4 | 27.6 | 33.8 | 38.5 | 44.0 | 50.6 | 57.9 | 66.7 | 78.9 | 86.8 | 96.3 |
| | 100 | 15.6 | 17.8 | 22.2 | 26.4 | 31.9 | 36.3 | 41.4 | 47.6 | 54.6 | 63.4 | 74.3 | 81.9 | 91.4 |
| | 125 | 14.6 | 16.6 | 20.1 | 23.6 | 28.4 | 32.1 | 36.5 | 41.9 | 48.0 | 55.7 | 65.9 | 72.6 | 81.0 |
| | 150 | 14.1 | 15.8 | 18.9 | 21.8 | 26.0 | 29.4 | 33.2 | 37.7 | 43.4 | 50.3 | 59.2 | 65.3 | 73.0 |
| | 175 | 13.7 | 15.2 | 18.2 | 20.7 | 24.4 | 27.3 | 30.8 | 35.1 | 39.9 | 46.1 | 54.5 | 59.8 | 66.7 |
| | 200 | 13.3 | 14.8 | 17.5 | 20.0 | 23.3 | 25.8 | 28.9 | 32.9 | 37.3 | 43.1 | 50.4 | 55.6 | 62.1 |
| 25 | 50 | 31.8 | 38.7 | 49.1 | 60.3 | 74.9 | 88.0 | 102 | 117 | 146 | 179 | 217 | 245 | 275 |
| | 60 | 28.5 | 35.2 | 44.5 | 53.8 | 66.6 | 74.8 | 89.1 | 104 | 121 | 141 | 178 | 206 | 237 |
| | 70 | 26.2 | 32.1 | 41.1 | 49.7 | 60.4 | 69.1 | 78.4 | 92.2 | 109 | 128 | 151 | 168 | 199 |
| | 80 | 24.4 | 29.7 | 38.1 | 46.2 | 56.5 | 63.4 | 73.0 | 83.5 | 96.9 | 116 | 139 | 155 | 172 |
| | 90 | 23.0 | 28.0 | 35.5 | 43.3 | 52.8 | 59.8 | 67.6 | 78.2 | 90.0 | 104 | 126 | 142 | 160 |
| | 100 | 21.9 | 26.2 | 33.4 | 40.8 | 50.0 | 56.1 | 64.1 | 73.0 | 84.8 | 98.5 | 115 | 130 | 147 |
| | 125 | 19.8 | 23.6 | 29.4 | 35.9 | 43.9 | 49.9 | 56.8 | 64.6 | 74.6 | 86.3 | 101 | 113 | 125 |
| | 150 | 18.6 | 21.6 | 27.0 | 32.3 | 39.7 | 44.9 | 51.3 | 58.8 | 67.5 | 77.8 | 91.7 | 101 | 112 |
| | 175 | 17.9 | 20.3 | 25.0 | 30.1 | 36.3 | 41.2 | 46.8 | 53.6 | 62.0 | 72.0 | 84.3 | 92.7 | 103 |
| | 200 | 17.2 | 19.4 | 23.5 | 28.2 | 34.1 | 38.0 | 43.6 | 49.6 | 57.3 | 66.7 | 78.4 | 86.7 | 96.0 |
| 40 | 50 | 59.9 | 73.4 | 98.8 | 121 | 163 | 198 | 233 | 270 | 312 | 360 | 422 | 468 | 520 |
| | 60 | 54.0 | 66.3 | 84.0 | 108 | 133 | 162 | 198 | 237 | 278 | 326 | 385 | 424 | 467 |
| | 70 | 49.9 | 60.7 | 77.6 | 94.5 | 120 | 139 | 163 | 203 | 245 | 292 | 350 | 389 | 432 |
| | 80 | 46.3 | 56.1 | 71.2 | 87.1 | 108 | 127 | 147 | 169 | 211 | 258 | 314 | 354 | 398 |
| | 90 | 43.2 | 53.0 | 67.1 | 81.3 | 99.0 | 115 | 135 | 157 | 181 | 224 | 279 | 319 | 363 |
| | 100 | 40.7 | 49.9 | 63.0 | 76.3 | 93.4 | 106 | 124 | 146 | 170 | 198 | 244 | 285 | 328 |
| | 125 | 36.0 | 43.8 | 56.1 | 67.5 | 82.1 | 93.1 | 107 | 122 | 143 | 170 | 204 | 227 | 252 |
| | 150 | 33.0 | 39.6 | 50.4 | 61.2 | 74.3 | 84.3 | 95.6 | 110 | 127 | 147 | 176 | 199 | 224 |
| | 175 | 30.6 | 36.6 | 46.3 | 55.9 | 68.3 | 77.6 | 87.9 | 101 | 115 | 135 | 159 | 175 | 196 |
| | 200 | 28.9 | 34.2 | 42.7 | 51.8 | 63.1 | 72.1 | 82.0 | 93.2 | 108 | 124 | 147 | 163 | 181 |
| **$Q'_y{}^1$ (kN)** | | 21.5 | 26.9 | 32.3 | 37.7 | 43.1 | 48.5 | 53.9 | 59.2 | 64.6 | 70.0 | 75.4 | 80.8 | 86.2 |

Notes:
1. $Q_r$ is the lesser of: $Q_{ry} = Q'_y K_{SF} K_T J_Y J_O H$ (rivet capacity)
   $Q_{rw} = Q'_w K_D K_{SF} K_T J_O H$ (wood capacity)
2. $Q_r$ is the factored lateral resistance for 2 groups of 2 rows of rivets as shown below. Rivet spacing, minimum end and edge distances (mm) are also shown below. For other connection configurations refer to Clause 10.7 of CSA O86. Minimum unloaded end distance is 50 mm.
3. L = rivet length

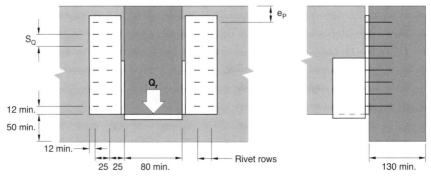

# Timber Rivet Selection Tables

## Beam Hanger

L = **90**mm

$Q'_w{}^1$ (kN)

Rivets per row, $n_c$

| $S_q$ | $e_p$ | 4 | 5 | 6 | 7 | 8 | 9 | 10 | 11 | 12 | 13 | 14 | 15 | 16 |
|---|---|---|---|---|---|---|---|---|---|---|---|---|---|---|
| 15 | 50 | 27.6 | 33.8 | 43.3 | 52.1 | 63.2 | 71.8 | 82.2 | 94.6 | 108 | 129 | 156 | 173 | 195 |
| | 60 | 25.3 | 30.4 | 38.9 | 47.0 | 57.3 | 64.8 | 74.1 | 84.5 | 97.8 | 114 | 133 | 150 | 171 |
| | 70 | 23.5 | 28.3 | 35.8 | 42.9 | 52.5 | 59.9 | 67.9 | 78.0 | 89.2 | 103 | 123 | 135 | 150 |
| | 80 | 22.3 | 26.5 | 33.3 | 39.9 | 48.5 | 55.5 | 63.3 | 72.5 | 82.8 | 96.2 | 113 | 125 | 140 |
| | 90 | 21.5 | 25.1 | 31.4 | 37.2 | 45.5 | 51.8 | 59.2 | 68.0 | 77.9 | 89.7 | 106 | 117 | 130 |
| | 100 | 21.0 | 24.0 | 29.9 | 35.5 | 42.8 | 48.8 | 55.6 | 64.1 | 73.5 | 85.2 | 100 | 110 | 123 |
| | 125 | 19.6 | 22.4 | 27.0 | 31.7 | 38.2 | 43.2 | 49.2 | 56.3 | 64.5 | 74.9 | 88.7 | 97.6 | 109 |
| | 150 | 18.9 | 21.3 | 25.4 | 29.3 | 35.0 | 39.5 | 44.7 | 50.7 | 58.4 | 67.6 | 79.6 | 87.8 | 98.3 |
| | 175 | 18.4 | 20.4 | 24.5 | 27.8 | 32.8 | 36.7 | 41.4 | 47.2 | 53.7 | 62.0 | 73.3 | 80.5 | 89.7 |
| | 200 | 17.9 | 19.9 | 23.5 | 26.9 | 31.3 | 34.7 | 38.9 | 44.2 | 50.2 | 58.0 | 67.8 | 74.7 | 83.5 |
| 25 | 50 | 42.7 | 52.0 | 66.0 | 81.1 | 101 | 118 | 137 | 158 | 197 | 241 | 292 | 329 | 370 |
| | 60 | 38.3 | 47.3 | 59.9 | 72.4 | 89.7 | 101 | 120 | 140 | 163 | 190 | 239 | 278 | 319 |
| | 70 | 35.3 | 43.2 | 55.2 | 66.9 | 81.3 | 93.0 | 105 | 124 | 147 | 172 | 203 | 226 | 267 |
| | 80 | 32.9 | 40.0 | 51.3 | 62.2 | 75.9 | 85.3 | 98.2 | 112 | 130 | 156 | 186 | 208 | 232 |
| | 90 | 31.0 | 37.6 | 47.8 | 58.3 | 71.0 | 80.4 | 90.9 | 105 | 121 | 140 | 169 | 191 | 215 |
| | 100 | 29.5 | 35.3 | 44.9 | 54.9 | 67.3 | 75.5 | 86.3 | 98.2 | 114 | 133 | 155 | 175 | 198 |
| | 125 | 26.7 | 31.7 | 39.6 | 48.3 | 59.1 | 67.2 | 76.4 | 86.9 | 100 | 116 | 136 | 152 | 169 |
| | 150 | 25.1 | 29.1 | 36.3 | 43.5 | 53.4 | 60.4 | 69.0 | 79.0 | 90.8 | 105 | 123 | 136 | 151 |
| | 175 | 24.1 | 27.3 | 33.7 | 40.4 | 48.8 | 55.5 | 63.0 | 72.2 | 83.4 | 96.8 | 113 | 125 | 139 |
| | 200 | 23.2 | 26.1 | 31.7 | 37.9 | 45.9 | 51.2 | 58.6 | 66.8 | 77.1 | 89.7 | 105 | 117 | 129 |
| 40 | 50 | 80.5 | 98.7 | 133 | 163 | 219 | 267 | 314 | 364 | 420 | 484 | 567 | 629 | 700 |
| | 60 | 72.7 | 89.2 | 113 | 145 | 179 | 217 | 267 | 318 | 374 | 438 | 518 | 570 | 628 |
| | 70 | 67.2 | 81.6 | 104 | 127 | 162 | 187 | 220 | 273 | 329 | 393 | 470 | 523 | 581 |
| | 80 | 62.3 | 75.5 | 95.8 | 117 | 145 | 171 | 197 | 227 | 284 | 347 | 423 | 476 | 535 |
| | 90 | 58.1 | 71.2 | 90.3 | 109 | 133 | 155 | 182 | 211 | 244 | 301 | 375 | 430 | 488 |
| | 100 | 54.7 | 67.2 | 84.8 | 103 | 126 | 143 | 167 | 197 | 229 | 266 | 328 | 383 | 442 |
| | 125 | 48.4 | 58.9 | 75.4 | 90.9 | 110 | 125 | 144 | 164 | 193 | 229 | 275 | 305 | 339 |
| | 150 | 44.3 | 53.3 | 67.8 | 82.4 | 99.9 | 113 | 129 | 148 | 171 | 197 | 236 | 267 | 302 |
| | 175 | 41.1 | 49.2 | 62.3 | 75.2 | 91.9 | 104 | 118 | 136 | 155 | 182 | 214 | 236 | 264 |
| | 200 | 38.9 | 46.1 | 57.5 | 69.8 | 84.9 | 97.0 | 110 | 125 | 145 | 167 | 198 | 219 | 243 |
| $Q'_y{}^1$ (kN) | | 24.3 | 30.3 | 36.4 | 42.5 | 48.5 | 54.6 | 60.6 | 66.7 | 72.8 | 78.8 | 84.9 | 91.0 | 97.0 |

**7**

Fastenings

Notes:
1. $Q_r$ is the lesser of: $Q_{ry} = Q'_y K_{SF} K_T J_Y J_O H$ (rivet capacity)
   $Q_{rw} = Q'_w K_D K_{SF} K_T J_O H$ (wood capacity)
2. $Q_r$ is the factored lateral resistance for 2 groups of 2 rows of rivets as shown below. Rivet spacing, minimum end and edge distances (mm) are also shown below. For other connection configurations refer to Clause 10.7 of CSA O86. Minimum unloaded end distance is 50 mm.
3. L = rivet length

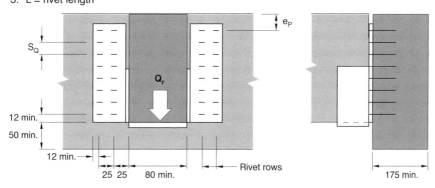

# 7.7 Shear Plates and Split Rings

## General

Shear plates and split rings are commonly used with either bolts or lag screws in heavy timber and glulam construction. These connectors distribute lateral forces over a larger bearing area than bolts or lag screws alone, resulting in higher resistance values.

Shear plates and split rings are installed in grooves that are precut into the wood member. Special grooving tools are used to accurately machine the grooves to specified tolerances (refer to Table 10.3.1B of CSA O86) since a poor fit will reduce the resistance of the connection.

Split rings and shear plates are marketed in imperial dimensions only. Galvanizing must be used in wet service conditions. Washers used in connector joints should conform to the requirements in Table 7.13.

Table 7.13
**Minimum washer dimensions for split ring and shear plate connections (mm)**

| Washer Type | 2-1/2" dia. split ring with 1/2" dia. bolt | | 4" dia. split ring with 3/4" dia. bolt | | 2-5/8" dia. shear plate and 4" dia. shear plate with 3/4" dia. bolt | | 4" dia. shear plate with 7/8" dia. bolt | |
|---|---|---|---|---|---|---|---|---|
| | thickness | outside dimension | thickness | outside dimension | thickness | outside dimension | thickness | outside dimension |
| Square plate | 3.2 | 50 | 4.8 | 75 | 6.4 | 75 | 6.4 | 90 |
| Round plate | 3.2 | 50 | 4.8 | 75 | 6.4 | 75 | 6.4 | 90 |
| Ogee | 3.2 | 55 | 4.8 | 75 | 6.4 | 75 | 6.4 | 90 |
| Malleable iron | 3.2 | 55 | 4.8 | 75 | 6.4 | 75 | 6.4 | 90 |

## Shear Plates

Shear plates are available in 2-5/8" and 4" diameters. The 2-5/8" shear plate is used with a 3/4" diameter bolt or lag screw, and the 4" size may be used with either a 3/4" or 7/8" diameter bolt or lag screw. The 2-5/8" shear plate is available in flange depths of 0.42" or 0.35", but CSA O86 only references the commonly available smaller depth. Shear plates are primarily used in steel-to-wood connections such as in a wood truss with steel gusset plates. However, shear plates may be used back-to-back in wood-to-wood connections whenever it is advantageous to have connectors flush with the wood face for ease of erection.

Figure 7.12
**Shear plates**

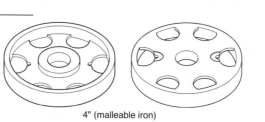

4" (malleable iron)

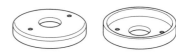

2-5/8" (pressed steel)

7

Fastenings

### Split Rings

Split rings are for use in wood-to-wood joints and are available in 2-1/2" and 4" diameters. The 2-1/2" split ring is for use with a 1/2" diameter bolt or lag screw and the 4" split ring requires a 3/4" diameter bolt or lag screw. Split rings bear against both sides of the groove, and the tapered edges of the ring allow for a tight fitting joint.

Figure 7.13
**Split ring**

### Analysis of Shear Plate and Split Ring Joints

Shear plates and split rings act on the faces of wood members. Often it is necessary to construct a free body diagram of the connection in order to determine the magnitude and direction of the force in each connector. An example of a free body diagram for a multileaf truss connection is shown in Figure 7.14. Note that the connector group on the near side of the tension diagonal has a force of 17.3 kN acting at 30° to the grain while on the far side the force is 10 kN at 60° to the grain.

Figure 7.14
**Free body diagram for a typical multi-leaf truss connection**

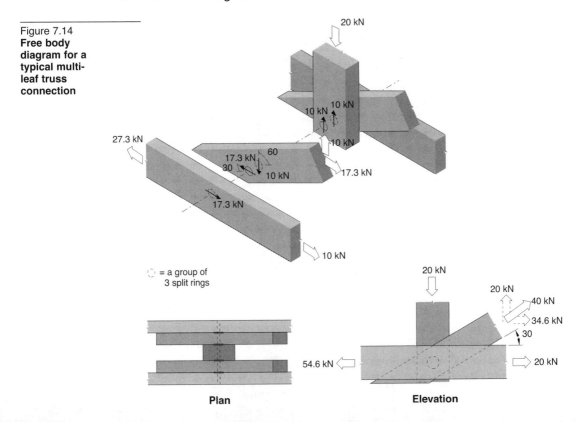

The connectors in the interface between the chord and the diagonal web must be designed for a 17.3 kN force acting at 0° on the chord face and at 30° on the diagonal web face. Similarly, the connector group between the vertical and diagonal webs must be designed for a 10 kN force acting at 0° on the vertical web face and at 60° to the diagonal web face. Generally, the face that has the largest angle of load to grain will govern the design.

## Design

Shear plates and split rings must be designed so that the factored lateral resistance of the connection is greater than or equal to the factored lateral load.

The lateral resistance of shear plates is equal to the resistance of the wood or the resistance of the steel, whichever is lower. The resistance of split rings depends only on the resistance of the wood.

### Factored Resistance of Wood (Split Rings and Shear Plates)

The resistance of the wood depends upon the angle of load to grain and is calculated as follows:

$$P_r = \phi\, p_u\, n_{Fe}\, n_R\, K'\, J'\, J_S \quad \text{for parallel to grain loading}$$

$$Q_r = \phi\, q_u\, n_{Fe}\, n_R\, K'\, J' \quad \text{for perpendicular to grain loading}$$

$$N_r = \frac{P_r Q_r}{P_r \sin^2 \theta + Q_r \cos^2 \theta} \quad \begin{array}{l}\text{for loading at an angle } \theta \text{ to grain.}\\ N_r \text{ may also be determined from Table 7.1.}\end{array}$$

where:

$\phi\, p_u$ and $\phi\, q_u$ are basic factored lateral resistances given in Tables 7.14 and 7.15

$n_{Fe}$ = effective number of fasteners per row, given in Tables 7.17 and 7.18

$n_R$ = number of rows

$K'$, $J'$ and $J_S$ are modification factors given below

### Factored Resistance of Steel (Shear Plates Only)

The resistance of the steel $N_{Sr}$ is limited by the bearing capacity of the shear plate and the shear capacity of the bolt. It is calculated as follows:

$$N_{Sr} = N_{Su}\, n_F\, n_R$$

where:

$N_{Su}$ = maximum factored resistance per shear plate, given in Table 7.16

$n_R$ = number of rows

$n_F$ = number of fasteners per row

7

Fastenings

## Modification Factors

The composite modification factors $K'$, $J'$ and $J_S$ adjust the basic factored lateral resistance for the actual conditions of use and are calculated as follows:

$$K' = K_D K_{SF} K_T$$
$$J' = J_C J_T J_O J_P$$
$$J_S = \text{side plate factor for 4" diameter shear plates}$$

where:

$K_D$ = duration of load factor

$K_{SF}$ = service condition factor

$K_T$ = fire-retardant treatment factor

$J_C$ = minimum configuration factor

$J_T$ = thickness factor

$J_O$ = factor for connector orientation in grain

$J_P$ = factor for lag screw penetration

In many cases $K'$, $J'$ and $J_S$ will equal 1.0. Review the following checklist to determine if each modification factor is equal to 1.0 for the actual conditions of use. Where a factor does not equal 1.0, determine the appropriate value and calculate $K'$ and $J'$.

## Additional Design Considerations

Split rings and shear plates remove considerable material from the connecting members, which must be considered in the design of the members. Section 7.1 contains information on the area of material removed due to boring and grooving.

Where shear plates or split rings are used in eccentric connections or where the connection exerts a shear force on a wood member, the shear resistance of the member must be checked as outlined in Section 7.1.

Steel side plates must be designed to adequately resist the factored loading in accordance with CSA S16.

# Checklist: **Shear Plates and Split Rings** ✅

1. $K_D$ = 1.0 where the loading is "standard" term
   = 1.15 for short term loading (e.g., dead plus wind)
   = 0.65 for permanent loads (e.g., dead loads alone)

2. $K_{SF}$ = 1.0 where the service conditions are "dry" and the lumber is seasoned
   (moisture content ≤ 15%) prior to fabrication
   = 0.8 for unseasoned lumber in dry service conditions
   = 0.67 for wet service conditions

3. $K_T$ = 1.0 when the wood is not treated with a fire retardant or other
   strength-reducing chemical.

   For wood treated with a fire retardant or other strength-reducing
   chemicals, see the Commentary for further guidance.

4. $J_C$ = 1.0 where connector spacing, end distance and edge distance meet the
   minimum values shown in Figure 7.15

   For reduced spacing, end distance or edge distance, calculate $J_C$ as the
   least of the following values and apply this factor to all connectors:

   $J_{C1}$ = factor for end distance given in Table 7.19
   $J_{C2}$ = factor for edge distance given in Table 7.20
   $J_{C3}$ = factor for spacing given in Tables 7.21 and 7.22

5. $J_T$ = 1.0 where the member thickness meets the minimum value shown in
   Figure 7.15

   For reduced thickness refer to Table 10.3.4 of CSA O86.

6. $J_O$ = 1.0 where the shear plates or split rings are installed in side grain
   = 0.67 when used in end grain

7. $J_P$ = 1.0 where the lag screw penetration is at least the "standard" number of
   shank diameters shown in Table 7.23, or $J_P$ = 1.0 when bolts are used.
   Lag screws must be installed in accordance with Section 7.5

   For reduced penetration, calculate $J_P$ as shown in Table 7.23

8. $J_S$ = 1.0 where split rings or 2-5/8" shear plates are used or when steel side
   plates are used with 4" shear plates
   = 0.9 when wood side plates are used with 4" shear plates

**7**

Fastenings

### Example 1: Shear Plates

Determine the number of shear plates required for the truss heel connection shown below (dimensions in mm). The bottom chord is unseasoned 140 × 191 mm Douglas-fir and the steel side plates are 6 mm thick. Use 4" diameter shear plates both sides with 3/4" diameter bolts. Dry service conditions apply and the truss supports dead loads plus snow load.

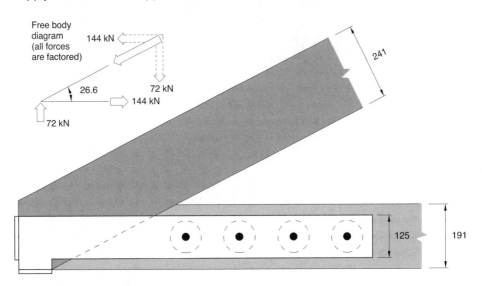

### Modification Factors

$K_D$ = 1.0 (duration of load is standard)

$K_{SF}$ = 0.8 (service conditions are dry, but material is unseasoned)

$K_T$ = 1.0 (material is not treated with a fire retardant)

$J_C$ = 1.0 (least value of $J_{C1}$, $J_{C2}$, $J_{C3}$)

    For $J_{C1}$ = 1.0 use end distance ≥ 180 mm

    For $J_{C2}$ = 1.0 use edge distance ≥ 65 mm

    For $J_{C3}$ = 1.0 use spacing ≥ 230 mm

$J_T$ = 1.0 (member thickness > 89 mm)

$J_O$ = 1.0 (connections are used in side grain)

$J_P$ = 1.0 (lag screws are not used)

$J_S$ = 1.0 (steel side plates used)

Therefore:

    $K'$ = 1.0 × 0.8 × 1.0 = 0.8

    $J'$ = 1.0 × 1.0 × 1.0 × 1.0 = 1.0

**Calculation**

$T_f$ = 144 kN

Resistance of wood:

$P_r = \phi \, p_u \, n_{Fe} \, n_R \, K' \, J' \, J_S$

$\phi \, p_u$ = 29.4 kN from Table 7.15

$n_R$ = 1.0

$K'$ = 0.8

$J'$ = 1.0

$P_r$ = 29.4 × $n_{Fe}$ × 1.0 × 0.8 × 1.0 × 1.0 = 23.5 $n_{Fe}$

Resistance of steel:

$N_{Sr} = N_{Su} \, n_F \, n_R$

$N_{Su}$ = 28 kN from Table 7.16

$N_{Sr}$ = 28 $n_F$ × 1 = 28 $n_F$

Therefore, required $n_{Fe}$ = $\dfrac{144}{23.5}$ = 6.1 total

or

$n_{Fe}$ per side = 3.05

Try four shear plates per side and check $n_{Fe}$ from Table 7.18

$A_m$ = 26740 mm$^2$

$A_s$ = 2 × 6 × 125 = 1500 mm$^2$

$A_m/A_s$ = 17.8

$n_{Fe}$ = 3.76 per side

$P_r$ = 23.5 × 2 × 3.76 = 177 kN

Check $N_{Sr}$:

$N_{Sr}$ = 28 × 2 × 4 = 224 kN > 144 kN          *Acceptable*

**7**

Fastenings

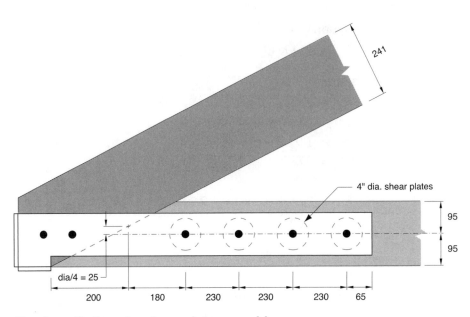

dia/4 = 25

| 200 | 180 | 230 | 230 | 230 | 65 |

4" dia. shear plates

95

95

241

**Use four 4" diameter shear plates per side.**

### Example 2: Split Rings

Check the resistance of the split rings in the near face of the tension diagonal shown below (dimensions in mm). This member is part of the truss connection shown in Figure 7.14. The wood is unseasoned 64 mm thick by 235 mm deep S-P-F and the connectors are 2-1/2" split rings. The loading is due to dead loads plus snow load.

### Modification Factors

$K_D$ = 1.0 (load duration is standard)

$K_{SF}$ = 0.8 (wood will be unseasoned at fabrication, service condition is dry)

$K_T$ = 1.0 (wood is untreated)

$J_{C1}$ = 0.92 (loaded end distance is 190 mm, thickness is < 130 mm)

$J_{C2}$ = 0.98 (loaded edge distance = 60 mm)

$J_{C3}$ = 0.75 (for 90 mm spacing and $\beta$ = 60°)
    = 1.0 (for 120 mm spacing and $\beta$ = 30°)
    = 1.0 (for 150 mm spacing and $\beta$ = 10°)

Therefore, $J_C$ = lowest of $J_{C1}$, $J_{C2}$, $J_{C3}$ = 0.75

$J_T$ = 1.0 (thickness > 51 mm for connectors on two faces)

$J_O$ = 1.0 (connectors are in side grain)

$J_P$ = 1.0 (bolts are used)

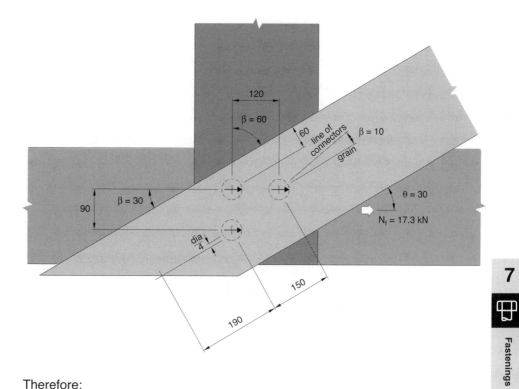

Therefore:

$$K' = 1.0 \times 0.8 \times 1.0 = 0.8$$
$$J' = 0.75 \times 1.0 \times 1.0 \times 1.0 = 0.75$$

## Calculation

$$P_r = \phi\, p_u\, n_{Fe}\, n_R\, K'\, J'$$
$$Q_r = \phi\, q_u\, n_{Fe}\, n_R\, K'\, J'$$
$$\phi\, p_u = 13.8 \text{ kN from Table 7.13}$$
$$\phi\, q_u = 10.2 \text{ kN}$$

For one split ring:

$$n_R = 1$$
$$n_{Fe} = 1.0$$
$$P_r = 13.8 \times 0.8 \times 0.75 = 8.28 \text{ kN}$$
$$Q_r = 10.2 \times 0.8 \times 0.75 = 6.12 \text{ kN}$$

7

Fastenings

For one row of two split rings:

$$N_R = 1$$
$$N_{Fe} = 2.0$$
$$P_r = 13.8 \times 1 \times 2.0 \times 0.8 \times 0.75 = 16.6 \text{ kN}$$
$$Q_r = 10.2 \times 1 \times 2.0 \times 0.8 \times 0.75 = 12.2 \text{ kN}$$

Since the capacity of each connector in the joint is identical, the total joint capacity is equal to the sum of the connector capacities:

$$P_r = 8.28 + 16.6 = 24.9 \text{ kN}$$
$$Q_r = 6.12 + 12.2 = 18.3 \text{ kN}$$

Note that if the connector row capacities of the joint were unequal, the total joint capacity would normally be calculated by multiplying the total number of connectors by the lowest maximum capacity connector.

Using Table 7.1, determine $N_r$ for $\theta = 30°$:

$$Q_r/P_r = 18.3/24.9 = 0.73$$
$$X = 0.91$$
$$N_r = 24.9 \times 0.91 = 22.7 \text{ kN} > 17.3 \text{ kN} \qquad \textit{Acceptable}$$

Note that the split rings should also be checked for loading at 0° to the grain on the chord face. In this case the connector resistance on the chord face is higher than on the diagonal web face.

**The connection is adequate.**

Table 7.14
**Basic factored lateral resistance for split rings (kN)**

|  |  | 2-1/2" dia. split ring | | 4" dia. split ring | |
|---|---|---|---|---|---|
| Species |  | $\phi\, p_u$ | $\phi\, q_u$ | $\phi\, p_u$ | $\phi\, q_u$ |
| D.Fir-L |  | 18.6 | 13.2 | 33.0 | 25.2 |
| Hem-Fir |  | 16.2 | 10.8 | 29.4 | 21.0 |
| S-P-F |  | 13.8 | 10.2 | 27.0 | 18.6 |
| Northern |  | 12.6 | 9.0 | 25.2 | 16.8 |

Note:
$P_r = \phi\, p_u\, n_{Fe}\, n_R\, K'\, J'$
$Q_r = \phi\, q_u\, n_{Fe}\, n_R\, K'\, J'$

Table 7.15
**Basic factored lateral resistance for shear plates (kN)**

|  | 2-5/8" dia. shear plate with 3/4" dia. bolt | | 4" dia. shear plate with 3/4" dia. bolt | | 4" dia. shear plate with 7/8" dia. bolt | |
|---|---|---|---|---|---|---|
| Species | $\phi\, p_u$ | $\phi\, q_u$ | $\phi\, p_u$ | $\phi\, q_u$ | $\phi\, p_u$ | $\phi\, q_u$ |
| D.Fir-L | 16.2 | 13.8 | 29.4 | 21.0 | 36.8 | 26.2 |
| Hem-Fir | 14.4 | 11.4 | 26.4 | 16.8 | 33.0 | 21.0 |
| S-P-F | 13.8 | 10.2 | 25.2 | 15.6 | 31.5 | 19.5 |
| Northern | 13.2 | 9.0 | 24.0 | 14.4 | 30.0 | 18.0 |

Note:
$P_r = \phi\, p_u\, n_{Fe}\, n_R\, K'\, J'$
$Q_r = \phi\, q_u\, n_{Fe}\, n_R\, K'\, J'$

**7**

Fastenings

Table 7.16
**Maximum factored resistance per shear plate $N_{Su}$ (kN)**

| Type of load | 2-5/8" dia. shear plate with 3/4" dia. bolt | 4" dia. shear plate with 3/4" dia. bolt | 4" dia. shear plate with 7/8" dia. bolt |
|---|---|---|---|
| Washers provided; no bearing on threaded portion of bolt | 18 | 32 | 43 |
| When bearing may occur on the threaded portion of the bolt | 16 | 28 | 38 |

Note:
$N_{Sr} = N_{Su}\, n_F\, n_R$

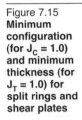

Figure 7.15
**Minimum
configuration
(for $J_C = 1.0$)
and minimum
thickness (for
$J_T = 1.0$) for
split rings and
shear plates**

**2-1/2" split rings
2-5/8" shear plates**

**4" split rings
4" shear plates**

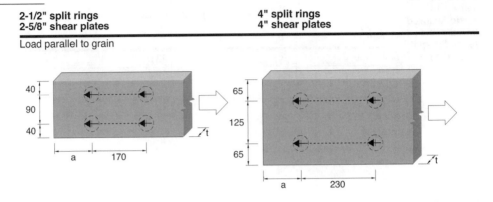

Load parallel to grain

Load perpendicular to grain

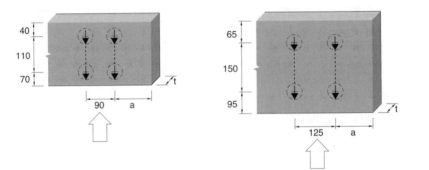

t = minimum thickness (mm)
a = end distance for tension members (mm)

| | |
|---|---|
| a = 210<br>when t < 130 | a = 270<br>when t < 130 |
| a = 140<br>when t  130 | a = 180<br>when t  130 |
| t = 51 for split rings on two faces<br>   38 for split rings on one face<br>   64 for shear plates on one or two faces | t = 76 for split rings on two faces<br>   38 for split rings on one face<br>   89 for shear plates on two faces<br>   44 for shear plates on one face |

Notes:
1. All dimensions are in mm.
2. Reduced end, edge and spacing dimensions are possible; see Tables 7.19, 7.20, 7.21
   and 7.22.

| Table 7.17 Effective number of fasteners per row $n_{Fe}$ for joints with wood side plates | Area ratio $A_m/A_s$ | The lesser of $A_m$ and $A_s$ | Actual number of fasteners in a row | | | | | | | | | | |
|---|---|---|---|---|---|---|---|---|---|---|---|---|---|
| | | | 2 | 3 | 4 | 5 | 6 | 7 | 8 | 9 | 10 | 11 | 12 |
| | 0.5 | < 8000 | 2.00 | 2.76 | 3.36 | 3.80 | 4.08 | 4.27 | 4.40 | 4.41 | 4.30 | 4.18 | 4.08 |
| | | 8001 to 12000 | 2.00 | 2.85 | 3.52 | 4.10 | 4.50 | 4.76 | 4.96 | 5.13 | 5.20 | 5.28 | 5.16 |
| | | 12001 to 18000 | 2.00 | 2.91 | 3.72 | 4.40 | 4.92 | 5.39 | 5.68 | 6.03 | 6.30 | 6.49 | 6.60 |
| | | 18001 to 26000 | 2.00 | 2.94 | 3.84 | 4.60 | 5.22 | 5.81 | 6.32 | 6.75 | 7.10 | 7.59 | 7.92 |
| | | 26001 to 42000 | 2.00 | 3.00 | 3.88 | 4.70 | 5.40 | 6.02 | 6.64 | 7.11 | 7.60 | 8.14 | 8.64 |
| | | > 42000 | 2.00 | 3.00 | 3.92 | 4.75 | 5.46 | 6.16 | 6.80 | 7.38 | 8.00 | 8.58 | 9.12 |
| | 1.0 | < 8000 | 2.00 | 2.91 | 3.68 | 4.25 | 4.68 | 4.97 | 5.20 | 5.31 | 5.40 | 5.39 | 5.28 |
| | | 8001 to 12000 | 2.00 | 2.94 | 3.76 | 4.45 | 5.04 | 5.46 | 5.76 | 5.94 | 6.10 | 6.16 | 6.12 |
| | | 12001 to 18000 | 2.00 | 3.00 | 3.88 | 4.65 | 5.34 | 5.95 | 6.40 | 6.84 | 7.20 | 7.48 | 7.68 |
| | | 18001 to 26000 | 2.00 | 3.00 | 3.96 | 4.80 | 5.52 | 6.23 | 6.80 | 7.47 | 8.00 | 8.58 | 9.00 |
| | | 26001 to 42000 | 2.00 | 3.00 | 4.00 | 4.85 | 5.64 | 6.37 | 7.04 | 7.65 | 8.40 | 9.02 | 9.60 |
| | | > 42000 | 2.00 | 3.00 | 4.00 | 4.95 | 5.76 | 6.51 | 7.28 | 7.92 | 8.70 | 9.46 | 10.2 |

Notes:
1. $A_m$ = gross cross-sectional area of main member, mm$^2$
   $A_s$ = sum of gross cross-sectional areas of wood side plates, mm$^2$
   Area ratio = the lesser of $A_m/A_s$ and $A_s/A_m$
2. For perpendicular to grain loading, the area of the main member may be taken as the product of the member thickness and the width of the fastener group. For a single row of fasteners, use the minimum parallel to grain spacing for $J_C = 1.0$ (shown in Figure 7.15) as the width of the fastener group.
3. For area ratios between 0.5 and 1.0 interpolate between tabulated values.
   For area ratios less than 0.5 extrapolate from tabulated values.
4. $n_{Fe}$ applies to shear plates, split rings and lag screws.

7

Fastenings

**Table 7.18**
**Effective number of fasteners per row $n_{Fe}$ for joints with steel side plates**

| Area ratio $A_m/A_s$ | $A_m$ | Actual number of fasteners in a row | | | | | | | | | | |
|---|---|---|---|---|---|---|---|---|---|---|---|---|
| | | 2 | 3 | 4 | 5 | 6 | 7 | 8 | 9 | 10 | 11 | 12 |
| 2 to 12 | 16000 to 26000 | 2.00 | 2.82 | 3.48 | 4.00 | 4.38 | 4.69 | 4.88 | 5.04 | 5.10 | 5.06 | 5.04 |
| | 26001 to 42000 | 2.00 | 2.88 | 3.68 | 4.35 | 4.86 | 5.25 | 5.60 | 5.94 | 6.20 | 6.38 | 6.60 |
| | 42001 to 76000 | 2.00 | 2.94 | 3.80 | 4.55 | 5.22 | 5.74 | 6.24 | 6.75 | 7.20 | 7.59 | 7.92 |
| | 76001 to 130000 | 2.00 | 2.97 | 3.88 | 4.75 | 5.52 | 6.23 | 6.88 | 7.56 | 8.10 | 8.69 | 9.36 |
| 12.1 to 18 | 26001 to 42000 | 2.00 | 2.94 | 3.76 | 4.50 | 5.10 | 5.60 | 6.00 | 6.30 | 6.70 | 6.82 | 6.96 |
| | 42001 to 76000 | 2.00 | 2.97 | 3.84 | 4.65 | 5.40 | 6.02 | 6.56 | 7.11 | 7.50 | 7.92 | 8.28 |
| | 76001 to 130000 | 2.00 | 3.00 | 3.92 | 4.75 | 5.64 | 6.44 | 7.12 | 7.74 | 8.30 | 8.80 | 9.36 |
| | > 130000 | 2.00 | 3.00 | 4.00 | 4.90 | 5.82 | 6.65 | 7.44 | 8.19 | 9.00 | 9.68 | 10.4 |
| 18.1 to 24 | 26001 to 42000 | 2.00 | 3.00 | 3.84 | 4.65 | 5.34 | 5.88 | 6.32 | 6.66 | 6.90 | 7.04 | 7.08 |
| | 42001 to 76000 | 2.00 | 3.00 | 3.88 | 4.70 | 5.52 | 6.23 | 6.88 | 7.47 | 8.00 | 8.36 | 8.76 |
| | 76001 to 130000 | 2.00 | 3.00 | 3.96 | 4.90 | 5.76 | 6.58 | 7.36 | 8.10 | 8.80 | 9.46 | 10.2 |
| | > 130000 | 2.00 | 3.00 | 4.00 | 5.00 | 5.88 | 6.72 | 7.60 | 8.37 | 9.20 | 10.1 | 10.9 |
| 24.1 to 30 | 26001 to 42000 | 2.00 | 2.94 | 3.76 | 4.50 | 5.10 | 5.60 | 5.92 | 6.21 | 6.50 | 6.71 | 6.96 |
| | 42001 to 76000 | 2.00 | 2.97 | 3.88 | 4.65 | 5.40 | 6.02 | 6.56 | 7.11 | 7.60 | 8.03 | 8.52 |
| | 76001 to 130000 | 2.00 | 3.00 | 3.92 | 4.80 | 5.64 | 6.44 | 7.12 | 7.83 | 8.50 | 9.13 | 9.72 |
| | > 130000 | 2.00 | 3.00 | 3.96 | 4.90 | 5.82 | 6.65 | 7.44 | 8.28 | 9.00 | 9.79 | 10.7 |
| 30.1 to 35 | 26001 to 42000 | 2.00 | 2.88 | 3.68 | 4.30 | 4.80 | 5.18 | 5.44 | 5.76 | 6.00 | 6.27 | 6.60 |
| | 42001 to 76000 | 2.00 | 2.94 | 3.80 | 4.50 | 5.16 | 5.67 | 6.08 | 6.48 | 6.80 | 7.15 | 7.44 |
| | 76001 to 130000 | 2.00 | 2.97 | 3.88 | 4.75 | 5.52 | 6.16 | 6.80 | 7.38 | 8.00 | 8.58 | 9.24 |
| | > 130000 | 2.00 | 3.00 | 3.92 | 4.85 | 5.70 | 6.51 | 7.20 | 8.01 | 8.70 | 9.46 | 10.2 |
| 35.1 to 42 | 26001 to 42000 | 2.00 | 2.85 | 3.56 | 4.10 | 4.50 | 4.83 | 5.04 | 5.22 | 5.30 | 5.39 | 5.52 |
| | 42001 to 76000 | 2.00 | 2.91 | 3.72 | 4.40 | 4.92 | 5.39 | 5.68 | 6.03 | 6.30 | 6.49 | 6.72 |
| | 76001 to 130000 | 2.00 | 2.94 | 3.84 | 4.65 | 5.34 | 5.95 | 6.48 | 7.02 | 7.60 | 8.03 | 8.52 |
| | > 130000 | 2.00 | 2.97 | 3.92 | 4.80 | 5.58 | 6.30 | 6.96 | 7.56 | 8.20 | 8.80 | 9.36 |

Notes:
1. $A_m$ = gross cross-sectional area of main member, $mm^2$
   $A_s$ = sum of gross cross-sectional area of steel side plates, $mm^2$
2. For perpendicular to grain loading, the area of the main member may be taken as the product of the member thickness and the width of the fastener group. For a single row of fasteners, use the minimum parallel to grain spacing for $J_C = 1.0$ (shown in Figure 7.15) as the width of the fastener group.
3. $n_{Fe}$ applies to shear plates, split rings and lag screws.

| Table 7.19 Factor for tension loading for split ring and shear plate end distance $J_{C1}$ | End distance, a (mm) | | | |
|---|---|---|---|---|
| | Member Thickness | | 2-1/2" split ring or 2-5/8" shear plate | 4" split ring or shear plate |
| | ≥ 130 mm | < 130 mm | | |
| | 65 | 100 | - | - |
| | 70 | 105 | 0.62 | - |
| | 75 | 115 | 0.65 | - |
| | 80 | 120 | 0.68 | - |
| | 85 | 130 | 0.70 | - |
| | 90 | 135 | 0.73 | 0.63 |
| | 95 | 145 | 0.76 | 0.65 |
| | 100 | 150 | 0.78 | 0.67 |
| | 105 | 160 | 0.81 | 0.69 |
| | 110 | 165 | 0.84 | 0.71 |
| | 115 | 175 | 0.86 | 0.73 |
| | 120 | 180 | 0.89 | 0.75 |
| | 125 | 190 | 0.92 | 0.77 |
| | 130 | 195 | 0.94 | 0.79 |
| | 135 | 205 | 0.97 | 0.82 |
| | 140 | 210 | 1.00 | 0.84 |
| | 145 | 220 | 1.00 | 0.86 |
| | 150 | 225 | 1.00 | 0.88 |
| | 155 | 235 | 1.00 | 0.90 |
| | 160 | 240 | 1.00 | 0.92 |
| | 165 | 250 | 1.00 | 0.94 |
| | 170 | 255 | 1.00 | 0.96 |
| | 175 | 265 | 1.00 | 0.98 |
| | 180 | 270 | 1.00 | 1.00 |

Notes:
1. For connections loaded in compression $J_C = 1.0$.
2. End distance is defined as follows.

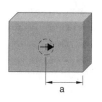

Straight cut

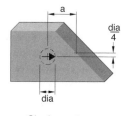

Sloping cut

7

Fastenings

Table 7.20
**Factor for split ring and shear plate edge distance $J_{C2}$**

| Edge distance [2] | 2-1/2" split ring or 2-5/8" shear plate | | | | 4" split ring or shear plate | | | |
| | Angle of load to grain $\theta°$ | | | | Angle of load to grain $\theta°$ | | | |
| e or $e_L$ | Unloaded edge | Loaded edge Angle of load to grain $\theta°$ | | | Unloaded edge | Loaded edge Angle of load to grain $\theta°$ | | |
| mm | 0 | 15 | 30 | 45 to 90 | 0 | 15 | 30 | 45 to 90 |
|---|---|---|---|---|---|---|---|---|
| 40 | 1.00 | - | - | - | - | - | - | - |
| 45 | 1.00 | 0.94 | 0.88 | 0.83 | - | - | - | - |
| 50 | 1.00 | 0.97 | 0.91 | 0.87 | - | - | - | - |
| 55 | 1.00 | 1.00 | 0.94 | 0.90 | - | - | - | - |
| 60 | 1.00 | 1.00 | 0.98 | 0.93 | - | - | - | - |
| 65 | 1.00 | 1.00 | 1.00 | 0.97 | 1.00 | - | - | - |
| 70 | 1.00 | 1.00 | 1.00 | 1.00 | 1.00 | 0.93 | 0.88 | 0.83 |
| 75 | 1.00 | 1.00 | 1.00 | 1.00 | 1.00 | 0.97 | 0.91 | 0.86 |
| 80 | 1.00 | 1.00 | 1.00 | 1.00 | 1.00 | 1.00 | 0.94 | 0.89 |
| 85 | 1.00 | 1.00 | 1.00 | 1.00 | 1.00 | 1.00 | 0.97 | 0.93 |
| 90 | 1.00 | 1.00 | 1.00 | 1.00 | 1.00 | 1.00 | 1.00 | 0.96 |
| 95 | 1.00 | 1.00 | 1.00 | 1.00 | 1.00 | 1.00 | 1.00 | 1.00 |
| 100 | 1.00 | 1.00 | 1.00 | 1.00 | 1.00 | 1.00 | 1.00 | 1.00 |

Notes:

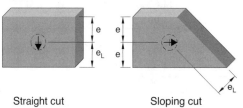

Straight cut          Sloping cut

1.  For intermediate angles, linear interpolation may be used.
2.  Edge distances are defined as follows (e = unloaded edge, $e_L$ = loaded edge).

| Table 7.21 Spacing $S_1$ (mm) of 2-5/8" shear plates and 2-1/2" split rings for $J_{C3} = 1.0$ | Angle between grain and line of connectors $\beta°$ | Angle of load to grain $\theta°$ | | | | | | | | | | | 60 to 90 |
|---|---|---|---|---|---|---|---|---|---|---|---|---|---|
| | | 0 | 5 | 10 | 15 | 20 | 25 | 30 | 35 | 40 | 45 | 50 | 55 | |
| | 0 | 170 | 163 | 157 | 150 | 143 | 137 | 130 | 123 | 117 | 110 | 103 | 97 | 90 |
| | 5 | 167 | 160 | 155 | 148 | 141 | 135 | 128 | 122 | 117 | 110 | 103 | 97 | 90 |
| | 10 | 163 | 158 | 152 | 147 | 140 | 134 | 127 | 121 | 116 | 110 | 103 | 97 | 90 |
| | 15 | 160 | 155 | 150 | 145 | 138 | 132 | 125 | 120 | 115 | 110 | 103 | 97 | 90 |
| | 20 | 152 | 148 | 144 | 140 | 134 | 129 | 123 | 119 | 115 | 110 | 103 | 97 | 90 |
| | 25 | 143 | 140 | 138 | 135 | 131 | 126 | 122 | 118 | 114 | 110 | 103 | 97 | 90 |
| | 30 | 135 | 133 | 132 | 130 | 127 | 123 | 120 | 117 | 113 | 110 | 103 | 97 | 90 |
| | 35 | 127 | 126 | 126 | 125 | 122 | 119 | 117 | 115 | 112 | 110 | 104 | 99 | 93 |
| | 40 | 118 | 119 | 119 | 120 | 118 | 116 | 113 | 112 | 111 | 110 | 106 | 101 | 97 |
| | 45 | 110 | 112 | 113 | 115 | 113 | 112 | 110 | 110 | 110 | 110 | 107 | 103 | 100 |
| | 50 | 107 | 109 | 110 | 112 | 110 | 110 | 108 | 108 | 108 | 108 | 106 | 103 | 100 |
| | 55 | 103 | 105 | 106 | 108 | 108 | 107 | 107 | 107 | 107 | 107 | 104 | 102 | 100 |
| | 60 | 100 | 102 | 103 | 105 | 105 | 105 | 105 | 105 | 105 | 105 | 103 | 102 | 100 |
| | 65 | 97 | 99 | 101 | 103 | 103 | 103 | 103 | 104 | 105 | 105 | 103 | 103 | 102 |
| | 70 | 93 | 96 | 99 | 102 | 102 | 102 | 102 | 103 | 104 | 105 | 104 | 104 | 103 |
| | 75 | 90 | 93 | 97 | 100 | 100 | 100 | 100 | 102 | 103 | 105 | 105 | 105 | 105 |
| | 80 | 90 | 93 | 96 | 98 | 99 | 99 | 100 | 102 | 103 | 105 | 105 | 106 | 107 |
| | 85 | 90 | 92 | 94 | 97 | 98 | 98 | 100 | 102 | 103 | 105 | 106 | 107 | 108 |
| | 90 | 90 | 92 | 93 | 95 | 97 | 98 | 100 | 102 | 103 | 105 | 107 | 108 | 110 |

Notes:

1. Minimum spacing $S_{min} = 90$ mm for $J_{C3} = 0.75$

2. For spacing S between $S_{min}$ and $S_1$:

$$J_{C3} = 0.75 + 0.25 \left[ \frac{S - 90}{S_1 - 90} \right]$$

3. Required spacing S for a value of $J_{C3}$ between 0.75 and 1.0:

$$S = \frac{(J_{C3} - 0.75) \times (S_1 - 90)}{0.25} + 90$$

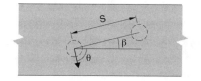

**7**

Fastenings

**Table 7.22**
**Spacing $S_1$ (mm) of 4" shear plates and 4" split rings for $J_{C3} = 1.0$**

| Angle between grain and line of connectors $\beta°$ | Angle of load to grain $\theta°$ | | | | | | | | | | | | 60 to 90 |
|---|---|---|---|---|---|---|---|---|---|---|---|---|---|
| | 0 | 5 | 10 | 15 | 20 | 25 | 30 | 35 | 40 | 45 | 50 | 55 | |
| 0 | 230 | 222 | 213 | 205 | 197 | 188 | 180 | 170 | 160 | 150 | 142 | 133 | 125 |
| 5 | 225 | 217 | 209 | 202 | 194 | 186 | 178 | 169 | 160 | 150 | 142 | 133 | 125 |
| 10 | 220 | 213 | 206 | 198 | 191 | 184 | 177 | 168 | 159 | 150 | 142 | 133 | 125 |
| 15 | 215 | 208 | 202 | 195 | 188 | 182 | 175 | 167 | 158 | 150 | 142 | 133 | 125 |
| 20 | 205 | 200 | 195 | 190 | 184 | 178 | 172 | 165 | 157 | 150 | 142 | 133 | 125 |
| 25 | 195 | 191 | 189 | 185 | 179 | 174 | 168 | 162 | 156 | 150 | 142 | 133 | 125 |
| 30 | 185 | 183 | 182 | 180 | 175 | 170 | 165 | 160 | 155 | 150 | 142 | 133 | 125 |
| 35 | 175 | 174 | 174 | 173 | 169 | 166 | 162 | 158 | 154 | 150 | 143 | 135 | 128 |
| 40 | 165 | 166 | 166 | 167 | 164 | 161 | 158 | 155 | 153 | 150 | 144 | 138 | 132 |
| 45 | 155 | 157 | 158 | 160 | 158 | 157 | 155 | 153 | 152 | 150 | 145 | 140 | 135 |
| 50 | 150 | 152 | 153 | 155 | 154 | 153 | 152 | 150 | 150 | 148 | 145 | 142 | 138 |
| 55 | 145 | 147 | 148 | 150 | 149 | 149 | 148 | 148 | 147 | 147 | 145 | 143 | 142 |
| 60 | 140 | 142 | 143 | 145 | 145 | 145 | 145 | 145 | 145 | 145 | 145 | 145 | 145 |
| 65 | 137 | 139 | 140 | 142 | 143 | 144 | 145 | 145 | 145 | 145 | 145 | 146 | 147 |
| 70 | 133 | 135 | 136 | 138 | 140 | 143 | 145 | 145 | 145 | 145 | 146 | 147 | 148 |
| 75 | 130 | 132 | 133 | 135 | 138 | 142 | 145 | 145 | 145 | 147 | 148 | 150 | |
| 80 | 128 | 131 | 133 | 135 | 138 | 141 | 143 | 144 | 145 | 145 | 147 | 148 | 150 |
| 85 | 127 | 129 | 132 | 135 | 137 | 139 | 142 | 143 | 144 | 145 | 147 | 148 | 150 |
| 90 | 125 | 128 | 132 | 135 | 137 | 138 | 140 | 142 | 143 | 145 | 147 | 148 | 150 |

Notes:

1. Minimum spacing $S_{min}$ = 125 mm for $J_{C3}$ = 0.75
2. For spacing S between $S_{min}$ and $S_1$:

$$J_{C3} = 0.75 + 0.25 \left[ \frac{S - 125}{S_1 - 125} \right]$$

3. Required spacing S for a value of $J_{C3}$ between 0.75 and 1.0:

$$S = \frac{(J_{C3} - 0.75) \times (S_1 - 125)}{0.25} + 125$$

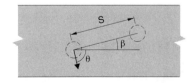

| Table 7.23 **Penetration factor for split rings and shear plates used with lag screws $J_p$** | | Penetration of lag screw into member receiving point (number of shank diameters) | | | | |
|---|---|---|---|---|---|---|
| Connector | Penetration | D.Fir-L | Hem-Fir | S-P-F | Northern | $J_p$ |
| 2-1/2" split ring 4" split ring or 4" shear plate | standard | 8 | 10 | 10 | 11 | 1.0 |
| | minimum | 3.5 | 4 | 4 | 4.5 | 0.75 |
| 2-5/8" shear plate | standard | 5 | 7 | 7 | 8 | 1.0 |
| | minimum | 3.5 | 4 | 4 | 4.5 | 0.75 |

Notes:

1. For intermediate penetrations, linear interpolation may be used for values of $J_p$ between 0.75 and 1.0.

2. When steel side plates are used with shear plates, use $J_p = 1.0$ for minimum penetration.

**7**

Fastenings

# 7.8    Truss Plates

## General

Truss plates are light gauge metal plates used to connect prefabricated light frame wood trusses. Truss plates are produced by punching light gauge galvanized steel (normally 16, 18 or 20 gauge) so that teeth protrude from one side (see Figure 7.16).

Figure 7.16
**Typical truss plate**

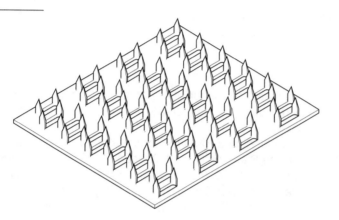

There are a number of truss plate manufacturers in Canada and each has its own proprietary tooth pattern. Truss plates are produced from sheet steel specified in ASTM standard A653/A653M. The steel is usually galvanized prior to punching.

Light frame trusses connected with truss plates should not be used in corrosive conditions or with fire-retardant treated lumber in wet service conditions. However, some manufacturers may recoat their plates for use in corrosive conditions.

## Installation

Truss fabrication is usually carried out at the fabricator's plant where the truss plates are embedded into the lumber with either a hydraulic press or a roller. CSA O86 specifies that the plates be installed in the following manner:

- The joints must be tight fitting with identical truss plates placed on opposing faces so that each plate is directly opposite the other.
- The truss plates are not deformed during installation.
- The teeth are normal to the surface of the lumber.
- The teeth must be fully embedded in the wood so that the plate is tight to the wood surface. However, the plate must not be embedded into the lumber deeper than half the plate thickness.
- The lumber below the truss plate does not contain wane, loose knots or knot holes.

**7**

Fastenings

## Establishment of Design Values for Truss Plates

Since truss plate configurations are proprietary, CSA O86 does not provide design values. Instead it requires that truss plates be tested in accordance with CSA Standard S347 *Method of Test for Evaluation of Truss Plates used in Lumber Joints*. Test results are listed in the *Manual of Evaluation Reports* published by the Canadian Construction Materials Centre (CCMC), Institute for Research in Construction, Ottawa, Ontario. The evaluation report also includes resistance values derived from the test results.

## Design

Truss design is usually the responsibility of the truss plate manufacturer. Most manufacturers are equipped with computer software that can rapidly design any truss configuration.

Design procedures and formulae for truss plate design are given in CSA O86. The Truss Plate Institute of Canada (TPIC) provides additional guidelines in their publication titled *Truss Design Procedures and Specifications for Light Metal Plate Connected Trusses – Limit States Design*.

In accordance with CSA O86, truss plates must be designed so that the following criteria are satisfied:

1. Factored ultimate lateral resistance of teeth $N_r \geq$ factored lateral load $N_f$

2. Factored tensile resistance of the plates $T_r \geq$ factored tensile force $T_f$

3. Factored shear resistance of the plates $V_r \geq$ factored shear force $V_f$

4. Factored lateral slip resistance $N_{rs} \geq$ specified lateral load $N_s$

CSA O86 specifies that truss plates must not be considered to be effective in transferring compression at a joint.

### Factored Lateral Resistance of Teeth

This may be calculated using the net area method or gross area method from the following formulae:

$$N_r = \phi \, n_u \, K' \, J_H \, A_N \text{ (net area method)}$$

or

$$N_r = 0.8 \, \phi \, n_u \, K' \, J_H \, A_G \text{ (gross area method)}$$

where:

$\phi$ = 0.9

$n_u$ = ultimate lateral resistance of teeth per unit net surface area of the plate (MPa). The value of $n_u$ is taken from the CCMC evaluation report and is dependent on the angle of load to grain and angle of load to plate axis as shown in Figure 7.17. The value of $n_u$ is normally given for a single plate.

$A_N$ = net area of plate coverage on the member (mm$^2$). This is defined as the total area of a member covered by a truss plate less the area within the distance from the end or edges of the member as shown in Figure 7.18.

$A_G$ = gross area of plate coverage, which is defined as the total area of a member covered by a truss plate.

$K'$ and $J_H$ are modification factors given below

**Factored Tensile Resistance of the Plate**

$$T_r = \phi\, t_p\, w_t$$

where:

$\phi$ = 0.6

$t_p$ = tensile resistance of plate per unit width perpendicular to the applied load (N/mm). The CCMC evaluation report provides $t_p$ values for loading parallel to the slots and loading perpendicular to the slots. The resistance value is normally given for a single plate.

$w_t$ = width of plate perpendicular to direction of loading.

**Factored Shear Resistance of the Plate**

$$V_r = \phi\, v_p\, w_s$$

where:

$\phi$ = 0.6

$v_p$ = shear resistance of the plate per unit of plate width along the line of the shear force (N/mm). The CCMC evaluation report provides $v_p$ values for tension and compression forces in various plate orientations.

$w_s$ = width of plate along the line of the shear force

**7**

Fastenings

**Factored Lateral Slip Resistance**

This may be calculated using the net area method or gross area method as follows:

$$N_{rs} = N_s K_{SF} A_N \text{ (net area method)}$$

or

$$N_{rs} = 0.8 N_s K_{SF} A_G \text{ (gross area method)}$$

where:

$N_s$ = lateral slip resistance of teeth per unit net surface area of the plate (MPa). The values of $N_s$ are taken from the CCMC evaluation report and are dependent on the angle of load to grain and the angle of load to plate axis as shown in Figure 7.17.

$A_N$ and $A_G$ are defined above.

$K_{SF}$ is a modification factor given below

## Modification Factors

The modification factors adjust the factored resistances for the actual conditions of use. The following factors apply to the design of truss plates:

$$K' = K_D K_{SF} K_T$$

$J_H$ = moment factor for heel connections of pitched trusses

where:

$K_D$ = duration of load factor

$K_{SF}$ = service condition factor

$K_T$ = fire-retardant treatment factor

For many joints the value of each factor will be equal to 1.0. Review the following checklist to determine if the factors equal 1.0 for the actual conditions of use. Where a factor does not equal 1.0, calculate the appropriate value and modify the factored resistance accordingly.

# Checklist: **Truss Plates** ✔

1. $K_D$ = 1.0 when the loading is "standard" term
   = 1.15 for short term loading (e.g., dead load plus wind)
   = 0.65 for permanent loads (e.g., dead loads alone)

2. $K_{SF}$ = 1.0 when the service conditions are "dry" and the lumber is seasoned
   (moisture content ≤ 15%) prior to fabrication
   = 0.8 for unseasoned lumber in dry service conditions
   = 0.67 for wet service conditions

3. $K_T$ = 1.0 when the wood is not treated with a fire retardant or other strength-reducing chemical.

   For wood treated with a fire retardant or other strength-reducing chemicals, see the Commentary for further guidance.

4. $J_H$ = 1.0 for any joint other than a heel connection in a pitched truss

   For the heel connection of a pitched truss, determine $J_H$ from Table 7.24

**7**

⊕

Fastenings

| Table 7.24 **Moment factor for heel connections of pitched trusses** $J_H$ | Slope of top chord, $\alpha°$ | $J_H$ |
|---|---|---|
| | $\alpha \le 14°$ | 0.85 |
| | $14° < \alpha \le 18.4°$ | 0.80 |
| | $18.4° < \alpha \le 22.6°$ | 0.75 |
| | $22.6° < \alpha \le 24.4°$ | 0.70 |
| | $\alpha > 24.4°$ | 0.65 |

## Example 1: Truss Plates

Check the adequacy of the tension splice shown below (dimensions in mm). The lumber is untreated kiln dried S-P-F. The truss is used in dry service conditions and the loading is due to snow and dead loads. The plate properties are as follows (per plate):

$$p_u = 1.50 \text{ MPa}$$
$$p_s = 1.60 \text{ MPa}$$
$$t_p = 310 \text{ N/mm}$$

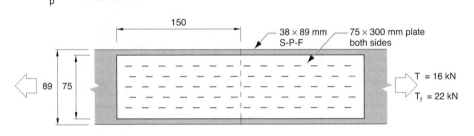

## Modification Factors

$$K_D = 1.0 \text{ (dead plus snow load)}$$
$$K_{SF} = 1.0 \text{ (dry service)}$$
$$K_T = 1.0 \text{ (dry service)}$$
$$J_H = 1.0 \text{ (not a heel connection)}$$

Therefore:

$$K' = 1.0$$

## Calculation

Check ultimate lateral resistance using gross area method:

$$
\begin{aligned}
N_r &= 0.8 \, \phi \, n_u \, K' \, J_H \, A_G \\
&= 0.8 \times 0.9 \times 1.50 \times 1.0 \times 1.0 \, (2 \times 75 \times 150) \\
&= 24.3 \times 10^3 \text{ N} \\
&= 24.3 \text{ kN} > 22 \text{ kN} \qquad\qquad\qquad \textit{Acceptable}
\end{aligned}
$$

Check tensile resistance of plate:

$$
\begin{aligned}
T_r &= \phi \, t_p \, w_p \\
&= 0.6 \times 310 \, (2 \times 75) \\
&= 27.9 \times 10^3 \text{ N} \\
&= 27.9 \text{ kN} > 22 \text{ kN} \qquad\qquad\qquad \textit{Acceptable}
\end{aligned}
$$

Check lateral slip resistance using gross area method:

$$N_{rs} = 0.8\ N_s\ K_{SF}\ A_G$$
$$= 0.8 \times 1.60 \times 1.0\ (2 \times 75 \times 150)$$
$$= 28.8 \times 10^3\ N$$
$$= 28.8\ kN > 16\ kN \qquad\qquad Acceptable$$

**The connection is adequate.**

Figure 7.17
**Angles of load
to grain and to
plate axis**

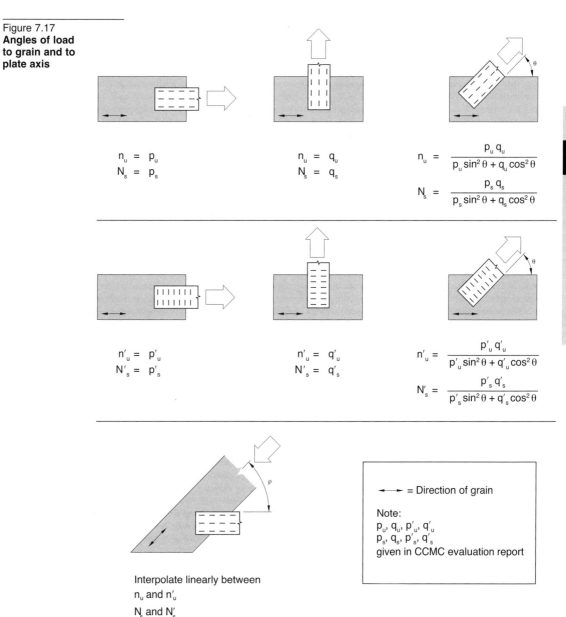

$n_u = p_u$
$N_s = p_s$

$n_u = q_u$
$N_s = q_s$

$n_u = \dfrac{p_u\, q_u}{p_u \sin^2 \theta + q_u \cos^2 \theta}$

$N_s = \dfrac{p_s\, q_s}{p_s \sin^2 \theta + q_s \cos^2 \theta}$

$n'_u = p'_u$
$N'_s = p'_s$

$n'_u = q'_u$
$N'_s = q'_s$

$n'_u = \dfrac{p'_u\, q'_u}{p'_u \sin^2 \theta + q'_u \cos^2 \theta}$

$N'_s = \dfrac{p'_s\, q'_s}{p'_s \sin^2 \theta + q'_s \cos^2 \theta}$

Interpolate linearly between
$n_u$ and $n'_u$
$N_s$ and $N'_s$

⟷ = Direction of grain

Note:
$p_u, q_u, p'_u, q'_u$
$p_s, q_s, p'_s, q'_s$
given in CCMC evaluation report

7

Fastenings

Figure 7.18
**End and edge distances for truss plate joints**

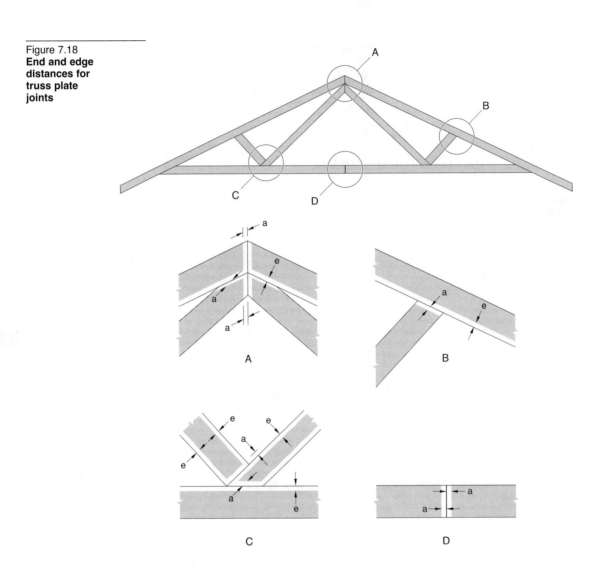

Note:
a = end distance = greater of 12 mm or 1/2 tooth length
e = edge distance = greater of 6 mm or 1/4 tooth length

# 7.9 Joist Hangers

## General

Joist hangers are produced by a number of manufacturers, each having their own proprietary designs.

Joist hangers are generally fabricated from 20, 18 or 16 gauge galvanized steel. Most joist hangers are the face-mount type, but top-mount hangers are available for heavier loads. Hangers are usually available for single, double or triple-ply joists ranging in size from 38 × 89 mm to 38 × 286 mm. Special hangers for wood I-joists and structural composite lumber are also readily available. Figure 7.19 shows a typical face mount and top mount joist hanger.

Figure 7.19
**Typical joist hangers**

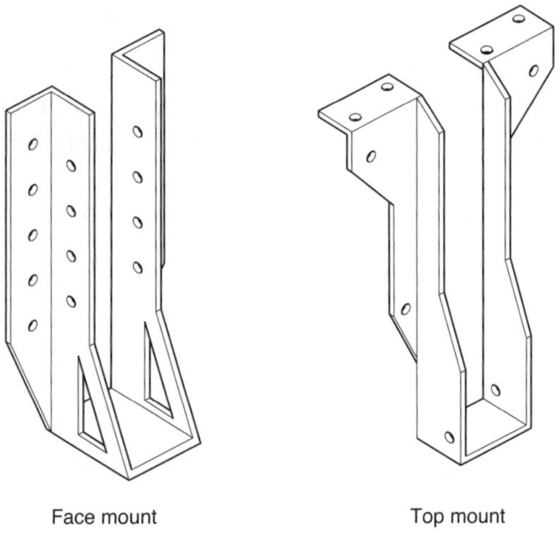

Face mount               Top mount

## Installation

Joist hangers are to be installed in accordance with the manufacturer's installation requirements. Where specifying a joist hanger, designers must ensure that the following conditions are satisfied:

- The hanger is at least half the depth of the joist and is capable of providing lateral support for the joist. If lateral support is not provided by the joist hanger, twisting must be prevented by some other means.
- The hanger is fastened to both the header and joist and nails or bolts used in the header and joist are the size specified and installed in accordance with the manufacturer's literature.
- Hangers used to support prefabricated wood I-joists are high enough to provide lateral stability to the top flange of the joist. If the joist hanger does not provide lateral support, bearing stiffeners may be required.
- Backer blocks are provided between the web and face mount hangers where prefabricated I-joists are used as the header.
- Where a prefabricated wood I-joist is supporting a top mount hanger, filler blocks are used between the top and bottom flange of the I-joist. The blocks are to be tight to the bottom of the top flange.

**7**

**Fastenings**

## Establishment of Design Values for Joist Hangers

Since joist hangers are proprietary, CSA O86 provides a method for determining design values but does not provide the design values in the Standard. Instead it requires that joist hangers be tested in accordance with ASTM Standard D 1761 *Standard Test Methods for Mechanical Fasteners in Wood*. Test results are listed in the *Manual of Evaluation Reports* published by the Canadian Construction Materials Centre (CCMC), Institute for Research in Construction, Ottawa, Ontario. The evaluation report also includes resistance values derived from the test results.

## Design

Design values for joist hangers are published by the manufacturer. CSA O86 gives design procedures and formulae for joist hangers and requires the effect of the factored loads to be less than or equal to the factored resistance of the hanger.

The factored resistance of joist hangers is calculated from the following formula:

$$N_r = \phi \, n_u K'$$

where:

$\phi$ = 0.6

$n_u$ = ultimate resistance of the hanger. The value of $n_u$ is taken from the CCMC evaluation report.

$K'$ = composite modification factor given below

### Modification Factors

The modification factors adjust the factored resistances for the actual conditions of use. The following factors apply to the design of joist hangers:

$$K' = K_D K_{SF} K_T$$

where:

$K_D$ = duration of load factor. Note that no increase for short term duration is permitted where the ultimate resistance is determined by the strength of the steel. Check with the manufacturer for appropriate short term $K_D$ values.

$K_{SF}$ = service condition factor. For hangers connected with nails see section 7.2. For hangers connected with bolts see section 7.3.

$K_T$ = fire-retardant treatment factor

= 1.0 when the wood is not treated with a fire retardant or other strength-reducing chemical. For wood treated with a fire retardant or other strength-reducing chemicals, see the Commentary for further guidance.

# 7.10    Framing Anchors

## General

Framing anchors are light gauge steel angles or clips, which may be used in place of toe nailing to provide a stronger connection. Framing anchors are proprietary products and are available from a number of manufacturers.

Most framing anchors are manufactured from 20 or 18 gauge galvanized steel with pre-drilled nail holes. Many manufacturers supply special nails, which are 1-1/4" or 1-1/2" long with a diameter equivalent to that of a 3" nail.

Some of the most common anchors are shown in Figure 7.20. The tie-down type anchors are used to provide an uplift connection for light frame trusses, rafters and joists. The angle-type anchors are often used in beam-post connections.

Figure 7.20
**Framing
anchors**

**7**

Fastenings

*Type:*
All purpose
framing anchor

*Application:*
Suits many
framing
applications

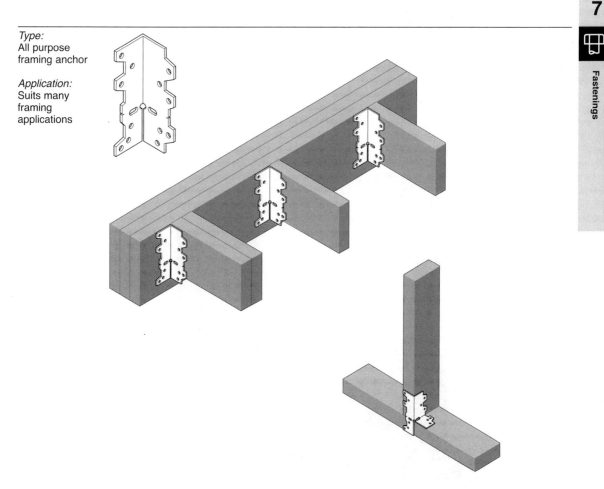

*Type:*
Tie-down
framing anchor

*Application:*
Specially
designed
for wall
applications
in cases of
high uplift
due to wind

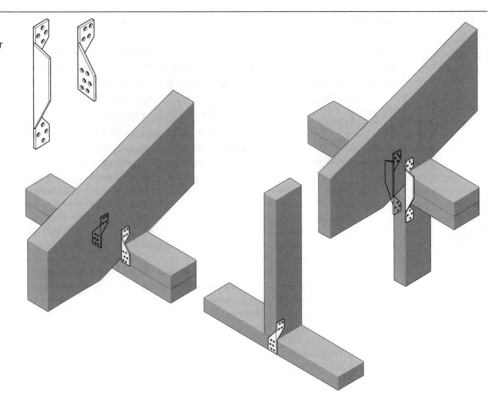

*Type:*
Triple grip
framing anchor

*Application:*
For wall framing

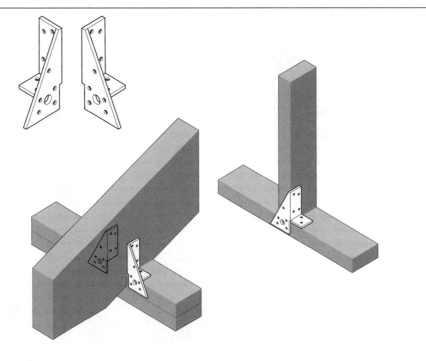

*Type:*
Truss and rafter
anchor

*Application:*
For fastening
trusses and
rafters to wall
plates

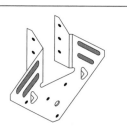

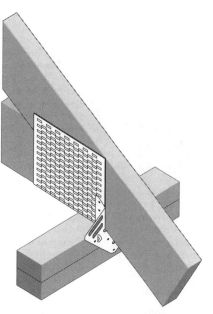

*Type:*
Straps

*Application:*
For resisting
wind and
earthquake
loads

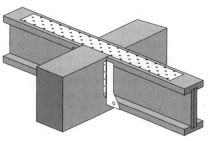

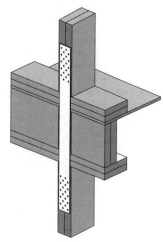

*Type:*
Framing angle

Application:
For post
and beam
anchorage

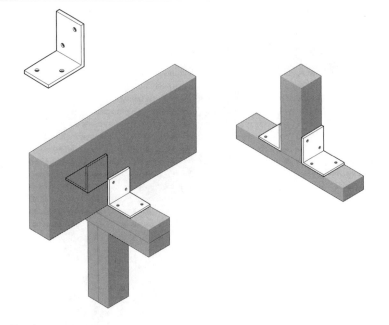

## Design

Most manufacturers publish design data for their framing anchors, including design values in Limit States Design format consistent with CSA O86 procedures.

The number and size of nails specified by the manufacturer must be used for the published values to be valid. Also, the framing anchor must be used with the species of wood assumed in the development of the allowable loads. When a different wood species is to be used, adjust the listed capacity by ratio of the nail resistance of the species used to the nail resistance of the given species.

# 7.11    Typical Connection Details

### General

Once wood connections have been designed to adequately transfer all loads (see Sections 7.1 to 7.7 of this manual), they must be properly detailed to take into account important additional "serviceability" requirements, which include consideration of shrinkage and swelling, notching effects, decay prevention and lateral restraint at supports. These requirements are described below.

It should be noted that the details that are included in this section will apply to many common connection configurations.

### Notching

Wherever possible, joints that cause tension perpendicular to grain stresses should be avoided. This occurs for example in cases where simple beams have been notched on the tension side at the supports (see Details 7.46 and 7.48). In this case, tension perpendicular to grain stresses can be caused by prying action caused by secondary moments.

### Decay Prevention

Where moisture is allowed to accumulate in connections, it can lead to decay problems (see Detail 7.42). Moisture barriers, flashing and other protective features should be used to prevent moisture or free water from being trapped. Preservative treatments are recommended when wood is fully exposed to the weather without roof cover.

Adequate site drainage must always be provided, all metals should be protected against corrosion by use of corrosive-resistant metals or resistant coatings or platings.

**7**

Fastenings

## Lateral Restraint at Supports

Lateral restraint to prevent displacement and rotation must be provided at points of bearing for all beams with a depth-to-width ratio greater than 2.5. Some usual methods of providing restraint are illustrated below.

Figure 7.21
**Fire cut beam restrained from lateral rotation by wedged blocking**

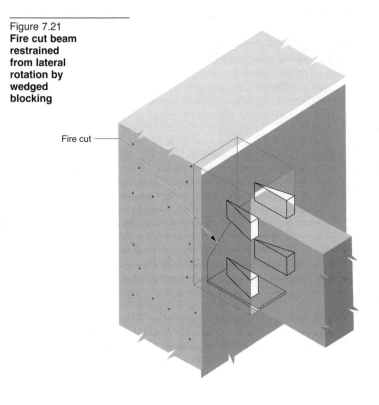

Fire cut

## Support on Masonry or Concrete

A fire cut is provided at the end of the beam to protect the masonry or concrete wall should the ends of the beam rotate and collapse in fire conditions.

Figure 7.22
**Beam
restrained
from lateral
rotation by clip
angles**

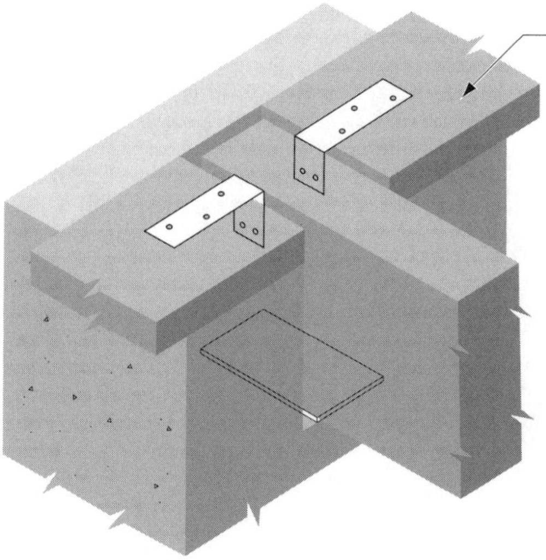

Wood sill plate

Note: Do not fasten clip angles to the beam. Shrinkage movement should not be restrained.

7

Fastenings

## Support on Columns

Beams supported on columns may be restrained against displacement and rotation by purlins framing into the side of the beam. The purlins should be securely connected or braced so that they do not move or sway when loaded axially.

Figure 7.23
**Beam restrained from lateral rotation by purlins**

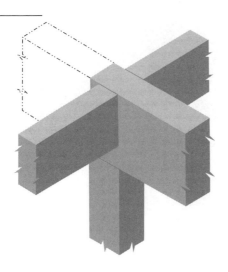

# Typical Connection Details

## Beam to Masonry

Detail 7.1

This standard anchorage to a masonry wall resists both uplift and lateral forces. The bearing plate should be a minimum of 6 mm thick when required to distribute the load over a larger area of masonry. Clearance should be maintained between the wall and end of the beam to allow for ventilation.

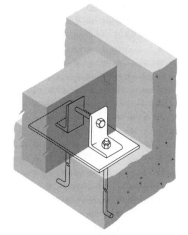

Detail 7.2

Should loading on the masonry not require the bearing plate to extend beyond the edge of the beam, this connection may be used. The bearing plate prevents the migration of moisture from the wall to the beam and should be at least 3 mm thick.

**7**

**Fastenings**

Detail 7.3

This arrangement may be used as an alternative to Detail 7.1. The bolt holes in the bearing plate should be oversized to permit final alignment. The side plates may be extended out to allow easy installation of timber rivets if the wall continues up above the beam.

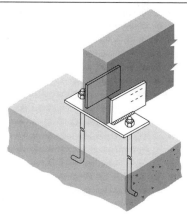

# Typical Connection Details

## Beam to Masonry

Detail 7.4    This U-shaped anchorage is suitable where adequate masonry bearing is provided under the beam and the pilaster is not wide enough to receive outside anchor bolts.

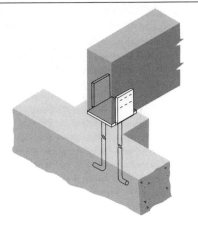

Detail 7.5    This simple anchorage for shallow beams (up to 600 mm deep) resists both uplift and minor lateral forces. Top of beam may be counterbored to provide a flush surface.
This detail should be avoided where shrinkage may occur.

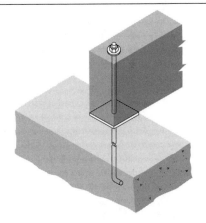

Detail 7.6    The slotted holes in the steel side plates allow for the slight horizontal movement that accompanies vertical deflection under live load in curved and tapered beams. The length of the slot required varies with the span and rise of the beam.

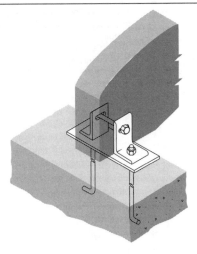

# Typical Connection Details

## Beam to Column

Detail 7.7

The simplest connection for a beam continuous over a column is a steel dowel driven through a hole drilled partially or fully through the beam. Rotation of the column is to be prevented at the base or by other framing.

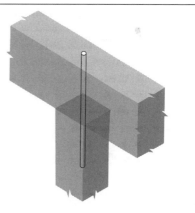

Detail 7.8

Uplift is resisted by this standard beam-to-column connection. The shear plates and dowel are only included when lateral forces are to be resisted, in which case some form of bracing would be required. A separate bearing plate may be included when the cross section of the column does not provide adequate bearing for the beam.

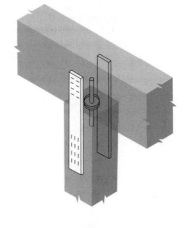

Detail 7.9

Beam loads are transferred to columns by shear-plate- or timber-rivet-connected hangers in multi-storey applications with continuous columns. If bolts are used, beams must be slotted to allow for nuts and bolt heads.

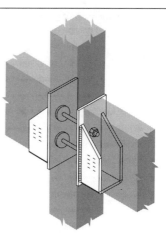

# Typical Connection Details
## Beam to Column

Detail 7.10        This concealed connection utilizes a steel plate in
                   the sawn kerf. Machine bolt heads and nuts may
                   be countersunk and plugged.

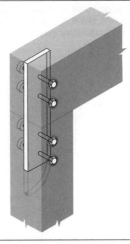

Detail 7.11a       When the beam and column are of different
                   widths, welded assemblies as shown may be
                   used to transfer loads effectively. For multi-storey
                   buildings with beams continuous through the
                   columns, these weldments may be used on both
                   the top and bottom of the beam.

Detail 7.11b       A variation of Detail 7.11a.

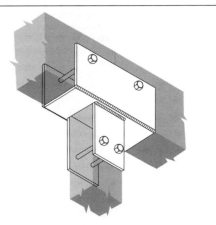

# Typical Connection Details

## Beam to Column

Detail 7.12

These connections offer alternatives for connecting beams that splice over columns. If the cross section of the column is insufficient for beam bearing, a steel bearing plate may be used to distribute the load. An alternate detail is to provide a dapped splice plate on top of the beam and fasten with lag screws (with or without shear plates). In this case, holes should be slotted to avoid restraining beam rotation.

Detail 7.13

Continuous or spliced beams are connected to the U-shaped column cap by bolts or timber rivets through the side plates. The cap is welded to the steel column. A continuous beam may be anchored by bolts or lag screws through the bottom plate.

Detail 7.14

For use in multi-storey buildings with continuous beams, this detail uses clip angles and bearing plates to distribute the load over the required bearing area. Bolts or lag screws may be used in lieu of timber rivets.

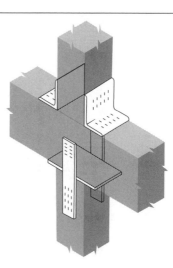

**7**

Fastenings

# Typical Connection Details

## Column to Base

Detail 7.15

This simple base connection, which typically uses a 19 mm diameter dowel, is effective when uplift and lateral forces are negligible. A base plate of at least 3 mm thickness prevents moisture transfer from the concrete support.

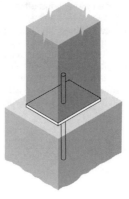

Detail 7.16a

These connections resist both uplift and lateral loading. The vertical leg of the angle may be increased as necessary for greater end distance or multiple bolting. Where bearing requires the base plate to be larger than the column, the base plate thickness will depend on the area over which the load is distributed, but should not be less than 6 mm.

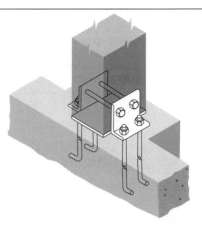

Detail 7.16b

A variation of Detail 7.16a.

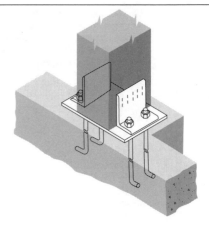

# Typical Connection Details

## Column to Base

Detail 7.17

A U-shaped anchorage to a concrete support will resist both uplift and lateral loads. A 3 mm bearing plate is sometimes used.

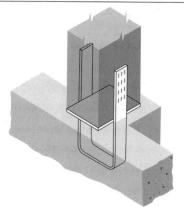

Detail 7.18

If concrete pedestal dimensions are limited, and the cross section of the column is adequate for bearing on the concrete, this connection is suggested. Some uplift and horizontal forces may be resisted. The end of the column must be countersunk to receive the anchor bolt and nut.

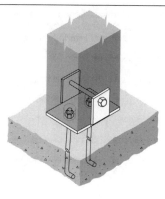

7

Fastenings

# Typical Connection Details

## Purlin to Beam

Detail 7.19

Connections in Details 7.19 to 7.21 are sometimes fabricated from standard 6 mm (min.) rolled
steel angles and plates with a minimum of cutting
and welding. The longer angle leg faces the
purlin, providing maximum end distance for the
purlin fasteners, and facilitating transfer of longitudinal forces through the beam.

This connection is recommended for purlins of
moderate depth where support for two members
is required.

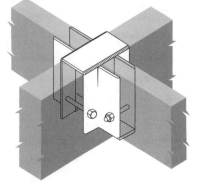

Detail 7.20

One-sided connections are well served by this
arrangement, which uses timber rivets. Loads for
standard hangers are provided in Section 7.6.

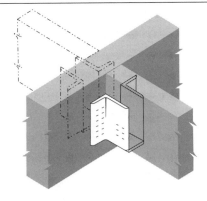

Detail 7.21

Purlins or beams of greater depth may be
connected by hangers as shown. The clip angles
prevent rotation of the end of the suspended
beam. However, they should not be bolted to it.

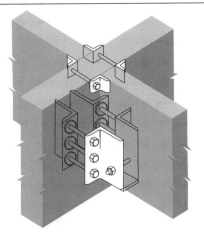

# Typical Connection Details
## Purlin to Beam

Detail 7.22

The rectangular shape of the centre gusset provides anchorage for, and prevents rotation of, the purlin in this semi-concealed connection. The bearing plate may be recessed into the bottom of the purlin to provide a flush detail. The pin is shorter than the width of the purlin and the holes are plugged after installation of the pin.

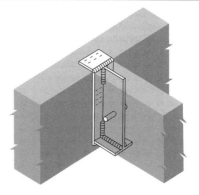

Detail 7.23

This welded and bent plate hanger is suitable to support moderate loads. The purlins should be raised above the top of the beam for hanger clearance.

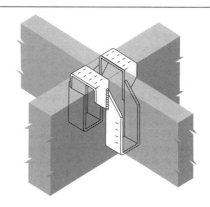

**7**

Fastenings

Detail 7.24a

Clips are used to fasten purlins supported or spliced on top of a beam or arch. Appropriate end and edge distances for the fasteners must be provided.

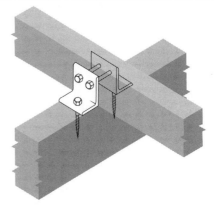

# Typical Connection Details

## Purlin to Beam

---

Detail 7.24b    A variation of Detail 7.24a.

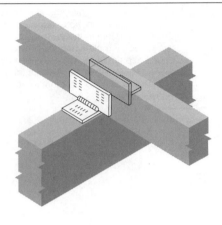

---

Detail 7.25a    For ridge purlins supported on the top of an arch, bent plates are used in lieu of the clip angles shown in Detail 7.24a. The arch peak is cut to provide a horizontal bearing surface for the ridge purlin. The usual arch peak connection (Details 7.30 to 7.32) must also be provided.

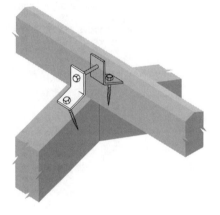

---

Detail 7.25b    A variation of Detail 7.25a.

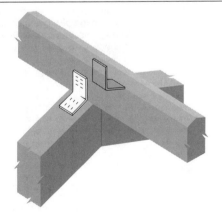

# Typical Connection Details

## Purlin to Beam

Detail 7.26a

For ridge purlins set between arches, the purlin hanger may be combined with the peak connection. The wide plates on each arch face are fastened to the arch and transmit shear and axial forces between the arch halves.

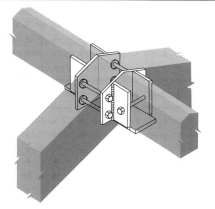

Detail 7.26b

A variation of Detail 7.26a.

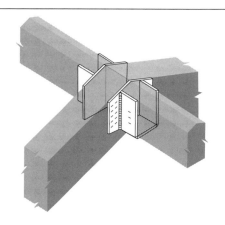

**7**

Fastenings

# Typical Connection Details

## Cantilevered-suspended Beam

Detail 7.27

The most common hanger is arranged so that the rod or bolt is in tension, with plate washers providing the necessary bearing area. This arrangement avoids concentrated shear stresses by using a sloped cut. Sloped cuts should be within lines drawn at 60° from the ends of the plate washers. The horizontal cut is made at mid-depth.

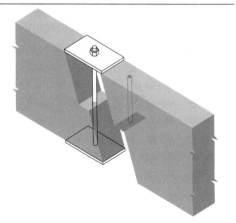

Detail 7.28

Moderate to heavy loads may be supported by this hanger detail where the vertical reaction of the supported member is transferred to the upper bearing plate by side plates. Rotation of the hanger is resisted by bearing on the edges of the top plates, which are dapped into the members. The bolts through the extended side plates resist both the separation force developed by eccentricity, and any axial tension to be transferred between the beams.
Bolt holes should be slotted vertically to avoid restraint of shrinkage.

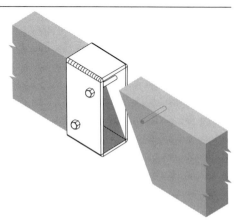

Detail 7.29

In this simple saddle connection, which is suitable for light to moderate loads, the beam ends are cut at an angle. Rotation is resisted by bolts through the side plates. No dapping is required.

# Typical Connection Details
## Arch Peak

Detail 7.30

For steep arches with rafter slopes of 20° or more, this connection transfers both horizontal and vertical loads. Two shear plates back to back are drawn together with a machine bolt or threaded rod with washers counterbored or dapped into the arch. Bevelling the arch peak tips helps prevent local crushing, and a butt plate between arch end cuts helps prevent interlocking of end grain.

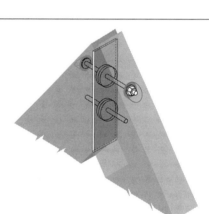

Detail 7.31

When vertical shear is too great for one pair of shear plates, or where the depth of section requires restraint for alignment, additional shear plates with a 19 mm diameter by 225 mm long dowel may be used. A butt plate between arch end cuts helps prevent interlocking of end grain.

7

Fastenings

Detail 7.32

For arches with a low rafter slope, the rod lengths for the connections shown in Details 7.31 and 7.32 become excessive. Here, shear plates with a 19 mm diameter by 225 mm long dowel in conjunction with steel side plates and through bolts provide a suitable detail. A butt plate between arch end cuts helps prevent interlocking of end grain.

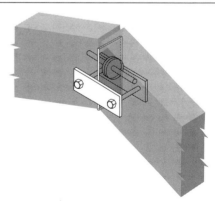

# Typical Connection Details

## Arch Base to Support

Detail 7.33

These connections must transfer horizontal loads to a tie rod or other restraint.

This is the most common connection between an arch base and the foundation, and forms the basic design for the variations shown in Details 7.34 and 7.35. Loads must be transferred from the base shoe to the foundation by the anchor bolts. This detail is suitable to resist horizontal thrusts of about 50 kN. A concealed shoe may be made by slotting the arch along its centreline, and using a single plate in the slot in lieu of the side plates.

Detail 7.34

In this arrangement, the anchor bolts need not transfer the horizontal thrust. The short rod stub is threaded to receive a turnbuckle, and the arch base is counterbored to receive the anchor bolts and nuts.

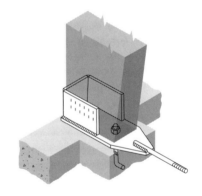

Detail 7.35

This detail has the tie rod extending through the arch, and anchored by a nut and washer on the threaded part of the rod at the back face of the shoe. Again, the arch base is counterbored to receive the anchor bolts. This detail may be used when the floor construction can accommodate the tie rod, as in the case of standard joist framing.

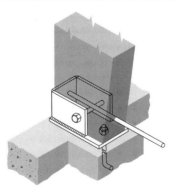

# Typical Connection Details

## Arch Base to Support

Detail 7.36

Arches may be anchored to a glulam floor beam in this fashion. The base below the arch leg must be sufficient to properly distribute the load onto the beam. Bolts and shear plates may be used in lieu of timber rivets. Alternatively, the floor beam may stop at the inside face of the arch leg, with the vertical reaction being taken directly into the bearing support.

Detail 7.37

Anchorage to a steel beam is similar to the detail shown in Detail 7.36.

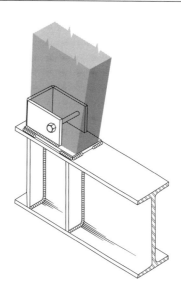

**7**

**Fastenings**

# Typical Connection Details

## Arch Base to Support

Detail 7.38    A smaller foundation arch may not require a true
hinge at the base. This detail may be used with
or without an elastomeric bearing pad as required
by the degree of anticipated rotation. Weep holes
or a slot should be provided at the lower (inside)
faceplate to allow drainage of any moisture inside
the shoe.

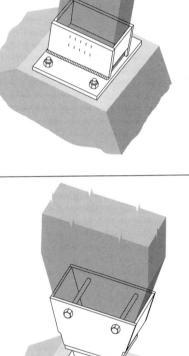

Detail 7.39    A true hinge connection should be provided for
long span or deep section arches if the rotation
at the base is too excessive for an elastomeric
bearing pad. The fasteners to the arch may be
required to resist uplift as well as shear. Again,
drainage at the lower inside face plate should be
provided.

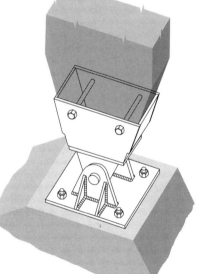

# Typical Connection Details

## Moment Splice

Detail 7.40

This connection detail provides for the maximum lever arm between splice plates. Direct thrust is transferred through a 3 mm pressure plate between the ends of the members to avoid end grain penetration of fibres. Shear forces are transferred through pairs of shear plates and 19 mm diameter by 225 mm long dowels in the member end faces. Lag screws or bolts together with shear plates may also be used with this connection.

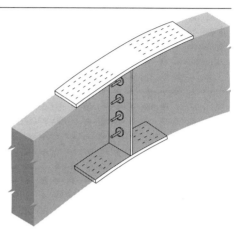

Detail 7.41

Similar in application to the connection in Detail 7.40, this moment connection utilizes fasteners on the side faces of the members. Other loads are transferred in the same manner as described for Detail 7.40.

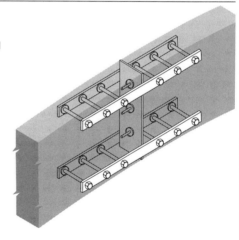

7

Fastenings

# Problem Connections

## Column Bases

Detail 7.42    In an effort to conceal a column base connection, the base is shown set below the floor slab. This detail will allow moisture to migrate into the wood, and may lead to decay.

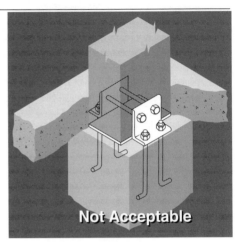

Detail 7.43a    A steel "bucket shoe" will encase the wood below the level of the slab and protect the wood against moisture as long as the top of the shoe projects slightly above the slab.

Detail 7.43b    Alternative arrangements provide for the column base to be raised to the slab level, and a steel plate used as a moisture barrier. In this case, a base trim may be used if it is necessary to conceal the hardware.

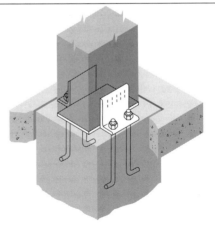

# Problem Connections

## Beam to Column

Detail 7.44   When connecting deep beams to columns, it is important to avoid details where the distance from the top of the column to the uppermost bolt location is more than 300 mm.

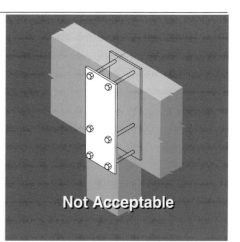

Detail 7.45   The recommended arrangement provides for a separate plate with slotted holes to keep the top of the beams aligned.

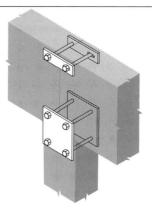

7

Fastenings

# Problem Connections

## Beam Bearing on Masonry

Detail 7.46    Clearance considerations sometimes limit the depth of beam, which may project above the bearing level. Stress concentrations at the notch may lead to splitting at this location (refer to notch factor, page 56).

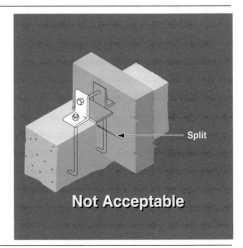

Split

**Not Acceptable**

Detail 7.47a    A beam hanger will provide support for the beam at the lower face. A 13 mm clearance should be maintained between the horizontal notched face of the beam and the plate bearing on the masonry.

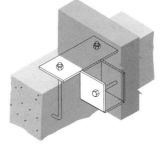

Detail 7.47b    It may be possible to lower the bearing elevation of the masonry support either along the full length of the wall, or at least at the bearing point as a pocket. In this case, the notch is eliminated altogether.

# Problem Connections

## Beam Bearing on Masonry

Detail 7.48

This bearing condition reflects similar constraints to those shown in Detail 7.46.

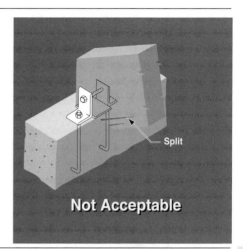

Split

Not Acceptable

Detail 7.49a

For comments, see Detail 7.47a.

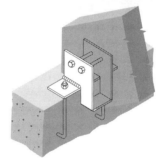

Detail 7.49b

For comments, see Detail 7.47b.

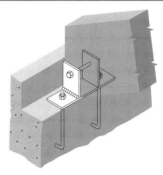

**7**

Fastenings

# Problem Connections

## Hanger to Underside of Beam

Detail 7.50    Hangers or straps that support significant loads
and are connected near the bottom of the
supporting beam may lead to splitting at the
connector group.

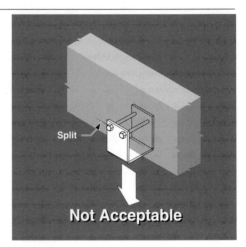

Detail 7.51    Such hangers should be connected into the
upper third of the supporting member, or replaced
by a saddle type hanger that would transfer all
the load to the top surface of the beam.

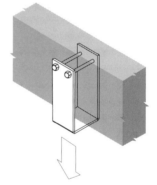

# Problem Connections

## Hanger to Side of Beam

Detail 7.52

Deep beam hangers that have fasteners installed in the side plates toward the top of the supported beam may promote splits at the fastener group should the wood member shrink and lift from the bottom of the beam hanger because of the support provided by the fastener group.

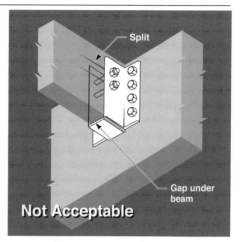

Detail 7.53

Provide a lower side plate connection for the supported beam, and if the top of the beam is not laterally restrained by other means such as decking or sheathing, keeper plates or separate clip angles without a fastener should be used.

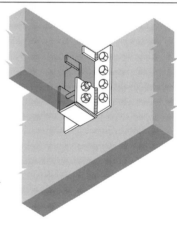

**7**

Fastenings

# Applications

Light wood trusses provide a very economical and easily erected roof structure for long span farm and commercial buildings as well as common residential applications.

Wood structures often serve a decorative function as in these large scale but intricate canopies over restaurant and lounge areas in a hotel atrium.

Since glulam may be curved, creative applications are possible such as in this marina clubhouse where the trusses have been used to support a roof whose exterior shape resembles a billowing sail.

As in the above photograph, curved glulam mambers allow the designer considreable scope to develop innovative structures.

Plywood
stressed-skin
panels used in
residential
roofing applica-
tions provide
the option of
additional living
space.

Concrete form-
work makes
extensive use
of Douglas Fir
Plywood. A
number of
forming panels
have surface
coatings and
sealed edges to
make them
impervious to
oil and water.

Glulam ribs form the domed roof for a mosque.

Long span wood I-joists supported by glulam frames allow large column free areas in this custom home.

Size limitations must be investigated when shipping large members such as these arches. In this case, cradles were used to support the frames in such a manner as to meet the clearance restrictions.

Swimming pool enclosures, as shown using pitched-tapered beams, are an excellent application for wood construction due to its ability to perform well over a long period of time in high humidity conditions.

# 8.1 General Information

Preceding chapters provide the resource with which to design a wide range of wood components. These elements may be incorporated into structures framed entirely of wood, or as a part of buildings that make use of several structural materials.

The *National Building Code of Canada (NBCC)* sets out guidelines for the use of wood in applications that extend well beyond the traditional residential and small building sector (see Chapter 10). The *NBCC* allows wood to be used as the structural framing in four storey buildings, and wood cladding for buildings designated to be of non-combustible construction.

## Light Wood Framing

Wood frame construction is an economical choice for the construction of low rise buildings, and makes use of lumber in a range of grades and dimensions. Prefabrication of components such as wall and roof panels, even complete homes or office units are efficient extensions of this framing technique.

The increasingly wide distribution of the light frame trusses and wood I-joists with standardized connection hardware, as well as glulam and structural composite lumber (SCL) beams and columns, has enhanced the competitive position of wood products for many structures that previously utilized other structural materials.

Applications ranging from shopping centres, plazas, service and maintenance buildings, to institutional and municipal facilities (all of which are illustrated in CWC *Design Plans, Case Studies, and Fact Sheets)* are making increasing use of these products either singly or in combination with other materials. The ready availability of product, ease of handling, on-site trimming options all using one framing crew can create considerable savings.

It is possible to completely frame and sheathe many of these buildings with wood components, including the use of preserved wood foundations. Integration with other materials such as steel and masonry construction is also very straightforward. Ducts and services are easily accommodated.

Wood I-joists and flat wood trusses have had a significant impact on the manner in which wood components have been incorporated into these projects. These members provide a very efficient secondary framing alternative to the open web steel joist. Residential and office floor applications up to about 10 m spans are generally served by in-stock products. Deeper sections are readily available for spans up to approximately 13 m. Distribution outlets usually stock I-joists and SCL beams and headers in lengths of about 15 to 20 m. I-joists and SCL members are often shipped in stock lengths for on-site trimming and installation to layouts shown on drawings prepared by either the building designer or the supplier. Instructions as to the requirements for web stiffeners, allowable web hole sizes, blocking, hanger types and other framing and header requirements are often provided on these drawings, in addition to procedures set out in the installation guides prepared by the manufacturer.

Close manufacturing tolerances in the production of wood I-joists and SCL materials result in uniform dimensions and low moisture content. The long lengths available can reduce the number of pieces to be handled on a project, as well as provide multiple span opportunities.

**8**

**Applications**

Assembly fire-resistance ratings for combinations of wood I-joists and trusses with various claddings are available from the manufacturers of these products. Similar ratings for framing lumber sections are set out in the *NBCC* (see Chapter 10 of this manual).

Floors sheathed with plywood or waferboard are often covered with a slurry of lightweight concrete prior to the application of finishes to enhance acoustic performance and provide other benefits. The sound transmission classification ratings are given in Appendix A-9.10.3.1.B of the *NBCC*.

## Heavy Timber Construction

A structural timber frame may be sized to satisfy the requirements of Part 3 of the *NBCC* for heavy timber construction. This aspect may be used to advantage in post and beam construction, where the exposed framing contributes an aesthetic as well as structural function.

Traditionally, post and beam construction utilized large solid timbers that were connected with mortise and tenon joints locked into place with hardwood pegs. The frames were stabilized by diagonal braces. While a number of specialized manufacturers still duplicate these classic techniques, metal brackets, shear plates and split rings with bolts are more commonly used as connectors in variations of this framing technique as it is applied to both residential and commercial applications, for reasons of ease of fabrication, and consequent economy. Particular attention must be paid to the anticipated seasoning effects of sawn timber when planning the arrangement and connection of the larger members in post and beam construction.

Hybrid post and beam and wood frame construction features the exposed heavy timber components, but allows insulation to be placed in the wall space, with finishes applied to both the inner and outer faces of the studs.

The following sections provide examples of wood components in practical and economical applications. Some design techniques for a number of the members are offered as a guide to the reader.

# 8.2  Curved Glulam

## General

Curved glulam members are used in applications such as pedestrian bridge girders, tied arches, foundation arches, and pitched-tapered beams. Arches are discussed in Section 8.3 and pitched-tapered beams in Section 8.4.

Glulam beams in excess of 7 m in length are usually manufactured with a standard pre-camber that approximates the in-service deflection indicated in Table 8.1. The values given in Table 8.1 are guidelines based on experience and are not code requirements.

Table 8.1
**Suggested camber for glulam beams**

| Application | Camber | |
| | All types of beams | Single span only |
| | Deflection due to dead load plus: | Empirical: |
|---|---|---|
| Roof beam | 50% snow load | 4 mm per m of span |
| Floor beam | 25% live load | 2 mm per m of span |
| Bridge girder | 200% live load | not used |

For design purposes, a beam is generally considered to be straight unless the camber is greater than 5% of the span. This small amount of curvature does not usually result in an increase in manufacturing costs.

## Radial Stress

The design of glulam pitched-tapered beams and curved members of minimum radii is usually governed by radial stresses.

When the bending moment tends to decrease the curvature (increase the radius) of the member, the radial stress is tension perpendicular to grain. When the bending moment tends to increase the curvature (decrease the radius) of the member, the radial stress is compression perpendicular to grain.

## Effect of Curvature

The thickness of laminating stock required for a curved glulam member is determined by the minimum radius of curvature in accordance with Table 8.2.

For reasons of economy, curved members should be designed to utilize the greatest possible lamination thickness. A member manufactured from standard 38 mm lamstock will be more economical than one made up from 19 mm lamstock. Non-standard laminations of less than 19 mm thickness are prepared from re-surfaced 19 mm lamstock, thus a larger volume of material is required to manufacture the required section.

The curving process creates residual stresses that reduce the bending moment resistance of the member. The factor $K_X$ accounts for this effect.

**8**

**Applications**

Table 8.2
**Minimum radius of curvature and curvature factor $K_X$**

| Lamination thickness t mm | | Minimum radius of curvature, mm | | Curvature factor $K_X$ | |
|---|---|---|---|---|---|
| | | Tangent ends | Curved ends | Tangent ends | Curved ends |
| Standard | 38 | 8400 | 10800 | 0.959 | 0.975 |
| | 19 | 2800 | 3800 | 0.908 | 0.950 |
| Non-standard | 35 | 7400 | 9500 | 0.955 | 0.973 |
| | 32 | 6300 | 8500 | 0.948 | 0.972 |
| | 29 | 5600 | 7300 | 0.946 | 0.968 |
| | 25 | 4600 | 6200 | 0.941 | 0.967 |
| | 16 | 2300 | 3000 | 0.903 | 0.943 |
| | 13 | 1800 | 2200 | 0.896 | 0.930 |
| | 10 | 1200 | 1400 | 0.861 | 0.898 |
| | 6 | 800 | 800 | 0.888 | 0.888 |

Note:

$$K_X = 1 - 2000 \left[ \frac{t}{R_I} \right]^2$$

where:

$t$ = lamination thickness and
$R_I$ = radius of curvature of innermost lamination.

## Design

Curved glulam members, including beams and arches, must be designed so that the following criteria are satisfied:

1. Factored bending moment resistance based on radial tension strength $M_{rt} \geq$ factored bending moment $M_f$

2. Factored bending moment resistance based on bending strength $M_{rb} \geq$ factored bending moment $M_f$

3. Where bending is combined with compression, the following interaction equation must be satisfied

$$\frac{M_f}{M_{rb}} + \frac{P_f}{P_r} \leq 1.0$$

where:

$M_{rb}$ = factored bending moment resistance based on bending strength
$P_r$ = factored compressive resistance for combined bending and axial load
$M_f$ = factored bending moment
$P_f$ = factored compressive force

4. Adequate shear resistance must be provided.

    a) For arches (and beams < 2.0 m³ in volume) the factored shear resistance $V_r$ ≥ factored shear force $V_f$

    b) For beams (any volume) the factored shear resistance $W_r$ ≥ sum of all factored loads acting on the beam $W_f$

5. Maximum deflection ≤ deflection criteria ($E_s I ≥ E_s I_{REQ'D}$)

**Factored Resistances**

The factored resistances may be calculated as indicated below. Where values are obtained from the Beam Selection Tables, review the checklists in Section 2.4 and modify the tabulated resistances if necessary.

1. a) The factored bending moment resistance based on radial tension strength is calculated from the following formula:

$$M_{rt} = \phi F_{tp} \frac{2}{3} A R_C K_{Ztp} \text{ (N·mm)}$$

    b) At the apex of double-tapered members only, the factored bending moment resistance based on radial tension strength is the lesser of the value given in (a) and the following formula. Double-tapered members include pitched-tapered beams and tudor arches.

$$M_{rt} = \phi F_{tp} S K_{Ztp} K_R \text{ (N·mm)}$$

where:

$\phi F_{tp}$ = factored tensile strength perpendicular to grain, given in Table 8.3 (MPa)

$S$ = section modulus (mm³)

$A$ = area (mm²)

$K_{Ztp}$ = size factor, given in Table 8.4

$K_R$ = radial stress factor

$$= \left[ A + B \left[ \frac{d_A}{R_C} \right] + C \left[ \frac{d_A}{R_C} \right]^2 \right]^{-1}$$

A,B,C = constants, given in Table 8.5

$d_A$ = depth at the apex (mm)

$R_C$ = radius of curvature at centreline (mm)

**8**

Applications

2. The factored bending moment resistance based on bending strength is calculated as follows:

$$M_{rb} = \text{the lesser of } M'_r \, K_L \, K_X \, K_M \text{ or } M'_r \, K_{Zbg} \, K_X \, K_M \text{ (kN} \bullet \text{m)}$$

where:

$M'_r$ = factored bending moment resistance from the Beam Selection Tables (Section 2.4) (kN•m). For intermediate depths interpolate values in the ratio of the section moduli.

$K_L$ = lateral stability factor (Section 2.5)

$K_{Zbg}$ = glulam size factor in bending (Section 2.5)

$K_X$ = curvature factor, applicable to curved portions only (refer to Table 8.2)

$K_M$ = 1.0 for all locations except at the apex of curved double-tapered members

$= \dfrac{1}{1 + 2.7 \tan \alpha}$ at the apex of curved double-tapered members

$\alpha$ = defined in Table 8.4

3. The factored compressive resistance $P_r$ for combined bending and axial load is calculated in accordance with Chapter 5.

4. a) The factored shear resistance $V_r$ is given in the Beam Selection Tables (Section 2.4). Use linear interpolation for intermediate depths.

   b) The factored shear resistance $W_r$ may be calculated as follows:

$$W_r = 0.72 \, V_r \, C_V \, Z^{-0.18} \text{ (kN)}$$

where:

$V_r$ = factored shear resistance given in the Beam Selection Tables

$C_V$ = shear load coefficient, given in Clause 6.5.7.4 of CSA O86.1

$Z$ = beam volume (m³)

5. The bending stiffness $E_S I$ is given in the Beam Selection Tables. $E_S I$ may be interpolated by the ratio of the moments of inertia.

| Table 8.3 Factored tensile strength perpendicular to grain $\phi\,F_{tp}$ (MPa) | | Dry service condition | | | Wet service condition | | |
|---|---|---|---|---|---|---|---|
| | | Load duration | | | Load duration | | |
| | Species | Stnd. | Perm. | Short term | Stnd. | Perm. | Short term |
| | D.Fir-L, Hem-Fir | 0.747 | 0.486 | 0.859 | 0.635 | 0.413 | 0.730 |
| | Spruce-Pine | 0.459 | 0.298 | 0.528 | 0.390 | 0.253 | 0.449 |

| Table 8.4 Size factor for tension perpendicular to grain $K_{Ztp}$ | | Loading | |
|---|---|---|---|
| | Member | Uniformly distributed | All other |
| | Constant depth, curved | $\dfrac{24}{\left(AR_c\beta\right)^{0.2}}$ | $\dfrac{20}{\left(AR_c\beta\right)^{0.2}}$ |
| | Double-tapered, curved | $\dfrac{35}{\left(AR_c\beta\right)^{0.2}}$ | $\dfrac{22}{\left(AR_c\beta\right)^{0.2}}$ |

Notes:
1. A = maximum cross-sectional area of member (mm²)
2. $R_C$ = radius of curvature at centreline of member (mm)
3. $\beta$ = enclosed angle in radians (see below) and is calculated as follows:
   a) For curved double-tapered members, $\beta$ is measured between points of tangency. $\beta$ can be conservatively estimated as twice $\alpha$ in radians (see below).
   b) For other curved uniform section members, $\beta$ is measured between points where the factored bending moment is 85% of the maximum factored bending moment.

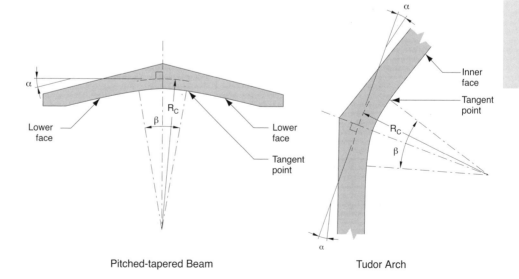

Pitched-tapered Beam                    Tudor Arch

8

Applications

| Table 8.5 Values of constants for radial stress factor $K_R$ | Angle $\alpha°$ | Value of constant | | |
|---|---|---|---|---|
| | | A | B | C |
| | 2.5 | 0.01 | 0.17 | 0.13 |
| | 5 | 0.02 | 0.13 | 0.19 |
| | 7.5 | 0.03 | 0.09 | 0.22 |
| | 10 | 0.04 | 0.08 | 0.21 |
| | 15 | 0.06 | 0.06 | 0.17 |
| | 20 | 0.09 | 0.06 | 0.14 |
| | 25 | 0.12 | 0.06 | 0.12 |
| | 30 | 0.16 | 0.06 | 0.11 |

Note:
Refer to Table 8.4 for definition of angle $\alpha$.

# 8.3 Timber Arches

## General

Arches may be manufactured from a number of components ranging from trussed wood members to glulam. The most practical construction utilizes glulam since it may be manufactured in a great variety of shapes and sizes. The only practical limitations are:

- Minimum radius of curvature, which determines the thickness of laminations required.
- Transportation restrictions, which may limit the overall length and height of curved members. The total shipping height should not typically exceed 4.75 m for rail or 4 m for road shipment, but may vary with location of manufacturing plant and project site. The designer should consult with manufacturers or shipping companies for larger projects since particular configurations of the member or restrictions of the transportation corridor may define other limits.

## Arch Types and Profiles

A number of the arch shapes in common usage are shown in the following summary, however, other configurations may be devised.

1. Foundation arches have the arch springing at or near the floor level, with the horizontal thrust resisted by buttressed foundations or structural ties within or below the floor construction.

| Arch type | Typical spans | Common applications | |
|---|---|---|---|
| Circular | 20 to 80 m<br><br>Rise is 20% to 50% of span | Arenas, halls curling rinks, warehouses | 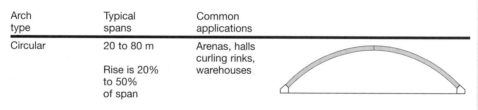 |
| Parabolic | 15 to 30 m<br>High rise arches | Feature structures, commercial buildings, churches |  |

| Arch type | Typical spans | Common applications | |
|---|---|---|---|
| Segmental (Gothic) | 10 to 40 m | Agricultural storage, commercial buildings | |
| Tudor | 10 to 25 m | Churches, pool enclosures, arenas, auditoria, commercial buildings | |
| A-frame | 10 to 80 m | Industrial, storage and commercial buildings, churches | |

2. Tied arches have the arch springing at eaves level, with the horizontal thrust resisted by a glulam or steel tie that is suspended from the arch to prevent sagging of the tie.

| Arch type | Typical spans | Common applications | |
|---|---|---|---|
| Bowstring | 15 to 40 m radius equal to span | Curling rinks, arenas, gymnasia, warehouses, commercial buildings | |

| Arch type | Typical spans | Common applications | |
|---|---|---|---|
| Straight-leg tied | 5 to 15 m | Recreational buildings, pool enclosures | |

## Design Considerations

Glulam arches are generally designed as three-hinged arches and manufactured with each half arch as a single continuous unit. Moment splices involving field assembly may be required in large arches to satisfy manufacturing and/or shipping limitations (see Section 7.11).

Long span circular arches, and short span segmental tied arches may be designed as two-hinged members. Again, consideration should be given to the need for moment splices.

Glulam arches should be designed to meet the criteria given in Section 8.2. The following points should also be considered:

1. The guidelines of the depth-to-width ratio for members subjected to combined loading (refer to Chapter 5).

2. Sections of arches in bending and compression must be checked for adequacy about both axes between points of lateral support.

3. The effective length used to determine the slenderness ratio of a member is the distance between points of contraflexure, or one hinge and the point of contraflexure, or between hinges in the absence of contraflexure points.

4. The extent of lateral deflection (sway) under wind loads. Excessive sway may cause damage to other structural or cladding components.

The following design example is for a three-hinged Tudor arch. However, the suggested design method is equally applicable to other arch types.

**8**

**Applications**

### Example 1: Tudor Arch

The glulam Tudor arch, for a church, shown below is to be designed for the following conditions:

- normal importance category building
- arch spacing = 4.0 m
- specified dead load = 0.8 kPa
- specified ground snow load = 2.7 kPa
- specified rain load = 0.2 kPa

- specified wind pressure = 0.55 kPa
- small, uniformly distributed openings
- exposure factor = 1.0
- wind loads uniformly distributed on vertical legs

- dry service condition
- untreated
- rafter laterally supported by decking
- vertical leg laterally supported by wall framing

Use 24f-EX D.Fir-L glulam with 19 mm laminations and 2800 mm radius of curvature.

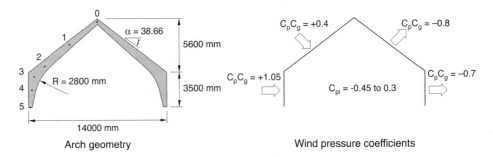

Arch geometry                                    Wind pressure coefficients

### Calculation

The arch was analyzed using a plane frame analysis program. The maximum member end forces at the critical locations are shown in Table 8.6. The maximum factored reactions are given in Table 8.7. Try a width of 130 mm and calculate the required depths, rounded to the nearest multiple of 19 mm, at each location as follows:

1. Determine the required depth at the base as governed by shear. From the Beam Selection Tables, try d = 285 mm

$$V_r \; = \; \frac{41.5 + 47.4}{2} \; = 44.5 \text{ kN} > 42.9 \text{ kN} \qquad\qquad \textit{Acceptable}$$

Therefore, select d = 285 mm

Table 8.6
**Maximum factored member end forces**

| Location | Joint | Shear force kN | Shear force load combination | Axial force kN | Bending moment kN•m | Combined bending and axial load combination |
|---|---|---|---|---|---|---|
| Peak | 0 | + 38.0 | $1.25D + 1.5S_u$ | + 39.2 | + 0 | $1.25D + 1.5S_u$ |
| Mid point of rafter | 1 | - 11.3 | $1.25D + 1.4W$ | + 43.2 | + 61.6 | $1.25D + 1.5S_u$ |
| Upper tangent point | 2 | - 45.4 | $1.25D + 1.5S_B$ | + 43.4 | - 99.2 | $1.25D + 1.4W + 0.5S_B$ |
| Haunch | 3 | - 60.0 | $1.25D + 1.5S_u$ | + 100 | - 106 | $1.25D + 1.5S_B$ |
|  |  |  |  | + 6.7 | + 21.0 | $1.25D + 1.4W$ |
| Lower tangent point | 4 | + 42.9 | $1.25D + 1.5S_B$ | + 111 | - 81.7 | $1.25D + 1.5S_B$ |

Notes:
1. D = dead load, $S_B$ = balanced snow load, $S_u$ = unbalanced snow, W = wind load
2. Positive moments produce tension on inside face.
   Positive axial forces are compressive.
   Positive shear forces are inward at the lower end and outward at the upper end of the member.
3. In the determination of critical load combinations, duration of load has been taken into consideration using $K_D$ = 1.15 for wind load cases and $K_D$ = 1.0 for snow load cases.

Table 8.7
**Maximum factored reactions**

| Location | Joint | Horizontal reaction kN | Horizontal reaction load case | Vertical reaction kN | Vertical reaction load case |
|---|---|---|---|---|---|
| Peak | 0 | 42.9 | $1.25D + 1.5S_B$ | 23.3 | $1.25D + 1.5S_u$ |
| Base | 5 | 42.9 | $1.25D + 1.5S_B$ | 111 | $1.25D + 1.5S_B$ |

Notes:
1. D = dead load, $S_B$ = balanced snow load, $S_u$ = unbalanced snow load
2. Positive vertical reactions are upward.
   Positive horizontal reactions are outward at the peak and inward at the base of the arch.

**8**

Applications

2. Determine the required depth at the lower tangent point

$$K_L = K_{Zbg} = 1.0$$
$$M_{rb} = M'_r K_X K_M$$
$$K_X = 0.908 \text{ (Table 8.2)}$$
$$K_M = 1.0 \text{ (Section 8.2)}$$
$$P_r = \phi F_{cb} A K_{Zc} K_C \text{ ($\phi F_{cb}$ values are given in Table 5.2)}$$

To determine $P_r$ the unsupported length and the effective depth must be known. It is conservative to take the straight line distance between the base and the peak as the unsupported length, and the depth at the tangent point as the effective depth:

$$K_e L = 1.0 \times 11500 = 11500 \text{ mm}$$

Estimate depth as span/30 = 14000/30 = 467 mm

Therefore, try 130 × 456 mm and check the interaction equation. Obtain $M'_r$ from the Beam Selection Tables, and calculate $P_r$ using Tables 5.2 and 5.3.

| Section | $M'_r$ kN•m | $M_{rb}$ kN•m | $C_c$ | $F_{cb}$ MPa | $F_{cb}/E'$ ×10⁻⁶ | $P_r$ kN | $\dfrac{M_f}{M_{rb}} + \dfrac{P_f}{P_r}$ |
|---|---|---|---|---|---|---|---|
| 130 × 456 | 124 | 113 | 25.2 | 24.2 | 75.7 | 550 | 0.93 |
| 130 × 437 | 114 | 104 | 26.3 | 24.2 | 75.7 | 495 | 1.01 |

Therefore, select d = 456 mm, although in some cases d = 437 mm could be acceptable.

3. Determine the required depth at the upper tangent point

For ease of fabrication the upper and lower tangent points are usually made the same depth. Therefore, try d = 456 mm. Since the governing load case is 1.25D + 1.4W + 0.5S_B, $M_r$ and $P_r$ values must be modified for short term loading.

| Section | $M'_r$ kN•m | $M_{rb}$ kN•m | $C_c$ | $F_{cb}$ MPa | $F_{cb}/E'$ ×10⁻⁶ | $P_r$ kN | $\dfrac{M_f}{M_{rb}} + \dfrac{P_f}{P_r}$ |
|---|---|---|---|---|---|---|---|
| 130 × 456 | 143 | 130 | 25.2 | 27.8 | 87.1 | 585 | 0.84 |

Therefore, select d = 456 mm.

4. Determine the required depth at the midpoint of the rafter

Since the rafter section is not curved $K_X = K_M = 1.0$ and $M'_r = M_{rb}$. Try d = 380:

| Section | $M'_r$ kN•m | $C_c$ | $F_{cb}$ MPa | $F_{cb}/E'$ ×10⁻⁶ | $P_r$ kN | $\dfrac{M_f}{M_{rb}} + \dfrac{P_f}{P_r}$ |
|---|---|---|---|---|---|---|
| 130 × 380 | 86.2 | 25.2 | 24.2 | 75.7 | 458 | 0.81 |
| 130 × 361 | 77.8 | 25.2 | 24.2 | 75.7 | 435 | 0.89 |
| 130 × 342 | 69.8 | 25.2 | 24.2 | 75.7 | 413 | 0.99 |

Therefore, select d = 342 mm.

5. Determine the required depth at the peak

From the Beam Selection tables, interpolate between depths of 228 and 266 mm to obtain the shear resistance for d = 247 mm:

$$V_r = \frac{41.5 + 35.6}{2} = 38.6 \text{ kN} > 23.3 \text{ kN} \qquad\qquad Acceptable$$

6. Verify that the depth at the peak is adequate for a factored vertical reaction of 23.3 kN. Use the connection shown in Detail 7.32 in Section 7.11.

Try two pairs of 2-5/8" diameter shear plates back to back.

$\theta = 90 - 38.66 = 51.3°$

$P_r = \phi\, p_u\, n_{Fe}\, n_R\, K'\, J'$

$Q_r = \phi\, q_u\, n_{Fe}\, n_R\, K'\, J'$

$\phi\, p_u = 16.2$ kN (Table 7.13)

$\phi\, q_u = 13.8$ kN (Table 7.13)

$n_{Fe} = 2.0$

$n_R = 1$

$K' = 1.0$

$J_O = 0.81$ (linear interpolation between $J_O = 1.0$ at 0° and $J_O = 0.67$ at 90°)

$J' = 0.81\, J_C$

$P_r = 16.2 \times 2 \times 0.81 \times J_C = 26.2\, J_C$ (kN)

$Q_r = 13.8 \times 2 \times 0.81 \times J_C = 22.4\, J_C$ (kN)

8

Applications

Using Table 7.1:

$$\frac{Q_r}{P_r} = \frac{22.4}{26.2} = 0.85$$

$$X = 0.90$$

$$N_r = 26.2 \times 0.90 \, J_C = 23.6 \, J_C \text{ kN} > 23.3 \text{ kN} \qquad \textit{Acceptable}$$

Therefore, $J_{Cmin} = \dfrac{23.3}{23.6} = 0.99$

Use $J_C = 1.0$ and calculate the required end distance, edge distance and spacing as shown below (mm).

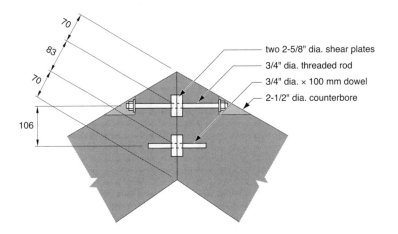

required loaded edge distance = 70 mm (Table 7.18)
required spacing along vertical face = 106 mm (Table 7.19)
required spacing perpendicular to grain = 106 sin 51.3° = 83 mm
total depth required = 2 × 70 + 83 = 223 mm < 247 mm    *Acceptable*

7. Check the moment resistance based on radial tension strength at the haunch

a) The depth at the haunch may be calculated from arch geometry as shown below (dimensions in mm):

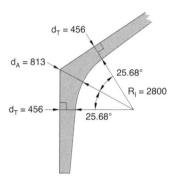

check $\dfrac{d}{b} = \dfrac{813}{130} = 6.3 < 7$        *Acceptable*

b) Using d = 813 mm calculate the lesser of $M_{rt}$ and compare to maximum positive moment:

$$M_{rt} = \phi \, F_{tp} \, S \, K_{Ztp} \, K_R$$

$$M_{rt} = \phi \, F_{tp} \, \frac{2}{3} A \, R_C \, K_{Ztp}$$

$\phi \, F_{tp} = 0.859$ MPa (Table 8.3)

$$S = \frac{130 \times 813^2}{6} = 14.3 \times 10^6 \text{ mm}^3$$

$$A = 130 \times 813 = 106 \times 10^3 \text{ mm}^2$$

$$R_C = 2800 + \left[\frac{813}{2}\right] = 3206 \text{ mm}$$

$$K_{Ztp} = \frac{35}{\left(A \, R_C \, \beta\right)^{0.2}} = \frac{35}{\left[130 \times 813 \times 3206 \times \dfrac{51.3° \times \pi}{180}\right]^{0.2}} = 0.70$$

$$K_R = \left[0.12 + 0.06\left[\frac{813}{3206}\right] + 0.12\left[\frac{813}{3206}\right]^2\right]^{-1} = 7.00$$

$$M_{rt} = 0.859 \times 14.3 \times 0.70 \times 7.00$$
$$= 60.2 \text{ kN} \bullet \text{m} > 21.0 \text{ kN} \bullet \text{m} \qquad \qquad \textit{Acceptable}$$

$$M_{rt} = 0.859 \times \frac{2}{3} \times 106 \times 3206 \times 0.70 \times 10^{-3}$$

$$= 136 \text{ kN} \bullet \text{m} > 21.0 \text{ kN} \bullet \text{m} \qquad \qquad \textit{Acceptable}$$

8. Calculate trial arch dimensions

In the calculation of arch dimensions the depth at the base and peak are limited by the following rules established through experience:

- The slope between a tangent point and peak or base should not exceed 3.5°.
- The depth at peak or base should be at least 0.63 of the tangent depth to limit deflection.
- The taper from upper tangent point to peak should be uniform.

Using these rules the trial arch dimensions are as follows:

| Location | Joint | Depth mm | Comment |
|---|---|---|---|
| Peak | 0 | 285 | Must be $\geq$ 0.63 of depth at pt. 2 |
| Mid point of rafter | 1 | 371 | For uniform taper |
| Upper tangent point | 2 | 456 | Same as pt. 4 for ease of fabrication |
| Haunch | 3 | 818 | From geometry |
| Lower tangent point | 4 | 456 | As per design |
| Base | 5 | 342 | Slope from pt. 4 to pt. 5 limited to 3.5° |

9. Using the trial dimensions the amount of sway under lateral load cases may be checked using a plane frame analysis program. In this example the amount of sway at the eave was found to be 51 mm, which may be unacceptable. The frame may be stiffened by adding laminations. For example, by increasing the peak depth to 342 mm, the tangent depths to 532 mm and the base depth to 418 mm, the sway is reduced to 33 mm.

**Use 130 mm wide 24f-EX D.Fir-L glulam with depths varying from 342 mm at the base to 285 mm at the peak with a 456 mm depth at the tangent points provided the sway is acceptable.**

# 8.4    Pitched-tapered Beams

## General

Glulam can be shaped to provide a vaulted ceiling using pitched-tapered beams. Beams of this type are commonly used in swimming pool enclosures, churches, community halls, gymnasia, showrooms and similar structures. A typical pitched-tapered beam is shown in Figure 8.1.

It is advisable to limit the beam slope to about 15°. This is due to the magnitude of radial tension stresses for steeply sloped shapes, resulting in much larger and less economical beams. Other design considerations include:

- A minimum radius of curvature for the innermost lamination of not less than 8400 mm for standard 38 mm laminations, or 2800 mm if 19 mm laminations are used.
- The depth to width ratio at the apex should be limited to 7:1 for reasons of lateral stability.
- Horizontal deflection at the end of the beam must be accommodated. In many cases a slotted end connection will serve this function.
- Since the radial stress governs in most cases, 20f-E is an appropriate stress grade.

**8**

**Applications**

Figure 8.1
**Pitched-tapered beam geometry**

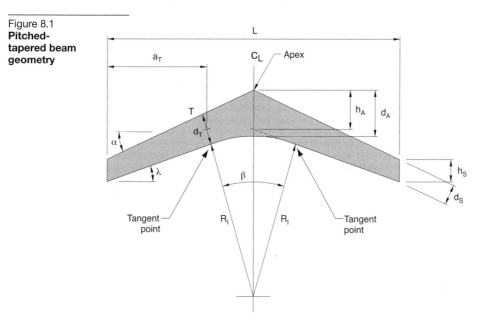

## Design Procedure

Pitched-tapered beams must be designed to meet the criteria outlined in Section 8.2. However, a direct design procedure is not possible since the size of the beam affects the moment resistance based on radial tension strength. Therefore, the procedure outlined below is recommended.

1. Determine the depth required at the apex for $M_{rt} > M_f$

    a) Calculate the equivalent factored moment $M_{fe}$ at the apex as follows:

$$M_{fe} = X_1 X_2 X_3 M_f$$

where:

    $M_f$ = factored bending moment at apex

    $X_1$ = constant for species, service condition and load duration, from Table 8.8

    $X_2$ = constant for loading conditions, from Table 8.9

    $X_3$ = constant for member width, from Table 8.9

    b) Select the required depth at the apex from Tables 8.10 or 8.11 so that $M_{rt} \geq M_{fe}$. The tabulated values have been calculated using $\beta = 2\alpha$ since the angle $\beta$ is not known, while the roof slope $\alpha$ is known. Since $\beta$ is generally less than $2\alpha$, this is conservative.

    c) Check that $d/b \leq 7$. If not, use a larger width and recalculate the required depth.

2. Check the bending moment resistance $M_{rb}$ at the apex

    a) Obtain $M'_r$ from the Beam Selection Tables after reviewing the checklist and making any necessary modifications.

    b) Calculate $M_{rb}$ as follows:

$$M_{rb} = \text{lesser of } M'_r K_L K_X K_M \text{ or } M'_r K_{Zbg} K_X K_M$$

where:

    $K_X$ = is given in Table 8.2

$$K_M = \frac{1}{1 + 2.7 \tan \alpha}$$

    $\alpha$ = roof slope

    c) Check that $M_{rb} \geq M_f$. If $M_{rb}$ is not adequate, select a larger depth and recheck.

3. a) Use the Beam Selection Tables to select a depth at the support $d_S$ so that $V_r \geq V_f$. Review the checklist prior to using the tables and modify the tabulated $V_r$ values if necessary.

   b) Check that the beam volume is less than 2.0 m³. If not then verify that:

   $$W_r \geq W_f$$

where:

   $W_r$ = shear resistance
   
        = $0.72 \ V_r \ C_v \ Z^{-0.18}$ (kN)

   $W_f$ = sum of all factored loads acting on the beam (kN)

   $V_r$ = shear resistance calculated in (a) above (kN)

   $C_v$ = shear load coefficient, given in Table 8.12

   $Z$ = beam volume (m³)

If the shear resistance $W_r$ is inadequate, then select a larger size and recheck.

**8**

**Applications**

4. Check the bending moment resistance $M_{rb}$ at the tangent point

   a) Calculate the slope $\lambda°$ of the underside of the beams as follows:

   $$\sin \lambda = \frac{2}{1+4K_2^2}\left[K_1 - 2K_2 \sqrt{0.25 - K_1^2 + K_2^2}\right]$$

where:

   $$K_1 = \frac{R_l + d_S}{L}$$

   $$K_2 = \frac{R_l + d_A}{L} - \frac{\tan \alpha}{2}$$

   $L$ = span (mm)

   $R_l$ = radius of curvature of innermost lamination (mm)

   $d_S$ = depth at support (mm)

   $d_A$ = depth at the apex (mm)

b) Calculate the depth at the tangent point $d_T$ and its location along the length of the beam $a_T$ as follows:

$$d_T = \frac{\cos\alpha}{\cos(\alpha - \lambda)}(R_l + d_A) - R_l \text{ (mm)}$$

$$a_T = \frac{L}{2} - \sin\lambda \left[ R_l + \frac{d_T}{2} \right] \text{ (mm)}$$

c) Determine the factored bending moment $M_f$ at a distance from the support $a_T$.

d) Determine the moment resistance $M_r$ using the Beam Selection Tables. Review the checklist prior to using the tables and modify the tabulated values if necessary. Where the depth $d_T$ is not listed in the tables, take the closest depth and multiply the corresponding $M_r$ value by the ratio of the section moduli.

e) Calculate $M_{rb}$ as follows ($K_X$ is given in Table 8.2):

$$M_{rb} = M_r K_X$$

f) Check that $M_{rb} > M_f$. If not, increase the depth.

5. Check deflection
Deflection calculations for pitched-tapered beams depend on the varying moments of inertia. An approximate solution for members subject to uniformly distributed loading follows. This solution predicts slightly greater deflection values than the exact solution.

a) Using the values of $d_A$, $d_S$ and the angle $\lambda°$, calculate the following values:

$$h_S = \frac{d_S}{\cos\alpha}$$

$$h_A = h_S + \frac{L}{2}[\tan\alpha - \tan\lambda]$$

$$u = \frac{h_A}{h_S}$$

b) Determine the bending stiffness $E_S I_A$, based on the depth $h_A$ from the Beam Selection Tables. Review the checklist prior to using the tables and modify the values if necessary. Where the depth $h_A$ is not listed in the tables, take the closest depth and multiply by the ratio of the moments of inertia.

c) Calculate the vertical deflection $\Delta_V$ at the centre as follows:

$$\Delta_V = \frac{5w \, L^4}{384 \, E_S I_A} K_\Delta \text{ (mm)}$$

where:

$w$ = uniformly distributed load (kN/m)

$L$ = span (mm)

$K_\Delta$ = deflection factor, given in Table 8.13

$E_S I_A$ = bending stiffness at apex (N·mm²)

d) The horizontal deflection $\Delta_H$ may be estimated as follows:

$$\Delta_H = \Delta_V \frac{2 \tan \alpha}{\cos \alpha} \text{ (mm)}$$

e) Compare $\Delta_V$ and $\Delta_H$ to the appropriate deflection criteria.

8

Applications

## Example 1: Pitched-tapered beams

Design a pitched-tapered glulam roof beam for the following conditions:

- 12 m span
- 10° roof slope
- specified snow load = 6.5 kN/m (strength)
                     = 5.9 kN/m (serviceability)
- specified dead load = 3.0 kN/m
- wet service condition
- untreated
- laterally supported by roof decking
- no ceiling below

Use 20f-E grade D.Fir-L with 38 mm laminations. The minimum radius of curvature for this lamination thickness is 8400 mm.

## Calculation
1. Determine the depth required at the apex for radial tension strength

$$w_f = (1.25 \times 3.0) + (1.5 \times 6.5) = 13.5 \text{ kN/m}$$

$$M_f = \frac{w_f L^2}{8} = \frac{13.5 \times 12.0^2}{8} = 243 \text{ kN·m}$$

Try b = 175 mm:

$$X_1 = 1.176 \text{ (Table 8.8)}$$
$$X_2 = 1.00 \text{ (Table 8.9)}$$
$$X_3 = 0.788 \text{ (Table 8.9)}$$

$$
\begin{aligned}
M_{fe} &= X_1 X_2 X_3 M_f \\
&= 1.176 \times 1.00 \times 0.788 \times 243 \\
&= 225 \text{ kN·m}
\end{aligned}
$$

From Table 8.10 select $d_A = 1064$:

$$M_{rt} = 229 \text{ kN·m} > 225 \text{ kN·m} \qquad \textit{Acceptable}$$
$$d/b < 7 \qquad \textit{Acceptable}$$

2. Check bending moment resistance at the apex

$$M_{rb} = M_r K_X K_M$$

$$M'_r = 761 \times 0.8 = 609 \text{ kN·m (from Beam Selection Tables and modified for wet service)}$$

$$K_{Zbg} = 0.901 \text{ for } L = 12 \text{ m and } B = 175 \text{ mm (from Table 2.11)}$$

$$M_r = 609 \times 0.901$$

$$= 549 \text{ kN·m}$$

$$K_X = 0.959 \text{ (from Table 8.2)}$$

$$K_M = \frac{1}{1+2.7\tan10°} = 0.677$$

$$M_{rb} = 549 \times 0.959 \times 0.677$$

$$= 356 \text{ kN·m} > 243 \text{ kN·m} \qquad\qquad Acceptable$$

Therefore, use $d_A = 1064$ mm at the apex.

3. a) Determine the depth required at the support:

$$V_f = \frac{w_f L}{2} = \frac{13.5 \times 12.0}{2} = 81.0 \text{ kN}$$

From Beam Selection Tables, try 175 × 456 mm and modify for wet service conditions:

$$V_r = 95.8 \times 0.87 = 83.3 \text{ kN} > 81.0 \text{ kN} \qquad\qquad Acceptable$$

b) Check that the beam volume is less than 2.0 m³:

$$Z = \frac{d_A + d_S}{2} \times \frac{bL}{\cos10°}$$

$$= \frac{1.064 + 0.456}{2} \times \frac{0.175 \times 12.0}{\cos10°}$$

$$= 1.62 \text{ m}^3 < 2.0 \text{ m}^3$$

Therefore, use $d_S = 456$ mm at the supports.

**8**

**Applications**

4. Check bending moment at the tangent point

$$K_1 = \frac{R_I + d_S}{L} = \frac{8400 + 456}{12000} = 0.738$$

$$K_2 = \frac{R_I + d_A}{L} - \frac{\tan\alpha}{2} = \frac{8400 + 1064}{12000} - \frac{\tan 10°}{2} = 0.701$$

$$\sin\lambda = \frac{2}{1 + 4K_2^2}\left[K_1 - 2K_2\sqrt{0.25 - K_1^2 + K_2^2}\right]$$

$$= \frac{2}{1 + 4 \times 0.701^2}\left[0.738 - 2 \times 0.701\sqrt{0.25 - 0.738^2 + 0.701^2}\right]$$

$$= 0.0783$$

$$\lambda = \sin^{-1} 0.0783 = 4.49°$$

$$d_T = \frac{\cos\alpha}{\cos(\alpha - \lambda)}(R_I + d_A) - R_I$$

$$= \frac{\cos 10°}{\cos(10° - 4.49°)}(8400 + 1064) - 8400$$

$$= 963 \text{ mm}$$

$$a_T = \frac{L}{2} - \sin\lambda\left[R_I + \frac{d_T}{2}\right]$$

$$= \frac{12000}{2} - 0.0783\left[8400 + \frac{963}{2}\right]$$

$$= 5300 \text{ mm}$$

$$M_f = 81.0 \times 5.30 - \frac{13.5 \times 5.30^2}{1} = 240 \text{ kN}\Sigma\text{m}$$

$$M_{rb} = M_r K_X K_M$$

From the Beam Selection Tables, obtain $M'_r$ for d = 950 mm, modify for wet service and $K_{Zbg}$ and calculate $M_r$ for $d_T$ = 963 mm.

$$M_r = 606 \times 0.8 \times 0.901 \times \left[\frac{963}{950}\right]^2 = 449 \text{ KN}\bullet\text{m}$$

$$M_{rb} = 449 \times 0.959 \times 1.0$$
$$= 430 \text{ kN}\bullet\text{m} > 238 \text{ kN}\bullet\text{m} \qquad\qquad \textit{Acceptable}$$

5. Check deflection

$$h_S = \frac{456}{\cos 10°} = 463 \text{ mm}$$

$$h_A = h_S + \frac{L}{2}(\tan\alpha - \tan\lambda) = 463 + \frac{12000}{2}(\tan 10° - \tan 4.49°) = 1050 \text{ mm}$$

$$u = \frac{h_A}{h_S} = \frac{1050}{463} = 2.27$$

From Beam Selection Tables, select $E_S I$ for $d_A = 1064$ mm and calculate $E_S I_A$:

$$E_S I_A = 218000 \times 10^9 \times \left[\frac{1050}{1064}\right]^3$$

$$= 210000 \times 10^9 \text{ N} \bullet \text{mm}^2$$

$$\Delta_V = \frac{5w L^4}{384 E_S I_A} K_\Delta$$

$$K_\Delta = 1.904 \text{ (from Table 8.13)}$$

For total load:

$$\Delta_V = \frac{5 \times 8.9 \times 12000^4 \times 1.904}{384 \times 210000 \times 10^9}$$

$$= 21.7 \text{ mm} < L/180 \qquad\qquad\qquad Acceptable$$

For live load:

$$\Delta_V = 21.7 \times \frac{5.9}{9.5} = 13.5 \text{ mm} < \frac{L}{240} \qquad\qquad Acceptable$$

Total horizontal deflection:

$$\Delta_H = \Delta_V \frac{2\tan\alpha}{\cos\alpha} = 21.7 \times \frac{2\tan 10°}{\cos 10°} = 7.8 \text{ mm}$$

8

Applications

Therefore, allow for a possible horizontal movement of 8 mm.

**Use a 175 mm wide 20f-E D.Fir-L beam varying in depth from 456 mm at the support to 963 mm at the tangent point to 1064 mm at the apex as shown below.**

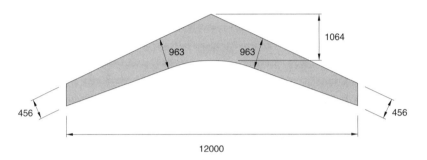

Table 8.8
**Constant X$_1$**

| Species | Service condition | Load duration | | |
|---|---|---|---|---|
| | | Standard | Permanent | Short term |
| D. Fir-L, Hem-Fir | Dry | 1.000 | 1.538 | 0.870 |
| | Wet | 1.176 | 1.809 | 1.023 |
| Spruce-Pine | Dry | 1.627 | 2.503 | 1.415 |
| | Wet | 1.915 | 2.946 | 1.665 |

Table 8.9a
**Constant X$_2$**

| Loading condition | X$_2$ |
|---|---|
| Uniformly distributed load * | 1.000 |
| All other types of loading | 1.591 |

Note:
* Over the entire span.

Table 8.9b
**Constant X$_3$**

| Member width b mm | X$_3$ |
|---|---|
| 80 | 1.475 |
| 130 | 1.000 |
| 175 | 0.788 |
| 215 | 0.669 |
| 265 | 0.566 |
| 315 | 0.493 |
| 365 | 0.438 |

**8**

Applications

| Table 8.10 Bending moment resistance at apex $M_{rt}$ (kN•m) for 38 mm laminations ($R_l$ = 8400 mm) | Depth at apex mm | $M_{rt}$ (kN•m) | | | | | |
|---|---|---|---|---|---|---|---|
| | | Roof slope $\alpha°$ | | | Roof slope | | |
| | | 5 | 10 | 15 | 1:12 | 2:12 | 3:12 |
| | 342 | 70.9 | 36.1 | 23.1 | 71.6 | 36.5 | 23.5 |
| | 380 | 83.5 | 43.2 | 27.8 | 84.4 | 43.7 | 28.2 |
| | 418 | 96.8 | 50.8 | 32.8 | 97.8 | 51.4 | 33.3 |
| | 456 | 110 | 58.8 | 38.2 | 112 | 59.5 | 38.7 |
| | 494 | 125 | 67.2 | 43.9 | 126 | 68.0 | 44.4 |
| | 532 | 139 | 76 | 49.8 | 141 | 76.9 | 50.5 |
| | 570 | 154 | 85.2 | 56.1 | 156 | 86.2 | 56.8 |
| | 608 | 169 | 94.7 | 62.6 | 171 | 95.8 | 63.4 |
| | 646 | 184 | 105 | 69.4 | 187 | 106 | 70.3 |
| | 684 | 200 | 115 | 76.5 | 202 | 116 | 77.5 |
| | 722 | 216 | 125 | 83.8 | 218 | 127 | 84.9 |
| | 760 | 232 | 136 | 91.4 | 234 | 137 | 92.6 |
| | 798 | 248 | 147 | 99.2 | 251 | 148 | 100 |
| | 836 | 264 | 158 | 107 | 267 | 160 | 109 |
| | 874 | 280 | 169 | 115 | 284 | 171 | 117 |
| | 912 | 296 | 181 | 124 | 300 | 183 | 125 |
| | 950 | 313 | 193 | 132 | 317 | 195 | 134 |
| | 988 | 329 | 205 | 141 | 333 | 207 | 143 |
| | 1026 | 345 | 217 | 150 | 350 | 219 | 152 |
| | 1064 | 362 | 229 | 159 | 367 | 232 | 161 |
| | 1102 | 378 | 242 | 169 | 384 | 244 | 171 |
| | 1140 | 395 | 254 | 178 | 400 | 257 | 180 |
| | 1178 | 411 | 267 | 188 | 417 | 270 | 190 |
| | 1216 | 428 | 280 | 198 | 434 | 283 | 200 |
| | 1254 | 444 | 292 | 208 | 451 | 296 | 210 |
| | 1292 | 461 | 305 | 218 | 467 | 309 | 220 |
| | 1330 | 477 | 319 | 228 | 484 | 322 | 231 |
| | 1368 | 493 | 332 | 238 | 501 | 335 | 241 |
| | 1406 | 510 | 345 | 249 | 517 | 349 | 252 |
| | 1444 | 526 | 358 | 259 | 534 | 362 | 262 |
| | 1482 | 542 | 372 | 270 | 551 | 376 | 273 |
| | 1520 | 558 | 385 | 281 | 567 | 389 | 284 |
| | 1558 | 574 | 399 | 292 | 584 | 403 | 295 |
| | 1596 | 590 | 412 | 303 | 600 | 417 | 306 |
| | 1634 | 606 | 426 | 314 | 616 | 430 | 317 |

Notes:
1. $M_{rt}$ is the lesser of the following formulae (refer to Section 8.2):

$$M_{rt} = \phi \, F_{tp} \, 2/3 \, A \, R_C \, K_{Ztp}$$
$$M_{rt} = \phi \, F_{tp} \, S \, K_{Ztp} \, K_R$$

2. In the calculation of $K_R$ (refer to Clause 6.5.6.6.3 of CSA O86.1), the constants A, B and C were linearly interpolated and rounded to two decimal places.

| Table 8.11 Bending moment resistance at apex $M_{rt}$ (kN•m) for 19 mm laminations ($R_1$ = 2800 mm) | Depth at apex mm | $M_{rt}$ (kN•m) | | | | | |
|---|---|---|---|---|---|---|---|
| | | Roof slope $\alpha°$ | | | Roof slope | | |
| | | 5 | 10 | 15 | 1:12 | 2:12 | 3:12 |
| | 342 | 59.6 | 37.4 | 25.9 | 60.4 | 37.8 | 26.2 |
| | 380 | 68.1 | 43.8 | 30.7 | 69.0 | 44.3 | 31.1 |
| | 418 | 76.6 | 50.4 | 35.8 | 77.7 | 51.0 | 36.2 |
| | 456 | 85.1 | 57.2 | 41.1 | 86.3 | 57.8 | 41.6 |
| | 494 | 93.5 | 64.1 | 46.6 | 94.9 | 64.8 | 47.1 |
| | 532 | 102 | 71.1 | 52.2 | 103 | 71.9 | 52.7 |
| | 570 | 110 | 78.1 | 58.0 | 112 | 79.0 | 58.6 |
| | 608 | 118 | 85.2 | 63.9 | 120 | 86.1 | 64.5 |
| | 646 | 126 | 92.3 | 70.0 | 128 | 93.3 | 70.6 |
| | 684 | 134 | 99.3 | 76.1 | 137 | 100 | 76.7 |
| | 722 | 142 | 106 | 82.3 | 145 | 108 | 82.9 |
| | 760 | 150 | 113 | 88.5 | 153 | 115 | 89.2 |
| | 798 | 157 | 121 | 94.9 | 160 | 122 | 95.5 |
| | 836 | 165 | 128 | 101 | 168 | 129 | 102 |
| | 874 | 172 | 134 | 108 | 176 | 136 | 108 |
| | 912 | 180 | 141 | 114 | 183 | 143 | 115 |
| | 950 | 187 | 148 | 121 | 191 | 150 | 121 |
| | 988 | 194 | 155 | 127 | 198 | 157 | 128 |
| | 1026 | 201 | 162 | 134 | 206 | 164 | 134 |
| | 1064 | 208 | 168 | 140 | 213 | 170 | 140 |
| | 1102 | 215 | 175 | 147 | 220 | 177 | 147 |
| | 1140 | 222 | 182 | 153 | 227 | 184 | 153 |
| | 1178 | 229 | 188 | 159 | 234 | 190 | 160 |
| | 1216 | 235 | 195 | 166 | 241 | 197 | 166 |
| | 1254 | 242 | 201 | 172 | 248 | 203 | 173 |
| | 1292 | 248 | 207 | 179 | 255 | 210 | 179 |
| | 1330 | 255 | 214 | 185 | 261 | 216 | 185 |
| | 1368 | 261 | 220 | 192 | 268 | 222 | 192 |
| | 1406 | 268 | 226 | 198 | 275 | 229 | 198 |
| | 1444 | 274 | 232 | 205 | 281 | 235 | 204 |
| | 1482 | 280 | 238 | 211 | 288 | 241 | 211 |
| | 1520 | 287 | 244 | 217 | 294 | 247 | 217 |
| | 1558 | 293 | 250 | 224 | 301 | 253 | 223 |
| | 1596 | 299 | 256 | 230 | 307 | 259 | 229 |
| | 1634 | 305 | 262 | 236 | 313 | 265 | 236 |

**8**

**Applications**

Notes:
1. $M_{rt}$ is the lesser of the following formulae (refer to Section 8.2):
$M_{rt} = \phi\, F_{tp}\, 2/3\, A\, R_C\, K_{Ztp}$
$M_{rt} = \phi\, F_{tp}\, S\, K_{Ztp}\, K_R$
2. In the calculation of $K_R$ (refer to Clause 6.5.6.6.3 of CSA O86.1), the constants A, B and C were linearly interpolated and rounded to two decimal places.

Table 8.12
**Shear load coefficient $C_V$ for tapered beams with uniformly distributed loads**

| $\dfrac{L}{d_s}$ | $m = 2\dfrac{(d_A - d_S)}{L}$ | | | | | |
|---|---|---|---|---|---|---|
| | 0.20 | 0.10 | 0.05 | 0.00 | - 0.04 | - 0.08 |
| 10 | 4.40 | 4.49 | 4.32 | 3.97 | 3.58 | 2.42 |
| 15 | 4.09 | 4.26 | 4.16 | 3.77 | 3.13 | 0.93 |
| 20 | 3.95 | 4.11 | 4.08 | 3.69 | 2.40 | 0.23 |
| 30 | 3.83 | 3.93 | 3.99 | 3.58 | 0.91 | - |

Note:
For other loading conditions refer to Clause 6.5.7.4 of CSA O86.1.

Table 8.13
**Deflection factor $K_\Delta$**

| u | $K_\Delta$ |
|---|---|
| 1.1 | 1.083 |
| 1.2 | 1.163 |
| 1.3 | 1.242 |
| 1.4 | 1.318 |
| 1.5 | 1.393 |
| 1.6 | 1.466 |
| 1.7 | 1.537 |
| 1.8 | 1.607 |
| 1.9 | 1.675 |
| 2.0 | 1.742 |
| 2.1 | 1.808 |
| 2.2 | 1.872 |
| 2.3 | 1.935 |
| 2.4 | 1.997 |
| 2.5 | 2.057 |
| 2.6 | 2.117 |
| 2.7 | 2.176 |
| 2.8 | 2.233 |
| 2.9 | 2.290 |
| 3.0 | 2.346 |
| 3.1 | 2.401 |

# 8.5 Pyramidal, Domed and A-frame Buildings

## General

Wood components are used in a number of configurations and combinations to construct domes, pyramidal forms with varying numbers of sides, and A-frame structures for a wide variety of uses from public assembly to storage.

The design of many of these structures will be assisted by the use of a three-dimensional frame analysis program. Such a program will permit a thorough investigation of the distribution of forces through the structure and an indication of the expected deflections due to a range of loading combinations. Individual components are designed in accordance with the procedures set out in Chapters 2 to 8 of this manual.

Segmented plywood stressed-skin panels have been used to provide economical and easily erected buildings for sand and salt storage. Larger structures for ore, sugar, phosphate and other materials usually incorporate straight or curved glulam members as the main structural elements.

Because wood is superior to many other construction materials in resisting chemical attack, it is well suited for storage and process buildings for corrosive products.

## Pyramidal Buildings

Shown below is an example of a square based pyramid. The base form may also be hexagonal, octagonal or another number of sides. The hip and secondary framing members are usually of glulam. The secondary framing may be arranged perpendicular to the outside walls and run up the sloped roof plane, or to span between the hip members and run concentrically to the outer walls.

The spacing of these members will depend on the choice of sheathing or framing. The structure is usually exposed in this type of building application and often makes use of plank decking for aesthetic reasons. In this case, the Decking Selection Tables in Section 2.2 may be used to determine the appropriate spacing of supports for various thicknesses of deck. Other options include joists or wood I-joists framing over or into the sides of the secondary members to support drywall or other ceiling materials.

Lateral forces at the base of the hip members are usually resisted by perimeter beams or steel ties in the line of the outer walls. When a steel tie is used, the effect of the elongation of the tie under load must be investigated for any possible effect on other structural components or masonry construction.

**Square based pyramid**

*Typical spans:*
10 to 30 m
wall length

*Common applications:*
Churches, showrooms, commercial, auditoria

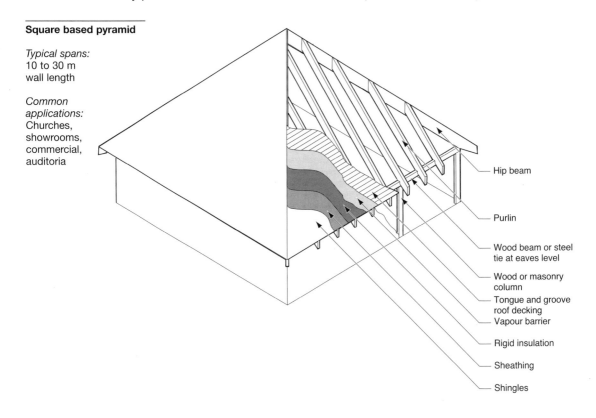

Hip beam

Purlin

Wood beam or steel tie at eaves level

Wood or masonry column

Tongue and groove roof decking

Vapour barrier

Rigid insulation

Sheathing

Shingles

## Domes

The ability to curve large glulam members allows the development of a very efficient frame profile, which at the same time creates an appropriate enclosure for cone-shaped storage piles. In most applications radial glulam members support glulam or heavy timber secondary framing, which in turn supports wood joists and plywood or composite sheathing. This shape of building very effectively supports conveyor loads applied at the peak. A three-dimensional analysis to include the "ring purlins" as part of the frame design will contribute to a more efficient structure. Base reactions are usually resisted in the foundations, which range from buttressed piers to ring beams as part of a tank wall.

**Domes**

*Typical spans:*
15 to 60 m dia.

*Common applications:*
Storage buildings

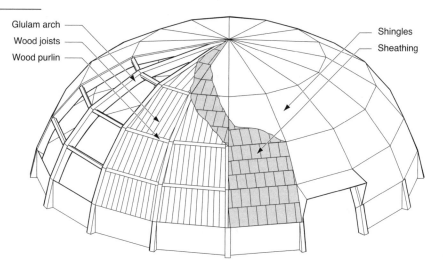

Glulam arch

Wood joists

Wood purlin

Shingles

Sheathing

**8**

**Applications**

## A-Frames

This basic frame has a wide range of applications where ease of construction and economy are important. Very large spans are possible and often provide the most economical option to frame large storage and process buildings.

For the smaller structures, sawn lumber, glulam and SCL components may be suitable for frame members. These members support plank decking or joist and sheathing. In designing these structures, consideration should be given to the protection of frame legs, which may be exposed to the weather.

A-frame buildings in excess of a 10 m span usually incorporate glulam frames spaced from 4 to 6 m. Framing between these members is often prefabricated stressed-skin panels, but may incorporate purlins and plank decking.

Again, the shape of the frame is very efficient and can easily incorporate a conveyor below the peak without compromising storage capacity. Buildings in excess of 200 m in length have been constructed utilizing this type of frame. The leg may be either straight or curved to suit the application. Spans in excess of 60 m will usually require a field-connected splice due to shipping restrictions. Glulam fabricators will be able to offer valuable advice based on previous experience in the design of these buildings.

**A-frames**

*Typical spans:*
10 to 80 m

*Common applications:*
Residences, commercial and storage buildings, churches

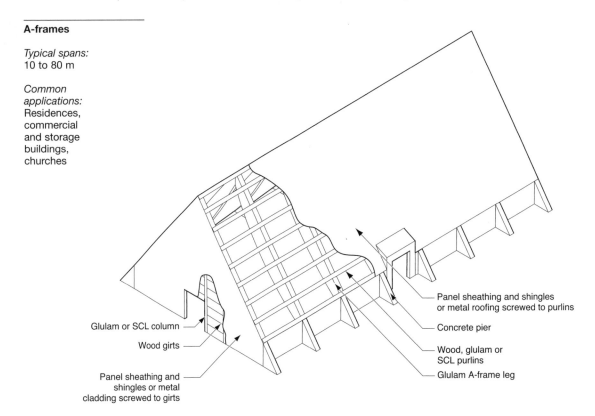

Glulam or SCL column

Wood girts

Panel sheathing and shingles or metal cladding screwed to girts

Panel sheathing and shingles or metal roofing screwed to purlins

Concrete pier

Wood, glulam or SCL purlins

Glulam A-frame leg

# 8.6 Heavy Timber Trusses

## General

Heavy timber trusses are usually exposed and take advantage of the heavy timber rating afforded to members meeting the minimum dimensional requirements as set out in *NBCC* 1995. Timber trusses can be constructed in a wide variety of shapes to suit particular architectural requirements or maximum economy.

The most common forms of heavy timber trusses are discussed below.

### Bowstring

The bowstring truss is very efficient under balanced loading conditions since the web forces are small. However, this roof shape is prone to significant snow accumulation on the leeward side of the roof (unbalanced loading), which results in higher web forces and larger connections. A tapered build-up at the peak or eave will alter the profile sufficiently to reduce the severity of the snow accumulation.

The radius of curvature of the top chord is most often equal to the span, creating a rise of 0.134 × span. The top chord is usually manufactured from glulam due to the curvature required.

**8**

Applications

**Bowstring trusses**

*Typical spans:*
15 to 50 m

*Common applications:*
Arenas, storage buildings

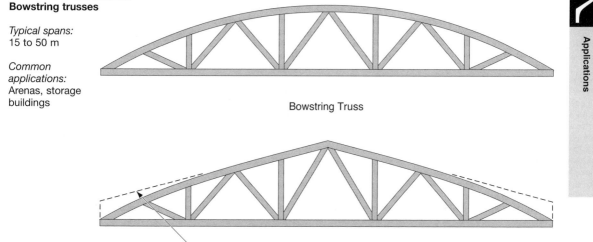

Bowstring Truss

Optional buildup

Variation of
Bowstring Truss Design

## Parallel Chord

These trusses are usually the least efficient since web forces are high, requiring the connections to be somewhat complex and expensive. Economies can be realized, however, in multiple span applications for large buildings where a flat roof is desired. A span-to-depth ratio of between 8:1 and 10:1 results in the greatest economy and stiffness.

**Parallel chord (flat) trusses**

*Typical spans:*
8 to 30 m

*Common applications:*
Indusrial and storage buildings

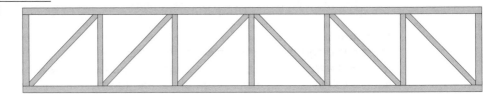

## Pitched

Pitched trusses are generally more efficient than flat trusses but less efficient than bowstring trusses. A pitched truss may be manufactured from a range of wood products since no curvature of the top chord is required. A number of different web systems may be utilized. A span-to-depth ratio of 5:1 to 6:1 is usually employed.

**Pitched trusses**

*Typical spans:*
8 to 30 m

*Common applications:*
Indusrial, agri-cultural and storage buildings, public assem-bly, gymnasia

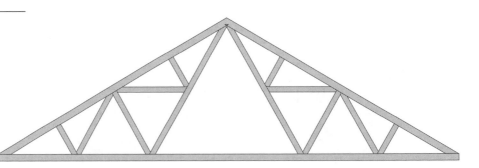

## Truss Components

The wide range of truss types and profiles possible, together with a number of relatively new products such as the timber rivet and structural composite lumber (SCL), have expanded the scope of applications for trusses in recent years. The following are the most common materials specified for use in truss manufacture. For proprietary products such as SCL, the manufacturer should be contacted for recommended applications.

### Chords

Glulam is generally used for truss chords since it is available in long lengths and may be curved to almost any shape required. SCL has the same advantage of high strength and long lengths but is not available in curved sections. Sawn timber may be suitable for shorter span applications but may involve splicing for the longer lengths generally required for these truss members. Chords are most often made up of one member (monochord) when manufactured from glulam, and multiple members when using sawn timber.

### Webs

Sawn timber is normally used for web members. However, glulam may be substituted if consistent appearance is a factor. Steel rods are sometimes used where force reversal does not occur.

### Joints

The selection of the connectors will depend on the materials selected for the truss chords and webs. Split rings and bolts are suitable for wood-to-wood connections, shear plates and bolts for metal-to-wood load transfer. Timber rivets with steel side plates can significantly reduce the connection fabrication and assembly time for truss work.

## Truss Spacing

The greatest possible spacing between trusses is usually the most economical but will be determined by such considerations as building layout, architectural requirements and the nature of the secondary framing system proposed. An analysis of various truss spacings and secondary framing alternatives should be undertaken before a final configuration is selected.

## Design Considerations

Trusses designed in accordance with the provisions of the *NBCC* are subject to a number of loading patterns and load combinations. Forces in the members will often be subject to reversal. Attention must be paid to the design of both members and connections as a result of these conditions.

Chord members will be subject to bending in addition to axial forces when the load is applied uniformly along the chord. In the top chords of bowstring trusses, eccentric moments due to the product of the axial force and the

8

Applications

eccentricity will oppose the moment resulting from the applied load. The eccentricity between the centreline of the chord and a straight line between panel points may be estimated as:

$$e = \frac{a^2}{8R}$$

where:

 e = eccentricity

 a = distance between panel points

 R = radius of top chord

The degree of end fixity of truss members is somewhere between a pinned end and a fixed end. For simplicity, members are generally assumed to behave as if they were pin connected with the effective length equal to the distance between panel points.

Good practice dictates that truss joints should be designed to minimize eccentricities. Where eccentricity is unavoidable, joints must be checked for adequate horizontal shear capacity as outlined in Section 7.1.

Consideration should be given to a period of seasoning for sawn timbers used in truss manufacture. Project scheduling may render this procedure impractical, however, it will permit a 25% increase in connection capacity over unseasoned timber and reduce the effects of shrinkage.

Splices in chord members should be made between panel points wherever possible. When compression splices in chords transfer forces in direct bearing, a 3 mm steel separator plate should be installed between bearing surfaces to prevent interlocking of end grain.

Heel connections transfer the horizontal load component from the top chord of a bowstring or pitched truss and from the end diagonal of a parallel chord truss to the bottom chord. Welded steel assemblies are generally used for this purpose. Either the top chord or diagonal bears directly on a steel heel plate to which straps are welded to transfer load via shear plates or timber rivets to the bottom chord.

## Camber Recommendations

For bowstring and pitched trusses usually only the bottom chord is cambered. Consequently, the effective depth of the truss should be modified accordingly in stress computations. Both top and bottom chords are cambered for flat trusses.

The following formula provides an empirical guideline for calculating pre-camber dimensions for different truss types.

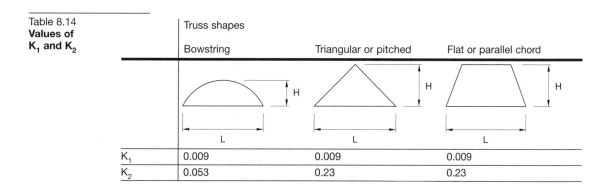

Table 8.14
**Values of**
**$K_1$ and $K_2$**

| Truss shapes | | |
|---|---|---|
| Bowstring | Triangular or pitched | Flat or parallel chord |
| $K_1$ | 0.009 | 0.009 | 0.009 |
| $K_2$ | 0.053 | 0.23 | 0.23 |

$$\text{Camber} = \frac{K_1 L^3}{H} + \frac{K_2 L^2}{H} \text{ (mm)}$$

where:

$L$  = Truss span (m)

$H$  = Truss rise (m)

Values for $K_1$ and $K_2$ for three truss types are listed in Table 8.14.

**Permanent Bracing**

Bracing is required to provide resistance to lateral loadings and to ensure that the trusses are held in position. Restraint is required both parallel and perpendicular to the plane of the trusses.

Lateral forces acting in the plane of the truss can be resisted by one of the following systems:

1. Knee bracing between the truss and supporting column

2. Columns integral with the truss to provide a rigid frame

3. Diaphragm action of the roof sheathing

4. Permanent horizontal bracing panels

In system 3 and 4, intermediate or end walls may be used to transfer shear loads to the foundations.

Lateral loads acting perpendicular to the plane of the truss are normally transferred to the sidewalls by the diaphragm action of the roof sheathing. Adequate connections at the perimeter of the diaphragm must be provided in each case.

**8**

**Applications**

In the absence of rigid frame or diaphragm action, a horizontal bracing system in the plane of either the top or bottom chord must be used. Such bracing systems must be supplemented by veritical cross bracing between the trusses to ensure that forces are transferred to the appropriate planes.

Stability bracing consists of vertical cross bracing in alternate bays and continuous lines of T-struts between bottom chords. This system should be used in addition to a bracing system designed to resist lateral loads. The struts should be spaced so that the slenderness ratio of the bottom chord is less than 50, with a maximum spacing being 10 m.

### Erection Bracing

Adequate erection bracing should be designed in accordance with sound engineering principles to suit the selected erection procedure by an engineer engaged by the erector.

# 8.7        Light Frame Trusses

## General

Light frame wood trusses are widely used in residential, agricultural and commercial construction. Light frame wood trusses are prefabricated by pressing galvanized steel truss plates into wood members that are precut and assembled in a jig (refer to Section 7.8). Many sizes of plates are manufactured to suit any shape or size of truss or load to be carried. Most trusses are fabricated using 38 × 64 mm to 38 × 184 mm visually graded and machine stress-rated lumber.

## History

Traditionally, light frame wood roof structures have been built on site using rafters, ceiling joists and collar ties. These components create a simple truss where the rafters act as the top chord; the ceiling joist functions as the bottom chord and the collar tie acts as a compressive strut. This system is simple to build but is labour intensive and limited to use on relatively short spans.

The rafter and ceiling joist approach led to the development of site-built light trusses using nailed plywood gussets. This system provided longer spans but required considerable time to build the trusses. About the same time, multi-leaf trusses were also being built using the split ring connector.

Most light trusses are now built using the metal connector plate that was developed in the United States in the 1950s. The popularity of this system grew rapidly since trusses could be prefabricated using highly efficient production techniques and machinery. In addition, metal plate connected trusses could be built for use on long or short spans.

In 1972, truss plate manufacturers in Canada formed the Truss Plate Institute of Canada (TPIC). There are also a number of regional fabricator associations in British Columbia, Alberta, Saskatchewan/Manitoba, Ontario, Quebec and Atlantic Canada. The Canadian Wood Truss Association (CWTA) is a national organization representing truss fabricators.

## Truss Shapes

Light trusses may be manufactured to suit virtually any roof profile. Truss shape and size is restricted only by manufacturing capabilities, shipping limitations and handling considerations. Some of the most common truss shapes are described below. Many of these shapes can be designed for a variety of bearing conditions such as simple or multiple spans. Cantilevers and overhangs can also be provided at one or both ends. Flat trusses may be designed for bottom chord bearing or top chord bearing where the supporting beam is to be hidden. The following are the most common shapes using industry terminology. The web arrangement is done at the detailed design state.

8

Applications

| | Triangular | These trusses may be simple span, multiple bearing, or cantilevered. Where the truss height exceeds approximately 3 m, a piggyback system (see below) may be needed due to transportation restrictions. |
|---|---|---|
| | Mono | This shape may be simple span, multiple span, or cantilevered. Top chord bearing is possible. |
| | Inverted | The inverted truss is used to provide a vaulted ceiling along a portion of the span. |
| | Cut-off (Bobtail, Stubend) | This shape may be used where a triangular truss will not fit. |
| | Dual Slope | This truss provides an asymmetric roof slope. |
| | Ridge Truss | The ridge truss provides a stepped roof appearance. |
| | Piggyback | The piggyback truss is a combination of a gable end truss on top of a hip truss, which can be transported in two sections. It is used when a single triangular truss is too large to transport. |

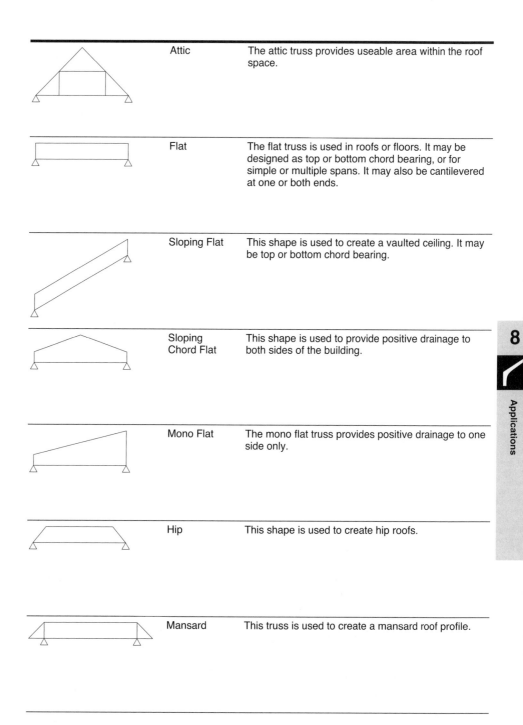

| | | |
|---|---|---|
| | Attic | The attic truss provides useable area within the roof space. |
| | Flat | The flat truss is used in roofs or floors. It may be designed as top or bottom chord bearing, or for simple or multiple spans. It may also be cantilevered at one or both ends. |
| | Sloping Flat | This shape is used to create a vaulted ceiling. It may be top or bottom chord bearing. |
| | Sloping Chord Flat | This shape is used to provide positive drainage to both sides of the building. |
| | Mono Flat | The mono flat truss provides positive drainage to one side only. |
| | Hip | This shape is used to create hip roofs. |
| | Mansard | This truss is used to create a mansard roof profile. |

8

Applications

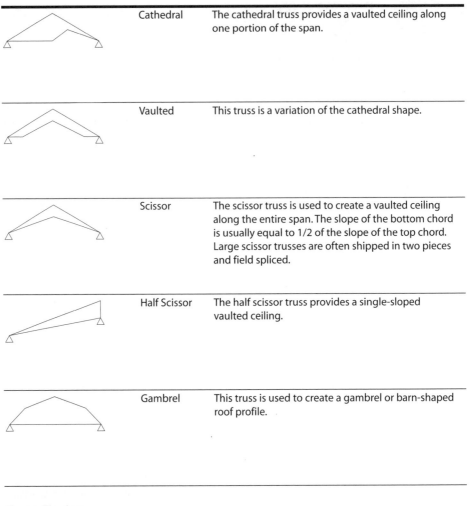

| | Cathedral | The cathedral truss provides a vaulted ceiling along one portion of the span. |
| | Vaulted | This truss is a variation of the cathedral shape. |
| | Scissor | The scissor truss is used to create a vaulted ceiling along the entire span. The slope of the bottom chord is usually equal to 1/2 of the slope of the top chord. Large scissor trusses are often shipped in two pieces and field spliced. |
| | Half Scissor | The half scissor truss provides a single-sloped vaulted ceiling. |
| | Gambrel | This truss is used to create a gambrel or barn-shaped roof profile. |

## Truss Design

Typically, the building designer or builder will contract with the truss fabricator, who will supply a truss layout and structural design of the trusses. The truss plate manufacturer's engineer usually reviews and seals the individual truss designs on behalf of the truss fabricator. Most of the design requirements are based on CSA O86, and either Part 4 or Part 9 of the *NBCC*, whichever is applicable. In addition, members of TPIC use additional design criteria contained in their publication titled *Truss Design Procedures and Specifications for Light Metal-Plate-Connected Wood Trusses (Limit States Design).*

The TPIC procedures depend on the type of construction. However, the design of the connections is carried out in accordance with CSA O86 regardless of the building type as discussed below:

### Houses and Small Buildings

Trusses for houses and small buildings are designed in accordance with TPIC Truss Design Procedures and Specifications for Light Metal-Plate-Connected Wood Trusses as referenced in Part 9 of the *NBCC*.

### Commercial or Industrial Buildings

Trusses for commercial or industrial construction, and some other small buildings, are governed by the requirements of Part 4 of *NBCC,* and are designed in accordance with CSA O86.

### Agricultural Buildings

Trusses for agricultural buildings are also designed in accordance with Part 4 of *NBCC* and CSA O86 with some modifications based on the *Canadian Farm Building Code* where it is accepted.

### Building Design Considerations

The building designer does not generally design the truss, but must provide the truss designer with design loads and building layout information. Generally, the structural framing drawings should include load diagrams or descriptions of applicable *NBCC* loadings plus any special loading conditions.

The building designer should also be concerned with the structure that supports the trusses. Bearing walls must be designed for uniform loading and for concentrated loads under girder trusses. Headers and lintels should also be designed to support the loading applied by the trusses.

The building designer should also ensure that all connections between the trusses and support framing, such as hangers and uplift anchors, accommodate horizontal, vertical or other reactions and displacements.

For light frame trusses, specification of temporary bracing is typically the responsibility of the building contractor and the truss erector. For trusses with large spans (over 18 m span) and with special requirements, it is recommended that the building contractor should retain professional assistance on the site to ensure adequate bracing is in place for the safety of the workers during erection. Specification of permanent bracing is typically the responsibility of the building designer. Temporary bracing is required to keep the trusses plumb, assure correct truss spacing and prevent them from tipping in the wind during erection. Permanent bracing is required to ensure that the trusses are integrated into the overall building system to; prevent buckling of web members loaded in compression, share loads between adjacent trusses and transfer lateral forces to diaphragms. Figure 8.2 illustrates standard bracing methods recommended by TPIC.

**8**

Applications

Figure 8.2a
**Step 1:**
**Bracing first**
**truss**

Long span trusses are braced securely at the end of the building. Shorter trusses can be supported laterally by a single gable end brace. The ground braces should be located directly in line with all rows of top chord continuous lateral bracing, otherwise the top chord of the first truss can bend sideways and allow the trusses to shift, putting a substantial strain on all connections of the bracing system. Scabs should not be nailed to the end of the building to brace the first truss. These scabs can break off or pull out, thus allowing a total collapse.

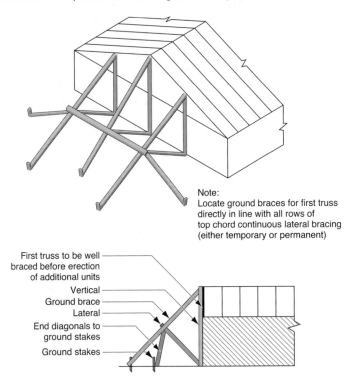

Note:
Locate ground braces for first truss
directly in line with all rows of
top chord continuous lateral bracing
(either temporary or permanent)

First truss to be well
braced before erection
of additional units

Vertical

Ground brace

Lateral

End diagonals to
ground stakes

Ground stakes

Figure 8.2b
**Step 2:**
**Cross-bracing**
**subsequent**
**trusses to**
**prevent**
**buckling**

As trusses are continously set in place, sufficient temporary bracing is applied to hold the trusses plumb, in alignment and secure untill permanent bracing, decking and/or sheathing can be installed. Temporary bracing should not be less than 38 × 89 mm lumber and should be as long as possible. The use of short spacer pieces of lumber between adjacent trusses is not considered a means of bracing. Temporary bracing should be nailed with two 3-1/2" double headed nails at every intersection with the braced members. The practice of removing bracing to adjust spacing of trusses as sheathing is applied can cause trusses to topple if a key connection is removed at the wrong time. Therefore, exact spacing of trusses should be maintained as temporary bracing is applied. Cross bracing should be installed as soon as the first few trusses are in place, in the vertical plane, between trusses, together with continuous lateral braces fastened to the top and bottom chords to prevent the trusses from toppling.

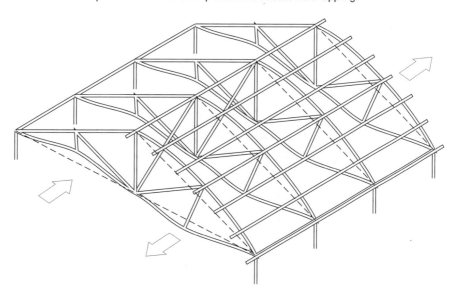

**8**

**Applications**

Figure 8.2c
**Step 3:**
**Temporary**
**bracing of top**
**chord plane**

Truss top chords are very susceptible to lateral buckling before they are braced or sheathed. Continuous lateral bracing shold be installed within 150 mm of the ridge line or centre line and at approximatly 2.4 to 3 m intervals between the ridge line of sloped trusses or centre line of flat trusses and the eaves. Diagonals, set at 45 between the lateral bracing, form the required stability of the top chord. On longer span trusses, lateral bracing and diagonals may require closer spacing. If possible the continuous lateral bracing should be located on the underside of the top chord so that it does not have to be removed as sheathing is applied. This will ensure that the trusses are held securely during installation of the decking. Bracing lumber should be no less than 38 × 89 mm by 3.05 m long.

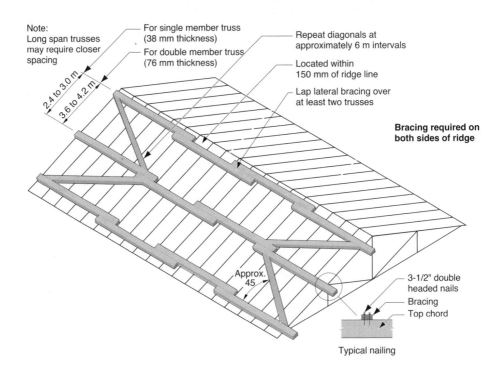

Note:
Long span trusses may require closer spacing

For single member truss (38 mm thickness)
For double member truss (76 mm thickness)

Repeat diagonals at approximately 6 m intervals

Located within 150 mm of ridge line

Lap lateral bracing over at least two trusses

**Bracing required on both sides of ridge**

2.4 to 3.0 m
3.6 to 4.2 m

Approx. 45

3-1/2" double headed nails
Bracing
Top chord

Typical nailing

Figure 8.2d
**Step 4:**
**Temporary**
**bracing of web**
**member plane**

Temporary bracing of the web member plane is usually installed at the same location specified on the engineering plan for permanent bracing. Permanent lateral web bracing should be called out on the truss design to reduce the buckling length of the individual web members. The bracing can form part of the temporary and permanent web bracing system. Sets of diagonal bracing should not be spaced more than 6 m apart (clear space between end of one set of braces and start of another set).

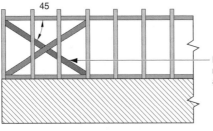

45

Diagonal bracing to be 38 × 89 mm minimum nailed with two 3-1/2" nails at each end and each intermediate member

Figure 8.2e
**Step 5:**
**Temporary**
**bracing of**
**bottom chord**
**plane**

To hold the proper spacing of the bottom chord, continuous lateral bracing at no greater than 2.4 to 3 m on centre along truss length is used for the full length of the building, secured to the bottom chord. Diagonal bracing at 45 between laterals will stabalize this bracing system. The bracing is usually left in place to become part of the permanent bracing system. Once the temporary bracing is properly installed, permanent bracing and decking can be installed. Concentrated loads from sheathing or roofing material should not be placed on trusses. These loads should be spread evenly over a large area to prevent overloading of any one truss. A limit of eight sheets of plywood should be placed on any pair of trusses and should be located adjacent to the supports.

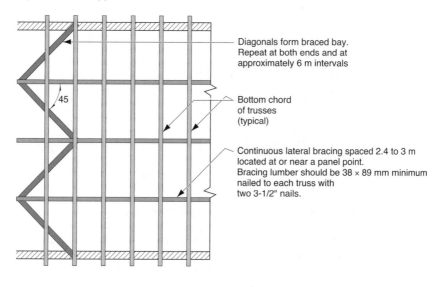

Diagonals form braced bay.
Repeat at both ends and at
approximately 6 m intervals

Bottom chord
of trusses
(typical)

Continuous lateral bracing spaced 2.4 to 3 m
located at or near a panel point.
Bracing lumber should be 38 × 89 mm minimum
nailed to each truss with
two 3-1/2" nails.

Note:
Where lateral bracing is shown on the truss design drawings, it must be installed so that truss will support design loads.

8

Applications

Figure 8.2f
**Step 6:**
**Permanent**
**bracing of top**
**chord plane**
**(large**
**buildings)**

If plywood floor or roof sheathing is properly applied with staggered joints and adequate nailing, a continous diaphragm action is developed to resist lateral movement at the top chord, and additional bracing in the plane is generally not required. Some metal roofing materials may act as a diaphragm when properly lapped and nailed, but selection and use of these materials is at the discretion of the building designer. If purlins are used, spaced not to exceed the buckling length at the top chord, diagonal bracing should be applied to the underside of the top chord to prevent lateral shifting of the purlins. The diagonal bracing should be installed on both sides of the ridge line in all end bays. If the building exceeds 18 m in length, this bracing should be repeated at intervals not exceeding 6 m.

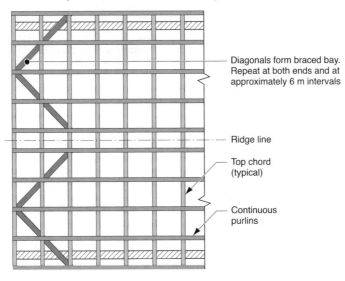

Diagonals form braced bay. Repeat at both ends and at approximately 6 m intervals

Ridge line

Top chord (typical)

Continuous purlins

Figure 8.2g
**Step 7:**
**Permanent**
**lateral bracing**
**to web**
**member or**
**bottom chord**
**plane (all**
**buildings)**

Permanent bracing in web and bottom chord planes is usually applied as temporary bracing (Steps 4 and 5). Lateral bracing of compression web members is a typical method to prevent buckling. The method used to anchor the lateral bracing must be specified by the designer. Bottom chord bracing helps to maintain truss spacing, also can resist buckling caused by stress reversal. Multiple-bearing or cantilevered trusses can result in compressive forces in bottom chords.

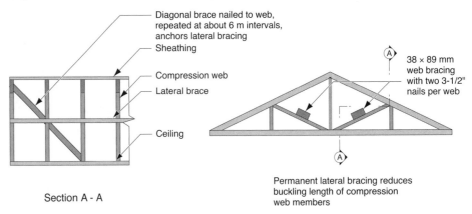

Diagonal brace nailed to web, repeated at about 6 m intervals, anchors lateral bracing

Sheathing

Compression web

Lateral brace

Ceiling

38 × 89 mm web bracing with two 3-1/2" nails per web

Section A - A

Permanent lateral bracing reduces buckling length of compression web members

Note:
Where lateral bracing is shown on the truss design drawings, it must be installed so that truss will support design loads.

# 8.8 Permanent Wood Foundations

## General Information

The permanent wood foundation (PWF) is a load bearing stud wall system designed for below grade use in accordance with CSA Standard S406 *Construction of Preserved Wood Foundations.* Three basic types of PWFs are depicted in Figure 8.3: concrete slab or wood sleeper floor basement, suspended wood floor basement and an unexcavated or partially excavated crawl space.

Figure 8.3
**Types of PWFs**

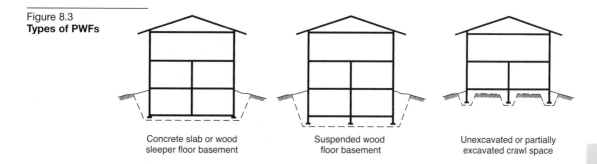

| Concrete slab or wood sleeper floor basement | Suspended wood floor basement | Unexcavated or partially excavated crawl space |

## Lumber
Lumber used in PWFs is produced in accordance with CSA Standard O141 *Softwood Lumber.* All structural members in a PWF must be No.2 grade or better. Typical stud sizes are 38 × 89 mm, 38 × 140 mm and 38 × 184 mm.

## Plywood
Plywood used as exterior wall sheathing in PWFs is an unsanded, exterior type with at least four plies and is limited to certain species for reasons of treatability and structural performance. It should, in all other regards, conform to CSA Standard O121, *Douglas Fir Plywood (DFP),* or CSA Standard O151, *Canadian Softwood Plywood (CSP).* Minimum plywood thickness requirements are shown in Table 8.15.

Table 8.15
**Plywood sheathing requirements**

| Plywood alignment on wall | Stud spacing, mm | Maximum backfill heights, m for plywood thickness | | |
|---|---|---|---|---|
| | | 12.5 mm | 15.5 mm | 18.5 mm |
| Face grain perpendicular to studs | 300 | 2.9 | 3.2 | 3.2 |
| | 400 | 2.2 | 2.6 | 3.2 |
| Face grain parallel to studs | 300 | 2.1 | 2.7 | 3.0 |
| | 400 | 1.3 | 2.0 | 2.2 |

Notes:
1. Backfill height is the distance from the top of the footing plate to grade level.
2. Plywood thicknesses shown are for unsanded sheathing grade plywood having at least four plies.
3. Four-ply plywood shall be installed with face grain perpendicular to studs.

8

Applications

## Preservative Treatment and Certification

With certain exceptions, all lumber and plywood used in PWFs must be preservative treated in accordance with CSA Standard O80.15, *Preservative Treatment of
Wood for Building Foundation Systems, Basements and Crawl Spaces by Pressure
Process.* CSA O80.15 provides for a higher retention of preservative in the wood
than is normal for treatment of wood in ground contact. Not all species are treatable and lumber used in PWFs must conform to the list of treatable species given
in Table 8.16. Designers can determine that treatable species are used by specifying that lumber and plywood be identified by the qualification mark for PWFs.

CSA Standard O322, *Procedure for Certification of Pressure-Treated Wood
Materials for use in Preserved Wood Foundations* is used to qualify treating
plants by recognized inspection agencies for stamping treated PWF material. A
facsimile of this stamp is shown in Figure 8.4 and should appear on all structural
lumber and sheathing used in a PWF where treated material is required.

| Table 8.16 **Treatable lumber species** | Species combinations | Treatable species | Grade stamp identification |
|---|---|---|---|
| | D.Fir-L | Coast Douglas fir | D Fir (N) |
| | Hem-Fir | Western hemlock | W Hem(N) or Hem-Fir(N) |
| | | Amabilis fir | Am Fir(N) or Hem-Fir(N) |
| | S-P-F | Lodgepole pine | L Pine(N) |
| | | Jack Pine | J Pine(N) |
| | | Alpine Fir | Alpine Fir(N) |
| | | Balsam Fir | B Fir(N) |
| | Northern | Red pine | R Pine(N) |
| | | Western white pine | W.W.Pine |
| | | Eastern white pine | East White Pine or (EW Pine) (N) |
| | | Eastern hemlock | Hem-Tam (N) |

Notes:
1.  Douglas fir lumber is restricted to Pacific coast Douglas fir, in conformance with CSA O80.15.
2.  Hem-Fir is the only species combination where all species are suitable for preservative treatment.

Figure 8.4
**Example of
qualification
mark**

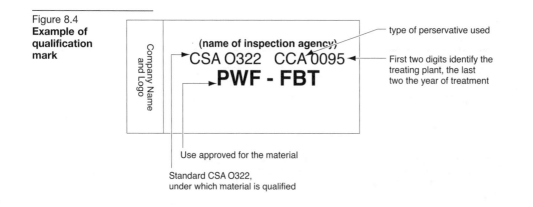

Designers should be aware that the appearance of other treated wood products is similar to PWF material. However, treated wood products not intended for PWFs do not have the same degree of treatment and do not normally conform to the more stringent requirements for PWFs.

### Fasteners and Connectors

Nails used in PWFs must be in accordance with CSA B111. Hot dipped galvanized or stainless steel nails are required for all treated material.

Framing anchors and straps should be used wherever the magnitude of loads is such that it is impractical to transfer the loads through nailing alone.

CSA S406 gives details on construction methods and fastening techniques that are applicable for use in typical PWFs.

## Design

### Studs

Provided that the PWF studwall is adequately braced by the floor structure at the top and bottom, and where practically no surcharge exists, the following formulae may be used for design (refer to Figure 8.5). These formulae are applicable to PWFs with concrete slab or wood sleeper floors. For suspended floors refer to CSA O86 Section A.5.5.12.

**8**

**Applications**

Figure 8.5
**Dimensions and loading of PWF studs with concrete slab or wood sleeper floors (without surcharge)**

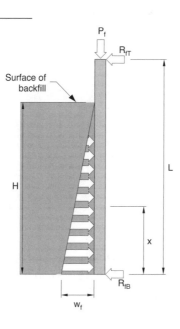

L = stud length (mm)
x = location of maximum moment (mm)
H = height of backfill (mm)

1. The studs must be designed to satisfy the following interaction equation

$$\frac{M_f + P_f \Delta}{M_r} + \left(\frac{P_f}{P_r}\right)^2 \le 1.0$$

where:

$M_f$ = maximum factored bending moment

$$= \frac{w_f H^2}{6L}\left[L - H + \frac{2}{3}\sqrt{\frac{H^3}{3L}}\right]$$

$w_f$ = factored loading (N/mm)
   = 1.5 × specified lateral soil pressure (kN/m$^2$) × stud spacing (m)

$P_f$ = factored axial load on stud (N)

$M_r$ = factored bending moment resistance taken from Joist Selection Tables in Section 2.3 modified for permanent load duration ($K_D = 0.65$) and treatment factor for preservative treated, incised lumber used in dry service conditions ($K_T = 0.75$) (kN•m).

$P_r$ = factored compressive resistance parallel to grain taken from Table 8.17 ($K_D = 1.0$) ($K_T = 0.75$) (N).

The deflection used to estimate the secondary moment $P_f\Delta$ may be calculated as follows:

$$\Delta = \frac{w_f(L-x)}{360 E_S I L H} K_\Delta \text{ (mm)}$$

where:

$K_\Delta$ = 10 H$^3$ (2 L - x) x - 3 H$^5$ + K$_2$

$K_2$ = $\dfrac{3L}{L-x}(H-x)^5$   when x ≤ H

$K_2$ = 0 when x > H

$x$ = $H - \sqrt{\dfrac{H^3}{3L}}$

$E_S I$ = bending stiffness taken from Joist Selection Tables and modified for treatment factor for preservative treated, incised lumber used in dry service conditions ($K_T = 0.90$) (N•mm$^2$).

2. Maximum deflection under specified loads $\leq$ deflection criteria (actual $E_s I \geq$ required $E_s I$)

Maximum deflection $\Delta$ may be calculated using the formula given above with $x = 0.45L$ and using specified rather than factored soil loads. Generally $L/300$ is used as a deflection criterion.

3. Factored shear resistance $V_r \geq$ factored shear force $V_f$

Maximum longitudinal shear is calculated as follows:

$$V_f = \frac{w_f H}{2} \left[ \frac{H}{3L} - \left[ \frac{H-d}{H} \right]^2 \right]$$

where:

$d$ = depth of stud (mm)

Factored shear resistance $V_r$ may be obtained from the Joist Selection Tables. The tabulated values must be modified for permanent load duration ($K_D = 0.65$) and treatment factor for preservative treated, incised lumber used in dry service conditions ($K_T = 0.75$).

4. Factored resistance at support $\geq$ factored reaction $R_f$

The factored reaction at the top and bottom of the foundation wall may be calculated from the following expressions:

$$R_{fT} = \frac{w_f H^2}{6L}$$

$$R_{fB} = \frac{w_f H}{2L} \left[ L - \frac{H}{3} \right]$$

where:

$R_{fT}$ = inward reaction at top of stud (N)
$R_{fB}$ = inward reaction at bottom of stud (N)

Nails or framing anchors may be used to connect the studs to their supports. Design information is provided in Chapter 7.

Typically, the lateral loads on a wood foundation wall are based on well-drained soil having an equivalent fluid pressure of 4.7 kN/m$^2$ per metre of depth. This is permitted by the *National Building Code of Canada (NBCC)* for average stable soils with Part 9 buildings. In accordance with the *NBCC*, the lateral soil load is combined with other loads using a load factor of 1.5.

**8**

**Applications**

## Service Conditions

Provided the permanent wood foundation is built in accordance with CSA S406 the service conditions for studs and fasteners may be considered to be dry. The service conditions for the plywood, however, are wet.

## Footings for PWFs

Footings for PWFs may consist of a wood footing plate (single member or composite wood-plywood) on a granular drainage layer, or a concrete strip footing. In either case, the footing must be wide enough so that the allowable bearing capacity of the soil is not exceeded. For the footing plate, the load is considered to be distributed at an angle of 30° to the vertical through the granular layer. For the concrete footing, provision must be made for passage of moisture through or under the footing into the granular drainage layer beneath the structure.

In accordance with CSA S406, wood footing plates must extend beyond the width of the bottom wall plate to provide a seat for the sheathing. They should not however extend more than 50 mm on either side of the wall in order to minimize tension perpendicular to grain.

Concrete strip footings should be constructed in accordance with the appropriate building code.

Table 8.17
Factored compressive resistance for studs used in preserved wood foundations $P_r$ (kN)

| Species | Grade | 2.4 m long (8 ft.) stud | | | | 3.0 m long (10 ft.) stud | | | |
|---------|-------|-------------------------|------|------|------|--------------------------|------|------|------|
| | | Depth of stud mm | | | | Depth of stud mm | | | |
| | | 89 | 140 | 184 | 235 | 89 | 140 | 184 | 235 |
| D.Fir-L | Sel Str | 21.3 | 58.5 | 87.9 | 117 | 13.4 | 45.7 | 76.0 | 107 |
| | No. 1/ No.2 | 16.8 | 44.3 | 65.7 | 87.0 | 10.7 | 35.2 | 57.4 | 80.1 |
| Hem-Fir | Sel Str | 20.7 | 55.3 | 82.2 | 109 | 13.2 | 43.6 | 71.6 | 100 |
| | No. 1/ No.2 | 17.9 | 47.0 | 69.5 | 92.1 | 11.5 | 37.4 | 60.9 | 84.8 |
| S-P-F | Sel Str | 17.7 | 46.3 | 68.3 | 90.3 | 11.4 | 36.9 | 59.9 | 83.3 |
| | No. 1/ No.2 | 14.8 | 37.5 | 54.7 | 72.0 | 9.62 | 30.3 | 48.3 | 66.6 |
| Northern | Sel Str | 14.1 | 39.4 | 59.6 | 79.9 | 8.81 | 30.5 | 51.3 | 72.9 |
| | No. 1/ No.2 | 12.2 | 32.6 | 48.5 | 64.5 | 7.75 | 25.7 | 42.3 | 59.2 |

Note:
Tabulated values are valid for the following conditions:
* standard term loading (dead plus snow or occupancy)
* dry service conditions
* incised lumber
* studs effectively pinned and laterally restrained at both ends and prevented from buckling about weak axis by wall sheathing
* wall system consisting of 3 studs spaced no farther apart than 610 mm
* 38 mm thick studs

## Racking Resistance

Foundation walls may be subjected to racking loads, for example, loads acting in a direction parallel to the wall to create shearing forces in the plane of the wall (see Figure 8.6).

Figure 8.6
**The effect of unequal backfill heights**

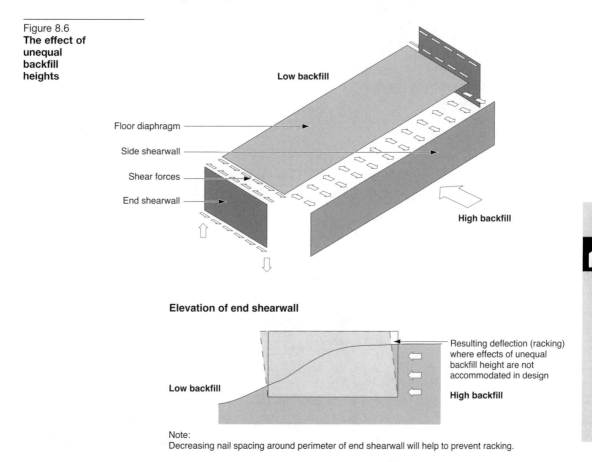

For rectangular shaped foundations, the net differential force F acting normal to the top of the wall having the greater depth of backfill is determined as follows:

$$F = \frac{e_f\, L_t}{6\, L}\left(H_1^3 - H_2^3\right)$$

where:

$H_1$ = height of backfill on the side of the structure with greatest depth of backfill (m)

$H_2$ = height of backfill on the side of the structure opposite the side with greatest depth of backfill (m)

$L_t$ = length of the structure having greatest depth of backfill (m)

L = length of the studs in the PWF (m)

$e_f$ = equivalent factored fluid weight of soil (kN/m³)

The net backfill force F is transferred to the floor system, which acts as a horizontal diaphragm to distribute it to the adjacent end walls of the building. For rectangular buildings, the racking load on each foundation end wall due to the differential backfill heights is, therefore, one-half of the differential force F. In order to resist this force, the designer must then ensure that the factored shear resistance of the nailed panel to stud connection $v_r$ is adequate as follows:

$$v_r \geq \frac{F}{2 L_W}$$

$$\geq \frac{e_f L_t}{12 L L_w}\left(H_1^3 - H_2^3\right)$$

Therefore, the maximum cubic difference in backfill height is expressed as follows:

$$\frac{e_f L_t}{6 L}\left(H_1^3 - H_2^3\right) \leq \frac{12 \, v_r \, L}{e_f \dfrac{L_t}{L_w}}$$

where:

$v_r$ = factored diaphragm shear resistance of nailed panel (kN/m)

$v_r$ = $\phi \, V_d \, J_{Sp} \, J_n$ (kN/m)

$\phi$ = 0.7

$V_d$ = $v_d \, (K_D \, K_{SF})$ (kN/m)

$v_d$ = specified shear strength for shear walls (kN/m)

$L_W$ = length of shear panel parallel to the direction of the factored load (m)

$K_D$ = load duration factor. For lateral soil loads assume a permanent load duration ($K_D$ = 0.565 when using Diaphragm Selection Tables in Chapter 9).

$K_{SF}$ = service condition factor.
= 1.0 for dry service conditions with the seasoned moisture content ≤ 15% at the time of fabrication
= 0.8 for unseasoned lumber in dry service conditions,
= 0.67 for wet service conditions, regardless of seasoning

$J_{Sp}$ = species factor

$J_n$ = nail diameter factor.

For additional information on wood foundations, refer to the CWC publication *Permanent Wood Foundations*. This guide to wood foundation construction covers major topics such as site preparation, footings, structural integrity of wall systems, moisture barriers and backfilling.

# 8.9        Stressed-skin Panels

### General

The stressed-skin panel is an efficient structural component. It has a plywood or OSB skin (flange) glued to the top of longitudinal lumber members (webs), and sometimes also to the bottom. The flanges and webs act as a single structural unit in carrying loads.

Stressed-skin panels may be designed in accordance with CSA O86 using plywood or OSB and lumber or glued-laminated timber only. When designed with both a top and bottom skin and filled with insulation, the stressed-skin panel also provides excellent thermal values and a ready-to-finish ceiling.

The various components of a typical stressed-skin panel are shown in Figure 8.7 below.

Figure 8.7
**Typical
stressed-skin
panel**

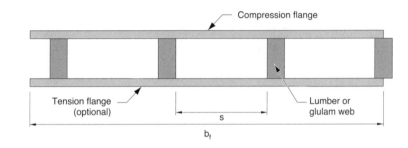

### Selection of Panel Geometry

Selection of panel geometry is an iterative process. The following recommendations may make the selection easier:

1. The strong axis of the panels is typically oriented parallel to the webs.

2. The compression flange should be no thinner than 9.5 mm for roof uses. Sheathing thicker than 12.5 mm is seldom used for this application.

3. The compression flange should be no thinner than 12.5 mm for floor uses.

4. Webs are spaced at about 400 mm on centre. This spacing is reduced to about 300 mm on centre with a 9.5 mm compression flange.

5. Lumber depth, species and grade are to be selected before proceeding with the design sequence in the next section.

8

Applications

## Design

The design sequence that follows provides guidance for the design of stressed-skin panels. CSA O86 provides design procedures for determining the resistance of stressed-skin panels. Additional design information can be obtained from the Canadian Plywood Association or the Structural Board Association.

1. Select trial section geometry.

2. Calculate panel section properties.

To account for the different materials that compose a stressed-skin panel, a transformed section is calculated.

3. Design for strength. Stressed-skin panels must be designed so that the following criteria are satisfied:

Factored buckling resistance of compression flange $\geq TL_f$

Factored transverse bending resistance $\geq \dfrac{TL_f\, s^2}{12}$

Factored transverse planar shear resistance $\geq \dfrac{TL_f\, s}{2}$

Factored bending resistance of compression flange $\geq \dfrac{TL_f\, \ell_p^2}{8}$

Factored bending resistance of tension flange $\geq \dfrac{TL_f\, \ell_p^2}{8}$

Factored bending resistance of web $\geq \dfrac{TL_f\, \ell_p^2}{8}$

Factored shear resistance at neutral plane $\geq \dfrac{TL_f\, \ell_p}{2}$

Factored shear resistance at flange-web interface $\geq \dfrac{TL_f\, \ell_p}{2}$

where:

$TL_f$ = total factored load (kN/m$^2$)

$s$ = clear spacing of webs (m)

$\ell_p$ = overall panel span in direction of webs (m)

$b_f$ = width of panel face (mm)

For checking transverse conditions, it is assumed that panel acts as a beam fixed at both ends under a uniformly distributed load. For checking longitudinal conditions, it is assumed that the panel acts as a simple beam (single span) under a uniformly distributed load.

4. Design for deflection. The effects of the specified load must not exceed the corresponding limits. The following limits are provided for guidance; however, other specified limits may be in effect.

a) Transverse deflection of compression flange:

$$\Delta = \frac{(L+D)\,s^4}{384\,B_b}$$

Suggested deflection limits: web spacing/180 for roofs
web spacing/360 for floors

where:

$B_b$ = bending stiffness of compression flange ($N \bullet mm^2/mm$)

b) Deflection of panel:

$$\Delta = \frac{(L+D)\,5\ell_p^4}{384\,X_G\,(EI)_e}$$

Suggested deflection limits: panel span/180 for roofs
panel span/360 for floors

where:

$(EI)_e$ = effective stiffness of panel ($N \bullet mm^2$)

$X_G$ = panel geometry factor = $1 - 4.8\left[\dfrac{s}{\ell_p}\right]^2$

8

Applications

## Structural Insulated Panels

Increasingly, proprietary structural insulated panels (SIPs) are being used in construction. Structural insulated panels are composed of a thick plastic foam layer sandwiched between two structural wood panel faces. They are used in residential and low-rise commercial structures as roof panels, wall panels and occasionally floor panels. There are many different of types of structural insulated panels and each manufacturer provides engineering design information. Typically, SIPs are custom manufactured to match specific building plans.

# 8.10 Concrete Formwork

### General

Formwork in concrete construction refers to the assembly required to give the desired shape to a structural or architectural element. It consists of the elements forming the contact surface with the liquid concrete and includes stiffeners, braces, ties and support members. The applications are varied, but some of the basic systems are shown in Figure 8.8.

The selection of formwork materials should be based on maximum overall operating economy consistent with safety and the quality of finish required.

Formwork costs can be substantially reduced by using certain standard dimensions. Beams and columns should have the same outside dimensions from foundation to roof, allowing beam and column forms to be re-used without alteration. A column should preferably be the same width as a beam framing into it. The column form then becomes a rectangular or square box with no cutouts, and the slab forms do not require cutting at the column corners.

It is highly desirable that columns, beams, stairwells and other items be so dimensioned that 1220 × 2440 mm (or 4' × 8') panels of plywood can be cut with a minimum of waste. If column centres are set so that the distance between faces of beams is a multiple of 1220 mm plus an allowance to facilitate panel removal, whole panels of plywood may be used without cutting for slab forms.

### Materials

#### Plywood

CANPLY EXTERIOR Douglas Fir Plywood (DFP) and Canadian Softwood Plywood (CSP) may be used for formwork. CANPLY EXTERIOR plywood meets the requirements of CSA Standard O121 *Douglas Fir Plywood* or CSA Standard O151 *Canadian Softwood Plywood,* plus the additional requirements specified in the CANPLY *Mill Guide.* They are available as unsanded plywood in Select, Select-Tight Face or Sheathing grades. DFP is also available as sanded plywood in Good One Side (G1S) or Good Two Sides (G2S) grades. Design capacities for use as concrete formwork, incorporating adjustment factors for wet service conditions and short term duration of load, are provided for various types of plywood in Tables 8.18 and 8.19. For sanded plywood, capacities were developed by the Canadian Plywood Association using procedures accepted in CSA O86 for unsanded plywood. For information on using CSP, contact the Canadian Plywood Association.

There are also a number of proprietary panels that are specially constructed to provide greater strength and stiffness for concrete formwork. Canadian Plywood Association mills produce COFI FORM and COFI FORM PLUS panels, which are available in sanded and unsanded grades and as overlaid or coated panels. Other panels equivalent to these products are also available.

All proprietary concrete forming panels are edge-sealed and surface overlaid or coated to make them impervious to oil and water. They are usually supplied surface treated with a release agent.

For a smooth architectural finish, overlaid and sanded grades are recommended (COFI FORM PLUS, COFI FORM, sanded DFP). Where a smooth

**8**

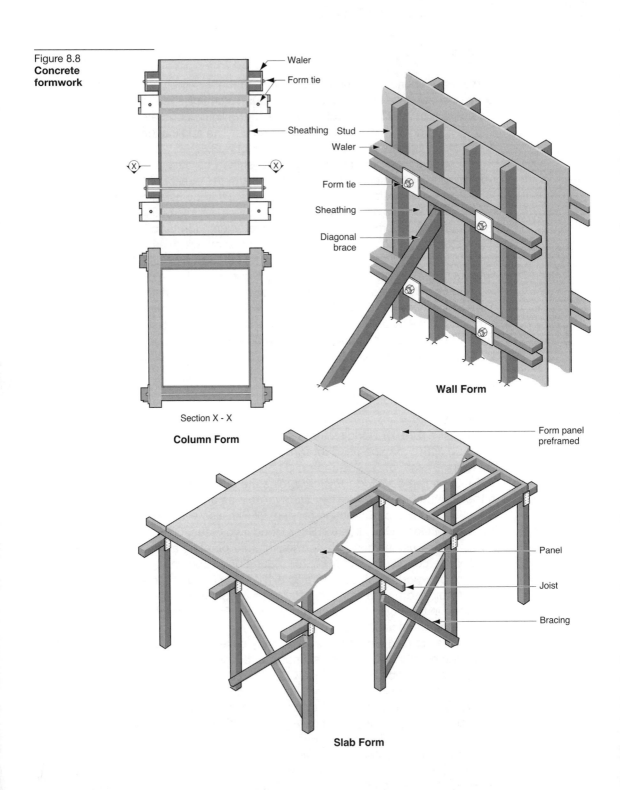

Figure 8.8
**Concrete formwork**

Waler

Form tie

Sheathing   Stud

Waler

Form tie

Sheathing

Diagonal brace

Section X - X

**Column Form**

**Wall Form**

Form panel preframed

Panel

Joist

Bracing

**Slab Form**

finish is not required (for economy), unsanded grades are recommended (Unsanded DFP).

A release agent should be applied to plywood prior to pouring concrete if the panel is not pretreated.

## OSB

For reasons of economy, standard grades of OSB sheathing are sometimes used in applications where forms cannot be retrieved after concrete has been poured. An example is a bridge deck with internal voids. Designers should be aware of the potential for thickness expansion in standard grades of OSB in wet service conditions; there are not yet any wet service condition factors for OSB in CSA O86. OSB form panels are sometimes designed by assuming standard term loading and a temporary wet service condition factor of 0.75.

Proprietary OSB panels specially manufactured for use as concrete forms are also available. These panels are specially designed and manufactured to limit deformation and swelling and can be used for multiple concrete pours.

For additional information on the use of OSB panel as concrete form work, contact the Structural Board Association.

## Framing Materials

Framing materials are very often 38 × 89 mm, 38 × 140 mm or 38 × 184 mm joists for floor slabs and 38 × 89 mm or 38 × 140 mm studs for wall forms. For larger projects, 89 × 89 mm and 89 × 140 mm members are often used. Walers are generally made from 38 × 140 mm material, usually in pairs to carry the loads from the studs to the form ties. Stringers built up from 38 × 140 mm or larger lumber are common. Shores may be wood posts or tubular steel frames.

## Formwork Hardware

Form hardware is used to anchor forms to each other or to some existing fixed structure. Examples of formwork hardware are shown in Figure 8.9.

Modern hardware has provisions for removing steel ends from an exposed surface so that unsightly rust marks will not appear later. Very often they combine spacing of the form with the tensile function. There are four types of form ties:

- Break-back ties that come in flat bar or round rod and are held against the walers by one or more wedges. They have a notch of some kind to allow the tie to break between 25 and 50 mm back from the exposed face when the tie is twisted.
- She-bolts and threaded rods can be made for any desired set-back. Their advantage is that the she-bolt, with its female end threaded to receive the tie that is left in the concrete, can be reused a number of times.
- Tapered bolts are useful because no ties are left in the form. If used with care, these bolts can be reused many times. Each bolt length is restricted for use on a small range of concrete widths. Tapered bolts cannot be used on structures that hold water.

**8**

**Applications**

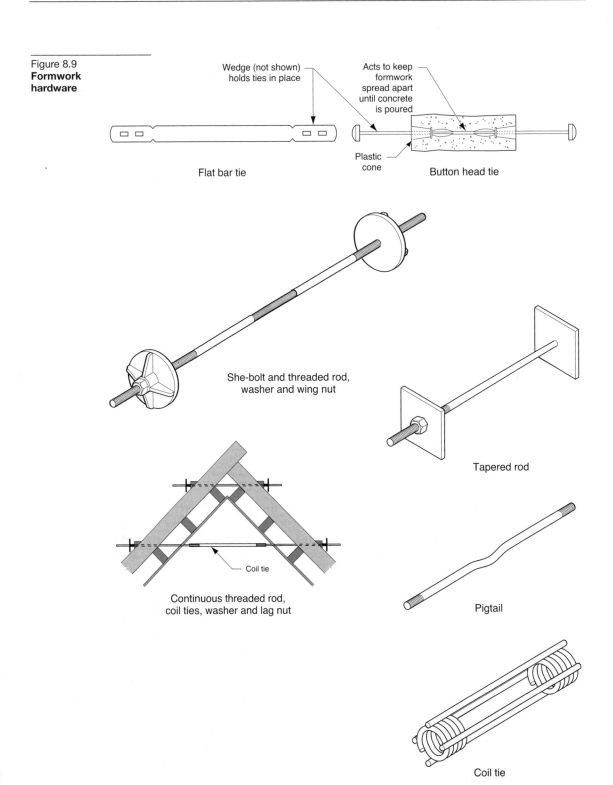

Figure 8.9
**Formwork
hardware**

Wedge (not shown)
holds ties in place

Acts to keep
formwork
spread apart
until concrete
is poured

Flat bar tie

Plastic
cone

Button head tie

She-bolt and threaded rod,
washer and wing nut

Tapered rod

Coil tie

Continuous threaded rod,
coil ties, washer and lag nut

Pigtail

Coil tie

- Continuous threaded rods can be used with ordinary handled nuts and washers or she-bolts. This system consists of two coils attached to each other by two or four bars and fitted over the threaded rods. No sitework is required other than cutting the rod to the desired length. A plastic pipe sleeve is usually fitted over the rod to permit reuse.
- Coil ties, consisting of a bent wire in a threaded pattern, are often used in forms for water tanks.

## Fabrication

It is economical to fabricate as much of the formwork as possible on the ground, making sections as large as can be conveniently handled by the lifting equipment or workers available.

Horizontal joints between panels may be backed up by headers or nailing strips to eliminate leakage and produce a smoother joint. Some contractors overcome the joint problem in high quality finish concrete surfaces by taping joints with thin, pressure-sensitive plastic tape.

## Loading

Concrete formwork must be designed for vertical and lateral loads due to the weight of the concrete, as well as for wind pressure or any other anticipated load. Vertical loads for formwork are given in CSA S269.1 and CSA S269.2. Lateral loading is covered in CSA S269.3.

## Design

### General Considerations

In the calculation of the factored loading, the weight of concrete should be taken as a live load (principal load factor, $\alpha_L = 1.5$) since the load is not permanently applied to the formwork.

Wood members in concrete formwork are generally designed for the following conditions:

- Short term loading ($K_D = 1.15$) unless the materials have been exposed to a duration of load greater than 7 days (see Table 11.25)
- System Case 1 ($K_H = 1.1$) for three or more studs or joists spaced no further apart then 610 mm
- Wet service conditions for panels in contact with concrete

### Framing

Studs, joists, walers and stringers must be designed to meet the criteria outlined in Section 2.3. Posts and bracing members must be designed as outlined in Chapter 3.

**8**

**Applications**

**Plywood**

Plywood formwork must be designed so that the following criteria are satisfied:

- Factored bending moment resistance $M_r \geq$ factored bending moment $M_f$
- Factored planar shear capacity $V_{rp} \geq$ factored shear force $V_f$
- Maximum deflection $\leq$ deflection criteria

The Plywood Formwork Selection Tables provide the specified design pressure that satisfies the above criteria for various span and thickness combinations. The tables apply to plywood construction with any number of plies permitted by the applicable standard or specification.

The tabulated values were developed using a finite element model; however, for designs outside of the selection tables, the specified design pressure may be calculated from the following formulae:

1. Specified design pressure governed by bending capacity

$$w_b = \frac{\phi\, M \times 10^3}{\alpha_L \times 0.1071 \times L_1^2}$$

where:

$w_b$ = specified design pressure applied as uniformly distributed load over four equal spans and conservative for three or more equal spans (kN/m$^2$)

$\phi$ = 0.95

$M$ = specified strength capacity in bending from Table 8.18 or 8.19 (N•mm/mm)

$\alpha_L$ = 1.50

$L_1$ = centre-to-centre span (mm)

2. Specified design pressure governed by planar shear capacity

$$w_s = \frac{\phi\, V \times 10^3}{\alpha_L \times 0.607 \times L_2}$$

where:

$w_s$ = specified design pressure applied as uniformly distributed load over four equal spans and conservative for three or more equal spans (kN/m$^2$)

$\phi$ = 0.95

$V$ = specified strength capacity in planar shear from Table 8.18 or 8.19 (N/mm)

$\alpha_L$ = 1.50

$L_2$ = clear span (mm)

3. Specified design pressure governed by deflection

$$w_\Delta = \frac{\Delta_{max} \times 10^3}{\left[\dfrac{0.0064\, L_2^4}{EI}\right] + \left[\dfrac{C\, L_2^2}{GA}\right]}$$

where:

$w_\Delta$ = specified design pressure uniformly distributed over three or more equal spans and governed by bending and shear deflection ($kN/m^2$)

$\Delta_{max}$ = maximum deflection (mm)

$L_2$ = clear span (mm)

$EI$ = specified bending stiffness from Table 8.18 or 8.19 ($N \bullet mm^2/mm$)

$C$ = shear deflection constant from Table 8.20

$GA$ = planar shear rigidity from Table 8.18 or 8.19 (N/mm)

8

Applications

**Table 8.18
Design capacities[1] for CANPLY certified exterior plywood applied as concrete formwork**

Design capacities per 1 mm width

Face grain oriented **perpendicular** to supports

| Type of plywood | Nominal panel thickness mm | Number of plies | Bending moment M N•mm/mm | Planar shear V N/mm | Bending stiffness EI × 10⁶ N•mm²/mm | Planar shear rigidity GA N/mm |
|---|---|---|---|---|---|---|
| Overlaid, sanded, or unsanded COFI FORM PLUS | 12.5 | 5 | 518 | 9.95 | 1.53 | 974 |
| | 15.5 | 5 | 724 | 12.5 | 2.68 | 1200 |
| | 17.5 | 7 | 933 | 12.5 | 3.93 | 1290 |
| | 19 | 7 | 1080 | 13.2 | 4.90 | 1490 |
| | 21 | 7 | 1190 | 14.3 | 5.82 | 1470 |
| Overlaid or sanded COFI FORM | 14 | 5 | 481 | 9.31 | 1.64 | 913 |
| | 17 | 6,7 | 668 | 9.31 | 2.83 | 1040 |
| | 19 | 6,7 | 830 | 10.3 | 3.72 | 1140 |
| Sanded DOUGLAS FIR PLYWOOD | 17 | 5,6,7 | 600 | 8.54 | 2.51 | 503 |
| | 19 | 5,6,7 | 705 | 9.82 | 3.26 | 588 |
| | 21 | 7 | 1080 | 10.2 | 5.35 | 785 |
| | 24 | 7 | 1370 | 12.5 | 7.84 | 753 |
| | 27 | 9 | 1870 | 14.5 | 11.8 | 951 |
| | 30 | 9 | 2090 | 16.3 | 14.7 | 953 |
| Unsanded COFI FORM | 12.5 | 5 | 500 | 7.87 | 1.53 | 923 |
| | 15.5 | 5 | 698 | 10.5 | 2.66 | 1120 |
| | 18.5 | 6,7 | 951 | 10.5 | 4.36 | 1210 |
| | 20.5 | 6,7 | 1140 | 11.4 | 5.65 | 1350 |
| Unsanded DOUGLAS FIR PLYWOOD | 15.5 | 4,5 | 677 | 6.69 | 2.62 | 531 |
| | 18.5 | 5,6,7 | 890 | 9.39 | 4.08 | 648 |
| | 20.5 | 5,6,7 | 1020 | 10.3 | 5.49 | 658 |
| | 22.5 | 6,7,9 | 1420 | 11.4 | 7.98 | 854 |
| | 25.5 | 7,9 | 1720 | 13.2 | 10.5 | 842 |
| | 28.5 | 9 | 2290 | 15.4 | 15.5 | 1060 |
| | 31.5 | 9,11 | 2570 | 16.7 | 19.3 | 1050 |

Notes:
1. All capacities adjusted for wet service conditions. Bending moment and planar shear capacities adjusted for short term duration of loading.
2. All capacities are recommended by the Canadian Plywood Association using the lowest section properties for construction of any number of plies in the table.

Table 8.19
**Design capacities[1] for CANPLY certified exterior plywood applied as concrete formwork**

Design capacities per 1 mm width

Face grain oriented **parallel** to supports

| Type of plywood | Nominal panel thickness mm | Number of plies | Bending moment M N•mm/mm | Planar shear V N/mm | Bending stiffness EI × 10^6 N•mm²/mm | Planar shear rigidity GA N/mm |
|---|---|---|---|---|---|---|
| Overlaid, sanded, or unsanded COFI FORM PLUS | 12.5 | 5 | 282 | 5.25 | 0.505 | 711 |
| | 15.5 | 5 | 444 | 6.23 | 0.999 | 890 |
| | 17.5 | 7 | 682 | 10.2 | 2.08 | 1080 |
| | 19.0 | 7 | 792 | 11.5 | 2.68 | 1100 |
| | 21.0 | 7 | 950 | 12.2 | 3.45 | 1260 |

Notes:
1. All capacities adjusted for wet service conditions. Bending moment and planar shear capacities adjusted for short term duration of loading.
2. All capacities are recommended by the Canadian Plywood Association.

Table 8.20
**Shear deflection constant C**

| Face grain orientation | Nominal panel thickness range | Centre to centre span between supports | Shear deflection constant C |
|---|---|---|---|
| Perpendicular to supports | 12.5 to 14 mm | All | 0.190 |
| | 15.5 to 18.5 mm | All | 0.170 |
| | 19 to 28.5 mm | All | 0.160 |
| | 30 to 31.5 mm | All | 0.155 |
| Parallel to supports | 12.5 mm only | All | 0.230 |
| | 15.5 mm only | All | 0.220 |
| | 17.5 to 21 mm | 200 to 399 mm | 0.200 |
| | | 400 to 800 mm | 0.240 |

Note:
Shear deflection constants for face grain oriented parallel to supports are applicable for COFI FORM PLUS only.

**8**

Applications

# Plywood Formwork Selection Tables

## CFP　COFI FORM PLUS

| Face grain orientation | Deflection limit | Centre to centre of supports L mm | Design pressure[1] for the indicated plywood thickness kN/m² | | | | |
|---|---|---|---|---|---|---|---|
| | | | 12.5 mm | 15.5 mm | 17.5 mm | 19 mm | 21 mm |
| Perpendicular to support | L/270 | 100 | 172 | 216 | 216 | 227 | 247 |
| | | 150 | 95 | 119 | 119 | 126 | 137 |
| | | 200 | 66 | 83 | 83 | 87 | 94 |
| | | 300 | 33 | 48 | 51 | 54 | 58 |
| | | 400 | 15 | 25 | 32 | 39 | 42 |
| | | 600 | 4.7 | 8.0 | 11 | 13 | 15 |
| | | 800 | 2.1 | 3.5 | 4.9 | 6.1 | 7.0 |
| Perpendicular to support | L/360 | 100 | 172 | 216 | 216 | 227 | 247 |
| | | 150 | 95 | 119 | 119 | 126 | 137 |
| | | 200 | 66 | 83 | 83 | 87 | 94 |
| | | 300 | 25 | 40 | 49 | 54 | 58 |
| | | 400 | 11 | 19 | 24 | 29 | 33 |
| | | 600 | 3.6 | 6.0 | 8.2 | 10 | 12 |
| | | 800 | 1.5 | 2.6 | 3.7 | 4.5 | 5.2 |
| Parallel to support | L/270 | 100 | 91 | 107 | 176 | 199 | 211 |
| | | 150 | 50 | 59 | 97 | 110 | 117 |
| | | 200 | 35 | 41 | 67 | 76 | 81 |
| | | 300 | 13 | 24 | 40 | 46 | 50 |
| | | 400 | 5.7 | 10 | 18 | 22 | 27 |
| | | 600 | 1.7 | 3.2 | 5.8 | 7.2 | 9.1 |
| | | 800 | 0.7 | 1.4 | 2.5 | 3.1 | 4.0 |
| Parallel to support | L/360 | 100 | 91 | 107 | 176 | 199 | 211 |
| | | 150 | 50 | 59 | 97 | 110 | 117 |
| | | 200 | 34 | 41 | 67 | 76 | 81 |
| | | 300 | 10 | 18 | 30 | 35 | 43 |
| | | 400 | 4.3 | 7.8 | 14 | 16 | 21 |
| | | 600 | 1.3 | 2.4 | 4.4 | 5.4 | 6.8 |
| | | 800 | 0.5 | 1.0 | 1.9 | 2.4 | 3.0 |

Note:
1. Plywood must be continous over 3 or more supports. Supports to be 38 mm or larger. Design pressure is the specified loading, not the factored loading.

# Plywood Formwork Selection Tables

## Sanded DFP

**DFP**

| Face grain orientation | Deflection limit | Centre to centre of supports L mm | Design pressure[1] for the indicated plywood thickness kN/m² | | | | | |
|---|---|---|---|---|---|---|---|---|
| | | | 17 mm | 19 mm | 21 mm | 24 mm | 27 mm | 30 mm |
| Perpendicular to support | L/270 | 100 | 146 | 169 | 175 | 214 | 248 | 280 |
| | | 150 | 81 | 93 | 97 | 118 | 137 | 155 |
| | | 200 | 56 | 64 | 67 | 82 | 95 | 107 |
| | | 300 | 33 | 40 | 41 | 51 | 59 | 66 |
| | | 400 | 17 | 22 | 30 | 36 | 43 | 48 |
| | | 600 | 6.2 | 8.2 | 12 | 15 | 21 | 23 |
| | | 800 | 2.9 | 3.8 | 5.8 | 7.4 | 10 | 12 |
| Perpendicular to support | L/360 | 100 | 146 | 169 | 175 | 214 | 248 | 280 |
| | | 150 | 81 | 93 | 97 | 118 | 137 | 155 |
| | | 200 | 56 | 64 | 67 | 82 | 95 | 107 |
| | | 300 | 25 | 31 | 41 | 47 | 59 | 66 |
| | | 400 | 13 | 17 | 24 | 27 | 36 | 39 |
| | | 600 | 4.7 | 6.1 | 9.2 | 11 | 15 | 17 |
| | | 800 | 2.2 | 2.8 | 4.4 | 5.6 | 7.9 | 9.1 |

## Unsanded DFP

**DFP** **8**

Applications

| Face grain orientation | Deflection limit | Centre to centre of supports L mm | Design pressure[1] for the indicated plywood thickness kN/m² | | | | | | |
|---|---|---|---|---|---|---|---|---|---|
| | | | 15.5 mm | 18.5 mm | 20.5 mm | 22.5 mm | 25.5 mm | 28.5 mm | 31.5 mm |
| Perpendicular to support | L/270 | 100 | 113 | 159 | 175 | 195 | 226 | 265 | 287 |
| | | 150 | 63 | 88 | 97 | 108 | 125 | 147 | 159 |
| | | 200 | 43 | 61 | 67 | 75 | 86 | 101 | 110 |
| | | 300 | 27 | 38 | 41 | 46 | 53 | 63 | 68 |
| | | 400 | 17 | 25 | 28 | 33 | 39 | 45 | 49 |
| | | 600 | 6.2 | 9.4 | 11 | 15 | 18 | 24 | 27 |
| | | 800 | 2.9 | 4.5 | 5.5 | 7.6 | 9.1 | 13 | 15 |
| Perpendicular to support | L/360 | 100 | 113 | 159 | 175 | 195 | 226 | 265 | 287 |
| | | 150 | 63 | 88 | 97 | 108 | 125 | 147 | 159 |
| | | 200 | 43 | 61 | 67 | 75 | 86 | 101 | 110 |
| | | 300 | 24 | 34 | 38 | 46 | 53 | 63 | 68 |
| | | 400 | 13 | 19 | 21 | 28 | 31 | 42 | 45 |
| | | 600 | 4.7 | 7.1 | 8.4 | 11 | 13 | 18 | 20 |
| | | 800 | 2.2 | 3.3 | 4.1 | 5.7 | 6.9 | 9.5 | 11 |

Note:
1. Plywood must be continous over 3 or more supports. Supports to be 38 mm or larger. Design pressure is the specified loading, not the factored loading.

# Plywood Formwork Selection Tables

## CF   Sanded COFI FORM

| Face grain orientation | Deflection limit | Centre to centre of supports L mm | Design pressure[1] for the indicated plywood thickness kN/m² 14 mm | 17 mm | 19 mm |
|---|---|---|---|---|---|
| Perpendicular to support | L/270 | 100 | 162 | 162 | 178 |
| | | 150 | 90 | 90 | 99 |
| | | 200 | 62 | 62 | 68 |
| | | 300 | 32 | 38 | 42 |
| | | 400 | 16 | 25 | 31 |
| | | 600 | 5.2 | 8.2 | 10 |
| | | 800 | 2.2 | 3.6 | 4.7 |
| Perpendicular to support | L/360 | 100 | 162 | 162 | 178 |
| | | 150 | 90 | 90 | 99 |
| | | 200 | 62 | 62 | 68 |
| | | 300 | 27 | 38 | 42 |
| | | 400 | 12 | 18 | 23 |
| | | 600 | 3.9 | 6.2 | 7.8 |
| | | 800 | 1.7 | 2.7 | 3.5 |

## CF   Unsanded COFI FORM

| Face grain orientation | Deflection limit | Centre to centre of supports L mm | Design pressure[1] for the indicated plywood thickness kN/m² 12.5 mm | 15.5 mm | 18.5 mm | 20.5 mm |
|---|---|---|---|---|---|---|
| Perpendicular to Support | L/270 | 100 | 137 | 182 | 183 | 199 |
| | | 150 | 76 | 101 | 101 | 110 |
| | | 200 | 52 | 70 | 70 | 76 |
| | | 300 | 32 | 43 | 43 | 47 |
| | | 400 | 15 | 24 | 31 | 34 |
| | | 600 | 4.7 | 7.8 | 12 | 15 |
| | | 800 | 2.0 | 3.4 | 5.3 | 6.7 |
| Perpendicular to Support | L/360 | 100 | 137 | 182 | 183 | 199 |
| | | 150 | 76 | 101 | 101 | 110 |
| | | 200 | 52 | 70 | 70 | 76 |
| | | 300 | 24 | 38 | 43 | 47 |
| | | 400 | 11 | 18 | 25 | 31 |
| | | 600 | 3.5 | 5.8 | 8.7 | 11 |
| | | 800 | 1.5 | 2.6 | 3.9 | 5.0 |

Note:
1. Plywood must be continous over 3 or more supports. Supports to be 38 mm or wider. Design pressure is the specified loading, not the factored loading.

# Shearwalls
# and
# Diaphragms

A stud wall consisting of panel sheathing and framing lumber may also be designed to act as a shear-wall, eliminating the need for an internal bracing system.

Both the end
and side walls
of this building
have been
designed to act
as shearwalls.

Hold-down
connections in
shearwalls are
designed to
resist uplift
forces caused
by lateral loads.

# 9.1     General Information

A shearwall or diaphragm is a plate-type structural element used to resist lateral loads such as wind or seismic forces. Generally, the term "diaphragm" is applied to a horizontal element such as a floor or roof; the term "shearwall", to a vertical element such as a wall or partition. Diaphragms may also be curved or sloping depending on the roof shape.

    The action of wood diaphragms and shearwalls in bracing a simple box-like building subjected to wind load is illustrated in Figure 9.1. The side walls, simply supported between roof and foundation, are assumed to transfer half of the total wind load to roof level. The roof diaphragm, acting as a horizontal beam, transmits the load to the end shearwalls, which in turn transfer the load to the foundations.

Figure 9.1
**Shearwall and diaphragm action**

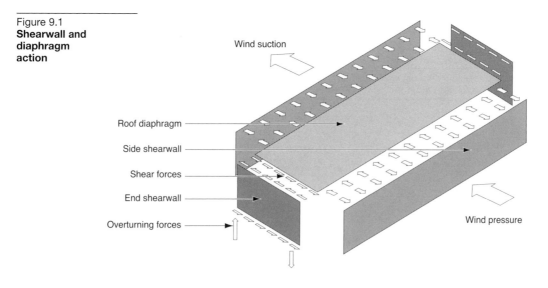

Wind suction

Roof diaphragm

Side shearwall

Shear forces

End shearwall

Overturning forces

Wind pressure

**9**

Shearwalls and Diaphragms

## Behaviour

Shearwalls and diaphragms behave similarly to a deep I-beam, where the sheathing acts as a web resisting the shear forces, while the chord members carry the axial forces that resist the applied bending moment (refer to Figure 9.2).

    The shear force transmitted from the diaphragm to the shearwall is considered to be uniformly distributed at the ends of the diaphragm. The perimeter members at the end of the diaphragm, known as struts, transfer the shear forces to the shearwall below. Struts that bridge over openings in the attached shearwall are called drag struts and transfer the diaphragm shear to the adjacent wall sections.

## Sheathing

Plywood, OSB and waferboard are used for sheathing in shearwall and diaphragm construction. Plywood used in shearwalls and diaphragms conforms to CSA O121, *Douglas Fir Plywood* (DFP), or CSA O151, *Canadian Softwood Plywood* (CSP). OSB and waferboard conform to CSA Standard O452.0, *Design Rated OSB*, CSA O325, *Construction Sheathing*, or CSA O437.0, *OSB and Waferboard*.

CSA O325 is a performance based standard for panel products (See Chapter 2), and provides panel marks for use in roof, floor or wall construction. Table 9.1 provides equivalence between tabulated thickness in the Diaphragm and Shearwall tables and panel marks for CSA O325 OSB.

**Table 9.1 Equivalent panel marks for use with diaphragm and shearwall selection tables**

| Diaphragm selection tables | | Shearwall selection tables | |
|---|---|---|---|
| Minimum nominal thickness (mm) | Minimum panel mark for CSA O325 OSB | Minimum nominal thickness (mm) | Minimum panel mark for CSA O325 OSB |
| 7.5 | 2R20 | 7.5 | 2R20 |
| 9.5 | 2R24 | 9.5 | 2R24 |
| 11.0 | 1R24/2F16 | 11.0 | 1R24/2F16 |
| 12.5 | 2R32/2F16 | 12.5 | 2R32/2F16 or 1F16 |
| 15.5 | 2R40/2F20 or 1F20 | 15.5 | 2R40/2F20 |
| 18.5 | 2R48/2F24 or 1F24 | | |

Shear panels using plywood, OSB or waferboard must consist of sheets of 1200 × 2400 mm or larger, except that one or two smaller sheets may be used near the boundaries. Panels less than 300 mm wide must have blocking at all panel joints. A minimum gap of 2 mm shall be left between panels to accomodate swelling. Framing members in shearwalls and diaphragms constructed with plywood, OSB or waferboard must be at least 38 mm wide and spaced no greater than 600 mm apart.

Shearwalls and diaphragms may also be constructed from plank decking or 19 mm lumber sheathing. These materials are most effective when laid diagonally due to triangulated (truss) action.

Figure 9.2
**Free body
diagram of a
shearwall and
diaphragm**

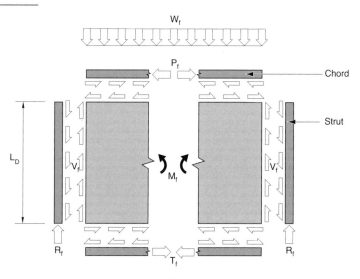

Plan of diaphragm

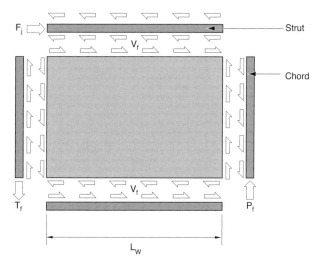

Elevation of shearwall segment

# 9.2       Diaphragm Design

## Shear Resistance

The diaphragm sheathing and its connection to the framing members must be designed so that the factored shear resistance of the diaphragm per unit length, $v_r$, is equal to or greater than the maximum shear force in the diaphragm per unit length, $v_f$. The maximum shear force, $V_f$, can be obtained from the beam analysis of the diaphragm and is typically greatest at the diaphragm supports. The maximum shear force is assumed to be uniformly distributed over the full depth of the diaphragm parallel to the applied load, $L_D$, and $v_f = V_f/L_D$.

The shear resistance of wood diaphragms is a function of the strength of the sheathing, the connection of the sheathing to the framing members, the configuration of the panels and blocking at the panel edges. Tabulated diaphragm shear values, based originally on tests of plywood diaphragms, have been extended to OSB and waferboard diaphragms, based on test data. Diaphragms with thicker sheathing are generally stronger than diaphragms with thinner sheathing, except where the strength of the diaphragm is limited by the capacity of the nail.

If the nails used to construct the diaphragms are not common wire nails, the strength of the diaphragm must be adjusted using the $J_n$ factor. Alternate nails must meet the limitations in Table 9.3, and the minimum nail penetration requirements given in the Diaphragm Selection Tables. Nails must not be placed within 9 mm of the edge of the panel, or over-driven more than 15 percent of the panel thickness.

## Chords

The diaphragm chord members must be designed so that the factored compressive and tensile resistance is greater than or equal to the maximum factored axial force. The axial force in each member may be calculated as follows:

$$P_f \text{ and } T_f = \frac{M_f}{h}$$

where:

$P_f$ = maximum factored compressive force (kN)

$T_f$ = maximum factored tensile force (kN)

$M_f$ = maximum factored bending moment (kN•m)

$h$ = centre to centre distance between chords (m)

In most cases the compressive resistance will be higher than the tensile resistance since the chord is laterally supported. Tensile resistances for various member sizes are given in the Tension Member Selection Tables in Chapter 4.

For wood frame walls, the double top plate of the wall is typically used as the chord member of the diaphragm. The plate members are lapped with staggered end joints and connected together by nailing or bolting (refer to Figure 9.3). Alternatively, a continuous header or trimmer joist may be used as the chord.

**9**

Shearwalls and Diaphragms

## Struts

Struts are members designed to transfer diaphragm shear forces to the supporting walls parallel to the lateral loads. Struts become chords when the lateral loading is applied perpendicular to the supporting walls. Therefore, the struts and splices in the struts should be designed to carry the strut forces or chord forces, whichever are critical.

Where a drag strut also functions as a header, it must be designed for the appropriate combination of vertical and axial loads.

**Figure 9.3**
**Chord splice**
**details**

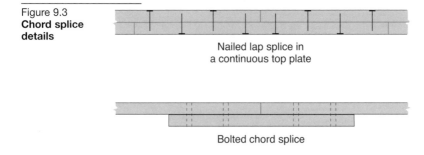

Nailed lap splice in
a continuous top plate

Bolted chord splice

## Connection Details

All of the components of the shearwall and diaphragm system must be adequately fastened together so that the structure acts as an effective unit. The following connection details are suggested for wood frame construction. For anchorage to concrete or masonry shearwalls, refer to CSA O86 Sections 9.3.5.1 and 9.3.5.2.

### Sheathing-to-Chord

Where the sheathing is not directly connected to the chord, a path for the transfer of shear forces is necessary in order for the chord to develop its axial force. The shear flow $q_f$ between the sheathing and the chord may be calculated as:

$$q_f = \frac{V_f}{h}$$

where:

$V_f$ = factored shear force in sheathing (kN)

$h$ = centre-to-centre distance between chords (m)

The shear flow is maximum at the support and follows the shape of the shear force diagram.

For wood frame walls with the top plate acting as the chord, this connection may be made by nailing to the header, which is in turn toe-nailed to the top plates, or connected by a framing anchor (refer to Figure 9.4). This connection also provides diaphragm-to-shearwall anchorage for lateral loading parallel to the wall.

## Sidewall-to-Diaphragm (Walls Perpendicular to Lateral Loads)

The lateral forces perpendicular to the wall must be transfered from the wall studs to the diaphragm. In wood frame walls, the top plate (chord) is end-nailed to the studs. Where the joists are perpendicular to the wall, the top plate may either be toe-nailed to the joist or connected with a framing anchor (see Figure 9.4). Where the joists are parallel to the wall, blocking is toe nailed or anchored to the plate and the sheathing is nailed to the blocking (see Figure 9.4).

Figure 9.4
**Diaphragm connection details**

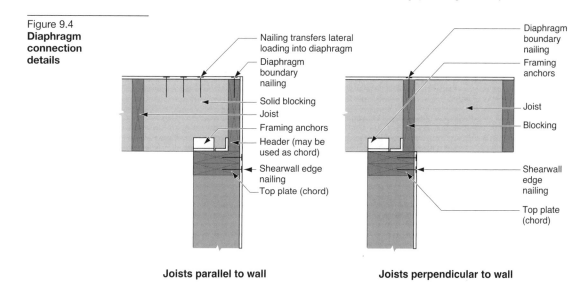

Joists parallel to wall                              Joists perpendicular to wall

## Diaphragm-to-Shearwall (Walls Parallel to Lateral Loads)

At the diaphragm edge the plywood is nailed to a joist (or blocking), which in turn must be connected to the top plate of the shear wall. This may be accomplished by toe-nailing the blocking or joist to the wall plate, or by fastening with a framing anchor.

## Corner Connections

The perimeter members – struts and chords – should be connected at the corners of the diaphragm. Where the top plate of the wall acts as the strut and chord, this may be done by lapping and nailing the plates at the corner. Heavier connections may be provided by using steel straps and nails or steel plates and bolts.

## Deflection

Typically wood diaphragms are designed assuming that they are single span members spanning between vertical supports; i.e. the diaphragms are assumed to be flexible. A rigid diaphragm is assumed to act as a multiple span continuous bending member. The assumptions about diaphragm flexibility affect the distribution of shear forces to the supporting members (see the

**9**

Shearwalls and Diaphragms

Commentary). To assess if a diaphragm is flexible or rigid, the deflection of the diaphragm must be determined.

The following formula may be used to estimate the deflection of simply supported, blocked diaphragms:

$$\Delta_d = \frac{5v_sL^3}{96E\,AL_D} + \frac{v_sL}{4B_v} + 0.0006Le_n \qquad \text{for diaphragms}$$

where:

$\Delta_d$ = lateral deflection at mid-span (mm)

$v_s$ = maximum shear force per unit length due to specified lateral loads (N/mm)

$L$ = diaphragm span (mm)

$A$ = cross-sectional area of chord members (mm$^2$)

$E$ = modulus of elasticity of chords (MPa)

$L_D$ = depth of diaphragm (mm)

$B_v$ = shear-through-thickness rigidity (N/mm) (refer to Table 7.3 of CSA O86)

$e_n$ = nail deformation for a particular load per nail (mm) (refer to Table 9.2)

**Table 9.2**
**Deformation $e_n$ for shearwall and diaphragm calculations**

| Load per nail[1] N | Nail length (in.) | Deformation, $e_n$ mm | | |
|---|---|---|---|---|
| | | 2 | 2-1/2 | 3 |
| | Gauge | 11-3/4 | 10 | 9 |
| | Diameter (mm) | 2.84 | 3.25 | 3.66 |
| 300 | | 0.46 | 0.29 | 0.23 |
| 400 | | 0.76 | 0.46 | 0.35 |
| 500 | | 1.20 | 0.64 | 0.49 |
| 600 | | 1.89 | 0.88 | 0.66 |
| 700 | | 2.97 | 1.21 | 0.86 |
| 800 | | | 1.70 | 1.13 |
| 900 | | | 2.33 | 1.48 |
| 1000 | | | | 1.95 |

Notes:
1. Load per nail = $v_s$ s
   where:
   $v_s$ = maximum specified shear force per unit length along diaphragm boundary or top of shearwall
   s = nail spacing along the boundary of an interior panel
2. Adapted from the Uniform Building Code (International Conference of Building Officials, Whittier, California).

## Openings and Discontinuities

Most diaphragms have openings to accommodate pipes, ductwork, elevators, stairwells and skylights. These openings must be adequately reinforced with framing members and connections to transfer the shear forces around the opening.

## Torsional Loading

In addition to the lateral seismic forces experienced by the structure, torsional effects may also be introduced due to eccentricity between the centres of mass and resistance, and due to accidental eccentricities. For symmetric structures with rigid diaphragms, the *National Building Code of Canada* requires the designer to use a minimum eccentricity of 10% of the plan building dimension perpendicular to the seismic load. Guidance on the design of the structures with flexible diaphragms is provided in the *Structural Commentaries to the National Building Code of Canada*. For these structures, accidental torsion should be taken into account by using a minimum eccentricity of 5% of the plan building dimension perpendicular to the seismic load to design the vertical elements. Torsional effects for wind loads are considered using the partial wind load provisions in the *National Building Code of Canada* or through the low rise wind load provisions in the *Structural Commentaries to the National Building Code of Canada*.

The commentary provides guidance on structures to be designed without a shearwall on one side. Three-sided wood structures can be designed provided that all the lateral forces can be safely transferred to the ground, no excessive deformations of the structure will occur as a result of torsion, and the dimensions of the structure meet the following restrictions:

- Depth of the diaphragm normal to the open wall must not exceed 7.5 m.
- Depth-to-width ratio must not be greater than 1:1 for one-storey buildings and 1:1.5 for buildings over one-storey in height. However, the depth-to-width ratio may be increased to 2:1 for plywood, waferboard or strandboard diaphragms where calculations show that deflections can be tolerated.

## Modification Factors

The tabulated resistance values for diaphragms are based upon the following formula and modification factors. When using the tables, be certain that the structure conforms exactly with the modification factors used in the tables; if not, use the factors below to adjust the tabulated values.

$$v_r = \phi \, V_d \, J_{sp} \, J_n$$

where:

$$\phi = 0.7$$
$$V_d = v_d \, (K_D \, K_{SF}) \; (kN/m)$$

**9**

Shearwalls and Diaphragms

$V_d$ = specified shear strength per unit length for shear walls or diaphragms (kN/m)

$K_D$ = load duration factor. The tabulated resistances are based on short term loading such as wind or earthquake loads ($K_D$ = 1.15). For permanent load duration multiply the tabulated values by 0.565. For standard term loads multiply the tabulated resistances by 0.870.

$K_{SF}$ = service condition factor for fastenings. The tabulated resistances are based on lumber that has been seasoned prior to fabrication (moisture content $\leq$ 15%) and being used in dry service conditions ($K_{SF}$ = 1.0). For unseasoned lumber in dry service conditions, multiply the tabulated values by $K_{SF}$ = 0.8. For wet service conditions, regardless of the lumber seasoning, multiply the resistances by $K_{SF}$ = 0.67.

$J_{sp}$ = species factor for framing material. It is incorporated into the tables.

$J_n$ = nail diameter factor. The tabulated resistances are based on diaphragms constructed with common wire nails. For diaphragms constructed with alternate nails, having a smaller diameter than the common nail in the tables and meeting the requirements in Table 9.3, $J_n$ is less than 1.0.

$$= \left(\frac{d_p}{d_c}\right)^2$$

$d_p$ = diameter of the nail being considered

$d_c$ = diameter of the common wire nail given in the tables.

| Table 9.3 **Requirements for using the nail diameter factor $J_n$** | Common wire nail diameter used in the tables, $d_c$ mm | Minimum nail diameter for alternate nail mm | Minimum yield strength for alternate nail MPa |
|---|---|---|---|
| | 2.84 | 2.27 | 660 |
| | 3.25 | 2.60 | 635 |
| | 3.66 | 2.93 | 615 |

# Checklist: **Diaphragms** ✔

To verify that the tabulated resistance values are valid for the diaphragm being designed the following questions should be asked (the appropriate modification factor is given in brackets):

1. Is load duration "short term" ($K_D$)?

2. Is the service conditon "dry" and are the framing members seasoned prior to fabrication (moisture content $\leq$ 15%) ($K_{SF}$)?

3. Is the diaphragm constructed with common wire nails?

If the answer to any of these questions is no, refer to the description of modification factors and adjust the tabulated values. Otherwise, the Diaphragm Selection Tables can be used directly.

### Example 1: Roof Diaphragm

Design the roof diaphragm shown below for the following conditions:

- one storey warehouse framed with S-P-F lumber
- building height = 4 m
- CSP plywood thickness (based on gravity loads) = 12.5 mm
- wind governs in north-south direction
- earthquake governs in east-west direction
- dry service conditions
- flexible diaphragm

**9**

Shearwalls and Diaphragms

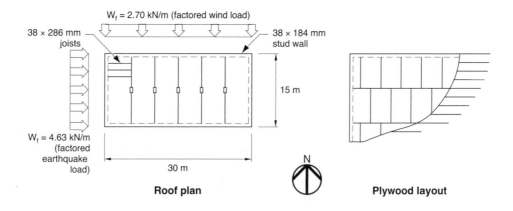

$W_f = 2.70$ kN/m (factored wind load)

38 × 286 mm joists

38 × 184 mm stud wall

15 m

$W_f = 4.63$ kN/m (factored earthquake load)

30 m

N

**Roof plan**                    **Plywood layout**

**Calculation**

Shear force along east and west walls:

$$v_f = \frac{w_f L}{2L_D} = \frac{2.70 \times 30.0}{2 \times 15} = 2.70 \text{ kN/m}$$

Shear force along north and south walls:

$$v_f = \frac{w_f L}{2L_D} = \frac{4.63 \times 15.0}{2 \times 30} = 1.16 \text{ kN/m}$$

1. Design of sheathing

From the Diaphragm Selection Tables, try 12.5 mm plywood with 3.25 mm diameter (2-1/2" long) common wire nails. The plywood layout is Case 2 for the wind load along the north wall and Case 4 for the earthquake load along the west wall. Using an unblocked diaphragm with nails spaced at 150 mm at the diaphragm boundary and at all panel edges, the factored shear resistance for both load cases is:

$$v_r = 3.16 \text{ kN/m} > 2.70 \text{ kN/m} \qquad\qquad \textit{Acceptable}$$

Note that 2-1/2" nails spaced at 300 mm on centre along intermediate framing members are also required.

2. Design of chords

The top plate of the 38 × 140 mm stud wall will be used as chord members. By inspection, the bending moment in the north-south direction will govern.

$$M_f = \frac{w_f L^2}{8} = \frac{2.70 \times 30.0^2}{8} = 304 \text{ kN} \cdot \text{m}$$

$$h = 15.0 - 0.140 = 14.9 \text{ m}$$

Therefore,

$$T_f = P_f = \frac{M_f}{h} = \frac{304}{14.9} = 20.4 \text{ kN}$$

Although the chord will consist of a double top plate, one piece must be able to carry the entire 20.4 kN load at splice locations in tension chords. Assuming that nails will be used to fasten chord members, the area of the chords is not reduced.

From the Tension Member Selection Tables check 38 × 140 mm No.1/No.2 grade S-P-F sawn lumber for short term loading ($K_D = 1.15$):

$$T_r = 34.2 \times 1.15 = 39.3 \text{ kN} > 20.4 \text{ kN} \qquad\qquad \textit{Acceptable}$$

Since the chord is fully laterally braced along its length by the wall sheathing and by the roof sheathing, buckling of the chord due to compression is not possible and tension controls the design.

3. Design of splice in tension chord

Try 3-1/2" common wire nails:

$$T_f = 20.4 \text{ kN}$$
$$N_r = \phi \, n_u \, J_Y \, n_F \, n_{Se} \, K' \, J'$$

Therefore,

$$n_F = \frac{T_f}{\phi \, n_u \, J_Y \, n_{Se} \, K' \, J'}$$

$\phi \, n_u J_Y$ = 0.720 kN (from Table 7.3)
$K_D$ = 1.15 (short term load duration)
$J_B$ = 1.6 (nails used in single shear and clinched on far side)
$J_D$ = 1.0 (nails used in chord member, not sheathing)
$K'$ = $K_D \, K_{SF} \, K_T$ = 1.15
$J'$ = $J_Y \, J_E \, J_A \, J_B \, J_D$ = 1.6

$$n_F = \frac{T_f}{\phi \, n_u \, J_Y \, n_{Se} \, K' \, J'} = \frac{20.4}{0.720 \times 1 \times 1.15 \times 1.6}$$

$$= 15.4 \text{ nails}$$

Therefore, use 16 nails in two staggered rows between each butt joint. If butt joints are 1.83 m apart the nail spacing and end distance is approximately 110 mm, which is acceptable (refer to Figure 7.4). The nailing may be reduced near the ends of the chords.

4. Shearwall and diaphragm connections

The details shown in Figure 9.4 may be used to transfer shear and lateral forces between the diaphragm and the walls. The spacing of nails or framing anchors must be calculated so that the resistance of the connection exceeds the applied forces.

**Use 12.5 mm plywood with 2-1/2" nails spaced at 150 mm along the diaphragm boundary and all panel edges. No blocking is required. The chords are two 38 × 140 mm No.1/No.2 grade S-P-F members lapped and nailed with sixteen 3-1/2" clinched nails spaced at 110 mm on centre.**

**9**

Shearwalls and Diaphragms

# Diaphragm Selection Tables

## DF-L    Factored Shear Resistance $v_r$ (kN/m)

| Common wire nail diameter mm | Minimum naill penetration in framing mm | Minimum nominal panel thickness[2] mm | Minimum width of framing member mm | Blocked | | | | Unblocked | |
|---|---|---|---|---|---|---|---|---|---|
| | | | | Nail spacing (mm) at diaphragm boundaries (all cases) and at continuous panel edges parallel to load (cases 3 and 4)[1] | | | | Nails spaced 150 mm maximum at supported panel ends[1] | |
| | | | | 150 | 100 | 64 | 50[3] | Load perp. to unblocked edges and continuous panel joints (Case 1) | All other configurations (Cases 2, 3 and 4) |
| | | | | Nail spacing at other panel edges (mm) | | | | | |
| | | | | 150 | 150 | 100 | 75 | | |
| 2.84 | 31 | 7.5 | 38 | 3.70 | 4.91 | 7.33 | 8.29 | 3.30 | 2.42 |
| | | | 64 | 4.19 | 5.47 | 8.29 | 9.42 | 3.70 | 2.74 |
| | | 9.5 | 38 | 4.03 | 5.47 | 8.21 | 9.18 | 3.62 | 2.74 |
| | | | 64 | 4.59 | 6.12 | 9.18 | 10.4 | 4.03 | 3.06 |
| 3.25 | 38 | 9.5 | 38 | 5.23 | 7.00 | 10.5 | 11.9 | 4.75 | 3.54 |
| | | | 64 | 5.88 | 7.89 | 11.8 | 13.4 | 5.23 | 3.94 |
| | | 11 | 38 | 5.55 | 7.41 | 11.0 | 12.6 | 5.07 | 3.70 |
| | | | 64 | 6.28 | 8.29 | 12.5 | 14.1 | 5.55 | 4.19 |
| | | 12.5 | 38 | 5.88 | 7.89 | 11.6 | 13.1 | 5.23 | 3.94 |
| | | | 64 | 6.60 | 8.77 | 13.1 | 14.8 | 5.80 | 4.35 |
| 3.66[4] | 41 | 12.5 | 38 | 6.36 | 8.45 | 12.6 | 14.3 | 5.55 | 4.19 |
| | | | 64 | 7.08 | 9.42 | 14.2 | 16.1 | 6.36 | 4.75 |
| | | 15.5 | 38 | 7.00 | 9.34 | 14.0 | 15.9 | 6.28 | 4.75 |
| | | | 64 | 7.89 | 10.5 | 15.8 | 18.0 | 7.00 | 5.23 |
| | | 18.5 | 64 | | 14.1 * | 20.4 * | | | |
| | | | 89 | | 16.4 * | 23.5 * | | | |

Notes:
1. Nails along intermediate framing members are to be the same size as used at the panel edges and spaced at 300 mm on centre.
2. For Construction Sheathing OSB, Table 9.1 provides an equivalence between tabulated thicknesses and panel mark.
3. Framing at adjoining panel edges are 64 mm nominal (or a built-up column composed of two 38 mm nominal width framing members connected to transfer the factored shear force), or wider and nails are staggered.
4. Framing at adjointing panel edges are 64 mm nominal (or a built-up column composed of two 38 mm nominal width framing members connected to transfer the factored shear force), or wider and nails are staggered when spaced 75 mm or less on centre.
* Two lines of fasteners are required.

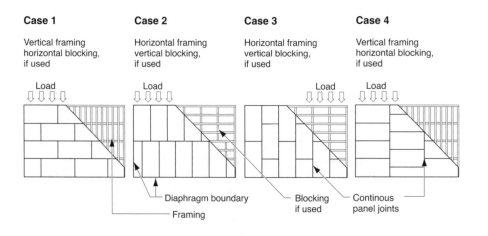

| Case 1 | Case 2 | Case 3 | Case 4 |
|---|---|---|---|
| Vertical framing horizontal blocking, if used | Horizontal framing vertical blocking, if used | Horizontal framing vertical blocking, if used | Vertical framing horizontal blocking, if used |

Diaphragm boundary
Framing
Blocking if used
Continuous panel joints

# Diaphragm Selection Tables

## Factored Shear Resistance $v_r$ (kN/m) H-F

| Common wire nail diameter mm | Minimum naill penetration in framing mm | Minimum nominal panel thickness[2] mm | Minimum width of framing member mm | Blocked | | | | Unblocked | |
|---|---|---|---|---|---|---|---|---|---|
| | | | | Nail spacing (mm) at diaphragm boundaries (all cases) and at continuous panel edges parallel to load (cases 3 and 4)[1] | | | | Nails spaced 150 mm maximum at supported panel ends[1] | |
| | | | | 150 | 100 | 64 | 50[3] | Load perp. to unblocked edges and continuous panel joints (Case 1) | All other configurations (Cases 2, 3 and 4) |
| | | | | Nail spacing at other panel edges (mm) | | | | | |
| | | | | 150 | 150 | 100 | 75 | | |
| 2.84 | 31 | 7.5 | 38 | 3.33 | 4.42 | 6.59 | 7.46 | 2.97 | 2.17 |
| | | | 64 | 3.77 | 4.93 | 7.46 | 8.48 | 3.33 | 2.46 |
| | | 9.5 | 38 | 3.62 | 4.93 | 7.39 | 8.26 | 3.26 | 2.46 |
| | | | 64 | 4.13 | 5.51 | 8.26 | 9.35 | 3.62 | 2.75 |
| 3.25 | 38 | 9.5 | 38 | 4.71 | 6.30 | 9.49 | 10.7 | 4.27 | 3.19 |
| | | | 64 | 5.29 | 7.10 | 10.7 | 12.0 | 4.71 | 3.55 |
| | | 11 | 38 | 5.00 | 6.67 | 9.93 | 11.3 | 4.56 | 3.33 |
| | | | 64 | 5.65 | 7.46 | 11.2 | 12.7 | 5.00 | 3.77 |
| | | 12.5 | 38 | 5.29 | 7.10 | 10.4 | 11.8 | 4.71 | 3.55 |
| | | | 64 | 5.94 | 7.90 | 11.8 | 13.3 | 5.22 | 3.91 |
| 3.66[4] | 41 | 12.5 | 38 | 5.72 | 7.61 | 11.3 | 12.9 | 5.00 | 3.77 |
| | | | 64 | 6.38 | 8.48 | 12.8 | 14.5 | 5.72 | 4.27 |
| | | 15.5 | 38 | 6.30 | 8.40 | 12.6 | 14.3 | 5.65 | 4.27 |
| | | | 64 | 7.10 | 9.42 | 14.2 | 16.2 | 6.30 | 4.71 |
| | | 18.5 | 64 | | 12.7 * | 18.4 * | | | |
| | | | 89 | | 14.8 * | 21.2 * | | | |

Notes:
1. Nails along intermediate framing members are to be the same size as used at the panel edges and spaced at 300 mm on centre.
2. For Construction Sheathing OSB, Table 9.1 provides an equivalence between tabulated thicknesses and panel mark.
3. Framing at adjoining panel edges are 64 mm nominal (or a built-up column composed of two 38 mm nominal width framing members connected to transfer the factored shear force), or wider and nails are staggered.
4. Framing at adjointing panel edges are 64 mm nominal (or a built-up column composed of two 38 mm nominal width framing members connected to transfer the factored shear force), or wider and nails are staggered when spaced 75 mm or less on centre.
* Two lines of fasteners are required.

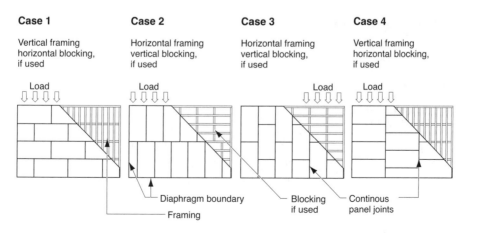

| Case 1 | Case 2 | Case 3 | Case 4 |
|---|---|---|---|
| Vertical framing horizontal blocking, if used | Horizontal framing vertical blocking, if used | Horizontal framing vertical blocking, if used | Vertical framing horizontal blocking, if used |

Load

Diaphragm boundary

Framing

Blocking if used

Continous panel joints

9

Shearwalls and Diaphragms

# Diaphragm Selection Tables

 **S-P-F** ## Factored Shear Resistance $v_r$ (kN/m)

| Common wire nail diameter mm | Minimum naill penetration in framing mm | Minimum nominal panel thickness[2] mm | Minimum width of framing member mm | Blocked | | | | Unblocked | |
|---|---|---|---|---|---|---|---|---|---|
| | | | | Nail spacing (mm) at diaphragm boundaries (all cases) and at continuous panel edges parallel to load (cases 3 and 4)[1] | | | | Nails spaced 150 mm maximum at supported panel ends[1] | |
| | | | | 150 | 100 | 64 | 50[3] | Load perp. to unblocked edges and continuous panel joints (Case 1) | All other configurations (Cases 2, 3 and 4) |
| | | | | Nail spacing at other panel edges (mm) | | | | | |
| | | | | 150 | 150 | 100 | 75 | | |
| 2.84 | 31 | 7.5 | 38 | 2.96 | 3.93 | 5.86 | 6.63 | 2.64 | 1.93 |
| | | | 64 | 3.35 | 4.38 | 6.63 | 7.53 | 2.96 | 2.19 |
| | | 9.5 | 38 | 3.22 | 4.38 | 6.57 | 7.34 | 2.90 | 2.19 |
| | | | 64 | 3.67 | 4.89 | 7.34 | 8.31 | 3.22 | 2.45 |
| 3.25 | 38 | 9.5 | 38 | 4.19 | 5.60 | 8.44 | 9.53 | 3.80 | 2.83 |
| | | | 64 | 4.70 | 6.31 | 9.47 | 10.7 | 4.19 | 3.16 |
| | | 11 | 38 | 4.44 | 5.92 | 8.82 | 10.0 | 4.06 | 2.96 |
| | | | 64 | 5.02 | 6.63 | 10.0 | 11.3 | 4.44 | 3.35 |
| | | 12.5 | 38 | 4.70 | 6.31 | 9.27 | 10.5 | 4.19 | 3.16 |
| | | | 64 | 5.28 | 7.02 | 10.5 | 11.8 | 4.64 | 3.48 |
| 3.66[4] | 41 | 12.5 | 38 | 5.09 | 6.76 | 10.0 | 11.5 | 4.44 | 3.35 |
| | | | 64 | 5.67 | 7.53 | 11.4 | 12.9 | 5.09 | 3.80 |
| | | 15.5 | 38 | 5.60 | 7.47 | 11.2 | 12.8 | 5.02 | 3.80 |
| | | | 64 | 6.31 | 8.37 | 12.6 | 14.4 | 5.60 | 4.19 |
| | | 18.5 | 64 | | 11.3 * | 16.4 * | | | |
| | | | 89 | | 13.1 * | 18.8 * | | | |

Notes:
1. Nails along intermediate framing members are to be the same size as used at the panel edges and spaced at 300 mm on centre.
2. For Construction Sheathing OSB, Table 9.1 provides an equivalence between tabulated thicknesses and panel mark.
3. Framing at adjoining panel edges are 64 mm nominal (or a built-up column composed of two 38 mm nominal width framing members connected to transfer the factored shear force), or wider and nails are staggered.
4. Framing at adjoining panel edges are 64 mm nominal (or a built-up column composed of two 38 mm nominal width framing members connected to transfer the factored shear force), or wider and nails are staggered when spaced 75 mm or less on centre.
* Two lines of fasteners are required.

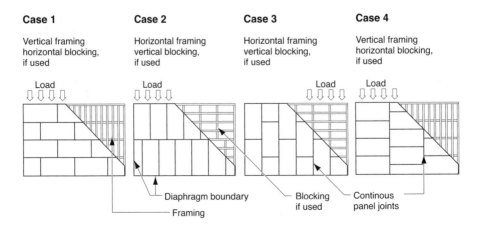

**Case 1**

Vertical framing horizontal blocking, if used

**Case 2**

Horizontal framing vertical blocking, if used

**Case 3**

Horizontal framing vertical blocking, if used

**Case 4**

Vertical framing horizontal blocking, if used

Load

Load

Load

Load

Diaphragm boundary

Framing

Blocking if used

Continous panel joints

# Diaphragm Selection Tables

## Factored Shear Resistance $v_r$ (kN/m) **Nor**

| Common wire nail diameter mm | Minimum naill penetration in framing mm | Minimum nominal panel thickness[2] mm | Minimum width of framing member mm | Blocked | | | | Unblocked | |
|---|---|---|---|---|---|---|---|---|---|
| | | | | Nail spacing (mm) at diaphragm boundaries (all cases) and at continuous panel edges parallel to load (cases 3 and 4)[1] | | | | Nails spaced 150 mm maximum at supported panel ends[1] | |
| | | | | 150 | 100 | 64 | 50[3] | Load perp. to unblocked edges and continuous panel joints (Case 1) | All other configurations (Cases 2, 3 and 4) |
| | | | | Nail spacing at other panel edges (mm) | | | | | |
| | | | | 150 | 150 | 100 | 75 | | |
| 2.84 | 31 | 7.5 | 38 | 2.59 | 3.44 | 5.13 | 5.80 | 2.31 | 1.69 |
| | | | 64 | 2.93 | 3.83 | 5.80 | 6.59 | 2.59 | 1.92 |
| | | 9.5 | 38 | 2.82 | 3.83 | 5.75 | 6.42 | 2.54 | 1.92 |
| | | | 64 | 3.21 | 4.28 | 6.42 | 7.27 | 2.82 | 2.14 |
| 3.25 | 38 | 9.5 | 38 | 3.66 | 4.90 | 7.38 | 8.34 | 3.32 | 2.48 |
| | | | 64 | 4.11 | 5.52 | 8.28 | 9.35 | 3.66 | 2.76 |
| | | 11 | 38 | 3.89 | 5.18 | 7.72 | 8.79 | 3.55 | 2.59 |
| | | | 64 | 4.40 | 5.80 | 8.73 | 9.86 | 3.89 | 2.93 |
| | | 12.5 | 38 | 4.11 | 5.52 | 8.11 | 9.19 | 3.66 | 2.76 |
| | | | 64 | 4.62 | 6.14 | 9.19 | 10.4 | 4.06 | 3.04 |
| 3.66[4] | 41 | 12.5 | 38 | 4.45 | 5.92 | 8.79 | 10.0 | 3.89 | 2.93 |
| | | | 64 | 4.96 | 6.59 | 10.0 | 11.3 | 4.45 | 3.32 |
| | | 15.5 | 38 | 4.90 | 6.54 | 9.80 | 11.2 | 4.40 | 3.32 |
| | | | 64 | 5.52 | 7.33 | 11.0 | 12.6 | 4.90 | 3.66 |
| | | 18.5 | 64 | | 9.86 * | 14.3 * | | | |
| | | | 89 | | 11.5 * | 16.5 * | | | |

Notes:
1. Nails along intermediate framing members are to be the same size as used at the panel edges and spaced at 300 mm on centre.
2. For Construction Sheathing OSB, Table 9.1 provides an equivalence between tabulated thicknesses and panel mark.
3. Framing at adjoining panel edges are 64 mm nominal (or a built-up column composed of two 38 mm nominal width framing members connected to transfer the factored shear force), or wider and nails are staggered.
4. Framing at adjointing panel edges are 64 mm nominal (or a built-up column composed of two 38 mm nominal width framing members connected to transfer the factored shear force), or wider and nails are staggered when spaced 75 mm or less on centre.
* Two lines of fasteners are required.

| Case 1 | Case 2 | Case 3 | Case 4 |
|---|---|---|---|
| Vertical framing horizontal blocking, if used | Horizontal framing vertical blocking, if used | Horizontal framing vertical blocking, if used | Vertical framing horizontal blocking, if used |

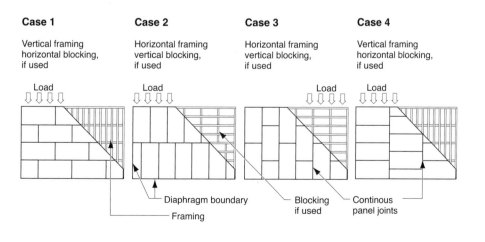

9

Shearwalls and Diaphragms

# 9.3 Shearwall Design

### Shear Resistance

The shear resistance of wood shearwalls is based on the strength and connection of wood-based panels and gypsum wallboard panels. Other construction details such as blocking at panel edges and hold-down connections also affect the shear resistance.

#### Plywood, OSB and Waferboard Sheathing

Tabulated shear values, based on tests of plywood shearwalls, have been extended to OSB and waferboard shearwalls, based on test data. Shearwalls with thicker sheathing are generally stronger than shearwalls with thinner sheathing, except where the strength of the shearwall is limited by the capacity of the nail.

If the nails used to construct the shearwalls are not common wire nails, the strength of the shearwall must be adjusted using the $J_n$ factor. Alternate types of nails must meet the limitations in Table 9.3, and the minimum nail penetration requirements given in the Shearwall Selection Tables. Nails must not be placed within 9 mm of the edge of the panel, or over-driven more than 15 percent of the panel thickness.

#### Type X (fire-rated) Gypsum Wallboard Sheathing

CSA O86 includes limited design provisions for shearwalls constructed with gypsum wallboard conforming only to Type X (fire-rated) in accordance with ASTM C36. Shearwalls using gypsum wallboard must consist of 1200 X 2400 mm or larger sheets, except that one or two smaller sheets may be used near the boundaries. Nails or screws used to attach the gypsum wallboard to the studs cannot be placed within 9 mm of the edge of the panel.

The shear resistance of gypsum wallboard shearwalls is a function of the thickness of the gypsum wallboard panels, the connection of the panels to the framing members, and the effects of hold-down connections and blocking at the panel edges.

When gypsum wallboard panels are considered in earthquake resistance, the applicable National Building Code of Canada seismic force modification factor, $R_d$, is 2. Resistance values are limited to shearwalls used in storey heights of 3.6 m or less and only apply to gypsum wallboard resisting loads of short term duration such as wind or earthquake.

Gypsum wallboard panels must be used in combination with structural wood-based panels either in the same shearwall or in parallel shearwalls, with a balanced spatial distribution of the gypsum wallboard and wood-based panels resisting shear in a given direction in a particular storey. The factored shear resistance of gypsum wallboard used in resisting the storey shear force cannot be greater than the percentage given in Table 9.4.

**9**

Shearwalls and Diaphragms

Table 9.4
**Maximum percentage of total shear forces resisted by gypsum wallboard in a storey**

| Storey | 4-storey building | 3-storey building | 2-storey building | 1-storey building |
|--------|-------------------|-------------------|-------------------|-------------------|
| 4th | 80 | – | – | – |
| 3rd | 60 | 80 | – | – |
| 2nd | 40 | 60 | 80 | – |
| 1st | 40 | 40 | 60 | 80 |

## Unblocked Shearwalls

Design provisions for unblocked shearwalls were introduced in the 2001 edition of CSA O86 based on shearwall tests using structural wood-based panels (see the Commentary). Blocking is not required for structural wood-based panel shearwalls where the specified shear strength is adjusted by the strength adjustment factor $J_{ub}$ factor (Table 9.5), and the following conditions are met:

- wood-based panels are applied horizontally;
- the maximum height of the shearwall, $H_S$, is 2.44 m; and
- the maximum stud spacing is 600 mm and details are in accordance with Table 9.5.

Table 9.5
**Strength adjustment factor[1], $J_{ub}$, for horizontally sheathed unblocked shearwalls[2]**

| Nail spacing at supported edges mm | Nail spacing at intermediate studs mm | Stud spacing (mm) | | | |
|---|---|---|---|---|---|
| | | 300 | 400 | 500 | 600 |
| 150 | 150 | 1.0 | 0.8 | 0.6 | 0.5 |
| 150 | 300 | 0.8 | 0.6 | 0.5 | 0.4 |

Notes:
1. Strength adjustment factor is only be applicable to horizontally sheathed structural wood-based panels
2. Strength adjustment factor is applied to the specified shear strength of blocked shearwall with nails spaced at 150 mm on centre around panel edges and 300 mm on centre along intermediate framing members.
3. Maximum height of shearwall is 2.44 m
4. Unblocked shearwalls using gypsum wallboard are assigned specified strengths in the Gypsum Panel Shearwall Selection Table.

## Shearwalls with Multiple Layers

Shearwalls may be constructed with:

- wood-based panels on both sides;
- gypsum panels on both sides; or
- wood-based panels on one side and gypsum panels on the opposite side.

The factored shear resistance of panels on both sides of the same shearwall may be added together. Where wood structural panel are applied over 12.7 mm or 15.9 mm thick gypsum wallboard, the shear resistance of the wood-based panel may be considered in the shearwall design, provided minimum nail penetration requirements are met. In all other cases with multiple layers of panels on the same side of the shearwall, only the shear resistance of the panel closest to the studs is considered in design.

**Shearwalls With Segments**

Where shearwalls have openings for windows or doors, only the full height shearwall segments between the openings and at the ends of the shearwalls are considered in the shearwall design. Where the height of the shearwall segment, $H_s$, measured from the bottom of the bottom plate to the top of the top plate, is greater than 3.5 times the length of the shearwall segment, $L_w$, the segment is not included in the resistance calculation.

A shearwall is designed to resist the sum of factored shear forces from upper storey shearwalls and diaphragms. Where materials or construction details vary between shearwall segments, the capacity of the shearwall may either be conservatively estimated based on the minimum segment capacity. Alternatively the total factored shear force on the shearwall, F, may be distributed to each of the segments based on the relative strength of each segment.

The shearwall sheathing and the connection of the sheathing to the framing members must be designed so that the factored shear resistance of the shearwall segment per unit length, $v_r$, is equal to or greater than the maximum shear force in the shearwall segment per unit length, $f_j$. The maximum shear force is assumed to be uniformly distributed the full length of the shearwall segment parallel to the applied load, $L_w$, and $f_j = F_j/L_w$.

Capacity of shearwalls may vary with load direction and shearwalls must be designed for lateral loads acting in opposite directions. The resistance on the shearwall in each direction must be greater than the corresponding lateral load.

**Shearwall Segments Without Hold-downs**

Traditionally, shearwalls have been designed using chords and hold-down connections at the ends of all shearwall segments. Hold-downs are designed to transfer the chord segment overturning force, $T_f$, to the shearwall or foundation below. CSA O86 includes provisions for design of shearwall segments without hold-down connections.

Without hold-downs, the overturning tension force is transferred from the top wall plate to the bottom wall plate through the shearwall sheathing. Since a portion of the shearwall sheathing is used to resist the overturning force, the shear capacity of the sheathing is reduced. Even though hold-down anchors are not used, anchorage is still required to transfer the uplift force from the wall plate to the foundation or shearwall below (see Commentary).

In some cases, hold-down connections may be placed at one end of a shearwall segment. Where the load is from the end of the segment that contains the hold-down, overturning uplift forces will be resisted by the hold-down. When the load is from the direction opposite the hold-down, the sheathing resists overturning uplift forces. The shear capacity of the shearwall segment is multiplied by the hold-down factor, $J_{hd}$, which must be calculated for loads acting in opposite directions.

**9**

**Shearwalls and Diaphragms**

Hold-down connections are not required for shearwall segments where the specified strength is adjusted by the $J_{hd}$ factor, and the following conditions are met:

- the sum of the factored basic shear resistances on both sides of the shearwall, $V_{hd}/L_W$, < 8.3 kN/m;
- shear resistance of the wood-based panel, $v_r$, is based on nail diameters ≤ 3.25 mm; and edge panel nail spacing ≥ 100 mm;
- the maximum height of the shearwall, $H_s$, is 3.6 m; and
- the factored uplift restraint force at the bottom of the end stud of the shearwall segment, $P_j$, is ≥ 0.

$J_{hd}$ is calculated as:

Case 1

$J_{hd}$ = 1.0 where there is sufficient dead load to resist overturning uplift forces or hold-down connections resist all of the overturning force.

Case 2

Where there is no net uplift at the top of the shearwall segment due to overturning and there is no hold-down connection at the bottom of the shearwall segment to resist overturning:

$$J_{hd} = \sqrt{1 + 2\frac{P_j}{V_{hd}} + \left(\frac{H_s}{L_W}\right)^2} - \left(\frac{H_s}{L_W}\right) < 1.0$$

where:

$P_j$ = factored uplift restraint force at the bottom of the end stud of the segment calculated as shown below (kN)

$V_{hd}$ = sum of the factored basic shear resistances on both sides of the shearwall segment calculated with $J_{hd}$ = 1.0 (kN)

     = $\Sigma(v_r\, J_n\, J_{ub} + v_{rg}) \times L_W$

$H_s$ = height of the shearwall segment measured from the bottom of the bottom plate to the top of the top plate (m)

$L_W$ = Length of the shearwall segment (m)

Case 3

Where hold-downs are provided at the bottom wall plate to resist overturning forces but the sheathing is in tension at the top of the shearwall segment due to overturning forces from upper storeys:

$$J_{hd} = \frac{V_{hd} + P_t}{V_{hd}} \le 1.0$$

where:

$P_t$ = factored uplift restraint force at the top of the end stud of the segment calculated as shown below (kN)

**Note:** $P_t < 0$

$V_{hd}$ = sum of the factored basic shear resistances on both sides of the shearwall segment calculated with $J_{hd} = 1.0$ (kN) (see above)

Calculation of overturning restraint forces, $P_j$ and $P_t$, and overturning force, $R_j$, is illustrated in Figure 9.6.

$P_{tj}$ = factored uplift restraint force at the top of the end stud of the segment (kN)

$P_j$ = factored uplift restraint force at the bottom of the end stud of the segment (kN)

$R_j$ = resultant overturning force at the end of the shearwall segment (kN)

$q_j$ = the factored uniform dead load at the top of the shearwall (kN/m)

$q_{wj}$ = the factored uniform dead load of the wall (kN/m)

**In the top storey of a structure:**

$P_{tj}$ = the factored roof dead load acting at the top of the end stud in the shearwall segment (kN)

$P_j$ = $P_{tj}$ + the factored wall dead load acting at the bottom of the end stud in the shearwall segment (kN)

$$R_j = \frac{F_j (H_s + d)}{L_w} - P_j \quad (kN)$$

where:

$F_j$ = factored shear force on the shearwall segment

$$= F \times \frac{V_{rs}}{\Sigma V_{rs}}$$

$F$ = the total factored shear force on the shearwall (kN)

$V_{rs}$ = the factored shear resistance of the shearwall segment (kN)

$$= V_{hd} J_{hd}$$

$\Sigma V_{rs}$ = the sum of the factored shear resistances for all of the shearwall segments in the shearwall (kN)

$H_s + d$ = the total storey height (m)

**9**

Shearwalls and Diaphragms

**In the lower storeys of a structure:**

$P_{tj}$ = the factored floor dead load acting on the top of the end stud in the shearwall segment minus $R_j$ from the storey above (kN)

$P_j$ = $P_{tj}$ + the factored wall dead load acting at the bottom of the end stud in the shearwall segment (kN)

$$R_j = \frac{F_j\,(H_s + d)}{L_w} - P_j \quad (kN)$$

Figure 9.5
**Steps in Calculation of $J_{hd}$**

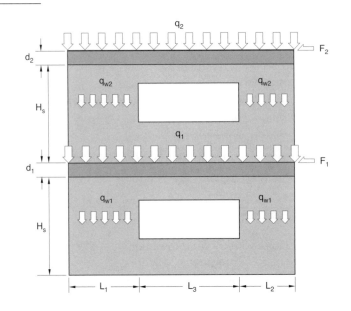

Steps:
Calculate $J_{hd}$ for all segments of the upper storey shearwall before proceeding to the next lower storey.
1. Divide the shearwall into segments ($L_1$, $L_2$)
2. Calculate the dead load to resist overturning at the top of the segments ($P_{tj}$), and the bottom of the segments ($P_j$).
3. Calculate $J_{hd}$ for each of the segments.
4. Calculate the shear resistance of each segment ($V_{rs}$).
5. Distribute the storey shear load (F) to the segments based on their relative resistance.
6. Calculate the resultant overturning force at the end of each segment ($R_j$).
7. Repeat steps 2 to 6 for lateral loads acting in the opposite direction.
8. Repeat steps 1 to 7 for each lower storey shearwall.

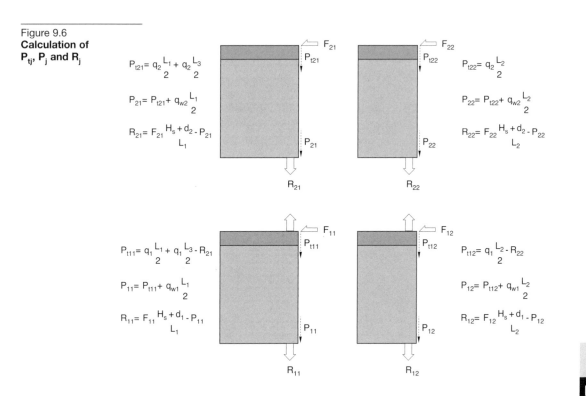

Figure 9.6
**Calculation of**
**$P_{tj}$, $P_j$ and $R_j$**

$$P_{t21} = q_2 \frac{L_1}{2} + q_2 \frac{L_3}{2}$$

$$P_{21} = P_{t21} + q_{w2} \frac{L_1}{2}$$

$$R_{21} = F_{21} \frac{H_s + d_2}{L_1} - P_{21}$$

$$P_{t22} = q_2 \frac{L_2}{2}$$

$$P_{22} = P_{t22} + q_{w2} \frac{L_2}{2}$$

$$R_{22} = F_{22} \frac{H_s + d_2}{L_2} - P_{22}$$

$$P_{t11} = q_1 \frac{L_1}{2} + q_1 \frac{L_3}{2} - R_{21}$$

$$P_{11} = P_{t11} + q_{w1} \frac{L_1}{2}$$

$$R_{11} = F_{11} \frac{H_s + d_1}{L_1} - P_{11}$$

$$P_{t12} = q_1 \frac{L_2}{2} - R_{22}$$

$$P_{12} = P_{t12} + q_{w1} \frac{L_2}{2}$$

$$R_{12} = F_{12} \frac{H_s + d_1}{L_2} - P_{12}$$

## Resistance to Overturning

### Chords

Resistance to overturning is provided by shearwall chord members at the ends of the shearwall segments. The chord members must be designed so that the factored compression and tensile resistance is greater than or equal to maximum factored axial load. The axial force in each chord member due to overturning is calculated as follows:

$$P_f \text{ and } T_f = \frac{F_j (H_s + d)}{h}$$

where:

$P_f$ = factored compressive force due to overturning (kN)

$T_f$ = factored tensile force due to overturning (kN)

$F_j$ = the factored shear force on the shearwall segment (kN)

$H_s + d$ = the total storey height (m)

$h$ = centre-to-centre distance between chord members (m)

Where hold-down connections are used to resist overturning, the end studs in the shearwall segment must be designed to resist the maximum

**9**

Shearwalls and Diaphragms

factored tensile force $T_f$. Tensile resistances for various member sizes are given in the Tension Member Selection Tables in Chapter 4. Where hold-down connections are not used to resist uplift, the end studs in the segment do not have to be designed to resist $T_f$, because the forces are transferred through the sheathing.

The end studs in the segment, acting in compression, must be designed as chord members to resist $P_f$ in addition to the factored gravity loads that they support. Compression resistance of studs is given in Chapter 3. For members without hold-down connections, $P_f$ is calculated using $h = L_W - 0.3$ m.

## Hold-Down Connections

Hold-down connections are used to anchor the shearwall chords to the shearwall or foundation below. This may be done using a hold-down bracket and bolts as shown in Figure 9.7.

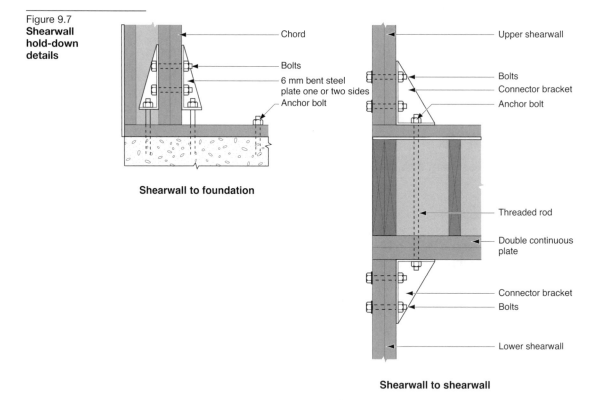

Figure 9.7
**Shearwall
hold-down
details**

**Shearwall to foundation**

**Shearwall to shearwall**

## Anchorages

Where hold-down connections are not used, the forces in the shearwall sheathing will cause uplift in the bottom plate of the shearwall. The uplift forces from the bottom plate are transferred to the shearwall or the foundation below using anchorages. Anchorages between shearwalls may consist of washers and threaded rods (see Figure 9.8 and Table 9.6). Bottom plates may be anchored to the foundation using anchor bolts.

Anchorages must be located within 300 mm of the end of the shearwall segment and be capable of resisting the resultant overturning force at the end of the segment, $R_j$, calculated in accordance with Figure 9.6.

Figure 9.8
**Anchorages**

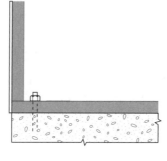

**Shearwall to foundation**

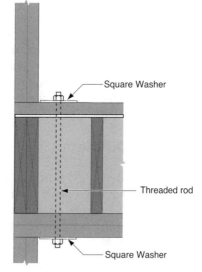

**Shearwall to shearwall**

Table 9.6
**Factored tensile resistance of shearwall to shearwall anchorage (kN)**

| Bolt or rod diameter[1] | Washer size | Species of wall plates | Tensile resistance of anchorage |
|---|---|---|---|
| 1/2 in. | 64 mm x 5 mm thick square washer | D. Fir-L | 26.3 |
|  |  | Hem-Fir | 18.5 |
|  |  | S-P-F | 21.3 |
|  |  | Northern | 14.1 |
| 5/8 in. | 70 mm x 6 mm thick square washer | D. Fir-L | 33.8 |
|  |  | Hem-Fir | 22.2 |
|  |  | S-P-F | 25.6 |
|  |  | Northern | 16.9 |
| 3/4 in. | 76 mm x 6 mm thick square washer | D. Fir-L | 39.9 |
|  |  | Hem-Fir | 26.2 |
|  |  | S-P-F | 30.2 |
|  |  | Northern | 19.9 |

Note:
1. Capacity based on ASTM A307 bolts.
2. Capacity based on short duration load ($K_D$ = 1.15). For normal duration load, multiply tabulated values by 0.87.

## Shear Transfer

Shear forces in the shearwall must be transferred to lower storey shearwalls or the foundation. This may be accomplished through the connection of the bottom plate of upper storey shearwalls to the floor framing, where the floor

**9**

Shearwalls and Diaphragms

framing is properly connected to lower storey shearwall (see Figure 9.4). The connection between the floor framing and the lower storey shearwall must be capable of resisting the combined shear forces of the upper storey shearwall and the floor diaphragm.

Oversized (longer) sheathing panels may be used to connect upper storey shearwalls to lower storey shearwalls through the floor rim joist or end joist. In this approach, space must be left between the upper and lower storey shear panels to accommodate movement of the rim joist, and nails must be staggered to prevent splitting of plates.

Anchor bolts are used to transfer the shear force from the lower storey shearwalls to the foundation. Anchor bolts are illustrated in Figure 9.7 and may be designed using the Wood to Concrete Bolt Selection Table in Chapter 7.

## Deflection

Deflection formulas are not available for unblocked shearwalls, shearwalls without hold-downs or gypsum wallboard shearwalls. The following formula may be used to assess the deflection of blocked wood shearwall segments with hold-down connections:

$$\Delta_s = \frac{2v_s H_s^3}{3EAL_W} + \frac{v_s H_s}{B_v} + 0.0025 H_s e_n + \frac{H_s}{L_W}\Delta_a$$

where:

$\Delta_s$ = horizontal in-plane deflection of top of shearwall (mm)

$v_s$ = maximum shear force per unit length due to specified lateral loads (N/mm)

$H_s$ = shearwall height (mm)

$E$ = modulus of elasticity of chords (MPa)

$A$ = cross-sectional area of chord members (mm$^2$)

$L_W$ = length of shearwall segment (mm)

$B_v$ = shear-through-thickness rigidity (N/mm) (see Table 7.3 of CSA O86)

$e_n$ = nail deformation for a particular load per nail (mm) (see Table 9.2)

$\Delta_a$ = deflection due to anchorage details (rotation and slip at hold-down connections) (mm) (refer to manufacturer's literature)

## Modification Factors

The tabulated resistance values for diaphragms are based upon the following formula and modification factors. When using the tables, be certain that the structure conforms exactly with the modification factors used in the tables; if not, use the factors below to adjust the tabulated values.

# Checklist: **Shearwalls** ✔

To verify that the tabulated resistance values are valid for the shearwall being designed the following questions should be asked (the appropriate modification factor is given in brackets):

1. Is load duration "short term" ($K_D$)?

2. Is the service conditon "dry" and are the framing members seasoned prior to fabrication (moisture content ≤ 15%) ($K_{SF}$)?

3. Is the wood-based panel shearwall constructed with common wire nails ($J_n$)?

4. Is the wood-based panel shearwall blocked ($J_{ub}$)?

5. Is there sufficient dead load to resist overturning or are hold-down connections provided to resist all of the overturning forces ($J_{hd}$)?

If the answer to any of these questions is no, refer to the description of modification factors and adjust the tabulated values. Otherwise, the Shearwall Selection Tables can be used directly.

**9**

Shearwalls and Diaphragms

For shearwalls constructed with wood-based panels:

$$v_r = \phi V_d J_{sp} J_n J_{ub} J_{hd}$$

For shearwalls constructed with gypsum wallboard panels:

$$v_{rg} = \phi v_{dg} J_{hd}$$

where:

$\phi$ = 0.7

$V_d$ = $v_d (K_D K_{SF})$ (kN/m)

$v_d$ = specified shear strength per unit length for wood-based panel shearwalls (kN/m)

$K_D$ = load duration factor. The tabulated resistances are based on short term loading such as wind or earthquake ($K_D$ = 1.15). For shearwalls of wood-based panels under permanent load duration multiply the tabulated values by 0.565; and under standard term loads multiply the tabulated resistances by 0.870. Gypsum wallboard is only considered effective in resisting short duration loads.

$K_{SF}$ = service condition factor for fastenings. The tabulated resistances are based on lumber that has been seasoned prior to fabrication (moisture content 15%) and being used in dry service conditions ($K_{SF}$ = 1.0). In the case of shearwalls of wood-based panels using unseasoned lumber in dry service conditions, multiply the tabulated values by $K_{SF}$ = 0.8; and for wet service conditions, regardless of the lumber seasoning, multiply the resistances by $K_{SF}$ = 0.67. Gypsum wallboard is not permitted in wet service conditions.

$J_{sp}$ = species factor for framing material. It is incorporated into the tables.

$J_n$ = nail diameter factor. The tabulated resistances for wood-based panels are based on shearwalls constructed with common wire nails. For shearwalls constructed with alternate nails, having a smaller diameter than the common nail in the tables and meeting the requirements in Table 9.3, $J_n$ is less than 1.0.

$$= \left(\frac{d_p}{d_c}\right)^2$$

$d_p$ = diameter of the alternate nail being considered

$d_c$ = diameter of the common wire nail given in the tables.

$J_{ub}$ = factor for unblocked shearwalls from Table 9.5

$J_{hd}$ = hold-down factor. Where there is sufficient dead load to resist overturning or hold-down connections provided to resist uplift due to overturning $J_{hd}$ = 1.0. Where hold-down connections are not provided, $J_{hd}$ is calculated using Case 2 or Case 3 equations on page 472 and 473.

$v_{dg}$ = specified shear strength for shearwalls constructed with gypsum sheathing (kN/m)

## Example 1: Shearwalls

Design the shearwalls shown below for wind loading under the following conditions:

- two storey office building framed with S-P-F lumber studs spaced at 400 mm
- OSB wall sheathing is applied directly to the studs
- dry service conditions
- factored roof diaphragm reaction ($F_2$) = 20 kN
- factored floor diaphragm reaction = 40 kN ($F_1$= 40 + 20 = 60 kN)
- roof and floor framing parallel to the wall
- walls do not support any roof loads ($q_2$ = 0 kN/m)
- walls support a factored floor dead load of 0.5 kN/m (including a 0.85 dead load factor) ($q_1$ = 0.5 kN/m)
- walls are 3 m high with a specified dead load of 0.35 kPa
- depth of the roof and floor framing is 0.3 m

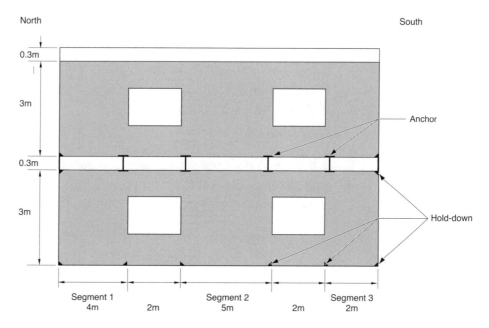

North                      South

0.3m

3m

Anchor

0.3m

3m

Hold-down

Segment 1        Segment 2        Segment 3
4m       2m       5m       2m       2m

**Calculation**

1. Design of sheathing and anchorages

9.5 mm sheathing is required to resist wind loads on the face of the wall. Since the sheathing is applied directly to the studs spaced at 400 mm, design values for 11 mm sheathing may be used. 12.5 mm gypsum is applied to the inside of the wall. The OSB and gypsum panel edges are supported by framing or blocking. The designer wishes to minimize the number of hold-down connections required by using them only at the end of the wall in the top storey and around all openings in the bottom storey.

## Second storey

The wall must be designed to resist wind from the north and south. From the Wood-Based Panel Shearwall Selection Table for S-P-F framing, select 11.0 mm OSB with 2-1/2" (3.25 mm diameter) common nails spaced at 150 mm. From the Shearwall Selection Table for Gypsum select 12.5 mm gypsum wallboard with nails or screws spaced at 200 mm for blocked walls.

$$v_r = 4.19 \text{ kN/m}$$
$$v_{rg} = 0.98 \text{ kN/m}$$

Note: Since the following conditions are met, wall segments may be designed without hold-down connections:

- wall height, $(H_s) < 3.6$ m;
- $v_r + v_{rg} < 8.3$ kN/m; and
- $v_r$ is based on nail diameter $\leq 3.25$ mm and edge panel nail spacing is $\geq 100$ mm.

**9**

Shearwalls and Diaphragms

For each of the second storey shearwall segments calculate $V_{hd}$, $P_j$, $J_{hd}$ and $V_{rs}$ for north and south wind directions.

where:

$$V_{hd} = \Sigma(v_r\, J_n\, J_{ub} + v_{rg})L_W$$
$$= (4.19 \times 1.0 \times 1.0 + 0.98) \times L_W$$
$$= 5.17\, L_W$$

$P_t$ = 0 (the wall does not support any load from the roof)

$q_w$ = (3 m x 0.35 kPa) x 0.85

    = 0.89 kN/m

$$P_j = P_t + q_w\, \frac{L_W}{2}$$

$J_{hd}$ = 1.0 if a hold-down is used to resist overturning

$$= \sqrt{1 + 2\, \frac{P_j}{V_{hd}} + \left(\frac{H_s}{L_W}\right)^2} - \left(\frac{H_s}{L_W}\right) \le 1.0 \text{ without a hold-down}$$

$$V_{rs} = V_{hd}\, J_{hd}$$

Second storey shearwall segments, hold-down factors ($J_{hd}$) and shear resistances ($V_{rs}$)

|  |  | Segment 1 | Segment 2 | Segment 3 |
|---|---|---|---|---|
|  | $L_W$ (m) | 4 | 5 | 2 |
|  | $V_{hd}$ (kN) | 20.7 | 25.8 | 10.3 |
| Wind from the North | $P_t$ (kN) | 0 | 0 | 0 |
|  | $P_j$ (kN) | 1.78 | 2.23 | 0.89 |
|  | Hold-down* | Yes | No | No |
|  | $J_{hd}$ | 1 | 0.638 | 0.350 |
|  | $V_{rs}$ (kN) | 20.7 | 16.5 | 3.62 |
| Wind from the South | $P_t$ (kN) | 0 | 0 | 0 |
|  | $P_j$ (kN) | 1.78 | 2.23 | 0.89 |
|  | Hold-down* | No | No | Yes |
|  | $J_{hd}$ | 0.567 | 0.638 | 1 |
|  | $V_{rs}$ (kN) | 11.7 | 16.5 | 10.3 |

*   indicates there is a hold-down anchor on the tension side to resist overturning

Determine if the shear capacity of the shearwall is adequate and distribute the shear force to each of the shearwall segments, $F_j$, based on the relative strength of each segment. Calculate the uplift force, $R_j$, at the end of each segment.

For wind from the north:

$\Sigma V_{rs} = 40.8$ kN $> 20$ kN                                          *Acceptable*

For wind from the south:

$\Sigma V_{rs} = 38.5$ kN $> 20$ kN                                          Acceptable

$$F_j = F \times \frac{V_{rs}}{\Sigma V_{rs}} \text{ (kN)}$$

$$R_j = \frac{F_j \times (H_s + d)}{L_W} - P_j \text{ (kN)}$$

Second storey shearwall segments, shear forces $(F_j)$ and uplift forces $(R_j)$

|                        |            | Segment 1 | Segment 2 | Segment 3 |
|------------------------|------------|-----------|-----------|-----------|
| Wind from the North    | $F_j$ (kN) | 10.1      | 8.09      | 1.77      |
|                        | $R_j$ (kN) | 6.59      | 3.11*     | 2.04*     |
| Wind from the South    | $F_j$ (kN) | 6.08      | 8.55      | 5.36      |
|                        | $R_j$ (kN) | 3.24*     | 3.42*     | 7.96      |

\*   Anchorages are required to transfer $R_j$ from the bottom wall plate to the top wall plate of the first storey.

The maximum force that must be transferred by the anchors is 3.42 kN. From Table 9.6, the capacity of 1/2 in. diameter rod with 64 mm x 5 mm thick square washers bearing on S-P-F wall plates is 21.3 kN.                    *Acceptable*

## First storey

The wall must be designed for wind from the north and south. From the Wood-Based Panel Shearwall Selection Table for S-P-F, select 11.0 mm OSB with 2-1/2" (3.25 mm diameter) common nails spaced at 100 mm. From the Shearwall Selection Table for Gypsum select 12.5 mm gypsum wallboard with nails or screws spaced at 200 mm for blocked walls.

$v_r = 6.12$ kN/m

$v_{rg} = 0.98$ kN/m

Since the following conditions are met, wall segments may be designed without hold-down connections:

- wall height, $(H_s) < 3.6$ m;
- $v_r + v_{rg} < 8.3$ kN/m; and
- $v_r$ is based on nail diameter $\leq 3.25$ mm and edge panel nail spacing is $\geq 100$ mm.

**9**

Shearwalls and Diaphragms

For each of the first storey shearwall segments calculate $V_{hd}$, $P_t$, $P_j$, $J_{hd}$ and $V_{rs}$ for north and south wind directions.

where:

$$V_{hd} = \Sigma(v_r J_n J_{ub} + v_{rg})L_W$$
$$= (6.12 \times 1.0 \times 1.0 + 0.98)L_W$$
$$= 7.10\ L_W$$

$P_t$ = 0.5 kN/m (tributary length of wall) – $R_j$ from 2nd storey

$q_w$ = 0.89 kN/m

$$P_j = P_t + q_w \frac{L_W}{2}$$

Hold-down connections are used at the bottom of all segments

$J_{hd}$ = 1.0 if there are hold-downs at the top and bottom of the segment to resist overturning

= 1.0 where $P_t$ is positive

$$= \frac{V_{hd} + P_t}{V_{hd}} \quad \text{where } P_t \text{ is negative}$$

$$V_{rs} = V_{hd} J_{hd}$$

Lower storey shearwall segments, hold-down factors ($J_{hd}$) and shear resistances ($V_{rs}$)

| | | Segment 1 | Segment 2 | Segment 3 |
|---|---|---|---|---|
| | $L_W$ (m) | 4 | 5 | 2 |
| | $V_{hd}$ (kN) | 28.4 | 35.5 | 14.2 |
| Wind from the North | $R_j$ from 2nd Storey (kN) | 6.59 | 3.11 | 2.04 |
| | Tributary wall length for $P_t$ (m) | 4/2 = 2 | 5/2+2/2 = 3.5 | 2/2+2/2 = 2 |
| | $P_t$ (kN) | -5.59 | -1.36 | -1.04 |
| | $P_j$ (kN) | -3.81 | 0.864 | -0.148 |
| | Hold-down* | Top and Bottom | Bottom | Bottom |
| | $J_{hd}$ | 1 | 0.962 | 0.927 |
| | $V_{rs}$ (kN) | 28.4 | 34.1 | 13.2 |
| Wind from the South | $R_j$ from 2nd Storey (kN) | 3.24 | 3.42 | 7.96 |
| | Tributary wall length for $P_t$ (m) | 4/2+2/2 = 3 | 5/2+2/2 = 3.5 | 2/2 = 1 |
| | $P_t$ (kN) | -1.74 | -1.67 | -7.46 |
| | $P_j$ (kN) | 0.041 | 0.555 | -6.57 |
| | Hold-down* | Bottom | Bottom | Top and Bottom |
| | $J_{hd}$ | 0.939 | 0.953 | 1 |
| | $V_{rs}$ (kN) | 26.6 | 33.8 | 14.2 |

\*    indicates hold-down anchors on the tension side to resist overturning

Determine if the shear capacity of the shearwall is adequate and distribute the shear force to each of the shearwall segments, $F_j$, based on the relative strength of each segment. Calculate the uplift force, $R_j$, at the end of each segment.

For wind from the north:

$\Sigma V_{rs}$= 75.7 kN > 60 kN                                              *Acceptable*

For wind from the south:

$\Sigma V_{rs}$= 74.7 kN > 60 kN                                              *Acceptable*

Lower storey shearwall segments, shear forces $(F_j)$ and uplift forces $(R_j)$

|                     |            | Segment 1 | Segment 2 | Segment 3 |
|---------------------|------------|-----------|-----------|-----------|
| Wind from the North | $F_j$ (kN) | 22.5      | 27.1      | 10.4      |
|                     | $R_j$ (kN) | 22.4      | 17.0      | 17.4      |
| Wind from the South | $F_j$ (kN) | 21.4      | 27.2      | 11.4      |
|                     | $R_j$ (kN) | 17.6      | 17.4      | 25.4      |

## 2. Design of chord members

Locate the hold-down connections approximately 150 mm from the edge of the wall to allow room for installation.

For shearwall segments with hold-down connections at both ends, the moment arm to determine the force in the tension and compression chords is:

   $h \quad = L_W - (2 \times 0.15)$

For shearwall segments without hold-down connections, the end studs in the segment are not required to be designed as tension chords. The end studs in a shearwall segment without hold-down connections must be designed as compression members using the moment arm:

   $h \quad = L_W - 0.3$

The overturning force is calculated as follows:

$$P_f \text{ and } T_f = \frac{F_j (H_s + d)}{h}$$

9

Shearwalls and Diaphragms

Second storey chord forces

|  |  | Segment 1 | Segment 2 | Segment 3 |
|---|---|---|---|---|
| Wind from the North | $F_j$ (kN) | 10.1 | 8.09 | 1.77 |
|  | h tension (m) | 4-0.15 = 3.85 | N/A | N/A |
|  | h comp. (m) | 4-0.15 = 3.85 | 5-0.3 = 4.70 | 2-0.3 = 1.70 |
|  | $T_f$ (kN) | 8.69 | N/A | N/A |
|  | $P_f$ (kN) | 8.69 | 5.68 | 3.44 |
| Wind from the South | $F_j$ (kN) | 6.08 | 8.55 | 5.36 |
|  | h tension (m) | N/A | N/A | 2-0.15 =1.85 |
|  | h comp. (m) | 4-0.3 = 3.70 | 5-0.3 = 4.70 | 2-0.15 = 1.85 |
|  | $T_f$ (kN) | N/A | N/A | 9.56 |
|  | $P_f$ (kN) | 5.42 | 6.00 | 9.56 |

Typically studs are doubled at openings. See design of chords for the first storey. Two 38 x 140 mm No.1/No.2 grade S-P-F studs are adequate.

First storey chord forces

|  |  | Segment 1 | Segment 2 | Segment 3 |
|---|---|---|---|---|
| Wind from the North | $F_j$ (kN) | 22.5 | 27.1 | 10.4 |
|  | h (m) | 4-2 x 0.15 = 3.70 | 5-2 x 0.15 = 4.70 | 2-2 x 0.15 = 1.70 |
|  | $T_f$ and $P_f$ (kN) | 20.1 | 19.0 | 20.3 |
| Wind from the South | $F_j$ (kN) | 21.4 | 27.2 | 11.4 |
|  | h (m) | 4-2 x 0.15 = 3.70 | 5-2 x 0.15 = 4.70 | 2-2 x 0.15 = 1.70 |
|  | $T_f$ and $P_f$ (kN) | 19.1 | 19.1 | 22.2 |

Assume that the chords will be anchored using 1/2" diameter bolts. Using the Tension Member Selection Tables, try two 38 × 140 mm No.1/No.2 grade S-P-F. The tabulated resistance must be modified for short term loading and area reduction due to bolt holes:

$$T_r = 2 \times 34.2 \times 1.15 \times \frac{(140 - 12.7 - 2)}{140}$$

$$= 70.4 \text{ kN} > 22.2 \text{ kN} \qquad \textit{Acceptable}$$

Check the chord member for compression using the Compression Member Selection Tables. In a stud wall, the studs are loaded to capacity under live and dead loads. The additional member in the chord should be capable of resisting the overturning force.

$$P_r = 1 \times 38.4$$

$$= 38.4 \text{ kN} > 22.2 \text{ kN} \qquad \textit{Acceptable}$$

Note that for this particular design case the selection tables do not give a correct value of $P_r$; however, it is sufficiently accurate to illustrate that the member is more than adequate for compression.

3. Design first storey anchorage connection

The chord members will be anchored to the foundation with a bolted bracket as shown in Figure 9.7. Try two 1/2" diameter bolts in double shear.

$$P_r = P'_r n_S n_F K' J'$$

$P'_r n_S$ = 11.4 kN interpolating from Bolt Selection Tables using member thickness = 2 × 38 mm = 76 mm

$n_F$ = 2

$K_D$ = 1.15

$K'$ = 1.15

$J'$ = 0.86

$P_r$ = 11.4 × 2 × 1.15 × 0.86

= 22.5 kN > 22.2 kN                    *Acceptable*

From Figure 7.5, the minimum required end distance is 127 mm and the minimum required spacing is 51 mm.

The anchor bolts must also be designed to carry the tensile force, and it may be found that two 1/2" diameter bolts are adequate.

The anchor bolts that fasten the bottom plate to the foundation must be designed to resist the shear force along the bottom of the wall.

**Use 9.5 mm OSB with 2-1/2" nails spaced at 150 mm on centre for the second storey shearwall and 100 mm on centre for the first storey shearwall in combination with 12.5 mm gypsum wallboard with nails or screws spaced at 200 mm on centre. The chords are two 38 x 140 mm No.1/No.2 grade S-P-F members, anchored with two 1/2" diameter bolts at the first storey.**

**9**

*Shearwalls and Diaphragms*

# Shearwall Selection Tables

**Wood-Based Panel**

## Factored Shear Resistance $v_r$ (kN/m)

| Stud species | Minimum nominal panel thickness mm | Minimum nail penetration in framing mm | Common nail size Length in. | Diameter mm | Panels applied directly to framing Nail spacing at panel edges (mm) 150 | 100 | 75 | 50 |
|---|---|---|---|---|---|---|---|---|
| D. Fir-L | 7.5++ | 31 | 2 | 2.84 | 3.94 | 5.88 | 7.65 | 9.82+ |
| | 9.5 | 31 | 2 | 2.84 | 4.35 | 6.60 | 8.53 | 11.2+ |
| | 9.5 | 38 | 2-1/2 | 3.25 | 4.83* | 7.00* | 8.94* | 11.6*+ |
| | 11 | 38 | 2-1/2 | 3.25 | 5.23* | 7.65* | 9.82* | 12.8*+ |
| | 12.5 | 38 | 2-1/2 | 3.25 | 5.72 | 8.29 | 10.7 | 14.0+ |
| | 12.5 | 41 | 3 | 3.66 | 6.76 | 10.1 | 13.1+ | 16.8+ |
| | 15.5 | 41 | 3 | 3.66 | 7.41 | 11.2 | 14.6+ | 19.1+ |
| Hem-Fir | 7.5++ | 31 | 2 | 2.84 | 3.55 | 5.29 | 6.88 | 8.84+ |
| | 9.5 | 31 | 2 | 2.84 | 3.91 | 5.94 | 7.68 | 10.1+ |
| | 9.5 | 38 | 2-1/2 | 3.25 | 4.35* | 6.30* | 8.04* | 10.4*+ |
| | 11 | 38 | 2-1/2 | 3.25 | 4.71* | 6.88* | 8.84* | 11.5*+ |
| | 12.5 | 38 | 2-1/2 | 3.25 | 5.14 | 7.46 | 9.64 | 12.6+ |
| | 12.5 | 41 | 3 | 3.66 | 6.09 | 9.06 | 11.8+ | 15.1+ |
| | 15.5 | 41 | 3 | 3.66 | 6.67 | 10.1 | 13.1+ | 17.2+ |
| S-P-F | 7.5++ | 31 | 2 | 2.84 | 3.16 | 4.70 | 6.12 | 7.86+ |
| | 9.5 | 31 | 2 | 2.84 | 3.48 | 5.28 | 6.83 | 8.95+ |
| | 9.5 | 38 | 2-1/2 | 3.25 | 3.86* | 5.60* | 7.15* | 9.27*+ |
| | 11 | 38 | 2-1/2 | 3.25 | 4.19* | 6.12* | 7.86* | 10.2*+ |
| | 12.5 | 38 | 2-1/2 | 3.25 | 4.57 | 6.63 | 8.57 | 11.2+ |
| | 12.5 | 41 | 3 | 3.66 | 5.41 | 8.05 | 10.5+ | 13.5+ |
| | 15.5 | 41 | 3 | 3.66 | 5.92 | 8.95 | 11.7+ | 15.3+ |
| Northern | 7.5++ | 31 | 2 | 2.84 | 2.76 | 4.11 | 5.35 | 6.87+ |
| | 9.5 | 31 | 2 | 2.84 | 3.04 | 4.62 | 5.97 | 7.83+ |
| | 9.5 | 38 | 2-1/2 | 3.25 | 3.38* | 4.90* | 6.25* | 8.11*+ |
| | 11 | 38 | 2-1/2 | 3.25 | 3.66* | 5.35* | 6.87* | 8.96*+ |
| | 12.5 | 38 | 2-1/2 | 3.25 | 4.00 | 5.80 | 7.49 | 9.80+ |
| | 12.5 | 41 | 3 | 3.66 | 4.73 | 7.04 | 9.19+ | 11.8+ |
| | 15.5 | 41 | 3 | 3.66 | 5.18 | 7.83 | 10.2+ | 13.4+ |

++ 9.5 mm minimum recommended when applied directly to framing as exterior siding

* The values for 9.5 mm and 11.0 mm panels applied directly to the framing may be increased to values shown respectively for 11.0 mm and 12.5 mm panels, provided studs are spaced at a maximum of 400 mm on centre.

+ Framing at adjoining panel edges is 64 mm lumber (or two 38 mm wide framing members connected to transfer factored shear force) or wider, and nails are staggered.

Notes:
1. Panel edges backed with 38mm or wider framing. Panels are installed either horizontally or vertically with nails spaced at 300 mm on centre along intermediate supports.
2. Where panels are applied on both faces of a wall and nail spacing is less than 150 mm on centre on either side, panel joints are offset to fall on different members or framing are 64 mm or thicker and nails on each side shall be staggered.
3. For panels applied over 12.7 mm or 15.9 mm gypsum wallboard, specified shear strength for the same thickness panel applied directly to framing may be used as long as minimum nail penetration (in the framing) is satisfied.
4. For Construction Sheathing OSB, product specification also includes a panel mark identifying a end-use rating. Table 9.1 provides an equivalence between tabulated thicknesses and panel marks.

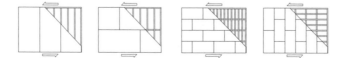

# Shearwall Selection Tables

## Factored Shear Resistance $v_r$ (kN/m) — Gypsum Panel

| Minimum nominal panel thickness mm | Minimum nail[2] and screw[3] penetration in framing mm | Wall construction | Panels applied directly to framing | | | | | | | | |
|---|---|---|---|---|---|---|---|---|---|---|---|
| | | | 400 mm stud spacing | | | 500 mm stud spacing | | | 600 mm stud spacing | | |
| | | | Fastener spacing at panel edges (mm) | | | Fastener spacing at panel edges (mm) | | | Fastener spacing at panel edges (mm) | | |
| | | | 200 | 150 | 100 | 200 | 150 | 100 | 200 | 150 | 100 |
| 12.5 | 19 | Unblocked | 0.84 | 0.98 | 1.1 | 0.67 | 0.78 | 0.90 | 0.50 | 0.59 | 0.67 |
| 12.5 | 19 | Blocked | 0.98 | 1.2 | 1.5 | 0.98 | 1.2 | 1.5 | 0.98 | 1.2 | 1.5 |
| 15.9 | 19 | Unblocked | 1.1 | 1.2 | 1.5 | 0.84 | 0.95 | 1.2 | 0.63 | 0.71 | 0.88 |
| 15.9 | 19 | Blocked | 1.2 | 1.5 | 1.8 | 1.2 | 1.5 | 1.8 | 1.2 | 1.5 | 1.8 |

Notes:
1. Gypsum wallboard is only considered effective in resisting loads of short term duration. Gypsum wallboard is not permitted in wet service conditions.
2. Gypsum board application nails – ring thread as specified in CSA Standard B111.
3. Gypsum board screws – Type W as specified in ASTM C1002
4. Fasteners spaced at maximum 300 mm on centre along intermediate framing members.
5. Maximum storey shear force does not exceed the values in Table 9.4.
6. Table may only be used where storey height does not exceed 3.6 m.
7. Where gypsum wallboard is included in earthquake resistance, the seismic force modification factor, R, is 2.

9

Shearwalls and Diaphragms

# Design for
# Fire Safety

Performance-
based
requirements in
the NBCC are
based on fire
tests such as
this test on an
exterior wall
assembly.

A floor assembly being tested to establish a Fire-resistance rating.

# 10.1     General Information

The design requirements for fire protection in Canadian building construction are found in Part 3, *Use and Occupancy,* of the *National Building Code of Canada (NBCC).* They are largely based on experience but in recent years have been revised to a more "performance based" approach. "Performance based" means the establishment of acceptance criteria related closely to the end use conditions of the product or system.

Significant changes included in the 1995 *NBCC* reduced the fire-resistance ratings required for exterior wood stud walls and increased by 50% the maximum areas permitted for wood frame construction when the building is sprinklered. In some cases, instead of increasing floor areas, buildings can be built an additional storey in height compared to what was permitted in the 1990 *NBCC.*

Research into fire protection engineering principles and building system behaviour in fire conditions will form the basis for many of the performance-based changes to the *NBCC* related to fire safety. This research evaluates the expected level of safety provided by various building systems. The Society of Fire Protection Engineers continues to be one of the leading organizations directing activities in this developing engineering field.

This section provides general background to *NBCC* requirements related to fire safety and fire resistance affecting the design of combustible and noncombustible construction, where both loadbearing and non-loadbearing wood components can be used.

The minimum requirements for building construction contained in the *NBCC* are based on the characteristics of each type of occupancy and an assessment of their impact on life safety. For example, the range of activities and location of occupants during 24-hour, seven-day weekly periods; the response capabilities of the occupants; occupancy fire hazards and expected fire loading all affect life safety.

In its simplest terms, fire protection is required for three objectives:

- structural stability under fire conditions
- protection against fire spread
- safe means of egress

Structural stability under fire conditions is characterized by the fire-resistance rating assigned to the structural assembly. The *NBCC* relates fire-resistance ratings to the intended occupancy, size and type of the structure. The rating is the major fire safety factor affecting structural design choices in wood. The methods used to determine fire-resistance ratings of building components are discussed in Sections 10.4 and 10.5.

Although protection against fire spread and safe means of egress are beyond the scope of this manual, there is a discussion of flame-spread ratings in Sections 10.6. Fire protection systems in a building typically include both passive and active systems. Passive systems include escape routes or "exits" that are provided to ensure a means of escaping a life-threatening situation and fire compartments to ensure a safer environment during a fire for the building

**10**

Design for Fire Safety

occupants. The life safety for occupants of other areas, away from the room of fire origin, depends on isolating the fire by walls and floor assemblies designed as fire separations and shielding access to exits from the fire. Active systems such as automatic fire sprinklers and fire alarm systems enhance occupant safety by providing detection, early warning and control/suppression of fire.

## 10.2      Definitions

The following terms are used throughout Part 3 of the *NBCC* and this text in discussing fire safety in building construction. Section 1.3 of the *NBCC* defines other applicable words and phrases.

**Building Area** means the greatest horizontal area of a building above grade within the outside surface of exterior walls or within the outside surface of exterior walls and the centreline of firewalls.

**Building Height** (in storeys) means the number of storeys contained between the roof and the floor of the first storey.

**Combustible** means that a material fails to meet the acceptance criteria of CAN4-S114, *Standard Method of Test for Determination of Noncombustibility in Building Materials.*

**Combustible Construction** means that type of construction that does not meet the requirements for noncombustible construction.

**Fire Compartment** means an enclosed space in a building that is separated from all other parts of the building by enclosing construction. This provides a fire separation that has a required fire-resistance rating.

**Fire-resistance Rating** means the time in hours or minutes that a material or assembly of materials will withstand the passage of flame and the transmission of heat when exposed to fire under specified conditions of test and performance criteria, or as determined by extension or interpretation of information derived therefrom as prescribed in the *NBCC.*

**Fire-retardant Treated Wood** means wood or a wood product that has had its surface-burning characteristics, such as flame-spread, rate of fuel contribution, and density of smoke developed, reduced by impregnation with fire-retardant chemicals.

**Fire Separation** means a construction assembly that acts as a barrier against the spread of fire. (A fire separation may or may not have a fire-resistance rating.)

**Firewall** means a type of fire separation of noncombustible construction that subdivides a building or separates adjoining buildings to resist the spread of fire and that has a fire-resistance rating as prescribed in the *NBCC* and has structural stability to remain intact under fire conditions for the required fire rated time.

**First Storey** means the uppermost storey having its floor level not more than 2 m above grade.

10

Design for Fire Safety

**Flame-spread Rating** means an index or classification indicating the extent of spread of flame on the surface of a material or an assembly of materials as determined in a standard fire test as prescribed in the *NBCC.*

**Grade** (as applying to the determination of building height) means the lowest of the average levels of finished ground adjoining each exterior wall of a building, except that localized depressions such as for vehicle or pedestrian entrances need not be considered in the determination of average levels of finished ground. (See **First Storey**)

**Heavy Timber Construction** means that type of combustible construction in which a degree of fire safety is attained by placing limitations on the sizes of wood structural members and on thickness and composition of wood floors and roofs and by the avoidance of concealed spaces under floors and roofs.

**Major Occupancy** means the principal occupancy for which a building or part thereof is used or intended to be used, and shall be deemed to include subsidiary occupancies that are an integral part of the principal occupancy.

**Noncombustible** means that a material meets the acceptance criteria of CAN4-S114 *Standard Method of Test for Determination of Noncombustibility in Building Materials.*

**Noncombustible Construction** means that type of construction in which a degree of fire safety is attained by the use of noncombustible materials for structural members and other building assemblies.

# 10.3    Wood Construction

Wood construction is permitted for use in buildings containing the occupancies covered by the *NBCC* depending on a variety of factors. The major factors dictating where wood is permitted are the major occupancy classification, building height and building area.

Subsection 3.2.2 of the *NBCC* provides specific details for determining the permitted type of construction, minimum fire-resistance ratings, internal fire protection (sprinklers) and firefighting access (streets faced) required for the structure.

Table 10.1 below gives several examples of the size of buildings permitted to be wood frame or heavy timber construction for various major occupancies. Many conditions can affect this Table; in general, however, the buildings described are required to have a fire-resistance rating (FRR) of 45 minutes for floors, roofs and loadbearing elements (except as noted). For roof assemblies, the required fire-resistance rating only applies where the building is not sprinklered.

The maximum building area for a sprinklered wood frame building is significantly higher than that permitted for a similar building that is not sprinklered. A sprinklered building is required to face only one street to provide access for firefighting. For an unsprinklered building, the size of the building can be increased by providing street access on two or three sides. Where greater building size is desired, firewalls can also be built between individual building areas, each of which can have the maximum area shown in Table 10.1. Four storey residential construction is required to be sprinklered regardless of area or type of construction.

Many wood frame components, typically non-loadbearing, can be used in buildings that are currently required in Subsection 3.2.2 of the *NBCC* to be of noncombustible construction. This includes permitting wood studs in partitions and exterior walls, raised wood floors of unlimited area and wood roof assemblies over concrete decks. Subsection 3.1.5 of the *NBCC* describes these and many other instances where wood products can be used in any building of noncombustible construction.

Roof assemblies of heavy timber construction are permitted to be used on any building required to be of noncombustible construction up to two storeys in building height, provided the building is protected by a sprinkler system. Other permitted uses of heavy timber arches, columns and beams in noncombustible construction are covered in Subsection 3.2.2 of the *NBCC*.

Further information on wood construction requirements may be found in Canadian Wood Council's *Fire Safety Design in Buildings* – A reference for applying the National Building Code of Canada fire safety requirements in building designs. Designers may also use CodeCHEK, an interactive web design tool that provides wood construction requirements based on the size, type, access and location of the building. CodeCHEK is located on the CWC web site at www.cwc.ca.

**10**

Design for Fire Safety

Table 10.1a
**Examples of maximum building area permitted per floor**

| Major occupancy Group | Division | Use | Building height in storeys | Number of sides with access & sprinklering | Maximum building area per floor[1] m² |
|---|---|---|---|---|---|
| **A** | | **Assembly** | | | |
| | 1 | Performing arts[2] | 1 | 1, sprinklered | unlimited |
| | 2 | Other (schools, restaurants) | 2 | 1, unsprinklered | 800 |
| | | | | 2, unsprinklered | 1000 |
| | | | | 3, unsprinklered | 1200 |
| | | | | 1, sprinklered | 2400 |
| | | | 1 | 1, unsprinklered | 1600 |
| | | | | 2, unsprinklered | 2000 |
| | | | | 3, unsprinklered | 2400 |
| | | | | 1, sprinklered | 4800 |
| | 3 | Arenas | 1 | 1, unsprinklered | 2400 |
| | | | | 2, unsprinklered | 3000 |
| | | | | 3, unsprinklered | 3600 |
| | | | | 1, sprinklered | 7200[3] |
| | 4 | Outdoor viewing (no FRR)[4] | – | 3, unsprinklered | unlimited |
| **B** | | **Institutional** | | | |
| | 2 | Hospitals, nursing homes[1] | 2 | 1, sprinklered | 1600 |
| | | | 1 | 1, sprinklered | 2400 |
| **C** | | **Residential** | | | |
| | | Apartments, hotels, motels | 3 | 1, unsprinklered | 600 |
| | | | | 2, unsprinklered | 750 |
| | | | | 3, unsprinklered | 900 |
| | | | | 1, sprinklered | 1800 |
| | | | 2 | 1, unsprinklered | 900 |
| | | | | 2, unsprinklered | 1125 |
| | | | | 3, unsprinklered | 1350 |
| | | | | 1, sprinklered | 2700 |
| | | | 1 | 1, unsprinklered | 1800 |
| | | | | 2, unsprinklered | 2250 |
| | | | | 3, unsprinklered | 2700 |
| | | | | 1, sprinklered | 5400 |
| **C** | | **Residential (1 hr FRR)** | | | |
| | | Apartments, hotels, motels | 4[1] | 1, sprinklered | 1800 |
| | | | 3 | 1, unsprinklered | 800 |
| | | | | 2, unsprinklered | 1000 |
| | | | | 3, unsprinklered | 1200 |
| | | | | 1, sprinklered | 2400 |
| | | | 2 | 1, unsprinklered | 1200 |
| | | | | 2, unsprinklered | 1500 |
| | | | | 3, unsprinklered | 1800 |
| | | | | 1, sprinklered | 3600 |
| | | | 1 | 1, unsprinklered | 2400 |
| | | | | 2, unsprinklered | 3000 |
| | | | | 3, unsprinklered | 3600 |
| | | | | 1, sprinklered | 7200 |

Notes:
1. In general, buildings described are of wood frame construction and are required to have 45-minute fire-resistance rating (FRR), or be of Heavy Timber construction (exceptions noted).
2. Occupant load limited to 300 persons.
3. Building requires no fire-resistance rating.
4. Occupant load limited to 1500 persons. Limiting distance ≥ 6m.

Table 10.1b
**Examples of maximum building area permitted per floor**

| Major occupancy Group | Division | Use | Building height in storeys | Number of sides with access & sprinklering | Maximum building area per floor[1] $m^2$ |
|---|---|---|---|---|---|
| **D** | | **Business and Personal Services** | | | |
| | | Offices | $4^2$ | 1, sprinklered | 3600 |
| | | | 3 | 1, unsprinklered | 1600 |
| | | | | 2, unsprinklered | 2000 |
| | | | | 3, unsprinklered | 2400 |
| | | | | 1, sprinklered | 4800 |
| | | | 1 | 1, unsprinklered | 4800 |
| | | | | 2, unsprinklered | 6000 |
| | | | | 3, unsprinklered | 7200 |
| | | | | 1, sprinklered | 14400 |
| **E** | | **Mercantile** | | | |
| | | Stores, supermarkets | $4^2$ | 1, sprinklered | 1800 |
| | | | 3 | 1, unsprinklered | 800 |
| | | | | 2, unsprinklered | 1000 |
| | | | | 3, unsprinklered | 1500 |
| | | | | 1, sprinklered | 2400 |
| | | | 1 | 1, unsprinklered | 1500 |
| | | | | 2, unsprinklered | 1500 |
| | | | | 3, unsprinklered | 1500 |
| | | | | 1, sprinklered | 7200 |
| **F** | | **Industrial** | | | |
| | 1 | High hazard | 2 | 1, sprinklered | 1200 |
| | | | 1 | 1, sprinklered | 2400 |
| | | | $1^3$ | 1, unsprinklered | 800 |
| | 2 | Medium hazard | 4 | 1, sprinklered | 2400 |
| | | | 3 | 1, sprinklered | 3200 |
| | | | 2 | 1, sprinklered | 4800 |
| | | | 1 | 1, sprinklered | 9600 |
| | 3 | Low hazard | 4 | 1, unsprinklered | 1200 |
| | | | | 2, unsprinklered | 1500 |
| | | | | 3, unsprinklered | 1800 |
| | | | | 1, sprinklered | 3600 |
| | | | 1 | 1, unsprinklered | 4800 |
| | | | | 2, unsprinklered | 6000 |
| | | | | 3, unsprinklered | 7200 |
| | | | | 1, sprinklered | 14400 |

Notes:
1. In general, buildings described are of wood frame construction and are required to have 45-minute fire-resistance rating (FRR), or be of Heavy Timber construction (exceptions noted).
2. One hour FRR.
3. No FRR.
4. For sprinklered options, access is required on one side only.

**10**

Design for Fire Safety

# 10.4     Fire-resistance Rating

Fire-resistance rating is the time that a component will withstand passage of heat and flame under standard test conditions. No two actual building fires will be exactly the same with respect to the amount and rate of heat developed; however, the fire-resistance rating determined in a fire test provides a relative assessment of a component's ability to confine a fire or continue to perform a structural function.

Minimum fire-resistance ratings required for major structural components are found in Subsection 3.2.2 of the *NBCC*. For wood construction, these minimum rating requirements range from 0 to 60 minutes. In smaller buildings where occupant load is low, exiting is direct to the exterior, and access is open for firefighting, no fire-resistance rating is required. In other cases, such as separations between major occupancies (see Subsection 3.1.3 of *NBCC*), a two hour fire-resistance rating could be required. Many wood frame assemblies (walls, roofs and floors) meet this range (0 to 2 hours) of fire-resistance rating requirements.

The fire-resistance ratings of building components can be determined in several ways (see *NBCC* Subsection 3.1.7). For a specific type of assembly, the rating may be determined by conducting a standard fire test in accordance with the Underwriters' Laboratories of Canada Standard CAN4-S101 *Standard Methods of Fire Endurance Tests of Building Construction and Materials* or its equivalent (see *NBCC* Subsection 2.5.3). Alternatively, the fire-resistance rating may be assigned on the basis of the requirements contained in Appendix D *(Fire Performance Ratings)* of the *NBCC*. The method referred to in Appendix D, the "Component Additive Method" for light frame assemblies, is described in Section 10.5 along with the method for calculating fire-resistance ratings for glulam beams and columns.

In the fire-resistance test, a full-scale assembly is exposed to a standardized test fire. The fire-resistance rating is that time when:

- the average temperature on the side of the assembly not exposed to the test fire increases by 139°C, or
- flame or gases hot enough to ignite cotton wool waste pass through the assembly, or
- the assembly fails to carry its design load.

Detailed information on a large number of tested assemblies with different fire-resistance ratings is contained in the list of Equipment and Materials – Fire Resistance published by Underwriters' Laboratories of Canada. Examples of the type of information contained in the ULC Listings are shown in Figures 10.1 and 10.2. Information on other tested assemblies can be obtained from the Gypsum Association, Underwriters' Laboratories Inc., Factory Mutual Corporation and from specific manufacturers of structural components (see **Additional Readings** at end of chapter).

Article 3.1.4.5 of the *NBCC* permits the use of heavy timber construction in buildings where combustible construction is required to have a 45 minute fire-resistance rating. Heavy timber construction is also permitted to be used in large noncombustible buildings in certain occupancies. To be acceptable, the components of the building must comply with the minimum dimension and

**10**

Design for Fire Safety

installation requirements specified in Article 3.1.4.6. Heavy timber construction is afforded this recognition because of its performance record under actual fire exposure and its acceptance as a fire-safe method of construction.

The minimum fire-resistance rating requirements specified in Part 3 of the *NBCC* for various occupancies were based in part on work by S.H. Ingberg. Ingberg looked at how a real fire involving the contents of a room (the fuel load of an occupancy) compared to the standard fire used in test furnaces. If the area under the curve of a time *vs.* temperature graph of a real fire was equal to that under the standard test time-temperature curve then the fires would have equal "fire severity". The expected fuel loads for each occupancy and Ingberg's theory on equivalencies were used as input to establish minimum fire-resistance requirements.

More recent research has shown that many other factors influence fire severity. These include compartment ventilation, thermal characteristics of compartment linings, area of compartment boundaries and the height of the compartment. Work in developing a more theoretical approach to calculating fire growth within compartments has grown significantly over the last 20 to 25 years. With advances in computer technology, mass and energy transfer processes from ignition to the fully developed stage of a fire can be analyzed. As a result, more can be learned about fire growth in a compartment leading to more reliable information about fire performance in buildings (Cote, 1991; DiNenno, 1988; Drysdale, 1985).

Figure 10.1
**(Reprinted by permission of Underwriters' Laboratories of Canada)**

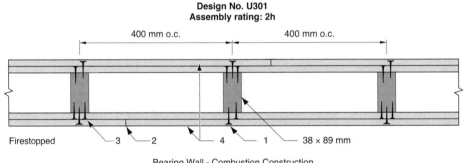

**Design No. U301**
**Assembly rating: 2h**

400 mm o.c.          400 mm o.c.

Firestopped        3     2        4      1        38 × 89 mm

Bearing Wall - Combustion Construction
(Finish Rating - 66 minutes)

1. Nailheads: Exposed or covered with joint finisher.
2. Joints: Exposed or covered with tape and joint finisher.
3. Nails: 51 mm, cement-coated flathead.
4. Gypsum Wallboard: (Guide No. 40U18.23),15.9 mm thick applied in two layers.
   Base layer placed vertically with joints butted over studs and nailed to studs 150 mm on centre. Face layer applied horizontally with joint finisher cement and nailed 300 mm on centre temporarily to base layer until cement sets. All joints in face layers staggered with joints in base layers and with joints on opposite sides.

Canadian Gypsum Company, A Division of CGC Inc.
Domtar Inc.

Figure 10.2
**(Reprinted by permission of Underwriters' Laboratories of Canada)**

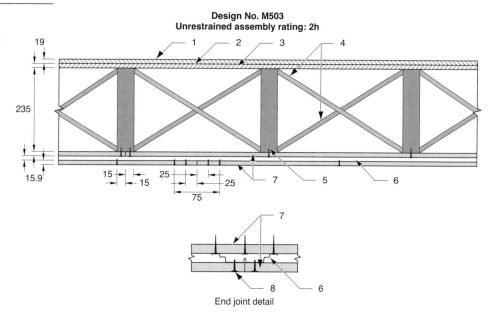

Design No. M503
Unrestrained assembly rating: 2h

7

8          6

End joint detail

Combustion Construction
(Finish Rating - 75 minutes)

1. Finish Flooring: 19 × 89 mm T & G flooring laid perpendicular to joists or 15.5 mm select sheathing grade T & G phenolic bonded Douglas Fir plywood with face grain perpendicular to joists and joints staggered.
2. Building Paper (optional): Commercial sheathing material, 0.25 mm thick.
3. Sub-flooring: 19 × 140 mm T & G boards laid diagonally to joists or 12.5 mm unsanded sheathing grade phenolic bonded Douglas Fir plywood with face grain perpendicular to joists and joints staggered.
4. Bridging: 19 × 64 mm.
5. Wood Joists: 38 × 235 mm spaced 400 mm on centre, firestopped.
6. Furring Channel: Resilient, formed of 0.5 mm electrogalvanized steel as shown, spaced 600 mm on centre perpendicular to joists. Channels overlapped at splice 38 mm and fastened to each joist with 63 mm common nails. Minimum clearance of channels to walls, 20 mm. Additional pieces 1500 mm long placed immediately adjacent to channels at end of joints of second layers; ends to extend 150 mm beyond each side of end joint.
7. Gypsum Wallboard: (Guide No. 40U18.23). 15.9 mm thick, 1200 mm wide. First layer of wallboard installed with long dimension perpendicular to joists and end joints of boards located at the joists. Nailed to joists with uncoated 63 mm box nails spaced 180 mm on centre. All nails located 15 mm minimum distance from the edges and ends of the board. Second layer of wallboard secured to furring channels by 25 mm long wallboard screws. Second layer installed with long dimension perpendicular to the furring channels and centre line of boards located under a joist and so placed that the edge joint of this layer is not in alignment with the end joint of the first layer. Secured to furring channels with wallboard screws 300 mm on centre with additional screws 75 mm from side joints. End joints of wallboard fastened at additional furring channels as shown in end-joint detail. All screws located 25 mm minimum distance from edges of boards.
   ATLANTIC GYPSUM, a Division of the Lundrigans-Comstock Limited
   DOMTAR INC.
   GEORGIA PACIFIC CORPORATION
   WESTROC INDUSTRIES LIMITED
8. Wallboard screws: Type S Phillips self-drilling and self-tapping 25 mm long.
9. Joint System (not shown): Paper tape embedded in cementitious compound over joints and exposed nail heads covered with compound, with edges of compound feathered out.

**10**

Design for Fire Safety

# 10.5 Determining Fire-resistance Ratings

The *NBCC* permits a designer to assign a fire-resistance rating to a material, product or assembly on the basis of Appendix D *(Fire Performance Ratings)* of the *NBCC.* For light frame assemblies, this provides an alternative to testing under the standard fire-resistance test, CAN4-S101. In the case of heavy timber construction, a designer may calculate the fire-resistance rating of glulam members for use where a fire-resistance rating of greater than 45 minutes is required.

Table A-9.10.3.1.A – Fire and Sound Resistance of Walls, was updated in the 1995 edition of the *NBCC* to reflect the results of a major NRC/industry research project on the fire and sound performance of walls. Although Part 3 does not directly reference Table A.9.10.3.1.A, the fire-resistance ratings listed were determined on the basis of tests conducted with the NBCC referenced fire standard, CAN4-S101. A majority of the listings are based on actual tests while some of the fire resistance ratings have been conservatively extrapolated.

Since the publication of the 1995 NBCC, numerous fire and acoustic tests have been done on floor assemblies and Table A-9.10.3.1.B was revised in the Fourth Revisions and Errata in April 2002 to reflect the results of the first phase of work.

The calculation methods that are discussed below are developed on the basis of data generated from numerous fire tests. The methods are applicable only to assemblies constructed from generic materials, or, in other words, material for which a nationally-recognized standard exists.

## Light Frame Assemblies

The calculation method for light frame assemblies relates to the fire performance of a wall assembly on the basis of fire exposure on one side only. For a floor or roof assembly, the method is based on fire performance when the fire exposure is from below.

The calculation method, termed the "Component Additive Method", in Appendix D of the *NBCC*, can be used to assign a fire-resistance rating of up to 1.5 hours. The ratings apply to non-loadbearing partitions, loadbearing wood frame walls, floors and roofs.

Simply put, the fire-resistance rating of a wood frame assembly is calculated by adding the time assigned to the protective membrane (wallboard/ceiling) on the "fire side" to the time assigned to the structural framing members. Additional time can be added for such things as reinforcement of the membrane or provision of some types of insulation within the assembly.

Table 10.2 lists the time assigned in the *NBCC* Appendix to various wall and ceiling membranes. These times are based on the ability of the membrane to stay in place during the standard fire test. Table 10.3 lists the times assigned in the Appendix to various framing members. These are based on the time between failure of the protective membrane and the collapse of the assembly.

For fire-resistance-rated interior partitions, the *NBCC* requires rating from both sides. The component additive method assumes that the wall assembly will be symmetrical in design with equivalent membrane protection on both sides. If the membranes differ, the fire-resistance rating must be determined on the basis of the membrane assigned the lowest time. In this calculation, no contribution to

10

Design for Fire Safety

the fire-resistance rating is assigned for the membrane(s) on the non-fire-exposed side.

For exterior walls, which are required to be rated from the inside only, the assembly need not be symmetrical, provided there is an exterior membrane consisting of sheathing and cladding and the spaces between the studs are filled with insulation conforming to CSA Standard A101-M, *Thermal Insulation, Mineral Fibre, for Buildings,* having a mass of not less than 1.22 kg/m$^2$ of wall surface.

For floor and roof assemblies, which are rated on the basis of fire exposure from below, the upper membrane must consist of one of the combinations listed in Table 10.4, or it may be any membrane in Table 10.2 assigned a time of at least 15 minutes. For the purposes of this requirement, it is not necessary to comply with Note 1 of Table 10.2. The times assigned to wallboard differ in cases where the fire-resistance rating of a floor or roof assembly is determined on the basis of the contribution of the ceiling membrane only *(NBCC* Article 3.6.4.2) and not on the complete assembly. These values are listed in Table 10.5.

**Table 10.2**
**Time assigned for contribution of panel membranes**

| Description of finish | Time minutes |
|---|---|
| 11.0 mm Douglas Fir plywood phenolic bonded | 10[1] |
| 14.0 mm Douglas Fir plywood phenolic bonded | 15[1] |
| 12.7 mm Type X gypsum wallboard | 25 |
| 15.9 mm Type X gypsum wallboard | 40 |

Note:
1. Non-loadbearing walls only, stud cavities filled with mineral wool conforming to CSA Standard A101-M, *Thermal Insulation, Mineral Fibre, for Buildings* and having a mass of not less than 2 kg/m$^2$, with no additional credit for insulation according to Table D-2.3.4.D. in Appendix D of the *NBCC.*

**Table 10.3**
**Time assigned for contribution of wood frame members**

| Description of frame | Time assigned to frame minutes |
|---|---|
| Wood studs 400 mm o.c. maximum | 20 |
| Wood studs 600 mm o.c. maximum | 15 |
| Wood floor and roof joists 400 mm o.c. maximum | 10 |
| Wood roof and floor truss assemblies 600 mm o.c. maximum | 5 |

**Table 10.4**
**Flooring or roofing over wood joists or trusses**

| Type of assembly | Structural members | Subfloor or roof deck | Finish flooring or roofing |
|---|---|---|---|
| Floor | Wood joists or trusses | 12.5 mm plywood or 17 mm T & G softwood | Hardwood or softwood flooring on building paper |
| | | | Resilient flooring, parquet floor, felted synthetic-fibre floor coverings, carpeting,or ceramic tile on 8 mm thick panel-type underlay |
| | | | Ceramic tile on 30 mm mortar bed |
| Roof | Wood joists or trusses | 12.5 mm plywood or 17 mm T & G softwood | Finish roofing material with or without insulation |

The reader is directed to Appendix D of the *NBCC* for specific details on other important features regarding fasteners, wallboard orientation and structural member descriptions, which have to be followed in applying this calculation method.

**Table 10.5**
**Fire-resistance rating for membranes (membrane method of calculation)**

| Description of membrane | Fire-resistance rating minutes |
|---|---|
| 15.9 mm Type X gypsum wallboard with at least 75 mm mineral wool batt insulation above wallboard | 30 |
| 19 mm gypsum-sand plaster on metal lath | 30 |
| Double 14.0 mm Douglas Fir plywood phenolic bonded | 30 |
| Double 12.7 mm Type X gypsum wallboard | 45 |
| 25 mm gypsum-sand plaster on metal lath | 45 |
| Double 15.9 mm Type X gypsum wallboard | 60 |
| 32 mm gypsum-sand plaster on metal lath | 60 |

Note:
Values shown apply where the assembly fire-resistance rating is to be determined on the basis of the membrane only, not the complete assembly.

## Examples of Fire-Resistance Rating Calculations

### Example 1
Determine the fire-resistance rating of an interior partition with 12.7 mm Type X gypsum wallboard (GWB) on both sides of wood studs spaced at 400 mm on centre.

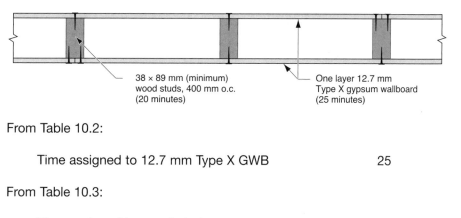

38 × 89 mm (minimum) wood studs, 400 mm o.c. (20 minutes)

One layer 12.7 mm Type X gypsum wallboard (25 minutes)

From Table 10.2:

Time assigned to 12.7 mm Type X GWB      25

From Table 10.3:

Time assigned to wood studs      20

**Fire-resistance rating of interior partition:**      **45 minutes**

**10**

Design for Fire Safety

## Example 2

Determine the fire-resistance rating of a wood stud exterior wall assembly with 12.7 mm Type X gypsum wallboard on the interior side and plywood sheathing and wood shingle siding on the exterior with the studs spaced at 400 mm on centre.

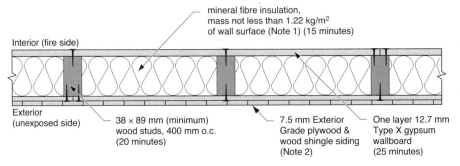

mineral fibre insulation,
mass not less than 1.22 kg/m² of wall surface (Note 1) (15 minutes)

Interior (fire side)

Exterior
(unexposed side)

38 × 89 mm (minimum)
wood studs, 400 mm o.c.
(20 minutes)

7.5 mm Exterior
Grade plywood &
wood shingle siding
(Note 2)

One layer 12.7 mm
Type X gypsum
wallboard
(25 minutes)

Notes:
1. If the exterior wall cavity is uninsulated or insulated with any other type of insulation, the exterior sheathing would have to be identical to the interior gypsum wallboard membrane and the FRR revised accordingly.
2. This combination could be replaced with any other combination of sheathing and exterior cladding permitted by the NBCC without revising the FRR.

From Table 10.2:

| | |
|---|---|
| Time assigned to 12.7 mm Type X GWB | 25 |

From Table D-2.3.4.D in Appendix D of *NBCC:*

| | |
|---|---|
| Time assigned to mineral fibre insulation | 15 |

From Table 10.3:

| | |
|---|---|
| Time assigned to wood studs at 400 mm on centre | 20 |
| **Fire-resistance rating of exterior wall:** | **60 minutes** |

## Example 3

Determine the fire-resistance rating of a wood truss floor assembly with a ceiling of 15.9 mm Type X gypsum wallboard and trusses spaced at 600 mm on centre.

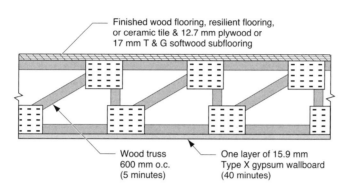

Finished wood flooring, resilient flooring, or ceramic tile & 12.7 mm plywood or 17 mm T & G softwood subflooring

Wood truss 600 mm o.c. (5 minutes)

One layer of 15.9 mm Type X gypsum wallboard (40 minutes)

From Table 10.2:

Time assigned to 15.9 mm Type X gypsum wallboard          40

From Table 10.3:

Time assigned to wood trusses                                             5

**Fire-resistance rating of wood truss floor assembly:      45 minutes**

**10**

Design for Fire Safety

## Example 4

Determine the fire-resistance rating of a wood joist floor assembly with a ceiling of one layer of 15.9 mm Type X gypsum wallboard and joists spaced at 400 mm on centre.

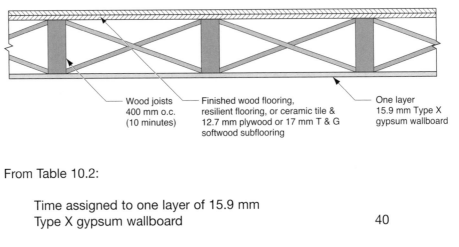

Wood joists
400 mm o.c.
(10 minutes)

Finished wood flooring,
resilient flooring, or ceramic tile &
12.7 mm plywood or 17 mm T & G
softwood subflooring

One layer
15.9 mm Type X
gypsum wallboard

From Table 10.2:

| | |
|---|---|
| Time assigned to one layer of 15.9 mm Type X gypsum wallboard | 40 |

From Table 10.3:

| | |
|---|---|
| Time assigned to wood joists at 400 mm on centre | 10 |
| **Fire-resistance rating of wood joist floor assembly:** | **50 minutes** |

### Glulam Beams and Columns

When exposed to fire, wood undergoes thermal degradation and produces a layer of char. Under standard fire test conditions, the constant across-grain char rate of most wood species is approximately 0.66 mm/min. (White, 1988). Although this char layer acts as an insulator and thereby protects the unburnt portion of the wood, the char has no residual strength. As the char depth increases, the cross-sectional area of the member decreases to a point when the member fails to carry the design load. A number of studies have looked at the pyrolysis and combustion of wood products (Bender, 1985; Hadvig, 1981; Hall, 1971; Schaffer 1967, 1986). Models to calculate the fire-resistance rating of wood assemblies have been developed that predict char depth, temperature distribution in the unburnt part of the member, and the strength properties of wood at elevated temperatures (White, 1995).

The information provided below on the calculation of the fire-resistance rating of glulam beams and columns was developed by Lie (1977) and is based on data from fire tests on timber beams and columns. Under this procedure, beams and columns may be assigned a fire-resistance rating on the basis of exposure to fire from three or four sides. Based on this approach the fire-resistance rating in minutes of glulam beams and columns is based on:

$$FRR = 0.1\,f\,B\left[4 - 2\frac{B}{D}\right] \quad \text{for beams exposed to fire on 4 sides}$$

$$FRR = 0.1\,f\,B\left[4 - \frac{B}{D}\right] \quad \text{for beams exposed to fire on 3 sides}$$

$$FRR = 0.1\,f\,B\left[3 - \frac{B}{D}\right] \quad \text{for columns exposed to fire on 4 sides}$$

$$FRR = 0.1\,f\,B\left[3 - \frac{B}{2D}\right] \quad \text{for columns exposed to fire on 3 sides}$$

where:

- $f$ = the load factor shown in Figure 10.3
- $B$ = the full dimension of the smaller side of the beam or column in mm before exposure to fire
- $D$ = the full dimension of the larger side of the beam or column in mm before exposure to fire

**Example**

Determine the fire-resistance rating of a glulam beam exposed on three sides having dimensions of 175 × 380 mm and stressed to 80% of its factored bending moment resistance.

- $B$ = 175 mm
- $D$ = 380 mm

From Figure 10.3, f = 1.075 for a beam designed to carry a factored load equal to 80% of factored bending moment resistance.

$$
\begin{aligned}
t &= 0.1\,f\,B\left[4 - \frac{B}{D}\right] \\[6pt]
&= 0.1 \times 1.075 \times 175 \times \left[4 - \frac{175}{380}\right]
\end{aligned}
$$

**Total fire-resistance rating = 66.6 minutes.**

This beam could be used to support a wood frame floor assembly having a one-hour fire-resistance rating.

10

Design for Fire Safety

Figure 10.3
**Load factor for glulam fire-resistance calculations (NBCC, 1995)**

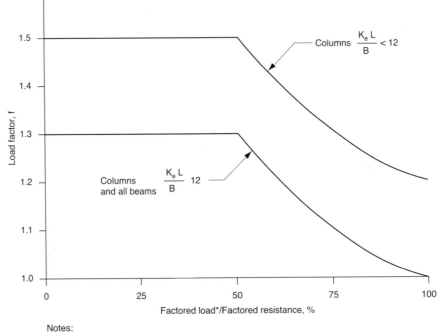

Notes:
1. $K_e$ = Effective length factor
2. L = Unsupported length of a column in mm
3. B = Smaller side of a beam or column in mm (before fire exposure)
4. The full dimension of the beam, before exposure to the fire, is used in the fire-resistance calculation
* In the case of beams, use factored bending moment in place of factored load.

# 10.6 Flame-spread Ratings

Flame-spread ratings are used in the *NBCC* primarily to regulate use of interior finish materials (Subsection 3.1.12) to reduce the probability of rapid fire spread on surfaces of walls and ceilings. They are also used to control the degree of combustibility of materials that may be used in some assemblies and types of construction. The standard test method also provides smoke developed classifications, used in conjunction with flame-spread ratings to regulate use of interior finish materials where smoke is of major fire safety importance, such as in high buildings regulated by Subsection 3.2.6.

The test method required by *NBCC* to determine flame-spread and smoke developed ratings for materials is the "25-Foot" or "Steiner" tunnel test outlined in Underwriters' Laboratories of Canada (ULC) Standard CAN4-S102 *Standard Method of Test for Surface Burning Characteristics of Building Materials and Assemblies.* This method arbitrarily assigns flame-spread ratings of 0 and 100 to asbestos cement board and red oak respectively; all other materials tested are assigned a rating relative to these two materials. Other test methods may be used if the authority having jurisdiction is satisfied that comparable results are obtained.

Dressed lumber and most plywoods have a flame-spread rating of 150 or less and therefore can be used as interior finish in any building. Fire-retardant treated wood, with a flame-spread rating of 25, qualifies for use as an interior finish in such areas as exits, public corridors and certain parts of high buildings where finishes with low flame-spread ratings are required. Fire-retardant coatings also can be used on wood products to meet the *NBCC* flame-spread rating requirements. The ULC List of Equipment and Materials contains specific proprietary listings for various wood products including those that are fire-retardant treated and fire-retardant coated.

In general, the *NBCC* requires the flame-spread rating of interior wall and ceiling finishes to be no more than 150. There are specific occupancies and locations in buildings that have stricter requirements (see Table 10.6). Table 10.7 lists a number of typical flame-spread ratings and smoke developed classifications for various wood species.

**10**

Design for Fire Safety

Table 10.6
**Maximum flame-spread ratings for walls and ceilings**

| Occupancy, location or element | Maximum flame-spread rating for walls and ceilings | |
|---|---|---|
| | Sprinklered | Unsprinklered |
| Group A, Division 1 occupancies including doors, skylights, glazing and light diffusers and lenses | 150 | 75 |
| Group B occupancies | 150 | 75 |
| Exits | 25 | 25 |
| Lobbies described in 3.4.4.2.(2) of *NBCC* | 25 | 25 |
| Covered vehicular passageways, except for roof assemblies of heavy timber construction in such passageways | 25 | 25 |
| Vertical service spaces | 25 | 25 |

| Table 10.7<br>**Typical flame-<br>spread ratings<br>and smoke<br>developed<br>classifications<br>of wood** | Species[1] | Flame-<br>spread | Smoke<br>developed |
|---|---|---|---|
| | Douglas Fir plywood (6 mm) | 118 | 80 |
| | with medium density overlay | 140 | 150 |
| | Douglas fir | 75-100 | * |
| | Amabilis fir | 69 | 58 |
| | Eastern white pine | 85 | 122 |
| | Lodgepole pine | 93 | 210 |
| | Maple flooring | 104 | 157 |
| | Pacific coast yellow cedar | 78 | 90 |
| | Red pine | 142 | 229 |
| | Select red oak flooring | 100 | 100 |
| | Sitka spruce | 74 | 74 |
| | Walnut | 130-140 | * |
| | Western hemlock | 60-75 | * |
| | Western red cedar | 73 | 98 |
| | Western white pine | 75 | * |
| | White spruce | 65 | * |

Notes:
1. All species other than plywood and flooring are 19 mm lumber.
* Not determined

The flame-spread ratings of wood interior finishes and flooring materials may also be determined from information contained in *NBCC* Appendix D, *Fire-Performance Ratings,* Tables D-3.1.1.A and D-3.1.1.B. In Table D-3.1.1.A, lumber, regardless of species, and plywood made of Douglas fir, poplar and spruce are assigned a flame-spread rating of 150 or less.

Traditional flooring materials such as hardwood flooring are less prone to igniting and burning in a fire than synthetic carpeting and have never been regulated by flame-spread requirements, except for high-rise buildings. With the exception of exits and services spaces, the flame-spread rating requirements for floor surfaces in high-rise buildings can be met by wood flooring without the use of any fire-retardant treatments or coatings.

## 10.7   Fire-retardant Treated Wood

Fire-retardant treated wood (frtw) is wood that is impregnated with fire-retardant chemicals under pressure. Besides meeting a flame-spread rating of 25 in the standard "tunnel" test, frtw shows no progressive burning when the test is extended from 10 minutes to 30 minutes. Wood products that are covered with fire-retardant coatings to achieve a flame-spread rating of 25 are not considered frtw because the coatings are not as permanent, being surface treatments, and are not listed on the basis of this extended 30-minute test.

Frtw can be used as interior finish where a flame-spread rating of 25 is required. It is also used structurally in roof assemblies. Subsection 3.2.2 of *NBCC* lists a number of occupancies where frtw roof systems can be used in one storey buildings as an alternative to using 45 minute fire-resistance rated wood frame construction or unrated noncombustible construction. The frtw roof system is not required to have a fire-resistance rating, but the assembly must be able to meet the conditions of acceptance of the ULC test method CAN/ULC-S126 *Standard Method of Test for Fire-Spread Under Roof-Deck Assemblies.* In buildings where such a roof assembly is used, the permitted maximum areas of the building are reduced by 50%.

Fire-retardant treated wood can also be used on the exterior of large noncombustible buildings either as fascia on one storey buildings or as cladding on buildings up to six storeys in height. For the latter applications, the cladding assembly must pass a large scale vertical flame-spread test as described in Subsection 3.1.5 of the *NBCC*. For these exterior applications, the frtw must show no increase in flame-spread rating in the tunnel test after having been exposed to an accelerated weathering test.

The use of fire-retardant treatments results in some reduction in the strength properties of wood products. Treatment factors to be applied to the strength properties of lumber can be determined by appropriate testing. See the CSA O86 Commentary for further information.

**10**

Design for Fire Safety

# References

Bender, D.A., F.E. Woeste, E.L. Schaffer, and C.M. Marx. 1985. Reliability Formulation for the Strength and Fire Endurance of Glued-laminated Beams. Res. Pap. FPL 460, USDA Forest Service, Forest Product Lab., Madison, WI.

Cote, A.E. and J.L. Linville. 1997. Fire Protection Handbook, 18th Edition. National Fire Protection Association, Quincy, MA.

DiNenno, P.J. et al. 1995. SFPE Handbook of Fire Protection Engineering; 2nd Edition. Society of Fire Protection Engineers, National Fire Protection Association, Quincy, MA.

Drysdale, D. 1999. An Introduction to Fire Dynamics 2nd Edition. John Wiley & Sons Ltd., Chichester, U.K.

Hadvig, S. 1981. Charring of Wood in Building Fires. Technical University of Denmark, Lyngby.

Hall, G.S., R.G. Saunders, R.T. Allcorn, P.E. Jackman, M.W. Hickey and R. Fitt. 1971. Fire Performance of Timber - A Literature Survey. Timber Research and Development Association, High Wycombe, U.K.

Lie, T.T. 1977. A Method for Assessing the Fire Resistance of Laminated Timber Beams and Columns. Can. J. of Civil Eng., 4, 161.

Schaffer, E.L. 1967. Charring Rates of Selected Woods - Tranverse to Grain. Res. Pap. FPL 69, USDA Forest Service, Forest Product Lab., Madison, WI.

Schaffer, E.L. et al. 1986. Strength Validation and Fire Endurance of Glued-laminated Timber Beams. Res. Pap. FPL 467, USDA Forest Service, Forest Products Lab., Madison, WI.

White, R.H. 1995. Analytical Methods for Determining Fire Resistance of Timber Members. Section 4, Chapter 11 SFPE Handbook of Fire Protection Engineering, SFPE, Quincy, MA.

## Additional Readings

**10**

Browne, F.L.. 1958. Rep. No. 2136, USDA Forest Services, Forest Product Lab., Madison, WI.

Commentary on Part 3 (Use and Occupancy) of the National Building Code of Canada 1990, National Research Council of Canada, Ottawa, ON.

Criteria for Use in Extension of Data from Fire Endurance Tests. 1988. ULC Subject C263(e)-M88, Underwriters' Laboratories of Canada, Scarborough, ON.

Ferguson, R.S. Principles of Fire Protection Applied in Part 3: Use and Occupancy, National Building Code of Canada. Technical Paper No. 272, Division of Building Research, (Now Institute for Research in Construction) National Research Council of Canada, Ottawa, ON.

Fire Resistance Classifications of Building Constructions. 1942. Building Materials and Structures. Report BMS 92, National Bureau of Standards (now National Institute of Standards and Technology), Washington, DC.

Fire Resistance Design Manual. GA-600-2000, Gypsum Association, 16th Edition, 810 First Street NE - #510 Washington, DC.

Fire Resistance Directory. Underwriters' Laboratories Inc., 333 Pfingsten Road, Northbrook, IL 60062.

Fire Safety Design in Buildings. 1996. (A reference for applying the National Building Code of Canada fire safety requirements in building design). Canadian Wood Council, Ottawa, ON.

Fitzgerald, Dr. R.W. 1997. Fundamentals of Firesafe Building Design. NFPA Fire Protection Handbook, 18th Edition, Section 1, Chapter 2. National Fire Protection Association, Quincy, MA.

Design for Fire Safety

FM Specification Tested Products Guide. 1989. Factory Mutual Corporation, P8016, 1151 Boston-Providence Turnpike, Norwood, MA.

Galbreath, M. 1966. Fire Endurance of Light Framed and Miscellaneous Assemblies. Technical Paper No. 222, Division of Building Research (NOW Institute for Research in Construction), National Research Council of Canada. Ottawa, ON.

Guidelines on Fire Ratings of Archaic Materials and Assemblies. 1980. Rehabilitation Guideline #8, U.S. Department of Housing and Urban Development, Germantown, Maryland.

Harmathy, T.Z. 1972. A New Look at Compartment Fires Part I and II. Fire Technology, Vol. 8, Nos. 3 and 4, National Fire Protection Association, Quincy, MA.

Harmathy, T.Z. 1960. Fire Test of a Wood Partition, Fire Study No. 3, Division of Building Research, National Research Council of Canada, Ottawa, ON.

Ingberg, S.H. 1928. Test of the Severity of Building Fires. NFPA Quarterly, Vol. 22, No. 1, National Fire Protection Association, Quincy, MA.

List of Equipment and Materials Volume II, Building Construction. Underwriters' Laboratories of Canada, Scarborough, ON.

1994 Certification Listings. Warnock Hersey, Mississauga, ON.

Quintiere, J.G. Growth of Fire in Building Compartments. Fire Standards and Safety, ASTM STP614, A.F. Robertson ed. American Society for Testing and Materials. Philadelphia, PA.

Schaffer, E.L. 1966. Review of Information Related to the Charring Rate of Wood. Res. Note FPL-145, USDA Forest Service, Forest Product Lab., Madison, WI.

Shaw, J.R. 1997. Fire Retardant and Flame Resistant Treatments of Cellulosic Materials. NFPA Fire Protection Handbook, 18th Edition, Section 4, Chapter 4. National Fire Protection Association, Quincy, MA.

SFPE. 2000. Engineering Guide to Performance-Based Fire Protection. National Fire Protection Association, Quincy, MA.

Standard Guide for Extension of Data from Fire Endurance Tests. ASTM E2032, 1999. American Society for Testing and Materials, West Conshohocken, PA.

Standard Method of Test for Fire Spread Under Roof-Deck Assemblies. CAN/ULC-S126, Underwriters' Laboratories of Canada, Scarborough, ON.

Standard Method of Test for Surface Burning Characteristics of Building Materials and Assemblies. CAN/ULC-S102, Underwriters' Laboratories of Canada, Scarborough, ON.

Standard Methods of Fire Endurance Tests of Building Construction and Materials. CAN4-S101-M89, 1st Edition , Underwriters' Laboratories of Canada, Scarborough, ON.

Thomas, P.H. Some Problem Aspects of Fully Developed Room Fires. Fire Standards and Safety, ASTM STP614, A.F. Robertson, ed. American Society for Testing and Materials. Philadelphia, PA.

Watts, Jr., John M.1991. Systems Concept for Building Firesafety. NFPA Fire Protection Handbook, 17th Edition, Section 1, Chapter 3. National Fire Protection Association, Boston, MA.

# Reference
# Information

11

REF

# 11.1 General Information

This section contains reference information pertaining to the following topics:

# Lumber

Table 11.1
**Commercial
species
combinations
of lumber**

| Species combination | Abbreviations as used in manual | Species included in combination | Characteristics | Colour ranges |
|---|---|---|---|---|
| Douglas Fir-Larch | DF-L or D.Fir-L | Douglas fir Western larch | - high degree of hardness<br>- good resistance to decay | reddish brown to yellowish |
| Hem-Fir | H-F or Hem-Fir | Pacific coast hemlock Amabilis fir | - works easily<br>- takes paint well<br>- holds nails well<br>- good gluing characteristics | yellow brown to white |
| Spruce-Pine-Fir | S-P-F | Spruce (all species except Coast sitka spruce) Jack pine Lodgepole pine Balsam fir Alpine fir | - works easily<br>- takes paint well<br>- holds nails well<br>- good gluing characteristics<br>- light weight, soft | white to pale yellow |
| Northern Species | Nor or North | Western red cedar | - exceptional resistance to decay<br>- high in appearance qualities<br>- works easily<br>- takes fine finishes<br>- lowest shrinkage | red cedar:<br>reddish brown heartwood<br>light sapwood |
| | | Red pine | - works easily<br>- easily treated with preservatives | reddish to pale brown heartwood |
| | | Ponderosa pine | - takes finish well<br>- holds nails well<br>- holds screws well<br>- seasons with little checking or cupping | pale yellow colour sapwood |
| | | Western white pine Eastern white pine | - softest of Canadian pines<br>- works easily<br>- finishes well<br>- doesn't tend to split or splinter<br>- hold nails well<br>- low shrinkage<br>- takes stains, paints, varnishes well | creamy white to light straw brown heartwood almost white sapwood |
| | | Trembling aspen Largetooth aspen Balsam poplar | - works easily<br>- finishes well<br>- holds nails well | almost white to greyish-white |
| | | Any other Canadian species graded in accordance with the NLGA rules | | |

**11**

**REF**

Reference Information

## Lumber Grading

Grading is the sorting of lumber by visual or mechanical means according to strength, appearance and end use. The sorting is identified by the grade stamp on the lumber.

The National Lumber Grades Authority publishes the *NLGA Standard Grading Rules for Canadian Lumber* in accordance with the provisions of CSA Standard O141 *Softwood Lumber.* Under this uniform rule, all Canadian lumber, regardless of species or source, is graded the same way and bears the same grade names.

The grading rule covers several categories of dimension lumber (38 to 102 mm in smaller dimension), each intended for specific purposes in light frame construction, as well as categories for decking, beams and stringers, and posts and timbers. All grade descriptions for the dimension lumber categories have been standardized throughout Canada and the United States. There are some minor differences of grade description in other categories of lumber between these grading rules. The scope of lumber categories for visually graded lumber is summarized in Table 11.2.

Responsibility for the overall supervision of grading and the control and certification of grading agencies in Canada are vested in the Canadian Lumber Standards Accreditation Board. Control of grading and the issue of grade stamps are the responsibility of various grading agencies in Canada for the species of wood grown in each region.

The grading rule establishes maximum permitted size of characteristics for each grade of lumber. The size and location of knots and splits, slope of grain, wane, warp, stain and manufacturing imperfections are some of the factors that must be considered as each piece of lumber is graded.

Each grade mark or stamp used in Canada contains the initials or logo of the regional association responsible for grading. In addition, stamps indicate the grades and species of the piece of lumber, often by means of an abbreviation.

The grading of lumber by mechanical means is another accepted method of grading lumber. There are two classifications of machine graded lumber in NLGA Special Products Standard SPS 2: *Machine Stress Rated Lumber* (MSR) and *Machine Evaluated Lumber* (MEL).

MEL lumber and MSR lumber are basically interchangeable except that the minimum (5th percentile) modulus of elasticity (MOE) for MSR lumber is limited to 0.82 times the grade mean value, whereas for MEL lumber it is limited to 0.75 times the grade mean. This results in slightly different compressive capacities using the column formulae for the two products.

Both MEL and MSR lumber may be produced using nondestructive stiffness-measuring machines. In a typical machine of this sort, forces are applied on both sides of the lumber, on the flat, with deflection measured every 150 mm along the length of each piece. Stiffness is calculated and recorded by a computer, and from this, strength is assessed by correlation methods. From this information, a grade is assigned. The lumber can be processed at speeds up to 365 m per minute, including being stamped with an MSR or MEL grade mark.

It is also possible to use machines that do not measure stiffness, alone or in conjunction with a stiffness-measuring machine, to produce MSR and MEL lumber, provided that the qualification and ongoing quality control demonstrate that the product meets the requirements of the standard.

Standard sizes for dimension lumber, timber and boards are given in Tables 11.5, 11.6 and 11.7, respectively.

Specified strengths for visual, MSR and MEL grades of lumber are given in Tables 11.8 to 11.12. The designer should be aware that CSA O86 has assigned identical specified strengths to No.1 and No.2 grade lumber. This is based on the results of the Canadian Wood Council's Lumber Properties Program, in which extensive testing was carried out on full size pieces of dimension lumber from across Canada. Throughout the manual this grade category is referred to as No.1/No.2; however, an appropriate specification is "No.2 and Better".

Table 11.2
**Guide to NLGA grades of visually graded lumber**

| Lumber product | Grade category | Sizes mm | Grades | Principal uses |
|---|---|---|---|---|
| Dimension lumber | Structural Light Framing, Joists and Planks | 38 to 89 wide 38 to 89 deep | Select Structural No.1 No.2 No.3 | Trusses, rafters, joists, engineered uses and general construction |
| | Light Framing | 38 to 89 wide 38 to 89 deep | Construction Standard Utility* Economy* | General construction uses such as rafters, studs, plates, blocking and bracing |
| | Stud | 38 to 89 wide 38 to 140 deep | Stud Economy Stud* | Studs for interior or exterior walls |
| Decking | Decking | 38 to 89 deep 140 (nominal) and wider | Select Commercial | Roof and floor decking |
| Timber | Beams and Stringers | 114 and wider depth more than 51 greater than width | Select Structural No.1 No.2 Standard* Utility* | Heavy beams |
| | Posts and Timbers | 114 × 114 and larger, depth not more than 51 greater than width | Select Structural No.1 No.2 Standard* Utility* | Columns |

Note:
* Specified strengths have not been assigned to these grades (i.e., they are not "stress grades").

**Plank Decking**

Select grade is used for applications where good strength and fine appearance are desired.

The characteristics of Select grade are given in Table 11.3. These provisions may apply to the exposed face (except where noted), although all or nearly all of the permissible characteristics of the grade are never present in maximum size or number in any one piece. Any piece with an unusual combination of characteristics that seriously affects normal serviceability is excluded from the grade.

Commercial grade is used for the same purposes as Select grade when appearance and strength requirements are not as critical. Its characteristics are given in Table 11.4, although all or nearly all of the permissible characteristics of the grade are never present in maximum size or number in any one piece. Any piece with an unusual combination of characteristics that seriously affects normal serviceability is excluded from the grade.

For a full description of Select and Commercial grade characteristics refer to NLGA *Standard Grading Rules for Canadian Lumber.* A lumber shipment is considered to meet grading requirements if 95% of a given shipment is of the said grade or better.

| Table 11.3 **Permitted characteristics for Select grade plank decking** | Category | Permitted characteristics |
|---|---|---|
| | Growth | medium stained wood |
| | | small holes, equivalent to chipped knots |
| | | slope of grain not to exceed 1 in 10 |
| | | medium bark pockets |
| | | sound and tight knots on exposed face |
| | | knots well spaced, not larger than approximately 60 mm in diameter permitted both wide faces for 38 × 140 mm nominal and 83 mm for 38 × 184 mm nominal. |
| | | in occasional pieces, unsound knots, if tight and not exceeding 38 mm in diameter, are permitted if medium checks not through the piece and do not exceed 2 in a 4 m length or equivalent smaller. |
| | | spike and narrow face knots are permitted if judged to have no more effect on strength than other knots. |
| | | chipped and/or broken-out knots not larger than approximately 19 mm in diameter are permitted if not through the piece and do not exceed 2 in a 4 m length. |
| | | on unexposed face and edges, hit and miss skips or wane approximately 1/3 of the face width, pecky spots in narrow streaks, skips 10% of exposed face in occasional pieces and other characteristics not interfering with the intended use are permitted |
| | Seasoning | medium checks |
| | | occasional short splits |
| | | occasional light crook |
| | Manufacturing | tongue 2 mm narrow on occasional pieces |
| | | medium torn grain |
| | | very light skips, maximum 10% of face in occasional pieces |

| Table 11.4 **Permitted characteristics for Commercial grade plank decking** | Category | Permitted characteristics |
|---|---|---|
| | Growth | stained wood |
| | | holes, 25 mm |
| | | slope of grain not to exceed 1 in 8, full length |
| | | bark or pitch pockets |
| | | unsound wood and/or peck not exceeding approximately 1/3 of any face |
| | | shake not serious |
| | | occasional crook medium |
| | | knots well spaced not larger than approximately 73 mm permitted on both wide faces for 38 × 140 mm nominal and 95 mm for 38 × 184 mm nominal |
| | | spike and narrow knots are permitted if judged to have no more effect on strength than other knots |
| | | chipped and/or broken-out knots or portions of knots not larger than approximately 38 mm in diameter are permitted if not through the piece |
| | | on unexposed face and edges wane approximately 1/3 of the face and other characteristics not interfering with intended use. |
| | Seasoning | checks |
| | | splits approximately 1/6 of the length |
| | Manufacturing | tongue 2 mm narrow |
| | | torn grain |
| | | hit and miss skips |
| | | wane approximately 1/6 of the face width |

**11**

**REF**

Reference Information

## Fingerjoined Lumber

Fingerjoined lumber is dimension lumber into which finger profiles have been machined (see Figure 11.1). The pieces are then end-glued together.

With fingerjoining, the length of a piece of lumber is not limited by tree size: joists and rafters over 12 m long can be produced.

This process also allows the removal of strength reducing defects, resulting in better use and conservation of wood fibre.

Canadian fingerjoined lumber is manufactured in conformance with NLGA Special Products Standards SPS 1, *Fingerjoined Structural Lumber,* or SPS 3, *Fingerjoined Stud Lumber-Vertical Use Only.*

Fingerjoined lumber manufactured to the requirements of SPS 1 is interchangeable with non-fingerjoined lumber of the same species, grade and length, and can be used for joists, rafters and other applications. Fingerjoined lumber manufactured according to SPS 3 can only be used as vertical end-loaded members in compression (i.e. wall studs), where bending or tension loading components do not exceed short term duration, and where the moisture content of the wood will not exceed 19%. SPS 3 lumber is manufactured in sizes up to 38 × 140 mm, in lengths up to 3.66 m.

All fingerjoined lumber manufactured to the Canadian NLGA Standards carries a grade stamp indicating:

- the species or species combination identification
- the seasoning designation (S-Dry or S-Green)
- the registered symbol of the grading agency
- the grade
- the mill identification
- the NLGA standard number and the designation SPS 1 CERT FGR JNT (certified finger joint) or SPS 3 CERT FGR JNT VERTICAL USE ONLY (certified finger joint for vertical use only).

Figure 11.1
**Fingerjoined lumber**

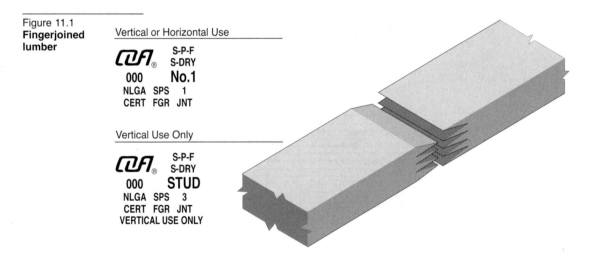

Vertical or Horizontal Use

*CU7*®    S-P-F
           S-DRY
000    No.1
NLGA  SPS  1
CERT  FGR  JNT

Vertical Use Only

*CU7*®    S-P-F
           S-DRY
000    STUD
NLGA  SPS  3
CERT  FGR  JNT
VERTICAL USE ONLY

| Table 11.5 **Dimension lumber sizes and section properties** | Nominal size in. | Surfaced Green (S-Grn) size in. | Surfaced Dry (S-Dry) size in. | Metric (S-Dry) size mm | Area $\times 10^3$ mm$^2$ | $I_x$ (major axis) $\times 10^6$ mm$^4$ | $S_x$ (major axis) $\times 10^3$ mm$^3$ |
|---|---|---|---|---|---|---|---|
| | 2 × 2 | 1-9/16 × 1-9/16 | 1-1/2 × 1-1/2 | 38 × 38 | 1.45 | 0.18 | 9.22 |
| | 3 | 2-9/16 | 2-1/2 | 64 | 2.42 | 0.81 | 25.6 |
| | 4 | 3-9/16 | 3-1/2 | 89 | 3.39 | 2.23 | 50.2 |
| | 6 | 5-5/8 | 5-1/2 | 140 | 5.32 | 8.66 | 124 |
| | 8 | 7-1/2 | 7-1/4 | 184 | 7.02 | 19.8 | 215 |
| | 10 | 9-1/2 | 9-1/4 | 235 | 8.95 | 41.2 | 351 |
| | 12 | 11-1/2 | 11-1/4 | 286 | 10.9 | 74.1 | 518 |
| | 3 × 3 | 2-9/16 × 2-9/16 | 2-1/2 × 2-1/2 | 64 × 64 | 4.03 | 1.35 | 42.7 |
| | 4 | 3-9/16 | 3-1/2 | 89 | 5.65 | 3.72 | 83.6 |
| | 6 | 5-5/8 | 5-1/2 | 140 | 8.87 | 14.4 | 207 |
| | 8 | 7-1/2 | 7-1/4 | 184 | 11.7 | 33.0 | 359 |
| | 10 | 9-1/2 | 9-1/4 | 235 | 14.9 | 68.6 | 584 |
| | 12 | 11-1/2 | 11-1/4 | 286 | 18.1 | 123 | 864 |
| | 4 × 4 | 3-9/16 × 3-9/16 | 3-1/2 × 3-1/2 | 89 × 89 | 7.90 | 5.21 | 117 |
| | 6 | 5-5/8 | 5-1/2 | 140 | 12.4 | 20.2 | 289 |
| | 8 | 7-1/2 | 7-1/4 | 184 | 16.4 | 46.3 | 502 |
| | 10 | 9-1/2 | 9-1/4 | 235 | 20.9 | 96.1 | 818 |
| | 12 | 11-1/2 | 11-1/4 | 286 | 25.4 | 173 | 1210 |

Notes:
1. 38 mm (2") lumber is readily available as S-Dry.
2. S-Dry Lumber is surfaced at a moisture content of 19% or less.
3. After drying, S-Grn lumber sizes will be approximately the same as S-Dry lumber.
4. Tabulated metric sizes are equivalent to imperial S-Dry sizes, rounded to the nearest millimetre.
5. Shrinkage is accounted for in given design values: therefore S-Dry sizes are used in design.

**11**

**REF**

Reference Information

| Table 11.6 | Nominal size in. | Surfaced Green (S-Grn) size in. | Metric size mm | Area × 10³ mm² | $I_x$ (major axis) × 10⁶ mm⁴ | $S_x$ (major axis) × 10³ mm³ |
|---|---|---|---|---|---|---|
| **Timber sizes and section properties** | 6 × 6 | 5-1/2 × 5-1/2 | 140 × 140 | 19.5 | 31.7 | 454 |
| | 8 | 7-1/2 | 191 | 26.6 | 80.5 | 845 |
| | 10 | 9-1/2 | 241 | 33.7 | 164 | 1360 |
| | 12 | 11-1/2 | 292 | 40.8 | 290 | 1990 |
| | 14 | 13-1/2 | 343 | 47.9 | 469 | 2740 |
| | 16 | 15-1/2 | 394 | 55.0 | 710 | 3610 |
| | 18 | 17-1/2 | 445 | 62.1 | 1020 | 4600 |
| | 8 × 8 | 7-1/2 × 7-1/2 | 191 × 191 | 36.3 | 110 | 1150 |
| | 10 | 9-1/2 | 241 | 46.0 | 223 | 1850 |
| | 12 | 11-1/2 | 292 | 55.6 | 396 | 2710 |
| | 14 | 13-1/2 | 343 | 65.3 | 640 | 3730 |
| | 16 | 15-1/2 | 394 | 75.0 | 969 | 4920 |
| | 18 | 17-1/2 | 445 | 84.7 | 1390 | 6270 |
| | 20 | 19-1/2 | 495 | 94.4 | 1930 | 7790 |
| | 10 × 10 | 9-1/2 × 9-1/2 | 241 × 241 | 58.2 | 283 | 2340 |
| | 12 | 11-1/2 | 292 | 70.5 | 501 | 3430 |
| | 14 | 13-1/2 | 343 | 82.7 | 811 | 4730 |
| | 16 | 15-1/2 | 394 | 95.0 | 1230 | 6230 |
| | 18 | 17-1/2 | 445 | 107 | 1770 | 7950 |
| | 20 | 19-1/2 | 495 | 120 | 2440 | 9870 |
| | 12 × 12 | 11-1/2 × 11-1/2 | 292 × 292 | 85.3 | 607 | 4150 |
| | 14 | 13-1/2 | 343 | 100 | 981 | 5720 |
| | 16 | 15-1/2 | 394 | 115 | 1490 | 7550 |
| | 18 | 17-1/2 | 445 | 130 | 2140 | 9620 |
| | 20 | 19-1/2 | 495 | 145 | 2960 | 11900 |

Notes:
1. Timbers are always surfaced green.
2. Tabulated metric sizes are equivalent to imperial dimensions.

**Table 11.7**
**Boards: Imperial and metric sizes, seasoned and unseasoned**

| Dimension | | Imperial measure | | | Metric measure | |
|---|---|---|---|---|---|---|
| | | Nominal in. | Dry in. | Green in. | Dry mm | Green mm |
| Thickness | 1 | | 3/4 | 25/32 | 19 | 20 |
| | 1-1/4 | | 1 | 1-1/32 | 25 | 26 |
| | 1-1/2 | | 1-1/4 | 1-9/32 | 32 | 33 |
| | 2 | | 1-1/2 | 1-9/16 | 38 | 40 |
| Width | 2 | | 1-1/2 | 1-9/16 | 38 | 40 |
| | 3 | | 2-1/2 | 2-9/16 | 64 | 65 |
| | 4 | | 3-1/2 | 3-9/16 | 89 | 90 |
| | 5 | | 4-1/2 | 4-5/8 | 114 | 117 |

**Table 11.8**
**Specified strengths and modulus of elasticity (MPa) for Structural Joists and Planks, Structural Light Framing and Stud grade lumber**

| Species combination | Grade | Bending at extreme fibre $f_b$ | Longi-tudinal shear $f_v$ | Compression | | Tension | Modulus of elasticity | |
|---|---|---|---|---|---|---|---|---|
| | | | | Parallel to grain $f_c$ | Perpen-dicular to grain $f_{cp}$ | Parallel to grain $f_t$ | E | $E_{05}$ |
| D.Fir-L | Sel Str | 16.5 | 1.9 | 19.0 | 7.0 | 10.6 | 12500 | 8500 |
| | No.1/No.2 | 10.0 | 1.9 | 14.0 | 7.0 | 5.8 | 11000 | 7000 |
| | No.3/Stud | 4.6 | 1.9 | 4.6 | 7.0 | 2.1 | 10000 | 5500 |
| Hem-Fir | Sel Str | 16.0 | 1.6 | 17.6 | 4.6 | 9.7 | 12000 | 8500 |
| | No.1/No.2 | 11.0 | 1.6 | 14.8 | 4.6 | 6.2 | 11000 | 7500 |
| | No.3/Stud | 7.0 | 1.6 | 7.0 | 4.6 | 3.2 | 10000 | 6000 |
| S-P-F | Sel Str | 16.5 | 1.5 | 14.5 | 5.3 | 8.6 | 10500 | 7500 |
| | No.1/No.2 | 11.8 | 1.5 | 11.5 | 5.3 | 5.5 | 9500 | 6500 |
| | No.3/Stud | 7.0 | 1.5 | 7.0 | 5.3 | 3.2 | 9000 | 5500 |
| Northern | Sel Str | 10.6 | 1.3 | 13.0 | 3.5 | 6.2 | 7500 | 5500 |
| | No.1/No.2 | 7.6 | 1.3 | 10.4 | 3.5 | 4.0 | 7000 | 5000 |
| | No.3/Stud | 4.5 | 1.3 | 4.5 | 3.5 | 2.0 | 6500 | 4000 |

**11**

**REF**

Reference Information

Table 11.9
**Specified strengths and modulus of elasticity (MPa) for Beams and Stringers**

| Species combination | Grade | Bending at extreme fibre $f_b$ | Longi- tudinal shear $f_v$ | Compression Parallel to grain $f_c$ | Compression Perpen- dicular to grain $f_{cp}$ | Tension Parallel to grain $f_t$ | Modulus of elasticity E | $E_{05}$ |
|---|---|---|---|---|---|---|---|---|
| D.Fir-L | Sel Str | 19.5 | 1.5 | 13.2 | 7.0 | 10.0 | 12000 | 8000 |
| | No.1 | 15.8 | 1.5 | 11.0 | 7.0 | 7.0 | 12000 | 8000 |
| | No.2 | 9.0 | 1.5 | 7.2 | 7.0 | 3.3 | 9500 | 6000 |
| Hem-Fir | Sel Str | 14.5 | 1.2 | 10.8 | 4.6 | 7.4 | 10000 | 7000 |
| | No.1 | 11.7 | 1.2 | 9.0 | 4.6 | 5.2 | 10000 | 7000 |
| | No.2 | 6.7 | 1.2 | 5.9 | 4.6 | 2.4 | 8000 | 5500 |
| S-P-F | Sel Str | 13.6 | 1.2 | 9.5 | 5.3 | 7.0 | 8500 | 6000 |
| | No.1 | 11.0 | 1.2 | 7.9 | 5.3 | 4.9 | 8500 | 6000 |
| | No.2 | 6.3 | 1.2 | 5.2 | 5.3 | 2.3 | 6500 | 4500 |
| Northern | Sel Str | 12.8 | 1.0 | 7.2 | 3.5 | 6.5 | 8000 | 5500 |
| | No.1 | 10.3 | 1.0 | 6.0 | 3.5 | 4.6 | 8000 | 5500 |
| | No.2 | 5.9 | 1.0 | 3.9 | 3.5 | 2.2 | 6000 | 4000 |

Notes:
1. Specified strengths for beams and stringers are based on loads applied to the narrow face. When beams and stringers are subject to loads applied to the wide face, the specified strengths for bending at the extreme fibre and modulus of elasticity shall be multiplied by the following factors:

| | $f_b$ | E or $E_{05}$ |
|---|---|---|
| Select Structural | 0.88 | 1.00 |
| No.1 or No.2 | 0.77 | 0.90 |

2. Beam and stringer grades listed in this Table are not graded for continuity (see Clause 5.5.3.of CSA O86).

Table 11.10
**Specified strengths and modulus of elasticity (MPa) for Posts and Timbers**

| Species combination | Grade | Bending at extreme fibre $f_b$ | Longi-tudinal shear $f_v$ | Compression | | Tension | Modulus of elasticity | |
|---|---|---|---|---|---|---|---|---|
| | | | | Parallel to grain $f_c$ | Perpen-dicular to grain $f_{cp}$ | Parallel to grain $f_t$ | E | $E_{05}$ |
| D.Fir-L | Sel Str | 18.3 | 1.5 | 13.8 | 7.0 | 10.7 | 12000 | 8000 |
| | No.1 | 13.8 | 1.5 | 12.2 | 7.0 | 8.1 | 10500 | 6500 |
| | No.2 | 6.0 | 1.5 | 7.5 | 7.0 | 3.8 | 9500 | 6000 |
| Hem-Fir | Sel Str | 13.6 | 1.2 | 11.3 | 4.6 | 7.9 | 10000 | 7000 |
| | No.1 | 10.2 | 1.2 | 10.0 | 4.6 | 6.0 | 9000 | 6000 |
| | No.2 | 4.5 | 1.2 | 6.1 | 4.6 | 2.8 | 8000 | 5500 |
| S-P-F | Sel Str | 12.7 | 1.2 | 9.9 | 5.3 | 7.4 | 8500 | 6000 |
| | No.1 | 9.6 | 1.2 | 8.7 | 5.3 | 5.6 | 7500 | 5000 |
| | No.2 | 4.2 | 1.2 | 5.4 | 5.3 | 2.6 | 6500 | 4500 |
| Northern | Sel Str | 12.0 | 1.0 | 7.5 | 3.5 | 7.0 | 8000 | 5500 |
| | No.1 | 9.0 | 1.0 | 6.7 | 3.5 | 5.3 | 7000 | 5000 |
| | No.2 | 3.9 | 1.0 | 4.1 | 3.5 | 2.5 | 6000 | 4000 |

| Table 11.11 Specified strengths and modulus of elasticity (MPa) for 38 mm thick machine stress-rated (MSR) lumber | Grade | Bending at extreme fibre $f_b$ | Compression parallel to grain $f_c$ | Tension parallel to grain 89 to 184 mm $f_t$ | Over 184 mm[4] $f_t$ | Modulus of elasticity E |
|---|---|---|---|---|---|---|
| | 1200F$_b$-1.2E | 17.4 | 15.1 | 6.7 | - | 8300 |
| | 1350F$_b$-1.3E | 19.5 | 16.9 | 8.4 | - | 9000 |
| | 1450F$_b$-1.3E | 21.0 | 17.3 | 9.0 | - | 9000 |
| | 1500F$_b$-1.4E | 21.7 | 17.5 | 10.1 | - | 9700 |
| | 1650F$_b$-1.5E | 23.9 | 18.1 | 11.4 | - | 10300 |
| | 1800F$_b$-1.6E | 26.1 | 18.7 | 13.2 | - | 11000 |
| | 1950F$_b$-1.7E | 28.2 | 19.3 | 15.4 | - | 11700 |
| | 2100F$_b$-1.8E | 30.4 | 19.9 | 17.7 | - | 12400 |
| | 2250F$_b$-1.9E | 32.6 | 20.5 | 19.6 | - | 13100 |
| | 2400F$_b$-2.0E | 34.7 | 21.1 | 21.6 | - | 13800 |
| | 2550F$_b$-2.1E | 36.9 | 21.7 | 23.0 | - | 14500 |
| | 2700F$_b$-2.2E | 39.1 | 22.3 | 24.1 | - | 15200 |
| | 2850F$_b$-2.3E | 41.3 | 22.9 | 25.8 | - | 15900 |
| | 3000F$_b$-2.4E | 43.4 | 23.5 | 26.9 | - | 16500 |

The following MSR grades provide a modulus of elasticity with higher corresponding strengths. For these MSR grades, qualification and daily quality control for tensile strength are required.

| Grade | $f_b$ | $f_c$ | $f_t$ (89 to 184 mm) | $f_t$ (Over 184 mm) | E |
|---|---|---|---|---|---|
| 1400F$_b$-1.2E | 20.3 | 17.1 | 9.0 | 9.0 | 8300 |
| 1600F$_b$-1.4E | 23.2 | 17.9 | 10.7 | 10.7 | 9700 |
| 1650F$_b$-1.3E | 23.9 | 18.1 | 11.4 | 11.4 | 9000 |
| 1800F$_b$-1.5E | 26.1 | 18.7 | 14.6 | 14.6 | 10300 |
| 2000F$_b$-1.6E | 29.0 | 19.5 | 14.6 | 14.6 | 11000 |
| 2250F$_b$-1.7E | 32.6 | 20.5 | 19.6 | 19.6 | 11700 |
| 2250F$_b$-1.8E | 32.6 | 20.5 | 19.6 | 19.6 | 12400 |
| 2400F$_b$-1.8E | 34.7 | 21.1 | 21.6 | 21.6 | 12400 |

Notes:
1. Tabulated values are based on standard term duration of load and dry service conditions.
2. The size factor $K_Z$ for MSR lumber shall be 1.0, except that $K_{Zv}$ is given in Table 5.4.5, $K_{Zcp}$ is determined in accordance with Clause 5.5.7.5, and $K_{Zc}$ is calculated in accordance with Clause 5.5.6.2.2.
3. Compression perpendicular to grain and shear values are the same as for corresponding values for visually stress-graded lumber taken from Table 5.3.1A for the appropriate group, with the exceptions:
   • The compression perpendicular specified strength is 6.5 MPa for S-P-F MSR lumber with E value of 12400 MPa or higher.
   • The compression perpendicular specified strength is 5.3 MPa for Hem-Fir MSR lumber with E value of 10300 to 11700 MPa or 6.5 MPa with E value of 12400 or higher.
4. The tension design values for narrow widths may be assigned to these sizes, provided the lumber is subject to the appropriate level of qualification and daily quality control testing for tension strength as specified in NLGA SPS 2.

| Table 11.12 Specified strengths and modulus of elasticity (MPa) for 38 mm thick machine evaluated lumber (MEL) | Grade | Bending at extreme fibre $f_b$ | Compression parallel to grain $f_c$ | Tension parallel to grain $f_t$ | Modulus of elasticity E |
|---|---|---|---|---|---|
| | M-10 | 20.3 | 17.1 | 9.0 | 8300 |
| | M-11 | 22.4 | 17.7 | 9.5 | 10300 |
| | M-12 | 23.2 | 17.9 | 9.5 | 11000 |
| | M-13 | 23.2 | 17.9 | 10.7 | 9700 |
| | M-14 | 26.1 | 18.7 | 11.2 | 11700 |
| | M-15 | 26.1 | 18.7 | 12.3 | 10300 |
| | M-18 | 29.0 | 19.5 | 13.5 | 12400 |
| | M-19 | 29.0 | 19.5 | 14.6 | 11000 |
| | M-21 | 33.3 | 20.7 | 15.7 | 13100 |
| | M-22 | 34.0 | 20.9 | 16.8 | 11700 |
| | M-23 | 34.7 | 21.1 | 21.3 | 12400 |
| | M-24 | 39.1 | 22.3 | 20.2 | 13100 |
| | M-25 | 39.8 | 22.5 | 22.4 | 15200 |
| | M-26 | 40.6 | 22.7 | 20.2 | 13800 |

Notes: See Table 11.11 notes.

# Glulam

## Grades of Glulam

There are two classifications or grade categories for glulam:

- **Stress Grade** defines specified strengths of the material.
- **Appearance Grade** defines the quality of finish on the exposed surfaces of the member (not related to the Stress Grade of the material).

All glulam is manufactured as an Exterior Grade product using waterproof glue (usually a resorcinol). Stress and appearance grades are described in Tables 11.13 and 11.14, respectively.

The lumber laminations are not graded to the same rules as regular lumber, but rather conform to the grading rules contained in CSA Standard O122 *Structural Glued-Laminated Timber*. Each lamination is visually graded based on the examination of both faces of the piece, and then assigned one of four grades: B, B-F, D, or C. Specified laminations are tested non-destructively by machine to establish required minimum E (modulus of elasticity) values. Laminations of higher grades, such as B and B-F, are used in the top and bottom portions of glulam beams and arches where bending stress is greatest. Standard lamination thicknesses for glulam are 19 and 38 mm.

Specified strengths for glulam are given in Table 11.15.

**Table 11.13**
**Glulam stress grades**

| Stress grade | | Species | Description |
|---|---|---|---|
| Bending grades | 20f-E and 20f-EX | D.Fir-L or Spruce-Pine | Used for members subjected to bending as the principal stress, such as beams and arches. |
| | 24f-E and 24f-EX | D.Fir-L or Hem-Fir | Specify EX when members subject to positive and negative moments or when members subject to combined bending and axial load. |
| Compression grades | 16c-E | D.Fir-L | Used for members stressed principally in axial compression, such as columns. |
| | 12c-E | Spruce-Pine | |
| Tension grades | 18t-E | D.Fir-L | Used for members stressed principally in axial tension, such as bottom chords of trusses. |
| | 14t-E | Spruce-Pine | |

**Table 11.14**
**Glulam appearance grade requirements**

| Requirement | Appearance grade | | |
|---|---|---|---|
| | Industrial | Commercial | Quality |
| Laminations may contain natural growth characteristics allowed in specified grades of laminating stock. | Yes | Yes | Yes |
| Tight knots and stain are permitted on exposed surfaces. | Yes | Yes | Yes |
| Sides shall be surfaced true to specified dimensions. | Yes | Yes | Yes |
| Planer misses along individual laminations shall be patched with replacement stock. Exposed surfaces shall be sanded smooth and shall be free of glue. | No | Yes | Yes |
| Wane, pitch pockets, loose knots, knot holes and voids on exposed surfaces shall be replaced by wood inserts or non-shrinking waterproof filling material. | No | No | Yes |
| Slightly broken knots, slivers, torn grain and checks shall be filled. | No | No | Yes |

Table 11.15
**Specified strengths and modulus of elasticity (MPa) for glulam**

| | | D.Fir-L 20f-E | 20f-EX | 24f-E | 24f-EX | 18t-E | 16c-E |
|---|---|---|---|---|---|---|---|
| Bending-positive moment | $f_b$ | 25.6 | 25.6 | 30.6 | 30.6 | 24.3 | 14.0 |
| Bending-negative moment | $f_b$ | 19.2 | 25.6 | 23.0 | 30.6 | 24.3 | 14.0 |
| Longitudinal shear | $f_v$ | 2.0 | 2.0 | 2.0 | 2.0 | 2.0 | 2.0 |
| Compression parallel to grain | $f_c$ | 30.2* | 30.2* | 30.2* | 30.2* | 30.2 | 30.2 |
| Compression parallel to grain combined with bending | $f_{cb}$ | 30.2* | 30.2* | 30.2* | 30.2 | 30.2 | 30.2 |
| Compression perp. to grain a) Compression face bearing | $f_{cp}$ | 7.0 | 7.0 | 7.0 | 7.0 | 7.0 | 7.0 |
| b) Tension face bearing | | 7.0 | 7.0 | 7.0 | 7.0 | 7.0 | 7.0 |
| Tension at net section | $f_{tn}$ | 20.4* | 20.4 | 20.4* | 20.4 | 23.0 | 20.4 |
| Tension at gross section | $f_{tg}$ | 15.3* | 15.3 | 15.3* | 15.3 | 17.9 | 15.3 |
| Tension perp. to grain | $f_{tp}$ | 0.83 | 0.83 | 0.83 | 0.83 | 0.83 | 0.83 |
| Modulus of elasticity | E | 12400 | 12400 | 13100 | 13100 | 13800 | 12400 |

| | | Spruce-Pine 20f-E | 20f-EX | 14t-E | 12c-E | Hem-Fir 24f-E | 24-EX |
|---|---|---|---|---|---|---|---|
| Bending-positive moment | $f_b$ | 25.6 | 25.6 | 24.3 | 9.8 | 30.6 | 30.6 |
| Bending-negative moment | $f_b$ | 19.2 | 25.6 | 24.3 | 9.8 | 23.0 | 30.6 |
| Longitudinal shear | $f_v$ | 1.75 | 1.75 | 1.75 | 1.75 | 1.75 | 1.75 |
| Compression parallel to grain | $f_c$ | 25.2* | 25.2* | 25.2* | 25.2* | - | - |
| Compression parallel to grain combined with bending | $f_{cb}$ | 25.2* | 25.2* | 25.2* | 25.2* | - | - |
| Compression perp. to grain a) Compression face bearing | $f_{cp}$ | 5.8 | 5.8 | 5.8 | 5.8 | 4.6 | 7.0 |
| b) Tension face bearing | | 5.8 | 5.8 | 5.8 | 5.8 | 7.0 | 7.0 |
| Tension at net section | $f_{tn}$ | 17.0* | 17.0 | 17.9 | 17.0 | 20.4* | 20.4 |
| Tension at gross section | $f_{tg}$ | 12.7* | 12.7 | 13.4 | 12.7 | 15.3* | 15.3 |
| Tension perp. to grain | $f_{tp}$ | 0.51 | 0.51 | 0.51 | 0.51 | 0.83 | 0.83 |
| Modulus of elasticity | E | 10300 | 10300 | 10700 | 9700 | 13100 | 13100 |

Note:
* The use of this stress grade for this primary application is not recommended.

**11**

**REF**

Reference Information

# Guide Specifications

## 1. General

### 1.1 Related Work Specified Elsewhere

1.1.1 Supply and installation of anchor bolts or anchorage units embedded in concrete.

1.1.2 Supply and installation of anchor bolts or anchorage units embedded in brickwork or concrete block work.

1.1.3 Grouting of bearings.

1.1.4 Connections shown on drawings, or specified welded to work supplied in other Sections.

1.1.5 Structural steel columns.

1.1.6 Wood plank decking (see note 1).

1.1.7 Paints, stains, sealers other than shop applied.

### 1.2 Shop Drawings

1.2.1 Submit shop drawings in accordance with contract procedures specified elsewhere.

1.2.2 Shop drawings shall indicate the following:

1.2.2.1 All dimensions

1.2.2.2 Material grade (stress designation)

1.2.2.3 Surface finish (sawn),
Appearance grade (glulam)

1.2.2.4 Shop applied finishes

1.2.2.5 Fabrication details

1.2.2.6 Connection details, materials, sizes and finishes.

### 1.3 Delivery, Storage and Handling

1.3.1 All materials shall be delivered to the site in consultation with the supplier and contractor to suit the construction schedule.

1.3.2 All materials shall be stored level on the site and shall be raised off the ground, stacked using separating spacers, and covered with a waterproof material. In the case of wrapped members, the wrapping shall be slit on the underside to prevent the accumulation of condensation.

1.3.3 Members that will be exposed to view in the finished building shall be handled using nylon or fabric slings to prevent surface damage.

## 2. Products

### 2.1 Materials

2.1.1 Specify for structural sheathing:

2.1.1.1 Type of sheathing (Plywood, OSB or Waferboard)

2.1.1.2 Species or manufacturing standard and grade.

2.1.1.3 Preservative treatment required, if any (see note 2).

2.1.2 Specify for sawn lumber:

2.1.2.1 Grade of material required and appropriate grading rule (NLGA Standard Grading Rules for Canadian Lumber).

2.1.2.2 Species required for the application.

2.1.2.3 Manufacture (dressed or rough sawn)

2.1.2.4 Preservative treatment required, if any.

2.1.3 Specify for glulam:

2.1.3.1 Qualification of manufacturer. Glulam shall be manufactured by a plant approved by the Canadian Standards Association under the requirements of CSA O177.

2.1.3.2 Certificate of conformance. Supply the purchaser on request with a certificate confirming that the material has been manufactured in a plant meeting the requirements of the qualification code CSA O177. Plants qualifying under this code shall manufacture glulam in accordance with the requirements of CSA O122, according to the design requirements of CSA O86.

2.1.3.3 Species required for the application.

2.1.3.4 Stress grade (Refer to Table 11.13)

2.1.3.5 Appearance grade: Industrial, Commercial, Quality.

2.1.3.6 Shop applied finishes.

2.1.3.7 Wrapping requirements

2.1.4 Specify for SCL:

2.1.4.1 Design values developed in conformance with CSA O86.

2.1.4.2 Manufacturer to provide upon request: the Material Evaluation Report listed in the *Registry of Product Evaluations* published by the Canadian Construction Material Centre (CCMC), or a certificate confirming that the material has been manufactured under a quality assurance program supervised by an independent third-party certification organization.

2.1.4.3 Install in accordance with manufacturer's guidelines.

2.1.4.4 Preservative treatment required, if any.

2.1.5 Specify for I-joists:

2.1.5.1 Design values developed in conformance with CSA O86.

2.1.5.2 Manufacturer to provide upon request: the Material Evaluation Report listed in the *Registry of Product Evaluations* published by the Canadian Construction Material Centre (CCMC), or a certificate confirming that the material has been manufactured under a quality assurance program supervised by an independent third-party certification organization.

2.1.5.3 Install in accordance with manufacturer's guidelines.

2.1.6 Specify for steel for connections:

2.1.6.1 Structural steel for connections shall conform to Specifications CSA S16 and shall be new material conforming to CSA specification CAN3 G40.21 Grade 300W

2.1.6.2 Structural steel shall be prime coated with paint to specification CGSB 85-GP-14M *Painting Steel Surfaces Exposed to Normally Dry Weather.* (Alternative types of corrosion protection may be used. Specify type.)

2.2 Fabrication (for framed materials)

2.2.1 Specify for all materials:

2.2.1.1 All members to be fabricated in accordance with specifications and approved shop drawings.

2.2.1.2 All members to be suitably marked for identification.

2.2.1.3 Splicing and jointing in locations other than shown on the drawings shall not be permitted.

2.2.2 Specify for sawn lumber:

2.2.2.1 Liberally apply sealer to all exposed end grain surfaces after fabrication.

2.2.3 Specify for glulam:

2.2.3.1 Apply specified shop sealer to all surfaces after fabrication. Double treat end grain surfaces.

3. Erection

3.1 Prior to site erection, examine all site conditions relating to this section of work to ensure that they are acceptable for a satisfactory installation. Report any discrepancies to the architect (engineer).

3.2 The erection contractor's engineer shall ensure that all structural lumber and connections will sustain any erection loadings that may occur with an adequate factor of safety.

**11**

**REF**

Reference Information

3.3 Members shall fit together properly, without trimming, cutting or any other unauthorized modifications. Report any discrepancies to the architect (engineer).

Notes :
1.  Wood plank decking is often supplied by the structural wood supplier.
2.  Preservative treatment of structural wood sheathing is limited to plywood sheathing.

## Composite Products

Most of the materials discussed in this manual are either graded to national grading rules or manufactured to CSA Standards.

Products such as SCL and I-joists are proprietary. Although design values may vary for these products, they are established using procedures in Clause 13 of CSA O86. To ensure that proprietary products have been manufactured under a quality assurance program supervised by an independent third-party certification organization, manufacturers typically have their products evaluated under the guidelines of the Canadian Construction Material Centre (CCMC). Products meeting the CCMC guidelines receive an Evaluation Number and Evaluation Report for the product, including design values, and are listed in the *Registry of Product Evaluations* published by the Canadian Construction Material Centre (CCMC), Institute for Research in Construction (NRC), Ottawa, Canada.

Until recently most structural composite lumber members, as well as glulam beams and columns, were manufactured to order and shipped pre-framed, complete with connection hardware to project sites. Now, stocks of a wide range of products are maintained in many locations across the country, and materials are often supplied as stock lengths for framing by the end-user on the job.

It is important that qualified professional engineering design be provided at some point in the supply sequence to ensure that appropriate loadings and all other aspects of good design are applied to the product selection. Manufacturers of these composite products provide member capacity tables that may be acceptable to building authorities as proper product documentation for simple and easily described loading applications. Any loading conditions outside these tables will require a specific design by a professional engineer employed by either the consumer or the manufacturer.

Since these products often provide span and load carrying capacities well beyond the range of standard framing connections and procedures, in most cases it will be necessary to provide layout drawings to define product placement, bearing and connection details. Engineered drawings are essential for projects in which loadings and spans exceed the limits of the simple design cases described in product literature. These drawings must be provided to the job site prior to the commencement of installation of materials.

In the case of projects that involve the supply of such structural members, material specifications commonly appear in the standard form of construction specifications.

# Fastenings

| Type of washer | Rod or bolt dia. mm | Hole Dia. mm | Outside dimension mm | Bearing area mm$^2$ | Thickness mm | Mass per 100 pieces kg | Pieces per 100 kg |
|---|---|---|---|---|---|---|---|
| Malleable iron | 12 | 16 | 64 | 2970 | 6 | 7.71 | 1300 |
| | 16 | 20 | 70 | 3350 | 8 | 10.43 | 960 |
| | 20 | 22 | 76 | 4000 | 11 | 14.06 | 720 |
| | 22 | 26 | 89 | 5680 | 11 | 16.78 | 600 |
| | 24 | 29 | 102 | 7480 | 13 | 28.12 | 360 |
| Cut [1] | 12 | 14 | 35 | 840 | 3 | 1.75 | 5700 |
| | 16 | 18 | 45 | 1290 | 4 | 3.49 | 2900 |
| | 20 | 21 | 51 | 1680 | 4 | 4.54 | 2200 |
| | 22 | 24 | 57 | 2130 | 4 | 6.49 | 1550 |
| | 24 | 29 | 64 | 2520 | 4 | 7.94 | 1260 |
| Round plate [2] | 12 | 14 | 64 | 2970 | 5 | 10.89 | 920 |
| | 20 | 21 | 76 | 4190 | 6 | 20.41 | 500 |
| | 22 | 24 | 83 | 4900 | 8 | 30.39 | 320 |
| Square plate | 12 | 14 | 64 | 3870 | 5 | 14.06 | 720 |
| | 16 | 18 | 70 | 4650 | 6 | 22.68 | 450 |
| | 20 | 21 | 76 | 5480 | 6 | 26.76 | 380 |
| | 22 | 24 | 83 | 6390 | 8 | 39.46 | 255 |
| | 24 | 29 | 89 | 7290 | 10 | 53.52 | 190 |
| Ogee [3] | 12 | 14 | 64 | 2970 | 13 | 15.88 | 630 |
| | 16 | 18 | 76 | 3550 | 16 | 29.03 | 345 |
| | 20 | 22 | 89 | 3810 | 19 | 48.53 | 206 |
| | 22 | 24 | 102 | 6580 | 22 | 66.68 | 150 |
| | 24 | 30 | 102 | 7480 | 25 | 84.82 | 118 |

Notes:
1. Cut washers cannot be used with shear plates and split rings.
2. For use with shear plates and split rings. These washers are larger than cut washers and are necessary for drawing up a number of connectors on a single bolt without cupping and damage of the washer. They are often preferred to square plate washers for more pleasing appearance.
3. These washers, because of their thickness, resist cupping better than malleable iron washers.

**11**

**REF**

Reference Information

| Table 11.17 **Lag screw dimensions** | Dimensions of lag screws, mm | | Nominal diameter, in. | | | | |
|---|---|---|---|---|---|---|---|
| | | | 1/4 | 3/8 | 1/2 | 5/8 | 3/4 |
| All lengths | Shank dia. | | 6.4 | 10 | 13 | 16 | 19 |
| | Root dia. | | 4.4 | 6.7 | 9.4 | 11.9 | 14.7 |
| | Unthread. tip len. | | 4.8 | 6.4 | 7.9 | 9.5 | 11.1 |
| | Head height | | 4.4 | 6.4 | 8.3 | 10.7 | 12.7 |
| | Head width | | 9.5 | 14.3 | 19.1 | 23.8 | 28.6 |

| Table 11.18 **Lag screw hole dimensions** | Length in. | C.B.[1] dia. | Dimensions for lag screw holes, mm | | | | |
|---|---|---|---|---|---|---|---|
| | | | 6.4 | 10 | 13 | 16 | 19 |
| | All lengths | L.H.[2] dia. D.Fir-L | 5 | 6.7 | 10 | 12 | 15 |
| | | L.H. dia. All other species | 3 | 6 | 9 | 10 | 13 |
| | 3 | Depth Hole | 72 | 70 | 68 | 67 | 65 |
| | | Depth C.B. | 26 | 26 | 26 | 26 | 26 |
| | 3-1/2 | Depth Hole | 84 | 83 | 81 | 79 | 78 |
| | | Depth C.B. | 32 | 32 | 32 | 32 | 32 |
| | 4 | Depth Hole | 97 | 95 | 94 | 92 | 90 |
| | | Depth C.B. | 38 | 38 | 38 | 38 | 38 |
| | 4-1/2 | Depth Hole | | 108 | 107 | 105 | 103 |
| | | Depth C.B. | | 45 | 45 | 45 | 45 |
| | 5 | Depth Hole | | 120 | 119 | 117 | 116 |
| | | Depth C.B. | | 51 | 51 | 51 | 51 |
| | 6 | Depth Hole | | 146 | 145 | 143 | 141 |
| | | Depth C.B. | | 64 | 64 | 64 | 64 |
| | 7 | Depth Hole | | 171 | 170 | 168 | 167 |
| | | Depth C.B. | | 77 | 77 | 77 | 77 |
| | 8 | Depth Hole | | 196 | 195 | 194 | 192 |
| | | Depth C.B. | | 89 | 89 | 89 | 89 |
| | 9 | Depth Hole | | 222 | 221 | 219 | 217 |
| | | Depth C.B. | | 102 | 102 | 102 | 102 |
| | 10 | Depth Hole | | 248 | 246 | 244 | 243 |
| | | Depth C.B. | | 114 | 114 | 114 | 114 |
| | 11 | Depth Hole | | | 271 | 270 | 268 |
| | | Depth C.B. | | | 127 | 127 | 127 |
| | 12 | Depth Hole | | | 297 | 295 | 294 |
| | | Depth C.B. | | | 153 | 153 | 153 |

Notes:
1. C.B. = counterbore
2. L.H. = lead hole
3. For lag screws longer than 12", depth of hole equals nominal length less 5 mm and depth of counterbore C.B. equals half the nominal length.

## Table 11.19
**Split ring and shear plate dimensions**

Split rings

| Nominal diameter | 2-1/2" | 4" |
|---|---|---|
| Bolt diameter | 1/2" | 3/4" |
| Inside diameter at centre when installed | 64.5 mm | 103.1 mm |
| Thickness of metal at centre | 4.1 mm | 4.9 mm |
| Depth of metal (width of ring) | 19.0 mm | 25.4 mm |
| Mass per 100 split rings | 12.7 kg | 31.8 kg |

Shear plates

| Nominal diameter | 2-5/8" | 4" | 4" |
|---|---|---|---|
| Material | pressed steel | malleable iron | malleable iron |
| Diameter of plate | 66.5 mm | 102.1 mm | 102.1 mm |
| Diameter of bolt hole | 20.6 mm | 20.6 mm | 23.9 mm |
| Thickness of plate | 4.4 mm | 5.1 mm | 5.1 mm |
| Depth of flange | 10.7 mm | 15.7 mm | 15.7 mm |
| Mass per 100 shear plates | 15.9 kg | 40.8 kg | 40.8 kg |

## Table 11.20
**Machine bolt and nut dimensions**

| Bolt diameter in. | Hex bolt height | | Width across | |
|---|---|---|---|---|
| | Head mm | Nut mm | Flats mm | Corners mm |
| 1/2 | 8 | 12 | 19 | 22 |
| 5/8 | 10 | 14 | 24 | 28 |
| 3/4 | 12 | 17 | 29 | 33 |
| 7/8 | 14 | 19 | 34 | 39 |
| 1 | 16 | 22 | 38 | 44 |
| 1-1/8 | 18 | 25 | 43 | 50 |
| 1-1/4 | 20 | 27 | 48 | 55 |
| 1-1/2 | 24 | 33 | 58 | 66 |
| 1-3/4 | 28 | 38 | 67 | 77 |
| 2 | 31 | 44 | 77 | 88 |

| Bolt diameter in. | Square bolt height | | Width across | |
|---|---|---|---|---|
| | Head mm | Nut mm | Flats mm | Corners mm |
| 1/2 | 9 | 12 | 21 | 30 |
| 5/8 | 11 | 14 | 26 | 36 |
| 3/4 | 13 | 17 | 29 | 41 |
| 7/8 | 15 | 20 | 34 | 48 |
| 1 | 17 | 23 | 38 | 54 |
| 1-1/8 | 19 | 26 | 43 | 61 |
| 1-1/4 | 22 | 28 | 48 | 68 |
| 1-1/2 | 26 | 34 | 58 | 81 |
| 1-3/4 | 30 | 39 | 67 | 95 |
| 2 | 34 | 45 | 77 | 108 |

**11**

**REF**

Reference Information

**Table 11.21**
**Machine bolt and nut threaded length and mass**

Finished hex bolts
Minimum thread length T (mm) and mass M (kg) per 100, without nuts

ASTM A307 bolt diameter, in.

| Bolt length* under head in. | 1/2 T | M | 5/8 T | M | 3/4 T | M | 7/8 T | M | 1 T | M |
|---|---|---|---|---|---|---|---|---|---|---|
| 4 | 32 | 11.5 | 38 | 18.2 | 44 | 27.2 | 51 | 38.4 | 57 | 51.3 |
| 4-1/2 | 32 | 12.8 | 38 | 20.2 | 44 | 30.0 | 51 | 42.3 | 57 | 56.4 |
| 5 | 32 | 14.0 | 38 | 22.1 | 44 | 32.9 | 51 | 46.1 | 57 | 61.4 |
| 6 | 32 | 16.6 | 38 | 26.1 | 44 | 38.6 | 51 | 53.9 | 57 | 71.5 |
| 6-1/2 | 38 | 17.8 | 44 | 28.1 | 51 | 41.4 | 57 | 57.7 | 63 | 76.6 |
| 7 | 38 | 19.1 | 44 | 30.0 | 51 | 44.2 | 57 | 61.6 | 63 | 81.6 |
| 8 | 38 | 21.6 | 44 | 34.0 | 51 | 49.9 | 57 | 69.3 | 63 | 91.7 |
| 9 | 38 | 24.1 | 44 | 37.9 | 51 | 55.6 | 57 | 77.1 | 63 | 101.8 |
| 10 | 38 | 26.7 | 44 | 41.9 | 51 | 61.3 | 57 | 84.8 | 63 | 111.9 |
| 11 | 38 | 29.2 | 44 | 45.8 | 51 | 67.0 | 57 | 92.5 | 63 | 122.0 |
| 12 | 38 | 31.7 | 44 | 49.8 | 51 | 72.6 | 57 | 100.3 | 63 | 132.1 |
| 13 | 38 | 34.2 | 44 | 53.7 | 51 | 78.3 | 57 | 108.0 | 63 | 142.2 |
| 14 | 38 | 36.8 | 44 | 57.7 | 51 | 84.0 | 57 | 115.3 | 63 | 152.3 |
| 15 | 38 | 39.3 | 44 | 61.6 | 51 | 89.7 | 57 | 123.5 | 63 | 162.4 |
| Hex nuts | - | 1.70 | - | 13.32 | - | 15.40 | - | 18.62 | - | 12.8 |

* Some lengths available on special order only. Check with local supplier before specifying bolts, especially larger lengths.

**Table 11.22**
**Lag screw mass**

Approximate mass (kg) per 100 pieces

Nominal diameter of lag screws, in.

| Nominal length of lag screws in. | 1/4 | 5/16 | 3/8 | 1/2 | 5/8 | 3/4 | 7/8 | 1 |
|---|---|---|---|---|---|---|---|---|
| 3 | 1.71 | 2.88 | 4.13 | 8.07 | 13.79 | 21.36 | 31.12 | 42.37 |
| 4 | 2.22 | 3.68 | 5.26 | 10.12 | 17.06 | 26.08 | 37.60 | 50.80 |
| 5 | | 4.48 | 6.40 | 12.2 | 20.28 | 30.84 | 44.13 | 59.42 |
| 6 | | 5.26 | 7.53 | 14.24 | 23.54 | 35.56 | 50.35 | 67.59 |
| 7 | | | 8.66 | 16.28 | 26.76 | 40.32 | 57.15 | 76.20 |
| 8 | | | 9.80 | 18.37 | 30.03 | 45.04 | 63.50 | 84.37 |
| 9 | | | 10.93 | 20.41 | 33.29 | 49.90 | 69.85 | 92.99 |
| 10 | | | 12.16 | 22.63 | 36.79 | 54.88 | 76.66 | 102.1 |
| 11 | | | | 24.72 | 40.32 | 60.33 | 83.91 | 111.1 |
| 12 | | | | 26.76 | 43.59 | 64.86 | 90.26 | 119.7 |

**Table 11.23**
**Timber rivet mass**

| Length mm | Length in. | Approximate mass (kg) per 100 pieces |
|---|---|---|
| 40 | 1-1/2 | 0.57 |
| 50 | 2 | 0.77 |
| 65 | 2-1/2 | 0.93 |
| 75 | 3 | 1.08 |
| 90 | 3-1/2 | 1.25 |

# Miscellaneous

## Duration of Load

Wood-based materials have the ability to support larger loads for short periods of time than for longer periods. This effect is taken into account by the load duration factor $K_D$. Table 11.25 describes the three load duration cases specified by CSA O86 and the $K_D$ values.

The values for short term and standard term apply as long as the dead load is not greater than the design live load. When the dead load is greater than five times the live load, the $K_D$ for permanent loading must be applied. For standard term loads where the dead load is greater than the live load, $K_D$ may be calculated as follows:

$$K_D = 1.0 - 0.5 \log \left[ \frac{D}{P_s} \right] \geq 0.65$$

where:

$D$ = dead load

$P_s$ = specified standard term load based on S and L loads acting alone or in combination

= S, L, S + 0.5L or 0.5S + L

$S$ = snow load calculated using an importance load factor equal to 1.0

$L$ = live load due to use and occupancy

In the calculation of resistance to dead loads plus combinations of live loads, $K_D$ is controlled by the live load with the shortest duration. Table 11.24 illustrates this concept for a number of common load cases. When designing a member or connection, each possible combination should be evaluated using the appropriate $K_D$ value to determine which combination will govern the design.

**11**

**REF**

Reference Information

Table 11.24
**Value of $K_D$ for various load combinations**

| Load combination | $K_D$ |
|---|---|
| D | 0.65 |
| D + S | 1.0 |
| D + L | 1.0 |
| D + S + L | 1.0 |
| D + W | 1.15 |
| D + E | 1.15 |
| D + S or L + W | 1.15 |
| D + S + L + E | 1.15 |

where:

D = dead load
S = snow load
L = live load due to use and occupancy
W = wind load
E = loads due to earthquakes

| Table 11.25 **Duration of loading** | Duration of loading | $K_D$ | Description |
|---|---|---|---|
| | Short term | 1.15 | Short term loading means that condition of loading where the duration of the specified loads is not expected to last more than 7 days continuously or cummulatively throughout the life of the structure. |
| | | | Examples include wind loads, earthquake loads, falsework and formwork as well as impact loads. |
| | Standard term | 1.00 | Standard term means that condition of loading where the duration of specified loads exceeds that of short term loading, but is less than permanent loading. |
| | | | Examples include snow loads, live loads due to occupancy, wheel loads on bridges, and dead loads in combination with all of the above. |
| | Permanent | 0.65 | Permanent duration means that condition of loading under which a member is subjected to a more or less continous specified load. |
| | | | Examples include dead loads or dead loads plus live loads of such character that they are imposed on the member for as long a period of time as the dead loads themselves. Such loads include those usually occuring in tanks or bins containing fluids or granular material; loads on retaining walls subject to lateral pressure such as earth; floor loads where the specified load may be expected to be continuously applied such as those in buildings for storage of bulk materials. Loads due to fixed machinery should be considered to be permanent. |

Note:
1. For OSB subject to permanent loads, protected from direct exposure to moisture but exposed to intermittent high temperature and humidity conditions, $K_D$ shall be 0.45.

## Service Conditions

The term "service condition" as applied to wood construction may be defined as the environment in which the structural member is expected to function during its lifetime and is taken to be the worst condition that, in the judgement of the designer, might exist for a long enough period to affect the structure .

Designers must determine the service condition for each contemplated structure so that they can select the proper design strength and determine whether or not preservative treatment is warranted.

Environments under which wood may be expected to serve can be separated into four general classes as follows:

- dry
- wet
- hot
- corrosive vapour, or a combination of the above

Any piece of wood will give up or take on moisture from the surrounding atmosphere until the moisture content has come to a balance with that of the atmosphere (moisture content is expressed as the percentage of moisture by weight, based on the oven dry weight of the wood). The moisture content of the wood at this point of balance is called the equilibrium moisture content. Table 11.26 provides the equilibrium moisture content of wood for various combinations of relative humidity and temperature. The following remarks are intended as a general guide in the determination of the proper design strengths and desirability of pressure treatment.

### Dry Service Conditions
Service conditions are considered to be dry when the average equilibrium moisture content is 15% or less over a year and does not exceed 19% at any time.

Wood contained within the interior of dry, heated or unheated buildings has generally been found to have a moisture content of between 6 and 14% according to the season and location. As a rule, wood that is used in exterior construction in protected or semi-protected locations, such as under roof or porch canopies or overhangs, or in locations where it is wet only for short periods and dry most of the time, will have an equilibrium moisture content of not more than 15%, and dry design strengths may be used.

**11**

**REF**

Reference Information

Table 11.26a
**Relative humidity (RH %) and equilibrium moisture content (EMC %) vs. dry-bulb temperature and wet-bulb depression (°C)[1]**

| Temp. dry-bulb °C | | Difference between wet- and dry-bulb temperatures (°C) | | | | | | | | | | | | | | |
|---|---|---|---|---|---|---|---|---|---|---|---|---|---|---|---|---|
| | | 0.5 | 1.0 | 1.5 | 2.0 | 2.5 | 3.0 | 3.5 | 4.0 | 4.5 | 5.0 | 6.0 | 7.0 | 8.0 | 9.0 | 10.0 |
| 0 | RH | 91 | 82 | 73 | 64 | 56 | 47 | 39 | 31 | 22 | 14 | | | | | |
| | EMC | 20.5 | 17.0 | 14.3 | 12.2 | 10.5 | 9.0 | 7.6 | 6.3 | 4.9 | 3.5 | | | | | |
| 5 | RH | 93 | 86 | 79 | 72 | 65 | 58 | 51 | 45 | 38 | 32 | 19 | 6 | | | |
| | EMC | 21.6 | 18.4 | 15.9 | 14.0 | 12.3 | 10.9 | 9.7 | 8.5 | 7.5 | 6.5 | 4.4 | 1.9 | | | |
| 10 | RH | 94 | 88 | 82 | 76 | 71 | 65 | 60 | 54 | 49 | 44 | 33 | 23 | 14 | 4 | |
| | EMC | 22.4 | 19.5 | 17.2 | 15.3 | 13.7 | 12.4 | 11.2 | 10.2 | 9.3 | 8.4 | 6.8 | 5.2 | 3.5 | 1.3 | |
| 15 | RH | 95 | 90 | 85 | 80 | 75 | 70 | 66 | 61 | 57 | 52 | 44 | 35 | 27 | 19 | 12 |
| | EMC | 23.0 | 20.3 | 18.1 | 16.3 | 14.8 | 13.6 | 12.4 | 11.5 | 10.6 | 9.8 | 8.3 | 7.0 | 5.8 | 4.5 | 3.0 |
| 20 | RH | 96 | 91 | 87 | 83 | 78 | 74 | 70 | 66 | 62 | 59 | 51 | 44 | 37 | 30 | 24 |
| | EMC | 23.4 | 20.9 | 18.8 | 17.1 | 15.7 | 14.4 | 13.4 | 12.4 | 11.5 | 10.8 | 9.4 | 8.2 | 7.2 | 6.2 | 5.2 |
| 25 | RH | 96 | 92 | 88 | 84 | 81 | 77 | 74 | 70 | 67 | 63 | 57 | 50 | 44 | 38 | 33 |
| | EMC | 23.6 | 21.2 | 19.3 | 17.7 | 16.3 | 15.1 | 14.0 | 13.1 | 12.3 | 11.5 | 10.2 | 9.1 | 8.1 | 7.2 | 6.4 |
| 30 | RH | 96 | 93 | 89 | 86 | 83 | 79 | 76 | 83 | 70 | 67 | 61 | 55 | 50 | 44 | 39 |
| | EMC | 23.7 | 21.5 | 19.6 | 18.0 | 16.7 | 15.5 | 14.5 | 13.6 | 12.8 | 12.1 | 10.8 | 9.7 | 8.8 | 8.0 | 7.2 |
| 35 | RH | 97 | 93 | 90 | 87 | 84 | 81 | 78 | 75 | 72 | 69 | 64 | 59 | 54 | 49 | 44 |
| | EMC | 23.7 | 21.5 | 19.8 | 18.2 | 16.9 | 15.8 | 14.8 | 13.9 | 13.1 | 12.5 | 11.2 | 10.2 | 9.3 | 8.5 | 7.8 |
| 40 | RH | 97 | 94 | 91 | 88 | 85 | 82 | 80 | 77 | 74 | 72 | 67 | 62 | 57 | 53 | 48 |
| | EMC | 23.6 | 21.5 | 19.8 | 18.3 | 17.1 | 16.0 | 15.0 | 14.1 | 13.4 | 12.7 | 11.5 | 10.5 | 9.6 | 8.8 | 8.1 |
| 45 | RH | 97 | 94 | 91 | 89 | 86 | 83 | 81 | 78 | 76 | 73 | 69 | 64 | 60 | 56 | 52 |
| | EMC | 23.4 | 21.4 | 19.7 | 18.3 | 19.1 | 16.0 | 15.1 | 14.2 | 13.5 | 12.8 | 11.6 | 10.6 | 9.8 | 9.0 | 8.4 |
| 50 | RH | 97 | 95 | 92 | 89 | 87 | 84 | 82 | 80 | 77 | 75 | 71 | 66 | 62 | 58 | 54 |
| | EMC | 23.1 | 21.2 | 19.6 | 18.2 | 17.0 | 16.0 | 15.0 | 14.2 | 13.5 | 12.8 | 11.7 | 10.7 | 9.9 | 9.2 | 8.5 |
| 55 | RH | 97 | 95 | 92 | 90 | 88 | 85 | 83 | 81 | 78 | 76 | 72 | 68 | 64 | 60 | 57 |
| | EMC | 22.8 | 20.9 | 19.4 | 18.0 | 16.9 | 15.8 | 15.0 | 14.2 | 13.4 | 12.8 | 11.7 | 10.7 | 9.9 | 9.2 | 8.6 |
| 60 | RH | 98 | 95 | 93 | 90 | 88 | 86 | 84 | 82 | 79 | 77 | 73 | 69 | 66 | 62 | 59 |
| | EMC | 22.4 | 20.6 | 19.1 | 17.8 | 16.7 | 15.7 | 14.8 | 14.0 | 13.3 | 12.7 | 11.6 | 10.7 | 9.9 | 9.2 | 8.6 |
| 65 | RH | 98 | 95 | 93 | 91 | 89 | 87 | 84 | 82 | 80 | 78 | 74 | 71 | 67 | 64 | 60 |
| | EMC | 22.0 | 20.3 | 18.8 | 17.5 | 16.4 | 15.5 | 14.6 | 13.9 | 13.2 | 12.6 | 11.5 | 10.6 | 9.8 | 9.1 | 8.5 |
| 70 | RH | 98 | 96 | 93 | 91 | 89 | 87 | 85 | 83 | 81 | 79 | 75 | 72 | 68 | 65 | 62 |
| | EMC | 21.6 | 19.9 | 18.5 | 17.2 | 16.2 | 15.2 | 14.4 | 13.6 | 13.0 | 12.4 | 11.3 | 10.4 | 9.7 | 9.0 | 8.5 |
| 75 | RH | 98 | 96 | 94 | 92 | 90 | 88 | 86 | 84 | 82 | 80 | 76 | 73 | 70 | 66 | 63 |
| | EMC | 21.1 | 19.5 | 18.1 | 16.9 | 15.9 | 15.0 | 14.1 | 13.4 | 12.9 | 12.2 | 11.1 | 10.3 | 9.5 | 8.9 | 8.4 |
| 80 | RH | 98 | 96 | 94 | 92 | 90 | 88 | 86 | 84 | 82 | 82 | 77 | 74 | 71 | 67 | 64 |
| | EMC | 20.6 | 19.1 | 17.7 | 16.6 | 15.5 | 14.7 | 13.9 | 13.2 | 12.5 | 11.9 | 10.9 | 10.1 | 9.4 | 8.8 | 8.2 |
| 85 | RH | 98 | 96 | 94 | 92 | 90 | 88 | 87 | 85 | 83 | 81 | 78 | 75 | 72 | 68 | 66 |
| | EMC | 20.1 | 18.6 | 17.3 | 16.2 | 15.2 | 14.3 | 13.6 | 12.9 | 12.3 | 11.7 | 10.7 | 9.9 | 9.2 | 8.6 | 8.1 |
| 90 | RH | 98 | 96 | 94 | 92 | 91 | 89 | 87 | 85 | 84 | 82 | 79 | 76 | 72 | 69 | 67 |
| | EMC | 19.6 | 18.1 | 16.9 | 15.8 | 14.8 | 14.0 | 13.3 | 12.6 | 12.0 | 11.4 | 10.5 | 9.7 | 9.0 | 8.4 | 7.9 |
| 95 | RH | 98 | 96 | 94 | 93 | 91 | 89 | 99 | 86 | 84 | 83 | 79 | 76 | 73 | 70 | 68 |
| | EMC | 19.1 | 17.7 | 16.4 | 15.4 | 14.5 | 13.7 | 12.9 | 12.3 | 11.7 | 11.2 | 10.3 | 9.5 | 8.8 | 8.2 | 7.7 |
| 100 | RH | 98 | 96 | 95 | 93 | 91 | 90 | 88 | 86 | 85 | 83 | 80 | 77 | 74 | 71 | 69 |
| | EMC | 18.5 | 17.2 | 16.0 | 15.0 | 14.1 | 13.3 | 12.6 | 12.0 | 11.4 | 10.9 | 10.0 | 9.2 | 8.6 | 8.0 | 7.5 |

Note:
1. This table is adapted from *Canadian Woods,* prepared by the Canadian Forest Service, and is reproduced by permission of Natural Resources Canada.

Table 11.26b
**Relative humidity (RH %) and equilibrium moisture content (EMC %) vs. dry-bulb temperature and wet-bulb depression (°C)[1]**

| Temp. dry-bulb °C | | Difference between wet- and dry-bulb temperatures (°C) | | | | | | | | | | | | | | |
|---|---|---|---|---|---|---|---|---|---|---|---|---|---|---|---|---|
| | | 11.0 | 12.0 | 13.0 | 14.0 | 15.0 | 16.0 | 17.0 | 18.0 | 19.0 | 20.0 | 22.0 | 24.0 | 26.0 | 28.0 | 30.0 |
| 0 | | | | | | | | | | | | | | | | |
| 5 | | | | | | | | | | | | | | | | |
| 10 | | | | | | | | | | | | | | | | |
| 15 | RH | 4 | | | | | | | | | | | | | | |
| | EMC | 1.3 | | | | | | | | | | | | | | |
| 20 | RH | 17 | 11 | 5 | | | | | | | | | | | | |
| | EMC | 4.1 | 2.9 | 1.6 | | | | | | | | | | | | |
| 25 | RH | 27 | 22 | 16 | 11 | 7 | | | | | | | | | | |
| | EMC | 5.6 | 4.8 | 3.9 | 3.0 | 1.9 | | | | | | | | | | |
| 30 | RH | 34 | 29 | 25 | 16 | 12 | 12 | 8 | 4 | | | | | | | |
| | EMC | 6.5 | 5.8 | 5.2 | 4.5 | 3.8 | 3.0 | 2.2 | 1.3 | | | | | | | |
| 35 | RH | 40 | 36 | 31 | 27 | 23 | 20 | 16 | 13 | 9 | 6 | | | | | |
| | EMC | 7.1 | 6.5 | 5.9 | 5.4 | 4.8 | 4.3 | 3.7 | 3.1 | 2.4 | 1.7 | | | | | |
| 40 | RH | 44 | 40 | 36 | 33 | 29 | 26 | 22 | 19 | 16 | 13 | 8 | 2 | | | |
| | EMC | 7.5 | 7.0 | 6.4 | 5.9 | 5.5 | 5.0 | 4.5 | 4.1 | 3.6 | 3.1 | 2.0 | 0.7 | | | |
| 45 | RH | 48 | 44 | 40 | 37 | 34 | 30 | 27 | 24 | 22 | 19 | 14 | 9 | 4 | | |
| | EMC | 7.8 | 7.3 | 6.8 | 6.3 | 5.9 | 5.5 | 5.1 | 4.7 | 4.3 | 3.9 | 3.1 | 2.2 | 1.2 | | |
| 50 | RH | 51 | 47 | 44 | 40 | 37 | 34 | 31 | 29 | 26 | 23 | 18 | 14 | 10 | 6 | 2 |
| | EMC | 8.0 | 7.5 | 7.0 | 6.5 | 6.1 | 5.8 | 5.4 | 5.0 | 4.7 | 4.4 | 3.7 | 3.0 | 2.3 | 1.5 | 0.6 |
| 55 | RH | 53 | 50 | 47 | 43 | 40 | 38 | 35 | 32 | 30 | 27 | 22 | 18 | 14 | 19 | 7 |
| | EMC | 8.0 | 7.5 | 7.1 | 6.7 | 6.3 | 5.9 | 5.6 | 5.3 | 5.0 | 4.7 | 4.1 | 3.5 | 2.9 | 2.3 | 1.7 |
| 60 | RH | 55 | 52 | 49 | 46 | 43 | 40 | 38 | 35 | 33 | 30 | 26 | 22 | 18 | 14 | 11 |
| | EMC | 8.1 | 7.6 | 7.0 | 6.7 | 6.4 | 6.0 | 5.7 | 5.4 | 5.1 | 4.8 | 4.3 | 3.8 | 3.3 | 2.8 | 2.3 |
| 65 | RH | 57 | 54 | 51 | 48 | 45 | 43 | 40 | 38 | 35 | 33 | 29 | 25 | 21 | 17 | 14 |
| | EMC | 8.0 | 7.6 | 7.1 | 6.8 | 6.4 | 6.1 | 5.8 | 5.5 | 5.2 | 4.9 | 4.4 | 4.0 | 3.5 | 3.1 | 2.7 |
| 70 | RH | 59 | 56 | 53 | 50 | 47 | 45 | 42 | 40 | 37 | 35 | 31 | 27 | 23 | 20 | 17 |
| | EMC | 8.0 | 7.5 | 7.1 | 6.7 | 6.4 | 6.1 | 5.8 | 5.5 | 5.2 | 5.0 | 4.5 | 4.1 | 3.7 | 3.3 | 2.9 |
| 75 | RH | 60 | 57 | 54 | 52 | 49 | 47 | 44 | 42 | 39 | 37 | 33 | 29 | 26 | 23 | 19 |
| | EMC | 7.9 | 7.4 | 7.0 | 6.6 | 6.3 | 6.0 | 5.7 | 5.5 | 5.2 | 5.0 | 4.5 | 4.1 | 3.8 | 3.4 | 3.1 |
| 80 | RH | 61 | 59 | 56 | 53 | 51 | 48 | 46 | 44 | 41 | 39 | 35 | 31 | 28 | 25 | 22 |
| | EMC | 7.7 | 7.3 | 6.9 | 6.6 | 6.2 | 5.9 | 5.7 | 5.4 | 5.2 | 4.9 | 4.5 | 4.1 | 3.8 | 3.5 | 3.1 |
| 85 | RH | 63 | 60 | 57 | 55 | 52 | 50 | 47 | 45 | 43 | 41 | 37 | 33 | 30 | 27 | 24 |
| | EMC | 7.6 | 7.2 | 6.8 | 6.4 | 6.1 | 5.8 | 5.6 | 5.3 | 5.1 | 4.9 | 4.5 | 4.1 | 3.8 | 3.5 | 3.2 |
| 90 | RH | 64 | 61 | 59 | 56 | 54 | 51 | 49 | 47 | 45 | 43 | 39 | 35 | 32 | 28 | 25 |
| | EMC | 7.4 | 7.0 | 6.7 | 6.3 | 6.0 | 5.7 | 5.5 | 5.2 | 5.0 | 4.8 | 4.4 | 4.1 | 3.7 | 3.4 | 3.2 |
| 95 | RH | 65 | 62 | 60 | 57 | 55 | 53 | 50 | 48 | 46 | 44 | 40 | 37 | 33 | 30 | 27 |
| | EMC | 7.3 | 6.9 | 6.5 | 6.2 | 5.9 | 5.6 | 5.4 | 5.1 | 4.9 | 4.7 | 4.3 | 4.0 | 3.7 | 3.4 | 3.1 |
| 100 | RH | 66 | 63 | 61 | 58 | 56 | 54 | 52 | 49 | 47 | 45 | 42 | 38 | 35 | 32 | 29 |
| | EMC | 7.1 | 6.7 | 6.3 | 6.0 | 5.7 | 5.5 | 5.2 | 5.0 | 4.8 | 4.6 | 4.3 | 3.9 | 3.6 | 3.3 | 3.1 |

**11**

**REF**

Reference Information

Note:
1. This table is adapted from *Canadian Woods,* prepared by the Canadian Forest Service, and is reproduced by permission of Natural Resources Canada.

## Wet Service Conditions

Wet service conditions are any conditions other than dry.

When determining the proper strengths to use in exterior construction, the geographical location must be considered. Although year-round dry service conditions might exist in many inland areas, the same structure situated in certain localities along or near the coast might have to be designed for wet service conditions.

Wet conditions of use will apply also to severe conditions such as in bridges, docks, marine structures, and boat framing. They apply in general to all framing subject to severe wetting or soaking where there is little or no possiblity of the wood being dry for substantial periods of time. Immediate proximity to earth or bodies of water will produce these conditions.

Similar conditions may prevail in some covered structures such as barns, swimming pools and certain chemical plants, where venting and air circulation are such that the moisture content of the air is almost always high and a state of low moisture equilibrium is seldom attained. Wet service conditions also occur in crawl spaces and other areas that are enclosed and contain a moisture source such as soil.

## Use of Preservatives

A pressure preservative treatment for wood is sometimes necessary in order to obtain an adequate service life. Where wood is alternately wet and dry because of contact with the ground or water, or when the equilibrium moisture content exceeds 20% for prolonged periods, a decay hazard exists. In the case of contact with salt water, there is a possiblity of marine borer attack. Under such circumstance a suitable preservative pressure treatment in accordance with the requirements of CSA O80 should be considered.

## Temperature

Most strength properties of dry wood (12% M.C.) decrease slightly with increases in temperature. This change in properties is greater with increased moisture content.

Exposure to exceptionally high temperatures for a short length of time will result in a temporary weakening of timber, which will become permanent if this exposure is prolonged. Specified strengths contain a built-in factor to provide for a range of temperatures up to about 50°C. Design values for dry service conditions should be used where the maximum temperature will not exceed 50°C. Where prolonged exposure to higher temperatures may be expected, design values should be reduced to the values for wet conditions of use or otherwise modified according to the judgement of the engineer.

## Chemical Effects

Wood is often superior to other common construction materials in resisting chemical attack. Hence, it has many applications in chemical processing and storage, as well as industrial buildings where corrosive fumes may exist (potash and sugar storage). The chemical resistance of wood will depend upon the type of chemical process, temperature, humidity and pH values involved.

Acids have a hydrolytic action on the cellulose of woods and are likely to cause permanent loss of strength if the pH value is low or very low. The rate of hydrolysis depends on the temperature increase. Generally, softwoods show better resistance to acids than do hardwoods. Organic acids such as acetic, formic, lactic and boric do not cause significant damage at room temperatures. Strong acids such as nitric, hydrochloric, and highly acidic salts (such as zinc chloride), cause substantial loss of strength.

Both softwoods and hardwoods offer low resistance to alkaline solutions. Alkalis with pH values below 10 and held at room temperature appear to have little weakening effect on wood if duration of exposure is moderate. Contact of wood with strongly alkaline solutions should be avoided.

Processes involving corrosive chemicals at high temperature permitting the escape of corrosive vapours of gases, such as chlorine, do cause gradual loss of strength in wood through absorption of moisture into the wood. Similarly, processes producing acidic deposits may hydrolyze the wood if permitted to remain on the surface.

Whenever there is a possiblity of chemical attack, the type and concentration of chemical likely to come in direct contact with the wood should be determined. In some cases protective coatings or treatment can eliminate or reduce this harmful effect.

## Dimensional Changes in Wood

### Effects of Moisture Content

Dimensional change with changes in moisture content should be considered in the design of structures. When moisture content is reduced, wood shrinks across the grain; when moisture content increases, transverse dimensions increase. Longitudinal shrinkage is usually negligible.

No dimensional changes occur at moisture contents above about 24%, a condition known as the fibre saturation point. Between 24% and 0% (oven dry) shrinkage is approximately as shown in Table 11.27. Wood will eventually reach an equilibrium moisture content dependent upon the average temperatures and humidity conditions in which it is installed, (refer to Table 11.26).

Variations in climatic conditions across Canada will affect the equilibrium moisture content of timber both indoors and outdoors. The values given in Table 11.26 are typical and do not represent extreme conditions. In extreme conditions, moisture contents may differ from those shown by about 3% in exterior locations, and by about 2% in interior locations.

Wood installed at a moisture content equal to the in service equilibrium moisture content will not change dimensions significantly. Seasoning of wood to the exact moisture content for expected service conditions is usually not practical, and even the prediction of service conditions may be difficult. By taking a few reasonable precautions most adverse effects of shrinkage can be minimized.

In all buildings, the arrangement of wood members should be organized to minimize the effects of shrinkage.

**11**

**REF**

Reference Information

## Thermal Effects

The coefficient of linear thermal expansion in the longitudinal direction of wood is from one-tenth to one-third of the values for metals, concrete, and glass. While the values in the transverse directions are larger than in the longitudinal direction, they are still usually less than those of other structural materials.

The approximate coefficients of linear thermal expansion for Douglas fir are:

| Longitudinal | Tangential | Radial |
|---|---|---|
| $4 \times 10^{-6}$ per °C | $40 \times 10^{-6}$ per °C | $27 \times 10^{-6}$ per °C |

It is usually unnecessary to consider thermal expansion in wood structures, since dimensional changes caused by thermal effects will be insignificant compared to those caused by variations in moisture content.

**Table 11.27**
**Timber shrinkage across the grain**

| | Percent shrinkage from 24% moisture content (M.C.) | | | | | |
|---|---|---|---|---|---|---|
| | To 15% M.C. (exterior locations above ground) | | To 12% M.C. (interiors of unheated buildings) | | To 6% M.C. (interiors of dry heated buildings) | |
| Species | Max. per piece | Average | Max. per piece | Average | Max. per piece | Average |
| Douglas fir | 2.8 | 2.3 | 3.7 | 3.0 | 5.6 | 4.6 |
| Western hemlock | 3.2 | 2.6 | 4.2 | 3.5 | 6.4 | 5.2 |
| Western red cedar | 1.7 | 1.2 | 2.2 | 1.6 | 3.4 | 2.5 |
| Eastern and western spruce | 3.0 | 2.0 | 4.0 | 2.7 | 6.0 | 4.0 |
| Eastern hemlock | 2.6 | 2.0 | 3.4 | 2.6 | 5.2 | 4.0 |
| Red pine | 2.2 | 1.8 | 3.0 | 2.4 | 4.4 | 3.5 |

## Significance of Checking

### General

Checking of wood is due to differential shrinkage of the fibres in the inner and outer portions of a member and is associated with rapid lowering of the moisture content at and near the surface of the member. Differential shrinkage causes tensile stresses perpendicular to the grain in the outer portions of the member, which may exceed the fibre strength and result in checking.

If wood is dried slowly enough to permit a very gradual transmission of moisture from the inner core to the outer surfaces, the tensile stress perpendicular to grain in the outer portion will be less than the corresponding fibre strength and no checking should occur. However, some seasoning checks may occur when timbers are installed under conditions of low relative humidity that require rapid adjustment to a much lower equilibrium moisture content.

Minor checks confined to the surface areas of a wood member very rarely have any effect on the strength of the member. Deep checks could be significant if they occur at a point of high shear stress. Checks in columns are not of structural importance, unless the check develops into a through split that will increase the slenderness ratio ($C_c$) of the column.

### Glulam

One of the major advantages of glulam is its freedom from major checking due to the exclusive use of kiln dried lumber in its fabrication. Glulam members glued within the range of moisture contents set out in CSA O122 (7 to 15%) approximate the moisture content in normal use, thereby minimizing checking.

Rapid changes in moisture content after gluing will result in shrinkage or swelling that might develop stresses in both the glued joint and the wood. In many instances good design minimizes these changes; for example, the outlet registers of a forced hot air heating system should not direct hot air onto members. The use of sealers, paints, etc., retard, but do not prevent moisture changes. Care is required during transit, storage and throughout all stages of building construction to avoid rapid changes in the moisture content of glulam members. Such changes could occur as a result of the sudden application of heat to buildings under construction in cold weather.

Differences in the shrinkage rate of the individual glued laminations tend to concentrate shrinkage stresses at or near the glue lines. For this reason, when checking does occur, it is usually adjacent to glue lines. The presence of wood fibre separation in the laminations of checked members indicates there is adequate glue bond and not delamination.

Site conditions often require that laminated members be stored on the construction site. They should be stored on edge and protected from rain and sunshine by a loosely fitting cover such as tarpaulin.

If small surface checks are considered to mar the appearance, it is customary to fill them with a suitable wood filler and refinish the surface as required, but only after the inner portion of the member has reached the same moisture content as that of the outer surfaces. Otherwise, the inner portion may be subjected to excessive tensile stresses perpendicular to grain, which could result in further hidden checking inside. It is therefore recommended to delay any filling of surface checks for not less than a year after checking has been observed.

If reasonable care to prevent rapid drying or adequate sealers are not applied, large checks or even splits could occur, which may require structural repair. Such repairs can be undertaken with the guidance of a qualified timber engineer, perhaps by epoxy injection or by mechanical means.

When large checks have developed that do not impair the strength of the member they should be sealed with a highly flexible sealer such as silicone.

### Sawn Lumber

The specified shear strengths of sawn lumber have been developed to consider the maximum amount of checking or splitting permitted by the applicable grading rule. Since the strength of wood increases with dryness, the enlargement of checks when dryness is increased may not affect the shear strength of the member.

**11**

**REF**

Reference Information

## Preservative Treatment

In applications where wood is subject to biological deterioration, the decay resistance of wood must be considered. Chemically treating wood is the most common method for ensuring long service life in harsh environments. Properly preservative-treated wood can have 5 to 10 times the service life of untreated wood. This extension of service life can save a significant portion of Canada's annual log harvest.

There are two basic methods of treating: with and without pressure. Non-pressure methods are the application of preservative by brushing, spraying or dipping the piece to be treated. These superficial treatments do not result in deep penetration or large absorption of preservative, and are typically restricted to field treatment during construction. Deeper more thorough penetration is achieved by driving the preservative into the wood cells with pressure. Various combinations of pressure and vacuum are used to force adequate levels of chemical into the wood.

### Conditions of Use Requiring Wood Preservation

The principal biological wood-destroying agencies are decay fungi, insects such as termites and carpenter ants and marine borers.

Four factors are necessary to the life and activity of wood-destroying fungi:

- suitable food (the wood itself),
- a sustained wood moisture content of about 20% or more, as found in many outdoor structures,
- air, and
- a favourable temperature; fungi grow over wide temperature ranges, and while they are most active under warm conditions, cold weather inhibits but does not eliminate them

Pressure treating with an approved preservative removes the food supply by making it poisonous to the fungi and wood-destroying insects such as termites.

Sea water in many parts of the world including the Atlantic and Pacific Coasts of Canada contains marine borers, which burrow into the wood for shelter and food. Attack by marine borers can effectively be prevented by pressure treating timber with heavy retentions of preservative.

The manufacture and application of wood preservatives are governed by the Canadian Standards Association O80 standards: a collection of more than 32 different standards based on the commodity being treated (lumber, plywood, glulam, wood for preserved wood foundations, etc.) These standards dictate the wood species that may be treated, the allowable preservatives and the retention and penetration of preservative in the wood that must be achieved for the commodity or application.

The CSA O80 standards for wood treating are "results based"; the quality of the treated wood is easily measured by sampling after processing. The standards specify full instructions for sampling, penetration and retention tests and their analysis. Most treating plants have on-site labs in which they analyze core borings taken from the treated wood to determine how much preservative is present.

Third-party quality control is also available through independent inspection agencies, such as those certified by the Canadian Wood Preservers Bureau (CWPB). These agencies inspect treated products for preservative penetration and retention and stamp them to indicate that they meet required standards.

For more information contact the CWPB at the following address:

Canadian Wood Preservers' Bureau
c/o Canadian Institute of Treated Wood
202 – 2141 Thurston Drive
Ottawa, ON
K1G 6C9

## Preservative Types

Each type of preservative has certain distinct advantages and the preservative used should be determined by the end use of the material. Health Canada's Pest Management Regulatory Agency is responsible for the registration of pesticides in Canada. Since the regulatory status of wood preservatives is being constantly reviewed, one should contact the Agency or the local authorities if the use of a particular preservative for a specific application is in question.

Information on wood preservatives can be found on the Canadian Institute of Treated Wood web site at **www.citw.org** or the Canadian Wood Council/Forintek durable wood web site at **www.durable-wood.com**.

**11**

**REF**

Reference Information

## Deflection Factors

Figure 11.2 provides deflection factors for a number of common load configurations. Using the formulae below, these factors can be used to calculate the mid-span deflection and/or the required $E_S I$ for L/360 deflection.

For single load cases:

$$\Delta = \frac{W L^3}{E_S I} K_\Delta$$

$$E_S I_{REQ'D} = W L^2 K_{360}$$

For multiple load cases:

$$\Delta = \frac{\Sigma (W K_\Delta) L^3}{E_S I}$$

$$E_S I_{REQ'D} = \Sigma (W K_{360}) L^2$$

where:

$\Delta$ = mid-span deflection (mm)

$E_S I_{REQ'D}$ = required $E_S I$ for L/360 deflection (mm$^4$)

L = span (mm)

W = total specified load (N)

$\Sigma (W K_\Delta)$ = sum of load $\times$ $K_\Delta$ for each load case

$\Sigma (W K_{360})$ = sum of load $\times$ $K_{360}$ for each load case

Figure 11.2a
**Deflection factors**

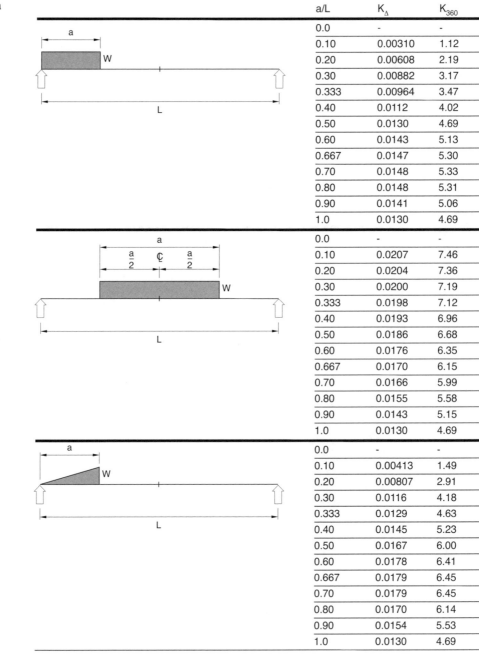

| a/L | $K_\Delta$ | $K_{360}$ |
|---|---|---|
| 0.0 | - | - |
| 0.10 | 0.00310 | 1.12 |
| 0.20 | 0.00608 | 2.19 |
| 0.30 | 0.00882 | 3.17 |
| 0.333 | 0.00964 | 3.47 |
| 0.40 | 0.0112 | 4.02 |
| 0.50 | 0.0130 | 4.69 |
| 0.60 | 0.0143 | 5.13 |
| 0.667 | 0.0147 | 5.30 |
| 0.70 | 0.0148 | 5.33 |
| 0.80 | 0.0148 | 5.31 |
| 0.90 | 0.0141 | 5.06 |
| 1.0 | 0.0130 | 4.69 |
| 0.0 | - | - |
| 0.10 | 0.0207 | 7.46 |
| 0.20 | 0.0204 | 7.36 |
| 0.30 | 0.0200 | 7.19 |
| 0.333 | 0.0198 | 7.12 |
| 0.40 | 0.0193 | 6.96 |
| 0.50 | 0.0186 | 6.68 |
| 0.60 | 0.0176 | 6.35 |
| 0.667 | 0.0170 | 6.15 |
| 0.70 | 0.0166 | 5.99 |
| 0.80 | 0.0155 | 5.58 |
| 0.90 | 0.0143 | 5.15 |
| 1.0 | 0.0130 | 4.69 |
| 0.0 | - | - |
| 0.10 | 0.00413 | 1.49 |
| 0.20 | 0.00807 | 2.91 |
| 0.30 | 0.0116 | 4.18 |
| 0.333 | 0.0129 | 4.63 |
| 0.40 | 0.0145 | 5.23 |
| 0.50 | 0.0167 | 6.00 |
| 0.60 | 0.0178 | 6.41 |
| 0.667 | 0.0179 | 6.45 |
| 0.70 | 0.0179 | 6.45 |
| 0.80 | 0.0170 | 6.14 |
| 0.90 | 0.0154 | 5.53 |
| 1.0 | 0.0130 | 4.69 |

**11**

**REF**

Reference Information

Figure 11.2b
**Deflection factors**

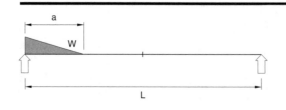

| a/L | $K_\Delta$ | $K_{360}$ |
|---|---|---|
| 0.0 | - | - |
| 0.10 | 0.00207 | 0.745 |
| 0.20 | 0.00410 | 1.48 |
| 0.30 | 0.00603 | 2.17 |
| 0.333 | 0.00664 | 2.39 |
| 0.40 | 0.00781 | 2.81 |
| 0.50 | 0.00938 | 3.38 |
| 0.60 | 0.0107 | 3.85 |
| 0.667 | 0.0114 | 4.11 |
| 0.70 | 0.0117 | 4.22 |
| 0.80 | 0.0125 | 4.49 |
| 0.90 | 0.0129 | 4.64 |
| 1.0 | 0.0130 | 4.69 |

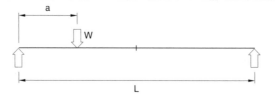

| a/L | $K_\Delta$ | $K_{360}$ |
|---|---|---|
| 0.0 | - | - |
| 0.05 | 0.00311 | 1.12 |
| 0.1 | 0.00617 | 2.22 |
| 0.15 | 0.00909 | 3.27 |
| 0.167 | 0.0100 | 3.61 |
| 0.20 | 0.0118 | 4.26 |
| 0.25 | 0.0143 | 5.16 |
| 0.30 | 0.0165 | 5.94 |
| 0.333 | 0.0177 | 6.39 |
| 0.40 | 0.0197 | 7.08 |
| 0.45 | 0.0205 | 7.39 |
| 0.50 | 0.0208 | 7.50 |

# Beam Diagrams and Formulae*

## Simple Beam

---

**1.**
**Uniformly distributed load**

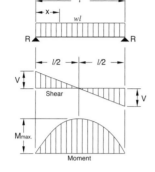

$$R = V \dots\dots\dots\dots\dots\dots\dots = \frac{wl}{2}$$

$$V_x \dots\dots\dots\dots\dots\dots\dots = w\left(\frac{l}{2} - x\right)$$

$$M \text{ max. (at center)} \dots\dots\dots\dots = \frac{wl^2}{8}$$

$$M_x \dots\dots\dots\dots\dots\dots\dots = \frac{wx}{2}(l - x)$$

$$\Delta \text{ max. (at center)} \dots\dots\dots\dots = \frac{5\,wl^4}{384\,EI}$$

$$\Delta_x \dots\dots\dots\dots\dots\dots\dots = \frac{wx}{24\,EI}(l^3 - 2lx^2 + x^3)$$

---

**2.**
**Load increasing uniformly to one end**

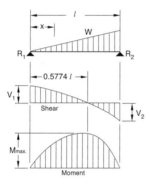

$$R_1 = V_1 \dots\dots\dots\dots\dots\dots = \frac{W}{3}$$

$$R_2 = V_2 \text{ max} \dots\dots\dots\dots\dots = \frac{2W}{3}$$

$$V_x \dots\dots\dots\dots\dots\dots\dots = \frac{W}{3} - \frac{Wx^2}{l^2}$$

$$M \text{ max. } \left(\text{at } x = \frac{l}{\sqrt{3}} = 0.5774l\right) \dots\dots = \frac{2Wl}{9\sqrt{3}} = 0.1283\,Wl$$

$$M_x \dots\dots\dots\dots\dots\dots\dots = \frac{Wx}{3l^2}(l^2 - x^2)$$

$$\Delta \text{ max.} \left(\text{at } x = l\sqrt{1 - \sqrt{\frac{8}{15}}} = 0.5193l\right) = 0.01304\,\frac{Wl^3}{EI}$$

$$\Delta_x \dots\dots\dots\dots\dots\dots\dots = \frac{Wx}{180EI\,l^2}(3x^4 - 10l^2x^2 + 7l^4)$$

---

**3.**
**Load increasing uniformly to centre**

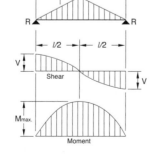

$$R = V \dots\dots\dots\dots\dots\dots\dots = \frac{W}{2}$$

$$V_x \left(\text{when } x < \frac{l}{2}\right) \dots\dots\dots\dots = \frac{W}{2l^2}(l^2 - 4x^2)$$

$$M \text{ max. (at center)} \dots\dots\dots\dots = \frac{Wl}{6}$$

$$M_x \left(\text{when } x < \frac{l}{2}\right) \dots\dots\dots\dots = Wx\left(\frac{1}{2} - \frac{2x^2}{3l^2}\right)$$

$$\Delta \text{ max. (at center)} \dots\dots\dots\dots = \frac{Wl^3}{60\,EI}$$

$$\Delta_x \left(\text{when } x < \frac{l}{2}\right) \dots\dots\dots\dots = \frac{Wx}{480\,EI\,l^2}(5l^2 - 4x^2)^2$$

**11**

**REF**

Reference Information

Note:
* By kind permission of the American Institute of Steel Construction.

# Beam Diagrams and Formulae*

## Simple Beam

---

**4.**
**Uniform load partially distributed**

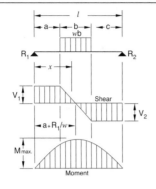

$R_1 = V_1$ (max. when a < c) . . . . $= \dfrac{wb}{2l}(2c + b)$

$R_2 = V_2$ (max. when a > c) . . . . $= \dfrac{wb}{2l}(2a + b)$

$V_x$ (when x > a and < (a + b)) . . . $= R_1 - w(x - a)$

M max. (at $x = a + \dfrac{R_1}{w}$) . . . . . . . $= R_1\left(a + \dfrac{R_1}{2w}\right)$

$M_x$ (when x < a) . . . . . . . . . $= R_1 x$

$M_x$ (when x > a and < (a + b)) . . . $= R_1 x - \dfrac{w}{2}(x - a)^2$

$M_x$ (when x > (a + b)) . . . . . . $= R_2(l - x)$

---

**5.**
**Uniform load partially distributed at one end**

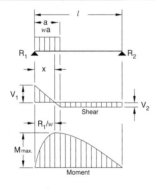

$R_1 = V_1$ max. . . . . . . . . . . . . $= \dfrac{wa}{2l}(2l - a)$

$R_2 = V_2$ . . . . . . . . . . . . . . . $= \dfrac{wa^2}{2l}$

V (when x < a) . . . . . . . . . $= R_1 - wx$

M max. (at $x = \dfrac{R_1}{w}$) . . . . . . . . $= \dfrac{R_1{}^2}{2w}$

$M_x$ (when x < a) . . . . . . . . . . $= R_1 x - \dfrac{wx^2}{2}$

$M_x$ (when x > a) . . . . . . . . . . $= R_2(l - x)$

$\Delta_x$ (when x < a) . . . . . . . . . . $= \dfrac{wx}{24\,EIl}(a^2(2l-a)^2 - 2ax^2(2l-a) + lx^3)$

$\Delta_x$ (when x > a) . . . . . . . . . . $= \dfrac{wa^2(l - x)}{24\,EIl}(4xl - 2x^2 - a^2)$

---

**6.**
**Uniform load partially distributed at each end**

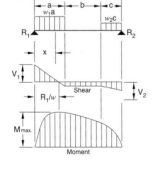

$R_1 = V_1$ . . . . . . . . . . . . . . . $= \dfrac{w_1 a(2l - a) + w_2 c^2}{2l}$

$R_2 = V_2$ . . . . . . . . . . . . . . . $= \dfrac{w_2 c(2l - c) + w_1 a^2}{2l}$

$V_x$ (when x < a) . . . . . . . . . . . $= R_1 - w_1 x$

$V_x$ (when x > a and < (a + b)) . . . $= R_1 - w_1 a$

$V_x$ (when x > (a + b)) . . . . . . . $= R_2 - w_2(l - x)$

M max. (at $x = \dfrac{R_1}{w_1}$ when $R_1 < w_1 a$) $= \dfrac{R_1{}^2}{2w_1}$

M max. (at $x = l - \dfrac{R_2}{w_2}$ when $R_2 < w_2 c$) $= \dfrac{R_2{}^2}{2w_2}$

$M_x$ (when x < a) . . . . . . . . . . $= R_1 x - \dfrac{w_1 x^2}{2}$

$M_x$ (when x > a and < (a + b)) . . . $= R_1 x - \dfrac{w_1 a}{2}(2x - a)$

$M_x$ (when x > (a + b)) . . . . . . . $= R_2(l - x) - \dfrac{w_2(l - x)^2}{2}$

---

Note:
* By kind permission of the American Institute of Steel Construction.

# Beam Diagrams and Formulae*

## Simple Beam

---

**7.**
**Concentrated load at centre**

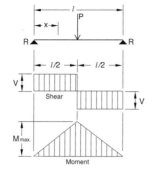

$$R = V \dots\dots\dots\dots\dots = \frac{P}{2}$$

$$M \text{ max. (at point of load)} \dots\dots = \frac{Pl}{4}$$

$$M_X \text{ (when } x < \tfrac{l}{2}) \dots\dots\dots = \frac{Px}{2}$$

$$\Delta \text{ max. (at point of load)} \dots\dots = \frac{Pl^3}{48\,EI}$$

$$\Delta_X \text{ (when } x < \tfrac{l}{2}) \dots\dots\dots = \frac{Px}{48\,EI}\,(3l^2 - 4x^2)$$

---

**8.**
**Concentrated load at any point**

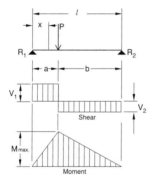

$$R_1 = V_1 \text{ (max. when } a < b) \dots\dots = \frac{Pb}{l}$$

$$R_2 = V_2 \text{ (max. when } a > b) \dots\dots = \frac{Pa}{l}$$

$$M \text{ max. (at point of load)} \dots\dots = \frac{Pab}{l}$$

$$M_X \text{ (when } x < a) \dots\dots\dots = \frac{Pbx}{l}$$

$$\Delta \text{ max.} \left(\text{at } x = \sqrt{\tfrac{a(a+2b)}{3}} \text{ when } a > b\right) = \frac{Pab\,(a+2b)\sqrt{3a\,(a+2b)}}{27\,EI\,l}$$

$$\Delta_a \text{ (at point of load)} \dots\dots\dots = \frac{Pa^2b^2}{3\,EI\,l}$$

$$\Delta_X \text{ (when } x < a) \dots\dots\dots = \frac{Pbx}{6\,EI\,l}\,(l^2 - b^2 - x^2)$$

---

**11**

**REF**

Reference Information

---

**9.**
**Two equal concentrated loads symmetrically placed**

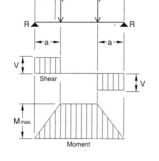

$$R = V \dots\dots\dots\dots\dots = P$$

$$M \text{ max. (between loads)} \dots\dots = Pa$$

$$M_X \text{ (when } x < a) \dots\dots\dots = Px$$

$$\Delta \text{ max. (at center)} \dots\dots\dots = \frac{Pa}{24\,EI}\,(3l^2 - 4a^2)$$

$$\Delta_X \text{ (when } x < a) \dots\dots\dots = \frac{Px}{6\,EI}\,(3la - 3a^2 - x^2)$$

$$\Delta_X \text{ (when } x > a \text{ and } < (l-a)) \dots = \frac{Pa}{6\,EI}\,(3lx - 3x^2 - a^2)$$

---

Note:
* By kind permission of the American Institute of Steel Construction.

# Beam Diagrams and Formulae*

## Simple Beam

---

**10.**
Two equal
concentrated
loads placed at
quarter points

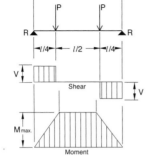

$$R = V \ldots\ldots\ldots\ldots\ldots\ldots = P$$

$$M \text{ max. (between loads)}\ldots\ldots = \frac{Pl}{4}$$

$$\Delta \text{ max. (at center)}\ldots\ldots\ldots = \frac{11\,Pl^3}{384\,EI}$$

---

**11.**
Two equal
concentrated
loads placed at
third points

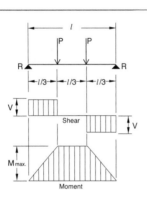

$$R = V \ldots\ldots\ldots\ldots\ldots\ldots = P$$

$$M \text{ max. (between loads)}\ldots\ldots = \frac{Pl}{3}$$

$$\Delta \text{ max. (at center)} \ldots\ldots\ldots = \frac{23\,Pl^3}{648\,EI}$$

---

**12.**
Two equal
concentrated
loads placed at
quarter and mid
points

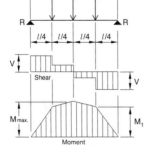

$$R = V \ldots\ldots\ldots\ldots\ldots = \frac{3P}{2}$$

$$M \text{ max. (at center)} \ldots\ldots\ldots = \frac{Pl}{2}$$

$$M_1 \ldots\ldots\ldots\ldots\ldots\ldots = \frac{3\,Pl}{8}$$

$$\Delta \text{ max. (at center)} \ldots\ldots\ldots = \frac{19\,Pl^3}{384\,EI}$$

Note:
* By kind permission of the American Institute of Steel Construction.

# Beam Diagrams and Formulae*

## Simple Beam

**13.**
Three equal concentrated loads symmetrically placed: 1/3 span spacing

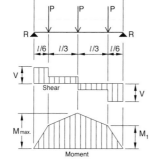

$$R = V \ldots\ldots\ldots\ldots = \frac{3P}{2}$$

$$M \text{ max. (at center)} \ldots\ldots = \frac{5\,Pl}{12}$$

$$M_1 \ldots\ldots\ldots\ldots = \frac{Pl}{4}$$

$$\Delta \text{ max. (at center)} \ldots\ldots = \frac{53\,Pl^3}{1296\,EI}$$

**14.**
Four equal concentrated loads symmetrically placed: equal spacing

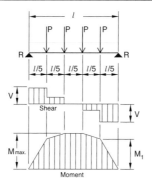

$$R = V \ldots\ldots\ldots\ldots = 2P$$

$$M \text{ max. (along center } \tfrac{l}{5} ) \ldots\ldots = \frac{3\,Pl}{5}$$

$$M_1 \ldots\ldots\ldots\ldots = \frac{2\,Pl}{5}$$

$$\Delta \text{ max. (at center)} \ldots\ldots = \frac{63\,Pl^3}{1000\,EI}$$

**15.**
Four equal concentrated loads symmetrically placed: 1/4 span spacing

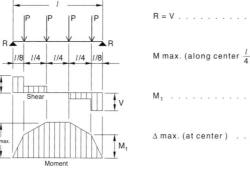

$$R = V \ldots\ldots\ldots\ldots = 2P$$

$$M \text{ max. (along center } \tfrac{l}{4} ) \ldots\ldots = \frac{Pl}{2}$$

$$M_1 \ldots\ldots\ldots\ldots = \frac{P}{4}$$

$$\Delta \text{ max. (at center)} \ldots\ldots = \frac{151\,Pl^3}{3072\,EI}$$

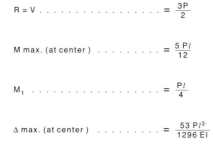

11

REF

Reference Information

Note:
* By kind permission of the American Institute of Steel Construction.

# Beam Diagrams and Formulae*

## Simple Beam

**16.**
Two equal
concentrated
loads
unsymmetrically
placed

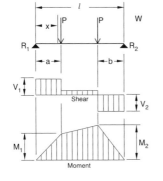

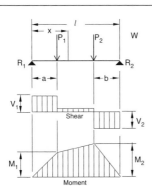

$$R_1 = V_1 \text{ (max. when } a < b) \ldots \ldots = \frac{P}{l}(l - a + b)$$

$$R_2 = V_2 \text{ (max. when } a > b) \ldots \ldots = \frac{P}{l}(l - b + a)$$

$$V_x \text{ (when } x > a \text{ and} < (l - b)) \ldots \ldots = \frac{P}{l}(b - a)$$

$$M_1 \text{ (max. when } a > b) \ldots \ldots \ldots = R_1 a$$

$$M_2 \text{ (max. when } a < b) \ldots \ldots \ldots = R_2 b$$

$$M_x \text{ (when } x < a) \ldots \ldots \ldots \ldots = R_1 x$$

$$M_x \text{ (when } x > a \text{ and} < (l - b)) \ldots = R_1 x - P(x - a)$$

**17.**
Two unequal
concentrated
loads
unsymmetrically
placed

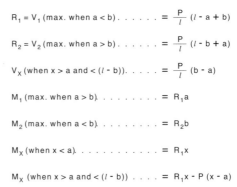

$$R_1 = V_1 \ldots \ldots \ldots \ldots \ldots = \frac{P_1(l - a) + P_2 b}{l}$$

$$R_2 = V_2 \ldots \ldots \ldots \ldots \ldots = \frac{P_1 a + P_2(l - b)}{l}$$

$$V_x \text{ (when } x > a \text{ and} < (l - b)) \ldots \ldots = R_1 - P_1$$

$$M_1 \text{ (max. when } R_1 < P_1) \ldots \ldots \ldots = R_1 a$$

$$M_2 \text{ (max. when } R_2 < P_2) \ldots \ldots \ldots = R_2 b$$

$$M_x \text{ (when } x < a) \ldots \ldots \ldots \ldots = R_1 x$$

$$M_x \text{ (when } x > a \text{ and} < (l - b)) \ldots = R_1 x - P_1(x - a)$$

## Beam Fixed at one end, Supported at Other

**18.**
Uniformly
distributed load

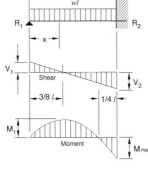

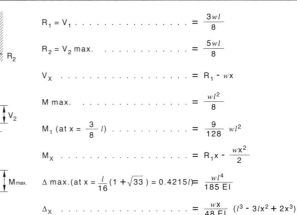

$$R_1 = V_1 \ldots \ldots \ldots \ldots \ldots = \frac{3wl}{8}$$

$$R_2 = V_2 \text{ max.} \ldots \ldots \ldots \ldots = \frac{5wl}{8}$$

$$V_x \ldots \ldots \ldots \ldots \ldots \ldots = R_1 - wx$$

$$M \text{ max.} \ldots \ldots \ldots \ldots \ldots = \frac{wl^2}{8}$$

$$M_1 \left(\text{at } x = \frac{3}{8}l\right) \ldots \ldots \ldots = \frac{9}{128}wl^2$$

$$M_x \ldots \ldots \ldots \ldots \ldots \ldots = R_1 x - \frac{wx^2}{2}$$

$$\Delta \text{ max.} \left(\text{at } x = \frac{l}{16}(1 + \sqrt{33}) = 0.4215l\right) = \frac{wl^4}{185\, EI}$$

$$\Delta_x \ldots \ldots \ldots \ldots \ldots \ldots = \frac{wx}{48\, EI}(l^3 - 3lx^2 + 2x^3)$$

Note:
* By kind permission of the American Institute of Steel Construction.

# Beam Diagrams and Formulae*

## Beam Fixed at one end, Supported at Other

**19.**
**Concentrated**
**load at centre**

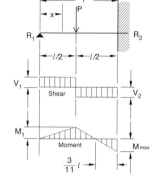

$R_1 = V_1 \dots\dots\dots\dots\dots = \dfrac{5P}{16}$

$R_2 = V_2 \text{ max.} \dots\dots\dots\dots = \dfrac{11P}{16}$

$M \text{ max. (at fixed end)} \dots\dots\dots = \dfrac{3Pl}{16}$

$M_1 \text{ (at point of load)} \dots\dots\dots = \dfrac{5Pl}{32}$

$M_x \left(\text{when } x < \dfrac{l}{2}\right) \dots\dots\dots = \dfrac{5Px}{16}$

$M_x \left(\text{when } x > \dfrac{l}{2}\right) \dots\dots\dots = P\left(\dfrac{l}{2} - \dfrac{11x}{16}\right)$

$\Delta \text{ max.} \left(\text{at } x = l\sqrt{\dfrac{1}{5}} = 0.4472l\right) \dots = \dfrac{Pl^3}{48\,EI\,\sqrt{5}} = 0.009317\,\dfrac{Pl^3}{EI}$

$\Delta_x \text{ (at point of load)} \dots\dots\dots = \dfrac{7Pl^3}{768\,EI}$

$\Delta_x \left(\text{when } x < \dfrac{l}{2}\right) \dots\dots\dots = \dfrac{Px}{96\,EI}(3l^2 - 5x^2)$

$\Delta_x \left(\text{when } x > \dfrac{l}{2}\right) \dots\dots\dots = \dfrac{P}{96\,EI}(x - l)^2\,(11x - 2l)$

**20.**
**Concentrated**
**load at any point**

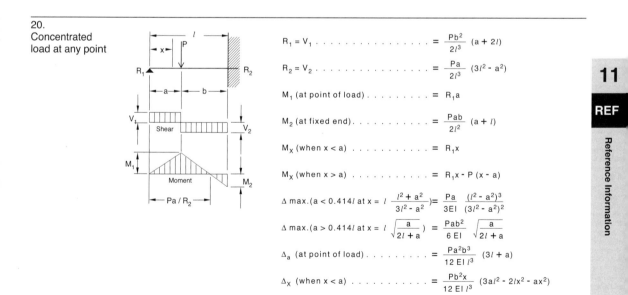

$R_1 = V_1 \dots\dots\dots\dots\dots = \dfrac{Pb^2}{2l^3}(a + 2l)$

$R_2 = V_2 \dots\dots\dots\dots\dots = \dfrac{Pa}{2l^3}(3l^2 - a^2)$

$M_1 \text{ (at point of load)} \dots\dots\dots = R_1 a$

$M_2 \text{ (at fixed end)} \dots\dots\dots\dots = \dfrac{Pab}{2l^2}(a + l)$

$M_x \text{ (when } x < a) \dots\dots\dots\dots = R_1 x$

$M_x \text{ (when } x > a) \dots\dots\dots\dots = R_1 x - P(x - a)$

$\Delta \text{ max.} \left(a < 0.414l \text{ at } x = l\,\dfrac{l^2 + a^2}{3l^2 - a^2}\right) = \dfrac{Pa}{3EI}\dfrac{(l^2 - a^2)^3}{(3l^2 - a^2)^2}$

$\Delta \text{ max.} \left(a > 0.414l \text{ at } x = l\sqrt{\dfrac{a}{2l + a}}\right) = \dfrac{Pab^2}{6EI}\sqrt{\dfrac{a}{2l + a}}$

$\Delta_a \text{ (at point of load)} \dots\dots\dots = \dfrac{Pa^2b^3}{12\,EI\,l^3}(3l + a)$

$\Delta_x \text{ (when } x < a) \dots\dots\dots\dots = \dfrac{Pb^2x}{12\,EI\,l^3}(3al^2 - 2lx^2 - ax^2)$

$\Delta_x \text{ (when } x > a) \dots\dots\dots\dots = \dfrac{Pa}{12\,EI\,l^3}(l - x)^2(3l^2x - a^2x - 2a^2l)$

**11**

**REF**

Reference Information

Note:
* By kind permission of the American Institute of Steel Construction.

# Beam Diagrams and Formulae*

## Beam Fixed at Both Ends

---

**21.**
**Uniformly distributed loads**

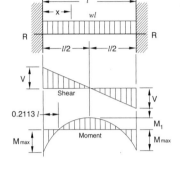

$R = V \dots\dots\dots\dots\dots\dots = \dfrac{wl}{2}$

$V_X \dots\dots\dots\dots\dots\dots = w\left(\dfrac{l}{2} - x\right)$

$M \text{ max. (at ends)} \dots\dots\dots = \dfrac{wl^2}{12}$

$M_1 \text{ (at center)} \dots\dots\dots\dots = \dfrac{wl^2}{24}$

$M_X \dots\dots\dots\dots\dots\dots = \dfrac{w}{12}(6lx - l^2 - 6x^2)$

$\Delta \text{ max. (at center)} \dots\dots\dots = \dfrac{wl^4}{384\,EI}$

$\Delta_X \dots\dots\dots\dots\dots\dots = \dfrac{wx^2}{24\,EI}(l - x)^2$

---

**22.**
**Concentrated load at centre**

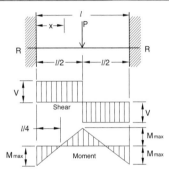

$R = V \dots\dots\dots\dots\dots\dots = \dfrac{P}{2}$

$M \text{ max. (at center and ends)} \dots\dots = \dfrac{Pl}{8}$

$M_X \left(\text{when } x < \dfrac{l}{2}\right) \dots\dots\dots = \dfrac{P}{8}(4x - l)$

$\Delta \text{ max. (at center)} \dots\dots\dots = \dfrac{Pl^3}{192\,EI}$

$\Delta_X \dots\dots\dots\dots\dots\dots = \dfrac{Px^2}{48\,EI}(3l - 4x)$

---

**23.**
**Concentrated load at any point**

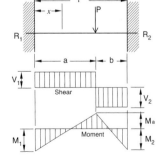

$R_1 = V_1 \text{ (max. when } a < b) \dots\dots = \dfrac{Pb^2}{l^3}(3a + b)$

$R_2 = V_2 \text{ (max. when } a > b) \dots\dots = \dfrac{Pa^2}{l^3}(a + 3b)$

$M_1 \text{ (max. when } a < b) \dots\dots\dots = \dfrac{Pab^2}{l^2}$

$M_2 \text{ (max. when } a > b) \dots\dots\dots = \dfrac{Pa^2b}{l^2}$

$M_a \text{ (at point of load)} \dots\dots\dots = \dfrac{2Pa^2b^2}{l^3}$

$M_X \text{ (when } x < a) \dots\dots\dots\dots = R_1 x - \dfrac{Pab^2}{l^2}$

$\Delta \text{ max. (when } a > b \text{ at } x = \dfrac{2al}{3a + b}) = \dfrac{2Pa^3b^2}{3EI\,(3a + b)^2}$

$\Delta_a \text{ (at point of load)} \dots\dots\dots = \dfrac{Pa^3b^3}{3EI\,l^3}$

$\Delta_X \text{ (when } x < a) \dots\dots\dots = \dfrac{Pb^2x^2}{6\,EI\,l^3}(3al - 3ax - bx)$

Note:
* By kind permission of the American Institute of Steel Construction.

# Beam Diagrams and Formulae*

## Cantilevered Beam

---

**24.**
**Load increasing uniformly to fixed end**

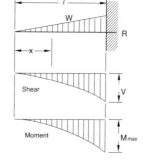

$$R = V \dots\dots\dots\dots\dots = W$$

$$V_X \dots\dots\dots\dots\dots = W\frac{x^2}{l^2}$$

$$M \text{ max. (at fixed end)} \dots\dots\dots = \frac{Wl}{3}$$

$$M_X \dots\dots\dots\dots\dots = \frac{Wx^3}{3\,l^2}$$

$$\Delta \text{ max. (at free end)} \dots\dots\dots = \frac{Wl^3}{15\,EI}$$

$$\Delta_X \dots\dots\dots\dots\dots = \frac{W}{60\,EI\,l^2}\ (x^5 - 5l^4x + 4l^5)$$

---

**25.**
**Uniformly distributed load**

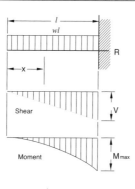

$$R = V \dots\dots\dots\dots\dots = wl$$

$$V_X \dots\dots\dots\dots\dots = wx$$

$$M \text{ max. (at fixed end)} \dots\dots\dots = \frac{wl^2}{2}$$

$$M_X \dots\dots\dots\dots\dots = \frac{wx^2}{2}$$

$$\Delta \text{ max. (at free end)} \dots\dots\dots = \frac{wl^4}{8\,EI}$$

$$\Delta_X \dots\dots\dots\dots\dots = \frac{w}{24\,EI}\ (x^4 - 4l^3x + 3l^4)$$

---

**26.**
**Beam fixed at one end, free to deflect vertically but not rotate at other – uniformly distributed load**

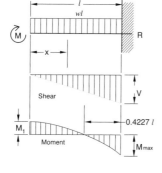

$$R = V \dots\dots\dots\dots\dots = wl$$

$$V_X \dots\dots\dots\dots\dots = wx$$

$$M \text{ max. (at fixed end)} \dots\dots\dots = \frac{wl^2}{3}$$

$$M_1 \text{ (at deflected end)} \dots\dots\dots = \frac{wl^2}{6}$$

$$M_X \dots\dots\dots\dots\dots = \frac{w}{6}\ (l^2 - 3x^2)$$

$$\Delta \text{ max. (at deflected end)} \dots\dots\dots = \frac{wl^4}{24\,EI}$$

$$\Delta_X \dots\dots\dots\dots\dots = \frac{w\,(l^2 - x^2)^2}{24\,EI}$$

**11**

**REF**

Reference Information

Note:
* By kind permission of the American Institute of Steel Construction.

# Beam Diagrams and Formulae*

## Cantilevered Beam

**27.**
**Concentrated load at any point**

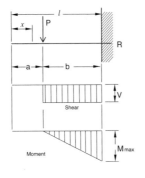

$R = V$ (when $x < a$) . . . . . . . . . $= P$

$M$ max. (at fixed end) . . . . . . . . $= Pb$

$M_x$ (when $x > a$) . . . . . . . . . $= P(x - a)$

$\Delta$ max. (at free end) . . . . . . . . $= \dfrac{Pb^2}{6\,EI}\,(3l - b)$

$\Delta a$ (at point of load) . . . . $= \dfrac{Pb^3}{3EI}$

$\Delta_x$ (when $x < a$) . . . . . . . . . $= \dfrac{Pb^2}{6\,EI}\,(3l - 3x - b)$

$\Delta_x$ (when $x > a$) . . . . . . . . . $= \dfrac{P(l-x)^2}{6\,EI}\,(3b - l + x)$

**28.**
**Concentrated load at free end**

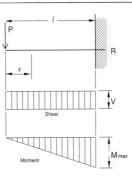

$R = V$ . . . . . . . . . . . . . . . $= P$

$M$ max. (at fixed end) . . . . . . . . $= Pl$

$M_x$ . . . . . . . . . . . . . . . . $= Px$

$\Delta$ max. (at free end) . . . . . . . . $= \dfrac{Pl^3}{3\,EI}$

$\Delta_x$ . . . . . . . . . . . . . . . $= \dfrac{P}{6\,EI}\,(2l^3 - 3l^2x + x^3)$

**29.**
**Beam fixed at one end, free to deflect vertically but not rotate at other – concentrated load at deflected end**

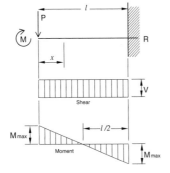

$R = V$ . . . . . . . . . . . . . . . $= P$

$M$ max. (at both ends) . . . . . . . $= \dfrac{Pl}{2}$

$M_x$ . . . . . . . . . . . . . . . . $= P\left(\dfrac{l}{2} - x\right)$

$\Delta$ max. (at deflected end) . . . . . . $= \dfrac{Pl^3}{12\,EI}$

$\Delta_x$ . . . . . . . . . . . . . . . $= \dfrac{P(l-x)^2}{12\,EI}\,(l + 2x)$

Note:
* By kind permission of the American Institute of Steel Construction.

# Beam Diagrams and Formulae*

## Beam Overhanging one Support

**30.**
Uniformly
distributed load

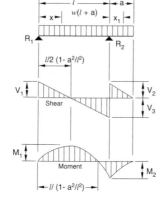

$R_1 = V_1 \dots\dots\dots\dots\dots = \dfrac{w}{2l}(l^2 - a^2)$

$R_2 = V_2 + V_3 \dots\dots\dots\dots = \dfrac{w}{2l}(l + a)^2$

$V_2 \dots\dots\dots\dots\dots\dots\dots = wa$

$V_3 \dots\dots\dots\dots\dots\dots = \dfrac{w}{2l}(l^2 + a^2)$

$V_x \text{ (between supports)} \dots\dots = R_1 - wx$

$V_{x_1} \text{ (for overhang)} \dots\dots\dots = w(a - x_1)$

$M_1 \left(\text{at } x = \dfrac{l}{2}\left(1 - \dfrac{a^2}{l^2}\right)\right) \dots\dots = \dfrac{w}{8l^2}(l + a)^2(l - a)^2$

$M_2 \text{ (at } R_2\text{)} \dots\dots\dots\dots = \dfrac{wa^2}{2}$

$M_x \text{ (between supports)} \dots\dots = \dfrac{wx}{2l}(l^2 - a^2 - xl)$

$M_{x_1} \text{ (for overhang)} \dots\dots\dots = \dfrac{w}{2}(a - x_1)^2$

$\Delta_x \text{ (between supports)} \dots\dots = \dfrac{wx}{24Eil}(l^4 - 2l^2x^2 + lx^3 - 2a^2l^2 + 2a^2x^2)$

$\Delta_{x_1} \text{ (for overhang)} \dots\dots\dots = \dfrac{wx_1}{24EI}(4a^2l - l^3 + 6a^2x_1 - 4ax_1^2 + x_1^3)$

---

**31.**
Uniformly
distributed load
on overhang

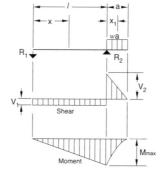

$R_1 = V_1 \dots\dots\dots\dots\dots = \dfrac{wa^2}{2l}$

$R_2 = V_1 + V_2 \dots\dots\dots\dots = \dfrac{wa}{2l}(2l + a)$

$V_2 \dots\dots\dots\dots\dots\dots = wa$

$V_{x_1} \text{ (for overhang)} \dots\dots\dots = w(a - x_1)$

$M \text{ max. (at } R_2\text{)} \dots\dots\dots\dots = \dfrac{wa^2}{2}$

$M_x \text{ (between supports)} \dots\dots\dots = \dfrac{wa^2x}{2l}$

$M_{x_1} \text{ (for overhang)} \dots\dots\dots = \dfrac{w}{2}(a - x_1)^2$

$\Delta \text{ max. } \left(\text{between supports at } x = \dfrac{l}{\sqrt{3}}\right) = \dfrac{wa^2l^2}{18\sqrt{3}\,EI} = 0.03208\dfrac{wa^2l^2}{EI}$

$\Delta \text{ max. (for overhang at } x_1 = a) \dots = \dfrac{wa^3}{24\,EI}(4l + 3a)$

$\Delta_x \text{ (between supports)} \dots\dots = \dfrac{wa^2x}{12\,EI\,l}(l^2 - x^2)$

$\Delta_{x_1} \text{ (for overhang)} \dots\dots\dots = \dfrac{wx_1}{24EI}(4a^2l + 6a^2x_1 - 4ax_1^2 + x_1^3)$

**11**

**REF**

Reference Information

Note:
* By kind permission of the American Institute of Steel Construction.

# Beam Diagrams and Formulae*

## Beam Overhanging one Support

---

**32.**
**Concentrated load at end of overhang**

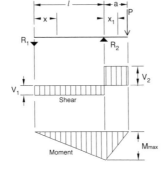

$$R_1 = V_1 \ldots\ldots\ldots\ldots = \frac{Pa}{l}$$

$$R_2 = V_1 + V_2 \ldots\ldots\ldots = \frac{P}{l}(l + a)$$

$$V_2 \ldots\ldots\ldots\ldots\ldots = P$$

$$M \text{ max. (at } R_2) \ldots\ldots\ldots = Pa$$

$$M_x \text{ (between supports)}\ldots\ldots = \frac{Pax}{l}$$

$$M_{x_1} \text{ (for overhang)}\ldots\ldots\ldots = P(a - x_1)$$

$$\Delta \text{ max. (between supports at } x = \frac{l}{\sqrt{3}}) = \frac{Pal^2}{9\sqrt{3}\,EI} = 0.06415\frac{Pal^2}{EI}$$

$$\Delta \text{ max. (for overhang at } x_1 = a) \ldots = \frac{Pa^2}{3\,EI}(l + a)$$

$$\Delta_x \text{ (between supports)}\ldots\ldots\ldots = \frac{Pax}{6\,EI\,l}(l^2 - x^2)$$

$$\Delta_{x_1} \text{ (for overhang)}\ldots\ldots\ldots = \frac{Px_1}{6\,EI}(2al + 3ax_1 - x_1^2)$$

---

**33.**
**Uniformly distributed load between supports**

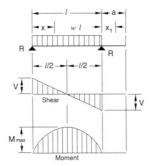

$$R = V \ldots\ldots\ldots\ldots\ldots = \frac{wl}{2}$$

$$V_x \ldots\ldots\ldots\ldots\ldots = w\left(\frac{l}{2} - x\right)$$

$$M \text{ max. (at center)} \ldots\ldots = \frac{wl^2}{8}$$

$$M_x \ldots\ldots\ldots\ldots\ldots = \frac{wx}{2}(l - x)$$

$$\Delta \text{max. (at center)} \ldots\ldots\ldots = \frac{5wl^4}{384\,EI}$$

$$\Delta_x \ldots\ldots\ldots\ldots\ldots = \frac{wx}{24\,EI}(l^3 - 2lx^2 + x^3)$$

$$\Delta_{x_1} \ldots\ldots\ldots\ldots\ldots = \frac{wl^3x_1}{24EI}$$

---

**34.**
**Concentrated load at any point between supports**

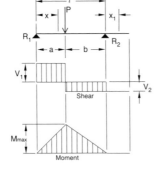

$$R_1 = V_1 \text{ (max. when } a < b) \ldots\ldots = \frac{Pb}{l}$$

$$R_2 = V_2 \text{ (max. when } a > b) \ldots\ldots = \frac{Pa}{l}$$

$$M \text{ max. (at point of load)} \qquad = \frac{Pab}{l}$$

$$M_x \text{ (when } x < a) \ldots\ldots\ldots\ldots = \frac{Pbx}{l}$$

$$\Delta \text{max. (at } x = \sqrt{\frac{a(a + 2b)}{3}} \text{ when } a > b) = \frac{Pab(a + 2b)\sqrt{3a(a + 2b)}}{27\,EI\,l}$$

$$\Delta a \text{ (at point of load)} \ldots\ldots\ldots = \frac{Pa^2b^2}{3\,EI\,l}$$

$$\Delta_x \text{ (when } x < a) \ldots\ldots\ldots\ldots = \frac{Pbx}{6\,EI\,l}(l^2 - b^2 - x^2)$$

$$\Delta_x \text{ (when } x > a) \ldots\ldots\ldots\ldots = \frac{Pa(l - x)}{6\,EI\,l}(2lx - x^2 - a^2)$$

$$\Delta_{x_1} \ldots\ldots\ldots\ldots\ldots = \frac{Pabx_1}{6\,EI\,l}(l + a)$$

---

Note:
* By kind permission of the American Institute of Steel Construction.

# Beam Diagrams and Formulae*

## Continuous Beam

### 35.
Two equal spans – uniform load on one span

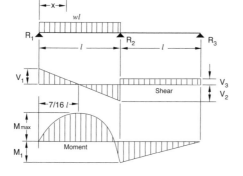

$$R_1 = V_1 \dots\dots\dots\dots\dots = \frac{7}{16} wl$$

$$R_2 = V_2 + V_3 \dots\dots\dots\dots = \frac{5}{8} wl$$

$$R_3 = V_3 \dots\dots\dots\dots\dots = -\frac{1}{16} wl$$

$$V_2 \dots\dots\dots\dots\dots\dots = \frac{9}{16} wl$$

$$M \text{ max. (at } x = \frac{7}{16} l) \dots\dots = \frac{49}{512} wl^2$$

$$M_1 \text{ (at support } R_2) \dots\dots\dots = \frac{1}{16} wl^2$$

$$M_x \text{ (when } x < l) \dots\dots\dots = \frac{wx}{16} (7l - 8x)$$

$$\Delta \text{ max. (0.472 } l \text{ from } R_1) \dots\dots = 0.0092 \frac{wl^4}{EI}$$

### 36.
Two equal spans – concentrated load at centre of one span

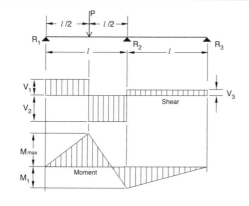

$$R_1 = V_1 \dots\dots\dots\dots\dots = \frac{13}{32} P$$

$$R_2 = V_2 + V_3 \dots\dots\dots\dots = \frac{11}{16} P$$

$$R_3 = V_3 \dots\dots\dots\dots\dots = -\frac{3}{32} P$$

$$V_2 \dots\dots\dots\dots\dots\dots = \frac{19}{32} P$$

$$M \text{ max. (at point of load)} \dots\dots = \frac{13}{64} Pl$$

$$M_1 \text{ (at support } R_2) \dots\dots\dots = \frac{3}{32} Pl$$

$$\Delta \text{ max. (0.480 } l \text{ from } R_1) \dots\dots = 0.015 \frac{Pl^3}{EI}$$

### 37.
Two equal spans – concentrated load at any point

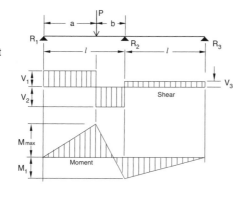

$$R_1 = V_1 \dots\dots\dots\dots\dots = \frac{Pb}{4l^3} (4l^2 - a(l + a))$$

$$R_2 = V_2 + V_3 \dots\dots\dots\dots = \frac{Pa}{2l^3} (2l^2 + b(l + a))$$

$$R_3 = V_3 \dots\dots\dots\dots\dots = -\frac{Pab}{4l^3} (l + a)$$

$$V_2 \dots\dots\dots\dots\dots\dots = \frac{Pa}{4l^3} (4l^2 + b(l + a))$$

$$M \text{ max. (at point of load)} \dots = \frac{Pab}{4l^3} (4l^2 - a(l + a))$$

$$M_1 \text{ (at support } R_2) \dots\dots = \frac{Pab}{4l^2} (l + a)$$

**11**

**REF**

Reference Information

Note:
* By kind permission of the American Institute of Steel Construction.

# Beam Diagrams and Formulae*

## Continuous Beam

**38.**
**Three equal spans – one end span unloaded**

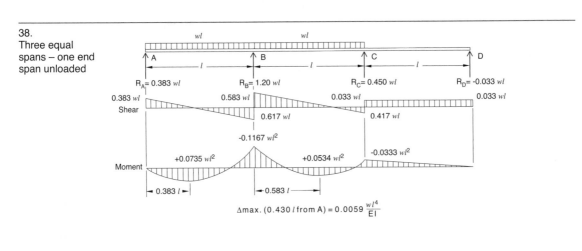

$\Delta$max. (0.430 $l$ from A) = 0.0059 $\frac{wl^4}{EI}$

**39.**
**Three equal spans – end spans loaded**

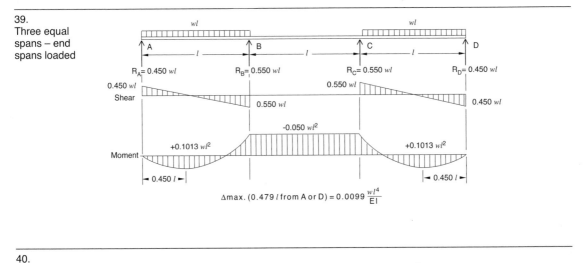

$\Delta$max. (0.479 $l$ from A or D) = 0.0099 $\frac{wl^4}{EI}$

**40.**
**Three equal spans – all spans loaded**

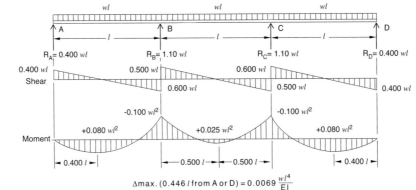

$\Delta$max. (0.446 $l$ from A or D) = 0.0069 $\frac{wl^4}{EI}$

Note:
* By kind permission of the American Institute of Steel Construction.

# Beam Diagrams and Formulae*

## Moving Loads

41.
One
concentrated
moving load

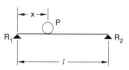

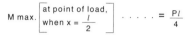

$R_1$ max. $= V_1$ max. (at x = 0). . . . . = P

$$M \text{ max.} \begin{bmatrix} \text{at point of load,} \\ \text{when } x = \dfrac{l}{2} \end{bmatrix} \dots \dots = \frac{Pl}{4}$$

---

42.
Two equal
concentrated
moving loads

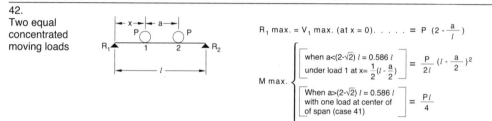

$R_1$ max. $= V_1$ max. (at x = 0). . . . . $= P \left( 2 - \dfrac{a}{l} \right)$

$$M \text{ max.} \begin{cases} \begin{bmatrix} \text{when } a<(2-\sqrt{2})\ l = 0.586\ l \\ \text{under load 1 at } x = \dfrac{1}{2}\left(l - \dfrac{a}{2}\right) \end{bmatrix} = \dfrac{P}{2l}\left(l - \dfrac{a}{2}\right)^2 \\[3ex] \begin{bmatrix} \text{When } a>(2-\sqrt{2})\ l = 0.586\ l \\ \text{with one load at center of} \\ \text{of span (case 41)} \end{bmatrix} = \dfrac{Pl}{4} \end{cases}$$

---

43.
Two unequal
concentrated
moving loads

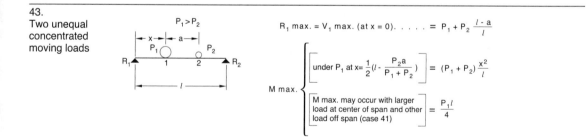

$R_1$ max. $= V_1$ max. (at x = 0). . . . . $= P_1 + P_2 \dfrac{l - a}{l}$

$$M \text{ max.} \begin{cases} \begin{bmatrix} \text{under } P_1 \text{ at } x = \dfrac{1}{2}\left(l - \dfrac{P_2 a}{P_1 + P_2}\right) \end{bmatrix} = (P_1 + P_2)\dfrac{x^2}{l} \\[3ex] \begin{bmatrix} \text{M max. may occur with larger} \\ \text{load at center of span and other} \\ \text{load off span (case 41)} \end{bmatrix} = \dfrac{P_1 l}{4} \end{cases}$$

Note:
* By kind permission of the American Institute of Steel Construction.

## NBCC Vibration Criterion

In addition to deflection criteria for joists, Part 9 of the *National Building Code of Canada (NBCC)* includes a vibration criterion. The calculations for the span tables in Part 9 use the following simplified static analysis method of estimating vibration-acceptable spans:

1. The span $S_i$ that results in a 2 mm deflection of a single joist supporting a 1 kN concentrated load at midspan is calculated.

2. The span $S_i$ is multiplied by a factor K to determine the "vibration-controlled" span for the entire floor system.

The K factor is determined as follows:

$$\ln(K) = A - B \ln\left[\frac{S_i}{S_{184}}\right] + G$$

where:

$A$ = factor for subfloor sheathing thickness (Table 11.28)

$B$ = factor for bridging of joists (Table 11.28)

$G$ = factor for connection of subfloor to joists (Table 11.29)

$S_i$ = span that results in a 2 mm deflection of the joist in question under a 1 kN concentrated midpoint load

$S_{184}$ = span that results in a 2 mm deflection of a 38 × 184 mm joist of same species and grade as the joist in question under 1 kN concentrated midpoint load.

Note: For sawn lumber, the ratio $\dfrac{S_i}{S_{184}}$ is equivalent to the joist depth in mm divided by 184.

The limiting value of K, $K_3$, occurs when the corresponding vibration-controlled span is equal to 3 m. This results in a limiting system deflection of 2 mm. When the calculated vibration controlled span is less than 3 m, $K_3$ must be determined and the vibration-controlled span recalculated. For typical floor joist sizes (38 × 184 mm, 38 × 235 mm) the vibration-controlled spans are usually greater than 3 m and $K_3$ need not be determined for these cases.

For span tables based on vibration, the designer is advised to consult the span tables provided in Part 9 of the *NBCC*. The Canadian Wood Council has published extended span tables for various floor system configurations, which may be of use to the designer.

The following design examples are provided to illustrate the application of the vibration criterion. Designers must also check strength and deflection.

### Example 1: Vibration

Check the acceptability, based on vibration, of a 3 m span for 38 × 184 mm S-P-F No.1/No.2 floor joists assuming a basic floor system.

For the basic floor:

- 15.5 mm subfloor sheathing thickness
- 400 mm joist spacing
- joists are strapped only
- subfloor sheathing nailed to joists

### Calculation

$$A = 0.25 \text{ (Table 11.28)}$$
$$B = 0.33 \text{ (Table 11.28)}$$
$$G = 0 \text{ (Table 11.29)}$$

$$S_i = \sqrt[3]{\frac{48 \, \Delta \, E_s I}{P}}$$

$$= \sqrt[3]{\frac{48 \times 2 \times 187 \times 10^9}{1000}}$$

$$= 2620 \text{ mm}$$

$$S_{184} = 2.62 \text{ m}$$

$$\ln(K) = A - B \ln\left[\frac{S_i}{S_{184}}\right] + G$$

$$= 0.25 - 0.33 \ln(1) + 0$$
$$= 0.25$$
$$K = e^{0.25} = 1.28$$

Vibration-controlled span = $K \, S_i$
$$= 1.28 \times 2.62 \text{ m}$$
$$= 3.35 \text{ m} > 3 \text{ m} \qquad \textit{Acceptable}$$

**38 × 184 mm S-P-F No.1/No.2 joists spanning 3 m is acceptable for floor vibration using the basic floor system.**

**11**

**REF**

Reference Information

### Example 2: Vibration

Calculate the vibration-controlled span for 38 × 235 mm D.Fir-L No.1/No.2 floor joists spaced at 400 mm using the following floor system:

- 19 mm subfloor sheathing thickness
- 400 mm joist spacing
- joists are bridged and strapped
- subfloor sheathing field-glued to joists

### Calculation

$$A = 0.42 \text{ (Table 11.28)}$$
$$B = 0.41 \text{ (Table 11.28)}$$
$$G = 0.10 \text{ (Table 11.29)}$$

$$S_i = \sqrt[3]{\frac{48 \, \Delta \, E_s I}{P}}$$

$$= \sqrt[3]{\frac{48 \times 2 \times 452 \times 10^9}{1000}}$$

$$= 3510 \text{ mm}$$

$$S_{184} = \sqrt[3]{\frac{48 \times 2 \times 217 \times 10^9}{1000}}$$

$$= 2750 \text{ mm}$$

$$\ln(K) = A - B \ln \left[ \frac{S_i}{S_{184}} \right] + G$$

$$= 0.42 - 0.41 \ln \left[ \frac{3.51}{2.75} \right] + 0.10$$

$$= 0.420$$

$$K = e^{0.420} = 1.52$$

Vibration-controlled span = $K \, S_i$
$$= 1.52 \times 3.51 \text{ m}$$
$$= 5.34 \text{ m}$$

Vibration-controlled span = 5.34 m

**The vibration-controlled span is 5.34 m.**

| Table 11.28 **Factor for sheathing thickness A and factor for bridging B** | | Factor A | | | | | | Factor B |
|---|---|---|---|---|---|---|---|---|
| | | 15.5 mm subfloor | | | 19.0 mm subfloor | | | |
| | | Joist spacing (mm) | | | Joist spacing (mm) | | | |
| | Floor description | 300 | 400 | 600 | 300 | 400 | 600 | |
| General case | | | | | | | | |
| | Strapping[1] | 0.30 | 0.25 | 0.20 | 0.36 | 0.30 | 0.24 | 0.33 |
| | Bridging | 0.37 | 0.31 | 0.25 | 0.45 | 0.37 | 0.30 | 0.38 |
| | Strapping and bridging | 0.42 | 0.35 | 0.28 | 0.50 | 0.42 | 0.33 | 0.41 |
| Ceiling attached to wood furring[2] | | | | | | | | |
| | No bridging | 0.39 | 0.33 | 0.24 | 0.42 | 0.36 | 0.27 | 0.34 |
| | Bridging | 0.49 | 0.44 | 0.38 | 0.51 | 0.46 | 0.40 | 0.37 |
| Concrete topping[3] | | 0.58 | 0.51 | 0.41 | 0.62 | 0.56 | 0.47 | 0.35 |

Notes:
1. Gypsum board attached directly to joists can be considered equivalent to strapping.
2. Wood furring means 19 × 89 mm boards not more than 600 mm on centre, or 19 × 64 mm boards not more than 300 mm on centre. For all other cases, see Table A-9.23.4.1.A.
3. 30 to 51 mm normal weight concrete (not less than 20 MPa) placed directly on the subflooring.

| Table 11.29 **Factor for connection of subfloor G** | Floor description | Factor G |
|---|---|---|
| | Floors with nailed subfloor | 0 |
| | Floor with field-glued subfloor[1], vibration-controlled span greater than 3 m | 0.10 |
| | Floor with field-glued subfloor[1], vibration-controlled span 3 m or less | 0.15 |

Note:
1. Subfloor glued to floor joists with elastomeric adhesive complying with CGSB Standard 71-GP-26M, *Standard for Adhesives for Field-gluing Plywood to Lumber Framing for Floor Systems.*

**11**

**REF**

Reference Information

# Drawings

### Contract Drawings (Architectural and/or Structural Drawings)

Contract drawings and the associated specifications are generally prepared for the client by the architect and/or structural engineer. They should contain complete and detailed information about the arrangement of the structure and the location, size, shape and length of all structural members. Connections should either be detailed completely, or the design loads and member reactions provided to allow the connections to be designed by others.

All information regarding requirements for sealer, stains, wrapping and fire retardant or preservative treatment should be noted.

Specifications for stress grades, finishes and any camber requirements should be noted for each member.

### Erection (Layout) Drawings

These drawings are generally prepared by the wood fabricator as a presentation of member layout and designation. They should show the location of all members and provide details of the required connections. A list of the connecting steel and hardware should appear either on this drawing or on a separate material list. All components should be clearly identified to minimize the possibility of error during assembly or erection.

### Shop (Detail) Drawings

Shop drawings are normally prepared by the wood supplier, but may be furnished by the purchaser. These drawings are prepared to show all dimensions and framing details necessary for each member. Information concerning stress grades, finishes and cambers should be shown. It is useful to indicate the direction in which a particular member end or face should be aligned by marking it "north", for example, to avoid confusion on the jobsite.

### Approvals

Erection and sometimes shop drawings are normally submitted to the purchaser, and via the purchaser to the consultants for approval. The purchaser should verify that the submitted drawings are in accordance with the requirements of the contract drawings and specifications, particularly with regard to overall dimensions. Member dimensions are the responsibility of the supplier. At least one set of erection drawings and/or shop drawings should be returned to the supplier by the purchaser within an agreed upon time period, with a notation signifying either:

1. Approval without change
2. Approval subject to changes indicated
3. Request for a revision and re-submission prior to fabrication or supply

Normally four sets of final erection and/or shop drawings incorporating any changes that have been made are issued to the purchaser for construction purposes. All materials should be supplied in accordance with the details shown on these final drawings. This drawing issue will normally bear the signed stamp of a professional engineer and should indicate the extent of design work for which he or she is responsible.

### Member Designation

Each member should bear a piece mark, which is also shown on both the erection and shop drawing. All pieces bearing the same piece mark are inter-changeable, and conversely, no two pieces that differ in any way should bear the same designation.

Piece marks usually consist of a prefix designating the type of member, followed by a number: e.g., beams markings might be shown as B1, B2, B3, etc. If two members differ only in that they are right-hand or left-hand, they are usually so marked: e.g., B1L and B1R. If there are only small differences in a standard member, a letter may be suffixed: e.g., B2, B2A, B2B, etc. Steel parts are marked in the same manner. Hardware such as bolts and timber connectors are not piece marked.

When two pieces are matched in the shop and are to be similarly matched in the field, each piece should bear a separate mark so that they may be identified and assembled properly.

### Clearances

The following clearances should be observed in detailing:

*   Bolt holes in wood and steel should be no more than 2 mm oversize; anchor bolt holes may require additional clearance.
*   Holes for drift pins should be 0.8 to 1 mm smaller than the drift pin itself.
*   Holes for lag screws in softwood should be bored in accordance with the dimensions provided in Table 7.8.
*   Daps should be 2 mm greater in size than the member that frames into the dap.
*   Side clearances between a member and the steel shoe or hanger should be at least 2 mm.
*   Where a member must frame exactly between two fixed points, an end clearance of 2 mm should be provided at each end.

### Dimensioning

Standard dimensioning practice should be followed. All dimensions should be in mm, except where components are not available in S.I. units, such as bolts and other timber connectors, which have been referenced in this manual in Imperial units.

Whenever possible, holes should be located on gauge lines, which are referenced along with other framing dimensions to the same datum plane.

All members should be described by their cross section and length. The radius and inner edge of curved members should be shown, except that when the radius is large as in a cambered beam, ordinates may be shown instead. Where only the centre ordinate for the nominal camber of a curved beam is given, the beam will normally be cambered to a parabolic profile.

Where a member is symmetrical about a centre line, the symmetry should be noted on the centre line, and dimensions given on one side only, referenced to the centreline.

### Material Lists Notes, and Special Data

A material list is necessary to completely summarize the items required to complete the work. As mentioned earlier, this list may appear on the actual drawing, or may accompany the drawing on separate sheets. Further, a summary of the hardware, listing the bolts, washers, shear plates, split rings, plates, or welded assemblies required at each connection should be shown opposite the drawing of the framing detail.

All additional data required to properly describe the materials required are to be shown on these drawings.

The abbreviations shown in Table 11.30 and symbols given in Figure 11.3 are commonly used in wood detailing. It is usual to spell out a description in full the first time an item is used on a drawing, and thereafter refer to the abbreviation. Other abbreviations and symbols may be used provided they are fully explained.

Figure 11.3a
**Drafting symbols**

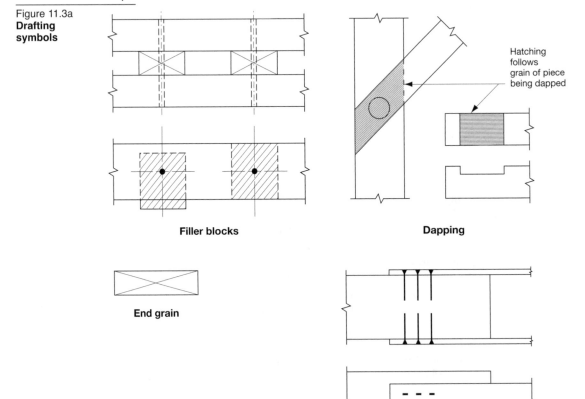

**Filler blocks**              **Dapping**

Hatching follows grain of piece being dapped

**End grain**

**Timber rivets**

Figure 11.3b
**Drafting
symbols**

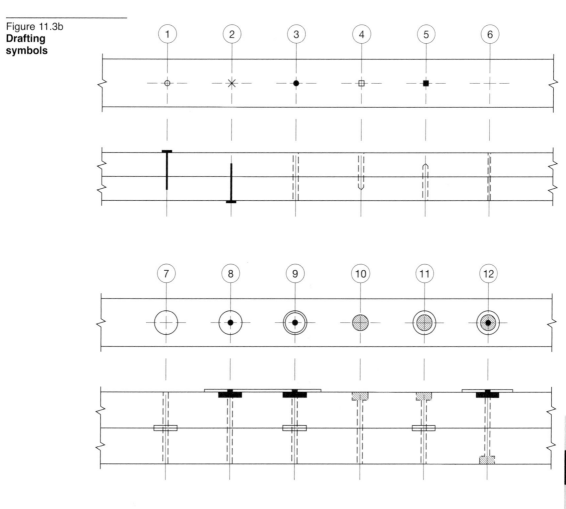

Explanation of symbols

For all symbols, indicate sizes and quantities required on drawings

1.   Nail, spike or timber rivet, near side
2.   Nail, spike or timber rivet, far side
3.   Machine bolt
4.   Lag screw, near side
5.   Lag screw, far side
6.   Drift pin
7.   One or more split rings and bolt
8.   One or more shear plates and bolt
9.   Split rings and shear plates on same bolt
10.  Counterbore for bolt
11.  Split rings and counterbore
12.  Shear plates and counterbore

Note:
Where mixed sizes occur or the above symbols do not provide a clear explanation of the connection, a detail
showing the hardware should be drawn.

11

REF

Reference Information

**Table 11.30**
**Standard drafting abbreviations**

| Term | Abbreviation |
|---|---|
| Air Dried | AD |
| Angle(s) | L,Ls |
| Beveled Siding | BEV SID |
| Block | BLK |
| Chamfer | CHFR |
| Counterbore | C.B. |
| Countersink | CSK |
| Cut Washer | C.W. |
| Dressed 4 Sides | D4S |
| Drift | Dr. |
| Far Side | F.S. |
| Galvanized | GALV |
| Glulam (Timber) Rivet | G.R. |
| Joist | JST |
| Kiln Dried | KD |
| Lag Screw | L.S. |
| Laminated Veneer Lumber | LVL |
| Lamination | Lam. |
| Lumber | LBR,Lbr |
| Machine Bolt | M.B. |
| Machine Stress Rated | MSR |
| Malleable Iron Washer | M.I.W. |
| Moisture Content | MC |
| Near Side | N.S. |
| Ogee (cast) Washer | O.G. |
| On Centre | O.C. |
| Parallel Strand Lumber | PSL |
| Pieces | Pcs. |
| Plate | PL or ℞ |
| Plate Washer | PLW |
| Precision End Trimmed | PET |
| Sawn | Swn |
| Select | SEL |
| Shear Plate | SH.℞ |
| Sheet | SHT |
| Siding | SID |
| Split Ring | S.R. |
| Square Edge | SQ E |
| Stringer | STGR |
| Structural Composite Lumber | SCL |
| Surfaced 4 Sides | S4S |
| Threaded Rod | THR R |
| Tie Rod | T.R. |
| Turnbuckle | T.B. |
| Tongue and Groove | T&G |
| Vee one Side, two edges | V1S2E |

Table 11.31a
**Mass and weight of materials**

| Substance | kg/m³ | N/m³ |
|---|---|---|
| Wood, Air Dry[1] | | |
| Cedar, Eastern, Western | 350 | 3500 |
| D.Fir-Larch | 490 | 4800 |
| D.Fir-Larch, glued-laminated | 490 | 4800 |
| Hem-Fir | 460 | 4500 |
| Spruce-Pine-Fir | 420 | 4100 |
| Spruce-Pine, glued-laminated | 440 | 4300 |
| 2.0E and higher S-P-F MSR (or MEL) | 500 | 4900 |
| 1.2E to 1.9E S-P-F MSR (or MEL) | 420 | 4100 |
| Birch, Yellow | 690 | 6800 |
| Maple, Hard (sugar & black) | 730 | 7200 |
| Oak, Red | 690 | 6800 |
| Oak, White | 750 | 7400 |
| | | |
| Metals, Alloys | | |
| Aluminium Cast, Hammered | 2640 | 25900 |
| Brass, Cast, Rolled | 8550 | 83900 |
| Copper | 8900 | 87300 |
| Iron, Cast, Pig | 7200 | 70700 |
| Iron, Wrought | 7760 | 76200 |
| Lead | 11360 | 111500 |
| Steel, Rolled | 7850 | 77000 |
| | | |
| Liquids | | |
| Gasoline | 670 | 6600 |
| Oils | 920 | 9000 |
| Water, Fresh | 1000 | 9800 |
| Water, Ice Form | 900 | 8800 |
| Water, Sea | 1000 | 10000 |
| | | |
| Earth, etc. Excavated | | |
| Earth, Wet | 1600 | 15700 |
| Earth, Dry | 1200 | 11800 |
| Sand and Gravel, Wet | 1920 | 18900 |
| Sand and Gravel, Dry | 1680 | 16500 |
| | | |
| Masonry | | |
| Cinder Concrete Fill | 960 | 9400 |
| Concrete, Cinder | 1610 | 15800 |
| Concrete, Slag | 2080 | 20400 |
| Concrete, Stone | 2300 | 22600 |
| Concrete, Reinforced Stone | 2400 | 23600 |

| Substance | kg/m³ | N/m³ |
|---|---|---|
| Brick Masonry, Soft | 1760 | 17300 |
| Brick Masonry, Common | 2000 | 19600 |
| Brick Masonry, Pressed | 2240 | 22000 |
| | | |
| Other Solids | | |
| Asphaltum | 1300 | 12700 |
| Pitch | 1100 | 10800 |
| Tar, Bituminous | 1200 | 11800 |
| Glass, Common | 2500 | 24500 |
| Glass, Plate or Crown | 2580 | 25300 |
| Paper | 920 | 9000 |
| Grain, Wheat | 770 | 7500 |
| Grain, Barley | 610 | 6000 |

| Substance | | kg/m² | N/m² |
|---|---|---|---|
| Flooring, Actual Thickness | | | |
| Hardwood | 20 mm | 19 | 190 |
| Concrete | 1 mm | 2.5 | 23 |
| Cinder Concrete | 1 mm | 2 | 17 |
| Vinyl Tile | 3 mm | 7 | 70 |
| Cork Tile | 2 mm | 2 | 20 |
| Rubber Tile or Asphalt Tile | 5 mm | 10 | 100 |
| Ceramic Tile or Quarry Tile | 20 mm | 54 | 530 |
| Carpets | | 10 | 100 |
| Terazzo | 25 mm | 90 | 900 |
| Mortar Base | 25 mm | 49 | 480 |
| Mastic Base | 25 mm | 39 | 380 |
| Wood Block (Treated) | 25 mm | 19 | 190 |
| | | | |
| Roofing | | | |
| Felt and Gravel | 3 ply | 26 | 260 |
| Felt and Gravel | 4 ply | 30 | 290 |
| Felt and Gravel | 5 ply | 32 | 310 |
| Felt without Gravel | 3 ply | 14 | 140 |
| Felt without Gravel | 4 ply | 17 | 170 |
| Felt without Gravel | 5 ply | 19 | 190 |
| Roll Roofing | | 5 | 50 |
| Cedar Shingles | | 10 | 100 |
| Asbestos Shingles | | 14 | 134 |
| Asphalt Shingles | | 12 | 120 |
| Slate Shingles | 6 mm | 46 | 450 |

**11**

**REF**

Reference Information

Note :
1.  For pressure-treated wood add retention to the weight of air dry material.

Table 11.31b
**Mass and weight of materials**

| Substance | kg/m² | N/m² |
|---|---|---|
| Clay or Tile Shingles | 68 | 670 |
| Rubberoid | 2 | 20 |
| Corrugated Steel (16 ga.) 1.5 mm | 16 | 160 |
| Corrugated Steel (20 ga.) 0.9 mm | 10 | 100 |
| Corrugated Steel (24 ga.) 0.6 mm | 7 | 70 |
| Turnall Cavity Roof | 54 | 530 |
| Aluminum (24 ga.)  0.6 mm | 2 | 20 |
| **Wall Covering** | | |
| Marble, Marble Wainscoting | 73 | 720 |
| Stucco | 49 | 480 |
| Glazed Tile | 88 | 860 |
| Wood Particle Board 6 mm | 4 | 40 |
| **Insulation, per mm Thickness** | | |
| Loose Insulation | 0.05 | 0.5 |
| Vermiculite, Porous Glass | 0.40 | 4.0 |
| Rockwool Batts | 0.02 | 0.2 |
| Fibreglass Batts | 0.02 | 0.2 |
| Fibreglass Sheets | 0.29 | 2.8 |
| Fibreboard (Donnacona, Tentest) | 0.31 | 3.0 |
| Cork Board | 0.15 | 1.5 |
| Sprayed Limpet | 0.20 | 2.0 |
| Styrofoam | 0.04 | 0.4 |
| Dyfoam | 0.06 | 0.6 |
| **Walls, per mm Thickness** | | |
| Brick | 1.8 | 17.7 |
| Glass Brick | 1.0 | 9.6 |
| Hollow Gypsum Block | 0.6 | 6.2 |
| Concrete Block | 1.5 | 14.4 |
| Cinder Concrete Block | 1.0 | 9.6 |
| Haydite Block | 1.1 | 10.5 |
| Limestone | 2.7 | 26.3 |
| Non-bearing Hollow Clay Tile | 0.9 | 8.6 |

| Substance | kg/m² | N/m² |
|---|---|---|
| Bearing Hollow Clay Tile | 1.1 | 11.0 |
| Terra Cotta Tile | 1.2 | 12.0 |
| Stone | 2.7 | 26.3 |
| **Partitions and Ceilings** | | |
| 19 × 64 mm Strapping at 300 mm | 2 | 20 |
| 38 × 89 mm Studs at 400 mm | 7 | 70 |
| Wood or Metal Lath | 10 | 100 |
| Plaster, per mm Thickness | 1.5 | 15 |
| Lightweight Plaster, per mm Thickness | 1 | 10 |
| Plasterboard 12 mm | 10 | 100 |
| Acoustic Tile 12 mm | 4 | 40 |
| Clay Tile, per mm Thickness | 0.9 | 8.6 |
| Gypsum Block, per mm Thickness | 0.6 | 6.2 |
| Gyproc 12 mm | 10 | 100 |
| Tectum, per mm Thickness | 0.4 | 4 |
| **Miscellaneous** | | |
| Porete Slab      per mm | 1.3 | 13 |
| Haydite Slab      per mm | 1.9 | 19 |
| Aerocrete Slab      per mm | 0.9 | 9 |
| Durisol Roof Plank  per mm | 1.1 | 11 |
| Plastic Sheet      6 mm | 7 | 70 |
| Skylight (glass and frame) | 59 | 580 |
| Windows, Wood Frame | 24 | 240 |
| Windows, Steel Frame | 39 | 380 |
| Trafford Tile      7 mm | 17 | 170 |
| Corrugated Asbestos      6 mm | 16 | 160 |
| Densite      6 mm | 12 | 120 |
| Glass (single strength) | 6 | 60 |
| Glass (double strength) | 8 | 80 |
| Glass      6 mm | 16 | 160 |
| Siporex      6 mm | 0.6 | 6 |
| Stramit      50 mm | 9 | 90 |

Table 11.32
**Dead load of wood joists (N/m²)**

| Seasoned D.Fir-L Joist size (mm) | Joist spacing (mm) | | | |
|---|---|---|---|---|
| | 300 | 400 | 500 | 600 |
| 38 × 89 | 60 | 50 | 40 | 30 |
| 38 × 140 | 90 | 70 | 60 | 50 |
| 38 × 184 | 120 | 90 | 80 | 60 |
| 38 × 235 | 160 | 120 | 100 | 80 |
| 38 × 286 | 200 | 140 | 120 | 100 |

**Table 11.33**
**Dead load of sheathing and decking (N/m²)**

| Thickness | Cedar | S-P-F | D.Fir-L | Any species |
|---|---|---|---|---|
| 19 mm sheathing | 70 | 80 | 100 | |
| 38 mm decking | 130 | 170 | 200 | |
| 64 mm decking | 220 | 280 | 340 | |
| 89 mm decking | 310 | 390 | 480 | |
| Plywood per mm of thickness | - | - | - | 5 |
| OSB/waferboard per mm of thickness | - | - | - | 7 |

**Figure 11.4**
**Properties of geometric sections**

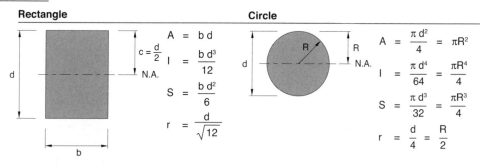

**Rectangle**

$$A = b\,d$$
$$I = \frac{b\,d^3}{12}$$
$$S = \frac{b\,d^2}{6}$$
$$r = \frac{d}{\sqrt{12}}$$
$$c = \frac{d}{2}$$

**Circle**

$$A = \frac{\pi\,d^2}{4} = \pi R^2$$
$$I = \frac{\pi\,d^4}{64} = \frac{\pi R^4}{4}$$
$$S = \frac{\pi\,d^3}{32} = \frac{\pi R^3}{4}$$
$$r = \frac{d}{4} = \frac{R}{2}$$

**Equal rectangles**

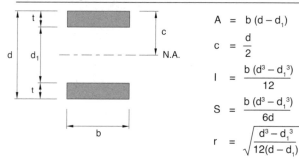

$$A = b\,(d - d_1)$$
$$c = \frac{d}{2}$$
$$I = \frac{b\,(d^3 - d_1^3)}{12}$$
$$S = \frac{b\,(d^3 - d_1^3)}{6d}$$
$$r = \sqrt{\frac{d^3 - d_1^3}{12(d - d_1)}}$$

**Unequal rectangles**

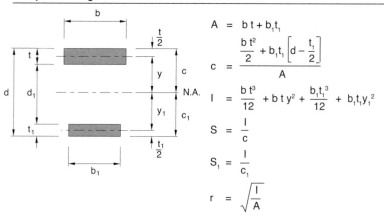

$$A = b\,t + b_1 t_1$$
$$c = \frac{\dfrac{b\,t^2}{2} + b_1 t_1 \left[d - \dfrac{t_1}{2}\right]}{A}$$
$$I = \frac{b\,t^3}{12} + b\,t\,y^2 + \frac{b_1 t_1^3}{12} + b_1 t_1 y_1^2$$
$$S = \frac{I}{c}$$
$$S_1 = \frac{I}{c_1}$$
$$r = \sqrt{\frac{I}{A}}$$

**11**

**REF**

Reference Information

| Table 11.34 **Metric units conversion factors** | Metric unit | Imperial equivalent |
|---|---|---|
| | **Length** | |
| | 1 millimetre (mm) | = 0.0393701 inch |
| | 1 metre (m) | = 39.3701 inches |
| | | = 3.28084 feet |
| | | = 1.09361 yards |
| | 1 kilometre (km) | = 0.621371 mile |
| | **Length/Time** | |
| | 1 metre per second (m/s) | = 3.28084 feet per second |
| | 1 kilometre per hour (km/h) | = 0.621371 mile per hour |
| | **Area** | |
| | 1 square millimetre (mm$^2$) | = 0.001550 square inch |
| | 1 square metre (m$^2$) | = 10.7639 square feet |
| | 1 hectare (ha) | = 2.47105 acres |
| | 1 square kilometre (km$^2$) | = 0.386102 square mile |
| | **Volume** | |
| | 1 cubic millimetre (mm$^3$) | = 0.0000610237 cubic inch |
| | 1 cubic metre (m$^3$) | = 35.3147 cubic feet |
| | | = 1.30795 cubic yards |
| | 1 millilitre (mL) | = 0.0351951 fluid ounce |
| | 1 litre (L) | = 0.219969 gallon |
| | **Mass** | |
| | 1 gram (g) | = 0.0352740 ounce |
| | 1 kilogram (kg) | = 2.20462 pounds |
| | 1 tonne (t)(= 1000 kg) | = 1.10231 tons (2000 lbs.) |
| | | = 2204.62 pounds |
| | **Mass/Volume** | |
| | 1 kilogram per cubic metre (kg/m$^3$) | = 0.0622480 pound per cubic foot |
| | **Force** | |
| | 1 newton (N) | = 0.224809 pound-force |
| | **Stress** | |
| | 1 megapascal (MPa) (=1 N/mm$^2$) | = 145.038 pounds-force per sq. in. |
| | **Loading** | |
| | 1 kilonewton per sq. metre (kN/m$^2$) | = 20.8854 pounds-force per sq. ft. |
| | 1 kilonewton per metre (kN/m) (=1 N/mm) | = 68.5218 pounds-force per ft. |
| | **Moment** | |
| | 1 kilonewton-metre (kN•m) | = 737.562 pound-force ft. |
| | **Miscellaneous** | |
| | 1 joule (J) | = 0.00094781 Btu |
| | 1 joule (J) | = 1 watt-second |
| | 1 watt (W) | = 0.00134048 electric horsepower |
| | 1 degree Celsius (°C) | = 32 + 1.8 (°C) degrees Farenheit |

Notes:
1. 9.80665 Newton = 1.0 Kilogram × 9.80665 m/s$^2$ (International Standard Gravity Value)
2. 1.0 Pascal = 1.0 Newton per square metre

| Table 11.35 **Imperial units conversion factors** | Imperial unit | | Metric equivalent |
|---|---|---|---|
| | **Length** | | |
| | 1 inch | = | 25.4 mm |
| | | = | 0.0254 m |
| | 1 foot | = | 0.3048 m |
| | 1 yard | = | 0.9144 m |
| | 1 mile | = | 1.60934 km |
| | **Length/Time** | | |
| | 1 foot per second | = | 0.3048 m/s |
| | 1 mile per hour | = | 1.60934 km/h |
| | **Area** | | |
| | 1 square inch | = | 645.16 mm$^2$ |
| | 1 square foot | = | 0.0929030 m$^2$ |
| | 1 acre | = | 0.404686 ha |
| | 1 square mile | = | 2.58999 km$^2$ |
| | **Volume** | | |
| | 1 cubic inch | = | 16387.1 mm$^3$ |
| | 1 cubic foot | = | 0.0283168 m$^3$ |
| | 1 cubic yard | = | 0.764555 m$^3$ |
| | 1 fluid ounce | = | 28.4131 mL |
| | 1 gallon | = | 4.54609 L |
| | **Mass** | | |
| | 1 ounce | = | 28.3495 g |
| | 1 pound | = | 0.453592 kg |
| | 1 ton (2000 lbs.) | = | 0.907185 t |
| | 1 pound | = | 0.0004539 t |
| | **Mass/Volume** | | |
| | 1 pcf | = | 16.1085 kg/m$^3$ |
| | **Force** | | |
| | 1 pound | = | 4.44822 N |
| | **Stress** | | |
| | 1 psi | = | 0.00689476 MPa |
| | **Loading** | | |
| | 1 psf | = | 0.0478803 kN/m$^2$ |
| | 1 plf | = | 0.0145939 kN/m |
| | **Moment** | | |
| | 1 pound-force ft. | = | 0.00135582 kN·m |
| | **Miscellaneous** | | |
| | 1 Btu | = | 1055.06 J |
| | 1 watt-second | = | 1 J |
| | 1 horsepower | = | 746 W |
| | 1 degree Farenheit | = | (°F - 32)/1.8 °C |

Notes:
1. 9.80665 Newton = 1.0 Kilogram × 9.80665 m/s$^2$ (International Standard Gravity Value)
2. 1.0 Pascal = 1.0 Newton per square metre

# CSA Commentary

**12**

**COM**

# 12.1     Reliability-based Design

Ricardo O. Foschi[1]

The 1984 edition of CSA Standard O86.1, *Engineering Design in Wood,* was the first version in limit states design (LSD) format. That edition was primarily a "soft conversion", resulting in the same member sections as in working stress design. Design recommendations included in the 1989 edition, and expanded in the 1994 and 2001 editions, have been derived partly from principles of reliability-based (or probabilistic) design. The general objective of such an approach is to develop safe design guidelines by considering, in a consistent manner, all the uncertainties involved in the design process.

Any design problem includes the interaction of several variables. For example, the design of a beam under combined bending and axial loads involves the beam's axial and bending strengths, the modulus of elasticity, the beam dimensions and the loads themselves. Some of these variables may be known with more certainty than others. Test results provide information on strength and stiffness, surveys permit the development of statistics on maximum expected loads and duration of load pulses, and fabrication tolerances can be used to quantify the uncertainty in dimensions.

Most design variables are random in nature, and reliability-based design procedures take these uncertainties into account by using principles of probability theory. In general the design problem can be written in terms of a "performance function" $G(X_1, X_2,..., X_N)$, which is a function of the N design variables X. Some of these variables influence the "demand" D on the system, and some others characterize the "capacity" C to withstand the demand.

If the function G is written, by convention, as

$$G = C - D \qquad\qquad\qquad (Eq.\ 1)$$

non-performance of the system is indicated by negative values of G. That is, the combination of variables leads to demands greater than the capacity and G < 0. Conversely, G > 0 implies performance as intended, and G = 0 corresponds to the "limit state" between performance and non-performance. The probability of non-performance can be calculated as the probability of the event G < 0.

This probability calculation can be performed using a well established computer algorithm (Madsen, 1986). This algorithm computes the reliability index $\beta$.

The computer algorithm can be adjusted for the distribution of the random variables. For example, maximum annual snow loads are better represented by extreme-type probability distributions. The algorithm can also be adjusted for correlated variables. For example, tests show that the bending strength and the modulus of elasticity of wood are positively correlated (it is likely that a stronger piece is also stiffer).

The algorithm used for the calculation of $\beta$ was implemented in the computer program RELAN, which was developed at the University of British Columbia. This is a general program for First Order Reliability Analysis, implementing the Rackwitz-Fiessler algorithm for non-normal variables (Madsen, 1986) and the work of Der Kiureghian (1986) for handling the correlation between variables.

[1] Professor, Department of Civil Engineering, University of British Columbia, Vancouver, British Columbia

**12**

**COM**

CSA Commentary

Since the algorithm produces the reliability index $\beta$, a graph can be constructed relating $\beta$ to the resistance factor $\phi$. The resistance factor is assigned to a specified material property, and accounts for variability of dimensions and properties, workmanship, type of failure and uncertainty in the prediction of resistance. A typical graph is shown in Figure 12.1.

A target value for $\beta$ for an adequate level of safety can be used as shown in Figure 12.1 to obtain the required value for $\phi$ in design.

The curve in Figure 12.1 will not be the same if the species, grade or beam size are changed, or if the snow load record is modified by changing the location, or if occupancy loads are considered instead of snow, or if the ratio of dead to live nominal loads is changed. Since only one parameter is being calibrated ($\phi$), it is impossible to achieve the same level of reliability for all cases.

The study of the performance function G shows how reliability can depend on the random variables. In a sense, G represents the actual structural behaviour, while the design equation is a conventional means of obtaining structural dimensions using nominal loads and strengths, with adjusting factors calibrated to ensure an adequate reliability. The calibration of these factors is done by a simultaneous study of the function G and the probability that $G < 0$.

The different adjusting factors have been computed to ensure a reliability level comparable to that of steel structures and to provide for a nearly uniform reliability across different applications. For lumber, as an example, the design guidelines result in nearly uniform reliability across species, grades and sizes.

Figure 12.1
**Typical relationship of reliability index $\beta$ to the resistance factor $\phi$**

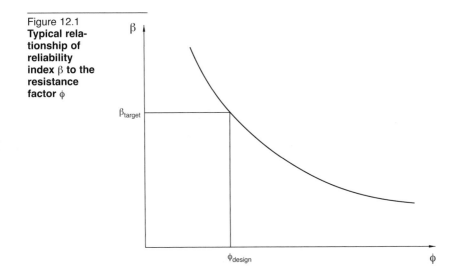

To illustrate the calibration procedure, consider the case of a simple beam under short term uniform loading.

Let:

R = bending strength, MPa
a random variable for given beam size, species and grade

D = dead or permanent distributed load, N/m
a random variable because material weights are estimates

Q = distributed live load maximum over the service life of the beam, N/m a random variable because of uncertainty in the estimation of this extreme load

L = beam span, m

B, H = beam cross-section dimensions, m

$D_n$ = nominal or "design" dead load, N/m, usually obtained by using average weights for materials

$Q_n$ = nominal or "design" live loads, N/m, (for example, specified return load for snow at a given location)

$R_o$ = "characteristic" or "specified" bending strength for the beam, a lower percentile (the fifth) of the distribution of bending strength R

Assuming linear elastic behaviour to failure for the limit state of bending strength, the performance function G can be written as:

$$G = R - (D + Q) \times \frac{6\,L^2}{8\,B\,H^2} \qquad \text{(Eq. 2)}$$

while the format for the design equation in the Code is:

$$(1.25\,D_n + 1.50\,Q_n) \times \frac{6\,L^2}{8\,B\,H^2} = \phi\,R_o \qquad \text{(Eq. 3)}$$

The factors 1.25 and 1.50 in this design equation are load factors common to all materials, but the factor $\phi$ is calibrated so that use of Eq. 3 ensures a proper reliability level.

Eq. 3 permits writing:

$$Q_n \times \frac{6\,L^2}{8\,B\,H^2} = \frac{\phi\,R_o}{1.25\,\gamma + 1.50} \qquad \text{(Eq. 4)}$$

where the constant $\gamma$ is the ratio between the nominal dead load and the nominal live load:

$$\gamma = \frac{D_n}{Q_n} \qquad \text{(Eq. 5)}$$

**12**

**COM**

CSA Commentary

The failure function G of Eq. 2 can also be written as

$$G = R - Q_n \times \frac{6L^2}{8BH^2}\left[\frac{D}{Q_n} + \frac{Q}{Q_n}\right] \qquad \textit{(Eq. 6)}$$

Eq. 4 can now be used to modify the performance function G in terms of the resistance factor $\phi$. Introducing Eq. 4 into Eq. 6,

$$G = R - \frac{\phi R_o}{1.25\,\phi + 1.50} \times (\gamma\,d + q) \qquad \textit{(Eq. 7)}$$

where d and q represent, respectively, the dead and live loads normalized with respect to their corresponding design values:

$$d = \frac{D}{D_n} \;\; ; \;\; q = \frac{Q}{Q_n} \qquad \textit{(Eq. 8)}$$

Given statistical information on the random variables R, d and q, Eq. 7 can be used to study the probability of G < 0 for different values of the resistance factor $\phi$.

For the example, Figure 12.2 shows the $\beta$ - $\phi$ relationships for lumber, averaged over three species, two grades and two sizes, when different cases for snow and occupancy loads are considered. The factor $\phi$ specified in the Standard has been chosen to provide an average reliability comparable to steel beams, over the range of species, sizes and grades, for five snow locations and two occupancy loads (offices and residential), for a nominal dead/live load ratio of 0.25 (representative of light frame buildings). The resistance factor $\phi$ = 0.90 provides an average reliability index $\beta$ = 2.6 for a design life of 30 years with an overall range 2.4 < $\beta$ < 2.9. (Note: this range is slightly larger than shown in Figure 12.2, due to the effect of material variability.)

A similar procedure has been followed for all other limit states whether related to strength or serviceability.

The reliability calculations used the latest data available, both for strengths and loads. For lumber strength and stiffness, for example, the data were obtained from the lumber properties testing program conducted by the Canadian Wood Council. The data included short-duration testing results in bending, tension and compression. Models for live loads were taken from snow loadings provided by the National Research Council of Canada.

Due consideration was also given to situations where non-performance may occur in different modes. For example, shear strength of beams is strongly controlled by the presence or absence of end splits. Two types of performance functions in shear have been considered, to study the probability of non-performance, under the assumption of no splits as well as when these cracks are considered. (See discussion under 12.4, *Sawn Lumber*.)

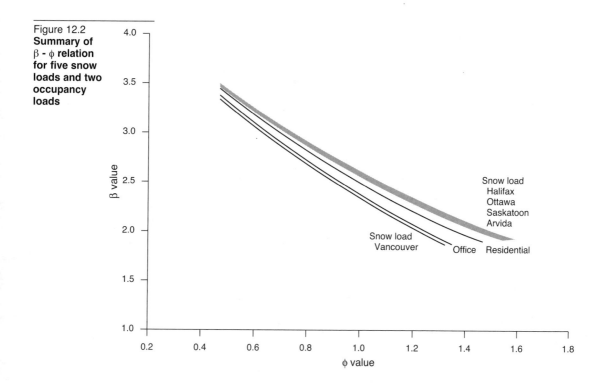

Figure 12.2
**Summary of β - φ relation for five snow loads and two occupancy loads**

The formulation of the performance functions G made use of research on the behaviour of wood structures. For example, in the case of columns axially loaded:

$$G = P_{max} - P \qquad (Eq.\ 9)$$

where P is the applied end load (demand) and $P_{max}$ is the column resistance (capacity). $P_{max}$ depends on the slenderness of the column, the modulus of elasticity, the compression and tensile strength, and the amount of end eccentricity for the load P. Furthermore, the behaviour of wood in compression is nonlinear. The calculation of $P_{max}$ was carried out by a finite element analysis which closely approximated the column's behaviour at all slenderness ratios.

The complete set of research results used in the background calculations for the Standard have been compiled in Foschi 1989.

**12**

**COM**

CSA Commentary

### References

Der Kiureghian, A. and P.L. Liu. 1986. Structural Reliability Under Incomplete Probability Information. J. Engineering Mechanics Division, ASCE, EM1.

Foschi, R.O. et al. 1989. Reliability-Based Design of Wood Structures. Structural Research Series, Report No. 34, University of British Columbia, Vancouver, BC.

Madsen, H.O. et al. 1986. Methods of Structural Safety. Prentice-Hall, Inc. Englewood Cliffs, N.J.

## 12.2　Load Duration

One of the distinctive characteristics of wood is that its strength is influenced by the intensity and duration of the applied load. In some sense, this phenomenon is similar to that of fatigue in metals. In wood, however, strength loss is observed even under static loading of a given intensity.

Should the applied stress be sustained, the strength loss phenomenon may cause failure after a given time. It is important to quantify this "load duration" effect to ensure reliability throughout the structure's service life when subjected to various loading sequences.

The load duration effect is treated in design as an adjustment to the design stress. These adjustments were based on experimental results collected at the US Forest Products Laboratory, Madison, WI, during the 1940s. These experiments were conducted with small Douglas fir specimens, free of defects, tested in bending.

Using these results, a curve (called the "Madison curve") was developed in earlier standards to explain load duration effects on strength (Wood, 1960). Based on the curve, short term strengths from ramp-load tests (lasting from two to ten minutes) were divided by 1.62 to estimate long term strengths corresponding to a ten year load duration. This ten year reference point was termed "normal" duration, corresponding to loads normally encountered in floors of residential, business, commercial and assembly occupancies.

For shorter cumulative durations, the design stresses were adjusted upward. For example, the effect of snow loads over the service life of the structure was made equivalent to a two month continuous application, for a factor of 1.15. A downward adjustment of 0.90 was applied when a permanent load lasted for the entire life of the structure (longer than ten years).

Research conducted at the University of British Columbia during the early 1970s using long term bending tests of Douglas fir lumber in structural sizes, showed that the load duration effect for material with defects was substantially different from that of small, clear specimens. The new research showed that the strength degradation was, overall, less severe than predicted from the earlier tests.

These results were later replicated by Forintek Canada Corp., using 38 × 140 mm No.2 and Better hemlock lumber in bending, and, more recently, two qualities and two sizes (38 × 89 mm and 38 × 184 mm) of spruce lumber also in bending. Long term tests of spruce lumber in tension and laterally restrained compression have replicated the findings in bending. All these data were used in the development of design guidelines.

Other experimental results have been obtained from long term shear testing using small torque tubes and from bending tests of plywood and waferboard.

All of the experiments have been conducted using an applied constant stress, at different fractions of the average strength obtained in a short term test of one minute average duration. The measured variable has been the time to failure. Because service loads are not generally constant during the life of the structure, studies were conducted to develop the means to predict times to failure for load sequences of varying intensity.

Following the procedures used in metal fatigue to predict number of cycles to failure, the process leading to failure in wood was modified as an accumulation of damage. The damage variable was defined as being zero at the beginning of load application and reaching one at failure. A process model was postulated to represent the speed with which damage would accumulate and this rate was assumed dependent both on the intensity of the applied stress and the magnitude of the damage already accumulated. As a consequence, damage under a constant load grows in a nonlinear fashion; slow at the beginning and accelerating as failure nears.

Parameters in the damage accumulation model were assumed to be random variables to represent the variability in long term performance across specimens. Research at the University of British Columbia (Foschi, 1989) calibrated the model parameters using the particular experimental load history and showed that the proposed damage accumulation model fit the experimental trends.

The advantage of an accumulation model is that it permits the prediction of damage produced by an arbitrary random load sequence. The model was thus used in computer simulations to estimate the damage that would be produced in a beam of given dimensions by a combination of dead and snow loads at the end of a service life of 30 years. This damage $\alpha_{30}$ can be used to estimate the reliability of the design at the end of the service life. Defining the performance function G as:

$$G = 1.0 - \alpha_{30} \qquad\qquad (Eq.\ 10)$$

the possibility of non-performance, or probability of $G < 0$, corresponds to the probability that the damage $\alpha_{30}$ exceeds 1.0 and the beam fails at or before the end of the service life. The dimensions of the beam can then be adjusted to reduce such probability to acceptable levels.

In the Standard, the duration of load effect is taken into account by modifying the short term characteristic or specified strength. The following example shows the manner in which the adjustment factor $K_D$ was obtained for the case of lumber in bending:

1. A curve relating reliability index $\beta$ and the resistance factor $\phi$ was developed as previously discussed, using the results of short term strength tests. This curve is shown as (I) in Figure 12.3;

2. A curve relating reliability index $\beta$ and the resistance factor $\phi$ was developed by computer simulations, using the performance function G from Eq. 10, and different sequences of loads over a period of 30 years. This curve (Curve (II) in Figure 12.3) reflects the effect of load duration. The resistance factor $\phi$ must be reduced from that of curve (I) to maintain consistent reliability under long term loading.

3. The adjustment factor $K_D$ to be applied to the short term resistance factor is determined from the ratio of the $\phi$ values from curves (I) and (II) at the same reliability level.

The adjustment factor is always less than 1.0, since it is applied to the short term strength.

Figure 12.3
**Effect of load duration on β - φ relationship**

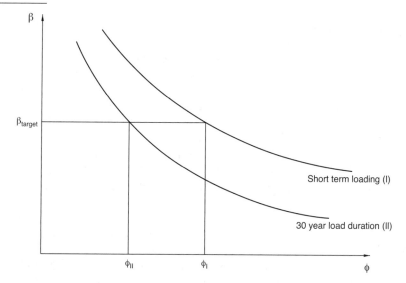

The adjustment factor was obtained for snow loads recorded in different locations across Canada, using statistics on snow magnitude and duration provided by the National Research Council of Canada. Also, the adjustment factor was obtained for two types of occupancy live loads, corresponding to office and residential uses. Finally, the factor was obtained for constant loads lasting 30 years, 7 days, 1 day and 1 hour. All research results are reported in Foschi 1989.

The effect of load duration is most severe for permanent loads. For such loads, the adjustment factor is 0.50 (the characteristic short term strength must be reduced by 50%). As the duration of the constant load is shortened, the adjustment is less severe.

Combinations of permanent and live loads like snow or occupancy are less severe than permanent (dead) loads only. The results of $K_D$ studies for these cases showed a dependency on the magnitude of the ratio between design dead load and design live load. Regardless of the type of the live load (snow or occupancy) a factor of 0.80 can be used with sufficient accuracy where the design dead load is less than or equal to the design live load.

The factor $K_D$, which is to be used when considering the superposition of dead and several distinct live loads (snow + wind or snow + earthquake), is controlled by the live load of the shortest duration.

The $K_D$ factors described above form the basis for those actually shown in CSA O86. This describes three classes of load duration: Short Term, Standard Term and Permanent. Standard Term load duration includes all snow and occupancy load cases, to which a $K_D = 0.80$ should apply. For simplicity, this factor has already been included in the specified strengths, resulting in a specified $K_D = 1.00$ for Standard Term loadings as shown in the following table.

|  | Calculated $K_D$ | $K_D$ in CSA O86 |
|---|---|---|
| Short Term | 0.9 to 1.0 | 1.15 |
| Standard Term | 0.8 | 1.00 |
| Permanent | 0.5 | 0.65 |

**12**

**COM**

CSA Commentary

Accordingly, the factor in CSA O86 for Permanent loads is 0.65, and for Short Term (wind, earthquake, formwork, impact) is 1.15. These factors for Short and Standard Term apply as long as the dead load is not greater than the design live load. When the design dead load is more than five times the design live load, the factor $K_D$ for Permanent Term must be applied. CSA O86 provides for a linear interpolation of the factor $K_D$ in intermediate cases.

The adjustment factors $K_D$ can be considered to be a reliable estimate of the load duration effect for lumber, given that the bulk of the experimental data was collected for that particular product. Without the benefit of a similar database, factors $K_D$ for other applications (glulam beams, connectors, panel products) must be considered to be approximations. However, it is recommended that the same adjustment factors be used until further testing is carried out.

### References

Foschi, R.O. et al. 1989. Reliability-Based Design of Wood Structures. Structural Research Series, Report No. 34, University of British Columbia, Vancouver, BC.

Wood, L. 1960. Relation of Strength of Wood to Duration of Load. U.S. Dept. of Agric., Forest Products Lab, Report No. 1916, Madison, WI.

# 12.3    System Modification Factors and Floor Vibration

## System Factor

Given the variability in properties of wood members when taken in isolation, it is important to consider their performance in a system when studying reliability, so as to not unduly penalize design. Earlier editions of the design standard used the name "Load Sharing Factor" for this, and assigned the value 1.15 to bending members. However, load sharing is only part of the picture in designing wood systems.

More recent editions of the Standard include system modification factors $K_H$ that may be used for typical wood frame systems with repetitive members all sharing the applied load. An example of such a structure is a floor supported by multiple joists, covered by plywood or waferboard panels fastened to the joists.

These systems are typically designed using a single member equation, considering only one isolated joist. The system modification factor compensates for this simplification and maintains the reliability level that was calibrated for a single member.

Justification for the factor $K_H$ stems from three considerations:

1. The reliability analysis of each member requires the calculation of the stresses that the member is actually carrying as part of the structure. These stresses can be estimated very conservatively by considering the member in isolation from the system and taking into account only the tributary area for the applied load. A better estimate of the stresses can be obtained by analyzing the system as a redundant structure, taking into account the effect that members and system components have on each other. In a load-sharing system the effect of other members will be related to the relative stiffness of the components.

2. The composite action of the sheathing and fasteners enhances the performance of each member in the system. This is reflected in the system modification factors.

3. The factor also accounts for the reduced probability that weaker members be placed in the location of higher stresses in a repetitive system.

Research was carried out for repetitive systems in bending, of the type found in floors or flat roofs using lumber joists or rafters, with nailing or adhesives connecting the lumber to sheathing, under uniformly distributed loads. The factor $K_H$ depends strongly on several variables: sheathing thickness, ratio of sheathing bending stiffnesses in directions parallel and perpendicular to the joists, fastener stiffness, variability in modulus of elasticity between members, variability in bending strength between members, magnitude and variability of the applied loads, and the statistical correlation between member stiffness and bending strength.

The factor $K_H$ is much less dependent on variables that are considered in the design equation, such as joist depth and joist spacing.

**12**

**COM**

CSA Commentary

The factor $K_H$ also depends on the definition of performance (in this case, bending failure for the joists or rafters). One definition may consider failure of the most stressed joist, with stresses calculated from a structural analysis of the system. Another, more stringent definition defines system performance as no failure in any joist.

The first definition follows the philosophy of single member design with due account of system-induced stresses. The second is a first level of a more sophisticated system design. One of the major differences between results from the two approaches is that the second is influenced by the number of joists since the greater the number of joists in a floor, the greater the chances of having included a weaker one.

Research conducted at the University of British Columbia (Foschi 1989) describes in detail the calculation of $K_H$ for this type of system, and Figure 12.4 shows the procedure. A floor configuration was chosen by selecting the number of joists, their dimensions, stiffness and spacing, and the type and stiffness of fasteners. The reliability index $\beta$ corresponding to selected floor spans was computed for the complete structure using a computer analysis of the stresses in the floor, as shown by Curve (I) in Figure 12.4; and for a single joist carrying load on its tributary area, as shown by Curve (II).

For a given target reliability, the ratio between the corresponding spans from Curves (I) and (II) was used to obtain the system factor $K_H$. For uniformly distributed loads, this factor is the ratio of the squares of the corresponding spans.

Using the first definition of performance (single member approach), the range for $K_H$ when considering: three species of lumber (Douglas fir, Hem-fir and S-P-F), two sizes (38 × 184 mm and 38 × 235 mm), three grades (Select Structural, No.2 and No.3), four plywood sheathing thicknesses (9.5 to 18.5 mm) and three loading conditions (two snows and one occupancy) was:

$$1.41 \leq K_H \leq 1.77$$

with an overall average $K_H = 1.63$ and a coefficient of variation (COV) of 4.5%. The highest values corresponded to the thicker sheathing. The results were obtained for a joist spacing of 400 mm, with nominal nailing (stiffness of 2.10 MN/m) with a spacing of 200 mm. Lumber data was obtained from the Canadian Wood Council lumber properties testing program.

The calculations were performed for a distributed load with a mean of 2.0 kN/m² (40 psf), and a (COV) of 30%. The values of $K_H$ are smaller if the mean of the load is increased: for 7.0 kN/m² (140 psf), values are approximately 15% smaller.

The average overall for the more stringent performance requirement of no joist failures, was $K_H = 1.43$.

CSA O86 specifies a value of $K_H = 1.40$ to be applied to all configurations for this type of floor/roof construction.

A value of $K_H = 1.10$ must be used when the cover is made of essentially one-directional elements perpendicular to the joists or rafters (for example, timber decking).

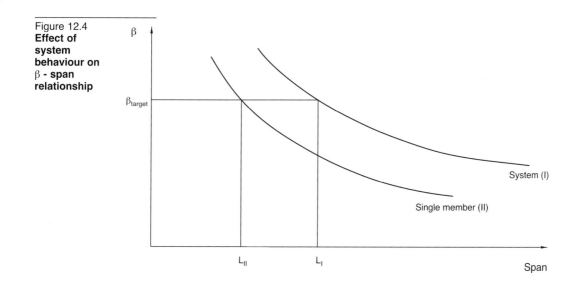

Figure 12.4
**Effect of system behaviour on β - span relationship**

No increase in the resistance factor ($K_H = 1.0$) is allowed if the cover is made of essentially one-directional elements parallel to the joists or rafters. Thus, for a roof with main beams, purlins, and timber decking perpendicular to the purlins, a factor $K_H = 1.10$ may be applicable for the purlin design but $K_H = 1.0$ applies for the main beams.

Research has not covered load sharing systems other than the ones described above. Thus, modification factors for a system of parallel chord trusses in a floor or for a system of pitched trusses in a roof have not been studied yet with the same detail. For these cases, the Standard includes a 10% increase factor.

The factor $K_H$ has been computed using short term strengths, since the duration of load adjustment ($K_D$) can apply equally to the single member as well as the repetitive member system.

**Floor Vibration**

Appendix A4.5.5 was added to the 2001 edition of CSA O86 to provide basic information relating to vibration performance of wood-framed floor systems.

Floor vibration is a serviceability limit state that reflects people's satisfaction with the performance of a floor. People may consider floor performance to be unsatisfactory when:
- cabinet contents and materials on shelves or tables vibrate when someone walks across the floor,
- a person walking across the floor is felt by another person sitting down, and
- the floor appears to be bouncy when walking on it.

Point load deflection and natural frequency are two criteria that have been used to assess the vibration performance of wood frame floors. Depending on the span, construction and weight of the floor, one or a combi-

**12**

**COM**

CSA Commentary

nation of the two criteria may be a better indicator of vibration performance and occupant satisfaction.

On short-span, lightweight floors, each footfall by a walking person results in a relatively large change in deflection, with a small transient vibration. The transient vibration may or may not be sensed, depending on the amplitudes and damping. In conventional short span floors, point load deflection has been used to represent vibration performance.

On long-span, heavier mass floors, which are stiffer systems, the deflection taking place under the action of an individual person is small in comparison to the transient vibration generated by a walking person. In some cases, natural frequency of the floor may assist in understanding vibration performance.

It should be recognized that information on floor performance is difficult to analyze and interpret for reasons of measurement issues, subjectivity of opinions about acceptability, construction variables, information gaps and other factors.

References for further reading are listed below.

## References

ATC Design Guide 1. Minimizing Floor Vibration. 1999. Applied Technology Council. Redwood City, CA. Prepared for ATC by D.E. Allen, D.M. Onysko and T.M. Murray.

Dolan, J.D., Murray, T.M., Johnson, J.R., Runte, D. and Shue, B.C. 1999. Preventing Annoying Wood Floor Vibrations. Journal of Structural Engineering. American Society of Civil Engineers, Vol. 125, No. 1, pp. 19-24.

Foschi, R.O. 1989. Reliability-Based Design of Wood Structures. Structural Research Series, Report No. 34, University of British Columbia, Vancouver, BC.

Hu, L.J. and Tardif, Y. 2000. Effectiveness of Strong-back Wood-I-blocking for Improving Vibration Performance of Engineered Wooden Floors, . In Proceedings of the World Conference on Timber Engineering. Whistler, BC.

ISO Standard 2631-2, 1989. Evaluation of Human Exposure to Whole-Body Vibration – Part 2: Human Exposure to Continuous and Shock Induced Vibrations in Buildings (1 to 80 Hz). International Standards Organization.

Onysko, D.M., Hu, L.J., Jones, E.D. and Di Lenardo, B. 2000. Serviceability Design of Residential Wood Framed Floors in Canada. In Proceedings of the World Conference on Timber Engineering. Whistler, BC.

Onysko D.M. 1988. Performance Criteria for Residential Floors Based on Consumer Responses. International Conference on Timber Engineering, Seattle, WA [Forest Products Society, V1, 1988 pp. 736-745].

Smith, I. and Chui, Y.H. 1988. Design of Lightweight Wooden Floors to Avoid Human Discomfort. Canadian Journal of Civil Engineering, pp. 254-262.

# 12.4    Sawn Lumber

J.D. Barrett[1]

### Clause 5.1 – Scope

Design procedures and design values provided in the Sawn Lumber section apply to structural lumber meeting the requirements of the National Lumber Grades Authority grading rules (NLGAa, 2000) and the requirements of CSA Standard O141, *Softwood Lumber*.

### Clause 5.2 – Materials

CSA Standard O141 establishes basic provisions for lumber grading to be carried out under the supervision of grading agencies that are accredited by an independent body to ensure consistent accuracy of grading. In Canada, the accreditation is carried out by the Canadian Lumber Standards Accreditation Board.

   The Standard includes the principal grade classifications and sizes of softwood lumber for structural use. It also provides a common basis of classification, measurement, grading and grade-marking of rough and dressed sizes of various items of lumber, including boards, dimension and timbers. Hardwood species may also be classified, graded and grade stamped under the same provisions.

   CSA O141 identifies nominal and minimum sizes for structural lumber in the dry and green conditions. Dry lumber is defined as lumber seasoned to a moisture content of 19% or less at the time of manufacture.

### Clause 5.3 – Specified Strengths

The basis for lumber specified strengths has evolved from tests of small clear pieces of wood to full-size lumber ("in-grade") testing, where the latter method has been adopted internationally as the basis for engineering properties of structural lumber. In-grade test data on dimension lumber has been used since the 1980 edition of CSA O86 as the basis for tension design values, since the 1984 edition for bending design values, and since the 1989 edition for compression parallel to grain design values. Tests of small clear wood are still used to determine dimension lumber properties such as relative density, horizontal shear, and compression perpendicular to grain, since these properties are less dependent on wood characteristics such as knots and slope of grain.

   The in-grade lumber database was used to establish relationships between characteristic properties and specified strengths through reliability procedures. These relationships are documented in a CSA Special Publication on *Standard Practice Relating Specified Strengths of Structural Members to Characteristic Structural Properties*.

**12**

**COM**

CSA Commentary

[1] Department of Wood Science, University of British Columbia, Vancouver, British Columbia

### Traditional Methodology

Design values for lumber were developed traditionally from tests of small clear specimens free from strength-reducing defects such as knots, slope of grain, splits and holes. Small clear test data for Canadian softwood and hardwood species are summarized in Jessome (1977), and also in the American Society for Testing and Materials (ASTM) Standard D 2555, *Standard Methods for Establishing Clear Wood Strength Values* (ASTM, 2000).

ASTM Standard D 245, *Standard Methods for Establishing Structural Grades and Related Allowable Properties for Visually Graded Lumber*, has provided the basis for deriving allowable lumber design properties from small clear wood data. These methods are still used for some types of visually graded structural lumber such as beams and stringers, and posts and timbers. Also, as noted above, some design values for dimension lumber are still based on small clear test data.

Where the small clear wood method is used, design values in Canada have typically been based on the weakest species in a commercial species combination. Fifth percentile strength properties are calculated using the assumption that clear wood properties are normally distributed. These fifth percentile strength properties are modified to account for differences between the small clear test specimen data and the strength and stiffness of full-size members subjected to long term loads and in-service climate conditions. These resulting values are further reduced for effects of characteristics such as slope-of-grain, knots, splits and cracks to determine design values for individual grades and sizes of structural lumber.

In some countries, lumber design values are still determined by the small clear wood procedures, based on a single set of reference strength data. The success of this clear wood approach can be traced to its simplicity in application and the history of successful performance of structures designed using these values.

### CWC Full-Size Lumber Properties Program

With the introduction of the limit states design philosophy, the CSA Committee for Engineering Design in Wood adopted the philosophy that design values for structural wood products should be based on full-size structural tests of members ("in-grade" testing) as used in building construction wherever feasible. Bending and tension design values in the 1984 edition were derived from in-grade test data developed from studies conducted by Madsen and co-workers during the late 1970s (Madsen, 1992) on behalf of the National Lumber Grades Authority, (NLGA). Tension values based on this work were first implemented in the 1980 edition of the Standard. This first major in-grade testing program established bending and tension parallel to grain strength and mean modulus of elasticity data for the three major commercial species groups (D Fir-L, Hem-Fir and S-P-F) using a proof loading approach; i.e., breaking only the weaker pieces.

Following this, the Canadian lumber industry conducted a major research program through the Canadian Wood Council Lumber Properties Project for bending, tension and compression parallel to grain strength properties of 38 mm thick (nominal 2") dimension lumber of all commercially important Canadian species groups. The CWC project was part of a cooperative program with the US industry. The basis for sampling and testing was coordinated with the North American In-grade Testing Committee recommendations that later evolved into ASTM consensus standards.

Lumber samples in three sizes (38 by 89 mm, 38 by 184 mm and 38 by 235 mm) were selected across the full Canadian growing regions for the three largest-volume commercial species groups: Spruce-Pine-Fir (S-P-F), Douglas Fir-Larch (D Fir-L) and Hem-Fir. Select Structural, No.1, No.2, No.3, as well as light framing grades, were sampled and tested in bending. Select Structural, No.1 and No.2 grades were evaluated in tension and compression parallel to grain. Several lesser-volume species were evaluated at lower sampling intensities for two grades (Select Structural and No.2) and three sizes (38 by 89 mm, 38 by 140 mm and 38 by184 mm).

After the test samples were conditioned to approximately 15% moisture content, they were sent to the Forintek Canada Corp. laboratory in Vancouver, BC. Short term flexural stiffness properties, and ultimate bending, tension, and compression parallel to grain strengths were tested in accordance with ASTM Standard D 4761, *Standard Test Methods for Mechanical Properties of Lumber and Wood-Base Structural Material* (ASTM, 2000).

The dimension lumber database was examined to establish trends in bending, tension and compression property relationships as affected by member size and grade. These studies provided a basis for extending the results to the full range of dimension lumber grades and member sizes specified in CSA O86.

A detailed description of the research programs and a discussion of the results were presented in an ASTM Workshop on the North American In-grade Testing Program (FPRS, 1989). Further discussion of the Canadian testing program and its results appears in a book titled *Canadian Lumber Properties* (Barrett and Lau, 1994).

Compression perpendicular to grain design values are derived directly from the ASTM D 245 procedures. However, since the 1994 Standard, the relationship between compression perpendicular to grain and wood density was recognized in setting the design values (See commentary on Clause 5.5.7).

Shear capacity of dimension lumber bending members has traditionally been based on the assumption that every member contained a full-length split. Actual crack length distributions were measured for all lumber evaluated in the in-grade testing program. The crack length distribution data was used in conjunction with a fracture mechanics failure model to study the reliability of dimension lumber members subjected to bending loads (Lau, 1988). These reliability analyses were used to develop shear design procedures that were more consistent with the in-grade testing philosophy.

### Clause 5.3.1 – Visually Stress-Graded Lumber

The National Lumber Grades Authority (NLGAa, 2000) *Standard Grading Rules for Canadian Lumber* classify visually graded structural lumber into specific categories defined by end use applications and member size. CSA O86 provides design values for three classes of visually graded lumber: Dimension Lumber, Beams and Stringers, and Posts and Timbers.

**12**

**COM**

CSA Commentary

## Dimension Lumber

The NLGA grading rules further classify dimension lumber into four categories: Structural Light Framing, Structural Joists and Planks, Light Framing and Studs. Dimension lumber is surfaced to thicknesses from 38 to 102 mm and widths of 38 mm or more. Lumber is typically specified in metric actual dimensions (or imperial nominal dimensions). Table A5.5.2 in CSA O86 lists green and dry sizes for dimension lumber and timbers.

Relationships between categories, grades and member sizes are shown in Table 5.2.2.1 of the Standard. Within a category, permissible grade characteristics such as knots, slope of grain, splits, cracks and wane are defined by grading rule requirements (NLGAa, 2000). Since grade characteristics vary with category as well as the grade, design values are also category- and grade-dependent.

Specified strengths for dimension lumber, given in Table 5.3.1.A. of CSA O86, were based mainly on results from the CWC Lumber Properties Project. These strength values have been derived in accordance with limit states design philosophy. The specified strength values for bending, tension, compression parallel to the grain, shear strength and modulus of elasticity are derived from reliability principles (Lau, 1988; Foschi, 1989). Compression perpendicular to grain values are based on ASTM D 245 procedures.

Specified strengths, derived from full-size tests, were modified to Standard Term duration of load. The specified strengths for the Standard Term duration, which applies for snow loads and occupancy loads, are 80% of the short term static test strengths obtained from full-size tests.

Specified strengths for the species group identified as Northern were derived from the weakest species tested to provide a basis for design using any Canadian commercial species.

The CWC in-grade testing program confirmed that design values for No.1 and No.2 grades of dimension lumber were not significantly different so these two grades are assigned the same specified strengths. The testing programs also resulted in No.3 and Stud grades being assigned the same specified strengths. Design values for dimension lumber (except light framing and machine stress-rated lumber), beams and stringers, posts and timbers apply to a member width of about 300 mm. Specified strengths for other member widths are derived using the appropriate size factor (Table 5.4.5 in CSA O86), with the exception of the Light Framing grades.

The Light Framing grades (i.e., Construction, Standard) apply to lumber 89 mm or narrower, so the design values in Table 5.3.1B are tabulated on an 89 mm basis and size factors are not used except for compression properties. Sizes of Light Framing grades other than 38 by 89 mm were assigned different design values in previous editions of CSA O86, based on analysis of the small clear wood approach. In the 2001 edition of CSA O86, however, values for the other Light Framing grade sizes were changed to be equivalent to the 38 by 89 mm design values, on the basis of the relationships between in-grade data of relevant sizes and grades of lumber.

## Beams and Stringers

Timbers with a width more than 51 mm (2") greater than the thickness are classified as Beams and Stringers. Actual sizes of Beams and Stringers are typically 13 mm (1/2") less than the nominal imperial sizes. A nominal 8 by 12" member would be graded in the Beams and Stringers category and have actual dimensions 191 by 292 mm (7-1/2" by 11-1/2"). Limited tests of full-size Beams and Stringers in bending demonstrated that the design values derived from the small clear specimen approach were conservative.

Specified strengths for Beams and Stringers (Table 5.3.1.C in CSA O86) were revised in 1989 to recognize the available test data for timbers (Madsen, 1982). The revised design values incorporate higher compression parallel to grain strengths and a size effect factor based upon evaluations of the bending, compression and tension property relationships as well as size effects derived from the 38 mm dimension lumber program. Specified strengths were added for a No.2 grade in the Beams and Stringers category in 1989.

Beams and Stringers are graded primarily for use in bending, assuming that the member will be loaded on the narrow face. Larger knots are permitted at the centre and at the ends of the wide face. When these members are used on the flat, the specified strengths and modulus of elasticity must be reduced using the factors tabulated in the footnote to Table 5.3.1.C.

The tabulated values apply to dry service conditions and Standard Term load duration. Since these sections are typically supplied in the green condition and seasoning occurs rather slowly, caution must be exercised to prevent over-loading in compression while the members are in the green state. If overloading is anticipated prior to seasoning, the specified strengths should be modified to accommodate wet use conditions.

## Posts and Timbers

Posts and Timbers are graded primarily for use in compression but they may also be used in applications where bending and tension design stresses occur. These members are essentially square cross sections where the maximum difference between the width and thickness is 51 mm (2"). Actual sizes are typically 13 mm (1/2") less than the nominal imperial sizes. Post and Timbers are graded so that the maximum permissible knot size may occur at any location across a face or along the length of the member. In rectangular sections the wider face determines the maximum knot size.

As with Beams and Stringers, care must be taken not to overload these members in compression prior to seasoning if specified strengths for the dry service condition are applied.

Limited bending strength data developed by the in-grade testing were used to update specified strengths for Posts and Timbers in 1989 considering the size effects and property relationships of the CWC Lumber Properties Program.

## Fingerjoined Lumber

Design data specified in the Standard for visually graded dimension lumber are applicable to fingerjoined lumber of the same species, grade and member size if

**12**

**COM**

CSA Commentary

the fingerjoined product is produced and grade stamped in accordance with requirements of SPS 1: *NLGAa Special Products Standard for Fingerjoined Structural Lumber* (NLGAc, 2000). Fingerjoined lumber meeting the requirements of SPS 1 may be used interchangeably for unjoined material of the same species, grade and member size.

### Remanufactured Lumber

Lumber that is ripped or otherwise reduced in cross-section size or member length in a manner that may lower the grade of the remanufactured member(s) must be regraded and grade stamped in accordance with the requirements of the National Lumber Grades Authority and CSA Standard 0141 *Softwood Lumber.*

### Clause 5.3.2 – Machine Stress-Rated and Machine Evaluated Lumber

### Property Classification

Machine stress-rated (MSR) lumber is sawn lumber that has been evaluated by mechanical stress-rating equipment and meets the product requirements specified in NLGA SPS 2 *Special Product Standard for Machine Stress-Rated Lumber* (NLGAb, 2000). SPS 2 specifies requirements for visual characteristics, property requirements, quality control procedures and the grade marking requirements for MSR lumber. MSR lumber is distinguished from visually graded lumber in that each piece is non-destructively evaluated usually by a mechanical evaluation for modulus of elasticity (E) and each piece is grade marked to indicate the E, and bending property ($F_b$) rating.

Other properties may also be marked on the piece if they are qualified and monitored as part of the quality control process.

Machine evaluated lumber (MEL) is a similar product, that is also nondestructively evaluated by a grading machine, and conforms to requirements for MSR lumber with the exception that the lower 5th percentile E value must equal or exceed 0.75 (rather than 0.82 for MSR lumber) times the characteristic mean E for the grade.

The $F_b$-E grade designations for MSR lumber (e.g., 1650$F_b$-1.5E) were established to correspond to allowable design stresses for MSR lumber in imperial units (psi). The $F_b$-E grade descriptors were the allowable design values assigned for bending (psi) and modulus of elasticity ($\times 10^6$ psi) in the working stress design standard. In limit states design, the grade descriptor generally does not relate directly to the design values (specified strengths) for the grade.

SPS 2 requires that qualification and quality control samples of MSR and MEL lumber meet minimum structural property requirements. For a particular grade, the property requirements for bending, tension and compression parallel to grain strength and modulus of elasticity are the same for all species.

The property requirements for mean E, fifth percentile E and fifth percentile of bending strength specified in SPS 2 must be qualified and checked using quality control programs based on full-size structural evaluations of samples selected from each days production. In some cases, tensile strength must also be part of the quality control.

## MSR and MEL Lumber Properties

In North America, machine graded lumber has been available only in 38 mm (nominal 2") thicknesses. The largest volumes of production occur in 89 and 140 mm widths. The Standard provides specified strength properties for 22 MSR $F_b$-E classifications and of these the 1450$F_b$-1.3E, 1650$F_b$-1.5E, 1800$F_b$-1.6E, 2100$F_b$-1.8E and 2400$F_b$-2.0E grades are produced in substantial quantities by Canadian mills. There are also 14 grades of MEL lumber in the Standard.

Full-size tests have been conducted in bending and tension parallel to grain for 38 × 89 mm, Spruce-Pine-Fir MSR lumber in the five commonly produced grades, as part of the CWC Lumber Properties Project. These evaluations confirmed the property specifications for MSR lumber given in SPS 2 for Spruce-Pine-Fir in tension and bending, as determined by in-grade testing. SPS 2 specifies limitations on visual characteristics as well as minimum property requirements. Visual characteristics typically are limited to the No.2 visual grade level or better. In the higher grades, edge knots are more severely limited to ensure that design values are attained.

Resistances and duration of load factors have been adopted in the Standard for sawn lumber based on reliability analysis. Thus, specified tension strengths for MSR lumber were calibrated to maintain approximately the same sections as permitted in the 1984 Standard. Specified bending strengths adopted in the 1984 Standard are retained, increasing the factored bending capacity for roof and floor applications.

The size effect factor for bending strength is $K_z = 1.0$ for MSR and MEL lumber. The grade minimum bending strengths are specified and verified with the quality control process in SPS 2. Grading parameters are varied to ensure that the MOE and bending strength requirements are satisfied independently of member width or species. Studies of tension-to-bending and compression-to-bending property relationships allow the tension and compression specified strengths to be defined in relation to the bending strength.

In the 1994 edition of CSA O86, compression parallel to grain design values were modified in view of the in-grade compression/bending relationships determined for visually graded lumber, and limited data on MSR lumber. This information showed that compression parallel to grain was under-rated for lower grades of machine rated lumber, and slightly over-rated for higher grades. In addition, the size factor for compression ($K_{Zc}$) was applied to MSR and MEL design formulae.

Shear and compression perpendicular to grain specified strengths were derived using procedures adopted for visually graded lumber. Thus, these values are generally species-dependent and the specified strengths are tabulated for the appropriate species in Table 5.3.1A of CSA O86. For Spruce-Pine-Fir machine graded lumber of 12,400 MPa or higher E values, and for Hem-Fir machine graded lumber of 10,300 MPa or higher E values, the compression perpendicular design values have been increased. This relates to the higher density values for these grades (See Appendix A10.1 of the Standard).

## Clause 5.4 – Modification Factors

### Clause 5.4.1 – Load Duration Factor, $K_D$

Effects of long term constant loads on time-to-failure behaviour of visually graded lumber have been studied extensively in the 1970s and 1980s. Results from these studies have been used to calibrate duration of load models (damage models), which can be used to predict member behaviour under typical load combinations encountered in buildings.

Studies of full-size dimension lumber members show that duration of load effects are relatively consistent across species, grades and member sizes. Based on these studies the CSA committee has concluded that previous duration of load adjustments for structural wood products, based on small clear specimen studies, were unnecessarily conservative. Since the 1989 Standard the duration of load factors have been based on studies of full-size member behaviour and snow load, occupancy load and permanent load models adopted for reliability studies of wood and other structural materials. These factors are unchanged in later editions.

### Clause 5.4.2 – Service Condition Factor, $K_S$

Wood shrinks as the moisture content is reduced below the fibre saturation point. The fibre saturation point ($M_p$) is that moisture content at which the wood cell walls are fully saturated but there is no free water in the cell cavities. Drying below this fibre saturation point then removes water from the cell walls and the cell wall shrinkage results in changes in member width and thickness. The fibre saturation point varies with species and can be dependent on the method of measurement. For sawn lumber the fibre saturation point is typically assumed to be between 25 and 30%. More specific information can be found in handbooks (Forest Products Laboratory, 1999 and Bodig, 1982).

Natural climatic variation in temperature and relative humidity causes changes in moisture content of wood products. Strength and stiffness properties of wood products generally increase with drying below the fibre saturation point.

The tabulated specified strengths are derived assuming that sawn lumber will be used in a dry service condition, where the average moisture content of a member over a year averages 15% or less and does not exceed 19%.

Shrinkage of sawn lumber is different for width and thickness. For engineering purposes, expressions generally used to calculate the section geometry changes are:

$$S_w = 6.031 - 0.215 \, M \qquad (Eq.\ 11)$$
$$S_t = 5.062 - 0.181 \, M \qquad (Eq.\ 12)$$

where:

$S_w$ = the percent shrinkage in width from the fibre saturation point

$S_t$ = the percent shrinkage in thickness from the fibre saturation point

$M$ = moisture content, (%)

Studies of strength and stiffness changes of dimension lumber due to moisture content have been used to predict the effect of moisture content on lumber properties (Barrett and Lau, 1994). When calculating a member capacity or stiffness, increases in strength properties more than compensate for shrinkage. As a result, member capacities and stiffness are generally higher for dry service conditions than wet service conditions. The wet service condition factors take into account both the shrinkage effects and the property differences between green and dry service conditions. The service condition factors in Table 5.4.2 of CSA O86 provide a convenient method of incorporating the effect of service conditions in design calculations while allowing calculations to be based on the product standard dry sizes.

### Clause 5.4.3 – Treatment Factor, $K_T$

Full-size tests have shown that strength and stiffness properties of 38 mm dimension lumber are reduced if the lumber is both incised and treated (Palka, et al, 1984; Palka, et al, 1992; and Lam and Morris, 1991). Preservative treatments themselves appear to have little effect on structural properties. However, when the 38 mm members are incised and then treated and re-dried, significant structural property decreases occur. Based on these full-size tests the CSA Standard specifies that the modulus of elasticity and specified strength values of sawn lumber 89 mm or less in thickness must be modified for incising and preservative treatment as shown in Table 5.4.3.

Investigations of the influence of incising and treating on the strength properties of larger sections did not demonstrate any consistent reductions. In addition, some of the earlier work was done using incising methods that are no longer practiced. For dimension lumber, incising is done typically to a density of no more than 10,000 incisions per square metre, and a depth of no more than 10 mm. Evaluation of incisor methods summarized in Lam and Morris (1991), and Morris, Morrell and Ruddick (1994) and review of current industry practices led to a modification of the dry-service strength reduction factor from 0.7 to 0.75 in the 2001 edition of CSA O86.

Fire-retardant treatments also reduce strength properties of structural lumber. In past editions of CSA O86, the effect was identified as a 10% reduction, however, the chemical formulations used today are different from earlier formulations and behave differently, particularly at elevated temperatures. As a result, CSA O86 no longer includes specific treatment factors for fire-retardant wood, but continues to require that the effects of the treatment be considered in design. Information on appropriate adjustments should be obtained from the company that provides the treatment.

CSA O86 requires that tests be carried out on the effects of fire-retardants, or any other potentially strength-reducing chemicals used with lumber, to determine an appropriate treatment factor. The tests must take into account the service conditions of the treated lumber. In particular, elevated temperatures for prolonged periods are known to reduce the strength of fire-retardant treated wood.

**12**

**COM**

CSA Commentary

ASTM Standard D 5664 *Standard Test Method for Evaluating the Effects of Fire-Retardant Treatments and Elevated Temperatures on Strength Properties of Fire-Retardant Treated Lumber* (ASTM, 2000), provides a standard test protocol for evaluating the strength reducing effects of fire retardants. Three test procedures are given in ASTM Standard D 5664:

- Test Procedure 1 uses small clear speciemens to evaluate the effects of fire-retardant treatments on bending, tension parallel, compression parallel, and horizontal shear properties at room temperature. These test results could be used to develop $K_T$ factors for treated wood used at room temperature.
- Test Procedure 2 uses small clear specimens to assess the effects of fire-retardant treatments on bending and tension parallel properties over the course of a prolonged exposure to elevated temperatures. These test results could be used to develop $K_T$ factors for treated wood used at elevated temperatures. Treated wood used in roof framing would normally be exposed to high temperatures for prolonged periods of time.
- Test Procedure 3 is an optional test which uses full-size test specimens to modify the results from Procedures 1 and 2 for size effects.

The test standard stipulates what data needs to be presented in the final report. The test standard does not give procedures for developing $K_T$ factors.; however, it provides a framework to be used in developing these factors. Additional information on developing $K_T$ factors is given in ASTM Standard D6305 *Standard Practice for Calculating Bending Strength Design Adjustment Factors for Fire-Retardant-Treated Plywood Sheathing* (ASTM, 2000).

### Clause 5.4.4 – System Factor, $K_H$

Wood structural systems such as floors, walls and roofs incorporating essentially parallel members providing mutual support due to the structural redundancy of the system, have a higher structural capacity than predicted from the single member analogue upon which most design equations are based. The interaction of members in redundant floor and roof systems comprising panel materials and sawn lumber framing members has been extensively studied (See Section 12.3 of commentary). These studies have provided a better understanding of relationships between the stresses and deformations calculated using single member design models and those actually induced in systems.

CSA O86 recognizes two different degrees of structural interaction (Case 1 and Case 2) for which factors are tabulated. System factors for Case 1 apply when the system consists of three or more essentially parallel members spaced not more than 610 mm apart and arranged to mutually support the load. Thus, Case 1 is analogous to the systems description adopted in earlier standards for which a so-called load-sharing factor would have applied. Case 1 applies to systems such as wood trusses where the relationships between member forces are complex, or to conventional framing applications such as tongue and groove decking, that do not meet the specifications of Case 2. For Case 1 the Standard permits a 10% increase in specified strengths for bending, shear, compression parallel and tension parallel to grain.

System factors can be significantly greater than permitted in Case 1 for many common wood floor, roof and wall systems used in light frame structures. However, the magnitude of the system factor will vary with member size and spacing, the member stiffness and strength variability, the correlation between stiffness and strength properties, sheathing thickness, nail properties, nailing pattern and many other factors. For the standard, the CSA committee has chosen to adopt a system factor that can be applied over a wide range of structural configurations provided the structural system meets the requirements for a Case 2 system.

For Case 2, different system factors are applied for visually graded and machine stress-rated lumber. MSR lumber grades have a lower variability in strength and stiffness properties and the lower variability in properties results in lower system factors.

### Clause 5.4.5 – Size Factor, $K_Z$

The dependence of apparent material strength on the member size and loading condition and the type of test specimen is classified as a size effect phenomenon. Size effects exist to a greater or lesser extent in all structural materials.

Strength properties of sawn lumber members vary depending on the member size and loading conditions. Full-size evaluations of 38 mm dimension lumber conducted at a constant length-to-width ratio typically show that wider members have lower strengths. For constant width members, strength tends to decrease as member test length increases. The magnitude of the size effect will usually vary directly with the variability of strength properties. For visually graded sawn lumber, where the natural property variability is high, the size effects are significant (Barrett and Lau, 1994; FPRS, 1989; Madsen, 1986 and 1992; Lam, 1987; Barrett, 1989).

To maintain uniform safety levels across the range of member sizes and load cases it is necessary and convenient to adopt a reference strength for a particular member size and then to incorporate an adjustment factor for other member sizes in the design equation. Size factors for bending and shear depend on both the member width and thickness. For tension parallel to grain the size factor depends only on the larger dimension (i.e., the member width). For compression parallel to grain loading the size factor is a function of both column length and the member dimension in the direction of buckling (Clause 5.5.6 in CSA O86.1).

In the 2001 edition of CSA O86, the size factor is also applied to 64 by 89 mm and 89 by 89 mm lumber of No.1 or No.2 grade. This reflects a change in grading practice for these sizes of lumber, adding restrictions on knots at the edges of these lumber sizes.

## Clause 5.5 – Strength and Resistance

### Clause 5.5.1 – General

Design equations for bending moment resistance, shear resistance, and compressive and tensile resistance parallel to grain have been developed using reliability principles. (See Section 12.1 of the commentary for a discussion of reliability analysis.)

### Clause 5.5.2 – Sizes

(See Table A5.5.2 in CSA O86).

### Clause 5.5.3 – Continuity

This clause is specified to alert the designer to the fact that sawn timber members classed as Beams and Stringers are graded differently in the middle one-third of the member length. The middle one-third is required to have smaller knots than the remaining two-thirds since the grading rule anticipates that the majority of these members will be used in simply supported full-length applications.

### Clause 5.5.4 – Bending Moment Resistance

The factored bending moment resistance $M_r$ is derived following the same principles incorporated in earlier editions. Since the basis for duration of load adjustments is Standard Term, the specified strengths are reduced from short-term strengths by a factor of 0.8. The performance factor = 0.9 has been derived based on reliability calculations and in-grade full-size test data.

### Clause 5.5.5 – Shear Resistance

The factored shear resistance $V_r$ of a sawn lumber member is calculated using mechanics based procedures. A size factor $K_{Zv}$ is applied to account for the change in member shear capacity with member size. The size factor, which for simplicity is taken to be the same as the bending size factor, provides for substantial increases in shear capacities for smaller members.

The increase in member capacity reflects the results of surveys to determine the actual lengths of end splits in sawn members and also reflects the fact that few sawn members have structurally significant end splits.

Given the increases in tabulated shear capacities for smaller members, the adjustments for crack lengths included in the 1984 Standard have been deleted. Shear values for sawn lumber members were increased in the 2005 Supplement to CSA 086 based on full-size member shear test data.

Research at the University of New Brunswick (Smith and Springer, 1993; Smith et al, 1993) applied fracture mechanics principles to the problem of notched members. The model, which uses relative density to predict capacity of notched lumber beams, showed that the traditional shear calculation for notched beams tended to be unconservative in some cases; e.g., when the notch was fairly long. As a result, a new design procedure for notching effects (Clause 5.5.5.3) was introduced into the Standard.

This design procedure applies only to notches on the tension side at supports, and is identified as the notched shear force resistance calculation ($F_r$), to distinguish it from the shear calculation ($V_r$). Both calculations are required for notched members. A Figure (5.5.5.4) and Clause (5.5.5.5) have been added in the 2001 edition to help clarify the calculation; i.e., depth and length of the notch, length of support, force components. In interpreting the notched shear force calculation for sloped members, the reaction component normal to the member is generally used.

The notched shear force calculation also has a separate service condition factor, since this limit state is more sensitive to moisture content effects.

## Clause 5.5.6 – Compressive Resistance Parallel to Grain

The load capacity of columns depends on their slenderness ratio, $C_c$. Earlier versions of the standard differentiated between short, intermediate and long columns depending on the slenderness ratio. Requirements for sawn lumber were modified in 1989 to incorporate new research on column behaviour and resistance factors based on a reliability analysis, as have requirements for glued-laminated timber columns in the 1994 edition.

The variation in column capacity with slenderness is incorporated through the slenderness factor, $K_c$, which is a continuous function of the slenderness ratio, $C_c$. The slenderness factor $K_c = 1.0$ for $C_c = 0$, and decreases as $C_c$ increases to approach the value corresponding to the elastic buckling load at high slenderness ratios. $K_c$ is dependent upon the adjusted specified strength, $F_c$, and the fifth percentile of modulus of elasticity, $E_{05}$.

The factor $K_c$ modifies compression strength obtained from tests of members where lateral deflection or buckling was restrained. The adjusted specified strength $F_c$ must also be modified for effects of column dimensions using the factor $K_{Zc}$. Tests of structural size members show that specified strengths increased for narrower widths and shorter members.

The resistance factor = 0.8 has been selected to achieve adequate reliability for all combinations of species, grades and sizes of lumber. Reliability calculations are reported in Foschi (1989), and compared with test data from Buchanan (1984). The formula chosen for the Standard was a cubic Rankine-Gordon relation, based on Neubauer (1973) and Johns (1991). A nominal load eccentricity to represent random column deviations from straightness was assumed for reliability calculations. The load eccentricity was taken to be normally distributed (mean = 5% of member width, COV = 20%).

CSA O86 contains information on built-up columns (Clause 5.5.6.4), based on a design procedure described in Malhotra and Van Dyer (1978). The Standard also includes provisions for spliced built-up columns (Clause 5.5.6.6), based on Bohnhoff, et al (1991).

**12**

**COM**

CSA Commentary

## Clause 5.5.7 – Compressive Resistance Perpendicular to Grain

Specified bearing strengths applicable to the commercial species groups are derived from ASTM procedures for clear wood compression perpendicular to grain strength. The strength tabulated for individual species in ASTM D 2555 corresponds to the average stress in compression perpendicular to grain at the proportional limit, as determined by the ASTM D143 clear wood test procedure. This value is modified to a mean 1 mm (0.04") deformation limit using a formula in the Appendix of ASTM D2555.

In the 1994 edition, a relationship between mean compression perpendicular strength and mean oven-dry wood density was used to establish a consistent basis for bearing strengths for various products (visually graded lumber, machine rated lumber, glued-laminated timber).

The formula that was used to determine specified strengths was:

$$f_{cp} = 0.9 \, L \, (2243.8 \, D - 473.8)/M \qquad \qquad \textit{(Eq. 13)}$$

where:

  0.9    was applied to establish a lower tolerance limit

  $L$   = conversion factor to limit states design and standard term load duration
      = 1.8125

  $D$  = oven-dry relative density

  $M$  = conversion factor for metric units
      = 145.038

Note: Bearing strengths for higher grades of S-P-F or Hem-Fir MSR or MEL lumber are increased due to the higher density values for these grades. The NLGA grading rules include provisions for mills producing S-P-F MSR or MEL lumber to qualify for other relative density values based on tests and daily quality control, and marking the qualified density value on the lumber. In such cases, the NLGA rules allow the compression perpendicular design value to be determined based on the marked density value and the formula shown above, without the 0.9 tolerance limit.

The bearing design procedure was revised in the 1994 edition in three ways:

1. An additional check for "critical" bearing is required for loads applied to opposite sides of a member, within a distance "d" from the centre of the support (see Figure 12.5). In the critical case, the stress can extend through the full depth of the member, in contrast with the general beam case where the bearing stress is typically limited to the outer fibres of the bending member. Due to the increased volume under stress, and the resulting increase in probability of deformation over time, the resistance for the critical case (Clause 5.5.7.3) is multiplied by a factor of 2/3, based on work at Forintek Canada Corp (Lum, 1994 and 1995).

2. A size factor for bearing $K_{Zcp}$ was introduced to account for the effect of member orientation on resistance. Used in a flat orientation, wood has improved crushing resistance compared with edge orientation, due partly to

growth characteristics (Lum, 1994 and 1995). In developing design values, the worst grain orientation (45°) is assumed.

3. The duration of load factor was reintroduced into the bearing equation. This factor reflects the ability of wood to carry greater loads for shorter periods of time.

Figure 12.5
**Compression perpendicular to grain procedure (sawn lumber, glulam)**

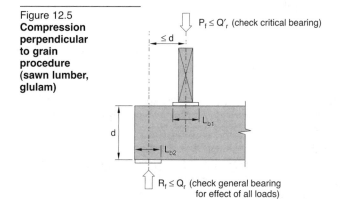

$P_f \leq Q'_r$ (check critical bearing)

$R_f \leq Q_r$ (check general bearing for effect of all loads)

In application of the critical bearing formula (Clause 5.5.7.3), there is room for interpretation. For example, research shows that the toothed connector plates used to join metal-plated wood trusses provide increased compression perpendicular to grain resistance at supports (Bulmanis et al, 1983).

The factored compressive resistance perpendicular to grain $Q_r$ is directly proportional to the bearing area except for cases where the bearing capacity may be increased by the bearing factor $K_B$. The bearing factor adjusts the tabulated specified strengths to recognize the fact that bearing resistance at locations of wood to wood or metal to wood bearing may be substantially higher than the tabulated values under certain special circumstances as defined in the Standard, due to the effect of wood fibres at the boundary of a bearing surface. In the critical bearing case, the bearing area may be calculated as an average of the top and bottom bearing surfaces (Clause 5.5.7.4).

### Clause 5.5.8 – Compressive Resistance at an Angle to Grain

The compressive resistance at an angle to grain, $N_r$, is calculated using the compressive resistance parallel to grain, $P_r$, the perpendicular to grain resistance, $Q_r$, and the Hankinson formula to derive, $N_r$, at any angle .

The factored compressive resistance parallel to grain, $P_r$, is calculated using the design equation for a simple compression member and assuming a slenderness factor $K_C = 1.0$. The expression for calculating the compressive resistance perpendicular to grain, $Q_r$, has been modified as described earlier.

**12**

**COM**

CSA Commentary

## Clause 5.5.9 – Tensile Resistance Parallel to Grain

The tensile resistance parallel to grain $T_r$ is calculated following the procedures used in the 1984 Standard. The performance factor = 0.9 has been selected based on reliability studies (Foschi, 1989). Specified tension strengths, like bending and compression strengths, apply to members with a width of approximately 290 mm. For narrower widths the specified strengths are increased by the size factor, $K_{Zt}$, and for wider members the specified strengths are decreased.

## Clause 5.5.10 – Resistance to Combined Bending and Axial Load

This clause provides interaction equations that must be satisfied when designing members subjected to combined axial and bending loads. These interaction equations are identical to those used in earlier Standards.

For members subjected to combined bending and axial compression the total factored bending moment, $M_f$, should include the additional moment generated by the so-called P-Δ effect. When a laterally deflected member is subjected to an axial factored compressive force, $P_f$, then the moment generated within the member due to the axial load is the P-Δ effect. This moment must be considered when calculating the total factored moment to be used in the interaction equation.

CSA O86 includes two cases where a different form of the interaction equation is permitted: Clauses 5.5.13 and A5.5.12. In both of these cases, the axial term is permitted to be squared to provide a more accurate solution as reported in Buchanan (1984), and Johns and Buchanan (1982). The first case applies to wood trusses, based on recent research results, and the second case applies to preserved wood foundations.

## Clause 5.5.12 – Preserved Wood Foundations

The provisions in Clause 5.5.12 that waived the use of the $K_T$ factor in the design of wood foundation studs have been deleted in the 2001 edition. The resulting design of wood foundation studs is consistent with design of other wood systems in the standard. Other changes to wood foundation design are given in Appendix A5.5.12.6: squared term in the interaction formula, and specific guidance in the footnote regarding application of the duration of load factor.

## Clause 5.5.13 – Sawn Lumber Design for Specific Truss Applications

Clause 5.5.13 was added in the 2001 edition to provide a more accurate methodology for the design of certain types of metal plate-connected wood trusses. Appendix A5.5.13 provides detailed commentary on this section.

# References

American Society for Testing and Materials (ASTM). 2000. Annual Book of Standards. Vol. 04.10 Wood. West Conshohocken, PA.

Barrett, J.D. and H. Griffin. 1989. Size Effects for Canadian 2-inch (38 mm) Dimension Lumber. Proceedings of CIB Meeting. Berlin, East Germany.

Barrett, J.D. and W. Lau. 1994. Canadian Lumber Properties. Canadian Wood Council, Ottawa, ON.

Bodig, J. and B. Jayne. 1982. Mechanics of Wood and Wood Composites. Van Nostrand Reinhold Company Inc. New York, NY.

Bohnhoff, D.R., R.C. Moody, S.P. Verrill and L.F. Shirek. 1991. Bending Properties of Reinforced and Unreinforced Spliced Nail-Laminated Posts. Res. Pap. FPL-RP-503. USDA Forest Service, Forest Products Laboratory, Madison, Wisconsin.

Buchanan, A.H. 1984. Strength Model and Design Methods for Bending and Axial Interaction in Timber Members. Ph.D. Thesis, Department of Civil Engineering, University of British Columbia.

Bulmanis, N.S., H.A. Latos, and F.J. Keenan. 1983. Improving the bearing strength of supports of light wood trusses. Canadian Journal of Civil Engineering, Vol. 10, pp. 306-312.

Forest Products Laboratory. 1999. Wood handbook– Wood as an Engineering Material. Gen Tech Report FPL-GTR-113. Madison, WI: US Department of Agriculture, Forest Service, Forest Products Laboratory. 463 p.

Forest Products Research Society (FPRS). 1989. In-Grade Testing of Structural Lumber. Proceedings of the ASTM Workshop on the North American In-Grade Testing Program. Forest Products Research Society. Madison, WI.

Foschi, R.O. et al. 1989. Reliability-Based Design of Wood Structures. Structural Research Series, Report No. 34, Department of Civil Engineering, University of British Columbia.

Jessome, A. 1977. Strength and related properties of woods grown in Canada. Forestry Technical Report 21. Eastern Forest Products Laboratory. Ottawa, ON (now Forintek Canada Corp., Vancouver, BC).

Johns, K.C. 1991. A Continuous Design Formula for Timber Columns. Canadian Journal of Civil Engineering, Vol. 18, 617-623.

Johns, K.C. and A.H. Buchanan. 1982. Strength of timber members in combined bending and axial loading. Boras, Sweden: International Union of Forest Research Organizations, Proceedings IUFRO Wood Engineering Group S5.02. 343-368.

Lam, F. 1987. Effect of Length on Tensile Strength of Lumber. Forintek Canada Corp. Vancouver, BC.

Lam, F. and P. Morris. 1991. Effect of Double-Density Incising on Bending Strength of Lumber. Forest Products Journal, Vol. 41, No.9, pp. 43-47.

Lau, W., J.D. Barrett and R.O. Foschi. 1988. Performance Factors for Lumber in Shear (Single-member, Short-term Strength). Reliability of Wood Structures Research Project. Report No. 9. Department of Civil Engineering, University of British Columbia.

Lum, C. 1995. Compression Perpendicular-to-Grain Design in CSA O86.1-94. Report to Forestry Canada, No. 14. Project No. 1510K018, Forintek Canada Corp., Vancouver, BC.

Lum, C. 1994. Rationalizing Compression Perpendicular-to-Grain Design. Report to Forestry Canada, No. 13. Project No. 1510K018, Forintek Canada Corp., Vancouver, BC.

Madsen, B. 1992. Structural Behaviour of Timber. Timber Engineering Ltd. North Vancouver, BC.

Madsen, B. and A.H. Buchanan. 1986. Size Effects in Timber Explained by a Modified Weakest Link Theory. Canadian Journal of Civil Engineering, 13:218-232.

Madsen, B. and T. Stinson. 1982. In-grade Testing of Timber Four or More Inches in Thickness. Department of Civil Engineering. University of British Columbia.

**12**

**COM**

CSA Commentary

Malhotra, S.K. and D.B. Van Dyer. 1978. Rational Approach to the Design of Built-Up Timber Columns. Wood Science, Vol. 9, No. 4.

Morris, P.I., J.J. Morrell and J.N.R. Ruddick. 1994. A review of incising as a means of improving treatment of sawnwood. International Research Group (IRG) on Wood Preservation. Document No. IRG/WP/94-40019. Stockholm, Sweden.

National Lumber Grades Authority (NLGAa). 2000. NLGA Standard Grading Rules for Canadian Lumber. National Lumber Grades Authority. Vancouver, BC.

National Lumber Grades Authority (NLGAb). 2000. SPS2 NLGA Special Product Standard For Machine Graded Lumber. Vancouver, BC.

National Lumber Grades Authority (NLGAc). 2000. SPS 1 NLGA Special Product Standard for Fingerjoined Structural Lumber. Vancouver, BC.

Neubauer, L.W. 1973. A Realistic and Continuous Wood Column Formula. Forest Products Journal, Vol. 23, No. 3, pp. 38-44.

Palka, L.C., J.D. Barrett, R.S. Smith and J.N.R. Ruddick. 1984. Effect of Incising and Pressure Preservative Treatments upon Selected Strength Properties of Commercial Dimension Lumber. Forintek Canada Corp. Project No. 2-50-68-584.

Palka, L.C., P.I. Morris and D.C. Walser. 1992. Bending Strength Properties of Incised and Preservative Treated Commercial 2x4 Western Lumber. Forintek Canada Corp., Vancouver, BC.

Smith, I. and G. Springer. 1993. Consideration of Gustaffson's Proposed Eurocode 5 Failure Criterion for Notched Timber Beams. Canadian Journal of Civil Engineering, Vol. 20, No. 6, Dec. 1993, pp 1030-1036.

Smith, I., L. Poulin, L.J. Hu, and Y.H. Chui. 1993. Characterisation of Critical Support Reactions for Lumber Joists with an End Notch on the Tension Face. Paper prepared for CSA O86. U. of New Brunswick, Fredericton, N.B.

# 12.5     Glulam

D. Himmelfarb[1] and G.A. Dring[2]

## Clause 6.1 – Scope

Glued-laminated timber (glulam) is a manufactured product. As such it retains some of the basic characteristics of the parent material from which it is created. This material is tested, graded and arranged to create a new material with characteristics that can be varied to suit the end purpose.

Lumber meeting special requirements for moisture content and surfacing tolerance is stiffness rated, visually graded and assembled with adhesive into timbers that are longer, wider and stronger than can be obtained from the parent material. The result may be straight or curved, with rectangular, square or I-shaped cross sections. Laminating stock of similar characteristics are assembled to produce members of uniform strengths for specific types of end uses. Glulam has been widely used for many years to provide reliable structures in Canada and in other countries.

Because the characteristics of the finished glulam member depend on quality of manufacture, the product must conform to CSA Standard O122, *Structural Glued-Laminated Timber,* and laminating plants must be qualified in accordance with CSA Standard O177, *Qualification Code for Manufacturers of Structural Glued-Laminated Timber.* Only material meeting the requirements of CSA O122 may be assigned the specified strengths given in Table 6.3 of CSA O86.

## Clause 6.2 – Materials

### Species
Glulam is widely available in both Douglas Fir-Larch or Spruce-Pine species groups. Douglas Fir-Larch is a brown to reddish colour with white sapwood. Spruce and lodgepole pine are light yellow brown to white in colour and jack pine is light orange brown to white.

Spruce-Pine glulam is somewhat lighter and easier to handle and work in the field but is more subject to damage from slings and rough handling than the harder and denser Douglas Fir-Larch.

Douglas Fir-Larch has a higher natural decay resistance than spruce or pine and is more suitable in moist service conditions. Under conditions requiring pressure treatment, Douglas Fir-Larch is typically chosen.

Hem-Fir/D. Fir-L has similar characteristics to Douglas Fir-Larch but is available only on special order. This species combination was developed during a period when Douglas fir was in short supply and is not likely to be widely available unless these conditions recur.

The standard depths for glulam vary in multiples of 38 mm for straight members and for curved members with radii greater than 10800 mm, or as small as 8400 mm if members have tangent ends.

[1] Timber West Engineering Ltd., Edmonton, Alberta

[2] G.A.Dring & Associates, Structural Wood Eng. Design & Inspection, Boissevain, Manitoba

**12**

**COM**

CSA Commentary

The standard depths vary in multiples of 19 mm for radii between 3800 and 10800 mm, or as small as 2800 mm if members have tangent ends. For radii smaller than these limits see Table A6.5.5 of CSA O86.

Tangent end means that a length of straight glulam is located between the cut end and the nearest tangent to the curve. For minimum radii this length must be at least 32 times the lamination thickness.

Tangent ends are commonly used in curved members, since the production of true curved ends requires special manufacturing techniques which increase the cost of the members. Often a curved outer shape is achieved by trimming the member to the desired radius during finishing.

### Clause 6.2.1 – Stress Grades

The various grades of glulam were developed to make the most efficient use of available material.

The bending grade 20f-E or 24f-E is intended for use in simple beams or where high reverse moments do not occur (i.e., short cantilever spans). The 20f-EX or 24f-EX grade is intended for use in continuous beams, wind columns and arches where large moments can occur in either direction.

Normally the 20f-E grade should be chosen for typical beam applications. The 24f-E grade requires more high grade material and may command a premium price, which is usually only justified for very large members where the high bending strength maintains practical sections, or architectural requirements demand smaller sizes.

The 16c-E and 12c-E column grades are both widely available and suitable for axial stresses.

The 18t-E grade is intended only for conditions where a high resistance to tension stress is required. Its greater content of high grade material will likely command a premium price.

### Clause 6.2.2 – Appearance Grades

In glulam the second level of grades, appearance grades, are sometimes mistakenly related to strength. In fact, since appearance grade refers only to surface finish, any stress grade can be obtained in any desired appearance grade.

The appearance grades are:

- Industrial Grade:
  This grade is intended for conditions where the timber is to be hidden from view or if appearance is of little importance. It receives no finishing other than planing and chamfering of the corners.

- Commercial Grade:
  This grade is intended for use where appearance is important but economy is also a consideration. It would normally be used in cottages, commercial establishments and small recreational buildings such as gymnasia and

swimming pools. This grade is planed, chamfered, all excess glue is removed and its surface is sanded.

- Quality Grade:
  This grade is intended for use in buildings such as homes, schools and churches where appearance is of prime importance. It is planed, chamfered, and all open defects, slivers and checks are filled to give a smooth flat surface, and then it receives a high quality sanding.

In all of the grades, the natural characteristics of the wood are permitted to show.

### Clause 6.3 – Specified Strengths

The specified strengths in bending, tension, and tension perpendicular to grain are calibrated to the values given in CSA O86-M84 (Working Stress Design). The decision to retain this calibration is based on the record of glulam structures over more than 40 years, and the lack of substantial new test data. Resistance to snow loading was used as the benchmark for calibration.

The specified strengths in longitudinal shear and compression parallel to grain are based on the results of reliability studies. (See the Commentary to Clauses 6.5.7 and 6.5.8).

The specified strengths in compression perpendicular to grain are, in general, based on the values used for sawn lumber. (See the Commentary to Clause 6.5.9).

### Clause 6.4 – Modification Factors

### Clause 6.4.1 – Load Duration Factor, $K_D$

The effect of the length of time that a load remains on a member has been shown to be similar for various sizes and species of wood. As such, the effect is considered to be a characteristic of the parent material, and the same duration of load factors were adopted for glulam as for sawn lumber.

### Clause 6.4.2 – Service Condition Factor, $K_S$

The effect of moisture is considered to be a characteristic of the parent material independent of both the laminating process and the waterproof glue that is used in the process. This clause then, is similar to that for sawn wood products.

Glulam is normally used in larger sections than sawn lumber. These sections contain frequent gluelines that are relatively impermeable to moisture. The effect of these factors in retarding moisture pick-up is recognized in Clause 6.4.2.2 by allowing the designer to choose a modification factor other than that given in Table 6.4.2 based on judgment of the moisture exposure and the specified protection methods. Caution should be exercised in coastal regions or microclimates where relative humidity may be high for prolonged periods.

**12**

**COM**

CSA Commentary

Untreated Douglas Fir-Larch glulam has demonstrated good performance under adverse moisture conditions, such as due to poor roof maintenance, provided that the moisture was not retained for long periods of time.

### Clause 6.4.3 – System Factor, $K_H$

The system factor is only rarely applicable to glulam structures as the members are normally spaced farther than 610 mm apart.

### Clause 6.4.4 – Treatment Factor, $K_T$

Preservative treatments are not considered to have a deleterious effect on glulam members provided that the members are not incised. The incising process causes a reduction in the moment of inertia of the cross-section, and therefore can reduce the strength and stiffness of glulam members. The magnitude of the incising effect depends on the incising depth, density, and tooth geometry used. Small beam sizes are more effected than large beam sizes.

In the case of fire-retardant treatments, the previous practice of multiplying the specified strength values by a factor of 0.90 has been discontinued. The current edition requires that the treatment factor for fire-retardant and other potentially strength-reducing chemicals be based on documented test results. It should be noted that the effect of fire-retardant treatment may vary, depending on the strength property tested and the treatment chemical used. For glulam members, the effect of the treatment on the strength of the end-joints within the laminations should also be considered.

The treatment of glulam members with water-borne chemicals after gluing is not permitted. Water-borne treatments, followed by subsequent re-drying, cause large changes to the moisture content of the wood. Dimensional changes occur in response to these changes in moisture content. If glulam members are treated with water-borne chemicals after gluing, these dimensional changes create both shear and tension perpendicular to grain stresses at the lamination boundaries, which may result in excessive checking or splitting of the member. Oil-borne treatments do not cause dimensional changes, and therefore this limitation does not apply to oil-borne chemical treatments.

### Clause 6.5 – Strength and Resistance

Glulam's strength is based to a considerable degree on the ability to place stronger laminations in areas where higher stresses will occur. This effect can be achieved most efficiently in beams, due to the high variation in stress intensity, provided that loading is in a plane perpendicular to the plane of the laminations.

In beams loaded parallel to the plane of the laminations, the beam lay-up has little or no effect but there is still a considerable increase in strength due to the effect of laminating different pieces of lumber together, and load sharing forced by the glue bond. Although the true strength is considered to be higher, a conservative value equal to that of No.2 grade lumber is applied where glulam is stressed in bending by forces acting parallel to the laminations.

Orientation of laminations has no effect in tension and compression members that are free of bending stresses.

### Clause 6.5.6.3 – Lateral Stability Conditions

Consideration of the effect of the lateral restraint of the compression face of glulam beams is separated into two parts. Where the beam is shallow (d/b < 2.5) or where the compression edge is restrained throughout its length by a rigid diaphragm, the unsupported length is considered to be zero.

A suitable rigid diaphragm is generally considered to be formed by 64 or 89 mm decking in which the pieces are edge-nailed to each other, or by a diaphragm-forming panel sheathing such as plywood, waferboard or strand-board (OSB). Boards and 38 mm decking are not edge-nailed and are not considered to provide an adequate diaphragm unless they have diaphragm-forming sheathing nailed to the deck either directly or through strapping.

Where rectangular glulam members are carrying both axial and bending loads, the lateral restraint conditions default to the same rules as are applied to sawn timber.

Where lateral restraint cannot be provided, a modification factor $K_L$ must be determined and applied to the moment resistance. The method used, the same as in previous standards, is based on the work of Hooley and Madsen (1964).

### Clause 6.5.6.5. Moment Resistance

### Clause 6.5.6.5.1
A significant change from previous editions of the standard is the introduction of a size factor for bending.

There is both experimental evidence and theoretical justification for the use of a size factor. Foschi (1993) concluded that the bending strength of glulam beams is controlled by the tensile strength of the end-joints used in the outer tension laminations. That is to say, their variability in strength, their number, and their location. Foschi conducted tests on both end-joints and beams manufactured by Canadian laminators. The end-joint test data demonstrated a coefficient of variation of approximately 20%. The value of the exponent in the size factor equation is directly related to this level of variability. The reference beam size, (i.e. the beam size resulting in a $K_{Zbg}$ value of 1.0), corresponds to the 130 mm x 610 mm x 9100 mm beam size tested.

The size factor given in the standard includes the effect of both length and width. The length of the tension zone relates to the number of end-joints present. The width term is in recognition of the fact that wider end-joints have somewhat lower strength because of the greater influence of manufacturing variability.

As noted in Clause 6.5.6.5.1, the length " L" to be used in the size factor equation, is the length of the beam segment from point of zero moment to point of zero moment. This defines the length of the tension zone. For simple span beams, "L" is equal to the beam length. For beams with one or more points of inflection (typically multi-span and cantilevered beams) there exists more than one beam segment. In these cases , "L" is less than the overall beam length.

**12**

**COM**

CSA Commentary

The moment resistance, as modified by $K_{Zbg}$, must be calculated for each beam segment and compared to the maximum factored moment within that segment.

The size factor, $K_{Zbg}$, is not to be applied cumulatively with the lateral stability factor, $K_L$. The size factor is associated with stresses on the tension side of the beam, whereas the lateral stability factor is associated with stresses on the compression side of the beam.

### Clause 6.5.6.5.2

One of the advantages of glulam is the ease with which it can be fabricated into curved shapes. The act of forming the wood to these shapes as well as the shapes themselves give rise to non-standard stress distributions, which must be considered in design. The first of these was quantified by Wilson (1939) and allows for the residual stresses induced when curving the individual laminations during fabrication. The modification factor $K_X$ allows for this effect.

### Clause 6.5.6.5.3

Instead of being curved during lamination, the surface of a beam may be sawn to provide a tapered or double tapered section for architectural or drainage purposes. This results in a member where the upper and lower surfaces are not parallel. The resulting reduction in bending capacity is accounted for in Clause 6.5.6.5.3, which applies to both straight and curved members.

### Clause 6.5.6.6  Radial Resistance

Another effect of curvature is the introduction of perpendicular to grain stress in service. Where bending moment tends to decrease curvature, the stresses are tension perpendicular to grain. The maximum values of these stresses are computed using methods described in Foschi (1970).

Barrett, Foschi and Fox (1975) showed that the resistance of the member decreased with an increase in the volume of the curved tapered section of the member. This resulted in the size factor that appears in the formula for resistance to tension perpendicular to grain. For those members, such as arches, where long curved sections may either have no tangent or where the moment reverses at some point in the curve, the effective volume should be taken between points where the moment is equal to 85% of its maximum value.

Although compression perpendicular to grain forces exist where the bending moment tends to increase the curvature, the capacity of wood in this direction is many times that for tension perpendicular to grain and the probability of an overstress is remote.

### Clause 6.5.7 – Shear Resistance

The resistance to horizontal shear of glulam members is based on the work of Foschi and Barrett (1975) who found that the resistance of Douglas fir varied depending on both the volume of the member and the loading pattern. For members less than 2.0 m$^3$ in volume a simplified method may be used. The simplified method in Clause 6.5.7.2.1 is the same as that used for sawn lumber, wherein a factored shear is calculated, neglecting loads within the depth of the member from the support, and compared to the factored resistance of the member. If the resistance is insufficient, either a greater section can be chosen to increase the resistance, or a second check can be made using the detailed method of Clause 6.5.7.3.

In the detailed method the total factored load on the beam is compared to the resistance calculated by a formula, which accounts for the influence of volume and loading pattern. In many cases, particularly for short heavily loaded beams, this method results in increased resistance. Large long-span beams however, will have lower resistance than would be given by the simpler formula. Based on the results of reliability studies (Foschi et al.,1989), the constant term in equation 6.5.7.3 has been revised from 0.60 to 0.48. This was done to achieve a reliability index $\beta$ equivalent to that used for bending properties.

As a result of the combined effects of volume and loading pattern, the principal of superposition does not apply when calculating the shear load co-efficient ($C_v$). For those conditions not given in Tables 6.5.7.4.A to F, the shear load coefficient must be calculated according to the method of Clause 6.5.7.4.

Prior to the 1994 edition of the Standard, the equation given in Clause 6.5.7.4(d)(ii) included adjustments for both impact and duration of load factors (normally applied to the design loads and specified strength values respectively). These adjustments resulted in the difference between the constant term in the equations for stationary and moving loads (i.e., 1.825 vs 2.310 in editions of the Standard prior to 1994). The current clause has all "hidden" adjustments removed and therefore the equations for stationary and moving loads are identical.

Table 6.5.7.4F was revised in 1994 to incorporate the above noted change and to include a number of vehicle live loads frequently used for bridge design.

Notching of glulam beams is limited to the ends of the members for bearing over a support. For beams notched at support locations, a notch factor ($K_N$) calculated in accordance with Clause 6.5.7.2.2 must be applied to the factored shear resistance. Clause 6.5.7.2.2 limits the depth of notching to 25% of the beam depth. For notches located at the tension side at supports, it is recommended that designers apply a more restrictive limit. The *National Design Specification for Wood Construction*, published by the American Forest and Paper Association, limits tension side notches at supports to 10% of the member depth.

**Clause 6.5.8 – Compressive Resistance Parallel To Grain**

The calculation of compressive resistance parallel to grain for glulam columns uses the same design approach as sawn lumber columns (5.5.6).

The design procedures are based on research into the behaviour of wood columns (Johns, 1991) and full-scale column tests conducted by Forintek Canada Corp. (Karacabeyli, 1992). The traditional "short", "intermediate" and "long" column equations are replaced by a single continuous column formula.

The slenderness factor $K_C$ which accounts for the effect of column slenderness on compressive resistance, is expressed in terms of a cubic Rankine-Gordon relationship. An empirical curve shape parameter (the constant

**12**

**COM**

CSA Commentary

term of 35 in the denominator) has been selected to make the new curve follow the Euler curve at high values of slenderness. In the calculation of the slenderness factor, the average MOE reported in Table 6.3 is reduced by a factor of 0.87 to a near minimum property value, $E_{05}$.

The values for specified strength parallel to grain ($f_c$) given in Table 6.3 are derived from the results of compression tests conducted on laterally restrained Spruce-Pine glulam columns (i.e. $K_C = 1.0$). The corresponding values for Douglas fir glulam are based on data relating the compressive strength of Douglas fir to Spruce-Pine lamstock.

Based on the results of reliability calculations the committee chose a $\phi$ value of 0.8 to provide a satisfactory level of reliability. As part of the reliability analysis, the effect of member volume on compressive strength was accounted for by means of a size factor, $K_{Zcg}$. This factor appears in the equations for both the factored compressive resistance and the slenderness factor, reflecting the fact that longer columns have lower compressive resistance due to the combined effect of buckling and reduced compressive strength.

The formula for $K_{Zcg}$ given in the standard has been calibrated to a reference column size of 127 mm by 152 mm by 2540 mm. This corresponds to the column size tested by Forintek to establish the specified strength in compression parallel to grain. In the absence of test data for columns of lesser volume, the upper limit for $K_{Zcg}$ has been changed from the value of 1.3 given in the 1994 edition of the Standard to the current value of 1.0.

Although the reliability calculations included a nominal load eccentricity (to account for out-of-straightness) the designer is required to consider bending moments due to eccentrically applied loads when sizing glulam columns. In this case, the provisions of Clause 6.5.12 apply.

### Clause 6.5.9 – Compressive Resistance Perpendicular To Grain (Bearing)

Design values assigned to sawn lumber have been adopted for use in Section 6 with one exception. The value for Spruce-Pine glulam is about 10% higher than that used for S-P-F sawn lumber. Specified strength values in compression perpendicular to grain for both glulam and sawn lumber are derived from an equation which relates the compressive stress at a deformation of 1 mm to oven-dry specific gravity (i.e. relative density). To be representative of the lumber grades used in glulam manufacture, a relative density value of 0.44 was chosen for Spruce-Pine glulam. This differs from the value of 0.42 used for S-P-F sawn lumber and thus the difference in design values. To reflect the similar calibration procedures used for sawn lumber a $\phi$ value of 0.8 has been chosen.

The equation given in Clause 6.5.9.2 is the same bearing resistance calculation found in previous versions of the standard. The intent of the clause is to limit deformation at points of bearing.

A "size factor" for bearing ($K_{Zcp}$) has been added to account for the effect of growth ring orientation on the specified strength in compression perpendicular to grain. Specified strength values given in Table 6.3 are based on a worst case orientation of 45°. Lumber loaded perpendicular to the wide faces (i.e. on flat) results in a random growth ring orientation and therefore higher bearing strength. In the case of glulam design, bearing stresses are usually applied perpendicular to the wide faces and $K_{Zcp}$ will generally be equal to 1.15. Vertically laminated beams would be an exception to this rule as the load is applied perpendicular to the narrow faces of the laminations.

Although bearing resistance in accordance with Clause 6.5.9.2 has traditionally been considered a serviceability limit state, duration of load adjustments have been retained to compensate for long term deformations which may occur as a result of the application of permanent loads.

Clause 6.5.9.3 requires the designer to limit the bearing stress resulting from loads applied near the supports to two-thirds of the value permitted for bearing on contact surfaces (Clause 6.5.9.2). Research has shown that such loads are transferred to the support by compression perpendicular to grain stresses as opposed to shear stresses (Lum, 1994). The intent of the clause is therefore to protect against the occurrence of: a) rolling shear failures and b) excessive deformation resulting from the application of compression perpendicular to grain stress over a large volume of wood (see Figure 12.5). The value of $f_{cp}$ corresponding to compression face bearing from Table 6.3 must be used with Clause 6.5.9.3 to be consistent with the species combinations specified in CSA O122.

### Clause 6.5.11 – Tensile Resistance Parallel To Grain

Tensile strength has been calibrated to resistance levels set in 1976. At that time there were indications that there was a volume effect in tension (i.e., reduced tension strength for members of greater volume). To compensate, the allowable stress for the gross section was decreased but that for the net section was retained because the volume was too small to warrant an additional reduction beyond the reduction for stress concentration. As the specified resistance for the gross section is less than that for net section, two checks are required for tensile resistance (at net and gross section).

### Connection Design With Glulam

Connection design is covered in the section on fastenings but following are some principles that either apply mainly to glulam or deserve emphasis.

Any problems with glulam are usually associated with connections. This is the point of interface with other members, materials or climates. Connections can create discontinuities in protective coating. They can also be more rigid and unyielding than glulam and conduct heat more readily than the glulam.

Deterioration should be avoided by good detailing of drainage, flashing and air barriers to either eliminate or limit contact with moisture-laden air.

The large size of glulam members makes shrinkage due to drying greater than the tolerances inherent in many connections. Designers should avoid connections with fastenings widely spaced perpendicular to the grain, especially where joined together with a more rigid steel plate, or a wood member stressed parallel to the grain. Instead, they should create a cluster of connections close together, and as near as possible to a bearing.

**12**

**COM**

CSA Commentary

Figure 12.6
**Arch peak
connection
with three sets
of shear plates
spaced
perpendicular
to grain**

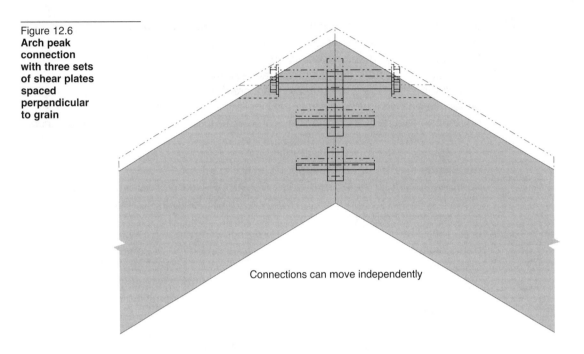

Figure 12.6
**Arch peak connection with three sets of shear plates spaced perpendicular to grain**

Connections can move independently

If connections must be spaced out perpendicular to the grain, separate them so that they may move independently or design them so that the wood can shrink without seriously impairing their function. An example of the first would be three sets of shear plates at the peak of an arch (Figure 12.6) and of the latter, a vertical tie-down bolt at a beam seat.

Most problems that have occurred with glulam members have been caused by poor connection fit. The most common is a beam suspended above its seat by the connectors. This condition is initiated by poorly fitting connections and compounded by shrinkage during drying. The resulting loads on the connections cause splitting of the ends of the beam. This problem can be remedied by shimming and/or grouting of the beam seat.

### Bolts and Lag Screws

Where connections are between different materials supplied by different sources, the bolt holes should be drilled on site. Where this cannot be done, the connections and the glulam should both come from the same supplier and tolerance for misalignment should be provided.

Lag screws are useful where inserted into deep members but they must be installed by turning with a wrench. Lubrication with a liquid soap or other non-petroleum lubricant, proper pilot drilling and power wrenches can aid installation.

Split rings and shear plates are most useful when used in pairs on opposite sides of members or in small groups. It is advisable to inspect these connections to ensure that the connectors were, in fact, installed. Specifications should require that shear plates be installed in the factory at the time of fabrication.

Split rings and shear plates are very useful where two cut faces are subject to shear such as arch peak connections, or a wind column to a beam. When the shear resistance is in the plane of shear, the cut faces can be held together with a simple tension tie rather than a complex connection resisting the shear eccentrically. Shear plates are also useful in rod bracings to take the component of the force in the plane of the glulam.

### Timber Rivets

Timber rivets, also known as glulam rivets, were developed more than 35 years ago. They have been the subject of continuous research and improvement with new applications being developed to the present.

Some general cautions with respect to timber rivets:

- If possible, each job should use only one length of timber rivet to avoid using the wrong length in a particular connection. Rivets must be driven with their wide face parallel to the grain. Care should be taken to ensure that the connection is properly placed, as a completed connection is extremely difficult to remove.

- When driving timber rivets, safety glasses should be worn to guard against particles of the galvanizing and because the hardened rivet can break if struck wrongly. Rivets should be seated firmly but not hammered flush, which might allow them to pull through the plate.

- The effort of driving timber rivets can be eased greatly by the use of pneumatic or electric drivers or rivetting guns.

Timber rivets have few fit-up problems, are very efficient and are readily field-inspected. They can be installed with an ordinary hammer and produce a connection with a neat textured patch instead of large bolt heads. They require little or no plant fabrication, thus lowering initial costs, and they greatly reduce site problems.

### Truss Plates

Truss plates are currently not widely used for glulam since their capacity is much below that of these large members. The development of new designs using these efficient connections may make them more feasible in the future. Nail-on plates are useful for attaching bracing or as tie down plates at columns.

### Nails

Nails are used in glulam construction to attach smaller members to the glulam and, as such, the capacity is limited by the side members.

**12**

**COM**

CSA Commentary

## References

American Forest and Paper Association, ANSI/AFPA NDS-1997 National Design Specification for Wood Construction.

Barrett, J.D., R.O. Foschi and S.P. Fox. 1975. Perpendicular-to-Grain Strength of Douglas Fir. Canadian Journal of Civil Engineering, Vol. 2, No. 1, pp. 50-57.

Foschi, R.O. et al. 1989. Reliability-Based design of Wood Structures. Structural Research series, Report No.34, University of British Columbia, Vancouver, B.C., pp 267-272.

Foschi, R.O. 1993. Design recommendations for Timber Bridges, Report No.1. Report to CSA-S6 Committee.

Foschi, R.O. and J.D. Barrett. 1975. Longitudinal Shear Strength of Douglas Fir. Canadian Journal of Civil Engineering, Vol. 3, No. 2, pp. 198-208.

Foschi, R.O. and S.P. Fox. 1970. Radial Stresses in Curved Timber Beams. Journal of the Structural Divison, Proceedings of American Society of Civil Engineers, Vol. 96, No. ST10.

Hooley, R.F. and B. Madsen. 1964. Lateral Stability of Glued Laminated Beams. Journal of the Structural Division, Proceedings of American Society of Civil Engineers, Vol. 90, No. ST3, pp. 201-218.

Johns, K.C. 1991. A Continuous Design Curve for Timber Columns. Canadian Journal of Civil Engineering. Vol. 18, pp. 617-623.

Karacabeyli, E. 1992. Non-Residential Applications for Glulam. Report to Forestry Canada, Forintek Canada Corp. Project No. 1510K014, Vancouver, BC.

Lum, C. 1994. Rationalizing Compression Perpendicular-To-Grain Design. Report to Forestry Canada, No. 13. Forintek Canada Corp. Project No. 1510K018, Vancouver, BC.

Wilson T.R.C. 1939. The Glued Laminated Wooden Arch. U.S. Department of Agriculture Technical Bulletin No. 691, pp. 118-119.

# 12.6 Structural Panels

C.K.A. Stieda[1] and Dominique Janssens[2]

### Clause 7.1 – Scope

The scope of this section has been broadened to include Construction Sheathing OSB (oriented strandboard) in addition to unsanded Douglas Fir Plywood, Canadian Softwood Plywood, and Design Rated OSB.

Information on the design of composite building components using either plywood or OSB structural panels in combination with lumber or glued-laminated timber is found in Section 8 of the standard.

### Clause 7.2 – Materials

CSA O86 provides strength and stiffness values for four qualities of structural panels: unsanded plywood manufactured in accordance with CSA Standard O121 *Douglas Fir Plywood* (DFP); unsanded plywood manufactured in accordance with CSA Standard O151 *Canadian Softwood Plywood* (CSP); Design Rated OSB manufactured in accordance with CSA Standard O452 *Design Rated OSB*; and additionally with this latest edition for Construction Sheathing OSB manufactured in accordance with CSA Standard O325 *Construction Sheathing*.

### Clause 7.2.1 – Plywood

The plywood product standards recognize two types of panel lay-ups: Standard Construction and Modified Construction. The standards also distinguish between sanded and unsanded grades. Panel thickness, species requirements, minimum number of plies and limits for the thickness of individual plies are prescribed for both sanded and unsanded grades. CSA O86 provides strength values only for unsanded grades of Standard Construction.

For Douglas Fir Plywood, CSA O121 requires that the faces and backs of a panel are Douglas fir. Veneer for inner plies can be any one of 18 listed species, including Douglas fir, western hemlock, and most spruce, pine and fir species in Canada.

Most species that are allowed as inner plies for DFP are also allowed by CSA O151 as face or back plies for CSP. Exceptions are western white pine, ponderosa pine and balsam fir, which are allowed in inner plies only. In addition, CSA O151 also permits the use of the following eastern Canadian species as face or back plies: tamarack, eastern white pine, red pine, eastern hemlock. Balsam poplar and trembling aspen, two hardwood species, are restricted to use as inner plies in CSP. Yellow cedar can be used as face, back or inner ply in CSP, but not in DFP.

Both standards define three grades of veneer (A, B and C). Grade A represents a high-quality surface and restricts any type of open defect in Douglas fir veneer to pin knots not more than 5 mm in diameter. There are also restrictions on the use of filler for splits, and the type of split and patches. These restrictions are relaxed for a B-grade veneer. C-grade veneer permits the presence of certain sizes of knots and knot-holes, which can be up to 50 mm in size measured across the grain.

[1] Consultant, former research scientist with Forintek Canada Corp., Vancouver, British Columbia

[2] Technical Director, Structural Board Association, Toronto, Ontario

**12**

**COM**

CSA Commentary

The strength values published in CSA O86 are for Sheathing Grade panels based on lay-ups containing only C-grade veneers. These strength values can also be used safely for plywood grades of higher quality.

Since the effectiveness of plywood can only be maintained through long-lasting bonding of veneers, CSA O121 and CSA O151 require that test specimens be subjected to moisture conditioning cycles, then tested in shear. If all or most of the shear failure takes place in the wood, the plywood meets the bond requirements.

The product standards require that panels be marked in a specific manner. All plywood panels conforming to either CSA O121 or CSA O151 are marked legibly and durably to designate the manufacturer, the bond type (EXTERIOR), the species (DFP) or (CSP), the standard (CSA O121 or CSA O151) and the grade. Unsanded plywood of Standard Construction will show the full name or an abbreviated grade mark (shown in Table 12.2).

**Table 12.2 Grade marking for standard constructions of unsanded plywood**

| Grade name | Abbreviated grade marks | |
| | CSA O121 | CSA O151 |
| | Douglas Fir Plywood (DFP) | Canadian Softwood Plywood (CSP) |
| Select Tight Face | SELECT TIGHT FACE | – |
| | SELECT TF | – |
| | SEL TF | – |
| Select | SELECT | SELECT |
| Sheathing | SHEATHING | SHEATHING |
| | SHG | SHG |

## Clause 7.2.2.1 – Design Rated OSB

The CSA O452 series of standards on design-rated OSB consists of three parts: Specifications (CSA O452.0), Test Methods (CSA O452.1) and Quality Assurance requirements (CSA O452.2). A commentary is given in a fourth part (CSA O452.3). The O452 series of standards pertain to OSB panels intended for use in engineered design applications.

Unlike CSA O121 and CSA O151, which are product standards that prescribe specific arrangements of veneers for each plywood thickness, CSA O452 is a performance standard for evaluating short term basic structural capacities of OSB.

CSA O452.0 Specifications describe the design rating process, which includes establishment of a mill-specific manufacturing specification and certification of the mill quality system by an independent third party. Initial qualification for a particular panel type requires that all design-rated OSB conforms to the property requirements for unsanded Grade O-2 panels given in CSA O437. CSA standard 0437, *OSB and Waferboard*, is a product standard that includes various grades. CSA O452 then outlines the establishment of control values for various physical and mechanical properties. Instead of specifying a particular set of manufacturing conditions, the standard establishes a classification system for the basic structural capacities of certain types of panels. Three types of design-rated OSB panels are recognized by the standard, i.e.: Type 1 (STANDARD), Type 2 (PLUS), and Type 3 (PROPRIETARY).

STANDARD (Type 1) design-rated OSB can be manufactured to any one of three rating grades for each of seven nominal thicknesses. Rating grades are designated as A,B and C with rating grade A having the largest specified bending capacity and bending stiffness for each nominal thickness category. Rules for assigning design ratings to qualified products based on qualification tests are given in CSA O452.

Similar to plywood manufacture, where different veneer lay-ups can be used for the same nominal panel thickness to provide different design values, OSB manufacture provides the opportunity to use raw material resources and equipment capability at an optimum level.

For plywood, producers have agreed to base strength values on the weakest species available to them, and the thickness and number of plies used in a particular panel lay-up. In contrast, a larger range of manufacturing variables can influence the structural properties of OSB. A performance type of standard therefore is a more appropriate standard for OSB.

CSA O86 also provides for design with PLUS (type 2) panels. For PLUS panels, one or more specific properties chosen by the manufacturer can be greater than those of a corresponding STANDARD panel. These properties have to be at least 10% greater than the corresponding properties in Table 7.3C of CSA O86. PLUS panels have to be marked with the percentage increase over the corresponding property value given in Table 7.3C.

Finally CSA O86 also recognizes PROPRIETARY panels, provided that the manufacture of these Type 3 design-rated OSB panels meets the quality control and certification requirements of CSA O452. These PROPRIETARY panels are not intended for general use, instead they are specifically designed to be used as part of an engineered building component, such as an I-beam. The design Standard therefore does not give strength values for these panels. Neither does the performance standard CSA O452 require that design properties for these panels be marked on the panel; instead the manufacturer is required to provide a Certificate of Conformance from an independent third-party certification organization for any panels marked as PROPRIETARY. Additional information on design-rated OSB may be found in CSA 0452.3, *Design Rated OSB: Commentary*.

## Clause 7.2.2.2 – Construction Sheathing OSB

This edition of the standard adds design values and procedures for OSB panels certified to meet the requirements of CSA Standard O325.0, *Construction Sheathing*. CSA O325.0 is a performance standard for wood-based panels such as plywood, OSB or waferboard, which are qualified for use in typical floor, roof and wall sheathing applications. This standard was first published in 1988 and has been referenced in Part 9 of the *National Building Code of Canada* (NBCC) since 1990. Panels are stamped with panel marks denoting the span rating and an appropriate end use, as opposed to a nominal thickness stamped on plywood or other OSB panels, such as those certified to CSA Standard O437. There is a

**12**

**COM**

CSA Commentary

relationship between a given panel mark and its corresponding predominant nominal thickness, although other thicknesses can be produced for a given panel mark, as explained in the Appendix of CSA O86. Besides the panel mark, the NBCC also requires that the grade stamp indicates that the panel adhesives are suitable for exterior exposure.

## Clause 7.3 – Specified Capacities

The strength and stiffness of structural panels are given in terms of capacities for specific panel thicknesses rather than in terms of unit stresses. This obviates the need for publishing section properties for panels and the designer is able to identify the panel thickness required. Strength and stiffness are given in terms of capacities per unit width of panel with the exception of planar shear which is given in MPa.

## Clause 7.3.1 – Plywood

The specified capacities for nominal plywood thicknesses of 7.5 to 20.5 mm are the same as those published in the 1994 issue of CSA O86. Added to these are capacities for DFP and CSP for panel thicknesses ranging from 22.5 to 31.5 mm. These thicker plywood panels provide more options for combinations of plies. As a consequence there is a greater range of strength and stiffness capacities for these thicker panels that are available to the designer.

The specified strength capacities for unsanded DFP and CSP are based on the results of in-grade tests of plywood by the Council of Forest Industries of British Columbia (Parasin, A.V. et al 1985; Smith, G.R. 1974). These tests represent the strength of over 1700 panels.

Tests were carried out to determine the ultimate strength of plywood in bending, tension, compression, shear-through-thickness, planar shear and bearing. Modulus of elasticity and modulus of rigidity were also determined for all properties, except for planar shear and bearing.

For each species, panel thickness, and orientation, the data were reduced to unit strengths for individual plies stressed in a direction parallel to the grain. These unit strengths were then combined for the various thicknesses, species and orientations of commercial panels.

Table 12.3
**Nominal
coefficients of
variation CV**

| Strength property | CV% |
|---|---|
| Modulus of Rupture, 3-, 4-plies 0° DFP | 25 |
| Modulus of Rupture, all other lay-ups and species | 20 |
| Tension, single ply | 40 |
| Tension, multiple plies | 30 |
| Compression | 20 |
| Shear-Through-Thickness | 15 |
| Planar Shear | 20 |

The fifth percentile exclusion values were calculated as a point estimate using the normal distribution assumption [$x_{05} = x_{mean} (1 - 1.645 CV)$], where $x_{mean}$ equals the mean of the observed strength values. Based on an examination of full data distributions from various sources, the following nominal coefficients of variation (CV), (shown in Table 12.3), were used for the calculation of the fifth percentile exclusion value $x_{05}$ of plies.

The resulting fifth percentile values were modified for load duration by a factor of 0.8 to establish the specified strengths.

The effect on strength of combining various species in one plywood lay-up was considered by Stieda (1974).

Studies by Wilson (1976) indicated that the strength of small, clear plywood bending specimens was 50 to 60% greater than that of large-size, in-grade bending specimens. Later studies by Bier (1984b) indicated that plywood manufactured from clear veneer differed little in strength regardless of specimen size. It must therefore be concluded that the size effect for bending strength observed by Wilson was primarily caused by the presence of defects in large-size panels.

Since the plywood strength values in the Standard are based on the results of tests with in-grade material, these strength values are characteristic for large specimen sizes. Wilson (1977) observed that 300 mm wide in-grade bending specimens were approximately 11% lower in strength than 900 mm wide specimens. This observation can probably be explained by the fact that grading rules for knots in plywood are not related to the size of the plywood. A knot with a given diameter therefore will have a greater effect on a narrow strip of plywood than on a full-width panel.

## Clause 7.3.2.1 – Design Rated OSB

Specified capacities for the strength and stiffness of STANDARD (Type 1) design-rated OSB are given in Table 7.3C. Nominal thicknesses range from 9.5 to 28.5 mm. For each nominal thickness, specified strength and stiffness values for three grades are given. Capacities are given for two panel directions. The 0° direction in Table 7.3C refers to the direction of the alignment of the strands in the face layers of a panel. For a 1220 × 2440 mm panel, this usually will be in the longer direction. The 90° orientation then refers to the direction of the shorter panel dimension.

For the 0° direction, specified strength capacities and stiffnesses for bending, axial tension and axial compression decrease from a maximum value for an A rated panel to a minimum for a C rated panel. Specified capacities for the 90° direction of Type 1 (STANDARD) OSB panels are the same for the three grades, as are the specified shear properties of these panels in both directions.

Tests have been carried out at Forintek to verify the certification process given in CSA O452 for design-rated OSB panels (Lucuik, 1992). The results of these tests were summarized by Karacabeyli (1993).

## Clause 7.3.2.4 – Construction Sheathing OSB

Specified capacities for the strength and stiffness of sheathing and single floor grades of Construction Sheathing OSB are given in Table 7.3D. Minimum nominal thicknesses range from 9.5 to 28.5 mm. For each nominal thickness, specified strength and stiffness capacities are given for two panel directions. The 0° direction in Table 7.3D refers to the direction of the alignment of the strands in the face layers or major axis of a panel. For a 1220 by 2440 mm panel, this usually will be in the longer dimension. The 90° orientation then refers to the direction of the shorter panel dimension, or minor axis.

Two different sets of values are given for panels marked for sheathing or single floor applications. Sheathing grade panels are often identified with a combination of roof and floor end uses. Shear-through thickness strengths and capacities are identical in the 0° and 90° directions.

Panels certified to CSA O325 were sampled from a national selection of Canadian OSB mills, non-destructively evaluated for bending stiffness at the Alberta Research Council and ranked to determine the lower half of the sample test panels. These identified samples were then tested by Forintek and ARC in accordance with accepted CSA and ASTM test methods for engineering strength and stiffness properties in bending, axial tension and compression, shear in-plane and through-thickness. Test results were then adjusted to climatic conditions of 20°C and 80% RH, followed by reliability normalization procedures.

These values were then compared to the OSB design values published in the U.S. by APA, the Engineered Wood Association (1995), after adjusting to limit states design format and appropriate moisture conditions. With the exception of axial stiffness values, the tabulated values in Table 7.3D can be traced back to the APA values. For axial stiffness values, the test data were found to be less than the values published by APA and as a result the tabulated numbers were equated to those found in Table 7.3C for equivalent thicknesses of Design Rated OSB. The Appendix to CSA O86 contains additional material about the panel marks and equivalent thicknesses for panels conforming to CSA O325.

Results of the test program are summarized in unpublished SBA reports by Forintek (Karacabeyli and Lum, 1998 and 1999) and the Alberta Research Council (Wasylciw, 1998)

## Clause 7.4 – Modification Factors

Strength and stiffness properties of structural panels, like those of all other wood-based building products, are affected by the length of time a load is applied to a structural component, moisture content and chemical treatment. Other factors may also apply, depending on the application.

## Clause 7.4.1 – Load Duration Factor, $K_D$

Experimental studies on the effect of constant loading on the bending strength of waferboard were carried out at Forintek (Palka et al, 1990) and on plywood at the US Forest Products Laboratory (Laufenberg et al, 1994). OSB has evolved from the waferboard product that was manufactured in the eighties and tested in the studies reported by Palka. In the absence of additional data on OSB, a conservative approach was to base duration of load factors on the waferboard research.

The results on waferboard were analyzed by Foschi (1993). He concluded that for dry conditions the same duration of load factors that are used for lumber and plywood (Table 4.3.1.2 of the Standard) could also be used for waferboard and OSB, with one exception.

The duration of load tests indicated that the waferboard specimens were sensitive to intermittent high temperatures or high humidity conditions (Palka, 1990), even though they were protected from direct exposure to moisture. Based on these results for waferboard, the Standard prescribes a reduced duration of load factor for permanent loading on design-rated OSB. For loads in excess of 50% of the OSB panel capacity and where the panels are subjected to intermittent high temperatures of up to 65°C and high humidity conditions, the duration of load factor for permanent loading has been set at 0.45, instead of the 0.65 used for other wood products.

To clarify how such climatic conditions affect OSB, the Structural Board Association commissioned a creep-rupture study, carried out at a number of research sites in North America (Tichy, 1997).

In a separate study conducted by Forintek for the SBA, it was also established that the load duration factors in CSA O86 were applicable to CSA O325 OSB panels in dry service conditions (Karacabeyli, 1998).

## Clause 7.4.2 – Service Condition Factor, $K_S$

The strength of wood is affected by moisture content. There have been a number of studies on the relationship between moisture content and strength of Douglas Fir Plywood using full-size specimens. The results of these studies have been compiled and analyzed by Palka (1982). In general, the strength of plywood increases as moisture content decreases from 30% to a maximum strength at about 10%. For compression strengths, the maximum occurs at very low moisture content, and for shear-through-thickness and stiffness, the maximum was observed at approximately 5% moisture content.

Detailed studies of the effect of wet service conditions on the strength and stiffness of OSB have not yet been carried out. The Standard's provisions therefore apply only to OSB used in dry service conditions.

Plywood strength capacities published in the Standard are based for the most part on strength tests carried out at 15% moisture content and the published values are intended for use at that moisture content. Field observations indicate that, for a given temperature and relative humidity, the equilibrium moisture content of plywood is lower than that of lumber. For example, at 20°C dry-bulb temperature and 80% relative humidity, the equilibrium moisture content of lumber will be about 16% whereas that of plywood will be about 14%.

For wet service conditions (moisture content greater than or equal to 30%) the Standard provides two reduction factors: 0.80 for specified strengths and 0.85 for specified stiffness and rigidity.

### Clause 7.4.3 – Treatment Factor, $K_T$

Plywood can be chemically treated to improve resistance to decay or to fire. Preservative treatment must be done by a pressure process, in accordance with CSA O80 standards.

There were a few early studies of the effect of preservative treatments on the strength of plywood. Wise (1952) reported that creosote does not weaken wood. Countryman (1957) studied Douglas Fir Plywood and concluded that treatment with regular Wolmann salts affected strength properties only slightly. Also, field experience with known preservative treatments appeared to be satisfactory. A treatment factor of $K_T = 1.0$ has therefore been assigned to preservative treated plywood.

On the other hand, some fire-retardant treatments used in North America have resulted in significant reductions in the strength of plywood, particularly in locations having elevated temperatures (LeVan, 1989). There have been studies of the strength-reducing effect of fire retardants (King, 1961), but with changes in the chemical composition of fire retardants, these studies are no longer applicable. CSA O86 requires that tests be carried out on the effects of fire retardants, or any other potentially strength-reducing chemicals used with structural panels, to determine an appropriate treatment factor. Standards on *Evaluating the Mechanical Properties of Fire-Retardant Treated Softwood Plywood Exposed to Elevated Temperatures* (ASTM D 5516), and for *Calculating Bending Strength Design Adjustment Factors for Fire-Retardant Treated Plywood Sheathing* (ASTM D 6305) have been developed by ASTM (See also the Commentary on Clause 5.4.3).

There have not yet been reported studies on the effects of chemical treatments on structural properties of OSB.

### Clause 7.4.4 – Stress Joint Factor, $X_J$

The stress-joint factor $X_J$ is intended for structural panels used in I-beams, box beams or stressed-skin panels. The factor therefore is referenced in Clause 8.3 of CSA O86. Only scarf-joints manufactured with resorcinol or phenol-resorcinol adhesives meeting the requirements of CSA O112.7 and having scarf slopes ranging from 1:12 to 1:4 are included in these provisions.

Since it is conceivable that a designer might want to use scarf-joined panels for uses other than I-beams, box-beams or stressed skin panels, Tables 7.4.4.1 and 7.4.4.2 are included in the general provisions of Chapter 7.

Research work at the University of New Brunswick developed information that led to the derivation of appropriate values for stress joint factors for glued OSB scarf and butt joints. Table 7.4.4.1 contains values for OSB scarf joints, and Table 7.4.4.2 contains values for OSB to OSB and OSB to lumber splice joints (Chui, 1997).

### Clause 7.4.5 Factor $K_F$ for Preserved Wood Foundations

The end use factor $K_F$ for preserved wood foundations applies only to bending strength, and to the planar shear resistance associated with bending. This factor calibrates to the field performance of plywood in wall systems of preserved wood foundations, and is restricted to plywood spans of not more than 815 mm. Normally, plywood panels are supported at spacings of not more than 410 mm for these uses. Provisions are included only for plywood, as this is currently not an application suitable for OSB.

### Clause 7.5 – Resistance of Structural Panels

Structural reliability of plywood was analyzed and reported by the Council of Forest Industries of British Columbia (Parasin, 1988), and of design-rated OSB by Foschi (1992), reported by the Structural Board Association. Reliability considerations were also included in the testing program on Construction Sheathing OSB (Karacabeyli, 1999).

The basic reliability approach described in 12.1 of this Commentary was used for panels. Distributions of strength and stiffness values were examined and it was determined that a normal distribution would best represent the available plywood data, whereas for OSB a two-parameter Weibull distribution was chosen.

The available plywood strength data had a coefficient of variability (CV) ranging from 15 to 20%, based on the full distribution. For OSB, the target CV was also about 15%.

The reliability index $\beta$ for a given loading condition is a function of the probability distribution for that load condition, the type of strength distribution for the structural panel, the coefficient of variation for that distribution and the resistance factor $\phi$.

The resistance factor $\phi$ chosen for structural panels in CSA O86 is 0.95 for all properties except one. The exception is plywood of 3- and 4-ply construction, where stressed in tension perpendicular to the orientation of the face grain. For this particular case, the Standard requires a $\phi$ of 0.6. The specified capacities for structural panels given in CSA O86, when multiplied by $\phi$, result in reliability indices of 2.6 to 2.8.

Foschi (1992) has shown that, while the reliability index $\beta$ for specific loading conditions for plywood is slightly different from design-rated OSB, the average of these reliability coefficients for residential, office and snow loads across Canada are the same.

Lum (1999) reported that previous analyses have shown that the use of the Vancouver snow load consistently provided a lower or more conservative estimate of the structural reliability, in his evaluation of the lower tail of the strength distribution with the limited test data available for construction sheathing OSB.

**12**

**COM**

CSA Commentary

**Stiffness**

Elastic properties of structural panels in the Standard are given in terms of stiffness (EI) for a cross section based on a 1 mm wide strip.

For plywood in bending, this stiffness is equal to the product of the modulus of elasticity (E) of the individual plies parallel to the fibre and the second moment of area (I) of all effective plies parallel to the fibre. The 1984 allowable stress version of CSA O86 (now withdrawn) gave the modulus of elasticity and the second moment of area for the various plywood thicknesses and constructions as separate values. The limit states design standard gives the bending stiffness in the two panel directions, for each plywood thickness and construction.

For OSB the bending stiffness is defined as the product of the applied bending moment and the corresponding panel radius (CSA, 1993).

Similarly the Standard provides a panel stiffness for axial loading, which consists of the product of modulus of elasticity and the effective cross-sectional area, A. For plywood, the effective cross-sectional area is based on the plies oriented in the same direction as the applied forces. For OSB, it is the total cross section.

For shear displacements due to shear-through-thickness stresses, the Standard provides a rigidity value $B_v$, which is calculated as the product of the modulus of rigidity for shear-through-thickness and the total thickness of the panel.

The units of the tabulated bending stiffness are N·mm$^2$/mm; for axial and shear-through-thickness stiffness, the units are N/mm.

Studies carried out at COFI (Parasin, 1983) indicate that for plywood the modulus of rigidity for planar shear is about 1 to 2% of that for shear-through-thickness. A rough estimate of this modulus of rigidity for plywood can be obtained by dividing the tabulated shear-through-thickness rigidity by the corresponding thickness and using 1% of the resulting modulus of rigidity.

No serviceability design equations for structural panels are provided in CSA O86. However, deflections and other deformations can be calculated by the usual engineering equations together with the mean stiffness values given in Tables 7.3A to D. For serviceability limit states (deflections and shear deformations) a resistance factor of 1.0 tends to result in a reliability index of about 2.0.

## Clause 7.5.1 – Stress Orientation

Both plywood and OSB are orthotropic materials, i.e. with different strength and stiffness properties in the two principal directions. For plywood, these differences are the result of placing veneers during the manufacture of the panels in such a way that the fibre orientation in at least one of the veneers is at right angles to that in an adjacent veneer. For OSB, the surface layer strands are aligned in the same direction as the panel, whereas inner layer strands are aligned at right angles or randomly.

As a result of this orientation of veneers or strands two distinct strength axes can be identified in these panels. The panel orientation with the greater unit stiffness and unit strength in bending has been designated as the major axis of the structural panel, that with the lesser stiffness and strength as the minor axis.

The panel strength values given in CSA O86 are for directions parallel and perpendicular to the major strength axis of the structural panels. The Standard does not provide information on the strength of panels in any other directions.

Kollmann (1951) reported results of plywood tensile strength tests at intermediate angles to the face plies. According to the results of these tests on birch plywood, the minimum strength occurred where the face grain orientation was approximately at 45° to the direction of the applied tensile stresses. These results were confirmed by Bier (1984a) for softwood plywood. Similar results would be expected if OSB were to be tested in directions at an angle to the major axis.

### Clause 7.5.4 – Planar Shear

For planar shear (or rolling shear, as it is sometimes called) the Standard provides strength values for two cases: bending and direct shear stress.

The first case results from transverse shear forces in a panel that is subject to bending (Stieda, 1983). For this case the Standard provides a transverse shear capacity $v_{pb}$ for each panel thickness in N/mm of panel width.

The second case arises where panels are subject to in-plane forces (where forces are transferred from one member to another, such as through a glued gusset plate). To determine the minimum plate size the designer needs to know the shear capacity $v_{pf}$ for such a gusset plate.

The critical plies for planar shear stresses are always oriented at 90 to the in-plane shear stresses. The unit strength in planar shear is dependent on the thickness of plies perpendicular to the stress. For plywood lay-ups where the ply thickness at the critical location can equal or exceed 4.2 mm, the unit strength is 0.55 MPa. If the lay-up only allows plies less than 4.2 mm in thickness, tests show that a higher planar shear strength can be used.

For plywood, the Standard provides separate planar shear strength values in the two principal directions, and the designer also has to consider the number of plies for the plywood thickness to be used. The specified planar shear strength for Douglas Fir Plywood (DFP) and Canadian Softwood Plywood (CSP) are identical, since most species that can be used in the core of a DFP panel are also permitted in the core of a CFP panel.

For design-rated OSB, each panel thickness has one in-plane shear capacity regardless of rating grade or panel orientation. For construction sheathing OSB, in-plane shear values vary slightly from one panel mark to another as well as for the two principal directions. OSB tables also have values for bending planar shear capacities.

### Clause 7.5.8 Compression Perpendicular to Grain

The tabulated values for compression perpendicular to grain were updated to reflect decisions made during the previous code cycle and were revised for both plywood and design rated OSB. (Tables 7.3A,B,C). No additional testing data were gathered for construction sheathing OSB, and subsequently the values for design rated OSB were adopted in Table 7.3D.

**12**

**COM**

CSA Commentary

# References

APA, the Engineered Wood Association. 1995. Design Capacities of APA Performance Rated Structural-Use Panels. Technical Note N375B.

American Society for Testing and Materials (ASTM).2000. Annual Book of Standards. Vol. 04.10 Wood. West Conshohocken, PA.

Bier, H. 1984a. Strength Properties of Pinus Radiata Plywood at Angles to Face Grain. New Zealand Journal of Forestry Science, 14(3):349-367.

Bier, H. 1984b. Pinus Radiata Plywood: Influence of Panel Width and Loading Method on Bending Properties. New Zealand Journal of Forestry Science. 14(3):400-403.

Canadian Standards Association. 1978. Canadian Softwood Plywood. CSA O151. Rexdale, ON.

Canadian Standards Association. 1978. Douglas Fir Plywood. CSA O121. Rexdale, ON.

Canadian Standards Association. 1993. Design Rated OSB. O452 Series. Rexdale, ON.

Chui, YH and Schneider, M. 1996. Performance of Glued Structural OSB Joints. University of New Brunswick, NSERC/SBA project progress report (Oct 1995 – May 1996)). Fredericton, NB.

Chui, YH and Schneider, M. 1997. Performance of Glued Structural OSB Joints. University of New Brunswick, NSERC/SBA project progress report (Oct 1996 – Mar 1997). Fredericton, NB.

Countryman, D. 1957. Effect on Plywood Strength of Preservative Treatment. Douglas-Fir Plywood Association Laboratory Report 74.

Foschi, R.O. 1993. Duration of Load Factors for OSB. Report prepared for the Structural Board Association. Toronto, ON.

Foschi, R.O. 1992. Reliability-Based Performance Factors for OSB. Report prepared for the Structural Board Association. Toronto, ON.

Karacabeyli, E, 1998, CSA-O325 OSB Design Values: Long Term Performance, Forintek Canada Corp. Report prepared for the Structural Board Association. Toronto, ON.

Karacabeyli, E. and W. Deacon. 1993. Summary of Short-Term Test Results for Waferboard and Oriented Strandboard. Report prepared for the Structural Board Association. Forintek Canada Corp. Vancouver, BC.

Karacabeyli, E. and Lum, C. 1999. CSA-O325 OSB Design Values: Strength and Stiffness Capacities (Final Report), Forintek Canada Corp. Confidential report prepared for the Structural Board Association. Toronto, ON.

King, E.G., Jr. and D.A. Matteson, Jr. 1961. Effect of Fire-Retardant Treatment on the Strength of Plywood. American Plywood Association Laboratory Report 90. Tacoma, WA.

Kollmann, F. 1951. Technologie des Holzes und der Holzwerkstoft. Springer Verlag, Berlin, p.692.

Laufenberg, T., L.C. Palka and J.D. McNatt. 1994. In Consolidation of Information of Strength and Creep of Oriented Strandboard (OSB) Panels. Report prepared for the Canadian Forest Service. Forintek Canada Corp. Vancouver, BC.

LeVan, S. and M. Collet. 1989. Choosing and Applying Fire-Retardant-Treated Plywood and Lumber for Roof Designs. US Forest Service, FPL General Technical Report, FPL-GTR-62.

Lucuik, M. 1992. Engineering Properties of OSB: Phase-2, Verification of Draft Industry Standard. Report prepared for the Structural Board Association. Forintek Canada Corp., Ottawa, ON

Lum, C. and Karacabeyli, E., 1998, CSA-O325 Design Values: Summary Report for the Engineering Properties Tests. Forintek Canada Corp. Report prepared for the Structural Board Association. Toronto, ON.

Lum, C. 1998. Planar and Through-the-thickness Shear tests on Oriented Strand Board (Data Report). Forintek Canada Corp. Report prepared for the Structural Board Association. Toronto, ON.

Palka, L.C. and B. Rovner. 1990. Long-Term Strength of Canadian Commercial Waferboard 5/8-inch Panels in Bending. Report prepared for Forestry Canada. Forintek Canada Corp. Vancouver, BC.

Palka, L.C. 1982. A Proposed Model of the Effect of Moisture Content on the Mechanical Properties of Sheathing-Grade Douglas-Fir Plywood in Structural Use of Woods in Adverse Environments. edited by R.W. Meyer and R.M. Kellogg, Van Nostraad, New York, pp. 100-116.

Parasin, A.V. 1983. Strength Properties of 9.5 mm 3-Ply and 15.5 mm 5-Ply Western White Spruce Sheathing Grade Plywood. Council of Forest Industries of British Columbia, Report 130. Vancouver, BC.

Parasin, A.V. and C.K.A. Stieda. 1985. Recommendations for Allowable Stresses for Canadian Softwood Plywood. Council of Forest Industries of British Columbia, Report 131. Vancouver, BC.

Parasin, A.V. 1988. Structural Reliability Analysis of Plywood. Council of Forest Industries of British Columbia, Report 144. Vancouver, BC.

Smith, G.R. 1974. The Derivation of Allowable Unit Stresses for Unsanded Grades of Douglas Fir Plywood. Council of Forest Industries of British Columbia, Report 105. Vancouver, BC.

Stieda, C.K.A. 1974. Bending Strength and Stiffness of Multiple Species Plywood. Proceedings CIB W18, Paper 3-4-2.

Stieda, C.K.A. 1983. Planar Shear Capacity of Plywood in Bending. Proceedings CIB W18, Paper 16-4-1.

Stieda, C.K.A. and A.V. Parasin. 1985. Recommendations for Allowable Stresses for Douglas Fir Plywood. Council of Forest Industries of British Columbia, Report 134. Vancouver, BC.

Tichy, R. 1997. Creep and Creep Rupture of OSB, TMI, Inc. Report prepared for the Structural Board Association. Toronto, ON.

Wasylciw, W. and Mirbach, C. 1998. SBA Mill Panel Testing: Phase I and Addendum. Alberta Research Council. Report prepared for the Structural Board Association. Toronto, ON.

Wasilciw, W. and Mirbach, C. 1998. SBA Mill Panel Testing: Phase 2. Alberta Research Council. Report prepared for the Structural Board Association. Toronto, ON.

Wilson, C.R. 1976. Comparison of the Size and Type of Specimen and Type of Test on Plywood Bending Strength and Stiffness. Proceedings CIB W18, Paper 6-4-2.

Wilson, C.R. and A.V. Parasin. 1977. Comparison of the Effect of Specimen Size on the Flexural Properties of Plywood Using the Pure Moment Test. Proceedings CIB W18, Paper 7-4-4.

Wise, L.E. and E.C. Jahn. 1952. Wood Chemistry, Vol. 1, 2nd Edition. American Chemical Society Monograph. Reinhold Publishing Corp. New York.

# 12.7 Composite Building Components

C.K.A. Stieda[1] and Dominique Janssens[2]

## Clause 8.1 – Scope

Lumber and panel materials can be joined together to form new building components. Such components can be constructed either by nailing or by gluing. This Clause covers only glued composite components that are not manufactured by a proprietary process. Proprietary structural wood products are covered by Clause 13 of this Standard.

Fabrication specifications should stipulate the method by which pressure should be applied to hold the lumber and panel material in place until the adhesive has set. This is often done by nailing. Any shear resistance that might be developed by nails used for nail-gluing cannot be considered in the design, since the glue joint is relatively rigid.

Information on the strength of nailed-only composite building components is available from such organizations as the Council of Forest Industries of British Columbia (COFI, 1981).

The Standard provides for design of two specific types of composite building components; glued panel web beams and stressed skin panels. Since the design equations are largely based on engineering mechanics, these equations can be applied equally to building components containing plywood or OSB webs or face skins. This edition of the standard was modified to allow the use of OSB as sheathing material in composite building components covered by this clause.

## Clause 8.2 – Materials

The components, which can be lumber and/or glulam, plywood and/or OSB must be glued using either resorcinol or a phenol-resorcinol resin meeting requirements set out in CSA O112.7. Casein glues, which were allowed for dry service conditions in previous standards, are no longer permitted because of the possibility of exposure to water during construction.

[1] Consultant, former research scientist with Forintek Canada Corp., Vancouver, British Columbia

[2] Technical Director, Structural Board Association, Toronto, Ontario

## Clause 8.3 – Stress-Joint Factor $X_J$

To provide continuity in standard size plywood or OSB panels used in composite components, it becomes necessary to end-join panels for constructions more than 3.05 m long, and often for panels more than 2.44 m long. However OSB panels can be specified in long lengths up to 7.3 m by special order.

Clause 8 has specific requirements for the construction of such end-joints between structural panels. Stress-joint factors ($X_J$) are provided to modify the strength capacities of panels. Since scarf-joints could occasionally be used for applications other than stressed-skin panels or box- and I-beams, the stress-joint factor is found in Clause 7 of the Standard.

**12**

**COM**

CSA Commentary

## Clause 8.5 – Plywood and OSB Web Beams

### Clause 8.5.1 – General

Beams having an I- or a box-section can readily be constructed with plywood or OSB and lumber. Where the panel meets the lumber, the panel must be glued to the lumber over its whole length. Such composite building components have been used successfully for many years in Canada and other countries.

More recently prefabricated wood I-joists have become common, consisting of a web (plywood, waferboard or most frequently oriented strandboard), flanges (lumber or laminated veneer lumber), and proprietary joints in the webs and between the web and flanges. These products are generally used in repetitive member applications, such as joists or rafters. These products are covered under Clause 13 of CSA O86, and not under Clause 8.

### Clause 8.5.2 – Effective Stiffness

The design of the panel box- or I-beam is based on the assumption that cross sections that are plane before bending remain that way as bending takes place, so that strains at any given cross section are directly proportional to their distance from the neutral axis of the beam. The design also assumes elastic behaviour, so that stresses at any given distance from the centroid of the cross section are proportional to the modulus of elasticity of the materials present at that location.

In the case of asymmetrical cross sections, the stiffnesses of the various parts of the composite can affect the location of the neutral axis.

Calculations of moment carrying capacity, shear capacity and deflection are simplified by the concept of effective stiffness of the beam $(EI)_e$. The effective stiffness is expressed in terms of the axial panel stiffness of $B_a$ given in Tables 7.3A to 7.3D of the Standard, and the flange stiffness. The flange stiffness, of course, can readily be calculated from the dimensions and the elastic properties of the lumber flanges.

### Clauses 8.5.3 to 8.5.5 – Bending and Shear Resistance

As in previous issues of CSA O86, the factored bending moment resistance is based on either the compression or tension capacity of the section.

Web shear-through-thickness and flange-web shear are calculated using the effective stiffness. In the case of flange-web shear, it is assumed that the strength of the glue bond between the lumber flange and the panel web exceeds that of the wood itself. Therefore, the limiting capacity is either the planar shear strength of the panel or the shear strength of the wood.

The resistance factor for composite beams is based on those resistance factors appropriate for the various materials used in the beams.

Where three or more beams meeting the requirements of the Standard are used parallel to each other and spaced not more than 610 mm apart to support the applied loads, a system factor $K_H$ of 1.10 applies (Case 1). It must be noted, however, that the system factor $K_H$ introduced in Clause 8.5 can only be used to modify the specified compressive and tensile strength of the lumber flanges of box- or I-beams.

## Clause 8.5.6 – Deflection

The relatively thin webs of plywood box- and I-beams generate shear stresses that are greater than those in lumber or glued laminated wood beams of rectangular cross section and comparable height. These stresses result in shear deformation of the web and, as a consequence, in deflection (Newlin, 1924; Cziesielski, 1965; Stieda, 1967; Booth, 1977). This shear deflection must be added to deflection caused by the applied bending moment.

Deflection due to bending moment is calculated in the usual manner using the effective stiffness $(EI)_e$ of the beam. Shear deflection is based on specified stiffness, rigidity and a shear coefficient $X_S$. This shear coefficient is given for a range of flange-depth to beam-depth ratios and web-thickness to beam-width ratios and is reproduced from Payne (1969).

Until 1984 the Standard only provided for calculation of shear deflections for three load cases. Since that time, the equation for this calculation has been generalized to include any conceivable load case for simply supported beams.

## Clause 8.5.7 – Lateral Stability of Panel Web Beams

The expressions for the bending resistance of composite beams given in CSA O86 are based on the assumption that the beam will only deflect in the plane defined by the applied loads. For certain cross-sectional dimensions, however, lateral deflections and rotations can take place.

In the case of box- and I-sections, the various combinations of web and flange dimensions make it impractical to reduce the results of the theory of elasticity to simple design rules. However, the Standard does provide some basic rules for the degree of lateral support required, depending on the ratios of moments of inertia about two axes.

If these rules are not applied, the designer must carry out a detailed analysis. Stieda (1968) has formulated a finite element solution for such an investigation. The lateral stiffness required for the analysis of lateral stability can be calculated readily for I- and box-beams. For plywood box sections, numerical values of the torsional rigidity for a range of cross-sectional dimensions have been calculated using a finite element approach (Stieda, 1969).

Approximations of the critical load can be obtained by considering the compression flange as a column. This approach has been suggested by COFI (Payne, 1969). Empirical rules were developed based on the relative stiffness about the two major principal axes for a symmetrical cross section.

**12**

**COM**

CSA Commentary

## Clause 8.6 – Stressed Skin Panels

### Clause 8.6.1 – General

Floor and roof constructions consisting of longitudinal ribs of lumber with plywood or OSB glued to the top and bottom of the lumber are referred to as stressed-skin panels. These panels usually are 1.22 m wide, the width of the panel sheet. Ribs commonly are of standard lumber sizes and can be spaced to suit the requirements of the design. Ribs and flanges form an integral part of the cross section.

The engineering theory of bending assumes that plane cross sections remain plane during bending. This is not the case with stressed-skin panels. During bending the panel between the ribs will deform. As a result, at some distance away from the ribs, the panel will be stressed less than over the longitudinal ribs. This phenomenon is known as shear lag and was investigated in detail by Foschi (1969b). At first, shear lag was considered in design by calculating an effective width as a function of plywood thickness. Foschi (1970) showed that the ratio of rib height to rib spacing, and rib height to panel length, had a far greater effect on shear lag than did plywood thickness. The 1976 edition of CSA O86 therefore introduced a geometry modification factor for bending.

More detailed methods of design of stressed-skin panels have also been proposed by Mazur (1968), Kuenzi (1976) and Smith (1979), and reviewed by Booth (1976).

Three of the modification factors given in Clause 8 are not material specific. They are geometric reductions for panel geometry, shear modification and shear section, and apply to plywood and OSB alike.

### Clause 8.6.2 – Effective Stiffness

Effective stiffness is calculated to account for asymmetry in the panel construction.

### Clauses 8.6.3.1 to 8.6.3.7 – Bending and Shear Resistance

To determine moment carrying capacity of a stressed-skin panel, three strengths have to be considered separately: that of the tension flange, the compression flange and the lumber web. The capacity is calculated in the usual manner and then multiplied by the geometry reduction factor $X_G$ to account for the effect of shear lag.

The compression flange also has to be checked to ensure that no buckling will take place. This phenomenon has been studied by Foschi (1969a). For a uniformly distributed load, the Appendix includes a buckling equation based on Foschi's work. Since there was no information available regarding a buckling coefficient for OSB, Clause 8.6.3.4 was rewritten per the provisions of the European STEP program, (Raadschelders,1995), to avoid buckling of the compression flange, while the existing clause was moved to the Appendix and restricted to plywood skins.

To determine the shear capacity of a stressed-skin panel, three locations have to be checked: the lumber at the neutral axis of the panel, the attachment of the flange to the lumber web on the compression side and on the tension side. In these calculations, corresponding (matched) values of $Q_w$, $B_a$ and y must be used. The factored shear resistance based on the shear strength of the lumber is calculated as in Clause 5.

When calculating the shear resistance of the glued attachment between panel and lumber, both the shear strength of the lumber and that of both panel flanges have to be considered together with their appropriate resistance factors. The values of $y_t$ or $y_c$ corresponding to the value of $B_a$ must be used. The Standard assumes that the bond between panel and lumber is adequate and that failure will occur in the wood or panel but not in the adhesive holding the two together.

As a result of shear lag, the actual shear at the lumber-panel interface is less than would be calculated using the engineering theory of bending (Foschi, 1969b). CSA O86 therefore allows an increase in the factored shear resistance.

This increase is a function of the contact area between lumber and panel and the clear spacing of the ribs. In the case of lumber shear strength at the rib-flange interface the shear modification factor has been set to 2. This last increase is not based on any consideration of joint geometry, but simply reflects the fact that shear stresses published for lumber are greatly reduced from test values to allow for possible checking at the neutral axis of lumber.

The strength modification factors for duration of load $K_D$, service conditions $K_S$ and chemical treatment $K_T$ are the same as those for plywood, OSB or lumber respectively.

Other applicable modification factors are the stress joint factor $X_J$, the panel geometry reduction factor $X_G$ and the shear modification factor $X_V$ discussed in Clause 8.5.

## Clause 8.6.3.8 – Deflection

Shear lag in stressed-skin panels reduces panel stiffness (Foschi, 1969a and b). The panel geometry reduction factor accounts for this effect, resulting in a small increase in the calculated deflection.

**12**

**COM**

CSA Commentary

# References

APA, the Engineered Wood Association. 1990. Design and Fabrication of Plywood Stressed-Skin Panels. Supplement 3, Plywood Design Specification (Revised 1996). Tacoma, WA.

Bach, L and Cheng, J. 1990. Full Scale Tests of OSB Faced Stressed Skin Panels. In proceedings 1990 Annual Conference and 1st Biennial Environmental Specialty Conference. Canadian Society for Civil Engineering.

Booth, L.G., C.B. Pierce and M.K. Surendranath. 1976. A Comparative Study of Three Methods of Designing Plywood Stressed Skin Panels. International Union of Forest Research Organizations, Wood Engineering Group. Proceedings of Meeting in Blokhus/Denmark; v.1.

Booth, L.G. 1977. Shear Deflections of Box and I-Beams Formed from Flanges and Webs with Different Bending and Shear Moduli. Journal of the Institute of Wood Science 7(6-42):37-44.

COFI. 1981. Nailed Plywood Beams. Council of Forest Industries of British Columbia. Vancouver, BC., pp. 8.

Cziesielski, E. 1965. Ermittlung des Schubwiderstandes Symmetrischer I-und Hohlkastenquerschnitte Sowie Symmetrischer und Unsymmetrischer Winkelquerschnitte. Bautechnik, 42(7):232-237.

Foschi, R.O. 1969a. Buckling of the Compressed Skin of a Plywood Stressed-Skin Panel with Longitudinal Stiffeners. Canadian Forestry Service, Publication No. 1265.

Foschi, R.O. 1969b. Stress Distribution in Plywood Stressed-Skin Panels with Longitudinal Stiffeners. Canadian Forestry Service, Publication No. 1261.

Foschi, R.O. 1970. Rolling Shear Failure of Plywood in Structural Components. FPL, Canadian Forestry Service, Information Report VP-X-67. Vancouver, BC.

Kuenzi, E.W. and J.J. Zahn. 1975. Stressed-Skin Panel Deflections and Stresses. USDA Forest Service, Research Paper FPL 251.

Mazur, S.J. 1967. Shear Strain Energy and Shear Deflection Constants. Studies in Structural Engineering, No. 1. Nova Scotia Technical College. Halifax, NS.

Newlin, J.A. and G.W. Trayer. 1924. Deflections of Beams with Special Reference to Shear Deformations. USFPL Report No. 1309. Reaffirmed March 1956.

Payne, R.J. Editor. 1969. Plywood Construction Manual. Council of Forest Industries of British Columbia. Vancouver, BC.

Raadschelders, J and Blass, H. 1995. Stressed Skin Panels, Lecture B10, STEP/Eurofortech An initiative under the EU Comett Programme.

Smith, I. 1979. Analysis of Plywood Stressed Skin Panels with Rigid or Semi-Rigid Connections. CIB W18, Paper No. 11-4-1.

Stieda, C.K.A. 1967. A Shear Stiffness Factor for Plywood Box Beams. Forest Products Laboratory (Canada). Information Report VP-X-31. Vancouver, BC.

Stieda, C.K.A. 1968. The Lateral Stability of Timber Beams and Arches. Doctoral Thesis, University of London.

Stieda, C.K.A. 1969. A Finite Element Solution for the Torsional Rigidity of Box Beams. Forestry Branch, Canada. Departmental Publication No. 1255.

# 12.8    Shearwalls and Diaphragms

Erol Karacabeyli[1] and Chun Ni[2]

### Clause 9.1 – Scope

Design procedures for shearwalls and diaphragms were first introduced into CSA O86 in 1989. Clause 9 addresses the two major contributors to lateral forces; i.e., high wind and seismic (earthquake) loads. In wood-frame structures, the lateral forces are transmitted through diaphragms such as roofs and floors to supports, provided generally by shear walls, and in turn to the lower stories and the foundation.

The most common design method for diaphragms is based on the assumption that horizontal bending moments are carried by the edge members and horizontal shear by the sheathing between the edge members. This design approach is sometimes referred to as the girder analogy (Applied Technology Council, 1981). Sheathing acts as the web to resist the shear in diaphragms, and the edge members act as the flanges to resist induced tension or compression forces.

For shearwalls, which may be considered to be deep vertical cantilever beams, the flanges are subjected to tension and compression while the webs resist the shear. It is important that all elements, including the flange members, connections at intermediate floors, and the connection to the foundation be detailed and sized for the induced forces.

### Clause 9.2 – Materials

Materials that can be used for the construction of diaphragms and shear walls are referenced to the other clauses of the Standard. For panel products, this includes all structural panel types referenced in Clause 7 for plywood (CSA O121 *Douglas Fir Plywood* and CSA O151 *Canadian Softwood Plywood*), and OSB (Types 1 and 2 Design Rated OSB in accordance with CSA Standard O452.0, and Construction Sheathing OSB in accordance with CSA Standard O325.0). In addition, it is acceptable to use OSB and waferboard meeting the requirements of CSA O437.0, and gypsum wallboard confirming to Type X (fire-rated) in ASTM Standard C36.

The majority of OSB panels produced in Canada are Construction Sheathing panels manufactured to CSA Standard O325. Construction Sheathing OSB panels were tested in shear walls at Forintek and at APA, the Engineered Wood Association. They were found to provide similar level of performance as nailed shearwalls sheathed with plywood panels in dry service conditions, and consequently are recognized in this edition of the Standard by allowing the use of CSA-O325 OSB in the nailed shearwalls or diaphragms Tables 9.5.1A and 9.5.2 (Karacabeyli and Ni, 1998; Rose, 1998; Skaggs, 1995). Since these tables are tabulated on the basis of minimum nominal panel thickness, an equivalency table (Table 9.5.3) is included to allow the designer to equate panel marks for Construction Sheathing OSB to tabulated thickness. Additional information can be found in the Commentary to Clause 7 and the Appendix A7.2.2.2 of the Standard.

[1] Manager, Engineering Forintek Canada Corp., Vancouver, British Columbia

[2] Research Scientist Forintek Canada Corp., Vancouver, British Columbia

**12**

**COM**

CSA Commentary

## Clause 9.3.2 - Resistance to Overturning

The lateral load capacities of shearwalls depend on the amount of uplift restraint available to resist the overturning moment. If hold-downs are used or factored dead loads are sufficient to prevent overturning, every nail along the perimeter of the panels contributes to the lateral capacity and the maximum lateral load capacities can be reached. However, if no hold-downs are used and factored dead loads are not sufficient to prevent overturning, nails along the bottom plate at the tension end take the uplift forces due to overturning moment, therefore the lateral load capacity of the shearwall is reduced. A new methodology, which accounts for the partial or full restraint against overturning in shearwall segments was developed and implemented in the 2001 edition of the Standard. Further details are given in the Commentary on Clause 9.4.5.

## Clause 9.3.3 - Shearwalls with Segments

In this edition, the lateral load capacity of a shearwall is determined as the sum of the lateral load capacities of full-height shearwall segments. This applies to shearwalls with openings, and also to shearwalls with different construction (dissimilar materials, thickness or nail spacing) along the length of the shear-walls. For shearwalls with openings, the lateral load capacities of the segments vary depending on whether hold-downs are applied around openings.

For shearwalls with openings, for simplicity, the lateral load capacities of sheathing above and below openings are ignored. For shearwalls with different construction along the length of the shearwalls, the uplift restraint contribution from adjacent shearwall segments is also ignored.

## Clause 9.3.4.2 - Two-Sided Shearwall

Tissel (1990) showed that where a shearwall is sheathed with the same type of wood-based panels on both sides, the load carrying capacity of the wall is approximately twice the capacity of a wall sheathed on only one side. To develop this capacity, sheathing should be installed with staggered panel joints; or, if sheathing is nailed to both sides of the wood members without staggered joints, it should be attached to 64 mm thick lumber (or two 38 by 89 members adequately fastened together).

Karacabeyli and Ceccotti (1996) tested shearwalls that were sheathed with: a) OSB on one side only; b) gypsum wallboard (GWB) on one side only; and c) OSB on one side and GWB on the other side. They concluded that up to a 30 mm horizontal displacement level, the load-displacement curves of a single-sided OSB sheathed wall (Case a) and single-sided GWB sheathed wall (Case b) could be superimposed to determine the lateral resistance of a Case c wall. They also reported that the combined OSB and GWB sheathed wall had a greater ultimate lateral load resistance with respect to the single-sided OSB sheathed wall, although the ductility was reduced.

The above test results suggested that the lateral load capacities were cumulative whether same or different sheathing was applied on both sides.

Summing shear capacities of wood-based panels and gypsum wallboard is recommended under the following conditions:

i) a lower force modification factor (R = 2) is adopted to account for the reduced ductility;

ii) application is limited to platform frame construction only; and

iii) percentage of storey shear force resisted by GWB walls is limited so that, in the first two stories of 3-4 storey buildings, the length of wood-based shear-walls will be similar compared to the R = 3 case where the contribution of gypsum wallboard walls is neglected.

Note: More discussion on R values can be found under section 9.5.4, Force Modification Factors (R).

### Clause 9.4.3 - Species Factor for Framing Material, $J_{sp}$

The species factor for framing material, $J_{sp}$, used in Clause 9.5.1 is based on tests by Stieda (1990) of the strength and stiffness of plywood-to-wood nailed joints. The joints tested were made from Douglas Fir-Larch, Hem-Fir, Spruce-Pine-Fir, and Western Cedar lumber, connected to Canadian Softwood Plywood sheathing of various thicknesses using common round wire nails. Specimens were either assembled dry and tested dry or assembled wet and tested wet. This work formed the basis for the species factor for framing material, $J_{sp}$, in this edition of the Standard. Based on the minimum ratios between the ultimate capacities, the following values are recommended for visually graded framing lumber: 1.0 for Douglas Fir-Larch, 0.90 for Hem-Fir, 0.80 for Spruce-Pine-Fir, and 0.70 for Northern species. Values are also given for glued-laminated timber and MSR (or MEL) lumber.

### Clause 9.4.4 - Strength Adjustment Factor for Unblocked Shearwalls, $J_{ub}$

In some applications such as exterior wall sheathing, the wood-based panels may be applied horizontally to the wall frame without blocking. Although design values were provided for unblocked diaphragms in previous editions of the Standard, design values were not available for unblocked shearwalls.

The load carrying capacity of an unblocked shearwall is a function of the nail spacing and framing spacing (Tissell, 1990). Typical failures observed in tests of unblocked walls were along the unblocked horizontal joint where the nails either withdrew from the framing members or pulled through the panel.

The specified shear strength for an unblocked shearwall can be expressed as a percentage of the specified shear strength of a reference blocked shearwall with 150 mm perimeter nail spacing and 610 mm stud spacing, based on the following observations from APA (Tissell, 1990) and Forintek (Ni et al, 2000) studies:

a) For both 406 mm and 610 mm stud spacing, the average capacity of unblocked shearwalls with 150 mm nail spacing at supported edges and 300 mm nail spacing at intermediate studs was approximately 80% of the average capacity of unblocked shearwalls with 150 mm nail spacing both at supported edges and at intermediate studs, and

b) For 100 mm nail spacing at supported edges and at intermediate studs, unblocked shearwalls with 406 mm stud spacing had approximately 150% of the capacities of unblocked shearwalls with 610 mm stud spacing. This indicated that the capacities of unblocked shearwalls were inversely related to stud spacing.

A strength adjustment factor for unblocked shearwalls, $J_{ub}$, was introduced in the 2001 edition based on the above findings.

## Clause 9.4.5 - Hold-down Effect Factor for Shearwall Segments, $J_{hd}$

Hold-downs are mechanical connections that transfer overturning forces from chords of shearwalls to lower-storey shearwalls or the foundation below. Where hold-downs are not used, overturning tension forces may be transferred through the sheathing on shearwalls; however, this reduces the shear capacity of the shearwall segment. The reduction in shear capacity is calculated using the $J_{hd}$ factor.

Earlier editions required all shearwalls to be designed and detailed to transfer forces around the openings, and did not provide any guidance on the design of shearwalls without hold-downs at openings. Framing and connections were required to transfer all forces around the openings. The design capacity of the shearwalls was assumed to be the sum of the capacities of all of the shearwall segments that did not contain openings. This design procedure is continued in the present edition, but a new procedure has been added for design of shearwalls without hold-downs around openings.

Sugiyama (1981) proposed an empirical equation to calculate the lateral load carrying capacity and the stiffness of shearwalls without hold-downs around openings. This empirical equation forms the basis of the perforated shearwall (shearwalls with openings) design method which appears in other codes and standards, such as the *Standard Building Code 1994, Revised Edition* (SBC, 1994) and the *Wood Frame Construction Manual for One- and Two-Family Dwellings – 1995 High Wind Edition* (WFCM, 1995). Although Sugiyama's empirical equation was found to predict conservatively the load carrying capacity of the shearwalls with openings (Johnson and Dolan, 1996), it did not provide a design procedure for calculating a clear load path for shearwalls between stories.

Forintek developed a mechanics-based design method for shearwalls with openings (Ni et al, 1998, Ni and Karacabeyli, 2000). This method accounts for the overturning restraints at the ends of shearwall segments, and provides a load path design procedure for shearwalls between stories. The method is compatible with the traditional engineering approach for calculating the load carrying capacities of shearwalls with openings. Comparison between the Forintek method and test results from Dolan and Heine (1997a, 1997b) showed that the method conservatively predicted the wall capacities.

## Clause 9.4.5.1 - Shearwall Segments with Hold-downs to Resist All Overturning Tension Forces

Shearwall segments with hold-down devices designed to resist the factored uplift forces at the bottom and at the top of the segments are assigned $J_{hd} = 1.0$. A steel threaded rod may be used as a hold-down device. For shearwall segments with factored dead loads that are sufficient to resist overturning, $J_{hd}$ is also unity.

## Clause 9.4.5.2 - Shearwall Segments without Hold-downs

The background information behind the mechanics-based approach for this clause was developed by Ni and Karacabeyli (2000). The uplift restraint force, P, is defined as the sum of: a) resultant force from upper storeys (negative if it is a net uplift force); and b) forces due to dead weight in that storey. An example is given in Figure 9.4.5.2.

Where factored dead loads are not sufficient to prevent overturning, and no hold-downs are used, anchorage on the bottom plate within 300 mm from both ends of the shearwall segment is required to transfer the uplift force to the top plate of the shearwall below or to the foundation. In this case $J_{hd}$ will be less than unity.

The factored shear resistance of the shearwall is determined for lateral loads in opposite directions.

## Clause 9.4.5.3 – Shearwall Segments with Hold-downs Only at the Bottom of the Segment

The top of a shearwall segment in the top storey in a building is not subject to overturning forces. For storeys below the top storey, overturning forces from the upper storeys can create uplift at the top of the segment. A hold-down is required at the top of the shearwall to resist this uplift; or the shearwall sheathing is required to transfer the tension force, thus reducing the shear capacity of the shearwall segment. In such cases, where a hold-down is used at the bottom but not at the top of the segment, $J_{hd}$ will be less than unity.

The factored shear resistance of the shearwall is determined for lateral loads in both directions.

## Clause 9.4.5.4 - Shearwall Segments With Hold-downs Only on One Side

For a shearwall segment with hold-downs only on the right or left side of the segment, the $J_{hd}$ factor is calculated based on the following:

a) Clause 9.4.5.1 if the segment is designed to resist all the uplift forces due to overturning; or
b) Clause 9.4.5.2 if the segment does not have a hold-down connection on the tension side of the segment; or

**12**

**COM**

CSA Commentary

c) Clause 9.4.5.3 if a hold-down is used only at the bottom of the tension side of a lower-storey segment, with uplift at the top of the segment.

The factored shear resistance of the shearwall is determined for lateral loads in opposite directions.

## Clause 9.4.5.5 - Conditions for Shearwall Segments With $J_{hd} < 1.0$

Additional requirements in this Clause are intended to limit the application of provisions in Clauses 9.4.5.2, 9.4.5.3 and 9.4.5.4 to the configurations of the full-size tests. As additional data become available, those limitations are expected to be reviewed in future editions.

## Clause 9.5.1 - Shear Resistance of Nailed Shearwalls

The specified shear strengths of shearwalls in CSA O86.1-94 were derived from allowable shear forces published for rated sheathing in the Uniform Building Code (UBC, ICBO 1997). The 1994 edition provided shearwall design values for a limited combination of panel thicknesses and nail diameters. In the current edition of CSA O86, the specified shear strengths have been expanded to cover a wider range of combinations of nail diameters and panel thicknesses.

The allowable shear force for a shearwall in the Uniform Building Code (UBC) is approximately equal to the average ultimate load carrying capacity of a tested shearwall divided by a load factor of 3. The UBC values were confirmed through shearwall tests conducted by APA (Adams, 1987; Tissell, 1990). Because the UBC allowable shear forces have remained unchanged since 1967, the 1997 UBC (ICBO, 1997) allowable shear forces were used as a basis to develop specified shear strengths for CSA O86.

Specified strengths $(V_{LSD})$ for shearwalls in CSA O86.1-94 were derived from UBC allowable stresses $(V_{ASD})$ using $V_{LSD} = 1.863 V_{ASD}$ This conversion was based on the premise that the results of wind design in 1990 should be the same as for the previous edition of the National Building Code of Canada.

Except for the few modifications noted below, the same approach was followed to derive the specified shear strength values for the 2001 edition of CSA O86.

To provide options that are more evenly distributed for horizontal diaphragms, the specified shear strength values for nail spacing at 64 mm at diaphragm boundaries were replaced with values for nail spacing at 75 mm. For this purpose, specified shear strength values for nail spacing at 75 mm at diaphragm boundaries are derived based on linear interpolation between values for nail spacings at 50 mm and 100 mm.

### Stud spacing
Under specific test conditions, panels have been observed to buckle locally under lateral loads. The buckling of wall panels is influenced by panel orientation and thickness, and stud spacing (Källsner, 1995). The effects of stud spacing on the performance of the shearwalls were evaluated by Tissell (1990). It was

found that the ultimate load carrying capacity of shearwalls with studs 406 mm on center was slightly greater than identically sheathed walls with studs spaced 610 mm on center. However, there was no clear difference for shearwalls sheathed with 15.5 mm with studs spaced at 406 mm and 610 mm on center. Based on these findings, the provisions in the UBC were adopted with a slight modification (note 4 in Table 9.5.1A).

## Power nails

The specified shear strength values in Tables 9.5.1A and 9.5.1B of CSA O86.1-94 were only applicable to horizontal diaphragms and shearwalls built with common nails. The Standard did not provide any guidance on how to assign a shear strength value to shearwalls using power nails with smaller diameters. Since the use of power nails has become the common practice in the field and is the preferred method to construct shearwalls, guidance for the use of power nails was needed in the Standard. Tests indicated that the shearwalls using 8d power nails were as strong as or stronger than those built with 8d common nails (Ficcadenti et al., 1997).

In the BOCA report NER-272 (1997), design properties for a broad range of power nails and sheathing thickness are given for both shearwalls and diaphragms. The design properties were factored in direct proportion to the joint (sheathing-to-framing) capacities.

A study conducted by Chui (1998) revealed a large variation in nail diameters among different proprietary brands of power-driven nails for the same length. Using yield theory (Whale et al, 1987), a reduction factor that is a function of nail diameter was obtained (Chui et al, 2000), and implemented in Appendix A9.5.1 of the 2001 edition.

## Framing members

Splitting of the bottom plate of the shear walls has been observed in tests as well as in structures subjected to earthquakes. Splitting of plates can be caused by the rotation of individual sheathing panels inducing uplift forces through the nails at one end of the panel and downward forces at the other end. With the upward forces from the nails and a downward force from the anchor bolt, the sill plate acts like a cantilever beam and cross-grain bending stresses are introduced.

Splitting can be prevented by use of large, sufficiently stiff plate washers. In the case of close nail spacing, to guard against the potential to split studs particularly where two panels meet, a note was added to the shearwalls and diaphragm tables in the 2001 edition that for 50 mm nail spacing (and also for 75 mm spacing for nails with 3.66 mm diameter), 64 mm or wider lumber (or two 38 mm framing members properly connected to transfer the factored shear force) are required to be used, with staggered panel joints.

**12**

**COM**

CSA Commentary

## Clause 9.5.2 - Shear Resistance of Nailed Diaphragms

Development of specified shear strengths for diaphragms followed the same approach as for shearwalls. In this edition, diaphragms with a panel thickness of 11 mm and 18.5 mm were included to provide more options in design.

## Clause 9.5.4 - Nailed Shearwalls Using Gypsum Wallboard

The lateral load resistance of gypsum wallboard was not recognized in the CSA O86.1-94. However, the Uniform Building Code (ICBO, 1997) allows the use of gypsum wallboard to resist lateral loads induced by earthquake or wind. Where gypsum wallboard is used in combination with nailed plywood shearwalls, a force modification factor, R, equal to 2 for the entire building was found to be appropriate for designing wood frame residential buildings (Ceccotti and Karacabeyli, 2000). Specified shear strength values for gypsum wallboard shearwalls with nail spacing 200 mm on the panel edges were introduced into the Standard based on this work. The specified shear strength values were increased by 25 and 50 percent for gypsum wallboard shearwalls with nail spacing 150 mm and 100 mm on the panel edges, respectively. The use of this design procedure for shearwalls of gypsum wallboard is restricted to Type X (fire rated) wallboard conforming to ASTM Standard C36, and also to platform frame construction where the height of a storey does not exceed 3.6 m.

### Force Modification Factors (R)

Most building codes contain force modification factors that account for the energy dissipating characteristics of the structural system under earthquake loads. In Part 4 of the National Building Code of Canada (NBCC), force modification factors or R factors are provided for various types of lateral force resisting systems in steel, concrete, masonry and timber. The R factors for timber structures were first implemented in the 1990 edition of NBCC and were initially selected so that designs of lateral force resisting systems would be consistent with the observed performance history.

A methodology for assessment of seismic design parameters for a wood-frame shearwall system was developed by Ceccotti and Karacabeyli (2000). This methodology consisted of a test program of shearwalls and the application of non-linear time history analyses to a 4-storey wood-frame building that was designed to resist the seismic requirements for Vancouver BC. Analyses included 28 selected earthquake accelerograms that were scaled upwards until a maximum Peak Ground Acceleration (PGA max) was reached where the shear wall reached a near collapse state. The 28 values of PGA max were found to be greater than the design PGA of 0.23 g, indicating the adequacy of the current design procedures (R = 3) for the particular shear walls investigated. These results were supported by the historical performance of platform-frame wood construction in past earthquakes (Rainer and Karacabeyli, 2000). The influence of gypsum wallboard on the behaviour of the shearwalls was also evaluated in the Cecotti and Karacabeyli study, resulting in the new force modification factor R = 2 for walls composed of a mixture of wood-based and gypsum panels. The effect of the flexible floor diaphragm model was considered separately and found to have a relatively small effect on the ultimate capacity of the building analyzed.

**Horizontal Distribution of Shear**

Traditionally light frame wood buildings have been designed by a hybrid approach where two assumptions have been made: a) diaphragms are modeled as flexible elements; and b) closely spaced walls on a line are considered to act as a unit (i.e. rigidly connected).

A different approach to assessing diaphragm rigidity was presented in NHERP (BSSC, 1997) as follows:

*"Diaphragms shall be defined as flexible for the purposes of distribution of story shear and torsional moment when the maximum lateral deformation of the diaphragm is more than two times the average story drift of the associated story determined by comparing the computed maximum in-plane deflection of the diaphragm itself under lateral load with the story drift of adjoining vertical-resisting elements under equivalent tributary lateral load. Other diaphragms shall be defined as rigid."*

The flexible diaphragm assumption simplifies the analysis and allows lateral forces to be distributed to the vertical elements (mainly shearwalls) of the lateral load resisting system by tributary area methods. In this case, the diaphragm can be visualized as a single-span beam supported on rigid supports. Another method of distributing loads to shearwalls uses a continuous beam analogy. Although rotation of the diaphragm may occur because lines of vertical elements have different stiffnesses, the diaphragm is not considered stiff enough to redistribute lateral forces through rotation, and consequently torsional effects are neglected.

Analytical methods relating to rigidity, rotation and torsional behaviour of diaphragms affect the way loads are assumed to be distributed to supporting elements, including shearwalls. For rigid diaphragms, the loads are assumed to be distributed according to the stiffness of the shearwalls. Torsional response of certain structures due to irregular stiffness at a given level can be very important.

In reality, most wood diaphragms behave as semi-rigid elements, neither fully flexible nor fully rigid. To account for this fact, SEAOC (1997) published an "Envelope Approach" that suggested two analyses be performed: the first analysis used the traditional flexible diaphragm assumptions, and the second analysis was based on rigid diaphragm assumptions. The lateral load-resisting system could then be designed for the most severe forces produced by either assumption. It is important to note, however, that because of the difficulties in determining the stiffness of the various elements, the use of rigid diaphragm assumptions may not be significantly better than the traditional flexible diaphragm assumptions.

**Distribution to Shearwall Segments**

After the applied loads are distributed to lines of shearwalls, the next step is to determine how to distribute the forces to shearwall segments within each line.

Some practitioners distribute lateral forces to the shearwall segments in

**12**

**COM**

CSA Commentary

proportion to the lengths of the wall segments, such that each segment carries the same unit load. This makes the assumption that wall segment stiffnesses are in proportion to the wall segments' lengths. This is a reasonable assumption for a line of shearwall segments with similar configuration and ductility as they will have the same displacements at a given load level.

On the other hand, for a line of shearwall segments with different configurations (for example with or without hold-downs, different unit load per nail due to sheathing, nail sizes or spacing), the assumption that stiffness is proportional to the wall length may not be valid. It would be preferred to determine the distribution of load to the wall segments on the basis of the stiffness of segments. Until the deflection equations become available for all types of shear walls and diaphragms, in this edition of the Standard, the distribution of lateral forces in a line of shearwall segments is determined in proportion to the strength of the segments. Research work is underway to develop stiffness of shearwalls so that this distribution can be made by using stiffnesses of the wall segments.

### Structures Without a Shearwall on one Side
Provisions for the lateral resistance of buildings that are open on one side were removed from the 1994 edition of the 2001 edition, pending development of more comprehensive shearwall design provisions. However, the information from the previous edition may be useful in some applications and is provided here for reference purposes. Designers may also wish to use more sophisticated models to assess torsional effects on these types of structures.

Structures meeting the limitations below may be designed without a shearwall of one storey on one side. The diaphragm supported by the remaining walls is required to be sheathed with diagonal boards or plywood, OSB, or waferboard. Otherwise, structures having one side without a shearwall may be permitted if it can be demonstrated that all lateral forces can be safely transferred to the ground and that no excessive deformations of the structure will occur as a result of torsion.

### Limitations on Length of Unsupported Edge and Depth-to-Width Ratio of Diaphragms
a) Except as given in (b) and (c), the depth of the diaphragm normal to the open side of the structure should not exceed the lesser of 7.5 m and two thirds of the diaphragm width.
b) For one storey wood-framed structures the depth normal to the open side should not exceed the lesser of 7.5 m and the diaphragm width.
c) Where calculations show that diaphragm deflections can be tolerated, the depth normal to the open side may be increased, and the depth-to-width ratio may be increased to:
   i)  1.5:1 for diaphragms using single layer diagonal sheathing; or,
   ii) 2:1 for diaphragms using nailed double layer diagonal sheathing or nailed plywood, OSB, or waferboard sheathing.

The intent of these provisions is to restrict building depth to 7.5 m for structures with one open side only in cases where lateral deflections were not calculated. If the lateral deflections are calculated and shown to be acceptable, and provided that the building conforms to specified aspect ratios, no restrictions on the absolute depth are intended.

### Deflections of Shearwalls and Diaphragms
The deflection of a shearwall may be calculated as:

$$d = \frac{2vH^3}{3EAb} + \frac{vH}{B_v} + 0.0025He_n + \frac{H}{b}d_a$$

where:

$A$ = area of boundary element cross section, mm²

$B_v$ = shear-through-thickness rigidity of sheathing, N/mm

$b$ = wall width, mm,

$d$ = deflection at the top of the wall, mm

$d_a$ = deflection due to anchorage details (rotation and slip at hold-down bolts)

$E$ = elastic modulus of boundary element (vertical member at shearwall boundary), N/mm²

$e_n$ = nail deformation, mm

$H$ = wall height, mm

$v$ = maximum shear due to factored design loads at the top of the wall, N/mm

This formula was developed based on engineering principles. Based on APA findings, it provides a reasonable estimate of shearwalls due to loads applied in the factored resistance shear range. The above formula is applicable to blocked wood-based panel shearwalls with hold-downs at both ends. No formula is available for unblocked shearwalls, shearwalls without hold-downs, and gypsum wallboard shearwalls.

The lateral deflection y of a simply supported diaphragm can be assessed by the following formula:

$$y = \frac{5vL^3}{96EAb} + \frac{vL}{4B_v} + 0.0006Le_n$$

where:

$A$ = area of flange cross section, mm²

$B_v$ = shear-through-thickness rigidity of sheathing, N/mm

$b$ = diaphragm width, mm,

**12**

**COM**

CSA Commentary

$E$ = elastic modulus of flange, N/mm$^2$

$e_n$ = nail deformation, mm

$L$ = diaphragm length, mm

$v$ = maximum shear due to factored design loads in the direction under consideration, N/mm

$y$ = lateral deflection at mid-span, mm

The first part of the equation represents the deflection due to bending, assuming that only the flanges carry the bending moment. The second part of the equation represents the shear deformation of the panels forming the web of the diaphragm. The third part represents the relative movement of panels due to the deformation of nails along panel boundaries. The formula is applicable to blocked diaphragms uniformly nailed throughout, but is not applicable to unblocked diaphragms.

# References

Adams, N.R. 1987. Plywood Shear Walls. APA Research Report 154. P.O. Box 11700, Tacoma, Washington.

Applied Technology Council, 1981. Guidelines for the Design of Horizontal Wood Diaphragms. Berkeley, CA

BOCA. 1997. Pneumatic or mechanically driven staples, nails, p-nails and allied fasteners for use in all types of building construction. Report No. NER-272, International Staple, Nail and tool Association. 435 North Michigan Avenue, Suite 1717, Chicago, Illinois.

BSSC. 1997. NEHRP recommended provisions for seismic regulations for new buildings and other structures, Part 1: Provisions (FEMA 302), 1997 edition. Building Seismic Safety Council, Washington, D.C.

Ceccotti, A. Karacabeyli, E. 2000. Dynamic Analysis of Nailed Wood-Frame Shear Walls. 12th World Conference of Earthquake Engineering. Auckland, New Zealand.

Chui, Y.H. 1998. Comparison of bending properties and joint performance made with hammer-driven and power-driven nails. Report prepared for Forintek Canada Corp, Wood Science and Technology Center, University of New Brunswick. Fredericton, NB, Canada.

Chui, Y.H., Ni, C., Karacabeyli, E. 2000. Derivation of modification factor for design capacities of diaphragms and shearwalls with non-standard nail sizes. Report prepared for CSA O86 committee. CSA, 1994. Engineering Design in Wood (Limit States Design). Canadian Standards Association. Toronto, ON.

Dolan, J.D., Heine, C.P. 1997a. Monotonic tests of wood-frame shear walls with various openings and base restraint configurations. VPI&SU Report No. TE-1997-001, Department of Wood Science and Forests Products, Virginia Polytechnic Institute and State University. Blacksburg, Virginia.

Dolan, J.D., Heine, C.P. 1997b. Sequential phased displacement cyclic tests of wood-frame shear walls with various openings and base restraint configurations. VPI&SU Report No. TE-1997-002, Department of Wood Science and Forests Products, Virginia Polytechnic Institute and State University. Blacksburg, VA.

Ficcadenti, S.J., Castle, T.A., Sandercock, D.A., Kazanjy, R.K., 1997. Laboratory testing to investigate pneumatically driven box nails for the edge nailing of 3/8" thick plywood shear walls. The 1997 SEAOC Convention, CA.

ICBO, 1997. Uniform Building Code, Volume 2. International Conference of Building Officials, 5360 Warkman Mill Road, Whittier. California.

Johnson, A.C., Dolan, J.D. 1996. Performance of long shear walls with openings. International Wood Engineerings Conference. New Orleans. Vol 2: p337-344.

Källsner, B., 1995. Racking strength of wall diaphragms – discussion of the Eurocode 5 approach. CIB-W18/28-102-2, International Council for Building Research Studies and Documentation Working Commission W18 – Timber Structures, Copenhagen, Denmark.

Karacabeyli, E., Ceccotti, A., 1997. Seismic force modification factors for the design of multi-story wood-frame platform construction. Wood Design Workshop, Department of Wood Science, University of British Columbia. Vancouver, BC.

Karacabeyli, E., Ceccotti, A. 1996. Test results on the lateral resistance of nailed shear walls. Proceedings of the International Wood Engineering Conference, Louisiana State University. Baton Rouge, LA.

Karacabeyli, E. Ni, C. 1998 CSA-O325 OSB Design Values: SBA Shear Wall Tests (Final Report). Prepared for Structural Board Association. Forintek Canada Corp. Vancouver, BC.

12

COM

CSA Commentary

Ni, C., Karacabeyli, E. Ceccotti, A. 1998. Design of shear walls with openings under lateral and vertical loads. International Conference on Timber Engineering, PTEC'99. Rotorua, New Zealand.

Ni, C., Karacabeyli, E. 2000. Effect of overturning restraint on performance of shear walls. World Timber Engineering Conference. Whistler, BC

Ni, C., Karacabeyli, E. Ceccotti, A. 2000. Lateral load capacities of horizontal sheathed unblocked shear walls. CIB-W18 paper.

Rainer, J.H., and E. Karacabeyli. 2000. Performance of Wood-frame building construction in earthquakes. Special Publication No.40. Forintek Canada Corp. Vancouver, BC.

Rose, J. 1998. Preliminary Testing of Wood Structural Panel Shear Walls Under Cyclic (Reversed) Loading. APA Research Report 158. APA Technical Services Division. Tacoma, WA.

SBC. 1994. Standard Building Code – Revised Edition, Southern Building Code Congress International. Birmingham, AL.

SEAOC, 1997. Seismic Design Manual. Volumes I and II. Structural Engineers Association of California. Sacramento, CA.

Skaggs, T. 1995. Summary of OSB Sheathed Shear Wall and Small Specimen Static Bending Tests, a Report to CSA O86 Panel Subcomittee, APA Report APA95-24. APA Technical Services Division. Tacoma, WA.

Stieda, A.K.A., 1990. The lateral resistance of nailed plywood-to-wood connections. Forintek Internal Report, Project No. 54-43D-216, Forintek Canada Corp. – West Laboratory, 2665 East Mall, Vancouver, BC.

Sugiyama, H. 1981. The evaluation of shear strength of plywood-sheathed walls with openings, Mokuzai Kogyo (Wood Industry), Vol.36, Vol.7.

Tissell, J.R., 1990. Structural panel shear walls. APA Research Report 154, P.O. Box 11700, Tacoma, WA.

Whale, L.R.J., Smith, I., Larsen, H.J., 1987. Design of nailed and bolted joints proposals for the revision of existing formulae in draft Eurocode 5 and the CIB code. Proceedings of CIB-W18A meeting, Dublin, Ireland.

WFCM. 1996. Wood Frame Construction Manual for One- and Two- Family Dwellings – SBC High Wind Edition. American Forest and Paper Association. Washington, D.C.

# 12.9 Fastenings

I.Smith[1] and P. Quenneville[2]

## Clause 10.1 – Scope

Clause 10 applies to split ring and shear plate connectors, bolts, drift pins, lag screws, timber rivets, truss plates, nails and spikes. Other types of fastenings, including many proprietary products, are used in wood design and construction. Designers can contact manufacturers of proprietary products for fastening design information for those products.

Failure modes for wood connections are complex and vary from connection to connection. Thus the Standard gives guidance on the number of fastenings required and the placement of individual fasteners in the connection.

In the 2001 edition of CSA O86, the following changes were made to Part 10:

- The values for fire-retardant treatment of fastenings have been deleted to be consistent with the remainder of the Standard,
- The end distance definition for timber connectors is no longer dependent on the number of shear planes,
- The embedment strength of concrete in wood-to-concrete bolted connections has been modified to reflect recent research results,
- The steel plate embedment strength in bolted and lag screw connections has been updated to be consistent with S16,
- A minimum penetration requirement was added to lag screws,
- The "timber rivet" designation is now used for glulam rivets, and
- The withdrawal resistance of nails has been updated in light of recent studies.

## Clause 10.2 – General Requirements

## Clause 10.2.1 – All Fastenings

## Clause 10.2.1.4 – Shear Depth

[1] Professor, Faculty of Forestry and Environmental Management, Frederickton, New Brunswick

[2] Associate Professor, Civil Engineering Department, Royal Military College of Canada Kingston, Ontario

Where a wood member is loaded at an angle to grain, the load results in a shear force component causing tension stress perpendicular to the grain of the member. Where the load is imposed by a fastening group, this stress is presumed to be greatest at the extreme boundary of the fastening group. Clause 10.2.1.4 therefore defines an "effective shear depth" $d_e$ that must be used instead of the total member depth d when checking for member shear resistance.

## Clause 10.2.1.5 – Service Condition Factor, $K_{SF}$

Table 10.2.1.5 gives the moisture service condition factor $K_{SF}$ for fastenings. The Table identifies two aspects of connection resistance that may be affected

**12**

**COM**

CSA Commentary

by moisture service conditions. First, wood tends to be weaker when wet, so wood connections used in wet service conditions generally have less resistance than those used in dry service conditions.

Second, where fasteners are installed in wood which will dry in service, or where the moisture conditions change seasonally in service, shrinkage damage may occur. The effects of this shrinkage damage are accounted for in the design, by the service condition factor.

The service condition factors for timber rivets were modified in the 1994 edition of the Standard, reflecting data collected in the Forintek timber rivet research project (Karacabeyli et. al., 1995). The $K_{SF}$ value for rivets installed in seasoned material and used in wet service conditions was reduced to 0.8 from 0.85, and values for rivet connections assembled in unseasoned material were added. Rivet withdrawal in wet service conditions should be avoided.

### Clause 10.2.1.6 – Load Duration Effects

The cumulative time that a load is applied to a wood joint affects both the ultimate strength and the joint deformation (slip). Traditionally the ultimate strength of wood joints is assumed to have the same duration of load behaviour as that of wood itself, and the fastener parts (usually steel) are assumed to have no duration of load effects.

Most load duration research has been done on sawn lumber. To be consistent with sawn lumber and other wood-based materials, the same load duration definitions and factors given in Table 4.3.2.2 of the Standard are applied to fastening design.

Load duration factors are unchanged from the 1989 edition of the Standard. In the 1989 edition there were major changes to the Fastenings section, as well as other sections, reflecting new load duration data. These changes are explained in the 1990 commentary (Turnbull, 1990).

### Clause 10.2.1.7 – Treatment Factor, $K_T$

Some chemical fire retardants have been shown to cause wood strength loss, thus affecting the ductility and strength of fastenings in wood-based materials. CSA O86 requires that tests be carried out on the effects of fire retardants, or any potentially strength-reducing chemicals used with wood-based materials to determine an appropriate treatment factor. Additional information on the effects of fire-retardant treatment can be found in Clauses 5.4.3., 6.4.4 and 7.4.3 of the Standard and the corresponding Commentary sections.

### Clause 10.2.2.3.4 – Groups of Fastenings

The total strength of a joint with a small group of fastenings has been assumed traditionally to be the product of the strength of a single fastener times the number of fasteners. This assumption of equal loads on each fastener was the basis of early design standards.

However, tests on large, heavily loaded joints have shown that each joint can have a total load capacity significantly lower than the strength of one fastener times the number of fasteners. A theoretical analysis by Lantos (1969), based on assumed elasticity of timbers end-connected by wood or steel side members under tension, showed that the end fasteners in each row could carry above-average loads whereas the middle fasteners could carry below-average loads. This was confirmed by researchers such as Cramer (1968), and empirically by comparison of calculated values with the results of tests.

Tables 10.2.2.3.4A and B list factors to be used for determining the resistance of joints made with two or more shear plates, split rings or lag screws. The group effect for bolts and timber rivets are incorporated in the design equations. Relatively ductile joints made with truss plates, nails or spikes are considered less vulnerable to this effect. For these fastenings, group factors are not applied.

## Clause 10.2.2.4 – Washers

Clause 10.2.2.4 requires washers between wood and the head (or nut) of a bolt, or lag screw, unless a steel strap or plate is used. Standard cut washers are sufficient with bolts and lag screws used alone for lateral loads, but when used with split ring or shear plate connectors they require bigger, thicker washers to draw the connectors into full wood contact. Otherwise the standard washer may deform, leading to non-uniform bearing stresses and crushing of the wood.

Table 10.2.2.4.1 specifies the minimum special washer sizes to be used with various applications. Malleable iron washers, ogee washers or steel plate washers are recommended for special applications.

## Clause 10.2.2.5 – Net Section

In adjacent rows, bolt holes and connector grooves must be spaced so that stress concentrations in the wood do not further reduce member strength, or else the holes or grooves must be considered to occur at the same net section.

Clause 10.2.2.5 defines how far fastenings in adjacent rows must be set apart in order not to be considered at the same critical section.

## Clause 10.3 – Split Ring and Shear Plate Connectors

## Clause 10.3.1 – General

Shear plates and split rings are circular steel connectors which are installed in specially cut wood grooves to provide a large diameter connection near the wood surface. Design data apply to those connectors dimensioned as in Table 10.3.1.A and placed in grooves accurately machined in the wood as dimensioned in Table 10.3.1.B.

Split ring connectors (2-1/2" or 4" diameter) are manufactured from hot-rolled carbon steel SAE 1010, meeting the requirements of the Society of Automotive Engineers Handbook. Shear plate connectors may be either pressed

**12**

**COM**

CSA Commentary

steel or malleable iron. The steel shear plates (2-5/8" diameter) are manufactured from hot-rolled carbon steel SAE 1010. The manufacturing reference for malleable iron shear plates (4" diameter) is to ASTM Standard A47, Grade 32510 or ASTM Standard A47M, Grade 22010.

## Clause 10.3.3 – Distance Factors

The location and relative position of connectors in members affects connector resistance. Factors which must be considered in the geometry of a joint made with split ring or shear plate connectors are:

- the angle of load to grain,
- the thickness of the members to be joined,
- whether one or two faces of the member is to receive connectors,
- the distance between the connector and the edge of the wood member measured perpendicular to the grain,
- the distance between the connector and the end of the wood member measured parallel to the grain,
- the centre-to-centre spacing of connectors,
- whether the connector is in side grain or end grain, and
- the group effect as discussed in Clause 10.2.2.3.4

Scholten (1944) established the original spacing requirements for shear plates and split rings. Erki and Huggins (1983) conducted tests on shear plates in glulam billets with steel side plates. These tests did not completely confirm the Lantos (1969) analytical models used to develop the group modification factor as given in Tables 10.2.2.3.4. To compensate for these results, the required loaded end distance for members less than 130 mm thick was increased in 1984 to reduce the probability of tensile failure in multiple-connector joints. A further modification in 1989 specified that the increased end distance applied to 130 mm or thicker members with 2 shear planes, or 65 mm or thicker members with one shear plane in a joint.

In the 1995 edition, Table 10.3.3B was modified to reflect research on end distance effects in compression (Quenneville, Charron and Van Dalen, 1993). This research indicated that the end distance did not affect the connection capacity for members loaded in compression. Based on this research, the $J_C$ factor in Table 10.3.3B is always 1.0 for members loaded in compression. Minimum end distances for members in compression are 70 mm for 2-1/2″ split rings or 2-5/8″ shear plates and 90 mm for 4″ split rings or shear plates. For thinner members, the end distances increase to 105 and 135 mm respectively. The research indicates that these end distances are conservative for the thinner members.

In the 2001 edition of CSA O86, the requirements for end distance in tension were modified in light of more recent research (Quenneville and Sauvé, 1998) that showed the strength of these connectors in members loaded in tension parallel-to-grain, when related to the end distance, was not further influenced by the number of shear planes. The end distance requirements are now as they were in the 1984 edition of O86.

### Clause 10.3.6 – Lateral Resistance

Scholten (1944) tested split ring and shear plate connectors in several species using three-member joints. His data showed that strengths parallel and perpendicular to grain were proportional to the applicable bearing strength of the wood. To make use of this data, mean regression lines were developed for each loading mode and each connector type and size.

In the 1984 limit states design edition of CSA O86, parallel to grain connector capacities were determined by calculating lower fifth percentile values from the mean ultimate strength regressions, then dividing by 1.6 to adjust to the 1984 "normal load duration" strengths (Anonymous, 1982). In 1989, the duration of load adjustment was changed (Turnbull, 1990).

Perpendicular to grain compressive connector resistance values were calibrated directly from the Douglas fir values given in earlier working stress standards (Anonymous, 1982). These resistance values are based on proportional limit strengths rather than ultimate strengths. The calibrated connector values were then adjusted for other species in proportion to perpendicular to grain compressive strength ratios.

Table 10.3.6C gives maximum values for shear plates in case the joint is limited by the shear strength of the bolt.

### Clause 10.4 – Bolts

### Clause 10.4.1 – General

In the pre-1994 editions of the Standard, resistance values for bolts were presented in tabular format. In the 1989 edition of CSA O86, the tables were developed using the fastening yield equations that were adopted as the basis for bolt design, and were presented in the Appendix. For many design cases, using the tables rather than the formulae resulted in conservative designs. In the 1994 edition, the formulae were presented in Clause 10.4 and the tables were eliminated. A more comprehensive set of bolt design tables is published in Chapter 7.

Design information in the Standard is limited to bolts conforming to the requirements of ASTM Standard A307. Threaded rods meeting the requirements of ASTM A307 may be designed and used in lieu of bolts. Use of fasteners with higher yield strengths, however, may result in more brittle failure modes and thus less conservative designs.

Bolt holes are usually pre-drilled in wood before the joints are assembled. This sequence requires some over sizing of holes to allow insertion of the bolts without damage. The upper limit on hole oversize prevents excessive slip, and the lower limit prevents assembly damage.

## Clause 10.4.2. – Member Thickness

With the change in format, the actual thicknesses of the connection members are used in the formulae in Clause 10.4.4.2. The member thickness needs to be defined when calculating the group effect $J_G$ in Clause 10.4.4.1. In this case, the member thickness is defined as the thickness of the thinnest wood member in the connection.

Clause 10.4.2.3 covering wood to concrete connections, first added to the 1994 edition of the Standard, applies to the design of sill plate and anchor bolt connections. Recent studies on wood-to-concrete bolted connections loaded parallel-to-grain (Stieda et al., 1997) and on connections loaded perpendicular-to-grain (Quenneville and Mohammad, 1999), showed that it was conservative to use an embedment strength of 125 MPa for concrete and an assumed thickness equal to the penetration of the anchor bolt. This new design method is independent of a check on concrete or masonry capacity for the connector, using the appropriate concrete or masonry design codes. Figure 12.7 illustrates how Clause 10.4.2.3 would be interpreted.

Figure 12.7
**Member thickness for anchor bolt connections**

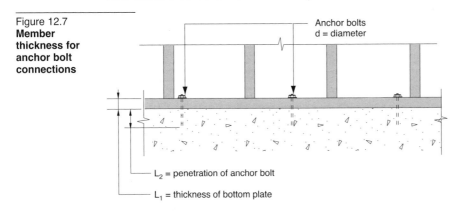

Anchor bolts
d = diameter

$L_2$ = penetration of anchor bolt

$L_1$ = thickness of bottom plate

## Clause 10.4.3 – Placement of Bolts in Joints

The minimum bolt spacing, end and edge distances were originally based on work by Trayer (1932). Joint configuration can affect the resistance of connections, particularly when bolts load a member parallel to the grain. Spacing between bolts in a row, and end distance are used in the group effect calculation.

Clause 10.4.3.2.3 prohibits use of a "single steel splice plate" when the distance between the outermost rows of bolts exceeds 125 mm. This is intended to apply to parallel-to-grain joints. Alternatively, the designer can specify two or more narrow parallel splice plates so that swelling and shrinking of the wood will not introduce stresses across the grain.

## Clause 10.4.4 – Lateral Resistance

Basic lateral resistance values for a single bolt ($p_u$ for loading parallel to grain, and $q_u$ for loading perpendicular) were formerly based on Trayer (1932). CSA O86 developed $p_u$ and $q_u$ from a method proposed originally by Johansen (1949) and subsequently refined by Larsen (1973). Larsen's prediction equations assumed that a dowel connection (including bolts) could fail by full bearing (i.e., crushing) in one or more wood members (for bolts with low l/d ratios), or by bending of the bolt (for bolts with high l/d ratios) accompanied by local wood crushing near the member interfaces.

In the 1989 edition of CSA O86, $p_u$ and $q_u$ values were based on modified forms of Larsen's equations by Whale et. al. (1987) and presented in tabular format in the body of the standard.

In the 1994 edition, the Whale et. al. (1987) equations were presented in Clause 10.4.4.2. Also, there were revisions to the embedding strengths of wood, the bolt yield strength in bending and the bolt-bearing strength of steel side plates. The equations in Clause 10.4.4.2 give resistance values per shear plane for a single bolt.

Single shear connections use the minimum of equations a, b, d, e, f, and g to determine $p_u$ or $q_u$. For double shear connections, $p_u$ or $q_u$ is calculated as the minimum of equations a, c, d or g. For connections with more than 3 members, the connection should be analyzed as a series of three member joints, and the most conservative value in the series should be used.

In the 2001 edition, the embedment strength of the steel plate has been modified so that the bolt-to-steel plate bearing resistance obtained in O86 yields identical results to the ones in S16 for the same failure mode. The 3.75 factor used to determine the plate embedment strength is the result of 3 over 0.8. The factor 3 is taken from S16, and the 0.8 is the factor used to obtain $F_1$. The designer still has the responsibility to check the other steel plate failure modes using S16.

The equations do not consider wood splitting and shear failure modes; these are currently addressed by group and spacing factors: $J_G$, $J_L$ and $J_R$ in Clause 10.4.4.1. These factors were incorporated in 1989 and were conservative estimates based on research by Massé et. al. (1988) and Yasumura et. al. (1987). The factor $J_G$ does not apply to wood-to-concrete connections.

Although bolted joints under loads perpendicular to grain have not been recently studied, they are assigned the same $J_R$ factors as bolts loaded parallel to grain.

## Clause 10.5 – Drift Pins

Drift pins were first introduced in 1989. Clause 10.5 is essentially unchanged from that edition of the Standard. Since drift pin lateral resistance is based on bolt values, editorial changes were made to reflect the changes in bolt design format. Design information in the Standard is based on 16 to 25 mm (5/8" to 1") diameter drift pins made from round mild steel conforming to ASTM Standard A307 or CSA Standard CAN3-G40.21.

**12**

**COM**

CSA Commentary

Drift pins are round steel dowels that do not have heads and are not threaded. The ends are tapered or shaped so that the pin may be easily driven into pre-bored holes with minimum damage to the wood. Drift pin holes are pre-bored with the members aligned and held in place. With hole alignment thus assured, the hole diameter is slightly undersized to give a tight fit when the pins are driven in. This provides friction, drawing the members tightly together during assembly. The holes are between 0.8 mm and 1.0 mm smaller than the diameter of the drift pin.

Drift pins must be slightly shorter than the combined depth of each pair of members to be pinned. This prevents interference between the pins in successive layers as they are tightened together.

Drift pin size and spacing rules are based on a 90° joint using four 20 mm pins to secure pairs of 200 mm wide timbers, a typical cribwork joint as shown in CSA O86 Figure 10.5.5.

### Clause 10.5.6 – Lateral Resistance

As a conservative measure, due to uncertainties associated with field installation, the lateral resistance for drift pins was set at 0.6 times that of bolts. The group and spacing factors for bolts have not been applied to connections made with drift pins, for practical reasons.

### Clause 10.6 – Lag Screws

### Clause 10.6.1 – General

Lag screws (or lag bolts) are generally used where through-bolts are not practical. Lag screws may be loaded laterally or in withdrawal, in side or end grain, with wood or steel side plates. End-grain loading in withdrawal is discouraged because of the inherent weakness and susceptibility to splitting of this type of joint.

The manufacturing reference for lag screws is the ANSI/ASME Standard B18.2.1 which is the current North American standard.

The lateral load resistance of lag screws in this Clause applies to a single shear connection. Use of lag screws for connector joints is covered in Clause 10.3.5.

### Clause 10.6.2 – Placement of Lag Screws in Joints

In general, the same minimum spacing, end distances, edge distances and net sections for bolts apply to lag screw joints. However, lag screw holes, where drilled in place with proper lead holes, do not present the same lack-of-fit problems as bolt holes drilled prior to assembly. It is important that lag screws be installed with a wrench; use of non-petroleum-based lubricants eases the insertion of lag screws, contributing to a better fit.

## Clause 10.6.3 – Penetration of Lag Screws

Increasing the length of penetration of a lag screw beyond a critical point does not increase either the strength or stiffness of the connection. Clause 10.6.3.2 gives the maximum lengths of penetration which are allowed to be used in the calculation of lateral resistance. The penetrations are a function of shank diameter and species. In the 2001 version of O86, a clause (10.6.3.3) was added to impose a 5d lower limit on the penetration of lag screws.

Normally, at the strength limit state (Clause 10.6.6), maximum penetration results in a "type f" failure. With this failure mode, an increase in the length of penetration into the main member ($l_2$) does not result in increased connection capacity. The same maximum penetration limitations are used when calculating joint slip (Appendix A10.6.3.3).

## Clause 10.6.5 – Withdrawal Resistance

The basic resistance values for lag screws loaded in withdrawal from side grain were developed using proprietary unpublished data from tests on five species (redwood, white pine, Douglas fir, southern yellow pine and white oak) with seven sizes of lag screws and six replications for each combination. Withdrawal resistance was directly proportional to the length of the threaded portion of the lag screw excluding the length of the tapered tip. As well, withdrawal resistance was directly proportional to $d^{0.75}$ and $G^{1.5}$ (d = shank diameter and G = wood relative density) (Anonymous, 1982).

The service condition factor for lag screws was adopted from tests on flat-head wood screws. The tests indicated that these factors could be adequate for lag screws in a continuously wet environment (Cockrell, 1933).

## Clause 10.6.6 – Lateral Resistance

In previous Canadian limit states design standards (1984,1989), lag screw joints were governed by either strength or serviceability limit states, with the serviceability limit state used to prevent slips exceeding 0.8 mm at specified loads. In the 1994 edition of the Standard, the European Yield Model, (Larsen, 1973, Whale et. al., 1987) was adopted for lag screws and the slip criteria was moved to the Appendix. The European Yield Model provides an estimate of the ultimate capacity of a lag screw connection.

In the 2001 edition, a factor was added to the $P_r$ and $Q_r$ equations in clause 10.6.6.1.1 to take into account the effect of reduced penetration and resulting reduced capacity. The full lateral load capacity is obtained for a penetration of 8d and is reduced by 37.5% at a penetration of 5d. Also, the embedment strength of the steel side plate has been modified so that the lag screw-to-steel plate bearing resistance obtained in O86 yields identical results to the ones in S16 for the same failure mode. The 3.75 factor used to determine the plate embedment strength is the result of 3 over 0.8. The 3 factor is taken from S16, and the 0.8 is the factor used to obtain $F_1$. The designer still has the responsibility to check the other steel plate failure modes using S16.

**12**

**COM**

CSA Commentary

Lateral deformation of a lag screw connection under specified loads can still be estimated using Appendix A10.6.3.3.

In cases where stiffness must be estimated for analysis, or where stiffness should be controlled, the designer should use the Appendix. As well, research (Newlin and Gahagan, 1938) has indicated that lag screws loaded laterally tend to reach a point of permanent deformation at about 0.8 to 1.0 mm. This limit should be avoided to prevent permanent deformation.

The same yield equations (Whale et. al., 1987) are used for lag screws and bolts. Lag screws are only considered for single shear connections and the equations are presented accordingly. The wood embedding strength is the same as for bolts. The lag screw yield strengths depend on diameter, such that higher yield strengths are applicable to smaller diameter lag screws.

Lateral slip resistance values (in Appendix A10.6.3.3) were based on mean published values by Newlin and Gahagan (1938) and unpublished test data. The tests indicated that slip resistance values were proportional to shank diameter, depth of penetration in the main member and wood relative density. Unpublished tests indicate that steel side plates increase joint stiffness by a factor of 1.5 over wood side plates. Therefore a $J_Y$ factor of 1.5 is applied when checking lateral slip resistance parallel to grain for joints with steel side plates.

## Clause 10.7 – Timber Rivets (also known as Glulam Rivets)

Timber rivets are high strength steel nails originally developed to connect glued-laminated timber through pre-drilled steel plates. Timber rivet joints offer flexibility of design and efficiency of load transfer in wood.

In the 1994 edition, additions to the timber rivet clause included the following: design values for use in solid sawn timber, withdrawal values, and design values for use with plates thinner than 4.8 mm.

These design values were based on extensive tests carried out by Karacabeyli et al. (1995). Both lateral and withdrawal tests were undertaken for a variety of species under different service conditions.

## Clause 10.7.1 – General

The rivets have a flattened-oval shank section and a wedge-shaped head. Dimensions are standardized as illustrated in Figure 10.7.1.1. When driven through the pre-drilled steel plate and into the timber beyond, the tapered heads wedge tightly in the holes. This prevents any movement of the heads within the plate, thus increasing both strength and stiffness of the joint.

The flattened shank section is 3.2 × 6.4 mm and must be driven with the wider dimension parallel to the wood grain. This minimizes wood splitting and optimizes the lateral resistance, whether loads are parallel or perpendicular to grain.

Timber rivets are supplied hot-dip galvanized, whereas the plates are usually custom-made and may be galvanized depending on the service conditions. Clause 10.7.1.4 states that the minimum thickness of steel side plate to be used with timber rivet connections is 3.2 mm. This is reduced from the previous minimum of 4.8 mm. Side plates thinner than 6.4 mm result in less fixity and consequently rivet bending capacity is reduced. The research (Karacabeyli et. al., 1995) has confirmed that the side plate factors of 0.9 and 0.8 are applicable to 4.8 and 3.2 mm plates respectively. Corrosion may be a consideration where thinner plates are used (the minimum recommended thickness of unprotected steel plates subjected to corrosion is 4.5 mm).

Although the Standard does not provide a limit on the maximum plate thickness, plates which are too thick decrease the penetration of the rivet into the wood member and reduce the wood capacity of the connection. Table 10.7.2.3 has been calculated assuming a side plate thickness of 6.3 mm. These tabular values could be reduced, particularly for smaller rivets, if thicker side plates were considered.

Glued-laminated timber is manufactured using dry wood. Therefore, it is unlikely that timber rivets will be installed in wet glulam material, reducing the possibility of splitting in service at timber rivet connections. Moisture content of solid sawn material is not as consistent as glulam, and has somewhat decreased resistance to splitting, leading to some precautionary clauses in the Standard.

Clause 10.7.1.5 includes a note with guidance on installation procedures for timber rivet connections. Rivets should be installed progressively from the outside of the connection to the interior of the connection. Experience has shown that this procedure helps to prevent splitting.

Clause 10.7.1.9 includes provision for the seldom-used condition where rivets in a two-sided connection (plates on both sides of a member) are long enough to penetrate beyond the midpoint of the member. In this case, rivets on both sides are required to be spaced apart as though they were all driven from one side. Capacities are calculated on the more conservative basis of the spacing between rivets from both sides at the centre of the member. This spacing requirement was adopted in lieu of specific research information. In no case is the rivet penetration permitted to exceed 70% of the wood member thickness.

Clause 10.7.1.10 was added to minimize the possibility of splitting where timber rivets are installed in wet wood. Tests (Karacabeyli et. al., 1995) indicated that splitting was not a problem for rivets installed in green material that was subsequently allowed to dry, where the width of the rivet group perpendicular to grain was restricted.

## Clause 10.7.2 – Lateral Resistance

Design of glulam timber joints is based primarily on Foschi and Longworth (1975). The theory describes and quantifies two main modes of failure, in the rivets and in the wood. The ultimate capacity is limited either by rivet shank bending combined with localized wood crushing at the rivets, or by the wood strength (shear or tension) surrounding the rivet group. Due to this variety in failure modes, the design of timber rivet joints is a trial-and-error process, optimizing the joints in relation to the sizes of the timbers and the forces to be resisted.

In the case of the rivet bending failure mode, the formulae for basic parallel and perpendicular design resistance values $P_Y$ and $Q_Y$ were obtained by dividing the mean theoretical values from Foschi and Longworth's work by 1.6

**12**

**COM**

CSA Commentary

to account for variability of rivet yielding values. Because the original rivet steel specification had later been modified to eliminate the possibility of hydrogen embrittlement in environments of high temperature and humidity, a slightly softer rivet resulted. Thus the capacities governed by nail bending were multiplied by a factor of 0.88. These values were further modified in 1989 to accommodate load duration calibrations (Turnbull, 1990). In the 1994 Standard, the $K_{SF}$ and $K_T$ factors were applied to rivet capacity.

In the 1989 edition, Karacabeyli and Fraser (1990) compared the lateral strengths of timber rivets in Spruce glulam to Douglas fir glulam, loaded parallel and perpendicular to grain. Based on this data, a species factor "H" was adopted in the 1989 Standard to accommodate timber rivet design in Spruce-Pine glulam.

In 1994, the "H" factor was renamed the material factor, and it was expanded to include the various species groups of sawn timbers, as well as glulam. Material factors for timbers were established based on tests in Douglas fir, Hem-Fir and Spruce-Pine-Fir solid sawn members (Karacabeyli et. al., 1995). To simplify the design, the same "H" factor is applied to all strength criteria parallel and perpendicular to grain.

Due to the complexity of equations for lateral strength resistance parallel to grain, the basic unfactored values for a wide range of rivet lengths, rivet spacings and sizes of rivet groups are given in Table 10.7.2.3 of the Standard. For values beyond the range of the table, see Appendix A10.7.2.3.

In the 1989 and earlier editions, tables included both rivet and wood capacity values parallel to grain. In 1994, this approach was changed so that the values in Table 10.7.2.3 were based on wood capacity only; rivet capacity must be calculated separately, providing a more accurate result.

### Clause 10.7.3 – Withdrawal Resistance

Design of timber rivets for withdrawal loads was added in the 1994 edition of CSA O86. Design values are based on research by Karacabeyli et. al., (1995). Rivet withdrawal tests were undertaken to investigate the effect of species, condition of wood when fabricated, density and waiting period before testing. Tests were for short duration loads and limited to material that was dry at the time testing. The design values for timber rivets loaded in withdrawal are conservative estimates of the data, and are limited to dry service conditions for short term and standard term load durations.

Withdrawal values are a function of the number of rivets in the connection and the length of penetration of the rivets. For simplicity, only two unit with-drawal values are given: one for glulam and one for sawn timber. The same values are independent of the species used. The withdrawal values were adopted for both short and standard duration loads; therefore, the duration factor is not applicable to these design values.

### Clause 10.8 – Truss Plates

### Clause 10.8.1 – General

Truss plates are toothed metal-plate connectors used to assemble pieces of dimension lumber into roof and floor trusses. Truss plates are produced by punching light gauge galvanized steel (normally 16, 18 or 20 gauge) so that teeth protrude from one side. The pattern of teeth in the plate varies by manufacturer.

Truss plates must be produced from galvanized sheet steel conforming to the standards specified in 10.8.1.3.

Because the sheet steel used for truss plates is relatively thin, corrosion of the plates could reduce its performance. The Standard contains restrictions on use in corrosive environments and, in particular, prohibits use in the highly corrosive environment where fire-retardant treated wood is exposed to moisture.

Truss plates are installed at every joint of a light frame wood truss. Truss plate sizes vary considerably depending on the loads which must be transfered at the connection. Truss fabrication is carried out at a plant where the truss plates are embedded into the lumber with either a hydraulic press or a roller.

To meet the design requirements of the Standard, the plates must be installed in the following manner:

- the joints must be tight fitting with identical truss plates placed on opposite faces so that each plate is directly opposite the other,
- the truss plates are not deformed during installation,
- the teeth are normal to the surface of the lumber,
- the teeth must be fully embedded in the wood so that the plate is tight to the wood surface; however, the plate must not be embedded into the lumber deeper than half of the plate thickness, and
- the lumber below the truss plate does not contain wane, loose knots, or knot holes.

Truss plates must be tested in accordance with CSA Standard S347, *Method of Test for Truss Plates used in Lumber Joints.* Test results for commercially used plates are listed in the *Registry of Product Evaluations* published by the Canadian Construction Materials Centre (CCMC), Institute for Research in Construction, Ottawa, Ontario. The evaluation reports also include resistance values derived from the tests.

The resistance per tooth varies little within a given manufacturer's range of plate sizes, and usually the larger plates are tested, resulting in a generally conservative strength value per tooth for the smaller plates.

### Clause 10.8.2 – Design

Due to the proprietary nature of truss plates, specific resistance values for truss plates are not given in the Standard. Instead, the Standard outlines procedures for deriving resistance values based on required tests. The resulting resistance

**12**

**COM**

CSA Commentary

values are normally used by the truss plate manufacturer who usually has the responsibility for truss design.

Truss plates transfer forces in tension or shear or both. Those forces may act in various directions depending on the geometry of the joint. Truss plates are also used in compression joints, mainly to keep the truss together and in alignment during handling, erecting and for stress reversal situations. The main compression forces are transferred by wood-to-wood bearing for which tightly fitted joints are essential.

With truss plate joints that are relatively short in the direction of the load, failure occurs when the teeth yield and then withdraw from the wood. Failures of this type are governed by the "lateral resistance of the teeth". With longer plates, the failure mode can change to tension failure across the most critical net section of the plate. This failure mode is resisted by the "tensile resistance of the plates". A third failure mode involves shear of the plate, usually indicated by diagonal buckling of the plate followed by tooth withdrawal or tensile tearing of the steel along the shear line. This is governed by the "shear resistance of the plate".

CSA S347 requires four types of tests: lateral resistance of the teeth, tensile resistance of the plates, ultimate tensile strength of the steel from which the plates are stamped, and shear resistance of the plates. To determine lateral resistance of the teeth, plates are tested with the primary axis of the plate oriented parallel and perpendicular to the direction of load, and loaded parallel and perpendicular to the grain for a total of four different test configurations. For design, intermediate orientations of plate to load are obtained by linear interpolation; for intermediate orientation of grain to load, the familiar Hankinson formula is used (see Clauses 10.8.3.2.2 and 10.8.4.3), as with other fastenings.

CSA O86 gives procedures for converting the test results into design values. In accordance with the Standard, truss plates must be designed so that the following criteria are satisfied:

1. Factored ultimate lateral resistance of the teeth, $N_r \geq$ factored lateral load $N_f$

2. Factored tensile resistance of the plate $T_r \geq$ factored tensile force $T_f$

3. Factored shear resistance of the plates $V_r \geq$ factored shear force $V_f$

4. Lateral slip resistance $N_{rs} \geq$ specified lateral load $N_s$

**Clause 10.8.3 – Factored Resistance of Truss Plates**

For LSD methodology, the resistance of elements and fastenings at the "strength limit state" is based on the low end of the strength distribution (i.e., generally the lower fifth percentile). The tests to determine lateral resistance of truss plate teeth are conducted using wood specimens with below-average density, in accordance with CSA S347, so relatively few tests are required. With only ten replications of tests for the lateral resistance of the teeth, the design value is based on the average of the three lowest values. This basic resistance value is divided by

1.6 as a traditional estimate of the effect of load duration. The published resistance factor for ultimate lateral resistance of the teeth is 0.9 instead of 0.7, in accordance with the 1989 revisions to duration of load (Turnbull, 1990).

To evaluate "tensile resistance of the plate", it is recognized that the plate material supplied for testing may be stronger than actually used to fabricate roof trusses. The tensile strength of specimens of unstamped plate material is compared with the specified minimum strength for the grade of steel used, and the ratio is used to convert the plate tension design values to what they would be if steel of the minimum strength had been used for the test plates. Due to the low variability associated with this failure mode, design values are the average of the two lowest of three corrected test values. Duration of load does not apply.

For the "shear resistance of the plates", the test standard requires that the plates be tested at angular increments of 15°, plate-axis-to-shear-line. At each shear angle, the average of these replications is corrected for the ultimate tensile strength of the plate material. The test standard further requires that the plates be large enough to ensure a plate shear failure along the joint rather than a failure in the teeth. A number of other test conditions are specified (i.e., lumber density, species, moisture content, over- or under-pressing, time from fabrication to testing, end and edge distances, plate size). Quaile and Keenan (1979) have discussed the effects of these factors and the reasons for the manner of their specification in the Standard. Design values are determined on the same basis as tension values.

Clause 10.8.3.2.4 was modified in the 1998 Supplement to CSA O86 to reflect the fact that the shear resistance of the plate depends also on whether the applied forces result primarily in tension or compression on the joint. The appropriate shear resistance value should be used for either case.

## Clause 10.8.4 – Lateral Slip Resistance

Slip resistance is a mandatory part of truss plate design in accordance with current industry practice. At the serviceability limit state, the mean value of the load at 0.8 mm deformation, divided by a factor of 1.4 is used. The factor of 1.4 calibrates design values to previous issues of the Standard.

## Clause 10.9 – Nails and Spikes

This clause provides lateral and withdrawal resistance values for common nails, spiral nails and spikes as described in CSA B111. Other nail-type fastenings not so described (such as staples) may also be used if supporting test data are available.

Changes to clause 10.9 for the 1994 edition of the Standard were largely editorial in nature. Design provisions for nail connections using oriented strandboard (OSB) were added.

In the 2001 edition, the withdrawal resistance of nails was amended in light of recent studies. As a result, Table 10.9.5.2 has been revised.

**12**

**COM**

CSA Commentary

## Clause 10.9.2 – Joint Configuration

The spacings for round wire nails are based on Ramos (1960), and crack propagation experiments by Lau and Tardiff (1987). These minimum requirements have been established to limit strength reductions as a result of splitting of the wood. The tabulated minimum nail spacings parallel to grain were set at double the maximum crack lengths caused during driving, as observed by Lau and Tardiff (1987). Different species are assigned different spacing requirements, based on the experimental results.

Very dry wood has a greater tendency to split when nails are driven into it. Therefore, spacing requirements for nails and spikes are limited to wood which is greater than 10% moisture content when nailed. This is not intended, however, to restrict use with products such as plywood or OSB, which are typically at lower moisture contents than solid wood.

Figure 10.9.2.1 of the Standard illustrates the spacing rules as applied to wood-to-wood joints connected at various angles, and shows how extra nails may be added on the diagonals between nails (Clause 10.9.2.1)

Clause 10.9.2.3 states that plywood or OSB of at least three nail diameters in thickness can be used for side plates, as compared to a thickness of five nail diameters for lumber. This allows the designer to use the lateral strength values of Table 10.9.2.2 as a basis for design of plywood-to-lumber joints and OSB-to-lumber joints. The design approach for OSB is based on experimental work by Mohammad and Smith, (1993).

## Clause 10.9.3 – Joint Design

In the first Canadian LSD Standard (1984), nail joints were designed for strength and serviceability limit states, with the serviceability limit state intended to prevent slips exceeding 0.4 mm at specified loads.

Considering the wide range of nail and spike sizes covered in the Standard, it was decided that a slip of only 0.4 mm, while quite satisfactory for small nails, was too restrictive for larger nails and spikes. Therefore the serviceability requirements were removed in the 1989 edition of the Standard and a formula adapted from a draft of the Eurocode V (Crubilé et. al., 1986) was added as Appendix A10.9.3.2. This permitted designers to estimate the in-service deformation of nailed joints. The formula is limited to specified loads of up to 1/3 of the ultimate load. Designers are advised to use this in cases where stiffness must be estimated for analysis, or where joint slip should be controlled.

## Clause 10.9.4 – Lateral Resistance

The modes of failure for a nailed joint have been described and quantified by Johansen (1949), subsequently modified and reported by Larsen (1977). The theory, similar to that for bolts, estimates the ultimate strength of a joint based on the yielding moment of the nail and the embedding strength of the wood. Because it assumes plastic behaviour of the joint elements, the theory applies only to the ultimate strength of the joint.

For a two-member connection, four different failure modes are identified:

1. Wood crushing in both members before the nail yields (stiff nail, thin members),

2. Wood failure in only the thinner member,

3. A combination of wood failure in both members with nail yielding in the thicker member, and

4. A failure that is governed by nail yielding and wood failures in both members.

Where nail yielding has occurred, an additional axial force based on the withdrawal resistance of the nail is added to the basic formulation.

The calculation of the basic resistance values given in Table 10.9.4 was based on assumptions of a nominal side plate thickness equal to 1/3 of the nail length, and a minimum side plate thickness of 1/6 of the nail length, where all members of the joint were of the same wood material. Clause 10.9.3.5 of the Standard requires that the factored resistance be based on the weakest member in the connection.

The material properties considered were the embedding strength of the wood and the yielding moment of the nail. The wood embedding strength was taken as 1.1 times the small clear compression parallel to grain strength (Larsen, 1973). A near-minimum embedding value was used for each species group. The nail yielding moment was based on a formula used in the Danish Timber Code.

For each nail size and species group, the mode of failure was found by calculating the limiting load capacity from the group of yield equations. In 1984, tabular values of unit lateral resistance were obtained by dividing the limiting theoretical load by 1.6 to account for load duration. In the 1989 Standard, these values were adjusted to accommodate the changed basis for load duration and the resistance value was reduced from 0.7 to 0.6.

Included in this clause are provisions for double shear where nails can penetrate two side plates and a main centre member. In particular, a minimum centre member thickness of 8 nail diameters is required for an "effective shear planes" factor of 1.8, and a centre member thickness of at least 11 nail diameters for a full double shear factor of 2.0, based on Turnbull (1987).

Although not stated, Clause 10.9.4 implies that multiple-shear joints could be designed with more than two shear planes provided the appropriate penetration requirements in main and connecting plate members are met.

For nails or spikes installed in side grain, connection resistance is assumed to be the same whether loaded parallel or perpendicular to the grain. Where nails are installed in end grain, only 67% of the side grain resistance is specified. Toenails are partially resisted in the end grain of the wood. Therefore, they have only 83% of the lateral resistance of a connection installed in the side grain.

Factors for service conditions are supported by research by Brock (1957) and by Welchert and Hinkle (1966).

**12**

**COM**

CSA Commentary

There are two other factors specific to nail and spike connections: $J_B$ for nail clinching and $J_D$ for diaphragm construction. In a two-member nailed connection, lateral resistance may be increased by 60% if the nail is clinched on the far side. (Crandall, 1959). The factor for nail clinching does not apply to three member connections, since the increase in resistance is covered by the $J_S$ factor.

The tabular values in the Standard are near-minimum resistance values. In diaphragm construction, many nails are used and the effects of variability of ultimate resistance are reduced. Therefore the resistance of nails used in diaphragms may be increased by 30%.

## Clause 10.9.5 – Withdrawal Resistance

The driving of a nail jams bent or broken wood fibres between the nail and other fibres. The fibres are forced aside as the nail enters the wood, exerting a squeezing action on the nail. It was commonly accepted that most of the withdrawal resistance of a nail was due to the jamming and wedging action of bent or broken fibres. Frictional withdrawal resistance depends on the bearing of these fibres on the nail surface.

Research has shown that the withdrawal resistance of a nail is a function of the length of penetration into the main member, the diameter of the nail and the specific gravity of the wood. With time, the displaced fibres around a driven nail relax and the withdrawal resistance is greatly reduced. This effect is more pronounced for nail connections subject to long term loads and cyclic moisture conditions. Therefore, withdrawal loading for nails is only permitted for short duration loads (wind and earthquake).

The equation used in the 2001 edition to relate the nail withdrawal resistance with the nail diameter (d) and the material's relative density (G) is based on McLain's model (McLain, 1997). The test strengths can be described using a normal distribution (Smith, 2000) and the average COV can be assumed to be 30%. With these assumptions, the factor to convert the mean strength to $5^{th}$ percentile characteristic strength is:

$$(1-1.645 \times 0.3) = 0.506.$$

Thefore the characteristic property, $y_w$, can be determined from:

$$
\begin{aligned}
y_w &= 0.506 \times (1.15 / 1.25) \times 0.62 \times 56.9 \times d^{0.82} \times G^{2.2} \\
&= 16.4 \times d^{0.82} \times G^{2.2}
\end{aligned}
$$

The 1.15/1.25 factor is to adjust the design value for duration of load. A delay between nailing and testing reduces the withdrawal resistance of smooth-shank nails. The effect of delay varies greatly between and within species. Data by Mack (1960) showed a 30% loss of withdrawal resistance after a delay of four months. Because of the delay effect, Table 10.9.5.2 is based on 62% of values estimated from the experimental results. The remaining factors are based on McLain's model.

Clause 10.9.5.2 gives a factor of 1.6 for improved withdrawal resistance where the nail is effectively clinched. This was adopted from Crandall's (1959) tests on clinched nails loaded laterally. It was assumed conservatively that nail clinching would be at least as effective in withdrawal as his tests showed for lateral strength.

Nails driven into end grain are not considered to resist any loads in withdrawal. Toe-nails are partially resisted in the end grain of the wood. Therefore, they have only 67% of the withdrawal resistance of a connection installed in the side grain.

The effect of seasoning in service is critical for nails loaded in withdrawal. As wet lumber dries, the fibres surrounding the nail relax, showing up to 75% loss of withdrawal resistance (Mack, 1960). Perkins (1971) found the same effect for nailed joints subject to continual wetting and drying. Therefore, Table 10.2.1.5 used to give a service condition factor of only 0.25 for nails in withdrawal following assembly with unseasoned wood (prior to 2001 edition). As it is generally accepted that the moisture change factor contains the influence of delay loading, the $K_{SF}$ value was adjusted in the 2001 edition, upward from the previous value of 0.25 to 0.4 (0.4 = 0.25 / 0.62) in Table 10.2.1.5. Nailed joints maintained in a continuously wet environment showed withdrawal strengths approximately 60% of those in a dry environment (Hellawell, 1965).

### Clause 10.10 – Joist Hangers

A new clause on joist hangers was added in the 1998 Supplement to CSA O86. Joist hangers are light-gauge steel framing connectors typically used to transfer load from a joist to a beam. Clause 10.10 is similar to Clause 10.8 on truss plates, in providing minimum requirements for determining design values for use with this Standard. Test results for hangers are listed in the *Registry of Product Evaluations* published by the Canadian Construction Materials Centre, Institute for Research in Construction, Ottawa, Ontario.

**12**

**COM**

CSA Commentary

# References

Anonymous. 1982. Improved Design of Fastenings in Timber Structures Based on Limit States Design Procedures. Unpublished report prepared by Morrison, Hershfield, Burgess & Huggins, Ltd., and sponsored by the Canadian Forestry Service.

Brock, G.R. 1957. The Strength of Nailed Joints. Forest Products Research Bulletin No. 41, Department of Science and Industrial Research, Charles Horisi, 5-11 Regent St., London, England.

Canadian Constructions Materials Centre. Evaluation Listings. Institute for Research in Construction, NRC, Ottawa, ON. (revised semi-annually)

Cockrell, R.A. 1933. A Study of the Screw-holding Properties of Wood. Technical Bulletin 44, New York State College of Forestry.

Cramer, C.O. 1968. Load Distribution in Multiple-Bolt Tension Joints. Journal of the Structural Division, American Society of Civil Engineering, ST-5, 5939: 1101-1117.

Crandall, C. 1959. Allowable Loads for 8d Nails. Forest Products Journal. 9(8): 250-262.

Crubilé, P., J. Ehlbeck, H. Brueninghoff, H.J. Larsen and J. Sunley. 1986. Eurocode V: Common Unified Rules for Timber Structures (Draft). Report prepared for the Commission of the European Communities."

DeGrace, R.F. 1986. Commentary on CSA Standard CAN3-086.1-M84 Engineering Design in Wood (limit states design). Canadian Standards Association. Special pub. 086.1.1-M1986, Rexdale, ON.

Erki, M.A., and M.W. Huggins. 1983. Load Capacity of Row and Shear Plate Connectors. Journal of Structural Engineering, American Society of Civil Engineers, No. 12, Vol. 109.

Foschi, R.O. and J. Longworth. 1975. Analysis and Design of Griplam Nailed Connections. Journal of the Structural Division, American Society of Civil Engineering. 101(ST12): 2537-2555.

Hellawell, C.R. 1965. Mechanical Fasteners and Timber Jointing in New Zealand from a Laboratory Viewpoint. International Symposium on Joints in Timber Structure. Timber Research and Development Association. New Zealand.

Johansen, K.W. 1949. Theory of Timber Connectors. Publications of the International Association of Bridge and Structural Engineering. No. 9: 249-262. Bern, General Secretariat.

Karacabeyli, E. and H. Fraser. 1990. Short-term strength of glulam rivet connections made with spruce and Douglas fir glulam, and Douglas fir solid timber. Can. J. Civ. Eng. 17, 166-172.

Karacabeyli, E., H. Fraser and W. Deacon. 1995. Lateral and withdrawal load resistance of glulam rivet connections made with sawn lumber. Unpublished report, Forintek Canada Corp., Vancouver, BC.

Lantos, G. 1969. Load Distribution in a Row of Fasteners Subjected to Lateral Load. Wood Science, No.3, Vol. 1, pp. 129-136.

Larsen, H.J. 1973. The Yield Load of Bolted and Nailed Joints. Proceedings, International Union of Forestry Research Organization meeting – 5th Congress. South Africa.

Larsen, H.J. 1977. K.W. Johansen's Nail Tests. Bygningsstatisk Meddelels No. 48: 9-30.

Lau, P.W.C. and Y. Tardiff. 1987. Cracks Produced by Driving Nails into Wood Effects of Wood and Nail Variables. Unpublished progress report, Building Systems Dept., Forintek Canada Corp., Ottawa, ON.

Mack, J.J. 1960. Grooved Nails. Australian Timber 26(8): 43-44, 46, 50, 131.

Massé, D.I., J.J. Salinas and J.E. Turnbull. 1988. Lateral Strength and Stiffness of Single and Multiple Bolts in Glued-laminated Timber Loaded Parallel to Grain. Unpublished contract. No. C-029, Eng. and Stat. Res. Centre, Research Branch, Agriculture Canada, Ottawa, ON.

McLain, T.E. 1997. Design axial withdrawal strength from wood : II. Plain-shank common wire nails. Forest Products Journal, 47(6):103-109.

Mohammad, M. and I. Smith. 1993. Load-Slip Response of Nailed OSB-to-Lumber Joints as Influenced by Moisture Conditioning. Proceedings, Annual Conference, Canadian Society for Civil Engineering.

Newlin, J.A. and J.M. Gahagan. 1938. Lag Screw Joints: Their Behavior and Design. U.S. Dept. of Agriculture Technical Bulletin No. 597

Perkins, P.H. 1971. Nail Withdrawal Resistance in Plantation Red Pine Grown in Indiana. Forest Products Journal 21(6): 29-32.

Quaile, A.T. and F.J. Keenan. 1979. Truss Plate Testing in Canada: Test Procedures and Factors Affecting Strength Properties. Proceedings, Metal Plate Wood Truss Conference, Forest Products Research Society.

Quenneville, J.H.P., J.G.A. Charron and K. Van Dalen. 1993. Effect of End Distance on the Resistance of Split Ring Connectors in Timber Joints Loaded in Compression. Canadian Journal of Civil Engineering. 20(5).

Quenneville, J.H.P and Mohammad, M. 1999. The Anchorage Strength of Bolted Wood-to-Concrete Connections Loaded Perpendicular-to-Grain. Royal Military College of Canada, report to the Canadian Wood Council, 1999.

Quenneville, J.H.P. and Sauvé, G. 1998. Strength and Behaviour of Full-Scale Split-Ring Connections. 5th World Conference on Timber Engineering, Montreux, Switzerland.

Ramos, A.N. 1960. Spacing of Sixpenny and Eightpenny Wire Nails in Douglas Fir Multi-nail Joints. U.S. Department of Agriculture, Forest Products Laboratory. Report No. 2155. Madison, WI.

Scholten, J.A. 1944. Timber Connector Joints, Their Strength and Design. U.S. Department of Agriculture Bulletin 865.

Smith, I., 2000. Some Nail Withdrawal Data and an Interpretation of it. Report to the CSA O86 Technical Committee. 44th Annual Meeting Book.

Stieda, C.K.A., Karacabeyli, E., Fraser, H. and Deacon, W. 1997. Lateral Strength of Bolted Wood-to-Concrete Connections, Forintek Project No. 1565K242, Korintek Canada Corp., Vancouver, BC.

Trayer, G.W. 1932. Bearing Strength of Wood Under Bolts. U.S. Department of Agriculture, Technical Bulletin No. 332.

Turnbull, J.E. 1987. Fastenings. Unpublished committee paper C-034, Eng. and Stat. Res. Centre, Research Branch, Agriculture Canada, Ottawa, ON.

Turnbull, J.E. 1990. Commentary on Clause 10 of CSA Standard CAN/CSA-O86.1-M89 Engineering Design in Wood (Limit States Design). Wood Design Manual (1990 edition). Canadian Wood Council, Ottawa, ON.

Welchert, W.T. and C.N. Hinkle. 1966. The Effect of Change in Moisture Content on the Strength of Nailed Wood Joints. Trans. of the American Society of Civil Engineering. 9(6): 774-6-781.

Whale, L.R.J., I. Smith and H.J. Larsen. 1987. Design of Nailed and Bolted Joints Proposals for the Revision of Existing Formulae in Draft Eurocode V and the CIB Code. International Council for Building Research Studies and Documentation Working Commission W18A. Paper No. 20-7-1.

Yasumura, M., T. Murota and H. Sakai. 1987. Ultimate Properties of Bolted Joints in Glued-laminated Timber. Report to the Working Commission W18 – Timber Structures. Dublin, Ireland.

**12**

**COM**

CSA Commentary

# 12.10    Proprietary Structural Wood Products

D. Rice[1]

### Clause 13.1 – Scope

Clause 13 is intended to apply to all proprietary structural wood products that meet the requirements of an appropriate consensus standard. Products currently covered under Clause 13 are manufactured under a quality assurance program supervised by an independent third-party certification organization (CO) to give assurance that the manufacturer has met all appropriate requirements of Clause 13 and the applicable referenced standard(s) and which is intended to provide evidence that design values are being maintained in ongoing production.

Clause 13 is intended to be used as a reference to help designers understand the origin of manufacturer's proprietary design values. The designer is not normally expected to calculate the proprietary design values using the equations provided herein. Proprietary design information including specified strengths and stiffness, application details and requirements, and installation guidelines are available from the manufacturer. Products designed in accordance with Clause 13 will provide a confidence level consistent with the intent of Part 4 of the *National Building Code of Canada* and with this Standard with respect to strength, serviceability and reliability.

The following items are considered essential requirements to permit a standard for proprietary structural wood products to be referenced in CSA O86 as the basis for their use in engineered wood structures.

- derivation based on a consensus standard developed through a recognized standards writing organization,
- consistent methodology for the development of structural capacities used by the manufacturers of a given type of proprietary structural wood product, and
- content to include as a minimum:
  - scope, definition, and references,
  - qualification procedures and methods for development of structural capacities and or design values,
  - minimum requirements of an appropriate "in house" manufacturing standard and quality assurance program, in association with a qualified third party CO,
  - a system for re-evaluation of recommended structural capacities.

Design values applicable to prefabricated wood I-joists and structural composite lumber products, as defined in this standard, are based on the capacities determined by the procedures of ASTM Standard D 5055 and ASTM Standard D 5456 respectively. It is the responsibility of the producer to determine design values. Judgement is required particularly when assessing design values from qualification tests. Design values need to consider potential low-line lot capacities to avoid marginal application performance or uneconomical reject rates in the quality assurance program.

[1] Manager of Product Acceptance Trus Joist, A Weyerhaeuser Business Boise, Idaho

ASTM Standard D 5055 has been adopted for reference in CSA O86 as an appropriate standard for establishing the requirements for prefabricated wood I-joists and their structural capacities. Some exceptions and additional requirements are noted in CSA O86.

CSA O452 has been adopted for reference in CSA O86 as an appropriate standard for establishing the requirements for Type 3 (Proprietary) Design Rated OSB Panels.

CSA Standard O325 has been adopted for reference in CSA O86 as an appropriate standard for establishing the requirements for OSB panel products designed and manufactured for protected construction uses such as roof, floor and wall sheathing in light frame construction. Other tests and criteria may be required to characterize CSA O325 panels for use as prefabricated wood I-joist web material.

ASTM Standard D 5456 has been adopted for reference in CSA O86 as an appropriate standard for establishing the requirements for structural composite lumber products and their structural capacities.

ASTM Standard D 5457 has been adopted for reference in CSA O86 as an appropriate standard for determining appropriate material property coefficients of variation ($CV_w$) of structural composite lumber products and prefabricated wood I-joists for use with Table 13.2.3.2 of CSA O86.

## Clause 13.2 – Prefabricated Wood I-Joists

Clause 13.2 contains engineering design requirements and appropriate adjustment factors for prefabricated wood I-joists for which design values based on structural capacities have been determined in accordance with ASTM Standard D5055.

## Clause 13.2.2.2 - Structural Panel Webs

The panel product conformance standards referenced in Clause 13.2.2.2 establish the basic requirements for panel sheathing products for use as structural roof, floor and wall sheathing. These products are also generally acceptable as prefabricated wood I-joist web panels. However, it is recommended that all prefabricated wood I-joist web panels be qualified and monitored through a quality assurance program supervised and approved by the qualified third party CO. Details of suitable qualification and quality assurance programs for web panels of prefabricated wood I-joists may be found in the most recent editions of *Quality Assurance Guidelines for Prefabricated Wood I-Joists*, by the Wood I-Joist Manufacturers Association, or the *APA EWS PRI-400 Performance Standard for Prefabricated Wood I-Joists*, by APA-Engineered Wood Systems.

## Clause 13.2.2.3 - Adhesives

One means of demonstrating equivalent performance is to evaluate alternative adhesives in accordance with the principles set forth in CSA O437.2, *Evaluation of Binder Systems for OSB and Waferboard*. CSA O437.2 provides a method of evaluating the performance of a binder system to be used in the manufacture of an OSB product in comparison to the performance of the same product manufactured using a known phenol formaldehyde resin adhesive.

In order to demonstrate adhesive equivalence, the procedures of CSA O437.2 need to be modified with respect to conditioning, aging and other appropriate durability issues and to be representative of the geometry of the wood furnish used in specific prefabricated wood I-joists. This method is not applicable to finger joints or web-to-web or web-to-flange joints of prefabricated wood I-joists.

## Clause 13.2.3 - Specified Strengths and Moduli of Elasticity

ASTM Standard D 5055 allows for the determination of shear capacities of prefabricated wood I-joists on the basis of prescribed qualification testing. Moment capacities are determined by one of the three following methods: (1) analytically, using the code listed axial capacity parallel to grain of flange material, (2) analytically, using the flange material axial capacity statistically determined on the basis of tests and (3) empirically, using the statistically determined moment capacity on the basis of prescribed full-scale tests. Additionally, ASTM Standard D 5055 includes requirements for the verification of the theoretical design capacities of the prefabricated wood I-joist.

For all materials, the limit states design (LSD) provisions of this edition of the Standard contain significant changes when compared to previous working stress design (WSD) versions. The primary changes which affect designs are changes in the traditional duration of load factor (DOL), the effects of factoring loads and resistance (specified strengths), and the use of reliability analysis.

The reliability normalization factors, $K_r$, in Table 13.2.3.2 are based on and derived in accordance with CSA Special Publication *Standard Practice Relating Specified Strengths of Structural Members to Characteristic Structural Properties*, providing equivalent target reliabilities, on a consistent basis, for derivation of specified strength's from characteristic values, for all products. A reliability index of 2.8 is used for all properties shown Table 13.2.3.2, with the exception of prefabricated wood I-joist shear that is based on a reliability index of 2.6. A scaling factor of 0.8, used to convert from test term to standard term, was applied to all properties listed in Table 13.2.3.2, with the exception of the factors for prefabricated wood I-joist shear which are based on a scaling factor of 0.7. The reliability normalization factors adjust not only to the target reliability, but also account for differences in scaling of shear capacities relative to bending or tension capacities. The scaling differences, embodied within the ASTM reduction factors for allowable stress design, must be preserved in order to continue to properly relate the specific test data basis to actual capacity basis, for all wood products.

## Clause 13.2.3.6 - Characteristic Values

ASTM Standard D 5055 does not define characteristic values for prefabricated wood I-joist strength properties. Clause 13.2.3.6 provides guidance to convert

**12**

**COM**

CSA Commentary

the design values developed in accordance with ASTM Standard D 5055 to appropriate characteristic values for use with this Clause.

### Clause 13.2.4 – Modification Factors

### Clause 13.2.4.1 – Duration of Load, $K_D$

The duration of load factors $K_D$ in Table 4.3.1.2 of the Standard are applicable for use with the specified strengths of prefabricated wood I-joists.

### Clause 13.2.4.2 – Service Condition, $K_S$

The specified strengths and stiffness of prefabricated wood I-joists are applicable for use under dry service conditions only. It is generally recommended that these products not be used in other than dry service conditions.

When these products are required for use in other environments, the specified strengths and stiffness must be modified by appropriate adjustments on the basis of the evaluation of the short and long-term effects of the particular environmental conditions.

Environmental conditions which result in high or fluctuating moisture content may affect material and product quality and may result in strength and stiffness adjustments different from those suitable for sawn lumber. Wet service condition use should be considered only when appropriate $K_S$ values for the individual prefabricated wood I-joist components may be determined from the clauses of this Standard, or when appropriate factors for specified strengths and stiffness are provided based on the documented results of tests that take into account the effects of time, temperature, and moisture content.

### Clause 13.2.4.3 – Treatment Factor, $K_T$

The specified strengths and stiffness of prefabricated wood I-joists are applicable for use with non-pressure impregnated products only. Pressure impregnating chemical treatments may affect material quality and result in the need for strength and stiffness adjustments different from those suitable for sawn lumber. Pressure impregnating chemical treatments should be permitted only when treatment adjustments for specified strengths and stiffness are based on the documented results of tests that take into account the effects of time, temperature and moisture content.

### Clause 13.2.4.4 - System Factor, $K_{HB}$

The allowable bending resistance increases for load sharing use were derived taking into consideration the coefficient of variation (COV) of the stiffness of various flange materials. The original theory justifying this type of increase seems to be based on the relative stiffness of the members and positive correlation between bending strength and stiffness. Logic indicates that as stiffness

COV decreases so would the load sharing. That is, as stiffness COV tends to zero, lack of differential deflection decreases load sharing.

For purposes of this Clause, it was determined that visually graded sawn lumber would have a stiffness COV of 18% and in that case the appropriate system factor would be 10% for sawn lumber as specified in Clause 5.4.4.1. It was judged that machine stress-rated and machine evaluated lumber stiffness COV would be 11% and structural composite lumber stiffness COV would be 7%. It was also judged that the system factors appropriate for machine stress-rated lumber, machine evaluated lumber and structural composite lumber would be proportional to the stiffness COV. This results in system factors of 7% for machine stress-rated and machine evaluated lumber and 4% for structural composite lumber. Determination of appropriate system factors for proprietary flange grades should be based on engineering judgement, stiffness COV of the material, and the guidelines described in ASTM Standard D6555. Resulting factors provided in Clause 13.2.4.4 are as follows:

| prefabricated wood I-joist flange | $K_{HB}$ |
|---|---|
| visually graded sawn lumber | 1.10 |
| machine stress-rated and machine evaluated lumber | 1.07 |
| structural composite lumber products | 1.04 |

### Clause 13.2.5 - Strength and Resistance

### Clause 13.2.5.2 - Lateral Stability Factor, $K_L$

Prefabricated wood I-joists require lateral support at points of bearing to prevent lateral displacement and rotation. Additionally, all compression edges require lateral support such as that provided by the permanent attachment of floor or roof sheathing in conformance with the applicable building code or, for other floor or roof decking products or systems, as determined by appropriate design procedures. For other applications such as long cantilevers or areas near intermediate bearing supports for continuous spans, lateral stability requirements should follow the recommendations of the manufacturer and should be determined on the basis of appropriate analytical and engineering principles and/or documented test data. When performing lateral stability calculations, only the compression flange material and geometric properties should be used.

### Clause 13.2.5.3 - Notches

Notches, holes, or cuts in the flanges of prefabricated wood I-joists will result in strength loss. Such notches, holes, or cuts are only permitted on the basis of the documented results of tests that take into account the effects of such notches, holes, or cuts.

## Clause 13.2.5.5 – Web Openings, Bearing Length and Web Stiffener Requirements

### Web Openings
Web openings (holes) are allowed only when appropriate documented test data is available from the manufacturer. ASTM Standard D 5055 provides details for determination of the effects of web openings.

### Bearing Length
Adequate bearing performance of prefabricated wood I-joists is dependent on more than perpendicular to grain bearing capacity of the flange materials and the supporting structure. ASTM Standard D 5055 prescribes qualification tests for the determination of the required bearing length. The prescribed tests include consideration of cross grain bending and tensile forces in the flanges, web stiffener nailing, flange-to-web glue joint strength, and perpendicular-to-grain bearing stresses. As a result, bearing lengths for prefabricated wood I-joists are based on empirical test results, rather than analytical calculations alone.

### Web Stiffeners
Web stiffeners are elements, generally sawn lumber, plywood, oriented strandboard (OSB) or structural composite lumber, that are oriented vertically in pairs and attached to opposite sides of the web member between the top and bottom flanges. They are generally installed with nails or staples loaded in double shear, with a minimum gap of 3 mm between the end of the web stiffener and the unloaded or non-bearing flange. If they are cut too long and require a force fit, the inherent prying action can fracture the critical glue joint between the web and the flange. No gap is allowed between the end of the web stiffener and the loaded or bearing flange.

Web stiffeners can be critical to the bearing capacity of a prefabricated wood I-joist and, when required, must be installed as per the manufacturer's instructions, which should be based on the testing required by ASTM Standard D 5055.

Web stiffeners perform two main functions: (1) they transfer a portion of the load from the web into the top of the bottom flange, reducing the load on the web-to-flange joint; and (2) they serve the implied function of reinforcing the web against buckling. Web stiffeners should not be used for vertical load transfer through the prefabricated wood I-joist at the bearing location since critical tolerances that are required for adequate performance are more stringent than can be expected under the best shop or field conditions.

ASTM Standard D 5055 provides the basis for determination of web stiffener requirements for bearing capacity for use with prefabricated wood I-joists. Special details such as concentrated loads may require web stiffeners at special locations. Loads may also be supported by connection to the web or on bottom flanges. The specific detail requirements should be based on documented test results.

### Clause 13.2.5.6 - Serviceability Limit States

The requirements for serviceability limit states in Clauses 4.1.3 and 4.5 of CSA O86, applicable to sawn lumber and glued-laminated timber, are also applicable to prefabricated wood I-joists. Maximum deflection limits are specified by code for all structural products.

ASTM Standard D 5055 establishes requirements for the determination of the stiffness and evaluation of the short term dry service creep characteristics of prefabricated wood I-joists. It also stipulates that any formula used for stiffness capacity calculations must accurately predict the combined effects of bending and shear deformation. Two commonly used methods of determining shear deflection are detailed in Clause 8.5.6 of CSA O86 and in *A Shear Stiffness Factor for Plywood Box Beams*, by C.K.A. Stieda. Appropriate deflection formulas for both, bending and shear are available from the manufacturers.

With very few exceptions, prefabricated wood I-joists are noncambered products. Use of these products in roof applications should be limited to sloped applications. A minimum slope of 1:50 is recommended.

### Clause 13.2.6 – Fastenings

### Clause 13.2.6.2 – Joist Hangers and Other Framing Connectors

Although there are numerous joist hangers and connectors available that appear compatible with prefabricated wood I-joists, some are not.

Hangers developed for conventional lumber or glued-laminated timber often use large nails spaced in a pattern that can split prefabricated wood I-joist flanges and web stiffeners. In addition to physical fit and load capacity, joist hanger selection for prefabricated wood I-joists should include consideration of nail length and diameter, nail location, joist bearing capacity, and the composition of the supporting member.

Because of the large and varied number of connector products available, the manufacturers of prefabricated wood I-joists must be consulted regarding the performance compatibility of joist hangers and other framing connectors with their products (See also Commentary on Clause 10.10).

### Clause 13.3 - Type 3 (Proprietary) Design-Rated OSB Panels

As explained in the Commentary on Clause 7, new engineering properties have been introduced in CSA O86 for design-rated OSB panels. Because of the nature of this product and mill processes, there are significant differences between the properties of products from different mills. For this reason, design values for OSB may be manufactured to fit into predetermined capacities, as in Clause 7, or may be manufactured to non-standard capacities.

12

CON

CSA Commentary

In the latter case, the product is termed Type 3 (Proprietary), and may be a non-standard thickness, or it may be the manufacturer's objective to use the full capacities of the product which may be significantly above a Type 1 or Type 2 grade level. A Certificate of Conformance is required for Proprietary OSB products. Clause 13.3 deals with this case.

### Clause 13.4 - Structural Composite Lumber Products

Clause 13.4 contains engineering design requirements and appropriate adjustment factors for structural composite lumber products for which characteristic values have been determined in accordance with ASTM Standard D 5456.

### Clause 13.4.2 – Adhesives

One means of demonstrating equivalent performance is to evaluate alternative adhesives in accordance with the principles set forth in CSA O437.2, *Evaluation of Binder Systems for OSB and Waferboard.* CSA O437.2 provides a method of evaluating the performance of a binder system to be used in the manufacture of an OSB product in comparison to the performance of the same product manufactured using a known phenol formaldehyde resin adhesive.

In order to demonstrate equivalence, the procedures of CSA O437.2 need to be modified with respect to conditioning, aging and other appropriate durability issues and to be representative of the geometry of the wood furnish used in specific structural composite lumber products.

### Clause 13.4.5 – Specified Strengths and Moduli of Elasticity

ASTM Standard D 5456 specifies the determination of characteristic values of structural composite lumber products. See the Commentary for Clause 13.2 for additional information.

### Clause 13.4.3.5 - Specified Compression Strength Perpendicular to Grain, $f_{cp}$

The characteristic value in compression perpendicular to grain as determined by ASTM Standard D 5456 is the average value at 1.0 mm deformation for compression perpendicular to grain from test results. To adjust from characteristic value to specified strengths, a factor of 1.09 (= load factor of 0.868 divided by $\phi$ of 0.80) was used. The load factor of 0.868 represents exact agreement with working stress design at a live load to dead load ratio of 4.0, when the traditional adjustment factor of 1.67 for compression perpendicular to grain is properly accounted for. This approach is similar to that adopted for sawn lumber in this Standard.

### Clause 13.4.4 - Modification Factors

### Clause 13.4.4.1 - Load Duration Factor, $K_D$

The load duration factors, $K_D$, in Table 4.3.2.2 of the Standard are applicable for use with the specified strengths of structural composite lumber products.

### Clause 13.4.4.2 - Service Condition Factor, $K_S$

The specified strengths and stiffness of structural composite lumber products are applicable for use under dry service conditions only. It is generally recommended that these products not be used in other than dry service conditions.

When these products are required for use in other environments, the specified strengths and stiffness must be modified by appropriate adjustments on the basis of the evaluation of the short and long-term effects of the particular environmental conditions.

Environmental conditions which result in high or fluctuating moisture content may affect material and product quality and may result in strength and stiffness adjustments different from those suitable for sawn lumber. Wet service condition use should be considered only when appropriate factors for specified strengths and stiffness are provided based on the documented results of tests that take into account the effects of time, temperature, and moisture content.

### Clause 13.4.4.3 - Treatment Factor, $K_T$

The specified strengths and stiffness of structural composite lumber products are applicable for use with non-pressure impregnated products only. Pressure impregnating chemical treatments may affect material quality and result in the need for strength and stiffness adjustments different from those suitable for sawn lumber. Pressure impregnating chemical treatments should be permitted only when treatment adjustments for specified strengths and stiffness are based on the documented results of tests that take into account the effects of time, temperature and moisture content.

### Clause 13.4.4.4 - System Factor, $K_H$

The system factor, $K_H$, for structural composite lumber products, was set at 1.04 to be consistent with the system factor specified for prefabricated wood I-joists with structural composite lumber flanges, as well as the system factor, $C_r$, as per a AF&PA's *LRFD Guideline for Structural Composite Lumber*.

### Clause 13.4.4.5 - Size Factor in Bending, $K_{Zb}$

The size factor in bending, $K_{Zb}$, is based on the provisions of section 6.4.1.3 and Annex A1 of ASTM Standard D 5456. The volumetric adjustments in Clauses 13.4.4.5 and 13.4.4.6 are intended to be performed by the manufacturer in determination of published and code evaluated properties and are not

**12**

**COM**

CSA Commentary

intended for general design use by a designer. Appropriate volumetric parameters, design information and limitations applicable to specific proprietary structural composite lumber products should be listed in the Registry of Product Evaluations, published by the Canadian Construction Materials Centre, Institute for Research in Construction, Ottawa, Ontario.

### Clause 13.4.4.6 - Size Factor in Tension, $K_{Zt}$

The size factor in tension, $K_{Zt}$, is based on the provisions of section 6.4.1.4 and Annex A1 of ASTM Standard D 5456. Also see the the Commentary for Clause 13.4.4.5.

### Clause 13.4.5 - Strength and Resistance

### Clause 13.4.5.3 - Notches

Notches, holes, or cuts in structural composite lumber products will result in strength loss. Such notches, holes, or cuts are only permitted on the basis of the documented results of tests that take into account the effects of such notches, holes, or cuts.

### Clause 13.4.5.4 - Shear Resistance

Presently there is no information available to support the use of a size factor in shear, $K_{Zv}$, other than 1.0. An ASTM committee is re-addressing the current test method for shear (the ASTM D245 shear revision proposal). This proposal also includes the determination of volumetric shear adjustments. A task group within the ASTM Standard D 5456 committee has been formed to monitor and review the results of the D245 shear proposal, to determine how it best applies to structural composite lumber products.

### Clause 13.4.5.5.3 - Factored Compressive Resistance Parallel to Grain

Presently there is no information available to support the use of a size factor in compression parallel to grain, other than $K_{Zc} = 1.0$.

### Clause 13.4.5.11 - Serviceability Limit States

The requirements for serviceability limit states in Clauses 4.1.3 and 4.5 of this Standard, applicable to sawn lumber and glued-laminated timber, are also applicable to structural composite lumber products. Maximum deflection limits are specified by code for all structural products.

With very few exceptions, structural composite lumber products are non-cambered. Use of these products in roof applications should be limited to sloped applications. A minimum slope of 1:50 is recommended.

## Clause 13.4.6 – Fastenings

Although there are numerous connectors available that appear to be compatible with structural composite lumber, some are not.

Hangers and other connectors such as split rings and truss plates developed for sawn lumber or glued-laminated timber can split structural composite lumber products in certain orientations, such as parallel to the gluelines, resulting in unacceptable or low performance. Manufacturers of structural composite lumber products must be consulted regarding the performance compatibility of connectors with their products.

The performance of nails, bolts and lag screws with structural composite lumber products is generally consistent with the performance of these connectors with sawn lumber and glued-laminated timber for the same density of material. However the specific product manufacturer should be consulted for appropriate guidance.

**12**

**COM**

CSA Commentary

## References

AF&PA. 1996. LRFD Guideline for Structural Composite Lumber. American Forest and Paper Association. Washington, DC.

APA. 2000. Performance Standard for Prefabricated Wood I-Joists. PRI-400. APA-Engineered Wood Systems, Tacoma, WA, USA.

ASTM. 2000. Evaluating System Effects in Repetitive-Member Wood Assemblies. Standard D 6555 American Society for Testing and Materials, West Conshohocken, PA.

Stieda, C.K.A. 1967. A Shear Stiffness Factor for Plywood Box Beams. Forest Products Laboratory (Canada). Information Report VP-X-31. Vancouver, BC.

WIJMA. 1999. Quality Assurance Guidelines for Prefabricated Wood I-Joists. Wood I-Joist Manufacturers Association.

## CAN/CSA-O86-01
### *A National Standard of Canada*
*(approved January 2003)*

# Engineering Design in Wood

*Reprinted June 2005. This reprint incorporates replacement pages issued as Update No. 1 (January 2003) and Supplement No. 1 (January 2005) into the original 2001 Standard.*

**CANADIAN STANDARDS ASSOCIATION**

**Standards Council of Canada**
**Conseil canadien des normes**

# Legal Notice for Standards

# CSA Standards Update Service

## CAN/CSA-O86-01
## Reprinted June 2005

**Title:** *Engineering Design in Wood* — originally published August 2001

**Revisions issued:** Update No. 1 — January 2003
Supplement No. 1 — January 2005

*If you are missing any General Instruction or Update, please contact CSA Information Products Sales or visit www.ShopCSA.ca.*

CAN/CSA-O86-01 originally consisted of **215 pages** (xix preliminary and 196 text), each dated **August 2001**. It now consists of the following pages:

| August 2001 | v, vi, ix–xix, 1–8, 21, 22, 29–36, 39–44, 47–52, 57–66, 69–86, 89, 90, 95–98, 101–158, 161, 162, 169–178, 181–190, 193, and 194 |
| --- | --- |
| **January 2003** | Cover and title page |
| **January 2005** | iii, iv, vii, viii, 9–20A, 23–28, 37, 38, 45, 46, 53–56, 67, 68, 87, 88, 91–94, 99, 100, 159, 160, 163–168, 179–180A, 191, 192, and 195–197 |
| **June 2005** | Copyright page |

**Note:** *The superseded pages have been gathered at the end of the Standard for reference. The replacement pages incorporated into the Standard are identified by date. Revisions made in the replacement pages in the body of the Standard are marked by the symbol delta (Δ) in the margin.*

Automatic notifications about any updates to this publication are available.

- To register for e-mail notifications, and/or to download any existing updates in PDF, enter the Online Store at **www.ShopCSA.ca** and click on **My Account** on the navigation bar. The **List ID** for this document is **2018509**.
- To receive printed updates, please complete and return the attached card.

✂ - - - - - - - - - - - - - - - - - - - - - - - - - - - - - - - - - - - - - - - - - - - - - - - - - - - - - - - - - - - - - - - - -

Name _____

Organization _____

Address _____

City _____

Province/State _____

Country _____ Postal/Zip Code _____

E-mail _____

I consent to CSA collecting and using the above information to send me updates relating to this publication.

*Visit CSA's policy on privacy at www.csagroup.org/legal to find out how we protect your personal information.*

## CAN/CSA-O86-01

**ASSOCIATION CANADIENNE DE NORMALISATION**
BUREAU CENTRAL DE L'INFORMATION
5060, SPECTRUM WAY, BUREAU 100
MISSISSAUGA ON  L4W 5N6
CANADA

**CANADIAN STANDARDS ASSOCIATION**
CONSOLIDATED MAILING LIST
5060 SPECTRUM WAY, SUITE 100
MISSISSAUGA ON  L4W 5N6
CANADA

*National Standard of Canada*
*(approved January 2003)*

*CAN/CSA-O86-01*
### *Engineering Design in Wood*

Prepared by

**CANADIAN STANDARDS**
**ASSOCIATION**

Approved by
*Standards Council of Canada*

Published in August 2001 by Canadian Standards Association
*A not-for-profit private sector organization*
5060 Spectrum Way, Suite 100, Mississauga, Ontario, Canada L4W 5N6
1-800-463-6727 • 416-747-4044

**Visit our Online Store at www.ShopCSA.ca**

Reprinted June 2005. This reprint incorporates replacement pages issued as Update No. 1 (January 2003) and Supplement No. 1* (January 2005) into the original 2001 Standard. The superseded pages have been gathered at the end of the Standard for reference. The replacement pages incorporated into the Standard are identified by date. Revisions made in the replacement pages in the body of the Standard are marked by the symbol delta ($\Delta$) in the margin.

*Supplement No. 1 contains major changes to make CAN/CSA-O86-01 consistent with the National Building Code of Canada (NBCC), 2005. The changes to Clause 4 of the Standard reflect changes adopted in the 2005 NBCC, including the companion load action approach, the separation of live load and snow load, and the rationalization of importance factors for building types and loads. Clause 4 also provides minimum load criteria for calculating deflection in wood members. Other revisions in the Supplement include increased specified shear values for sawn lumber; revised negative bending moment design values for glued-laminated timber; revisions to design values for structural sheathing OSB; and revisions to the clauses dealing with proprietary structural wood products. Additional information on compression perpendicular to grain capacity has been added in an appendix.*

ISBN 1-55436-094-3

(Copyright page replaced June 2005)

# Δ *Contents*

# *Technical Committee on Engineering Design in Wood*

| | | |
|---|---|---|
| **C.R. Wilson** | Carl R. Wilson & Associates Ltd., Vancouver, British Columbia | *Chair* |
| **G.C. Williams** | Timber Systems Limited, Markham, Ontario | *Vice-Chair* |
| **P. Trott** | Canadian Wood Council, Ottawa, Ontario | *Secretary* |
| **J.D. Barrett** | University of British Columbia, Vancouver, British Columbia | |
| **S. Boyd** | Quaile Engineering Ltd., Newmarket, Ontario | |
| **Y.H. Chui** | Wood Science and Technology Centre, Fredericton, New Brunswick | |
| **D.E. Darby** | Alberta Agriculture, Food and Rural Development, Lethbridge, Alberta | |
| **B. Di Lenardo** | NRC-Canadian Construction Materials Centre, Ottawa, Ontario | |
| **G.A. Dring** | G.A. Dring and Associates, Boissevain, Manitoba | |
| **R.A. Hewett** | Hewett Consulting, Nepean, Ontario | |
| **D. Himmelfarb** | Timber West Engineering Ltd., Edmonton, Alberta | |
| **B. Hintz** | Jager Industries Inc., Calgary, Alberta | |
| **M.J. Janotta** | Town of Richmond Hill, Building Services Division, Richmond Hill, Ontario | |
| **D. Janssens** | Structural Board Association, Willowdale, Ontario | |
| **K.C. Johns** | Université de Sherbrooke, Sherbrooke, Québec | |

| | | |
|---|---|---|
| **E. Jones** | Canadian Wood Council, Ottawa, Ontario | |
| **E. Karacabeyli** | Forintek Canada Corp., Vancouver, British Columbia | |
| **T.V. Leung** | Thomas Leung Structural Engineering Inc., Vancouver, British Columbia | |
| **B. Madsen** | Timber Engineering Ltd., North Vancouver, British Columbia | |
| **R. Malczyk** | Equilibrium Consulting Inc., Vancouver, British Columbia | |
| **N. Nagy** | Canadian Plywood Association, North Vancouver, British Columbia | |
| **P. Quenneville** | Royal Military College, Kingston, Ontario | |
| **D. Rice** | Trus Joist Technology Center, Boise, Idaho, USA | |
| **M. Ruflange** | Structurlam Products Ltd., Penticton, British Columbia | |
| **I. Smith** | University of New Brunswick, Fredericton, New Brunswick | |
| **R. Tiller** | Structural Design Inc., St. John's, Newfoundland | |
| **M.R. Lottamoza** | CSA, Toronto, Ontario | *Project Manager* |

# *Subcommittee on General Design*

| | | |
|---|---|---|
| **K.C. Johns** | Université de Sherbrooke,<br>Sherbrooke, Québec | *Chair* |
| **S. Boyd** | Quaile Engineering Ltd.,<br>Newmarket, Ontario | |
| **Y.H. Chui** | Wood Science and Technology Centre,<br>Fredericton, New Brunswick | |
| **B. Di Lenardo** | NRC-Canadian Construction Materials Centre,<br>Ottawa, Ontario | |
| **G.A. Dring** | G.A. Dring and Associates,<br>Boissevain, Manitoba | |
| **M.J. Janotta** | Town of Richmond Hill,<br>Building Services Division,<br>Richmond Hill, Ontario | |
| **E. Jones** | Canadian Wood Council,<br>Ottawa, Ontario | |
| **F. Lam** | University of British Columbia,<br>Vancouver, British Columbia | |
| **T.V. Leung** | Thomas Leung Structural Engineering Inc.,<br>Vancouver, British Columbia | |
| **N. Nagy** | Canadian Plywood Association,<br>North Vancouver, British Columbia | |
| **G.C. Williams** | Timber Systems Limited,<br>Markham, Ontario | |

# *Subcommittee on Sawn Lumber*

| | | |
|---|---|---|
| **J.D. Barrett** | University of British Columbia, Vancouver, British Columbia | *Chair* |
| **S. Boyd** | Quaile Engineering Ltd., Newmarket, Ontario | |
| **Y.H. Chui** | Wood Science and Technology Centre, Fredericton, New Brunswick | |
| **B. Craig** | Trus Joist, Delta, British Columbia | |
| **D.E. Darby** | Alberta Agriculture, Food and Rural Development, Lethbridge, Alberta | |
| **S. Goldie** | Vancouver, British Columbia | |
| **R.A. Hewett** | Hewett Consulting, Nepean, Ontario | |
| **B. Hintz** | Jager Industries Inc., Calgary, Alberta | |
| **M.J. Janotta** | Town of Richmond Hill, Building Services Division, Richmond Hill, Ontario | |
| **E. Jones** | Canadian Wood Council, Ottawa, Ontario | |
| **F. Lam** | University of British Columbia, Vancouver, British Columbia | |
| **T.V. Leung** | Thomas Leung Structural Engineering Inc., Vancouver, British Columbia | |
| **C. Lum** | Forintek Canada Corp., Vancouver, British Columbia | |
| **B. Madsen** | Timber Engineering Ltd., North Vancouver, British Columbia | |
| **A. Rozek** | National Lumber Grades Authority, New Westminster, British Columbia | |

# *Subcommittee on Glued-Laminated Timber*

| | | |
|---|---|---|
| **D. Himmelfarb** | Timber West Engineering Ltd., Edmonton, Alberta | *Chair* |
| **G.A. Dring** | G.A. Dring and Associates, Boissevain, Manitoba | |
| **E. Karacabeyli** | Forintek Canada Corp., Vancouver, British Columbia | |
| **B. Madsen** | Timber Engineering Ltd., North Vancouver, British Columbia | |
| **R. Malczyk** | Equilibrium Consulting Inc., Vancouver, British Columbia | |
| **M. Rufiange** | Structurlam Products Ltd., Penticton, British Columbia | |
| **G.C. Williams** | Timber Systems Limited, Markham, Ontario | |
| **B. Yeh** | APA, Tacoma, Washington, USA | |

# *Subcommittee on Panel Products*

# *Subcommittee on Fastenings*

| | | |
|---|---|---|
| **P. Quenneville** | Royal Military College,<br>Kingston, Ontario | *Chair* |
| **S. Boyd** | Quaile Engineering Ltd.,<br>Newmarket, Ontario | |
| **Y.H. Chui** | Wood Science and Technology Centre,<br>Fredericton, New Brunswick | |
| **G.A. Dring** | G.A. Dring and Associates,<br>Boissevain, Manitoba | |
| **D. Janssens** | Structural Board Association,<br>Willowdale, Ontario | |
| **E. Karacabeyli** | Forintek Canada Corp.,<br>Vancouver, British Columbia | |
| **K. Koo** | Jager Industries Inc.,<br>Bolton, Ontario | |
| **P. Lau** | Alpa Roof Truss Inc.,<br>Maple, Ontario | |
| **M. Lepper** | Canadian Wood Council,<br>Ottawa, Ontario | |
| **R. Malczyk** | Equilibrium Consulting Inc.,<br>Vancouver, British Columbia | |
| **D. Onysko** | DMO Associates,<br>Orléans, Ontario | |
| **H. Prion** | University of British Columbia,<br>Vancouver, British Columbia | |
| **D. Rice** | Trus Joist Technology Center,<br>Boise, Idaho, USA | |
| **I. Smith** | University of New Brunswick,<br>Fredericton, New Brunswick | |
| **G.C. Williams** | Timber Systems Limited,<br>Markham, Ontario | |

# Subcommittee on Proprietary Structural Wood Products

# *Task Force on Seismic Design in Wood*

| | | |
|---|---|---|
| **E. Karacabeyli** | Forintek Canada Corp., Vancouver, British Columbia | *Chair* |
| **C. Chiu** | Chiu Engineering, Vancouver, British Columbia | |
| **Y.H. Chui** | Wood Science and Technology Centre, Fredericton, New Brunswick | |
| **E. Jones** | Canadian Wood Council, Ottawa, Ontario | |
| **F. Lam** | University of British Columbia, Vancouver, British Columbia | |
| **T.V. Leung** | Thomas Leung Structural Engineering Inc., Vancouver, British Columbia | |
| **G. Newfield** | Read Jones Christofferson, Vancouver, British Columbia | |
| **C. Ni** | Forintek Canada Corp., Vancouver, British Columbia | |
| **H. Prion** | University of British Columbia, Vancouver, British Columbia | |
| **I. Smith** | University of New Brunswick, Fredericton, New Brunswick | |
| **R. Tiller** | Structural Design Inc., St. John's, Newfoundland | |

# *Preface*

This is the eighth edition of CSA Standard O86, *Engineering Design in Wood*. It is written in limit states design (LSD) format and supersedes the previous editions, published in 1994, 1989, 1984, 1980, 1976, 1970, and 1959, including their Supplements.

Editions of CSA Standard O86 published in 1959, 1970, 1976, 1980, and 1984 were all developed using working stress design (WSD) theory. The last WSD version, CSA Standard CAN3-O86-M84, *Engineering Design in Wood (Working Stress Design)*, existed concurrently with the first (1984) and second (1989) limit states design (LSD) versions, *Engineering Design in Wood (Limit States Design)*. The WSD version was withdrawn on publication of the 1994 LSD edition.

Three previous LSD editions were published in 1984, 1989, and 1994 with the CSA designation O86.1. Supplements to each of these editions were published in 1987, 1993, and 1998, respectively. Although this new edition continues to be based on the LSD method, the O86 designation has been reinstituted.

Major revisions in this 2001 edition are included in Clause 9, where specified strengths have been expanded to provide for construction OSB and gypsum. A mechanics-based design procedure has been included to provide criteria for shearwall segments with and without hold-downs and anchorages for shearwalls constructed of dissimilar materials of two layers, of two sides, and of blocked and unblocked diaphragms. In addition, more flexibility has been included for using the factors accounting for fastener capacities.

Other revisions include:

(a) for sawn lumber, additional guidance on dealing with vibration and elastic deflection of systems, revised notch criteria, and specified strengths for 89 × 89 mm light framing;
(b) for glulam, bending size factor for beams;
(c) for structural panels, specified strengths and modulus of elasticity for CSA O325 OSB and reference to panel mark equivalency;
(d) for composite building components, revised stress joint factors and engineering basis for the use of panels; and
(e) for connections, inclusion of withdrawal resistance for nails and spikes, design criteria for anchor bolts in concrete capacities, and updated references to truss plates standards.

Other minor revisions and refinements are found throughout the document, including the clauses dealing with proprietary structural wood products, the harmonization of the treatment factor for all materials, the design of preserved wood foundations, and the design of trusses.

This Standard was prepared by the Technical Committee on Engineering Design in Wood, under the jurisdiction of the Strategic Steering Committee on Structures (Design), and has been formally approved by the Technical Committee. This Standard has been approved as a National Standard of Canada by the Standards Council of Canada.

*August 2001*

**Notes:**
(1) *Use of the singular does not exclude the plural (and vice versa) when the sense allows.*
(2) *Although the intended primary application of this Standard is stated in its Scope, it is important to note that it remains the responsibility of the users of the Standard to judge its suitability for their particular purpose.*
(3) *This publication was developed by consensus, which is defined by CSA Policy governing standardization — Code of good practice for standardization as "substantial agreement. Consensus implies much more than a simple majority, but not necessarily unanimity". It is consistent with this definition that a member may be included in the Technical Committee list and yet not be in full agreement with all clauses of this publication.*
(4) *CSA Standards are subject to periodic review, and suggestions for their improvement will be referred to the appropriate committee.*
(5) *All enquiries regarding this Standard, including requests for interpretation, should be addressed to Canadian Standards Association, 5060 Spectrum Way, Suite 100, Mississauga, Ontario, Canada L4W 5N6.*

Requests for interpretation should

(a) define the problem, making reference to the specific clause, and, where appropriate, include an illustrative sketch;

(b) provide an explanation of circumstances surrounding the actual field condition; and

(c) be phrased where possible to permit a specific "yes" or "no" answer.

Committee interpretations are processed in accordance with the CSA Directives and guidelines governing standardization and are published in CSA's periodical Info Update, which is available on the CSA Web site at www.csa.ca.

# CAN/CSA-O86-01
# *Engineering Design in Wood*

## 1. Scope

This Standard provides criteria for the structural design and appraisal of structures or structural elements made from wood or wood products, including graded lumber, glued-laminated timber, unsanded plywood, oriented strandboard (OSB), composite building components, shearwalls and diaphragms, timber piling, pole-type construction, prefabricated wood I-joists, structural composite lumber products, preserved wood foundations, and their structural fastenings. The Standard employs the limit states design method.

## 2. Definitions, Symbols, Spacing Dimensions, and Reference Publications

### 2.1 Definitions

The following definitions apply in this Standard:

**Adhesive (glue)** — a substance capable of holding materials together by surface attachment for structural purposes.

**Analogue member** — the line representation of a truss member for the purposes of structural analysis.

**Aspect ratio of a shearwall segment** — the ratio of the height to the length of the segment.

**Basic structural capacity** — the numeric result of certain calculations specified in CSA Standard O452.0 to characterize the short-term mechanical engineering properties (at EMC at 20°C/80% RH) of a product, such as tensile capacity or shear capacity, based on test results for a sample undergoing qualification testing, and used to establish the specified capacities of design-rated OSB.

**Beam** — a timber whose larger dimension exceeds its smaller dimension by at least 51 mm; the beam is usually graded for use in bending with the load applied to the narrow face. (Grading rules sometimes designate beams as "beams and stringers".)

**Board** — a piece of lumber that is less than 38 mm in its smaller dimension.

**Butt joint** — a square joint between the ends of two pieces of wood or panel.

**Capacity** — in relation to prefabricated wood I-joists or structural composite lumber, the numeric value determined from strength and stiffness test data by calculations specified in ASTM Standard D 5055 or D 5456, respectively, carried out to characterize strength properties of I-joists or structural composite lumber or their component materials. The term is used in combination with a specific property, such as tensile capacity or shear capacity.
**Note:** *See also **Specified capacity** and **Basic structural capacity** for the term's application to panel products.*

**Certificate of conformance** — a document applicable to a design-rated OSB product issued by the certification organization. It certifies that the product meets the requirements of CSA Standard O452 Series and identifies its specified capacities determined in accordance with CSA Standard O452 Series.

**Certification organization (C.O.)** — an impartial body possessing the necessary competence and reliability to operate a certification system in which the interests of all parties concerned with the functioning of the system are represented, and accredited as such by agencies having a national mandate to accredit certification organizations operating within their countries' borders.
**Note:** *The Standards Council of Canada (SCC) has a national mandate to accredit certification organizations for operation in Canada.*

**Concentrically braced heavy timber space frame** — a structural system with an essentially complete timber space frame providing support for gravity loads and diagonal bracing with ductile connections resisting lateral loads.

**Density** — mass per unit volume.  In the case of wood, density is usually expressed as kilograms per cubic metre at a specified moisture content.

**Design rating** — a grade mark (consisting of a nominal thickness and a rating grade) assigned to a qualified OSB panel that indicates the panel's suitability for engineering design construction and that denotes a specific set of engineering property values for that panel.

**Diaphragm** — a horizontal or nearly horizontal system that acts to transmit lateral forces to the vertical resisting elements.  The term "diaphragm" includes horizontal bracing systems.

**Dimension lumber** — lumber 38 to 102 mm, inclusive, in its smaller dimension.

**Documented** — having written technical substantiation that the use of a particular material, design, practice, or construction method satisfies the intent of this Standard.

**Dressed size** — the cross-sectional dimensions in millimetres of lumber after planing.

**Drift pin** — a round mild steel bar, without head or threads, used to provide a laterally loaded connection between overlapping timbers in heavy engineering structures such as cribwork.

**Edge distance** — the distance from the edge of the member to the centre of the nearest fastening.

**End distance** — the distance measured parallel to the axis of a piece from the centre of a fastening to the square-cut end of the member.  In the case of a connector, if the end of the member is not square-cut, the end distance is taken from any point on the centre half of the connector diameter drawn perpendicular to the centreline of the piece to the nearest point on the end of the member measured parallel to the axis of the piece (see Figures 10.3.3A and 10.3.3B).

**Equilibrium moisture content** — the moisture content at which wood or wood products neither gain nor lose moisture when surrounded by air at a given relative humidity and temperature.

**Factored load** — the product of a specified load and its applicable load factor.

**Factored resistance** — the product of resistance and its applicable resistance factor.

**Fibre saturation point** — the moisture content at which the cell walls are saturated and the cell cavities are free of water; approximately 25–30% moisture content.

**Flat truss** — a truss in which the slope of the top chord does not exceed 2 in 12.

**Girder truss** — a truss that is used as a main supporting member for secondary framing systems such as other trusses, joists, or rafters.

**Glue** — see **Adhesive.**

**Glued-laminated timber (glulam)** — see **Structural glued-laminated timber.**

**Grade** — the designation of the quality of a piece of wood.

**Hold-down connection** — a connection at the corner of a shearwall or shearwall segment that is designed to provide a structural load path between the boundary chords of the segment and
(a) the foundation or beam supporting the shearwall; or
(b) the corresponding chord member of the shearwall segment above or below.

**Importance factor,** $\gamma$ — a factor applied to the factored loads other than dead load to take into account the consequences of collapse as related to the use and occupancy of the structure.

**Joist** — a piece of dimension lumber 114 mm or more in its larger dimension, intended to be loaded on its narrow face.

**Lamination** — a thin element of wood of appreciable width and length consisting of one or more pieces that may be joined end-to-end.

**Limit state** — a condition of a structure in which the structure ceases to fulfill the design function.

**Load combination factor,** $\Psi$ — a factor applied to the factored loads other than dead load to take into account the reduced probability of a number of loads from different sources acting simultaneously.

**Load duration** — the period of continuous application of a given load or the aggregate of periods of intermittent applications of the same load.

**Load factor,** $\alpha$ — a factor applied to a specified load that, for the limit state under consideration, takes into account the variability of the loads and load patterns.

**Lumber** —

   **Machine evaluated lumber** — structural lumber that has been graded by means of a nondestructive test and visual grading, conforming to the requirements for machine stress-rated lumber, with the exception that the process lower fifth percentile modulus of elasticity (MOE) equals or exceeds 0.75 times the characteristic mean MOE for the grade.

   **Machine stress-rated lumber** — structural lumber graded by means of a nondestructive test and visual grading, in accordance with the requirements of CSA Standard CAN/CSA-O141.

   **Rough lumber** — lumber as it comes from the saw.

   **Sawn lumber** — the product of a sawmill not further manufactured other than by sawing, resawing, passing lengthwise through a standard planing mill, and cross-cutting to length.

   **Structural lumber** — lumber in which strength is related to the anticipated end use as a controlling factor in grading or selecting.

   **Visually stress-graded lumber** — structural lumber that has been graded in accordance with the provisions of the NLGA *Standard Grading Rules for Canadian Lumber.*

**Lumber sizes** — under the metric system
(a) rough lumber is designated by its actual dry or green size;

(b) dressed dry (S-Dry) lumber is designated by its actual finished size;

(c) dressed green (S-Grn) dimension lumber is designated by its anticipated dry size at 19% moisture content;

(d) dressed green timber is designated by its actual green size; and

(e) sizes are rounded to the nearest millimetre.

**Major axis (major strength axis)** — the axis with the greater stiffness and strength in bending: for plywood, the direction parallel to the face grain; for OSB, the direction of alignment of the strands in the face layers of the panel.

**Mid-panel moment** — the maximum moment between panel points.

**Minor axis (minor strength axis)** — the axis with the lesser stiffness and strength in bending: for plywood, the direction perpendicular to the face grain; for OSB, the direction perpendicular to the alignment of the strands in the face layers of the panel.

**Moisture content** — the mass of water in wood expressed as a percentage of the mass of the oven-dry wood.

**Moment-resisting wood space frame** — a structural system with an essentially complete wood space frame providing support for gravity loads, with resistance to lateral loads provided primarily by flexural action of members.

**Nailed shear panel** — a nailed diaphragm or a nailed shearwall.

**OSB** — an acronym for oriented strandboard: that is, a strandboard panel containing layers of aligned strands, generally with the strands in the face layers aligned in the direction of the panel length. Panels are marked to show the direction of alignment of face layers.

    **Construction sheathing OSB** — OSB that has been certified to CSA Standard CAN/CSA-O325.0 for protected construction uses such as roof sheathing, wall sheathing, and floor sheathing in light frame construction applications and other permitted engineering applications in this Standard.

    **CSA O437 OSB** — OSB that meets the requirements of CSA Standard O437.0 (Grade O-2 or O-1) and that is recognized for use as sheathing for shearwalls and diaphragms within this Standard.

    **Design-rated OSB** — OSB panels qualified and certified for use in engineering design construction in accordance with CSA Standard O452 Series.

    **Type 1: STANDARD** — design-rated OSB meeting the minimum basic structural capacity values set in CSA Standard O452.0 for the rating grade.

    **Type 2: PLUS** — design-rated OSB having one or more properties assigned higher basic structural capacity values, in percentage, than the minimum set for the rating grade of the product.

    **Type 3: PROPRIETARY** — design-rated OSB with assigned proprietary specified capacity values determined in accordance with Clause 13.3.

**Panel length** — with respect to the design of lumber members in metal-plated trusses (see Clause 5.5.13), the distance between two adjacent panel points.

**Panel point** — with respect to the design of lumber members in metal-plated trusses (see Clause 5.5.13), a point representing the intersection of two or more analogue member lines and/or a normal line from a bearing surface.

**Panel point moment** — with respect to the design of lumber members in metal-plated trusses (see Clause 5.5.13), the moment computed at an analogue panel point.

**Perimeter member** — an element at edges of openings or at perimeters of shearwalls or diaphragms.

**Pitch** — the rise in run, usually expressed as a fraction of 12, of the upper surface of a roof member.

**Pitch break** — the point at which a truss chord member changes slope.

**Planar shear** — the shear that occurs in the plane of the panel. Also referred to as "shear-in-plane".

**Plank** — a piece of dimension lumber 114 mm or more in its larger dimension, intended to be loaded on its wide face.

**Ply** — a thin layer or sheet of wood (veneer), or several pieces laid with adjoining edges that may or may not be edge-glued, forming one layer in a plywood panel.

**Plywood** —

   **Regular unsanded grade** — any one of the following three grades: Select-Tight Face, Select, or Sheathing as defined in CSA Standards O121 and O151.

   **Standard construction** — panels that meet the requirements for standard constructions as defined in CSA Standards O121 and O151 and Clause A7.3.1 of this Standard.

**Pole-type construction** — a form of construction in which the principal vertical members are round poles or sawn timbers embedded in the ground and extending vertically above ground to provide both foundation and vertical framing members for the structure.

**Post** — a timber with its larger dimension not more than 51 mm greater than the smaller dimension, usually graded for use as a column. (Grading rules sometimes designate posts as "posts and timbers".)

**Prefabricated wood I-joist** — a structural member manufactured using structural lumber, structural glued-laminated timber, or structural composite lumber flanges, and structural panel webs, bonded together with exterior exposure adhesives, forming an "I" cross-sectional shape.
**Note:** *To avoid confusion with plywood web beams as defined in Clause 8.5, "prefabricated wood I-joist" refers to high-volume, mass-produced proprietary products primarily used as joists in the construction of floor and roof systems.*

**Resistance factor,** $\phi$ — a factor applied to the resistance of a member or connection for the limit state under consideration, which takes into account the variability of dimensions and material properties, quality of work, type of failure, and uncertainty in the prediction of resistance.

**Service condition** —

   **Dry service condition** — a climatic condition in which the average equilibrium moisture content of solid wood over a year is 15% or less and does not exceed 19%.

   **Wet service condition** — all service conditions other than dry.

**Serviceability limit states** — those states which restrict the intended use and occupancy of the structure; they include deflection, joint slip, vibration, and permanent deformation.

**Shearwall** — a stud wall system designed to resist lateral forces parallel to the plane of the wall (sometimes referred to as a vertical diaphragm or a structural wall). A shearwall may consist of one or more shearwall segments in the plane of the wall.

**Shearwall segment** — a section of a shearwall with uniform construction that forms a structural unit designed to resist lateral forces parallel to the plane of the wall.

**Shrinkage** — the decrease in the dimensions of wood or wood products due to a decrease of moisture content.

**Slab floor** — a basement floor system in which a concrete slab or equivalent provides lateral support at the bottom of the foundation studs.

**Slenderness ratio for beams** — the ratio used in lateral stability calculations of a bending member.

**Slenderness ratio for compression members** — the ratio of the effective length of a compression member to its actual dimensions.

**Slip resistance of a connection** — a serviceability state; a resistance that corresponds to a specific level of slip.

**Space frame** — a three-dimensional structural system without structural stud walls that is composed of members interconnected so as to function as a complete self-contained unit with or without the aid of horizontal diaphragms or floor bracing systems.

**Spacing of fastenings** — the distance between fastenings measured between centres.

**Specified capacity** — the assigned strength capacity, or stiffness or rigidity capacity, for use in the prediction of strength resistance or deflection.

**Specified loads** — those loads defined in the appropriate building code, or those loads determined by use and occupancy for structures other than buildings, or such larger loads as may be selected for the design.

**Specified strength** — the assigned strength for use in the prediction of strength resistance.

**Stiffener** — a piece of wood of rectangular cross-section that extends between the inner surfaces of the top and bottom flanges of a plywood web beam, and is glued or otherwise fastened to the webs.

**Strandboard** — a mat-formed structural panel made of specialized wood wafers having a length at least twice their width.

**Strength limit states** — those states concerning safety, including the maximum load-carrying capacity, overturning, sliding, fracture, and deterioration.

**Strength resistance of a connection** — a resistance based on the geometry and on the ultimate load-carrying capacity of the structural materials of a connection.

**Stressed skin panel** — a form of construction in which the outer skin, in addition to its normal function of providing a surface covering, acts integrally with the frame members, contributing to the strength of the unit as a whole.

**Structural composite lumber** — the wood product that is either laminated veneer lumber (LVL) or parallel strand lumber (PSL), manufactured for use in structural applications and bonded with exterior exposure adhesives.

**Laminated veneer lumber (LVL)** — a composite of wood veneer sheet elements and adhesive manufactured with wood fibres primarily oriented along the length of the member. The veneer elements do not exceed 6.4 mm in thickness.

**6**

**Parallel strand lumber (PSL)** — a composite of wood strand elements and adhesive manufactured with wood fibres primarily oriented along the length of the member. The strand elements do not exceed 6.4 mm in thickness and have an average length of at least 150 times their least dimension.

**Structural glued-laminated timber** — the wood product that is made by bonding under pressure graded laminating stock whose grain is essentially parallel and that meets the requirements of CSA Standard CAN/CSA-O122.

**Structural panel** — in this Standard, plywood and OSB panels of specific grades and quality to which specified capacities have been assigned, or are assignable, e.g., standard constructions of regular grades of unsanded Douglas Fir plywood and Canadian Softwood plywood manufactured and marked in accordance with CSA Standards O121 and O151, and design-rated OSB manufactured, marked, and certified for use in engineered design construction in accordance with CSA Standard O452.0.

**Stud wall system** — a structural system without a complete vertical load-carrying space frame. Stud walls provide support for all gravity loads. Studs are spaced not more than 610 mm on centre.

**Suspended floor** — a basement floor system in which a floor assembly is attached to continuous foundation studs at a point above the bottom of the studs.

**Timber** — a piece of lumber 114 mm or more in its smaller dimension.

**Timber connector** — a metal ring or plate that, by being embedded in adjacent wood faces or in one wood face, acts in shear to transmit loads from one timber to another or from a timber to a bolt and, in turn, to a steel plate or another connector.

**Truss plate** — a light steel plate fastening, intended for use in structural lumber assemblies, that may have integral teeth of various shapes and configurations.

**Waferboard** — a mat-formed structural panel made predominantly of wood wafers of a minimum and controlled length, a controlled thickness, and a variable or predetermined width, bonded together with a waterproof and boilproof binder. Waferboard meets the requirements of CSA Standard O437.0 (Grade R-1) and is recognized for use as sheathing for shearwalls and diaphragms within this Standard.

**Wood preservation** —

**Preservative treatment** — impregnation under pressure with a wood preservative.

**Wood preservative** — any suitable substance that is toxic to fungi, insects, borers, and other living wood-destroying organisms.

## 2.2  Symbols
The following symbols are used throughout this Standard. Deviations from these usages and additional nomenclature are noted where they appear.

$A$ = cross-sectional area, mm$^2$

$A_b$ = bearing area, mm$^2$

$A_g$ = gross cross-sectional area, mm$^2$

$A_n$ = net cross-sectional area, mm$^2$

$B_a$ = specified axial stiffness of structural panels, N/mm (Tables 7.3A, 7.3B, 7.3C, and 7.3D)

$B_b$ = specified bending stiffness of structural panels, N•mm$^2$/mm (Tables 7.3A, 7.3B, 7.3C, and 7.3D)

$B_r$ = factored buckling resistance for plywood assemblies, $kN/m^2$ (Clause A8.6.3.4)

$B_v$ = specified shear-through-thickness rigidity of structural panels, N/mm (Tables 7.3A, 7.3B, 7.3C, and 7.3D)

$b$ = width of member, mm

$b_p$ = width of structural panel, mm

$C_B$ = slenderness ratio for bending members

$C_C$ = slenderness ratio for compression members

$d$ = depth of member, mm

$d_F$ = diameter of fastening, mm

$d_p$ = depth of structural panel in plane of bending, mm

$E$ = specified modulus of elasticity, MPa

$E_{05}$ = modulus of elasticity for design of compression members, MPa

$E_S$ = modulus of elasticity for stiffness calculations, MPa (Clause 4.5.1)

$(EI)_e$ = effective stiffness of structural panel assemblies, $N \bullet mm^2$ (Clause 8.5.2 and 8.6.2)

$f_b$ = specified strength in bending, MPa

$f_c$ = specified strength in compression parallel to grain, MPa

$f_{cp}$ = specified strength in compression perpendicular to grain, MPa

$f_f$ = specified notch shear force resistance, MPa

$f_t$ = specified strength in tension parallel to grain at net section, MPa

$f_{tg}$ = specified strength in tension parallel to grain at gross section of glued-laminated timber, MPa

$f_{tp}$ = specified strength in tension perpendicular to grain, MPa

$f_v$ = specified strength in shear, MPa

$I$ = moment of inertia, $mm^4$

$J$ = factors affecting capacity of fastenings, used with appropriate subscripts (Clause 10)

$J_{hd}$ = hold-down effect factor for shearwall segments (Clause 9.4.5)

$K_B$ = bearing factor (Clause 5.5.7.6)

$K_C$ = slenderness factor for compression members (Clauses 5.5.6.2.3 and 6.5.8.5)

$K_D$ = load duration factor (Clause 4.3.2 and Table 4.3.2.2)

$K_E$ = end fixity factor for spaced compression members (Clause A5.5.6.3.7)

$K_F$ = foundation factor for plywood (Clause 7.4.5)

$K_H$ = system factor (Clause 4.3.5)

$K_L$ = lateral stability factor for bending members (Clause 4.3.7)

$K_M$ = bending capacity modification factor (Clause 5.5.13.5)

$K_N$ = notch factor (Clauses 5.5.5.4 and 6.5.7.2.2)

$K_R$ = radial stress factor (Clause 6.5.6.6.3)

$K_S$ = service condition factor for sawn lumber, glued-laminated timber, plywood, design-rated OSB, poles, and piling (Clause 4.3.3)

$K_{Sb}$ = service condition factor for bending

$K_{Sc}$ = service condition factor for compression parallel to grain

$K_{Scp}$ = service condition factor for compression perpendicular to grain

$K_{SE}$ = service condition factor for modulus of elasticity

$K_{SF}$ = service condition factor for fastening

$K_{St}$ = service condition factor for tension parallel to grain

$K_{Stp}$ = service condition factor for tension perpendicular to grain

$K_{Sv}$ = service condition factor for shear

$K_T$ = treatment factor (Clause 4.3.4.1)

$K_X$ = curvature factor for glued-laminated timber (Clause 6.5.6.5.2)

$K_Z$ = size factor (Clause 5.4.5 and Table 5.4.5)

$K_{Zb}$ = size factor for bending for sawn lumber

$K_{Zbg}$ = size factor for bending for glued-laminated timber (Clause 6.5.6.5.1)

$K_{Zc}$ = size factor for compression for sawn lumber (Clauses 5.5.6.2.3 and 5.5.13.3.3)

$K_{Zcg}$ = size factor for compression for glued-laminated timber (Clause 6.5.8.4.2)

$K_{Zcp}$ = size factor for bearing (Clauses 5.5.7.5 and 6.5.9.2)

$K_{Zt}$ = size factor for tension for sawn lumber

$K_{Ztp}$ = size factor for tension perpendicular to grain for glued-laminated timber (Table 6.5.6.6.1)

$K_{Zv}$ = size factor for shear for sawn lumber (Clause 5.4.5.3)

$L$ = length, mm

$L_e$ = effective length, mm

$L_p$ = length of penetration of fastening into main member, mm

$\ell$ = span, mm

$M_f$ = factored bending moment, N•mm

$M_r$ = factored bending moment resistance, N•mm

$m_p$ = specified strength capacity of structural panels in bending, N•mm/mm (Tables 7.3A, 7.3B, 7.3C, and 7.3D)

$N_r$ = factored compressive resistance at an angle to grain, N; or

= factored lateral strength resistance of fastenings at an angle to grain, N or kN

$N_{rs}$ = factored lateral slip resistance of fastenings at an angle to grain, N

$N_s$ = lateral slip resistance of fastenings at an angle to grain, N

$N_u$ = lateral strength resistance of fastenings at an angle to grain, N or kN

$n_F$ = number of fastenings in a group

$P_f$ = factored axial load in compression, N

$P_r$ = factored compressive resistance parallel to grain, N; or

= factored lateral strength resistance of fastenings parallel to grain, N or kN

$P_{rs}$ = factored lateral slip resistance of fastenings parallel to grain, N

$P_{rw}$ = factored withdrawal resistance of fastenings from side grain, N

$P_u$ = lateral strength resistance of fastenings parallel to grain, N or kN

$p_p$ = specified strength capacity of structural panels in axial compression, N/mm (Tables 7.3A, 7.3B, 7.3C, and 7.3D)

$Q_r$ = factored compressive resistance perpendicular to grain or to plane of plies, N; or

= factored lateral strength resistance of fastenings perpendicular to grain, N or kN

$Q_{rs}$ = factored lateral slip resistance of fastenings perpendicular to grain, N

$Q_u$ = lateral strength resistance of fastenings perpendicular to grain, N or kN

$q_p$ = specified strength capacity of structural panels in bearing, MPa (Tables 7.3A, 7.3B, 7.3C, and 7.3D)

R = radius of curvature at centreline of member, mm (Figure 6.5.6.6.3)

S = section modulus, $mm^3$

$T_f$ = factored axial load in tension, N

$T_r$ = factored tensile resistance parallel to grain, N

$t_p$ = specified strength capacity of structural panels in axial tension, N/mm (Tables 7.3A, 7.3B, 7.3C, and 7.3D)

$V_f$ = factored shear force, N

$V_{hd}$ = factored basic shear resistance calculated with $J_{hd}$ = 1.0, kN (Clause 9.4.5)

$V_r$ = factored shear resistance, N; or

= factored shear-through-thickness resistance of structural panels, N

$V_{rp}$ = factored planar shear resistance of structural panels, N

$V_{rs}$ = factored shear resistance of a shearwall segment, kN (Clause 9.5)

$v_p$ = specified strength capacity of structural panels in shear-through-thickness, N/mm (Tables 7.3A, 7.3B, 7.3C, and 7.3D)

$v_{pb}$ = specified strength capacity of structural panels in planar shear (due to bending), N/mm (Tables 7.3A, 7.3B, 7.3C, and 7.3D)

$v_{pf}$ = specified strength capacity of structural panels in planar shear (due to in-plane forces), MPa (Tables 7.3A, 7.3B, 7.3C, and 7.3D)

$W_f$ = factored total load, N

w = specified total uniformly distributed load, $kN/m^2$

X = factors affecting capacities of plywood and plywood assemblies, used with appropriate subscripts (Clause 8)

Z = volume, $m^3$

Δ  γ  — Deleted

φ  = resistance factor

Δ  ψ  — Deleted

## 2.3 Spacing Dimensions

For the purpose of this Standard, the following apply:
(a) Centre-to-centre member spacing dimensions may be used interchangeably:
    (i)   300 mm and 305 mm;

    (ii)  400 mm and 406 mm; and

    (iii)  600 mm and 610 mm.

(b)  Panel dimensions may be used interchangeably:

    (i)  1200 mm and 1220 mm; and

    (ii)  2400 mm and 2440 mm.

## Δ 2.4 Reference Publications

This Standard refers to the following publications and where such reference is made it shall be to the edition listed below, including all amendments published thereto.

### CSA Standards

B111-1974 (R2003),
*Wire Nails, Spikes, and Staples;*

G40.20-04/G40.21-04,
*General requirements for rolled or welded structural quality steel/Structural quality steel;*

CAN/CSA-O15-90 (R2004),
*Wood Utility Poles and Reinforcing Stubs;*

CAN3-O56-M79 (R2001),
*Round Wood Piles;*

O80 Series-97 (R2002),
*Wood Preservation;*

    O80.15-97 (R2002),
    *Preservative Treatment of Wood for Building Foundation Systems, Basements, and Crawl Spaces by Pressure Processes;*

O112 Series-M1977 (R2001),
*CSA Standards for Wood Adhesives;*

    O112.6-M1977 (R2001),
    *Phenol and Phenol-Resorcinol Resin Adhesives for Wood (High-Temperature Curing);*

    O112.7-M1977 (R2001),
    *Resorcinol and Phenol-Resorcinol Resin Adhesives for Wood (Room- and Intermediate-Temperature Curing);*

    O112.9-04,
    *Evaluation of adhesives for structural wood products (exterior exposure);*

O121-M1978 (R2003),
*Douglas Fir Plywood;*

CAN/CSA-O122-M89 (R2003),
*Structural Glued-Laminated Timber;*

CAN/CSA-O141-91 (R2004),
*Softwood Lumber;*

O151-M1978 (R2003),
*Canadian Softwood Plywood;*

O153-M1980 (R2003),
*Poplar Plywood;*

CAN/CSA-O177-M89 (R2003),
*Qualification Code for Manufacturers of Structural Glued-Laminated Timber;*

O322-02,
*Procedure for Certification of Pressure-Treated Wood Materials for Use in Preserved Wood Foundations;*

CAN/CSA-O325.0-92 (R2003),
*Construction Sheathing;*

O437 Series-93 (R2001),
*Standards on OSB and Waferboard;*

    O437.0-93 (R2001),
    *OSB and Waferboard;*

O452 Series-94 (R2001),
*Design Rated OSB;*

    O452.0-94 (R2001),
    *Design Rated OSB: Specifications;*

S307-M1980 (R2001),
*Load Test Procedure for Wood Roof Trusses for Houses and Small Buildings;*

S347-99 (R2004),
*Method of Test for Evaluation of Truss Plates Used in Lumber Joints;*

CAN/CSA-S406-92 (R2003),
*Construction of Preserved Wood Foundations.*

**ANSI/ASME\* Standard**
B18.2.1-1996,
*Square and Hex Bolts and Screws, Inch Series.*

**ASTM† Standards**
A 36/A 36M-04,
*Carbon Structural Steel;*

A 47/A 47M-99,
*Ferritic Malleable Iron Castings;*

A 307-03,
*Carbon Steel Bolts and Studs, 60 000 PSI Tensile Strength;*

A 653/A 653M-03,
*Specification for Steel Sheet, Zinc-Coated (Galvanized) or Zinc-Iron Alloy-Coated (Galvannealed) by the Hot-Dip Process;*
**Note:** *ASTM Standards A 653/A 653M replace ASTM Standards A 446/A 446M. Their chemical and mechanical requirements are the same.*

C 36/C 36M-03,
*Gypsum Wallboard;*

C 1002-01,
*Steel Self-Piercing Tapping Screws for the Application of Gypsum Panel Products or Metal Plaster Bases to Wood Studs or Steel Studs;*

D 1761-88 (2000),
*Mechanical Fasteners in Wood;*

D 5055-04,
*Establishing and Monitoring Structural Capacities of Prefabricated Wood I-Joists;*

D 5456-01,
*Evaluation of Structural Composite Lumber Products;*

D 5457-93 (1998),
*Computing the Reference Resistance of Wood-Based Materials and Structural Connections for Load and Resistance Factor Design;*

E 8-04,
*Standard Test Methods for Tension Testing of Metallic Materials.*

**Canadian Geotechnical Society Publication**
*Canadian Foundation Engineering Manual,* 1992.

**Canadian Wood Council**
CWC, *Commentary,* 2001 (in *Wood Design Manual*);

*Standard Practice Relating Specified Strengths of Structural Members to Characteristic Structural Properties,* April 2001.

**National Research Council Canada**
*CCMC Registry of Product Evaluations* (published annually);

*National Building Code of Canada,* 2005;

*User's Guide — NBC 2005 Structural Commentaries (Part 4).*

**NIST‡ Standard**
PS2-92,
*Performance Standard for Wood-Based Structural-Use Panels.*

**NLGA§ Publications**
*Standard Grading Rules for Canadian Lumber,* 2003;

SPS 1-2003,
*Special Products Standards on Finger-Joined Structural Lumber;*

SPS 2-2003,
*Special Products Standards on Machine Stress-Rated Lumber.*

**SAE** Publication**
*SAE Handbook,* 2004.

**Truss Plate Institute of Canada**
TPIC-1996,
*Truss Design Procedures and Specifications for Light Metal Plate Connected Wood Trusses.*

*American National Standards Institute/American Society of Mechanical Engineers.
†American Society for Testing and Materials.
‡National Institute of Standards and Technology.
§National Lumber Grades Authority.
**Society of Automotive Engineers.

# 3. Objectives and Design Requirements

## 3.1 Objective

The objective of the provisions in this Standard is the achievement of acceptable assurances that the structure, when correctly designed and built, will be fit for the intended use.

## 3.2 Limit States

The structure or portion thereof is considered fit for use when the structure, its components, and its connections are designed such that the requirements of Clauses 3.3, 4.1.2, and 4.1.3 are satisfied.

## 3.3 Design Requirements

### 3.3.1 Structural Adequacy

All members shall be so framed, anchored, tied, and braced together as to provide the strength and rigidity necessary for the purpose for which they are designed. All structural members shall be of adequate size and quality to carry all loads and other forces that can be reasonably expected to act upon them during construction and use without exceeding the strength or serviceability limit states.

### 3.3.2 New or Special Systems of Design and Construction

New or special systems of design or construction of wood structures or structural elements not already covered by this Standard may be used where such systems are based on analytical and engineering principles, or reliable test data, or both, that demonstrate the safety and serviceability of the resulting structure for the purpose intended.

### 3.3.3 Structural Integrity

The general arrangement of the structural system and the interconnection of its members shall provide positive resistance to widespread collapse of the system due to local failure.

### 3.3.4 Basis of Design

Design in accordance with this Standard is based on the assumption that
(a) the specified loads are realistic in size, kind, and duration;
(b) the wood product is normal for its species, kind, and grade;
(c) consideration is given to service conditions, including possible deterioration of members and corrosion of fastenings;
(d) the temperature of the wood does not exceed 50°C, except for occasional exposures to 65°C;
(e) the design is competent, fabrication and erection are good, grading and inspection are reliable, and maintenance is normal; and
(f) wood products are used as graded or manufactured for a designated end use.

### 3.3.5 Quality of Work

The quality of work in fabrication, preparation, and installation of materials shall conform throughout to accepted good practice.

### 3.3.6 Design Drawings

#### 3.3.6.1

Where design drawings are required they shall be drawn to a scale adequate to convey the required information. The drawings shall show a complete layout of the structure or portion thereof that is the subject of the design, with members suitably designated and located, including dimensions and detailed descriptions necessary for the preparation of shop and erection drawings. Governing heights, column centres, and offsets shall be dimensioned.

### 3.3.6.2

Design drawings shall designate the design standards used, as well as material or product standards applicable to the members and details depicted.

### 3.3.6.3

When needed for the preparation of shop drawings, the governing loads, reactions, shears, moments, and axial forces to be resisted by all members and their connections shall be shown on drawings or supplemental material, or both.

### 3.3.6.4

If camber is required for beams, girders, or trusses, the magnitude of such camber shall be specified on the design drawings.

# 4. General Design

Δ ## 4.1 Ultimate and Serviceability Limit States

### 4.1.1 Method of Analysis

The load effect on all members and connections shall be determined in accordance with recognized methods of analysis generally based on assumptions of elastic behaviour.

Δ ### 4.1.2 Ultimate Limit States

Design for ultimate limit states shall include
(a) establishing the value of the effect of the factored loads individually and with the load combinations specified in Clause 4.2; and
(b) confirming by rational means that for each load effect in Item (a), the factored load effect does not exceed the corresponding factored resistance, as determined in accordance with the appropriate clauses of this Standard.

### 4.1.3 Serviceability Limit States

Design for serviceability limit states shall include
Δ (a) establishing the value of the effect of the specified loads individually and with the load combinations specified in Clause 4.2; and
(b) confirming by rational means that for each load effect in Item (a), the structural effect falls within the limits specified in the appropriate clauses of this Standard.

### 4.1.4 Resistance Factors

The resistance factors, $\varphi$, are given in the appropriate sections of this Standard for all applicable limit states for wood members and fastenings.

## 4.2 Specified Loads, Load Effects, and Load Combinations

Δ ### 4.2.1 Buildings

Except as provided for in Clause 4.2.2, the specified loads, load effects, and combinations to be considered in the design of a building and its elements shall be those given in Clauses 4.2.3 and 4.2.4.
**Note:** *Specified loads, load effects, and combinations specified herein are in accordance with the provisions of the* National Building Code of Canada, *2005, its* Structural Commentaries on Part 4, *and the* Canadian Foundation Engineering Manual.

## 4.2.2 Other Structures

Where load requirements other than those in Clause 4.2.1 are specified, the appropriateness of the applicable factored resistance in this Standard shall be considered.

△ **4.2.3 Specified Loads**

### 4.2.3.1 Loads to be Considered

Specified loads shall include the following wherever applicable, and minimum specified values of these loads shall be increased to account for dynamic effects where applicable:

(a) D — dead load due to weight of members; the weight of all materials of construction incorporated into the building to be supported permanently by the member, including permanent partitions and allowance for nonpermanent partitions; the weight of permanent equipment;

(b) E — load due to earthquake, including the effect of the importance factors in Clause 4.2.3.2;

(c) L — live load due to intended use and occupancy, including loads due to cranes and the pressure of liquids in containers;

(d) S — load due to snow, including ice and associated rain, and also including the effect of the importance factors in Clause 4.2.3.2;

(e) W — load due to wind, including the effect of the importance factors in Clause 4.2.3.2;

(f) H — permanent load due to lateral earth pressure, including groundwater;

(g) P — permanent effects caused by prestress; and

(h) T — load due to contraction or expansion caused by temperature changes, shrinkage, moisture changes, creep in component materials, movement due to differential settlement, or combinations thereof.

### 4.2.3.2 Importance Factors

For the purpose of determining the specified S, W, or E loads of Clause 4.2.3.1, importance factors shall be applied in accordance with Table 4.2.3.2.

**Note:** *For further information on specified loads and importance factors, see the* National Building Code of Canada, *2005.*

△

## Table 4.2.3.2
## Importance Factors for Determining S, W, or E Loads

| Importance category | Importance factors for snow loads, $I_S$ | | Importance factors for wind loads, $I_W$ | | Importance factors for earthquake loads, $I_E$ | |
|---|---|---|---|---|---|---|
| | Ultimate limit state | Serviceability limit state | Ultimate limit state | Serviceability limit state | Ultimate limit state | Serviceability limit state |
| Low | 0.8 | 0.9 | 0.8 | 0.75 | 1.0 | N/A |
| Normal | 1.0 | 0.9 | 1.0 | 0.75 | 1.0 | N/A |
| High | 1.15 | 0.9 | 1.15 | 0.75 | 1.3 | N/A |
| Post-disaster | 1.25 | 0.9 | 1.25 | 0.75 | 1.5 | N/A |

△ **4.2.4 Load Combinations**

△ **4.2.4.1 Load Combinations for Ultimate Limit States**

The effect of factored principal plus companion loads shall be determined in accordance with the load combinations in Table 4.2.4.1. The applicable combination shall be that which results in the most unfavourable effect.

Δ

## Table 4.2.4.1
## Load Combinations for Ultimate Limit States

| Case | Principal loads* | Companion loads |
|------|------------------|-----------------|
| 1 | 1.4D | |
| 2 | (1.25D† or 0.9D) + 1.5L‡ | 0.5S§ or 0.4W |
| 3 | (1.25D† or 0.9D) + 1.5S | 0.5L§** or 0.4W |
| 4 | (1.25D† or 0.9D) + 1.4W | 0.5L** or 0.5S |
| 5 | 1.0D + 1.0E | 0.5L§** + 0.25S§ |

*Refer to the National Building Code of Canada, 2005, for loads due to lateral earth pressure (H), prestress (P), and imposed deformation (T).
†Refer to the National Building Code of Canada, 2005, for a dead load (D) for soil.
‡The principal load factor of 1.5 for a live load (L) may be reduced to 1.25 for liquids in tanks.
§Refer to the National Building Code of Canada, 2005, for loads on exterior areas.
**The companion load factor of 0.5 for a live load (L) shall be increased to 1.0 for storage occupancies, equipment areas, and service rooms.*

Δ **4.2.4.2 Load Combinations for Serviceability Limit States**

The effect of principal plus companion loads shall be determined in accordance with the load combinations in Table 4.2.4.2. The applicable combination shall be that which results in the most unfavourable effect.

Δ

## Table 4.2.4.2
## Load Combinations for Serviceability Limit States

| Case | Principal loads | Companion loads |
|------|-----------------|-----------------|
| 1 | 1.0D* | |
| 2 | 1.0D* + 1.0L | 0.5S† or 0.4W |
| 3 | 1.0D* + 1.0S | 0.5L† or 0.4W |
| 4 | 1.0D* + 1.0W | 0.5L or 0.5S |

*Dead loads include permanent loads due to lateral earth pressure (H) and prestress (P).
†Refer to the National Building Code of Canada, 2005, for loads on exterior areas.*

Δ **4.2.4.3 —** *Deleted*

Δ **4.2.4.4 —** *Deleted*

Δ **4.2.4.5 —** *Deleted*

## 4.3 Conditions and Factors Affecting Resistance

Δ **4.3.1 General**

Specified strengths and capacities for materials and fastenings shall be multiplied by the modification factors in this clause and the appropriate materials or fastening clauses.

**Note:** *The basis for derivation of specified strengths for sawn lumber members is described in the Canadian Wood Council's Standard Practice Relating Specified Strengths of Structural Members to Characteristic Structural Properties. The principles described therein have also been used to guide derivations for other products in this Standard.*

## 4.3.2 Load Duration Factor, $K_D$

### 4.3.2.1 Specified Strengths and Capacities

The specified strengths and capacities given in this Standard are based on the standard-term duration of the specified loads.

### 4.3.2.2 Load Duration Factor

Except as specified in Clause 4.3.2.3, the specified strengths and capacities shall be multiplied by a load duration factor, $K_D$, in accordance with Table 4.3.2.2, but not exceeding 1.15.

**Table 4.3.2.2**
**Load Duration Factor, $K_D$**

| Duration of loading | $K_D$ | Explanatory notes |
|---|---|---|
| Short term | 1.15 | Short-term loading means that condition of loading where the duration of the specified loads is not expected to last more than 7 days continuously or cumulatively throughout the life of the structure.<br>  Examples include wind loads, earthquake loads, falsework, and formwork, as well as impact loads. |
| Standard term | 1.00 | Standard term means that condition of loading where the duration of specified loads exceeds that of short-term loading, but is less than permanent loading.<br>  Examples include snow loads, live loads due to occupancy, wheel loads on bridges, and dead loads in combination with all of the above. |
| Permanent | 0.65 | Permanent duration means that condition of loading under which a member is subjected to more or less continuous specified load.<br>  Examples include dead loads or dead loads plus live loads of such character that they are imposed on the member for as long a period of time as the dead loads themselves. Such loads include those usually occurring in tanks or bins containing fluids or granular material, loads on retaining walls subjected to lateral pressure such as earth, and floor loads where the specified load may be expected to be continuously applied, such as those in buildings for storage of bulk materials. Loads due to fixed machinery should be considered to be permanent. |

**Note:** *Duration of load may require professional judgment by the designer. Explanatory notes in this table provide guidance to designers about the types of loads and load combinations for which each modification factor should be applied.*

Δ **4.3.2.3 Permanent Load Factor**

For standard-term loads where D is greater than the specified standard-term load, $P_s$, the permanent load factor may be used, or the factor may be calculated as

$$K_D = 1.0 - 0.50 \log \left( \frac{D}{P_s} \right) \geq 0.65$$

where
D  = specified dead load
$P_s$  = specified standard-term load based on S and L loads acting alone or in combination
   = S, L, S + 0.5L, or 0.5S + L, where S is determined using an importance factor equal to 1.0.

### 4.3.2.4 Combined Loads

When the total specified load is made up of loads acting for different durations, the design shall be based on the most severe combination. The appropriate load duration factor shall be taken into account for each load combination.

### 4.3.3 Service Condition Factor, $K_S$

Where materials or fastenings are used in service conditions other than dry, specified strengths and capacities shall be multiplied by the service condition factor, $K_S$, in the appropriate materials or fastening clauses.

### 4.3.4 Preservative and Fire-Retardant Treatment Factor, $K_T$

#### 4.3.4.1 General

Except as permitted in Clause 4.3.4.4, specified strengths and capacities shall be multiplied by the treatment factor, $K_T$, in the appropriate materials or fastenings clause.

#### 4.3.4.2 Preservative Treatment

When conditions conducive to decay or other deterioration are likely to occur in the case of permanent structures, wood should be pressure-treated with preservative in accordance with the requirements of the CSA Standard O80 Series. If possible, all boring, grooving, cutting, and other fabrication should be completed before treatment. Fabrication that is carried out after pressure treatment shall be treated locally in accordance with the CSA Standard O80 Series.

#### 4.3.4.3 Untreated Wood

Untreated wood in permanent structures shall not be in direct contact with masonry, concrete, or soil when moisture transfer can occur. Any method that eliminates transfer of moisture, e.g., a minimum of 10 mm air space around a member in a wall, shall be considered adequate protection.

#### 4.3.4.4 Fire-Retardant Treatment

Where wood is impregnated with fire-retardant or other strength-reducing chemicals, $K_T$ shall be determined in accordance with the results of appropriate tests or shall not exceed the value of $K_T$ tabulated in the appropriate clause.

### Δ 4.3.5 System Factor, $K_H$

Specified strengths may be multiplied by a system factor, $K_H$, as specified in Clauses 5.4.4, 6.4.3, 13.2.4.4, and 13.4.4.4.

**Note:** *See Clause A4.3.5 for additional information on system factors.*

### Δ 4.3.6 Size Factor, $K_Z$

Where size influences the specified strengths of members, the specified strengths shall be multiplied by the size factor, $K_Z$, in accordance with Clauses 5.4.5, 6.5.6., 6.5.8, 6.5.9, 13.2.5.1, and 13.4.4.6.

**Note:** *See the Canadian Wood Council's Commentary.*

### 4.3.7 Lateral Stability Factor, $K_L$

The effect of width-to-depth ratios and of the degree of lateral support on the factored bending moment resistance is specified in Clauses 5.5.4.2 and 6.5.6.4.

### 4.3.8 Reduction in Cross-Section

#### 4.3.8.1 Net Section

The net section, obtained by deducting from the gross section the area of all material removed by boring, grooving, dapping, notching, or other means, shall be checked in calculating the strength capacity of a member.

#### 4.3.8.2 Limitation

In no case shall the net section be less than 75% of the gross section.

Δ **4.4  Resistance to Seismic Loads**

The factored resistance required for seismic loading may be obtained by the use of shearwalls and diaphragms (Clause 9). Where concentrically braced heavy timber space frames or moment-resisting wood space frames are used to provide seismic resistance, fastenings such as nails, bolts, lag screws, or glulam rivets as specified in Clause 10 shall be detailed to provide ductile connections.
**Note:** *Split rings and shear plates are not generally considered to provide ductile connections.*

## 4.5  Serviceability Requirements

### 4.5.1  Modulus of Elasticity

The modulus of elasticity for stiffness calculations, $E_S$, shall be taken as

$$E_S = E(K_{SE}K_T)$$

where
$E$   = specified modulus of elasticity, MPa
$K_{SE}$ = service condition factor
$K_T$  = treatment factor

Δ **4.5.2  Elastic Deflection**

The elastic deflection of structural members under the load combinations for serviceability limit states shall not exceed 1/180 of the span. For members having cambers equalling at least dead load deflection, the additional deflection due to live, snow, and wind loads shall not exceed 1/180 of the span. Deflection under the load combinations for serviceability limit states shall be limited to avoid damage to structural elements or attached nonstructural elements.
**Note:** *See Clause A4.5.2 for additional information on deflection of a wood frame system under static loads.*

Δ **4.5.3  Permanent Deformation**

Structural members that support permanent loads in excess of 50% of the load combinations for serviceability limit states shall be designed to limit permanent deformation. In lieu of a more accurate evaluation of acceptable deflection limits, an upper limit of 1/360 of the span shall be imposed on the elastic deflection due to permanent loads.

### 4.5.4  Ponding

Roof framing systems shall be investigated by rational analysis to ensure adequate performance under ponding conditions unless
(a) the roof surface is provided with sufficient slope toward points of free drainage to prevent accumulation of rain water; or
(b) for a simply supported system subjected to a uniformly distributed load, the following condition is satisfied:

$$\frac{\Sigma\Delta}{w} < 65$$

where
$\Sigma\Delta$ = sum of deflections due to this load, mm, of all the components of the system (decking, secondary beams, primary beams, etc)
$w$  = total uniformly distributed load, kN/m$^2$

Δ **4.5.5  Vibration**

Special consideration shall be given to structures subjected to vibration to ensure that such vibration is acceptable for the use of the structure.
**Note:** *See Clause A4.5.5 for information on floor vibration. Additional information can be found in the commentary on serviceability criteria for deflections and vibrations in the* User's Guide — NBC 2005 Structural Commentaries (Part 4)*.*

# 5. Sawn Lumber

## 5.1 Scope

Design tables, data, and methods specified in Clause 5 apply only to structural lumber complying with the requirements of CSA Standard CAN/CSA-O141.

## 5.2 Materials

### 5.2.1 Identification of Lumber

#### 5.2.1.1 General

Design in accordance with this Standard is predicated on the use of lumber that is graded in accordance with the NLGA *Standard Grading Rules for Canadian Lumber* and identified by the grade stamp of an association or independent grading agency in accordance with the provisions of CSA Standard CAN/CSA-O141.

**Note:** *A list of approved agencies may be obtained from the Canadian Lumber Standards Accreditation Board.*

#### 5.2.1.2 Canadian Lumber

In this Standard, Canadian species are designated according to species combinations given in Table 5.2.1.2, which reflects marketing practice. These combinations should be used for general design purposes.

**Note:** *The designer is strongly advised to check availability of species, grade, and sizes before specifying.*

#### 5.2.1.3 US Lumber

For US commercial species combinations graded in accordance with the *National Grading Rule for Dimension Lumber,* the design data may be determined using the species combination equivalents in Table 5.2.1.3.

## Table 5.2.1.2
## Species Combinations

| Species combinations | Stamp identification | Species included in the combination |
|---|---|---|
| Douglas Fir-Larch | D Fir-L (N) | Douglas Fir, Western Larch |
| Hem-Fir | Hem-Fir (N) | Pacific Coast Hemlock, Amabilis Fir |
| Spruce-Pine-Fir | S-P-F | Spruce (all species except Coast Sitka Spruce), Jack Pine, Lodgepole Pine, Balsam Fir, Alpine Fir |
| Northern Species | North Species | Any Canadian species graded in accordance with the NLGA rules |

**Notes:**

**(1)** *Names of species in this Table are standard commercial names. Additional information on botanical names and other common names is given in CSA Standard CAN/CSA-O141.*

**(2)** *The NLGA* Standard Grading Rules for Canadian Lumber *contains many species designations not shown in this Table. If the species can be identified, however, it may be possible to group it in one of the species combinations, for purposes of assigning specified strengths.*

## Table 5.2.1.3
## Lumber Species Equivalents

| US combination | Equivalent Canadian combination |
|---|---|
| Douglas Fir-Larch | Douglas Fir-Larch |
| Hem-Fir | Hem-Fir |
| Southern Pine | Spruce-Pine-Fir |

**Note:** *The NLGA* Standard Grading Rule for Canadian Lumber *incorporates the* National Grading Rules for Dimension Lumber, *a uniform set of grade descriptions and other requirements for softwood dimension lumber that form a required part of all softwood lumber grading rules in the United States. Thus, all dimension lumber throughout Canada and the United States is graded to uniform requirements.*

## 5.2.2 Lumber Grades and Categories

## 5.2.2.1 Visually Stress-Graded Lumber

Table 5.2.2.1 lists categories, limiting dimensions, and structural grades for which design data are assigned in this Standard. These grades are specified in the NLGA *Standard Grading Rules for Canadian Lumber*.

## Table 5.2.2.1
## Visual Grades and Their Dimensions

| Grade category | Smaller dimension, mm | Larger dimension, mm | Grades |
|---|---|---|---|
| Light Framing | 38 to 89 | 38 to 89 | Construction, Standard |
| Stud | 38 to 89 | 38 or more | Stud |
| Structural Light Framing | 38 to 89 | 38 to 89 | Select Structural No. 1, No. 2, No. 3 |
| Structural Joists and Planks | 38 to 89 | 114 or more | Select Structural No. 1, No. 2, No. 3 |
| Beam and Stringer | 114 or more | Exceeds smaller dimension by more than 51 | Select Structural No. 1, No. 2 |
| Post and Timber | 114 or more | Exceeds smaller dimension by 51 or less | Select Structural No. 1, No. 2 |
| Plank Decking | 38 to 89 | 140 or more | Select, Commercial |

### 5.2.2.2 Machine Stress-Rated (MSR) and Machine Evaluated Lumber (MEL)

Design data specified in this Standard apply to lumber graded and grade-stamped in accordance with NLGA Special Product Standard SPS 2, and identified by the grade stamp of a grading agency accredited for grading by mechanical means.

**Note:** *A list of accredited agencies may be obtained from the Canadian Lumber Standards Accreditation Board.*

### 5.2.3 Finger-Joined Lumber

Design data specified in this Standard apply to finger-joined lumber that has been produced and grade-stamped in accordance with NLGA Special Product Standard SPS 1.

### 5.2.4 Remanufactured Lumber

Dimension lumber and timbers that are resawn or otherwise remanufactured shall be regraded in accordance with Clause 5.2.1.

### 5.2.5 Mixed Grades

When mixed grades are used, the specified strength shall be that of the grade having the lowest value.

## 5.3 Specified Strengths

### 5.3.1 Visually Stress-Graded Lumber

#### 5.3.1.1

The specified strengths (MPa) for visually stress-graded lumber are tabulated as follows:
(a) structural joist and plank, structural light framing, and stud grade categories of lumber in Table 5.3.1A;
(b) light framing grades in Table 5.3.1B;
(c) beam and stringer grade categories of lumber in Table 5.3.1C; and
(d) post and timber grade categories of lumber in Table 5.3.1D.

## 5.3.1.2

The specified strengths (MPa) for plank decking shall be derived from Table 5.3.1A using the following grade equivalents:

| Decking grade | Equivalent lumber grade |
|---|---|
| Select | Select Structural |
| Commercial | No. 2 |

## 5.3.2 Machine Stress-Rated and Machine Evaluated Lumber

The specified strengths (MPa) for machine stress-rated lumber are given in Table 5.3.2. The specified strengths (MPa) for machine evaluated lumber are given in Table 5.3.3. Specified strengths in shear are not grade-dependent and shall be taken from Table 5.3.1A for the appropriate species.

Δ

### Table 5.3.1A
### Specified Strengths and Modulus of Elasticity for Structural Joist and Plank, Structural Light Framing, and Stud Grade Categories of Lumber (MPa)

| Species identification | Grade | Bending at extreme fibre, $f_b$ | Longi-tudinal shear, $f_v$ | Compression Parallel to grain, $f_c$ | Compression Perpen-dicular to grain, $f_{cp}$ | Tension parallel to grain, $f_t$ | Modulus of elasticity E | Modulus of elasticity $E_{05}$ |
|---|---|---|---|---|---|---|---|---|
| D Fir-L | SS | 16.5 | | 19.0 | | 10.6 | 12 500 | 8 500 |
| | No. 1/No. 2 | 10.0 | 1.9 | 14.0 | 7.0 | 5.8 | 11 000 | 7 000 |
| | No. 3/Stud | 4.6 | | 4.6 | | 2.1 | 10 000 | 5 500 |
| Hem-Fir | SS | 16.0 | | 17.6 | | 9.7 | 12 000 | 8 500 |
| | No. 1/No. 2 | 11.0 | 1.6 | 14.8 | 4.6 | 6.2 | 11 000 | 7 500 |
| | No. 3/Stud | 7.0 | | 7.0 | | 3.2 | 10 000 | 6 000 |
| S-P-F | SS | 16.5 | | 14.5 | | 8.6 | 10 500 | 7 500 |
| | No. 1/No. 2 | 11.8 | 1.5 | 11.5 | 5.3 | 5.5 | 9 500 | 6 500 |
| | No. 3/Stud | 7.0 | | 7.0 | | 3.2 | 9 000 | 5 500 |
| Northern | SS | 10.6 | | 13.0 | | 6.2 | 7 500 | 5 500 |
| | No. 1/No. 2 | 7.6 | 1.3 | 10.4 | 3.5 | 4.0 | 7 000 | 5 000 |
| | No. 3/Stud | 4.5 | | 4.5 | | 2.0 | 6 500 | 4 000 |

**Note:** *Tabulated values are based on the following standard conditions:*
*(a) 286 mm larger dimension;*
*(b) dry service conditions; and*
*(c) standard-term duration of load.*

## Table 5.3.1B
## Specified Strengths and Modulus of Elasticity for Light Framing Grades (MPa) Applicable to Sizes 38 by 38 mm to 89 by 89 mm

| Species identification | Grade | Bending at extreme fibre, $f_b$ | Longitudinal shear, $f_v$ | Compression Parallel to grain, $f_c$ | Perpendicular to grain, $f_{cp}$ | Tension parallel to grain, $f_t$ | Modulus of elasticity E | $E_{05}$ |
|---|---|---|---|---|---|---|---|---|
| D Fir-L | Const. | 13.0 | 3.2 | 16.0 | 7.0 | 6.6 | 10 000 | 5 500 |
|  | Stand. | 7.3 |  | 13.1 |  | 3.7 | 9 000 | 5 000 |
| Hem-Fir | Const. | 14.3 | 2.7 | 16.9 | 4.6 | 7.0 | 10 000 | 6 000 |
|  | Stand. | 8.0 |  | 13.9 |  | 3.9 | 9 000 | 5 500 |
| S-P-F | Const. | 15.3 | 2.6 | 13.1 | 5.3 | 6.2 | 9 000 | 5 500 |
|  | Stand. | 8.6 |  | 10.8 |  | 3.5 | 8 000 | 5 000 |
| Northern | Const. | 9.9 | 2.2 | 11.9 | 3.5 | 4.5 | 6 500 | 4 000 |
|  | Stand. | 5.5 |  | 9.8 |  | 2.5 | 6 000 | 3 500 |

**Notes:**
**(1)** The size factor $K_Z$ for light framing grades shall be 1.00, except that $K_{Zc}$ shall be calculated in accordance with Clause 5.5.6.2.2, and $K_{Zcp}$ shall be determined in accordance with Clause 5.5.7.5.
**(2)** Tabulated values are based on the following standard conditions:
(a) 89 mm width (except for compression properties);
(b) dry service conditions; and
(c) standard-term duration of load.

Δ

# Table 5.3.1C
## Specified Strengths and Modulus of Elasticity for Beam and Stringer Grades (MPa)

| Species identification | Grade | Bending at extreme fibre,* $f_b$ | Longi-tudinal shear, $f_v$ | Compression Parallel to grain, $f_c$ | Perpen-dicular to grain, $f_{cp}$ | Tension parallel to grain, $f_t$ | Modulus of elasticity E | $E_{05}$ |
|---|---|---|---|---|---|---|---|---|
| D Fir-L | SS | 19.5 | | 13.2 | | 10.0 | 12 000 | 8 000 |
| | No. 1 | 15.8 | 1.5 | 11.0 | 7.0 | 7.0 | 12 000 | 8 000 |
| | No. 2 | 9.0 | | 7.2 | | 3.3 | 9 500 | 6 000 |
| Hem-Fir | SS | 14.5 | | 10.8 | | 7.4 | 10 000 | 7 000 |
| | No. 1 | 11.7 | 1.2 | 9.0 | 4.6 | 5.2 | 10 000 | 7 000 |
| | No. 2 | 6.7 | | 5.9 | | 2.4 | 8 000 | 5 500 |
| S-P-F | SS | 13.6 | | 9.5 | | 7.0 | 8 500 | 6 000 |
| | No. 1 | 11.0 | 1.2 | 7.9 | 5.3 | 4.9 | 8 500 | 6 000 |
| | No. 2 | 6.3 | | 5.2 | | 2.3 | 6 500 | 4 500 |
| Northern | SS | 12.8 | | 7.2 | | 6.5 | 8 000 | 5 500 |
| | No. 1 | 10.8 | 1.0 | 6.0 | 3.5 | 4.6 | 8 000 | 5 500 |
| | No. 2 | 5.9 | | 3.9 | | 2.2 | 6 000 | 4 000 |

*Specified strengths for beams and stringers are based on loads applied to the narrow face. When beams and stringers are subject to loads applied to the wide face, the specified strength for bending at the extreme fibre and the specified modulus of elasticity shall be multiplied by the following factors:*

| | $f_b$ | E or $E_{05}$ |
|---|---|---|
| *Select Structural* | *0.88* | *1.00* |
| *No. 1 or No. 2* | *0.77* | *0.90* |

**Notes:**

**(1)** *Beams and stringers have a smaller dimension of at least 114 mm, with a larger dimension more than 51 mm greater than the smaller dimension.*

**(2)** *An approximate value for modulus of rigidity may be estimated at 0.065 times the modulus of elasticity.*

**(3)** *With sawn members thicker than 89 mm that season slowly, care should be exercised to avoid overloading in compression before appreciable seasoning of the outer fibre has taken place; otherwise, compression strengths for wet service conditions shall be used.*

**(4)** *Beam and stringer grades listed in this table are not graded for continuity (see Clause 5.5.3).*

**(5)** *Tabulated values are based on the following standard conditions:*

*(a) 343 mm larger dimension for bending and shear, 292 mm larger dimension for tension and compression parallel to grain;*

*(b) dry service conditions; and*

*(c) standard-term duration of load.*

Δ

## Table 5.3.1D
## Specified Strengths and Modulus of Elasticity
## for Post and Timber Grades (MPa)

| Species identification | Grade | Bending at extreme fibre, $f_b$ | Longi-tudinal shear, $f_v$ | Compression | | Tension parallel to grain, $f_t$ | Modulus of elasticity | |
| | | | | Parallel to grain, $f_c$ | Perpen-dicular to grain, $f_{cp}$ | | E | $E_{05}$ |
|---|---|---|---|---|---|---|---|---|
| D Fir-L | SS | 18.3 | | 13.8 | | 10.7 | 12 000 | 8 000 |
| | No. 1 | 13.8 | 1.5 | 12.2 | 7.0 | 8.1 | 10 500 | 6 500 |
| | No. 2 | 6.0 | | 7.5 | | 3.8 | 9 500 | 6 000 |
| Hem-Fir | SS | 13.6 | | 11.3 | | 7.9 | 10 000 | 7 000 |
| | No. 1 | 10.2 | 1.2 | 10.0 | 4.6 | 6.0 | 9 000 | 6 000 |
| | No. 2 | 4.5 | | 6.1 | | 2.8 | 8 000 | 5 500 |
| S-P-F | SS | 12.7 | | 9.9 | | 7.4 | 8 500 | 6 000 |
| | No. 1 | 9.6 | 1.2 | 8.7 | 5.3 | 5.6 | 7 500 | 5 000 |
| | No. 2 | 4.2 | | 5.4 | | 2.6 | 6 500 | 4 500 |
| Northern | SS | 12.0 | | 7.5 | | 7.0 | 8 000 | 5 500 |
| | No. 1 | 9.0 | 1.0 | 6.7 | 3.5 | 5.3 | 7 000 | 5 000 |
| | No. 2 | 3.9 | | 4.1 | | 2.5 | 6 000 | 4 000 |

**Notes:**

**(1)** *Posts and timbers have a smaller dimension of at least 114 mm, with a larger dimension not more than 51 mm greater than the smaller dimension.*

**(2)** *Posts and timbers graded to beam and stringer rules may be assigned beam and stringer strength.*

**(3)** *An approximate value for modulus of rigidity may be estimated at 0.065 times the modulus of elasticity.*

**(4)** *With sawn members thicker than 89 mm that season slowly, care should be exercised to avoid overloading in compression before appreciable seasoning of the outer fibre has taken place; otherwise, compression strengths for wet service conditions shall be used.*

**(5)** *Tabulated values are based on the following standard conditions:*
*(a) 343 mm larger dimension for bending and shear, 292 mm larger dimension for tension and compression parallel to grain;*
*(b) dry service conditions; and*
*(c) standard-term duration of load.*

Δ

## Table 5.3.2
### Specified Strengths and Modulus of Elasticity for Machine Machine Stress-Rated Grades 38 mm Thick by All Widths (MPa)

| Grade | Bending at extreme fibre, $f_b$ | Modulus of elasticity, E | Tension parallel to grain, $f_t$ | | Compression | |
|---|---|---|---|---|---|---|
| | | | 89 to 184 mm | >184 mm† | Parallel to grain, $f_c$ | Perpendicular to grain,* $f_{cp}$ |
| 1200F$_b$-1.2E | 17.4 | 8 300 | 6.7 | — | 15.1 | 5.3 |
| 1350F$_b$-1.3E | 19.5 | 9 000 | 8.4 | — | 16.9 | 5.3 |
| 1450F$_b$-1.3E | 21.0 | 9 000 | 9.0 | — | 17.3 | 5.3 |
| 1500F$_b$-1.4E | 21.7 | 9 700 | 10.1 | — | 17.5 | 5.3 |
| 1650F$_b$-1.5E | 23.9 | 10 300 | 11.4 | — | 18.1 | 5.3 |
| 1800F$_b$-1.6E | 26.1 | 11 000 | 13.2 | — | 18.7 | 5.3 |
| 1950F$_b$-1.7E | 28.2 | 11 700 | 15.4 | — | 19.3 | 5.3 |
| 2100F$_b$-1.8E | 30.4 | 12 400 | 17.7 | — | 19.9 | 6.5 |
| 2250F$_b$-1.9E | 32.6 | 13 100 | 19.6 | — | 20.5 | 6.5 |
| 2400F$_b$-2.0E | 34.7 | 13 800 | 21.6 | — | 21.1 | 6.5 |
| 2550F$_b$-2.1E | 36.9 | 14 500 | 23.0 | — | 21.7 | 6.5 |
| 2700F$_b$-2.2E | 39.1 | 15 200 | 24.1 | — | 22.3 | 6.5 |
| 2850F$_b$-2.3E | 41.3 | 15 900 | 25.8 | — | 22.9 | 6.5 |
| 3000F$_b$-2.4E | 43.4 | 16 500 | 26.9 | — | 23.5 | 6.5 |

*The following MSR grades provide a modulus of elasticity with higher corresponding strengths. For these MSR grades, qualification and daily quality control for tensile strength are required.*

| Grade | Bending at extreme fibre, $f_b$ | Modulus of elasticity, E | Tension parallel to grain 89 to 184 mm | Tension parallel to grain >184 mm† | Parallel to grain, $f_c$ | Perpendicular to grain,* $f_{cp}$ |
|---|---|---|---|---|---|---|
| 1400F$_b$-1.2E | 20.3 | 8 300 | 9.0 | 9.0 | 17.1 | 5.3 |
| 1600F$_b$-1.4E | 23.2 | 9 700 | 10.7 | 10.7 | 17.9 | 5.3 |
| 1650F$_b$-1.3E | 23.9 | 9 000 | 11.4 | 11.4 | 18.1 | 5.3 |
| 1800F$_b$-1.5E | 26.1 | 10 300 | 14.6 | 14.6 | 18.7 | 5.3 |
| 2000F$_b$-1.6E | 29.0 | 11 000 | 14.6 | 14.6 | 19.5 | 5.3 |
| 2250F$_b$-1.7E | 32.6 | 11 700 | 19.6 | 19.6 | 20.5 | 5.3 |
| 2250F$_b$-1.8E | 32.6 | 12 400 | 19.6 | 19.6 | 20.5 | 6.5 |
| 2400F$_b$-1.8E | 34.7 | 12 400 | 21.6 | 21.6 | 21.1 | 6.5 |

*Compression perpendicular to grain values are for S-P-F MSR (all grades) and Hem-Fir MSR lumber with E grade of 10 300 MPa or higher. For other species or grades, use corresponding values for visually stress-graded lumber taken from Table 5.3.1A for the appropriate group.

†The tension design values for narrow widths may be assigned to these sizes, provided the lumber is subject to the appropriate level of qualification and daily quality control testing for tension strength, as specified in NLGA SPS 2.

**Notes:**

**(1)** Tabulated values are based on standard-term duration of load and dry service conditions.

**(2)** The size factor $K_Z$ for MSR lumber shall be 1.00, except that $K_{Zv}$ is given in Table 5.4.5, $K_{Zcp}$ is determined in accordance with Clause 5.5.7.5, and $K_{Zc}$ is calculated in accordance with Clause 5.5.6.2.2.

## Table 5.3.3
## Specified Strengths and Modulus of Elasticity for Machine Evaluated Lumber Grades 38 mm Thick by All Widths (MPa)

| Grade | Bending at extreme fibre, $f_b$ | Modulus of elasticity, E | Tension parallel to grain, $f_t$ | Compression Parallel to grain, $f_c$ | Perpendicular to grain,* $f_{cp}$ |
|---|---|---|---|---|---|
| M-10 | 20.3 | 8 300 | 9.0 | 17.1 | 5.3 |
| M-11 | 22.4 | 10 300 | 9.5 | 17.7 | 5.3 |
| M-12 | 23.2 | 11 000 | 9.5 | 17.9 | 5.3 |
| M-13 | 23.2 | 9 700 | 10.7 | 17.9 | 5.3 |
| M-14 | 26.1 | 11 700 | 11.2 | 18.7 | 5.3 |
| M-15 | 26.1 | 10 300 | 12.3 | 18.7 | 5.3 |
| M-18 | 29.0 | 12 400 | 13.5 | 19.5 | 6.5 |
| M-19 | 29.0 | 11 000 | 14.6 | 19.5 | 5.3 |
| M-21 | 33.3 | 13 100 | 15.7 | 20.7 | 6.5 |
| M-22 | 34.0 | 11 700 | 16.8 | 20.9 | 5.3 |
| M-23 | 34.7 | 12 400 | 21.3 | 21.1 | 6.5 |
| M-24 | 39.1 | 13 100 | 20.2 | 22.3 | 6.5 |
| M-25 | 39.8 | 15 200 | 22.4 | 22.5 | 6.5 |
| M-26 | 40.6 | 13 800 | 20.2 | 22.7 | 6.5 |

*Compression perpendicular to grain values are for S-P-F MEL (all grades) and Hem-Fir MEL lumber with E grade of 10 300 MPa or higher. For other species or grades, use corresponding values for visually stress-graded lumber taken from Table 5.3.1A for the appropriate group.

**Notes:**
(1) Tabulated values are based on standard-term duration of load and dry service conditions.
(2) The size factor $K_Z$ for MEL lumber shall be 1.00, except that $K_{Zv}$ is given in Table 5.4.5, $K_{Zcp}$ is determined in accordance with Clause 5.5.7.5, and $K_{Zc}$ is calculated in accordance with Clause 5.5.6.2.2.

## 5.4 Modification Factors

### 5.4.1 Load Duration Factor, $K_D$
The specified strength of lumber shall be multiplied by a load duration factor, $K_D$, as given in Clause 4.3.2.2.

### 5.4.2 Service Condition Factor, $K_S$
The specified strength of lumber shall be multiplied by a service condition factor, $K_S$, as given in Table 5.4.2.

### 5.4.3 Treatment Factor, $K_T$

#### 5.4.3.1
The specified strength of lumber shall be multiplied by a treatment factor, $K_T$, as given in Table 5.4.3.

#### 5.4.3.2
For lumber treated with fire-retardant or other strength-reducing chemicals, strength and stiffness capacities shall be based on the documented results of tests that shall take into account the effects of time, temperature, and moisture content. Test procedures shall meet the requirements of Clause 3.3.2.
**Note:** The effects of fire retardant treatments can vary depending on manufacturing materials and processes. See the Canadian Wood Council's Commentary for additional explanation.

## 5.4.4 System Factor, $K_H$

### 5.4.4.1 Case 1

Specified strengths for sawn lumber members in a system consisting of three or more essentially parallel members spaced not more than 610 mm apart and so arranged that they mutually support the applied load may be multiplied by the system factor for Case 1 given in Table 5.4.4.

**Note:** *Case 1 applies to systems of closely spaced structural components such as light-frame trusses, composite building components, and glued-laminated timbers. Case 1 may also apply to some conventional joist and rafter systems where the framing details do not meet the requirements of Clause 5.4.4.2.*

### 5.4.4.2 Case 2

Specified strengths for sawn lumber used in a system of solid joists, rafters, or studs meeting the requirements of Clause 5.4.4.1 may be multiplied by the system factor for Case 2 given in Table 5.4.4, provided that the following additional conditions are met:

(a) the joists, rafters, or studs are sheathed with plywood, waferboard, or OSB of minimum 9.5 mm thickness, or with 17 mm minimum thickness lumber in combination with panel covering such as underlayment or with wood finish flooring; and

(b) the sheathing or subfloor is attached to the members to provide a minimum stiffness equivalent to that provided by 2 in common nails at 150 mm centres at edges of sheathing panels, and 300 mm centres elsewhere.

**Note:** *Case 2 applies to systems such as conventional light-frame wood floor, roof, and wall systems using dimension lumber framing members and minimum required sheathing and fastenings. Tabulated Case 2 system factors are to be applied to single-member section properties and cannot be used in conjunction with augmented section properties based on analysis of partial composite action between lumber and sheathing.*

### 5.4.4.3

For lumber in built-up beams consisting of two or more individual members of the same depth that are fastened or glued together so the beam will deflect as a unit, specified strengths may be multiplied by the system factor, $K_H$, given in Table 5.4.4.

## 5.4.5 Size Factor, $K_Z$

### 5.4.5.1

Some specified strengths of visually stress-graded lumber vary with member size and shall be multiplied by a size factor, $K_Z$, in accordance with Table 5.4.5.

**Note:** *See Clauses 5.4.5.2 and 5.4.5.3 for exceptions.*

### 5.4.5.2

The size factor, $K_Z$, for light framing grades shall be 1.00, except that $K_{Zc}$ shall be calculated in accordance with Clause 5.5.6.2.2, and $K_{Zcp}$ may be determined in accordance with Clause 5.5.7.5.

### 5.4.5.3

The size factor, $K_Z$, for machine stress-rated lumber and machine evaluated lumber shall be 1.00, except that $K_{Zv}$ shall be as given in Table 5.4.5, $K_{Zc}$ shall be calculated in accordance with Clause 5.5.6.2.2, and $K_{Zcp}$ may be determined in accordance with Clause 5.5.7.5.

## Table 5.4.2
## Service Condition Factors, $K_S$

| $K_S$ | Property | Dry service conditions | Wet service conditions: sawn lumber, piling, and poles of least dimension | |
|---|---|---|---|---|
| | | | 89 mm or less | Over 89 mm |
| $K_{SB}$ | Bending at extreme fibre | 1.00 | 0.84 | 1.00 |
| $K_{Sv}$ | Longitudinal shear | 1.00 | 0.96 | 1.00 |
| $K_{Sc}$ | Compression parallel to grain | 1.00 | 0.69 | 0.91 |
| $K_{Scp}$ | Compression perpendicular to grain | 1.00 | 0.67 | 0.67 |
| $K_{St}$ | Tension parallel to grain | 1.00 | 0.84 | 1.00 |
| $K_{SE}$ | Modulus of elasticity | 1.00 | 0.94 | 1.00 |

## Table 5.4.3
## Treatment Factor, $K_T$

| Product | Dry service conditions | Wet service conditions |
|---|---|---|
| Untreated lumber | 1.00 | 1.00 |
| Preservative-treated, unincised lumber | 1.00 | 1.00 |
| Preservative-treated, incised lumber of thickness 89 mm or less, for | | |
| (a) modulus of elasticity | 0.90 | 0.95 |
| (b) other properties | 0.75 | 0.85 |
| Fire-retardant-treated lumber | See Clause 5.4.3.2 for effects of fire-retardant treatment. | |

## Table 5.4.4
## System Factor, $K_H$

| For specified strength in | Case 1* | Case 2† Visually graded | MSR | Built-up beams |
|---|---|---|---|---|
| Bending | 1.10 | 1.40 | 1.20 | 1.10 |
| Longitudinal shear | 1.10 | 1.40 | 1.20 | 1.10 |
| Compression parallel to grain | 1.10 | 1.10 | 1.10 | 1.00 |
| Tension parallel to grain | 1.10 | N/A | N/A | 1.00 |
| All other properties | 1.00 | 1.00 | 1.00 | 1.00 |

*See Clause 5.4.4.1 for conditions applying to Case 1.
†See Clause 5.4.4.2 for conditions applying to Case 2.
N/A = not applicable

## Table 5.4.5
## Size Factor, $K_Z$, for Visually Stress-Graded Lumber

| Larger dimension (mm) | Bending and shear $K_{Zb}$, $K_{Zv}$ | | | Tension parallel to grain $K_{Zt}$ | Compression perpendicular to grain $K_{Zcp}$ | Compression parallel to grain $K_{Zc}$ | All other properties |
|---|---|---|---|---|---|---|---|
| | Smaller dimension (mm) | | | | | | |
| | 38 to 64 | 89 to 102 | 114 or more | All | All | All | All |
| 38 | 1.7 | — | — | 1.5 | | | 1.0 |
| 64 | 1.7 | — | — | 1.5 | See Clause 5.5.7.5 | *Value computed* | 1.0 |
| 89 | 1.7 | 1.7 | — | 1.5 | | *using formula in* | 1.0 |
| 114 | 1.5 | 1.6 | 1.3 | 1.4 | | *Clause 5.5.6.2.2* | 1.0 |
| 140 | 1.4 | 1.5 | 1.3 | 1.3 | | | 1.0 |
| 184 to 191 | 1.2 | 1.3 | 1.3 | 1.2 | | | 1.0 |
| 235 to 241 | 1.1 | 1.2 | 1.2 | 1.1 | | | 1.0 |
| 286 to 292 | 1.0 | 1.1 | 1.1 | 1.0 | | | 1.0 |
| 337 to 343 | 0.9 | 1.0 | 1.0 | 0.9 | | | 1.0 |
| 387 or larger | 0.8 | 0.9 | 0.9 | 0.8 | | | 1.0 |

# 5.5 Strength and Resistance

## 5.5.1 General

Clause 5.5 contains design data and methods that apply to sawn lumber of rectangular cross-section.

## 5.5.2 Sizes

### 5.5.2.1

Except as provided in Clause 5.5.2.2, the standard dry size rounded to the nearest millimetre (net dimension) of lumber shall be used.

### 5.5.2.2

In conjunction with Tables 5.3.1C and 5.3.1D, green manufactured sizes may be used for all service conditions.

**Notes:**

**(1)** *In developing specified strengths in this Standard, variables of moisture content and shrinkage, and their relationship to strength and stiffness, have been taken into account. Standard sizes and net dimensions of structural lumber and timbers are given in CSA Standard CAN/CSA-O141.*

**(2)** *Sizes rounded to the nearest millimetre are given in Table A5.5.2.*

## 5.5.3 Continuity

Beam and stringer grades shall not be designed for continuity in determining requirements for bending resistance, unless regraded along the full length of the member. Continuity may be considered in deflection and shear calculations whether the lumber is regraded or not.

**Note:** *Beam and stringer grades listed in Table 5.3.1C are not graded for continuity.*

## 5.5.4 Bending Moment Resistance

### 5.5.4.1 General

The factored bending moment resistance, $M_r$, of sawn members shall be taken as

$M_r = \phi F_b S K_{Zb} K_L$

where
$\phi$    = 0.9
$F_b$   = $f_b(K_D K_H K_{Sb} K_T)$
$f_b$    = specified strength in bending (Tables 5.3.1A to 5.3.1D, 5.3.2, and 5.3.3), MPa
$K_{Zb}$  = size factor in bending (Clause 5.4.5)
$K_L$    = lateral stability factor (Clause 5.5.4.2)

## 5.5.4.2  Lateral Stability Factor, $K_L$

### 5.5.4.2.1
The lateral stability factor, $K_L$, may be taken as unity when lateral support is provided at points of bearing to prevent lateral displacement and rotation, provided that the maximum depth-to-width ratio of the member does not exceed the following values:

4:1    if no additional intermediate support is provided;
5:1    if the member is held in line by purlins or tie rods;
6.5:1  if the compressive edge is held in line by direct connection of decking or joists spaced not more
       than 610 mm apart;
7.5:1  if the compressive edge is held in line by direct connection of decking or joists spaced not more
       than 610 mm apart and adequate bridging or blocking is installed at intervals not exceeding
       eight times the depth of the member; or
9:1    if both edges are held in line.

Alternatively, $K_L$ may be calculated in accordance with the requirements of Clause 6.5.6.4.

### 5.5.4.2.2
For built-up beams consisting of two or more individual members of the same depth, the ratio in Clause 6.5.6.3.1 may be based on the total width of the beam, provided that the individual members are fastened together securely at intervals not exceeding four times the depth.

## 5.5.5  Shear Resistance

### 5.5.5.1  General
The factored shear resistance, $V_r$, of sawn members shall be taken as

$$V_r = \phi F_v \frac{2A_n}{3} K_{Zv}$$

where
$\phi$    = 0.9
$F_v$    = $f_v(K_D K_H K_{Sv} K_T)$
$f_v$    = specified strength in shear (Clauses 5.3.1 and 5.3.2), MPa
$A_n$    = net area of cross-section (Clause 4.3.8), mm$^2$
$K_{Zv}$  = size factor in shear (Clause 5.4.5)
**Note:** *For sawn members notched on the tension side at supports, see Clause 5.5.5.3.*

## 5.5.5.2  Loads near Supports
In the calculation of shear resistance the effect of all loads acting within a distance from a support equal to the depth of the member need not be taken into account.

## 5.5.5.3  Notches on the Tension Side at Supports
The factored notch shear force resistance at a notch on the tension side at supports, $F_r$, shall be taken as

$$F_r = \phi F_f A K_N$$

where

$\phi$ = 0.9

$F_f$ = $f_f(K_D K_H K_{Sf} K_T)$

$f_f$ = specified notch shear force resistance (Clause 5.5.5.5), MPa

= 0.50 for all sawn members

$K_{Sf}$ = service factor

= 1.00 for dry service

= 0.70 for wet service

A = gross cross-section area, mm$^2$

$K_N$ = notch factor (Clause 5.5.5.4)

**Note:** *Notches or abrupt changes of section will produce stress concentrations and should be avoided.*

## 5.5.5.4 Notch Factor

The notch factor for members of rectangular cross-sections shall be determined as follows:

$$K_N = \left[ 0.006d \left( 1.6 \left( \frac{1}{\alpha} - 1 \right) + \eta^2 \left( \frac{1}{\alpha^3} - 1 \right) \right) \right]^{-\frac{1}{2}}$$

where

d = depth of cross-section, mm

$\alpha$ = $1 - (d_n/d)$

$d_n$ = depth of notch measured normal to the member axis in accordance with Figure 5.5.5.4, mm, which must not exceed 0.25d

$\eta$ = e/d

e = length of notch measured parallel to the member axis, mm, from the centre of the nearest support to reentrant corner of notch (Figure 5.5.5.4). For a member notched over an end support, the length of support may be taken as the lesser of minimum required bearing length (Clause 5.5.7) or the actual bearing length. For a continuous member the length of support equals the actual bearing length.

**Note:** *Values of $K_N\sqrt{d}$ for selected combinations of $\alpha$ and $\eta$ are given in Table 5.5.5.4.*

## 5.5.5.5 Shear Force at Notches

In the calculation of notch shear force resistance, the associated applied force is the factored shear force in the member at the support. The shear force is calculated using the component of the force normal to the member axis. Consideration of the notch shear force resistance concerns avoidance of fracture at a reentrant corner of a notch and does not negate the need to ensure that the residual cross-section at a notch can resist the factored shear force.

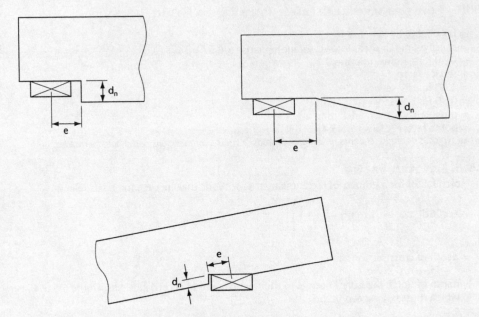

**Figure 5.5.5.4**
**Determination of Length and Depth of Notch**

**Table 5.5.5.4**
**Values of $K_N \sqrt{d}$**

| η | α | | | | |
|---|---|---|---|---|---|
| | 0.75 | 0.80 | 0.85 | 0.90 | 0.95 |
| 0.15 | 17.2 | 19.9 | 23.7 | 29.9 | 43.5 |
| 0.20 | 16.8 | 19.5 | 23.3 | 29.4 | 42.8 |
| 0.25 | 16.4 | 19.0 | 22.8 | 28.8 | 42.0 |
| 0.30 | 15.9 | 18.5 | 22.2 | 28.1 | 41.0 |
| 0.35 | 15.4 | 18.0 | 21.5 | 27.3 | 39.9 |
| 0.40 | 14.9 | 17.4 | 20.9 | 26.5 | 38.8 |
| 0.45 | 14.3 | 16.8 | 20.2 | 25.7 | 37.6 |
| 0.50 | 13.8 | 16.2 | 19.5 | 24.8 | 36.4 |
| 0.60 | 12.7 | 15.0 | 18.1 | 23.1 | 34.0 |
| 0.70 | 11.8 | 13.9 | 16.8 | 21.5 | 31.7 |
| 0.80 | 10.9 | 12.8 | 15.6 | 20.0 | 29.6 |
| 0.90 | 10.1 | 11.9 | 14.5 | 18.7 | 27.6 |
| 1.00 | 9.36 | 11.1 | 13.5 | 17.4 | 25.8 |
| 1.20 | 8.15 | 9.70 | 11.8 | 15.3 | 22.7 |
| 1.40 | 7.20 | 8.57 | 10.5 | 13.6 | 20.2 |
| 1.60 | 6.42 | 7.66 | 9.39 | 12.1 | 18.1 |
| 1.80 | 5.79 | 6.91 | 8.48 | 11.0 | 16.4 |
| 2.00 | 5.26 | 6.29 | 7.72 | 10.0 | 14.9 |

**Notes:**
**(1)** $\alpha = 1 - d_n/d$; $\eta = e/d$
**(2)** *Interpolation may be applied for intermediate values of α and η.*

## 5.5.6 Compressive Resistance Parallel to Grain

### 5.5.6.1 Effective Length

Unless noted otherwise, the effective length $L_e = K_eL$ shall be used in determining the slenderness ratio of compression members. Recommended effective length factors, $K_e$, for compression members are given in Table A5.5.6.1.

### 5.5.6.2 Simple Compression Members

#### 5.5.6.2.1 Constant Rectangular Cross-Section

The slenderness ratio, $C_c$, of simple compression members of constant rectangular section shall not exceed 50 and shall be taken as the greater of

$$C_c = \frac{\text{effective length associated with width}}{\text{member width}}$$

or

$$C_c = \frac{\text{effective length associated with depth}}{\text{member depth}}$$

#### 5.5.6.2.2 Factored Compressive Resistance Parallel to Grain

The factored compressive resistance parallel to grain, $P_r$, shall be taken as

$$P_r = \phi F_C A K_{Zc} K_C$$

where
$\phi = 0.8$
$F_C = f_c(K_D K_H K_{Sc} K_T)$
$f_c$ = specified strength in compression parallel to grain (Tables 5.3.1A to 5.3.1D, 5.3.2, and 5.3.3), MPa
$K_{Zc} = 6.3\ (dL)^{-0.13} \le 1.3$
    where
    $d$ = dimension in direction of buckling (depth or width), mm
    $L$ = length associated with member dimension, mm

#### 5.5.6.2.3 Slenderness Factor, $K_C$

The slenderness factor, $K_C$, shall be determined as follows:

$$K_C = \left[1.0 + \frac{F_c K_{Zc} C_c^3}{35 E_{05} K_{SE} K_T}\right]^{-1}$$

where
$E_{05} = 0.82E$ for MSR lumber
    $= 0.75E$ for MEL lumber
    = as specified in Tables 5.3.1A to 5.3.1D for visually graded lumber

### 5.5.6.3 Spaced Compression Members

Spaced compression members shall be designed in accordance with the requirements of Clause A5.5.6.3 using the specified strengths and adjustment factors for sawn lumber.

### 5.5.6.4 Built-up Compression Members

#### 5.5.6.4.1 General

Built-up rectangular compression members shall consist of two to five individual members of at least 38 mm thickness joined with nails or bolts, or bolts and split ring connectors. The factored compressive resistance of built-up compression members may be evaluated in accordance with Clauses 5.5.6.4.2 to 5.5.6.4.4, provided that the minimum values of end distance, edge distance, and spacing for fastenings conform to the appropriate requirements in Clause 10 and the maximum value of end distance does not exceed 1.2 times the minimum value. The factored compressive resistance of the built-up compression member may be taken as the greater of the values calculated according to Clause 5.5.6.4.2, 5.5.6.4.3, or 5.5.6.4.4, or the combined factored resistance of the individual pieces taken as independent members.

**Note:** *Slenderness ratios are calculated according to Clause 5.5.6.2.1 using the overall dimensions of the composite member or the dimensions of the individual pieces, as appropriate.*

## 5.5.6.4.2 Nailed Built-up Compression Members

The factored compressive resistance of a built-up compression member fastened together with nails or spikes may be taken as 60% of the compressive strength of a solid member of equivalent gross cross-sectional dimensions designed according to Clause 5.5.6.2, provided that the following requirements are satisfied:

(a) spacing of nails along the member length shall not exceed six times the thickness of the thinnest piece, and spacing perpendicular to the member length shall not exceed 20 times the nail diameter;

(b) all nails shall penetrate through at least 3/4 of the thickness of the last individual piece, and nails shall be driven alternately from either face of the built-up member along the length; and

(c) when the individual pieces of the built-up member are wider than three times their thickness, there shall be at least two rows of nails across the member width.

## 5.5.6.4.3 Bolted Built-up Compression Members

The factored compressive resistance of a built-up compression member fastened together by minimum 1/4 in diameter bolts may be taken as 75% of the compressive strength of a solid member of equivalent gross cross-sectional dimensions designed according to Clause 5.5.6.2, provided that the following requirements are satisfied:

(a) spacing of bolts along the member length shall not exceed six times the thickness of the thinnest piece, and spacing perpendicular to the member length shall not exceed 10 times the bolt diameter; and

(b) when the individual pieces of the built-up member are wider than three times their thickness, there shall be at least two rows of bolts across the member width.

## 5.5.6.4.4 Split-Ring-Connected Built-up Compression Members

The factored compressive resistance of a built-up compression member fastened together at intervals not exceeding six times the thickness of the thinnest piece by minimum 1/2 in diameter bolts and 2-1/2 in split-ring connectors may be calculated as having 80% of the compressive strength of a solid member of equivalent gross cross-sectional dimensions designed according to Clause 5.5.6.2.

## 5.5.6.4.5 Built-up Compression Members as Simple Compression Members

Except for spaced compression members, the factored compressive resistance of built-up compression members not meeting the requirements of Clauses 5.5.6.4.1 to 5.5.6.4.4 shall be taken as the combined factored compressive strength of the individual pieces considered as independent members.

## 5.5.6.4.6 Strong Axis Buckling

The strength reduction factors given in Clauses 5.5.6.4.2 to 5.5.6.4.4 may be omitted for buckling in the strong axis of the laminations.

## 5.5.6.5 Stud Walls

When stud walls are adequately sheathed on at least one side, as in light frame construction, the dimension of the stud normal to the sheathing may be used in calculating the slenderness ratio.

## 5.5.6.6  Spliced Built-up Compressive Members

### 5.5.6.6.1

Spliced nail-laminated built-up columns that are constructed in accordance with Figure 5.5.6.6 may be designed for axial loads and bending loads applied parallel to the wide face of the laminations in accordance with Clauses 5.5.6.6.2 and 5.5.6.6.3, provided that the following additional conditions are met:

(a) the spliced columns shall consist of three members, with nails penetrating all three members;

(b) the minimum overall splice length, L, shall be 1200 mm;

(c) the spliced columns shall be braced by sheathing, or purlins spaced at a maximum of 600 mm on centres in the direction perpendicular to the wide face of the laminations;

(d) minimum lamination size shall be 38 mm thick by 140 mm wide; and

(e) maximum lamination size shall be 38 mm thick by 184 mm wide.

### 5.5.6.6.2

The factored bending resistance shall be determined using Clause 5.5.10 based on equivalent members of the same size, grade, and species, using

(a) 40% of the factored bending resistance of an unspliced built-up beam in the splice region, R; and

(b) 100% of the factored bending resistance of an unspliced built-up beam outside of the splice region, R.

### 5.5.6.6.3

The factored compressive resistance in the direction parallel to the wide face of the laminations shall be determined using Clause 5.5.6.2.2 based on an $E_{05}$ value equal to 60% of the value for a simple compression member of the same species and grade.

**Note:** *Splicing of built-up members significantly reduces their stiffness and bending resistance, and should be avoided wherever possible.*

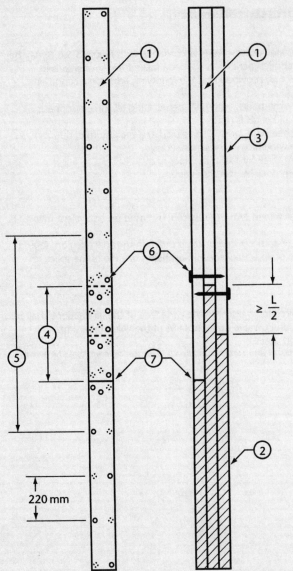

**Legend:**
1. 3 members, 38 mm thick
2. Treated wood portion, when required
3. Untreated wood portion
4. Splice length, L ≥ 1200 mm
5. Splice region, R = 1.5 L
6. Nails: 4-1/2 inch common wire nail hot-dip galvanized when used in treated wood; 6 per joint; 220 mm oc; 2 per row driven from alternate sides
7. Butt joints

**Figure 5.5.6.6**
**Spliced Built-up Columns**

Δ

## 5.5.7 Compressive Resistance Perpendicular to Grain

### 5.5.7.1 General
Factored bearing forces shall not exceed the factored compressive resistance perpendicular to grain determined in accordance with the provisions of Clauses 5.5.7.2 and 5.5.7.3.

### 5.5.7.2 Effect of All Applied Loads
The factored compressive resistance perpendicular to grain under the effect of all factored applied loads shall be taken as $Q_r$ in the following formula:

$$Q_r = \phi F_{cp} A_b K_B K_{Zcp}$$

where
$\phi$ = 0.8
$F_{cp}$ = $f_{cp}(K_D K_{Scp} K_T)$
$f_{cp}$ = specified strength in compression perpendicular to grain (Tables 5.3.1A to 5.3.1D, 5.3.2, and 5.3.3), MPa
$A_b$ = bearing area, mm$^2$
$K_B$ = length of bearing factor (Clause 5.5.7.6)
$K_{Zcp}$ = size factor for bearing (Clause 5.5.7.5)

### 5.5.7.3 Effect of Loads Applied near a Support
The factored compressive resistance perpendicular to grain under the effect of only those loads applied within a distance from the centre of the support equal to the depth of the member shall be taken as $Q_r'$ in the following formula:

$$Q_r' = (2/3)\phi F_{cp} A_b' K_B K_{Zcp}$$

where
$\phi$ = 0.8
$F_{cp}$ = $f_{cp}(K_D K_{Scp} K_T)$
$A_b'$ = average bearing area (see Clause 5.5.7.4)

### 5.5.7.4
Where unequal bearing areas are used on opposite surfaces of a member, the average bearing area shall not exceed the following:

$$A_b' = b\left(\frac{L_{b1} + L_{b2}}{2}\right), \text{ but } \leq 1.5b(L_{b1})$$

where
$b$ = average bearing width (perpendicular to grain), mm
$L_{b1}$ = lesser bearing length, mm
$L_{b2}$ = larger bearing length, mm

### 5.5.7.5 Size Factor for Bearing, $K_{Zcp}$
When the width of a member (dimension perpendicular to the direction of the load) is greater than the depth of the member (dimension parallel to the direction of the load), specified strength in compression perpendicular to grain may be multiplied by a size factor for bearing, $K_{Zcp}$, in accordance with Table 5.5.7.5.

## Table 5.5.7.5
## Size Factor for Bearing, $K_{Zcp}$

| Ratio of member width to member depth* | $K_{Zcp}$ |
|---|---|
| 1.0 or less | 1.00 |
| 2.0 or more | 1.15 |

*Interpolation applies for intermediate ratios.

### 5.5.7.6 Length of Bearing Factor, $K_B$

When lengths of bearing or diameters of washers are less than 150 mm, specified strengths in compression perpendicular to grain may be multiplied by a length of bearing factor, $K_B$, in accordance with Table 5.5.7.6, provided that
(a) no part of the bearing area is less than 75 mm from the end of the members; and
(b) bearing areas do not occur in positions of high bending stresses.

## Table 5.5.7.6
## Length of Bearing Factor, $K_B$

| Bearing length (parallel to grain) or washer diameter (mm) | Modification factor, $K_B$ |
|---|---|
| 12.5 and less | 1.75 |
| 25.0 | 1.38 |
| 38.0 | 1.25 |
| 50.0 | 1.19 |
| 75.0 | 1.13 |
| 100.0 | 1.10 |
| 150.0 or more | 1.00 |

### 5.5.8 Compressive Resistance at an Angle to Grain

The factored compressive resistance at an angle to grain shall be taken as

$$N_r = \frac{P_r Q_r}{P_r \sin^2\theta + Q_r \cos^2\theta}$$

where
$P_r$ = factored compressive resistance parallel to grain (Clause 5.5.6.2.2, assuming $K_C = 1.00$), N
$Q_r$ = factored compressive resistance perpendicular to grain (Clause 5.5.7.2), N
$\theta$ = angle between direction of grain and direction of load,°

### 5.5.9 Tensile Resistance Parallel to Grain

The factored tensile resistance, $T_r$, parallel to grain shall be taken as

$$T_r = \phi F_t A_n K_{Zt}$$

where
$\phi$ = 0.9
$F_t$ = $f_t(K_D K_H K_{St} K_T)$
$f_t$ = specified strength in tension parallel to grain (Tables 5.3.1A to 5.3.1D, 5.3.2, and 5.3.3), MPa
$A_n$ = net area of cross-section (Clause 4.3.8), mm$^2$
$K_{Zt}$ = size factor in tension (Clause 5.4.5)

## 5.5.10 Resistance to Combined Bending and Axial Load

Members subject to combined bending and compressive or tensile axial loads shall be designed to satisfy the appropriate interaction equation:

$$\frac{P_f}{P_r} + \frac{M_f}{M_r} \leq 1.0$$

or

$$\frac{T_f}{T_r} + \frac{M_f}{M_r} \leq 1.0$$

where

$P_f$ = factored compressive axial load

$P_r$ = factored compressive load resistance parallel to grain calculated in accordance with the requirements of Clause 5.5.6

$M_f$ = factored bending moment, taking into account end moments and amplified moments due to axial loads in laterally loaded members

$M_r$ = factored bending moment resistance calculated in accordance with the requirements of Clause 5.5.4

$T_f$ = factored tensile axial load

$T_r$ = factored tensile load resistance parallel to grain calculated in accordance with the requirements of Clause 5.5.9

## 5.5.11 Decking

### 5.5.11.1 General

To utilize continuity in the design of decking, the conditions specified in Clauses 5.5.11.2 to 5.5.11.5 shall apply.

### 5.5.11.2 Plank Decking

#### 5.5.11.2.1 Fastening Requirements

Material shall be 75 mm or more in width and shall be tongued and grooved or splined. Planks 38 mm or less in thickness shall be nailed to the supporting members with nails not shorter than twice the thickness of the plank and in no case less than 2-1/2 in. Planks thicker than 38 mm shall be toe-nailed to the supporting members with one 5 in toe-nail and face-nailed with one or more nails not less than 6 in in length. Planks 140 mm or less in width shall be nailed with two nails to each support. Planks more than 140 mm in width shall be nailed with three nails to each support.

#### 5.5.11.2.2 Butt Joints

In bridges, each plank shall extend over at least one support. In roofs and floors, planks not extending over at least one support in any span are permitted, provided that they are
(a) double tongue-and-groove planks more than 38 mm in thickness;
(b) flanked by planks that rest on both supports of that span; and
(c) separated by at least six planks in that span, each of which extends over at least one support.

### 5.5.11.3 Nail Laminated Decking

#### 5.5.11.3.1 Fastening Requirements

Material shall be 38 mm or more in thickness and 64 mm or more in width, and shall be laid on edge and spiked together. Nails used to spike the laminations together shall be at least 4 in long for 38 mm thickness laminations and 6 in long for 64 mm thickness laminations. Decking 140 mm or less in depth shall be spiked together with a staggered single row of nails at intervals of not more than 450 mm in the row. One nail shall be placed not more than 100 mm from the end of each lamination. Decking more than 140 mm in depth shall be spiked together with a staggered double row of nails at intervals of not more than 450 mm in each row.  Two nails shall be placed not more than 100 mm from the end of each lamination.  Each lamination shall be toe-nailed to each support with not less than 4 in nails.

### 5.5.11.3.2 Butt Joints
In bridges, each lamination shall extend over at least one support.  In roofs and floors, laminations not extending over at least one support in any span shall be flanked by laminations that rest on both supports of that span, and shall be separated by at least six laminations in that span, each of which extends over at least one support.

### 5.5.11.4 Deflection Calculations
For uniform design loads, decking deflections for the laying patterns described in Table 5.5.11.4 shall be calculated by the formulae given in Table 5.5.11.4.  For other loading conditions or laying patterns, deflections shall be calculated by recognized engineering formulae.

### 5.5.11.5 Bending
Bending moments for plank decking laid in a controlled, random pattern, as described in Table 5.5.11.4, shall be calculated on the basis of simple span moments.  For other deck patterns, bending moments shall be calculated on the basis of recognized engineering formulae.

### Table 5.5.11.4
### Laying Patterns and Deflection Formulae for Decking

| Pattern | Description | Deflection formula* |
|---|---|---|
| Simple span | All pieces bear on two supports only | $\Delta_1 = \dfrac{5w\ell^4}{384E_s I}$ |
| Controlled random | Decking continuous for three or more spans | |
| | End joints staggered in adjacent planks not less than 610 mm | |
| | Joints in same general line separated by at least two intervening courses | $\Delta_2 = 0.77\Delta_1$ |
| | End joints in first half of end spans avoided | |
| | Requirements of Clause 5.5.11.2.2 or 5.5.11.3.2 shall be met | |
| Continuous over two spans | All pieces bear on three supports | $\Delta_3 = 0.42\Delta_1$ |

*where
$\Delta$ = deflection, mm
$w$ = uniformly distributed specified load, kN/m$^2$
$\ell$ = span, mm
$E_S$ = modulus of elasticity, MPa
$I$ = moment of inertia of the decking, mm$^4$ per m of width

### 5.5.12 Preserved Wood Foundations

### 5.5.12.1 General
All lumber and plywood in preserved wood foundations shall be treated with a preservative in accordance with CSA Standard O80.15, except where exempted from treatment by CSA Standard CAN/CSA-S406.

The provisions for design of preserved wood foundations are predicated on the use of lumber and plywood identified by a certification mark on the material that confirms that treatment, where required, has been carried out by a plant certified under CSA Standard O322.

**Note:** *CSA Standard O322 outlines procedures for the certification of treatment plants and for the identification of wood* materials pressure-treated for use in preserved wood foundations. *Refer to Clause A5.5.12 for more details about wood wood foundations.*

## 5.5.12.2 Wall Footings

In the design of wall footings for preserved wood foundations, the specified strength in bending perpendicular to grain for wood footing plates that are wider than the bottom plates shall not exceed 1/3 the factored shear resistance. A granular layer, under footings, may be assumed capable of distributing the load transferred by the footing to the undisturbed soil at an angle of not more than 30° to the vertical.

## 5.5.13 Sawn Lumber Design for Specific Truss Applications

**Note:** *See also Clause A5.5.13.*

### 5.5.13.1 Scope

Design methods specified in Clause 5.5.13 apply only to fully triangulated metal-plate-connected wood roof trusses that meet the following conditions:
(a)  spacing not to exceed 610 mm;
(b)  clear span between inside face of supports not to exceed 12.20 m;
(c)  total truss length between outermost panel points not to exceed 18.0 m, with no single cantilever length exceeding 25% of the adjacent clear span; and
(d)  top chord pitch not less than 2 in 12.
   Clause 5.5.13 does not apply to girder, bowstring, semi-circular, or attic trusses (which have non-triangulated sections), or to flat or floor trusses.
**Note:** *The provisions of Clause 5.5.13 are predicated on the determination of load effects on members and connections in accordance with recognized methods of analysis such as those given in TPIC Truss Design Procedures.*

### 5.5.13.2 General

Except as modified in Clauses 5.5.13.3 to 5.5.13.5, truss member design shall be in accordance with the sawn lumber provisions of Clauses 5.5.1 to 5.5.10. Metal connector plate design shall be in accordance with Clause 10.8.

### 5.5.13.3 Compressive Resistance Parallel to Grain

#### 5.5.13.3.1

Unless otherwise required, the effective length, $L_e = K_e L_p$, shall be used in determining the slenderness ratio for truss compression members, where
$L_e$ = effective length of truss compression member
$K_e$ = effective length factor for truss compression member
$L_p$ = actual length of member between adjacent panel points
**Note:** *Effective length factors for compression members and conditions under which these factors apply may be found in TPIC Truss Design Procedures.*

#### 5.5.13.3.2

A compression chord member containing a metal-plate-connected splice may be considered continuous for a specific load case if the splice is located within ±10% of the panel length from an inflection point.

#### 5.5.13.3.3

The member length, L, used in Clause 5.5.6.2.2 to compute the factor $K_{zc}$ shall be the greater of the panel length or one-half the chord length between pitch breaks.

### 5.5.13.4 Compressive Resistance Perpendicular to Grain

Factored bearing forces shall not exceed the factored compressive resistance perpendicular to grain determined in accordance with the provisions of Clauses 5.5.7.2 and 5.5.7.3.
   The requirements of Clause 5.5.7.3 may be met by providing adequate bearing reinforcement against

the effects of concentrated bearing loads acting near a support.

**Note:** *Bearing reinforcing details using light-gauge metal plates that conform to Clause 10.8.1 may be found in TPIC Truss Design Procedures.*

## 5.5.13.5 Resistance to Combined Bending and Axial Load

Members subject to combined bending and compressive or tensile axial load shall be designed to satisfy the appropriate interaction equation:

$$\left(\frac{P_f}{P_r}\right)^2 + \frac{M_f}{K_M \, M_r} \leq 1.0 \quad \text{or} \quad \frac{T_f}{T_r} + \frac{M_f}{M_r} \leq 1.0$$

where

$P_f$ = factored compressive axial load

$P_r$ = factored compressive load resistance parallel to grain calculated in accordance with the requirements of Clauses 5.5.6 and 5.5.13.3

$M_f$ = factored bending moment. Unless mid-panel deflection of truss chords are limited to criteria such as in TPIC *Truss Design Procedures*, moments shall be amplified to account for the effects of axial loads on laterally loaded members

$K_M$ = bending capacity modification factor as defined in Table 5.5.13.5

$M_r$ = factored bending moment resistance calculated in accordance with the requirements of Clause 5.5.4

$T_f$ = factored tensile axial load

$T_r$ = factored tensile load resistance parallel to grain calculated in accordance with the requirements of Clause 5.5.9

### Table 5.5.13.5
### Bending Capacity Modification Factors, $K_M$, for Specific Truss Applications

| $K_M$* | Applicable condition |
|---|---|
| $\left[1.31 + 0.12\left(\dfrac{M_1}{M_2}\right)\right] \cdot \left(\dfrac{L_p}{d}\right)^{-\frac{1}{6}} \leq 1.3$ | Compression chord members continuous over one or more panel points, and where <br><br> $1.0 < \dfrac{M_1}{M_2} \leq 3.0$ |
| $\left[2.20 - 0.53\left(\dfrac{M_1}{M_2}\right) - 0.64\left(\dfrac{M_1}{M_2}\right)^2 + 0.41\left(\dfrac{M_1}{M_2}\right)^3\right] \cdot \left(\dfrac{L_p}{d}\right)^{-\frac{1}{6}} \leq 1.3$ | Compression chord members continuous over one or more panel points, and where <br><br> $-1.0 \leq \dfrac{M_1}{M_2} \leq 1.0$ |
| $1.67\left(\dfrac{L_p}{d}\right)^{-\frac{1}{6}} \leq 1.3$ | All other compression chord members |

*where

$M_1$ = maximum bending moment between panel points, N•mm

$M_2$ = maximum of the two panel point bending moments, N•mm

$L_p$ = actual length of the member between adjacent panel points, mm

$d$ = depth of the member between adjacent panel points, mm

**Note:** *The sign of the bending moments, $M_1$ and $M_2$, are retained in determining $K_M$. The factored bending moment, $M_f$, used in Clause 5.5.13.5 is the larger of the absolute values of $M_1$ and $M_2$.*

# 6. Glued-Laminated Timber (Glulam)

## 6.1 Scope

Characteristic strengths, design data, and methods specified in Clause 6 apply only to glued-laminated timber manufactured in accordance with CSA Standard CAN/CSA-O122.

## 6.2 Materials

### 6.2.1 Stress Grades

Design in accordance with Clause 6 is based on the use of the stress grades of glued-laminated timber given in Table 6.2.1.

**Note:** *The* National Building Code of Canada, Part 4, *requires that glued-laminated timber be fabricated in plants conforming to CSA Standard CAN/CSA-O177. A list of certified manufacturers may be obtained from the certifying agency or agencies providing certification service.*

### Table 6.2.1
### Glued-Laminated Timber Stress Grades

| Primary application | Wood species | | |
| | Douglas Fir-Larch | Spruce-Lodgepole Pine-Jack Pine | Hem-Fir and Douglas Fir-Larch |
| --- | --- | --- | --- |
| Bending members | 20f-E, 24f-E 20f-EX, 24f-EX | 20f-E 20f-EX | 24f-E 24f-EX |
| Compression members | 16c-E | 12c-E | |
| Tension members | 18t-E | 14t-E | |

Δ ## 6.2.2 Appearance Grades

### 6.2.2.1 General

Except as provided for in Clause 6.2.2.2, appearance grades as defined in CSA Standard CAN/CSA-O122 do not affect the specified strength.

### 6.2.2.2 Textured Finishes

Some manufacturers offer a variety of textured finishes. Designers are advised to check the availability of textured finishes before specifying.

Such finishes may change the finished sizes and tolerances given in CSA Standard CAN/CSA-O122. Depending on the degree of texturing, it may be necessary for the designer to compensate for any resulting reduction of cross-section and/or specified strength of the member.

## 6.3 Specified Strengths

The specified strengths for glued-laminated timber are given in Table 6.3.

Δ

## Table 6.3
## Specified Strengths and Modulus of Elasticity
## for Glued-Laminated Timber (MPa)

| | | Douglas Fir-Larch | | | | | |
|---|---|---|---|---|---|---|---|
| | | 24f-E | 24f-EX | 20f-E | 20f-EX | 18t-E | 16c-E |
| Bending moment (pos.) | $f_b$ | 30.6 | 30.6 | 25.6 | 25.6 | 24.3 | 14.0 |
| Bending moment (neg.) | $f_b$ | 23.0 | 30.6 | 19.2 | 25.6 | 24.3 | 14.0 |
| Longitudinal shear | $f_v$ | 2.0 | 2.0 | 2.0 | 2.0 | 2.0 | 2.0 |
| Compression parallel | $f_c$ | 30.2* | 30.2* | 30.2* | 30.2* | 30.2 | 30.2 |
| Compression parallel combined with bending | $f_{cb}$ | 30.2* | 30.2 | 30.2* | 30.2 | 30.2 | 30.2 |
| Compression perpendicular<br>— compression face bearing<br>— tension face bearing | $f_{cp}$ | <br>7.0<br>7.0 | <br>7.0<br>7.0 | <br>7.0<br>7.0 | <br>7.0<br>7.0 | <br>7.0<br>7.0 | <br>7.0<br>7.0 |
| Tension net section (See Clause 6.5.11) | $f_{tn}$ | 20.4* | 20.4 | 20.4* | 20.4 | 23.0 | 20.4 |
| Tension gross section | $f_{tg}$ | 15.3* | 15.3 | 15.3* | 15.3 | 17.9 | 15.3 |
| Tension perpendicular to grain | $f_{tp}$ | 0.83 | 0.83 | 0.83 | 0.83 | 0.83 | 0.83 |
| Modulus of elasticity | E | 13 100 | 13 100 | 12 400 | 12 400 | 13 800 | 12 400 |

| | | Spruce-Lodgepole Pine-Jack Pine | | | | Hem-Fir and Douglas Fir-Larch | |
|---|---|---|---|---|---|---|---|
| | | 20f-E | 20f-EX | 14t-E | 12c-E | 24f-E | 24-EX |
| Bending moment (pos.) | $f_b$ | 25.6 | 25.6 | 24.3 | 9.8 | 30.6 | 30.6 |
| Bending moment (neg.) | $f_b$ | 19.2 | 25.6 | 24.3 | 9.8 | 23.0 | 30.6 |
| Longitudinal shear | $f_v$ | 1.75 | 1.75 | 1.75 | 1.75 | 1.75 | 1.75 |
| Compression parallel | $f_c$ | 25.2* | 25.2* | 25.2 | 25.2 | — | — |
| Compression parallel combined with bending | $f_{cb}$ | 25.2* | 25.2 | 25.2 | 25.2 | — | — |
| Compression perpendicular<br>— compression face bearing<br>— tension face bearing | $f_{cp}$ | <br>5.8<br>5.8 | <br>5.8<br>5.8 | <br>5.8<br>5.8 | <br>5.8<br>5.8 | <br>4.6<br>7.0 | <br>7.0<br>7.0 |
| Tension net section (See Clause 6.5.11) | $f_{tn}$ | 17.0* | 17.0 | 17.9 | 17.0 | 20.4* | 20.4 |
| Tension gross section | $f_{tg}$ | 12.7* | 12.7 | 13.4 | 12.7 | 15.3* | 15.3 |
| Tension perpendicular to grain | $f_{tp}$ | 0.51 | 0.51 | 0.51 | 0.51 | 0.83 | 0.83 |
| Modulus of elasticity | E | 10 300 | 10 300 | 10 700 | 9700 | 13 100 | 13 100 |

*The use of this stress grade for this primary application is not recommended.

**Notes:**

(1) Designers are advised to check the availability of grades before specifying.

(2) Tabulated values are based on the following standard conditions:

(a) dry service conditions; and

(b) standard term duration of load.

## 6.4 Modification Factors

### 6.4.1 Load Duration Factor, $K_D$

The specified strength shall be multiplied by a load duration factor, $K_D$, in accordance with Clause 4.3.2.

### 6.4.2 Service Condition Factor, $K_S$

#### 6.4.2.1

Specified strengths for glued-laminated timber are tabulated for dry service conditions. For wet service conditions, tabulated values shall be multiplied by a service condition factor, $K_S$, in accordance with Table 6.4.2.

#### 6.4.2.2

Where glued-laminated members that may be exposed to free moisture are adequately protected, an intermediate value of $K_S$ between 1.00 and that listed in Table 6.4.2 may be used.

### 6.4.3 System Factor, $K_H$

Specified strengths for glued-laminated timber members in a system consisting of three or more essentially parallel members spaced not more than 610 mm apart and so arranged that they mutually support the applied load may be multiplied by a system factor, $K_H$, equal to 1.00 for tension parallel to grain, and 1.10 for all other strength properties.

### 6.4.4 Treatment Factor, $K_T$

For preservative treatment, the treatment factor for unincised glued-laminated timber may be taken as unity. For glued-laminated timber treated with fire-retardant or other potentially strength-reducing chemicals, strength and stiffness capacities shall be based on documented results of tests that shall take into account the effects of time, temperature, and moisture content. Test procedures shall meet the requirements of Clause 3.3.2. Treating of glued-laminated members with water-borne chemicals after gluing shall not be permitted.

### Table 6.4.2
### Service Condition Factors, $K_S$

| $K_S$ | For specified strength in | Glued-laminated timber | |
|---|---|---|---|
| | | Dry service conditions | Wet service conditions |
| $K_{Sb}$ | Bending at extreme fibre | 1.00 | 0.80 |
| $K_{Sv}$ | Longitudinal shear | 1.00 | 0.87 |
| $K_{Sc}$ | Compression parallel to grain | 1.00 | 0.75 |
| $K_{Scp}$ | Compression perpendicular to grain | 1.00 | 0.67 |
| $K_{St}$ | Tension parallel to grain | 1.00 | 0.75 |
| $K_{Stp}$ | Tension perpendicular to grain | 1.00 | 0.85 |
| $K_{SE}$ | Modulus of elasticity | 1.00 | 0.90 |

## 6.5 Strength and Resistance

### 6.5.1 Scope

Clause 6.5 contains design information and design formulae for glued-laminated timber members of rectangular cross-section.

## 6.5.2 Orientation

Design data for bending members specified in Clause 6.5 apply to horizontally laminated members, the wide faces of whose laminations are normal to the direction of load.

## 6.5.3 Vertically Glued-Laminated Beams

Vertically glued-laminated beams, the narrow faces of whose laminations are normal to the direction of load, shall be designed as a built-up system of sawn lumber members of No. 2 grade, in accordance with Clause 5.4.4.3.

## 6.5.4 Net Section

The net section, obtained by deducting from the gross cross-section the area of all material removed by boring, grooving, dapping, notching, or other means, shall be checked in calculating the strength capacity of a member. In no case shall the net section be less than 75% of the gross section.

## 6.5.5 Sizes

For design purposes the actual dry size rounded to the nearest millimetre (net dimension) shall be used for both dry and wet service conditions.

**Note:** *Standard sizes rounded to the nearest millimetre are given in Clause A6.5.5.*

## 6.5.6 Bending Moment Resistance

### 6.5.6.1 Members of Constant Cross-Section

The factored bending moment resistance of glued-laminated timber members of constant cross-section shall be determined in accordance with Clause 6.5.6.5.

### 6.5.6.2 Curved and/or Double-Tapered Members

In addition to the requirements of Clause 6.5.6.5, the factored bending moment resistance of rectangular curved and/or tapered glued-laminated timber members shall not exceed the value determined in accordance with Clause 6.5.6.6.

### 6.5.6.3 Lateral Stability Conditions

#### 6.5.6.3.1

For laterally unsupported glued-laminated timber bending members, the lateral stability factor, $K_L$, may be taken as unity, provided that the maximum depth-to-width ratio of the member does not exceed 2.5:1. If the ratio is greater than 2.5:1, lateral support shall be provided at points of bearing to prevent lateral displacement and rotation, and $K_L$ shall be determined in accordance with Clause 6.5.6.4.

#### 6.5.6.3.2

In the case of glued-laminated members of rectangular section subjected to combined bending and axial loads, the rules in Clause 5.5.4.2 may be applied.

#### 6.5.6.3.3

For two or more individual members of the same depth, the ratio in Clause 6.5.6.3.1 may be based on the total width of the beam, provided that the individual members are fastened together securely at intervals not exceeding four times the depth.

### 6.5.6.4 Calculation of Lateral Stability Factor, $K_L$

#### 6.5.6.4.1 Unsupported Length, $\ell_u$

When no additional intermediate support is provided, the unsupported length, $\ell_u$, shall be the distance between points of bearing or the length of the cantilever. When intermediate support is provided by purlins so connected that they prevent lateral displacement of the compressive edge of the bending member, the unsupported length shall be taken as the maximum purlin spacing, a.

### 6.5.6.4.2 Prevention of Lateral Displacement

When the compressive edge of the bending member is supported throughout its length so as to prevent lateral displacement, the unsupported length may be taken as zero. For decking to provide such support, it shall be fastened securely to the bending member and adjacent framing to provide a rigid diaphragm.

### 6.5.6.4.3 Slenderness Ratio, $C_B$

The slenderness ratio of a bending member shall not exceed 50 and shall be calculated as follows:

$$C_B = \sqrt{\frac{L_e d}{b^2}}$$

where
$L_e$ = effective length, mm, from Table 6.5.6.4.3

### Table 6.5.6.4.3
### Effective Length, $L_e$, for Bending Members

|  | Intermediate support | |
|---|---|---|
|  | Yes | No |
| **Beams** | | |
| Any loading | 1.92 a | 1.92 $\ell_u$ |
| Uniformly distributed load | 1.92 a | 1.92 $\ell_u$ |
| Concentrated load at centre | 1.11 a | 1.61 $\ell_u$ |
| Concentrated loads at 1/3 points | 1.68 a | |
| Concentrated loads at 1/4 points | 1.54 a | |
| Concentrated loads at 1/5 points | 1.68 a | |
| Concentrated loads at 1/6 points | 1.73 a | |
| Concentrated loads at 1/7 points | 1.78 a | |
| Concentrated loads at 1/8 points | 1.84 a | |
| **Cantilevers** | | |
| Any loading | | 1.92 $\ell_u$ |
| Uniformly distributed load | | 1.23 $\ell_u$ |
| Concentrated load at free end | | 1.69 $\ell_u$ |

**Note:** $\ell_u$ *and* a *are as defined in Clause 6.5.6.4.1.*

### 6.5.6.4.4 Calculation of Lateral Stability Factor, $K_L$

The lateral stability factor shall be determined as follows:
(a) when $C_B$ does not exceed 10

$K_L = 1.0$

(b) when $C_B$ is greater than 10, but does not exceed $C_K$

$$K_L = 1 - \frac{1}{3}\left(\frac{C_B}{C_K}\right)^4$$

where

$$C_K = \sqrt{\dfrac{0.97EK_{SE}K_T}{F_b}}$$

(c) when $C_B$ is greater than $C_K$, but does not exceed 50

$$K_L = \dfrac{0.65EK_{SE}K_T}{C_B^2 F_b K_X}$$

where
$F_b = f_b(K_D K_H K_{Sb} K_T)$
$f_b$ = specified strength in bending (Table 6.3), MPa
$K_X$ = curvature factor (Clause 6.5.6.5.2)

## 6.5.6.5 Moment Resistance

### 6.5.6.5.1
Except as provided for in Clauses 6.5.6.5.3 and 6.5.6.6, the factored bending moment resistance, $M_r$, of glued-laminated timber members shall be taken as the lesser of $M_{r1}$ or $M_{r2}$ calculated from

$$M_{r1} = \varphi F_b S K_X K_{Zbg} \quad \text{and} \quad M_{r2} = \varphi F_b S K_X K_L$$

where
$\varphi$ = 0.9
$F_b$ = $f_b (K_D K_H K_{Sb} K_T)$
$f_b$ = specified strength in bending (Table 6.3), MPa
$K_L$ = lateral stability factor (Clause 6.5.6.4)
$K_X$ = curvature factor (Clause 6.5.6.5.2)
$K_{Zbg}$ = 1.03 (BL)$^{-0.18}$ ≤1.0
    where
    B = either the beam width (for single piece laminations) or the width of the widest piece (for multiple piece laminations), m
    L = length of beam segment from point of zero moment to point of zero moment, m
**Note:** *For beams with one or more points of inflection (i.e., multi-span beams and cantilevered beams), the size factor is calculated for each beam segment. The moment resistance for each beam segment as modified by the appropriate size factor is then compared to the maximum factored moment within that segment.*

### 6.5.6.5.2 Curvature Factor, $K_X$
For the curved portion only of glued-laminated timber members, the specified strength in bending shall be multiplied by the curvature factor.

$$K_X = 1-2000\left(\dfrac{t}{R}\right)^2$$

where
t = lamination thickness, mm
R = radius of curvature of the innermost lamination, mm

The minimum radius of curvature permitted for a given thickness of lamination shall conform to the provisions set forth in CSA Standard CAN/CSA-O122. (See Table A6.5.5.)
**Note:** *$K_X$ = 1.0 for straight members and the straight portion of curved members.*

## 6.5.6.5.3

At the apex of curved double-tapered members (pitched cambered beams), the factored bending moment resistance, $M_r$, shall be taken as the value obtained by the formula in Clause 6.5.6.5.1 divided by the factor [1 + 2.7 tan α], where α = slope of upper surface of member (roof slope) in degrees.

## 6.5.6.6 Radial Resistance

**Notes:**

**(1)** *The provisions of this clause apply to members of rectangular cross-section.*

**(2)** *Radial stresses occur in curved and/or double-tapered glued-laminated members and may limit their factored bending moment resistance.*

**(3)** *When the bending moment tends to decrease curvature (increase the radius), the corresponding radial stress is tension perpendicular to grain. When the bending moment tends to increase curvature (decrease the radius), the corresponding radial stress is compression perpendicular to grain.*

## 6.5.6.6.1

The factored bending moment resistance as governed by tension perpendicular to grain, $M_r$, shall be calculated by the following formula, but shall not be greater than the value determined in accordance with the requirements of Clauses 6.5.6.5.1 and 6.5.6.5.3. For double-tapered members, the additional requirement of Clause 6.5.6.6.2 shall also be satisfied.

$$M_r = \Phi F_{tp} \frac{2A}{3} R K_{Ztp}$$

where

$\phi$ = 0.9

$F_{tp}$ = $f_{tp}(K_D K_H K_{Stp} K_T)$

$f_{tp}$ = specified strength in tension perpendicular to grain (Table 6.3), MPa

R = radius of curvature at centreline of member, mm

$K_{Ztp}$ = size factor in tension perpendicular to grain (Table 6.5.6.6.1)

## Table 6.5.6.6.1
## Size Factor, $K_{Ztp}$, for Tension Perpendicular to Grain*

| Member | Loading | |
| --- | --- | --- |
| | Uniformly distributed | All other |
| Constant depth, curved | $\dfrac{24}{(AR\beta)^{0.2}}$ | $\dfrac{20}{(AR\beta)^{0.2}}$ |
| Double-tapered, curved | $\dfrac{35}{(AR\beta)^{0.2}}$ | $\dfrac{22}{(AR\beta)^{0.2}}$ |
| Double-tapered, straight | $\dfrac{36}{(Ad)^{0.2}}$ | $\dfrac{23}{(Ad)^{0.2}}$ |

*where

$A$ = maximum cross-sectional area of member, mm$^2$

$R$ = radius of curvature at centreline of member, mm

$\beta$ = enclosed angle in radians (1 radian = 57.3°)

**Notes:**

**(1)** *For curved double-tapered members, β is measured between points of tangency.*

**(2)** *For curved uniform section members, β is measured between the points where the factored bending moment is 85% of the maximum factored bending moment.*

## 6.5.6.6.2

For double-tapered members subjected to radial tension perpendicular to grain, the following additional requirement shall be satisfied:

$$M_r = \phi F_{tp} S K_{Ztp} K_R$$

where
$\phi$ = 0.9
$F_{tp}$ = $f_{tp}(K_D K_H K_{Stp} K_T)$
$f_{tp}$ = specified strength in tension perpendicular to grain (Table 6.3), MPa
$S$ = section modulus at apex, mm³
$K_{Ztp}$ = size factor in tension perpendicular to grain (Table 6.5.6.6.1)
$K_R$ = radial stress factor (Clause 6.5.6.6.3)

## 6.5.6.6.3

The radial stress factor, $K_R$, shall be taken as

$$K_R = \left[ A + B\left(\frac{d}{R}\right) + C\left(\frac{d}{R}\right)^2 \right]^{-1}$$

where
A,B,C = constants given in Table 6.5.6.6.3
d = maximum depth at apex, mm
R = radius of curvature at centreline of member, mm

### Table 6.5.6.6.3
### Values of Constants for Determination
### of Radial Stress in Double-Tapered
### Curved Members

| Angle α* | Value of constant | | |
|---|---|---|---|
| | A | B | C |
| 2°30′ | 0.01 | 0.17 | 0.13 |
| 5° | 0.02 | 0.13 | 0.19 |
| 7°30′ | 0.03 | 0.09 | 0.22 |
| 10° | 0.04 | 0.08 | 0.21 |
| 15° | 0.06 | 0.06 | 0.17 |
| 20° | 0.09 | 0.06 | 0.14 |
| 25° | 0.12 | 0.06 | 0.12 |
| 30° | 0.16 | 0.06 | 0.11 |

*See Figure 6.5.6.6.3.

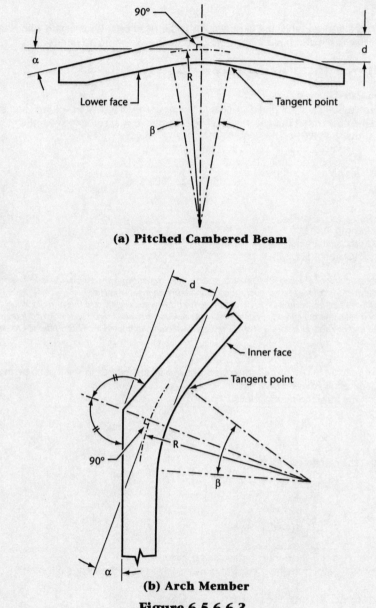

**(a) Pitched Cambered Beam**

**(b) Arch Member**

**Figure 6.5.6.6.3**
**Double-Tapered Member**

## 6.5.7 Shear Resistance

### 6.5.7.1 General

#### 6.5.7.1.1
The provisions of Clause 6.5.7 apply to members of rectangular cross-section only.

### 6.5.7.1.2

In the calculation of shear resistance in Clause 6.5.7.2.1, the effect of all loads acting within a distance from a support equal to the depth of the member need not be taken into account.

## 6.5.7.2 Factored Shear Resistance — Case 1

Δ ### 6.5.7.2.1 General

The factored shear resistance, $V_r$, of glued-laminated beams less than 2.0 m³ in volume, and of glued-laminated members other than beams, shall be determined in accordance with the provisions of Clause 6.5.7.3, or shall be taken as

$$V_r = \phi F_v \frac{2A_g}{3} K_N$$

where
$\phi$ = 0.9
$F_v$ = $f_v(K_D K_H K_{Sv} K_T)$
$f_v$ = specified strength in shear (Table 6.3), MPa
$A_g$ = gross cross-sectional area of member, mm²
$K_N$ = notch factor (Clause 6.5.7.2.2)

**Notes:**
**(1)** *Notches or abrupt changes of section will produce stress concentrations and should be avoided. The magnitude of these stress concentrations is reduced by gradual rather than abrupt changes of section.*
**(2)** *Calculation of factored shear resistance in accordance with these requirements and this formula follows an approximate method only, and may greatly underestimate the true factored shear resistance of glued-laminated members. For a more detailed and accurate calculation of shear resistance of glued-laminated members, refer to Clause 6.5.7.3.*

### 6.5.7.2.2

At the location of notches in rectangular members, the specified strength in shear shall be multiplied by a notch factor, $K_N$, determined as follows:
(a) for notches at the tension side at supports

$$K_N = \left(1 - \frac{d_n}{d}\right)^2$$

(b) for notches at the compression side

(i) for e>d, $\quad K_N = 1 - \dfrac{d_n}{d}$

(ii) for e<d, $\quad K_N = 1 - \dfrac{d_n e}{d(d - d_n)}$

where
$d_n$ = depth of notch, mm, which must not exceed 0.25d
$e$ = length of notch, mm, from inner edge of closest support to farthest edge of notch

Δ ### 6.5.7.3 Factored Shear Resistance — Case 2

The factored shear resistance, $V_r$, of glued-laminated beams including those that exceed the maximum volume restriction of Clause 6.5.7.2.1 shall not be less than the sum of all factored loads, $W_f$, acting on the beam and shall be taken as

$$V_r = \phi F_v 0.48 A_g K_N C_V Z^{-0.18} \geq W_f$$

where
$\phi$ = 0.9
$F_v$ = $f_v(K_D K_H K_{Sv} K_T)$

$f_v$ = specified strength in shear (Table 6.3), MPa
$A_g$ = gross cross-sectional area of member, mm²
$K_N$ = notch factor (Clause 6.5.7.2.2)
$C_V$ = shear load coefficient (Clause 6.5.7.4)
$Z$ = beam volume, m³

## 6.5.7.4 Shear Load Coefficient, $C_V$

For any load condition not shown in Tables 6.5.7.4A to 6.5.7.4F, the coefficient for simple span, continuous, or cantilevered beams of constant depth may be determined using the following procedure (the principle of superposition of loads does not apply):

(a) Construct the shear force diagram for the beam. If the beam is under moving concentrated loads, construct the diagram of the maximum shear forces occurring along the full length of the beam without regard to sign convention. (Positive and negative maximum shear forces both show positive.)

(b) Divide the total beam length, L, into n segments of variable lengths, $\ell_a$, such that within each segment there are neither abrupt changes nor sign changes in the shear force.

(c) For each segment determine
    (i) $V_A$ = factored shear force at beginning of segment, N;
    (ii) $V_B$ = factored shear force at end of segment, N; and
    (iii) $V_C$ = factored shear force at centre of segment, N;
and calculate the factor G in accordance with the formula

$$G = \ell_a \left[ V_A^5 + V_B^5 + 4V_C^5 \right]$$

(d) Determine the coefficient, $C_V$, in accordance with the following formulae:
    (i) for stationary loads

$$C_V = 1.825 W_f \left( \frac{L}{\Sigma G} \right)^{0.2}$$

where
$W_f$ = the total of all factored loads applied to the beam, N

    (ii) for moving loads

$$C_V = 1.825 W_f \left( \frac{L}{\Sigma G} \right)^{0.2}$$

where
$W_f$ = the total of all factored moving loads and all factored distributed loads applied to the beam, N

### Table 6.5.7.4A
### Shear Load Coefficient, $C_V$, for Simple Span Beams

| Number of equal loads equally and symmetrically spaced | r* | | | |
|---|---|---|---|---|
| | 0.0 | 0.5 | 2.0 | 10.0 and over |
| 1 | 3.69 | 3.34 | 2.92 | 2.46 |
| 2 | 3.69 | 3.37 | 3.01 | 2.67 |
| 3 | 3.69 | 3.41 | 3.12 | 2.84 |
| 4 | 3.69 | 3.45 | 3.21 | 2.97 |
| 5 | 3.69 | 3.48 | 3.28 | 3.08 |
| 6 | 3.69 | 3.51 | 3.34 | 3.16 |

$*r = \dfrac{total\ of\ concentrated\ loads}{total\ of\ uniform\ loads}$

## Table 6.5.7.4B
## Shear Load Coefficient, $C_V$, for Distributed Loads

| Type of loading | $P_{min}/P_{max}$ | | | | | |
|---|---|---|---|---|---|---|
| | 0.0 | 0.2 | 0.4 | 0.6 | 0.8 | 1.0 |
| | 3.40 | 3.55 | 3.63 | 3.67 | 3.69 | 3.69 |

## Table 6.5.7.4C
## Shear Load Coefficient, $C_V$, for Cantilevered Beams

| Beam type and loading | $L_1/L_2$ | $r^*$ | | | |
|---|---|---|---|---|---|
| | | 0.0 | 0.5 | 2.0 | 10.0 and over |
| $L = L_1 + L_2$ | 0.05 | 3.91 | 5.64 | 4.06 | 2.73 |
| | 0.10 | 4.13 | 5.19 | 3.07 | 2.08 |
| | 0.20 | 4.55 | 4.36 | 2.53 | 1.75 |
| | 0.30 | 4.88 | 3.83 | 2.31 | 1.62 |
| $L = L_2 + 2L_1$ | 0.05 | 4.13 | 6.19 | 7.13 | 4.86 |
| | 0.10 | 4.58 | 6.72 | 5.42 | 3.72 |
| | 0.20 | 5.50 | 6.90 | 4.49 | 3.17 |
| | 0.30 | 6.40 | 6.31 | 4.10 | 2.97 |

$$*r = \frac{total\ of\ concentrated\ loads}{total\ of\ uniform\ loads}$$

## Table 6.5.7.4D
## Shear Load Coefficient, $C_V$, for 2-Span Continuous Beams

| Loading case† | $L_1/L$ | $r^*$ | | | |
|---|---|---|---|---|---|
| | | 0.0 | 0.5 | 2.0 | 10.0 and over |
| | 0.2 | 4.09 | 3.04 | 2.35 | 2.01 |
| | 0.3 | 5.10 | 3.48 | 2.57 | 2.15 |
| | 0.4 | 6.09 | 3.96 | 2.82 | 2.32 |
| | 0.5 | 6.66 | 4.42 | 3.07 | 2.50 |

$$*r = \frac{total\ of\ concentrated\ loads}{total\ of\ uniform\ loads}$$

†Values shown correspond to the worst position for the concentrated loads

## Table 6.5.7.4E
## Shear Load Coefficient, $C_V$, for Tapered Beams — Uniformly Distributed Loads

| Beam case | $L/d_0$* | m | | | | | |
|---|---|---|---|---|---|---|---|
| | | 0.20 | 0.10 | 0.05 | 0.00 | −0.04 | −0.08 |
| $d_0$ ... $d_1$; $L$; $m = \dfrac{(d_1 - d_0)}{L}$ | 10 | 4.95 | 4.99 | 4.68 | 3.97 | — | — |
| | 20 | 4.46 | 4.63 | 4.54 | 3.69 | — | — |
| | 30 | 4.33 | 4.44 | 4.47 | 3.58 | — | — |
| $d_0$ ... $d_1$; $L$; $m = \dfrac{2(d_1 - d_0)}{L}$ | 10 | 4.40 | 4.49 | 4.32 | 3.97 | 3.58 | 2.42 |
| | 15 | 4.09 | 4.26 | 4.16 | 3.77 | 3.13 | 0.93 |
| | 20 | 3.95 | 4.11 | 4.08 | 3.69 | 2.40 | 0.23 |
| | 30 | 3.83 | 3.93 | 3.99 | 3.58 | 0.91 | — |

*To compute the ratio $L/d_0$, L and $d_0$ shall be in the same units.

## Table 6.5.7.4F
## Shear Load Coefficient, $C_V$, for Moving Loads

| Type of concentrated loads | Span, L (mm) | r* | | | | |
|---|---|---|---|---|---|---|
| | | 0.5 | 1.5 | 3.0 | 10.0 | 100.0 |
| P ; L | 10 000 | 2.65 | 2.12 | 1.90 | 1.71 | 1.62 |
| | 20 000 | 2.65 | 2.12 | 1.90 | 1.71 | 1.62 |
| | 30 000 | 2.65 | 2.12 | 1.90 | 1.71 | 1.62 |
| | 40 000 | 2.65 | 2.12 | 1.90 | 1.71 | 1.62 |
| P P ; 2400 | 10 000 | 2.87 | 2.38 | 2.17 | 1.98 | 1.90 |
| | 20 000 | 2.76 | 2.24 | 2.03 | 1.83 | 1.75 |
| | 30 000 | 2.72 | 2.20 | 1.98 | 1.79 | 1.70 |
| | 40 000 | 2.70 | 2.18 | 1.96 | 1.77 | 1.68 |
| $\frac{P}{3}$ P P P ; 4000 6000 6000 | 10 000 | 3.93 | 4.05 | 4.11 | 4.17 | 4.20 |
| | 20 000 | 3.39 | 3.13 | 2.99 | 2.86 | 2.80 |
| | 30 000 | 3.14 | 2.75 | 2.57 | 2.40 | 2.32 |
| | 40 000 | 3.03 | 2.59 | 2.40 | 2.21 | 2.13 |
| 0.3P 0.8P 0.8P P 0.8P ; 3600 6000 7200 1200 | 10 000 | 3.78 | 3.76 | 3.74 | 3.72 | 3.70 |
| | 20 000 | 3.40 | 3.13 | 3.00 | 2.86 | 2.79 |
| | 30 000 | 3.20 | 2.84 | 2.67 | 2.50 | 2.42 |
| | 40 000 | 3.08 | 2.66 | 2.47 | 2.29 | 2.21 |
| P P P P 0.44P ; 1200 7200 4200 1200 | 10 000 | 3.78 | 3.76 | 3.73 | 3.70 | 3.67 |
| | 20 000 | 3.24 | 2.90 | 2.73 | 2.58 | 2.50 |
| | 30 000 | 3.05 | 2.63 | 2.43 | 2.25 | 2.17 |
| | 40 000 | 2.96 | 2.51 | 2.31 | 2.12 | 2.03 |

*$r = \dfrac{\text{total of concentrated loads}}{\text{total of uniform loads}}$

## 6.5.8 Compressive Resistance Parallel to Grain

### 6.5.8.1 Effective Length, $L_e$

Unless noted otherwise, the effective length, $L_e = K_e L$, shall be used in determining the slenderness ratio of compression members.

Recommended effective length factors, $K_e$, for compression members are given in Table A5.5.6.1.

### 6.5.8.2 Slenderness Ratio, $C_C$

The slenderness ratio, $C_C$, of simple compression members of constant rectangular section shall not exceed 50 and shall be taken as the greater of

$$C_C = \frac{\text{effective length associated with width}}{\text{member width}}$$

or

$$C_C = \frac{\text{effective length associated with depth}}{\text{member depth}}$$

### 6.5.8.3 Variable Rectangular Cross-Section

Tapered rectangular compression members shall be designed for an effective width or depth equal to the minimum width or depth plus 0.45 times the difference between the maximum and minimum widths or depths. The factored compressive resistance determined in this manner shall not exceed the factored resistance based on the minimum dimensions in conjunction with a slenderness factor $K_C = 1.00$.

### 6.5.8.4 Factored Compressive Resistance Parallel to Grain

#### 6.5.8.4.1

Bending moments due to eccentrically applied axial loads shall be taken into account in accordance with Clause 6.5.12.

#### 6.5.8.4.2

The factored compressive resistance parallel to grain, $P_r$, shall be taken as

$$P_r = \phi F_c A K_{Zcg} K_C$$

where
$\phi$ = 0.8
$F_c$ = $f_c (K_D K_H K_{Sc} K_T)$
$f_c$ = specified strength in compression parallel to grain (Table 6.3), MPa
$K_{Zcg}$ = $0.68 (Z)^{-0.13} \leq 1.0$
    where
    $Z$ = member volume, m$^3$
$K_C$ = slenderness factor (Clause 6.5.8.5)

### 6.5.8.5 Slenderness Factor, $K_C$

The slenderness factor, $K_C$, shall be determined as follows:

$$K_C = \left[ 1.0 + \frac{F_c K_{Zcg} C_c^3}{35 E_{05} K_{SE} K_T} \right]^{-1}$$

where
$E_{05} = 0.87E$

## 6.5.8.6  Spaced Compression Members
Spaced compression members shall be designed in accordance with the requirements of Clause A5.5.6.3, using the specified strengths and modification factors appropriate for glued-laminated timber.

## 6.5.8.7  Built-up Compression Members
Built-up compression members shall be designed in accordance with the requirements of Clause 5.5.6.4, using the specified strengths and adjustment factors appropriate for glued-laminated timber.

## 6.5.9  Compressive Resistance Perpendicular to Grain (Bearing)

## 6.5.9.1  General
Factored bearing forces shall not exceed the factored compressive resistance perpendicular to grain determined in accordance with the provisions of Clauses 6.5.9.2 and 6.5.9.3.

## 6.5.9.2  Effect of All Applied Loads
The factored compressive resistance perpendicular to grain under the effect of all applied loads shall be taken as $Q_r$ in the following formula:

$$Q_r = \phi F_{cp} A_b K_B K_{Zcp}$$

where
$\phi$ = 0.8
$F_{cp}$ = $f_{cp}(K_D K_{Scp} K_T)$
$f_{cp}$ = specified strength in compression perpendicular to grain (Table 6.3), MPa
$A_b$ = bearing area, mm$^2$
$K_B$ = length of bearing factor (Clause 5.5.7.6)
$K_{Zcp}$ = size factor for bearing, where depth is thickness of lamination (Clause 5.5.7.5)

## 6.5.9.3  Effect of Loads Applied near a Support
The factored compressive resistance perpendicular to grain under the effect of only those applied loads acting within a distance from the centre of the support equal to the depth of the member shall be taken as $Q_r'$ in the following formula:

$$Q_r' = (2/3)\phi F_{cp} A_b' K_B K_{Zcp}$$

where
$\phi$ = 0.8
$F_{cp}$ = $f_{cp}(K_D K_{Scp} K_T)$
$f_{cp}$ = f-E grade value from Table 6.3 for compression face bearing strength, MPa
$A_b'$ = average bearing area (see Clause 6.5.9.4), mm$^2$

## 6.5.9.4  Bearing Area on Opposite Faces of a Member
Where unequal bearing areas are used on opposite surfaces of a member, the average bearing area shall not exceed the following:

$$A_b' = b\left(\frac{L_{b1} + L_{b2}}{2}\right), \text{ but } \leq 1.5\ bL_{b1}$$

where
b = average bearing width (perpendicular to grain), mm
$L_{b1}$ = lesser bearing length, mm
$L_{b2}$ = larger bearing length, mm

## 6.5.10 Compressive Resistance at an Angle to Grain

The factored compressive resistance at an angle to grain shall be calculated in accordance with the requirements of Clause 5.5.8, using the appropriate specified strengths and resistances for glued-laminated timber.

## 6.5.11 Tensile Resistance Parallel to Grain

The factored tensile resistance parallel to grain, $T_r$, shall be calculated as the lesser of

$$T_r = \phi F_{tn} A_n$$

or

$$T_r = \phi F_{tg} A_g$$

where
$\phi$ = 0.9
$F_{tn}$ = $f_{tn}(K_D K_H K_{St} K_T)$
$f_{tn}$ = specified strength in tension parallel to grain at the net section (Table 6.3), MPa
$A_n$ = net area of cross-section, $mm^2$
$F_{tg}$ = $f_{tg}(K_D K_H K_{St} K_T)$
$f_{tg}$ = specified strength in tension parallel to grain at the gross section (Table 6.3), MPa
$A_g$ = gross area of cross-section, $mm^2$

## 6.5.12 Resistance to Combined Bending and Axial Load

Members subject to combined bending and compressive or tensile axial loads shall be designed to satisfy the appropriate interaction equation:

$$\frac{P_f}{P_r} + \frac{M_f}{M_r} \leq 1.0 \quad \text{or}$$

$$\frac{T_f}{T_r} + \frac{M_f}{M_r} \leq 1.0$$

where
$P_f$ = factored compressive axial load
$P_r$ = factored compressive load resistance parallel to grain calculated in accordance with the requirements of Clause 6.5.8.4 using $F_{cb} = f_{cb}(K_D K_H K_{Sc} K_T)$
$M_f$ = factored bending moment, taking into account end moments and amplified moments due to axial loads in laterally loaded members
$M_r$ = factored bending moment resistance calculated in accordance with the requirements of Clause 6.5.6.5.1
$T_f$ = factored tensile axial load
$T_r$ = factored tensile load resistance parallel to grain calculated in accordance with the requirements of Clause 6.5.11

# 7. Structural Panels

## 7.1 Scope

Design equations, data, and construction requirements specified in Clause 7 apply to the materials specified in Clause 7.2.

Design equations and construction requirements for glued building components manufactured using structural panels are provided in Clause 8.

## 7.2 Materials

### 7.2.1 Plywood

The provisions in Clauses 7.3 to 7.5 apply to standard constructions of regular grades of unsanded Douglas Fir plywood manufactured and identified in accordance with CSA Standard O121 and to standard constructions of regular grades of unsanded Canadian Softwood plywood manufactured and identified in accordance with CSA Standard O151.

### 7.2.2 OSB

#### 7.2.2.1 Design-Rated OSB

The provisions in Clauses 7.3 to 7.5 apply to design-rated OSB Types 1, 2, and 3 that are qualified, certified for engineering uses, and identified in accordance with CSA Standard O452.0.
**Note:** *The designer is strongly advised to check availability before specifying.*

#### 7.2.2.2 Construction Sheathing OSB

The provisions in Clauses 7.3 to 7.5 also apply to OSB panels that are qualified and identified in accordance with CSA Standard CAN/CSA-O325.0, which pertains to wood-based panel products, designed and manufactured for protected construction uses such as roof sheathing, wall sheathing, and floor sheathing in light frame construction applications. Other tests and criteria may be required to characterize panels for special construction uses or other applications.
**Note:** *Construction Sheathing OSB is distinguished from other mat-formed panels by a mark showing the direction of face alignment. (See Clause A7.2.2.2 for additional information.)*

### 7.2.3 Adhesives for Stress Joints

Adhesives for stress joints for structural panels shall meet the requirements of CSA Standard O112.7.

## 7.3 Specified Capacities

### 7.3.1 Plywood

The specified capacities for minimum veneer layup for each plywood thickness are given for Douglas Fir plywood in Table 7.3A, and for Canadian Softwood plywood in Table 7.3B.
**Note:** *Information on thick panel layups is provided in Clause A7.3.1.*

### 7.3.2 OSB

#### 7.3.2.1

The specified capacities for Type 1 (Standard) design-rated OSB are given in Table 7.3C.

#### 7.3.2.2

The specified capacities for Type 2 (Plus) panels shall be the capacities for the designated design rating with the Plus properties increased by the designated percentage shown on the panel (and obtainable from the manufacturer).

#### 7.3.2.3

The specified capacities for Type 3 (Proprietary) panels are not given in the Standard, but shall be determined in accordance with Clause 13.3 and listed on the Certificate of Conformance required by CSA Standard O452.0.

## 7.3.2.4

The specified capacities for Construction Sheathing OSB conforming to CSA Standard CAN/CSA-O325.0 are given in Table 7.3D.

### Table 7.3A
### Specified Strength, Stiffness, and Rigidity Capacities for Standard Constructions of Regular Grades of Unsanded Douglas Fir Plywood (DFP)

| Nominal thickness, mm | No. of plies | Bending, $m_p$, N•mm/mm | | Axial tension, $t_p$, N/mm | | Axial compression, $p_p$, N/mm | | Shear-through-thickness, $v_p$, N/mm | Planar shear Bending, $v_{pb}$, N/mm | | Shear in-plane, $v_{pf}$, MPa | |
|---|---|---|---|---|---|---|---|---|---|---|---|---|
| | | Orientation of applied force relative to face grain | | | | | | | | | | |
| | | 0° | 90° | 0° | 90° | 0° | 90° | 0°& 90° | 0° | 90° | 0° | 90° |
| 7.5 | 3 | 180 | 38 | 97 | 23 | 130 | 40 | 20 | 3.7 | 1.2 | 0.72 | 0.72 |
| 9.5 | 3 | 270 | 59 | 97 | 28 | 130 | 50 | 24 | 3.9 | 1.4 | 0.55 | 0.72 |
| 12.5 | 4 | 420 | 130 | 97 | 55 | 130 | 96 | 30 | 5.5 | 2.8 | 0.55 | 0.72 |
| 12.5 | 5 | 560 | 200 | 130 | 71 | 170 | 79 | 30 | 7.3 | 3.7 | 0.72 | 0.72 |
| 15.5 | 4 | 750 | 230 | 160 | 72 | 200 | 130 | 40 | 6.6 | 3.6 | 0.55 | 0.72 |
| 15.5 | 5 | 770 | 280 | 130 | 71 | 170 | 79 | 36 | 9.4 | 4.9 | 0.72 | 0.72 |
| 18.5 | 5 | 1300 | 460 | 200 | 110 | 260 | 120 | 45 | 11.0 | 5.7 | 0.72 | 0.72 |
| 18.5 | 6 | 990 | 440 | 160 | 71 | 210 | 79 | 43 | 9.2 | 5.4 | 0.55 | 0.55 |
| 18.5 | 7 | 1100 | 450 | 160 | 110 | 210 | 120 | 43 | 9.7 | 7.1 | 0.72 | 0.72 |
| 20.5 | 5 | 1200 | 740 | 180 | 130 | 230 | 150 | 47 | 10.0 | 5.7 | 0.55 | 0.55 |
| 20.5 | 6 | 1100 | 550 | 170 | 71 | 220 | 79 | 47 | 10.0 | 6.5 | 0.55 | 0.55 |
| 20.5 | 7 | 1200 | 560 | 160 | 110 | 210 | 120 | 47 | 11.0 | 8.5 | 0.72 | 0.72 |
| 22.5 | 7 | 1600 | 640 | 190 | 110 | 240 | 130 | 52 | 12.0 | 9.8 | 0.72 | 0.72 |
| 22.5 | 8 | 1600 | 630 | 190 | 140 | 240 | 160 | 52 | 9.3 | 10.0 | 0.55 | 0.72 |
| 25.5 | 7 | 1900 | 1000 | 220 | 160 | 280 | 180 | 58 | 13.0 | 11.0 | 0.72 | 0.72 |
| 25.5 | 8 | 1900 | 850 | 190 | 160 | 240 | 180 | 58 | 11.0 | 12.0 | 0.55 | 0.72 |
| 25.5 | 9 | 2000 | 850 | 220 | 140 | 280 | 160 | 58 | 14.0 | 10.0 | 0.72 | 0.72 |
| 25.5 | 10 | 2000 | 910 | 250 | 140 | 330 | 160 | 58 | 14.0 | 7.8 | 0.72 | 0.55 |
| 28.5 | 8 | 2300 | 1200 | 200 | 200 | 260 | 230 | 65 | 12.0 | 14.0 | 0.55 | 0.72 |
| 28.5 | 9 | 2300 | 1000 | 220 | 140 | 280 | 160 | 65 | 16.0 | 12.0 | 0.72 | 0.72 |
| 28.5 | 10 | 2300 | 1100 | 250 | 140 | 330 | 160 | 65 | 16.0 | 9.2 | 0.72 | 0.55 |
| 28.5 | 11 | 2400 | 1200 | 250 | 180 | 330 | 200 | 65 | 15.0 | 12.0 | 0.72 | 0.72 |
| 31.5 | 8 | 2800 | 1700 | 240 | 250 | 320 | 280 | 71 | 13.0 | 16.0 | 0.55 | 0.72 |
| 31.5 | 9 | 2600 | 1500 | 240 | 190 | 310 | 210 | 71 | 17.0 | 13.0 | 0.72 | 0.72 |
| 31.5 | 10 | 2600 | 1300 | 250 | 140 | 330 | 160 | 71 | 18.0 | 11.0 | 0.72 | 0.55 |
| 31.5 | 11 | 2700 | 1300 | 250 | 180 | 330 | 200 | 71 | 17.0 | 14.0 | 0.72 | 0.72 |
| 31.5 | 12 | 2800 | 1400 | 250 | 210 | 330 | 240 | 71 | 13.0 | 14.0 | 0.55 | 0.72 |

*(Continued)*

## Table 7.3A (Concluded)

| Nominal thickness, mm | No. of plies | Bending stiffness, $B_b = EI$, N•mm$^2$/mm | | Axial stiffness (in tension or compression), $B_a = EA$, N/mm | | Shear-through-thickness rigidity, $B_v$, N/mm |
|---|---|---|---|---|---|---|
| | | Orientation of applied force relative to face grain | | | | |
| | | 0° | 90° | 0° | 90° | 0° & 90° |
| 7.5 | 3 | 440 000 | 17 000 | 70 000 | 24 000 | 4 600 |
| 9.5 | 3 | 840 000 | 33 000 | 70 000 | 30 000 | 5 500 |
| 12.5 | 4 | 1 700 000 | 190 000 | 70 000 | 57 000 | 6 900 |
| 12.5 | 5 | 1 700 000 | 350 000 | 94 000 | 47 000 | 6 900 |
| 15.5 | 4 | 3 800 000 | 430 000 | 110 000 | 75 000 | 9 100 |
| 15.5 | 5 | 3 000 000 | 630 000 | 94 000 | 47 000 | 8 400 |
| 18.5 | 5 | 6 000 000 | 1 300 000 | 140 000 | 73 000 | 10 000 |
| 18.5 | 6 | 4 600 000 | 1 300 000 | 120 000 | 47 000 | 9 800 |
| 18.5 | 7 | 4 900 000 | 1 400 000 | 120 000 | 71 000 | 9 800 |
| 20.5 | 5 | 6 300 000 | 2 600 000 | 130 000 | 89 000 | 11 000 |
| 20.5 | 6 | 5 900 000 | 1 900 000 | 130 000 | 47 000 | 11 000 |
| 20.5 | 7 | 6 200 000 | 2 000 000 | 120 000 | 71 000 | 11 000 |
| 22.5 | 7 | 8 800 000 | 2 500 000 | 130 000 | 75 000 | 12 000 |
| 22.5 | 8 | 9 100 000 | 2 500 000 | 130 000 | 95 000 | 12 000 |
| 25.5 | 7 | 12 000 000 | 4 800 000 | 160 000 | 110 000 | 13 000 |
| 25.5 | 8 | 12 000 000 | 4 100 000 | 130 000 | 110 000 | 13 000 |
| 25.5 | 9 | 13 000 000 | 4 100 000 | 160 000 | 95 000 | 13 000 |
| 25.5 | 10 | 13 000 000 | 4 400 000 | 180 000 | 95 000 | 13 000 |
| 28.5 | 8 | 16 000 000 | 7 000 000 | 140 000 | 140 000 | 15 000 |
| 28.5 | 9 | 16 000 000 | 5 700 000 | 160 000 | 95 000 | 15 000 |
| 28.5 | 10 | 17 000 000 | 6 100 000 | 180 000 | 95 000 | 15 000 |
| 28.5 | 11 | 17 000 000 | 6 400 000 | 180 000 | 120 000 | 15 000 |
| 31.5 | 8 | 22 000 000 | 11 000 000 | 180 000 | 170 000 | 16 000 |
| 31.5 | 9 | 21 000 000 | 9 400 000 | 170 000 | 120 000 | 16 000 |
| 31.5 | 10 | 21 000 000 | 8 200 000 | 180 000 | 95 000 | 16 000 |
| 31.5 | 11 | 22 000 000 | 8 500 000 | 180 000 | 120 000 | 16 000 |
| 31.5 | 12 | 22 000 000 | 9 000 000 | 180 000 | 140 000 | 16 000 |

**Notes:**
(1) *For specified stiffness in bending on edge, use axial stiffness values.*
(2) *Tabulated values are based on dry service conditions and standard-term duration of load.*
(3) *Specified strength in bearing (normal to plane of panel) $q_p$ = 4.5 MPa.*

## Table 7.3B
## Specified Strength, Stiffness, and Rigidity Capacities for Standard Constructions of Regular Grades of Unsanded Canadian Softwood Plywood (CSP)

| Nominal thickness, mm | No. of plies | Bending, $m_p$, N•mm/mm | | Axial tension, $t_p$, N/mm | | Axial compression, $p_p$, N/mm | | Shear-through-thickness, $v_p$, N/mm | Planar shear | | | |
|---|---|---|---|---|---|---|---|---|---|---|---|---|
| | | | | | | | | | Bending, $v_{pb}$, N/mm | | Shear in-plane, $v_{pf}$, MPa | |
| | | Orientation of applied force relative to face grain | | | | | | | | | | |
| | | 0° | 90° | 0° | 90° | 0° | 90° | 0°& 90° | 0° | 90° | 0° | 90° |
| 7.5 | 3 | 160 | 38 | 71 | 23 | 79 | 40 | 18 | 3.7 | 1.2 | 0.72 | 0.72 |
| 9.5 | 3 | 250 | 59 | 71 | 28 | 79 | 50 | 23 | 3.9 | 1.4 | 0.55 | 0.72 |
| 12.5 | 4 | 420 | 130 | 89 | 55 | 99 | 96 | 30 | 5.5 | 2.8 | 0.55 | 0.72 |
| 12.5 | 5 | 380 | 200 | 110 | 71 | 120 | 79 | 30 | 7.3 | 3.7 | 0.72 | 0.72 |
| 15.5 | 4 | 670 | 230 | 110 | 72 | 130 | 130 | 38 | 6.6 | 3.6 | 0.55 | 0.72 |
| 15.5 | 5 | 520 | 280 | 110 | 71 | 120 | 79 | 38 | 9.4 | 4.9 | 0.72 | 0.72 |
| 18.5 | 5 | 880 | 460 | 160 | 110 | 180 | 120 | 46 | 11.0 | 5.7 | 0.72 | 0.72 |
| 18.5 | 6 | 790 | 440 | 160 | 71 | 180 | 79 | 46 | 12.0 | 5.4 | 0.72 | 0.55 |
| 18.5 | 7 | 740 | 450 | 140 | 110 | 160 | 120 | 46 | 9.7 | 7.1 | 0.72 | 0.72 |
| 20.5 | 5 | 840 | 740 | 150 | 130 | 170 | 150 | 51 | 10.0 | 5.7 | 0.55 | 0.55 |
| 20.5 | 6 | 780 | 550 | 150 | 71 | 170 | 79 | 51 | 10.0 | 6.5 | 0.55 | 0.55 |
| 20.5 | 7 | 840 | 560 | 140 | 110 | 160 | 120 | 51 | 11.0 | 8.5 | 0.72 | 0.72 |
| 22.5 | 7 | 1100 | 640 | 160 | 110 | 180 | 130 | 56 | 12.0 | 9.8 | 0.72 | 0.72 |
| 22.5 | 8 | 1100 | 630 | 160 | 140 | 180 | 160 | 56 | 9.3 | 10.0 | 0.55 | 0.72 |
| 25.5 | 7 | 1300 | 1000 | 190 | 160 | 210 | 180 | 63 | 13.0 | 11.0 | 0.72 | 0.72 |
| 25.5 | 8 | 1400 | 850 | 160 | 160 | 180 | 180 | 63 | 11.0 | 12.0 | 0.55 | 0.72 |
| 25.5 | 9 | 1400 | 850 | 200 | 140 | 220 | 160 | 63 | 14.0 | 10.0 | 0.72 | 0.72 |
| 25.5 | 10 | 1500 | 910 | 230 | 140 | 260 | 160 | 63 | 14.0 | 7.8 | 0.72 | 0.55 |
| 28.5 | 8 | 1600 | 1200 | 170 | 200 | 200 | 230 | 71 | 12.0 | 14.0 | 0.55 | 0.72 |
| 28.5 | 9 | 1600 | 1000 | 200 | 140 | 220 | 160 | 71 | 16.0 | 12.0 | 0.72 | 0.72 |
| 28.5 | 10 | 1700 | 1100 | 230 | 140 | 260 | 160 | 71 | 16.0 | 9.2 | 0.72 | 0.55 |
| 28.5 | 11 | 1800 | 1200 | 230 | 180 | 260 | 200 | 71 | 15.0 | 12.0 | 0.72 | 0.72 |
| 31.5 | 8 | 2000 | 1700 | 220 | 250 | 250 | 280 | 78 | 13.0 | 16.0 | 0.55 | 0.72 |
| 31.5 | 9 | 1900 | 1500 | 220 | 190 | 250 | 210 | 78 | 17.0 | 13.0 | 0.72 | 0.72 |
| 31.5 | 10 | 1900 | 1300 | 230 | 140 | 260 | 160 | 78 | 18.0 | 11.0 | 0.72 | 0.55 |
| 31.5 | 11 | 2000 | 1300 | 230 | 180 | 260 | 200 | 78 | 17.0 | 14.0 | 0.72 | 0.72 |
| 31.5 | 12 | 2100 | 1400 | 230 | 210 | 260 | 240 | 78 | 13.0 | 14.0 | 0.55 | 0.72 |

*(Continued)*

## Table 7.3B (Concluded)

| Nominal thickness, mm | No. of plies | Bending stiffness, $B_b = EI$, N•mm²/mm | | Axial stiffness (in tension or compression), $B_a = EA$, N/mm | | Shear-through-thickness rigidity, $B_v$, N/mm |
|---|---|---|---|---|---|---|
| | | Orientation of applied force relative to face grain | | | | |
| | | 0° | 90° | 0° | 90° | 0° & 90° |
| 7.5 | 3 | 300 000 | 17 000 | 47 000 | 24 000 | 3 400 |
| 9.5 | 3 | 570 000 | 33 000 | 47 000 | 30 000 | 4 300 |
| 12.5 | 4 | 1 300 000 | 190 000 | 59 000 | 57 000 | 5 700 |
| 12.5 | 5 | 1 200 000 | 350 000 | 71 000 | 47 000 | 5 700 |
| 15.5 | 4 | 2 600 000 | 430 000 | 76 000 | 75 000 | 7 100 |
| 15.5 | 5 | 2 000 000 | 630 000 | 71 000 | 47 000 | 7 100 |
| 18.5 | 5 | 4 100 000 | 1 300 000 | 110 000 | 73 000 | 8 600 |
| 18.5 | 6 | 3 600 000 | 1 300 000 | 110 000 | 47 000 | 8 600 |
| 18.5 | 7 | 3 400 000 | 1 400 000 | 95 000 | 71 000 | 8 600 |
| 20.5 | 5 | 4 300 000 | 2 600 000 | 100 000 | 89 000 | 9 500 |
| 20.5 | 6 | 4 000 000 | 1 900 000 | 100 000 | 47 000 | 9 500 |
| 20.5 | 7 | 4 300 000 | 2 000 000 | 95 000 | 71 000 | 9 500 |
| 22.5 | 7 | 6 100 000 | 2 500 000 | 110 000 | 75 000 | 10 000 |
| 22.5 | 8 | 6 400 000 | 2 500 000 | 110 000 | 95 000 | 10 000 |
| 25.5 | 7 | 8 600 000 | 4 800 000 | 130 000 | 110 000 | 12 000 |
| 25.5 | 8 | 8 700 000 | 4 100 000 | 110 000 | 110 000 | 12 000 |
| 25.5 | 9 | 9 000 000 | 4 100 000 | 130 000 | 95 000 | 12 000 |
| 25.5 | 10 | 9 400 000 | 4 400 000 | 150 000 | 95 000 | 12 000 |
| 28.5 | 8 | 12 000 000 | 7 000 000 | 120 000 | 140 000 | 13 000 |
| 28.5 | 9 | 12 000 000 | 5 700 000 | 130 000 | 95 000 | 13 000 |
| 28.5 | 10 | 12 000 000 | 6 100 000 | 150 000 | 95 000 | 13 000 |
| 28.5 | 11 | 13 000 000 | 6 400 000 | 150 000 | 120 000 | 13 000 |
| 31.5 | 8 | 16 000 000 | 11 000 000 | 150 000 | 170 000 | 15 000 |
| 31.5 | 9 | 15 000 000 | 9 400 000 | 150 000 | 120 000 | 15 000 |
| 31.5 | 10 | 15 000 000 | 8 200 000 | 150 000 | 95 000 | 15 000 |
| 31.5 | 11 | 16 000 000 | 8 500 000 | 150 000 | 120 000 | 15 000 |
| 31.5 | 12 | 17 000 000 | 9 000 000 | 150 000 | 140 000 | 15 000 |

**Notes:**
**(1)** *For specified stiffness in bending on edge, use axial stiffness values.*
**(2)** *Tabulated values are based on dry service conditions and standard-term duration of load.*
**(3)** *Specified strength in bearing (normal to plane of panel) $q_p$ = 4.5 MPa.*

## Table 7.3C
## Specified Strength, Stiffness, and Rigidity Capacities
## for Type 1 (Standard) Design-Rated OSB*

| Nominal thickness, mm | Rating grade | Bending, $m_p$, N•mm/mm | | Axial tension, $t_p$, N/mm | | Axial compression, $p_p$, N/mm | | Shear-through-thickness, $v_p$, N/mm | Planar shear Bending, $v_{pb}$, N/mm | Shear in-plane, $v_{pf}$, MPa |
|---|---|---|---|---|---|---|---|---|---|---|
| | | Capacities relative to major axis*† | | | | | | | | |
| | | 0° | 90° | 0° | 90° | 0° | 90° | 0°& 90° | 0°& 90° | 0°& 90° |
| 9.5 | A | 290 | 90 | 79 | 38 | 79 | 38 | 30 | 4.1 | 0.64 |
| 9.5 | B | 240 | 90 | 63 | 38 | 63 | 38 | 30 | 4.1 | 0.64 |
| 9.5 | C | 190 | 90 | 47 | 38 | 47 | 38 | 30 | 4.1 | 0.64 |
| 11.0 | A | 390 | 120 | 91 | 44 | 91 | 44 | 35 | 4.7 | 0.64 |
| 11.0 | B | 320 | 120 | 73 | 44 | 73 | 44 | 35 | 4.7 | 0.64 |
| 11.0 | C | 260 | 120 | 55 | 44 | 55 | 44 | 35 | 4.7 | 0.64 |
| 12.5 | A | 500 | 160 | 100 | 50 | 100 | 50 | 40 | 5.3 | 0.64 |
| 12.5 | B | 420 | 160 | 83 | 50 | 83 | 50 | 40 | 5.3 | 0.64 |
| 12.5 | C | 330 | 160 | 62 | 50 | 62 | 50 | 40 | 5.3 | 0.64 |
| 15.5 | A | 770 | 240 | 130 | 62 | 130 | 62 | 50 | 6.6 | 0.64 |
| 15.5 | B | 640 | 240 | 100 | 62 | 100 | 62 | 50 | 6.6 | 0.64 |
| 15.5 | C | 510 | 240 | 77 | 62 | 77 | 62 | 50 | 6.6 | 0.64 |
| 18.5 | A | 1100 | 340 | 150 | 74 | 150 | 74 | 59 | 7.9 | 0.64 |
| 18.5 | B | 910 | 340 | 120 | 74 | 120 | 74 | 59 | 7.9 | 0.64 |
| 18.5 | C | 720 | 340 | 92 | 74 | 92 | 74 | 59 | 7.9 | 0.64 |
| 22.0 | A | 1600 | 480 | 180 | 88 | 180 | 88 | 70 | 9.4 | 0.64 |
| 22.0 | B | 1300 | 480 | 150 | 88 | 150 | 88 | 70 | 9.4 | 0.64 |
| 22.0 | C | 1000 | 480 | 110 | 88 | 110 | 88 | 70 | 9.4 | 0.64 |
| 28.5 | A | 2600 | 810 | 240 | 110 | 240 | 110 | 91 | 12.0 | 0.64 |
| 28.5 | B | 2200 | 810 | 190 | 110 | 190 | 110 | 91 | 12.0 | 0.64 |
| 28.5 | C | 1700 | 810 | 140 | 110 | 140 | 110 | 91 | 12.0 | 0.64 |

(Continued)

## Table 7.3C (Concluded)

| Nominal thickness, mm | Rating grade | Bending stiffness, $B_b = EI$, $N \cdot mm^2/mm$ | | Axial stiffness (in tension or compression), $B_a = EA$, $N/mm$ | | Shear-through-thickness rigidity, $B_v$, $N/mm$ |
|---|---|---|---|---|---|---|
| | | Capacities relative to major axis*† | | | | |
| | | 0° | 90° | 0° | 90° | 0°& 90° |
| 9.5 | A | 590 000 | 170 000 | 46 000 | 19 000 | 9 500 |
| 9.5 | B | 490 000 | 170 000 | 39 000 | 19 000 | 9 500 |
| 9.5 | C | 390 000 | 170 000 | 33 000 | 19 000 | 9 500 |
| 11.0 | A | 920 000 | 270 000 | 53 000 | 22 000 | 11 000 |
| 11.0 | B | 760 000 | 270 000 | 46 000 | 22 000 | 11 000 |
| 11.0 | C | 610 000 | 270 000 | 38 000 | 22 000 | 11 000 |
| 12.5 | A | 1 300 000 | 390 000 | 60 000 | 25 000 | 12 000 |
| 12.5 | B | 1 100 000 | 390 000 | 52 000 | 25 000 | 12 000 |
| 12.5 | C | 900 000 | 390 000 | 43 000 | 25 000 | 12 000 |
| 15.5 | A | 2 600 000 | 740 000 | 75 000 | 31 000 | 15 000 |
| 15.5 | B | 2 100 000 | 740 000 | 64 000 | 31 000 | 15 000 |
| 15.5 | C | 1 700 000 | 740 000 | 53 000 | 31 000 | 15 000 |
| 18.5 | A | 4 400 000 | 1 300 000 | 89 000 | 37 000 | 18 000 |
| 18.5 | B | 3 600 000 | 1 300 000 | 77 000 | 37 000 | 18 000 |
| 18.5 | C | 2 900 000 | 1 300 000 | 64 000 | 37 000 | 18 000 |
| 22.0 | A | 7 300 000 | 2 100 000 | 110 000 | 44 000 | 22 000 |
| 22.0 | B | 6 100 000 | 2 100 000 | 91 000 | 44 000 | 22 000 |
| 22.0 | C | 4 900 000 | 2 100 000 | 76 000 | 44 000 | 22 000 |
| 28.5 | A | 16 000 000 | 4 600 000 | 140 000 | 57 000 | 28 000 |
| 28.5 | B | 13 000 000 | 4 600 000 | 120 000 | 57 000 | 28 000 |
| 28.5 | C | 11 000 000 | 4 600 000 | 98 000 | 57 000 | 28 000 |

*For Type 2 Design-Rated OSB panels, tabulated specified capacities are increased by a percentage (see CSA Standard O452.0). For Type 3 Design-Rated OSB panels, specified capacities are proprietary (see Clause 13.3).

†Orientation of applied force relative to panel's long direction.

**Notes:**
**(1)** For specified stiffness in bending on edge, use axial stiffness values.
**(2)** Tabulated values are based on dry service conditions and standard-term duration of load.
**(3)** Specified strength in bearing (normal to plane of panel) $q_p = 4.2$ MPa.

Δ

# Table 7.3D
## Specified Strength, Stiffness, and Rigidity Capacities for Construction Sheathing OSB

| Panel mark (CSA O325) | Minimum nominal thickness,* mm | Bending, $m_p$ N•mm/mm | | Axial tension, $t_p$ N/mm | | Axial compression, $p_p$ N/mm | | Shear-through-thickness, $v_p$ N/mm | Planar shear Bending, $v_{pb}$ N/mm | | Shear in-plane, $v_{pf}$ MPa | |
|---|---|---|---|---|---|---|---|---|---|---|---|---|
| | | Capacities relative to major axis† | | | | | | | | | | |
| | | 0° | 90° | 0° | 90° | 0° | 90° | 0°& 90° | 0° | 90° | 0° | 90° |
| 2R24 | 9.5 | 180 | 57 | 53 | 18 | 62 | 54 | 42 | 3.8 | 2.4 | 0.60 | 0.38 |
| 1R24/2F16 | 11.0 | 240 | 68 | 60 | 30 | 71 | 54 | 46 | 4.4 | 2.4 | 0.60 | 0.33 |
| 2R32/2F16 | 12.0 | 270 | 100 | 65 | 38 | 77 | 67 | 50 | 4.8 | 3.0 | 0.60 | 0.38 |
| 2R40/2F20 | 15.0 | 460 | 160 | 67 | 48 | 92 | 87 | 55 | 6.1 | 3.8 | 0.61 | 0.38 |
| 2R48/2F24 | 18.0 | 630 | 240 | 92 | 59 | 110 | 94 | 60 | 7.8 | 4.4 | 0.65 | 0.37 |
| 1F16 | 15.0 | 310 | 100 | 60 | 43 | 87 | 78 | 47 | 5.2 | 3.3 | 0.52 | 0.33 |
| 1F20 | 15.0 | 360 | 150 | 67 | 48 | 92 | 87 | 54 | 6.1 | 3.9 | 0.61 | 0.39 |
| 1F24 | 18.0 | 480 | 230 | 77 | 59 | 110 | 94 | 59 | 7.8 | 4.5 | 0.65 | 0.37 |
| 1F32 | 22.0 | 640 | 400 | 92 | 75 | 140 | 130 | 64 | 9.2 | 6.4 | 0.63 | 0.44 |
| 1F48 | 28.5 | 1 200 | 720 | 130 | 110 | 180 | 150 | 85 | 14.0 | 10.0 | 0.73 | 0.55 |

*(Continued)*

## Table 7.3D (Concluded)

| Panel mark (CSA O325) | Minimum nominal thickness,* mm | Bending stiffness, $B_b = EI$, N•mm²/mm | | Axial stiffness (in tension or compression), $B_a = EA$, N/mm | | Shear-through-thickness rigidity, $B_v$, N/mm |
|---|---|---|---|---|---|---|
| | | Capacities relative to major axis† | | | | |
| | | 0° | 90° | 0° | 90° | 0° & 90° |
| 2R24 | 9.5 | 560 000 | 100 000 | 33 000 | 19 000 | 10 000 |
| 1R24/2F16 | 11.0 | 730 000 | 140 000 | 38 000 | 22 000 | 11 000 |
| 2R32/2F16 | 12.0 | 1 100 000 | 220 000 | 43 000 | 25 000 | 11 000 |
| 2R40/2F20 | 15.0 | 2 100 000 | 500 000 | 53 000 | 31 000 | 12 000 |
| 2R48/2F24 | 18.0 | 3 800 000 | 820 000 | 64 000 | 37 000 | 13 000 |
| 1F16 | 15.0 | 1 400 000 | 300 000 | 53 000 | 31 000 | 11 000 |
| 1F20 | 15.0 | 2 000 000 | 360 000 | 53 000 | 31 000 | 11 000 |
| 1F24 | 18.0 | 2 800 000 | 720 000 | 64 000 | 37 000 | 12 000 |
| 1F32 | 22.0 | 6 100 000 | 2 100 000 | 76 000 | 44 000 | 15 000 |
| 1F48 | 28.5 | 11 000 000 | 4 400 000 | 98 000 | 51 000 | 20 000 |

*The minimum nominal thickness shown on the panel mark can be 0.5 mm less than the values shown here.
†Orientation of applied force relative to panel's long direction.

**Notes:**

**(1)** For specified stiffness in bending on edge, use axial stiffness values.

**(2)** Tabulated values are based on dry service conditions and standard-term duration of load.

**(3)** Specified strength in bearing (normal to plane of panel) $q_p = 4.2$ MPa.

**(4)** Design values do not apply to panels marked W only.

## 7.4 Modification Factors

### 7.4.1 Load Duration Factor, $K_D$

#### 7.4.1.1
Except as detailed in Clause 7.4.1.2, the specified strength capacity values for structural panels shall be multiplied by a load duration factor, $K_D$, as given in Table 4.3.2.2.

#### 7.4.1.2
For OSB used in structures subject to permanent loads in excess of 50% of design capacity, protected from direct exposure to moisture, but exposed to intermittent high temperature and/or humidity conditions, the load duration factor shall be 0.45.

### 7.4.2 Service Condition Factor, $K_S$
The specified strength capacity values for structural panels shall be multiplied by a service condition factor, $K_S$, as given in Table 7.4.2.
**Note:** *OSB is specified for use under dry service conditions only.*

### Table 7.4.2
### Service Condition Factor, $K_S$

| Property to be modified | Plywood | | OSB |
| --- | --- | --- | --- |
| | Service conditions | | |
| | Dry | Wet | Dry |
| Specified strength capacity | 1.0 | 0.80 | 1.0 |
| Specified stiffness and rigidity capacities | 1.0 | 0.85 | 1.0 |

### 7.4.3 Treatment Factor, $K_T$
For preservative-treated plywood, $K_T = 1.0$. For other preservative-treated structural panels and structural panels treated with fire-retardant or other potentially strength-reducing chemicals, strength and stiffness capacities shall be based on the documented results of tests that shall take into account the effects of time, temperature, and moisture content. Test procedures and data shall meet the requirements of Clause 3.3.2.
**Note:** *See the Canadian Wood Council's* Commentary *for additional explanation.*

### 7.4.4 Stress Joint Factor, $X_J$

#### 7.4.4.1 Scarf Joints
Where scarf joints transmit forces from one panel to another, the specified strength capacity shall be multiplied by a stress joint factor, $X_J$, as given in Table 7.4.4.1. Construction requirements for scarf joints are given in Clause 8.4.3.

## Table 7.4.4.1
## Stress Joint Factor, $X_J$, for Scarf Joints

| Panel type | Slope of scarf | Tension, bending | Compression | Shear |
|---|---|---|---|---|
| Plywood | 1 in 12 | 0.85 | 1.00 | 1.00 |
| | 1 in 10 | 0.80 | 1.00 | 1.00 |
| | 1 in 8 | 0.75 | 1.00 | 1.00 |
| | 1 in 5 | 0.60 | 1.00 | — |
| OSB | 1 in 6 | 0.80 | 0.80 | 0.80 |
| | 1 in 5 | 0.70 | 0.70 | 0.70 |
| | 1 in 4 | 0.60 | 0.60 | 0.60 |

### 7.4.4.2  Butt Joints

Where structural panels are used as glued splice plates in butt joints to transmit forces from one panel to another or from one lumber piece to another, the specified strength of splice plates shall be multiplied by a stress joint factor, $X_J$, as given in Table 7.4.4.2.  Construction requirements for butt joints are given in Clause 8.4.4.

## Table 7.4.4.2
## Stress Joint Factor, $X_J$, for Butt Joints

| Main/ side member | Nominal thickness of panel splice plate, mm | One side Min. length of splice plate, mm | Tension | Compression, shear | Both sides Min. length of splice plate, mm | Tension | Compression, shear |
|---|---|---|---|---|---|---|---|
| Plywood/ | 7.5 | 200 | 0.67 | 1.00 | 200 | 0.85 | 1.00 |
| Plywood | 9.5 | 300 | 0.67 | 1.00 | 300 | 0.85 | 1.00 |
| | 12.5 | 350 | 0.67 | 1.00 | 350 | 0.85 | 1.00 |
| | 15.5–20.5 | 400 | 0.50 | 1.00 | 400 | 0.85 | 1.00 |
| OSB/ | 9.5–11.0 | 200 | 0.40 | 0.40 | 200 | 0.90 | 0.90 |
| OSB | | 650* | 0.70 | 0.70 | | | |
| | 12.5–18.5 | 200 | 0.30 | 0.30 | 200 | 0.85 | 0.85 |
| | | 800* | 0.50 | 0.50 | | | |
| Lumber/ | 9.5–11.0 | 200 | 0.60 | 0.60 | 200 | 0.90 | 0.90 |
| OSB | | 250* | 0.75 | 0.75 | | | |
| | 12.5–18.5 | 200 | 0.40 | 0.40 | 200 | 0.85 | 0.85 |
| | | 300* | 0.55 | 0.55 | | | |

*For intermediate OSB splice plate lengths, the stress joint factor shall be obtained by linear interpolation.

### 7.4.5  Factor $K_F$ for Preserved Wood Foundations

For plywood in preserved wood foundations supported at intervals not exceeding 815 mm, the end use factor for panel bending and planar shear shall be $K_F = 1.15$.  For all other properties, $K_F = 1.0$.

### 7.5  Resistance of Structural Panels

### 7.5.1  Stress Orientation

Structural panels are orthotropic materials, and the specified strength capacities used in calculations shall be those for the orientation of the face grain (plywood) or the orientation of the major axis (OSB) intended in the design.

## 7.5.2 Bending as a Panel

The factored bending resistance of a structural panel in the plane perpendicular to the plane of the panel shall be taken as

$$M_r = \phi M_p b_p$$

where
$\phi$ = 0.95
$M_p$ = $m_p(K_D K_S K_T K_F)$ for plywood
= $m_p(K_D K_S K_T)$ for OSB
$m_p$ = specified strength capacity in bending (plywood — Tables 7.3A and 7.3B; OSB — Tables 7.3C and 7.3D), N•mm/mm
$b_p$ = width of panel, mm

## 7.5.3 Bending on Edge

The factored bending resistance of structural panels loaded on edge in the plane of a panel that is adequately braced to prevent lateral buckling shall be taken as

$$M_r = \phi T_p \frac{d_p^2}{6}$$

where
$\phi$ = 0.95
$T_p$ = $t_p(K_D K_S K_T)$
$t_p$ = specified strength capacity in tension (plywood — Tables 7.3A and 7.3B; OSB — Tables 7.3C and 7.3D), N/mm
$d_p$ = depth of panel in plane of bending, mm

## 7.5.4 Planar Shear

### 7.5.4.1 Planar Shear Due to Bending

The factored resistance in planar shear for structural panels subjected to bending shall be taken as

$$V_{rp} = \phi V_{pb} b_p$$

where
$\phi$ = 0.95
$V_{pb}$ = $v_{pb}(K_D K_S K_T K_F)$ for plywood
= $v_{pb}(K_D K_S K_T)$ for OSB
$v_{pb}$ = specified strength capacity in planar shear (due to bending) (plywood — Tables 7.3A and 7.3B; OSB — Tables 7.3C and 7.3D), N/mm

### 7.5.4.2 Planar Shear in Structural Panel Splice or Gusset Plate

The factored resistance in planar shear developed by a glued structural panel splice or gusset plate, or by the splice plates at a structural panel butt joint, shall be taken as

$$V_{rp} = \phi V_{pf} A_c$$

where
$\phi$ = 0.95
$V_{pf}$ = $v_{pf}(K_D K_S K_T)$
$v_{pf}$ = specified strength capacity in planar shear (due to in-plane forces) (plywood — Tables 7.3A and 7.3B; OSB — Tables 7.3C and 7.3D), MPa
$A_c$ = contact area of splice or gusset plate on one side of joint, mm$^2$

## 7.5.5 Shear-through-Thickness of Structural Panel

### 7.5.5.1 Shear Due to Bending of Structural Panel on Edge

The factored resistance in shear through the thickness of a structural panel due to bending in the plane of the panel shall be taken as

$$V_r = \phi V_p \frac{2d_p}{3}$$

where

$\phi$ = 0.95

$V_p$ = $v_p(K_D K_S K_T)$

$v_p$ = specified strength capacity in shear-through-thickness (plywood — Tables 7.3A and 7.3B; OSB — Tables 7.3C and 7.3D), N/mm

### 7.5.5.2 Shear-through-Thickness in Structural Panel Splice or Gusset Plate

The factored shear-through-thickness resistance developed by a structural panel splice or gusset plate shall be taken as

$$V_r = \phi V_p L_G$$

where

$\phi$ = 0.95

$V_p$ = $v_p(K_D K_S K_T)$

$v_p$ = specified strength capacity in shear-through-thickness (plywood — Tables 7.3A and 7.3B; OSB — Tables 7.3C and 7.3D), N/mm

$L_G$ = length of splice or gusset plate subjected to shear, mm

## 7.5.6 Compression Parallel to Panel Edge

The factored compressive resistance parallel to a laterally supported panel edge shall be taken as

$$P_r = \phi P_p b_p$$

where

$\phi$ = 0.95

$P_p$ = $p_p(K_D K_S K_T)$

$p_p$ = specified strength capacity in axial compression (plywood — Tables 7.3A and 7.3B; OSB — Tables 7.3C and 7.3D), N/mm

## 7.5.7 Tension Parallel to Panel Edge

The factored tensile resistance parallel to a panel edge shall be taken as

$$T_r = \phi T_p b_n$$

where

$\phi$ = 0.95 for all plywood thicknesses and number of plies except 3- and 4-ply layups stressed perpendicular to face grain

= 0.60 for 3- and 4-ply plywood layups stressed perpendicular to face grain

= 0.95 for OSB

$T_p$ = $t_p(K_D K_S K_T)$

$t_p$ = specified strength capacity in axial tension (plywood — Table 7.3A and 7.3B; OSB — Tables 7.3C and 7.3D), N/mm

$b_n$ = net width of panel after cutting of holes, etc, mm

## 7.5.8 Compressive Resistance Perpendicular to Face (Bearing)

The factored bearing resistance normal to plane of panel shall be taken as

$$Q_r = \phi Q_p A_b$$

where
$\phi$ = 0.95
$Q_p$ = $q_p(K_D K_S K_T)$
$q_p$ = specified strength capacity in bearing normal to plane of panel (plywood — Tables 7.3A and 7.3B; OSB — Tables 7.3C and 7.3D), MPa
$A_b$ = bearing area, mm$^2$

# 8. Composite Building Components

## 8.1 Scope

Clause 8 provides design equations and data for glued composite building components using plywood, OSB, and lumber or glued-laminated timber. The design provisions apply, provided that glue joints are made in strict conformance to the requirements of the manufacturer of the adhesive used in the fabrication of these composite building components.

**Note:** *Clause 8 does not apply to proprietary structural wood products covered by Clause 13.*

## 8.2 Materials

### 8.2.1 General

The provisions in Clauses 8.3 to 8.6 apply to material as specified in Clause 5 for lumber, Clause 6 for glued-laminated timber, Clause 7 for plywood and OSB, and Clause 8.2.2 for adhesives.

### 8.2.2 Adhesives for Structural Components

Adhesives for the assembly of structural components shall meet the requirements of CSA Standard O112.7.

### 8.2.3 Lumber

The provisions in Clauses 8.3 to 8.6 apply to lumber that is graded in accordance with NLGA *Standard Grading Rules for Canadian Lumber* and identified by the grade stamp of an association or independent grading agency in accordance with the provisions of CSA Standard CAN/CSA-O141.

### 8.2.4 Glulam

The provisions in Clauses 8.3 to 8.6 apply to glued-laminated timber that is manufactured in accordance with CSA Standard CAN/CSA-O122.

## 8.3 Stress Joint Factor, X_J

### 8.3.1 Joint Requirements

Stress joint factors, $X_J$, in Clauses 8.3.2 and 8.3.3 apply to glued plywood and OSB stress joints fabricated according to the requirements of Clause 8.4.

### 8.3.2 Scarf Joints

The stress joint factor for plywood scarf joints across the face grain or for OSB scarf joints across the major axis stressed in tension, compression, or shear-through-thickness shall be as given in Table 7.4.4.1.

### 8.3.3 Butt Joints

### 8.3.3.1 General
For the length of splice plates perpendicular to the joint, the stress joint factors for butt joints across the face grain of plywood or the major axis of OSB stressed in tension, compression, or shear-through-thickness shall be as given in Table 7.4.4.2.

### 8.3.3.2 Butt Joints with Short Plywood Plates in Compression
For plywood butt joints with splice plates shorter than the minimum length shown in Table 7.4.4.2, the stress joint factor for compression shall be reduced in direct proportion to such reduction in length.

## 8.4 Construction Requirements for Stress Joints

### 8.4.1 Types of Stress Joints
Joints transmitting forces from one panel to another may be either scarf joints or butt joints.

### 8.4.2 Adhesives for Stress Joints
Adhesives for the assembly of stress joints shall meet the requirements of Clause 8.2.2.

### 8.4.3 Scarf Joints

### 8.4.3.1 Scarf Joints in Shear
The slope of plywood scarf joints shall be not steeper than 1:8. The slope of OSB scarf joints shall not be steeper than 1:4.

### 8.4.3.2 Scarf Joints in Tension, Compression, or Bending
The slope of plywood scarf joints shall be not steeper than 1:5. The slope of OSB scarf joints shall not be steeper than 1:4.

### 8.4.4 Butt Joints

### 8.4.4.1 Splice Plates for Butt Joints
Butt joints shall be backed on one or both sides of the panel by a panel splice plate of a type and grade at least equal to the panel being spliced. The splice plate shall be centred on the joints and glued to both panels meeting at the joint. The splice plate shall be oriented with its major axis perpendicular to the joint.

### 8.4.4.2 Splice Plate Thickness
Splice plates shall have a minimum thickness equal to that of the panel being spliced.

### 8.4.4.3 Butt Joints in Shear
Splice plates stressed in shear shall have a length in the direction perpendicular to the joint equal to 12 times the thickness of the butt-jointed panel and shall have a width equal to the full depth or width of the panel between framing members.

### 8.4.4.4 Butt Joints in Tension
Splice plates stressed in tension shall have a minimum length as shown in Table 7.4.4.2.

### 8.4.4.5 Butt Joints in Compression
Splice plates stressed in compression may have a length as shown in Table 7.4.4.2. For plywood joints, if shorter lengths are used, the strength of the joint shall be reduced as indicated in Clause 8.3.3.2.

## 8.5 Plywood and OSB Web Beams

### 8.5.1 General

A panel web beam shall have one or more plywood or OSB webs glued or nailed/glued at upper and lower edges to sawn lumber or glued-laminated timber flanges, with lumber stiffeners at intervals along the web to prevent buckling. (See Figure 8.5.1.)

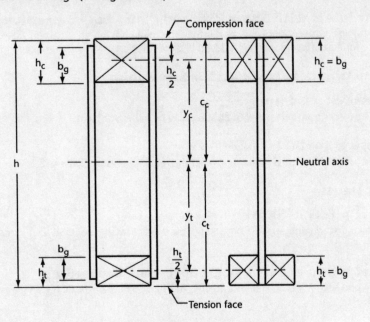

**Figure 8.5.1**
**Panel Web Beam Dimensions (mm)**

### 8.5.2 Effective Stiffness

The effective stiffness, $(EI)_e$, of a panel web beam shall be taken as

$$(EI)_e = (\Sigma B_a)K_S \frac{(c_t^3 + c_c^3)}{3} + (EI)_f K_{SE}$$

where
$(\Sigma B_a)$ = sum of axial stiffness of panel webs (Tables 7.3A, 7.3B, 7.3C, and 7.3D), N/mm
$K_S$    = service condition factor for web material (Table 7.4.2)
$(EI)_f$ = stiffness of flanges with respect to neutral axis of composite section, N/mm$^2$
$K_{SE}$  = service condition factor for modulus of elasticity of flange (Table 5.4.2 for sawn lumber and Table 6.4.2 for glulam)

### 8.5.3 Bending Resistance

The factored bending moment resistance of a panel web beam shall be the lesser of the factored resistance of the tension or compression flanges determined as follows:
(a) compression flange

$$M_r = \phi F_c K_{Zc} \frac{(EI)_e}{E K_{SE} c_c}$$

where
$\phi$ = 0.8 for sawn lumber
    = 0.9 for glulam
$F_c$ = $f_c(K_D K_{Sc} K_T K_H)$
$f_c$ = specified strength of flange in compression (Tables 5.3.1A to 5.3.1D, 5.3.2, and 5.3.3 for sawn lumber and Table 6.3 for glulam), MPa
$K_H$ = system factor (Clause 5.4.4 for sawn lumber and Clause 6.4.3 for glulam)
$K_{Zc}$ = size factor for compression for sawn lumber (Clause 5.4.5)
$E$ = modulus of elasticity of flange (Tables 5.3.1A to 5.3.1D, 5.3.2, and 5.3.3 for sawn lumber and Table 6.3 for glulam), MPa
$K_{SE}$ = service condition factor for modulus of elasticity of flange (Table 5.4.2 for sawn lumber and Table 6.4.2 for glulam)
$c_c$ = distance from neutral axis to compression face (Figure 8.5.1)

(b) tension flange

$$M_r = \phi F_t K_{Zt} \frac{(EI)_e}{E K_{SE} c_t}$$

where
$\phi$ = 0.9
$F_t$ = $f_t(K_D K_{St} K_T K_H)$
$f_t$ = specified strength of flange in tension (Tables 5.3.1A to 5.3.1D, 5.3.2, and 5.3.3 for sawn lumber and Table 6.3 for glulam), MPa
$K_{Zt}$ = size factor for tension for sawn lumber (Table 5.4.5)
$E$ = modulus of elasticity of flange (Tables 5.3.1A to 5.3.1D, 5.3.2, and 5.3.3 for sawn lumber and Table 6.3 for glulam), MPa
$c_t$ = distance from neutral axis to tension face (Figure 8.5.1)

## 8.5.4 Web Shear-through-Thickness
The factored shear resistance of the web of a panel web beam at its neutral axis shall be taken as

$$V_r = \phi V_p X_J \frac{(EI)_e}{E K_{SE} Q_f + 0.5(\Sigma B_a) K_S c_w^2}$$

where
$\phi$ = 0.95
$V_p$ = $(\Sigma v_p)(K_D K_S K_T)$
$\Sigma v_p$ = sum of specified strengths of all panel webs in shear-through-thickness (Tables 7.3A, 7.3B, 7.3C, and 7.3D), N/mm
$X_J$ = stress joint factor (Clause 8.3)
$E$ = modulus of elasticity of flange (Tables 5.3.1A to 5.3.1D, 5.3.2, and 5.3.3 for sawn lumber and Table 6.3 for glulam), MPa
$Q_f$ = moment of area of flange about neutral axis, mm³
$\Sigma B_a$ = sum of specified axial stiffness for all panel webs (Tables 7.3A, 7.3B, 7.3C, and 7.3D), N/mm
$c_w$ = greatest distance from neutral axis to outer edge of web, mm

## 8.5.5 Flange-Web Shear
The factored shear resistance of the glued area between the flange and web of a panel web beam shall be the lesser of the shear capacities of the web or flange components determined as follows:

$$V_{rp} = \phi V_g (\Sigma b_g X_v) \frac{(EI)_e}{E K_{SE} Q_f}$$

where
$\Sigma b_g$ = sum of contact widths between flange and web
$E$ = modulus of elasticity of flange (Tables 5.3.1A to 5.3.1D, 5.3.2, and 5.3.3 for sawn lumber and Table 6.3 for glulam), MPa

$Q_f$ = moment of area of flange about neutral axis, mm$^3$

(a) for web
$\phi$ = 0.95
$V_g$ = $v_{pf}(K_DK_SK_T)$
$v_{pf}$ = specified strength in planar shear (Tables 7.3A, 7.3B, 7.3C, and 7.3D), MPa
$X_v$ = shear modification factor (Figure 8.5.5)

(b) for flange
$\phi$ = 0.9
$V_g$ = $f_v(K_DK_{Sv}K_T)$
$f_v$ = specified strength in shear (Clauses 5.3.1 and 5.3.2 for sawn lumber and Table 6.3 for glulam), MPa
$X_v$ = 2.00

## 8.5.6 Deflection
Deflection shall be calculated as the sum of the deflections due to moment, using the effective stiffness, $(EI)_e$, determined in accordance with Clause 8.5.2, and due to shear as determined by the following formula:

$$\Delta_s = \frac{B_a M h^2 X_s}{B_v (EI)_e}$$

where
$B_a$ = specified axial stiffness (Tables 7.3A, 7.3B, 7.3C, and 7.3D), N/mm
$M$ = maximum bending moment due to specified loads, N/mm
$h$ = height of web beam (Figure 8.5.1), mm
$X_s$ = section shear coefficient (Figure 8.5.6)
$B_v$ = specified shear rigidity (Tables 7.3A , 7.3B, 7.3C, and 7.3D), N/mm

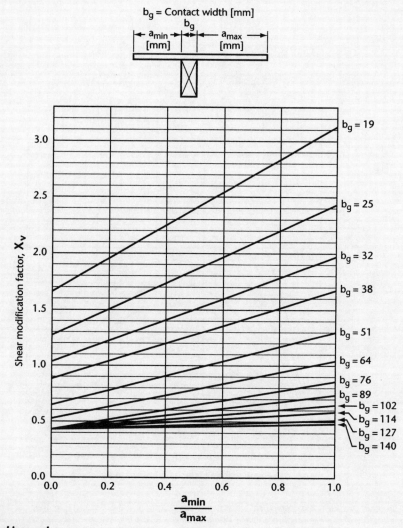

**Notes:**

**(1) Stressed skin panels**

At an inside web, $a_{min} = a_{max}$

At an outside web

$a_{min}$ = the overhang at the edge

$a_{max}$ = one-half the clear spacing between the outside web and the adjacent web

**(2) Panel web beams**

$a_{min} = 0$

**(3)** For all other cases (splice plates, etc), the unmodified specified strength capacity in planar shear shall be used.

**Figure 8.5.5**
**Shear Modification Factor, $X_v$**

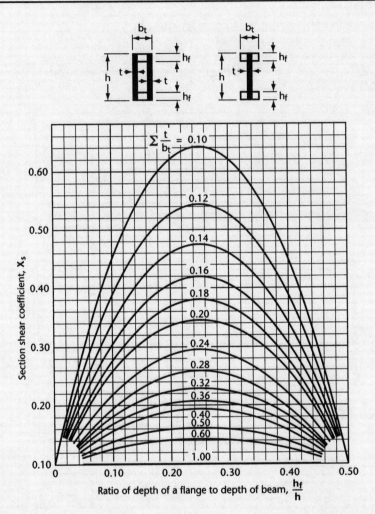

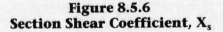

**Note:**

*The section shear coefficient is a geometrical property of a beam section that depends on the shape of the cross-section and arises because of nonuniform distribution of shearing stresses across the section. It can be derived using fundamental engineering theory and evaluated for any beam geometry from the formula.*

$$X_s = \frac{1}{I\,h^2} \int_{y=0}^{y=h} \frac{Q^2 dy}{b_x}$$

*where*
$X_s$ = *section shear coefficient*
$I$ = *moment of inertia (mm$^4$)*
$h$ = *overall beam depth (mm)*
$Q$ = *first moment of beam (mm$^3$)*
$b_x$ = *width of beam carrying the shear associated with Q (mm)*
*This figure is valid only for box and I-beams symmetrical about 2 axes.*

**Figure 8.5.6**
**Section Shear Coefficient, $X_s$**

## 8.5.7 Lateral Stability of Panel Web Beams

Lateral stability of a beam shall be determined by considering the flange as a column that tends to deflect sideways between points of support, or by application of one of the following rules:

(a) if the ratio of the moment of inertia of the cross-section about the neutral axis to the moment of inertia about the axis perpendicular to the neutral axis does not exceed 5:1, no lateral support is required;

(b) if the ratio of the moments of inertia is greater than 5:1 but does not exceed 10:1, the ends of the beam shall be held in position at the bottom flange at supports;

(c) if the ratio of the moments of inertia is greater than 10:1 but does not exceed 20:1, the beam shall be held in line at the ends;

(d) if the ratio of the moments of inertia is greater than 20:1 but does not exceed 30:1, one edge shall be held in line;

(e) if the ratio of the moments of inertia is greater than 30:1 but does not exceed 40:1, the beam shall be restrained by bridging or other bracing at intervals of not more than 2400 mm; or

(f) if the ratio of the moments of inertia is greater than 40:1, the compression flanges shall be fully restrained.

## 8.5.8 Stiffeners

Load distribution stiffeners shall be provided at reaction points and at the location of heavy concentrated loads. These stiffeners shall be adequately fastened to the webs and shall bear on the inner surfaces of the top and bottom flanges. The stiffeners shall be made as wide as the flanges, and their dimensions parallel to the span shall be adequate to support the applied concentrated loads or reactions. The cross-sectional area of a load-bearing stiffener shall be such that the factored resistance of the flange material perpendicular to grain is not less than the concentrated load or the reaction due to the factored loads.

## 8.5.9 Web Stabilizers

Web-stabilizing stiffeners shall be provided as necessary to prevent buckling of the webs.

## 8.6 Stressed Skin Panels

### 8.6.1 General

A stressed skin panel shall have continuous or spliced longitudinal web members and continuous or spliced panel flanges on one or both panel faces, with the flanges glued to the web members. (See Figure 8.6.1.)

### 8.6.2 Effective Stiffness

The effective stiffness, $(EI)_e$, of a stressed skin panel shall be taken as

$$(EI)_e = (EI)_w K_{SE} + b_f (B_{at} y_t^2 + B_{ac} y_c^2) K_S$$

where

$(EI)_w$ = stiffness of lumber webs, N•mm$^2$

$B_{at}$ = specified axial stiffness of tension flange ($B_a$ for appropriate panel thickness in Tables 7.3A, 7.3B, 7.3C, and 7.3D), N/mm

$B_{ac}$ = specified axial stiffness of compression flange (Tables 7.3A, 7.3B, 7.3C, and 7.3D), N/mm

$b_f, y_t, y_c$ = panel dimensions as per Figure 8.6.1, mm

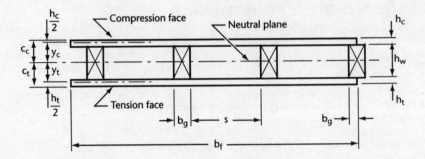

**Figure 8.6.1**
**Stressed Skin Panel Dimensions, mm**

## 8.6.3 Bending Resistance

### 8.6.3.1 Bending along Stressed Skin Panel Span

The factored bending moment resistance along the direction of the webs of a stressed skin panel shall be the least of the factored resistances of the tension or compression flanges or the web determined as follows:

(a) tension flange

$$M_r = \phi T_p X_J X_G \frac{(EI)_e}{B_a K_S c_t}$$

where
$\phi$ = 0.95
$T_p = t_p(K_D K_S K_T)$
$t_p$ = specified strength capacity of flange in axial tension (Tables 7.3A, 7.3B, 7.3C, and 7.3D), N/mm
$X_J$ = stress joint factor (Clause 8.3)
$B_a$ = specified axial stiffness (Tables 7.3A, 7.3B, 7.3C, and 7.3D), N/mm

(b) compression flange

$$M_r = \phi P_p X_J X_G \frac{(EI)_e}{B_a K_S c_c}$$

where
$\phi$ = 0.95
$P_p = p_p(K_D K_S K_T)$
$p_p$ = specified strength capacity of flange in axial compression (Tables 7.3A, 7.3B, 7.3C, and 7.3D), N/mm
$X_G$ = panel geometry reduction factor (Clause 8.6.3.2)

(c) web

$$M_r = \phi F_b K_{Zb} K_L X_G \frac{(EI)_e}{E K_{SE} c_w}$$

where
$\phi$ = 0.9
$F_b = f_b(K_D K_{Sb} K_T K_H)$
$f_b$ = specified strength in bending of webs (Tables 5.3.1A to 5.3.1D, 5.3.2, and 5.3.3 for sawn lumber and Table 6.3 for glulam), MPa

E = modulus of elasticity of web (Tables 5.3.1A to 5.3.1D, 5.3.2, and 5.3.3 for sawn lumber and Table 6.3 for glulam), MPa

$c_w$ = greatest distance from neutral axis to outer edge of web, mm

## 8.6.3.2 Panel Geometry Reduction Factor

The panel geometry reduction factor, $X_G$, shall be taken as

$$X_G = 1 - 4.8(s/\ell_p)^2$$

where

s = clear spacing between longitudinals, mm

$\ell_p$ = span of stressed skin panel, mm

**Note:** *This formula accounts for shear lag and is valid for values of $s/\ell_p$ ranging from 0.05 to 0.25.*

## 8.6.3.3 Bending Perpendicular to Panel Span

The factored bending resistance of the compression flange between web members shall be calculated using Clause 7.5.2.

## 8.6.3.4 Buckling of Compression Flange

The compression flange of a stressed skin panel shall be designed according to principles of engineering mechanics to prevent elastic buckling failure. If a detailed analysis is not made, such a condition is assumed to be met if

(a) s ≤50 $h_c$, for panels with their major axis parallel to the span ($\ell_p$); or

(b) s ≤40 $h_c$, for panels with their major axis perpendicular to the span ($\ell_p$)

where s and $h_c$ are as per Figure 8.6.1.

Clause A8.6.3.4 provides a detailed analysis for stressed skin panels with a plywood compression flange.

**Note:** *See Clause A8.6.3.4 for additional information on buckling of compression flanges.*

## 8.6.3.5 Shear in Plane of Plies

The factored planar shear resistance of the compression flange in a stressed skin panel shall be calculated using Clause 8.6.3.6.

## 8.6.3.6 Shear Resistance

The factored shear resistance at the neutral plane of a stressed skin panel shall be taken as

$$V_r = \phi F_v K_N K_{Zv} \frac{(EI)_e \Sigma b_g}{E K_{SE} \Sigma Q_w + B_a K_S b_f y}$$

where

$\phi$ = 0.9

$F_v$ = $f_v(K_D K_{Sv} K_T K_H)$

$f_v$ = specified strength in shear of webs (Clauses 5.3.1 and 5.3.2 for sawn lumber and Table 6.3 for glulam), MPa

$K_N$ = notch factor (Clauses 5.5.5.4 and 6.5.7.2.2)

$K_{Zv}$ = size factor in shear (Clause 5.4.5)

$b_g$ = contact width between flange and web (Figure 8.6.1)

E = modulus of elasticity of web (Tables 5.3.1A to 5.3.1D, 5.3.2, and 5.3.3 for sawn lumber and Table 6.3 for glulam), MPa

$\Sigma Q_w$ = sum of moments of area of all webs about neutral plane, $mm^3$

$B_a$ = specified axial stiffness (Tables 7.3A, 7.3B, 7.3C, and 7.3D), N/mm

$b_f$ = width of flange, mm

y = the greater value of $y_t$ or $y_c$, mm

## 8.6.3.7 Flange-Web Shear
The factored shear resistance of the glued area between the flange and the web of a stressed skin panel shall be taken as the lesser of the shear capacities based on flange or web components determined as follows:

$$V_{rp} = \phi V_g \frac{(EI)_e \Sigma (b_g X_v)}{B_a K_S b_p y}$$

where
$B_a$ = specified axial stiffness (Tables 7.3A, 7.3B, 7.3C, and 7.3D), N/mm
$y$ = the greater value of $y_t$ or $y_c$, mm,

and

(a) for flange
$\phi$ = 0.95
$V_g$ = $v_{pf}(K_D K_S K_T)$
$v_{pf}$ = specified strength capacity in planar shear (Tables 7.3A, 7.3B, 7.3C, and 7.3D), MPa
$X_v$ = shear modification factor (Figure 8.5.5)

(b) for web
$\phi$ = 0.9
$V_g$ = $f_v(K_D K_S K_T)$
$f_v$ = specified strength in shear (Clauses 5.3.1 and 5.3.2 for sawn lumber and Table 6.3 for glulam), MPa
$X_v$ = 2.00

## 8.6.3.8 Deflection
The deflection of stressed skin panels shall be calculated using the effective stiffness, $(EI)_e$, determined in accordance with Clause 8.6.2, multiplied by the panel geometry reduction factor, $X_G$, determined in accordance with Clause 8.6.3.2.

# 9. Shearwalls and Diaphragms

## 9.1 Scope
Clause 9 provides requirements and data for the design of wood structures subject to lateral forces.
**Note:** *Wind and earthquake loads are examples of lateral forces.*

## 9.2 Materials

### 9.2.1 General
The provisions in Clauses 9.3 to 9.5 apply to materials as specified in Clause 5 for lumber, Clause 6 for glued-laminated timber, Clause 7 for structural panels, and Clause 10 for fastenings, and to additional materials specified in Clause 9.2.2.

### 9.2.2 Additional Materials
The provisions in Clauses 9.3 to 9.5 are also applicable to OSB and waferboard manufactured to meet the requirements of CSA Standard O437.0, gypsum wallboard conforming to Type X (fire-rated) in ASTM Standard C 36, and Type 3 (proprietary) design-rated OSB as specified in Clause 13.3 of this Standard.

## 9.3 Design of Shearwalls and Diaphragms

### 9.3.1 General

#### 9.3.1.1 Standard Methods

Shearwalls and diaphragms may be designed using the provisions for nailed shear panels using structural wood panels, gypsum wallboard, and diagonally sheathed shear panels (Clauses 9.5.1 and 9.5.2).

#### 9.3.1.2 Alternative Methods

Alternative methods of analysis utilizing the factored lateral strength resistance of nails, spikes, or bolts to achieve ductility and the factored resistance of materials specified elsewhere in this Standard may be used, provided it can be demonstrated that such alternative methods of analysis are based on recognized principles of mechanics.

### 9.3.2 Resistance to Overturning

#### 9.3.2.1 Shearwall Segments with Hold-downs

Where the factored dead loads are not sufficient to prevent overturning, hold-down connections (see Figure 9.3.2(a)) shall be designed to resist the factored uplift forces and transfer the forces through a continuous load path to the foundation.

#### 9.3.2.2 Shearwall Segments without Hold-downs

Where the factored dead loads are not sufficient to prevent overturning, and hold-down connections are not used, anchorage (see Figure 9.3.2(b)) on the bottom plate within 300 mm from both ends of the shearwall segment shall transfer the uplift force "$R_{ij}$" (Clause 9.4.5.2) to the supporting structure (i.e., to the top plate of the shearwall below, or the foundation).

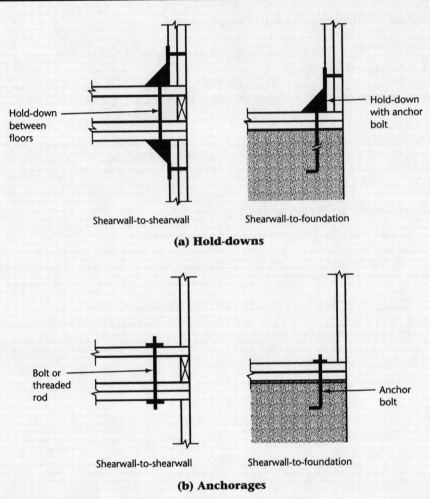

**(a) Hold-downs**

Hold-down between floors

Hold-down with anchor bolt

Shearwall-to-shearwall  Shearwall-to-foundation

Bolt or threaded rod

Anchor bolt

Shearwall-to-shearwall  Shearwall-to-foundation

**(b) Anchorages**

**Notes:**
**(1)** *These are examples only. Other types of hold-downs and anchorages may be used.*
**(2)** *Hold-downs as per Clause 9.3.2.1 provide a continuous direct load path, typically between upper storey shearwall chords and lower storey chords, beams, or foundations.*
**(3)** *Anchorages as per Clause 9.3.2.2 typically transfer loads from the sill plate of the upper storey shearwall segment to the lower storey top plates, beams, or foundations.*

**Figure 9.3.2
Examples of Hold-downs and Anchorages**

### 9.3.3 Shearwalls with Segments

### 9.3.3.1 General
The factored shear resistance of a shearwall shall equal the sum of the factored shear resistance of the wall segments determined according to Clause 9.5.1. The factored shear resistance of the shearwall shall be determined for lateral loads acting in opposite directions.

## 9.3.3.2 Shearwall Segment Aspect Ratio

The maximum aspect ratio (height-to-length ratio) of a shearwall segment shall be 3.5:1. The height is defined as the height from the underside of the bottom shearwall plate to the topside of the top shearwall plate within a storey.

## 9.3.3.3 Shearwalls with Openings

Shearwalls with openings shall be analyzed as the sum of the separate shearwall segments. The contribution of sheathing above and below openings shall not be included in the calculation of shearwall resistance.

## 9.3.3.4 Shearwalls with Dissimilar Materials

Except as allowed in Clause 9.3.3.5, shearwalls constructed with dissimilar materials, thicknesses, or nail spacings along the length of the shearwall shall be analyzed as the sum of the separate shearwall segments.

## 9.3.3.5 Alternative Method for Shearwalls with Dissimilar Materials

Shearwalls constructed with dissimilar materials, thicknesses, or nail spacings along the length of the shearwall may be analyzed, in accordance with Clause 9.5.1, as a shearwall of uniform construction, provided that the least value of $v_d K_D K_{SF} J_{ub} J_{sp}$ is assumed to apply over the entire shearwall.

## 9.3.4 Shearwalls with Multiple Layers

### 9.3.4.1 A Shearwall with Two Layers of Panels on One Side

The factored shear resistance for a shearwall with two layers of the same or different panels applied to one side is determined by the first (inside) layer of panels, except as allowed in Note 5 to Table 9.5.1A.

Δ    ### 9.3.4.2 Two-Sided Shearwall

The factored shear resistance from each side of the same shearwall is cumulative when panels of the same or different materials are applied on both sides.
**Note:** *See appropriate seismic force modification factor, $R_d$, in Clauses 9.5.3 and 9.5.4.*

## 9.3.5 Concrete or Masonry Wall Anchorage

### 9.3.5.1 Anchorage Design

Where wood roofs and floors are used to provide lateral support to concrete and masonry walls, they shall be anchored to these walls. The anchorage shall provide a direct connection between the walls and the roof or floor construction. The connections shall be capable of resisting the lateral force induced by the wall, but not less than 3 kN per lineal metre of the wall.

### 9.3.5.2 Anchorage Details

Anchorage of concrete or masonry walls shall not be accomplished by use of toe-nails or nails subject to withdrawal, nor shall wood ledgers be designed to resist tensile stresses perpendicular to grain.

## 9.3.6 Shearwall Anchorage

The anchor bolts to resist lateral forces shall be designed in accordance with Clause 10.

## 9.4 Modification Factors

### 9.4.1 Load Duration Factor, $K_D$

The specified shear strengths for wood-based shearwalls and diaphragms shall be multiplied by the load duration factor, $K_D$, given in Clause 4.3.2.
**Note:** *Specified shear strengths for gypsum wallboard shearwalls apply only to short-term load duration, and $K_D$ is not applicable.*

## 9.4.2 Service Condition Factor, $K_{SF}$

The specified shear strengths for wood-based shearwalls and diaphragms shall be multiplied by the service condition factor, $K_{SF}$, given in Table 10.2.1.5 for lateral loads on nails.

## 9.4.3 Species Factor for Framing Material, $J_{sp}$

The specified shear strengths for wood-based shearwalls and diaphragms shall be multiplied by the species factor for framing material, $J_{sp}$, as given in Table 9.4.3.

### Table 9.4.3
### Species Factor for Framing Material, $J_{sp}$

| $J_{sp}$ | Visually graded lumber | Glued-laminated timber | MSR (or MEL) E-Grade of S-P-F,* MPa |
|---|---|---|---|
| 1.0 | Douglas Fir-Larch | Douglas Fir-Larch | 13 800 to 16 500 |
| 0.9 | Hem-Fir | N/A | 12 400 to 13 100 |
| 0.8 | S-P-F | Spruce-Pine | 8300 to 11 700 |
| 0.7 | Northern Species | N/A | N/A |

*For other species of MSR or MEL lumber, use visually graded lumber values.*

## 9.4.4 Strength Adjustment Factor for Unblocked Shearwalls, $J_{ub}$

The specified shear strengths for horizontally sheathed unblocked shearwalls sheathed with wood-based panels shall be multiplied by the strength adjustment factor $J_{ub}$, as given in Table 9.4.4.

### Table 9.4.4
### Strength Adjustment Factor, $J_{ub}$,
### for Horizontally Sheathed Unblocked Shearwalls*

| Nail spacing at supported edges, mm | Nail spacing at intermediate studs, mm | Stud spacing, mm | | | |
|---|---|---|---|---|---|
| | | 300 | 400 | 500 | 600 |
| 150 | 150 | 1.0 | 0.8 | 0.6 | 0.5 |
| 150 | 300 | 0.8 | 0.6 | 0.5 | 0.4 |

*Specified shear strength of an unblocked shearwall shall be calculated by multiplying the strength adjustment factor by the specified shear strength of a blocked shearwall with 600 mm stud spacing, and with nails spaced at 150 mm on centre around panel edges and 300 mm on centre along intermediate framing members.*
**Note:** *Strength adjustment factor shall only be applicable to structural wood-based panels.*

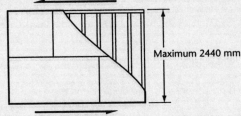

Maximum 2440 mm

Horizontal panels,
no blocking

## 9.4.5 Hold-down Effect Factor for Shearwall Segments, $J_{hd}$

### 9.4.5.1 Shearwall Segments with Hold-downs to Resist All Overturning Tension Forces

For shearwall segments with hold-down connections that are designed to resist all of the factored tension forces due to overturning

$J_{hd} = 1.0$

### 9.4.5.2 Shearwall Segments without Hold-downs

For shearwall segments without hold-down connections at either end, and that meet the requirements of Clauses 9.3.2.2 and 9.4.5.5 and the additional requirement that $P_{ij}$ is equal to or greater than zero

$$J_{nd} = \sqrt{1 + 2\frac{P_{ij}}{V_{hd}} + \left(\frac{H_s}{L_s}\right)^2} - \frac{H_s}{L_s} \leq 1.0$$

where
$P_{ij}$ = factored uplift restraint force for storey "i" at the bottom of the end stud of a shearwall segment "j", kN (see Figure 9.4.5.2)
$V_{hd}$ = factored basic shear resistance, kN
    = factored shear resistance of the shearwall segment calculated with $J_{hd} = 1.0$
$H_s$ = height of shearwall segment, m
$L_s$ = length of shearwall segment, m
**Note:** *The following terms, required to determine the value of the variables used in calculating $J_{hd}$, are illustrated in Figure 9.4.5.2:*
$q_i$ = *factored storey "i" dead load to resist overturning (includes only dead weight from current storey sill plate to next storey floor or roof), kN/m*
$R_{ij}$ = *resultant overturning force at storey "i", segment "j", kN*
$F_{ij}$ = *factored shear load at storey "i" on the shearwall segment "j", kN*

$$= F_i \frac{V_{rs}}{\Sigma V_{rs}}$$

$F_i$ = *total applied factored shear load on the shearwall at storey "i", kN*
$V_{rs}$ = *factored shear resistance of the shearwall segment calculated in accordance with Clause 9.5.1, kN*
$\Sigma V_{rs}$ = *sum of factored shear resistances, kN, for each segment in a shearwall*

### 9.4.5.3 Shearwall Segments with Hold-downs Only at the Bottom of the Segment

For a lower-storey shearwall segment with hold-down connections at the bottom of the shearwall segment and without hold-down connections at the top of the shearwall segment, where P is less than zero

$$J_{hd} = \frac{V_{hd} + P}{V_{hd}} \leq 1.0$$

where
$V_{hd}$ = factored basic shear resistance, kN
    = factored shear resistance of the shearwall segment calculated with $J_{hd} = 1.0$
P    = uplift restraint force at the top of the end stud of a shearwall segment, kN

## 9.4.5.4 Shearwall Segments with Hold-downs Only on One Side

For a shearwall segment with hold-down connections only on one side of the segment

(a) $J_{hd}$ shall be determined according to Clause 9.4.5.1 if designed to resist all tension forces due to overturning.

(b) $J_{hd}$ shall be determined according to Clause 9.4.5.2 if there is no hold-down on the tension side of the segment.

(c) $J_{hd}$ shall be determined according to Clause 9.4.5.3 if there is a hold-down only at the bottom of the tension side of a lower-storey segment.

## 9.4.5.5 Conditions for Shearwall Segments with $J_{hd}<1.0$

The conditions for calculating $J_{hd}$ in Clauses 9.4.5.2 to 9.4.5.4 are as follows:

(a) The maximum nail diameter shall be 3.25 mm, and the minimum nail spacing shall be 100 mm.

(b) The maximum specified shear strength, including both sides of a shearwall where applicable, shall be 10.3 kN/m.

(c) The height of the shearwall segment shall be less than 3.6 m.

## 9.5 Strength and Resistance

### 9.5.1 Shear Resistance of Nailed Shearwalls

The factored shear resistance of nailed shearwalls of structural wood-based panels, gypsum wallboard, or diagonal lumber sheathing, constructed in accordance with Clauses 9.5.3, 9.5.4, and 9.5.5, respectively, shall be determined as follows:

$$V_r = \Sigma V_{rs}$$

where

$V_{rs}$ = factored shear resistance for each shearwall segment along the length of the shearwall, kN

The factored shear resistance for a shearwall segment of structural wood-based panels or diagonal lumber sheathing shall be taken as

$$V_{rs} = \phi \, v_d K_D K_{SF} \, J_{ub} J_{sp} J_{hd} L_w$$

where

$\phi$ = 0.7

$v_d$ = specified shear strength for shearwall segment with plywood, OSB, or waferboard (Table 9.5.1A) or diagonal lumber sheathing (Clause 9.5.5), kN/m

$J_{ub}$ = strength adjustment factor for unblocked shearwalls (Clause 9.4.4)

$J_{sp}$ = species factor for framing material (Clause 9.4.3)

$J_{hd}$ = hold-down effect factor for shearwall segment (Clause 9.4.5)

$L_w$ = length of shearwall segment parallel to direction of factored load, m

The factored shear resistance for a shearwall segment of gypsum wallboard shall be taken as

$$V_{rs} = \phi \, v_d J_{hd} L_w$$

where

$\phi$ = 0.7

$v_d$ = specified shear strength for shearwall segment sheathed with gypsum wallboard (Table 9.5.1B), kN/m

$J_{hd}$ = hold-down effect factor for shearwall segment (Clause 9.4.5)

$L_w$ = length of shearwall segment parallel to direction of factored load, m

**Note:** See Clause A9.5.1 for additional information on shear resistance of nailed shearwalls.

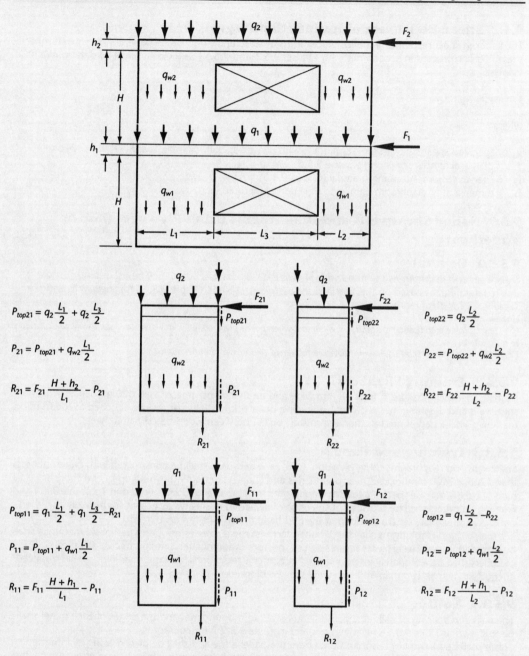

$$P_{top21} = q_2 \frac{L_1}{2} + q_2 \frac{L_3}{2}$$

$$P_{21} = P_{top21} + q_{w2} \frac{L_1}{2}$$

$$R_{21} = F_{21} \frac{H + h_2}{L_1} - P_{21}$$

$$P_{top22} = q_2 \frac{L_2}{2}$$

$$P_{22} = P_{top22} + q_{w2} \frac{L_2}{2}$$

$$R_{22} = F_{22} \frac{H + h_2}{L_2} - P_{22}$$

$$P_{top11} = q_1 \frac{L_1}{2} + q_1 \frac{L_3}{2} - R_{21}$$

$$P_{11} = P_{top11} + q_{w1} \frac{L_1}{2}$$

$$R_{11} = F_{11} \frac{H + h_1}{L_1} - P_{11}$$

$$P_{top12} = q_1 \frac{L_2}{2} - R_{22}$$

$$P_{12} = P_{top12} + q_{w1} \frac{L_2}{2}$$

$$R_{12} = F_{12} \frac{H + h_1}{L_2} - P_{12}$$

**Figure 9.4.5.2**
**Multi-Storey Shearwall Force Diagrams**

## 9.5.2 Shear Resistance of Nailed Diaphragms

The factored shear resistance of nailed diaphragms of structural wood-based panels or diagonal lumber sheathing constructed in accordance with Clauses 9.5.3 and 9.5.5, respectively, shall be determined as follows:

$$V_r = \phi\, v_d K_D K_{SF}\, J_{sp} L_D$$

where
$\phi$ = 0.7
$v_d$ = specified shear strength for diaphragms with plywood, OSB, or waferboard (Table 9.5.2) or diagonal lumber sheathing (Clause 9.5.5), kN/m
$J_{sp}$ = species factor for framing material (Clause 9.4.3)
$L_D$ = dimension of diaphragm parallel to direction of factored load, m

## 9.5.3 Nailed Shearwalls and Diaphragms Using Plywood, OSB, or Waferboard

### Δ 9.5.3.1 General

Shearwalls and diaphragms sheathed with plywood, OSB, or waferboard may be used to resist shear due to lateral forces based on the specified shear strength given in Table 9.5.1A for shearwalls and Table 9.5.2 for diaphragms.

**Notes:**
**(1)** Seismic force modification factor, $R_d$, is equal to 3 when nailed plywood, OSB, or waferboard shearwalls are considered to resist lateral loads.
**(2)** Table 9.5.3 provides an equivalence between tabulated thickness and panel marks.

### 9.5.3.2 Framing Members

Framing members shall be at least 38 mm wide and be spaced no greater than 600 mm apart in shearwalls and diaphragms. In general, adjoining panel edges shall bear and be attached to the framing members, and a gap of not less than 2 mm shall be left between wood-based panel sheets.

### 9.5.3.3 Framing and Panels

Shearwalls and diaphragms using plywood, OSB, or waferboard shall be constructed with panels not less than 1200 × 2400 mm, except near boundaries and changes in framing, where up to two short or narrow panels may be used. Panels for diaphragms shall be arranged as indicated in Table 9.5.2. Framing members shall be provided at the edge of all panels in shearwalls except horizontally sheathed unblocked shearwalls where blocking at the middle of the wall height is omitted.

Shearwalls and diaphragms shall be designed to resist shear stresses only, and perimeter members shall be provided to resist axial forces resulting from the application of lateral design forces. Perimeter members shall be adequately interconnected at corner intersections, and member joints shall be spliced adequately. Panels less than 300 mm wide shall be blocked.

### 9.5.3.4 Nailing

The nails and spacing of nails at shearwall and diaphragm boundaries and the edges of each panel shall be as shown in Table 9.5.1A for shearwalls and in Table 9.5.2 for diaphragms.

Nails shall be placed not less than 9 mm from the panel edge and shall be placed along all intermediate framing members at 300 mm on centre for floors, roofs, and shearwalls. Nails shall be firmly driven into framing members but shall not be over-driven into sheathing. For structural wood-based sheathing, nails shall not be over-driven more than 15% of the panel thickness.

### Δ 9.5.4 Nailed Shearwalls Using Gypsum Wallboard

Shearwalls using gypsum wallboard shall be constructed with panels not less than 1200 × 2400 mm, except near boundaries and changes in framing, where up to two short or narrow panels may be used.

Shearwalls sheathed with gypsum wallboard may be used to resist shear due to lateral forces based on the specified shear strength given in Table 9.5.1B for shearwalls.

Gypsum wallboard application nails or screws shall be placed not less than 9 mm from the panel edge.

Gypsum wallboard shall be used in combination with structural wood-based panels. The factored shear resistance of gypsum wallboard shall be equal to or less than the percentage of storey shear forces in Table 9.5.4. The application of gypsum wallboard shall be restricted to platform frame construction where the height of a storey does not exceed 3.6 m.

**Notes:**

**(1)** *Seismic force modification factor, $R_d$, is equal to 2 and system overstrength factor, $R_o$, is equal to 1.7 when gypsum wallboard is considered to resist lateral loads.*

**(2)** *There should exist a balanced spatial distribution of the gypsum wallboard and wood-based panels resisting shear in a given direction in a particular storey.*

## 9.5.5 Nailed Shearwalls and Diaphragms Using Diagonal Lumber Sheathing

### 9.5.5.1 General

Nailed shearwalls and diaphragms as described in Clauses 9.5.5.2 to 9.5.5.4 may be used to resist lateral forces. The specified shear strength, $v_d$, with a single layer of diagonally sheathed lumber (Clause 9.5.5.2) shall be taken as 8 kN/m; that for a double layer of diagonally sheathed lumber (Clause 9.5.5.3) as 24 kN/m.

### 9.5.5.2 Single-Layer Diagonal Sheathing

Single-layer diagonal sheathing shall be made up of 19 mm boards laid at an angle of approximately 45° to supports. Boards shall be nailed to each intermediate member with not less than two common nails (d = 3.25 mm) for 19 × 140 mm boards and three common nails (d = 3.25 mm) for 19 × 184 mm or wider boards. One additional nail shall be used in each board at shear panel boundaries.

End joints in adjacent rows of boards shall be staggered by at least one stud or joist space, and joints on the same support shall be separated by at least two rows of boards.

Shearwalls and diaphragms made up of 38 mm thick diagonal sheathing using common nails (d = 4.06 mm) may be used at the same shear values and in the same locations as for 19 mm boards, provided that there are no splices in adjacent boards on the same support and the supports are not less than 89 mm in depth or 64 mm in thickness.

### 9.5.5.3 Double-Layer Diagonal Sheathing

Double-layer diagonal sheathing shall conform to Clause 9.5.5.2 and shall consist of two layers of diagonal boards at 90° to each other on the same face of the supporting members.

### 9.5.5.4 Boundary Members

Diagonal sheathing produces a load component acting normal to the boundary members in the plane of the shear panel. Boundary members in diagonally sheathed shearwalls and diaphragms shall be designed to resist the bending stresses caused by the normal load component.

## 9.5.6 Moment Resistance of Nailed Shearwalls and Diaphragms

### 9.5.6.1 General

Except as provided in Clause 9.5.6.2, the factored moment resistance of nailed shearwalls and diaphragms shall be determined as

$$M_r = P_r h$$

where

$P_r$ = factored axial tension and compression resistance of the elements resisting chord forces with due allowance being made for joints, N

h = centre-to-centre distance between moment resisting elements, mm
 = centre-to-centre distance between diaphragm chords in the design of diaphragms, mm
 = centre-to-centre distance between stud chords in shearwall segments designed with hold-down connections at both ends of the shearwall segment, mm
 = length of shearwall segment minus 300 mm for shearwall segments designed without hold-down connections at both ends of the segment, mm

## 9.5.6.2 Moment Resistance for Shearwall Segments without Hold-downs

For shearwall segments without hold-downs, moment resistance calculation specifically for design of the tension chords shall not be required.

## 9.6 Detailing Requirements

### 9.6.1 General

All boundary members, chords, and struts of nailed shearwalls and diaphragms shall be designed and detailed to transmit the induced axial forces. The boundary members shall be fastened together at all corners.

### 9.6.2 Fastenings to Shearwalls and Diaphragms

Fastenings and anchorages capable of resisting the prescribed forces shall be provided between the shearwall or diaphragm and the attached components.

## Table 9.5.1A
## Specified Shear Strength, $v_d$, for Shearwalls with Framing of Douglas Fir-Larch (kN/m)

| Minimum nominal panel thickness, mm | Minimum nail penetration in framing, mm | Common nail diameter, mm | Panel applied directly to framing | | | |
|---|---|---|---|---|---|---|
| | | | Nail spacing at panel edges, mm | | | |
| | | | 150 | 100 | 75 | 50† |
| 7.5§ | 31 | 2.84 | 4.9 | 7.3 | 9.5 | 12.2 |
| 9.5 | 31 | 2.84 | 5.4 | 8.2 | 10.6 | 13.9 |
| 9.5 | 38 | 3.25 | 6.0* | 8.7* | 11.1* | 14.4* |
| 11.0 | 38 | 3.25 | 6.5* | 9.5* | 12.2* | 15.9* |
| 12.5 | 38 | 3.25 | 7.1 | 10.3 | 13.3 | 17.4 |
| 12.5 | 41 | 3.66‡ | 8.4 | 12.5 | 16.3 | 20.9 |
| 15.5 | 41 | 3.66‡ | 9.2 | 13.9 | 18.1 | 23.7 |

*The values for 9.5 mm and 11.0 mm panels applied directly to framing may be increased to values shown, respectively, for 11.0 mm and 12.5 mm panels, provided studs are spaced at a maximum of 400 mm on centre.

†Framing at adjoining panel edges shall be 64 mm lumber (or two 38 mm wide framing members connected to transfer the factored shear force) or wider, and nails shall be staggered where nails are spaced 50 mm on centre.
‡Framing at adjoining panel edges shall be 64 mm lumber (or two 38 mm width framing members connected to transfer the factored shear force), or wider and nails shall be staggered where nails of 3.66 mm diameter having penetration into framing of more than 41 mm are spaced 75 mm or less on centre.
§9.5 mm minimum recommended when applied directly to framing as exterior siding.

**Notes:**

**(1)** Tabulated values are applicable to nailed shear panels using structural wood-based panels based on dry service conditions and standard duration of load.

**(2)** All panel edges are backed with 38 mm or wider framing. Panels are installed either horizontally or vertically, with nails spaced at 300 mm on centre along intermediate framing members. For unblocked horizontal panels, see Clause 9.4.4.

**(3)** Where panels are applied on both faces of a wall and nail spacing is less than 150 mm on centre on either side, panel joints shall be offset to fall on different framing members or framing shall be 64 mm or thicker and nails on each side shall be staggered.

**(4)** For panels applied over 12.7 mm or 15.9 mm gypsum wallboard, specified shear strength for the same thickness panel applied directly to framing may be used as long as minimum nail penetration (in the framing) is satisfied.

**(5)** For shearwalls fabricated with nails having a diameter that deviates from those presented in the table (e.g., power-driven nails), consult Appendix A9.5.1 for an appropriate modification factor, which should be applied to the capacities given in the table.

**(6)** For construction sheathing OSB, product specification shall also include a panel mark identifying an end-use rating. Table 9.5.3 provides an equivalence between tabulated thicknesses and panel marks.

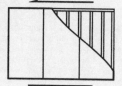
Vertical panels, no blocking

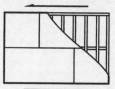
Horizontal panels, with blocking

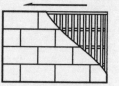
Horizontal panels, with blocking

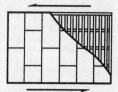
Vertical panels, with blocking

## Table 9.5.1B
## Specified Shear Strength, $v_d$, for Gypsum
## Wallboard Shearwalls (kN/m)

| Minimum nominal panel thickness, mm | Minimum nail and screw penetration in framing, mm | Wall construction | Panels applied directly to framing | | |
|---|---|---|---|---|---|
| | | | Nail and screw spacing at panel edges, mm | | |
| | | | 200 | 150 | 100 |
| 12.5 | 19 | Unblocked | 1.2 | 1.4 | 1.6 |
| 12.5 | 19 | Blocked | 1.4 | 1.7 | 2.1 |
| 15.9 | 19 | Unblocked | 1.5 | 1.7 | 2.1 |
| 15.9 | 19 | Blocked | 1.7 | 2.2 | 2.5 |

**Notes:**

**(1)** *Tabulated values are based on dry service conditions and are applicable to wood framing of all species. Values for unblocked walls are given for 400 mm stud spacing, and shall be reduced by 20% for 500 mm stud spacing, and 40% for 600 mm stud spacing. Values for blocked walls are applicable to stud spacings from 400 to 600 mm.*

**(2)** *Gypsum wallboard shall only be considered effective in resisting loads of short-term duration. Gypsum wallboard shall not be permitted in wet service conditions.*

**(3)** *Tabulated values apply when gypsum wallboard is applied to framing with nails conforming to CSA Standard B111, gypsum board application nails — ring threaded.*

**(4)** *Tabulated values apply when gypsum wallboard is applied to framing with wallboard screws conforming to ASTM Standard C 1002, Type W.*

**(5)** *Space nails and screws at maximum 300 mm on centre along intermediate framing members.*

## Table 9.5.2

## Specified Shear Strength, $v_d$ for Diaphragms with Framing of Douglas Fir-Larch (kN/m)

| Common nail diameter, mm | Minimum nail penetration in framing, mm | Minimum panel thickness, mm | Minimum width of framing member, mm | Blocked diaphragms — Nail spacing (mm) at diaphragm boundaries (all cases) and at continuous panel edges parallel to load (cases 3 and 4) | | | | Unblocked diaphragms — Nail spacing at 150 mm maximum at supported edges | |
|---|---|---|---|---|---|---|---|---|---|
| | | | | 150 | 100 | 64 | 50* | Load perp. to unblocked edges and continuous panel joints (case 1) | All other configurations (cases 2, 3, and 4) |
| | | | | Nail spacing at other panel edges, mm | | | | | |
| | | | | 150 | 150 | 100 | 75 | | |
| 2.84 | 31 | 7.5 | 38 | 4.6 | 6.1 | 9.1 | 10.3 | 4.1 | 3.0 |
| | | | 64 | 5.2 | 6.8 | 10.3 | 11.7 | 4.6 | 3.4 |
| | | 9.5 | 38 | 5.0 | 6.8 | 10.2 | 11.4 | 4.5 | 3.4 |
| | | | 64 | 5.7 | 7.6 | 11.4 | 12.9 | 5.0 | 3.8 |
| 3.25 | 38 | 9.5 | 38 | 6.5 | 8.7 | 13.1 | 14.8 | 5.9 | 4.4 |
| | | | 64 | 7.3 | 9.8 | 14.7 | 16.6 | 6.5 | 4.9 |
| | | 11.0 | 38 | 6.9 | 9.2 | 13.7 | 15.6 | 6.3 | 4.6 |
| | | | 64 | 7.8 | 10.3 | 15.5 | 17.5 | 6.9 | 5.2 |
| | | 12.5 | 38 | 7.3 | 9.8 | 14.4 | 16.3 | 6.5 | 4.9 |
| | | | 64 | 8.2 | 10.9 | 16.3 | 18.4 | 7.2 | 5.4 |
| 3.66† | 41 | 12.5 | 38 | 7.9 | 10.5 | 15.6 | 17.8 | 6.9 | 5.2 |
| | | | 64 | 8.8 | 11.7 | 17.7 | 20.0 | 7.9 | 5.9 |
| | | 15.5 | 38 | 8.7 | 11.6 | 17.4 | 19.8 | 7.8 | 5.9 |
| | | | 64 | 9.8 | 13.0 | 19.6 | 22.3 | 8.7 | 6.5 |
| | | 18.5 | 64 | — | 17.5‡ | 25.4‡ | — | — | — |
| | | | 89 | — | 20.4‡ | 29.2‡ | — | — | — |

*(Continued)*

# Table 9.5.2 (Concluded)

*Framing at adjoining panel edges shall be 64 mm lumber (or a built-up column composed of two 38 mm width framing members connected to transfer the factored shear force) or wider, and nails shall be staggered where nails are spaced 50 mm on centre.

†Framing at adjoining panel edges shall be 64 mm lumber (or two 38 mm width framing members connected to transfer the factored shear force) or wider, and nails shall be staggered where nails of 3.66 mm diameter having penetration into framing of more than 41 mm are spaced 75 mm or less on centre.

‡Two lines of fasteners are required.

**Notes:**

**(1)** Tabulated values are based on dry service conditions and standard-term duration of load, and apply to nailed shear panels using structural wood-based panels. Space nails 300 mm on centre along intermediate framing members.

**(2)** For diaphragms fabricated with nails having a diameter that deviates from those presented in the table (e.g., power-driven nails), consult Clause A9.5.1 for an appropriate modification factor, which should be applied to the capacities given in the table.

**(3)** For Construction Sheathing OSB, product specification shall also include a panel mark identifying an end-use rating. Table 9.5.3 provides an equivalence between tabulated thicknesses and panel marks.

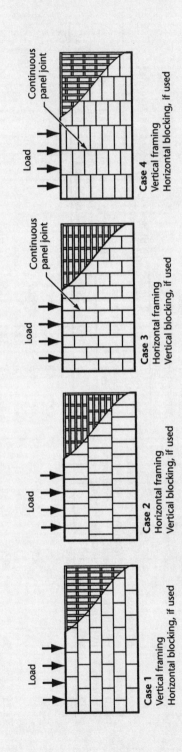

**Case 1**
Vertical framing
Horizontal blocking, if used

**Case 2**
Horizontal framing
Vertical blocking, if used

**Case 3**
Horizontal framing
Vertical blocking, if used

**Case 4**
Vertical framing
Horizontal blocking, if used

## Table 9.5.3
## Panel Marking Equivalence in Shearwall and Diaphragm Tables

| In shearwall Table 9.5.1A | | In diaphragm Table 9.5.2 | |
|---|---|---|---|
| Minimum nominal thickness, mm | Minimum panel mark | Minimum nominal thickness, mm | Minimum panel mark |
| 7.5 | 2R20 | 7.5 | 2R20 |
| 9.5 | 2R24 | 9.5 | 2R24 |
| 11.0 | 1R24/2F16 | 11.0 | 1R24/2F16 |
| 12.5 | 2R32/2F16 or 1F16 | 12.5 | 2R32/2F16 |
| 15.5 | 2R40/2F20 | 15.5 | 2R40/2F20 or 1F20 |
| | | 18.5 | 2R48/2F24 or 1F24 |

**Notes:**
**(1)** *For OSB panels rated to CSA Standard CAN/CSA-O325.0, the minimum nominal thickness may be 0.5 mm less than the thickness shown above. No adjustment to the tabulated shear strength values is required.*
**(2)** *For alternative panel marks meeting the minimum requirements, see Clause A7.2.2.2.*

Δ

## Table 9.5.4
## Maximum Percentage of Total Shear Forces
## Resisted by Gypsum Wallboard in a Storey

| Storey | Percentage of shear forces | | | |
|---|---|---|---|---|
| | 4-storey building | 3-storey building | 2-storey building | 1-storey building |
| 4th | 80 | — | — | — |
| 3rd | 60 | 80 | — | — |
| 2nd | 40 | 60 | 80 | — |
| 1st | 40 | 40 | 60 | 80 |

**Notes:**
**(1)** *A force modification factor of $R_d = 2.0$ and a system overstrength factor of $R_o = 1.7$ are used when gypsum wallboard sheathing is considered to resist lateral loads.*
**(2)** *Maximum storey height shall not exceed 3.6 m.*

# 10. Fastenings

## 10.1 Scope

Clause 10 provides criteria for the engineering design and appraisal of connections using split ring and shear plate connectors, bolts, drift pins, lag screws, timber rivets (also known as glulam rivets), truss plates, nails, spikes, and joist hangers.
**Note:** *Lateral resistance values for bolts, drift pins, and lag screws are based on relative density of the wood material. Reference density values are given in Table A10.1.*

## 10.2 General Requirements

### 10.2.1 All Fastenings
**Note:** *Joint details should be avoided where shrinkage of the wood can lead to excessive tension perpendicular to grain.*

### 10.2.1.1
The tables are predicated on the requirement that the projecting end of a member shall not be trimmed or otherwise altered in such a manner as to reduce the specified minimum end distance.

## 10.2.1.2
Under severe conditions conducive to corrosion, connection design should provide adequate protection.

## 10.2.1.3
Joints made using hard maple, soft maple, elm, beech, black oak, white oak, or birch may be assigned the same resistances as the D Fir-L species group.

## 10.2.1.4
Where a fastening or group of fastenings exerts a shear force on a member, the factored shear resistance of the member as calculated in Clauses 5.5.5 and 6.5.7 shall be based upon the dimension $d_e$ shown in Figure 10.2.1.4, instead of the dimension d.  Dimension $d_e$ is defined as the distance, measured perpendicular to the axis of the member, from the extremity of the fastening or group of fastenings to the loaded edge of the member.

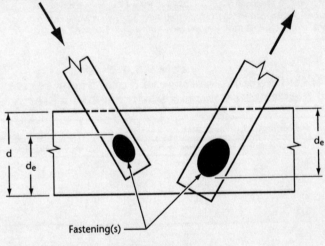

**Figure 10.2.1.4**
**Shear Depth**

### 10.2.1.5  Service Condition Factor, $K_{SF}$
The service condition factor, $K_{SF}$, for fastenings is given in Table 10.2.1.5.

### 10.2.1.6  Load Duration Factor, $K_D$
The load duration factor, $K_D$, for fastenings is given in Table 4.3.2.2.

### 10.2.1.7  Treatment Factor, $K_T$
For connections containing wood-based members treated with fire-retardant or other strength-reducing chemicals, strength capacities of connections shall be based on the documented results of tests that shall take into account the effect of time, temperature, and moisture content.  Test procedures shall meet the requirements of Clause 3.3.2.
**Note:** *The effects of fire-retardant treatments can vary depending on manufacturing materials and processes. See the Canadian Wood Council's* Commentary *for additional explanation.*

### 10.2.1.8
Joints shall be assembled so that the surfaces are brought into close contact.

## Table 10.2.1.5
## Service Condition Factor, $K_{SF}$, for Fastenings

| | Condition of lumber when fabricated | | | | | |
|---|---|---|---|---|---|---|
| | Seasoned (moisture content ≤ 15%) | | Unseasoned (moisture content > 15%) | | Joint detail* | Angle of load to grain |
| Service conditions | Dry | Wet | Dry | Wet | | |
| Timber rivets (also known as glulam rivets): | | | | | | |
| – lateral loads | 1.00 | 0.80 | 0.90 | 0.80 | All | All |
| – withdrawal loads | 1.00 | † | 0.60 | † | | |
| Split rings, shear plate connectors, truss plates | 1.00 | 0.67 | 0.80 | 0.67 | All | All |
| Bolts, drift pins, lag screws | 1.00 | 0.67 | 1.00 | 0.67 | A | All |
| | 1.00 | 0.67 | 1.00 | 0.67 | B | 0° |
| | 1.00 | 0.67 | 0.40 | 0.27 | B | 90° |
| | 1.00 | 0.67 | 0.40 | 0.27 | C | All |
| Nails: | | | | | | |
| – lateral loads | 1.00 | 0.67 | 0.80 | 0.67 | All | All |
| – withdrawal loads | 1.00 | 0.67 | 0.40 | 0.40 | All | 90° |

*where
A = single fastening or a single row parallel to grain with steel side plates
B = single row parallel to grain with wood side plates or two rows parallel to grain not more than 127 mm apart with a common wood splice plate, or multiple rows with separate wood or steel splice plates for each row
C = all other arrangements
†No data available for this condition.

# 10.2.2  Bolts, Lag Screws, Split Rings, and Shear Plate Connectors (General Requirements)

## 10.2.2.1  Inspection and Tightening
Structures that have been assembled with unseasoned or partially seasoned lumber or timbers shall be inspected regularly at intervals not exceeding 6 months until it becomes apparent that further shrinkage of the wood will not be appreciable, and at each inspection the fastenings shall be tightened sufficiently to bring the faces of the connected members into close contact without deformation.

## 10.2.2.2  Assembly
Grooves, daps, and holes shall be fabricated and oriented accurately in the contacting faces. Holes in steel plates shall be accurately placed to line up with holes in the adjoining wood and shall not be more than 2 mm larger than the bolt or lag screw diameters.

## 10.2.2.3  Group of Fastenings

### 10.2.2.3.1
A group of fastenings consists of one or more rows of fastenings of the same type and size arranged symmetrically with respect to the axis of the load.

### 10.2.2.3.2

A row of fastenings consists of one or more bolts, lag screws, or timber connector units of the same type and size aligned with the direction of the load (see Figure 10.4.3).

### 10.2.2.3.3

When fastenings in adjacent rows are staggered, and the distance between adjacent rows is less than 1/4 the distance between the closest fastenings in adjacent rows measured parallel to the rows, the adjacent rows shall be considered as one row for purposes of determining the resistance of the group. For a group of fastenings having an even number of rows, this principle shall apply to each pair. For a group of fastenings having an odd number of rows, the more conservative interpretation shall apply.

### 10.2.2.3.4

The modification factor, $J_G$, for groups of timber connectors and lag screws is given in Tables 10.2.2.3.4A and 10.2.2.3.4B.

### 10.2.2.3.5

The modification factors, $J_G$ and $J_R$, for groups of bolts are given in Clause 10.4.4.

## 10.2.2.4 Washers

### 10.2.2.4.1

A standard cut washer or its equivalent (see Table 10.2.2.4.1) or a metal strap of the same thickness as the washer shall be placed between the wood and the head and between the wood and the nut.

### 10.2.2.4.2

When a bolt head or nut bears directly on a steel plate, washers may be omitted.

### 10.2.2.4.3

All bolts or lag screws in axial tension or with a calculated tension component shall be provided with steel plate washers, standard ogee washers, or malleable iron washers under heads and nuts. The area of such washers shall be such that the bearing stress on the wood under the washer does not exceed the factored resistance in compression perpendicular to grain. If steel washers are used, the thickness shall be not less than one-tenth the diameter or one-tenth the length of the longer side of the washer.

## 10.2.2.5 Net Section

### 10.2.2.5.1

Resistance of joints made using bolts, lag screws, and split ring and shear plate connectors shall be checked for net section in accordance with Clause 4.3.8.

### 10.2.2.5.2

For a bolted or lag screw joint under parallel-to-grain loading, staggered adjacent bolts or lag screws shall be considered to be placed at the critical section unless their spacing centre-to-centre parallel to grain is more than eight bolt or lag screw shank diameters.

### 10.2.2.5.3

For connector joints, the area deducted from the gross section shall include the projected area of that portion of the connectors within the member and that portion of the bolt hole not within the connector projected area, located at the critical plane. Where connectors are staggered, adjacent connectors shall be considered as occurring in the same critical transverse plane unless their spacing centre-to-centre parallel to grain is more than two connector diameters.

## Table 10.2.2.3.4A
## Modification Factors, $J_G$, for Timber Connector and Lag Screw Joints with Wood Side Plates

| Area ratio* | The lesser of $A_m$ or $A_s$† | Number of fasteners in a row | | | | | | | | | | |
|---|---|---|---|---|---|---|---|---|---|---|---|---|
| | | 2 | 3 | 4 | 5 | 6 | 7 | 8 | 9 | 10 | 11 | 12 |
| 0.5 | <8000 | 1.00 | 0.92 | 0.84 | 0.76 | 0.68 | 0.61 | 0.55 | 0.49 | 0.43 | 0.38 | 0.34 |
| | 8 001–12 000 | 1.00 | 0.95 | 0.88 | 0.82 | 0.75 | 0.68 | 0.62 | 0.57 | 0.52 | 0.48 | 0.43 |
| | 12 001–18 000 | 1.00 | 0.97 | 0.93 | 0.88 | 0.82 | 0.77 | 0.71 | 0.67 | 0.63 | 0.59 | 0.55 |
| | 18 001–26 000 | 1.00 | 0.98 | 0.96 | 0.92 | 0.87 | 0.83 | 0.79 | 0.75 | 0.71 | 0.69 | 0.66 |
| | 26 001–42 000 | 1.00 | 1.00 | 0.97 | 0.94 | 0.90 | 0.86 | 0.83 | 0.79 | 0.76 | 0.74 | 0.72 |
| | >42 000 | 1.00 | 1.00 | 0.98 | 0.95 | 0.91 | 0.88 | 0.85 | 0.82 | 0.80 | 0.78 | 0.76 |
| 1.0 | <8 000 | 1.00 | 0.97 | 0.92 | 0.85 | 0.78 | 0.71 | 0.65 | 0.59 | 0.54 | 0.49 | 0.44 |
| | 8 001–12 000 | 1.00 | 0.98 | 0.94 | 0.89 | 0.84 | 0.78 | 0.72 | 0.66 | 0.61 | 0.56 | 0.51 |
| | 12 001–18 000 | 1.00 | 1.00 | 0.97 | 0.93 | 0.89 | 0.85 | 0.80 | 0.76 | 0.72 | 0.68 | 0.64 |
| | 18 001–26 000 | 1.00 | 1.00 | 0.99 | 0.96 | 0.92 | 0.89 | 0.85 | 0.83 | 0.80 | 0.78 | 0.75 |
| | 26 001–42 000 | 1.00 | 1.00 | 1.00 | 0.97 | 0.94 | 0.91 | 0.88 | 0.85 | 0.84 | 0.82 | 0.80 |
| | >42 000 | 1.00 | 1.00 | 1.00 | 0.99 | 0.96 | 0.93 | 0.91 | 0.88 | 0.87 | 0.86 | 0.85 |

*Area ratio = the lesser of $A_m/A_s$ or $A_s/A_m$
† $A_m$ = gross cross-sectional area of main member, mm²
$A_s$ = sum of gross cross-sectional areas of side members, mm²
**Note:** For area ratios between 0.5 and 1.0, interpolate between tabulated values. For area ratios less than 0.5, extrapolate from tabulated values.

## Table 10.2.2.3.4B
## Modification Factors, $J_G$, for Timber Connector and Lag Screw Joints with Steel Side Plates

| Area ratio $A_m/A_s$* | Am | Number of fasteners in a row | | | | | | | | | | |
|---|---|---|---|---|---|---|---|---|---|---|---|---|
| | | 2 | 3 | 4 | 5 | 6 | 7 | 8 | 9 | 10 | 11 | 12 |
| 2–12 | 16 000–26 000 | 1.00 | 0.94 | 0.87 | 0.80 | 0.73 | 0.67 | 0.61 | 0.56 | 0.51 | 0.46 | 0.42 |
| | 26 001–42 000 | 1.00 | 0.96 | 0.92 | 0.87 | 0.81 | 0.75 | 0.70 | 0.66 | 0.62 | 0.58 | 0.55 |
| | 42 001–76 000 | 1.00 | 0.98 | 0.95 | 0.91 | 0.87 | 0.82 | 0.78 | 0.75 | 0.72 | 0.69 | 0.66 |
| | 76 001–130 000 | 1.00 | 0.99 | 0.97 | 0.95 | 0.92 | 0.89 | 0.86 | 0.84 | 0.81 | 0.79 | 0.78 |
| 12–18 | 26 001–42 000 | 1.00 | 0.98 | 0.94 | 0.90 | 0.85 | 0.80 | 0.75 | 0.70 | 0.67 | 0.62 | 0.58 |
| | 42 001–76 000 | 1.00 | 0.99 | 0.96 | 0.93 | 0.90 | 0.86 | 0.82 | 0.79 | 0.75 | 0.72 | 0.69 |
| | 76 001–130 000 | 1.00 | 1.00 | 0.98 | 0.95 | 0.94 | 0.92 | 0.89 | 0.86 | 0.83 | 0.80 | 0.78 |
| | >130 000 | 1.00 | 1.00 | 1.00 | 0.98 | 0.97 | 0.95 | 0.93 | 0.91 | 0.90 | 0.88 | 0.87 |
| 18–24 | 26 001–42 000 | 1.00 | 1.00 | 0.96 | 0.93 | 0.89 | 0.84 | 0.79 | 0.74 | 0.69 | 0.64 | 0.59 |
| | 42 001–76 000 | 1.00 | 1.00 | 0.97 | 0.94 | 0.92 | 0.89 | 0.86 | 0.83 | 0.80 | 0.76 | 0.73 |
| | 76 001–130 000 | 1.00 | 1.00 | 0.99 | 0.98 | 0.96 | 0.94 | 0.92 | 0.90 | 0.88 | 0.86 | 0.85 |
| | >130 000 | 1.00 | 1.00 | 1.00 | 1.00 | 0.98 | 0.96 | 0.95 | 0.93 | 0.92 | 0.92 | 0.91 |
| 24–30 | 26 001–42 000 | 1.00 | 0.98 | 0.94 | 0.90 | 0.85 | 0.80 | 0.74 | 0.69 | 0.65 | 0.61 | 0.58 |
| | 42 001–76 000 | 1.00 | 0.99 | 0.97 | 0.93 | 0.90 | 0.86 | 0.82 | 0.79 | 0.76 | 0.73 | 0.71 |
| | 76 001–130 000 | 1.00 | 1.00 | 0.98 | 0.96 | 0.94 | 0.92 | 0.89 | 0.87 | 0.85 | 0.83 | 0.81 |
| | >130 000 | 1.00 | 1.00 | 0.99 | 0.98 | 0.97 | 0.95 | 0.93 | 0.92 | 0.90 | 0.89 | 0.89 |
| 30–35 | 26 001–42 000 | 1.00 | 0.96 | 0.92 | 0.86 | 0.80 | 0.74 | 0.68 | 0.64 | 0.60 | 0.57 | 0.55 |
| | 42 001–76 000 | 1.00 | 0.98 | 0.95 | 0.90 | 0.86 | 0.81 | 0.76 | 0.72 | 0.68 | 0.65 | 0.62 |
| | 76 001–130 000 | 1.00 | 0.99 | 0.97 | 0.95 | 0.92 | 0.88 | 0.85 | 0.82 | 0.80 | 0.78 | 0.77 |
| | >130 000 | 1.00 | 1.00 | 0.98 | 0.97 | 0.95 | 0.93 | 0.90 | 0.89 | 0.87 | 0.86 | 0.85 |
| 35–42 | 26 001–42 000 | 1.00 | 0.95 | 0.89 | 0.82 | 0.75 | 0.69 | 0.63 | 0.58 | 0.53 | 0.49 | 0.46 |
| | 42 001–76 000 | 1.00 | 0.97 | 0.93 | 0.88 | 0.82 | 0.77 | 0.71 | 0.67 | 0.63 | 0.59 | 0.56 |
| | 76 001–130 000 | 1.00 | 0.98 | 0.96 | 0.93 | 0.89 | 0.85 | 0.81 | 0.78 | 0.76 | 0.73 | 0.71 |
| | >130 000 | 1.00 | 0.99 | 0.98 | 0.96 | 0.93 | 0.90 | 0.87 | 0.84 | 0.82 | 0.80 | 0.78 |

*$A_m$ = gross cross-sectional area of main member, mm$^2$
$A_s$ = sum of gross cross-sectional area of steel side plates, mm$^2$

# Table 10.2.2.4.1
## Minimum Washer Sizes for Bolted, Lag Screw, and Timber Connector Joints

| Washer type | Use | Bolted or lag screw joints | | | Timber connector joints | | | | | |
|---|---|---|---|---|---|---|---|---|---|---|
| | | Rod or bolt diameter, $d_F$ in | Outside dimension, $d_o$, mm | Thickness, t, mm | 2-1/2 in split ring with 1/2 in bolt | | 4 in split ring with 3/4 in bolt | | 2-5/8 in shear plate and 4 in shear plate with 3/4 in bolt* | |
| | | | | | t, mm | $d_o$ mm | t, mm | $d_o$ mm | t, mm | $d_o$ mm |
| Standard cut (steel) | For bolts and lag screws only; too thin to resist any tensile loads | 1/2 | 35 | 3 | Cut washers not to be used with connectors | | | | | |
| | | 5/8 | 45 | 4 | | | | | | |
| | | 3/4 | 50 | 4 | | | | | | |
| | | 7/8 | 60 | 4 | | | | | | |
| | | 1 | 65 | 4 | | | | | | |
| Square plate (steel) | For connector or tensile load | 1/2 | 65 | 5 | | | | | | |
| | | 5/8 | 70 | 6 | | | | | | |
| | | 3/4 | 75 | 6 | 3.2 | 50 | 4.8 | 75 | 6.4 | 75 |
| | | 7/8 | 85 | 9 | | | | | | |
| | | 1 | 90 | 8 | | | | | | |
| Round plate (steel) | For any use, unless tensile loading develops enough stress to crush wood | 1/2 | 65 | 5 | | | | | | |
| | | 3/4 | 75 | 6 | 3.2 | 50 | 4.8 | 75 | 6.4 | 75 |
| | | 7/8 | 85 | 8 | | | | | | |

(Continued)

## Table 10.2.2.4.1 (Concluded)

| Washer type | Use | Bolted or lag screw joints | | | Timber connector joints | | | | | |
|---|---|---|---|---|---|---|---|---|---|---|
| | | Rod or bolt diameter, $d_r$, in | Outside dimension, $d_o$, mm | Thickness, t, mm | 2-1/2 in split ring with 1/2 in bolt t, mm | $d_o$, mm | 4 in split ring with 3/4 in bolt t, mm | $d_o$, mm | 2-5/8 in shear plate and 4 in shear plate with 3/4 in bolt* t, mm | $d_o$, mm |
| Ogee (cast iron) | Thicker and wider than normal or malleable iron washers; for increased stiffness and bearing strength | 1/2 | 65 | 13 | 3.2 | 55 | 4.8 | 75 | 6.4 | 75 |
| | | 5/8 | 75 | 16 | | | | | | |
| | | 3/4 | 90 | 19 | | | | | | |
| | | 7/8 | 100 | 22 | | | | | | |
| | | 1 | 100 | 25 | | | | | | |
| Malleable iron | Wider than normal washers; for added bearing strength | 1/2 | 65 | 6 | 3.2 | 55 | 4.8 | 75 | 6.4 | 75 |
| | | 5/8 | 70 | 8 | | | | | | |
| | | 3/4 | 75 | 11 | | | | | | |
| | | 7/8 | 90 | 11 | | | | | | |
| | | 1 | 100 | 13 | | | | | | |

*For 4 in shear plates used with 7/8 in bolts, $d_o$ is 90 mm.

**Note:** Square or round plate bevelled washers may be necessary when bolts project at an angle to the wood.

## 10.3 Split Ring and Shear Plate Connectors

### 10.3.1 General

#### 10.3.1.1 Connector Unit

For purposes of specifying connector resistance herein, a connector unit shall consist of one of the following, in any joint of any number of members:
(a) one split ring connector with its bolt or lag screw;
(b) one shear plate connector with its bolt or lag screw, used in conjunction with a steel strap or plate in a wood-to-metal joint; or
(c) two shear plate connectors used back-to-back in the contact faces of a wood-to-wood joint with their bolt or lag screw.

#### 10.3.1.2 Split Ring Connectors

Tabulated resistances and design methods for split ring connectors given in Clause 10.3 are for connectors whose dimensions are in accordance with Table 10.3.1A and that are manufactured from hot-rolled carbon steel, SAE 1010, meeting the requirements of the *SAE Handbook*. Each ring shall form a closed true circle with the principal axis of the cross-section of the ring metal parallel to the geometric axis of the ring. The ring shall be bevelled from the central portion toward the edges to a thickness less than that at midsection so that it will fit snugly in a precut groove, or such other means as to accomplish the equivalent performance shall be used. It shall be cut through in one place in its circumference to form a tongue and slot.

#### 10.3.1.3 Shear Plate Connectors

Tabulated resistances and design methods are for shear plate connectors whose dimensions are in accordance with Table 10.3.1A and that conform to either of the following:
(a) Pressed Steel Type: Pressed steel shear plates manufactured from hot-rolled carbon steel, SAE 1010, meeting the requirements of the *SAE Handbook*. Each plate shall be a true circle with a flange around the edge, extending at right angles to the face of the plate from one face only. The plate portion shall have a central hole and two small perforations on diametrically opposite sides of the hole, each midway from the centre and circumference; or
(b) Malleable Iron Type: Malleable iron shear plates manufactured in accordance with the requirements of ASTM Standard A 47, Grade 32510 (or ASTM Standard A 47M, Grade 22010). Each casting shall consist of a perforated round plate with a flange extending at right angles to the face of the plate and projecting from one face only. The plate portion shall have a central bolt hole, reamed to size where required, with an integral hub concentric to the bolt hole and extending from the same face as the flange.

### Table 10.3.1A
### Timber Connector Dimensions (mm)

| Split ring | 2-1/2 in | 4 in | |
|---|---|---|---|
| Inside diameter at centre when closed | 63.5 | 101.6 | |
| Thickness of steel at centre | 4.1 | 4.9 | |
| Depth of steel | 19.0 | 25.4 | |
| | 2-5/8 in | 4 in | |
| Shear plate | | 3/4 in bolt | 7/8 in bolt |
| Diameter of plate | 66.5 | 102.1 | 102.1 |
| Diameter of bolt hole | 20.6 | 20.6 | 23.9 |
| Thickness of plate | 4.3 | 5.1 | 5.1 |
| Depth of flange | 10.7 | 15.7 | 15.7 |

## 10.3.1.4  Connector Grooves

Dimensions of connector grooves and bolt hole sizes shall be in accordance with Table 10.3.1B.

### Table 10.3.1B
### Timber Connector Groove Dimensions (mm)

| Split ring groove | 2-1/2 in split ring | 4 in split ring |
|---|---|---|
| Bolt hole diameter | 14.3 | 20.6 |
| Inside diameter | 65.0 | 103.6 |
| Width | 4.6 | 5.3 |
| Depth | 9.8 | 13.1 |

| Shear plate groove | 2-5/8 in shear plate | 4 in shear plate | |
|---|---|---|---|
| | | 3/4 in bolt | 7/8 in bolt |
| A = 66.8 | 102.4 | 102.4 |
| B = — | 39.4 | 39.4 |
| C = 20.6 | 20.6 | 23.8 |
| D = — | 24.6 | 24.6 |
| E = 4.5 | 5.3 | 5.3 |
| F = 11.4 | 16.3 | 16.3 |
| G = 6.4 | 5.6 | 5.6 |
| H = — | 12.7 | 12.7 |
| I = 57.2 | 88.6 | 88.6 |

## 10.3.2  Service Condition Factor

The service condition factors in Table 10.2.1.5 are based on the moisture content within a depth of 20 mm from the connected surface.

## 10.3.3  Distance Factors

Connectors installed at any edge distance, end distance, or spacing less than the minimum for which a tabulated value appears in the appropriate columns of Tables 10.3.3A to 10.3.3C shall not be considered to provide resistance.  Factors for reduction of resistance for edge distance, end distance, and spacing shall be separately determined, and the lowest factor so determined for any one connector shall be applied to all connectors resisting a common force in a joint. (See Figures 10.3.3A and 10.3.3B.)

## Table 10.3.3A
## Values of $J_C$ for Timber Connector Edge Distance

| Edge distance, mm | 2-1/2 in split ring or 2-5/8 in shear plate | | | 4 in split ring or shear plate | | |
|---|---|---|---|---|---|---|
| | $\theta=15°$ | $\theta=30°$ | $\theta=45°$ to 90° | $\theta=15°$ | $\theta=30°$ | $\theta=45°$ to 90° |
| 45 | 0.94 | 0.88 | 0.83 | — | — | — |
| 50 | 0.97 | 0.91 | 0.87 | — | — | — |
| 55 | 1.00 | 0.94 | 0.90 | — | — | — |
| 60 | 1.00 | 0.98 | 0.93 | — | — | — |
| 65 | 1.00 | 1.00 | 0.97 | — | — | — |
| 70 | 1.00 | 1.00 | 1.00 | 0.93 | 0.88 | 0.83 |
| 75 | 1.00 | 1.00 | 1.00 | 0.97 | 0.91 | 0.86 |
| 80 | 1.00 | 1.00 | 1.00 | 1.00 | 0.94 | 0.89 |
| 85 | 1.00 | 1.00 | 1.00 | 1.00 | 0.97 | 0.93 |
| 90 | 1.00 | 1.00 | 1.00 | 1.00 | 1.00 | 0.96 |
| 95 | 1.00 | 1.00 | 1.00 | 1.00 | 1.00 | 1.00 |
| 100 | 1.00 | 1.00 | 1.00 | 1.00 | 1.00 | 1.00 |

**Notes:**

**(1)** At angle of load to grain $\theta=0°$, the minimum edge distance for the particular connector size gives a value of $J_C = 1.00$. For intermediate values of $\theta$, linear interpolation may be used.

**(2)** Values of $J_C$ apply to loaded edge distance only. Minimum edge distance for loaded or unloaded edge is 40 mm for 2-1/2 in split rings and 2-5/8 in shear plates, and 65 mm for 4 in split rings and shear plates.

## Table 10.3.3B
## Values of $J_C$ for Timber Connector End Distance

| End distance, mm | | Tension | |
|---|---|---|---|
| | | 2-1/2 in split ring or 2-5/8 in shear plate | 4 in split ring or shear plate |
| For members ≥130 mm thick | For members < 130 mm thick | $\theta = 0°–90°$ | $\theta = 0°–90°$ |
| 70 | 105 | 0.62 | — |
| 75 | 115 | 0.65 | — |
| 80 | 120 | 0.68 | — |
| 85 | 130 | 0.70 | — |
| 90 | 135 | 0.73 | 0.63 |
| 95 | 145 | 0.76 | 0.65 |
| 100 | 150 | 0.78 | 0.67 |
| 105 | 160 | 0.81 | 0.69 |
| 110 | 165 | 0.84 | 0.71 |
| 115 | 175 | 0.86 | 0.73 |
| 120 | 180 | 0.89 | 0.75 |
| 125 | 190 | 0.92 | 0.77 |
| 130 | 195 | 0.94 | 0.79 |
| 135 | 205 | 0.97 | 0.82 |
| 140 | 210 | 1.00 | 0.84 |
| 145 | 220 | 1.00 | 0.86 |
| 150 | 225 | 1.00 | 0.88 |
| 155 | 235 | 1.00 | 0.90 |
| 160 | 240 | 1.00 | 0.92 |
| 165 | 250 | 1.00 | 0.94 |
| 170 | 255 | 1.00 | 0.96 |
| 175 | 265 | 1.00 | 0.98 |
| 180 | 270 | 1.00 | 1.00 |

**Notes:**
**(1)** Values of $\theta$ shown are for angle of load to grain.
**(2)** For connectors loaded in compression, $J_C = 1.00$. Minimum end distances for connectors loaded in compression are those given in the table for connectors loaded in tension.

## Table 10.3.3C
# Timber Connector Spacing (mm) for Values of $J_C$ between 0.75 and 1.0

| Angle of load to grain, $\theta$ ° | Angle of connector row to grain, $\beta$ ° | Minimum spacing between connectors measured centre-to-centre, mm | | | |
|---|---|---|---|---|---|
| | | 2-1/2 in split rings and 2-5/8 in shear plates | | 4 in split rings and 4 in shear plates | |
| | | $J_C=0.75$ | $J_C=1.00$ | $J_C=0.75$ | $J_C=1.00$ |
| 0 | 0 | 90 | 170 | 125 | 230 |
| | 15 | 90 | 160 | 125 | 215 |
| | 30 | 90 | 135 | 125 | 185 |
| | 45 | 90 | 110 | 125 | 155 |
| | 60 | 90 | 100 | 125 | 140 |
| | 75 | 90 | 90 | 125 | 130 |
| | 90 | 90 | 90 | 125 | 125 |
| 15 | 0 | 90 | 150 | 125 | 205 |
| | 15 | 90 | 145 | 125 | 195 |
| | 30 | 90 | 130 | 125 | 180 |
| | 45 | 90 | 115 | 125 | 160 |
| | 60 | 90 | 105 | 125 | 145 |
| | 75 | 90 | 100 | 125 | 135 |
| | 90 | 90 | 95 | 125 | 135 |
| 30 | 0 | 90 | 130 | 125 | 180 |
| | 15 | 90 | 125 | 125 | 175 |
| | 30 | 90 | 120 | 125 | 165 |
| | 45 | 90 | 110 | 125 | 155 |
| | 60 | 90 | 105 | 125 | 145 |
| | 75 | 90 | 100 | 125 | 145 |
| | 90 | 90 | 100 | 125 | 140 |
| 45 | 0 | 90 | 110 | 125 | 150 |
| | 15 | 90 | 110 | 125 | 150 |
| | 30 | 90 | 110 | 125 | 150 |
| | 45 | 90 | 110 | 125 | 150 |
| | 60 | 90 | 105 | 125 | 145 |
| | 75 | 90 | 105 | 125 | 145 |
| | 90 | 90 | 105 | 125 | 145 |
| 60–90 | 0 | 90 | 90 | 125 | 125 |
| | 15 | 90 | 90 | 125 | 125 |
| | 30 | 90 | 90 | 125 | 125 |
| | 45 | 90 | 100 | 125 | 135 |
| | 60 | 90 | 100 | 125 | 145 |
| | 75 | 90 | 105 | 125 | 150 |
| | 90 | 90 | 110 | 125 | 150 |

**Note:** *Values of $J_C$ between 0.75 and 1.00 for intermediate connector spacings may be obtained by linear interpolation.*

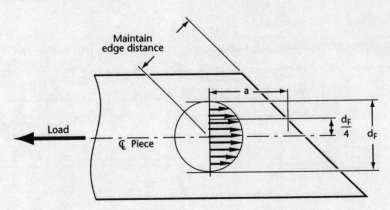

**Legend:**
a = End distance
$d_F$ = Connector diameter

**Figure 10.3.3A**
**End Distance for Member with Sloping End Cut**

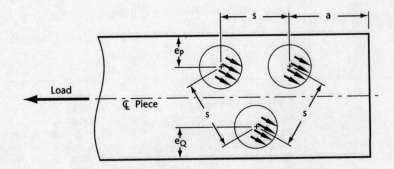

**Legend:**
a = End distance
$e_P$ = Unloaded edge distance
$e_Q$ = Loaded edge distance
s = Spacing

**Figure 10.3.3B**
**End Distance, Edge Distance, and Spacing**

## 10.3.4 Lumber Thickness

Connectors installed in lumber of a thickness less than the minimum specified in Table 10.3.4 for the connector type and use shall not be considered to provide resistance.

### Table 10.3.4
### Thickness Factor for Timber Connector, $J_T$

| Connector type and size | Number of faces of a piece containing connectors on a bolt | Thickness of piece, mm | $J_T$ |
|---|---|---|---|
| 2-1/2 in split ring | 1 | 38 | 1.00 |
|  |  | 25 | 0.85 |
|  | 2 | 51 | 1.00 |
|  |  | 38 | 0.80 |
| 4 in split ring | 1 | 38 | 1.00 |
|  |  | 25 | 0.65 |
|  | 2 | 76 | 1.00 |
|  |  | 64 | 0.95 |
|  |  | 51 | 0.80 |
|  |  | 38 | 0.65 |
| 2-5/8 in shear plate | 1 | 64 | 1.00 |
|  |  | 51 | 0.95 |
|  |  | 38 | 0.95 |
|  | 2 | 64 | 1.00 |
|  |  | 51 | 0.95 |
|  |  | 38 | 0.75 |
| 4 in shear plate | 1 | 44 | 1.00 |
|  |  | 38 | 0.85 |
|  | 2 | 89 | 1.00 |
|  |  | 76 | 0.95 |
|  |  | 64 | 0.85 |
|  |  | 51 | 0.75 |
|  |  | 44 | 0.65 |

## 10.3.5 Lag Screw Connector Joints

When lag screws instead of bolts are used with connectors, the resistance shall vary uniformly with penetration into the member receiving the point, from the full resistance for one connector unit with bolt for standard penetration to 0.75 times the full resistance for one connector unit with bolt for minimum penetration. Penetration shall be in accordance with Table 10.3.5 and shall be not less than the minimum value.

## Table 10.3.5
### Penetration Factor, $J_P$, for Split Rings and Shear Plates Used with Lag Screws

| Connector | Penetration | Penetration of lag screw into member receiving point (number of shank diameters) Species | | | | $J_P$ |
| | | Douglas Fir-Larch | Hem-Fir | Spruce-Pine-Fir | Northern Species | |
|---|---|---|---|---|---|---|
| 2-1/2 in split ring | Standard | 8 | 10 | 10 | 11 | 1.00 |
| 4 in split ring or 4 in shear plate* | Minimum | 3.5 | 4 | 4 | 4.5 | 0.75 |
| 2-5/8 in shear plate* | Standard | 5 | 7 | 7 | 8 | 1.00 |
| | Minimum | 3.5 | 4 | 4 | 4.5 | 0.75 |

*When steel side plates are used with shear plates, use $J_P = 1.0$.
**Note:** For intermediate penetrations, linear interpolation may be used for values of $J_P$ between 0.75 and 1.00.

## 10.3.6 Lateral Resistance

The factored lateral strength resistance of a split ring or shear plate connection, $P_r$, $Q_r$, or $N_r$, determined using equations (a), (b), and (c), shall be greater than or equal to the effect of the factored loads. The factored strength resistance per shear plate unit shall not exceed the values in Table 10.3.6C:

(a) For parallel-to-grain loading

$$P_r = \phi P_u n_F J_F$$

(b) For perpendicular-to-grain loading

$$Q_r = \phi Q_u n_F J_F$$

(c) For loads at angle, θ, to grain

$$N_r = \frac{P_r Q_r}{P_r \sin^2\theta + Q_r \cos^2\theta}$$

where
$\phi$ = 0.6
$P_u$ = $p_u (K_D K_{SF} K_T)$
$p_u$ = lateral strength resistance parallel to grain (Table 10.3.6A), kN
$J_F$ = $J_G J_C J_T J_O J_P$
$J_G$ = factor for groups of fastenings (Tables 10.2.2.3.4A and 10.2.2.3.4B)
$J_C$ = minimum configuration factor (Clause 10.3.3 and Tables 10.3.3A, 10.3.3.B, and 10.3.3C)
$J_T$ = thickness factor (Table 10.3.4)
$J_O$ = factor for connector orientation in grain
     = 1.00 for side grain installation
     = 0.67 for end grain and all other installations
$J_P$ = factor for lag screw penetration (Clause 10.3.5 and Table 10.3.5)
$Q_u$ = $q_u (K_D K_{SF} K_T)$
$q_u$ = lateral strength resistance perpendicular to grain (Table 10.3.6B), kN

## Table 10.3.6A
### Lateral Strength Resistance Parallel to Grain, p$_w$, of Timber Connector Unit (kN)

| Species | Split rings | | Shear plates | |
|---|---|---|---|---|
| | 2-1/2 in | 4 in | 2-5/8 in | 4 in |
| Douglas Fir-Larch | 31 | 55 | 27 | 49 |
| Hem-Fir | 27 | 49 | 24 | 44 |
| Spruce-Pine-Fir | 23 | 45 | 23 | 42 |
| Northern Species | 21 | 42 | 22 | 40 |

**Notes:**
**(1)** *Resistances of 4 in shear plates are for plates with 3/4 in bolts. For plates with 7/8 in bolts, resistances may be increased by 25%.*
**(2)** *Where wood side plates are used with 4 in shear plates, resistances are 90% of the tabulated resistances.*

## Table 10.3.6B
### Lateral Strength Resistance Perpendicular to Grain, q$_w$ of Timber Connector Unit (kN)

| Species | Split rings | | Shear plates | |
|---|---|---|---|---|
| | 2-1/2 in | 4 in | 2-5/8 in | 4 in |
| Douglas Fir-Larch | 22 | 42 | 23 | 35 |
| Hem-Fir | 18 | 35 | 19 | 28 |
| Spruce-Pine-Fir | 17 | 31 | 17 | 26 |
| Northern Species | 15 | 28 | 15 | 24 |

## Table 10.3.6C
### Maximum Factored Strength Resistance per Shear Plate Unit (kN)

| Type of load | 2-5/8 in shear plate | 4 in shear plate | |
|---|---|---|---|
| | | 3/4 in bolt | 7/8 in bolt |
| Washers provided; no bearing on threaded portion of the bolt | 18 | 32 | 43 |
| When bearing may occur on the threaded portion of the bolt | 16 | 28 | 38 |

## 10.4  Bolts

### 10.4.1  General

#### 10.4.1.1
Design requirements and data in Clause 10.4 for bolted joints are based upon the use of bolts conforming to the requirements of ASTM Standard A 307. When bolts are used with steel side plates, the side plates shall conform to the requirements of CSA Standard G40.21 or ASTM Standard A 36.
**Note:** *Alternatively, bolted joints may be used where their design conforms to the requirements of Clause 3.3.2.*

### 10.4.1.2
Bolt holes in wood shall be accurately aligned and drilled not less than 1.0 mm nor more than 2.0 mm larger than the bolt diameter.

## 10.4.2 Member Thickness

### 10.4.2.1 Wood Side Plates
In single and multiple shear connections, the member thickness in Clause 10.4.4.1 shall be that of the thinnest wood member.

### 10.4.2.2 Steel Side Plates
The member thickness in Clause 10.4.4.1 shall be that of the thinnest wood member. Steel side plates shall be of adequate thickness to resist the applied load.

### 10.4.2.3 Wood to Concrete
When a connection consists of one wood member attached to concrete or masonry, the connection shall be designed as a single shear connection utilizing the formulae in Clause 10.4.4. The wood member shall be considered the side member. The main member shall be assumed to have a thickness equal to the penetration of the bolt in the concrete or masonry. A value of 125 MPa shall be assigned to $f_2$. The concrete or masonry shall be of sufficient strength to resist the applied loads.

## 10.4.3 Placement of Bolts in Joints

### 10.4.3.1 Spacing of Bolts in a Row
In a row of bolts aligned with direction of load, regardless of direction of grain, and measured from centres of bolts (see Figure 10.4.3)
(a) for parallel-to-grain loading: minimum spacings shall be four times the bolt diameter; and
(b) for perpendicular-to-grain loading: spacing between bolts in a row perpendicular to grain shall be limited by the spacing requirements of the attached member or members (whether of wood loaded parallel to grain or of metal), but shall be not less than three diameters.

### 10.4.3.2 Row Spacing

#### 10.4.3.2.1
For parallel-to-grain loading, the spacing between rows shall be not less than twice the bolt diameter.

#### 10.4.3.2.2
For perpendicular-to-grain loading, the spacing between rows shall be at least 2-1/2 times the bolt diameter for a member thickness-to-diameter ratio of 2, and five times the bolt diameter for member thickness-to-diameter ratios of 6 or more. For ratios between 2 and 6, the spacing shall be obtained by linear interpolation.

#### 10.4.3.2.3
A single steel splice plate shall not be used for rows of bolts when the distance between the two outer rows exceeds 125 mm.

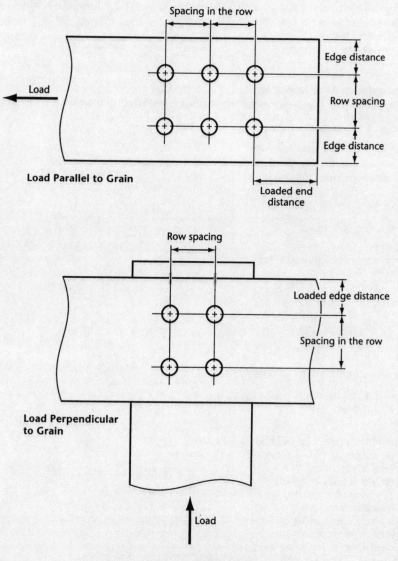

**Figure 10.4.3**
**Placement of Bolts in Joints**

### 10.4.3.3  End Distance

The end distance shall be at least
(a)  seven times the bolt diameter or 50 mm, whichever is greater, for the loaded end; or
(b)  four times the bolt diameter or 50 mm, whichever is the greater, for the unloaded end.

### 10.4.3.4  Edge Distance

For members loaded perpendicular to grain, the loaded edge distance shall be at least four times the
bolt diameter, and the unloaded edge distance shall be at least 1-1/2 times the bolt diameter.  For

members loaded parallel to grain, the edge distance shall be at least 1-1/2 times the bolt diameter, or half the distance between rows of bolts, whichever is greater.

## 10.4.4 Lateral Resistance

### 10.4.4.1

The factored lateral strength resistance of a bolted connection, $P_r$, $Q_r$, or $N_r$, varies directly with the number of shear planes and shall be greater than or equal to the effect of the factored loads:

(a) For parallel-to-grain loading

$$P_r = \phi \, P_u n_s n_F J_F$$

(b) For perpendicular-to-grain loading

$$Q_r = \phi Q_u n_s n_F J_R$$

(c) for loads at angle, $\theta$, to grain

$$N_r = \frac{P_r Q_r}{P_r \sin^2\theta + Q_r \cos^2\theta}$$

where
$\phi$ = 0.7
$P_u$ = $p_u(K_D K_{SF} K_T)$
$p_u$ = lateral strength resistance for parallel to grain loading (Clause 10.4.4.2), N
$n_s$ = number of shear planes
$J_F$ = $J_G J_L J_R$
$J_G$ = factor for two to maximum 12 bolts in a row

$$= 0.33\left(\frac{l}{d}\right)^{0.5}\left(\frac{s}{d}\right)^{0.2} N^{-0.3}, \text{ but is not greater than 1.0}$$

  where
  l   = member thickness (see Clause 10.4.2), mm
  s   = bolt spacing in the row, mm
  d   = bolt diameter, mm
  N   = number of bolts in a row
  **Note:** $J_G = 1.0$ *in cases with only one bolt per row, and in all wood-to-concrete connections.*
$J_L$ = factor for loaded end distance
    = 0.75 for end distance of 7d, or 1.0 for 10d (for intermediate values, interpolate linearly)
$J_R$ = factor for number of rows
    = 1.0 for 1 row, or for 1 bolt per row
    = 0.8 for 2 rows (2 or more bolts in a row)
    = 0.6 for 3 rows (2 or more bolts in a row)
$Q_u$ = $q_u(K_D K_{SF} K_T)$
$q_u$ = lateral strength resistance for perpendicular to grain loading (Clause 10.4.4.2), N

### 10.4.4.2

The unit lateral strength resistances, $p_u$ or $q_u$, (N per shear plane) shall be taken as the smallest value determined from formulae (a) to (g) as follows:
  For two-member connections, only formulae (a), (b), (d), (e), (f), and (g), are valid. For three-member connections, only formulae (a), (c), (d), and (g) are valid.

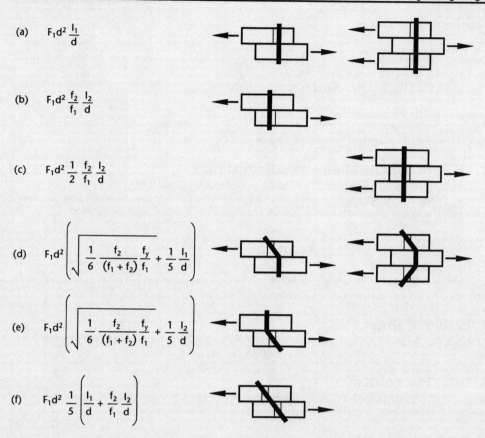

(a)    $F_1 d^2 \dfrac{l_1}{d}$

(b)    $F_1 d^2 \dfrac{f_2}{f_1} \dfrac{l_2}{d}$

(c)    $F_1 d^2 \dfrac{1}{2} \dfrac{f_2}{f_1} \dfrac{l_2}{d}$

(d)    $F_1 d^2 \left( \sqrt{\dfrac{1}{6} \dfrac{f_2}{(f_1 + f_2)} \dfrac{f_y}{f_1}} + \dfrac{1}{5} \dfrac{l_1}{d} \right)$

(e)    $F_1 d^2 \left( \sqrt{\dfrac{1}{6} \dfrac{f_2}{(f_1 + f_2)} \dfrac{f_y}{f_1}} + \dfrac{1}{5} \dfrac{l_2}{d} \right)$

(f)    $F_1 d^2 \dfrac{1}{5} \left( \dfrac{l_1}{d} + \dfrac{f_2}{f_1} \dfrac{l_2}{d} \right)$

(g)    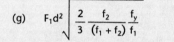 $F_1 d^2 \sqrt{\dfrac{2}{3} \dfrac{f_2}{(f_1 + f_2)} \dfrac{f_y}{f_1}}$

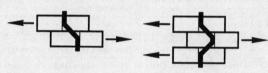

where
$F_1$ = $0.8 f_1$
d   = bolt diameter, mm
$l_1$   = side member thickness, mm
$f_2$   = embedding strength of main member, MPa
$l_2$   = main member thickness, mm
$f_1$   = embedding strength of side member, MPa
$f_y$   = bolt yield strength, MPa
    = 310 MPa for ASTM A 307 bolts

For wood member embedding strength:

f    = 63G (1–0.01d), for parallel-to-grain loading
     = 27.4G (1–0.01d), for perpendicular-to-grain loading
G   = mean relative density (Table A10.1)

For steel plate embedding strength:

f    $= 3.75 \times (\phi_{steel} / \phi_{wood}) \times F_u$
$\phi_{steel}$ = resistance factor for steel member in bolted connection
     = 0.67
$\phi_{wood}$ = resistance factor for wood member in bolted connection
     = 0.7
$F_u$   = ultimate tensile strength of steel
     = 400 MPa for ASTM A 36 steel
     = 450 MPa for G40.21M steel, grades 300W and 350W

## 10.4.5 Combined Lateral and Axial Resistance

Resistances are for loading acting perpendicular to the axis of a bolt. Connections shall also be of adequate size to resist the component parallel to the bolt axis. Washers or plates of adequate thickness and size to resist the factored load component parallel to the axis of the bolt shall be installed.

## 10.5 Drift Pins

### 10.5.1 General

Design requirements for drift pin joints are based on round mild steel bolt stock, 16–25 mm diameter, in accordance with ASTM Standard A 307 or CSA Standard G40.21.

### 10.5.2 Prebored Holes

Holes in timber shall be prebored not less than 0.8 mm nor more than 1 mm smaller than the drift pin diameter.

### 10.5.3 Drift Pin Points

The leading end of drift pins shall be chisel-pointed, conically tapered, hemispherical or otherwise shaped to permit driving into prebored holes with minimum damage to the wood.

### 10.5.4 Drift Pin Length

#### 10.5.4.1

Length of drift pins shall be equal to the sum of the depths of two superimposed members to be connected less 15 mm, and each drift pin shall be considered to give one shear plane. Figure 10.5.5 shows a typical drift pin connection in timber cribwork.

#### 10.5.4.2

Drift pin joints shall be used only where gravity or mechanical restraint prevents axial tension stress in the drift pins.

### 10.5.5 Size and Placement of Drift Pins in Joints

#### 10.5.5.1

Pin diameter shall not be greater than 1/10 of the width of the timbers to be connected.

#### 10.5.5.2

End and edge distance shall be at least 2-1/2 times the pin diameter.

#### 10.5.5.3

Spacing between pins in a row and between rows of pins shall be at least four times the pin diameter.

## 10.5.6 Lateral Resistance

The factored lateral strength of a drift pin connection, $P_r$, $Q_r$, or $N_r$, shall be greater than or equal to the effect of the factored loads:

(a) for parallel-to-grain loading

$$P_r = \phi(0.6P_u)n_F$$

(b) for perpendicular-to-grain loading

$$Q_r = \phi(0.6Q_u)n_F$$

(c) for loads at angle, θ, to grain

$$N_r = \frac{P_rQ_r}{P_r\sin^2\theta + Q_r\cos^2\theta}$$

where
$\phi$ = 0.7
$P_u$ = $p_u(K_DK_{SF}K_T)$
$p_u$ = lateral strength resistance for parallel-to-grain loading for bolts (Clause 10.4.4.2), N
$Q_u$ = $q_u(K_DK_{SF}K_T)$
$q_u$ = lateral strength resistance for perpendicular-to-grain loading for bolts (Clause 10.4.4.2), N

At any shear plane between two overlapping timbers, as shown in Figure 10.5.5, only two pins shall be counted as resisting the shear force.

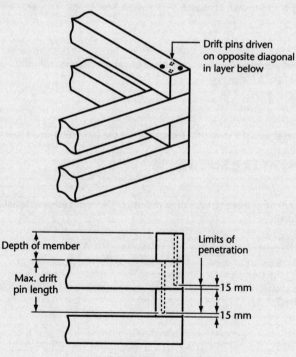

**Figure 10.5.5**
**Placement of Drift Pins**

## 10.6 Lag Screws

### 10.6.1 General

#### 10.6.1.1
Design requirements in Clause 10.6 for lag screw joints are based upon the use of lag screws of material conforming to the requirements of ANSI/ASME Standard B18.2.1.

#### 10.6.1.2
For purposes of specifying resistances of lag screw joints, values tabulated in this Standard shall apply to one lag screw either in withdrawal or in lateral resistance in a two-member joint.

### 10.6.2 Placement of Lag Screws in Joints

#### 10.6.2.1
Lag screw holes shall be in accordance with the following:
(a) the lead hole for the shank shall have the same diameter as the shank and the same depth as the length as the unthreaded shank; and
(b) the lead hole for the threaded portion shall have a diameter equal to 65–85% of the shank diameter for dense hardwoods, 60–75% of the shank diameter for Douglas Fir-Larch species, and 40–70% of the shank diameter for less dense species. The larger percentage figure in each range shall apply to screws of the greater diameters. The length of the lead hole shall be at least equal to the length of the threaded portion.

#### 10.6.2.2
The threaded portion of the screw shall be inserted in its lead hole by turning with a wrench, not by driving.

#### 10.6.2.3
Soap or other lubricant, not petroleum based, may be used on the screws or in the lead hole to facilitate insertion and prevent damage to the screw.

#### 10.6.2.4
The spacings, end distances, edge distances, and net section for lag screw joints shall be the same as for joints with bolts of a diameter equal to the shank diameter of the lag screw used (see Clause 10.4.2).

### 10.6.3 Penetration of Lag Screws

#### 10.6.3.1
In determining the penetration of a lag screw into a member, the reduced point shall not be considered a part of the threaded portion.

#### 10.6.3.2
The maximum lengths of penetration used in determination of lateral resistance are
(a) for Douglas Fir-Larch, nine times shank diameter;
(b) for Hem-Fir, 10 times shank diameter; and
(c) for S-P-F and Northern Species, 11 times shank diameter.

#### 10.6.3.3
For lag screws loaded laterally, the minimum length of penetration into the main member ($l_2$ in Clause 10.6.6.1.2) shall be no less than five times the shank diameter, d.

## 10.6.4 Side Members

### 10.6.4.1 Wood Side Plates
Thickness of wood side plates shall be at least twice the shank diameter of the lag screw.

### 10.6.4.2 Steel Side Plates
The stresses induced in the steel side plate and at the bearing of the lag screw on the plate shall not exceed the resistance of the steel used.

## 10.6.5 Withdrawal Resistance
The factored withdrawal resistance, $P_{rw}$ of a group of lag screws in a connection shall be greater than or equal to the effect of the factored loads:

$$P_{rw} = \phi Y_w L_t n_F J_E$$

where
$\phi$ = 0.6
$Y_w$ = $y_w(K_D K_{SF} K_T)$
$y_w$ = basic withdrawal resistance per millimetre of penetration (Table 10.6.5.1), N/mm
$L_t$ = length of penetration of threaded portion of lag screw in main member (Clause 10.6.3), mm
$J_E$ = end grain factor for lag screws
   = 0.75 in end grain, or
   = 1.00 for all other cases
**Note:** *Use of lag screws in end grain should be avoided whenever possible.*

### Table 10.6.5.1
### Basic Withdrawal Resistance for Lag Screws, $y_w$ (N/mm)

| Species group | Shank diameter, in | | | | | | | | |
|---|---|---|---|---|---|---|---|---|---|
| | 1/4 | 5/16 | 3/8 | 7/16 | 1/2 | 5/8 | 3/4 | 7/8 | 1 |
| Douglas Fir-Larch | 74 | 97 | 120 | 140 | 170 | 200 | 240 | 280 | 310 |
| Hem-Fir | 37 | 55 | 70 | 86 | 100 | 130 | 150 | 180 | 200 |
| S-P-F | 31 | 42 | 61 | 75 | 91 | 120 | 140 | 170 | 190 |
| Northern Species | 27 | 42 | 58 | 70 | 84 | 110 | 130 | 150 | 180 |

## 10.6.6 Lateral Resistance

### 10.6.6.1 Side Grain

#### 10.6.6.1.1
The factored lateral strength resistance of a lag screw connection, $P_r$, $Q_r$, or $N_r$, shall be greater than or equal to the effect of the factored loads:
(a) For parallel-to-grain loading

$$P_r = \phi P_u n_F J_c J_{PL}$$

(b) For perpendicular-to-grain loading

$$Q_r = \phi Q_u n_F J_c J_{PL}$$

(c) For loads at angle, θ, to grain

$$N_r = \frac{P_r Q_r}{P_r \sin^2\theta + Q_r \cos^2\theta}$$

where
$\phi$ = 0.6
$P_u$ = $p_u(K_D K_{SF} K_T)$
$p_u$ = lateral strength resistance for parallel-to-grain loading, N (Clause 10.6.6.1.2)
$J_G$ = factor for groups of fastenings (Tables 10.2.2.3.4A and 10.2.2.3.4B)
$J_{PL}$ = factor for reduced penetration
    = 0.625 for penetration of 5d and 1.0 for 8d (for intermediate values, interpolate linearly)
$Q_u$ = $q_u(K_D K_{SF} K_T)$
$q_u$ = lateral strength resistance for perpendicular-to-grain loading, N (Clause 10.6.6.1.2)

## 10.6.6.1.2

The unit lateral strength resistances, $p_u$ or $q_u$, shall be taken as the smallest value determined from formulae (a) to (f) as follows:

(a) $F_1 d^2 \dfrac{l_1}{d}$

(b) $F_1 d^2 \dfrac{f_2}{f_1} \dfrac{l_2}{d}$

(c) $F_1 d^2 \left( \sqrt{\dfrac{1}{6} \dfrac{f_2}{(f_1 + f_2)} \dfrac{f_y}{f_1} + \dfrac{1}{5} \dfrac{l_1}{d}} \right)$

(d) $F_1 d^2 \left( \sqrt{\dfrac{1}{6} \dfrac{f_2}{(f_1 + f_2)} \dfrac{f_y}{f_1} + \dfrac{1}{5} \dfrac{l_2}{d}} \right)$

(e) $F_1 d^2 \dfrac{1}{5} \left( \dfrac{l_1}{d} + \dfrac{f_2}{f_1} \dfrac{l_2}{d} \right)$

(f) $F_1 d^2 \sqrt{\dfrac{2}{3} \dfrac{f_2}{(f_1 + f_2)} \dfrac{f_y}{f_1}}$

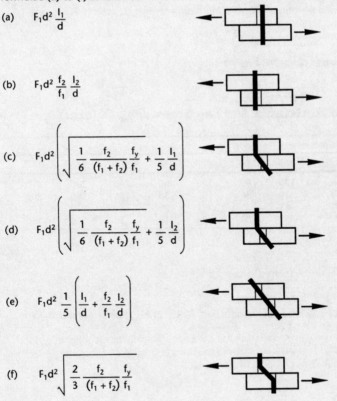

where
$F_1$ = $0.8f_1$
d = lag screw diameter, mm

$f_2$ = embedding strength of main member, MPa
= 63G(1–0.01d) for parallel-to-grain loading
= 27.4G(1–0.01d) for perpendicular-to-grain loading
G = mean relative density (Table A10.1)
$l_2$ = length of penetration into main member, mm (Clause 10.6.3)
$f_y$ = lag screw yield strength, MPa
= 480 MPa for 1/4 in diameter lag screws
= 410 MPa for 5/16 in diameter lag screws
= 310 MPa for 3/8 in or greater diameter lag screws

For wood side plates:

$f_1$ = embedding strength of side member, MPa
= 63G(1–0.01d) for parallel-to-grain loading
= 27.4G(1–0.01d) for perpendicular-to-grain loading
$l_1$ = side member thickness, mm (Clause 10.6.4.1)

For steel side plates:

$f_1$   = embedding strength of steel side plate, MPa
= 3.75 × ($\phi_{steel}$ / $\phi_{wood}$) × $F_u$
$\phi_{steel}$ = resistance factor for steel member in lag screw connection
= 0.67
$\phi_{wood}$ = resistance factor for wood member in lag screw connection
= 0.60
$F_u$   = ultimate tensile strength of steel
= 400 MPa for ASTM A 36 steel
= 450 MPa for CSA-G40.21M steel, grades 300W and 350W
$l_1$   = side plate thickness, mm

## 10.6.6.2 End Grain
Lateral resistance of lag screws inserted parallel to grain in the end grain of the main member shall be no greater than 2/3 of the lateral side grain resistance for perpendicular to grain if wood side plates are used. If steel side plates are used, lateral resistance shall be no greater than 1/2 of the lateral side grain resistance for perpendicular-to-grain loading in the main member.

## 10.6.6.3 Joint Deformation
Where the lateral deformation of lag screw joints is required for design, joint deformation may be estimated in accordance with Clause A10.6.6.3.

## 10.7 Timber Rivets (also known as Glulam Rivets)

### 10.7.1 General

### 10.7.1.1
Design methods and tabulated resistances given in Clause 10.7 are for timber rivets manufactured to have the properties shown below and used with steel side plates conforming to CSA Standard G40.21 or ASTM Standard A 36, and whose dimensions conform to Figure 10.7.1.1.

**Hardness**
Rockwell C32-39

**Ultimate tensile strength**
1000 MPa, minimum

**Finish**
Hot-dip galvanized

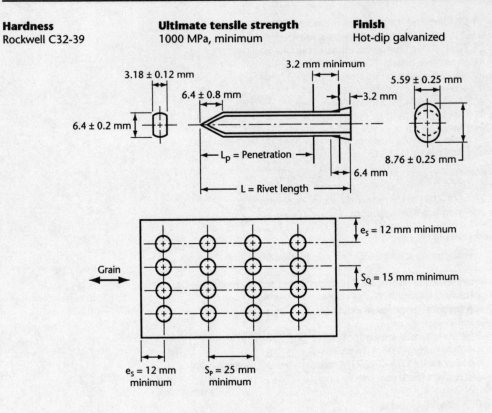

**Notes:**
**(1)** *Hole diameter: 6.7 mm minimum to 7.0 mm maximum.*
**(2)** *Tolerance in location of holes: 3 mm maximum in any direction.*
**(3)** *Orient wide face of rivets parallel to grain, regardless of plate orientation.*
**(4)** *All dimensions are prior to galvanizing, in millimetres.*

## Figure 10.7.1.1
## Steel Side Plates for Timber Rivets

### 10.7.1.2
For wet service conditions, side plates shall be hot-dip galvanized.

### 10.7.1.3
Design criteria for timber rivet joints apply to timber rivets that satisfy the requirements of
Clause 10.7.1.1 loaded in single shear or in withdrawal, with steel side plates, on Douglas Fir-Larch or
Spruce-Lodgepole Pine-Jack Pine glued-laminated timber manufactured in accordance with CSA
Standard CAN/CSA-O122, or on sawn lumber of 64 mm minimum thickness.

### 10.7.1.4
Side plates shall be of adequate cross-section to resist tension and compression forces, as well as buckling
at critical sections, but shall be not less than 3.2 mm in thickness.

## 10.7.1.5

Each rivet shall, in all cases, be placed with its major cross-sectional dimension aligned parallel to the grain. Design criteria are based on rivets driven through circular holes in the side plates until the conical heads are firmly seated, but rivets shall not be driven flush.

**Note:** *Timber rivets at the perimeter of the group should be driven first. Successive timber rivets should be driven in a spiral pattern from the outside to the centre of the group.*

## 10.7.1.6

Minimum spacing of rivets shall be 15 mm perpendicular to the grain and 25 mm parallel to the grain.

## 10.7.1.7

Minimum values for end and edge distance, as shown and noted in Figure 10.7.1.7, are listed in Table 10.7.1.7.

## 10.7.1.8

The maximum penetration of any rivet shall be 70% of the thickness of the wood member, whether driven on two faces or one face only. Except as permitted by Clause 10.7.1.9 for joints with rivets driven from opposite faces of a wood member, the rivet length shall be such that the points do not overlap.

**Table 10.7.1.7**
**Minimum End and Edge Distances for Timber Rivet Joints**

| Number of rivet rows, $n_R$ | Minimum end distance, a, mm | | Minimum edge distance, e, mm | |
|---|---|---|---|---|
| | Load parallel to grain | Load perpendicular to grain | Free edge, $e_P$ | Loaded edge, $e_Q$ |
| 1, 2 | 75 | 50 | 25 | 50 |
| 3–8 | 75 | 75 | 25 | 50 |
| 9, 10 | 100 | 80 | 25 | 50 |
| 11, 12 | 125 | 100 | 25 | 50 |
| 13, 14 | 150 | 120 | 25 | 50 |
| 15, 16 | 175 | 140 | 25 | 50 |
| 17 and greater | 200 | 160 | 25 | 50 |

**Note:** *End and edge distances are shown in Figure 10.7.1.7.*

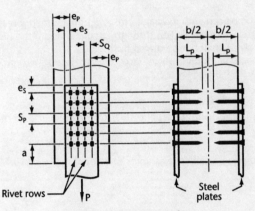

**Load parallel to grain**

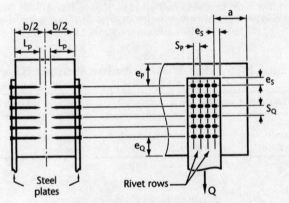

**Load perpendicular to grain**

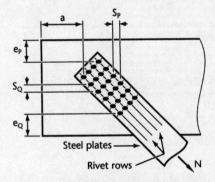

**Load at angle to grain**

**Figure 10.7.1.7**
**End and Edge Distances for Timber Rivet Joints**

## 10.7.1.9

For joints where rivets are driven from opposite faces of a wood member such that their points overlap, the minimum spacing requirements of Clause 10.7.1.6 shall apply to the distance between the rivets at their points. The total lateral resistance of the connection shall be calculated in accordance with Clause 10.7.2, considering the connection to be a one-sided timber rivet joint, with

(a) the number of rivets associated with the one plate equalling the total number of rivets at the joint; and

(b) $S_p$ and $S_Q$ determined as the distances between the rivets at their points.

## 10.7.1.10

For wet fabrication conditions in sawn lumber, the maximum dimension perpendicular to grain over which a rivet group spans shall not exceed 200 mm.

## 10.7.2 Lateral Resistance

### 10.7.2.1

A timber rivet joint (one plate and the rivets associated with it) in side grain shall be designed such that the factored lateral strength resistance of the joint is greater than or equal to the effect of the factored loads. Design of timber rivets loaded laterally is governed by either the ductile failure of the rivet or the brittle failure of the wood.

### 10.7.2.2

For loading parallel to grain, the factored lateral strength resistance, $P_r$, of the joint shall be

$$P_r = \phi P_u H$$

where
$\phi$ = 0.6
$P_u$ = lateral resistance parallel to grain (Clause 10.7.2.3), kN
$H$ = material factor
   = 1.00 for Douglas Fir-Larch glulam
   = 0.80 for Spruce-Lodgepole Pine-Jack Pine glulam
   = 0.50 for Douglas Fir-Larch sawn timber
   = 0.45 for Hem-Fir sawn timber
   = 0.40 for Spruce-Pine-Fir sawn timber
   = 0.35 for Northern Species sawn timber

### 10.7.2.3

The unit capacity per rivet joint parallel to grain, $P_u$, shall be calculated as the lesser of $P_y$ or $P_w$, as follows:
(a) $P_y = (1.09 L_p^{0.32} n_R n_C) J_Y K_{SF} K_T$ for rivet capacity

and

(b) $P_w = p_w K_D K_{SF} K_T$ for wood capacity

where
$L_p$ = length of penetration ( = overall rivet length – plate thickness – 3.2), mm (Figure 10.7.1.1)
$n_R$ = number of rows of rivets parallel to direction of load
$n_C$ = number of rivets per row
$J_Y$ = side plate factor
   = 1.00 for side plate thickness of 6.3 mm and more
   = 0.90 for side plate thickness between 4.7 and 6.3 mm
   = 0.80 for side plate thickness between 3.2 and 4.7 mm

$p_w$ = lateral resistance parallel to grain (Table 10.7.2.3), kN, using wood member
thickness for the member dimension in Table 10.7.2.3 for connections with
steel plates on opposite sides, and using twice the wood member thickness for the
member dimension in Table 10.7.2.3 for connections having only one plate
**Note:** *As an alternative, $p_w$ may be calculated in accordance with Clause A10.7.2.3.*

### 10.7.2.4
For loading perpendicular to grain, the factored lateral strength resistance, $Q_r$, of the joint shall be

$$Q_r = \phi Q_u H$$

where
$\phi$ = 0.6
$Q_u$ = lateral resistance perpendicular to grain (Clause 10.7.2.5), kN
$H$ = material factor (Clause 10.7.2.2)

### 10.7.2.5
The unit capacity per rivet joint perpendicular to grain, $Q_u$, shall be calculated as the lesser of $Q_y$ or $Q_w$, as follows:
(a) $Q_y = (0.62 L_p^{0.32} n_R n_C) J_Y K_{SF} K_T$ for rivet capacity

and

(b) $Q_w = (q_w L_p^{0.8} C_t) K_D K_{SF} K_T$ for wood capacity

where
$L_p, n_R, n_C, J_Y$ = variables specified in Clause 10.7.2.3
$q_w$ = value determined from Table 10.7.2.5A, kN
$C_t$ = factor determined from Table 10.7.2.5B
**Note:** *As an alternative, $q_w$ and $C_t$ may be calculated in accordance with Clause A10.7.2.3.*

### 10.7.2.6
For loading at an angle to the grain, $\theta$, the factored lateral resistance of the joint, $N_r$, shall be calculated
from
$$N_r = \frac{P_r Q_r}{P_r \sin^2\theta + Q_r \cos^2\theta}$$

where
$P_r$ = value determined in accordance with Clause 10.7.2.2
$Q_r$ = value determined in accordance with Clause 10.7.2.4

### 10.7.2.7
When timber rivets are used in end grain, the factored lateral resistance of the joint shall be 50% of that
for loading perpendicular to grain. When used in intermediate grain, the factored lateral resistance may
be increased linearly from the value calculated for end grain, up to 100% of the applicable parallel or
perpendicular to side grain value.

## 10.7.3 Withdrawal Resistance

### 10.7.3.1
The use of timber rivets loaded in withdrawal shall be permitted only for dry service conditions for short-
term and standard-term load durations.

**130**

## 10.7.3.2

The factored withdrawal resistance from the side grain, $P_{rw}$, of a timber rivet joint shall be greater than or equal to the effect of the factored loads

$$P_{rw} = \phi Y_w L_p n_R n_C$$

where

$\phi$       = 0.6

$Y_w$      = $y_w (K_{SF} K_T)$

$y_w$      = withdrawal resistance per millimetre of penetration, N/mm

        = 13 N/mm for glulam

        = 7 N/mm for sawn timber

$L_p, n_R, n_C$ = variables specified in Clause 10.7.2.3

# Table 10.7.2.3
## Values of $p_w$ (kN), Parallel to Grain for Timber Rivet Joints
### 40 mm rivets. Spacing: $S_p = 25$ mm; $S_Q = 25$ mm

| Member dimension,* mm | Rivets per row, $n_C$ | Number of rows, $n_R$ | | | | | | | | | |
|---|---|---|---|---|---|---|---|---|---|---|---|
| | | 2 | 4 | 6 | 8 | 10 | 2 | 14 | 16 | 18 | 20 |
| | 2 | 24 | 56 | 88 | 125 | 160 | 195 | 225 | 260 | 290 | 330 |
| | 4 | 35 | 74 | 110 | 155 | 200 | 240 | 270 | 310 | 350 | 390 |
| | 6 | 46 | 92 | 135 | 185 | 240 | 280 | 320 | 360 | 410 | 460 |
| | 8 | 58 | 108 | 160 | 215 | 270 | 320 | 370 | 410 | 460 | 520 |
| 80 | 10 | 68 | 125 | 180 | 245 | 310 | 370 | 410 | 460 | 510 | 580 |
| | 12 | 76 | 140 | 205 | 270 | 340 | 400 | 450 | 510 | 570 | 640 |
| | 14 | 84 | 155 | 220 | 300 | 370 | 440 | 490 | 560 | 630 | 710 |
| | 16 | 88 | 170 | 245 | 320 | 410 | 480 | 530 | 600 | 680 | 770 |
| | 18 | 98 | 185 | 270 | 350 | 430 | 510 | 570 | 640 | 730 | 810 |
| | 20 | 104 | 205 | 280 | 370 | 460 | 540 | 600 | 680 | 770 | 850 |
| | 2 | 31 | 62 | 72 | 88 | 112 | 130 | 150 | 180 | 235 | 290 |
| | 4 | 44 | 80 | 92 | 108 | 135 | 160 | 180 | 215 | 260 | 310 |
| | 6 | 60 | 98 | 112 | 130 | 165 | 190 | 215 | 250 | 310 | 360 |
| | 8 | 76 | 116 | 130 | 150 | 190 | 215 | 245 | 280 | 340 | 390 |
| 130 | 10 | 88 | 135 | 150 | 175 | 215 | 245 | 270 | 310 | 370 | 440 |
| | 12 | 100 | 150 | 170 | 195 | 240 | 270 | 300 | 350 | 410 | 480 |
| | 14 | 108 | 170 | 185 | 215 | 260 | 300 | 330 | 380 | 450 | 520 |
| | 16 | 114 | 185 | 205 | 235 | 290 | 330 | 360 | 410 | 500 | 580 |
| | 18 | 125 | 200 | 225 | 250 | 310 | 350 | 390 | 450 | 540 | 610 |
| | 20 | 135 | 220 | 240 | 270 | 330 | 380 | 420 | 490 | 590 | 660 |
| | 2 | 34 | 58 | 66 | 80 | 104 | 120 | 140 | 170 | 215 | 270 |
| | 4 | 50 | 74 | 84 | 100 | 125 | 150 | 170 | 200 | 245 | 290 |
| | 6 | 66 | 90 | 102 | 120 | 150 | 175 | 200 | 235 | 280 | 330 |
| | 8 | 84 | 108 | 120 | 140 | 175 | 200 | 225 | 260 | 310 | 360 |
| 175 | 10 | 98 | 125 | 140 | 160 | 200 | 225 | 250 | 290 | 350 | 410 |
| | 12 | 110 | 140 | 155 | 180 | 220 | 250 | 280 | 330 | 390 | 450 |
| | 14 | 120 | 155 | 175 | 200 | 245 | 280 | 310 | 360 | 420 | 490 |
| | 16 | 125 | 170 | 190 | 215 | 270 | 300 | 330 | 390 | 460 | 540 |
| | 18 | 140 | 185 | 205 | 235 | 290 | 330 | 360 | 420 | 510 | 570 |
| | 20 | 150 | 205 | 225 | 250 | 310 | 350 | 390 | 460 | 550 | 620 |
| | 2 | 34 | 56 | 66 | 80 | 102 | 118 | 135 | 165 | 215 | 270 |
| | 4 | 50 | 72 | 84 | 98 | 125 | 145 | 165 | 195 | 240 | 290 |
| | 6 | 66 | 90 | 100 | 118 | 150 | 170 | 195 | 230 | 280 | 320 |
| | 8 | 84 | 106 | 118 | 140 | 170 | 195 | 225 | 260 | 310 | 350 |
| 215 and greater | 10 | 98 | 120 | 135 | 155 | 195 | 225 | 250 | 290 | 340 | 400 |
| | 12 | 110 | 135 | 155 | 175 | 215 | 250 | 270 | 320 | 380 | 440 |
| | 14 | 120 | 155 | 170 | 195 | 240 | 270 | 300 | 350 | 410 | 480 |
| | 16 | 125 | 170 | 185 | 210 | 260 | 300 | 330 | 380 | 460 | 530 |
| | 18 | 140 | 185 | 200 | 230 | 280 | 320 | 360 | 410 | 500 | 560 |
| | 20 | 150 | 200 | 220 | 245 | 300 | 350 | 390 | 450 | 540 | 610 |

(See notes at end of Table.)                                    (Continued)

## Table 10.7.2.3 (Continued)

## 40 mm rivets.  Spacing: $S_p$ = 40 mm; $S_Q$ = 25 mm

| Member dimension,* mm | Rivets per row, $n_C$ | Number of rows, $n_R$ | | | | | | | | | |
|---|---|---|---|---|---|---|---|---|---|---|---|
| | | 2 | 4 | 6 | 8 | 10 | 12 | 14 | 16 | 18 | 20 |
| 80 | 2 | 27 | 64 | 100 | 140 | 185 | 225 | 260 | 300 | 340 | 380 |
| | 4 | 40 | 86 | 125 | 175 | 225 | 280 | 320 | 360 | 400 | 450 |
| | 6 | 52 | 106 | 155 | 215 | 270 | 330 | 370 | 410 | 470 | 530 |
| | 8 | 66 | 125 | 185 | 245 | 310 | 370 | 430 | 470 | 520 | 590 |
| | 10 | 76 | 145 | 210 | 280 | 350 | 420 | 480 | 530 | 590 | 660 |
| | 12 | 86 | 160 | 235 | 310 | 390 | 460 | 530 | 590 | 650 | 730 |
| | 14 | 94 | 180 | 250 | 340 | 420 | 510 | 580 | 640 | 720 | 810 |
| | 16 | 100 | 195 | 280 | 370 | 460 | 550 | 620 | 700 | 780 | 880 |
| | 18 | 110 | 215 | 310 | 400 | 490 | 590 | 670 | 740 | 830 | 930 |
| | 20 | 118 | 235 | 330 | 420 | 520 | 620 | 710 | 790 | 870 | 970 |
| 130 | 2 | 35 | 66 | 82 | 106 | 145 | 180 | 225 | 290 | 390 | 490 |
| | 4 | 50 | 94 | 118 | 150 | 205 | 250 | 310 | 380 | 500 | 590 |
| | 6 | 68 | 120 | 150 | 185 | 250 | 310 | 380 | 470 | 610 | 690 |
| | 8 | 86 | 150 | 180 | 225 | 300 | 370 | 450 | 540 | 680 | 770 |
| | 10 | 100 | 175 | 210 | 260 | 350 | 420 | 510 | 610 | 760 | 860 |
| | 12 | 112 | 200 | 240 | 290 | 390 | 480 | 560 | 690 | 840 | 950 |
| | 14 | 125 | 225 | 270 | 320 | 430 | 530 | 620 | 760 | 930 | 1050 |
| | 16 | 130 | 250 | 300 | 360 | 480 | 580 | 680 | 830 | 1010 | 1140 |
| | 18 | 145 | 270 | 320 | 390 | 520 | 630 | 750 | 910 | 1090 | 1210 |
| | 20 | 150 | 290 | 350 | 420 | 560 | 680 | 810 | 990 | 1140 | 1270 |
| 175 | 2 | 39 | 60 | 76 | 98 | 135 | 170 | 205 | 260 | 360 | 480 |
| | 4 | 56 | 88 | 110 | 135 | 190 | 235 | 280 | 350 | 470 | 590 |
| | 6 | 76 | 114 | 140 | 175 | 235 | 290 | 350 | 440 | 570 | 710 |
| | 8 | 96 | 140 | 170 | 205 | 280 | 340 | 410 | 500 | 650 | 790 |
| | 10 | 110 | 160 | 195 | 240 | 320 | 390 | 470 | 570 | 730 | 910 |
| | 12 | 125 | 185 | 225 | 270 | 360 | 440 | 520 | 640 | 810 | 1010 |
| | 14 | 135 | 210 | 250 | 300 | 400 | 490 | 580 | 710 | 900 | 1110 |
| | 16 | 145 | 230 | 280 | 330 | 440 | 540 | 630 | 770 | 990 | 1230 |
| | 18 | 160 | 250 | 300 | 360 | 480 | 580 | 700 | 850 | 1090 | 1310 |
| | 20 | 170 | 270 | 330 | 390 | 520 | 630 | 760 | 920 | 1190 | 1400 |
| 215 and greater | 2 | 39 | 60 | 74 | 96 | 130 | 165 | 205 | 260 | 360 | 480 |
| | 4 | 56 | 86 | 108 | 135 | 185 | 230 | 280 | 350 | 460 | 580 |
| | 6 | 76 | 112 | 135 | 170 | 235 | 290 | 350 | 430 | 560 | 700 |
| | 8 | 96 | 135 | 165 | 205 | 280 | 340 | 410 | 500 | 640 | 780 |
| | 10 | 110 | 160 | 190 | 235 | 320 | 380 | 470 | 560 | 710 | 890 |
| | 12 | 125 | 180 | 220 | 260 | 360 | 440 | 510 | 630 | 800 | 1000 |
| | 14 | 135 | 205 | 245 | 300 | 400 | 480 | 570 | 700 | 880 | 1090 |
| | 16 | 145 | 225 | 270 | 320 | 430 | 530 | 620 | 760 | 980 | 1210 |
| | 18 | 160 | 250 | 290 | 360 | 470 | 570 | 680 | 830 | 1080 | 1290 |
| | 20 | 170 | 270 | 320 | 380 | 510 | 620 | 740 | 910 | 1170 | 1410 |

*(See notes at end of Table.)*

*(Continued)*

## Table 10.7.2.3 (Continued)

## 40 mm rivets.  Spacing:  $S_p$ = 25 mm; $S_Q$ = 15 mm

| Member dimension,* mm | Rivets per row, $n_C$ | Number of rows, $n_R$ | | | | |
|---|---|---|---|---|---|---|
| | | 2 | 4 | 6 | 8 | 10 |
| 80 | 2 | 21 | 34 | 48 | 68 | 92 |
| | 4 | 31 | 44 | 60 | 86 | 114 |
| | 6 | 39 | 54 | 74 | 104 | 140 |
| | 8 | 46 | 64 | 88 | 120 | 160 |
| | 10 | 54 | 74 | 102 | 140 | 180 |
| | 12 | 62 | 84 | 116 | 155 | 205 |
| | 14 | 70 | 94 | 130 | 170 | 225 |
| | 16 | 78 | 104 | 140 | 190 | 245 |
| | 18 | 86 | 114 | 155 | 205 | 260 |
| | 20 | 92 | 125 | 165 | 220 | 290 |
| 130 | 2 | 24 | 34 | 46 | 66 | 86 |
| | 4 | 31 | 42 | 60 | 82 | 106 |
| | 6 | 39 | 54 | 74 | 98 | 130 |
| | 8 | 46 | 64 | 88 | 116 | 150 |
| | 10 | 54 | 74 | 100 | 130 | 170 |
| | 12 | 62 | 84 | 114 | 145 | 186 |
| | 14 | 70 | 94 | 125 | 165 | 205 |
| | 16 | 78 | 104 | 140 | 180 | 225 |
| | 18 | 86 | 114 | 150 | 195 | 245 |
| | 20 | 94 | 125 | 165 | 210 | 260 |
| 175 and greater | 2 | 24 | 34 | 46 | 64 | 84 |
| | 4 | 31 | 42 | 60 | 80 | 104 |
| | 6 | 39 | 54 | 74 | 96 | 125 |
| | 8 | 46 | 64 | 86 | 114 | 145 |
| | 10 | 54 | 74 | 100 | 130 | 165 |
| | 12 | 62 | 84 | 112 | 145 | 180 |
| | 14 | 70 | 94 | 125 | 160 | 200 |
| | 16 | 78 | 104 | 140 | 175 | 220 |
| | 18 | 86 | 114 | 150 | 190 | 235 |
| | 20 | 94 | 125 | 160 | 205 | 250 |

*(See notes at end of Table.)*                                                        *(Continued)*

## Table 10.7.2.3 (Continued)
### 65 mm rivets.  Spacing:  $S_p$ = 25 mm; $S_Q$ = 25 mm

| Member dimension,* mm | Rivets per row, $n_C$ | Number of rows, $n_R$ | | | | | | | | | |
|---|---|---|---|---|---|---|---|---|---|---|---|
| | | 2 | 4 | 6 | 8 | 10 | 12 | 14 | 16 | 18 | 20 |
| 130 | 2 | 27 | 64 | 98 | 140 | 180 | 220 | 250 | 290 | 330 | 370 |
| | 4 | 39 | 84 | 125 | 175 | 225 | 270 | 310 | 350 | 390 | 440 |
| | 6 | 52 | 104 | 150 | 210 | 270 | 320 | 360 | 410 | 460 | 520 |
| | 8 | 66 | 120 | 180 | 245 | 310 | 360 | 410 | 460 | 520 | 580 |
| | 10 | 76 | 140 | 205 | 280 | 350 | 410 | 460 | 520 | 580 | 650 |
| | 12 | 86 | 155 | 230 | 310 | 390 | 450 | 510 | 570 | 640 | 720 |
| | 14 | 94 | 175 | 250 | 340 | 420 | 500 | 560 | 630 | 710 | 800 |
| | 16 | 98 | 195 | 280 | 360 | 460 | 540 | 600 | 680 | 770 | 860 |
| | 18 | 110 | 210 | 300 | 390 | 490 | 570 | 650 | 720 | 820 | 920 |
| | 20 | 116 | 230 | 320 | 420 | 520 | 610 | 680 | 770 | 860 | 960 |
| 175 | 2 | 31 | 74 | 114 | 160 | 210 | 250 | 300 | 340 | 380 | 430 |
| | 4 | 44 | 96 | 145 | 200 | 260 | 310 | 350 | 400 | 460 | 520 |
| | 6 | 60 | 120 | 175 | 240 | 300 | 340 | 390 | 440 | 530 | 600 |
| | 8 | 76 | 140 | 210 | 270 | 330 | 370 | 420 | 480 | 560 | 640 |
| | 10 | 88 | 165 | 240 | 300 | 360 | 410 | 450 | 510 | 600 | 690 |
| | 12 | 100 | 180 | 270 | 320 | 390 | 440 | 480 | 550 | 640 | 740 |
| | 14 | 110 | 205 | 290 | 350 | 420 | 470 | 510 | 590 | 680 | 780 |
| | 16 | 114 | 225 | 320 | 370 | 450 | 500 | 540 | 620 | 730 | 840 |
| | 18 | 125 | 245 | 350 | 400 | 470 | 530 | 580 | 660 | 790 | 870 |
| | 20 | 135 | 270 | 370 | 420 | 500 | 560 | 610 | 700 | 830 | 930 |
| 215 | 2 | 35 | 82 | 125 | 160 | 205 | 235 | 270 | 320 | 410 | 490 |
| | 4 | 50 | 108 | 150 | 180 | 220 | 260 | 290 | 330 | 410 | 480 |
| | 6 | 68 | 135 | 170 | 200 | 250 | 280 | 320 | 370 | 440 | 510 |
| | 8 | 86 | 160 | 195 | 225 | 280 | 310 | 350 | 390 | 470 | 530 |
| | 10 | 100 | 185 | 215 | 245 | 300 | 340 | 370 | 420 | 500 | 580 |
| | 12 | 112 | 205 | 240 | 270 | 320 | 370 | 400 | 460 | 540 | 620 |
| | 14 | 120 | 225 | 260 | 290 | 350 | 390 | 430 | 490 | 570 | 650 |
| | 16 | 130 | 245 | 280 | 310 | 370 | 420 | 450 | 520 | 610 | 710 |
| | 18 | 145 | 270 | 290 | 330 | 390 | 440 | 480 | 550 | 660 | 730 |
| | 20 | 150 | 280 | 310 | 350 | 420 | 470 | 510 | 590 | 700 | 780 |
| 265 | 2 | 39 | 90 | 118 | 145 | 185 | 215 | 245 | 290 | 370 | 460 |
| | 4 | 56 | 112 | 135 | 160 | 200 | 235 | 260 | 300 | 370 | 440 |
| | 6 | 76 | 135 | 160 | 185 | 225 | 260 | 290 | 340 | 400 | 470 |
| | 8 | 96 | 155 | 180 | 205 | 250 | 280 | 310 | 360 | 430 | 480 |
| | 10 | 110 | 175 | 200 | 225 | 270 | 310 | 340 | 390 | 460 | 530 |
| | 12 | 125 | 195 | 215 | 245 | 300 | 330 | 360 | 420 | 490 | 570 |
| | 14 | 135 | 215 | 235 | 260 | 320 | 360 | 390 | 450 | 520 | 600 |
| | 16 | 145 | 230 | 250 | 280 | 340 | 380 | 410 | 470 | 560 | 650 |
| | 18 | 160 | 250 | 270 | 300 | 360 | 400 | 440 | 510 | 600 | 670 |
| | 20 | 170 | 260 | 290 | 320 | 380 | 430 | 470 | 540 | 640 | 720 |
| 315 and greater | 2 | 40 | 88 | 114 | 140 | 180 | 205 | 235 | 280 | 360 | 450 |
| | 4 | 60 | 110 | 130 | 155 | 195 | 225 | 250 | 290 | 360 | 420 |
| | 6 | 80 | 130 | 155 | 175 | 215 | 245 | 280 | 320 | 380 | 440 |
| | 8 | 100 | 150 | 170 | 195 | 240 | 270 | 300 | 340 | 410 | 460 |
| | 10 | 116 | 170 | 190 | 215 | 260 | 290 | 320 | 370 | 430 | 500 |
| | 12 | 130 | 185 | 205 | 230 | 280 | 320 | 350 | 400 | 470 | 540 |
| | 14 | 145 | 205 | 225 | 250 | 300 | 340 | 370 | 430 | 500 | 570 |
| | 16 | 150 | 220 | 240 | 270 | 320 | 360 | 390 | 450 | 540 | 620 |
| | 18 | 170 | 240 | 260 | 290 | 340 | 380 | 420 | 480 | 580 | 640 |
| | 20 | 175 | 250 | 270 | 300 | 360 | 410 | 450 | 520 | 620 | 690 |

*(See notes at end of Table.)*        *(Continued)*

## Table 10.7.2.3 (Continued)
## 65 mm rivets. Spacing: $S_p = 40$ mm; $S_Q = 25$ mm

| Member dimension,* mm | Rivets per row, $n_C$ | Number of rows, $n_R$ | | | | | | | | | |
|---|---|---|---|---|---|---|---|---|---|---|---|
| | | 2 | 4 | 6 | 8 | 10 | 12 | 14 | 16 | 18 | 20 |
| 130 | 2 | 31 | 72 | 114 | 160 | 205 | 250 | 300 | 340 | 380 | 430 |
| | 4 | 44 | 96 | 145 | 200 | 260 | 310 | 360 | 400 | 450 | 510 |
| | 6 | 60 | 120 | 175 | 240 | 310 | 370 | 420 | 470 | 530 | 600 |
| | 8 | 74 | 140 | 205 | 280 | 350 | 420 | 480 | 530 | 590 | 670 |
| | 10 | 86 | 160 | 235 | 310 | 390 | 480 | 540 | 600 | 660 | 750 |
| | 12 | 98 | 180 | 260 | 350 | 440 | 520 | 600 | 660 | 730 | 830 |
| | 14 | 108 | 200 | 290 | 390 | 480 | 580 | 650 | 720 | 810 | 910 |
| | 16 | 112 | 220 | 320 | 420 | 520 | 620 | 700 | 790 | 880 | 990 |
| | 18 | 125 | 240 | 350 | 450 | 560 | 670 | 760 | 840 | 940 | 1050 |
| | 20 | 130 | 260 | 370 | 480 | 590 | 700 | 800 | 890 | 990 | 1100 |
| 175 | 2 | 35 | 84 | 130 | 185 | 240 | 300 | 350 | 390 | 440 | 500 |
| | 4 | 52 | 112 | 165 | 230 | 300 | 360 | 420 | 470 | 520 | 590 |
| | 6 | 68 | 140 | 205 | 280 | 350 | 430 | 490 | 540 | 610 | 690 |
| | 8 | 86 | 165 | 240 | 320 | 410 | 490 | 560 | 620 | 690 | 780 |
| | 10 | 100 | 190 | 270 | 360 | 460 | 560 | 630 | 690 | 770 | 870 |
| | 12 | 114 | 210 | 310 | 410 | 510 | 660 | 700 | 770 | 850 | 960 |
| | 14 | 125 | 235 | 330 | 450 | 560 | 670 | 760 | 840 | 940 | 1060 |
| | 16 | 130 | 260 | 370 | 480 | 600 | 730 | 810 | 910 | 1020 | 1150 |
| | 18 | 145 | 280 | 400 | 520 | 650 | 770 | 880 | 970 | 1090 | 1220 |
| | 20 | 155 | 310 | 430 | 550 | 680 | 820 | 930 | 1030 | 1150 | 1270 |
| 215 | 2 | 40 | 94 | 140 | 185 | 250 | 310 | 380 | 440 | 490 | 560 |
| | 4 | 58 | 125 | 185 | 230 | 310 | 380 | 450 | 520 | 590 | 660 |
| | 6 | 76 | 155 | 220 | 270 | 360 | 440 | 530 | 610 | 690 | 780 |
| | 8 | 98 | 185 | 260 | 310 | 410 | 490 | 590 | 690 | 770 | 870 |
| | 10 | 112 | 210 | 290 | 340 | 450 | 540 | 640 | 770 | 860 | 970 |
| | 12 | 125 | 235 | 320 | 380 | 490 | 590 | 690 | 840 | 950 | 1080 |
| | 14 | 140 | 260 | 350 | 410 | 540 | 640 | 750 | 900 | 1050 | 1190 |
| | 16 | 145 | 290 | 380 | 440 | 570 | 690 | 800 | 960 | 1140 | 1290 |
| | 18 | 160 | 310 | 400 | 470 | 610 | 730 | 860 | 1030 | 1230 | 1370 |
| | 20 | 170 | 340 | 430 | 500 | 650 | 780 | 910 | 1100 | 1290 | 1430 |
| 265 | 2 | 44 | 94 | 130 | 170 | 230 | 280 | 350 | 440 | 550 | 620 |
| | 4 | 64 | 130 | 170 | 210 | 280 | 350 | 410 | 510 | 650 | 740 |
| | 6 | 86 | 160 | 205 | 245 | 330 | 400 | 480 | 590 | 760 | 860 |
| | 8 | 108 | 190 | 235 | 280 | 370 | 450 | 540 | 650 | 820 | 970 |
| | 10 | 125 | 220 | 260 | 310 | 420 | 500 | 590 | 710 | 890 | 1080 |
| | 12 | 140 | 245 | 290 | 340 | 450 | 540 | 630 | 770 | 970 | 1190 |
| | 14 | 155 | 270 | 320 | 370 | 490 | 590 | 690 | 830 | 1040 | 1270 |
| | 16 | 165 | 290 | 340 | 400 | 530 | 630 | 730 | 880 | 1130 | 1380 |
| | 18 | 180 | 320 | 370 | 430 | 560 | 670 | 790 | 950 | 1210 | 1450 |
| | 20 | 190 | 340 | 390 | 460 | 600 | 710 | 840 | 1020 | 1300 | 1550 |
| 315 and greater | 2 | 46 | 92 | 125 | 160 | 220 | 270 | 330 | 420 | 580 | 650 |
| | 4 | 68 | 125 | 165 | 200 | 270 | 330 | 400 | 490 | 640 | 780 |
| | 6 | 90 | 160 | 195 | 240 | 320 | 390 | 470 | 570 | 730 | 900 |
| | 8 | 114 | 185 | 225 | 270 | 360 | 430 | 520 | 620 | 790 | 960 |
| | 10 | 130 | 210 | 250 | 300 | 400 | 480 | 570 | 680 | 860 | 1060 |
| | 12 | 150 | 235 | 280 | 330 | 430 | 520 | 610 | 740 | 930 | 1150 |
| | 14 | 165 | 260 | 300 | 360 | 470 | 560 | 650 | 790 | 1000 | 1230 |
| | 16 | 170 | 280 | 330 | 380 | 500 | 600 | 700 | 840 | 1080 | 1340 |
| | 18 | 190 | 310 | 350 | 410 | 530 | 640 | 750 | 910 | 1160 | 1390 |
| | 20 | 200 | 330 | 370 | 430 | 570 | 680 | 800 | 970 | 1240 | 1490 |

*(See notes at end of Table.)* (Continued)

## Table 10.7.2.3 (Continued)

## 65 mm rivets. Spacing: $S_p = 25$ mm; $S_Q = 15$ mm

| Member dimension,* mm | Rivets per row, $n_C$ | Number of rows, $n_R$ | | | | |
|---|---|---|---|---|---|---|
| | | 2 | 4 | 6 | 8 | 10 |
| 130 | 2 | 24 | 36 | 50 | 72 | 100 |
| | 4 | 34 | 46 | 66 | 92 | 125 |
| | 6 | 42 | 58 | 80 | 110 | 150 |
| | 8 | 50 | 68 | 94 | 130 | 175 |
| | 10 | 58 | 80 | 110 | 150 | 195 |
| | 12 | 66 | 90 | 125 | 165 | 220 |
| | 14 | 76 | 102 | 140 | 185 | 240 |
| | 16 | 84 | 112 | 150 | 200 | 260 |
| | 18 | 92 | 125 | 165 | 220 | 280 |
| | 20 | 100 | 135 | 180 | 240 | 310 |
| 175 and greater | 2 | 26 | 36 | 50 | 72 | 100 |
| | 4 | 34 | 46 | 66 | 92 | 125 |
| | 6 | 42 | 58 | 80 | 110 | 150 |
| | 8 | 50 | 68 | 94 | 130 | 170 |
| | 10 | 58 | 80 | 110 | 150 | 195 |
| | 12 | 66 | 90 | 125 | 165 | 215 |
| | 14 | 76 | 102 | 135 | 185 | 240 |
| | 16 | 84 | 112 | 150 | 200 | 260 |
| | 18 | 92 | 125 | 165 | 220 | 280 |
| | 20 | 100 | 135 | 180 | 235 | 310 |

*(See notes at end of Table.)*

*(Continued)*

## Table 10.7.2.3 (Continued)
## 90 mm rivets.  Spacing:  $S_p = 25$ mm; $S_Q = 25$ mm

| Member dimension,* mm | Rivets per row, $n_C$ | Number of rows, $n_R$ | | | | | | | | | |
|---|---|---|---|---|---|---|---|---|---|---|---|
| | | 2 | 4 | 6 | 8 | 10 | 12 | 14 | 16 | 18 | 20 |
| 175 | 2 | 28 | 66 | 102 | 145 | 190 | 230 | 270 | 300 | 350 | 390 |
| | 4 | 40 | 86 | 130 | 180 | 235 | 280 | 320 | 360 | 410 | 460 |
| | 6 | 54 | 108 | 160 | 220 | 280 | 330 | 380 | 420 | 480 | 540 |
| | 8 | 68 | 125 | 190 | 250 | 320 | 380 | 430 | 480 | 540 | 610 |
| | 10 | 80 | 145 | 215 | 290 | 360 | 430 | 480 | 540 | 600 | 680 |
| | 12 | 90 | 165 | 240 | 320 | 400 | 470 | 540 | 600 | 670 | 750 |
| | 14 | 98 | 180 | 260 | 350 | 440 | 520 | 580 | 650 | 740 | 830 |
| | 16 | 104 | 200 | 290 | 380 | 480 | 560 | 620 | 710 | 800 | 900 |
| | 18 | 114 | 220 | 310 | 410 | 510 | 600 | 670 | 760 | 860 | 960 |
| | 20 | 120 | 240 | 340 | 430 | 540 | 630 | 710 | 810 | 900 | 1000 |
| 215 | 2 | 31 | 72 | 114 | 160 | 210 | 250 | 290 | 330 | 380 | 430 |
| | 4 | 44 | 96 | 145 | 200 | 260 | 310 | 350 | 400 | 450 | 510 |
| | 6 | 60 | 118 | 175 | 240 | 310 | 370 | 410 | 470 | 530 | 600 |
| | 8 | 76 | 140 | 205 | 280 | 350 | 420 | 470 | 530 | 590 | 670 |
| | 10 | 88 | 160 | 235 | 320 | 400 | 470 | 530 | 590 | 660 | 750 |
| | 12 | 98 | 180 | 260 | 350 | 440 | 520 | 590 | 660 | 730 | 830 |
| | 14 | 108 | 200 | 290 | 390 | 480 | 570 | 640 | 720 | 810 | 910 |
| | 16 | 114 | 220 | 320 | 420 | 520 | 620 | 690 | 780 | 880 | 990 |
| | 18 | 125 | 240 | 340 | 450 | 560 | 660 | 740 | 830 | 950 | 1050 |
| | 20 | 135 | 260 | 370 | 480 | 590 | 690 | 780 | 890 | 990 | 1100 |
| 265 | 2 | 34 | 80 | 125 | 180 | 235 | 280 | 330 | 370 | 420 | 480 |
| | 4 | 50 | 106 | 160 | 225 | 290 | 340 | 390 | 450 | 500 | 570 |
| | 6 | 66 | 130 | 195 | 270 | 340 | 410 | 460 | 520 | 590 | 670 |
| | 8 | 84 | 155 | 230 | 310 | 390 | 470 | 530 | 590 | 660 | 750 |
| | 10 | 98 | 180 | 260 | 350 | 440 | 500 | 550 | 610 | 700 | 800 |
| | 12 | 110 | 200 | 290 | 390 | 470 | 520 | 550 | 630 | 720 | 820 |
| | 14 | 120 | 225 | 320 | 410 | 490 | 540 | 570 | 650 | 740 | 840 |
| | 16 | 125 | 245 | 350 | 430 | 500 | 550 | 590 | 660 | 780 | 880 |
| | 18 | 140 | 270 | 380 | 440 | 520 | 570 | 610 | 690 | 810 | 890 |
| | 20 | 150 | 290 | 410 | 460 | 540 | 590 | 640 | 720 | 850 | 930 |
| 315 | 2 | 38 | 90 | 140 | 195 | 260 | 310 | 360 | 410 | 470 | 530 |
| | 4 | 54 | 118 | 175 | 245 | 320 | 380 | 430 | 490 | 560 | 630 |
| | 6 | 74 | 145 | 215 | 300 | 380 | 420 | 470 | 530 | 630 | 720 |
| | 8 | 94 | 170 | 250 | 320 | 390 | 430 | 470 | 520 | 610 | 680 |
| | 10 | 108 | 200 | 280 | 330 | 400 | 440 | 470 | 530 | 610 | 700 |
| | 12 | 120 | 220 | 310 | 340 | 410 | 450 | 480 | 540 | 630 | 720 |
| | 14 | 135 | 245 | 320 | 360 | 420 | 470 | 500 | 560 | 650 | 730 |
| | 16 | 140 | 270 | 340 | 370 | 440 | 480 | 510 | 580 | 680 | 770 |
| | 18 | 155 | 300 | 360 | 390 | 450 | 490 | 530 | 600 | 710 | 780 |
| | 20 | 165 | 320 | 370 | 400 | 470 | 510 | 560 | 630 | 740 | 820 |
| 365 and greater | 2 | 40 | 96 | 150 | 210 | 280 | 330 | 390 | 450 | 510 | 570 |
| | 4 | 60 | 125 | 190 | 270 | 340 | 410 | 450 | 520 | 600 | 680 |
| | 6 | 80 | 155 | 225 | 290 | 360 | 400 | 440 | 500 | 590 | 670 |
| | 8 | 100 | 180 | 250 | 300 | 360 | 400 | 430 | 490 | 570 | 640 |
| | 10 | 116 | 205 | 270 | 310 | 370 | 410 | 440 | 490 | 570 | 650 |
| | 12 | 130 | 230 | 290 | 320 | 380 | 420 | 450 | 510 | 590 | 670 |
| | 14 | 145 | 250 | 310 | 340 | 400 | 440 | 460 | 520 | 600 | 690 |
| | 16 | 150 | 280 | 320 | 350 | 410 | 450 | 480 | 540 | 630 | 720 |
| | 18 | 165 | 300 | 330 | 360 | 420 | 460 | 500 | 560 | 670 | 740 |
| | 20 | 175 | 310 | 350 | 370 | 440 | 480 | 520 | 590 | 700 | 770 |

*(See notes at end of Table.)* (Continued)

## Table 10.7.2.3 (Continued)
## 90 mm rivets.  Spacing:  $S_p = 40$ mm; $S_Q = 25$ mm

| Member dimension,* mm | Rivets per row, $n_C$ | Number of rows, $n_R$ | | | | | | | | | |
|---|---|---|---|---|---|---|---|---|---|---|---|
| | | 2 | 4 | 6 | 8 | 10 | 12 | 14 | 16 | 18 | 20 |
| 175 | 2 | 32 | 76 | 118 | 165 | 215 | 270 | 310 | 350 | 390 | 450 |
| | 4 | 46 | 100 | 150 | 205 | 270 | 330 | 380 | 420 | 470 | 530 |
| | 6 | 62 | 125 | 180 | 250 | 320 | 390 | 440 | 490 | 550 | 620 |
| | 8 | 78 | 145 | 215 | 290 | 370 | 440 | 510 | 550 | 620 | 700 |
| | 10 | 90 | 170 | 245 | 330 | 410 | 500 | 560 | 620 | 690 | 780 |
| | 12 | 102 | 190 | 270 | 370 | 460 | 550 | 630 | 690 | 760 | 860 |
| | 14 | 112 | 210 | 300 | 400 | 500 | 600 | 680 | 750 | 840 | 950 |
| | 16 | 118 | 230 | 330 | 430 | 540 | 650 | 730 | 820 | 910 | 1030 |
| | 18 | 130 | 250 | 360 | 470 | 580 | 700 | 790 | 870 | 980 | 1090 |
| | 20 | 140 | 280 | 390 | 500 | 610 | 730 | 830 | 930 | 1030 | 1150 |
| 215 | 2 | 35 | 84 | 130 | 180 | 235 | 290 | 340 | 390 | 430 | 490 |
| | 4 | 50 | 110 | 165 | 230 | 290 | 360 | 410 | 460 | 520 | 580 |
| | 6 | 68 | 135 | 200 | 270 | 350 | 430 | 490 | 540 | 600 | 680 |
| | 8 | 86 | 160 | 240 | 320 | 400 | 480 | 560 | 610 | 680 | 770 |
| | 10 | 100 | 185 | 270 | 360 | 450 | 550 | 620 | 680 | 760 | 860 |
| | 12 | 112 | 205 | 300 | 400 | 500 | 600 | 690 | 760 | 840 | 950 |
| | 14 | 120 | 230 | 330 | 440 | 550 | 660 | 750 | 830 | 930 | 1050 |
| | 16 | 130 | 250 | 360 | 480 | 600 | 720 | 800 | 900 | 1000 | 1130 |
| | 18 | 145 | 280 | 400 | 510 | 640 | 760 | 870 | 960 | 1080 | 1200 |
| | 20 | 150 | 300 | 420 | 540 | 670 | 810 | 910 | 1020 | 1130 | 1260 |
| 265 | 2 | 39 | 94 | 145 | 205 | 260 | 330 | 380 | 430 | 480 | 550 |
| | 4 | 56 | 125 | 185 | 250 | 330 | 400 | 460 | 510 | 580 | 650 |
| | 6 | 76 | 150 | 225 | 310 | 390 | 470 | 540 | 600 | 670 | 760 |
| | 8 | 96 | 180 | 260 | 350 | 450 | 540 | 620 | 680 | 760 | 860 |
| | 10 | 110 | 210 | 300 | 400 | 510 | 610 | 690 | 760 | 850 | 960 |
| | 12 | 125 | 230 | 340 | 450 | 560 | 670 | 770 | 850 | 940 | 1060 |
| | 14 | 135 | 260 | 370 | 500 | 610 | 740 | 840 | 930 | 1030 | 1170 |
| | 16 | 145 | 280 | 410 | 530 | 670 | 800 | 900 | 1010 | 1120 | 1270 |
| | 18 | 160 | 310 | 440 | 570 | 710 | 850 | 970 | 1070 | 1210 | 1340 |
| | 20 | 170 | 340 | 470 | 600 | 750 | 900 | 1020 | 1140 | 1260 | 1410 |
| 315 | 2 | 42 | 102 | 160 | 225 | 290 | 360 | 420 | 470 | 530 | 600 |
| | 4 | 62 | 135 | 205 | 280 | 360 | 440 | 510 | 570 | 630 | 720 |
| | 6 | 84 | 170 | 245 | 340 | 430 | 520 | 600 | 660 | 740 | 840 |
| | 8 | 106 | 200 | 290 | 390 | 490 | 600 | 680 | 750 | 830 | 940 |
| | 10 | 120 | 230 | 330 | 420 | 540 | 630 | 740 | 840 | 930 | 1050 |
| | 12 | 140 | 250 | 370 | 440 | 560 | 660 | 760 | 910 | 1030 | 1170 |
| | 14 | 150 | 280 | 400 | 460 | 590 | 700 | 790 | 950 | 1140 | 1290 |
| | 16 | 160 | 310 | 420 | 480 | 610 | 720 | 830 | 990 | 1240 | 1400 |
| | 18 | 175 | 340 | 440 | 500 | 640 | 750 | 870 | 1040 | 1320 | 1480 |
| | 20 | 185 | 370 | 460 | 520 | 670 | 790 | 920 | 1100 | 1390 | 1550 |
| 365 and greater | 2 | 46 | 102 | 175 | 240 | 310 | 390 | 460 | 510 | 580 | 650 |
| | 4 | 68 | 145 | 220 | 300 | 390 | 480 | 550 | 610 | 690 | 780 |
| | 6 | 90 | 180 | 270 | 350 | 460 | 550 | 640 | 710 | 800 | 910 |
| | 8 | 114 | 215 | 310 | 370 | 480 | 560 | 660 | 780 | 900 | 1020 |
| | 10 | 130 | 250 | 340 | 390 | 500 | 590 | 690 | 810 | 1010 | 1140 |
| | 12 | 150 | 270 | 360 | 410 | 530 | 620 | 710 | 850 | 1060 | 1260 |
| | 14 | 165 | 310 | 380 | 430 | 550 | 650 | 750 | 890 | 1100 | 1340 |
| | 16 | 170 | 340 | 400 | 450 | 580 | 680 | 780 | 930 | 1170 | 1430 |
| | 18 | 190 | 360 | 410 | 470 | 600 | 700 | 820 | 980 | 1240 | 1470 |
| | 20 | 200 | 380 | 430 | 490 | 630 | 740 | 860 | 1030 | 1310 | 1550 |

*(See notes at end of Table.)*

*(Continued)*

## Table 10.7.2.3 (Concluded)
## 90 mm rivets.  Spacing:  $S_p$ = 25 mm; $S_Q$ = 15 mm

| Member dimension,* mm | Rivets per row, $n_C$ | Number of rows, $n_R$ | | | | |
|---|---|---|---|---|---|---|
| | | 2 | 4 | 6 | 8 | 10 |
| | 2 | 25 | 36 | 52 | 74 | 100 |
| | 4 | 34 | 46 | 66 | 92 | 125 |
| | 6 | 42 | 58 | 80 | 112 | 150 |
| 175 | 8 | 50 | 70 | 96 | 130 | 175 |
| and | 10 | 60 | 80 | 110 | 150 | 200 |
| greater | 12 | 68 | 92 | 125 | 170 | 220 |
| | 14 | 76 | 102 | 140 | 185 | 245 |
| | 16 | 84 | 114 | 155 | 205 | 270 |
| | 18 | 94 | 125 | 165 | 225 | 290 |
| | 20 | 102 | 135 | 180 | 240 | 310 |

*Member dimension is identified as "b" in Figure 10.7.1.7 for connections with steel plates on opposite sides.  For connections having only one plate, member dimension is twice the thickness of the wood member.

**Note:** For intermediate sawn lumber dimensions, interpolation may be used.

## Table 10.7.2.5A
## Values of $q_w$ (kN), Perpendicular to Grain for Timber Rivet Joints
## Spacing: $S_p$ = 25 mm

| $S_Q$ | Rivets per row, $n_C$ | Number of rows, $n_R$ | | | | | | | |
|---|---|---|---|---|---|---|---|---|---|
| | | 1 | 2 | 3 | 4 | 5 | 6 | 8 | 10 |
| | 2 | 0.57 | 0.57 | 0.61 | 0.61 | 0.67 | 0.71 | 0.84 | 0.97 |
| | 3 | 0.57 | 0.57 | 0.61 | 0.63 | 0.66 | 0.70 | 0.82 | 0.93 |
| | 4 | 0.60 | 0.60 | 0.65 | 0.66 | 0.71 | 0.74 | 0.85 | 0.95 |
| | 5 | 0.63 | 0.63 | 0.69 | 0.70 | 0.75 | 0.78 | 0.89 | 0.99 |
| | 6 | 0.71 | 0.71 | 0.76 | 0.77 | 0.81 | 0.84 | 0.95 | 1.06 |
| | 7 | 0.77 | 0.77 | 0.82 | 0.82 | 0.87 | 0.89 | 1.00 | 1.11 |
| | 8 | 0.86 | 0.86 | 0.90 | 0.90 | 0.94 | 0.96 | 1.07 | 1.18 |
| | 9 | 0.91 | 0.91 | 0.97 | 0.97 | 1.01 | 1.03 | 1.13 | 1.25 |
| | 10 | 0.97 | 0.97 | 1.05 | 1.06 | 1.10 | 1.12 | 1.21 | 1.35 |
| 15 | 11 | 1.05 | 1.05 | 1.12 | 1.13 | 1.17 | 1.18 | 1.28 | 1.43 |
| | 12 | 1.14 | 1.14 | 1.21 | 1.21 | 1.24 | 1.25 | 1.38 | 1.52 |
| | 13 | 1.26 | 1.26 | 1.29 | 1.29 | 1.33 | 1.33 | 1.45 | 1.59 |
| | 14 | 1.42 | 1.42 | 1.40 | 1.37 | 1.42 | 1.44 | 1.54 | 1.68 |
| | 15 | 1.50 | 1.50 | 1.50 | 1.47 | 1.50 | 1.50 | 1.62 | 1.78 |
| | 16 | 1.61 | 1.61 | 1.62 | 1.60 | 1.60 | 1.58 | 1.71 | 1.89 |
| | 17 | 1.73 | 1.73 | 1.72 | 1.69 | 1.69 | 1.67 | 1.79 | 1.96 |
| | 18 | 1.88 | 1.88 | 1.85 | 1.80 | 1.80 | 1.77 | 1.87 | 2.04 |
| | 20 | 1.84 | 1.84 | 1.91 | 1.91 | 1.93 | 1.93 | 2.08 | 2.24 |
| | 2 | 0.67 | 0.67 | 0.70 | 0.69 | 0.75 | 0.79 | 0.93 | 1.08 |
| | 3 | 0.66 | 0.66 | 0.70 | 0.72 | 0.74 | 0.78 | 0.91 | 1.03 |
| | 4 | 0.70 | 0.70 | 0.75 | 0.75 | 0.80 | 0.83 | 0.94 | 1.06 |
| | 5 | 0.73 | 0.73 | 0.80 | 0.79 | 0.84 | 0.87 | 0.98 | 1.10 |
| | 6 | 0.82 | 0.82 | 0.87 | 0.86 | 0.91 | 0.94 | 1.05 | 1.18 |
| | 7 | 0.90 | 0.90 | 0.94 | 0.93 | 0.97 | 1.00 | 1.11 | 1.23 |
| | 8 | 1.01 | 1.01 | 1.04 | 1.02 | 1.06 | 1.08 | 1.19 | 1.31 |
| | 9 | 1.06 | 1.06 | 1.11 | 1.10 | 1.14 | 1.15 | 1.26 | 1.39 |
| | 10 | 1.13 | 1.13 | 1.20 | 1.20 | 1.24 | 1.25 | 1.34 | 1.50 |
| | 11 | 1.22 | 1.22 | 1.29 | 1.28 | 1.30 | 1.32 | 1.43 | 1.59 |
| 25 | 12 | 1.33 | 1.33 | 1.39 | 1.37 | 1.39 | 1.40 | 1.53 | 1.69 |
| | 13 | 1.47 | 1.47 | 1.48 | 1.45 | 1.48 | 1.49 | 1.61 | 1.77 |
| | 14 | 1.65 | 1.65 | 1.61 | 1.55 | 1.59 | 1.61 | 1.71 | 1.86 |
| | 15 | 1.75 | 1.75 | 1.72 | 1.66 | 1.68 | 1.68 | 1.80 | 1.97 |
| | 16 | 1.87 | 1.87 | 1.86 | 1.80 | 1.79 | 1.77 | 1.90 | 2.10 |
| | 17 | 2.02 | 2.02 | 1.97 | 1.91 | 1.89 | 1.87 | 1.98 | 2.18 |
| | 18 | 2.19 | 2.19 | 2.12 | 2.03 | 2.01 | 1.98 | 2.08 | 2.27 |
| | 20 | 2.14 | 2.14 | 2.19 | 2.15 | 2.17 | 2.16 | 2.31 | 2.49 |
| | 2 | 0.96 | 0.96 | 0.98 | 0.93 | 0.98 | 1.03 | 1.20 | 1.38 |
| | 3 | 0.95 | 0.95 | 0.98 | 0.96 | 0.98 | 1.02 | 1.16 | 1.32 |
| | 4 | 1.02 | 1.02 | 1.05 | 1.00 | 1.05 | 1.07 | 1.21 | 1.36 |
| | 5 | 1.06 | 1.06 | 1.11 | 1.06 | 1.11 | 1.13 | 1.26 | 1.41 |
| | 6 | 1.19 | 1.19 | 1.22 | 1.16 | 1.20 | 1.22 | 1.35 | 1.51 |
| | 7 | 1.30 | 1.30 | 1.32 | 1.24 | 1.28 | 1.30 | 1.43 | 1.58 |
| | 8 | 1.45 | 1.45 | 1.45 | 1.36 | 1.40 | 1.40 | 1.53 | 1.68 |
| | 9 | 1.53 | 1.53 | 1.55 | 1.47 | 1.50 | 1.50 | 1.61 | 1.79 |
| | 10 | 1.63 | 1.63 | 1.69 | 1.60 | 1.63 | 1.63 | 1.72 | 1.93 |
| 40 | 11 | 1.76 | 1.76 | 1.80 | 1.71 | 1.72 | 1.71 | 1.83 | 2.04 |
| | 12 | 1.92 | 1.92 | 1.94 | 1.83 | 1.84 | 1.82 | 1.96 | 2.17 |
| | 13 | 2.12 | 2.12 | 2.08 | 1.94 | 1.96 | 1.94 | 2.07 | 2.27 |
| | 14 | 2.39 | 2.39 | 2.25 | 2.07 | 2.10 | 2.09 | 2.20 | 2.39 |
| | 15 | 2.53 | 2.53 | 2.41 | 2.22 | 2.22 | 2.19 | 2.31 | 2.53 |
| | 16 | 2.70 | 2.70 | 2.61 | 2.41 | 2.36 | 2.30 | 2.44 | 2.69 |
| | 17 | 2.91 | 2.91 | 2.76 | 2.55 | 2.49 | 2.43 | 2.54 | 2.79 |
| | 18 | 3.17 | 3.17 | 2.97 | 2.72 | 2.66 | 2.58 | 2.66 | 2.91 |
| | 20 | 3.10 | 3.10 | 3.07 | 2.88 | 2.86 | 2.80 | 2.96 | 3.19 |

## Table 10.7.2.5B
## Values of Factor $C_t$

| $\dfrac{e_p}{(n_C-1)S_Q}$ | $C_t$ | $\dfrac{e_p}{(n_C-1)S_Q}$ | $C_t$ |
|---|---|---|---|
| 0.1 | 5.76 | 3.2 | 0.79 |
| 0.2 | 3.19 | 3.6 | 0.77 |
| 0.3 | 2.36 | 4.0 | 0.76 |
| 0.4 | 2.00 | 5.0 | 0.72 |
| 0.5 | 1.77 | 6.0 | 0.70 |
| 0.6 | 1.61 | 7.0 | 0.68 |
| 0.7 | 1.47 | 8.0 | 0.66 |
| 0.8 | 1.36 | 9.0 | 0.64 |
| 0.9 | 1.28 | 10.0 | 0.63 |
| 1.0 | 1.20 | 12.0 | 0.61 |
| 1.2 | 1.10 | 14.0 | 0.59 |
| 1.4 | 1.02 | 16.0 | 0.57 |
| 1.6 | 0.96 | 18.0 | 0.56 |
| 1.8 | 0.92 | 20.0 | 0.55 |
| 2.0 | 0.89 | 25.0 | 0.53 |
| 2.4 | 0.85 | 30.0 | 0.51 |
| 2.8 | 0.81 | | |

## 10.8 Truss Plates

## 10.8.1 General

### 10.8.1.1
Design requirements in Clause 10.8 for truss plate joints are for light-gauge metal plates that depend upon extended teeth or nails embedded into the wood to transfer load and that conform to the requirements of Clause 10.8.1.3.

### 10.8.1.2
The provisions of Clause 10.8 do not apply to the following situations:
(a) corrosive conditions; and
(b) the use of galvanized truss plates in lumber that has been treated with a fire retardant and that is used in wet service conditions or in locations prone to condensation.

### 10.8.1.3
Truss plates shall be manufactured from galvanized sheet steel conforming to Grades SQ230, SQ255, SQ275, HSLA I340, HSLA I410, HSLA II340, or HSLA II410 of ASTM Standard A 653/A 653M having the minimum properties given in Table 10.8.1.3.

## Table 10.8.1.3
## Minimum Properties of Steels Used for Truss Plates

| Grade | SQ230 | SQ255 | SQ275 | HSLA I340 or HSLA II340 | HSLA I410 or HSLA II410 |
|---|---|---|---|---|---|
| Ultimate tensile strength, MPa | 310 | 360 | 380 | 410 | 480 |
| Minimum yield, MPa | 230 | 255 | 275 | 340 | 410 |
| Elongation in 50 mm length at failure, % | 20 | 18 | 16 | 20 | 16 |

**Note:** Galvanizing may be carried out before manufacture and should be G90 coating class.

## 10.8.1.4
Joint design shall be based on tight-fitted joints with truss plates placed on opposing faces in such a way that, at each joint, the plates on opposing faces are identical and are placed directly opposite each other.

## 10.8.1.5
In cases where nail-on plates are used, the word "nail" should be read in place of "tooth".

## 10.8.1.6
Design criteria for truss plates are based on the following conditions:
(a) the plate is prevented from deforming during installation;
(b) the teeth are normal to the surface of the lumber;
(c) tooth penetration in joints is not less than that used in the tests referred to in Clause 10.8.1.9; and
(d) the lumber beneath the plate does not contain wane, loose knots, or knot holes.

## 10.8.1.7
Thickness of members used in joints shall be not less than twice the tooth penetration.

## 10.8.1.8
The primary axis of a truss plate, in the case of slotted truss plate tooth configurations, is parallel to the direction of slots in the plate. For rosette-style configurations, the primary axis is that axis of symmetry in which the tensile strength of the truss plate is the greatest.

## 10.8.1.9
Design requirements in Clause 10.8 are for truss plates that have been tested in accordance with CSA Standard S347 for the species group in which the plates are to be used.
**Note:** *Test results for such plates are listed in the* Registry of Product Evaluations, *published by the Canadian Construction Materials Centre, Institute for Research in Construction, Ottawa, Ontario.*

## 10.8.2 Design

### 10.8.2.1
Truss plate joints shall be designed such that
(a) for the strength limit state, the effect of factored loads is less than or equal to
    (i) the factored ultimate lateral resistance of the teeth;
    (ii) the factored tensile resistance of the plates; and
    (iii) the factored shear resistance of the plates; and
(b) for the serviceability limit state, the effect of specified loads is less than or equal to the lateral slip resistance of the teeth.

### 10.8.2.2
Truss plates shall not be considered to be effective in transferring compression loads at a joint.

### 10.8.2.3
Design of truss plate joints shall take into consideration
(a) species of lumber;
(b) orientation of plates relative to the applied load (Figure 10.8.2.3, angle ρ);
(c) direction of the applied load relative to the grain (Figure 10.8.2.3, angle θ); and
(d) orientation of plates relative to the applied shear force.

### 10.8.2.4
The factored ultimate lateral resistance and the lateral slip resistance of the teeth shall be expressed in terms of the surface area of the plates.

## 10.8.2.5

Surface area shall be based on the net area method using the test values, or on the gross area method using 80% of the test values, where
(a) the gross area is defined as the total area of a member covered by a truss plate; and
(b) the net area is defined as the total area of a member covered by a truss plate less the area within a given distance from the edge or end of the member, as shown in Figure 10.8.2.5. For net area calculation, the minimum end distance, "a", measured parallel to grain, shall be the greater of 12 mm or 1/2 the length of the tooth; the minimum edge distance, "e", measured perpendicular to grain, shall be the greater of 6 mm or 1/4 the length of the tooth.

## 10.8.2.6

The factored tensile resistance of the plates shall be expressed in terms of the dimension of the plate measured perpendicular to the line of action of the applied forces. The factored shear resistance shall be expressed in terms of the dimension of the plate measured along the line of action of the shearing forces.

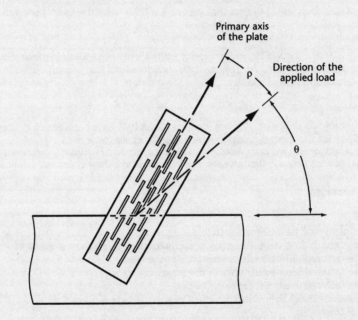

**Legend:**
θ = *angle between load direction and grain direction*
ρ = *angle between load direction and the primary axis of the plate*

### Figure 10.8.2.3
### Truss Plate, Load, and Grain Orientation

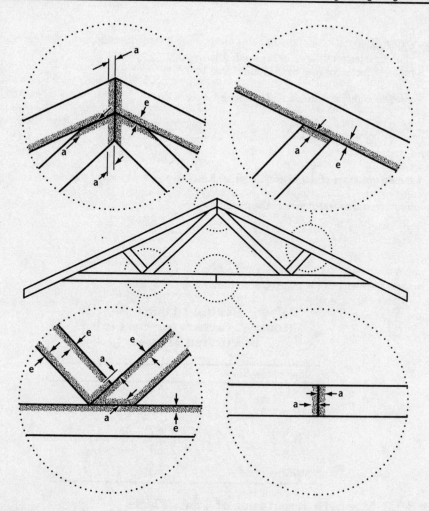

**Legend:**
a = *end distance*
e = *edge distance*

## Figure 10.8.2.5
## End and Edge Distances for Truss Plates

## 10.8.3  Factored Resistance of Truss Plates

### 10.8.3.1

For the strength limit state, the factored resistances of truss plates shall be determined as follows:
(a)  For factored ultimate lateral resistance of the teeth

$$N_r = \phi N_u J_H$$

where

$\phi$ = 0.9

$N_u$ = $n_u(K_D K_{SF} K_T)$

$n_u$ = ultimate lateral resistance of the teeth (Clause 10.8.3.2.2)

$J_H$ = moment factor for heel connection (Table 10.8.3.1)

(b) For factored tensile resistance of the plate

$T_r$ = $\phi t_p$

where

$\phi$ = 0.6

$t_p$ = tensile resistance of the plate (Clause 10.8.3.2.3)

(c) For factored shear resistance of the plate

$V_r$ = $\phi v_p$

where

$\phi$ = 0.6

$v_p$ = shear resistance of the plate (Clause 10.8.3.2.4)

### Table 10.8.3.1
### Moment Factors for Heel Joints
### of Pitched Trusses, $J_H$

| Slope of top chord | $J_H$ |
|---|---|
| <1/4 | 0.85 |
| >1/4 to 1/3 | 0.8 |
| >1/3 to 1/2.4 | 0.75 |
| >1/2.4 to 1/2.2 | 0.7 |
| >1/2.2 | 0.65 |

## 10.8.3.2 Strength Resistance of Truss Plates

### 10.8.3.2.1 Resistance Values for Plates and Teeth

Resistance values for plates and teeth shall be obtained from tests carried out in accordance with CSA Standard S347, where the resistance values are

(a) the average, divided by 1.6, of the three lowest of ten ultimate test values for lateral resistance of the teeth;

(b) the average of the two lowest of three corrected test values for tensile strength of the plate; and

(c) the average of the two lowest of three corrected test values for shear strength of the plate.

### 10.8.3.2.2 Ultimate Lateral Resistance of the Teeth

The ultimate lateral resistance of the teeth shall be calculated as follows:

(a) For loads parallel to the primary axis of the plate

$$n_u = \frac{p_u q_u}{p_u \sin^2\theta + q_u \cos^2\theta}$$

(b) For loads perpendicular to the primary axis of the plate

$$n'_u = \frac{p'_u q'_u}{p'_u \sin^2\theta + q'_u \cos^2\theta}$$

where

$p_u, q_u, p'_u, q'_u$ = ultimate lateral resistances determined in accordance with Clause 10.8.3.2.1(a), used with the following values of $\theta$ and $\rho$:

$p_u$ : $\theta = 0°$, $\rho = 0°$
$q_u$ : $\theta = 90°$, $\rho = 0°$
$p'_u$ : $\theta = 0°$, $\rho = 90°$
$q'_u$ : $\theta = 90°$ , $\rho = 90°$

where $\theta$ and $\rho$ are as shown in Figure 10.8.2.3.

When the primary axis of the plate is oriented at an angle other than parallel or perpendicular to the direction of the load, the resistance value shall be determined by linear interpolation between the values $n_u$ and $n'_u$.

## 10.8.3.2.3 Tensile Resistance

Tensile resistance of the plate, $t_p$, is determined both parallel and perpendicular to the direction of the applied load in accordance with Clause 10.8.3.2.1(b).

## 10.8.3.2.4 Shear Resistance

Shear resistance of the plate, $v_p$, is determined for specified angles of plate axis to load direction in accordance with Clause 10.8.3.2.1(c). For all other angles, shear resistance shall be determined by linear interpolation.

The shear resistance values for tensile mode of failure shall be used where the applied shear forces create tension in the plate. Where the applied forces create compression in the plate, the compressive shear values shall be used. Alternatively, the lower of the two shear resistances for an angle shall be used.

## 10.8.4 Lateral Slip Resistance

### 10.8.4.1

For the serviceability limit state, the lateral slip resistance of the teeth, $N_{rs}$, shall be determined as follows:

$$N_{rs} = N_s K_{SF}$$

where
$N_s$ = lateral slip resistance of the teeth (Clause 10.8.4.3)

### 10.8.4.2

Resistance values shall be obtained from tests carried out in accordance with CSA Standard S347, where the resistance values are the average of 10 test loads at 0.8 mm wood-to-wood slip divided by 1.4.

### 10.8.4.3

The lateral slip resistance of the teeth shall be calculated as follows:

(a) For loads parallel to the primary axis of the plate

$$N_s = \frac{p_s q_s}{p_s \sin^2\theta + q_s \cos^2\theta}$$

(b) For loads perpendicular to the primary axis of the plate

$$N'_s = \frac{p'_s q'_s}{p'_s \sin^2\theta + q'_s \cos^2\theta}$$

where
$p_s, q_s, p'_s, q'_s$ = lateral slip resistances determined in accordance with Clause 10.8.4.2, used with the following values of $\theta$ and $\rho$:

$p_s$ : $\theta = 0°$, $\rho = 0°$
$q_s$ : $\theta = 90°$, $\rho = 0°$
$p'_s$ : $\theta = 0°$, $\rho = 90°$
$q'_s$ : $\theta = 90°$, $\rho = 90°$

where $\theta$ and $\rho$ are as shown in Figure 10.8.2.3.

When the primary axis of the plate is oriented at an angle other than parallel or perpendicular to the direction of the load, the resistance value shall be determined by linear interpolation between the values $N_s$ and $N'_s$.

## 10.9 Nails and Spikes

### 10.9.1 General
Resistance values given in Clauses 10.9.2 to 10.9.5 apply only to common round steel wire nails and spikes and common spiral nails spiralled to head as defined in CSA Standard B111.
**Note:** *These provisions are not intended to preclude the use of other types of fastenings and other methods of loading the fastenings when appropriate supporting data are available.*

### 10.9.2 Joint Configuration

#### 10.9.2.1
For joints nailed at 10% wood moisture content or greater, minimum nail spacings in sawn lumber side plates and main members shall be as given in Table 10.9.2.1. Additional nails may be staggered on the intersection of diagonal lines drawn between rows of nails (see Figure 10.9.2.1).
**Note:** *When the moisture content of the wood is expected to be less than 10% at time of fabrication, minimum spacings and/or end and edge distances should be increased and holes should be predrilled to avoid splitting.*

## Table 10.9.2.1
## Minimum Spacings for Nails and Spikes

| Dimension* | | Minimum spacing (nail diameters) | |
|---|---|---|---|
| | | Douglas Fir-Larch, Hem-Fir, Western Cedar | Spruce-Pine-Fir, Northern Species |
| a | Spacing parallel to grain | 20 | 16 |
| b | End distance parallel to grain | 15 | 12 |
| c | Spacing perpendicular to grain | 10 | 8 |
| d | Edge distance perpendicular to grain | 5 | 4 |

*See Figure 10.9.2.1.

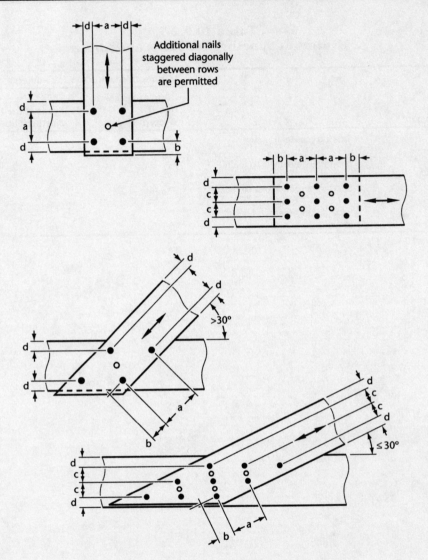

**Figure 10.9.2.1**
**Nail Spacings for Wood-to-Wood Joints**

### 10.9.2.2
Except as given in Clause 10.9.4, the length of penetration shall be at least eight nail diameters in the main member. For spiral nails, the diameter shall be taken as the effective diameter (see Table 10.9.4).

### 10.9.2.3
Side plate thickness shall be at least five diameters of the nail or spike for sawn lumber, or three diameters for plywood and OSB.

## 10.9.3 Joint Design

### 10.9.3.1

The factored lateral resistance for nails and spikes driven perpendicular to the grain shall be computed according to Clause 10.9.4.

### 10.9.3.2

Where the lateral deformation of nailed or spiked wood-to-wood joints, including structural panel-to-lumber joints, is required for design, joint deformation may be estimated in accordance with Clause A10.9.3.2.

### 10.9.3.3

The factored withdrawal resistance per millimetre of nail penetration when driven perpendicular to the grain shall be computed according to Clause 10.9.5.

### 10.9.3.4

Nails driven into end grain shall not be considered to carry load in withdrawal.

### 10.9.3.5

For a nailed joint having two different species, the factored resistance determined by either Clause 10.9.4 or 10.9.5 shall be based on the weaker species.

## 10.9.4 Lateral Resistance

The factored lateral strength resistance of the nail or spike connection, $N_r$, shall be greater than or equal to the effect of the factored loads:

$N_r = \phi N_u n_F J_F$

where
$\phi$ = 0.6
$N_u$ = $n_u(K_D K_{SF} K_T)$
$n_u$ = unit lateral strength resistance (Table 10.9.4), N
$J_F$ = $J_S J_Y J_E J_A J_B J_D$
$J_S$ = effective shear planes factor in three-member connections, where nails fully penetrate all members to obtain double shear and where the nails are either clinched on the far side or driven alternately from both sides
   = 2.00 where the centre member is at least 11 nail diameters in thickness, or
   = 1.80 where the centre member is at least 8 nail diameters in thickness; interpolate linearly for thicknesses between 8 and 11 nail diameters
   = 1.00 in two-member connections
$J_Y$ = side plate factor
   = 1.25 for steel side plates
   = 1.00 for wood side plates
$J_E$ = end grain factor
   = 0.67 for nailing into end grain, and
   = 1.0 in all other cases
$J_A$ = toe-nailing factor
   = 0.83 for toe-nailing, where toe-nails are started at approximately 1/3 the nail length from the end of the piece and driven at an angle of 30° to the grain of the member
   = 1.00 for cases other than toe-nailing
$J_B$ = nail clinching factor
   = 1.6 for nail clinching on the far side in a two-member connection
   = 1.0 if not clinched, or in three- or more member connections

$J_D$ = factor for diaphragm construction
   = 1.3 for nails and spikes used in diaphragm construction, or
   = 1.0 in all other cases

## Table 10.9.4
## Values for $n_u$ Unit Lateral Resistances for
## Round Wire Nails, Spikes, and Spiral Nails*, N

| Nail characteristics | | | | Species groups | | |
|---|---|---|---|---|---|---|
| Type | Length, inches | Gauge, No. | Diameter,* mm | Douglas Fir-Larch | Hem-Fir | Spruce-Pine-Fir, Northern Species |
| Common | 1 | 15 | 1.83 | 300 | 260 | 220 |
| wire | 1-1/8 | 15 | 1.83 | 300 | 260 | 220 |
| nails | 1-1/4 | 14 | 2.03 | 380 | 320 | 260 |
| | 1-1/2 | 13 | 2.34 | 510 | 420 | 350 |
| | 1-3/4 | 12 | 2.64 | 650 | 540 | 450 |
| | 2 | 11-3/4 | 2.84 | 780 | 650 | 530 |
| | 2-1/4 | 11 | 2.95 | 870 | 730 | 600 |
| | 2-1/2 | 10 | 3.25 | 1100 | 920 | 770 |
| | 2-3/4 | 10 | 3.25 | 1100 | 920 | 770 |
| | 3 | 9 | 3.66 | 1400 | 1200 | 1000 |
| | 3-1/4 | 9 | 3.66 | 1400 | 1200 | 1000 |
| | 3-1/2 | 8 | 4.06 | 1700 | 1500 | 1200 |
| | 4 | 6 | 4.88 | 2400 | 2000 | 1700 |
| | 4-1/2 | 5 | 5.38 | 2900 | 2400 | 2000 |
| | 5 | 4 | 5.89 | 3600 | 2900 | 2400 |
| | 5-1/2 | 3 | 6.40 | 4200 | 3500 | 2800 |
| | 6 | 2 | 7.01 | 5000 | 4100 | 3300 |
| Common | 4 | 3 | 6.40 | 4200 | 3500 | 2800 |
| spikes | 6 | 1 | 7.62 | 5500 | 4500 | 3700 |
| | 7 | 1 | 7.62 | 5500 | 4500 | 3700 |
| | 8 | 0 | 8.23 | 6600 | 5400 | 4500 |
| | 9 | 0 | 8.23 | 6600 | 5400 | 4500 |
| | 10 | 0 | 8.84 | 8000 | 6500 | 5700 |
| | 12 | 0 | 8.84 | 8000 | 6500 | 5700 |
| Common | 2-1/2 | 10-1/2 | 2.77 | 720 | 600 | 510 |
| spiral | 3 | 9-3/4 | 3.10 | 920 | 790 | 690 |
| nails | 3-1/4 | 9-3/4 | 3.10 | 920 | 790 | 690 |
| | 3-1/2 | 8 | 3.86 | 1600 | 1300 | 1100 |
| | 4 | 7 | 4.33 | 2000 | 1600 | 1400 |
| | 5 | 5 | 4.88 | 2400 | 2000 | 1700 |

*In this table, "diameter" for spiral nails is the effective diameter based on the projected lateral width.

## 10.9.5 Withdrawal Resistance

### 10.9.5.1
The use of nails and spikes loaded in withdrawal shall be permitted only for wind or earthquake loading.

## 10.9.5.2

The factored withdrawal resistance of the nail or spike connection, $P_{rw}$, shall be greater than or equal to the effect of the factored loads:

$$P_{rw} = \phi Y_w L_p n_F J_A J_B$$

where

$\phi$ = 0.6

$Y_w$ = $y_w(K_{SF}K_T)$

$y_w$ = withdrawal resistance per millimetre of penetration (for sawn lumber; see Table 10.9.5.2), N/mm

= $(16.4)(d)^{0.82}(G)^{2.2}$

where

d = nail diameter, mm

G = mean relative density based on oven-dry weight and volume (Table A10.1)

$L_p$ = length of penetration into main member, mm

$J_A$ = toe-nailing factor

= 0.67; or

= 1.00 for cases other than toe-nailing

$J_B$ = nail clinching factor

= 1.6 for nail-clinching on the far side of a two-member connection

= 1.0 if not clinched, or in three or more member connections

## Table 10.9.5.2
## Unit Withdrawal Resistance, $y_w$ (N/mm), for Round Wire Nails, Spikes, and Spiral Nails in Sawn Lumber

| Nail or spike diameter, mm | Douglas Fir-Larch | Hem-Fir | Spruce-Pine-Fir | Northern Species |
|---|---|---|---|---|
| 1.83 | 5.6 | 4.9 | 4.0 | 2.7 |
| 2.03 | 6.1 | 5.3 | 4.3 | 2.9 |
| 2.34 | 6.9 | 6.0 | 4.9 | 3.3 |
| 2.64 | 7.6 | 6.6 | 5.4 | 3.6 |
| 2.84 | 8.0 | 7.0 | 5.7 | 3.8 |
| 2.95 | 8.3 | 7.2 | 5.9 | 4.0 |
| 3.25 | 9.0 | 7.8 | 6.4 | 4.3 |
| 3.66 | 9.9 | 8.6 | 7.0 | 4.7 |
| 4.06 | 10.8 | 9.4 | 7.7 | 5.1 |
| 4.88 | 12.5 | 10.9 | 8.9 | 6.0 |
| 5.38 | 13.6 | 11.8 | 9.7 | 6.5 |
| 5.89 | 14.6 | 12.7 | 10.4 | 7.0 |
| 6.40 | 15.6 | 13.6 | 11.1 | 7.5 |
| 7.01 | 16.9 | 14.7 | 12.0 | 8.0 |
| 7.62 | 18.1 | 15.7 | 12.9 | 8.6 |
| 8.23 | 19.2 | 16.7 | 13.7 | 9.2 |
| 8.84 | 20.4 | 17.7 | 14.5 | 9.7 |

**Notes:**

**(1)** *Tabulated values will be conservative for spiral nails.*

**(2)** *For length of common wire nails or spikes, see Table 10.9.4.*

## 10.10 Joist Hangers

### 10.10.1 General

#### 10.10.1.1
Design requirements in Clause 10.10 for joist hangers are for proprietary mass-produced metal devices, usually cold-formed from light-gauge steel or welded from steel plate, that are used to transfer loads from a joist to a header or beam. The joist and header or beam may be sawn lumber, wood trusses, glued-laminated timber, prefabricated wood I-joists, or structural composite lumber.

#### 10.10.1.2
The provisions of Clause 10.10 do not apply under the following conditions:
(a) corrosive conditions;
(b) the use of galvanized joist hangers in lumber that has been treated with a fire retardant and that is used in wet service conditions or in conditions prone to condensation;
(c) joist hangers connected to headers or beams of other than wood-based materials; and
(d) special hangers having a skew in the horizontal or vertical plane, except skewed hangers with level bearing seats.

#### 10.10.1.3
The steel shall have a specified minimum ultimate and yield strength and have specified dimensional characteristics. Sheet steel shall be hot-dip galvanized.
**Note:** *Galvanizing may be carried out before manufacturing and should be minimum G90 galvanizing class.*

#### 10.10.1.4
The joist hanger shall be constructed to meet the following requirements:
(a) The height of the hanger shall be at least half the depth of the joist and be capable of providing lateral support for the joist unless the joist is prevented from twisting by other means.
(b) The hanger shall be fastened to both the joist and the header or beam. Where nails are used, the size and spacing shall be sufficient to prevent splitting of the wood. Where bolts are used, the spacing shall conform to Clause 10.4.
(c) Hangers used to support prefabricated wood I-joists that do not require bearing stiffeners shall be high enough to provide lateral stability to the top flange of the joist.
(d) Where a prefabricated wood I-joist is the header, backer blocks shall be provided between the web and face mount hangers.
(e) Where a prefabricated wood I-joist is supporting a top mount hanger, filler blocks shall be used between the top and bottom flange of the I-joist. The blocks shall be tight to the bottom of the top flange.

#### 10.10.1.5
Design requirements in Clause 10.10 are for joist hangers tested for vertical load capacity in accordance with ASTM Standard D 1761. A set of at least three tests (six hangers) shall be conducted for each possible variation of the hanger, wood material, and fasteners, including
(a) joist species, size, and type;
(b) header species, size, and type;
(c) joist hanger size and type; and
(d) fastener size, type, and spacing.
For sawn wood and glued-laminated timber joists and headers, the relative density of the material used in testing shall be no greater than 2% above the mean values shown in Table A10.1. For manufactured wood products, the relative density shall be no greater than 2% above the average of the population. The moisture content of sawn wood at the time of testing shall be 11–19%. For wood products that are manufactured, installed, and maintained at or below 15% moisture content, the tests shall be made at a moisture content of 8–15%. To allow for relaxation effects, a minimum period of 1 week shall elapse between assembly and testing of the specimens.

## 10.10.2 Design

### 10.10.2.1
Joist hangers shall be designed so that the effect of the factored loads is less than or equal to the factored resistance of the hanger.

### 10.10.2.2
For joist hangers attached to the face of a header or beam, the shear resistance of the header or beam shall be checked in accordance with Clause 10.2.1.4.

## 10.10.3 Factored Resistance of Joist Hangers

### 10.10.3.1 General
The factored resistance of joist hangers shall be as follows:

$$N_r = \phi \, N_u$$

where
$\phi$ = 0.6
$N_u = n_u \, (K_D K_{SF} K_T)$
$n_u$ = ultimate resistance of the hanger, per Clause 10.10.3.2
$K_D$ = the value determined in accordance with Clause 4.3.2, except that no increase for short-term duration shall be permitted where the ultimate resistance is determined by the strength of the steel

## 10.10.3.2 Ultimate Resistance of Joist Hangers
The ultimate resistance of joist hangers shall be obtained from vertical load tests on no less than three pairs of hangers, conducted in accordance with ASTM Standard D 1761. The ultimate resistance shall be calculated as the lesser of the following:
(a) except as provided in Item (b), the ultimate resistance shall be the lowest corrected ultimate load per hanger calculated in accordance with Clause 10.10.3.3, multiplied by 0.91;
(b) where ten pairs of hangers are tested, the ultimate resistance shall be the lowest corrected ultimate load per hanger calculated in accordance with Clause 10.10.3.3, multiplied by 1.2; or
(c) the average load per hanger at which the vertical movement between the joist and the header is 3 mm, multiplied by 2.42.
**Note:** Test results for hangers are listed in the Registry of Product Evaluations, published by the Canadian Construction Materials Centre, Institute for Research in Construction, Ottawa, Ontario.

## 10.10.3.3 Corrected Ultimate Load of Joist Hangers
The corrected ultimate load per hanger obtained from testing shall be calculated as one-half of the ultimate load per test assembly multiplied by the correction factor, CF, calculated from

$$CF = \frac{f_{u\ min}}{f_{u\ test}} \le 1.0$$

where
$f_{u\ min}$ = minimum specified ultimate tensile strength of the steel
$f_{u\ test}$ = ultimate tensile strength of the hanger steel measured in accordance with ASTM Standard E 8

# 11. Timber Piling

## 11.1 Scope
Design tables, data, and methods specified in Clause 11 apply only to the engineering design of piling,

complying with the requirements of CSA Standard CAN3-O56, as structural members; calculation of the bearing (supporting) capacity of the soil or rock is not included.

## 11.2 Materials

### 11.2.1 Preservative Treatment
Design data and methods specified in Clause 11 are based on the use of piling pressure-treated with preservative in accordance with the requirements of CSA Standard O80 Series, except as provided in Clause 11.2.2.
**Note:** *All species covered by CSA Standard CAN3-O56 are not necessarily suitable for pressure treatment with preservatives. Species of piles to be preservative-treated are restricted to those species listed in CSA Standard O80 Series.*

### 11.2.2 Untreated Piling
Design data and methods specified herein may also be applied to untreated piling used for temporary construction.

## 11.3 Specified Strengths
Specified strengths for round timber piles shall be as in Table 11.3.

## 11.4 Modification Factors
The modification factors in Clause 4.3.2.2 for duration of load and Clause 5.4.2 for service condition shall apply to timber piling specified strengths. No other modification factors shall apply.

## 11.5 Strength and Resistance

### 11.5.1 General
Timber piles may act as end-bearing piles or friction piles and shall be designed to transmit all the applied loads to supporting soil or rock.

### 11.5.2 Piles as Compression Members
Piles shall be considered to act as compression members. Where necessary, piles shall be designed to withstand factored bending moments and factored tensile forces due to uplift or other causes, in accordance with the appropriate provisions of Clause 5.

### 11.5.3 Effective Length
When the finished pile projects above ground level and is not secured against buckling by adequate bracing, the effective length shall be governed by the fixity conditions imposed on it by the structure it supports and by the nature of the ground into which it is driven. In firm soil, the lower point of contraflexure may be taken to be at a depth below ground level of about one-tenth of the exposed length. Where the top stratum is soft clay, or silt, this point may be taken at about one-half the depth of penetration into this stratum, but not less than one-tenth of the exposed length of the pile. Where a pile is wholly embedded, its carrying capacity is not limited by its strength as a long column. However, where there is a stratum of very soft soils or peat, piles shall be designed in accordance with Clause 11.5.5.

### 11.5.4 Embedded Portion

#### 11.5.4.1 General
That portion of a pile permanently in contact with soil or rock providing adequate lateral support shall be designed in accordance with Clause 5.5.6, using a slenderness factor $K_C = 1.00$.

## 11.5.4.2 End-Bearing Piles

The factored compressive resistance, $P_r$, of end-bearing piles shall be calculated for an area, A, equal to the minimum cross-sectional area of the pile.

## 11.5.4.3 Friction Piles

The factored compressive resistance, $P_r$, of friction piles shall be calculated over an area, A, equal to the cross-sectional area of the pile at a point 1/3 of the length of the embedded portion of the pile from the tip.

## 11.5.5 Unembedded Portion

The factored compressive resistance, $P_r$, of that portion of the pile in contact with air, water, or soils that do not provide adequate lateral support shall be calculated in accordance with Clause 5.5.6. The slenderness factor, $K_C$, shall be calculated using a slenderness ratio, $C_C$, determined in accordance with Clauses 12.5.2.5 and 12.5.2.6. Piles subject to eccentric or lateral loads shall be designed in accordance with Clause 5.5.10.

### Table 11.3
### Specified Strengths and Modulus of Elasticity
### for Round Timber Piles (MPa)

| Species | Bending at extreme fibre, $f_b$ | Longitudinal shear, $f_v$ | Compression parallel to grain, $f_c$ | Compression perpendicular to grain, $f_{cp}$ | Tension parallel to grain, $f_t$ | Modulus of elasticity | |
|---|---|---|---|---|---|---|---|
| | | | | | | E | $E_{05}$ |
| Douglas Fir, Western Larch | 20.1 | 1.4 | 18.7 | 7.7 | 13.6 | 11 000 | 7000 |
| Jack Pine | 18.1 | 1.5 | 15.6 | 5.2 | 11.6 | 7000 | 5000 |
| Lodgepole and Ponderosa Pine | 14.2 | 1.0 | 13.2 | 5.2 | 9.7 | 7000 | 5000 |
| Red Pine | 13.6 | 1.2 | 11.7 | 5.2 | 9.0 | 7000 | 5000 |

**Notes:**
**(1)** *Tabulated values are listed for dry service condition and standard-term duration of load.*
**(2)** *Timber piles using Southern Yellow Pine may be assigned the same resistances as the Douglas Fir-Larch species group.*

# 12. Pole-Type Construction

## 12.1 Scope

### 12.1.1 Round Poles

Design data and methods specified in Clause 12 apply only to the engineering design of round poles complying with the physical requirements, other than strength properties, of CSA Standard CAN/CSA-O15 as structural members in pole type structures; calculation of the bearing (supporting) capacity of the soil is not included.

### 12.1.2 Sawn Timbers

Sawn timbers used as poles shall comply with the requirements of Clause 5.

## 12.2 Materials

### 12.2.1 Preservative Treatment

Design data and methods specified in Clause 12 for poles and other wood components that are exposed to soil, moisture, inadequate ventilation, contact with masonry or concrete, or other conditions favourable to decay are predicated on the assumption that the poles, etc, are pressure-treated with preservatives in accordance with the requirements of CSA Standard O80 Series.

**Note:** *All species covered by CSA Standard CAN/CSA-O15 are not necessarily suitable for pressure treatment with preservatives. Species of poles to be preservative-treated are restricted to those species listed in the CSA Standard O80 Series.*

### 12.2.2 Short Poles

When round pole lengths are shorter than specified in CSA Standard CAN/CSA-O15 but meet all other requirements of that Standard, the same taper and the same minimum circumference at the top shall be used in calculations.

## 12.3 Specified Strengths

Specified strengths for round poles, except Eastern White Cedar, shall be 80% of the specified strengths for select structural grade beams and stringers of the appropriate species combination listed in Table 5.3.1C. Specified strengths for round Eastern White Cedar poles shall be 50% of the specified strengths for Select Structural grade beams and stringers of the species combination Northern Species.

## 12.4 Modification Factors

The specified strengths for round poles shall be modified by the same modification factors as for beams and stringers in Clause 5.

## 12.5 Strength and Resistance

### 12.5.1 General

Poles shall be designed to transmit all applied factored loads to the soil and shall be suitable for the soil conditions at the site.

### 12.5.2 Poles as Compression Members

#### 12.5.2.1 General

Where necessary, poles shall be designed to withstand factored bending moments and factored tensile forces due to uplift or other causes, in accordance with the appropriate provisions of Clause 5.

#### 12.5.2.2 Effective Length

Effective length shall be established in accordance with Clause 11.5.3.

#### 12.5.2.3 Embedded Portion

That portion of a pole permanently in contact with soil or rock providing adequate lateral support shall be designed in accordance with Clause 5.5.6, using the slenderness factor $K_C = 1.00$.

#### 12.5.2.4 Unembedded Portion

The factored compressive resistance, $P_r$, of the portion of a pole in contact with air, water, or soil that does not provide adequate lateral support shall be calculated in accordance with Clause 5.5.6. The slenderness factor, $K_C$, shall be calculated using a slenderness ratio, $C_C$, determined in accordance with Clauses 12.5.2.5 and 12.5.2.6. Poles subject to eccentric or lateral loads shall be designed in accordance with Clause 5.5.10.

## 12.5.2.5 Constant Nonrectangular Cross-Section

For nonrectangular compression members of constant section, $r \sqrt{12}$ shall be substituted for member width or depth in Clause 5.5.6, where r is the applicable radius of gyration of the cross-section of the member.

## 12.5.2.6 Variable Circular Cross-Section

The radius of gyration of round tapered compression members shall be calculated for an effective diameter equal to the minimum diameter plus 0.45 times the difference between the maximum and minimum diameters. The factored compressive resistance determined in this manner shall not exceed the factored resistance based on the minimum diameter in conjunction with a slenderness factor $K_C = 1.00$.

## 12.5.3 Poles as Bending Members

The factored bending moment resistance, $M_r$, of round members shall be taken as that of a square member having the same cross-sectional area. A tapered round member shall be considered as an equivalent square member of variable cross-section.

# 13. Proprietary Structural Wood Products

## 13.1 Scope

Clauses 13.2 to 13.4 provide design methods for proprietary structural wood products that conform to the applicable referenced standards and the additional requirements contained in Clause 13.

**Note:** *Clauses 13.2 to 13.4 are provided as a reference for designers to explain the origin of manufacturers' proprietary design values. In general, proprietary design values are published by the product manufacturer (i.e., proprietary design literature and/or CCMC Evaluation Reports within the CCMC Registry of Product Evaluations) with appropriate factors for specific applications. The designer is not normally expected to calculate the proprietary product properties using the equations provided herein. For applications where adjustments to design values may be warranted, the designer is recommended to seek guidance from the product manufacturer. For additional information on proprietary structural wood products in general, and prefabricated wood I-joists and structural composite lumber products in particular, see the Canadian Wood Council's Commentary.*

## 13.2 Prefabricated Wood I-Joists

## 13.2.1 General

Except as specified in Clause 13.2.2.2, all prefabricated wood I-joists for use under the provisions of this Standard shall meet the requirements of, and be evaluated for strength and stiffness in accordance with, ASTM Standard D 5055. Determination of characteristic values for design with prefabricated wood I-joists shall be in accordance with Clause 13.2.3.6.

All prefabricated wood I-joists for use under the provisions of Clause 13.2 shall bear the mark of a certification organization (C.O.) indicating certification by the C.O. as meeting the applicable requirements of Clause 13.2.

## 13.2.2 Materials

## 13.2.2.1 Flange Materials

The provisions of Clause 13.2 apply to flanges as specified in Clause 5 for sawn structurally graded lumber or Clause 6 for glued-laminated timber. Lumber not conforming to Clause 5 and structural composite lumber products may be used as flange material when such material is qualified by testing as specified in ASTM Standard D 5055.

## 13.2.2.2 Structural Panel Webs

Webs for prefabricated wood I-joists shall be manufactured from structural panels conforming to

CSA Standard O121, O151, O153 (Exterior Bond), CAN/CSA-O325.0, O437.0, or O452.0.
**Note:** *For additional information, see the Canadian Wood Council's* Commentary.

Δ **13.2.2.3 Adhesives**
Prefabricated wood I-joists shall be manufactured using
(a) material-specific adhesives conforming to CSA Standard O112.6 or O112.7; or
(b) alternative adhesives conforming to the performance-based Standard, CSA O112.9.
**Note:** *For additional information on equivalent adhesive systems, see the Canadian Wood Council's* Commentary.

## 13.2.3 Specified Strengths and Moduli of Elasticity

### 13.2.3.1 Specified Strength Parallel to Grain, $f_a$
The specified strength parallel to grain, $f_a$, shall be the lesser of the specified strength in tension parallel to grain, $f_t$, or the specified strength in compression parallel to grain, $f_c$, as defined in Clauses 13.2.3.2 and 13.2.3.3.

### 13.2.3.2 Specified Strength in Tension Parallel to Grain, $f_t$
The specified strength in tension parallel to grain, $f_t$, shall be determined in one of the following ways:
(a) where the flange material is sawn lumber conforming to Clause 5.2 or glued-laminated timber conforming to Clause 6.2 of this Standard, the specified strength in tension parallel to grain shall be determined from $f_t$ in Clause 5.3, or $f_{tg}$ in Clause 6.3, respectively; and
(b) where the flange material is not as described in Item (a), $f_t$ shall be taken as

$$f_t = t\,K_r$$

where
t  = the characteristic value for tension parallel to grain as defined in Clause 13.2.3.6, MPa
$K_r$ = reliability normalization factor for bending and tension from Table 13.2.3.2

## Table 13.2.3.2
## Reliability Normalization Factors, $K_r$
## (Applicable to Prefabricated Wood I-Joists
## and Structural Composite Lumber Products Only)

| $CV_w$* % | Bending and tension† | Compression parallel to grain‡ | Shear | |
|---|---|---|---|---|
| | | | Prefabricated wood I-joists | Structural composite lumber |
| 10 | 0.88 | 0.84 | 0.74 | 0.59 |
| 11 | 0.88 | 0.84 | 0.74 | 0.59 |
| 12 | 0.88 | 0.84 | 0.74 | 0.59 |
| 13 | 0.88 | 0.84 | 0.74 | 0.59 |
| 14 | 0.88 | 0.84 | 0.74 | 0.59 |
| 15 | 0.88 | 0.83 | 0.74 | 0.59 |
| 16 | 0.87 | 0.82 | 0.74 | 0.58 |
| 17 | 0.86 | 0.80 | 0.74 | 0.57 |
| 18 | 0.84 | 0.78 | 0.73 | 0.56 |
| 19 | 0.82 | 0.77 | 0.71 | 0.55 |
| 20 | 0.80 | 0.75 | 0.71 | 0.54 |
| 21 | 0.79 | 0.73 | 0.69 | 0.52 |
| 22 | 0.77 | 0.71 | 0.67 | 0.51 |
| 23 | 0.75 | 0.70 | 0.66 | 0.50 |
| 24 | 0.73 | 0.68 | 0.65 | 0.49 |
| 25 | 0.72 | 0.66 | 0.63 | 0.48 |

*$CV_w$ shall be determined in accordance with ASTM Standard D 5457.
†Applicable to structural composite lumber products in bending and tension. Also applicable to flanges of prefabricated wood I-joist flanges in compression as well as tension.
‡Applicable to structural composite lumber products in compression parallel to grain.
**Note:** See also the Canadian Wood Council's Commentary.

## 13.2.3.3 Specified Strength in Compression Parallel to Grain, $f_c$

The specified strength in compression parallel to grain shall be determined in one of the following ways:
(a) where the flange material is sawn lumber conforming to Clause 5.2 or glued-laminated timber conforming to Clause 6.2 of this Standard, the specified strength in compression parallel to grain shall be determined from $f_c$ in Clause 5.3, or $f_c$ in Clause 6.3, respectively; and
(b) where the flange material is not as described in Item (a), $f_c$ shall be taken as

$$f_c = c K_r$$

where
$c$ = the characteristic value for compression parallel to grain as defined in Clause 13.2.3.6, MPa
$K_r$ = reliability normalization factor for bending and tension from Table 13.2.3.2

## 13.2.3.4 Specified Shear Capacity, $V_c$

The specified shear capacity, $V_c$, shall be taken as

$$V_c = v K_r$$

where
v  = the characteristic value for shear as defined in Clause 13.2.3.6, N
$K_r$ = reliability normalization factor for shear for prefabricated wood I-joists from Table 13.2.3.2

## 13.2.3.5 Modulus of Elasticity

The modulus of elasticity of flange material shall be determined in one of the following ways:
(a) where the flange material is sawn lumber conforming to Clause 5.2 or glued-laminated timber conforming to Clause 6.2 of this Standard, the modulus of elasticity shall be determined from Clause 5.3 or Clause 6.3, respectively; and
(b) where the flange material is not as described in Item (a), the modulus of elasticity shall be the mean value of the modulus of elasticity determined from the test results required by ASTM Standard D 5055, Section 6.5.2.1.

## 13.2.3.6 Characteristic Values

(a) The maximum characteristic shear value, v, for prefabricated wood I-joists shall be the shear capacity as defined in ASTM Standard D 5055 and multiplied by 2.37.
(b) The maximum characteristic value in tension parallel to grain, t, for flanges of prefabricated wood I-joists shall be taken as
　(i) for sawn lumber, the flange tensile capacity as determined in ASTM Standard D 5055 multiplied by 2.1; and
　(ii) for structural composite lumber, the characteristic value in tension, $t_{SCL}$, from Clause 13.4.3.5.
(c) The maximum characteristic value in compression parallel to grain, c, for flanges of prefabricated wood I-joists shall be calculated from one of the following:
　(i) for sawn lumber, c shall be calculated from the following:

$$c = t \, (f_{c1}/ f_{t1})$$

where
$f_{t1}$ = closest assigned specified strength to $f_t$ in tension parallel to grain from Clause 5.3 of this Standard for the species and size tested in accordance with ASTM Standard D 5055
$f_{c1}$ = assigned specified strength in compression parallel to grain from Clause 5.3 of this Standard for the same grade, species, and size as $f_{t1}$

　(ii) for structural composite lumber, the characteristic value in compression, c, from Clause 13.4.3.4.
(d) For prefabricated wood I-joists with either sawn lumber or structural composite lumber flanges, when determined in accordance with the empirical method of Section 6.3.3 of ASTM Standard D 5055, the maximum characteristic value for moment capacity shall be based on the lower 5% tolerance limit with 75% confidence.

## 13.2.4 Modification Factors

### 13.2.4.1 Load Duration Factor, $K_D$

The specified strengths of prefabricated wood I-joists shall be multiplied by a load duration factor, $K_D$, as given in Clause 4.3.2.

### 13.2.4.2 Service Condition Factor, $K_S$

The specified strengths and stiffness of prefabricated wood I-joists described in Clause 13 are applicable for use in dry service conditions with $K_S = 1.0$.

### 13.2.4.3 Treatment Factor, $K_T$

The specified strengths and stiffness described in Clause 13 are applicable to untreated prefabricated wood I-joists with $K_T = 1.0$.

Δ **13.2.4.4  System Factor, $K_H$**

The system factor, $K_H$, for prefabricated wood I-joists shall be taken as 1.0.
**Note:** *For additional information, see Appendix X1.4.1 of ASTM Standard D 5055.*

## 13.2.5  Strength and Resistance

Δ **13.2.5.1  Bending Moment Resistance**

The factored bending moment resistance, $M_r$, of prefabricated wood I-joists shall be calculated using either

$$M_r = \phi\, f_a K_{LN} A_{net} Y\, (K_D K_S K_H K_T K_{Zt})\, K_L$$

or

$$M_r = \phi\, M_{cv}(K_D K_S K_H K_T)\, K_r K_L$$

where
$\phi$   = 0.90
$f_a$   = specified strength parallel to grain, per Clause 13.2.3.1, MPa
$K_{LN}$ = length adjustment factor, as defined in ASTM Standard D 5055 (see Clause A13.2.5.1)
$A_{net}$ = net area of one flange, excluding all areas of web material and rout, mm²
$Y$   = distance between the flange centroids, with the rout removed, mm
$K_S$   = service condition factor, as per Clause 13.2.4.2
$K_H$   = system factor, per Clause 13.2.4.4
$K_{Zt}$ = the size factor for tension parallel to grain, from Table 5.4.5, applicable only to visually stress-graded lumber used in accordance with Clause 13.2.3.1
$K_L$   = lateral stability factor, per Clause 13.2.5.2
$M_{cv}$ = the characteristic value for moment capacity as defined in Clause 13.2.3.6(d), N•m
$K_r$   = reliability normalization factor for bending and tension, from Table 13.2.3.2

**13.2.5.2  Lateral Stability Factor, $K_L$**

The lateral stability factor, $K_L$, shall be taken as unity when lateral support is provided at points of bearing, to prevent lateral displacement and rotation, and along all compression edges. Lateral support requirements and lateral stability factors for other applications such as continuous spans shall be based on analytical and engineering principles or documented test data, or both, that demonstrate the safe use of the product in the intended application.
**Note:** *For additional information on lateral stability, see the Canadian Wood Council's Commentary.*

**13.2.5.3  Notches**

Notching or cutting of the flanges of prefabricated wood I-joists shall not be permitted, unless such details have been evaluated and are demonstrated to be acceptable based on documented test data.

**13.2.5.4  Shear Resistance**

The factored shear resistance, $V_r$, of prefabricated wood I-joists shall be taken as

$$V_r = \phi V_c K_v$$

where
$\phi$  = 0.90
$V_c$ = specified shear capacity for a given brand and depth of prefabricated wood I-joist, in accordance with Clause 13.2.3.4, N
$K_v$ = $K_D K_S K_T$

Neglecting loads within a distance from the support equal to the depth of the member shall not be permitted, and any adjustments to the shear design value near the support shall be substantiated by independent testing to the shear capacity criteria in ASTM Standard D 5055.

## 13.2.5.5 Web Openings, Bearing Length, and Web Stiffener Requirements

Designers shall obtain information regarding web openings, bearing length, and web stiffener requirements from specific prefabricated wood I-joist manufacturers. The requirements for permitted web openings, minimum bearing length, and web stiffener details shall be determined in accordance with ASTM Standard D 5055.

**Note:** *For additional information, see the Canadian Wood Council's* Commentary.

## 13.2.5.6 Serviceability Limit States

Design of prefabricated wood I-joists for serviceability limit states shall be in accordance with Clauses 4.1.3 and 4.5. Deflection calculations shall include shear deformation.

The flange moduli of elasticity for stiffness calculations shall be taken as

$$E_s = E\,(K_{SE}\,K_{TE})$$

The effective stiffness, $EI_w$, of prefabricated wood I-joist web members employing structural panels in Clause 7.3 conforming to CSA Standard O121, O151, CAN/CSA-O325.0, or O452.0 shall be taken as

$$EI_w = \left(\sum B_a\right)\left(\frac{W_D{}^3}{12}\right) K_{SE}\,K_{TE}$$

The shear-through-thickness rigidity, $W_S$, of structural panels in Clause 7.3 used as web members of prefabricated wood I-joists and conforming to CSA Standard O121, O151, CAN/CSA-O325.0, or O452.0 shall be taken as

$$W_S = B_v\,K_{SG}\,K_{TG}$$

where
$E$ = specified modulus of elasticity, per Clause 13.2.3.5
$K_{SE}$ = service condition factor for modulus of elasticity
   = 1.0 for dry service condition (in accordance with Clause 13.2.4.2)
$K_{TE}$ = treatment factor for modulus of elasticity
   = 1.0 for untreated prefabricated wood I-joists (see Clause 13.2.4.3)
$B_a$ = axial stiffness (tension or compression) from Table 7.3A, 7.3B, 7.3C, or 7.3D, N/mm
$W_D$ = overall depth of the structural panel web, mm
$B_v$ = shear-through-thickness rigidity from Table 7.3A, 7.3B, 7.3C, or 7.3D, N/mm
$K_{SG}$ = service condition factor for shear-through-thickness rigidity
   = 1.0 for dry service condition (see Clause 13.2.4.2)
$K_{TG}$ = treatment factor for shear-through-thickness rigidity
   = 1.0 for untreated prefabricated wood I-joists (see Clause 13.2.4.3)

**Note:** *Axial web stiffness and web shear-through-thickness rigidity for products not covered by Table 7.3A, 7.3B, 7.3C, or 7.3D must be determined from appropriate standards or documented test data, which can be obtained from the prefabricated wood I-joist manufacturer.*

## 13.2.6 Fastenings

### 13.2.6.1 Nails

Nailed connections shall be designed in accordance with Clause 10.9.

### 13.2.6.2 Joist Hangers and Other Framing Connectors

The use of joist hangers and other framing connectors with prefabricated wood I-joists shall be based on documented test data.

**Note:** *Required details of use and attachment are available from the manufacturers. For additional information, see Clause 10.10 and the Canadian Wood Council's Commentary.*

## 13.3 Type 3 (Proprietary) Design-Rated OSB Panels

### 13.3.1 Manufacture

Type 3 (Proprietary) design-rated OSB structural panels shall be manufactured and their structural properties evaluated in accordance with the testing, quality control, and quality assurance and certification provisions of the CSA Standard O452 Series. Type 3 OSB structural panels may be of any thickness.

### 13.3.2 Panel Identification and Certificates of Conformance

Each Type 3 (Proprietary) OSB product shall be identified by a distinctive company product designation approved by the certification organization. Its compliance with the requirements in CSA Standard O452.0 for Type 3 products shall be verified by the Certificate of Conformance issued by the certification organization. The Certificate of Conformance shall identify the product designation, the nominal thickness, and the assigned specified capacities (see Clause 13.3.4).

### 13.3.3 Basic Structural Capacities

Nominal thicknesses and basic structural capacities from which specified design capacities are derived shall be determined in accordance with the CSA Standard O452 Series.

**Note:** *The basic structural capacities are the lower tolerance limits of the mean stiffness and of the lower fifth percentile of strength, determined from testing of the mechanical properties, and adjusted to dry service conditions.*

### 13.3.4 Specified Capacities

#### 13.3.4.1 Derivation

The specified capacities for stiffness and strength of Type 3 OSB structural panels shall be derived for each product from its basic structural capacities in accordance with Clauses 13.3.4.2 and 13.3.4.3.

#### 13.3.4.2 Specified Stiffness and Rigidity

The specified capacities for stiffness and rigidity for a Type 3 OSB panel shall be its basic structural capacities, rounded to two significant figures.

#### 13.3.4.3 Specified Strengths

The standard term specified strength capacities for a Type 3 OSB panel shall be equal to the basic strength capacities determined in accordance with the CSA Standard O452 Series multiplied by an adjustment factor of 0.8, and rounded to two significant figures.

#### 13.3.4.4 Application of Specified Capacities

The specified capacities determined by Clauses 13.3.4.1 to 13.3.4.3 for a Type 3 OSB structural panel may be used in design procedures for structural panels specified in this Standard.

### 13.3.5 Design Methods

Designs with Type 3 (Proprietary) design-rated OSB shall be in accordance with the modification factors and design methods for OSB structural panels (see Clauses 7.4 and 7.5).

## 13.4 Structural Composite Lumber Products

### 13.4.1 General
All structural composite lumber products for use under the provisions of this Standard shall be manufactured to, and evaluated for, characteristic values in accordance with the requirements of ASTM Standard D 5456.

All structural composite lumber products for use under the provisions of Clause 13.4, including products subjected to secondary processing operations, shall bear the mark of a certification organization (C.O.) indicating certification by the C.O. as meeting the applicable requirements of Clauses 13.4.2 to 13.4.6.

### Δ 13.4.2 Adhesives and Binder Systems

#### 13.4.2.1 Adhesives
Adhesives used in the manufacture of structural composite lumber products shall be
(a) material-specific adhesives conforming to CSA Standard O112.6 or O112.7; or
(b) alternative adhesives conforming to the performance-based Standard, CSA O112.9.

#### 13.4.2.2 Binder Systems
Binder systems shall demonstrate equivalent performance to the adhesives of Clause 13.4.2.1(a).
**Note:** *For additional information on equivalent adhesives, see the Canadian Wood Council's Commentary.*

### 13.4.3 Specified Strengths and Moduli of Elasticity

#### 13.4.3.1 General
Specified strengths and moduli of elasticity for structural composite lumber products for use with this Standard shall be established in accordance with Clauses 13.4.3.2 to 13.4.3.7.

#### 13.4.3.2 Specified Bending Strength, $f_b$
The specified bending strength, $f_b$, for structural composite lumber products shall be taken as

$$f_b = F_B K_r$$

where
$F_B$ = the characteristic value in bending as determined by ASTM Standard D 5456, MPa
$K_r$ = reliability normalization factor for bending and tension from Table 13.2.3.2

#### 13.4.3.3 Specified Shear Strength, $f_v$
The specified shear strength, $f_v$, for structural composite lumber products shall be taken as

$$f_v = v_{SCL} K_r$$

where
$v_{SCL}$ = the characteristic value in shear as determined by ASTM Standard D 5456, MPa
$K_r$ = reliability normalization factor for shear for structural composite lumber from Table 13.2.3.2

#### 13.4.3.4 Specified Compression Strength Parallel to Grain, $f_c$
The specified compression strength parallel to grain, $f_c$, for structural composite lumber products shall be taken as

$$f_c = c K_r$$

where
c   =   the characteristic value in compression parallel to grain as determined by ASTM Standard D 5456, MPa
$K_r$   =   reliability normalization factor for compression parallel to grain from Table 13.2.3.2

## 13.4.3.5  Specified Compression Strength, Perpendicular to Grain, $f_{cp}$
The specified compression strength perpendicular to grain, $f_{cp}$ (MPa), for structural composite lumber products shall not exceed the characteristic value for compression perpendicular to grain as determined by ASTM Standard D 5456, multiplied by 1.09.

## 13.4.3.6  Specified Tension Strength Parallel to Grain, $f_t$
The specified tension strength parallel to grain, $f_t$, for structural composite lumber products shall be taken as

$$f_t = t_{SCL}K_r$$

where
$t_{SCL}$   =   the characteristic value in tension parallel to grain as determined by ASTM Standard D 5456, MPa
$K_r$      =   reliability normalization factor for bending and tension from Table 13.2.3.2

## 13.4.3.7  Specified Modulus of Elasticity
The specified moduli of elasticity, E, for structural composite lumber products shall be the mean moduli as determined by ASTM Standard D 5456.

## 13.4.4  Modification Factors

### 13.4.4.1  Load Duration Factor, $K_D$
The load duration factors, $K_D$, as given in Clause 4.3.2 are applicable to the specified strengths of structural composite lumber products, provided that appropriate testing has been conducted that demonstrates the validity of those load duration factors for use with the structural composite lumber product.
**Note:** *See also the Canadian Wood Council's* Commentary.

### 13.4.4.2  Service Condition Factor, $K_S$
The specified strengths and stiffness of structural composite lumber products described in Clause 13.4.4 are applicable for use in dry service conditions with $K_S = 1.0$. If structural composite lumber products are to be used in other than dry service conditions, the specified strengths and stiffness shall be evaluated, including development of appropriate strength reduction factors, based on documented test results.

### 13.4.4.3  Treatment Factor, $K_T$
The specified strengths and stiffness described in Clause 13.4.4 are applicable to untreated structural composite lumber products with $K_T = 1.0$. Treatment adjustments for specified strengths and stiffness shall be based on the documented results of tests that shall take into account the effects of time, temperature, and moisture content.

### 13.4.4.4  System Factor, $K_H$
The system factor, $K_H$, permitted for structural composite lumber products used in a load-sharing system shall be 1.04.
   To qualify for the above increase, the structural composite lumber products shall be part of a wood-framing system consisting of at least three parallel members joined by transverse load distributing elements adequate to support the design load and shall not be spaced more than 610 mm on centre.

Δ  ### 13.4.4.5  Size Factor in Bending, $K_{Zb}$
The size factor in bending, $K_{Zb}$, for structural composite lumber products shall be taken as

$$K_{Zb} = \left(\frac{d_1}{d}\right)^{\frac{1}{n}}$$

where
$d_1$ = specified depth on which the published specified strength in bending, $f_b$, is based
$d$ = depth of application member
$n$ = parameter defined in Section 7.4.1.3 of ASTM Standard D 5456.

### 13.4.4.6 Size Factor in Tension, $K_{Zt}$

The size factor in tension, $K_{Zt}$, for structural composite lumber products shall be taken as

$$K_{Zt} = \left(\frac{L_1}{L}\right)^{\frac{1}{m}}$$

where
$L_1$ = base length between test grips, as tested in Section 5.5.2 of ASTM Standard D 5456
$L$ = end use length
$m$ = parameter determined in accordance with Annex A1 of ASTM Standard D 5456

## 13.4.5 Strength and Resistance

### 13.4.5.1 Bending Moment Resistance

The factored bending moment resistance, $M_r$, of structural composite lumber products shall be taken as

$$M_r = \phi F_b\, S K_{Zb}\, K_L$$

where
$\phi$ = 0.90
$F_b$ = $f_b (K_D K_H K_{Sb} K_T)$
$f_b$ = specified bending strength, per Clause 13.4.3.2, MPa
$K_{Zb}$ = size factor in bending, per Clause 13.4.4.5
$K_L$ = lateral stability factor, per Clause 13.4.5.2

### 13.4.5.2 Lateral Stability Factor, $K_L$

The lateral stability factor, $K_L$, for structural composite lumber products shall be determined in accordance with Clause 5.5.4.2.

### 13.4.5.3 Notches

The use of structural composite lumber products with notches or cuts shall not be permitted unless such details have been evaluated and are demonstrated to be acceptable based on documented test data.

### 13.4.5.4 Shear Resistance

The factored shear resistance, $V_r$, of structural composite lumber products shall be taken as

$$V_r = \phi F_v \frac{2A}{3} K_{Zv}$$

where
$\phi$ = 0.90
$F_v$ = $f_v (K_D K_{Sv} K_T)$
$f_v$ = specified shear strength of structural composite lumber products, per Clause 13.4.3.3, MPa
$A$ = cross-sectional area of member, mm$^2$
$K_{Zv}$ = 1.0

**Note:** *For additional information on size factor in shear, $K_{Zv}$, see the Canadian Wood Council's Commentary.*

## 13.4.5.5 Compressive Resistance Parallel to Grain

### 13.4.5.5.1 Effective Length, $L_e$

Unless noted otherwise, the effective length, $L_e = K_e L$, shall be used in determining the slenderness ratio of structural composite lumber products in compression.

Recommended effective length factors, $K_e$, for structural composite lumber products in compression are given in Table A5.5.6.1.

### 13.4.5.5.2 Slenderness Ratio, $C_C$

The slenderness ratio, $C_C$, of simple compression members of constant rectangular section shall not exceed 50 and shall be taken as the greater of

$$C_C = \frac{\text{effective length associated with width}}{\text{member width}}$$

or

$$C_C = \frac{\text{effective length associated with depth}}{\text{member depth}}$$

### 13.4.5.5.3 Factored Compressive Resistance Parallel to Grain

The factored compressive resistance parallel to grain, $P_r$, of structural composite lumber products shall be taken as

$$P_r = \phi F_c A K_C K_{Zc}$$

where
$\phi$ = 0.80
$F_c$ = $f_c (K_D K_{sc} K_T)$
$f_c$ = specified strength in compression parallel to grain, per Clause 13.4.3.4, MPa
$A$ = cross-sectional area of member, mm²
$K_C$ = slenderness factor, per Clause 13.4.5.6
$K_{Zc}$ = 1.0
**Note:** *For additional information on size factor in compression parallel to grain, $K_{Zc}$, see the Canadian Wood Council's Commentary.*

## 13.4.5.6 Slenderness Factor, $K_C$

The slenderness factor, $K_C$, shall be determined as follows:

$$K_c = \left[1.0 + \frac{F_c K_{Zc} C_C^3}{35 E_{05} K_{SE} K_T}\right]^{-1}$$

where
$E_{05}$ = 0.87E

## 13.4.5.7 Compressive Resistance Perpendicular to Grain (Bearing)

### 13.4.5.7.1 Maximum Loads

Factored bearing forces shall not exceed the factored compressive resistance perpendicular to grain in accordance with the provisions of Clauses 13.4.5.7.2 to 13.4.5.7.4.

### 13.4.5.7.2 Effect of All Applied Loads

The factored compressive resistance perpendicular to grain under the effect of all applied loads, $Q_r$, shall be taken as

$$Q_r = \phi F_{cp} A_b K_B K_{Zcp}$$

where
$\phi$ = 0.80
$F_{cp}$ = $f_{cp}(K_D K_S K_T)$
$f_{cp}$ = specified strength in compression perpendicular to grain, per Clause 13.4.3.5, MPa
$A_b$ = bearing area, $mm^2$
$K_B$ = length of bearing factor (Clause 5.5.7.6)
$K_{Zcp}$ = size factor for bearing (Clause 5.5.7.5)

## 13.4.5.7.3 Effect of Loads Applied near a Support
The factored compressive resistance perpendicular to grain under the effect of only those loads acting within a distance from the centre of the support equal to the depth of the member, $Q'_r$, shall be taken as

$$Q'_r = (2/3)\, \phi\, F_{cp} A'_b K_B K_{Zcp}$$

where
$\phi$ = 0.8
$F_{cp}$ = $f_{cp}(K_D K_S K_T)$
$f_{cp}$ = specified strength in compression perpendicular to grain, per Clause 13.4.3.5, MPa
$A'_b$ = average bearing area (see Clause 13.4.5.7.4), $mm^2$

## 13.4.5.7.4 Average Bearing Area
Where unequal bearing areas are used on opposite surfaces of a member, the average bearing area shall not exceed the following:

$$A'_b = b\left(\frac{L_{b1} + L_{b2}}{2}\right), \text{ but } \leq 1.5b(L_{b1})$$

where
b = average bearing width (perpendicular to grain), mm
$L_{b1}$ = lesser bearing length, mm
$L_{b2}$ = larger bearing length, mm

## 13.4.5.8 Compressive Resistance at an Angle to Grain
The factored compressive resistance at an angle to grain shall be calculated in accordance with the requirements of Clause 5.5.8, using the appropriate specified strengths and resistances for the proprietary grade of structural composite lumber products.

## 13.4.5.9 Tensile Resistance Parallel to Grain
The factored tensile resistance parallel to grain, $T_r$, of structural composite lumber products shall be taken as

$$T_r = \phi F_t A_n K_{Zt}$$

where
$\phi$ = 0.90
$F_t$ = $f_t(K_D K_{St} K_T)$
$f_t$ = specified strength in tension parallel to grain, per Clause 13.4.3.6, MPa
$A_n$ = net area, $mm^2$
$K_{Zt}$ = size factor in tension, per Clause 13.4.4.6

## 13.4.5.10  Resistance to Combined Bending and Axial Load

Members subject to combined bending and compressive or tensile axial loads shall be designed to satisfy the appropriate interaction equation:

$$\frac{P_f}{P_r} + \frac{M_f}{M_r} \leq 1.0$$

or

$$\frac{T_f}{T_r} + \frac{M_f}{M_r} \leq 1.0$$

where

$P_f$ = factored compressive axial load

$P_r$ = factored compressive resistance parallel to grain calculated in accordance with the requirements of Clause 13.4.5.5.3

$M_f$ = factored bending moment, taking into account end moments and amplified moments due to axial loads in laterally loaded members

$M_r$ = factored bending moment resistance calculated in accordance with the requirements of Clause 13.4.5.1

$T_f$ = factored tensile axial load

$T_r$ = factored tensile resistance parallel to grain calculated in accordance with the requirements of Clause 13.4.5.9

## 13.4.5.11  Serviceability Limit States

Design of structural composite lumber products for serviceability limit states shall be in accordance with Clauses 4.1.3 and 4.5.  Deflection calculations shall include shear deformation.

The member modulus of elasticity for stiffness calculations shall be taken as

$$E_s = E (K_{SE} K_{TE})$$

where

$E$ = specified modulus of elasticity, per Clause 13.4.3.7, MPa

$K_{SE}$ = service condition factor for modulus of elasticity

     = 1.0 for dry service condition, per Clause 13.4.4.2

$K_{TE}$ = treatment factor for modulus of elasticity

     = 1.0 for untreated structural composite lumber products, per Clause 13.4.4.3

The shear modulus or shear rigidity, $G_S$, for stiffness calculations shall be taken as

$$G_S = G (K_{SG} K_{TG})$$

where

$G$ = specified shear modulus or shear rigidity established by test or as published in a recognized reference for the structural composite lumber product wood species, MPa

$K_{SG}$ = service condition factor for shear modulus

     = 1.0 for dry service condition, per Clause 13.4.4.2

$K_{TG}$ = treatment factor shear modulus

     = 1.0 for untreated structural composite lumber products, per Clause 13.4.4.3

## 13.4.6  Fastenings

## 13.4.6.1  Joist Hangers

The use of joist hangers with a specific proprietary structural composite lumber product shall conform to the requirements of Clause 10.10.

## 13.4.6.2 Other Fastenings

The procedures and specified capacities for nails, bolts, lag screws, timber rivets, shear plates, truss plates, and split rings in Clause 10 may be used for the design of fastenings for a proprietary structural composite lumber product when testing has demonstrated the validity of those procedures and specified capacities for use with that product.

**Notes:**

**(1)** *Design information for some fasteners, primarily nails and joist hangers, applicable for use with specific proprietary structural composite lumber products are listed in the* Registry of Product Evaluations, *published by the Canadian Construction Materials Centre, Institute for Research in Construction, Ottawa, Ontario. Additional design information for fasteners for use with specific proprietary structural composite lumber products, including specified capacities, will be developed as test data becomes available. It is recommended that manufacturers list such additional design information for their products with the* Registry of Product Evaluations.

**(2)** *In the absence of design information for specific fasteners in specific proprietary structural composite lumber products as set out above, connections for structural composite lumber products should be limited to bearing-type arrangements.*

# *Appendix A*
# *Additional Information and Alternative Procedures*

**Notes:**
**(1)** *This Appendix is not a mandatory part of this Standard. Some clauses have been written in mandatory language to facilitate their adoption by anyone wishing to do so.*
**(2)** *Clause numbering within this Appendix corresponds to the clause numbering in the main body of the Standard.*

## A4.3.5 System Modification Factor, $K_H$

It is well known that the behaviour of a single member does not represent that of a system such as a floor or a flat roof with a number of joists or rafters. System behaviour can be accounted for in single member design by implementing system modification factors: $K_H$ for strength and $K_\Delta$ for serviceability. In this edition of the Standard, only $K_H$ has been quantified.

The system modification factor, $K_H$, is a function of the parameters that define the mechanical state and physical layout of the system. These parameters are the mean live load and its coefficient of variation, the mean modulus of rupture and its coefficient of variation, the mean modulus of elasticity and its coefficient of variation, the MOE-MOR correlation, the sheathing thickness, and the fastening stiffness. The Canadian Wood Council's *Commentary* contains further information on this method.

## A4.5.2 Elastic Deflection of Wood Light-Frame Systems under Static Loads

### A4.5.2.1 Wood Frame Deflection Calculations

Wood frame systems connected with sheathing or cladding on one or both sides deflect less than the joists, rafters, or studs carrying the same loads independently. Traditionally, however, deflection calculations have ignored this interaction and assumed that each framing member in these systems is loaded individually on its tributary area. The deflection criteria that evolved from this approach have provided satisfactory system performance based on calculated single member deflections.

It is possible to estimate system performance by calculating system factors greater than 1.0 as a ratio of system deflection to single member deflection. Caution should be used when implementing system factors in traditional design procedures. Where design procedures incorporate a system factor for deflection, there is a need to consider whether the system effects add to enhancements that are already present in traditional wood frame performance, before adjusting design procedure criteria.

### A4.5.2.2 Elastic Deflection of Stud Wall Systems under Wind Load

Typical wood stud wall systems sheathed with wood panel products and designed for a single member deflection of 1/360 of the span may satisfy the intent of masonry design specifications intended to limit the deflection of steel studs in high-rise buildings to 1/720 of the span.

For example, the actual deflection would be approximately half of the deflection calculated on a single member basis under the following conditions:
(a) lumber modulus of elasticity (see Table 5.3.1A) derived from visually graded lumber data;
(b) lumber used in a stud wall system (i.e., 38 × 89 mm or 38 × 140 mm) meeting minimum requirements for Case 2 system factor (see Clause 5.4.4.2);
(c) gypsum wallboard or structural sheathing attached to the inside face of the studs in accordance with minimum building code requirements; and
(d) cladding and secondary member wind loading based on the tributary area of a stud in a low-rise building.

## A4.5.5 Floor Vibration

Serviceability design of wood-framed floor systems, like other floor systems, has traditionally been addressed by limiting the computed joist deflection under a uniform load. For some floor systems and end uses, traditional criteria have provided satisfactory performance. However, these criteria do not always restrict floor vibration to the satisfaction of occupants. Vibration design of wood-framed floor systems has evolved from a single limitation on maximum uniform load deflection (e.g., 1/360 or 1/480 of span) to a dual check that adds a limitation on point load deflection (see, for example, National Building Code of Canada, Part 9).

While the point load deflection check has proven to be adequate for traditional sawn lumber joist floors, it does not adequately address the broad range of application variables that occur in engineered wood product floor systems. The span capabilities and optimization of engineered wood floor systems may merit a more refined analysis procedure. This may take the form of recommended maximum spans or calculation procedures.

Users are advised to exercise judgment in applying simplified criteria when attempting to limit objectionable floor vibrations in these systems. Particular emphasis should be placed on natural frequency (related to mass and stiffness), relative along-joist and across-joist system stiffnesses, and the effectiveness of between-joist bridging/blocking systems.

In addition to the guidance provided by the NRC's Structural Commentaries to Part 4 of the National Building Code of Canada, users are directed to the Canadian Wood Council's Commentary, to assist in their assessment of floor vibration issues for their specific applications.

## Table A5.5.2
## Minimum Dressed Sizes of Dimension Lumber and Timbers*

| Item | Smaller dimension, mm | | Larger dimension, mm | |
|---|---|---|---|---|
| | Dry | Green | Dry | Green |
| Dimension | 38 | 40 | 38 | 40 |
| lumber | 51 | 53 | 64 | 66 |
| | 64 | 66 | 89 | 91 |
| | 76 | 78 | 114 | 117 |
| | 89 | 91 | 140 | 143 |
| | 102 | 104 | 184 | 190 |
| | | | 235 | 241 |
| | | | 286 | 292 |
| | | | 337 | 343 |
| | | | 387 | 393 |
| Timbers | 114 | | 114 | |
| | 140 | | 140 | |
| | 165 | | 165 | |
| | 191 | | 191 | |
| | 216 | | 216 | |
| | 241 | | 241 | |
| | 292 | | 292 | |
| | 343 | | 343 | |
| | 394 | | 394 | |

*Sizes are rounded to the nearest whole millimetre and are based on CSA Standard CAN/CSA-O141.
**Notes:**
(1) Dry lumber is defined as lumber that has been seasoned or dried to a moisture content of 19% or less.
(2) Green lumber is defined as lumber having a moisture content in excess of 19%.

## A5.5.6.1 Effective Length Factor, $K_e$

### Table A5.5.6.1
### Minimum Design Values of Effective
### Length Factor, $K_e$, for Compression Members

| Degree of end restraint of compression member | Effective length factor, $K_e$ | Symbol |
|---|---|---|
| Effectively held in position and restrained against rotation at both ends | 0.65 | |
| Effectively held in position at both ends, restrained against rotation at one end | 0.80 | |
| Effectively held in position at both ends, but not restrained against rotation | 1.00 | |
| Effectively held in position and restrained against rotation at one end, and at the other restrained against rotation but not held in position | 1.20 | |
| Effectively held in position and restrained against rotation at one end, and at the other partially restrained against rotation but not held in position | 1.50 | |
| Effectively held in position at one end but not restrained against rotation, and at the other end restrained against rotation but not held in position | 2.00 | |
| Effectively held in position and restrained against rotation at one end but not held in position nor restrained against rotation at the other end | 2.00 | |

**Note:** *Effective length $L_e = K_e L$, where L is the distance between centres of lateral supports of the compression member in the plane in which buckling is being considered. At a base or cap detail, the distance shall be measured from the outer surface of the base or cap plate. The effective length factor, $K_e$, shall be not less than what would be indicated by rational analysis. Where conditions of end restraint cannot be evaluated closely, a conservative value for $K_e$ shall be used.*

## A5.5.6.3 Spaced Compression Members

### A5.5.6.3.1 General
Spaced compression members shall consist of two or more individual members joined with timber connectors and having spacer and end blocks as specified in Clauses A5.5.6.3.2, A5.5.6.3.3, and A5.5.6.3.4.

### A5.5.6.3.2 Spacer and End Blocks
Requirements for spacer and end blocks are as follows:
(a) End blocks shall be so placed that end and edge distances and spacing, as required in Clause 10 for the size and number of connectors, are maintained in end blocks and in individual members. Connectors shall be placed so that the limits according to Clause A5.5.6.3.3, depending on the fixity factor assumed,

are met. In compression members of trusses, a panel point that is stayed laterally may be considered as the end of the spaced member.

(b) A single spacer block shall be located within the middle 10% of the length of the compression members; when so located, connectors are not necessary for this block. When more than one spacer block is used, the distance between any two blocks shall not exceed one-half the distance between centres of connectors in the end blocks. The requirements for connectors shall be the same as for end blocks, when two or more spacer blocks are used.

(c) The thickness of spacer and end blocks shall be not less than that of the individual members of the spaced compression member, except that spacer and end blocks of a thickness between that of the individual members and one-half that thickness may be used, provided that the length of the blocks is made inversely proportional to the thickness in relation to the required length of full-thickness block. Spacer and end block sizes shall be adequate to develop the strength required by Clause 10.

### A5.5.6.3.3  Fixity Classes

Spaced compression members shall be classified as to end fixity either as condition "a" or condition "b", as follows (see Figure A5.5.6.3):

(a) for condition "a", the centroid of connectors or of the connector group in the end block shall be within one-twentieth of the length, L, from the end of the member; and

(b) for condition "b", the centroid of connectors or of the connector group in the end block shall be between one-twentieth and one-tenth of the length, L, from the end of the member.

### A5.5.6.3.4  Connectors in End Blocks

The connectors in each pair of contacting surfaces of end blocks and individual members at each end of a spaced compression member shall be at least of a size and number to provide a factored strength resistance (N) equal to the required cross-sectional area in square millimetres of one of the individual members multiplied by the appropriate end block constant listed in Table A5.5.6.3.

### A5.5.6.3.5

The slenderness ratio, $C_C$, of spaced compression members of uniform rectangular section shall not exceed 80 and shall be taken as

$$C_C = \frac{\text{actual length between points of lateral support}}{\text{least dimension of an individual member}}$$

### A5.5.6.3.6  Factored Compressive Resistance Parallel to Grain

The factored compressive load resistance, $P_r$, parallel to grain shall be taken as

$$P_r = \phi F_c A K_c K_{zc}$$

where

$\phi$ = resistance factor (Clause A5.5.6.3.7)

$F_c$ = $f_c (K_D K_{Sc} K_T)$

$f_c$ = specified strength in compression parallel to grain (Tables 5.3.1A and 5.3.3 for sawn lumber and Table 6.3 for glulam), MPa

$A$ = total cross-sectional area, mm$^2$

$K_C$ = slenderness factor (Clause A5.5.6.3.7)

$K_{zc}$ = size factor

= $6.3(dL)^{-0.13} < 1.3$ for sawn lumber

= 1.0 for glued-laminated timber

$d$ = member dimension in direction of buckling (depth or width), mm

$L$ = column length associated with member dimension, mm

## A5.5.6.3.7 Resistance Factor, φ, and Slenderness Factor, K$_C$

The resistance factor, φ, and the slenderness factor, K$_C$, shall be determined as follows:

φ = 0.80 for sawn lumber
= 0.90 for glued-laminated timber

(a) when C$_C$ does not exceed 10

K$_C$ = 1.00

(b) when C$_C$ is greater than 10 but does not exceed C$_K$

$$K_c = 1 - \frac{1}{3}\left(\frac{C_C}{C_K}\right)^4$$

$$C_K = \sqrt{\frac{0.76 E_{05} K_{SE} K_E K_T}{F_c}}$$

where
E$_{05}$ = the applicable value from Tables 5.3.1A to 5.3.1D for visually graded sawn lumber
= 0.82E for MSR lumber
= 0.87E for glued-laminated timber
K$_E$ = end fixity factor (see Clause A5.5.6.3.3)
= 2.50 for condition a
= 3.00 for condition b

(c) where C$_C$ is greater than C$_K$ but does not exceed 80

$$K_c = \frac{E_{05} K_{SE} K_E K_T}{k C_C^2 F_c}$$

where
k = 1.8 for sawn lumber
= 2.0 for glued-laminated timber

## A5.5.6.3.8 Design Check of Spaced Compression Members

The factored resistance determined by spaced compression member design shall be checked against the sum of factored resistances of individual members taken as simple compression members. In this check

$$C_C = \frac{\text{actual length between points of lateral support}}{\text{larger dimension of an individual member}}$$

The factored compressive resistance, P$_r$, shall be the smaller value obtained by the two methods of evaluation.

## A5.5.6.3.9 Combined Stresses

When axial compression in spaced compression members is combined with bending stresses, the provisions of Clause 5.5.10 shall be used only if the bending is in a direction parallel to the larger dimension of the individual member.

## Table A5.5.6.3
## End Block Constants for Spaced Compression Members, MPa

| $C_C$* | D Fir-L | Hem-Fir | S-P-F | Northern |
|---|---|---|---|---|
| 0–10 | 0.00 | 0.00 | 0.00 | 0.00 |
| 15 | 0.38 | 0.30 | 0.26 | 0.23 |
| 20 | 0.79 | 0.62 | 0.55 | 0.47 |
| 25 | 1.2 | 0.92 | 0.81 | 0.72 |
| 30 | 1.5 | 1.3 | 1.1 | 0.96 |
| 35 | 1.9 | 1.5 | 1.4 | 1.2 |
| 40 | 2.2 | 1.9 | 1.6 | 1.5 |
| 45 | 2.6 | 2.2 | 1.9 | 1.6 |
| 50 | 3.0 | 2.5 | 2.2 | 1.9 |
| 55 | 3.4 | 2.8 | 2.5 | 2.2 |
| 60–80 | 3.8 | 3.0 | 2.6 | 2.3 |

*Constants for intermediate values of $C_C$ may be obtained by straight-line interpolation.*

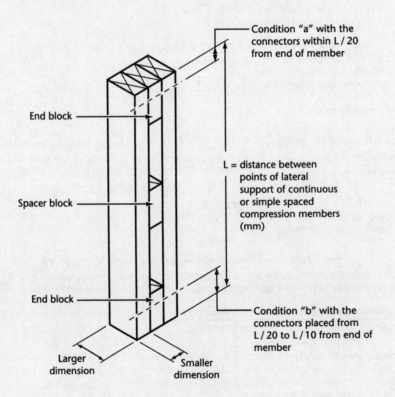

Condition "a" with the connectors within L / 20 from end of member

End block

Spacer block

L = distance between points of lateral support of continuous or simple spaced compression members (mm)

End block

Condition "b" with the connectors placed from L / 20 to L / 10 from end of member

Larger dimension    Smaller dimension

## Figure A5.5.6.3
## Spaced Compression Member (Connector Joined)

Δ **A5.5.7 Compression Perpendicular to Grain**

A relationship between mean compression perpendicular to grain strength and mean oven-dry wood density was introduced to establish a consistent basis for bearing strengths for various products in the 1994 edition of this Standard. It is as follows:

$$f_{cp} = 0.9 \, L \, (2243.8 \, D - 473.8) \, / \, M$$

where

$f_{cp}$ = specified compression perpendicular to grain strength, MPa
0.9 = factor applied to obtain a lower tolerance limit
L = conversion factor to limit states design (LSD) and standard-term load duration
    = 1.8125
D = mean oven-dry density (g/cm³)
M = conversion factor for metric units
    = 145.038

Tables 5.3.2 and 5.3.3 assign increased compression perpendicular to grain design values to specific grades of S-P-F or Hem-Fir machine-graded lumber, which have higher mean density than visually graded lumber of the same species (see Table A10.1).

The NLGA grading rules also include provisions for mills producing any grade of machine-graded lumber to qualify for other density values based on tests, daily quality control, and marking the qualified density value on the lumber. In these cases the NLGA rules provide for compression perpendicular values to be based on the marked density value and the formula shown above, without the 0.9 tolerance limit.

## A5.5.12 Preserved Wood Foundations

### A5.5.12.1

Studs for preserved wood foundations may be designed in accordance with recognized engineering methods. When assumed to be laterally supported, and when no surcharge exists, the formulae presented in Clauses A5.5.12.6 to A5.5.12.12 give conservative approximations of sufficient accuracy for practical construction. Dimensions used in the formulae are identified in Figure A5.5.12.1.

### A5.5.12.2

Studs for exterior foundation walls may be designed as members subjected to combined bending and axial compressive loading. Deflection due to lateral and axial loads should not exceed 1/300 of the unsupported height of the stud.

### A5.5.12.3

Sheathing for exterior foundation walls may be designed as simple bending members. The calculated maximum deflection at a point 300 mm above the bottom of the sheathing should not exceed 1/180 of the span of sheathing between studs. The nominal thickness of sheathing should not be less than 12.5 mm.

### A5.5.12.4

Floors and connections between floors and walls shall be designed to withstand loads imposed upon them by lateral soil pressure as well as floor loads appropriate for the occupancy.

### A5.5.12.5

Unequal pressure distribution may result from differing backfill heights on opposite sides of a building, openings in foundation walls, openings in floors at the top of foundation walls, or other causes. Framing members and sheathing shall be designed to resist loads resulting from unequal pressure distribution, by diaphragm action, or by other suitable means.

## A5.5.12.6

Combined bending and axial load effects may be evaluated using the formula

$$\frac{M_f + P_f \Delta}{M_r} + \left(\frac{P_f}{P_r}\right)^2 < 1.0$$

where

$M_f$ = maximum factored moment due to lateral load on stud, N•mm
$P_f$ = factored axial load on stud, N
$\Delta$ = deflection due to lateral load at point where $M_f$ is calculated, mm
$M_r$ = factored bending moment resistance, in accordance with Clause 5.5.4.1, N•mm
$P_r$ = factored compressive resistance, in accordance with Clause 5.5.6.2.2, N

**Notes:**
**(1)** A $K_D$ factor of 0.65 applies to the calculation of $M_r$, and a $K_D$ factor of 1.0 applies to the calculation of $P_r$.
**(2)** The value of $P_f \Delta$ represents secondary bending, which may be negligible.

## A5.5.12.7

The value of $M_f$ in Clause A5.5.12.6 is the maximum moment due to factored lateral load, and may be calculated using the following expression derived from recognized engineering formulae. At any point, x, above the floor the factored bending moment, $M_{fx}$ (N•mm), is

$$M_{fx} = \frac{w_f H^2}{6L}\left[(H-3a)\left(\frac{L-x}{H}\right) - L\left(\frac{H-Ax}{H}\right)^3\right]$$

where

$w_f$ = maximum factored lateral load per stud, N/mm
= maximum factored lateral soil pressure, N/mm², times stud spacing, mm
H, L, a, x = variables shown in Figure A5.5.12.1, mm

## A5.5.12.8

The following formulae may be used to determine the maximum factored moment, $M_f$, and its location, x:
(a) for wood sleeper and slab floors

$$M_f = \frac{w_f H^2}{6L}\left[L - H + \frac{2}{3}\sqrt{\frac{H^3}{3L}}\right]$$

and

$$x = H - \sqrt{\frac{H^3}{3L}}$$

(b) for suspended floors, both the moment between supports and the cantilever moment at the support should be checked using

$$M_f = \frac{w_f H^2}{6L} K_m$$

where

$$K_m = (H-3a)\left[K_1 + \frac{L+a-H}{H}\right] - LK_1^3$$

and between supports

$$K_1 = \sqrt{\frac{H - 3a}{3L}}$$

$$x = H - a - H\sqrt{\frac{H - 3a}{3L}}$$

at the support

$$K_1 = \frac{H - a}{H} \text{ and } x = 0$$

**Note:** *Values of $K_m$ for a range of backfill heights and typical wall dimensions are given in Table A5.5.12.8.*

## A5.5.12.9

Secondary moment is the term $P_f\Delta$ in Clause A5.5.12.6. The value of $\Delta$ may be calculated at any point, x, above the basement floor (see Figure A5.5.12.1), using the formula

$$\Delta = \frac{w_f(L - x)}{360EILH} K_\Delta$$

where

$$K_\Delta = [10H^2(H-3a)(2L-x)x-3(H-a)^5+K_2]$$

$$K_2 = \frac{3L}{L-x}(H-a-x)^5 \text{ when } x \leq H-a$$

$$= 0 \text{ when } X > H-a$$

E = modulus of elasticity of stud, MPa

I = moment of inertia of stud, mm⁴

$w_f$ = variable shown in Figure A5.5.12.1, N/mm

H, L, a = variables shown in Figure A5.5.12.1, mm

**Notes:**

**(1)** *Δ is normally calculated at the point where maximum moment occurs. If the maximum moment occurs at the support (due to cantilever effect), Δ = 0.*

**(2)** *Values of $K_\Delta$ for a range of backfill heights and typical wall dimensions are given in Table A5.5.12.8.*

## A5.5.12.10

Maximum deflection may be calculated from Clause A5.5.12.9 with x = 0.45L, and using specified rather than factored loads, to give a good approximation of the theoretical maximum deflection.

## A5.5.12.11

Maximum longitudinal shear may be calculated from the following expressions derived from recognized engineering formulae, and identified as the greatest value of $V_f$:

(a) for wood sleeper and slab floors at bottom of the foundation wall

$$V_f = \frac{w_f H}{2}\left[\frac{H}{3L}-\left(\frac{H-d}{H}\right)^2\right]$$

(b) for suspended floors

$$V_f = \frac{w_f H}{2}\left[\frac{H-3a}{3L}-\left(\frac{H-a-c}{H}\right)^2\right]$$

just above the suspended floor, and

$$V_f = \frac{w_f H}{2}\left[1-\left(\frac{H-a+c}{H}\right)^2\right]$$

just below the suspended floor

where

$V_f$ = factored shear force per stud, N

c = depth of stud + 1/2 of the joist depth, mm

d = depth of stud, mm

$w_f$ = variable shown in Figure A5.5.12.1, N/mm

H, L, a = variables shown in Figure A5.5.12.1, mm

## A5.5.12.12

Lateral restraint required at top of the foundation wall may be calculated from the following expressions:

(a) for wood sleeper and slab floors

$$R_T = \frac{w_f H^2}{6L}$$

(b) for suspended floors

$$R_T = \frac{w_f H}{2L}\left(\frac{H}{3} - a\right)$$

Lateral restraint required at the bottom of the foundation wall may be calculated from the following expressions:

(c) for wood sleeper and slab floors

$$R_B = \frac{w_f H}{2L}\left(L - \frac{H}{3}\right)$$

(d) for suspended floors

$$R_B = \frac{w_f H}{2L}\left(L + a - \frac{H}{3}\right)$$

where
$R_T$ = inward reaction at top of stud, N
$R_B$ = inward reaction at bottom of stud, N
$w_f$ = variable shown in Figure A5.5.12.1, N/mm
$H, L, a$ = variables shown in Figure A5.5.12.1, mm

## Table A5.5.12.8
### Moment and Deflection Coefficients, $K_m$ and $K_\Delta$, for Typical Values for L and a*

| Backfill height, H, mm | Slab floor $K_\Delta \times 10^{15}$ | | Suspended floor $K_\Delta \times 10^{15}$ | | |
|---|---|---|---|---|---|
| | At point of maximum moment | At x = 0.45L | At point of maximum moment | At x = 0.45L | $K_m$† |
| 400 | 0.85 | 2.5 | — | — | — |
| 600 | 3.8 | 8.4 | 0 | −14 | −3800 |
| 800 | 11 | 20 | 0 | −20 | −2300 |
| 1000 | 23 | 37 | 0 | −22 | −1600 |
| 1200 | 43 | 62 | 0 | −19 | −1100 |
| 1400 | 71 | 94 | 0 | −10 | −840 |
| 1600 | 110 | 130 | 0 | 6.3 | −660 |
| 1800 | 150 | 180 | 0 | 31 | −530 |
| 2000 | 200 | 230 | 0 | 64 | −430 |
| 2200 | 260 | 280 | 96 | 110 | 400 |
| 2400 | 320 | 340 | 150 | 150 | 430 |
| 2600 | — | — | 200 | 210 | 450 |
| 2800 | — | — | 270 | 260 | 450 |
| 3000 | — | — | 330 | 320 | 450 |

*Tabulated coefficients are for the cases where L = 2400 mm, a = 0 mm for a slab floor and L = 2500 mm, a = 500 mm for a suspended floor.*

†*Values for $K_m$ (last column) apply only to foundations with suspended floors. Tabulated are the greater of the calculated values for $K_m$ at the support (negative numbers) or between supports (positive numbers). $K_\Delta$ at the point of maximum moment (fourth column) is zero where moment at the support governs.*

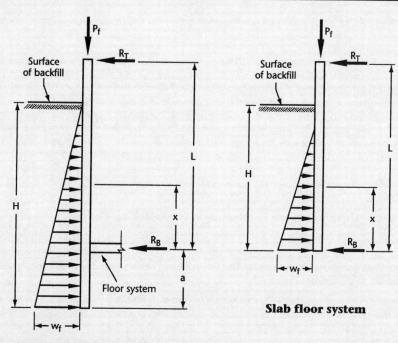

**Legend:**
L = *Stud length (mm)*
x = *Location of maximum moment (mm)*
H = *Height of backfill (mm)*

**Figure A5.5.12.1**
**Dimensions and Loading of Foundation Studs without Surcharge**

## A5.5.13  Sawn Lumber Design for Specific Truss Applications

### A5.5.13.1  Scope

**Fully triangulated** — The modified design procedures of Clause 5.5.13 are based on research reported by C. Lum, E. Jones, and B. Hintz *(Design of Wood Trusses for Small Buildings*, Proceedings of the International Wood Engineering Conference, New Orleans, LA, Vol. 1, 1996). They apply only to sawn lumber used in trusses where all of the members form a side of a triangle. In such a system, a bending failure at a panel point of a compression member would not normally result in collapse of the triangle. An attic truss is not a fully triangulated system. Also, the ends of top chords in top chord bearing trusses, and top chord overhangs (i.e., outward extensions of truss chords beyond the panel points) do not fall within the scope of Clause A5.5.13 and therefore are not considered part of the overall truss length.

**Clear span limitation** — The 12.2 m clear span limitation is consistent with that for snow loading for *National Building Code of Canada* (NBCC) Part 9 structures (NBCC, Subsection 9.4.2). When the 12.20 m span limit is exceeded or when other conditions are in effect, an 80% snow load factor must be used (i.e., the truss is designed as a Part 4 truss). When the 610 mm spacing limit is exceeded, the 80% snow load factor must be used and the $K_H$ factor in CSA Standard O86 is reduced from 1.1 to 1.0. Note that neither the CSA Standard S307 test nor the testing done in the research program is intended to address system effects.

**Truss configuration** — Clause A5.5.13 limits the applicability of Clause 5.5.13 to roof trusses with slopes that are similar to those trusses tested. Compared to the standard pitched chord trusses evaluated in the testing program, very low pitch (less than 2 in 12) roof and flat trusses have a higher axial force to bending moment ratio and are excluded from coverage in this Standard.

The overall length is a limit that the truss industry has traditionally used to place additional limits on design. The two limits, 12.20 m clear span and the 18.0 m overall length, provide a boundary between traditional residential spans and long span roof trusses. Below the 18.0 m overall truss length limit, the truss may consist of cantilevers and/or multiple clear spans, provided that no single span exceeds 12.20 m.

Girder, bowstring, semi-circular, attic, flat, and floor trusses continue to be designed to the balance of the Standard.

## A5.5.13.3 Compressive Resistance Parallel to Grain

**Effective length** — The Standard recommends effective length factors that it tabulates in Table A5.5.6.1. In addition, TPIC *Truss Design Procedures* contains specific recommendations for effective length of truss compression members. The selection of these factors depends on the load distribution and the type of structure.

**Compression chord splices** — For purposes of strength and deflection calculations, a compression chord splice may be considered continuous, provided that it is located at an inflection point for the load case being considered. To allow for changes in lumber length, the splice need only be within ±10% of the panel length from the inflection point. This allowance also recognizes that the location of the inflection point will depend on the loading condition.

**Size effects in compression** — In most cases, the member length for computing $K_{zc}$ is the panel length: between panel points, the axial force changes little compared with at the panel points. In cases where the axial stresses are high, relative to the bending stresses, resulting in relatively short panel lengths, and where the axial forces are relatively constant between adjacent panels, the member length for computing $K_{zc}$ should include several panels. One-half the chord length between pitch breaks has been judged to be sufficient to cover these cases.

A pitch break is a point along the chord analogue line where the slope of the chord changes.

## A5.5.13.4 Compressive Resistance Perpendicular to Grain

**Bearing reinforcement** — Bearing reinforcement consists of applying truss plates to both sides of a member that may be subjected to compression perpendicular to grain stresses through the depth of the member. Designs are also required to meet the basic bearing requirements of Clause 5.5.7.1. Testing to support this method of improving the bearing resistance is described in F.J. Keenan et al., "Improving the Bearing Strength of Supports of Light Wood Trusses", *Can. J. Civil Engineering,* 10 (1983), pp. 306–312.

## A5.5.13.5 Resistance to Combined Bending and Axial Load

**Interaction equation** — The modification to the axial ratio term was introduced to recognize the increase in bending capacity when a brittle material is subjected to axial compression in addition to bending. The $K_M$ factor is used to adjust the bending capacity for various moment configurations in the top chords. These two changes to the design of compression chords help to explain the satisfactory levels of safety observed in the test trusses.

No increase is permitted for combined tension and bending members, as the testing program was not designed to evaluate the performance of tension chord members.

**Amplified moments** — The proposed design procedures have been written to cover the general case where amplified moments are used. Although moment amplification should not be ignored, some structures may be accurately analyzed without having to use analysis methods that include moment amplification. An analysis of moment amplification in trusses indicated that mid-panel moments were more susceptible to P-delta effects, while panel point moments were less susceptible. Furthermore, the amount of moment amplification computed is sensitive to the type of structure and the analogue assumptions.

Results from the testing program suggests that the design procedure currently in use by TPIC results in trusses that exhibit satisfactory levels of performance. The TPIC design approach does not include moment amplification; however, the procedure does require that the mid-panel deflection be limited. This, in effect, limits the length of truss panels, even though the chord member may possess sufficient strength. If the deflection limitations in TPIC *Truss Design Procedures* are not used to limit panel length, the bending capacity modification factors, $K_M$, from Table 5.5.13.5 may not be appropriate.

**Bending capacity modification factor, $K_M$** — The $K_M$ factors calculated from Table 5.5.13.5 are based on analysis done by the UBC Wood Science Department (W. Lau, J.D. Barrett, F. Lam, *Chord Member Design Proposal*, University of British Columbia, Vancouver, 1995). In addition to being a function of the member's span-to-depth ratio, the $K_M$ factor also depends on the shape of the moment diagram.

A $K_M$ greater than 1 generally indicates a bending moment distribution with one or more inflection points in the member between panel points, and a panel point moment that is higher than the mid-panel moment.

For cases where the mid-panel moment is higher than the panel point moments or where the loading is such that there are no inflections points in the panel, the $K_M$ factor is generally less than 1.

For other cases where the structural analysis indicates zero moment at the panel points (i.e., $M_2 = 0$), the bending capacity increase will simply be a function of the span-to-depth ratio. This generally occurs at pitch breaks or panel point splices, where, although the bending moments may not be zero, designers traditionally assume a pin connection. However, a fictitious analogue member, such as that used to model a heel joint in a pitched chord truss, is considered to introduce a panel point moment in the heel. Therefore, the top chord of a king post truss can be assumed to be continuous over a panel point at the heel, but not at the peak.

The test trusses and trusses analyzed in the impact study, which are considered typical designs, result in values of $K_M$ up to 1.3. The upper limit on $K_M$ at 1.3 has been introduced to prevent extrapolation to higher values.

## A6.5.5 Standard Sizes for Glued-Laminated Timber

The standard dimensions for glued-laminated timber are as follows:
(a) widths of 80, 130, 175, 215, 265, 315, and 365 mm; and
(b) depths, as calculated for
    (i) straight or cambered members, in multiples of 38 mm; and
    (ii) members curved to a radius of curvature less than 10 800 mm, in multiples of the required lamination thickness (Table A6.5.5).
**Notes:**
**(1)** *Actual widths commercially available may vary.*
**(2)** *For widths greater than 365 mm, designers are advised to check availability before specifying.*

## Table A6.5.5
## Minimum Radius of Curvature

| Lamination thickness, mm | Minimum radius of curvature, mm | |
|---|---|---|
| | Tangent end* | Curved end |
| 38 Standard | 8400 | 10 800 |
| 19 Standard | 2800 | 3800 |
| 35 Non-standard | 7400 | 9500 |
| 32 | 6300 | 8500 |
| 29 | 5600 | 7300 |
| 25 | 4600 | 6200 |
| 16 | 2300 | 3000 |
| 13 | 1800 | 2200 |
| 10 | 1200 | 1400 |
| 6 | 800 | 800 |

*Tangent end requires a straight length of finished lamination beyond the tangent point of not less than 32 times the lamination thickness.*

## A7.2.2.2 Construction Sheathing OSB

As identified in its preface, CSA Standard CAN/CSA-O325.0 does not contain recommended engineering design values, nor does it suggest methods of calculating such values.

Design values contained in Table 7.3D for Construction Sheathing OSB certified to CSA Standard CAN/CSA-O325.0 are consistent with values developed by in-grade testing and supported by various organizations.

Certification organizations shall ensure that reference values for bending strength and bending stiffness of Construction Sheathing OSB certified to CSA Standard CAN/CSA-O325.0 are also consistent with the design values of this Standard.

OSB panels marked to CSA Standard CAN/CSA-O325.0 are technically equivalent to OSB panels marked to the U.S. NIST Standard PS2, which uses a different span rating designation.

## Table A7.2.2.2A
## Panel Marks for Construction Sheathing Products (CSA O325)

(a) Panel Marks

| End use marks | Span marks | | | | | |
|---|---|---|---|---|---|---|
| | 16 | 20 | 24 | 32 | 40 | 48 |
| | Recommended framing member spacing, mm | | | | | |
| | 400 | 500 | 600 | 800 | 1000 | 1200 |
| 1F | 1F16 | 1F20 | 1F24 | 1F32 | X | 1F48 |
| 2F | 2F16 | 2F20 | 2F24 | X | X | X |
| 1R | 1R16 | 1R20 | 1R24 | 1R32 | 1R40 | 1R48 |
| 2R | 2R16 | 2R20 | 2R24 | 2R32 | 2R40 | 2R48 |
| W | W16 | W20 | W24 | X | X | X |

X = Not available.

**Notes:**
**(1)** Panel marks comprise an end use mark (see (b) below) followed by the appropriate span mark (in inches), e.g., 2F24/W16.
**(2)** Multiple panel marks may be shown on panels qualified for more than one end use, e.g., 1R24/2F16 or 2R48/2F24/1F24.

**(3)** The span mark relates to the centre-to-centre spacing of supports (test span) used for the qualification testing of Construction Sheathing products. These spans are based on assumed end use and framing member spacings normally found in light wood-frame construction. The framing member itself shall be designed for the expected loads using recognized engineering procedures.

(b) End Use Marks

| For panels marked | Assumed end use |
|---|---|
| 1F | Subflooring |
| 2F | Subflooring used with panel-type underlay |
| 1R | Roof sheathing used without edge support |
| 2R | Roof sheathing used with edge support |
| W* | Wall sheathing |

*Panels marked W only are not permitted by this Standard.
**Note:** Panels marked 1 are usually stiffer than panels marked 2.

## Table A7.2.2.2B
## Relationship between Panel Mark and Nominal Thickness

| Panel mark | Nominal thickness, mm | | | | | | | | | | | |
|---|---|---|---|---|---|---|---|---|---|---|---|---|
| | 7.5 | 9.5 | 11 | 12 | 12.5 | 15 | 15.5 | 18 | 18.5 | 22 | 25 | 28.5 |
| 2R20 | P | | | | | | | | | | | |
| 2R24 | | P | A | A | A | | | | | | | |
| 1R24/2F16 | | | P | A | A | | | | | | | |
| 2R32/2F16 | | | | P | A | A | A | | | | | |
| 2R40/2F20 | | | | | | P | A | A | A | | | |
| 2R48/2F24 | | | | | | | | P | A | A | | |
| 1F16 | | | | | | P | A | | | | | |
| 1F20 | | | | | | P | A | | | | | |
| 1F24 | | | | | | | | P | A | | | |
| 1F32 | | | | | | | | | | P | A | |
| 1F48 | | | | | | | | | | | | P |

**Note:**
P — indicates the predominant nominal thickness for each panel mark.
A — indicates alternative nominal thicknesses that may be available for each panel mark. Check with suppliers regarding availability.

## A7.3.1 Plywood Specified Capacities
The specified capacities for plywood in Tables 7.3A and 7.3B are predicated on the following restrictions:
(a) In panels with an even number of plies, only a single pair of plies with grain parallel to each other is permitted.
(b) In panels of nominal thickness greater than 20.5 mm, the maximum outer ply thickness is 3 mm.
(c) In panels of nominal thickness greater than 20.5 mm, the maximum inner ply thickness is 4.2 mm.

## A8.6.3.4 Buckling of Plywood Compression Flange

For stressed skin panels with a plywood compression flange, the factored buckling resistance, expressed as the maximum factored load applied perpendicular to the compression flange, shall be taken as

$$B_r = \phi X_B \frac{(2h_w + h_t + h_c)(10^9)}{2(s\ell_p)^2}$$

where
$B_r$ = factored buckling resistance, $kN/m^2$
$\phi$ = 0.95
$X_B$ = buckling coefficient (Table A8.6.3.4)
$s$ = clear spacing between longitudinals, mm
$\ell_p$ = span of stressed skin panel, mm

**Note:** *This clause is not applicable to OSB compression flanges. Buckling coefficients have not been developed for OSB.*

### Table A8.6.3.4
### Buckling Coefficient, $X_B$, for the Plywood Compression Flange of Stressed Skin Panels, kN·m

| Unsanded plywood thickness (mm) | Face grain parallel to span | Face grain perpendicular to span |
|---|---|---|
| 7.5 | 23 | 53 |
| 9.5 | 59 | 110 |
| 12.5 | 160* | 240 |
| 15.5 | 350 | 470 |
| 18.5 | 610 | 790 |
| 20.5 | 880 | 1050 |

*For 12.5 mm, 3-ply plywood and face grain parallel to span, use $X_B$ = 120.*

## A9.5.1 Alternate Nails in Shearwalls

For shearwalls and diaphragms fabricated using nails having a diameter that deviates from the standard common nail diameter, and meeting the following criteria:
(a) the non-standard nail diameter is within 80% of that of a standard common nail; and
(b) the yield strength of the non-standard nail is at least
   (i)   660 MPa for nail diameter 2.34–2.84 mm;
   (ii)  635 MPa for nail diameter 2.64– 3.25 mm; and
   (iii) 615 MPa for nail diameter 2.95–3.66 mm.
The design capacities may be estimated by multiplying the capacities presented in Tables 9.5.1A and 9.5.2 by the multiplication factor given below:

$$\text{Multiplication factor} = \left(\frac{d_1}{d_2}\right)^2$$

where
$d_1$ = the non-standard nail diameter
$d_2$ = the standard nail diameter given in either Table 9.5.1A or 9.5.2
$d_1 < d_2$

## Table A10.1
## Relative Density Values

| Visually graded lumber | Glued-laminated timber | MSR (or MEL) E Grades of S-P-F* | Mean oven-dry relative density |
|---|---|---|---|
|  |  | 13 800–16 500 MPa | 0.50 |
| D Fir-Larch | D Fir-Larch, Hem-Fir† |  | 0.49 |
|  |  | 12 400–13 100 MPa | 0.47 |
| Hem-Fir | Hem-Fir† |  | 0.46 |
|  | Spruce-Pine |  | 0.44 |
| Spruce-Pine-Fir |  | 8300–11 700 MPa | 0.42 |
| Northern Species |  |  | 0.35 |

*For species of MSR or MEL lumber other than S-P-F, use visually graded lumber values.*
†*The outer laminations of Hem-Fir glulam consist of Douglas Fir-Larch; for this reason, use the relative density of Douglas Fir-Larch for Hem-Fir glulam where the fasteners do not pass through the inner laminations. In all other cases, use the visually graded lumber Hem-Fir density values.*

**Notes:**
**(1)** *Relative density values are listed above on a mean oven-dry weight and volume basis. In the fastenings equations, these values are modified to relate fastening capacities to fifth percentile density values on a 15% moisture volume basis.*
**(2)** *Where fastening capacity for bolts, drift pins, or lag screws in wood of a given relative density is not available, use the capacity in a lower relative density wood, or calculate capacity using the equations given in the Standard.*

## A10.6.3.3 Lateral Deformation of Lag Screw Joints

For a specified load, P, the lateral deformation of a lag screw joint may be estimated from

$$\Delta = \frac{P}{kdl_2 n_f}$$

where
$\Delta$ = lateral deformation, mm
$P$ = specified load on the connection, N
$k$ = lateral slip resistance of lag screw, MPa
    for   $\theta = 0°$ (parallel-to-grain loading)
        $k = k_P = (5.04G–0.29)J_Y J_{SF} J_G$
    for   $\theta = 90°$ (perpendicular-to-grain loading)
        $k = k_Q = (5.04G–0.29)J_Q J_{SF} J_G$
    for   $0° < \theta < 90°$ (angle-to-grain loading)
        $k = k_P k_Q/(k_P \sin^2\theta + k_Q \cos^2\theta)$
$J_Y$ = side plate factor
    = 1.5 for steel side plates
$J_Q$ = perpendicular-to-grain load factor (Table A10.6.3.3)
$J_G$ = factor for groups of fastenings (Tables 10.2.2.3.4A and 10.2.2.3.4B)
$G$ = mean relative density (Table A10.1)
$d$ = lag screw diameter, mm
$l_2$ = length of penetration into main member, mm (Clause 10.6.3)
$n_f$ = number of lag screws in connection

**Note:** *Lag screws loaded laterally tend to reach a point of permanent deformation at about 0.8 to 1.0 mm. This limit should be avoided to prevent permanent deformation.*

## Table A10.6.3.3
### Factor $J_Q$ for Perpendicular-to-Grain Loading of Lag Screws

| Lag screw diameter, in | $J_Q$ |
|---|---|
| 3/16 | 1.00 |
| 1/4 | 0.97 |
| 5/16 | 0.85 |
| 3/8 | 0.76 |
| 7/16 | 0.71 |
| 1/2 | 0.65 |
| 5/8 | 0.60 |
| 3/4 | 0.55 |
| 7/8 | 0.52 |
| 1 | 0.50 |

## A10.7.2.3 Analysis of Timber Rivet (Glulam Rivet) Joints: General Method for Douglas Fir-L Glulam

**Note:** *The following design formulae are derived from tests on timber rivet (also known as glulam rivet) joints in Douglas Fir-Larch glulam. For joints in other species of glulam, or in sawn timber, reduce the resulting strength resistance by the factor H in Clause 10.7.2.*

### A10.7.2.3.1 Parallel-to-Grain Loading

In Clause 10.7.2.3, the lateral strength resistance for wood capacity, $p_w$, kN, per joint parallel to grain is equal to the least value of the tensile strength of the timber, $P_t$, and the shear strength of the timber, $P_v$, determined as follows:

$$P_t = \frac{X_t f_{tn} S_Q (n_R - 1)}{K_t \beta_t E_t}$$

where
$X_t$ = adjustment factor for tension parallel = 1.41
$f_{tn}$ = specified strength in tension parallel to grain at net section (Table 6.3), MPa
$S_Q$ = rivet spacing perpendicular to grain (Figure 10.7.1.7), mm
$n_R$ = number of rows of rivets
$K_t$ = constant depending on $n_R$ and $n_C$ (Table A10.7.2.3A)
$n_C$ = number of rivets per row
$\beta_t$ = constant depending on $S_p$, $S_Q$, and $n_R$ (Table A10.7.2.3B)
$S_p$ = rivet spacing parallel to grain (Figure 10.7.1.7), mm
$E_t$ = constant depending on b and $L_p$ (Table A10.7.2.3C)
b = member dimension, mm; for connections with steel plates on opposite sides, member dimension is the width of the member; for connections having only one plate, member dimension is twice the width of the member.

$$P_v = \frac{X_v F_v L_p [S_p (n_c - 1) + 50]}{K_v \beta_v \gamma}$$

where
$X_v$ = adjustment factor for shear = 1.48
$F_v$ = $f_v (0.15 + 4.35 C_v)$, MPa
$f_v$ = longitudinal shear strength, MPa (Table 6.3)
$C_v$ = $(\beta_1 + \beta_2 \beta_3)^{-0.2}$

$$\beta_1 = \frac{1}{1300} L_p S_p (n_c - 1)\left[1 + 500\exp^{-0.52(S_Q - 12.5)}\right]$$

$$\beta_2 = 0.5 \times 10^{-16} L_p \left[(n_c - 1)S_p\right]^3 \left[(n_R - 1)S_Q\right]^{4.5}\exp^{-\left(\frac{a-50}{100}\right)}$$

Δ $\quad \beta_3 = \left(\frac{3\mu - 1}{2} + L_p\frac{1-\mu}{50}\right)^5 \left(1 - \exp^{\left(1.9 - 0.95\frac{b}{L_p}\right)}\right)^5$

$$\mu = 43.9\left[(n_c - 1)S_p\right]^{-0.4}\left[(n_R - 1)S_Q\right]^{-0.2}$$

$a$    = end distance (Figure 10.7.1.7), mm
$L_p$   = rivet penetration (Figure 10.7.1.1)
$K_v$   = constant depending on $n_R$ and $n_c$ (Table A10.7.2.3D)
$\beta_v$   = constant depending on $S_p$ and $S_Q$ (Table A10.7.2.3E)
$\gamma$   = $90.5 + 5.4\,L_p$

**Note:** *For cases where $b \le 175$ mm, $S_p = 40$ mm, $S_Q = 25$ mm, and $L_p \ge 55$ mm, $P_v$ will be greater than $P_t$.*

## A10.7.2.3.2 Perpendicular-to-Grain Loading

In Clause 10.7.2.5, the lateral strength resistance for wood capacity perpendicular to grain, $q_w$, may be determined from

$$q_w = \frac{23.3 X_{tp} f_{tp}\left[(n_R - 1)S_p\right]^{0.8}}{K_{tp}\beta_{tp}10^3\left[(n_c - 1)S_Q\right]^{0.2}}$$

where
$X_{tp}$ = adjustment factor for tension perpendicular = 1.45
$f_{tp}$ = specified strength in tension perpendicular to grain, MPa (Table 6.3)
$K_{tp}$ = constant depending on $n_R$ and $n_c$ (Table A10.7.2.3F)
$\beta_{tp}$ = constant depending on $S_p$ and $S_Q$ (Table A10.7.2.3G)

and the value of the factor, $C_t$, may be determined from

$$C_t = \frac{1}{\beta_D}\left[\frac{e_p}{(n_c - 1)S_Q}\right]^{-0.2}$$

where
$\beta_D$ = constant depending on $e_p/(n_c - 1)S_Q$ (Table A10.7.2.3H)
$e_p$ = unloaded edge distance, mm (Figure 10.7.1.7)

## Table A10.7.2.3A
## Values of $K_t$

| Rivets per row, $n_C$ | Number of rows, $n_R$ | | | | | | | | | |
|---|---|---|---|---|---|---|---|---|---|---|
| | 2 | 4 | 6 | 8 | 10 | 12 | 14 | 16 | 18 | 20 |
| 2 | 0.75 | 1.16 | 1.37 | 1.47 | 1.51 | 1.54 | 1.57 | 1.61 | 1.64 | 1.64 |
| 4 | 0.51 | 0.88 | 1.08 | 1.17 | 1.22 | 1.26 | 1.30 | 1.35 | 1.38 | 1.38 |
| 6 | 0.38 | 0.71 | 0.89 | 0.97 | 1.02 | 1.06 | 1.11 | 1.16 | 1.18 | 1.18 |
| 8 | 0.30 | 0.60 | 0.75 | 0.84 | 0.89 | 0.93 | 0.97 | 1.02 | 1.05 | 1.05 |
| 10 | 0.26 | 0.52 | 0.66 | 0.74 | 0.79 | 0.82 | 0.87 | 0.91 | 0.94 | 0.94 |
| 12 | 0.23 | 0.47 | 0.59 | 0.66 | 0.71 | 0.75 | 0.78 | 0.82 | 0.85 | 0.85 |
| 14 | 0.21 | 0.42 | 0.54 | 0.60 | 0.65 | 0.68 | 0.72 | 0.75 | 0.77 | 0.77 |
| 16 | 0.20 | 0.38 | 0.49 | 0.56 | 0.60 | 0.63 | 0.67 | 0.69 | 0.71 | 0.71 |
| 18 | 0.18 | 0.35 | 0.45 | 0.52 | 0.56 | 0.59 | 0.62 | 0.65 | 0.66 | 0.67 |
| 20 | 0.17 | 0.32 | 0.42 | 0.49 | 0.53 | 0.56 | 0.59 | 0.61 | 0.63 | 0.64 |
| 22 | 0.16 | 0.30 | 0.40 | 0.46 | 0.51 | 0.54 | 0.56 | 0.58 | 0.60 | 0.61 |
| 24 | 0.15 | 0.29 | 0.38 | 0.45 | 0.49 | 0.52 | 0.53 | 0.55 | 0.57 | 0.58 |
| 26 | 0.14 | 0.28 | 0.36 | 0.42 | 0.46 | 0.50 | 0.51 | 0.52 | 0.54 | 0.55 |

## Table A10.7.2.3B
## Values of $\beta_t$

| $S_P$, mm | $S_Q$, mm | Number of rows, $n_R$ | | | | | | | | | |
|---|---|---|---|---|---|---|---|---|---|---|---|
| | | 2 | 4 | 6 | 8 | 10 | 12 | 14 | 16 | 18 | 20 |
| 25 | 12.5 | 1.00 | 1.00 | 1.00 | 1.00 | 1.00 | 1.00 | 1.00 | 1.00 | 1.00 | 1.00 |
| | 15.0 | 1.11 | 1.06 | 1.04 | 1.02 | 1.02 | 1.01 | 1.01 | 1.01 | 1.01 | 1.01 |
| | 25.0 | 1.68 | 1.36 | 1.23 | 1.14 | 1.09 | 1.08 | 1.08 | 1.06 | 1.04 | 1.03 |
| | 32.0 | 2.03 | 1.54 | 1.34 | 1.22 | 1.14 | 1.10 | 1.09 | 1.07 | 1.06 | 1.05 |
| | 40.0 | 2.37 | 1.72 | 1.46 | 1.29 | 1.18 | 1.14 | 1.12 | 1.10 | 1.08 | 1.06 |
| 32 | 12.5 | 0.94 | 0.93 | 0.93 | 0.93 | 0.93 | 0.93 | 0.93 | 0.93 | 0.93 | 0.93 |
| | 15.0 | 1.05 | 0.99 | 0.97 | 0.95 | 0.95 | 0.94 | 0.94 | 0.94 | 0.94 | 0.94 |
| | 25.0 | 1.58 | 1.27 | 1.15 | 1.07 | 1.02 | 1.00 | 1.00 | 0.98 | 0.98 | 0.97 |
| | 32.0 | 1.90 | 1.44 | 1.26 | 1.14 | 1.06 | 1.02 | 1.01 | 0.99 | 0.98 | 0.98 |
| | 40.0 | 2.23 | 1.61 | 1.36 | 1.21 | 1.11 | 1.06 | 1.04 | 1.02 | 1.00 | 1.00 |
| 40 | 12.5 | 0.87 | 0.87 | 0.87 | 0.87 | 0.87 | 0.87 | 0.88 | 0.87 | 0.87 | 0.87 |
| | 15.0 | 0.97 | 0.92 | 0.90 | 0.89 | 0.88 | 0.88 | 0.88 | 0.88 | 0.88 | 0.88 |
| | 25.0 | 1.48 | 1.18 | 1.07 | 1.00 | 0.96 | 0.93 | 0.92 | 0.92 | 0.91 | 0.90 |
| | 32.0 | 1.78 | 1.34 | 1.17 | 1.06 | 0.99 | 0.96 | 0.94 | 0.93 | 0.93 | 0.92 |
| | 40.0 | 2.08 | 1.50 | 1.27 | 1.13 | 1.04 | 0.99 | 0.97 | 0.95 | 0.94 | 0.93 |
| 50 | 12.5 | 0.75 | 0.75 | 0.75 | 0.75 | 0.75 | 0.75 | 0.75 | 0.75 | 0.75 | 0.75 |
| | 15.0 | 0.84 | 0.79 | 0.77 | 0.76 | 0.76 | 0.76 | 0.76 | 0.75 | 0.75 | 0.77 |
| | 25.0 | 1.27 | 1.00 | 0.91 | 0.85 | 0.81 | 0.79 | 0.79 | 0.82 | 0.80 | 0.79 |
| | 32.0 | 1.54 | 1.14 | 1.00 | 0.91 | 0.85 | 0.82 | 0.82 | 0.85 | 0.83 | 0.82 |
| | 40.0 | 1.80 | 1.27 | 1.09 | 0.97 | 0.89 | 0.86 | 0.85 | 0.83 | 0.82 | 0.81 |

## Table A10.7.2.3C
## Values of $E_t$*

| Rivet penetration, $L_p$, mm | Width of glulam member, b (mm) | | | | | | |
|---|---|---|---|---|---|---|---|
| | 80 | 130 | 175 | 215 | 265 | 315 | 365 |
| 30 | 24.0 | 18.6 | 16.8 | 16.8 | 16.8 | 16.8 | 16.8 |
| 55 | 25.3 | 21.2 | 18.4 | 16.4 | 14.8 | 14.1 | 14.0 |
| 80 | 25.6 | 22.7 | 20.3 | 18.5 | 16.7 | 15.2 | 14.1 |

*For intermediate sawn timber widths, straight line interpolation or the following formula may be used to calculate $E_t$:

$$E_t = \frac{2\alpha_t \gamma}{L_P}$$

where

$\gamma = 90.5 + 5.4 L_p$

$\alpha_t = 1.0$ for $b \geq 6L_p$

$$= 1.0 + 0.155\left(3 - \frac{b}{2L_P}\right)^2 \quad \text{for } b < 6L_p$$

## Table A10.7.2.3D
## Values of $K_v$

| Rivets per row, $n_C$ | Number of rows, $n_R$ | | | | | | | | | |
|---|---|---|---|---|---|---|---|---|---|---|
| | 2 | 4 | 6 | 8 | 10 | 12 | 14 | 16 | 18 | 20 |
| 2 | 2.23 | 1.61 | 1.15 | 0.81 | 0.60 | 0.48 | 0.40 | 0.32 | 0.25 | 0.19 |
| 4 | 2.31 | 1.69 | 1.22 | 0.88 | 0.66 | 0.53 | 0.45 | 0.37 | 0.30 | 0.24 |
| 6 | 2.35 | 1.73 | 1.27 | 0.93 | 0.70 | 0.57 | 0.48 | 0.40 | 0.33 | 0.27 |
| 8 | 2.36 | 1.76 | 1.30 | 0.96 | 0.73 | 0.60 | 0.51 | 0.43 | 0.36 | 0.30 |
| 10 | 2.37 | 1.78 | 1.32 | 0.98 | 0.75 | 0.62 | 0.53 | 0.45 | 0.38 | 0.31 |
| 12 | 2.36 | 1.78 | 1.33 | 1.00 | 0.77 | 0.63 | 0.55 | 0.46 | 0.39 | 0.32 |
| 14 | 2.35 | 1.78 | 1.34 | 1.01 | 0.78 | 0.64 | 0.56 | 0.47 | 0.40 | 0.33 |
| 16 | 2.34 | 1.78 | 1.34 | 1.02 | 0.79 | 0.65 | 0.57 | 0.48 | 0.40 | 0.33 |
| 18 | 2.33 | 1.78 | 1.35 | 1.02 | 0.80 | 0.66 | 0.57 | 0.48 | 0.40 | 0.34 |
| 20 | 2.32 | 1.78 | 1.35 | 1.03 | 0.80 | 0.66 | 0.57 | 0.48 | 0.40 | 0.34 |
| 22 | 2.31 | 1.78 | 1.35 | 1.03 | 0.80 | 0.66 | 0.57 | 0.48 | 0.40 | 0.34 |
| 24 | 2.30 | 1.78 | 1.35 | 1.03 | 0.80 | 0.66 | 0.57 | 0.48 | 0.40 | 0.34 |
| 26 | 2.30 | 1.78 | 1.35 | 1.03 | 0.80 | 0.66 | 0.57 | 0.48 | 0.40 | 0.35 |

## Table A10.7.2.3E
## Values of $\beta_v$

| $S_{P}$, mm | $S_{Q}$, mm | Number of rows, $n_R$ | | | | | | | | | |
|---|---|---|---|---|---|---|---|---|---|---|---|
| | | 2 | 4 | 6 | 8 | 10 | 12 | 14 | 16 | 18 | 20 |
| 25 | 12.5 | 1.00 | 1.00 | 1.00 | 1.00 | 1.00 | 1.00 | 1.00 | 1.00 | 1.00 | 1.00 |
| | 15.0 | 1.00 | 0.97 | 0.95 | 0.95 | 0.94 | 0.94 | 0.94 | 0.93 | 0.93 | 0.93 |
| | 25.0 | 0.97 | 0.81 | 0.71 | 0.67 | 0.63 | 0.62 | 0.61 | 0.60 | 0.58 | 0.57 |
| | 32.0 | 0.95 | 0.72 | 0.57 | 0.51 | 0.44 | 0.43 | 0.42 | 0.40 | 0.38 | 0.35 |
| | 40.0 | 0.94 | 0.63 | 0.43 | 0.34 | 0.26 | 0.24 | 0.23 | 0.20 | 0.17 | 0.13 |
| 32 | 12.5 | 1.06 | 1.06 | 1.06 | 1.06 | 1.05 | 1.05 | 1.04 | 1.04 | 1.03 | 1.02 |
| | 15.0 | 1.05 | 1.02 | 1.00 | 0.99 | 0.97 | 0.97 | 0.96 | 0.95 | 0.94 | 0.93 |
| | 25.0 | 1.02 | 0.84 | 0.71 | 0.66 | 0.60 | 0.58 | 0.56 | 0.54 | 0.51 | 0.49 |
| | 32.0 | 1.02 | 0.75 | 0.58 | 0.50 | 0.42 | 0.40 | 0.38 | 0.36 | 0.33 | 0.30 |
| | 40.0 | 1.02 | 0.68 | 0.46 | 0.36 | 0.27 | 0.25 | 0.24 | 0.21 | 0.18 | 0.14 |
| 40 | 12.5 | 1.11 | 1.12 | 1.12 | 1.11 | 1.10 | 1.09 | 1.08 | 1.07 | 1.06 | 1.05 |
| | 15.0 | 1.11 | 1.08 | 1.05 | 1.03 | 1.01 | 1.00 | 0.98 | 0.97 | 0.96 | 0.94 |
| | 25.0 | 1.07 | 0.84 | 0.68 | 0.61 | 0.53 | 0.49 | 0.45 | 0.42 | 0.38 | 0.35 |
| | 32.0 | 1.10 | 0.79 | 0.60 | 0.51 | 0.42 | 0.40 | 0.37 | 0.34 | 0.31 | 0.27 |
| | 40.0 | 1.11 | 0.73 | 0.48 | 0.38 | 0.27 | 0.26 | 0.24 | 0.22 | 0.18 | 0.14 |
| 50 | 12.5 | 1.22 | 1.24 | 1.24 | 1.22 | 1.20 | 1.18 | 1.16 | 1.14 | 1.12 | 1.10 |
| | 15.0 | 1.23 | 1.21 | 1.18 | 1.15 | 1.12 | 1.10 | 1.08 | 1.06 | 1.04 | 1.02 |
| | 25.0 | 1.26 | 1.04 | 0.89 | 0.82 | 0.74 | 0.72 | 0.71 | 0.68 | 0.65 | 0.62 |
| | 32.0 | 1.27 | 0.93 | 0.71 | 0.61 | 0.52 | 0.50 | 0.48 | 0.46 | 0.42 | 0.39 |
| | 40.0 | 1.29 | 0.83 | 0.53 | 0.41 | 0.29 | 0.27 | 0.25 | 0.23 | 0.19 | 0.15 |

## Table A10.7.2.3F
## Values of $K_{tp}$

| Rivets per row, $n_C$ | Number of rows, $n_R$ | | | | |
|---|---|---|---|---|---|
| | 2 | 4 | 6 | 8 | 10 |
| 2 | 0.29 | 0.67 | 0.88 | 0.98 | 1.04 |
| 4 | 0.22 | 0.50 | 0.68 | 0.78 | 0.85 |
| 6 | 0.17 | 0.39 | 0.54 | 0.63 | 0.69 |
| 8 | 0.13 | 0.31 | 0.44 | 0.52 | 0.58 |
| 10 | 0.11 | 0.25 | 0.36 | 0.44 | 0.48 |
| 12 | 0.09 | 0.21 | 0.31 | 0.37 | 0.41 |
| 14 | 0.07 | 0.18 | 0.26 | 0.32 | 0.36 |
| 16 | 0.06 | 0.15 | 0.23 | 0.28 | 0.31 |
| 18 | 0.05 | 0.13 | 0.20 | 0.25 | 0.28 |
| 20 | 0.05 | 0.12 | 0.18 | 0.22 | 0.25 |

## Table A10.7.2.3G
## Values of $\beta_{tp}$

| $S_Q$, mm | $S_P$, mm | Number of rows, $n_R$ | | | | |
|---|---|---|---|---|---|---|
| | | 2 | 4 | 6 | 8 | 10 |
| 15 | 25 | 1.29 | 1.25 | 1.24 | 1.23 | 1.23 |
| | 40 | 1.76 | 1.61 | 1.49 | 1.45 | 1.40 |
| 25 | 25 | 1.00 | 1.00 | 1.00 | 1.00 | 1.00 |
| | 32 | 1.18 | 1.13 | 1.10 | 1.09 | 1.07 |
| | 40 | 1.36 | 1.27 | 1.20 | 1.17 | 1.14 |
| | 50 | 1.72 | 1.53 | 1.40 | 1.34 | 1.28 |
| 32 | 25 | 0.82 | 0.84 | 0.85 | 0.86 | 0.86 |
| | 32 | 0.97 | 0.96 | 0.94 | 0.93 | 0.93 |
| | 40 | 1.12 | 1.07 | 1.03 | 1.00 | 0.98 |
| | 50 | 1.42 | 1.29 | 1.20 | 1.15 | 1.10 |
| 40 | 25 | 0.63 | 0.68 | 0.70 | 0.71 | 0.71 |
| | 32 | 0.75 | 0.77 | 0.78 | 0.77 | 0.76 |
| | 40 | 0.87 | 0.86 | 0.84 | 0.83 | 0.82 |
| | 50 | 1.11 | 1.04 | 0.98 | 0.95 | 0.92 |

## Table A10.7.2.3H
## Values of $\beta_D$

| $\dfrac{e_P}{(n_C-1)S_Q}$ | $\beta_D$ | $\dfrac{e_P}{(n_C-1)S_Q}$ | $\beta_D$ |
|---|---|---|---|
| 0.1 | 0.275 | 1.0 | 0.83 |
| 0.2 | 0.433 | 1.2 | 0.88 |
| 0.3 | 0.538 | 1.4 | 0.92 |
| 0.4 | 0.60 | 1.6 | 0.95 |
| 0.5 | 0.65 | 1.8 | 0.97 |
| 0.6 | 0.69 | 2.0 | 0.98 |
| 0.7 | 0.73 | 2.4 | 0.99 |
| 0.8 | 0.77 | 2.8 and more | 1.00 |
| 0.9 | 0.80 | | |

**Note:** For $e_P/[(n_C-1)S_Q]$ between 0.1 and 0.3, $\beta_D$ is given to three significant digits due to the sensitivity in this range.

## A10.9.3.2 Lateral Deformation of Nailed and Spiked Wood-to-Wood Joints

For specified loads, P, not greater than $n_u/3$, the lateral deformation of nailed and spiked joints may be estimated from

$$\Delta = 0.5dK_m(P/n_u)^{1.7}$$

where
$\Delta$ = lateral deformation, mm
d = nail diameter, mm
$K_m$ = service creep factor (Table A10.9.3.2)
P = specified load per nail or spike, N
$n_u$ = unit lateral strength resistance (Table 10.9.4), N

### Table A10.9.3.2
### Service Creep Factors, $K_m$, for Nail and Spike Joints

| Load duration class | Moisture condition | | |
| --- | --- | --- | --- |
| | Nailed dry, loaded dry | Nailed wet, loaded dry | Nailed wet, loaded wet |
| Permanent | 1.5 | 2.0 | 3.0 |
| Standard | 1.2 | 1.5 | 2.0 |
| Short | 1.0 | 1.2 | 1.5 |

$\Delta$ **A13.2.5.1 Length Adjustment Factor, $K_{LN}$, Used to Determine Moment Resistance of Prefabricated Wood I-Joists**

The length adjustment factor is used by manufacturers to develop proprietary I-joist moment resistance values and is not intended as an adjustment factor for specific applications. $K_{LN}$ is taken from Section 6.3.1.5 of ASTM Standard D 5055 and is the lesser of 1.0 or the value computed as follows:

$$K_{LN} = \text{(stress distribution adjustment factor)} (L_1/L)^Z \leq 1.0$$

where
stress distribution adjustment factor = the adjustment of specified strength parallel to grain, $f_a$, from full-length constant stress (such as a tension test) to the reference stress condition (simple span and uniform load) = 1.15
$L_1$ = gauge length (distance between grips) used in tension tests, parallel to grain, for I-joist flange material
L = nominal I-joist span
= 18 times the joist depth
Z = a coefficient (see Table A13.2.5.1) that accounts for the variation in tensile strength of the flange material

Δ

## Table A13.2.5.1
## Exponent, Z, used in the Calculation of the
## Length Adjustment Factor for Prefabricated Wood I-Joists

| Coefficient of variation*†, % | Z‡ |
|---|---|
| ≤ 10 | 0.06 |
| 15 | 0.09 |
| 20 | 0.12 |
| 25 | 0.15 |
| ≥ 30 | 0.19 |

*Coefficient of variation is determined from the full test data set using the higher coefficient of variation attained from the tensile strength of flange material or the tensile strength of end joints.
†Coefficient of variation for tensile strength of flange material is taken as 20% for machine-graded lumber (including SPS-4 material) and 25% for visually graded lumber.
‡Interpolation between tabular values is permitted.

O86-01
**Engineering Design in Wood**

# CSA Standards Update Service

## O86-01
## August 2001

**Title:** *Engineering Design in Wood*
**Pagination: 215 pages** (xix preliminary and 196 text), each dated August 2001

Automatic notifications about any updates to this publication are available.

- To register for email notifications, and/or to download any existing updates in PDF, enter the Online Store at **www.csa.ca** and click on **My Account** on the navigation bar.

  The **List ID** for this document is **2012272**.

- To receive printed updates, please complete and return the attached card.

✂ - - - - - - - - - - - - - - - - - - - - - - - - - - - - - - - - - - - - - - - - - - - - - - - - -

Name _____

Organization _____

Address _____

City _____

Province/State _____

Country _____ Postal/Zip Code _____

Email _____

## O86-01

*CSA Standard*

*O86-01*
**Engineering Design in Wood**

**CANADIAN STANDARDS
ASSOCIATION**

Published in August 2001 by Canadian Standards Association
A not-for-profit private sector organization
178 Rexdale Boulevard, Toronto, Ontario, Canada M9W 1R3
1-800-463-6727 • 416-747-4044

Visit our Online Store at **www.csa.ca**

ISBN 1-55324-411-7

**Technical Editor:** Mike Lottamoza
**Managing Editor:** Gary Burford
**Production Manager:** Alison MacIntosh

**Administrative Assistant:** Elizabeth Hope
**Document Analyst:** Indira Kumaralagan
**Document Processor:** Hematie Hassan
**Editors:** Maria Adragna/Samantha Coyle/Sandra Hawryn/Ann Martin/John McConnell
**Graphics Coordinator:** Cindy Kerkmann
**Publishing System Coordinators:** Ursula Das/Grace Da Silva/Seetha Rajagopalan

# Contents

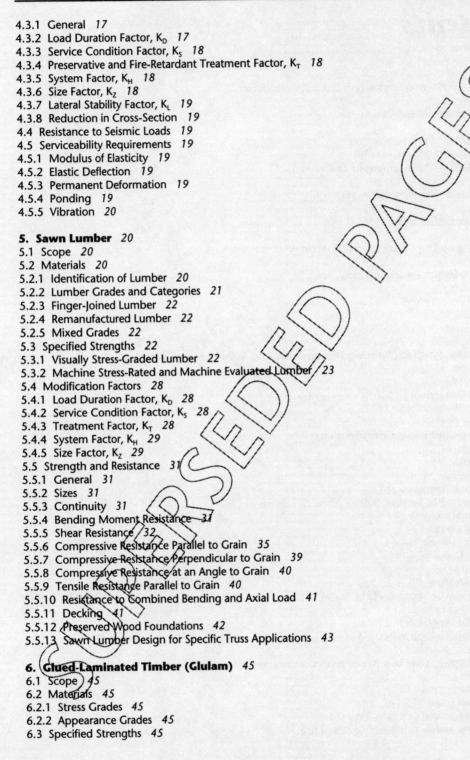

$K_{Sb}$ = service condition factor for bending

$K_{Sc}$ = service condition factor for compression parallel to grain

$K_{Scp}$ = service condition factor for compression perpendicular to grain

$K_{SE}$ = service condition factor for modulus of elasticity

$K_{SF}$ = service condition factor for fastening

$K_{St}$ = service condition factor for tension parallel to grain

$K_{Stp}$ = service condition factor for tension perpendicular to grain

$K_{Sv}$ = service condition factor for shear

$K_T$ = treatment factor (Clause 4.3.4.1)

$K_x$ = curvature factor for glued-laminated timber (Clause 6.5.6.5.2)

$K_Z$ = size factor (Clause 5.4.5 and Table 5.4.5)

$K_{Zb}$ = size factor for bending for sawn lumber

$K_{Zbg}$ = size factor for bending for glued-laminated timber (Clause 6.5.6.5.1)

$K_{Zc}$ = size factor for compression for sawn lumber (Clauses 5.5.6.2.3 and 5.5.13.3.3)

$K_{Zcg}$ = size factor for compression for glued-laminated timber (Clause 6.5.8.4.2)

$K_{Zcp}$ = size factor for bearing (Clauses 5.5.7.5 and 6.5.9.2)

$K_{Zt}$ = size factor for tension for sawn lumber

$K_{Ztp}$ = size factor for tension perpendicular to grain for glued-laminated timber (Table 6.5.6.6.1)

$K_{Zv}$ = size factor for shear for sawn lumber (Clause 5.4.5.3)

$L$ = length, mm

$L_e$ = effective length, mm

$L_p$ = length of penetration of fastening into main member, mm

$\ell$ = span, mm

$M_f$ = factored bending moment, N•mm

$M_r$ = factored bending moment resistance, N•mm

$m_p$ = specified strength capacity of structural panels in bending, N•mm/mm (Tables 7.3A, 7.3B, 7.3C, and 7.3D)

$N_r$ = factored compressive resistance at an angle to grain, N; or

= factored lateral strength resistance of fastenings at an angle to grain, N or kN

$N_{rs}$ = factored lateral slip resistance of fastenings at an angle to grain, N

$N_s$ = lateral slip resistance of fastenings at an angle to grain, N

$N_u$ = lateral strength resistance of fastenings at an angle to grain, N or kN

$n_F$ = number of fastenings in a group

$P_f$ = factored axial load in compression, N

$P_r$ = factored compressive resistance parallel to grain, N; or

= factored lateral strength resistance of fastenings parallel to grain, N or kN

$P_{rs}$ = factored lateral slip resistance of fastenings parallel to grain, N

$P_{rw}$ = factored withdrawal resistance of fastenings from side grain, N

$P_u$ = lateral strength resistance of fastenings parallel to grain, N or kN

$p_p$ = specified strength capacity of structural panels in axial compression, N/mm (Tables 7.3A, 7.3B, 7.3C, and 7.3D)

$Q_r$ = factored compressive resistance perpendicular to grain or to plane of plies, N; or

= factored lateral strength resistance of fastenings perpendicular to grain, N or kN

$Q_{rs}$ = factored lateral slip resistance of fastenings perpendicular to grain, N

$Q_u$ = lateral strength resistance of fastenings perpendicular to grain, N or kN

$q_p$ = specified strength capacity of structural panels in bearing, MPa (Tables 7.3A, 7.3B, 7.3C, and 7.3D)

$R$ = radius of curvature at centreline of member, mm (Figure 6.5.6.6.3)

$S$ = section modulus, mm$^3$

$T_f$ = factored axial load in tension, N

$T_r$ = factored tensile resistance parallel to grain, N

$t_p$ = specified strength capacity of structural panels in axial tension, N/mm (Tables 7.3A, 7.3B, 7.3C, and 7.3D)

$V_f$ = factored shear force, N

$V_{hd}$ = factored basic shear resistance calculated with $J_{hd}$ = 1.0, kN (Clause 9.4.5)

$V_r$ = factored shear resistance, N; or

= factored shear-through-thickness resistance of structural panels, N

$V_{rp}$ = factored planar shear resistance of structural panels, N

$V_{rs}$ = factored shear resistance of a shearwall segment, kN (Clause 9.5)

$v_p$ = specified strength capacity of structural panels in shear-through-thickness, N/mm (Tables 7.3A, 7.3B, 7.3C, and 7.3D)

$v_{pb}$ = specified strength capacity of structural panels in planar shear (due to bending), N/mm (Tables 7.3A, 7.3B, 7.3C, and 7.3D)

$v_{pf}$ = specified strength capacity of structural panels in planar shear (due to in-plane forces), MPa (Tables 7.3A, 7.3B, 7.3C, and 7.3D)

$W_f$ = factored total load, N

$w$ = specified total uniformly distributed load, kN/m$^2$

$X$ = factors affecting capacities of plywood and plywood assemblies, used with appropriate subscripts (Clause 8)

$Z$ = volume, m$^3$

$\gamma$ = importance factor (Clause 4.2.4.4)

$\varphi$ = resistance factor

$\psi$ = load combination factor (Clause 4.2.4.3)

## 2.3 Spacing Dimensions

For the purpose of this Standard, the following apply:
(a) Centre-to-centre member spacing dimensions may be used interchangeably:
  (i) 300 mm and 305 mm;

**10**

(ii)   400 mm and 406 mm; and

(iii)  600 mm and 610 mm.

(b) Panel dimensions may be used interchangeably:

(i)   1200 mm and 1220 mm; and

(ii)  2400 mm and 2440 mm.

## 2.4  Reference Publications

This Standard refers to the following publications and where such reference is made it shall be to the edition listed below, including all amendments published thereto.

**CSA Standards**

B111-1974 (R1998),
*Wire Nails, Spikes, and Staples;*

G40.20/G40.21-98,
*General Requirements for Rolled or Welded Structural Quality Steel/Structural Quality Steel;*

CAN/CSA-O15-90 (R2001),
*Wood Utility Poles and Reinforcing Stubs;*

CAN3-O56-M79 (R2001),
*Round Wood Piles;*

O80 Series-97,
*Wood Preservation;*

O80.15-97,
*Preservative Treatment of Wood for Building Foundation Systems, Basements, and Crawl Spaces by Pressure Processes;*

O112 Series-M1977 (R2001),
*CSA Standards for Wood Adhesives;*

O112.6-M1977 (R2001),
*Phenol and Phenol-Resorcinol Resin Adhesives for Wood (High-Temperature Curing);*

O112.7-M1977 (R2001),
*Resorcinol and Phenol-Resorcinol Resin Adhesives for Wood (Room- and Intermediate-Temperature Curing);*

O121-M1978 (R2001),
*Douglas Fir Plywood;*

CAN/CSA-O122-M89 (R2001),
*Structural Glued-Laminated Timber;*

CAN/CSA-O141-91 (R2001),
*Softwood Lumber;*

O151-M1978 (R2001),
*Canadian Softwood Plywood;*

O153-M1980 (R2001),
*Poplar Plywood;*

CAN/CSA-O177-M89 (R2001),
*Qualification Code for Manufacturers of Structural Glued-Laminated Timber;*

O322-1976 (R1999),
*Procedure for Certification of Pressure-Treated Wood Materials for Use in Preserved Wood Foundations;*

CAN/CSA-O325.0-92 (R2001),
*Construction Sheathing;*

O437 Series-93 (R2001),
*Standards on OSB and Waferboard;*

O437.0-93 (R2001),
*OSB and Waferboard;*

O452 Series-94 (R2001),
*Design Rated OSB;*

O452.0-94 (R2001),
*Design Rated OSB: Specifications;*

S307-M1980 (R2001),
*Load Test Procedure for Wood Roof Trusses for Houses and Small Buildings;*

S347-99,
*Method of Test for Evaluation of Truss Plates Used in Lumber Joints;*

CAN/CSA-S406-92 (R1998),
*Construction of Preserved Wood Foundations.*

*Standard Practice Relating Specified Strengths of Structural Members to Characteristic Structural Properties.* CSA Technical Committee on Engineering Design in Wood, November 2000. Available free of charge at www.csa.ca.

**ANSI/ASME* Standard**
B18.2.1-1996,
*Square and Hex Bolts and Screws, Inch Series.*

**ASTM† Standards**
A 36/A 36M-00a,
*Carbon Structural Steel;*

A 47/A 47M-99,
*Ferritic Malleable Iron Castings;*

A 307-00,
*Carbon Steel Bolts and Studs, 60 000 PSI Tensile Strength;*

A 653/A 653M-00,
*Specification for Steel Sheet, Zinc-Coated (Galvanized) or Zinc-Iron Alloy-Coated (Galvannealed) by the Hot-Dip Process;*
**Note:** *ASTM Standards A 653/A 653M replace ASTM Standards A 446/A 446M. Their chemical and mechanical requirements are the same.*
C 36/C 36M-99,
*Gypsum Wallboard;*

C 1002-00,
*Steel Self-Piercing Tapping Screws for the Application of Gypsum Panel Products or Metal Plaster Bases to Wood Studs or Steel Studs;*

D 1761-88 (2000),
*Mechanical Fasteners in Wood;*

D 5055-00,
*Establishing and Monitoring Structural Capacities of Prefabricated Wood I-Joists;*

D 5456-99a,
*Evaluation of Structural Composite Lumber Products;*

D 5457-93 (1998),
*Computing the Reference Resistance of Wood-Based Materials and Structural Connections for Load and Resistance Factor Design;*

E 8-00b,
*Standard Test Methods for Tension Testing of Metallic Materials.*

**Canadian Geotechnical Society Publication**
*Canadian Foundation Engineering Manual,* 1992.

**Canadian Wood Council**
CWC, *Commentary,* 2001 (in *Wood Design Manual*).

**National Research Council Canada**
CCMC *Registry of Product Evaluations* (published annually);

*National Building Code of Canada,* 1995;

*User's Guide — NBC 1995 Structural Commentaries (Part 4).*

**NIST‡ Standard**
PS2-92,
*Performance Standard for Wood-Based Structural-Use Panels.*

**NLGA§ Publications**
*Standard Grading Rules for Canadian Lumber,* 2000;

SPS 1-2000,
*Special Products Standards on Finger-Joined Structural Lumber;*

SPS 2-2000,
*Special Products Standards on Machine Stress-Rated Lumber.*

**SAE\*\* Publication**
*SAE Handbook,* 2000.

**Truss Plate Institute of Canada**
TPIC-1996,
*Truss Design Procedures and Specifications for Light Metal Plate Connected Wood Trusses.*

*\*American National Standards Institute/American Society of Mechanical Engineers.*
*†American Society for Testing and Materials.*
*‡National Institute of Standards and Technology.*
*§National Lumber Grades Authority.*
*\*\*Society of Automotive Engineers.*

# 3. Objectives and Design Requirements

## 3.1 Objective
The objective of the provisions in this Standard is the achievement of acceptable assurances that the structure, when correctly designed and built, will be fit for the intended use.

## 3.2 Limit States
The structure or portion thereof is considered fit for use when the structure, its components, and its connections are designed such that the requirements of Clauses 3.3, 4.1.2, and 4.1.3 are satisfied.

## 3.3 Design Requirements

### 3.3.1 Structural Adequacy
All members shall be so framed, anchored, tied, and braced together as to provide the strength and rigidity necessary for the purpose for which they are designed. All structural members shall be of adequate size and quality to carry all loads and other forces that can be reasonably expected to act upon them during construction and use without exceeding the strength or serviceability limit states.

### 3.3.2 New or Special Systems of Design and Construction
New or special systems of design or construction of wood structures or structural elements not already covered by this Standard may be used where such systems are based on analytical and engineering principles, or reliable test data, or both, that demonstrate the safety and serviceability of the resulting structure for the purpose intended.

### 3.3.3 Structural Integrity
The general arrangement of the structural system and the interconnection of its members shall provide positive resistance to widespread collapse of the system due to local failure.

### 3.3.4 Basis of Design
Design in accordance with this Standard is based on the assumption that
(a) the specified loads are realistic in size, kind, and duration;
(b) the wood product is normal for its species, kind, and grade;
(c) consideration is given to service conditions, including possible deterioration of members and corrosion of fastenings;
(d) the temperature of the wood does not exceed 50°C, except for occasional exposures to 65°C;
(e) the design is competent, fabrication and erection are good, grading and inspection are reliable, and maintenance is normal; and
(f) wood products are used as graded or manufactured for a designated end use.

### 3.3.5 Quality of Work
The quality of work in fabrication, preparation, and installation of materials shall conform throughout to accepted good practice.

### 3.3.6 Design Drawings

#### 3.3.6.1
Where design drawings are required they shall be drawn to a scale adequate to convey the required information. The drawings shall show a complete layout of the structure or portion thereof that is the subject of the design, with members suitably designated and located, including dimensions and detailed descriptions necessary for the preparation of shop and erection drawings. Governing heights, column centres, and offsets shall be dimensioned.

### 3.3.6.2

Design drawings shall designate the design standards used, as well as material or product standards applicable to the members and details depicted.

### 3.3.6.3

When needed for the preparation of shop drawings, the governing loads, reactions, shears, moments, and axial forces to be resisted by all members and their connections shall be shown on drawings or supplemental material, or both.

### 3.3.6.4

If camber is required for beams, girders, or trusses, the magnitude of such camber shall be specified on the design drawings.

# 4. General Design

## 4.1 Strength and Serviceability Limit States

### 4.1.1 Method of Analysis

The load effect on all members and connections shall be determined in accordance with recognized methods of analysis generally based on assumptions of elastic behaviour.

### 4.1.2 Strength Limit States

Design for strength limit states shall include
(a) establishing the value of the effect of the factored loads for the load combinations specified in Clause 4.2; and
(b) confirming by rational means that for each load effect in Item (a), the factored load effect does not exceed the corresponding factored resistance, as determined in accordance with the appropriate clauses of this Standard.

### 4.1.3 Serviceability Limit States

Design for serviceability limit states shall include
(a) establishing the value of the effect of the specified loads for the load combinations specified in Clause 4.2; and
(b) confirming by rational means that for each load effect in Item (a), the structural effect falls within the limits specified in the appropriate clauses of this Standard.

### 4.1.4 Resistance Factors

The resistance factors, $\phi$, are given in the appropriate sections of this Standard for all applicable limit states for wood members and fastenings.

## 4.2 Specified Loads, Load Effects, and Load Combinations

### 4.2.1 Buildings

Except as provided for in Clause 4.2.2, the specified loads, load effects, and combinations to be considered in the design of a building and its elements shall be those given in Clauses 4.2.3 and 4.2.4.
**Note:** *Specified loads, load effects, and combinations specified herein are in accordance with the provisions of the* National Building Code of Canada, *1995, its* Structural Commentaries on Part 4, *and the* Canadian Foundation Engineering Manual.

## 4.2.2 Other Structures

Where load requirements other than those in Clause 4.2.1 are specified, the appropriateness of the applicable factored resistance in this Standard shall be considered.

## 4.2.3 Specified Loads

Specified loads shall include the following wherever applicable, and minimum specified values of these loads shall be increased to account for dynamic effects where applicable:
(a) D — dead load due to weight of members; the weight of all materials of construction incorporated into the building to be supported permanently by the member, including permanent partitions and allowance for nonpermanent partitions; the weight of permanent equipment; forces due to prestressing;
(b) E — live load due to earthquake;
(c) L — live load due to static or inertial forces arising from intended use and occupancy (includes vertical loads due to cranes); snow, ice, and rain; earth and hydrostatic pressure;
(d) W — live load due to wind; and
(e) T — loads due to contraction or expansion caused by temperature changes, shrinkage, moisture changes, creep in component materials, movement due to differential settlement, or combinations thereof.

## 4.2.4 Load Effects and Combinations

## 4.2.4.1 Combinations Not Including Earthquake

For load combinations not including earthquake, the effect of factored loads is the structural effect due to the specified loads multiplied by load factors, $\alpha$, defined in Clause 4.2.4.2, a load combination factor, $\Psi$, defined in Clause 4.2.4.3, and an importance factor, $\gamma$, defined in Clause 4.2.4.4, and the factored load combination shall be taken as

$$\alpha_D D + \gamma \Psi [\alpha_L L + \alpha_w W + \alpha_T T]$$

## 4.2.4.2 Load Factors ($\alpha$)

Load factors, $\alpha$, for the strength limit states shall be taken as
$\alpha_D$  = 1.25, except that when the dead load resists overturning, uplift, or reversal of load, $\alpha_D = 0.85$;
$\alpha_L$  = 1.50;
$\alpha_w$  = 1.50; and
$\alpha_T$  = 1.25.
Load factors, $\alpha$, for serviceability limit states shall be 1.00.

## 4.2.4.3 Load Combination Factor ($\Psi$)

The load combination factor, $\Psi$, shall be taken as
(a)  1.00 when only one of L, W, and T acts;
(b)  0.70 when two of L, W, and T act;
(c)  0.60 when all of L, W, and T act.
The most unfavourable effect shall be determined by considering L, W, and T acting alone or in combination.

## 4.2.4.4 Importance Factor ($\gamma$)

The importance factor, $\gamma$, for strength limit states shall be not less than 0.80 for structures where it can be shown that collapse is not likely to cause injury or other serious consequences, and 1.00 for all other structures. The importance factor, $\gamma$, for serviceability limit states shall be 1.00.
**Note:** *Examples of buildings where it can be shown that collapse is not likely to cause injury or other serious consequences are buildings of low human occupancy, such as farm buildings, certain temporary facilities, and minor storage facilities.*

## 4.2.4.5 Combinations Including Earthquake

For load combinations including earthquake, the factored load combinations shall be taken as
$1.0D + \gamma(1.0E)$; and either
(a)  for storage and assembly occupancies, $1.0D + \gamma(1.0L + 1.0E)$; or
(b)  for all other occupancies, $1.0D + \gamma(0.5L + 1.0E)$.

## 4.3 Conditions and Factors Affecting Resistance

### 4.3.1 General

Specified strengths and capacities for materials and fastenings shall be multiplied by the modification factors in this clause and the appropriate materials or fastening clauses.

**Note:** *The basis for derivation of specified strengths for sawn lumber members is described in CSA Special Publication Standard Practice Relating Specified Strengths of Structural Members to Characteristic Structural Properties. The principles described therein have also been used to guide derivations for other products in this Standard.*

### 4.3.2 Load Duration Factor, $K_D$

#### 4.3.2.1 Specified Strengths and Capacities

The specified strengths and capacities given in this Standard are based on the standard-term duration of the specified loads.

#### 4.3.2.2 Load Duration Factor

Except as specified in Clause 4.3.2.3, the specified strengths and capacities shall be multiplied by a load duration factor, $K_D$, in accordance with Table 4.3.2.2, but not exceeding 1.15.

### Table 4.3.2.2
### Load Duration Factor, $K_D$

| Duration of loading | $K_D$ | Explanatory notes |
|---|---|---|
| Short term | 1.15 | Short-term loading means that condition of loading where the duration of the specified loads is not expected to last more than 7 days continuously or cumulatively throughout the life of the structure. Examples include wind loads, earthquake loads, falsework, and formwork, as well as impact loads. |
| Standard term | 1.00 | Standard term means that condition of loading where the duration of specified loads exceeds that of short-term loading, but is less than permanent loading. Examples include snow loads, live loads due to occupancy, wheel loads on bridges, and dead loads in combination with all of the above. |
| Permanent | 0.65 | Permanent duration means that condition of loading under which a member is subjected to more or less continuous specified load. Examples include dead loads or dead loads plus live loads of such character that they are imposed on the member for as long a period of time as the dead loads themselves. Such loads include those usually occurring in tanks or bins containing fluids or granular material, loads on retaining walls subjected to lateral pressure such as earth, and floor loads where the specified load may be expected to be continuously applied, such as those in buildings for storage of bulk materials. Loads due to fixed machinery should be considered to be permanent. |

**Note:** *Duration of load may require professional judgment by the designer. Explanatory notes in this table provide guidance to designers about the types of loads and load combinations for which each modification factor should be applied.*

### 4.3.2.3 Permanent Load Factor

For standard-term loads where D is greater than L, the permanent load factor may be used, or the factor may be calculated as

$$K_D = 1.0 - 0.50 \log\left(\frac{D}{L}\right) \geq 0.65$$

where
D = specified dead load
L = specified live load

### 4.3.2.4 Combined Loads

When the total specified load is made up of loads acting for different durations, the design shall be based on the most severe combination. The appropriate load duration factor shall be taken into account for each load combination.

### 4.3.3 Service Condition Factor, $K_S$

Where materials or fastenings are used in service conditions other than dry, specified strengths and capacities shall be multiplied by the service condition factor, $K_S$, in the appropriate materials or fastening clauses.

### 4.3.4 Preservative and Fire-Retardant Treatment Factor, $K_T$

### 4.3.4.1 General

Except as permitted in Clause 4.3.4.4, specified strengths and capacities shall be multiplied by the treatment factor, $K_T$, in the appropriate materials or fastenings clause.

### 4.3.4.2 Preservative Treatment

When conditions conducive to decay or other deterioration are likely to occur in the case of permanent structures, wood should be pressure-treated with preservative in accordance with the requirements of the CSA Standard O80 Series. If possible, all boring, grooving, cutting, and other fabrication should be completed before treatment. Fabrication that is carried out after pressure treatment shall be treated locally in accordance with the CSA Standard O80 Series.

### 4.3.4.3 Untreated Wood

Untreated wood in permanent structures shall not be in direct contact with masonry, concrete, or soil when moisture transfer can occur. Any method that eliminates transfer of moisture, e.g., a minimum of 10 mm air space around a member in a wall, shall be considered adequate protection.

### 4.3.4.4 Fire-Retardant Treatment

Where wood is impregnated with fire-retardant or other strength-reducing chemicals, $K_T$ shall be determined in accordance with the results of appropriate tests or shall not exceed the value of $K_T$ tabulated in the appropriate clause.

### 4.3.5 System Factor, $K_H$

Specified strengths may be multiplied by a system factor, $K_H$, as specified in Clauses 5.4.4 and 6.4.3.
**Note:** See Clause A4.3.5 for additional information on system factors.

### 4.3.6 Size Factor, $K_Z$

Where size influences the specified strengths of members, the specified strengths shall be multiplied by the size factor, $K_Z$, in accordance with Clauses 5.4.5, 6.5.6., 6.5.8, and 6.5.9.
**Note:** See the Canadian Wood Council's Commentary.

## 4.3.7 Lateral Stability Factor, $K_L$

The effect of width-to-depth ratios and of the degree of lateral support on the factored bending moment resistance is specified in Clauses 5.5.4.2 and 6.5.6.4.

## 4.3.8 Reduction in Cross-Section

### 4.3.8.1 Net Section

The net section, obtained by deducting from the gross section the area of all material removed by boring, grooving, dapping, notching, or other means, shall be checked in calculating the strength capacity of a member.

### 4.3.8.2 Limitation

In no case shall the net section be less than 75% of the gross section.

## 4.4 Resistance to Seismic Loads

The factored resistance required for seismic loading may be obtained by the use of shearwalls and diaphragms (Clause 9). Where concentrically braced heavy timber space frames or moment-resisting wood space frames are used to provide seismic resistance, fastenings such as nails, bolts, lag screws, or glulam rivets as specified in Clause 10 shall be used to provide ductile connections.

**Note:** *Split rings and shear plates are not generally considered to provide ductile connections.*

## 4.5 Serviceability Requirements

### 4.5.1 Modulus of Elasticity

The modulus of elasticity for stiffness calculations, $E_s$, shall be taken as

$$E_S = E(K_{SE}K_T)$$

where
$E$    = specified modulus of elasticity, MPa
$K_{SE}$ = service condition factor
$K_T$   = treatment factor

### 4.5.2 Elastic Deflection

The elastic deflection of structural members under the specified loads shall not exceed 1/180 of the span. For glued-laminated members having cambers equalling at least dead load deflection, the additional deflection due to specified live loads shall not exceed 1/180 of the span. Deflection under the specified loads shall be limited to avoid damage to structural elements or attached nonstructural elements.

**Note:** *See Clause A4.5.2 for additional information on deflection of a wood frame system under static loads.*

### 4.5.3 Permanent Deformation

Structural members that support continuously applied loads in excess of 50% of the total specified loads shall be designed to avoid excessive permanent deformation. In lieu of a more accurate evaluation of acceptable deflection limits, an upper limit of 1/360 of the span shall be imposed on the elastic deflection due to continuously applied loads. Special allowance shall be made in the design where permanent deformations can result in unsightly appearance or potential damage to adjacent elements of the building or structure.

### 4.5.4 Ponding

Roof framing systems shall be investigated by rational analysis to ensure adequate performance under ponding conditions unless
(a) the roof surface is provided with sufficient slope toward points of free drainage to prevent accumulation of rain water; or

(b) for a simply supported system subjected to a uniformly distributed load, the following condition is satisfied:

$$\frac{\Sigma\Delta}{w} < 65$$

where

$\Sigma\Delta$ = sum of deflections due to this load, mm, of all the components of the system (decking, secondary beams, primary beams, etc)

w   = total uniformly distributed load, kN/m$^2$

### 4.5.5 Vibration

Special consideration shall be given to structures subjected to vibration to ensure that such vibration is acceptable for the use of the structure.

**Note:** *See Clause A4.5.5 for information on floor vibration. Additional information can be found in the commentary on serviceability criteria for deflections and vibrations in the* User's Guide — NBC 1995 Structural Commentaries (Part 4).

# 5. Sawn Lumber

## 5.1 Scope

Design tables, data, and methods specified in Clause 5 apply only to structural lumber complying with the requirements of CSA Standard CAN/CSA-O141.

## 5.2 Materials

### 5.2.1 Identification of Lumber

#### 5.2.1.1 General

Design in accordance with this Standard is predicated on the use of lumber that is graded in accordance with the NLGA *Standard Grading Rules for Canadian Lumber* and identified by the grade stamp of an association or independent grading agency in accordance with the provisions of CSA Standard CAN/CSA-O141.

**Note:** *A list of approved agencies may be obtained from the Canadian Lumber Standards Accreditation Board.*

#### 5.2.1.2 Canadian Lumber

In this Standard, Canadian species are designated according to species combinations given in Table 5.2.1.2, which reflects marketing practice. These combinations should be used for general design purposes.

**Note:** *The designer is strongly advised to check availability of species, grade, and sizes before specifying.*

#### 5.2.1.3 US Lumber

For US commercial species combinations graded in accordance with the *National Grading Rule for Dimension Lumber,* the design data may be determined using the species combination equivalents in Table 5.2.1.3.

### 5.3.1.2

The specified strengths (MPa) for plank decking shall be derived from Table 5.3.1A using the following grade equivalents:

| Decking grade | Equivalent lumber grade |
|---|---|
| Select | Select Structural |
| Commercial | No. 2 |

## 5.3.2 Machine Stress-Rated and Machine Evaluated Lumber

The specified strengths (MPa) for machine stress-rated lumber are given in Table 5.3.2. The specified strengths (MPa) for machine evaluated lumber are given in Table 5.3.3. Specified strengths in shear are not grade-dependent and shall be taken from Table 5.3.1A for the appropriate species.

### Table 5.3.1A
### Specified Strengths and Modulus of Elasticity for Structural Joist and Plank, Structural Light Framing, and Stud Grade Categories of Lumber (MPa)

| Species identification | Grade | Bending at extreme fibre, $f_b$ | Longitudinal shear, $f_v$ | Compression Parallel to grain, $f_c$ | Compression Perpendicular to grain, $f_{cp}$ | Tension parallel to grain, $f_t$ | Modulus of elasticity E | Modulus of elasticity $E_{05}$ |
|---|---|---|---|---|---|---|---|---|
| D Fir-L | SS | 16.5 | | 19.0 | | 10.6 | 12 500 | 8 500 |
| | No. 1/No. 2 | 10.0 | 1.1 | 14.0 | 7.0 | 5.8 | 11 000 | 7 000 |
| | No. 3/Stud | 4.6 | | 4.6 | | 2.1 | 10 000 | 5 500 |
| Hem-Fir | SS | 16.0 | | 17.6 | | 9.7 | 12 000 | 8 500 |
| | No. 1/No. 2 | 11.0 | 0.9 | 14.8 | 4.6 | 6.2 | 11 000 | 7 500 |
| | No. 3/Stud | 7.0 | | 7.0 | | 3.2 | 10 000 | 6 000 |
| S-P-F | SS | 16.5 | | 14.5 | | 8.6 | 10 500 | 7 500 |
| | No. 1/No. 2 | 11.8 | 1.0 | 11.5 | 5.3 | 5.5 | 9 500 | 6 500 |
| | No. 3/Stud | 7.0 | | 7.0 | | 3.2 | 9 000 | 5 500 |
| Northern | SS | 10.6 | | 13.0 | | 6.2 | 7 500 | 5 500 |
| | No. 1/No. 2 | 7.6 | 0.9 | 10.4 | 3.5 | 4.0 | 7 000 | 5 000 |
| | No. 3/Stud | 4.5 | | 4.5 | | 2.0 | 6 500 | 4 000 |

**Note:** *Tabulated values are based on the following standard conditions:*
*(a) 286 mm larger dimension;*
*(b) dry service conditions; and*
*(c) standard-term duration of load.*

## Table 5.3.1B
## Specified Strengths and Modulus of Elasticity for Light Framing Grades (MPa) Applicable to Sizes 38 by 38 mm to 89 by 89 mm

| Species identification | Grade | Bending at extreme fibre, $f_b$ | Longi-tudinal shear, $f_v$ | Compression Parallel to grain, $f_c$ | Compression Perpendicular to grain, $f_{cp}$ | Tension parallel to grain, $f_t$ | Modulus of elasticity $E$ | Modulus of elasticity $E_{05}$ |
|---|---|---|---|---|---|---|---|---|
| D Fir-L | Const. | 13.0 | 1.9 | 16.0 | 7.0 | 6.6 | 10 000 | 5 500 |
|         | Stand. | 7.3  |     | 13.1 |     | 3.7 | 9 000  | 5 000 |
| Hem-Fir | Const. | 14.3 | 1.5 | 16.9 | 4.6 | 7.0 | 10 000 | 6 000 |
|         | Stand. | 8.0  |     | 13.9 |     | 3.9 | 9 000  | 5 500 |
| S-P-F   | Const. | 15.3 | 1.7 | 13.1 | 5.3 | 6.2 | 9 000  | 5 500 |
|         | Stand. | 8.6  |     | 10.8 |     | 3.5 | 8 000  | 5 000 |
| Northern| Const. | 9.9  | 1.5 | 11.9 | 3.5 | 4.5 | 6 500  | 4 000 |
|         | Stand. | 5.5  |     | 9.8  |     | 2.5 | 6 000  | 3 500 |

**Notes:**

**(1)** *The size factor $K_Z$ for light framing grades shall be 1.00, except that $K_{Zc}$ shall be calculated in accordance with Clause 5.5.6.2.2, and $K_{Zcp}$ shall be determined in accordance with Clause 5.5.7.5.*

**(2)** *Tabulated values are based on the following standard conditions:*

*(a) 89 mm width (except for compression properties);*

*(b) dry service conditions; and*

*(c) standard-term duration of load.*

## Table 5.3.1C
## Specified Strengths and Modulus of Elasticity
## for Beam and Stringer Grades (MPa)

| Species identification | Grade | Bending at extreme fibre,* $f_b$ | Longi-tudinal shear, $f_v$ | Compression Parallel to grain, $f_c$ | Perpen-dicular to grain, $f_{cp}$ | Tension parallel to grain, $f_t$ | Modulus of elasticity E | $E_{05}$ |
|---|---|---|---|---|---|---|---|---|
| D Fir-L | SS | 19.5 | | 13.2 | | 10.0 | 12 000 | 8 000 |
| | No. 1 | 15.8 | 0.9 | 11.0 | 7.0 | 7.0 | 12 000 | 8 000 |
| | No. 2 | 9.0 | | 7.2 | | 3.3 | 9 500 | 6 000 |
| Hem-Fir | SS | 14.5 | | 10.8 | | 7.4 | 10 000 | 7 000 |
| | No. 1 | 11.7 | 0.7 | 9.0 | 4.6 | 5.2 | 10 000 | 7 000 |
| | No. 2 | 6.7 | | 5.9 | | 2.4 | 8 000 | 5 500 |
| S-P-F | SS | 13.6 | | 9.5 | | 7.0 | 8 500 | 6 000 |
| | No. 1 | 11.0 | 0.7 | 7.9 | 5.3 | 4.9 | 8 500 | 6 000 |
| | No. 2 | 6.3 | | 5.2 | | 2.3 | 6 500 | 4 500 |
| Northern | SS | 12.8 | | 7.2 | | 6.5 | 8 000 | 5 500 |
| | No. 1 | 10.8 | 0.6 | 6.0 | 3.5 | 4.6 | 8 000 | 5 500 |
| | No. 2 | 5.9 | | 3.9 | | 2.2 | 6 000 | 4 000 |

*Specified strengths for beams and stringers are based on loads applied to the narrow face. When beams and stringers are subject to loads applied to the wide face, the specified strength for bending at the extreme fibre and the specified modulus of elasticity shall be multiplied by the following factors:

| | $f_b$ | E or $E_{05}$ |
|---|---|---|
| Select Structural | 0.88 | 1.00 |
| No. 1 or No. 2 | 0.77 | 0.90 |

**Notes:**
**(1)** Beams and stringers have a smaller dimension of at least 114 mm, with a larger dimension more than 51 mm greater than the smaller dimension.
**(2)** An approximate value for modulus of rigidity may be estimated at 0.065 times the modulus of elasticity.
**(3)** With sawn members thicker than 89 mm that season slowly, care should be exercised to avoid overloading in compression before appreciable seasoning of the outer fibre has taken place; otherwise, compression strengths for wet service conditions shall be used.
**(4)** Beam and stringer grades listed in this table are not graded for continuity (see Clause 5.5.3).
**(5)** Tabulated values are based on the following standard conditions:
(a) 343 mm larger dimension for bending and shear, 292 mm larger dimension for tension and compression parallel to grain;
(b) dry service conditions; and
(c) standard-term duration of load.

## Table 5.3.1D
## Specified Strengths and Modulus of Elasticity
## for Post and Timber Grades (MPa)

| Species identification | Grade | Bending at extreme fibre, $f_b$ | Longi-tudinal shear, $f_v$ | Compression | | Tension parallel to grain, $f_t$ | Modulus of elasticity | |
| | | | | Parallel to grain, $f_c$ | Perpen-dicular to grain, $f_{cp}$ | | $E$ | $E_{05}$ |
|---|---|---|---|---|---|---|---|---|
| D Fir-L | SS | 18.3 | 1.2 | 13.8 | | 10.7 | 12 000 | 8 000 |
| | No. 1 | 13.8 | 0.9 | 12.2 | 7.0 | 8.1 | 10 500 | 6 500 |
| | No. 2 | 6.0 | 0.9 | 7.5 | | 3.8 | 9 500 | 6 000 |
| Hem-Fir | SS | 13.6 | 1.0 | 11.3 | | 7.9 | 10 000 | 7 000 |
| | No. 1 | 10.2 | 0.7 | 10.0 | 4.6 | 6.0 | 9 000 | 6 000 |
| | No. 2 | 4.5 | 0.7 | 6.1 | | 2.8 | 8 000 | 5 500 |
| S-P-F | SS | 12.7 | 0.9 | 9.9 | | 7.4 | 8 500 | 6 000 |
| | No. 1 | 9.6 | 0.7 | 8.7 | 5.3 | 5.6 | 7 500 | 5 000 |
| | No. 2 | 4.2 | 0.7 | 5.4 | | 2.6 | 6 500 | 4 500 |
| Northern | SS | 12.0 | 0.8 | 7.5 | | 7.0 | 8 000 | 5 500 |
| | No. 1 | 9.0 | 0.6 | 6.7 | 3.5 | 5.3 | 7 000 | 5 000 |
| | No. 2 | 3.9 | 0.6 | 4.1 | | 2.5 | 6 000 | 4 000 |

**Notes:**
(1) *Posts and timbers have a smaller dimension of at least 114 mm, with a larger dimension not more than 51 mm greater than the smaller dimension.*
(2) *Posts and timbers graded to beam and stringer rules may be assigned beam and stringer strength.*
(3) *An approximate value for modulus of rigidity may be estimated at 0.065 times the modulus of elasticity.*
(4) *With sawn members thicker than 89 mm that season slowly, care should be exercised to avoid overloading in compression before appreciable seasoning of the outer fibre has taken place; otherwise, compression strengths for wet service conditions shall be used.*
(5) *Tabulated values are based on the following standard conditions:*
(a) *343 mm larger dimension for bending and shear, 292 mm larger dimension for tension and compression parallel to grain;*
(b) *dry service conditions; and*
(c) *standard-term duration of load.*

## Table 5.3.2
## Specified Strengths and Modulus of Elasticity for Machine Machine Stress-Rated Grades 38 mm Thick by All Widths (MPa)

| Grade | Bending at extreme fibre, $f_b$ | Modulus of elasticity, E | Tension parallel to grain, $f_t$ 89 to 184 mm | >184 mm | Compression Parallel to grain, $f_c$ | Perpendicular to grain,* $f_{cp}$ |
|---|---|---|---|---|---|---|
| 1200F$_b$-1.2E | 17.4 | 8 300 | 6.7 | — | 15.1 | 5.3 |
| 1350F$_b$-1.3E | 19.5 | 9 000 | 8.4 | — | 16.9 | 5.3 |
| 1450F$_b$-1.3E | 21.0 | 9 000 | 9.0 | — | 17.3 | 5.3 |
| 1500F$_b$-1.4E | 21.7 | 9 700 | 10.1 | — | 17.5 | 5.3 |
| 1650F$_b$-1.5E | 23.9 | 10 300 | 11.4 | — | 18.1 | 5.3 |
| 1800F$_b$-1.6E | 26.1 | 11 000 | 13.2 | — | 18.7 | 5.3 |
| 1950F$_b$-1.7E | 28.2 | 11 700 | 15.4 | — | 19.3 | 5.3 |
| 2100F$_b$-1.8E | 30.4 | 12 400 | 17.7 | — | 19.9 | 6.5 |
| 2250F$_b$-1.9E | 32.6 | 13 100 | 19.6 | — | 20.5 | 6.5 |
| 2400F$_b$-2.0E | 34.7 | 13 800 | 21.6 | — | 21.1 | 6.5 |
| 2550F$_b$-2.1E | 36.9 | 14 500 | 23.0 | — | 21.7 | 6.5 |
| 2700F$_b$-2.2E | 39.1 | 15 200 | 24.1 | — | 22.3 | 6.5 |
| 2850F$_b$-2.3E | 41.3 | 15 900 | 25.8 | — | 22.9 | 6.5 |
| 3000F$_b$-2.4E | 43.4 | 16 500 | 26.9 | — | 23.5 | 6.5 |

*The following MSR grades provide a modulus of elasticity with higher corresponding strengths. For these MSR grades, qualification and daily quality control for tensile strength are required.*

| Grade | | | | | | |
|---|---|---|---|---|---|---|
| 1400F$_b$-1.2E | 20.3 | 8 300 | 9.0 | 9.0 | 17.1 | 5.3 |
| 1600F$_b$-1.4E | 23.2 | 9 700 | 10.7 | 10.7 | 17.9 | 5.3 |
| 1650F$_b$-1.3E | 23.9 | 9 000 | 11.4 | 11.4 | 18.1 | 5.3 |
| 1800F$_b$-1.5E | 26.1 | 10 300 | 14.6 | 14.6 | 18.7 | 5.3 |
| 2000F$_b$-1.6E | 29.0 | 11 000 | 14.6 | 14.6 | 19.5 | 5.3 |
| 2250F$_b$-1.7E | 32.6 | 11 700 | 19.6 | 19.6 | 20.5 | 5.3 |
| 2250F$_b$-1.8E | 32.6 | 12 400 | 19.6 | 19.6 | 20.5 | 6.5 |
| 2400F$_b$-1.8E | 34.7 | 12 400 | 21.6 | 21.6 | 21.1 | 6.5 |

*Compression perpendicular to grain values are for S-P-F MSR (all grades) and Hem-Fir MSR lumber with E grade of 10 300 MPa or higher. For other species or grades, use corresponding values for visually stress-graded lumber taken from Table 5.3.1A for the appropriate group.*

**Notes:**
**(1)** Tabulated values are based on standard-term duration of load and dry service conditions.
**(2)** The size factor $K_z$ for MSR lumber shall be 1.00, except that $K_{Zv}$ is given in Table 5.4.5, $K_{Zcp}$ is determined in accordance with Clause 5.5.7.5, and $K_{Zc}$ is calculated in accordance with Clause 5.5.6.2.2.

## Table 5.3.3
## Specified Strengths and Modulus of Elasticity for Machine Evaluated Lumber Grades 38 mm Thick by All Widths (MPa)

| Grade | Bending at extreme fibre, $f_b$ | Modulus of elasticity, E | Tension parallel to grain, $f_t$ | Compression Parallel to grain, $f_c$ | Perpendicular to grain,* $f_{cp}$ |
|-------|-----|--------|------|------|-----|
| M-10 | 20.3 | 8 300 | 9.0 | 17.1 | 5.3 |
| M-11 | 22.4 | 10 300 | 9.5 | 17.7 | 5.3 |
| M-12 | 23.2 | 11 000 | 9.5 | 17.9 | 5.3 |
| M-13 | 23.2 | 9 700 | 10.7 | 17.9 | 5.3 |
| M-14 | 26.1 | 11 700 | 11.2 | 18.7 | 5.3 |
| M-15 | 26.1 | 10 300 | 12.3 | 18.7 | 5.3 |
| M-18 | 29.0 | 12 400 | 13.5 | 19.5 | 6.5 |
| M-19 | 29.0 | 11 000 | 14.6 | 19.5 | 5.3 |
| M-21 | 33.3 | 13 100 | 15.7 | 20.7 | 6.5 |
| M-22 | 34.0 | 11 700 | 16.8 | 20.9 | 5.3 |
| M-23 | 34.7 | 12 400 | 21.3 | 21.1 | 6.5 |
| M-24 | 39.1 | 13 100 | 20.2 | 22.3 | 6.5 |
| M-25 | 39.8 | 15 200 | 22.4 | 22.5 | 6.5 |
| M-26 | 40.6 | 13 800 | 20.2 | 22.7 | 6.5 |

*Compression perpendicular to grain values are for S-P-F MEL (all grades) and Hem-Fir MEL lumber with E grade of 10 300 MPa or higher. For other species or grades, use corresponding values for visually stress-graded lumber taken from Table 5.3.1A for the appropriate group.

**Notes:**
(1) Tabulated values are based on standard-term duration of load and dry service conditions.
(2) The size factor $K_z$ for MEL lumber shall be 1.00, except that $K_{Zv}$ is given in Table 5.4.5, $K_{Zcp}$ is determined in accordance with Clause 5.5.7.5, and $K_{Zc}$ is calculated in accordance with Clause 5.5.6.2.2.

## 5.4 Modification Factors

### 5.4.1 Load Duration Factor, $K_D$

The specified strength of lumber shall be multiplied by a load duration factor, $K_D$, as given in Clause 4.3.2.2.

### 5.4.2 Service Condition Factor, $K_S$

The specified strength of lumber shall be multiplied by a service condition factor, $K_S$, as given in Table 5.4.2.

### 5.4.3 Treatment Factor, $K_T$

#### 5.4.3.1
The specified strength of lumber shall be multiplied by a treatment factor, $K_T$, as given in Table 5.4.3.

#### 5.4.3.2
For lumber treated with fire-retardant or other strength-reducing chemicals, strength and stiffness capacities shall be based on the documented results of tests that shall take into account the effects of time, temperature, and moisture content. Test procedures shall meet the requirements of Clause 3.3.2.
**Note:** The effects of fire retardant treatments can vary depending on manufacturing materials and processes. See the Canadian Wood Council's Commentary for additional explanation.

## 5.5.6.6 Spliced Built-up Compressive Members

### 5.5.6.6.1

Spliced nail-laminated built-up columns that are constructed in accordance with Figure 5.5.6.6 may be designed for axial loads and bending loads applied parallel to the wide face of the laminations in accordance with Clauses 5.5.6.6.2 and 5.5.6.6.3, provided that the following additional conditions are met:

(a) the spliced columns shall consist of three members, with nails penetrating all three members;
(b) the minimum overall splice length, L, shall be 1200 mm;
(c) the spliced columns shall be braced by sheathing, or purlins spaced at a maximum of 600 mm on centres in the direction perpendicular to the wide face of the laminations;
(d) minimum lamination size shall be 38 mm thick by 140 mm wide; and
(e) maximum lamination size shall be 38 mm thick by 184 mm wide.

### 5.5.6.6.2

The factored bending resistance shall be determined using Clause 5.5.10 based on equivalent members of the same size, grade, and species, using

(a) 40% of the factored bending resistance of an unspliced built-up beam in the splice region, R; and
(b) 100% of the factored bending resistance of an unspliced built-up beam outside of the splice region, R.

### 5.5.6.6.3

The factored compressive resistance in the direction parallel to the wide face of the laminations shall be determined using Clause 5.5.6.2.2 based on an $E_{05}$ value equal to 60% of the value for a simple compression member of the same species and grade.

**Note:**  *Splicing of built-up members significantly reduces their stiffness and bending resistance, and should be avoided wherever possible.*

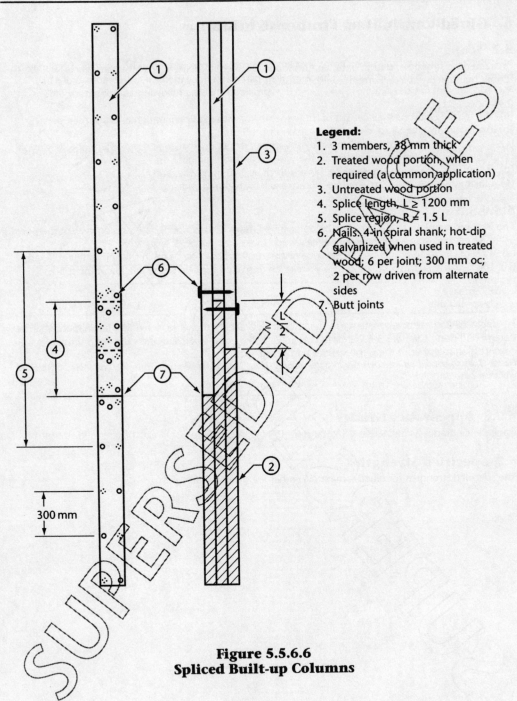

**Legend:**
1. 3 members, 38 mm thick
2. Treated wood portion, when required (a common application)
3. Untreated wood portion
4. Splice length, L ≥ 1200 mm
5. Splice region, R = 1.5 L
6. Nails: 4-in spiral shank; hot-dip galvanized when used in treated wood; 6 per joint; 300 mm oc; 2 per row driven from alternate sides
7. Butt joints

**Figure 5.5.6.6
Spliced Built-up Columns**

# 6. Glued-Laminated Timber (Glulam)

## 6.1 Scope

Characteristic strengths, design data, and methods specified in Clause 6 apply only to glued-laminated timber manufactured in accordance with CSA Standard CAN/CSA-O122.

## 6.2 Materials

### 6.2.1 Stress Grades

Design in accordance with Clause 6 is based on the use of the stress grades of glued-laminated timber given in Table 6.2.1.

**Note:** *The* National Building Code of Canada, Part 4, *requires that glued-laminated timber be fabricated in plants conforming to CSA Standard CAN/CSA-O177. A list of certified manufacturers may be obtained from the certifying agency or agencies providing certification service.*

### Table 6.2.1
### Glued-Laminated Timber Stress Grades

| Primary application | Wood species | | |
| | Douglas Fir-Larch | Spruce-Lodgepole Pine-Jack Pine | Hem-Fir and Douglas Fir-Larch |
| --- | --- | --- | --- |
| Bending members | 20f-E, 24f-E<br>20f-EX, 24f-EX | 20f-E<br>20f-EX | 24f-E<br>24f-EX |
| Compression members | 16c-E | 12c-E | |
| Tension members | 18t-E | 14t-E | |

### 6.2.2 Appearance Grades

Appearance grades as defined in CSA Standard CAN/CSA-O122 do not affect the specified strength.

## 6.3 Specified Strengths

The specified strengths for glued-laminated timber are given in Table 6.3.

## Table 6.3
## Specified Strengths and Modulus of Elasticity
## for Glued-Laminated Timber (MPa)

| | | Douglas Fir-Larch | | | | | |
|---|---|---|---|---|---|---|---|
| | | 24f-E | 24f-EX | 20f-E | 20f-EX | 18t-E | 16c-E |
| Bending moment (pos.) | $f_b$ | 30.6 | 30.6 | 25.6 | 25.6 | 24.3 | 14.0 |
| Bending moment (neg.) | $f_b$ | 14.0 | 30.6 | 14.0 | 25.6 | 24.3 | 14.0 |
| Longitudinal shear | $f_v$ | 2.0 | 2.0 | 2.0 | 2.0 | 2.0 | 2.0 |
| Compression parallel | $f_c$ | 30.2* | 30.2* | 30.2* | 30.2* | 30.2 | 30.2 |
| Compression parallel combined with bending | $f_{cb}$ | 30.2* | 30.2 | 30.2* | 30.2 | 30.2 | 30.2 |
| Compression perpendicular — compression face bearing — tension face bearing | $f_{cp}$ | 7.0 7.0 | 7.0 7.0 | 7.0 7.0 | 7.0 7.0 | 7.0 7.0 | 7.0 7.0 |
| Tension net section (See Clause 6.5.11) | $f_{tn}$ | 20.4* | 20.4 | 20.4* | 20.4 | 23.0 | 20.4 |
| Tension gross section | $f_{tg}$ | 15.3* | 15.3 | 15.3* | 15.3 | 17.9 | 15.3 |
| Tension perpendicular to grain | $f_{tp}$ | 0.83 | 0.83 | 0.83 | 0.83 | 0.83 | 0.83 |
| Modulus of elasticity | E | 13 100 | 13 100 | 12 400 | 12 400 | 13 800 | 12 400 |

| | | Spruce-Lodgepole Pine-Jack Pine | | | | Hem-Fir and Douglas Fir-Larch | |
|---|---|---|---|---|---|---|---|
| | | 20f-E | 20f-EX | 14t-E | 12c-E | 24f-E | 24-EX |
| Bending moment (pos.) | $f_b$ | 25.6 | 25.6 | 24.3 | 9.8 | 30.6 | 30.6 |
| Bending moment (neg.) | $f_b$ | 9.8 | 25.6 | 24.3 | 9.8 | 10.6 | 30.6 |
| Longitudinal shear | $f_v$ | 1.75 | 1.75 | 1.75 | 1.75 | 1.75 | 1.75 |
| Compression parallel | $f_c$ | 25.2* | 25.2* | 25.2 | 25.2 | — | — |
| Compression parallel combined with bending | $f_{cb}$ | 25.2* | 25.2 | 25.2 | 25.2 | — | — |
| Compression perpendicular — compression face bearing — tension face bearing | $f_{cp}$ | 5.8 5.8 | 5.8 5.8 | 5.8 5.8 | 5.8 5.8 | 4.6 7.0 | 7.0 7.0 |
| Tension net section (See Clause 6.5.11) | $f_{tn}$ | 17.0* | 17.0 | 17.9 | 17.0 | 20.4* | 20.4 |
| Tension gross section | $f_{tg}$ | 12.7* | 12.7 | 13.4 | 12.7 | 15.3* | 15.3 |
| Tension perpendicular to grain | $f_{tp}$ | 0.51 | 0.51 | 0.51 | 0.51 | 0.83 | 0.83 |
| Modulus of elasticity | E | 10 300 | 10 300 | 10 700 | 9700 | 13 100 | 13 100 |

*The use of this stress grade for this primary application is not recommended.

**Notes:**

(1) Designers are advised to check the availability of grades before specifying.

(2) Tabulated values are based on the following standard conditions:

(a) dry service conditions; and

(b) standard term duration of load.

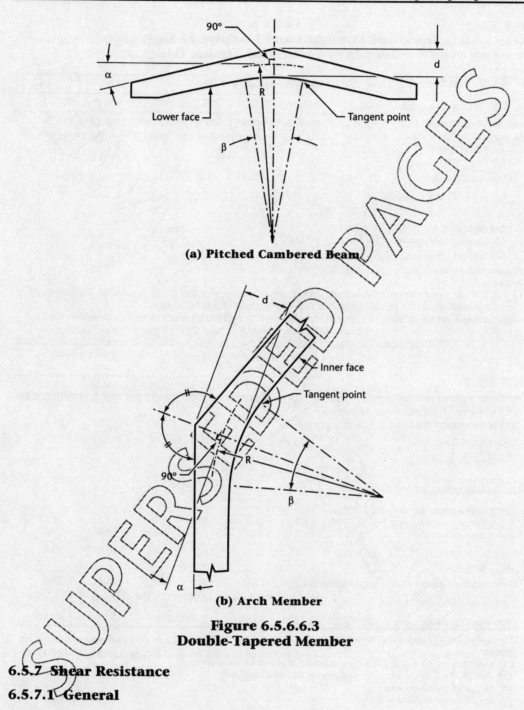

**(a) Pitched Cambered Beam**

**(b) Arch Member**

**Figure 6.5.6.6.3
Double-Tapered Member**

## 6.5.7 Shear Resistance

### 6.5.7.1 General

#### 6.5.7.1.1
The provisions of Clause 6.5.7 apply to members of rectangular cross-section only.

### 6.5.7.1.2

In the calculation of shear resistance in Clause 6.5.7.2.1, the effect of all loads acting within a distance from a support equal to the depth of the member need not be taken into account.

## 6.5.7.2 Factored Shear Resistance — Case 1

### 6.5.7.2.1 General

The factored shear resistance, $V_r$, of glued-laminated beams less than 2.0 $m^3$ in volume, and of glued-laminated members other than beams, shall be determined in accordance with the provisions of Clause 6.5.7.3, or shall be taken as

$$V_r = \phi F_v \frac{2A}{3} K_N$$

where

$\phi$ = 0.9
$F_v$ = $f_v(K_D K_H K_{Sv} K_T)$
$f_v$ = specified strength in shear (Table 6.3), MPa
$A$ = cross-sectional area of member, $mm^2$
$K_N$ = notch factor (Clause 6.5.7.2.2)

**Notes:**
**(1)** *Notches or abrupt changes of section will produce stress concentrations and should be avoided. The magnitude of these stress concentrations is reduced by gradual rather than abrupt changes of section.*
**(2)** *Calculation of factored shear resistance in accordance with these requirements and this formula follows an approximate method only, and may greatly underestimate the true factored shear resistance of glued-laminated members. For a more detailed and accurate calculation of shear resistance of glued-laminated members, refer to Clause 6.5.7.3.*

### 6.5.7.2.2

At the location of notches in rectangular members, the specified strength in shear shall be multiplied by a notch factor, $K_N$, determined as follows:
(a) for notches at the tension side at supports

$$K_N = \left(1 - \frac{d_n}{d}\right)^2$$

(b) for notches at the compression side

    (i) for $e > d$,    $K_N = 1 - \frac{d_n}{d}$

    (ii) for $e < d$,    $K_N = 1 - \frac{d_n e}{d(d - d_n)}$

where
$d_n$ = depth of notch, mm, which must not exceed 0.25d
$e$ = length of notch, mm, from inner edge of closest support to farthest edge of notch

## 6.5.7.3 Factored Shear Resistance — Case 2

The factored shear resistance, $V_r$, of glued-laminated beams including those that exceed the maximum volume restriction of Clause 6.5.7.2.1 shall not be less than the sum of all factored loads, $W_f$, acting on the beam and shall be taken as

$$V_r = \phi F_v 0.48 A K_N C_v Z^{-0.18} \geq W_f$$

where
$\phi$ = 0.9
$F_v$ = $f_v(K_D K_H K_{Sv} K_T)$

**54**                *August 2001*

$f_v$ = specified strength in shear (Table 6.3), MPa
A = cross-sectional area of member, mm²
$K_N$ = notch factor (Clause 6.5.7.2.2)
$C_v$ = shear load coefficient (Clause 6.5.7.4)
Z = beam volume, m³

## 6.5.7.4 Shear Load Coefficient, $C_V$

For any load condition not shown in Tables 6.5.7.4A to 6.5.7.4F, the coefficient for simple span, continuous, or cantilevered beams of constant depth may be determined using the following procedure (the principle of superposition of loads does not apply):

(a) Construct the shear force diagram for the beam. If the beam is under moving concentrated loads, construct the diagram of the maximum shear forces occurring along the full length of the beam without regard to sign convention. (Positive and negative maximum shear forces both show positive.)

(b) Divide the total beam length, L, into n segments of variable lengths, $\ell_a$, such that within each segment there are neither abrupt changes nor sign changes in the shear force.

(c) For each segment determine
(i) $V_A$ = factored shear force at beginning of segment, N;
(ii) $V_B$ = factored shear force at end of segment, N; and
(iii) $V_C$ = factored shear force at centre of segment, N;
and calculate the factor G in accordance with the formula

$$G = \ell_a \left[ V_A^5 + V_B^5 + 4V_C^5 \right]$$

(d) Determine the coefficient, $C_V$, in accordance with the following formulae:
(i) for stationary loads

$$C_V = 1.825 W_f \left( \frac{L}{\Sigma G} \right)^{0.2}$$

where
$W_f$ = the total of all factored loads applied to the beam, N

(ii) for moving loads

$$C_V = 1.825 W_f \left( \frac{L}{\Sigma G} \right)^{0.2}$$

where
$W_f$ = the total of all factored moving loads and all factored distributed loads applied to the beam, N

### Table 6.5.7.4A
### Shear Load Coefficient, $C_V$, for Simple Span Beams

| Number of equal loads equally and symmetrically spaced | r* | | | |
|---|---|---|---|---|
| | 0.0 | 0.5 | 2.0 | 10.0 and over |
| 1 | 3.69 | 3.34 | 2.92 | 2.46 |
| 2 | 3.69 | 3.37 | 3.01 | 2.67 |
| 3 | 3.69 | 3.41 | 3.12 | 2.84 |
| 4 | 3.69 | 3.45 | 3.21 | 2.97 |
| 5 | 3.69 | 3.48 | 3.28 | 3.08 |
| 6 | 3.69 | 3.51 | 3.34 | 3.16 |

*r = total of concentrated loads / total of uniform loads

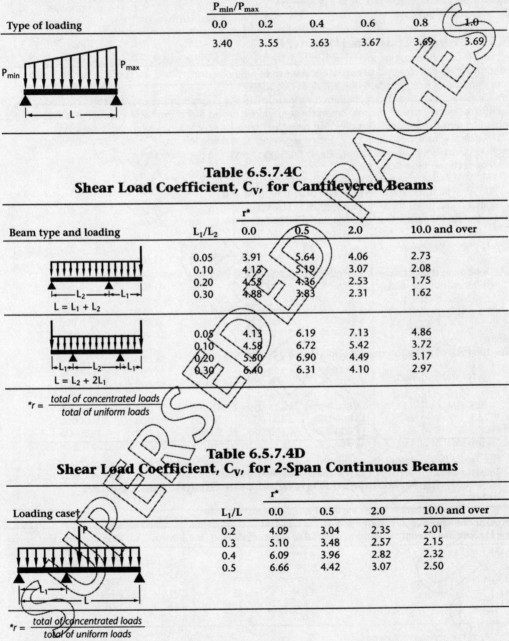

## Table 6.5.7.4B
### Shear Load Coefficient, $C_V$, for Distributed Loads

| Type of loading | $P_{min}/P_{max}$ | | | | | |
|---|---|---|---|---|---|---|
| | 0.0 | 0.2 | 0.4 | 0.6 | 0.8 | 1.0 |
| | 3.40 | 3.55 | 3.63 | 3.67 | 3.69 | 3.69 |

## Table 6.5.7.4C
### Shear Load Coefficient, $C_V$, for Cantilevered Beams

| Beam type and loading | $L_1/L_2$ | r* | | | |
|---|---|---|---|---|---|
| | | 0.0 | 0.5 | 2.0 | 10.0 and over |
| | 0.05 | 3.91 | 5.64 | 4.06 | 2.73 |
| | 0.10 | 4.13 | 5.19 | 3.07 | 2.08 |
| | 0.20 | 4.55 | 4.36 | 2.53 | 1.75 |
| | 0.30 | 4.88 | 3.83 | 2.31 | 1.62 |
| | 0.05 | 4.13 | 6.19 | 7.13 | 4.86 |
| | 0.10 | 4.58 | 6.72 | 5.42 | 3.72 |
| | 0.20 | 5.50 | 6.90 | 4.49 | 3.17 |
| | 0.30 | 6.40 | 6.31 | 4.10 | 2.97 |

$$*r = \frac{total\ of\ concentrated\ loads}{total\ of\ uniform\ loads}$$

## Table 6.5.7.4D
### Shear Load Coefficient, $C_V$, for 2-Span Continuous Beams

| Loading case† | $L_1/L$ | r* | | | |
|---|---|---|---|---|---|
| | | 0.0 | 0.5 | 2.0 | 10.0 and over |
| | 0.2 | 4.09 | 3.04 | 2.35 | 2.01 |
| | 0.3 | 5.10 | 3.48 | 2.57 | 2.15 |
| | 0.4 | 6.09 | 3.96 | 2.82 | 2.32 |
| | 0.5 | 6.66 | 4.42 | 3.07 | 2.50 |

$$*r = \frac{total\ of\ concentrated\ loads}{total\ of\ uniform\ loads}$$

† Values shown correspond to the worst position for the concentrated loads

## Table 7.3C (Concluded)

| Nominal thickness, mm | Rating grade | Bending stiffness, $B_b = EI$, N•mm²/mm | | Axial stiffness (in tension or compression), $B_a = EA$, N/mm | | Shear-through-thickness rigidity, $B_v$, N/mm |
|---|---|---|---|---|---|---|
| | | Capacities relative to major axis*† | | | | |
| | | 0° | 90° | 0° | 90° | 0° & 90° |
| 9.5 | A | 590 000 | 170 000 | 46 000 | 19 000 | 9 500 |
| 9.5 | B | 490 000 | 170 000 | 39 000 | 19 000 | 9 500 |
| 9.5 | C | 390 000 | 170 000 | 33 000 | 19 000 | 9 500 |
| 11.0 | A | 920 000 | 270 000 | 53 000 | 22 000 | 11 000 |
| 11.0 | B | 760 000 | 270 000 | 46 000 | 22 000 | 11 000 |
| 11.0 | C | 610 000 | 270 000 | 38 000 | 22 000 | 11 000 |
| 12.5 | A | 1 300 000 | 390 000 | 60 000 | 25 000 | 12 000 |
| 12.5 | B | 1 100 000 | 390 000 | 52 000 | 25 000 | 12 000 |
| 12.5 | C | 900 000 | 390 000 | 43 000 | 25 000 | 12 000 |
| 15.5 | A | 2 600 000 | 740 000 | 75 000 | 31 000 | 15 000 |
| 15.5 | B | 2 100 000 | 740 000 | 64 000 | 31 000 | 15 000 |
| 15.5 | C | 1 700 000 | 740 000 | 53 000 | 31 000 | 15 000 |
| 18.5 | A | 4 400 000 | 1 300 000 | 89 000 | 37 000 | 18 000 |
| 18.5 | B | 3 600 000 | 1 300 000 | 77 000 | 37 000 | 18 000 |
| 18.5 | C | 2 900 000 | 1 300 000 | 64 000 | 37 000 | 18 000 |
| 22.0 | A | 7 300 000 | 2 100 000 | 110 000 | 44 000 | 22 000 |
| 22.0 | B | 6 100 000 | 2 100 000 | 91 000 | 44 000 | 22 000 |
| 22.0 | C | 4 900 000 | 2 100 000 | 76 000 | 44 000 | 22 000 |
| 28.5 | A | 16 000 000 | 4 600 000 | 140 000 | 57 000 | 28 000 |
| 28.5 | B | 13 000 000 | 4 600 000 | 120 000 | 57 000 | 28 000 |
| 28.5 | C | 11 000 000 | 4 600 000 | 98 000 | 57 000 | 28 000 |

*For Type 2 Design-Rated OSB panels, tabulated specified capacities are increased by a percentage (See CSA Standard O452.0). For Type 3 Design-Rated OSB panels, specified capacities are proprietary (see Clause 13.3).
†Orientation of applied force relative to panel's long direction.

**Notes:**
**(1)** For specified stiffness in bending on edge, use axial stiffness values.
**(2)** Tabulated values are based on dry service conditions and standard-term duration of load.
**(3)** Specified strength in bearing (normal to plane of panel) $q_p$ = 4.2 MPa.

## Table 7.3D
## Specified Strength, Stiffness, and Rigidity Capacities for
## Construction Sheathing OSB

| Panel mark (CSA O325) | Minimum nominal thickness,* mm | Bending, $m_p$, N•mm/mm | | Axial tension, $t_p$, N/mm | | Axial compression, $p_p$, N/mm | | Shear-through-thickness, $v_p$, N/mm | Planar shear Bending, $v_p$, N/mm | | Shear in-plane, $v_p$, MPa | |
|---|---|---|---|---|---|---|---|---|---|---|---|---|
| | | Capacities relative to major axis† | | | | | | | | | | |
| | | 0° | 90° | 0° | 90° | 0° | 90° | 0° & 90° | 0° | 90° | 0° | 90° |
| 2R24 | 9.5 | 180 | 57 | 53 | 18 | 62 | 54 | 42 | 3.8 | 2.4 | 0.60 | 0.38 |
| 1R24/2F16 | 11.0 | 240 | 68 | 60 | 30 | 71 | 54 | 46 | 4.4 | 2.4 | 0.60 | 0.33 |
| 2R32/2F16 | 12.0 | 270 | 100 | 65 | 38 | 77 | 67 | 50 | 4.8 | 3.0 | 0.60 | 0.38 |
| 2R40/2F20 | 15.0 | 460 | 160 | 67 | 48 | 92 | 87 | 55 | 6.1 | 3.8 | 0.61 | 0.38 |
| 2R48/2F24 | 18.0 | 630 | 240 | 92 | 59 | 110 | 100 | 60 | 7.8 | 4.4 | 0.65 | 0.37 |
| | | | | | | | | | | | | |
| 1F16 | 15.0 | 310 | 100 | 60 | 43 | 87 | 78 | 47 | 5.2 | 3.3 | 0.52 | 0.33 |
| 1F20 | 15.0 | 360 | 150 | 67 | 48 | 92 | 87 | 54 | 6.1 | 3.9 | 0.61 | 0.39 |
| 1F24 | 18.0 | 480 | 230 | 77 | 59 | 110 | 100 | 59 | 7.8 | 4.5 | 0.65 | 0.37 |
| 1F32 | 22.0 | 640 | 400 | 92 | 75 | 140 | 130 | 64 | 9.2 | 6.4 | 0.63 | 0.44 |
| 1F48 | 28.5 | 1 200 | 720 | 130 | 110 | 280 | 270 | 85 | 14.0 | 10.0 | 0.73 | 0.55 |

*(Continued)*

## 9.3.3.2 Shearwall Segment Aspect Ratio

The maximum aspect ratio (height-to-length ratio) of a shearwall segment shall be 3.5:1. The height is defined as the height from the underside of the bottom shearwall plate to the topside of the top shearwall plate within a storey.

## 9.3.3.3 Shearwalls with Openings

Shearwalls with openings shall be analyzed as the sum of the separate shearwall segments. The contribution of sheathing above and below openings shall not be included in the calculation of shearwall resistance.

## 9.3.3.4 Shearwalls with Dissimilar Materials

Except as allowed in Clause 9.3.3.5, shearwalls constructed with dissimilar materials, thicknesses, or nail spacings along the length of the shearwall shall be analyzed as the sum of the separate shearwall segments.

## 9.3.3.5 Alternative Method for Shearwalls with Dissimilar Materials

Shearwalls constructed with dissimilar materials, thicknesses, or nail spacings along the length of the shearwall may be analyzed, in accordance with Clause 9.5.1, as a shearwall of uniform construction, provided that the least value of $v_d K_D K_{SF} J_{ub} J_{sp}$ is assumed to apply over the entire shearwall.

## 9.3.4 Shearwalls with Multiple Layers

## 9.3.4.1 A Shearwall with Two Layers of Panels on One Side

The factored shear resistance for a shearwall with two layers of the same or different panels applied to one side is determined by the first (inside) layer of panels, except as allowed in Note 5 to Table 9.5.1A.

## 9.3.4.2 Two-Sided Shearwall

The factored shear resistance from each side of the same shearwall is cumulative when panels of the same or different materials are applied on both sides.

**Note:** *See appropriate seismic force modification factor, R, in Clauses 9.5.3 and 9.5.4.*

## 9.3.5 Concrete or Masonry Wall Anchorage

## 9.3.5.1 Anchorage Design

Where wood roofs and floors are used to provide lateral support to concrete and masonry walls, they shall be anchored to these walls. The anchorage shall provide a direct connection between the walls and the roof or floor construction. The connections shall be capable of resisting the lateral force induced by the wall, but not less than 3 kN per lineal metre of the wall.

## 9.3.5.2 Anchorage Details

Anchorage of concrete or masonry walls shall not be accomplished by use of toe-nails or nails subject to withdrawal, nor shall wood ledgers be designed to resist tensile stresses perpendicular to grain.

## 9.3.6 Shearwall Anchorage

The anchor bolts to resist lateral forces shall be designed in accordance with Clause 10.

## 9.4 Modification Factors

## 9.4.1 Load Duration Factor, $K_D$

The specified shear strengths for wood-based shearwalls and diaphragms shall be multiplied by the load duration factor, $K_D$, given in Clause 4.3.2.

**Note:** *Specified shear strengths for gypsum wallboard shearwalls apply only to short-term load duration, and $K_D$ is not applicable.*

## 9.4.2 Service Condition Factor, $K_{SF}$
The specified shear strengths for wood-based shearwalls and diaphragms shall be multiplied by the service condition factor, $K_{SF}$, given in Table 10.2.1.5 for lateral loads on nails.

## 9.4.3 Species Factor for Framing Material, $J_{sp}$
The specified shear strengths for wood-based shearwalls and diaphragms shall be multiplied by the species factor for framing material, $J_{sp}$, as given in Table 9.4.3.

### Table 9.4.3
### Species Factor for Framing Material, $J_{sp}$

| $J_{sp}$ | Visually graded lumber | Glued-laminated timber | MSR (or MEL) E-Grade of S-P-F,* MPa |
|------|------------------------|------------------------|--------------------------|
| 1.0 | Douglas Fir-Larch | Douglas Fir-Larch | 13 800 to 16 500 |
| 0.9 | Hem-Fir | N/A | 12 400 to 13 100 |
| 0.8 | S-P-F | Spruce-Pine | 8300 to 11 700 |
| 0.7 | Northern Species | N/A | N/A |

*For other species of MSR or MEL lumber, use visually graded lumber values.

## 9.4.4 Strength Adjustment Factor for Unblocked Shearwalls, $J_{ub}$
The specified shear strengths for horizontally sheathed unblocked shearwalls sheathed with wood-based panels shall be multiplied by the strength adjustment factor $J_{ub}$, as given in Table 9.4.4.

### Table 9.4.4
### Strength Adjustment Factor, $J_{ub}$,
### for Horizontally Sheathed Unblocked Shearwalls*

| Nail spacing at supported edges, mm | Nail spacing at intermediate studs, mm | Stud spacing, mm | | | |
|---|---|---|---|---|---|
| | | 300 | 400 | 500 | 600 |
| 150 | 150 | 1.0 | 0.8 | 0.6 | 0.5 |
| 150 | 300 | 0.8 | 0.6 | 0.5 | 0.4 |

*Specified shear strength of an unblocked shearwall shall be calculated by multiplying the strength adjustment factor by the specified shear strength of a blocked shearwall with 600 mm stud spacing, and with nails spaced at 150 mm on centre around panel edges and 300 mm on centre along intermediate framing members.

**Note:** Strength adjustment factor shall only be applicable to structural wood-based panels.

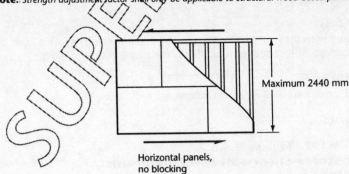

Maximum 2440 mm

Horizontal panels,
no blocking

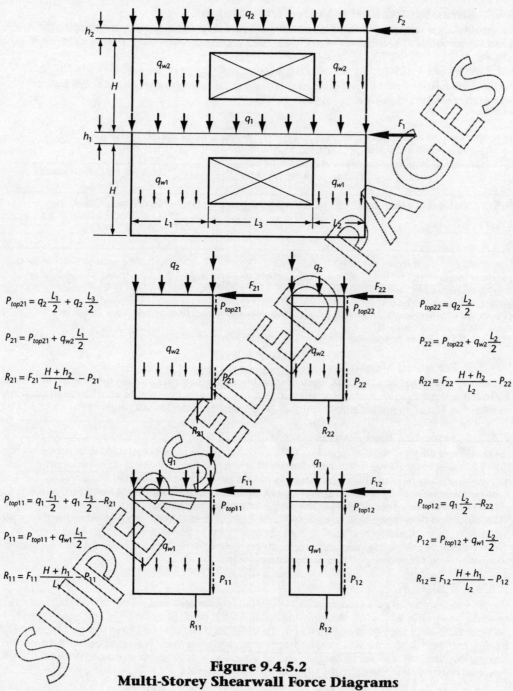

**Figure 9.4.5.2**
**Multi-Storey Shearwall Force Diagrams**

## 9.5.2 Shear Resistance of Nailed Diaphragms

The factored shear resistance of nailed diaphragms of structural wood-based panels or diagonal lumber sheathing constructed in accordance with Clauses 9.5.3 and 9.5.5, respectively, shall be determined as follows:

$$V_r = \phi \, v_d K_D K_{SF} \, J_{sp} L_D$$

where

$\phi$ = 0.7

$v_d$ = specified shear strength for diaphragms with plywood, OSB, or waferboard (Table 9.5.2) or diagonal lumber sheathing (Clause 9.5.5), kN/m

$J_{sp}$ = species factor for framing material (Clause 9.4.3)

$L_D$ = dimension of diaphragm parallel to direction of factored load, m

## 9.5.3 Nailed Shearwalls and Diaphragms Using Plywood, OSB, or Waferboard

### 9.5.3.1 General

Shearwalls and diaphragms sheathed with plywood, OSB, or waferboard may be used to resist shear due to lateral forces based on the specified shear strength given in Table 9.5.1A for shearwalls and Table 9.5.2 for diaphragms.

**Notes:**

**(1)** *Seismic force modification factor, R, is equal to 3 when nailed plywood, OSB, or waferboard shearwalls are considered to resist lateral loads.*

**(2)** *Table 9.5.3 provides an equivalence between tabulated thickness and panel marks.*

### 9.5.3.2 Framing Members

Framing members shall be at least 38 mm wide and be spaced no greater than 600 mm apart in shearwalls and diaphragms. In general, adjoining panel edges shall bear and be attached to the framing members, and a gap of not less than 2 mm shall be left between wood-based panel sheets.

### 9.5.3.3 Framing and Panels

Shearwalls and diaphragms using plywood, OSB, or waferboard shall be constructed with panels not less than 1200 × 2400 mm, except near boundaries and changes in framing, where up to two short or narrow panels may be used. Panels for diaphragms shall be arranged as indicated in Table 9.5.2. Framing members shall be provided at the edge of all panels in shearwalls except horizontally sheathed unblocked shearwalls where blocking at the middle of the wall height is omitted.

Shearwalls and diaphragms shall be designed to resist shear stresses only, and perimeter members shall be provided to resist axial forces resulting from the application of lateral design forces. Perimeter members shall be adequately interconnected at corner intersections, and member joints shall be spliced adequately. Panels less than 300 mm wide shall be blocked.

### 9.5.3.4 Nailing

The nails and spacing of nails at shearwall and diaphragm boundaries and the edges of each panel shall be as shown in Table 9.5.1A for shearwalls and in Table 9.5.2 for diaphragms.

Nails shall be placed not less than 9 mm from the panel edge and shall be placed along all intermediate framing members at 300 mm on centre for floors, roofs, and shearwalls. Nails shall be firmly driven into framing members but shall not be over-driven into sheathing. For structural wood-based sheathing, nails shall not be over-driven more than 15% of the panel thickness.

### 9.5.4 Nailed Shearwalls Using Gypsum Wallboard

Shearwalls using gypsum wallboard shall be constructed with panels not less than 1200 × 2400 mm, except near boundaries and changes in framing, where up to two short or narrow panels may be used.

Shearwalls sheathed with gypsum wallboard may be used to resist shear due to lateral forces based on the specified shear strength given in Table 9.5.1B for shearwalls.

Gypsum wallboard application nails or screws shall be placed not less than 9 mm from the panel edge.

Gypsum wallboard shall be used in combination with structural wood-based panels. The factored shear resistance of gypsum wallboard shall be equal to or less than the percentage of storey shear forces in Table 9.5.4. The application of gypsum wallboard shall be restricted to platform frame construction where the height of a storey does not exceed 3.6 m.

**Notes:**

**(1)** *Seismic force modification factor, R, is equal to 2 when gypsum wallboard is considered to resist lateral loads.*

**(2)** *There should exist a balanced spatial distribution of the gypsum wallboard and wood-based panels resisting shear in a given direction in a particular storey.*

## 9.5.5 Nailed Shearwalls and Diaphragms Using Diagonal Lumber Sheathing

### 9.5.5.1 General

Nailed shearwalls and diaphragms as described in Clauses 9.5.5.2 to 9.5.5.4 may be used to resist lateral forces. The specified shear strength, $v_d$, with a single layer of diagonally sheathed lumber (Clause 9.5.5.2) shall be taken as 8 kN/m; that for a double layer of diagonally sheathed lumber (Clause 9.5.5.3) as 24 kN/m.

### 9.5.5.2 Single-Layer Diagonal Sheathing

Single-layer diagonal sheathing shall be made up of 19 mm boards laid at an angle of approximately 45° to supports. Boards shall be nailed to each intermediate member with not less than two common nails (d = 3.25 mm) for 19 × 140 mm boards and three common nails (d = 3.25 mm) for 19 × 184 mm or wider boards. One additional nail shall be used in each board at shear panel boundaries.

End joints in adjacent rows of boards shall be staggered by at least one stud or joist space, and joints on the same support shall be separated by at least two rows of boards.

Shearwalls and diaphragms made up of 38 mm thick diagonal sheathing using common nails (d = 4.06 mm) may be used at the same shear values and in the same locations as for 19 mm boards, provided that there are no splices in adjacent boards on the same support and the supports are not less than 89 mm in depth or 64 mm in thickness.

### 9.5.5.3 Double-Layer Diagonal Sheathing

Double-layer diagonal sheathing shall conform to Clause 9.5.5.2 and shall consist of two layers of diagonal boards at 90° to each other on the same face of the supporting members.

### 9.5.5.4 Boundary Members

Diagonal sheathing produces a load component acting normal to the boundary members in the plane of the shear panel. Boundary members in diagonally sheathed shearwalls and diaphragms shall be designed to resist the bending stresses caused by the normal load component.

## 9.5.6 Moment Resistance of Nailed Shearwalls and Diaphragms

### 9.5.6.1 General

Except as provided in Clause 9.5.6.2, the factored moment resistance of nailed shearwalls and diaphragms shall be determined as

$$M_r = P_r h$$

where

$P_r$ = factored axial tension and compression resistance of the elements resisting chord forces with due allowance being made for joints, N

h = centre-to-centre distance between moment resisting elements, mm
  = centre-to-centre distance between diaphragm chords in the design of diaphragms, mm
  = centre-to-centre distance between stud chords in shearwall segments designed with hold-down connections at both ends of the shearwall segment, mm
  = length of shearwall segment minus 300 mm for shearwall segments designed without hold-down connections at both ends of the segment, mm

## 9.5.6.2 Moment Resistance for Shearwall Segments without Hold-downs

For shearwall segments without hold-downs, moment resistance calculation specifically for design of the tension chords shall not be required.

## 9.6 Detailing Requirements

### 9.6.1 General

All boundary members, chords, and struts of nailed shearwalls and diaphragms shall be designed and detailed to transmit the induced axial forces. The boundary members shall be fastened together at all corners.

### 9.6.2 Fastenings to Shearwalls and Diaphragms

Fastenings and anchorages capable of resisting the prescribed forces shall be provided between the shearwall or diaphragm and the attached components.

## Table 9.5.3
## Panel Marking Equivalence in Shearwall and Diaphragm Tables

| In shearwall Table 9.5.1A | | In diaphragm Table 9.5.2 | |
|---|---|---|---|
| Minimum nominal thickness, mm | Minimum panel mark | Minimum nominal thickness, mm | Minimum panel mark |
| 7.5 | 2R20 | 7.5 | 2R20 |
| 9.5 | 2R24 | 9.5 | 2R24 |
| 11.0 | 1R24/2F16 | 11.0 | 1R24/2F16 |
| 12.5 | 2R32/2F16 or 1F16 | 12.5 | 2R32/2F16 |
| 15.5 | 2R40/2F20 | 15.5 | 2R40/2F20 or 1F20 |
| | | 18.5 | 2R48/2F24 or 1F24 |

**Notes:**
**(1)** *For OSB panels rated to CSA Standard CAN/CSA-O325.0, the minimum nominal thickness may be 0.5 mm less than the thickness shown above. No adjustment to the tabulated shear strength values is required.*
**(2)** *For alternative panel marks meeting the minimum requirements, see Clause A7.2.2.2.*

## Table 9.5.4
## Maximum Percentage of Total Shear Forces
## Resisted by Gypsum Wallboard in a Storey

| Storey | Percentage of shear forces | | | |
|---|---|---|---|---|
| | 4-storey building | 3-storey building | 2-storey building | 1-storey building |
| 4th | 80 | — | — | — |
| 3rd | 60 | 80 | — | — |
| 2nd | 40 | 60 | 80 | — |
| 1st | 40 | 40 | 60 | 80 |

**Notes:**
**(1)** *A force modification factor of R = 2.0 is used when gypsum wallboard sheathing is considered to resist lateral loads.*
**(2)** *Maximum storey height shall not exceed 3.6 m.*

# 10. Fastenings

## 10.1 Scope
Clause 10 provides criteria for the engineering design and appraisal of connections using split ring and shear plate connectors, bolts, drift pins, lag screws, timber rivets (also known as glulam rivets), truss plates, nails, spikes, and joist hangers.
**Note:** *Lateral resistance values for bolts, drift pins, and lag screws are based on relative density of the wood material. Reference density values are given in Table A10.1.*

## 10.2 General Requirements

### 10.2.1 All Fastenings
**Note:** *Joint details should be avoided where shrinkage of the wood can lead to excessive tension perpendicular to grain.*

### 10.2.1.1
The tables are predicated on the requirement that the projecting end of a member shall not be trimmed or otherwise altered in such a manner as to reduce the specified minimum end distance.

## 10.2.1.2
Under severe conditions conducive to corrosion, connection design should provide adequate protection.

## 10.2.1.3
Joints made using hard maple, soft maple, elm, beech, black oak, white oak, or birch may be assigned the same resistances as the D Fir-L species group.

## 10.2.1.4
Where a fastening or group of fastenings exerts a shear force on a member, the factored shear resistance of the member as calculated in Clauses 5.5.5 and 6.5.7 shall be based upon the dimension $d_e$ shown in Figure 10.2.1.4, instead of the dimension d.  Dimension $d_e$ is defined as the distance, measured perpendicular to the axis of the member, from the extremity of the fastening or group of fastenings to the loaded edge of the member.

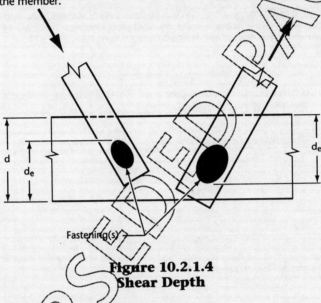

**Figure 10.2.1.4**
**Shear Depth**

## 10.2.1.5  Service Condition Factor, $K_{SF}$
The service condition factor, $K_{SF}$, for fastenings is given in Table 10.2.1.5.

## 10.2.1.6  Load Duration Factor, $K_D$
The load duration factor, $K_D$, for fastenings is given in Table 4.3.2.2.

## 10.2.1.7  Treatment Factor, $K_T$
For connections containing wood-based members treated with fire-retardant or other strength-reducing chemicals, strength capacities of connections shall be based on the documented results of tests that shall take into account the effect of time, temperature, and moisture content.  Test procedures shall meet the requirements of Clause 3.3.2.
**Note:** *The effects of fire-retardant treatments can vary depending on manufacturing materials and processes.  See the Canadian Wood Council's Commentary for additional explanation.*

## 10.2.1.8
Joints shall be assembled so that the surfaces are brought into close contact.

### 12.5.2.5 Constant Nonrectangular Cross-Section

For nonrectangular compression members of constant section, $r\sqrt{12}$ shall be substituted for member width or depth in Clause 5.5.6, where r is the applicable radius of gyration of the cross-section of the member.

### 12.5.2.6 Variable Circular Cross-Section

The radius of gyration of round tapered compression members shall be calculated for an effective diameter equal to the minimum diameter plus 0.45 times the difference between the maximum and minimum diameters. The factored compressive resistance determined in this manner shall not exceed the factored resistance based on the minimum diameter in conjunction with a slenderness factor $K_C = 1.00$.

### 12.5.3 Poles as Bending Members

The factored bending moment resistance, $M_r$, of round members shall be taken as that of a square member having the same cross-sectional area. A tapered round member shall be considered as an equivalent square member of variable cross-section.

## 13. Proprietary Structural Wood Products

### 13.1 Scope

Clauses 13.2 to 13.4 provide design methods for proprietary structural wood products that conform to the applicable referenced standards and the additional requirements contained in Clause 13.

**Note:** *Clauses 13.2 to 13.4 are provided as a reference for designers to explain the origin of manufacturers' proprietary design values. In general, proprietary design values are published by the product manufacturer (i.e., proprietary design literature and/or CCMC Evaluation Reports within the CCMC Registry of Product Evaluations) with appropriate factors for specific applications. The designer is not normally expected to calculate the proprietary product properties using the equations provided herein. For applications where adjustments to design values may be warranted, the designer is recommended to seek guidance from the product manufacturer. For additional information on proprietary structural wood products in general, and prefabricated wood I-joists and structural composite lumber products in particular, see the Canadian Wood Council's Commentary.*

### 13.2 Prefabricated Wood I-Joists

#### 13.2.1 General

Except as specified in Clause 13.2.2.2, all prefabricated wood I-joists for use under the provisions of this Standard shall meet the requirements of, and be evaluated for strength and stiffness in accordance with, ASTM Standard D 5055. Determination of characteristic values for design with prefabricated wood I-joists shall be in accordance with Clause 13.2.3.6.

All prefabricated wood I-joists for use under the provisions of Clause 13.2 shall bear the mark of a certification organization (C.O.) indicating certification by the C.O. as meeting the applicable requirements of Clause 13.2.

#### 13.2.2 Materials

##### 13.2.2.1 Flange Materials

The provisions of Clause 13.2 apply to flanges as specified in Clause 5 for sawn structurally graded lumber or Clause 6 for glued-laminated timber. Lumber not conforming to Clause 5 and structural composite lumber products may be used as flange material when such material is qualified by testing as specified in ASTM Standard D 5055.

##### 13.2.2.2 Structural Panel Webs

Webs for prefabricated wood I-joists shall be manufactured from structural panels conforming to CSA

Standard O121, O151, O153 (Exterior Bond), CAN/CSA-O325.0, O437.0, or O452.0.
**Note:** *For additional information, see the Canadian Wood Council's* Commentary.

### 13.2.2.3 Adhesives
Prefabricated wood I-joists shall be manufactured using
(a) adhesives conforming to CSA Standard O112.6 or O112.7; or
(b) an adhesive demonstrated to provide equivalent performance to the adhesives referenced in Item (a).
**Note:** *For additional information on equivalent adhesive systems, see the Canadian Wood Council's* Commentary.

## 13.2.3 Specified Strengths and Moduli of Elasticity

### 13.2.3.1 Specified Strength Parallel to Grain, $f_a$
The specified strength parallel to grain, $f_a$, shall be the lesser of the specified strength in tension parallel to grain, $f_t$, or the specified strength in compression parallel to grain, $f_c$, as defined in Clauses 13.2.3.2 and 13.2.3.3.

### 13.2.3.2 Specified Strength in Tension Parallel to Grain, $f_t$
The specified strength in tension parallel to grain, $f_t$, shall be determined in one of the following ways:
(a) where the flange material is sawn lumber conforming to Clause 5.2 or glued-laminated timber conforming to Clause 6.2 of this Standard, the specified strength in tension parallel to grain shall be determined from $f_t$ in Clause 5.3, or $f_{tg}$ in Clause 6.3, respectively; and
(b) where the flange material is not as described in Item (a), $f_t$ shall be taken as

$$f_t = t\, K_r$$

where
t  = the characteristic value for tension parallel to grain as defined in Clause 13.2.3.6, MPa
$K_r$ = reliability normalization factor for bending and tension from Table 13.2.3.2

## 13.2.4.4 System Factor, $K_{HB}$

Depending upon the type of flange material, prefabricated wood I-joists used in a load sharing system shall be permitted the following moment resistance adjustment increases:

| Prefabricated wood I-joist flange | $K_{HB}$ |
|---|---|
| Visually graded sawn lumber | 1.10 |
| Machine stress-rated and machine evaluated lumber | 1.07 |
| Structural composite lumber products | 1.04 |

To qualify for the above increase, the prefabricated wood I-joist shall be part of a wood-framing system consisting of at least three parallel prefabricated wood I-joists joined by transverse load distributing elements adequate to support the design load and shall be spaced not more than 610 mm on centre.

## 13.2.5 Strength and Resistance

### 13.2.5.1 Bending Moment Resistance

The factored bending moment resistance, $M_r$, of prefabricated wood I-joists shall be calculated using either

$$M_r = \phi \, F_t S K_L$$

or

$$M_r = \phi \, M_{cv} (K_D K_S K_{HB} K_T) \, K_r K_L$$

where

$\phi$ = 0.90

$F_t$ = $f_a(K_D K_S K_{HB} K_T K_{Zt})$

$f_a$ = specified strength parallel to grain, per Clause 13.2.3.1, MPa

$S$ = net section modulus, all web materials removed and, when appropriate, calculated as a transformed section, mm³

$K_L$ = lateral stability factor, per Clause 13.2.5.2

$K_{HB}$ = system factor, per Clause 13.2.4.4

$K_{Zt}$ = the size factor for tension parallel to grain, from Table 5.4.5, applicable only to visually stress-graded lumber used in accordance with Clause 13.2.3.1

$M_{cv}$ = the characteristic value for moment capacity as defined in Clause 13.2.3.6(d), N•m

$K_r$ = reliability normalization factor for bending and tension, from Table 13.2.3.2

### 13.2.5.2 Lateral Stability Factor, $K_L$

The lateral stability factor, $K_L$, shall be taken as unity when lateral support is provided at points of bearing, to prevent lateral displacement and rotation, and along all compression edges. Lateral support requirements and lateral stability factors for other applications such as continuous spans shall be based on analytical and engineering principles or documented test data, or both, that demonstrate the safe use of the product in the intended application.

**Note:** *For additional information on lateral stability, see the Canadian Wood Council's Commentary.*

### 13.2.5.3 Notches

Notching or cutting of the flanges of prefabricated wood I-joists shall not be permitted, unless such details have been evaluated and are demonstrated to be acceptable based on documented test data.

### 13.2.5.4 Shear Resistance

The factored shear resistance, $V_r$, of prefabricated wood I-joists shall be taken as

$$V_r = \phi V_c \, K_v$$

where
$\phi$ = 0.90
$V_c$ = specified shear capacity for a given brand and depth of prefabricated wood I-joist, in accordance with Clause 13.2.3.4, N
$K_v$ = $K_D K_S K_T$

Neglecting loads within a distance from the support equal to the depth of the member shall not be permitted, and any adjustments to the shear design value near the support shall be substantiated by independent testing to the shear capacity criteria in ASTM Standard D 5055.

## 13.2.5.5 Web Openings, Bearing Length, and Web Stiffener Requirements
Designers shall obtain information regarding web openings, bearing length, and web stiffener requirements from specific prefabricated wood I-joist manufacturers. The requirements for permitted web openings, minimum bearing length, and web stiffener details shall be determined in accordance with ASTM Standard D 5055.
**Note:** *For additional information, see the Canadian Wood Council's Commentary.*

## 13.2.5.6 Serviceability Limit States
Design of prefabricated wood I-joists for serviceability limit states shall be in accordance with Clauses 4.1.3 and 4.5. Deflection calculations shall include shear deformation.
The flange moduli of elasticity for stiffness calculations shall be taken as

$$E_s = E (K_{SE} K_{TE})$$

The effective stiffness, $EI_w$, of prefabricated wood I-joist web members employing structural panels in Clause 7.3 conforming to CSA Standard O121, O151, CAN/CSA-O325.0, or O452.0 shall be taken as

$$EI_w = \left(\sum B_a \left(\frac{W_D^3}{12}\right)\right) K_{SE} K_{TE}$$

The shear-through-thickness rigidity, $W_s$, of structural panels in Clause 7.3 used as web members of prefabricated wood I-joists and conforming to CSA Standard O121, O151, CAN/CSA-O325.0, or O452.0 shall be taken as

$$W_s = B_v K_{SG} K_{TG}$$

where
E = specified modulus of elasticity, per Clause 13.2.3.5
$K_{SE}$ = service condition factor for modulus of elasticity
   = 1.0 for dry service condition (in accordance with Clause 13.2.4.2)
$K_{TE}$ = treatment factor for modulus of elasticity
   = 1.0 for untreated prefabricated wood I-joists (see Clause 13.2.4.3)
$B_a$ = axial stiffness (tension or compression) from Table 7.3A, 7.3B, 7.3C, or 7.3D, N/mm
$W_D$ = overall depth of the structural panel web, mm
$B_v$ = shear-through-thickness rigidity from Table 7.3A, 7.3B, 7.3C, or 7.3D, N/mm
$K_{SG}$ = service condition factor for shear-through-thickness rigidity
   = 1.0 for dry service condition (see Clause 13.2.4.2)
$K_{TG}$ = treatment factor for shear-through-thickness rigidity
   = 1.0 for untreated prefabricated wood I-joists (see Clause 13.2.4.3)
**Note:** *Axial web stiffness and web shear-through-thickness rigidity for products not covered by Tables 7.3A, 7.3B, 7.3C, or 7.3D must be determined from appropriate standards or documented test data, which can be obtained from the prefabricated wood I-joist manufacturer.*

## 13.2.6 Fastenings

### 13.2.6.1 Nails
Nailed connections shall be designed in accordance with Clause 10.9.

### 13.2.6.2 Joist Hangers and Other Framing Connectors
The use of joist hangers and other framing connectors with prefabricated wood I-joists shall be based on documented test data.
**Note:** *Required details of use and attachment are available from the manufacturers. For additional information, see Clause 10.10 and the Canadian Wood Council's* Commentary.

## 13.3 Type 3 (Proprietary) Design-Rated OSB Panels

### 13.3.1 Manufacture
Type 3 (Proprietary) design-rated OSB structural panels shall be manufactured and their structural properties evaluated in accordance with the testing, quality control, and quality assurance and certification provisions of the CSA Standard O452 Series. Type 3 OSB structural panels may be of any thickness.

### 13.3.2 Panel Identification and Certificates of Conformance
Each Type 3 (Proprietary) OSB product shall be identified by a distinctive company product designation approved by the certification organization. Its compliance with the requirements in CSA Standard O452.0 for Type 3 products shall be verified by the Certificate of Conformance issued by the certification organization. The Certificate of Conformance shall identify the product designation, the nominal thickness, and the assigned specified capacities (see Clause 13.3.4).

### 13.3.3 Basic Structural Capacities
Nominal thicknesses and basic structural capacities from which specified design capacities are derived shall be determined in accordance with the CSA Standard O452 Series.
**Note:** *The basic structural capacities are the lower tolerance limits of the mean stiffness and of the lower fifth percentile of strength, determined from testing of the mechanical properties, and adjusted to dry service conditions.*

### 13.3.4 Specified Capacities

### 13.3.4.1 Derivation
The specified capacities for stiffness and strength of Type 3 OSB structural panels shall be derived for each product from its basic structural capacities in accordance with Clauses 13.3.4.2 and 13.3.4.3.

### 13.3.4.2 Specified Stiffness and Rigidity
The specified capacities for stiffness and rigidity for a Type 3 OSB panel shall be its basic structural capacities, rounded to two significant figures.

### 13.3.4.3 Specified Strengths
The standard term specified strength capacities for a Type 3 OSB panel shall be equal to the basic strength capacities determined in accordance with the CSA Standard O452 Series multiplied by an adjustment factor of 0.8, and rounded to two significant figures.

### 13.3.4.4 Application of Specified Capacities
The specified capacities determined by Clauses 13.3.4.1 to 13.3.4.3 for a Type 3 OSB structural panel may be used in design procedures for structural panels specified in this Standard.

## 13.3.5 Design Methods

Designs with Type 3 (Proprietary) design-rated OSB shall be in accordance with the modification factors and design methods for OSB structural panels (see Clauses 7.4 and 7.5).

## 13.4 Structural Composite Lumber Products

### 13.4.1 General

All structural composite lumber products for use under the provisions of this Standard shall be manufactured to, and evaluated for characteristic values in accordance with, the requirements of ASTM Standard D 5456.

All structural composite lumber products for use under the provisions of Clause 13.4, including products subjected to secondary processing operations, shall bear the mark of a certification organization (C.O.) indicating certification by the C.O. as meeting the applicable requirements of Clauses 13.4.2 to 13.4.6.

### 13.4.2 Adhesives

Structural composite lumber products shall be manufactured using
(a) adhesives conforming to CSA Standard O112.6 or O112.7; or
(b) an adhesive demonstrated to provide equivalent performance to the adhesives referenced in Item (a).

**Note:** *For additional information on equivalent adhesives, see the Canadian Wood Council's* Commentary.

### 13.4.3 Specified Strengths and Moduli of Elasticity

#### 13.4.3.1 General

Specified strengths and moduli of elasticity for structural composite lumber products for use with this Standard shall be established in accordance with Clauses 13.4.3.2 to 13.4.3.7.

#### 13.4.3.2 Specified Bending Strength, $f_b$

The specified bending strength, $f_b$, for structural composite lumber products shall be taken as

$$f_b = F_B K_r$$

where
$F_B$ = the characteristic value in bending as determined by ASTM Standard D 5456, MPa
$K_r$ = reliability normalization factor for bending and tension from Table 13.2.3.2

#### 13.4.3.3 Specified Shear Strength, $f_v$

The specified shear strength, $f_v$, for structural composite lumber products shall be taken as

$$f_v = v_{scl} K_r$$

where
$v_{scl}$ = the characteristic value in shear as determined by ASTM Standard D 5456, MPa
$K_r$ = reliability normalization factor for shear for structural composite lumber from Table 13.2.3.2

#### 13.4.3.4 Specified Compression Strength Parallel to Grain, $f_c$

The specified compression strength parallel to grain, $f_c$, for structural composite lumber products shall be taken as

$$f_c = c K_r$$

where
$c$ = the characteristic value in compression parallel to grain as determined by ASTM Standard D 5456, MPa

$K_r$ = reliability normalization factor for compression parallel to grain from Table 13.2.3.2

### 13.4.3.5 Specified Compression Strength, Perpendicular to Grain, $f_{cp}$

The specified compression strength perpendicular to grain, $f_{cp}$ (MPa), for structural composite lumber products shall not exceed the characteristic value for compression perpendicular to grain as determined by ASTM Standard D 5456, multiplied by 1.09.

### 13.4.3.6 Specified Tension Strength Parallel to Grain, $f_t$

The specified tension strength parallel to grain, $f_t$, for structural composite lumber products shall be taken as

$$f_t = t_{SCL} K_r$$

where

$t_{SCL}$ = the characteristic value in tension parallel to grain as determined by ASTM Standard D 5456, MPa
$K_r$ = reliability normalization factor for bending and tension from Table 13.2.3.2

### 13.4.3.7 Specified Modulus of Elasticity

The specified moduli of elasticity, E, for structural composite lumber products shall be the mean moduli as determined by ASTM Standard D 5456.

## 13.4.4 Modification Factors

### 13.4.4.1 Load Duration Factor, $K_D$

The load duration factors, $K_D$, as given in Clause 4.3.2 are applicable to the specified strengths of structural composite lumber products, provided that appropriate testing has been conducted that demonstrates the validity of those load duration factors for use with the structural composite lumber product.

**Note:** *See also the Canadian Wood Council's Commentary.*

### 13.4.4.2 Service Condition Factor, $K_S$

The specified strengths and stiffness of structural composite lumber products described in Clause 13.4.4 are applicable for use in dry service conditions with $K_S$ = 1.0. If structural composite lumber products are to be used in other than dry service conditions, the specified strengths and stiffness shall be evaluated, including development of appropriate strength reduction factors, based on documented test results.

### 13.4.4.3 Treatment Factor, $K_T$

The specified strengths and stiffness described in Clause 13.4.4 are applicable to untreated structural composite lumber products with $K_T$ = 1.0. Treatment adjustments for specified strengths and stiffness shall be based on the documented results of tests that shall take into account the effects of time, temperature, and moisture content.

### 13.4.4.4 System Factor, $K_H$

The system factor, $K_H$, permitted for structural composite lumber products used in a load-sharing system shall be 1.04.

To qualify for the above increase, the structural composite lumber products shall be part of a wood-framing system consisting of at least three parallel members joined by transverse load distributing elements adequate to support the design load and shall not be spaced more than 610 mm on centre.

### 13.4.4.5 Size Factor in Bending, $K_{Zb}$

The size factor in bending, $K_{Zb}$, for structural composite lumber products shall be taken as

$$K_{Zb} = \left(\frac{d_1}{d}\right)^{\frac{1}{m}} \left(\frac{L_1}{L}\right)^{\frac{1}{m}}$$

where
$d_1, L_1$ = depth and length of unit volume members
$d, L$ = depth and length of an application member
$m$ = parameter determined in accordance with Annex A1 of ASTM Standard D 5456.
**Note:** *For further information regarding depth and length of unit volume members, see ASTM Standard D 5456.*

### 13.4.4.6 Size Factor in Tension, $K_{Zt}$
The size factor in tension, $K_{Zt}$, for structural composite lumber products shall be taken as

$$K_{Zt} = \left(\frac{L_1}{L}\right)^{\frac{1}{m}}$$

where
$L_1$ = base length between test grips, as tested in Section 5.5.2 of ASTM Standard D 5456
$L$ = end use length
$m$ = parameter determined in accordance with Annex A1 of ASTM Standard D 5456.

## 13.4.5 Strength and Resistance

### 13.4.5.1 Bending Moment Resistance
The factored bending moment resistance, $M_r$, of structural composite lumber products shall be taken as

$$M_r = \phi F_b \, S K_{Zb} \, K_L$$

where
$\phi$ = 0.90
$F_b$ = $f_b \, (K_D \, K_H \, K_{Sb} \, K_T)$
$f_b$ = specified bending strength, per Clause 13.4.3.2, MPa
$K_{Zb}$ = size factor in bending, per Clause 13.4.4.5
$K_L$ = lateral stability factor, per Clause 13.4.5.2

### 13.4.5.2 Lateral Stability Factor, $K_L$
The lateral stability factor, $K_L$, for structural composite lumber products shall be determined in accordance with Clause 5.5.4.2.

### 13.4.5.3 Notches
The use of structural composite lumber products with notches or cuts shall not be permitted unless such details have been evaluated and are demonstrated to be acceptable based on documented test data.

### 13.4.5.4 Shear Resistance
The factored shear resistance, $V_r$, of structural composite lumber products shall be taken as

$$V_r = \phi \, F_v \, \frac{2A}{3} \, K_{Zv}$$

where
$\phi$ = 0.90
$F_v$ = $f_v \, (K_D \, K_{Sv} \, K_T)$
$f_v$ = specified shear strength of structural composite lumber products, per Clause 13.4.3.3, MPa
$A$ = cross-sectional area of member, mm$^2$
$K_{Zv}$ = 1.0

**Note:** *For additional information on size factor in shear, $K_{Zv}$, see the Canadian Wood Council's Commentary.*

**168**

## A5.5.12 Preserved Wood Foundations

### A5.5.12.1

Studs for preserved wood foundations may be designed in accordance with recognized engineering methods. When assumed to be laterally supported, and when no surcharge exists, the formulae presented in Clauses A5.5.12.6 to A5.5.12.12 give conservative approximations of sufficient accuracy for practical construction. Dimensions used in the formulae are identified in Figure A5.5.12.1.

### A5.5.12.2

Studs for exterior foundation walls may be designed as members subjected to combined bending and axial compressive loading. Deflection due to lateral and axial loads should not exceed 1/300 of the unsupported height of the stud.

### A5.5.12.3

Sheathing for exterior foundation walls may be designed as simple bending members. The calculated maximum deflection at a point 300 mm above the bottom of the sheathing should not exceed 1/180 of the span of sheathing between studs. The nominal thickness of sheathing should not be less than 12.5 mm.

### A5.5.12.4

Floors and connections between floors and walls shall be designed to withstand loads imposed upon them by lateral soil pressure as well as floor loads appropriate for the occupancy.

### A5.5.12.5

Unequal pressure distribution may result from differing backfill heights on opposite sides of a building, openings in foundation walls, openings in floors at the top of foundation walls, or other causes. Framing members and sheathing shall be designed to resist loads resulting from unequal pressure distribution, by diaphragm action, or by other suitable means.

### A5.5.12.6

Combined bending and axial load effects may be evaluated using the formula

$$\frac{M_f + P_f\Delta}{M_r} + \left(\frac{P_f}{P_r}\right)^2 < 1.0$$

where

$M_f$ = maximum factored moment due to lateral load on stud, N•mm
$P_f$ = factored axial load on stud, N
$\Delta$ = deflection due to lateral load at point where $M_f$ is calculated, mm
$M_r$ = factored bending moment resistance, in accordance with Clause 5.5.4.1, N•mm
$P_r$ = factored compressive resistance, in accordance with Clause 5.5.6.2.2, N

**Notes:**
**(1)** A $K_D$ factor of 0.65 applies to the calculation of $M_r$, and a $K_D$ factor of 1.0 applies to the calculation of $P_r$.
**(2)** The value of $P_f\Delta$ represents secondary bending, which may be negligible.

### A5.5.12.7

The value of $M_f$ in Clause A5.5.12.6 is the maximum moment due to factored lateral load, and may be calculated using the following expression derived from recognized engineering formulae. At any point, x, above the floor the factored bending moment, $M_{fx}$ (N•mm), is

$$M_{fx} = \frac{w_f H^2}{6L}\left[(H-3a)\left(\frac{L-x}{H}\right) - L\left(\frac{H-Ax}{H}\right)^3\right]$$

where

$w_f$ = maximum factored lateral load per stud, N/mm

= maximum factored lateral soil pressure, N/mm², times stud spacing, mm

H, L, a, x = variables shown in Figure A5.5.12.1, mm

## A5.5.12.8

The following formulae may be used to determine the maximum factored moment, $M_f$, and its location, x:

(a) for wood sleeper and slab floors

$$M_f = \frac{w_f H^2}{6L}\left[L - H + \frac{2}{3}\sqrt{\frac{H^3}{3L}}\right]$$

and

$$x = H - \sqrt{\frac{H^3}{3L}}$$

(b) for suspended floors, both the moment between supports and the cantilever moment at the support should be checked using

$$M_f = \frac{w_f H^2}{6L}K_m$$

where

$$K_m = (H - 3a)\left[K_1 + \frac{L + a - H}{H}\right] - LK_1^3$$

and between supports

$$K_1 = \sqrt{\frac{H - 3a}{3L}}$$

$$x = H - a - H\sqrt{\frac{H - 3a}{3L}}$$

at the support

$$K_1 = \frac{H - a}{H} \text{ and } x = 0$$

**Note:** *Values of $K_m$ for a range of backfill heights and typical wall dimensions are given in Table A5.5.12.8.*

## A5.5.12.9

Secondary moment is the term $P_f\Delta$ in Clause A5.5.12.6. The value of $\Delta$ may be calculated at any point, x, above the basement floor (see Figure A5.5.12.1), using the formula

$$\Delta = \frac{w_f(L - x)}{360EILH}K_\Delta$$

$$\beta_1 = \frac{1}{1300} L_p S_p (n_c - 1) [1 + 500 \exp^{-0.52(S_Q - 12.5)}]$$

$$\beta_2 = 0.5 \times 10^{-16} L_p [(n_c - 1)S_p]^3 [(n_R - 1)S_Q]^{4.5} \exp^{-\left(\frac{a-50}{100}\right)}$$

$$\beta_3 = \left( \frac{3\mu - 1}{2} + L_p \frac{1-\mu}{50} \right) 5^{\left( \gamma - \exp^{\left(1.9 - 0.95 \frac{b}{L_p}\right)^5} \right)}$$

$$\mu = 43.9[(n_c - 1)S_p]^{-0.4} [(n_R - 1)S_Q]^{-0.2}$$

$a$   = end distance (Figure 10.7.1.7), mm
$L_p$ = rivet penetration (Figure 10.7.1.1)
$K_v$ = constant depending on $n_R$ and $n_c$ (Table A10.7.2.3D)
$\beta_v$ = constant depending on $S_p$ and $S_Q$ (Table A10.7.2.3E)
$\gamma$   = 90.5 + 5.4 $L_p$

**Note:** *For cases where $b \le 175$ mm, $S_p = 40$ mm, $S_Q = 25$ mm, and $L_p \ge 55$ mm, $P_v$ will be greater than $P_t$*

## A10.7.2.3.2 Perpendicular-to-Grain Loading

In Clause 10.7.2.5, the lateral strength resistance for wood capacity perpendicular to grain, $q_w$, may be determined from

$$q_w = \frac{23.3 X_{tp} f_{tp}[(n_R - 1)S_p]^{0.8}}{K_{tp}\beta_{tp}10^3[(n_c - 1)S_Q]^{0.2}}$$

where
$X_{tp}$ = adjustment factor for tension perpendicular = 1.45
$f_{tp}$   = specified strength in tension perpendicular to grain, MPa (Table 6.3)
$K_{tp}$ = constant depending on $n_R$ and $n_c$ (Table A10.7.2.3F)
$\beta_{tp}$ = constant depending on $S_p$ and $S_Q$ (Table A10.7.2.3G)

and the value of the factor, $C_t$, may be determined from

$$C_t = \frac{1}{\beta_D} \left[ \frac{e_p}{(n_c - 1)S_Q} \right]^{-0.2}$$

where
$\beta_D$ = constant depending on $e_p/(n_c - 1)S_Q$ (Table A10.7.2.3H)
$e_p$   = unloaded edge distance, mm (Figure 10.7.1.7)

## Table A10.7.2.3A
## Values of $K_t$

| Rivets per row, $n_C$ | Number of rows, $n_R$ | | | | | | | | | |
|---|---|---|---|---|---|---|---|---|---|---|
| | 2 | 4 | 6 | 8 | 10 | 12 | 14 | 16 | 18 | 20 |
| 2 | 0.75 | 1.16 | 1.37 | 1.47 | 1.51 | 1.54 | 1.57 | 1.61 | 1.64 | 1.64 |
| 4 | 0.51 | 0.88 | 1.08 | 1.17 | 1.22 | 1.26 | 1.30 | 1.35 | 1.38 | 1.38 |
| 6 | 0.38 | 0.71 | 0.89 | 0.97 | 1.02 | 1.06 | 1.11 | 1.16 | 1.18 | 1.18 |
| 8 | 0.30 | 0.60 | 0.75 | 0.84 | 0.89 | 0.93 | 0.97 | 1.02 | 1.05 | 1.05 |
| 10 | 0.26 | 0.52 | 0.66 | 0.74 | 0.79 | 0.82 | 0.87 | 0.91 | 0.94 | 0.94 |
| 12 | 0.23 | 0.47 | 0.59 | 0.66 | 0.71 | 0.75 | 0.78 | 0.82 | 0.85 | 0.85 |
| 14 | 0.21 | 0.42 | 0.54 | 0.60 | 0.65 | 0.68 | 0.72 | 0.75 | 0.77 | 0.77 |
| 16 | 0.20 | 0.38 | 0.49 | 0.56 | 0.60 | 0.63 | 0.67 | 0.69 | 0.71 | 0.71 |
| 18 | 0.18 | 0.35 | 0.45 | 0.52 | 0.56 | 0.59 | 0.62 | 0.65 | 0.66 | 0.67 |
| 20 | 0.17 | 0.32 | 0.42 | 0.49 | 0.53 | 0.56 | 0.59 | 0.61 | 0.63 | 0.64 |
| 22 | 0.16 | 0.30 | 0.40 | 0.46 | 0.51 | 0.54 | 0.56 | 0.58 | 0.60 | 0.61 |
| 24 | 0.15 | 0.29 | 0.38 | 0.45 | 0.49 | 0.52 | 0.53 | 0.55 | 0.57 | 0.58 |
| 26 | 0.14 | 0.28 | 0.36 | 0.42 | 0.46 | 0.50 | 0.51 | 0.52 | 0.54 | 0.55 |

## Table A10.7.2.3B
## Values of $\beta_t$

| $S_P$, mm | $S_Q$, mm | Number of rows, $n_R$ | | | | | | | | | |
|---|---|---|---|---|---|---|---|---|---|---|---|
| | | 2 | 4 | 6 | 8 | 10 | 12 | 14 | 16 | 18 | 20 |
| 25 | 12.5 | 1.00 | 1.00 | 1.00 | 1.00 | 1.00 | 1.00 | 1.00 | 1.00 | 1.00 | 1.00 |
| | 15.0 | 1.11 | 1.06 | 1.04 | 1.02 | 1.02 | 1.01 | 1.01 | 1.01 | 1.01 | 1.01 |
| | 25.0 | 1.68 | 1.36 | 1.23 | 1.14 | 1.09 | 1.08 | 1.08 | 1.06 | 1.04 | 1.03 |
| | 32.0 | 2.03 | 1.54 | 1.34 | 1.22 | 1.14 | 1.14 | 1.12 | 1.10 | 1.08 | 1.05 |
| | 40.0 | 2.37 | 1.72 | 1.46 | 1.29 | 1.18 | 1.14 | 1.12 | 1.10 | 1.08 | 1.06 |
| 32 | 12.5 | 0.94 | 0.93 | 0.93 | 0.93 | 0.93 | 0.93 | 0.93 | 0.93 | 0.93 | 0.93 |
| | 15.0 | 1.05 | 0.99 | 0.97 | 0.95 | 0.95 | 0.94 | 0.94 | 0.94 | 0.94 | 0.94 |
| | 25.0 | 1.58 | 1.27 | 1.15 | 1.07 | 1.02 | 1.00 | 1.00 | 0.98 | 0.98 | 0.97 |
| | 32.0 | 1.90 | 1.44 | 1.26 | 1.14 | 1.06 | 1.02 | 1.01 | 0.99 | 0.98 | 0.98 |
| | 40.0 | 2.23 | 1.61 | 1.36 | 1.21 | 1.11 | 1.06 | 1.04 | 1.02 | 1.00 | 1.00 |
| 40 | 12.5 | 0.87 | 0.87 | 0.87 | 0.87 | 0.87 | 0.87 | 0.88 | 0.87 | 0.87 | 0.87 |
| | 15.0 | 0.97 | 0.92 | 0.90 | 0.89 | 0.88 | 0.88 | 0.88 | 0.88 | 0.88 | 0.88 |
| | 25.0 | 1.48 | 1.18 | 1.07 | 1.00 | 0.96 | 0.93 | 0.92 | 0.92 | 0.91 | 0.90 |
| | 32.0 | 1.78 | 1.34 | 1.17 | 1.06 | 0.99 | 0.96 | 0.94 | 0.93 | 0.93 | 0.92 |
| | 40.0 | 2.08 | 1.50 | 1.27 | 1.13 | 1.04 | 0.99 | 0.97 | 0.95 | 0.94 | 0.93 |
| 50 | 12.5 | 0.75 | 0.75 | 0.75 | 0.75 | 0.75 | 0.75 | 0.75 | 0.75 | 0.75 | 0.75 |
| | 15.0 | 0.84 | 0.79 | 0.77 | 0.76 | 0.76 | 0.76 | 0.76 | 0.75 | 0.75 | 0.75 |
| | 25.0 | 1.27 | 1.00 | 0.91 | 0.85 | 0.81 | 0.79 | 0.79 | 0.78 | 0.78 | 0.77 |
| | 32.0 | 1.54 | 1.14 | 1.00 | 0.91 | 0.85 | 0.82 | 0.82 | 0.80 | 0.80 | 0.79 |
| | 40.0 | 1.80 | 1.27 | 1.09 | 0.97 | 0.89 | 0.86 | 0.85 | 0.83 | 0.82 | 0.81 |

## Table A10.7.2.3G
## Values of $\beta_{tp}$

| $S_Q$, mm | $S_p$, mm | Number of rows, $n_R$ | | | | |
|---|---|---|---|---|---|---|
| | | 2 | 4 | 6 | 8 | 10 |
| 15 | 25 | 1.29 | 1.25 | 1.24 | 1.23 | 1.23 |
| | 40 | 1.76 | 1.61 | 1.49 | 1.45 | 1.40 |
| 25 | 25 | 1.00 | 1.00 | 1.00 | 1.00 | 1.00 |
| | 32 | 1.18 | 1.13 | 1.10 | 1.09 | 1.07 |
| | 40 | 1.36 | 1.27 | 1.20 | 1.17 | 1.14 |
| | 50 | 1.72 | 1.53 | 1.40 | 1.34 | 1.28 |
| 32 | 25 | 0.82 | 0.84 | 0.85 | 0.86 | 0.86 |
| | 32 | 0.97 | 0.96 | 0.94 | 0.93 | 0.93 |
| | 40 | 1.12 | 1.07 | 1.03 | 1.00 | 0.98 |
| | 50 | 1.42 | 1.29 | 1.20 | 1.15 | 1.10 |
| 40 | 25 | 0.63 | 0.68 | 0.70 | 0.71 | 0.71 |
| | 32 | 0.75 | 0.77 | 0.78 | 0.77 | 0.76 |
| | 40 | 0.87 | 0.86 | 0.84 | 0.83 | 0.82 |
| | 50 | 1.11 | 1.04 | 0.98 | 0.95 | 0.92 |

## Table A10.7.2.3H
## Values of $\beta_D$

| $\dfrac{e_p}{(n_C-1)S_Q}$ | $\beta_D$ | $\dfrac{e_p}{(n_C-1)S_Q}$ | $\beta_D$ |
|---|---|---|---|
| 0.1 | 0.275 | 1.0 | 0.83 |
| 0.2 | 0.433 | 1.2 | 0.88 |
| 0.3 | 0.538 | 1.4 | 0.92 |
| 0.4 | 0.60 | 1.6 | 0.95 |
| 0.5 | 0.65 | 1.8 | 0.97 |
| 0.6 | 0.69 | 2.0 | 0.98 |
| 0.7 | 0.73 | 2.4 | 0.99 |
| 0.8 | 0.77 | 2.8 and more | 1.00 |
| 0.9 | 0.80 | | |

**Note:** For $e_p/[(n_C-1)S_Q]$ between 0.1 and 0.3, $\beta_D$ is given to three significant digits due to the sensitivity in this range.

## A10.9.3.2 Lateral Deformation of Nailed and Spiked Wood-to-Wood Joints

For specified loads, P, not greater than $n_u/3$, the lateral deformation of nailed and spiked joints may be estimated from

$$\Delta = 0.5dK_m(P/n_u)^{1.7}$$

where
$\Delta$ = lateral deformation, mm
d   = nail diameter, mm
$K_m$ = service creep factor (Table A10.9.3.2)
P   = specified load per nail or spike, N
$n_u$ = unit lateral strength resistance (Table 10.9.4), N

### Table A10.9.3.2
### Service Creep Factors, $K_m$, for Nail and Spike Joints

| Load duration class | Moisture condition | | |
|---|---|---|---|
| | Nailed dry, loaded dry | Nailed wet, loaded dry | Nailed wet, loaded wet |
| Permanent | 1.5 | 2.0 | 3.0 |
| Standard | 1.2 | 1.5 | 2.0 |
| Short | 1.0 | 1.2 | 1.5 |

# Proposition de modification

N'hésitez pas à nous faire part de vos suggestions et de vos commentaires. Au moment de soumettre des propositions de modification aux normes CSA et autres publications CSA prière de fournir les renseignements demandés ci-dessous et de formuler les propositions sur une feuille volante. Il est recommandé d'inclure

- le numéro de la norme/publication
- le numéro de l'article, du tableau ou de la figure visé
- la formulation proposée
- la raison de cette modification.

# Proposal for change

CSA welcomes your suggestions and comments. To submit your proposals for changes to CSA Standards and other CSA publications, please supply the information requested below and attach your proposal for change on a separate page(s). Be sure to include the

- Standard/publication number
- relevant Clause, Table, and/or Figure number(s)
- wording of the proposed change
- rationale for the change.

**Nom/Name:** _____

**Affiliation:** _____

**Adresse/Address:** _____

_____

**Ville/City:** _____

**État/Province/State:** _____

**Pays/Country:** _____ **Code postal/Postal/Zip code:** _____

**Téléphone/Telephone:** _____ **Télécopieur/Fax:** _____

**Date:** _____

ISBN 1-55436-094-3

# Appendix

# List of Symbols

| Symbol | Meaning |
|--------|---------|
| A | Cross-sectional Area |
| a | Unloaded End Distance, Purlin Spacing |
| $A_b$ | Bearing Area, Area of Bolt |
| $A_G$ | Gross Cross-sectional Area |
| $a_L$ | Loaded End Distance |
| $A_m$ | Gross Cross-sectional Area of Main Member |
| $A_N$ | Net Area of Cross-section |
| $A_R$ | Area Reduced Due to Drilling, Boring, Grooving |
| $A_s$ | Sum of Gross Cross-sectional Areas of Side Members |
| b | Width of Member |
| B | Width of the Widest Lamination |
| $B_v$ | Shear through Thickness Rigidity |
| $C_c$ | Slenderness ratio |
| COFI | Council of Forest Industries of British Columbia |
| $C_V$ | Shear Load Coefficient |
| d | Depth of Member, Nail Diameter |
| D | Dead Load |
| $d_A$ | Depth at the Apex |
| $d_e$ | Shear Depth |
| $d_F$ | Fastening Diameter |
| $d_n$ | Depth of Notch |
| $d_S$ | Depth at Support |
| $d_T$ | Depth at the Tangent Point |
| e | Length of Notch, Edge Distance |
| E | Modulus of Elasticity, Specified Earthquake Load |
| $e_n$ | Nail Deformation |
| $e_L$ | Loaded Edge Distance |
| $E_s I$ | Bending Stiffness |
| F | Applied Shearwall Shear Force |
| $f_b$ | Specified Strength in Bending |
| $f_c$ | Specified Compressive Strength |
| $f_{cp}$ | Specified Compressive Strength Perpendicular to Grain |
| $F_c / E'$ | Strength to Stiffness Ratio |
| $f_f$ | Specified Notch Shear Resistance |
| $f_t$ | Specified Tensile Strength |
| $f_{tg}$ | Specified Tensile Strength at Gross Section |
| $f_{tn}$ | Specified Tensile Strength at Net Section |
| $f_{tp}$ | Specified Tensile Strength Perpendicular to Grain |

| Symbol | Meaning |
|--------|---------|
| $f_v$ | Specified Shear Strength |
| $G_A$ | Planar Shear Ridgidity |
| h | Distance Between Chords |
| H | Truss Rise, Height, Material Factor |
| I | Moment of Inertia |
| $J_A$ | Factor for Toe Nailing |
| $J_B$ | Factor for Nail Clinching |
| $J_C$ | Minimum Configuration Factor |
| $J_D$ | Factor for Diaphragm Construction |
| $J_E$ | Factor for Connecting into End Grain |
| $J_G$ | Group Factor |
| $J_H$ | Moment Factor for Heel Connections of Pitched Trusses |
| $J_L$ | Factor for Loaded End Distance |
| $J_n$ | Nail Diameter Factor |
| $J_O$ | Factor for Connector Orientation to Grain |
| $J_P$ | Factor for Lag Screw Penetration |
| $J_R$ | Factor for Number of Rows |
| $J_S$ | Side Plate Factor for 4 in. Shear Plates |
| $J_{sp}$ | Species Factor |
| $J_T$ | Thickness Factor |
| $J_y$ | Side Plate Factor |
| $J'$ | Composite Modification Factor |
| $K_B$ | Bearing Factor |
| $K_C$ | Slenderness Factor |
| $K_D$ | Duration of Load Factor |
| $K_\Delta$ | Deflection Factor |
| $K_e$ | Effective Length Factor |
| $K_H$ | System Factor |
| $K_L$ | Lateral Stability Factor |
| $K_N$ | Notch Factor |
| kN | Kilonewton |
| kN·m | Kilonewton metre |
| kN/m | Kilonewton per Metre |
| kPa | Kilopascals |
| $K_R$ | Radial Stress Factor |
| $K_S$ | Service Condition Factor |
| $K_{SF}$ | Service Condition Factor for Fastenings |
| $K_{span}$ | Deflection Factor for Decking Pattern |
| $K_T$ | Treatment Factor |
| $K_X$ | Curvature Factor |
| $K_Z$ | Size Factor |
| $K'$ | Composite Modification Factor |
| L | Length, Span, Live Load |

| Symbol | Meaning |
|--------|---------|
| $L_b$ | Unsupported Length in Direction of b, Bearing Length |
| $L_d$ | Unsupported Length in Direction of d |
| $L_e$ | Effective Length |
| $l_p$ | Span of Panel |
| $L_p$ | Length of Penetration |
| $L_t$ | Length of Penetration of Threads |
| $l_u$ | Unsupported Length |
| LVL | Laminated Veneer Lumber |
| $L_w$ | Length of PWF Shearwall |
| $L'_b$ | Average Bearing Length |
| m | Metre |
| Max. | Maximum |
| $M_f$ | Factored Bending Moment |
| $M_{fe}$ | Equivalent Factored Moment |
| Min. | Minimum |
| mm | Millimetre |
| MPa | Megapascals |
| $M_r$ | Factored Bending Moment Resistance |
| $M_{rb}$ | Factored Bending Moment Resistance based on Bending Strength |
| $M_{rt}$ | Factored Bending Moment Resistance based on Radial Tension Strength |
| $n_F$ | Number of Fastenings |
| $N_f$ | Factored Lateral Load |
| $n_{Fe}$ | Number of Effective Fastenings |
| $N_r$ | Factored Ultimate Lateral Resistance of Fastenings |
| $n_R$ | Number of Rows of Fastenings |
| $N_{rs}$ | Factored Lateral Slip Resistance of Fastenings |
| $N_S$ | Lateral Slip Resistance |
| $n_s$ | Number of Shear Planes |
| $n_{Se}$ | Effective Number of Shear Planes |
| $N_{Su}$ | Maximum Factored Resistance per Shear Plate |
| $n_u$ | Ultimate Lateral Resistance of Teeth per Unit |
| P | Uplift Restraint Force |
| $P_E$ | Euler Buckling Load |
| $P_f$ | Factored Axial Load |
| $P_r$ | Factored Compressive Resistance Parallel to Grain |
| PSL | Parallel Strand Lumber |
| PWF | Permanent Wood Foundation |
| $p_u$ | Lateral Resistance of Fastenings Parallel to Grain |

| Symbol | Meaning |
|--------|---------|
| $P'_r$ | Unit Factored Lateral Resistance of Fastenings Parallel to Grain, Maximum Combined Compressive Load |
| $P'_{rw}$ | Factored Withdrawal Resistance of Fastenings per mm of Penetration |
| Q | Specified Wind or Earthquake Load |
| $Q_f$ | Factored Compressive Force |
| $Q_r$ | Factored Compressive Resistance Perpendicular to Grain |
| $q_u$ | Factored Lateral Resistance of Fastenings Perpendicular to Grain |
| $Q'_r$ | Unit Factored Lateral Resistance of Fastenings Perpendicular to Grain |
| R | Radius of Curvature, Reaction, Overturning Force |
| $R_C$ | Radius of Curvature at Centreline of Member |
| $R_I$ | Radius of Curvature of Innermost Lamination |
| S | Snow Load, Section Modulus |
| SH ℔ | Shear Plate |
| SCL | Structural Composite Lumber |
| $S_p$ | Spacing of Fastenings Parallel to Grain |
| $S_Q$ | Spacing of Fastenings Perpendicular to Grain |
| $S_u$ | Unbalanced Snow |
| T | Specified Load Due to Temperature, Shrinkage & Settlement Effects |
| t | Lamination Thickness |
| $T_f$ | Factored Tensile Force |
| $TL_f$ | Total Factored Load |
| $t_p$ | Tensile Resistance of Truss Plate |
| $T_r$ | Factored Tensile Resistance Parallel to Grain |
| $T_{rN}$ | Factored Tensile Resistance at Net Area |
| T&G | Tongue and Groove |
| $v_d$ | Specified Shear Strength for Shearwalls |
| $v_f$ | Factored Shear Force per Unit Length |
| $V_f$ | Factored Shear Force |
| $v_p$ | Shear Resistance of Truss Plate |
| $V_r$ | Factored Shear Resistance |
| $v_r$ | Factored Shear Resistance per Unit Length |
| $v_s$ | Shear Force per Unit Length Due to Specified Loads |

| Symbol | Meaning |
|--------|---------|
| W | Wind Load |
| w | Uniformly Distributed Load |
| $w_{\Delta R}$ | Maximum Load Capacity Based on Deflection for Plank Decking |
| $W_f$ | Sum of all Factored Loads acting on the Beam |
| $w_{FR}$ | Maximum Load Capacity Based on Factored Moment Resistance for Plank Decking |
| $W_r$ | Factored Shear Resistance |
| $w_S$ | Width of Truss Plate along the Line of the Shear Force |
| $w_t$ | Width of Truss Plate Perpendicular to Direction of Loading |
| $X_1$ | Constant for Species |
| $X_2$ | Constant for Loading Conditions |
| $X_3$ | Constant for Member Width |
| $X_G$ | Panel Geometry Factor |
| Z | Beam Volume |
| $(EI)_e$ | Effective Stiffness of Panel |
| $\Delta$ | Deflection |
| $\theta$ | Angle of Load to Grain |
| $\Psi$ | Load Combination Factor |

# Index